LINCOLN CHRISTIAN COLLEGE AND SEMINARY

Marriages & Families

Making Choices and Facing Change

■ Third Edition ■

Mary Ann Lamanna
University of Nebraska at Omaha

Agnes Riedmann

Wadsworth Publishing Company
Belmont, California
A Division of Wadsworth, Inc.

Sociology Editor: Sheryl Fullerton
Special Projects Editor: Judith McKibben
Editorial Assistant: Cynthia Haus
Production Editor: Sandra Craig
Managing Designer: MaryEllen Podgorski
Print Buyer: Karen Hunt
Text Designer: Merle Sanderson
Copy Editor: Thomas L. Briggs
Photo Researcher: Lindsay Kefauver
Compositor: Graphic Typesetting Service
Cover: Walker & Bercu Design Studios

To our families,
especially Beth and Bill, Jr.,
Larry and Valerie

© 1988, 1985, 1981 by Wadsworth, Inc. All rights reserved. No part of this book may be reproduced, stored in a retrieval system, or transcribed, without the prior written permission of the publisher, Wadsworth Publishing Company, Belmont, California 94002, a division of Wadsworth, Inc.

Printed in the United States of America   56

    2   3   4   5   6   7   8   9   10

92   91   90   89   88

Library of Congress Cataloging-in-Publication Data

Lamanna, Mary Ann.
    Marriages and families : making choices and facing change / Mary Ann Lamanna, Agnes Riedmann.—3rd ed.
        p. cm.
        Bibliography: p.
        Includes indexes.
        ISBN 0-534-08664-0
        1. Marriage. 2. Family. 3. Remarriage. 4. Single people 5. Choice (Psychology) I. Riedmann, Agnes Czerwinski. II. Title.
HQ734.L22 1988
306.8—dc19   87-26231
                                                        CIP

About the Authors

Mary Ann Lamanna   received her bachelor's degree from Washington University, where she was elected to Phi Beta Kappa; her master's degree from the University of North Carolina, Chapel Hill; and her doctorate from the University of Notre Dame. She is Associate Professor of Sociology at the University of Nebraska at Omaha. She has two children, Larry, 23, and Valerie, 20.

Agnes Riedmann   attended Clarke College, Dubuque, and received her bachelor's degree from Creighton University and her master's degree in sociology from the University of Nebraska at Omaha. She is the author of several published short stories and poems and of *The Story of Adamsville* (Wadsworth), a science fiction novella written to supplement introductory sociology textbooks. She is currently pursuing a doctorate in sociology at the University of Nebraska and has received a one-year Fulbright award for demographic research at Australian National University, Canberra. She has two children, Beth, 22, and Bill, 21.

Contents
in Brief

Contents

Part IV

EXPERIENCING FAMILY COMMITMENT 344

Preface

We wrote—and have revised—this textbook with the belief that, although they are changing, marriage, families, and values are still important in contemporary American life. Our aim in the first edition was to help students question assumptions and long-held values and to reconcile conflicting ideas and values so that they could make knowledgeable choices throughout their lives. This continues to be our primary goal in the third edition. The best way of reaching this goal, we believe, is by providing sound facts and using a problem-solving approach.

An important part of our task is to call attention to some of the striking changes that have taken place in recent years in the American family and in its social and economic environment. In fact, we have reworded the book's subtitle—now *Making Choices and Facing Change*—to acknowledge that family choices are being made in a context that has continued to change in the years between the first and third editions.

The Book's Themes

Several themes are interwoven throughout this text: Marriage is changing from being an institution to being a relationship; there is an interplay between individual families and the larger society; and individuals make family-related choices throughout adulthood.

Making Choices Creating and maintaining marriages and families require many personal choices, and people continue to make decisions, even "big" ones, throughout their lives.

Handling Personal Problems Tension frequently exists between the individual and the social environment. Many personal troubles result from societal influences, values, or assumptions, inadequate societal support for family goals, or conflict between family values and individual values. By understanding some of these possible sources of tension and conflict, individuals can perceive their personal troubles more clearly and can work constructively toward solutions.

Focus on Relationships In the past, people tended to emphasize the dutiful performance of social roles in marriage and in the family structure. Today people are more apt to view marriages as committed relationships in which they expect to find companionship and intimacy. This book examines the implications of this shift in perspective.

The Themes Throughout the Life Course

The three themes are introduced in the Prologue, and they reappear throughout the text. We developed these themes by looking at the interplay between findings in the social sciences and the experiences of people of all ages around us. Some ideas for topics arose from the needs and concerns we perceived. We also observed many changes in the roles people play and in the ways they relate to each other. Neither the "old" nor the "new" roles and relationships seemed to us as stereotyped or as free of ambivalence and conflict as is often indicated in books and articles. The attitudes, behavior, and relationships of real people have a complexity that we have tried to portray in this book and that are especially visible in the photographs.

Interwoven with these themes is the concept of the life cycle: the idea that adults go through a sequence of stages and transitions during which they may reevaluate and restructure the chosen life course. For example, the book makes these points:

- Many people reexamine the decisions they have made about marriage and family not once or twice but throughout their lives.
- People's personal problems and their interaction with the social environment change as they and their marriages and families grow older.
- People reevaluate their relationships and their expectations for relationships as they and their marriages and families mature.
- Because marriage and family forms are so flexible today, people have the option of changing the style of their marriage throughout their lives.

This emphasis on the life course creates a comprehensive picture of marriages and families and enables this book to cover many topics that are new to marriage and family texts.

Marriages and Families: Making Choices

Making decisions about one's marriage and family, either knowledgeably or by default, begins in early adulthood and lasts into old age. People choose whether they will adhere to traditional beliefs, values, and attitudes about gender roles or will adopt more androgynous roles and relationships. They may clarify their sexual values and become more knowledgeable and comfortable with their sexuality. Women and men may choose to remain single or to marry, and they have the option today of staying single longer before marrying. Single people make choices about their sex lives, ranging from decisions to engage in sex for recreation to decisions to abstain from sex altogether. In the courtship process people choose between the more formal custom of dating and the less formal "getting together."

Once individuals choose their partners, they have to decide how they are going to structure their marriages and families. Will the partners be legally married? Will theirs be a dual-career marriage? Will they plan periods in which just the husband or just the wife works interspersed with times in which both work? Will they have children? Will other family members live with them—parents, for example? They will make these decisions not once but over and over during their lifetimes.

Within the marital relationship, couples choose how they will deal with conflicts. Will they try to ignore conflicts and risk devitalized relationships? Will they vent their anger in hostile, alienating, or physically violent ways? Or will they practice bonding ways of communicating and fighting—ways that emphasize sharing and can deepen intimacy?

How will the partners distribute power in the marriage? Will they work toward a no-power relationship in which the individual is more concerned with helping and supporting the other than with gaining a power advantage? How will the partners allocate work responsibilities in the home? What value will they place on their sexual lives together? Throughout their experience family members continually face decisions about how to balance each one's need for individuality with the need for togetherness.

Parents also have choices. In raising their children, they can assume the role of martyr or police officer, for example, or they can simply present themselves as human beings who have more experience than their youngsters and who are concerned about developing supportive, mutually cooperative relationships.

Many spouses face decisions about whether to divorce. They weigh the pros and cons, asking themselves which is the better alternative: living together as they are or separating? Even when a couple decides to divorce, there are choices to make: Will they try to cooperate as much as possible or insist on blame and revenge?

The majority of divorced individuals eventually face decisions about remarriage. And in the absence of cultural models, they choose how they will define step-relationships.

When families meet crisis—and every family will face *some* crisis—members have to make additional decisions. Will they view the crisis as a challenge to be met without blame or as an unfair and devastating blow?

An emphasis on knowledgeable decision making does not mean that individuals can completely control their lives. People can influence but never directly determine how those around them behave or feel about them. Partners cannot control each other's changes over time, nor can they avoid all accidents, illnesses, unemployment, deaths, or even divorces.

Families *can* control how they respond to such crises, however. Their responses will meet their own needs better when they refuse to react automatically and choose instead to act as a consequence of knowledgeable decision making.

New in This Edition

In response to our reviewers, students, and colleagues, to societal changes since our previous editions, and to subtle changes in our own perceptions about marriages and families, we have made numerous changes in the third edition. In keeping with the recognition that people do not follow predictable *life cycles,* we have omitted that term from the title. The concepts *life course* and *life spiral* may better fit reality—an idea that is discussed in Chapter 1.

We have reduced the number of chapters to seventeen and rearranged the chapters. Material from the former Chapter 19, "Balancing Individuality with Commitment," has been incorporated throughout the book because it is our growing conviction that this topic runs through virtually all issues in the text. The chapter on communication was reorganized to focus on family cohesiveness and communication in general in addition to communicating about conflicts. Because separation, divorce, and remarriage are critical processes for families, we have positioned these chapters after Chapter 15, "Family Crisis Management." The two chapters on sex have been integrated into one, Chapter 4, "Our Sexual Selves," and information on human sexual anatomy, conception, pregnancy, and childbirth, contraceptive techniques, sexually transmitted diseases, sexual dysfunctions, and sex therapy now appears in Appendixes A through F. Finally, to recognize the fact that people are people first and women or men second, we have reversed the order of Chapters 1 and 2. In this edition, Chapter 1 addresses choices that all of us, men and women, make throughout our lives. Chapter 2 focuses on how changing sex or gender roles affect those choices.

We have also added or increased coverage of emerging topics. For example, Chapter 2 now devotes less space to traditional feminine roles and more space to new research and information on masculine roles. This edition includes a discussion (in Chapter 10) of date or acquaintance rape. Chapter 4 now contains a lengthy exploration of

issues surrounding AIDS. Chapter 15 now discusses death in the family, particularly the death of a child, and explores the double ABC-X model of family stressors and strains. In Chapter 12, the discussion of surrogate motherhood was expanded, and some implications of the 1987 "Baby M" case were included.

To all the issues and topics we address throughout the text, we have added information—whenever it was available in the literature—on older families and on black and other minority families. For example, black wives' employment is addressed in Chapter 11, and black fertility rates are discussed in Chapter 12. We have also added more on family history. For example, Chapter 12 includes a discussion of historical developments and trends in birth control since the 1830s. In addition, we raise questions about family policy throughout the text.

Finally, we have thoroughly updated our research base, using the most current literature, research findings, and demographic data available.

Special Features of *Marriages and Families*

- **A broad, up-to-date research base.** The content is based on extensive research. More than 1,400 sources are cited, including many recent studies.
- **Interview case studies.** Agnes Riedmann talked with individuals of all ages about their experiences in marriages and families. These interviews appear as boxed excerpts, balancing and expanding topics presented in the chapters. We hope that the presentation of individuals' stories in their own words will help students to see their own lives more clearly and will encourage them to discuss and reevaluate their attitudes and values.
- **Enrichment material.** Boxed material drawn from classic research, new studies, popular social science, and journal articles supports and expands the chapter content.
- **Photographs.** Third edition photographs come from the real world. Many have been contributed by staff members and friends of Wadsworth. Rather than illustrating concepts in a direct way, these photos capture the richness and uniqueness of individuals and families. The flavor and texture of family relationships as they are actually lived emerge from these pages.
- **Pedagogical aids.** An outline of topics to be covered introduces each chapter. A large

number of charts and diagrams present current data in easily understood form. End-of-chapter study aids include a summary, a list of key terms, study questions, and annotated suggested readings. A comprehensive glossary defines and illustrates important terms.

Teaching and Learning Aids

To help students understand and remember all the facts, research, and information in the text, David Treybig of Baldwin-Wallace College has revised the *Study Guide* and *Test Items*.

- **Study Guide.** Each unit in the *Study Guide* parallels the format and organization of the text and includes a chapter overview, summary, list of key terms, list of key theories, completion exercises, true-false questions, answers to all exercises and questions and incorporates a short section on tips for effective studying in college.
- **Test Items.** This bank of over 1000 multiple-choice and true-false questions prepared by Dr. Treybig is drawn from all text materials and tests students' knowledge of facts, concepts, theories, and research. *Test Items* are available in book form and in computerized form. *Micro-Pac Test Bank*, a test-generating, editing, and authoring system for Apple II Series and IBM-PC and compatibles, is available for those with access to a computer. Wadsworth's *Tele-Testing Service* can generate tests for those without access to a computer. For more information please contact the Sales Service Department, Wadsworth Publishing Company, 10 Davis Drive, Belmont, Ca. 94002 (phone 415-595-2350).

A New Telecourse

Portrait of a Family is a new college-credit telecourse produced by the Southern California Consortium and offered in Fall 1988 by the PBS Adult Learning Service. *Marriages and Families*, Third Edition, was chosen as the text for the course on the basis of a national curriculum survey and consultation with a board of experienced marriage and family instructors. For more information please write (on school letterhead) to Ken Calhoun, Marketing Specialist, Southern California Consortium, 5400 Orange Avenue, Suite 215, Cypress, Ca. 90630.

Acknowledgments

This book is the result of a joint effort on our part; neither one of us could have conceptualized or written it alone. We want to thank some of the many people who helped us.

The people at Wadsworth Publishing Company have been professionally competent and a pleasure to work with. We are especially grateful to Sheryl Fullerton, sociology editor, who worked with us again to shepherd this edition to publication, providing professional guidance and personal support. Thanks also to Steve Rutter, vice president, for his vision of the project and his faith in us; to Judith McKibben, special projects editor, for her comments and help on each chapter; to Sandra Craig, senior production editor, for her skillful management of the production of the book; and to MaryEllen Podgorski, designer, for supervising the selection of photographs.

Special thanks go to Shirley Scritchfield, Creighton University, who lent Agnes Riedmann several personally owned issues of *Journal of Marriage and the Family* for what was to be a weekend and turned out to be several months. Agnes Riedmann also especially acknowledges her mother, Ann Langley Czerwinski, Ph.D., who helped significantly with this revision.

Sam Walker contributed to the book by entertaining Mary Ann Lamanna. Revision is a lengthy and wearing process, but movies, reggae, and Pefferoni's pizza did as much as anything to make completion of this third edition possible.

Reviewers gave us many helpful suggestions for revising the book, and although we have not incorporated all of their suggestions, we considered them all carefully and used many. The review process made a substantial contribution to the revision. Peter Stein and Norval Glenn were especially helpful. The reviewers were Carol Darling, Florida State University; James Dedic, Fullerton College; Norval Glenn, University of Texas, Austin; Lynda M. Glennon, Rollins College; C. J. Harris, Purdue University; Maggie P. Hayes, University of Oklahoma; Thomas B. Holman, Brigham Young University; Ross A. Klein, Iowa State University; Jerry Michel, Memphis State University; Lois T. Mickle, Oklahoma State University; Ann Page, Appalachian State University; Peter J. Stein, William Paterson College; Marilyn Story, University of Northern Iowa; Mary Poston Tanner, University of Tennessee, Chattanooga; David L. Treybig, Baldwin-Wallace College.

Students and faculty members who tell us of their interest in the book are a special inspiration.

To all of the people who gave their time and gave of themselves—interviewees, students, our families and friends—many thanks.

Mary Ann Lamanna
Agnes Riedmann

Prologue: A New Look at a Familiar World

*We are neither totally
victims of systems nor
totally captains of our
own souls.*

CATHERINE CHILMAN

Americans are enthusiastic yet apprehensive about marriage. More than 90 percent marry at some time during their lives. This percentage hasn't changed radically during this century; most Americans continue to seek lasting happiness in marriage. We continue to expect a family to provide us with a "haven in a heartless world" (Lasch, 1977).

Yet Americans have reason to be fearful about their chances of finding such happiness in marriage. The high divorce rate has called into question the stability of the institution. As far back as the late nineteenth century the great sociologist Emile Durkheim observed that "moral calmness and tranquility," once the promise of marriage, are replaced by "uneasiness" (1951:273). Some contemporary sociologists speak of "the reconceptualization of marriage as a nonpermanent relationship" (Safilios-Rothschild, 1983:306) and argue that the family has been so shaken up that "all bets are off" (Wiley, 1985:22). But amid this concern, we are hopeful.

One reason we continue to hope is because, in the words of sociologists Brigitte and Peter Berger, "We may assume that close significant relationships are important throughout life for the maintenance of identity and meaning." Moreover,

what is peculiar about the modern situation is that the marriage partner has been culturally defined as *the most significant other* in adult life. . . . Marriage occupies a privileged status among the significant validation relationships for adults in our society [Berger and Berger, 1983:165]. ▪

However, hoping alone won't make emotionally satisfying marriages, though it may help. Many American marriages can and do last. But maintaining a marriage requires work and commitment. It also requires knowledge of what you're doing, and that theme represents a good part of what this book is all about.

YOU AND *MARRIAGES AND FAMILIES*

This course is different from others you could be taking. It is not intended to prepare you for a particular occupation. Instead, it has two other goals: first, to make you more conscious of the personal decisions you must make throughout your life and of the cultural influences that affect those decisions; and second, to help you understand yourself and your family situations.

You'll see that we're going to use the term *family* rather loosely, so that we can talk about different sexual and family living arrangements in the United States today. For the institution of marriage and the family has been undergoing change, as the box "Some Facts About Today's Marriages and Families" suggests. In fact, the flexibility of the family has been vital to its success, as Americans have found ways to adapt it to contemporary life (Chilman, 1978a).

The flexibility that has allowed us to keep marriages and families as cherished institutions, however, has also created many new situations requiring serious decisions. As marriage has become less rigidly structured, people have made fewer choices "once and for all." Many people reexamine their decisions about marriage and family throughout the full course of their lives, continually reassessing and reevaluating their relationships. Thus, choice is an important emphasis of this book.

It's Your Choice

Not many years ago, people weren't as intent as they are today on choosing their own life-style. Many young men assumed their father's occupations without question; the majority of young women grew up to be homemakers as their mothers had been. Similarly, people expected to fall in love, marry, have children, raise them, and wait for grandchildren.

This pattern has changed. At every turn we must make choices. Will we marry young or embark on a career first? Will we marry at all? Do we believe in staying married even if we're unhappy? These are just a few of the choices people must make; there are many others. With few guidelines available, it can be difficult to know what is the right decision.

The Pressures and Freedom of Choosing

This book rests on the assumption that the best possible way for us to make decisions about our personal lives is to make them knowledgeably. It helps to know something about all the alternatives; it also helps to know what kinds of social pressures affect our decisions. As we'll soon see, people are influenced by the beliefs and values of their society. In a very real way, we and our personal decisions and attitudes are products of our environment.

But in just as real a way, people are free to influence society. If you don't agree with something in this text, you can write us; your opinion may influence ours. Similarly, every time you participate in class discussions, you help to shape the mood, tone, and content of the class. Individuals create social change by continually offering new insights to their groups.[1]

We can apply this view to the phenomenon of living together, or cohabitation. Not long ago, it was widely accepted that unmarried couples who lived together were "immoral." But in the seventies college students challenged university restrictions on cohabitation, and many people, students and nonstudents, young and old, chose to live together. As cohabitation rates increased, societal attitudes changed. Consequently, it is now less difficult for people to choose this option. While we are influenced by the society around us, we are also free to influence it. And we do that every time we make a choice.

Personal Troubles and Societal Influences

We've stated that a purpose of this text is to help people better understand themselves and their situations. One way to do this is to begin to see yourself as a member of society, not only influencing it but also being influenced by it.

People's private lives are affected by what is happening in the society around them. Many of

---

1. We have drawn this theme from Peter Berger and Thomas Luckmann, *The Social Construction of Reality* (1966). According to these social scientists, people *externalize* their own ideas, impressions, opinions, and ways of doing things (that is, they voice them or act them out). In the process of externalization, things may come to seem real, to become part of assumed common knowledge. For instance, "everyone knows" that friendly people are more likeable. Yet in France the person who is most liked is the one who has "reserve," a posture of aloof dignity: Friendly people are viewed as tasteless. (At the same time, individuals often internalize externalized impressions or points of view. They begin to believe that commonly held opinions are true—a process described in Chapter 1.)

their personal troubles are shared by others, and these troubles often reflect societal influences.[2] When a young mother, for example, feels lonesome and bored in the role of homemaker, her own lack of inventiveness may not be at issue as much as society's tendency to isolate her in this role. Similarly, when a family breadwinner is laid off from work, the cause may lie not in his or her lack of ambition, but in the economy's inability to provide jobs (see Figure P·1). This text assumes that people need to understand themselves (and their problems) in the context of the larger society.

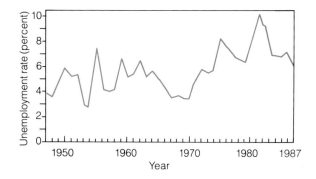

Figure P·1

Unemployment rate in the United States, 1947–87. To what extent can personal problems be viewed apart from their socioeconomic context? (Source: Data from Flaim, 1979; *New York Times*, August 1, 1982; Bureau of Labor Statistics, July 7, 1984; *New York Times*, Dec. 6, 1986; Klott, 1987)

CULTURAL VALUES AND PERSONAL CHOICES

People are free to make choices. But their alternatives are limited by their environment. In the United States before 1800, for example, relatively few couples considered using birth control to limit their family's size. But as cultural values began to encourage smaller families and as birth control technology became increasingly available, fertility began to decline (Wells, 1985:28–47). Individuals' choices depend in large part on the alternatives that exist in their social environment and on cultural values and attitudes toward those alternatives.

But cultural values can contradict one another. By the 1850s in the United States, for example, marriage guides included information on birth control techniques, and newspaper advertisements regularly offered various chemicals and mechanical devices that could be used to limit births. At the same time, federal legislation was passed in 1873 that limited the circulation of birth control information through the mail (Wells, 1985:50–51). American values—particularly those that pertain to marriages and families—are often contradictory. The result is that individuals often experience **ambivalence,** or mutually conflicting feelings or thoughts. This section examines two groups of contradictory American values that can create an ambivalence about marriages and families. The first are family values, or familism; the second, individualistic values.[3]

Family Values

Family values (familism) permeate American culture. These values, such as family togetherness, stability, and loyalty, focus on the family group as a whole.

Togetherness Many of us have an image of the ideal family relationship in which family members spend considerable time together and enjoy each other's company. The time that individual family members spend away from one another—at work, at school, or at play—is of secondary importance.

2. This theme is drawn from C. Wright Mills, *The Sociological Imagination.* In Mills's words people must begin to grasp the "problems of biography, of history and of their interactions within a society" (1959, 1973:6).

3. Such contradictory family and individual values are part of a general "value cleavage" growing out of changes in our society. Philip Slater (1976) in *The Pursuit of Loneliness* contrasts the "old" culture, which stresses social forms, with the "new" emphasis on personal expression. Ralph Turner (1976) points to a growing emphasis on acts of self-expression, as opposed to past self-realization through dutiful performance of accepted social roles.

BOX P · 1

SOME
FACTS
ABOUT
TODAY'S
MARRIAGES
AND
FAMILIES

Marriage and family aren't what they were back in the fifties. But they haven't changed as radically as some people feared they would—or thought they should. What do marriage and the family look like today?

1. People have been postponing marriage in recent years. Median age at first marriage, after a half century of decline, has been rising since the early sixties. The median age at first marriage for women, 23.3 years, is the highest since the government started keeping records in 1890, while for men it is higher (25.5 years) than in any year since 1900 (U.S. Bureau of the Census, 1986a).

2. In the 1960s, 96 percent of the adult population had married at one time; during the 1970s that figure dropped to 93 percent, and it is likely to go down to 90 percent for women born during the 1950s (Thornton and Freedman, 1983). This is still a high percentage, of course; most Americans do marry eventually.

3. Despite a slight decline in the remarriage rate in recent years, remarriages comprise an increasingly large proportion of all marriages. In 1982, 45 percent of all marriages were remarriages for one or both partners, compared to 33 percent in 1972 (U.S. National Center for Health Statistics, 1985a).

4. Unmarried-couple households tripled between 1970 and 1982 (U.S. Bureau of the Census, 1983a) and have continued to increase gradually since then. Just over 4 percent of all couples living together are unmarried (U.S. Bureau of the Census, 1986a).

5. Premarital sex has increased, especially among women. About two-thirds of ever-married women age 15–44 surveyed in 1982 had had sexual intercourse before marriage (U.S. National Center for Health Statistics, 1985c). Currently, an estimated 57 percent of unmarried American women have experienced intercourse by age 17 (Louis Harris poll, 1986).

6. The rate of illegitimate births is high, especially among adolescents and young adult women. The rate of illegitimate births rose to a peak in the mid-sixties, dropped in the seventies, and rose again in the late seventies to previously unseen levels. In 1983, 20 percent of all births were illegitimate, and 58 percent of all black births occurred outside legal marriage.

   Out-of-wedlock childbearing is now more concentrated among women in their twenties than among teenagers. This is partly because women in their twenties are less likely to be married than in the past, and partly because the aging of the baby-boom cohort (children born during the post–World War II "baby boom") means there are now fewer women in their teens and more in their twenties (U.S. National Center for Health Statistics, 1985b).

7. Overall, fertility has declined drastically since the fifties and early sixties. The total fertility rate (which represents the number of children born to a hypothetical typical woman) was 1.8 in 1984, compared to 2.9 in 1965 and over 3.6 in 1955 (U.S. Bureau of the Census, 1986b; 1987).

   Since the early 1970s women have delayed childbearing, so that an increasing number of women are having their first child in their thirties.

Parenthood is no longer taken for granted, and levels of childlessness among women in their thirties are higher than they have been for over thirty years. In 1984, 24 percent of women age 30–34 had not had any children, compared with 12 percent in 1970 (U.S. National Center for Health Statistics, 1985b).

8. About half of all families today contain no children under the age of 18 (U.S. Bureau of the Census, 1986b). These are couples who have no children yet or who do not plan to have children or couples whose children have reached 18 and have left home.

9. The rate of divorce has more than doubled since 1965, peaking in 1979 and dropping slightly since then (U.S. National Center for Health Statistics, 1986a). Consequently, the proportion of the population currently married has decreased. For example, the percentage of white males age 35–39 in intact (first or later) marriages fell from 85.7 percent in 1970 to 80.5 percent in 1980, while the percentage of black men dropped from 69.5 percent to 60.8 percent (Sanders, 1986).

Projections indicate that in the future less than 50 percent of marriages will last a lifetime, and 60 percent of second marriages are expected to end in divorce (Thornton and Freedman, 1983; Norton and Moorman, 1987).

10. As a consequence of divorce and unmarried parenthood, about one-quarter of all families with children had only one parent present in 1984 (U.S. Bureau of the Census, 1986a). Predictions are that "60 percent of today's 2-year-olds will have lived in a single-parent household by age 18" (Brophy, 1986).

The increasing number of single-parent households, 90 percent of which are female headed, are likely to have relatively low incomes. This "feminization of poverty," as some observers have called it, results mainly from the fact that separation and divorce reduce income for female-headed households in every income category, while the burden of maintaining the household and supporting children remains. For middle- and higher-income households, for example, divorce reduces household income by one-third and one-half, respectively (Weiss, 1984).

11. More mothers are either employed or returning to school. Currently, 55 percent of all women are in the labor force (U.S. Bureau of Labor Statistics, 1986a), and employment among married mothers of preschool children has increased significantly—from 18 percent in 1960 to 53.4 percent in 1985 (U.S. Bureau of the Census, 1986b).

12. More husbands accept the idea that they should share housework and participate more actively in child rearing. However, actual behavior falls far short of the ideal: One recent review concludes that "there is still strong support for a fundamental specialization and division of labor between husbands and wives" (Thornton and Freedman, 1983).

BOX P · 1

Continued

13. More and more people are living alone. The average size of a household in the United States dropped from 3.14 persons in 1970 to 2.71 in 1984 (U.S. Bureau of the Census, 1985a). This reflects at least three trends: first, smaller families due to declining fertility; second, an increase in single-parent households, which tend to be smaller; and third, a growing number of "nonfamily households," most of which are single-person households.

14. Young adults, however, are increasingly likely to be living with their parents. In 1984 the Census Bureau reported that 62 percent of men and 47 percent of women between the ages of 18 and 24 were still—or again—living at home. These percentages were up from 54 percent for men and 41 percent for women in 1970 (U.S. Bureau of the Census, 1985b). This trend seems to reflect not only economic changes (higher unemployment rate and lower real incomes) but also changes in marital patterns (high divorce rates and delayed marriage). For example, the proportion of women age 30–34 who had never married was more than twice as high in 1984 as in 1970.

15. The proportion of the population over age 65 has increased by one-third since 1960. The elderly maintain independent living arrangements as long as possible and, for the most part, maintain their own households or live with family members rather than in institutions. Fifty-three percent of people over 65 were husbands and wives in their own households (75 percent of men, 38 percent of women); 30 percent lived alone; 14 percent lived with other relatives, mostly children; and 2 percent lived with nonrelatives (U.S. Bureau of the Census, 1986b).

16. Americans are more optimistic about family life than they were at the beginning of the decade. Fifty-three percent of those questioned agreed that "family life for others has gotten better in the last fifteen years," compared with 37 percent who answered positively in 1980. Ninety-three percent report themselves "very satisfied" or "mostly satisfied" with their own family life in 1986 (Gallup, 1986).

Togetherness, in other words, represents an important part of family life.

Stability Despite the demands for societal change that came out of the late 1960s, most Americans are apprehensive about change. Journalists have made much of the nostalgia syndrome in which contemporary Americans yearn for the "good old days." On a more personal level we also resist change. Why must our parents sell the house we grew up in? Why must our good friends move away? For many of us, the family is an important source of stability, and we are disturbed when it is disrupted.

Loyalty Like stability and togetherness, loyalty is an American value. The group most deserving of our loyalty, we believe, is our family. Most of us who are married today have vowed publicly to stay with our partners as long as we live. We expect our partners, our parents, our children, and often even our more distant relatives to remain loyal to the family unit.

Loyalty, stability, and togetherness are American values that we have learned to associate with marriages and families. Because of these family values, home is sometimes considered "the place where you can scratch anywhere you itch."

Individualism

If the values just described were the only threads holding our cultural fabric together, family life might be simpler. Just as family values permeate our American society, however, so also do **individualistic values** of **self-fulfillment** and personal change, both of which are associated with a sense of urgency.

Self-Fulfillment Developing one's individual talents and interests is an American goal. We cherish success, not just because of its frequent financial benefits but also because it makes us feel good about ourselves. Many people attend college as an avenue to a personally satisfying occupation, or as an opportunity for self-development, or both. Adult education, running, reading, and midlife reentry into the work force are just a few other examples of experiences individuals pursue in the quest for self-fulfillment.

Personal Change Self-fulfillment implies personal change, a second value of individualism. Americans change jobs and areas of residence. They join clubs, and later, should their interests change, they join different clubs. Americans lose contact with old friends only to make new ones. As we modify our physical and social surroundings, we modify ourselves. We alter our interests, our opinions, and our attitudes. We call this self-modification *personal change.*

Urgency The values of individual fulfillment and personal growth are often associated with a sense of urgency. We all know "you only live once"; occasions for self-fulfillment may be at a premium. As Americans, a part of our cultural milieu is the belief that it's foolish to put off until tomorrow what we can do today.

A Family of Individuals

Personal growth and self-fulfillment in a climate of urgency are American values, just as are the family values of togetherness, stability, and loyalty. This juxtaposition of opposites creates a tension: Where is it leading us?

Sociologist Lucile Duberman argues that individualism may soon eclipse family values in America:

A new ideology is growing in this country and it exalts the individual. It impels us to reach more into ourselves and to rely on ourselves.... It urges us to withdraw from dependence on others, to avoid entanglements, and to keep our relationships temporary and tentative. Individualism ... is becoming the supreme ethic. Our struggle is to free ourselves from involvement with all others, including the family, and to recognize that others do not really understand who we are, what we want, why we do as we do, or what we hope to become. The key is oneself—nobody else, not even one's family can ultimately be considered trustworthy [1977:22]. ▪

Duberman's concern is echoed in the recent book *Habits of the Heart,* an important analysis of public and private life in contemporary America. Arguing that our culture's recent emphasis on self-fulfillment has undercut the traditional valuation of commitment and community, the authors warn:

If love and marriage are seen primarily in terms of psychological gratification, they may fail to fulfill their older social function of providing people with stable, committed relationships that tie them into the larger society.... Tensions between these partially conflicting conceptions of love and marriage are endemic in our society today [Bellah et al., 1985:85]. ▪

We echo the implication of this last sentence: People value both individualism *and* familism. Tension between individual gratification and commitment to others creates ambivalence about marriage and families. How much individual fulfillment can people pursue and still maintain family togetherness? Or conversely, how much personal freedom must be sacrificed in the act of marrying or becoming a parent?

Americans today have the difficult task of reconciling family and individualistic values. People can understand themselves better if they recognize that their ambivalence may well result from cultural contradictions. One source of this understanding is personal experience: Most of you have probably felt the opposing pulls of individual and family needs. But as we'll see in the next few paragraphs, personal experience does not always provide a foundation broad enough for important decisions.

■ This 1928 photograph of a Catholic wedding party is also a portrait of a small Lithuanian community in Pennsylvania, where everyone was related to or knew everyone else. Among the bridesmaids are two of the bride's five sisters. (Can you find them?) This couple had five children before the husband, a coal miner, left his wife a young widow. Wedding pictures tell different and similar stories; throughout this book, we'll examine changing patterns in the institution of marriage.

PERSONAL EXPERIENCE AND MYTH AND HOW TO SEE BEYOND THEM

Two basic ideas are probably becoming apparent. The first is how important it is for individuals to be knowledgeable about the family decisions they make. The second is that many forces influence those decisions. At the risk of further complicating the issue, it is worthwhile to examine a few more influences we must be aware of before we can become informed decision makers. The first of these is personal experience; the second, the popular mythology that exists about marriage and families.

The "Blinders" of Personal Experience

Most people grow up in some form of family and know something about what marriages and families are. But while personal experience provides us with information, it can also act as blinders. We assume that our own family is "normal" or typical. If you grew up in a large family, for example, in which a grandparent or an aunt or uncle shared your home, you probably assumed (for a short time at least) that everyone had a big family. Perceptions like this are usually outgrown at an early age, but there may be more subtle, not-yet-apparent differences between your family experience and that of others. For instance, the members of your family may spend a lot of time alone, perhaps reading, whereas in other families, if a family member—adult or child—is not talking with others around the kitchen table, it may be cause for alarm.

Personal experience, then, can make us think that most people's family lives are similar to our own when this is often not the case. The box "A Cross-Cultural Look at Marriages and Families" lists a number of differences between American families and those of other cultures.

In looking at marriage and family customs around the world, we can easily see the error of assuming that all marriage and family practices are like our own. But not only do the traditional American assumptions about family life not hold true in other places, they also frequently don't even describe our own society. Black, Hispanic, and Asian fami-

lies; Jewish, Protestant, and Catholic families; upper-class, middle-class, and lower-class families all represent some subtle (often not-so-subtle) differences in life-style (Wiseman, 1985). However, the tendency to use the most familiar yardstick for measuring things is a strong one; even social scientists have fallen victim to it.

Myth Versus Reality

As we have just seen, it can be a mistake to generalize too broadly from one's own family experience. Another frequent error is to accept the "truth" of myths.

Myths are cultural beliefs, often inaccurate, about the way things are. Myths can be dangerous. When they portray idealized behavior patterns, they often leave real people wondering what's wrong with themselves. Who hasn't felt guilty at some time about not being a model son, daughter, or parent?

We will look more closely at two myths about marriages and families. The first pertains to the "natural" form of families; the second, to the "ideal" relationship that exists in a "good" marriage.

Myth 1: The "Typical" Family For many Americans the word *family* creates a mental image of a couple with two children. They live in their own (mortgaged) home and own at least one car. While the mother may work either full- or part-time, the father is the principal breadwinner. This mythical family structure continues to seem real for many people.

Actually, there is statistically no natural American family (see Figure P-2). Only 28 percent of American households in 1985 took the form of the "typical" nuclear family (complete with married parents and their offspring). In 1986 only 20 percent of American families with children under 18 contained a father-breadwinner and mother-homemaker. Others were single-parent families or families with a working mother or unemployed father (Brophy, 1986).

Myth 2: The "Ideal" Marriage A second popular myth concerns the "ideal" marriage. Americans' expectations concerning marriages include the idea that people should and do marry only (or,

BOX P · 2

A CROSS-CULTURAL LOOK AT MARRIAGES AND FAMILIES

Some features of family life that we take for granted do not necessarily occur in all cultures. How many of the following statements have you assumed to be characteristic of what is "normal" or universal?

1. *Marriage is monogamous.* When we think of marriage we think of **monogamy,** the sexually exclusive union of one man and one woman. Actually, only 20 percent of the world's cultures insist on monogamous marriage. Many societies permit **polygamy** (a man's having more than one wife) and practice both polygamy and monogamy. In some societies adultery is accepted, though often limited to certain classes of partners.

2. *Young people select their own marriage partners.* Only a few societies allow young people to choose partners without the approval of parents or other relatives. Often, though not always, the child's preference is deferred to, at least somewhat.

3. *"Love" is universal and provides the basis for marriage.* Many Americans believe that marriage should be the outcome of falling in love, but love is not considered a reason for marriage in all cultures. The notion of romantic love seems to be a phenomenon peculiar to Western culture.

4. *The nuclear family is a separate economic unit.* We assume that members of a **nuclear family**—husband, wife, and children—share income, property, and expenses. They buy necessities together as a unit. In our society one or more adults work to support the nuclear family. Other relatives or adult children are usually not included in this economic pool. In other societies the economic unit is the extended family. In an **extended family** three or more generations, including, perhaps, relatives besides parents and children, share work and resources. In still other cases the wife and husband may each be

at the very least, primarily) for love. People anticipate that married lovers will become a "fused unity" in which individuals' identities will easily merge into one secure and happy "couple identity." According to the myth, true love will flourish effortlessly, "conquering all" and at the same time "fulfilling all needs for love, affection, romance, sex, companionship, and friendship" (Crosby, 1976:19). In Rubin Carson's words most people expect their marriage (or other deeply committed relationship) to act as "a kind of cornucopia whence all blessings flow" (1978:6).

This view of the ideal relationship is an especially dangerous myth. According to family therapist Linda Carson, " 'Happily ever after' may be one of the most misleading and therefore destructive

expressions in our literature" (in R. Carson, 1978:7). One of the most misleading aspects of the myth is the idea that things happen automatically. A woman married eighteen years expressed her views: "People go into marriages expecting them to 'work.' That's crazy! Marriages don't 'work.' You've got to *make* them work."

In sum, it is not a myth to say that love can flourish in a committed relationship—it can. But an emotionally strong relationship demands that both partners be aware of their own and each other's emotional and sexual needs, that they know how to communicate with each other supportively, and that they know how to deal effectively with conflict. We will address these topics throughout this text (particularly in Chapters 3 and 9).

economically self-sufficient. Among the Hopi Indians, for example, it is the wife who owns farmland, orchards, livestock, and water holes. They are not joint property.

5. *Families contain an economically dependent wife, with the husband as primary breadwinner.* We may think of working women as a new development, but in most societies wives produce food or other items as needed for household use, along with goods for the market. In West Africa, for example, women conduct most of the trading in the marketplace.

6. *The members of a nuclear family reside together.* We assume that one hallmark of a family is that its members live together. Yet in other cultures mothers and children do not always reside with fathers. The father may live next door or at some distance, or he may rotate among several wives.[4]

In what ways are expectations concerning marriage in other cultures more—and less—realistic than ours? Would you like to live where you couldn't choose your own marriage partner? Are there nuclear families in our society whose members do not reside together? Why?

---

4. For additional examples of cross-cultural variations in family life, see William N. Stephens, *The Family in Cross-Cultural Perspective* (New York: Holt, Rinehart & Winston, 1963); Stuart Queen and Robert W. Habenstein (eds.), *The Family in Various Cultures,* 4th ed. (Philadelphia: Lippincott, 1974); and M. Kay Martin and Barbara Voorhies, *Female of the Species* (New York: Columbia University Press, 1975).

Scientific Investigation: Removing Blinders

Separating myth from reality is essential to an understanding of oneself and one's options; so is seeing beyond one's personal experience. It is not always easy, however, to distinguish fact and myth or to perceive what kinds of life-styles other people are choosing, with what consequences.

Surveys One way of learning about a group is through a **survey,** which communicates with a representative sample. Questionnaires (forms filled out by the person being studied) and interviews (face-to-face questioning) are both examples of survey methods.

One of the goals of this book is to separate myth from reality, thus providing a broader, more accurate picture of contemporary marriage and family experiences. To do this, we rely on data gathered systematically from many sources through techniques of **scientific investigation,** from which it often is possible to generalize. The techniques— surveys, laboratory observation and experiments, naturalistic observation, case studies, longitudinal studies, historical and cross-cultural data—will be referred to throughout this text, so we will briefly describe them now.

Surveys are part of our everyday experience. When conducting scientific surveys, researchers either engage in face-to-face or telephone interviews or distribute questionnaires to be answered

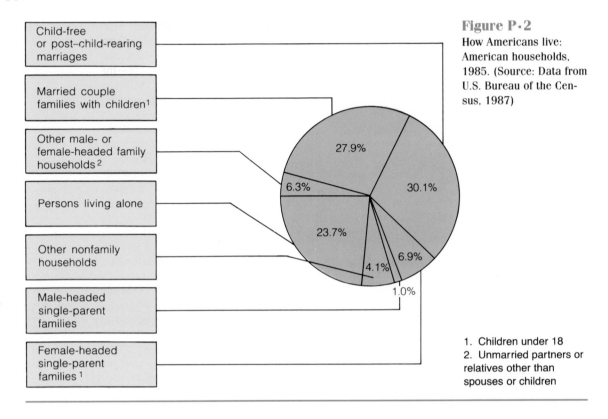

Figure P·2

How Americans live: American households, 1985. (Source: Data from U.S. Bureau of the Census, 1987)

Child-free or post–child-rearing marriages

Married couple families with children[1]

Other male- or female-headed family households[2]

Persons living alone

Other nonfamily households

Male-headed single-parent families

Female-headed single-parent families[1]

27.9%

30.1%

6.3%

23.7%

4.1%

6.9%

1.0%

1. Children under 18
2. Unmarried partners or relatives other than spouses or children

and returned. Questions are often structured so that after a statement, such as "I like to go places with my partner," the respondent has answers from which to choose. The possible responses might be: Always, Usually, Sometimes, Not very often, Never. Researchers spend much energy and time wording such "close-ended" questions so that, as much as possible, all respondents will interpret questions in the same way.

Interview questions can also be open-ended. For example, the question might be, "How do you feel about going places with your partner?" or "Tell me about going places with your partner." Many social scientists and respondents alike feel that open-ended questions give those answering more opportunity to express how they really feel or how they actually believe than do more structured survey questions, which require people to choose from a predetermined set of responses.

Once the returns are in, survey responses are counted and statistically analyzed, usually with computers. After the survey data have been ana-

lyzed, the scientists conducting the research begin to draw conclusions about the respondents' attitudes and feelings. Then the scientists must decide to whom their conclusions can be applied. Do they apply *only* to those whom they interviewed directly, for example, or to other people similar to the respondents? In order to ensure, moreover, that their conclusions can be generalized (applied to people other than those directly questioned), survey researchers do their best to ensure that their respondents will comprise a *representative sample* of the people they intend to draw conclusions about. Popular magazine surveys, for example, are seldom representative of the total American public. A survey on attitudes about premarital sex in *Cosmopolitan* or *Playboy* likely will yield different findings than one in *Family Living* or *Reader's Digest.* Consequently, it would not be scientifically accurate to generalize from a set of conclusions drawn from a *Playboy* or *Cosmopolitan* survey about how all American adults feel about premarital sex. In the same way, results from a survey in which all respondents are white, middle-class college students cannot be considered representative of Americans in general. Researchers and political pollsters may, however, use random samples, in which households or individuals are randomly selected from a comprehensive list (see Babbie, 1982, for a more detailed discussion). A random sample is considered to be representative of the population from which it is drawn. A national random sample of approximately 1,500 people can validly represent the U.S. population.

Survey research has certain advantages over other inquiry techniques. The main advantage is uniformity. Presumably, all respondents are asked exactly the same questions in the same way. Also, surveys are relatively efficient means of gathering large amounts of information. And, provided the sample is designed to be accurately representative, conclusions drawn from that information can be applied to a large number of people.

Surveys have disadvantages, too. Because they ask uniform or standardized questions, "surveys overlook the subtle varieties of attitudes and conditions that exist for people. The respondent who protests that none of the standardized answers is a satisfactory one presents a problem for survey research" (Babbie, 1977:62).

Other disadvantages of surveys result from respondents' tendency to say what they think they *should*, rather than what they actually believe. Social scientists refer to this problem as the tendency of respondents to give *normative answers*. If asked whether or how often physical abuse occurs in the home, for example, even—and perhaps especially—those who often engage in family violence might be reluctant to say so.

Another disadvantage of surveys, closely akin to the tendency of respondents to say what they think they should, is the tendency of respondents to forget or to reinterpret what happened in the past. (Because of this, social scientists recognize the value of longitudinal studies—studies in which the same group of respondents is surveyed or interviewed intermittently over a period of years.) For this reason most researchers agree that asking about attitudes or events that occurred in the past seldom yields valid results. Another disadvantage of surveys, again closely akin to respondents' tendency to give normative answers, is a problem particular to interviewer surveys. Depending on the sex, age, race, and general style of the person questioning you, you might tend, even without knowing

it, to give a certain response. Scientists call this tendency *interview effects of an interviewer*. Certain characteristics of the interviewer—age, sex, race, clothing style, hair length—may tend to elicit a certain kind of response. A 45-year-old male, for example, asked about his experience concerning sexual impotence, can be expected to reply differently to a male interviewer of 20 than he would to one of 60—or to a female of any age. Perhaps the most significant disadvantage of every research survey is that what respondents say may not accurately reflect what they do.

Laboratory Observation and Experiments

Because of the relative ease of conducting surveys, the flexibility of the format, and the availability of samples (even a classroom sample can provide useful information), surveys have been the primary source of information about family living. Other techniques are also used, however. In a laboratory observation or **experiment** behaviors are carefully monitored or measured under controlled conditions. These methods are particularly useful in measuring physiological changes associated with anger, fear, sexual response (as discussed in Chapter 4), or behavior that is difficult to report verbally—in family problem solving, for example.

The experimental technique is best explained by an example. In 1965 sociologist Elaine Walster was studying the topic of romantic love, particularly "love on the rebound." She hypothesized (made an educated guess) that whenever a person's self-esteem is lowered, because of a recently broken relationship or for some other reason, "a new relationship is actively sought out to regain self-esteem." She then set up an experiment to test her assumption. A group of young women volunteered to take part in an experiment described as an assessment of personality traits. On their way to the room where personality tests were to be given, each encountered a young man—presumably by accident. The young man began a conversation and asked the young woman for a date. Then the women did the official experiment, taking several personality tests. After completing them, they were shown the "results"—not their actual scores, but rather bogus scores assigned at random. The results given to some of the women were flattering, others were given negative evaluations. After the women looked over their results, they were asked for honest appraisals of several persons they knew or had just met. On the average, women whose self-esteem had been lowered by receiving negative "results" of the tests (experimental group) made a positive appraisal of the men who had approached them just before the experiment, whereas women whose self-esteem had been bolstered by the "results" (control group) gave a more neutral response. The researcher concluded that these outcomes supported the hypothesis (Walster, 1965).

This example can illustrate several features of experimental research. In an experiment subjects from a pool of similar participants will be randomly assigned to groups (experimental and control groups) that will be given different experiences (treatments) (the treatments in this experiment are the false high or low test results). If the two groups differ in their behavior according to some measure (here the measure is favorable evaluation of the young man), this outcome is presumed to be a result of the treatment, since no other differences are presumed to exist between the randomly assigned groups. The specific results of the lab experiment (that false negative ratings led to high ratings of the attractiveness of the young man) are considered to provide evidence for the more general hypothesis that low self-esteem leads to interest in a new relationship.

A true experiment has these features of random assignment and experimental manipulation of the important variable. Laboratory *observation*, on the other hand, simply means that behavior is *observed* in a laboratory setting, but does not involve random assignment or experimental manipulation of a variable. Experiments are often conducted in a laboratory setting because of the greater control possible. Some experiments, however, unlike the one described above, may be conducted in a field, or real-life, setting. A laboratory setting does permit more careful observation and measurement than a natural setting, however.

Experiments, like surveys, have both advantages and disadvantages. One advantage of experiments is that social scientists can observe human behavior directly, rather than depending, as they do in surveys, on what respondents *tell* them about what they think or do. The experimenter can control the experience of the subjects and can ensure, to some extent, the initial similarity of subjects in the two groups. A disadvantage of this research technique is that the behaviors being observed are taking place in an artificial situation. Walster's experiment, for example, relied on the assumption that getting a low score on a personality test was

equivalent to having recently broken an important romantic relationship. Whether the artificial or simulated testing situation is analogous to real life is debatable. The fact that the subject pool is often drawn from college classrooms and is not very representative of the general population is another limitation. And "volunteer" subjects may instead be draftees or may be recruited in response to financial incentives, raising questions about the authenticity of their responses.

Naturalistic Observation Of course, many aspects of human behavior and interaction just don't lend themselves to study in laboratory settings, so social scientists use another technique in an attempt to overcome virtually all artificiality (or as much as possible). In **naturalistic observation** the researcher lives with a family or social group or spends extensive time with family or group members, carefully recording their activities, conversations, gestures, and other aspects of everyday life. The researcher then attempts to discern family interrelationships and communication patterns and to draw implications and conclusions from them for understanding family behavior in general. The following passage gives the flavor of naturalistic observation done by a serious social scientist:

Around five-thirty in the afternoon we all left for a picnic at the lake in Latham Park. Preparations had been very hectic because Dr. and Mrs. Jones dawdled and delayed a great deal and did not plan. . . .

During the preparations Dr. Jones kept insisting that many things did not have to be done but Mrs. Jones insisted they did, and her way prevailed.

Dr. Jones did not help with the lunch dishes, so Mrs. Jones did them herself. . . .

Mrs. Jones asked her husband to weed the garden and pick some corn while she was shopping, and he kept busy doing that. Bobby and Jackie took me for a long walk. . . .

When we started to build a fire at the picnic grounds we discovered that Mrs. Jones had left the grate at home, so there was nothing on which to broil the hamburgers. Dr. Jones became abusive and called her an idiot. When he was out of earshot she admitted to me that she had been stupid to forget it. He called out to her that she really never wanted to go on picnics, anyway, and that the reason she forgot the grate was probably because she didn't want to go. Meanwhile she dished out orange drinks and potato chips to the famished children, who were gathered around her [Henry, 1971:27–28]. ▪

The principal advantage of naturalistic observation is that it allows us to view family behavior as it actually happens in its own natural—as opposed to artificial—setting. The most significant disadvantage of this tool is that findings and conclusions may be highly subjective. That is, what is recorded, analyzed, and assumed to be accurate depends on what one or very few observers think is significant. Another drawback to naturalistic observation, which you may have already recognized, is that it requires enormous amounts of time to observe only a few families. And these families may not be representative of family living in general. Perhaps because of these disadvantages, very few studies use these techniques.

Clinicians' Case Studies   A fourth way that we get information about families is from **case studies** compiled by clinicians—psychologists, psychiatrists, marriage counselors, and social workers, who counsel persons with marriage and family problems. As they see individuals, couples, or whole families over a period of time, these counselors become acquainted with communication patterns and other interaction within families. Clinicians offer us knowledge about family behavior and attitudes by describing cases to us or by telling us about their conclusions based on a series of cases.

The advantages of case studies are the vivid detail and realistic flavor that enable us to vicariously experience the family life of others. The insights of the clinicians can be helpful.

But case studies also have weaknesses. There is always a subjective or personal element in the way the clinician views the family. Inevitably, any one person has a limited viewpoint. The clinicians' professional training may also lead them to over- or underemphasize certain aspects of family life and to "see" family behavior in a certain way. For example, psychiatrists traditionally have tended to assume that the assertiveness or career interests of women caused the development of marital and sexual problems (Chesler, 1972).

Furthermore, persons who present themselves for counseling may differ in important ways from those who do not. Most obviously, they may have more problems. For example, although psychia-

trists have reported that homosexuals in therapy have many emotional difficulties, studies of males not in therapy have concluded that homosexuals are no more likely to have mental health problems than heterosexuals (Hooker, 1963).

Longitudinal Studies   Finally, **longitudinal studies** provide long-term information about individuals or groups, as a researcher or research group conducts follow-up investigations (by means of interviews or questionnaires), most often for several years after an initial study has been made. Observational or experimental studies could be repeated, but this is rarely done.

A study in which the same community, though not precisely the same individuals, is resurveyed would be considered a longitudinal study. The city of "Middletown" (Muncie, Indiana) was recently restudied by a research team (Caplow et al., 1982), some fifty years after the initial community study (Lynd and Lynd, 1929).

Historical and Cross-Cultural Data   The Middletown study of family life reached back into the nineteenth century through the use of historical records, a research approach that is becoming more and more common in the study of the family. Some interesting work by social historians on the family in France (Ariès, 1962) and in England (Laslett, 1969; Laslett and Wall, 1972) began to attract the interest of sociologists about twenty years ago. Conversely, more and more historians have adopted the quantitative methods characteristic of sociology. Family life of past times is presently being investigated by both historians and sociologists through the use of such documents as population and tax registers, diaries, advice manuals, legal documents and other archival materials, and popular literature.

Sociologists, especially those who place more emphasis on cross-cultural comparison than we do in this text, continue to look to anthropological fieldwork for information on family life and structure in societies in both developed and developing nations. They also make use of anthropological data that have been compiled in a systematic way, such as the Human Relations Area Files, in which various features of a multitude of societies are described in a standard format.

The Application of Scientific Techniques   All research tools "represent a compromise." Each "has its special strengths and weaknesses" (Babbie, 1977:62). The strengths of one research tool, however, can make up for the weaknesses of another. Findings that result from direct observations, for example, supplement survey reports in an important way. While the former allow scientists to observe actual behavior among a limited number of people, surveys provide information about attitudes and reported behavior about a vast number of persons. In order to get around the drawbacks of each technique, social scientists may combine two or more tools in their research (Denzin, 1970). Ideally, scientists examine one topic by several different methods. In general, the scientific conclusions in this text result from many studies and from various and complementary research tools. Despite the drawbacks and occasional blinders, the total body of information available from sociological, psychological, and counseling literature provides a reasonably accurate portrayal of marriage and family life today.

FAMILIES: A CONTEMPORARY DEFINITION

We have been talking about families throughout this prologue, and if one point has emerged clearly in your minds by now, it is probably that the term *family* is a broad one. What exactly is a family? We will use the following definition: A **family** is any sexually expressive or parent-child relationship in which (1) people live together with a commitment, in an intimate, interpersonal relationship; (2) the members see their identity as importantly attached to the group; and (3) the group has an identity of its own (Chilman, 1978a).

This definition is considerably less rigid than earlier social science definitions. Contrast it, for example, with that provided by Ernest Burgess and Harvey Locke, who, in their classic work, *The Family: From Institution to Companionship*, defined the family as "a group of persons united by the ties of marriage, blood, or adoption; constituting a single household; interacting and communicating with each other in their respective social roles (husband and wife, mother and father, son and daughter, brother and sister); and creating and maintaining a common culture" (1945:8). Notice the

emphasis on well-defined social roles and on legal and genetic ties ("marriage, blood, or adoption").

Social scientists continue to be concerned about the family's responsibly performing necessary social roles, such as child rearing. But many social scientists today (including us) refuse to limit families so precisely. According to the newer perspective, family members need not be bound by legal marriage or by blood or adoption, nor must they conform to "respective social roles." Thus, communes and cohabiting couples—both heterosexual and homosexual—may be considered families.[5] Nor do social scientists now believe that for a household to be a family *all* the roles mentioned—husband, wife, children—must be included. Single-parent households and childless unions are considered "families." And "roles" may be nontraditional: Social scientists no longer assume that a family has a male breadwinner and a female homemaker; and dual-career and reversed-role (working wife; "house husband") combinations are also considered to be families.

Another distinction between contemporary definitions and earlier ones has to do with family communication. While Burgess and Locke, for example, assume that family members communicate significantly with each other according to their respective social roles, the contemporary view stresses that significant family communication is not so constrained. Of course, wives, husbands, and other family members can and do communicate according to traditional family roles—or example, when parents discuss their child's schooling, dental visit, or behavior. But they also may communicate more intimately, confiding their private hopes, fears, and doubts, and, according to today's perspective, this is also significant family communication, even though it does not necessarily flow from family roles.

The two perspectives are alike in two significant ways. First, Burgess and Locke specify that family members live together. We would probably expand this definition to include commuter couples and noncustodial parents by saying that there is some living together or domesticity, though it may not be continuous. Second, Burgess and Locke pre-

---

5. This "liberalization" has affected others besides social scientists: Since June 1977, federal regulations permit unmarried low-income heterosexual and homosexual couples to qualify as families and live in public housing.

sume that family members are engaged in "creating and maintaining a common culture," a premise that corresponds to parts 2 and 3 of our contemporary definition. Family members still think of themselves as essential parts of a distinct and particular family group.

And the family can still be viewed as the ideal **primary group**—a term coined by sociologist Charles Horton Cooley (1909:23) almost eighty years ago to describe any group in which there is a close, face-to-face relationship.[6] In a primary group people communicate with one another as whole human beings. They laugh and cry together; they share experiences; they quarrel, too, because that's part of being close. The main reason people stay together in a primary group is simply that they want to. Primary groups give one the feeling of being accepted and liked for what one is.

MARRIAGES AND FAMILIES: THREE THEMES

Throughout this book we will develop three major themes. First, we acknowledge the tension between the individual and the societal environment and the many personal troubles that result from societal conditions or influences. Another source of conflict is the existence of contradictory cultural values. Second, we note the continuing need for decisions in family life. Creating and maintaining marriages and families require many personal decisions, and people continue to make decisions throughout their lives. Third, we recognize the shift in focus from institution to relationship that is taking place. Marriages and families have moved—and are still moving—away from emphasizing the performance of social roles. More and more people view marriages as committed relationships in which they expect to find companionship and intimacy.

You've probably already noted that these themes are interrelated. Because marriages and families are beginning to be seen more as relationships than institutions, for example, individuals make a greater

■ When asked to bring a photo of her family to school, the young girl shown here chose this one. The four people on the left live together; two are Molly's godmothers. Her parents, on the right, were their neighbors in Boston. Everyone in this contemporary West Coast "family" has relatives back East.

number of choices. These, in turn, help focus people's attention not only on family values, but also on individual values. As you continue reading, you'll see these themes intermittently surfacing.

Summary

This book rests on a few assumptions. The first is that as people adapt the institutions of marriage and family to contemporary American life, they make many personal decisions. The awareness that decision making is important leads to a second assumption—that it is best to make personal decisions knowledgeably, particularly when they pertain to marriage and family life. We begin to make

---

6. Another example of a primary group relationship is a close friendship. A *secondary* group, in contrast, is characterized by more distant, practical relationships.

decisions knowledgeably when we recognize that social pressures exist that influence our choices. One such pressure comes from cultural values. As Americans, we cherish both family values and individual values, and reconciling them is a continuing concern. Another source of social pressure is myths, which can cause people to have unrealistic expectations for themselves or their family. We can make personal decisions more knowledgeably if we realize that individuals can challenge popular myths and values.

Scientific investigation has been helpful both in debunking myths and in helping us to see beyond our personal experience. Statistics show that marriages and families today exist in many forms, and our definition of marriages and families reflects this flexibility.

Key Terms

family values (familism) *5*	nuclear family *12*
individualistic values *9*	extended family *12*
self-fulfillment *9*	scientific investigation *13*
myth *11*	family *18*
monogamy *12*	primary group *19*
polygamy *12*	

Suggested Readings

Babbie, Earl
1986   *The Practice of Social Research.* 4th ed. Belmont, Calif.: Wadsworth.
Respected textbook in sociological methods. Recommended for those who would like further discussion or clarification.

Bellah, Robert N., Richard Madsen, William M. Sullivan, Ann Swidler, and Steven M. Tipton
1985   *Habits of the Heart: Individualism and Commitment in American Life.* Berkeley: University of California Press.
Broad analysis of the American pursuit of happiness in relationships. The authors' position is that American individualism, especially as expressed in recent years, may undercut the commitment and community necessary for social life and personal satisfaction.

Caplow, Theodore, Howard M. Bahr, Bruce A. Chadwick, Reuben Hill, and Margaret Holmes Williamson

1982   *Middletown Families: Fifty Years of Change and Continuity.* Minneapolis: University of Minnesota Press.
Restudy of the famous Middletown community, which emphasizes the essential stability of the family since the turn of the century.

Cherlin, Andrew
1981   *Marriage, Divorce, Remarriage.* Cambridge, Mass.: Harvard University Press.
Chapter 4 presents data on black-white differences in family structure and discusses their causes.

Coward, Raymond T., and William M. Smith, Jr.
1981   *The Family in Rural Society.* Boulder, Colo.: Westview.
Interesting enough to be read by urbanites as well as those who are especially interested in rural life.

D'Antonio, William V., and Joan Aldous (eds.)
1983   *Families and Religions: Conflict and Change in Modern Society.* Beverly Hills, Calif.: Sage.
Interesting articles on the impact of religion on the family. The book includes articles on specific religions—white and black Protestantism, Judaism, Catholicism (including Hispanics), Mormonism, and the Unification Church (Moonies)—and also contains an article on "televangelism" and the family.

Gordon, Michael
1977   *The American Family: Past, Present, and Future.* New York: Random House.
Readable summary of the history of the American family putting current issues into an historical context.

Hess, Beth B.
1984   "Protecting the American family: Public policy, family, and the New Right." In *Families and Change,* edited by Rosalind G. Genovese, pp. 11–21. South Hadley, Mass.: Bergin and Garvey.
Analyzes the clash of liberal and religious conservative agendas for the family. The author writes from a liberal perspective but offers a detailed discussion that could serve as a useful reference for those with other views.

Lasch, Christopher
1977   *Haven in a Heartless World: The Family Beseiged.* New York: Basic Books.
A very critical look at sociology of the family and family therapy, which recapitulates the work of major figures in the field such as Burgess, Parsons, Waller, and Ogburn.

Mindel, Charles H., and Robert W. Habenstein (eds.)
1976   *Ethnic Families in America: Patterns and Variations.* New York: Elsevier.
This textbook examines a wide variety of American ethnic families. It is a valuable antidote to

"mainstream" (that is, white, middle-class) family social science.

Queen, Stuart A., Robert W. Habenstein, and Jill Quadagno (eds.)
1985   *The Family in Various Cultures.* 5th ed. New York: Harper & Row.
Series of articles on the family in various historical and contemporary societies.

Shorter, Edward
1975   *The Making of the Modern Family.* New York: Basic Books.
Historian's view of development in the western European family accompanying the change from a traditional to a modern social order. The family, in this view, has become less solid as it is now bound primarily by sentimental ties rather than community support.

Staples, Robert (ed.)
1986   *The Black Family: Essays and Studies.* 3d ed. Belmont, Calif.: Wadsworth.
This book, compiled by a black social scientist,

examines a variety of interesting issues reflecting the black family.

Stephens, William N.
1963   *The Family in Cross-Cultural Perspective.* New York: Holt, Rinehart & Winston.
A topically organized look at the family in various, mostly primitive, societies.

Thornton, Arland, and Deborah Freedman
1983   "The changing American family." *Population Bulletin,* v. 38. Washington, D.C.: Population Reference Bureau.
Summary and interpretation of current statistical data on the family. Best concise description of the American family today.

Willie, Charles Vert
1985   *Black and White Families: A Study in Complementarity.* Bayside, N.Y.: General Hall.
This book examines black and white families in a social-class context in terms of how they adapt to access or lack of access to opportunity.

I Married Partners as Individuals

People are increasingly aware that marriages and families are comprised of separate, unique individuals. Part One discusses marriage partners as individuals. Each person on earth is somehow unique—no two people in history have ever been exactly alike. That uniqueness stems partly from the fact that human beings are able to make choices. They have creativity and free wills; nothing they think or do is totally "programmed."

At the same time, all the individuals in a particular society share some things. They speak the same language, for example, and have similar religious beliefs and some common attitudes about work, education, and marriages and families.

Chapter 1 discusses some choices adults make over the course of their lives. While no two people's life trajectories are exactly the same, Americans tend to share certain periods of stability and of transition. The most important idea in Chapter 1 is that adults change. Because of this, marriages and families are not static: Every time one individual in a marital relationship changes, the relationship changes, however subtly. Throughout this text we will discuss some creative ways in which mates can alter their relationship in order to meet their changing needs.

Societal values and attitudes about gender roles (what is appropriate behavior for each sex) affect how individuals think and feel about and behave within their own marriages and families. Chapter 2 examines Americans' views about gender roles. You will see that, traditionally, our society has held different views about how men and women (and boys and girls) should behave. Yet through creative choices that people can make, these expectations and stereotypes are changing.

But change doesn't come about all at once; each of us probably carries some traditional ideas about gender roles, along with some newer ones. Chapter 2 points out how combining these two different sets of ideas can affect individual women and men. Through the remainder of the text, we'll touch on how combining traditional with contemporary ideas affects relationships, marriages, and families.

Remembering, then, that no two people are exactly alike—and that every adult continues to change—we will begin our study by looking at some (changing) beliefs, values, and attitudes about gender roles.

1 Choices Throughout Life

*Human nature is not a
machine to be built after
a model, and set to do
exactly the work
prescribed for it, but a
tree, which requires to
grow and develop itself
on all sides, according to
the tendency of the
inward forces which
make it a living thing.*
JOHN STUART MILL, 1859

Passages, Gail Sheehy's (1974) populariza- tion of scholarly work on adult development (Gould, 1977, 1978; Levinson, 1978), changed our belief (Schaie and Parham, 1976) that adult per- sonality is fixed so that the only significant devel- opmental period is early childhood. Adult person- ality development and sociology of aging have become important disciplines (Meyer, 1986; Riley, 1987) that have taught us a great deal about change over the life course. More and more people believe that all of life is a "flowing, changing process in which nothing is fixed" (Rogers, 1961:27). In other words, adult life is recognized as process rather than product.

Adults change. In this chapter we'll examine some choices and decisions that changing adults make throughout their lives. We'll look at the adult life course—the typical pattern of adult person- ality development and social roles over the life- span—and discuss some social and cultural fac- tors that influence choices throughout adulthood. And we'll examine some important ways in which the changes each individual goes through affect the course of a marriage partnership.

Individual choices are shaped by the social con- text in which they are made, so to begin with, we'll examine some social factors that influence adult decisions.

SOCIAL INFLUENCES AND PERSONAL CHOICES

As the Prologue points out, social factors influence people's personal choices in two ways. First, it is always easier to make the common choice; norms about appropriate behavior make the alternatives psychologically and socially difficult. For example, in the fifties, when the majority of middle-class women were stay-at-home mothers, a working mother was exposed to criticism and was vulner- able to feelings of guilt. She had difficulty arrang- ing child care and dealing with the hostility of ele- mentary schools. Now choosing to be a homemaker goes against the grain (Luker, 1984).

Second, social factors limit people's options. For example, American society has never offered fam- ilies the option of collective housekeeping. Despite some earlier experiments with communal cooking (Hayden, 1981), the decisive development in twen- tieth-century America has been the self-contained household in the suburbs (Wright, 1981). Nor has American society offered the options of legal polygamy or homosexual marriage. We are pres- ently waiting to learn whether the courts will endorse surrogate parenthood as an alternative for infertile couples.

What I really want is a real home ~~to~~ with nice furniture, also a van to drive. I also would like to give my son ~~out~~ what I didn't get in life. Which includes love.

Sharon D. Butts

Historical Events

The shift from a preindustrial to an industrial and bureaucratic society has changed the family dramatically. (Chapters 7 and 8 address this shift.)

Specific historical events, such as war, depression, and inflation, affect options and choices. Demographers speculate that the Vietnam War played a part in the rise in the American divorce rate in the sixties and seventies (Norton and Moorman, 1987). Many families, black and white, found

their lives much affected by school desegregation in the 1950s and 1960s (Lukas, 1985; Shange, 1985).

The work of sociologist Glen Elder (1977) and demographer Richard Easterlin (1980) reminds us that family life has been a different experience in the Great Depression, in the optimistic fifties, in the tumultuous sixties, and in the economically constricted eighties. In the Depression years, couples delayed marriage and parenthood and had far fewer children than they wanted. During World War II, married women were encouraged to get defense jobs, and they went to work in factories for the first time. Day care centers were popular; some women even left their youngsters with relatives in distant cities.

In the affluent fifties, young people could better afford to get married—and they did at younger and younger ages. They had large families, cared for by stay-at-home mothers. Divorce rates slowed their long-term increase (Easterlin, 1980). The expanding economy provided a sound basis for this family life. Today one person can no longer earn a "family wage" (Ehrenreich, 1983; Thurow, 1980). More and more wives must seek employment, regardless of their preference. Our constricting economy limits options for housing, hiring household help, and visiting geographically distant relatives, among other things. Some persons who might prefer to live alone, but cannot afford to, find themselves returning home to live with parents (Clemens and Axelson, 1985).

Historical change involves not only specific events but also short- or long-term change in basic indicators of human life. As recently as 100 years ago, one-third of our population died before reaching adulthood. Presently three-fourths of the U.S. population live to be 65, and many reach 85. Among the consequences of this increased longevity are more years invested in education, longer marriages for those who do not divorce, a longer period during which parents and children are both adults, more time in which to accumulate various experiences, and a long retirement (one-quarter of life) (Riley, 1987).

Race

In addition to specific historical events, race affects people's options and decisions. The impact of racial discrimination and economic disadvantage on the family is indicated by the fact that in 1984, 40.8 percent of black family groups with children under 18 had two parents present, compared to 79.9 percent of white family groups. Only 17 percent of white family groups were single-parent, female-headed families, and only 2.7 percent were maintained by never-married mothers, while among blacks these percentages were 55.9 percent and 28.1 percent, respectively (U.S. Bureau of the Census, 1986b; U.S. Bureau of the Census, 1985a).

One reason for this fairly dramatic trend toward female-headed households among blacks has been an attrition in the number of black husbands who can help support a wife and children. The decline of two-parent families among blacks is a post-World War II phenomenon. Contrary to popular belief, blacks managed to maintain a considerable degree of stable family life under slavery and after (Gutman, 1976). Even the movement to the urban north after World War I was not too disruptive; in 1925 five-sixths of black children lived in two-parent families (Cherlin, 1981). Black and white divergence in marital status has become most pronounced in the past twenty-five years (Cherlin, 1981). Experts disagree dramatically on the cause of the increase in female-headed households (Murray, 1984; Lemann, 1986; Cherlin, 1981; Norton, 1985), but we are convinced that the elimination of entry-level positions paying a family wage is responsible for high levels of black unemployment, which in turn preclude marriage or doom it from the start (Norton, 1985; Liebow, 1967). The fact that the typical black family had less than one-tenth of the assets of a white family (*Omaha World Herald*, July 19, 1986) will influence not only the economics but also the emotional atmosphere of those families, given our expectations of family providers (Scanzoni, 1970).

Marriage and family patterns vary among other racial and ethnic groups as well. The proportion of Hispanics who are married, for example, has remained about the same since 1970, and Hispanic fertility rates are the highest of all the major racial/ethnic groups (U.S. Bureau of the Census, 1986b). These trends probably have to do with the strong influence of the Catholic religion on Hispanic culture.

Social Class

Social class or status may be as important as race in affecting people's choices. Clearly, the distribution of wealth in the United States is skewed. In 1986 the Census Bureau reported that the top 12 percent of American families control almost 40 percent of household wealth. While the typical American family had a net worth of $32,667, the wealthiest 12 percent had a median net worth of $123,474 (*Omaha World Herald*, July 19, 1986:1). Money may not buy happiness. But it does afford a myriad of options, from educations at prestigious universities to vacations, household help, and family counseling.

Besides distinguishing families on the basis of income and/or assets, social scientists often distinguish between white- and blue-collar workers. **White-collar workers** include professionals, clerical workers, sales people, and so forth, who have traditionally worn white shirts to work. Working-class people, or **blue-collar workers,** are employed as mechanics, truckers, police officers, machine operators, factory workers, and so forth—jobs typically requiring uniforms.

Social scientists do not agree on whether blue- and white-collar workers have become more and more alike in their values and attitudes in recent decades; but it is certain that, in some ways, they look at life differently (Marciano, 1977; L. Rubin, 1976). Regarding marriage, for example, working-class couples tend to emphasize values associated with parenthood and job stability, whereas white-collar partners are more inclined to value companionship, self-expression, and communication (Fengler, 1973; L. Rubin, 1976). Other ways in which differing social-class perspectives affect marriages and families will be noted throughout this text.

Age Expectations

In the same way that historical events and social class influence choices, so do **age expectations.** When individuals shop for clothes, they sometimes wonder whether they are too old or too young to wear something they like. They are at least unconsciously aware that society views some attitudes and behaviors as appropriate for a given age and others as inappropriate. Despite growing diversity there is still generally—at least among the middle and upper classes—a "right time" to marry, to have children, to retire (Hogan and Astone, 1986:118). Among women who have left the labor force to have and rear children, there is a time (about age 36) when they are supposed to begin or return to college (Aldous, 1978:129; West, 1985).

Individuals are aware of their own life timing in relation to social expectations. Accordingly, they view themselves as "early," "late," or "on time" in family, occupational, and educational events. Because of this, age expectations act as "prods and brakes" on people's personal choices (Neugarten, 1977). For example, some spouses admit that their choice to marry was influenced by the feeling that it was time they were married.

Being early, late, or on time can affect one's options, also. For example, individuals choose from the largest pools of eligibles when looking for marriage partners when they are "on time." Looking for a partner "late"—especially for women in our society—means a narrower range of choices.

Some previously held expectations concerning age are changing. More and more young adults are postponing marriage until their late 20s and early 30s (Norton, 1983). And since the mid-1970s, white women have increasingly put off having children until their late 20s or 30s.

Social factors such as historical events and age limit people's options to some extent. But that does not mean that important life decisions (or even unimportant ones) are predetermined. Being conscious of social influences permits a more knowledgeable choice. Let's look more closely at two forms of decision making—choosing by default and choosing knowledgeably—along with their consequences.

CHOOSING BY DEFAULT

All people make choices, even when they are not aware of it. Such unconscious decisions are called **choosing by default.** Choices made by default are ones people make when they are not aware of all the alternatives or when they pursue the proverbial path of least resistance.

If you're taking this class, for example, but you're unaware that a class in modern dancing (which you would have preferred) is meeting at the same time, you have chosen *not* to take the class in modern dancing. You have done so by default, because you didn't find out about all the alternatives when you registered.

Another kind of decision by default occurs when people pursue a course of action primarily because it seems the easiest thing to do. Many times college students choose their courses by default. They arrive at registration only to find that the classes they had planned to take are closed. So they register for something they hadn't planned on, do pretty well, and continue in it just because that seems easier than rearranging their curriculum programs.

Many decisions concerning marriages and families are also made by default. Spouses may focus on career success, for example, to the neglect of their relationship, simply because this is what society expects of them. (Chapters 8 and 11 explore this further.)

While most of us have made at least some decisions by default, almost everyone can probably recall having the opposite experience: **choosing knowledgeably.**

CHOOSING KNOWLEDGEABLY

Today society offers many options. People can stay single or marry, they can choose to live together outside legal marriage; they can form communes; they can decide to divorce or to stay married. One important component of choosing knowledgeably is recognizing as many options or alternatives as possible. This text is designed in part to help you do that.

A second component in making knowledgeable choices is recognizing the social pressures that may influence personal choices. Sometimes people decide that they agree with socially accepted or prescribed behavior. They concur in the teachings of their religion, for example. Other times, though, people decide that they strongly disagree with socially prescribed beliefs, values, and standards. Whether they agree with such standards or not, once people recognize the force of social pressures, they are freer to choose whether to act in accordance with them.

A third aspect of making knowledgeable choices is considering the consequences of each alternative rather than just gravitating toward the one that initially seems most attractive. A couple deciding whether to move so that the husband can be promoted, for example, may want to list the consequences, both positive and negative, on paper. In the positive column the husband may have a higher position and earn more money, and the region to which they would move may have a friendlier climate. In the negative column the wife may have to give up or disrupt her career, and both husband and wife may have to leave relatives. Listing positive and negative consequences of alternatives— either mentally or on paper—helps one see the larger picture and thus make a more knowledgeable decision.

A fourth element in this process is personally clarifying one's values. In recent years counselors and others have given considerable attention to **values clarification**—becoming aware of one's own values and choosing to act consistently with those values. Society today holds up contradictory sets of values to people. Chapter 5 discusses the fact, for example, that today there are at least four standards of premarital sex ranging from abstinence to sex-for-recreation, even without personal affection. Or, to give another example, our society values full-time motherhood, at least for women with very young children, but it also values women who are "more than just housewives." Contradictory values can cause people to feel ambivalent about what they want for themselves (Merton, 1976).

Clarifying one's values involves cutting through this ambivalence in order to decide which of several orientations one more strongly values, at least for the present. To do this, it is important to respect what has been called "the gut factor"—the emotional dimension of decision making. Besides rationally considering alternatives, people have subjective, often almost visceral feelings about what "feels" right or wrong, good or bad. Respecting one's feelings is an important part of making the right decision. People who make choices only on the basis of rational considerations often regret their choices later (Hall and Hall, 1979:197–98).

One other component of decision making should be mentioned, and that is rechecking. Once a choice is made and a person acts on it, the process is not necessarily ended. People constantly recheck their decisions, as Figure 1•1 suggests, throughout the entire decision-making cycle, testing these decisions against their own subsequent feelings and against any changes in the environment.

An assumption underlying this discussion has been that individuals cannot have everything. Every time people make an important decision, they rule out alternatives—at least for the time being. Persons cannot simultaneously have the relative freedom of a child-free union and the gratification that often accompanies parenthood. One way people deal with this problem is to focus on some goals and values during one part of their lives, then turn their attention to different ones at other times (Komarovsky, 1977:229–39). As we shall see in the next section, choices throughout life often are made according to this pattern.

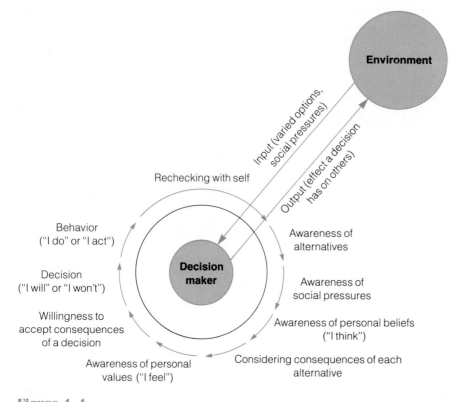

Figure 1·1
The cycle of knowledgeable decision making. (Source: Adapted from O'Neill and O'Neill, 1974)

PERSONAL CHOICES AND CHANGE

Gail Sheehy's best-seller *Passages* (1974) popularized the concept of the **adult life course.** For reasons we'll outline shortly, this view of personal choices and change has been subject to considerable criticism, and an alternative view, termed the **life spiral,** has emerged.

The Adult Life Course

Adults shape their lives. They structure life-styles for themselves. Then they step back to review and evaluate what they've created. (See Case Study

1·1, "An Inside View of Adult Change.") This sequence throughout adulthood of structuring one's life followed by self-examination makes up the concept adult life course. As the following overview shows, each stage presents a particular developmental challenge to the individual (see also Table 1·1).

Entering the Adult World The first stage in structuring one's life is **entering the adult world.** For the middle class this stage lasts roughly from age 18 to age 28. This stage, along with those that follow it, may occur some three to five years earlier for members of the working and lower classes.

Traditionally, marriage has served as a rite of passage marking the bride's and groom's entry into autonomous adulthood. There is evidence that how

TABLE 1·1 The Adult Life Course: Developmental Stages

Stage	Task
Entering the adult world (ages 18–28)	Establishing autonomy, establishing socially prescribed roles
Age-thirty transition (ages 28–32)	Assessing young adult accomplishments, changing or reaffirming goals
Settling down (ages 32–45)	Establishing a firm niche in society in a way that is personally meaningful
Midlife transition (begins ages 35–45)	Assessing accomplishments and goals, changing or reaffirming goals
Life's second half (begins ages 50–65)	Accepting limitations and mortality

Note: Age groupings are approximate; individuals vary greatly. The descriptive phrases *entering the adult world, midlife transition,* and *age-thirty transition* are from Levinson, 1978.

and at what age people enter the adult world has important consequences for the rest of their lives. Marrying early before completing one's education (especially high school) limits options for occupational and financial advancement (Otto, 1979). Teenage mothers, particularly those who leave their parents' homes, tend to not finish school, to take the lowest-paid jobs, and to be unemployed or on welfare, or both (Furstenberg, 1976).

If people between ages 18 and 22 are successful in declaring their independence, they *feel* separate and autonomous by the end of this first phase.

Age-Thirty Transition   Once people have begun to establish themselves in adult roles, an interesting psychological phenomenon often begins to take place. Like the artist who has completed some preliminary sketching, they find themselves stepping back to evaluate the lives they've begun to shape.

During the **age-thirty transition,** which lasts from about age 28 to age 32, people ask themselves "What is this life all about now that I am doing what I'm supposed to be doing?" (Gould, 1977:15; Reinke et al., 1985). They look around and note some of the things they feel they've been missing, perhaps things they always wanted to do but put off because they were too busy. Individuals may

■ For most of us, the adult life course will include the choice of marriage. But other transitions are less predictable: A year after his wedding, this man died in a plane crash; she later remarried.

CASE STUDY 1·1

AN INSIDE VIEW OF ADULT CHANGE

Mike is 41 years old. He has been married eighteen years and has three children, ages 17, 15, and 13. Here he talks about personal changes he has made during adulthood.

I came from a very rigid background. I was a very small child. I was only five feet two inches when I graduated from high school, and I had a very slight build. I think because of my size I grew up with an inferiority complex. Everyone was big. . . . I never measured up to the things my father said. And—this may be typical of the era I grew up in—one thing I could do better than anybody else I knew was drink. I started drinking when I was 13. I lived in a small town and they sold alcohol to just about anybody who could reach over the bar. And I was tall enough to do that! I drank heavy through high school and still managed to get pretty decent grades. But I flunked out of college [because of drinking]. . . .

When I flunked out of college I went into the service, and during that time my wife—she was my girlfriend then—went into and finished nurse's training. We got married when I got out of the service. I landed a good job with IBM, because what I had been doing in the military was electronically oriented.

At first the job was going fine. . . . But after a few years, my drinking got totally out of hand. I got to the point where I could no longer handle it. I started having blackouts. . . . My wife got to the point where she would no longer take this excessive drinking. She threatened divorce. And I said I would do something about my problem. . . .

I signed into an alcoholism treatment center and spent five weeks [there]. It changed my life. I now consider that place my birthplace, because my whole life has turned around since then. That was six years ago.

About a year after I [finished treatment], I decided I wanted to go back to school. I wanted to change my profession. I wanted to get out of data processing. So about a year ago, I left my job and started at my current job. I took a pay cut. But this new job gives me an opportunity to go back to school on a part-time basis. I am still in data processing by the way, but now I work for the university and I go to school. And I like that better. . . .

Part of the sobering up was that my wife and I were looking at each other for the first time after about fifteen years. And we found out that we really didn't know each other. We had some pretty big communication-type problems. At this point in my life, I was willing to seek out help, whereas during the drinking time in my life I would never admit to a problem that I couldn't solve.

But now I'm at the point where I believe a lot of people can help me better than I can help myself. So we started going to a marriage counselor, and we still do.... And for a while we had a separation.

I got an apartment. I didn't have a lot of money to play around with or anything. I mean I was (*laughs*) I really wasn't in a position to be a playboy or anything, but what [the apartment] provided was space for us to be apart. And we learned what I still believe is a very valuable lesson: that we need space away from each other for our own well-being.... I could come home to the apartment at night after work and do things that I wanted to do rather than seeing all the projects around the house that had to be done that I didn't have time to do—and I didn't have the frustration of it.

So things went so well through this separation that we—I think we both—really realized that we liked each other enough that we wanted this thing to work.... But being around each other all the time—we needed more space. So.... we sold our house in the suburbs and bought this huge house in the inner city.... It's been beautiful—the best thing we've ever done....

You know, I've gone through some radical changes in the last few years. I've gone from a Goldwater-type Republican to what some people would call a "bleeding heart liberal." That's a drastic political change! I've opened up, too, to so many new things. I was thinking just the other night—I'm taking swimming lessons down at the Y, and while I was doing a couple laps I was thinking... how much richer my life is now and how I couldn't really have perceived that before....

My wife and I are taking yoga lessons together now. And last semester I took a music appreciation course. Music Masterpieces. I had never had any experience with a symphony.... But I felt I was missing something, so I did that. Now my wife and I have season tickets to the symphony, and we go to concerts, and I love it. It's just another thing I'd never have known about if—I really don't have the time to do all the things I want to do now.

- What factors seem to have encouraged Mike's midlife crisis? In what other way(s) might he have responded to his wife's threatening divorce? What further changes can you predict for Mike as he continues through his adult life? How can a separation be a growth experience?

    While Mike was changing, his wife was herself involved in growing and changing. In Chapter 11 Mike describes his reactions to his wife's changes over her adult life.

decide to invest time and energy in hobbies or other interests that do not directly contribute to their work or family roles. Or they may begin to believe that society "pushed" them into roles that now seem restricting. Consequently, they may set about removing those roles from their lives.

Settling Down After the age-thirty transition, people begin the process of **settling down,** a step that culminates the first half of life. This phase usually lasts until the late 30s for women and to about age 45 for men. During this phase individuals invest themselves in whatever they have decided is important to them—work, family, friendships, leisure, community work. Becoming aware of a time squeeze, those in professional careers often look to success in their work as "one last chance to make it big" (Gould, 1977:15).

During this stage individuals may first see their parents as real people. They may change their perspectives and feelings about their parents, more fully appreciating and accepting them (Troll et al., 1979).

The Midlife Transition Having established themselves in work and family roles, adults in midlife begin to "restructure time in terms of time-left-to-live rather than time-since-birth" (Neugarten, 1977:43). Beginning as early as age 35 for women and about 45 for men, Americans emotionally become aware that their lives are "half over" (Jacques, 1977:318).

Facing the reality of "one's own eventual personal death" is the "central and crucial feature" of the **midlife transition** (Jacques, 1977:319). In this phase a heightened personal awareness of one's mortality precipitates the urgent desire to use one's remaining time wisely.

As a result, some people choose to modify their lives significantly during this passage. Individuals may divorce, remarry, or make major career shifts (Levinson, 1978:194). Others make less visible but equally significant changes. They may alter their moral or religious values appreciably, for example; or, once they have reexamined these values, they may make an even stronger commitment to them through the second half of life.

Life's Second Half In the second half of life, during a person's 50s and 60s, one must become resigned to finite time: "The die is cast" (Gould, 1977:15). Life is too short, people realize, to do all that they had hoped and planned. The major task of this stage is to accept that fact.

During life's second half many adults become experts and mentors to a new generation of novices. And in their 50s and 60s people often accomplish "a mellowing and warming up" (Gould, 1977:16) as they come to accept their limitations and weaknesses. Many people renew old family loyalties and relationships. They make more effort to visit sisters and brothers, for example, even at great distances, than they did in middle age (Troll et al., 1979). Some individuals respond to their increased awareness of finiteness in a less positive way, regretting their failures or shortcomings. For them, these and subsequent years may be marked by bitterness rather than acceptance.

Today more people are living into their 80s and beyond. But very little is known about development during those years. Psychologists do know, however, that development near the end of life involves coming to terms with decreasing social responsibilities and physical capabilities, and eventually with one's own death (Levinson, 1978:38–39).

All through life, people make choices and decisions that both result from and precipitate their changing. Many adults don't change very noticeably, however. They remain relatively constant in their basic interests, values, and attitudes. Some people consciously censor different or new experiences and ideas that could challenge their own. They avoid people, for example, who think or behave differently than they do. Still others become increasingly open to new experiences. They read books that suggest values they may not agree with, for example. But all adults change to some degree. As they do, their marriages and intimate relationships will also change. A later section explores how changing adults affect marriage and family living.

Criticisms of the Adult Life Course Model

Since the peak of its popularity in the 1970s, the adult life course model has been criticized on several grounds. For one thing, people who are taught to expect transitional crises may experience them for just that reason. Though some recent research suggests the validity of the age-30 transition among women (Reinke et al., 1985), such transitions may result as much from "self-fulfilling prophecy" as

I was and still am a wild woman.
I'm a positive Thinker.
I have a fairly high I.Q.
I'm not afraid of old age
I shake a fist at Death

This   NOT   This

Mary E. H.
Neville Manor

from individuals' developmental stages. That is, "The cultural attention given to such phenomena as the male mid-life crisis, through scientific 'knowledge,' through applications of it by the helping professions and through media promotions," may function to *create* such crises (Dannefer, 1984:110).

A second issue is the model's white, middle-class bias. Among young black women, for example, it seems likely that unmarried motherhood has become a more common path to adulthood than marriage is (Hogan and Astone, 1986:118). Put more generally, "Many persons do not conform to normative patterns in their life span transitions" (Hogan, 1985:70). Because many persons do not conform to the white, middle-class model, sociologists have proposed an alternative—the life spiral.

The Life Spiral The life spiral model of adult change is meant to better accommodate the variety of life-style choices people make today and to acknowledge that people do not necessarily enter certain stages "on time" (Etzkowitz and Stein, 1978). While some adults follow fairly traditional patterns, others shift from traditional to alternative patterns, and vice versa. People marry, divorce, and then remain single, for example. Or they live in communal groups and marry later. (See Case Study 1•2, "Estella: A Nontraditional Life-Style Now— with More Traditional Hopes for Later.") Another pattern involves people choosing and remaining in alternative life-styles; an example would be unmarried, cohabiting parenthood.

The term *spiral* conveys a sense of "the incorporation of traditional and alternative roles in the life course" (Etzkowitz and Stein, 1978:434) and the variations in a person's role commitments over the life course.

Although Etzkowitz and Stein do not make this connection, the life spiral idea leaves room for the observation that parents are often influenced by their children and may come to share the values of a later generation (Glass et al., 1986).

Both life spiral and adult life course models are important because they draw our attention to the inevitability of change in individuals and in their relationships throughout life.

Hard Choices That choices in adult development and social roles are contingent on opportunity and, to some degree, chance, is illustrated by sociologist Kathleen Gerson's research on women's role choices. She studied 63 women who were between 27 and 37 when interviewed in 1978–1979. Extensive and repeated interviews enabled Gerson to construct life histories and to trace adult development, particularly decisions about work and motherhood.

The women fell into four groups: two groups of women made role choices early in life and held to them. The other two groups are the most interesting for our purposes. These women had entered young adulthood with clear expectations for their lives. One set planned a rather conventional marriage and family; work would be an interim activity. The other group gave high priority to careers, regardless of any hopes for marriage and children.

But their lives turned out to be quite different from their expectations. Sometimes women who had planned careers met obstacles, often overt or covert discrimination. They became dissatisfied and pessimistic about their chances of realizing their original goals. Or they fell into very satisfying relationships and may also have found children more enjoyable than they had expected. Often this dissatisfaction and satisfaction combined to channel their movement into a more traditional family life-style. Here is one example:

Vicki was never especially oriented toward motherhood. Instead, since she was old enough to know who the police were, she wanted to be a policewoman. . . . Forced to take the best job she could find after high school, Vicki became a secretary-clerk. She also took the qualifying exam for police work and passed with high marks. No jobs were available, however. . . . In the meantime, she met and married Joe.

. . . She ultimately grew to hate working, for it usually involved taking orders from bosses she did not respect. . . . Joe also began to pressure her to have children. . . . After the birth of her first child, Vicki discovered that staying at home to rear a child was more important than her succession of boring, dead-end jobs. By her mid-thirties, she was a full-time mother of two. Today she has given up hope of becoming a policewoman, but in return for this sacrifice she feels she has gained the secure home life she never knew as a child [Gerson, 1985:18–19]. ■

Vicki's story illustrates a point we made earlier: Individuals can only choose options that are available in their society. At the time Vicki sought a job as a policewoman, probably few women were being hired, so she was not able to have the career she wanted. Other women may have been discouraged from working by the lack of child care or inadequate maternity-leave policies. In recent years women have been hired as policewomen in large numbers, partly as a consequence of the courts' support for affirmative action hiring practices (*Johnson* v. *Transportation Agency, Santa Clara County, California,* 1987); this change indicates that it is possible to create wanted options through changes in public policy. Making choices about family life may include political activity directed toward creating those choices. (We discuss family policy and family advocacy further in Chapter 14.)

Vicki's life course was redirected from a nontraditional to a traditional family life-style. Meanwhile, some of the women in Gerson's study who planned to marry and start families failed to develop permanent relationships or were not able to have children. Or they chanced onto career opportunities, particularly as women began to be included in formerly male-dominated positions. Or both. These women found themselves very involved in their careers and perhaps not married or not wanting to become a parent.

Elizabeth, the dutiful daughter, ... married a young engineer soon after college graduation. Within a few years, however, the marriage began to sour. Before she could fully assimilate the implications of her situation, she was divorced and out on her own for the first time in her life. Desperate for a paycheck, she wandered into an employment agency looking for a job, any job. They placed her in a small company, where she started as a receptionist and office manager. She quickly made herself indispensable and over a period of about five years worked her way up the organization to her present position of executive vice-president.

Elizabeth is now in her mid-thirties, and there appear to be few limits on how high she can rise. Despite her childhood expectations, home and family just do not fit with the commitments she has developed as an adult [Gerson, 1985:13]. ▪

The import of this study for our understanding of change over the course of life is that childhood socialization and early goals do not predict adult life-styles with much accuracy. The adult life course is determined by the interaction of the individual's goals, values, abilities, and motivation with the opportunities that present themselves. Throughout adulthood, individuals make a series of choices about their lives, and different individuals will respond differently to those options that are the product of a particular time. The development of adult life is a process of on-going decision and choice, early choices shaping later ones, within the possibilities of a particular historical time.

The case study "An Inside View of Adult Change" illustrates the continuing nature of personal change. Many of Mike's most important changes came not during childhood or adolescence but rather several years after marriage. The same is true, to varying degrees, for many adults.

CHANGING ADULTS AND THE COURSE OF FAMILY LIVING

The view of adult life as fluid rather than static affects both the way social scientists study family life and the way people view their own family situations. The social-scientific view of the course of family living has changed a great deal.

Family Development Theory

Family development theory is one foundation for our thinking about changes over the course of life. This perspective has been an important one in sociology of the family for many years (Duvall, 1957, 1977; Broderick, 1971; Duvall and Miller, 1985). It takes the family as the unit of analysis and begins with the formation of a family through marriage. Typical stages (see Figure 1·2) of family life are marked off by (1) the addition and subtraction of family members (through birth, death, and leaving home), (2) the various stages the children go through, and (3) changes in the family's connection with other social systems (retirement from work, for example). These succeed one another in

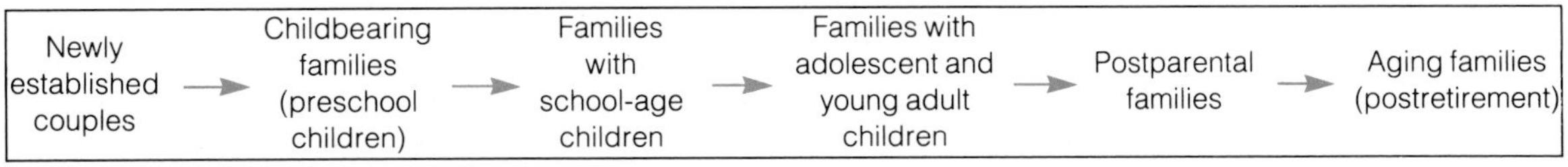

| Newly established couples | → | Childbearing families (preschool children) | → | Families with school-age children | → | Families with adolescent and young adult children | → | Postparental families | → | Aging families (postretirement) |

Figure 1·2
The traditional family life cycle.

CASE STUDY 1·2

ESTELLA: A NONTRADITIONAL LIFE-STYLE NOW— WITH MORE TRADITIONAL HOPES FOR LATER

Estella, 27, is an accountant with a major opera company. As you will see, she has created a rather unique life-style for herself. Single now, she seems to be enjoying herself even though she misses the companionship she hopes to find in marriage someday.

When I was deciding on my professional career, a big factor was that I was going to be single for a long time. I knew this because when I was in high school, I wasn't very attractive. I was overweight and very shy. I didn't date at all. I couldn't talk to boys. I knew I would be single for a while, a long while. So I knew I had to support myself, and I knew I had to find the money to do what I wanted to do. That was to travel and to find adventure and all those good things. Have my own apartment.

Not that I *wanted* to so much, you know. But I knew the single person was going to be with me, was somebody I was going to be for a while.... It bothered me; it still does. I still want to get married. I think that would be great! What I look for in marriage is the companionship.

Interviewer: How do you fill that need now?

Roommates or friends. I go out a lot. I go to a lot of arts events and to a lot of movies. I'm a big movie fan. Most of my friends are very interested in going to movies or the ballet or things like that. I just call up and say, "Let's go."

And when the singers are in town to do an opera, we go out. Last night I was out with them and the night before. I get to meet some very exciting people. I get to play with them, not just work with them professionally. I get to know them personally. In fact, the hairdresser for this show lives in Houston. We've just decided that I'm going to go down there this summer, and we'll drive over to Santa Fe. He's going to be doing an opera in Santa Fe. So, the traveling and getting to meet friends—it's great.

Now if I were married, my traveling would be curtailed. To take a month off like I did last May and go to Britain—you know, I could never have done that. One, the money would have gone somewhere else—a mortgage or something. My money would be out of my control. That is one of the things I don't look forward to in marriage.... Still, marriage would be nice someday. You know, it's always the commitment you want.

Interviewer: Tell me about your roommate.

My roommate, Frank, is male and gay. He's a university student in his last year. My ex-roommate was female, and she was moving. I like sharing expenses. I've had roommates most of my independent life, and I like it. You get nicer places cheaper. Frank was a friend of a friend. He'd been living alone and didn't like his apartment. By getting together we could find something we both liked and could afford. He found the apartment, and I liked it, so we did it.

It works for us. I can't say that if he were entertaining men in the apartment, it would work. I don't know. I don't entertain men at the apartment. . . . Except for one occasion when I did have a man stay overnight. It was a little awkward, and I told Frank later that I was sorry. But we both decided that if we would entertain, we were going to accept it from each other. We did talk about it. If he did bring home a guest, or if I did, that it would be tolerated, that we would work it out. We mentioned about meeting these folks in the bathrooms. . . .

Interviewer: Are the two of you good friends?

Very. I feel very comfortable. I made that comment to him just a couple days ago. I got home after work and just started rattling off to him. And later I said, "You know, this feels very comfortable. I thank you. I must tell you that you're the best roommate I've ever had." That's the truth. We can talk about little insignificant things, silly things, and yet we can talk about very deep things too. It's very comfortable.

Yesterday I was doing box office duty here all alone, and I was thirsty and bored. I called him at home and said, "I'm bored, talk to me." I said, "I'm thirsty. Can you bring down something, and can you bring a book with you?" He made hot water and brought tea in a thermos. He got into his cold car, took a break from his studies, and came down. He made my afternoon, let me tell you.

Interviewer: Do you go out together?

We do. Mostly for lunches. We haven't gone out to a lot of movies together lately, but we did for a long time. He likes to play videogames. I make an effort to accompany him. I'm not so crazy about them but he's very good about going to things that I like. It's like I can enjoy his enjoyment and he can enjoy mine.

He's always interested in hearing about my trips, for example. In 1982 I went to England for a month. Then I went to New York, and another time to Florida for five days. For the England trip, I traveled to London alone and met my aunt there. Then we traveled together. That was great fun. It was wonderful!

Interviewer: Do you ever feel lonely?

No, I don't. Oh, on certain occasions you do. You get melancholy, and you would love to have somebody there to snuggle up with. That's the one thing I miss. I don't have anybody to snuggle with. Frank doesn't like to be hugged or touched.

■ How does Estella's story illustrate the fact that individuals may choose different life-styles at different stages in their adult lives? How do social factors like age and income affect her life-style?

an orderly progression and have their requisite "developmental tasks," the activities required by or characteristic of each stage. For example, the honeymoon couple must establish a sexual relationship and a home of its own. If the developmental tasks of a particular stage are not successfully completed, adjustment in the next stage will be impaired.

Social Scientists and the Family Life Course The family development perspective assumes that family structure and family life follow certain conventional patterns. Sexual relations are established after marriage, all families have children and don't divorce, husbands are breadwinners, nuclear families live separately, and so on. Social scientists with a family development perspective have regarded the course of family living as a family life cycle in which unchanging adults married, had children, and eventually launched them into the world (see Figure 1•2). These stages in the family life cycle were followed by the **empty nest** stage—during which the couple inhabited a house empty of children—and eventually retirement. Gradual changes in marital happiness were explained primarily—and in many cases *only*—according to the ages of a couple's children (Rollins and Feldman, 1970).

By the 1970s social scientists had begun to recognize the importance of other influences besides children. Rollins and Feldman surveyed husbands and wives in 799 middle-class families in Syracuse, New York. One of their important conclusions was that occupational experiences of husbands might influence marital satisfaction more than the presence or developmental level of children (Rollins and Feldman, 1970:27). More recently, social scientists have examined the relationship between the family life course and stages in either or both partners' work careers (Voydanoff, 1980). Chapter 11 explores this topic in detail.)

That the course of people's careers might affect marital happiness was an important realization among family social scientists. Nevertheless, the focus remained on social roles. (These social scientists also suggested that wives' satisfaction was probably related to their parenthood role, just as their husbands' happiness was related to their careers.) Rollins and Feldman did not perceive the people they surveyed as individuals so much as entities filling the socially prescribed family roles.

This focus is changing as we become more aware of the dynamics of adult development. More recently, sociologist Glen Elder has argued that the life course of families must be studied in terms of interdependent individuals living together and communicating. Families are not simply husbands and wives engaged in performing parent and occupational roles; they are married individuals who have careers and perhaps other outside interests. Family living thus becomes a situation in which multiple life courses must be coordinated (Elder, 1977).

Family Members/Family Living

Family members have become less predictable than in the past. The course of family living results in large part from decisions and choices two individual adults make, both moving in their own ways and at their own paces through their own lives. One consequence of this is that one's marriage is no longer as likely to be permanent, as we'll see in Chapter 16. Assuming that partners' respective beliefs, values, and behaviors mesh fairly well at marriage, any change in either spouse is likely to adversely affect the fit. If both husband and wife change little over the years, their match can remain mutually satisfying. But if one or both change considerably over time, the danger exists that they will grow apart instead of together. A couple does not necessarily move in parallel paths through the various stages of their lives, nor do they always enter the same stage at the same time. A challenge for contemporary relationships is to integrate divergent personal change into the relationship.

One reason the concept of family life cycle seems less and less accurate is that an individual's life choices and changes are neither automatic nor easy. Transition periods can be turbulent times in which rigorous self-appraisal leads to self-doubt, impatience, and anger. This can be highly disruptive to a family. A tendency is to blame the spouse for all one's own feelings of failure and misery: "If it weren't for her, I'd have been in management (or made vice-president) by now"; or "If it weren't for him, I wouldn't have an expired teaching certificate." An aging husband, for example, who misses the energy of his youth, may believe it is his wife, not the aging process itself, that makes him act and feel old. As a result, he may find a younger partner who makes him "feel young again."

■ Alone, together: Sharing a comfortable compromise in separateness and togetherness, this couple balances individual and common interests.

How can partners make it through all these changes and still stay together? Two guidelines may be helpful. The first is for people to take responsibility for their own past choices and decisions rather than blaming previous "mistakes" on their mates. The second is for individuals to be aware that married life is far more complex than the traditional image portrayed by the family life cycle. It helps to recognize that the spouse in transition may be difficult to live with for a while. It helps also to make decisions knowledgeably, not by default. A relationship needs to be flexible enough to allow for each partner's individual changes—to allow family members some degree of freedom. At the same time, we must remind ourselves of the benefits of family living.

Finding Freedom Within Families

Expressing one's individuality within the context of a family requires one to negotiate innumerable day-to-day issues. How much privacy can each person be allowed at home? What things and places in the family dwelling belong just to one particular individual? What family activities should be scheduled, how often, and when? What outside friendships and activities can a family member have?

Family Rhythms of Separateness and Togetherness In every family members regulate personal privacy (Kantor and Lehr, 1975). Members come together for family rituals, such as playing games or watching television, but they also need and want to spend time alone. For example, adolescents who have their own bedrooms might spend considerable time there using stereo equipment and headphones to block out family interaction. Freedom from excessive demands is another aspect of privacy. In some families individuals may feel they "never get any peace and quiet" (Gove et al., 1979:65).

The amount and degree of privacy a family member gets frequently depend on how much power each member wields. Powerful members can more readily regulate family interaction to give themselves space and time alone. For example, a parent might send the children outside or to another room, but the children cannot send the parent away.

Being shortchanged on privacy is associated with irritability, weariness, family violence, poor family relationships, and emotional distance from one's spouse.

In addition to the issue of privacy, each family member has feelings about what possessions and spaces are hers or his and are not to be violated without permission (Kantor and Lehr, 1975). We use the term **territoriality** for this reservation of space and defense of objects and places against their use by others.

Time represents another important dimension of family life. A factor that helps determine an individual's freedom is the timing of family activities. Even when all members agree on activities, they must still agree on their sequence: "Should we go swimming before lunch or after?" How often activities should take place and how long they should last are all matters for negotiation (Kantor and Lehr, 1975:78–89). Each family member has personal feelings about timing. For a small child, hearing a story five times may be just the beginning; for the parent, twice may be more than enough. Staying at a party until the wee hours might feel good to one spouse; the other might prefer to call it quits earlier. Working out a common rhythm for dialogue, sexual expression, and joint activities can be difficult for spouses, particularly when a "night person" marries a "morning person" (Cromwell et al., 1976; Adams and Cromwell, 1978).

In all intimate relationships partners alternately move toward each other, then back away to reestablish a sense of individuality or separateness. The needs of different individuals vary, of course, and so do the temporary or permanent balances that couples and families strike between togetherness and individuality.

"Family life in any form has both costs and benefits.... Belonging to any group involves some loss of personal freedom" (Chilman, 1978a). Indirectly, at least, we've addressed some costs of family living. But families provide the seminal function of providing people a place to belong.

Families as a Place to Belong

Whether families are traditional or newer in form (such as communes or cohabiting partnerships), they create a "place to belong" in at least two ways. First, families create *boundaries*, both physical and psychological, between themselves and the rest of the world. Whether in multiple- or single-family dwellings, families in virtually all cultures mark off some physical space that is private and theirs alone (Boulding, 1976). Family members determine "what kinds of things are allowed to enter the family space and under what conditions and what kinds of items are simply not permitted admission" (Kantor and Lehr, 1975:68).

With an idea of how the external world resembles and differs from the family interior, family members screen off certain aspects of the larger, outside culture. They put up fences so that they can barbeque or sunbathe in privacy, for example, and they prevent certain people, books, pictures, words, and topics of conversation from entering the family interior. Spouses may screen each other's friends, and parents may screen their children's friends. Family members may patrol one another's activities, so that a child or a spouse is accompanied by another family member when leaving the family home, in order to provide safety from the real or imagined hazards of the outside world. They may also keep a kind of "border patrol" or "watch" on strangers or others approaching or telephoning the house (Kantor and Lehr, 1975:70).

A second way families create a place to belong is by performing an **archival family function.** That is, families create, store, preserve, and pass on particular objects, events, or rituals that members consider relevant to their personal identities and to maintaining the family as a unique existential reality or group (Weigert and Hastings, 1977:1173–74). The archives contain a variety of symbols:

■ All family photo albums resemble each other, celebrating good times and rites of passage with snapshots and formal poses. Literally and symbolically, they help preserve a family's identity.

There are snapshots of happy times, posed and unposed (apparently never snapshots of sad times); family movies of celebrations or rites of passage or vacations; ... artifacts from infancy or childhood transmuted into relics of lost and sweet identities; symbols of recognition and achievement such as diplomas; ... pointed anecdotes about infancy or youth which reinforce a particular identity as the reckless one, the always helpful one, or the unlucky one ("Remember the time you accidentally broke two of Mr. Jones's porch windows!"); and various ... symbols which function almost like debts binding one to past relationships with the implication of potential future obligations ("Here is part of the plaster cast from your left leg which you broke in sixth grade, when I had to care for you at home for six weeks—remember that when I am unable to walk around by myself anymore"). [Weigert and Hastings, 1977:1174] ▪

Family archives and boundaries help create a family identity, which in turn becomes integrated into each family member's personal identity (Weigert and Hastings, 1977).

Summary

It is now widely recognized that change and development continue throughout adult life. People make choices, either actively and knowledgeably or by default, that determine the courses of their own lives. These choices are influenced by a number of factors, including age expectations, religion, social class, gender, and current events.

Adult life can be seen as a sequence of stages during which people structure their life course. These stages are followed by more turbulent periods of transition when adults step back to evaluate their goals and accomplishments. Entering the adult world, settling down, and life's second half may be seen as stages; the age-thirty transition and the midlife transition are periods of self-appraisal.

Traditionally, social scientists measured the stages of both the adult's life and the "family life cycle" according to family changes, such as the birth of children and retirement. But the independent changes each adult experiences also affect family life profoundly. While families fill the important function of providing members a place to belong, finding personal freedom within families is an ongoing, negotiated process.

Key Terms

age expectations *28*	age-thirty transition *31*
choosing by default *28*	settling down *34*
choosing knowledgeably *29*	midlife transition *34*
	midlife transition *34*
values clarification *29*	empty nest *40*
adult life course *30*	archival family
life spiral *30*	function *42*
entering the adult world *30*	

Study Questions

1. Some people think that little change occurs in people's personalities after young adulthood, while others think that change also occurs throughout adulthood. How do you feel about this? Are there as many changes in adulthood? Are they as important as changes earlier in life?
2. What are some of the social factors that influence people's choices? How do these factors operate? Does the fact that social factors limit people's options mean that important life decisions are predetermined? Why or why not?
3. What are the components of knowledgeable decision making? How does knowledgeable choosing differ from choosing by default? How might the consequences be different? Give some examples of the two forms of decision making.
4. What are the major components of each stage of the adult life cycle? How are the stages alike? How are they different?
5. How has the view of adult life as fluid rather than static affected the way social scientists study family life?
6. How does the concept *adult life course* differ from *family life course* and *life spiral*?
7. What is territoriality, and why does it need to be negotiated among family members?
8. What is the archival function of families? How important is it?

Suggested Readings

Aldous, Joan
1978 *Family Careers.* New York: Wiley.
Textbook analyzing the family from the life-cycle perspective that makes an effort to integrate individual and family development. New edition forthcoming.

Brunner, Marguerite Ashworth
1979 *Pass It On: How to Make Your Own Family Keepsakes.* Rochester, Wash.: Sovereign Books.
Ideas for ways to enrich the family archives in the current generation.

Duvall, Evelyn M., and Brent C. Miller
1985 *Marriage and Family Development.* 6th ed. New York: Harper & Row.
Family development textbook whose senior author is one of the pioneers of this framework.

Easterlin, Richard
1987 *Birth and Fortune.* 2d rev. ed. Chicago: University of Chicago Press.
Data-based analysis of how cohort size (how many people were born at the same time) affects economic opportunity, chance of marrying, chance of divorcing, crime rate, mental health, and so on.

Elder, Glen H., Jr.
1977 "Family history and the life course." *Journal of Family History* 2 (4) (Winter):279–304.
This scholarly article outlines some distinctive ways that societal and historical factors, such as the Great Depression of the 1930s, affect individual and family life courses. If you are not familiar with professional social-scientific jargon, this article will be difficult to read.

Levinson, Daniel J.
1978 *The Seasons of a Man's Life.* New York: Knopf.
Levinson is a Yale professor of psychology who researched the adult life cycle for years before journalist Gail Sheehy popularized the concept. (Some of Sheehy's book is based on Levinson's work.) Levinson describes specific developmental periods in adult men's lives, and male readers especially should be able to identify with the feelings and experiences the author describes.

Lukas, J. Anthony
1985 *Common Ground: A Turbulent Decade in the Lives of Three American Families.* New York: Knopf.
How school desegregation in Boston affects a black family, a working-class white family, and a white middle-class family.

Norton, Eleanor Holmes
1985 "Restoring the traditional black family." *New York Times Magazine,* June 2:43ff.
Connects changes in the black family to economic trends.

Rubin, Lillian B.
1979 *Women of a Certain Age: The Midlife Search for Self.* New York: Harper & Row.
Interview-based study of "empty nest" women that is readable and optimistic.

Shange, Ntozake
1985 *Betsey Brown: A Novel.* New York: St. Martin's Press.
About a black girl growing up in St. Louis in the fifties, describing the year school integration disrupted lives. This novel considers the stress created in black families by racism and court-ordered integration and by class conflict within the black community.

Sheehy, Gail
1974 *Passages: Predictable Crises of Adult Life.* New York: Bantam.
A journalistic account of transitions throughout the adult life cycle, based on psychological research. While Levinson's book (see above) is about men, Sheehy discusses both sexes' "predictable crises" and may even emphasize women's.
1981 *Pathfinders.* New York: Morrow.
Another readable book that could be considered a sequel to *Passages,* this work examines the lives of people who chose to make significant changes in adulthood.

Sorensen, A. B., F. E. Weinert, and L. R. Sherrod
1986 *Human Development and the Life Course: Multidisciplinary Perspectives.* Hillsdale, N.J.: Erlbaum.
Scholarly articles on adult development and the life course for those who would like to learn more about this perspective.

Troll, Lillian E.
1975 *Early and Middle Adulthood: The Best Is Yet to Be—Maybe.* Monterey, Calif.: Brooks/Cole.
One volume in the *Life Span Human Development Series,* this little book discusses, in academic style, physical, intellectual, and personality development during middle adulthood with implications for married and family living. The book examines husband-wife roles, parenting, grandparenting, adults as children, and adult development in the job world.

2 Changing Gender Roles

*No individual and no
society can benefit from
a circumstance in which
men fear intimacy and
women fear
impersonality.*

ALICE S. ROSSI, "Gender and
Parenthood"

The two chapters in Part I focus on the choices people make, and the kinds of influences that affect their choices. This chapter deals especially with one important influence: the expectations associated with being male or female in our society. Gender influences virtually every aspect of people's relations with one another. And gender affects one's **self-concept**: the basic feelings people have about themselves, their abilities, and their worth.

We will discuss some traditional and emerging aspects of women's and men's roles. We will examine the influence of both genetics and cultural environment on gender-associated behavior: Do people learn to behave "appropriately" as men or women, or are they born that way? We'll also discuss what can happen as individuals choose to change their attitudes, expectations, and behaviors with regard to gender roles. To begin, we will review some character traits traditionally associated with masculinity and femininity.

INSTRUMENTAL MEN/EXPRESSIVE WOMEN

Traditionally, the number of traits on which women and men have been said to differ is virtually inexhaustible. Men are believed to be aggressive, independent, unemotional, objective, and not easily influenced by others' opinions. They "know their way around," make decisions comfortably, and are self-confident, logical, competitive, and ambitious. People don't expect men to express feelings of tenderness easily (Broverman et al., 1972:63).

Women are said to be talkative, warm, gentle, and aware of others' feelings. Women are not considered to be as naturally ambitious or competitive as men (Broverman et al., 1972:63). In short, people have traditionally perceived men as active and women as passive.

Social scientists use two other terms to differentiate these traditional character traits: instrumental and expressive. **Instrumental character traits** are associated with masculinity and enable one to accomplish difficult tasks or goals. Instrumental traits, such as competitiveness, self-confidence, logic, and nonemotionality, are supposedly natural to men and help them provide for their families successfully.

A relative absence of instrumental traits has traditionally been thought to characterize women. **Expressive character traits** are perceived as more feminine. These traits include warmth, sensitivity to the needs of others, and the ability to express tender feelings. Relative to women, men have been perceived as lacking in these characteristics (Broverman et al., 1972:66–67). Today, even as attitudes about gender-related traits are changing, to some extent these cultural beliefs remain.[1] In a recent study 128 college students rated the "desirable" man and "desirable" woman as similar on 42 out of 54 attributes; attitudes were egalitarian. However, stereotypes about "typical" men and women remained; men and women were thought to differ on 53 out of the 54 items (Ruble, 1983).

It is important to recognize here that individual men and women probably perceive themselves as less extremely "masculine" or "feminine" than the general stereotypes (Rosenkrantz et al., 1968). Research shows, for example, that children raised in families in which the mother works outside the home or has more power in relation to her husband tend to view women as more competent than do children raised in families where only the father is breadwinner and head of the household (Broverman et al., 1972; Van Fossen, 1977). To a significant degree, nevertheless, virtually all people internalize gender-related attitudes and expectations (Rosenkrantz et al., 1968; Bem, 1975:62).

Inasmuch as people believe that women and men have different gender-linked character traits, they expect males and females to behave in ways consistent with these traits. As sociologist Talcott Parsons wrote:

The adult feminine role [is] anchored primarily in the internal affairs of the family, as wife, mother and manager of the household, while the role of the adult male is primarily anchored in the occupational world, in his job and through it by his status-giving and income-earning functions for the family [1955:14–15]. ■

Feminine and masculine character traits, then, become prescriptions for behavior. We call such prescribed behavior **gender roles.** The next two sections discuss some traditional and emerging aspects of masculine and feminine gender roles.

"His" Role

The traditional gender role for males is demanding. A man must be successful, strong, self-assured, smart—and never afraid. Men can live up to these expectations in various ways. They can be successful in their careers, accumulating such symbols of their competitive achievement as wealth, fame, positions of leadership, or expensively dressed wives or mistresses (David and Brannon, 1976:90). Whatever their occupational success, many men command authority and respect because they are the principal family breadwinners. (Chapters 7 and 10 examine this further.)

Success is but one dimension of the male gender role (Pleck and Pleck, 1980; Franklin, 1984). Rather than show affection or express feelings of tenderness, men learn to be "strong and silent" (Balswick and Peek, 1977:222–29). This inexpressiveness is often a major barrier to intimacy in marriage. (Gender differences in communications are discussed in Chapter 9.)

Another aspect of the male gender role emphasizes adventure, sometimes coupled with the need to humiliate, outwit, or defeat. "Real" men, our culture holds, "give 'em hell" (at least sometimes).[2] Young boys learn to give 'em hell in such sports as boxing, hockey, and football (David and Brannon, 1976:200). Adult men give 'em hell in war, barroom brawls, daring driving, or playing or watching sports. Overemphasizing this aspect of the male role can have tragic results; in our society men are more frequently involved in criminal assault and have higher rates of accidental death than women do. As the figures in Table 2•1 illustrate, both black and white males in all age categories die from motor vehicle and other accidents, as well as from suicide and homicide, three to four times more often than do females.

---

1. In her book *Women and Dualism* (1979) Lynda Glennon pointed out the pitfalls of dichotomous thinking about human behavior. She viewed instrumental and expressive traits and behaviors as human qualities that exist apart from gender. In traditional thinking, however, we have tied them closely to gender, labeling expressive behavior as "feminine" and instrumental behavior as "masculine." But by severing the cultural cognitive link between instrumental and expressive behaviors and gender, men and women can be free to display valued qualities without being labeled "masculinized" or "feminized." We can further abandon dichotomous thinking by conceiving of a synthesis or combination of instrumental and expressive characteristics in the same person, as in the androgynous person discussed later in this chapter.

---

2. Sociologist William Goode points out that descriptions of the masculine role may be oversimplified. "The male role prescriptions that commonly appear in the literature do not describe correctly," for example, "the male ideal in Jewish culture, which embodied a love of music, learning, and literature; an avoidance of physical violence; an acceptance of tears and sentiment, nurturance, and a sensitivity to others' feelings" (1982: 135).

■ Like father, like son: Many males continue to follow the dictates of their traditional gender role; part of "his" role involves being strong, self-assured—and inexpressive.

All these elements of the hypothetical male gender role—ambition, inexpressiveness, the "give 'em hell" tradition—can cause problems for men when they try to live up to them, as the case study "An Inside View of Masculinity" points out.

For several reasons the traditional male gender role is no longer a valid model. The fundamental shift in the United States in the late twentieth century from an industrial to a service-based economy has had important effects on the masculine role.

For many men unemployment, or the fear of unemployment, has made the traditional family-provider role precarious and thereby less fulfilling. Then, too, the nature of work has changed. The increasing prevalence of white-collar office work over blue-collar jobs has required men to develop cooperative behavior patterns rather than physical strength or mechanical ability. Avenues other than work through which men have traditionally established their masculine credentials are also being under-

CASE STUDY 2·1

AN INSIDE VIEW OF MASCULINITY

The following is from an essay written by a male student of marriage and family in his 20s. He spent six years in the Marine Corps and served in Vietnam. Here he looks back at his childhood and the pressures he felt to conform to the traditional male role. Ironically, as you will see, it was his Marine Corps experience during the 1960s that led him to view the traditional masculine stereotype as more myth than reality.

Growing up to be a man has been confusing and frustrating. From the time I was very young until now, I had to live with the idea of how things should be, not how they are.

As a young boy, I was brought up in the traditional male role, with constant pressure on what I should be, not what I am. In grammar school, I began to believe that power was everything. No matter what you said, if you could back it up with power, you were right. So I went out to prove I was powerful. There were triumphs and defeats, but I did get my point across—that I was a force to be reckoned with.

What I eventually achieved was splitting up the people I knew into two groups: people I could push around, and people that could push me around. . . .

I rallied all the kids on my block to attack the kids on the next block. We made swords out of wood, used garbage cans as shields, and went into battle. We threw rocks. What a thrill it was to lead the troops to battle. . . .

As I got older, I did other things to prove my masculinity. I would hitch a ride on a freight train and climb the highest trees, all to prove I was daring and brave. I would do things that I would never do without someone watching, all the time never letting anyone know I was afraid of the ferris wheel. I couldn't tolerate being called a "sissy" or a "fraidy cat." That just wasn't what they called a man.

In high school I participated in the roughest sports. Being on the football team was proof in itself that I had to be a man. . . . I wrestled because the people who wrestled would tease the basketball players about playing a sissy sport. I ran the 880 in track because it was referred to as a long, grueling sprint. Wrestling built up the muscles, football was a definite man's sport, and track demonstrated endurance. All of these served as my identity. I even took woodshop one year, not because I was interested in working with wood, but I felt that a man should know how to do it.

There were certain things I liked to do, but I would do them privately until I could feel out the crowd to see if they would fit into the acceptable standards of being a man. One was art. I became very accomplished as an oil painter, but I would only paint the things that men would be interested in—paintings of football scenes and the like. . . .

I remember the first time I felt I was in love. The girl and I were both 14. I met her at a Little League baseball game. She was watching her brother, and I was watching her. I used to walk to her house to see her. I was playing the he-man game. I was so afraid of saying the things that I felt for fear she would think I was a sissy. I also felt that I had never been really close to anyone before, and I didn't know how to act. At the time I didn't realize that girls were going to play such a large part of proving my manliness. We ran around for about six months. I never even kissed her—something I never overlooked in later relationships. . . .

Now I feel that maybe at the time I actually resented girls. When I was younger, men didn't get mushy. When I was asked as a small boy if I was going to get married, I would promptly say no! I would chase little girls with worms or anything I felt they wouldn't like. All my friends did the same because there was a feeling of not getting too close to [girls], for fear they would try to get you to play house. . . .

When I got out of high school, I made my most drastic move ever to prove my manliness. I joined the Marines. What could be more manly than that? Everyone knows the Marine Corps builds men, and I felt I could use more building.

It wasn't until I got in the Marine Corps that I realized that I could get close to men. In boot camp and in Nam I found out these people felt the same way I did. They had the same self-doubts and were trying to satisfy the same needs. It wasn't until this time that I found out that other people are not all living up to the myth. I got answers and true, gut feelings from these guys, and I found out there was nothing wrong with me. We had all been victims of having to live up to a standard that never existed in the first place.

■ How does this essay illustrate both masculine and feminine stereotypes? As a little boy, this young man saw getting too close to girls as dangerous because girls "try to get you to play house." Does this situation have a parallel for older male-female dating relationships? (Chapter 6 answers this question.) What limits did the writer impose on himself by trying to live up to the masculine myth? What kind of courage did it take for him to write this essay?

TABLE 2·1 Death Rates from Accidents and Violence, 1984, by Sex and Race (per 100,000 population in specified group, age adjusted)

Cause of Death	White	Black
Male		
Motor vehicle accidents	28.4	27.2
All other accidents	22.9	37.5
Suicide	19.7	11.2
Homicide	8.2	50.8
Female		
Motor vehicle accidents	10.9	7.6
All other accidents	7.6	12.5
Suicide	5.6	2.3
Homicide	2.9	11.0

SOURCE: U.S. National Center for Health Statistics, 1986d:34.

mined. For example, "The traditional status of the heroic warrior no longer awaits soldiers in the current age of nuclear and high-tech warfare" (Brod, 1986:46).

As we'll see later in this chapter, many of these gender-role expectations for males are changing accordingly. Traditional gender-role expectations for females are often no more suited to contemporary reality than those for men.

"Her" Role

The traditional female gender role assumes that women need to be taken care of by men; in return they offer emotional support and sexual availability. Fortunate to have a man in her life, the woman acts as helpmate, encouraging and cheering the man's accomplishments, and perhaps bearing and rearing "his" children.

This role *may* have been appropriate in the last century. But—if for no other reason than population or demographic changes—the female gender role no longer fits the traditional model. Today women can expect to share fewer of their years with husbands and/or children. The rising divorce

rate, discussed in Chapter 16, is one reason for this. But even if she stays married, a woman can expect to spend almost ten years as a widow, compared with just under four years in 1900 (Uhlenberg, 1980).

Moreover, married women are having fewer (if any) children, and many women are finished with childbearing and child rearing at a relatively early age. In addition, women (and men) live longer today than in the past. Since 1970 those over age 65 have experienced a fairly dramatic increase in longevity, due largely to new treatments for heart and cerebrovascular diseases (Crimmins, 1984). Consequently, by 1984 U.S. life expectancy at birth among whites was 71.8 for males and 78.8 for females; among blacks those figures were 67.3 and 75.2, respectively. The Social Security Administration now projects a life expectancy at birth for females in 2080 of 94.2 years (U.S. Bureau of the Census, 1986b; Crimmins, 1984)!

Because they have fewer children and live longer, women today can expect to spend more years outside the mother role. Then, too, the image women may have of a satisfying grandmotherhood in later life is rapidly becoming outdated. Geographic mobility, divorce, and remarriage distance children from grandparents. And increased longevity means that what grandchildren there are will have to satisfy the needs not only of grandparents but also of great-grandparents and possibly even great-great-grandparents (Deegan, 1986).

As with the traditional male gender role, many elements of the female stereotype are inaccurate, as psychologists Eleanor Maccoby and Carol Jacklin demonstrated (1974). After reviewing all the psychological research on sex differences from 1966 through the early 1970s, they found little evidence for many of the differences people often assume exist: Girls are not necessarily more social, more suggestible, less motivated to achieve, or less analytical; nor do they have lower self-esteem than boys. Maccoby and Jacklin did find some differences between boys and girls; for example, girls tend to be more verbal, and boys tend to be better at math and at visual-spatial tasks. But even these differences were not true of young children. The researchers suggest that these discrepancies result more from differences in socialization (explained later in this chapter) than from inborn differences. The only difference between boys and girls that clearly seemed to Maccoby and Jacklin to be biologically based was in aggressiveness. The term

■ Besides bearing and rearing children, women have customarily been responsible for maintaining family traditions and holiday rituals, as this mother and daughter are doing for a Thanksgiving dinner. Although this new mother may expect to treat her twins the same, society has different expectations for this girl and boy.

aggressiveness here refers to physical or verbal hostility and attempts to injure another, not simply competitiveness.

Maccoby and Jacklin concluded that there is not enough evidence to tell whether many other traits, such as competitiveness, general activity level, timidity, nurturance, and dominance, are biologically based or a result of social influences.[3] This

last characteristic, dominance, is one that merits special note, for it is a cultural trait that has traditionally shaped personal relationships between men and women.

MALE DOMINANCE

Are the different culturally prescribed personality traits and role expectations of women and men equally valued by society? Research suggests that, on the whole, male traits have been more highly valued. When psychiatrists, psychologists, and social work professionals were asked what traits the "mentally healthy adult" (sex unspecified) should possess, the traits they listed were almost identical to those considered ideal for the "mentally healthy *male*," and sharply different from those of the

---

3. Conclusions that can be drawn from Maccoby and Jacklin's research review are limited by the fact that much of the research on gender differences was done on children only and not on adults. Until psychologists felt the influence of the women's movement, they were not interested enough to design studies specifically to explore gender differences. Much psychological research on adults simply used males as generic humans, with results we now realize are limited (Gilligan, 1982). Researchers were apt to include both sexes in their research on children, but not in their research on adults.

"mentally healthy *female*" (Broverman et al., 1972:71; Gilligan, 1982).

Our society is not as patriarchal or male dominated as a traditional agricultural society or some contemporary Latin American, Asian, or Moslem societies, in which women may not be allowed to work outside their homes or to participate in public life. But our society is not egalitarian either. That male qualities have been more highly valued than female qualities indicates some degree of male dominance in our society. While there is some suggestion that the relative evaluation of masculine and feminine qualities may be shifting (Silvern and Ryan, 1983), women's participation in economic and political life is still characterized by striking disadvantages. Our society, therefore, can best be characterized as moderately patriarchal, or male dominant.

Male dominance is the cultural idea of masculine superiority whereby men exercise the most control and influence over society's members. Male dominance is deeply rooted in our own historical tradition, as, for example, the *unity of person principle* indicates. Under English common law, which applied in America, married couples were not separate individuals but became one, with the woman's role clearly subordinate. A wife could not institute a lawsuit or execute a valid contract without her husband. After marriage all personal property owned by a wife came under the exclusive control of her husband. "He could spend her money, including wages, sell her slaves or stocks, and appropriate her clothing and jewelry.... He made all managerial decisions concerning her lands and tenements and controlled the rents and profits" (Salmon, 1986:15). While these property laws were repealed in the nineteenth century, the unity of person principle was not overturned until 1960 (*U.S. v. Dege*, 1960).

As a group, women do not enjoy an equal share of money, power, or prestige, even though they account for slightly more than half the population. They are entering the labor force in record numbers, and female admissions to professional schools have increased dramatically. But the majority continue to fill relatively low-paid **pink-collar jobs**, comprising, for example, over 95 percent of dental hygienists, preschool teachers, secretaries, receptionists, typists, domestic servants, and registered nurses (Hacker, 1986:30).

Where women are professionals, they tend to be in the lower-ranking and lower-paying professions. Even in the same occupation women earn less than men (Quinn, 1983; Hacker, 1986). (In Chapter 11 we discuss pink-collar work.)

Full-time women workers earn only 65 percent of what male workers earn. Women are members of political bodies much less frequently than are men. While the proportion of women in state legislatures has risen to 15.5 percent in 1985 (from 4 percent in 1969), there has not been a corresponding increase in the election of women to Congress, where women hold 4.5 percent of the seats according to a study conducted by the Rutgers Center for the American Woman and Politics (Tomasson, 1987). Such restriction of women to the lower ranks of power and reward is the result of direct discrimination, traditional socialization that limits women's choices and goals, and structural barriers such as women's greater responsibility for home and child care and males' priority in job-related geographic moves.

The essence of male dominance lies in the fact that for centuries men have been defined as normal, standard, or ideal human beings, while women have been viewed as different from men. Simone de Beauvoir has observed that man is defined as a human being while woman is defined as "other." Whenever a woman tries to behave as a human being she is accused of trying to emulate the male. As Figure 2•1 shows, even a woman's posture is culturally restricted. In our society women traditionally learn to sit in "ladylike" positions, while men are permitted to relax and sit comfortably.

Male dominance has a long tradition (as we'll see in the discussion of patriarchy in Chapter 7) that is rooted in the prehistoric agricultural revolution. Until fairly recently it was virtually unquestioned. One influential person who gave great credence to male dominance was Sigmund Freud.

Sigmund Freud on Male Dominance

Sigmund Freud (1856–1939) was an Austrian physician and the founder of psychoanalysis. He enunciated what he considered to be a scientific theory of femininity, which powerfully reinforced age-old prejudices and which continues to influence individuals and male-female relationships even today.

Freud assumed the biological, sexual, and moral inferiority of women. This assumption is evident in

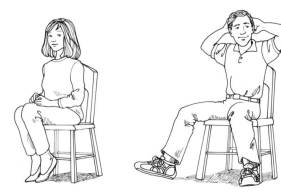

Figure 2·1
Body posture. Typical body postures of men and women reveal the more restricted, unassertive behavior expected of women. By contrast, men are expected to be more expansive and self-confident. (Source: Adapted from Frieze et al., 1978:330)

his well-known description of the phenomenon of **penis envy.** At about age 4, Freud theorized, girls and boys make an important discovery: Boys have a penis, and girls don't. They react differently. Boys assume that little girls are inferior to them—an assumption that persists throughout later stages of development. Girls, on the other hand, are envious. They devalue themselves and all other women. While never completely resigned to their femininity, most women, according to Freud, get some relief from this envy with the birth of their first baby.[4]

Freud's theory of femininity has been rigorously criticized. These data were gathered from the dreams and childhood memories of patients in psychoanalysis, yet were applied to mentally healthy adults. On those grounds alone their validity is questionable, but there are other reasons as well. Another criticism is the cultural limitedness of his viewpoint. Freud, like most nineteenth-century Western males, made the conscious and unconscious assumption of male dominance: The male

is the norm; the female is an inadequate, biologically inferior male. Freud described the **clitoris,** for instance, as an underdeveloped male organ. (Later writers have pointed out that he never referred to the penis, in contrast, as a "bloated clitoris" [Rotkin, 1973]; nor was a case ever made for male "womb envy"!)

A final criticism of Freud's work is that he largely ignored social context. It is true even today, for example, that some parents desire and value boy babies more than they do girls. But this seems to be because a boy is more likely to carry on the family name, not because the mother wants to possess a penis. Also, when girls wish they were boys, their reasons probably have more to do with the higher prestige and power associated with masculinity than the penis itself (Lynn, 1969). Freud's assumption that genetic physiological factors alone determine women's and men's attitudes has been capsulized "anatomy is destiny." In the following discussions we'll see whether this assumption is supported by evidence.

IS ANATOMY DESTINY?

Individuals' sexual identity involves both the physiology with which they were born and the attitudes and behavior by which they present themselves as either female or male. The word **sex** refers only to male or female physiology. Sex includes the different chromosomal, hormonal, and anatomical components of males and females at birth. We use the term **gender** far more broadly, to describe attitudes and behavior associated with and expected of the two sexes.

With this distinction, one can ask what aspects of gender-associated behavior depend on physiology and what aspects people have learned. For example, is the desire to paint one's fingernails something females but not males are born with? Are males biologically destined to be more instrumental and powerful than females? Or do women and men learn their behavior?

Advocates of the genetic basis for gender-related differences today invoke varied arguments to support their beliefs. Some find "proof" for inborn differences in religious works such as the Bible; various religious groups see gender roles as sacred and ordained by God. Scientific arguments are provided by **ethologists,** who study human beings as

---

4. As they grow up, they are able to partially adjust. The "vaginal orgasm"—a myth that has been debunked by Masters and Johnson, as discussed in Chapter 4—provides one substitute: taking a man's penis temporarily into the vagina. Another partial substitute, childbearing, also provides some relief from penis envy.

an evolved animal species. Ethologists note male dominance among most primates, arguing that *Homo sapiens* inherited this condition through evolutionary processes. Ethologists also argue that the prehistoric male's greater size and strength let him perform instrumental tasks (such as hunting and defense) better and that these roles are the basis of the political and familial controls that have become genetically established in all societies. Specifically, ethologists attribute masculine instrumentality and dominance to the male sex hormone, testosterone (Goldberg, 1973).[5]

Most sociologists disagree with these ethologists.[6] They stress the extent to which culture nurtures and shapes gender roles. A classic study of

anthropologist Margaret Mead's is important here (1935). Mead (1901–1978) observed a number of primitive tribes in New Guinea. She found that gender-related personality traits differed among three tribes in particular. Among the Arapesh both men and women were gentle, passive, warm, and nurturing people. In the Mundugumor tribe both men and women were aggressive, hostile, and uninterested in nurturing children. Mead did find gender-related differences among the Tchambuli: Tchambuli men were emotional and dependent, while the women were dominant, impersonal, and managerial. Mead concluded that apart from individual differences, gender-related character traits and roles are more apt to result from cultural learning than from genetics (1935).[7]

An Interactive Influence

Today there is growing evidence that gender-linked characteristics result from the interaction of cultural learning and biology. Some of the most striking research in this regard is that of John Money and Anke Ehrhardt at Johns Hopkins University Hospital in Baltimore.

Money and Ehrhardt studied **hermaphrodites,** persons whose genitalia cannot be clearly identified as either female or male at birth. Their research supported arguments for both socialization and genetics as influences on behavior. For the argument for socialization, Money and Ehrhardt found that the most crucial factor in these infants' ultimate self-perception as girls or boys, and later as women or men, was their **assignment** (at birth or shortly after, hermaphrodites are often arbitrarily assigned a sex identity and are then

---

5. **Hormones** are chemical substances secreted into the bloodstream by the endocrine glands; they influence the activities of cells, tissues, and body organs. Sex hormones are secreted by male or female gonads, or sex glands. The primary male sex hormone is testosterone, produced in the male testes. Females secrete testosterone also, but in smaller amounts. The primary female hormones are estrogen and progesterone, secreted by the female ovaries.

Sex hormones influence sexual dimorphism: sex-related differences in body structure and size, muscle development, fat distribution, hair growth, and voice quality. Various researchers report findings that testerosterone levels correlate positively with tendencies toward physical and verbal aggression, although not necessarily with desire for achievement or competitiveness (Bardwick, 1971).

6. Some sociologists, however, have attempted to provide scientific support for the notion that women should not have careers. Sociologists such as Talcott Parsons maintained that instrumental roles for men and expressive roles for women were functional for society. Parsons and colleagues (Parsons and Bales, 1955) maintained that clear specialization of roles was necessary for group (family) survival, that the family would disintegrate if the wife became "competitive" with the husband by taking a serious interest in outside work, and that only one person (the husband) should link the family to other social institutions such as the economy and the polity.

For many years sociology textbooks advocated traditional roles as socially beneficial and conducive to better marriages (Ehrlich, 1971). The evidence does not support this point of view, as male expressiveness is an important contributor to marital happiness (Laws, 1971). Cross-cultural evidence shows that instrumental and expressive tasks are not rigidly segregated by gender (Crano and Aranoff, 1975), nor, according to Marwell's theoretical analysis, are they functional in advanced societies (Marwell, 1975). Much instrumental activity is apparent in historical descriptions of women's actual roles in the European family, which involved a high ratio of productive (market-oriented) work compared to child care or domestic chores until at least the nineteenth century (Tilly and Scott, 1978).

---

7. Mead's work has recently been criticized in a book by anthropologist Derek Freeman (Freeman, 1983), who spent six years in Samoa in the 1960s. His criticism is specific to Mead's work in Samoa (Mead, 1928), and he portrays a vastly different Samoa, raising questions about the validity of Mead's work. While Freeman's attack has generated a great deal of interest and some of his points have been accepted, other reviewers have pointed out that *all* participant observation, not only Mead's, has a subjective character. Addressing the more general issue of Freeman's apparent attempt to discredit the notion of cultural (rather than biological) influences on behavior, noted anthropologist Marvin Harris wrote: "The bottom line of [Freeman's] attempt to discredit the Boasian position ('nurture' as well as 'nature') by toppling Margaret Mead is a fat zero" (Harris, 1983:27). The issue continues to be debated.

■ Is anatomy destiny? Some individuals seem to shape their own destinies more than others do. Consider this Olympic gymnast and her exceptional coordination of grace and strength. How much of her athletic ability is inherent and how much is learned?

treated accordingly). Hermaphrodites assigned *male* grow up to think and behave as men, while those assigned *female* grow up to think and behave as women (Money and Ehrhardt, 1974).

Money and Ehrhardt also found evidence for genetic influence. Androgynized females (female infants who had been exposed prenatally to a greater amount of the male sex hormone androgen through drugs taken by the mother) were much more apt than normal girls to be tomboys. They were more likely to be athletic, play with boys, assert themselves, compete, and reject feminine adornment. They tended to be uninterested in either dolls or babies. As adult women, they were ori-

ented more toward careers than toward marriage. Such masculinization, the researchers concluded, probably results from the action of male sex hormones on the developing fetus (Money and Ehrhardt, 1974). Some biologists have noted the possibility that parents' awareness of their daughters' exposure to masculine hormones may have affected the parents' behavior toward their daughters, so that Money and Ehrhardt's findings cannot be presumed to be solely biological in origin (Bleier, 1984).

A more recent study investigated the relationship between testosterone concentration and gender-role identity among females (Baucom and Besch, 1985). Eighty-four women students completed masculinity and femininity scales, which are questionnaire items designed to indicate the extent to which the individual's personality traits were similar to the expressive (feminine) or instrumental (masculine) roles discussed earlier in the chapter. Testosterone concentration was determined from samples of their saliva. The researchers found that women characterized by "the stereotypic feminine personality" had a relatively low level of testosterone, while females with more stereotypically masculine traits had somewhat higher levels. Hormones may predispose one to "appropriate" gender-related behavior.

Social and psychological factors—what's happening in one's environment—can also influence hormone secretion levels. For example, hormone levels directing a new mother's ability to produce milk are influenced by her culturally learned attitudes toward nursing (Bardwick, 1971:80). Environmental factors can cause increased secretion of the sex hormone involved (Rossi, 1977). When a teenager steals a car to go for a joy ride, the action may stimulate increased secretions of testosterone. (This may in turn result in a greater tendency to act aggressively in the future.)

These facts point to what sociologist Alice Rossi (1977; 1984) has called the interactive influence of both "nature" (genetics) and "nurture" (learning) on sex-linked attitudes and behavior.[8] In Rossi's words,

It makes no sense to view biology and social experience as separate domains contesting for election as "primary causes." Biological processes unfold in a cultural context, and are themselves malleable, not stable and inevitable. So too, cultural processes take place within and through the biological organism; they do not take place in a biological vacuum [1984:10]. ■

---

8. We do not discuss recent research on possible differences in brain organization of females and males because much of it is new and has not yet been evaluated by critics. See McGuinness and Pribram (1979) for a review arguing the existence of differences. An exchange of views on the implications of biological research for gender roles appeared in recent issues of the feminist journal *Signs* and is worth reading for further information on this issue. We can expect new research in this area to have an impact on the debate about gender roles and their origins (Rogers and Walsh, 1982; DeBold and Luria, 1983; Rogers, 1983; Baker, 1980; Rossi, 1984).

The potential to be nurturing, expressive, and emotionally supportive may be greater in more female than male infants because of the action of female hormones even before birth. At the same time, prenatal effects of male hormones may give male infants greater potential for aggression. Beginning at birth, however, and throughout their lives, males and females learn sex-appropriate roles. It's important to recognize that cultural learning can either reinforce (as seems to be the case in our society) or minimize whatever genetic tendencies exist.

Male-dominant societies reinforce any genetic tendencies toward female expressivity and male aggression that may exist at birth. We'll see how this happens in the following section.

GENDER AND SOCIALIZATION

Societal attitudes influence how we behave. As people in a given society learn to talk, think, and feel, they **internalize** cultural attitudes; that is, they make the attitudes their own. Besides attitudes, people internalize cultural expectations about how to behave. The process by which society influences members to internalize attitudes and expectations is called **socialization.** In various ways society socializes people to adhere, often unconsciously, to culturally acceptable sex roles. We'll examine in some detail how language, family, and school function in gender socialization.

The Power of Language

You are probably already aware of how our language accentuates male-female differences rather than similarities. Soon after birth, most infants receive either a masculine or a feminine name. From that day on, gender identity is stamped on the individual so thoroughly that people who want to avoid gender identification (for instance, through the mail or in phone book listings) must use their initials only.

In addition to names, pronouns, adjectives, and nouns remind people that males and females are different: People use the pronouns *she* and *he*; doctors may tell new mothers, "You have a lovely little girl," or a "sturdy boy"; people speak of chairmen and cleaning ladies. Through language, then, people learn that males and females are essentially different.

Family and School

Parents treat female and male infants differently. When a new father lifts his baby boy, he'll probably jostle it a little; if it's a girl, he'll be more likely to cuddle it (Lewis, 1972:54). One study of mothers' reactions to infants (actually, a single infant) found that women were likely to hand "Adam" (dressed in blue pants) a toy train, and that they more often smiled and cooed at "Beth" (the same infant dressed in pink) and offered her a doll (Will et al., 1975).

The father will continue to play a bit more roughly with his son than with his daughter (Chafetz, 1974). As a toddler Mary will probably have a doll; by this time Johnny may already have his first football. In fact, boys have more toys—"toys that encourage activities directed away from home—toward sports, cars, animals, and the military—and the girls [have more] objects that encourage activities toward the home" (Rheingold and Cook, 1975:463, cited in Richardson, 1981:45–46).

When Mary reaches junior high school, other parents will probably call her to baby-sit; John, in turn, will be encouraged to get a paper route or mow lawns. This differential treatment will continue into Mary's and John's adulthood. Middle-aged mothers admit that they expect more attention and help from their grown daughters than from sons (Troll et al., 1979).

Parents do vary, however, and it appears that children of working mothers have less traditional views of gender roles. Not only are daughters of working mothers more supportive of less traditional roles (Van Fossen, 1977), but sons, too, are more likely to be more favorable toward women's entering the labor force (Powell and Steelman, 1982).

There has been some change over the last ten years. Some interesting nonsexist children's books are becoming available, and television is beginning to depict women in nontraditional roles more often than in the past. Data from the Detroit Area Study comparing the 1953 survey responses with those of 1971 and 1976 find parents much more likely to think both boys and girls should wash the car, make beds, and dust (O. Duncan, 1982). High school sen-

iors surveyed nationwide in 1976 and 1977 revealed that most of the girls expected to work outside the home for most of their adult lives, and many girls expected to work in high-level occupations. Moreover, nearly as many girls (72 percent) as boys (76 percent) expected work to be central to their lives. Deckard concluded that although changes in gender roles are likely to be spread unevenly across the population for some time (with some segments of society changing more than others), still a significant beginning has been made in acquainting children and young adults with the possibility of finding nontraditional (and more suitable) roles for themselves (Deckard, 1983:57–58).[9]

Identification and Learning Gender Roles

Socialization can take place in many ways—through punishment, imitation, or reward, for instance.[10]

According to David Lynn's gender-role socialization theory, the processes by which girls and boys internalize gender roles are different (Lynn, 1969). To understand why, it's important first to know what is meant by identification. **Identification** refers to a strong emotional attachment for a particular person ("model"), coupled with the desire to be like that person.

Lynn asserts that in infancy both males and females usually establish their initial and principal

---

9. In support of this conclusion, a recent study of working-class women found "overall attitudes toward the women's movement were surprisingly positive" (Ferree, 1983:496). "The . . . majority . . . see the relevance of the movement primarily in terms of future generations" (Ferree, 1983:493).

10. There are three gender-role socialization theories explaining how children develop a gender identity: social learning theory (parents reinforce desired behavior), modeling/identification theory (children learn gender roles by observing their parents), and Kohlberg's cognitive or self-socialization theory (children classify themselves as boys or girls by age 3, then search for clues as to appropriate behavior in the culture generally—mass media, for example—or in their particular social world). All three of these theories have insufficient or contradictory evidence—as do the Lynn (1969) and Chodorow (1978) theories, which we have chosen as most interesting to present. Readers who wish to pursue this topic, which has a substantial literature, should refer to Maccoby and Jacklin (1974), Richardson (1981), or Vander Zanden (1981).

identification with their mother and that neither gender ever completely loses this identification. But although girls and boys both begin by identifying with their mother, the similarities do not continue. When little Mary seeks to imitate her mother (or a female caretaker, if her mother works outside the home), she will be rewarded and praised. In contrast, little Johnny cannot imitate his mother. In order to learn appropriate gender-related behavior, he must weaken his initial emotional identification. Early in his life adults begin to admonish him for imitating "feminine" ways. Mary is permitted to dress up in her mother's clothes, for example, but her brother is chastised for doing the same thing.

To complicate matters further, Johnny's father is probably absent during most of Johnny's waking hours and consequently is unable to provide a strong role model. Thus, Johnny must piece together a cultural definition of masculinity from television, books, movies, peers, and a series of directions and reprimands from parents, teachers, and others. For the greater portion of Johnny's childhood, he learns masculinity primarily by being told what he is *not* to be. Because of this, says Lynn, and because internalizing the male gender role necessitates their shifting their initial identification from their mothers, boys may have difficulty learning to feel they are "really" boys. Many remain anxious throughout their lives, continually feeling called on to "prove their masculinity." Moreover, they learn hostility toward femininity and often, consequently, toward women (Lynn, 1969:64).

There are other implications of these two different methods of early gender-role learning. According to Lynn, the fact that Mary can learn by imitation and positive reinforcement (that is, positive praise and encouragement for desired behavior), while John has to make a mental effort to figure out his role, itself contributes to their different behaviors as adults. Throughout their lives females rely more on affection or demonstrate a greater need for affiliation. But because of the early mental exercise essential to learning their gender role, males develop greater problem-solving abilities (Lynn, 1969). And because they must weaken their identification with their mothers, males develop attitudes of independence more readily than do females (Bardwick, 1971).

It should be noted here that although boys initially experience greater difficulty in internalizing their gender role, they soon become aware of the higher value placed on masculinity (Broverman et al., 1972). Girls, as might be expected, do not have the same experience with reference to the feminine role. Indeed, a larger number of girls wish they were boys than vice versa.

A more recent theory of socialization, outlined in Nancy Chodorow's *The Reproduction of Mothering* (1978), is very similar to Lynn's in that it emphasizes the girl's continued attachment to the mother and the boy's break with this attachment. Chodorow goes further in drawing out the implications of this for limiting adult relationships. She also predicts the possible results if roles were changed. (See Box 2•1.)

Both Lynn's and Chodorow's theories, along with what we know about the more general influences of families, schools, and language in gender-role socialization, help explain how and why men tend to develop instrumental character traits, and women expressive ones. The question arises: Does internalizing this dichotomy allow people to feel as good as possible about themselves?

To answer this question, it is necessary to understand what is involved in feeling good about oneself. To do that, we will explore what is meant by self-concept. *Self-concept*, you may recall, refers to basic feelings people have about themselves, their talents, abilities, and worth. Persons with a positive self-concept enjoy an inner sense of worth. Recognizing their strengths and weaknesses, they accept themselves for what they are (Maslow, 1956). People whose self-concepts are not so positive are more unsure about their abilities and about their value as persons. Because they don't like or trust themselves as much as they could, they doubt whether others truly love or even like them.

Erik Erikson on Developing a Positive Self-Concept

How do people come to have a positive or a negative self-concept? According to psychologist Erik Erikson (1902–), people are not born with a sense of their own worth but develop one as they mature.

Acquiring a positive self-concept is a process that involves internalizing certain necessary attitudes, and this must take place in several sequential stages. The first of these is **trust**, the feeling, usually developed during infancy, that one can rely on oneself and others to provide for one's needs. After learning trust, individuals must acquire a sense of **autonomy**, the experience of self-control and self-direction, usually developed during toddlerhood. Autonomous people know and take care of their own needs and wants and can assert themselves with others to satisfy legitimate needs. They try not to let events or other people's opinions control their own actions or the course of their lives. Those who do not learn autonomy experience self-doubt and feelings of inferiority.

Next, people must learn to enjoy and be truly proud of their abilities and talents. They have to develop those talents. Only then can they acquire a sense of **identity**. By identity Erikson meant that individuals develop some sense of inner sameness. They "know who they are" throughout their endeavors and pursuits, no matter how varied these may be. They have a sense of continuity and consistency as persons.

Once people acquire a sense of identity, Erikson theorized, they are ready to choose **intimacy.** Erikson defined intimacy as the capacity to commit oneself to a particular other and to stick with this commitment, in spite of personal sacrifices, while sharing one's inner self with the other. The opposite of intimacy is **isolation**, which Erikson (1963) described as the result of engineering distance between oneself and others and of avoiding relationships that could lead to disclosure of inner feelings.

For people to feel good about themselves, then, they must trust themselves and others and be convinced of their own worth. They must be autonomous and reasonably independent, able to remain true to themselves in the face of rejection or unpopularity. And they must be able to engage in deep emotional relationships based on intimacy and self-disclosure. But expectations for women foster emotional dependency; they neglect to develop attitudes of autonomy, initiative, and industry. In fact, Erikson himself expected women to defer their identity formation until after they established intimacy with a potential marital partner so that the woman's identity would be fitted to her husband's personality and life-style (Erikson, 1964). At the same time, expectations for men exaggerate achievement and success and discourage expressiveness and intimacy and interdependence. One consequence is that their capacity to feel good about themselves is limited. But what effect do traditional gender role expectations have on women and men, and on their relationships with one another?

Females: Turning Against the Self

"Dying was one of the few controversial things my mother ever did," wrote journalist Jane Howard in *A Different Woman* (1973:23). In a lifetime of living for others, Howard's mother had never learned autonomy. To the degree that women adopt attitudes and behaviors that have traditionally been designated feminine, they are relatively deficient in autonomy.

The implications of these conclusions relate to Erikson's view. People who neither feel autonomous nor actualize individual talents and capacities, according to Erikson, suffer from feelings of inferiority. Such negative emotions are particularly evident among women. Women are more likely than men to feel depressed, bored, empty, dissatisfied with life, inadequate, and excessively guilty (Gove and Tudor, 1973). Suicide attempts are between six and ten times more common in women's lives than in men's (although men are more likely to succeed in suicide efforts and therefore have a higher suicide rate). Women also experience higher rates of mental illness (see Figure 2•2) and are particularly prone to depression (Scarf, 1979). Women, then, seem to be much more likely than men in our society to exhibit behavior characterized as "turning against the self" (Frieze et al., 1978:260).

Males: Stress and Isolation

Traditional gender expectations can also be seen as limiting men. Overemphasis on productivity, competition, and achievement creates anxiety or emotional stress, which may contribute to males' shorter life expectancy (see Figure 2•2). Discussing stress-related physical diseases, Janet Chafetz argues that "the pressures on males to 'succeed' in a highly competitive world of work creates tremendous stress; in the final analysis, few males can ever sit back and say, 'I've arrived; I am a success; now I can relax'" (1978:65). Chafetz continues:

So strong is the work and success ethic for males in our society that even millionaires feel compelled to "produce." ... Among the large numbers of males doing less competitive but more repetitive labor, the pressure persists day in, day out, year after year, in highly alienating work [that]

BOX 2 · 1

**CHODOROW'S
THEORY OF
GENDER**

Gender is a central organizing principle of all societies. But women and men, argues Nancy Chodorow, are not born with a sense of gender. They develop such through interaction with their families and other socializing agents.

The process of becoming someone in the world, a male or female someone, begins in infancy with a sense of "oneness," a "primary identification" that all infants make with the person responsible for their early care. Emerging from this phase, every child faces the challenge of separation: distinguishing *self* from *other*. If the separation is too early, violent, or abrupt (and this is more often the case for boys), the child loses a capacity for "relatedness"—for intimacy. If the separation is too late, ambivalent, or grudging (and this is more often the case for girls), the child lacks a strong enough sense of self.

Because women are the primary caretakers of children, that first "other" is almost without exception female. Both daughters and sons make their "primary identification" with a woman—and this provides their earliest sense of gender....

The task of separation, which is full of stress and anxiety for both sexes, is more difficult for a boy, on two counts. First, a heterosexual mother is more likely to experience a son than a daughter as a sexual "other." A boy must reject feelings of overwhelming love, attachment, and dependence on his mother that are charged by the sexual current between mother and son. At the same time, he must also learn that he is *not female,* and his feelings are charged by his sense that they are feminine and not masculine....

The particular nature of life in a traditional nuclear family heightens the conflicts that child and mother experience at this period. They are relatively isolated; there are usually no other strong adult figures, and particularly often, because of their long hours of work and lack of involvement in fathering, no men to diffuse the child's passionate dependence on, yearning for, fear of, and anger at the mother. At the same time, absent fathers become symbols of separateness and independence....

The dilemma of the boy-child meshes neatly with society's devaluation of women, mothering, and the domestic sphere in general. His reward for making the break is "identification with his father and with the superiority of masculine ... prerogatives." Contempt for women not only helps free the boy from his mother "but also from the femininity within himself. It therefore becomes entangled with the issue of masculinity and is generalized to all women." From their dominant position in society, "men have the means to ... institutionalize their unconscious defenses against repressed yet strongly experienced developmental conflicts."

A daughter does not have the same experience as a son in relation to her mother. She is female, her mother is female, and her sense of gender and self is

SOURCE:
Judith Thurman, *Ms.,*
September, 1982:35–36.
Based on Nancy Chodorow,
1978.

more continuous and positive. A daughter's feeling of "oneness" lasts longer than a son's and is less threatening. She emerges from the pre-Oedipal stage with a capacity for "relatedness" that a boy loses or suppresses in his struggle against his maternal identification. As a result, Nancy Chodorow suggests, the emotional life of a girl is richer and her sense of self is less problematic.... The capacity for "relatedness" is necessary and appropriate for "women's role" in the family, her "concern about children and attunement to masculine needs." The "denial of relatedness" prepares men for "their" work in the public sphere, which in modern societies "is likely to be contractual and specifically delineated."

But the traditional nuclear family, even as it creates these positive capacities, creates a different set of emotional binds and stumbling blocks for daughters. Mothers tend to perceive their sons as "other" from the beginning and to give them greater emotional freedom. They also tend to identify, and in many cases to overidentify, with their daughters, making it difficult for the daughters to develop a clearly defined sense of self.... A boy's early bond with his mother is re-created in his adult sexual relationships with women. A girl is expected to transfer her "primary love" from a female to a male object. The absence of fathers in the nuclear family, their inaccessibility to daughters, intensifies the ambivalence....

Women's exclusive mothering, particularly in the context of a nuclear family, creates difficulties with women for both sexes. Both girls and boys "come to expect a mother's"—and hence a woman's—"unique capacities for sacrifice, caring, and mothering, and to associate women with their own fears of repression and powerlessness." At the same time, the emotional needs and capacities of men and women evolve in radically different and tragically incompatible ways. "Too much mother" makes men resentful and defensive toward women and creates their search for "nonthreatening, undemanding, dependent, even infantile" sexual partners. It also leads them to deny their own relational needs and to be intolerant of those needs in their female partners. "Too much mother" creates problems of autonomy for girls, and an ongoing struggle for separation....

Nancy Chodorow speculates on the results of a more equitable parenting arrangement. First, she suggests, the presence of more than one primary caretaker would diffuse the intensity of the mother-child relationship. Second, a mother who has a meaningful life outside the home, and other nurturing adult relationships, is not so likely to overinvest in her children. Third, a boy raised partly by a father or men would "not develop fears of *maternal* omnipotence and expectations of *women's* unique self-sacrificing qualities." This would also relieve men of the need to defend their masculinity so fiercely from the woman within....

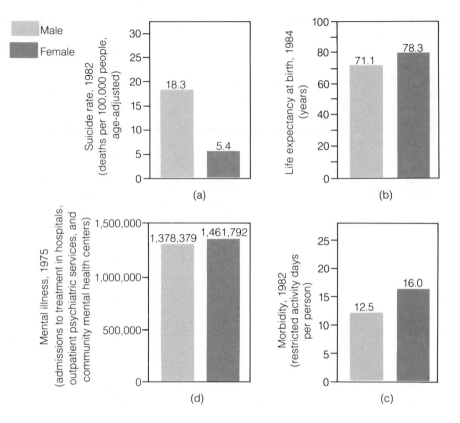

Figure 2·2

Some indicators of gender-associated stress. Stress on *males* is evidenced by a *high suicide rate* and by a *lower life expectancy*. These may be partly due to genetic factors, but they also reflect the pressures of the breadwinner role, a generally less sheltered life-style (Stoll, 1978), less openness to emotional support from others (Jourard, 1964), and less sensitivity to internal cues of impending illness (Jourard, 1964). Stress on *women* (especially married women) is reflected in higher rates of *mental illness* and *morbidity* (illness, but not death). Women's nurturant role, which requires women to put meeting others' needs ahead of meeting their own (Gove and Hughes, 1979), seems to be at least partly responsible. Women's increased participation in the labor force has not been reflected in higher death rates or stress-related illness except for an increase in lung cancer. Alcoholism has not increased among women generally, although it has among cohabiting females and those who are divorced, separated, or never married (*Omaha World Herald,* May 21, 1984), according to a national survey conducted in 1981. One can argue that lack of change in the death rate is only temporary, but at this point we simply don't know the long-term impact on health of changes in men's and women's roles. (Sources: (a) U.S. Bureau of the Census, 1986b:74; (b) U.S. Bureau of the Census, 1986b:68; (c) U.S. Bureau of the Census, 1986b:114; (d) Cockerham, 1981:203)

results from the gender role requirement that they provide for their families the best they possibly can in material things [1978:56]. ▪

The masculine role not only requires that men undergo pressure for success but also encourages them to discount or ignore their anxiety and physical symptoms of stress (Jourard, 1976). Men also learn to hide emotions of vulnerability, tenderness, and warmth when they are in public. But it is difficult to maintain one personality in public and another in private. Consequently, inexpressiveness often becomes a general way of behaving. "Men thus reject half their personalities" (David and Brannon, 1976:49–50). Hiding tender feelings, men cannot share their inner selves. Hence, they block avenues to intimacy, isolating themselves (Shapiro, 1984; McGill, 1985). Isolation, like the lack of autonomy, limits people's potential to feel positive about themselves.

Inasmuch as they have internalized gender expectations, both women and men are limited in important ways. To the extent that they are constrained by these roles and expectations, men and women find it more difficult to develop positive self-concepts, and this makes it harder to fully experience intimate relationships. The view of these authors is that human relationships are flexible and that gender identification can limit relationships in many cases. An alternative that we believe may increase a couple's potential for intimacy is described in the following section.

Androgyny: An Alternative

Androgyny (a term formed from the Greek words *andro*, meaning "male," and *gyne*, "female") is the social and psychological condition by which individuals can think, feel, and behave both instrumentally and expressively. In other words, androgynous persons evidence the positive qualities traditionally associated with both masculine and feminine roles. In a modern, complex society people need to be assertive and self-reliant and also to depend on one another for emotional support. By allowing people both to develop their talents and capacities and to be emotionally expressive, androgyny can greatly expand the range of behavior open to everyone, permitting people to cope more effectively with diverse situations (Bem, 1975:62).

An important part of the social change advocated and often acted upon in the 1960s and 1970s was the notion that traditional gender roles should be replaced by an androgynous model for both women and men. Some segments of society are more comfortable with a move toward androgynous roles than are others. Some families are more likely, by design or as an unintended by-product of their circumstances, to socialize their children toward androgyny. One study in the early 1970s compared daughters of employed mothers with those of homemakers. The researchers found that the former saw men and women as significantly more alike in both "competency" and "warmth expressiveness" (Broverman et al., 1972).

Research suggests that parents continue to allocate household chores—both the amount and kinds—to their children differentially, that is, according to their sex. But more highly educated parents are less likely to accept a traditional sex-typed division of labor for their children (White and Brinkerhoff, 1981). Moreover, the number of boys and girls in a family may influence how chores are distributed. Families with all girls, for example, more readily assign traditional male-child tasks—mowing the grass and taking out the garbage—to girls than do families with at least one boy (Brody and Steelman, 1985).

Gender and Race

Our comments about changing American gender roles are based on white Anglo patterns. But gender roles are also at issue among black Americans. The politics of racial and sexual oppression and liberation has a complex history; leaders and organizations dedicated to blacks' and women's causes have sometimes worked together and at other times have been at odds (Giddings, 1984). Class differences and conflicts of interest between immigrant and established groups complicate the historical picture (Davis, 1981).

Today many observers, black and white, view the contemporary women's movement as a white middle-class creation, with origins in the recent historical experience of educated upper middle-class homemakers (Friedan, 1963) and New Left activists (Evans, 1978). How women of color are to be incorporated in this movement is seen as problematic, though viewed as desirable by feminist organizations and by black feminists (Joseph,

■ Skill with a hammer, handy with a skillet: To Colin, who learned these useful skills from his uncle and mother, being a good cook is a matter of pride and practicality, not androgyny.

1984). But some find the women's movement irrelevant to blacks and other women of color to the extent that it focuses on psychological oppression or on professional women's opportunities. Black women have always labored in the productive economy under duress or out of financial necessity and did not experience the enforced delicacy of women in the Victorian period. Nor were they ever "housewives," so much of the feminist critique of that role seems irrelevant to black women (Davis, 1981; Giddings, 1984). To others, the black power or civil rights movement and the women's or feminist movement appear to have collided (see Box 2▪2, "Black Power—For Men Only?").

A goal of the black power movement has been socioeconomic, political, and psychological parity for black men. In fact, using the simple indicator

of life expectancy, one can argue that black males are a uniquely disadvantaged group. As black psychiatrist Alvin Poussaint states, "Being a black man in America is a high-risk adventure" (1982:37). The life expectancy of black men is about four years less than that of white men and eight years less than that of black women (eleven years less than that of white women). In addition to high infant mortality rates and high adult death rates from illness and as homicide victims, black men have higher rates of mental hospitalization than the other three groups, higher rates of alcoholism and drug abuse than black women, and high rates of unemployment and imprisonment (Poussaint, 1982; Staples, 1982).

One response to the obvious disadvantage of black men in particular, and blacks in general, is

■ Some black Americans find conflicts in the goals of the civil rights movement and the women's movement. For Coretta Scott King, human rights take priority over race and gender.

to treat gender discrimination as less pressing than racial discrimination, particularly in view of the image of black women as "strong" and black society as "matriarchal." A sometimes concurrent theme is that "black men must regain a leadership position and take control of their households" (Ransford and Miller, 1983:49). The evidence does *not* support this image of black society and the black family as matriarchal, or female dominated (Staples, 1971; Wallace, 1979), but the image has persisted nevertheless, with some important consequences. This ideology encourages black women to support black male authority in the home and in politics, or at least to subordinate issues of sexism to issues of racism.

Nevertheless, we have come to expect more egalitarian gender roles among blacks in some areas,

for black women have traditionally had to work outside their homes, and work hard at that. Angela Davis's interpretation of historical data suggests that the more egalitarian roles reported in some research on black marriages (McDonald, 1980; Gray-Little, 1982) are rooted in qualities of strength and competence developed by black women in the slave period. Furthermore, black women did not experience the debilitating nineteenth-century removal of women from productive working lives to lives characterized by fragility and dependence (Davis, 1981).

It is difficult to assess current goals and opinions of the black community, partly because blacks do not speak with one voice. Some blacks (Joseph and Lewis, 1981; Davis, 1981) argue that race and class are both important. Davis is critical of "the

BOX 2 · 2

BLACK POWER—FOR MEN ONLY?

In her book *Black Macho and the Myth of the Super-woman*, black feminist Michele Wallace explores sex roles in the black community through history and in contemporary America. Following are some excerpts from that book, which has generated strong responses, some affirming Wallace, some harshly critical.

I am saying, among other things, that for perhaps the last fifty years there has been a growing distrust, even hatred, between black men and black women. It has been nursed along not only by racism on the part of whites but also by an almost deliberate ignorance on the part of blacks about the sexual politics of their experience in this country.

As the Civil Rights Movement progressed, little attention was devoted to an examination of the historical black male/female relationship, except for those aspects of it that reinforced the notion of the black man as the sexual victim of "matriarchal" tyranny. The result has been calamitous. The black woman has become a social and intellectual suicide; the black man, unintrospective and oppressive. . . .

Though I am a black feminist, and that label rightly suggests that I feel black men could stand substantial improvement, I still find it difficult to blame them alone. Black men have had no greater part than black women in perpetuating the ignorance with which they view one another. The black man, however, particularly since the Black Movement, has been in the position to define the black woman. He is the one who tells her whether or not she is a woman and what it is to be a woman. And therefore, whether he wishes to or not, he determines her destiny as well as his own.

Though originally it was the white man who was responsible for the black woman's grief, a multiplicity of forces act upon her life now and the black man is one of the most important. The white man is downtown. The black man lives with her. He's the head of her church and may be the principal of her local school or even the mayor of the city in which she lives.

She is the workhorse that keeps his house functioning, she is the foundation of his community, she raises his children, and she faithfully votes for him

SOURCE: Wallace, 1979:13–15.

---

ideological snare of insisting that one struggle is absolutely more important than the other" (1981:44). Michele Wallace (1979) claims black attention for feminism by pointing to the greater poverty and unemployment and burden of care falling to black women. But other voices give the racial struggle clear primacy (Green, 1982; anonymous reviewer). Also, just as white middle-class and working-class men and women vary in their attitudes and behavior, so do class differences among blacks affect gender-role attitudes and behavior.

We can look at public opinion polls for some assessment of comparative attitudes of blacks and whites toward gender roles. A recent study explores current attitudes toward gender roles among blacks and whites of middle and lower classes (Ransford and Miller, 1983). Based on NORC surveys of a national sample[11] for the years 1974–78, the

---

11. The National Opinion Research Center at the University of Chicago conducts regular surveys of a random sample of the population. These form the basis for various attitude studies of the U.S. population.

in elections, goes to his movies, reads his books, watches him on television, buys in his stores, solicits his services as doctor, lawyer, accountant.

She has made it quite clear that she has no intention of starting a black woman's liberation movement. One would think she was satisfied, yet she is not. The black man has not really kept his part of the bargain they made when she agreed to keep her mouth shut in the sixties. When she stood by silently as he became a "man," she assumed that he would subsequently grant her her long overdue "womanhood," that he would finally glorify and dignify black womanhood just as the white man had done for the white woman. But he did not. . . . She too was angry, but paralyzed by the feeling that she had no right to be.

Therefore her strange numbness, her determination, spoken or unspoken, to remain basically unquestioning of the black man's authority and thereby seemingly supportive of all he has done, even that which has been abusive of her. She is in the grip of Black Macho and it has created within her inestimable emotional devastation.

The black woman's silence is a new silence. She knows that. Not so long ago it would have been quite easy to find any number of black women who would say with certainty, "A nigga man ain't shit." Perhaps more to the point, there has been from slavery until the Civil Rights Movement a thin but continuous line of black women who have prodded their sisters to self-improvement. These women were of the opinion that being a woman did not exempt one from responsibility. Just like a man, a woman had to struggle to deliver the race from bondage and uplift it. In their time a woman's interest in herself was not automatically interpreted as hostile to men and their progress, at least not by black people. Day to day these women, like most women, devoted their energies to their husbands and children. When they found time, they worked on reforms in education, medicine, housing, and their communities through their organizations and churches. Little did they know that one day their activities would be used as proof that the black woman has never known her place and has mightily battled the black man for his male prerogative as head of the household.

research indicated little difference between black and white women. That is, black women's attitudes today are neither more nor less feminist than white women's.

Interestingly, however, according to this study, black and white men are differently affected by having had employed mothers. For white men, having had an employed mother is associated with stronger feminist attitudes, as these mothers provided a model for new roles. The reverse is true for blacks. It is possible that black children resented seeing their mothers working outside their homes since black mothers worked primarily in low-paying, low-status domestic and service occupations and often did not have the choice of remaining at home to care for children. As adults, these children may have come to value domesticity or to resist economic exploitation through acceptance of more domestic roles for women. In this framework domestic roles for women—attention to one's own family—would be self-fulfilling rather than restrictive. Black men who prefer traditional roles for women may see themselves as protective, in a position at last to provide the traditional family life-style that has been so highly valued in our society (Richards-Ekeh, 1984).

In general, black men have more traditional attitudes than do white men, especially with regard to the idea that a woman's place is in the home and to the suitability of women for politics. Black males who identify themselves as middle class are even more traditional than lower-class black males. We do not know whether these differences are recent or long-standing, so we cannot assess the impact of black power on gender-role differences. In fact, any discussion of gender roles among blacks at present is based on a very limited body of research.

Research on gender roles among other racial and ethnic groups is even more limited. We can expect this situation to change because recognition of this limitation and the keen interest of minorities themselves have sparked new research. As we see with blacks, our perspective on the roles of women (and men) is expanded by increasing our awareness of cultural diversity.

For example, native Americans have a complex heritage that varies by tribe, but may include a matrilineal tradition in which women owned, and may still own, houses, tools, and agricultural land. Still, native American women face some of the same problems of women generally, particularly a lack of political power dating from the reorganization of Indian life in the 1920s. Recently they have begun to regain this power: A woman serves as chief of the Cherokee nation, and in the 1986 Navajo elections women gained 72 of the 327 local offices, the most since the 1920s. Women have advanced educationally as well, receiving 62 percent of the Navajo tribal scholarships (Robbins, 1987). "'There has been a revitalization of the role of women in the Cherokee nation,'" according to Chief Wilma Mankiller (quoted in Robbins, 1987). Asserting a spiritual dimension to the emergence of female leadership in Indian tribes, Avis Arthcambault, a Lakota/Gros Ventre social worker, states, "'This is all in the prophesies, that the spirit of the woman is emerging and is a strong force right now'" (Robbins, 1987).

Native Americans face some of the most severe social and economic pressures in our society, including high rates of poverty and extensive alcoholism and unemployment among Indian men. Women are central in keeping family and tribe together. Despite traditions that sometimes limit women's leadership and religious restrictions that exclude family planning and abortion in some tribes, tradition may also strengthen the native American woman's role:

It is by upholding tradition that American Indian women seem to have preserved a tribal life despite the devastations of alcoholism. "If it wasn't for the women, their intestinal fortitude in keeping our traditions going, we would have disbanded as a tribe a long time ago," claims Alfred Benalli, Navajo director of an alcoholism program [Robbins, 1987]. ▪

This brief discussion of gender roles among blacks and native Americans indicates the enormous diversity of responses to the women's movement among racial and economic groups. "To understand the black woman is not to understand the chicana," as Nieto notes (1974:42). A thorough discussion of gender in the racial/ethnic, class, and religious communities of American society is beyond the scope of this book, and interested readers are urged to pursue the courses in black studies, ethnic studies, and women's and men's studies available at many universities.

CHANGING GENDER ROLES— WHERE ARE WE AND WHAT HAS IT BROUGHT US?

Changes in gender roles and gender-role socialization thus occur unevenly throughout society. Moreover, such changes have had differing consequences for women and men. During the 1970s there was evidence of a move toward androgyny, despite people's ambivalence as they addressed these changes. But in general, the outlook was positive: People believed in the future and in the benefits of androgyny. In the 1980s, however, serious new concerns have been raised, as we shall see.

The 1970s: Growing Evidence of Androgyny

The idea that men and women should become more androgynous was accepted by about half the general public, according to a *New York Times*–CBS poll taken in 1977. That poll concluded that 48 percent of Americans preferred shared marriage roles in which "the husband and wife both have jobs, both do housework and both take care of the children." It was a slim majority, however—43 percent chose more traditional marriage, with the husband as the provider and the wife as the child rearer (Meislin, 1977:75).

Nevertheless, change in gender roles was apparent as part of a long-term trend arising out of such demographic trends as smaller family size (fewer home responsibilities) and a changing economy in which women workers are needed (Cherlin, 1981). The feminist movement in the 1960s both reflected and helped to accelerate these changes (Mason et al., 1976), which were also set in motion by the declining sex ratio, that is, ratio of men to women in a society (see Chapter 5), and by the "contraceptive revolution" (Heer and Grossbard-Schechtman, 1981).

A 1970 *Louis Harris* poll (see Figure 2·3) asked women what they thought were "the two or three most enjoyable things about being a woman today." Asking the same question in 1983, the *Times* reported marked changes. In 1970, 53 percent answered "being a mother and raising a family"; by 1983 only 28 percent did. In 1970 only 9 percent answered "career, jobs, pay"; in 1983 that figure rose to 26 percent. In 1970, 14 percent responded "general rights and freedoms"; in 1983, 32 percent responded this way (*The New York Times*, Dec. 4, 1983).

Pollster and psychologist Daniel Yankelovich found profound changes in social norms, many of them affecting marriages and families (1981). He interviewed several hundred people in cities across the country about their values and goals, especially as compared to their parents'. He also conducted a random sample (about 1,500 people) of the American population and reviewed other poll data and research. Change was reflected in responses to surveys over the years. For example, while only about a third of a national sample of Americans in 1970 and 1971, respectively, agreed that both sexes are responsible for the care of small children or that it was all right for wives and husbands to take separate vacations, more than half agreed in 1980. (See Figure 2·4.)

Sociologist John Scanzoni found that men and women saw themselves as having both instrumen-

Women on Womanhood

"What do you think are the two or three most enjoyable things about being a woman today?"

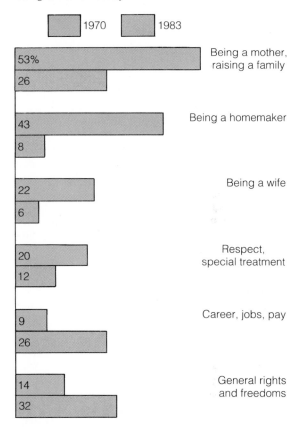

Figure 2·3
Jobs rival family life in poll of U.S. women
(Source: *The New York Times*, Dec. 4, 1983)

tal and expressive qualities. Married men viewed themselves as *more* instrumental than women, but there was no difference between the married men and women surveyed on the degree of expressiveness they attributed to themselves. The younger (college) men and women in the study did not differ in instrumentality, so Scanzoni predicted eventual convergence between men and women in instrumental and expressive qualities (Scanzoni, 1975). The road to convergence would be marked by ambivalence, however.

1. Disapprove of a married woman earning money if she has a husband capable of supporting her

2. Four or more children is the ideal number for a family

    Two children is the ideal

3. For a woman to remain unmarried she must be "sick," "neurotic," or "immoral"

4. Would vote for a qualified woman nominee for president

5. Agree that both sexes are responsible for the care of small children

6. Approve of husband and wife taking separate vacations

7. Would go on working for pay even if they didn't have to

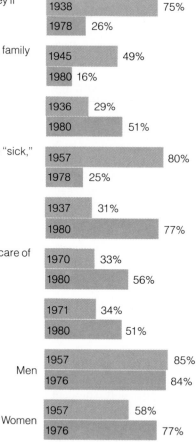

	1938	75%
	1978	26%
	1945	49%
	1980	16%
	1936	29%
	1980	51%
	1957	80%
	1978	25%
	1937	31%
	1980	77%
	1970	33%
	1980	56%
	1971	34%
	1980	51%
Men	1957	85%
	1976	84%
Women	1957	58%
	1976	77%

Figure 2·4

Changing norms. (Sources: Yankelovich, 1981:91–93, based on Yankelovich, Skelly and White; Gallup; NORC; ABC/Harris; and Institute for Survey Research [University of Michigan] surveys)

Ambivalence

This ambivalence can be illustrated by looking more closely at one element of male dominance: success. Contemporary husbands are expected both to "succeed" and to express tender emotions, but these two qualities may inherently conflict with one another. Expressing tender emotions involves being open enough that others can see one's doubts, fears, and feelings of vulnerability. But in our society, for the most part, showing vulnerability does not facilitate successful competition. On the contrary, in making it to the top, it helps if one appears totally competent and confident rather than unsure (David and Brannon, 1976). This conflict can be a source of ambivalence for men.

Men also experienced ambivalence with regard to women's changing roles. In one study of sixty-two senior men in an Ivy League college, sociologist Mirra Komarovsky found that many men felt torn between an internalized need to feel dominant over women and emerging egalitarian values. While the male students had generally overcome their earlier fear of women as intellectual equals, they still assumed that their women would play a supportive and secondary role. One man wrote that it is necessary for women to develop careers; otherwise, they "get hung up with tranquilizers, because they have no outlet for their abilities." But he went on to state that a woman's "work shouldn't interfere with or hurt [her husband's] career in any way. He should not sacrifice his career to hers" (Komarovsky, 1977:237).

It was not only the men in her sample who had internalized the traditional expectations for male dominance. Komarovsky talked with several students who claimed that *women* stood in the way of more equal relations between the sexes. These students perceived that while women wanted men to be sensitive and emotionally expressive, they also wanted them to be self-assured and dominant. As a result, Komarovsky concluded that nearly half the men interviewed felt anxious about their ability to play the emerging masculine role (Komarovsky, 1976:126–55).

In writing about men's roles, we also need to state the obvious: Men are not all alike. The traditional role and the men's liberation movement, which seeks to incorporate more expressive and nurturant elements into men's lives and personalities, are primarily constructions of the white middle-class. Minority men, gay men, and working-class men have not benefited from the privileges or experienced the dominance taken for granted by white middle- and upper-class men. Their experiences are different in many respects. For example, working-class fathers typically do not offer themselves as role models to their sons; the opposite is true: " 'If you ever wind up in that steel mill like me, I'm gonna hit you right over the head. Don't be foolish. Get yourself a schooling. Stay out of the steel mill or you'll wind up the same way I did' " (Terkel, 1977:55, cited in Kimmel, 1986:18).

Presentation of a new model of masculinity to a member of a racial, ethnic, or class group excluded from, but encouraged to strive for, the status provided by the old model may create a complex and ambivalent response. For gay men, issues of sexuality and the integration of sexual preference into one's life as a whole are likely to take priority over concern about men's roles in general. The male role and corresponding attitudes toward women presented by the gay community are likely to depart from the traditional model. Men look not only to general American culture for their models of masculinity and attitudes toward women but also to their particular class, racial/ethnic, religious, or other social group, and these models may be conflicting.

Ambivalence may exist even among those men who are committed to changing the male role. According to Kann, "American men have inherited the privileges of patriarchy which enable them to experiment with new sensibilities without incurring major risks to their well-being" (1986:33). Male self-interest may mean that men's liberation is not necessarily supportive of women's liberation:

Let me be bolder, I would suggest as a rule of thumb that men's immediate self-interest rarely coincides with feminist opposition to patriarchy. Consider that men need money and leisure to carry out their experiments in self-fulfillment. Is it not their immediate interest to monopolize the few jobs that promise affluence and autonomy by continuing to deny women equal access to them? Further, men need social space or freedom from constraints for their experiments. Why should they commit themselves to those aspects of feminism that reduce men's social space? It is one thing to try out the joys of parenting, for example, but quite another to assume sacrificial responsibility for the pains of parenting. Is it not men's immediate self-interest to strengthen the cultural presumption that women are the prime parents and thus the ones who must diaper, chauffeur, tend middle-of-the-night illnesses, launder, and so forth? [Kann, 1986:32]. ■

Women may also experience a great deal of ambivalence. Women today are often expected both to assume primary responsibility for nurturing others and to pursue their own achievement—goals that can conflict. This conflict is more than psychological. It is in part a consequence of our society's failure to provide support for working mothers in the form of maternity leave, day care, and family allowances. Virtually all Western European nations allow women to take extended maternity leave without losing jobs and seniority, and they pay the family a small stipend toward the support of each child. In contrast, American women are faced with a forced choice of job *or* baby, or they deal individually with problems of pregnancy, recovery from birth, and early child care as best they can. Adequate job performance, let alone career achievement, is difficult under such conditions regardless of the woman's ability (Hewlett, 1986).

Furthermore, feminists have disagreed about androgyny as a model for women and men in our society. Some continue to emphasize equal treatment of men and women and to encourage nonsexist child rearing that would produce similarity in personality between men and women. Others seek to acknowledge biological differences and celebrate a women's culture that rejects individual ambition to emphasize communitarian values and women's nurturing capacity (Mitchell and Oakley, 1986; Stacey, 1986).

Old patterns are difficult to alter. This is true for women and men, both of whom are often torn between what they have learned to value from the past and newer ideas. (We will explore in more detail change in roles related to work [Chapter 11], childbearing [Chapter 12], child rearing [Chapter 13], sexuality [Chapter 4], and communication [Chapter 9].) In this context we need to explore a serious emerging issue: Is it androgyny we have been approaching—or narcissism?

The 1980s: Androgyny or Narcissism?

Narcissism means, generally, undue admiration for or concern with oneself, without regard for the well-being of others. Its source lies in Greek mythology, in the story of a young man named Narcissus, who, having spurned the love Echo offered him, pined away in admiration of his own image in a pool of water and was eventually transformed into the flower that bears his name. (Echo, by the way, pined away too until nothing but her voice remained.)

According to Christopher Lasch (1980), among others, ours is a narcissistic culture in which anxious, self-indulgent people seek meaning in life while doubting virtually everything historically deemed meaningful. The narcissist "praises respect for rules and regulations in the secret belief that they do not apply to himself. Acquisitive in the sense that his cravings have no limits, he ... demands immediate gratification and lives in a state of restless, perpetually unsatisfied desire" (Lasch, 1980:xxvi). What has this to do with androgyny?

Androgyny, you will recall, implies incorporating characteristics of both masculine and feminine roles. To the extent that people do that, they become both autonomous and somehow committed; they blend ambition with the willingness and ability to nurture. But to the extent that people—even in the name of changing gender roles—pursue autonomy or personal ambition to the neglect of intimate commitment and/or nurturing responsibilities, they are being narcissistic, not androgynous.

There is evidence of androgyny today. The National Organization for Changing Men, for example, formally organized in 1981, is dedicated to challenging patriarchal attitudes and behaviors through ongoing task groups concerned with such issues as pornography and "ending men's violence" (National Organization for Changing Men, 1986).

At the same time, however, men are increasingly choosing neither marriage nor child-rearing responsibilities. Studying census and *Current Population Reports* data for men age 20–49, sociologists David Eggebeen and Peter Uhlenberg concluded that "a substantial reorganization" of (white) men's lives occurred between 1960 and 1980. Men spent 43 percent less time in family environments where young children were present (from an average of 12.34 years in 1960 to 7.0 years in 1980). They spent 49 percent more time outside of marriage (from 6.28 years in 1960 to 9.34 years in 1980). In both cases the bulk of the change occurred between 1970 and 1980. White males experienced only a 5 percent increase in time outside of marriage between 1960 and 1970, but a 42 percent increase between 1970 and 1980 (1985:253).

Recognizing this trend, Alice Rossi expresses concern about "this gender gap in embeddedness in the caring institutions of society," warning that it carries broad political and social deviance implications:

One may not go as far as French social scientist Gaston Bouthol (1969), who argues that the best predictor of war is a surplus in the number of young unattached males, but sociologists need no reminder that the same subpopulation group predominates in sexual violence, alcohol and drug abuse, crime and social deviance. Unattached males roam the interstices between socially cohesive groups, kill and are themselves killed and maimed, but the machine cultures of the West have shown no inventiveness in developing new social institutions capable of providing individual loyalty and social integration. Our only answers have been armies and prisons [1984:4–5]. ■

Implications for the family are equally worrisome. Changing gender-role expectations may have all but absolved men of traditional provider responsibilities, leaving divorced and never-married mothers to do double-duty as both breadwinners and nurturers (Weitzman, 1985; Ehrenreich, 1983). (Chapters 13 and 16 address this issue.) Moreover, there is growing concern that children's needs will have declining priority at community and public policy levels. Only a minority of political constituents may be rearing children; and single legislators may be less likely to interest themselves in child-welfare issues (Rossi, 1984:4; Eggebeen and Uhlenberg, 1985:256–57). Concern has also been expressed about the conflict between women's (legitimate) work goals and the need for supporting day care and children's need for a flexible, responsive, loving, and stable social environment, often lacking in available day care (Suransky, 1982). Probably neither sex has a monopoly on narcissism, and our hope may lie in recognizing that fact and in resolving to cooperate even in the face of ambivalence.

Egalitarian Relationships—Can They Work?

Can relationships based on equality work? First, we need to address what we mean by "work." If we mean to imply permanence, the answer for individual couples is that this is entirely possible, although less likely than in the past. Permanence has become less likely for many reasons (discussed in Chapter 16), one of which is spouses' lessened practical dependence on each other due to their more androgynous roles.

But if by "work" we mean cooperation and caring, our answer is that, while changing gender roles may make things problematic in this time of transition, there is hope based on our willingness to do certain things. The first requirement is to recognize an increased, not lessened, need for commitment. The narcissist, chronically bored and restlessly searching "instantaneous intimacy," fears commitment (Lasch, 1980:40). But "just as the person makes no definitive gift of himself, he has definitive title to nothing" (Durkheim, 1951:271). For an egalitarian—or any—relationship to work, we have to commit ourselves to making the effort. (Chapter 3 discusses commitment in detail.)

The second requirement is to appreciate that, in the face of change, both men and women may be, to paraphrase sociologist William Goode, hurt and angry. A "deep" and "complex source of male anger" relates to a central male role, that of jobholder and breadwinner:

Most men . . . see their job as not yielding much intrinsic satisfaction, not being fun in itself, but they pride themselves on the hard work and personal sacrifice they make as breadwinners. In the male view, men make a gift of all this to their wives and children.
Now they are told that it was not a gift, and they have not earned any special deference for it. In fact, their wives earned what they received, and indeed nothing is owing. If work was a sacrifice, they are told, so were all the services, comforts, and self-deprivations women provided. Whatever the justice of either claim, clearly if you think you are giving or sacrificing much to make gifts to someone over a period of time, and then you learn he or she feels the gifts were completely deserved, or the countergifts are asserted to have been as great and no gratitude or special debt was incurred, you are likely to be hurt or angry [Goode, 1982:139–140]. ■

Christopher Lasch, commenting on what he sees as "the escalating war between men and women" (1980:189), points out that formerly sexual antagonism "was tempered not only by chivalric, paternalistic conventions but by a more relaxed acceptance of the limitations of the other sex. Men and women acknowledged each other's shortcomings without making them the basis of a comprehensive indictment" (195). According to Lasch, a woman today rightly asks for no less than "a combination of sex, compassion, and intelligent understanding" (196–97). But because she is often repeatedly disappointed in this quest, she, too, is hurt and angry.

A third, and related, requirement for equal or egalitarian relationships to work, then, is to recognize that change is slow and may, in fact, never be complete. In Lasch's opinion "the abolition of sexual tensions is an unworthy goal in any case; the point is to live with them more gracefully than we have lived with them in the past" (206). This, we believe, is not only possible but necessary.

To encourage couples contemplating androgyny and, hence, role-sharing marriages, we take note of a small but interesting study. Social scientist Linda Haas's (1980) research with thirty-one role-sharing couples in Madison, Wisconsin, indicates that, in fact, such a model is workable. This is not a large or a randomly selected sample. Nor is it one that is typical of all segments of society: Most respondents were between ages 26 and 30 and were either being educated for or were engaged in professional fields, particularly social service or the humanities. About half had no children; the other half had preschoolers.

Haas found these couples to be equitably sharing breadwinner, domestic, maintenance, kinship, child-care, and decision-maker roles. Noting that two-career couples do not necessarily share marital roles equally and that the husband's career may dominate, Haas did not find this to be so among her respondents. In this sample "the husband and wife are equally responsible for earning family income; the wife's employment is not considered more optional or less desirable than the husband's. Consequently the spouses' occupations are equally important and receive equal status, or at least the occupation which has more status is not determined by notions of the intrinsic supremacy of one sex over the other" (Haas, 1980:290). Other marital roles besides breadwinning may be differentially filled by wife or husband (that is, one may cook, the other clean). But in no case were these specializations sex determined.

Interestingly enough, couples did not adopt role sharing for ideological reasons, but rather out of dissatisfaction with traditional roles as previously experienced in their current marriage, in a past marriage, or as observed in their parents' marriages. Generally, role sharing had developed at the initiative of the wife. Spouses told of benefits to themselves as individuals. These included the wife's being able to work outside the home for personal fulfillment; freedom for either partner to quit outside employment for a time to pursue other interests; relief from stress and the overwork of being primarily responsible for either housework and children or for economic support; and greater economic independence for both partners. (Chapter 11 examines work and family roles and, among other things, notes that few couples—even two-career couples—achieve true role sharing. Housework, for example, tends to remain the woman's responsibility. The couples in Haas's study shared even that role, however.)

Besides benefits to themselves as persons, partners saw benefits to the family as a whole. For one thing, their greater personal happiness contributed to familial happiness. Beyond that, couples saw diminished female resentment of the male's power, along with increased communication and intimacy. They felt they had more in common because they had experienced the difficulties of both the marketplace and homemaking. They enjoyed time spent together in domestic chores, saw improvement in parent-child relationships because of less stress on the woman and increased male contact with the children, and felt greater financial security.

We have pointed out people's ambivalent responses to changing roles; Haas's study presents a positive model of couples who tell of personal and family gains from androgyny or egalitarian role sharing.

Summary

In our society men are encouraged to behave instrumentally, and women expressively. Biology plays some part in gender differentiation, as hormonal levels are sometimes linked to behavior. Also, cultural learning, or socialization, plays a role in teaching gender-related behavior.

Socialization can either emphasize or deemphasize inborn behavior differences. In our society socialization has emphasized genetic differences. Through language and family, school, and other influences, people internalize attitudes and behaviors that exaggerate men's instrumentality and women's expressiveness. People also internalize attitudes of male dominance.

A traditional division of labor offers the advantage of familiarity and clarity. However, the limitation of the expressive role to women in a traditional relationship limits the communication and intimacy that many couples want from marriage today. The economic dependence of the wife creates power imbalances that have a negative psychological and sexual impact on the quality of married life. Furthermore, changed social conditions—concern about population control, for example, and the problems and demands of a postindustrial economy, along with problems of poverty and the support of women alone with children or in their old age—make it necessary for women to work outside the home and consequently call for some change in the allocation of familial responsibilities.

Insofar as persons are not encouraged to explore both the instrumental and expressive sides of their personalities, they limit their potential. An alternative is androgyny, the model by which people think, feel, and behave both expressively and instrumentally. The current trend toward androgyny causes ambivalence and some tension, but it also offers hope for better understanding and communication between the sexes.

Key Terms

self-concept *47*
instrumental character
    traits *47*
expressive character
    traits *47*
gender roles *48*
male dominance *54*
sex *55*
gender *55*
ethologist *55*
socialization *58*
identification *59*
trust *60*
autonomy *61*
identity *61*
intimacy *61*
isolation *61*
androgyny *65*
narcissism *74*

Study Questions

1. What are some of the traits generally associated with males in our society? What traits are associated with females? How do these affect our expectations about the ways men and women behave?
2. Briefly describe Freud's theory of male dominance. What are some important criticisms of this theory?
3. Although Freud's theory of male dominance is not generally accepted today, women continue to occupy a minority status in our society. What are some examples of this lower status?
4. What evidence is used to demonstrate the influence of heredity on gender-linked behavior? To show the influence of the cultural environment? Describe the research and findings of Money and Ehrhardt on this issue.
5. How are people socialized to adhere, often unconsciously, to culturally acceptable gender roles? Can you give some examples of how you were socialized into your gender role?
6. Discuss Lynn's theory of gender-role learning. How does it help to explain how and why men tend to develop instrumental character traits, and women expressive ones?
7. Briefly, what is meant by *self-concept*? What are some of the ways in which gender affects one's self-concept? How does this tend to limit both men and women in acquiring positive self-concepts?
8. Describe Erik Erikson's theory of how people acquire a positive self-concept. Do Erikson's stages describe your own development?
9. It has been said that masculine and feminine roles are polar opposites, that opposites attract, and that this results in intimate marital relationships. Do you agree with these statements? Why or why not?
10. Explain the concept of androgyny as an alternative to traditional gender roles. How might a marriage of androgynous partners differ from a traditional marital relationship? Why might people in our society feel ambivalent about androgyny?
11. How does androgyny differ from narcissism?

Suggested Readings

Bem, Sandra
1975 "Androgyny vs. the tight little lives of fluffy women and chesty men." *Psychology Today* 9 (Sept):58–62.
1977 "Beyond androgyny: Some presumptuous prescriptions for a liberated sexual identity." Pp. 204–21 in Arlene Skolnick and Jerome H. Skolnick (eds.), *Family in Transition: Rethinking Marriage, Sexuality, Child Rearing, and Family Organization.* 2nd ed. Boston: Little, Brown.

Both of these articles (the first is written in a livelier style) argue that traditional gender roles are limiting and that androgyny allows persons to be freer and more fully human.

Bleier, Ruth
1984   *Science and Gender: A Critique of Biology and Its Theories of Women.* Elmsford, N.Y.: Pergamon.
Review of the evidence for possible biological bases of gender roles.

Chodorow, Nancy
1978   *The Reproduction of Mothering: Psychoanalysis and the Sociology of Gender.* Berkeley: University of California Press.
Important recent theory of gender role socialization.

David, Deborah S., and Robert Brannon (eds.)
1976   *The Forty-Nine Percent Majority: The Male Sex Role.* Reading, Mass.: Addison-Wesley.
The first few years of the 1970s focused on the limitations of the traditional feminine role, but almost nothing was written on the masculine role. These editors—a sociologist and a psychologist respectively—managed to compile a reader around a conceptualization of the male role. We find it fascinating and easy to read.

Doyle, James A.
1983   *The Male Experience.* Dubuque, Iowa: Wm. C. Brown.
Comprehensive analysis of the male role, drawing on sociology, psychology, economics, history, and popular culture.

Ehrenreich, Barbara
1983   *The Hearts of Men: American Dreams and the Flight from Commitment.* New York: Anchor-Doubleday.
Argues that "the male revolt" from the breadwinner role preceded and inspired both feminist and antifeminist movements.

Farrell, Warren
1974   *The Liberated Man.* New York: Random House.
Farrell's theses are that the "Ten Commandments" of traditional masculinity (for example, "Thou shalt not have other egos before thee"; "Thou shalt have an answer to all problems at all times") severely limit men and that women's liberation would mean men's liberation.

Ferree, Myra Marx
1983   "The women's movement in the working class." *Sex Roles* 9:493–505.

Freeman, Jo
1984   *Women: A Feminist Perspective.* 3d ed. Palo Alto, Calif.: Mayfield.
Classic feminist reader touching many aspects of women's lives.

Giddings, Paula
1984   *When and Where I Enter: The Impact of Black Women on Race and Sex in America.* New York: Morrow.
History of black women in America.

Gilligan, Carol
1982   *In a Different Voice: Psychological Theory and Women's Development.* Cambridge, Mass.: Harvard University Press.
Influential book built on the observation that human development research and theory has been based on males. The inclusion of women recasts our thinking about the value of various qualities such as individuality and autonomy, caring and responsibility.

Green, Rayna
1980   "Native American women." *Signs* 6:248–67.

Hewlett, Sylvia Ann
1986   *A Lesser Life: The Myth of Women's Liberation in America.* New York: Morrow.
Hewlett's description of the feminist movement is inaccurate, but her personal story articulates the dilemma of today's woman who wants both career and family—there's been no adaptation of our society to this very widespread need.

Lewis, Robert A., and Robert E. Salt (eds.).
1986   *Men in Families.* Beverly Hills: Sage.

Lewis, Robert A., and Marvin B. Sussman (eds.).
1986   *Men's Changing Roles in the Family.* New York: Haworth Press.
Up-to-date research.

Margolis, Maxine L.
1984   *Mothers and Such: Views of American Women and Why They Changed.* Berkeley: University of California Press.
History of women's roles in America, including a discussion of why housework takes longer than it used to.

Mirande, Alfreda, and Evangelina Enriquez
1978   *La Chicana: The Mexican-American Women.* Chicago: University of Chicago Press.
Significant analysis of the status of chicana women based on historical, literary, and sociological materials.

Pleck, Elizabeth, and Joseph Pleck
1980   *The American Man.* Englewood Cliffs, N.J.: Prentice-Hall.
Sociological and historical treatment of the various aspects of masculinity in America, from early "agrarian patriarchy" (1630–1820) through "the commercial age" (1820–1860), the "strenuous life" (1861–1919), and "companionate providing" (1920–1965).

Pleck, Joseph
1981   *The Myth of Masculinity.* Cambridge, Mass.: MIT Press.
Scholarly review of research and presentation of a new theory of gender roles.

Staples, Robert
1982   *Black Masculinity: The Black Male's Role in American Society.* Santa Barbara, Calif.: Black Scholar Press.
Respected sociologist of the black family takes a look at the male role.
1983   *The Black Woman in America: Sex, Marriage, and the Family.* Chicago: Nelson Hall.
Staples analyzes the black woman's role in the context of familial relationships in the black community.

II Becoming Partners

I ndividuals form relationships and "fall in love." The various facets of choosing partners and falling in love—or not falling in love—are addressed in Part Two. "Falling in love"—indeed, the word *love* itself—has vastly different meanings to different people. In Chapter 3 you'll see what the authors (backed, we think, by counseling psychologists) mean by *love.* Loving is a caring, responsible, and sharing relationship involving deep feelings. Loving is not a romantic fictionalizing of the beloved, but a commitment to intimacy. Intimacy involves disclosing one's inner feelings, a process that is always emotionally risky. For this reason, the people who are most capable of intimate loving are those who first love themselves or have high self-esteem. Chapter 3 explores ways to work actively on building self-esteem.

Chapter 4 describes the sexual aspects of our selves and of our partnerships. A sexual relationship can be a profound way to communicate love, because partners literally and symbolically shed their protective coverings. While it doesn't necessarily have to, sexual expressiveness can symbolically communicate a couple's mutual commitment to self-disclosure. Chapter 4 describes two sexual scripts, or ways that Americans tend to view sex: the traditional (or patriarchal) script, which centers around male dominance; and an emerging, expressive script that focuses on intimacy—both psychic and sexual—as a relationship between equals.

But not everyone chooses to "fall in love," and among those who do, not all couples' intimate relationships lead to marriage. Chapter 5 discusses being single. Although more and more people are choosing to remain single, you will see that *not* becoming partners takes courage in our society: Americans expect young people to marry. Chapter 5 also reviews some beliefs and values that singles have about sex. There are several conflicting sexual standards in the United States today: Adhering to any one of them involves making conscious, knowledgeable choices.

But even though more people are single today, the majority will choose a marriage partner at least once. Chapter 6 examines the process of choosing a spouse and influences on that process. It also shows how one goal in becoming partners—gaining a loved one's commitment to getting married—can conflict with the essence of intimacy—honest self-disclosure.

3 Loving Ourselves and Others

> *Love is an active power in man; a power which breaks through the walls which separate man from his fellow men, which unites him with others; love makes him overcome the sense of isolation and separateness, yet it permits him to be himself, to retain his integrity. In love the paradox occurs that two beings become one and yet remain two.*
>
> ERICH FROMM, *The Art of Loving*

Americans tend to believe that "everything's better with love." We marry and remarry for love. But when asked what love is, most of us have trouble answering. Love *is* hard to define; in attempting to do so, we "toy with mystery." Our view here is that love is "the will to extend one's self for the purpose of nurturing." Because it involves the will, "love implies choice. We do not have to love. We choose to love" (Peck, 1978:81–83).

In this chapter we'll discuss the need for loving in today's society and describe one writer's view of some styles love takes. We'll examine what love is (and isn't). We'll explore the idea that self-esteem, or loving oneself, is a prerequisite to loving others. We begin by looking at what love means in impersonal, modern society.

PERSONAL TIES IN AN IMPERSONAL SOCIETY

We say that modern society is impersonal because so much of the time we are encouraged to think and behave in ways that deny our emotional need to be cared for and to care for others (Bellah et al., 1985). An impersonal society exaggerates the rational aspect of human beings and tends to ignore people's feelings and their need for affection and human contact. We expect people to leave their friends and relatives to move to job-determined new locations because it is an economically efficient way of organizing production and management. Salespersons and service employees (airline hostesses, for example) may be required to display certain emotions and repress others as part of their job (Hochschild, 1983). Only recently have we considered the emotional toll this takes.[1]

---

1. This impersonality of modern society has been a principal concern of sociologists since sociology first appeared as a distinct discipline in the Western world, roughly at the time of the Industrial Revolution. During this period of demographic transition when, due to sharply declining mortality rates, population began to increase dramatically, social theorists became concerned with how people would fare in the emerging rational, bureaucratic world. In France Émile Durkheim's *Division of Labor in Society,* first published in 1894, argued that people had once been held together by common beliefs—often religious—and sentiments "born of resemblances" (106). In such societies solidarity was "mechanical"; the concept of individuality as we know it did not exist (130). As more people inhabited the world, traveled, and/or moved into cities, common resemblances diminished, and sacred beliefs and practices took on a less religious or commonly held character. As a result, individuality emerged. A danger, however, was that "the individual becomes the object for a [new] sort of religion." As "we erect a cult" dedicated to personal autonomy (172), society is increasingly characterized by anomie, that is, normlessness and feelings of isolation.

According to Max Weber, a German contemporary of Durkheim, any emerging individuality would, ironically, be "depersonalized," or nonemotional. Weber noted the growing rationalization or bureaucratization of society in which formal (legal-rational) rules and regulations were replacing

Much of modern living is characterized by brief or pragmatic secondary relationships that encourage superficiality and anonymity.

In the context of this impersonality, most people search for at least one feeling, caring person with whom to share their private time. Some find love and nourish it; some don't discover loving at all. But we all need it. Physicians point out that loving enhances physical health (Lynch, 1977); and many psychologists insist that loving is essential for emotional survival. It helps confirm a person's sense of individual worth.

We can see that love is highly important to people, perhaps especially in today's world. For all its importance, however, love is frequently misunderstood. Before defining what love is, we'll look at a few relationships in which certain feelings are often mistaken for love.

---

the prior authority of tradition and personal charisma. While this might be a necessary development in a densely populated world, the unfortunate tendency was toward "levelling," or depersonalization. An emerging "spirit of formalistic impersonality" meant that people would interact in an "iron cage" of obedient, orderly passivity, "without hatred or passion, and hence without affection or enthusiasm" (Weber, 1948:340).

Georg Simmel, another early social theorist, also addressed this issue. In one essay that focused on the trend toward urbanization, Simmel recognized that the metropolis "grants to the individual a kind and an amount of personal freedom which has no analogy whatsoever under any conditions" (1950:416). But that freedom is not without costs. Simmel describes the indifference that exists in the metropolis, characterized by a rationality that yields a "blasé attitude," an "unmerciful matter-of-factness" (411–14).

Contemporary thinkers have continued to warn against extreme rationality and individuality. For example, Erich Fromm (1947, 1975) argues that the modern attitude of "man for himself" is ethically inappropriate, while Herbert Marcuse (1964) worries that humans have become "one-dimensional," bereft of emotive caring. Peter Berger (Berger et al., 1973) builds on Weber's analysis of bureaucracy by arguing that today's individual is characterized by a "homeless mind," and Christopher Lasch (1980) writes that we inhabit a "culture of narcissism."

We stated in the Prologue that one theme of this text is the tension between individual and family (or interpersonal) values. It is probably safe to say that none of us could comfortably return to the kind of solidarity or group cohesiveness characteristic of preindustrial societies, in which tribal, group, or family values predominated to the virtual exclusion of individuality. At the same time, we believe that elevating individuality to a "religion" whereby, ironically, sacrifice becomes sin can only beget isolation and loneliness. This chapter reflects that position.

SOME THINGS LOVE ISN'T

Love is not the creating of the beloved in our imaginations. Nor does loving imply inordinate self-sacrifice. And loving is not the continual attempt to get others to feel or do what we want them to—although each of these ideas is frequently mistaken for love. We'll examine these misconceptions in detail.

Romanticizing

A country-western singer croons, "She could kiss the ground in the winter time and make a flower grow." The line is an example of **romanticizing**: imagining or fabricating many qualities of the person we want to love.

Romanticizing, or "romantic love," has often been confused with erotic love, or "eros," discussed later in this chapter. This is because romanticizing, like eros, often involves strong sexual desires. The two are not synonymous, however. Romanticizing involves falling in love with an image rather than with a real person. Romanticizers may imagine, for example, that their ideal lover would never become irritable or put on excess weight.

Romanticizing also involves many myths. Some of these are that most people truly love but once in their lives, and that somewhere there is the "ideal" mate for each person. Romanticizers tend to believe that a person "knows it" when he or she meets the ideal mate, and that as long as they are in love, nothing one partner does will make the other really angry. Common interests between partners are often considered unimportant. Convinced that "true" love conquers all, romanticizers feel that they will automatically adjust to being together (Knox, 1971). Romanticizing is not love, however, because romanticizers imagine partners' qualities rather than seeing, and accepting, their partners as they really are.

Romance can be, and often is, a first step toward love. But it may be so only if one realizes that the romantic experience of falling in love is "invariably temporary" (Peck, 1978:84; Fromm, 1956).

No matter whom we fall in love with, we sooner or later fall out of love if the relationship contin-

■ Whose picture did you pin up when you were 13? Romanticizing—often a young person's first step toward love—includes falling in love with an image, not a real person. Frequently figures of fantasy are literally images like the photos on the walls of this bedroom.

ues long enough. This is not to say that we invariably cease loving the person with whom we fell in love. But it is to say that the feeling of ecstatic lovingness that characterizes the experience of falling in love always passes. . . .

Once again [the lovers feel like] two separate individuals. At this point they begin either to dissolve the ties of their relationship or to initiate the work of real loving [Peck, 1978:84–88]. ■

Psychologist Daniel Goldstine and his colleagues (1977) maintain that, if intimate relationships are to last, they must go through three stages: falling in love, disappointment and, finally, acceptance (see Box 3•1).

Martyring

A second thing that love isn't is martyring. **Martyring** involves maintaining relationships by giving others more than one receives in return. Martyrs usually have good intentions; they believe that loving involves doing unselfishly for others without voicing their own needs in return. Consequently, they seldom feel that they receive genuine affection. Martyrs do more for the relationship—or feel that they do—than their partners.

Martyrs may

1. offer to do things for others that others can, should, or would prefer to do for themselves;

BOX 3 · 1

LOVE
IN THREE
STAGES

Psychologist Daniel Goldstine and his colleagues popularized their theory of love in three stages in the best-selling paperback *The Dance-Away Lover* (1977). In Goldstine's view, based on clinical experience, intimate relationships go through three stages: falling in love, disappointment, and acceptance.

STAGE I: FALLING IN LOVE

A person who is falling in love feels good about himself, good about his partner, and good about his relationship—so good that he's tempted to believe that the relationship will realize his fantasies and transform his life....

But under these circumstances, a person's vision of his partner is doubly distorted. His perception is colored by his selective attention; his desire to seek out and attend to what he finds admirable in the other and to blank out whatever is discreditable.

Both partners strive to be their finest selves and they're apt to be at their most appealing in the context of Stage I.... Stage I usually displays people to advantage because it leads them to relinquish, temporarily, many of their ill-favored defenses....

But the bleak fact is that Stage I is necessarily fleeting. Over time, satiation dilutes the intense pleasure the partners originally found in being together. Real-world obligations encroach on the relationship. As evidence of each other's shortcomings piles up, and as the relationship begins to exact visible costs, mutual idealization gives way to mutual disillusionment. With the dimming of Stage I sparkle, any underlying ambivalence about intimacy begins to reassert itself....

One phase of a long-term process, Stage I constitutes the most romantic, but not the most enduring, version of coupled love. Stage I should be appreciated for what it is—a very special experience, and not mistaken for what it isn't—a paradigm to which all experiences of love should conform. Delightful in and of itself, a Stage I doesn't ensure that a relationship has a potential to endure or flourish.... [But] evanescent of itself, Stage I can leave a couple a valuable legacy—the knowledge that they can create pleasure together—that will help them to keep their relationship a source of satisfaction to them both.

STAGE II: DISAPPOINTMENT

Stage II of a couple relationship begins in disappointment. Conflicts and failures pile up, the letdown settles in, and a couple begins to realize that their relationship is not bringing them the fulfillment they'd hoped for....

In Stage II every couple discovers that there are crucial ways in which their operating procedures do not mesh, and crucial features of each other they find neither creditable nor lovable. The question then becomes, "What do I do about all those things about him that I don't like, things he can't change—his jokes, his values?..."

SOURCE:
Goldstine et al.,
1977:155–241.

It is difficult to be subjected to someone else's flaws and limitations without questioning the wisdom of the commitment to that person. It can also be difficult to keep from using such discreditable discoveries about a person as weapons against him....

Stage II means mutual disapproval, the more painful because it's unexpected. The most concentrated dose of approval people usually get comes when they're falling in love. A major proof of the rightness of a new relationship is the fact that the partner "makes me feel so good." But gradually, the appreciation turns to criticism....

The anxiety and the resentment that mark Stage II often provoke people to behavior they have trouble accepting in themselves.... Usually a person holds his partner responsible for the unappetizing changes that have been wrought in him....

The issue of who's at fault obscures the fact that people almost invariably behave badly in Stage II. One of the reasons they do so is because they have realized that their couple relationship is never going to give them the things they truly want....

A little perspective may help to take some of the edge off all that misery. The troubles a person experiences in Stage II do not necessarily have prognostic significance; they don't necessarily mean that he's made a bad choice of partners or that he won't be able to relate successfully to someone else. Furthermore, these troubles should not be allowed to obscure the bearable or the agreeable aspects of the relationship. There are ups and downs within Stage II, and it's possible, with persistence and goodwill, to reach "a place beyond resentment," a place where concord is not banality, and where harmony is not the simple absence of discord.

STAGE III: ACCEPTANCE

A Stage III couple has brought their expectations for their relationship into some kind of equilibrium with their everyday lives. Frustrations and anxieties don't stop, but these no longer trigger doubts about their future as a couple. That's settled. Each knows, and knows the other knows, that they're here to stay....

For a relationship to reach Stage III, changes on the level of behavior and feeling are invariably necessary.... In order that their relationship may flourish, a couple must relinquish threatening strategies like mutual blame—and they must learn some way of responding helpfully to each other's needs....

Changes in behavior and feeling must ultimately be accompanied by further changes in expectations. The person who asks his couple relationship to fill the conventional romantic bill is guaranteed disappointment....

The Stage III couple has learned to accept themselves as lovable people.... Known, and appreciated, a person is free to become most fully himself or herself. He can trust his partner, and the slow accumulation of trust over the years spent together enables the Stage III couple to share an unrivaled intimacy, an intimacy not of illusion, but of achieved, earned knowledge.

2. be reluctant to suggest what they would like, concerning recreation or entertainment, for example, and leave decisions to the other;
3. allow the other to be constantly late for engagements and never protest directly;
4. work on helping loved ones develop talents and interests while neglecting their own;
5. be sensitive to others' feelings and problems while hiding their own disappointments and hurts.

While it sounds noble, there's a catch to martyring. Aware that they're not receiving as much as they're giving, martyrs grow angry (Walster et al., 1974), even though they seldom express their anger directly. (In Chapter 9 we will discuss how unexpressed anger can damage a loving relationship.) Psychologists tell us that martyrs often think "it is better to be wanted as a victim than to not be wanted at all" (Szasz, 1976:62). The reluctance of martyrs to express even legitimate needs is damaging to a relationship, for it prevents openness and intimacy.

Martyring has other negative consequences. Social psychologists have been researching the concept of equity, the balance of rewards and costs to the partners in a relationship. In love relationships and marriage, as well as in other relationships, people seem most comfortable when things are fair or equitable, that is, when partners are reasonably well balanced in terms of what they are giving to and getting from the relationship. (We will discuss this theoretical perspective, termed *exchange theory*, in Chapter 6.) According to interviews with more than 600 women and men who were dating, living together, or married (Walster, Walster, and Traupman, 1978):

Couples with equitable relationships were more content and happy than were other couples. Those men and women who knew they were getting far *more* than they deserved were uneasy—they were less happy, and a lot more guilty than were their peers. It appears that lovers who are "too good" to their partners are really not doing them any favor. Of course, those men and women who felt they were getting *less* than they deserved were in even worse shape—they were a lot less content, a lot less happy, and a lot angrier than were their peers [Walster and Walster, 1978:143]. ■

Manipulating

Manipulators follow this maxim: If I can get him (or her) to do what I want done, then I'll be sure he (or she) loves me. **Manipulating** means seeking to control the feelings, attitudes, and behavior of one's partner or partners in underhanded ways rather than by assertively stating one's case. Manipulating is not the same thing as love. Manipulators may

1. ask others to do things for them that they could do for themselves, and generally expect to be waited on;
2. assume that others will (if they "really" love them) be happy to do whatever the manipulators choose, not only regarding recreation, for example, but also in more important matters;
3. be consistently late for engagements ("if he [or she] will wait patiently for me, he [or she] loves me");
4. want others to help them develop their interests and talents, but seldom think of reciprocating.

Manipulators, like martyrs, do not believe that they are lovable or that others can "really" love them; that is why they feel a continual need to test their partner. Aware that they are exploiting others, habitual manipulators often experience guilt. They try to relieve this guilt by minimizing or finding fault with their loved one's complaints (Walster et al., 1974). "You don't really love me," they may accuse. Manipulating, along with the guilt that often accompanies it, can destroy a relationship.

You may already have noticed that martyring and manipulating complement each other. Martyrs and manipulators are often attracted to each other, forming what family counselor John Crosby calls **symbiotic relationships**—where each partner depends on the other for a sense of self-worth (Crosby, 1976:42). Often, such symbiotic relationships are quite stable. Should one symbiotic partner learn to stand on his or her own two feet, however, the relationship is less likely to last. For, as Crosby explains, "There is no such thing as half-symbiosis" (1976:42).

Manipulating, martyring, and romanticizing are all sometimes mistaken for love. But they are not love, for one simple reason: All three relationships share a refusal to accept oneself or one's partner realistically—a quality we'll examine in greater detail later in this chapter.

Identifying what love *is* may not be as easy as identifying what it is not. Loving relationships can take many forms, or "personalities," just as the individuals in a relationship can. Before defining specific characteristics of love, therefore, we will look at a number of ways people can love each other, depending on their own needs, situations, and personalities.

SOME CONTEMPORARY LOVE STYLES

People can love each other in different ways. They can love passionately, quietly, pragmatically, and even playfully. In this section we'll look at some contemporary **love styles**, that is, distinctive characteristics or personalities that loving or love-like relationships can take. Notice that the word *love-like* is included in this definition: Not all love styles necessarily apply to genuine loving. (In fact, one of the styles we discuss below—mania—is not really loving at all.)

The classification of love styles we use here was developed by social scientist John Lee, based on interviews he conducted with 112 respondents, half male and half female (Lee, 1973). All were white and of Canadian or English descent. Lee used terminology borrowed from his knowledge of classical language and literature to distinguish six love styles: eros, storge, pragma, agape, ludus, and mania. In real life no loving relationship is entirely one style or another—people incorporate different aspects of several styles into their relationships.[2]

Eros

Eros (pronounced "air-ohs") is a Greek word meaning "love"; it forms the root of our word *erotic*. This love style is characterized by intense emotional attachment and powerful sexual feelings or desires. Erotic partners experience an immediate, strong attraction upon first meeting. Lee's respondents recalled physical symptoms of excitement, such as sweating, stomach churning, and increased rates of breathing, on first beholding their beloveds. When erotic couples establish sustained relationships, these are characterized by continued active interest in sexual and emotional fulfillment, plus the development of intellectual rapport. Some sociologists (e.g., Udry, 1974) argue that the emotional intensity of eros can be a binding force that carries a couple through family crises.

Storge

Storge (pronounced "stór-gay") is an affectionate, companionate style of loving. Taken from the Greek root word *stoa*, meaning "impassive," this love style focuses on deepening mutual commitment, respect, and friendship over time. Whereas eros emphasizes emotional intensity and sexual passion, storge does not. Sexual intimacy may result as partners develop increasing understanding of one another. The storgic lover's basic attitude to his or her partner is one of familiarity: "I've known you a long time, seen you in many moods" (Lee, 1973:87).

Pragma

Pragma (pronounced "prág-mah") is the root word for *pragmatic;* in Greek it means "thing done." Pragmatic love emphasizes the practical element in human relationships, particularly in marriages. Pragmatic love involves rational assessment of a potential partner's assets and liabilities. Here a relationship provides a practical base for both economic and emotional security. A pragmatic partner might remarry, for example, to replace his or her children's absent parent or because it's "time to settle down."

Agape

Agape (pronounced "ah-gáh-pay") is a Greek word meaning "love feast." Agape emphasizes unselfish concern for the beloved. A partner attempts to fill

---

2. Even though Lee's typology has intrigued many counselors and social scientists, independent research has not yet clearly supported the division of love experience into these styles (Hatkoff, 1977; Murstein, 1980). We nevertheless find this typology a useful way of thinking about love.

■ "She's crazy about him." That's a common way to describe someone "in love," but what does it mean? Two ways of expressing love are eros and mania.

the other's needs even when that means some personal sacrifice. Lovers gain satisfaction through working for the well-being of the beloved. Often called *altruistic love*, agape emphasizes nurturing others with little conscious desire for return other than the intrinsic satisfaction of having loved and cared for someone else.

Ludus

Ludus (pronounced "lewd-us") focuses on love as play or fun. The word means "game" in Latin: It is the root of our word *ludicrous*, which means to cause laughter. According to Lee, this love style does not tend to lead to marriage or long-term commitment, as ludus emphasizes the recreational aspects of sexuality and the enjoyment of many sexual partners rather than searching for one seri-

ous relationship. Of course, ludic flirtation and playful sexuality may be part of a more committed relationship based on one of the other love styles.

Mania

Mania, a Greek word, designates a wild or violent mental disorder, an obsession or craze. Like ludus, it does not usually lead to a long-term commitment. Mania rests on strong sexual attraction and emotional intensity, as does eros. It differs from eros, however, in that manic partners are extremely jealous and moody, and their need for attention and affection is insatiable. Manic lovers alternate between euphoria and depression. The slightest lack of response from the love partner causes anxiety and resentment; any small sign of warmth evokes enormous relief. Mania does not usually last very long, and when it ends, it often does so abruptly. In his films Woody Allen is usually a manic lover.

These variations, particularly the contrast between erotic and manic lovers, may be related to childhood experiences with parents. "Those who are secure describe their love relationships as happy and trusting, while the anxious lovers report that they frequently become obsessed by their lovers, are prone to intense jealousy, and undergo extreme emotional highs and lows," according to psychologists Philip Shaver and Cindy Hazan (Goleman, 1985b). Research by Shaver and Hazan indicated that about half their sample of 540 people aged 15 to 82 evidenced a secure style of loving, while the remainder divided into anxious clingers and those who avoided romantic attachments. These variations were closely associated with childhood experiences of security or insecurity (Goleman, 1985b).

These six love styles represent different ways people can feel about and behave toward one another in love-like relationships. In real life a relationship is never entirely one style, and the same relationship may be characterized, at different times, by features of several styles. Lovers can be erotic or pragmatic. Loving can assume qualities of quiet understanding and respect, along with playfulness. However, these love styles do not define what loving is. We'll turn next to a definition.

WHAT IS LOVE?

Love exists between parents and children, and between persons of the same and opposite sexes. Love may or may not involve sexuality. When it does involve sexuality, love can be heterosexual or homosexual. **Love** is a deep and vital emotion resulting from significant need satisfaction, coupled with a caring for and acceptance of the beloved, and resulting in an intimate relationship. We'll discuss each part of this definition in detail.

Love Is a Deep and Vital Emotion

An **emotion** is a strong feeling, arising without conscious mental or rational effort, that motivates an individual to behave in certain ways. Loving par-

ents, for example, will be motivated to see what is wrong if their child begins to cry. Anger, reverence, and fear are some other emotions, and they also evoke certain behaviors. When people get angry, for instance, they may feel like screaming or throwing things. Emotions are sometimes difficult for social scientists to come to grips with. Yet, even the most careful of researchers was able to find "the poetry of love" in his psychological data. The part of the brain associated with fantasy rather than rationality was most closely connected with emotional response and spontaneous behavior toward others (McClelland, 1986).

Liking Versus Loving   In defining love as an emotion, it is important to distinguish it from another, similar feeling—liking. **Liking** is not as powerful as loving, and research indicates that liking may be more rational—a result of thinking rather than feeling.

Social psychologist Zick Rubin investigated the differences between liking and loving. He found that people like others whom they respect, evaluate highly, or who seem to share similar values, attitudes, or social class. Liking often involves recognition of an individual's socially desirable qualities—believing that someone is unusually well-adjusted or capable of good judgment, for instance (Z. Rubin, 1973). Loving, however, is different. Research has generally found the overriding component of love to be its emotional intensity (Murstein, 1980). It involves emotional closeness and attachment to a person thought to be unique and indefinably special. Lovers often feel that they can confide "almost anything" to each other or that, if they were lonely, their "first thought" would be to seek out their beloved (Z. Rubin, 1973).

Another social psychologist who studied the emotional aspect of love is Elaine Walster, and she, too, distinguished love from liking, labeling them "passionate love" and "companionate love," respectively (Walster and Walster, 1978). While liking is sensible and rational and increases in accordance with partners' similarities, loving is less predictable. Furthermore, Walster found that passion between lovers often develops in irrational or illogical ways. "Passion sometimes develops under conditions that would seem more likely to provoke aggression and hatred than love. For example,... individuals experience intense love for those who have rejected them" (Walster, 1974:279). Walster hypothesized (with some support from her research) that negative emotions can arouse passion because they cause a heightened emotional state. This is not to imply that passion is always negatively generated; both positive and negative emotions heighten the passionate component of loving. Though not all research psychologists agree with Walster's interpretation of her data (Kenrick and Cialdini, 1977), there is some support for her theory. Many counseling psychologists maintain that conflict may heighten rather than weaken the emotion of loving (e.g., Bach and Deutsch, 1970), because, properly resolved, conflict can generate greater mutual knowledge and intimacy as the partners reveal themselves in their effort to resolve their differences.

R. S. Cimbalo and colleagues synthesized Rubin's loving/liking types and Walster's passionate love/companionate love dichotomy in their investigation of the course of love over time. They found that passion decreased in relation to the length of time a couple had been married:

Length of time married	Passionate love "score"
0–3 years	98.40
4–6 years	88.90
7–9 years	85.20
10–17 years	84.04

However, the companionate love a couple felt remained uniformly high (Cimbalo et al., 1976). This study has significant methodological weaknesses—it uses a small, unrepresentative sample and does not really follow the course of love over time, but rather depends on a comparison of different couples with different lengths of marriage. Looking at the whole body of research on love, however, Walster and Walster conclude that

although passionate love loses its fight against time, companionate love does not. The friend/lover who shored up our self-esteem, shared our attitudes and interests, kept us from feeling lonely, reduced our anxiety, and helped us get the things we wanted early in the relationship continues to be appreciated many years later [1978:126]. ■

New research expands upon these notions, but presents a more complex picture. Psychologist Robert Sternberg believes that the qualities most important to a lasting relationship are not so visible in the early stages. In his research on relationships varying in length from one month to thirty-six years he found three components of love: intimacy, passion, and commitment. "'Passion is the quickest to develop, and the quickest to fade.... Intimacy develops more slowly, and commitment more gradually still'" (quoted in Goleman, 1985b). Passion peaks early in the relationship, but continues at a stable lower level and is important to the long-term maintenance of the relationship. Intimacy, which includes understanding each other's needs, listening and supporting each other, and sharing common values, becomes increasingly important. In its most emotional form intimacy may not always be visible, but it emerges when the relationship is interrupted—for example, by travel, sickness, or death. Commitment is essential, but a commitment without intimacy and passion is hollow. In other words, all these elements of love are important. Because these components each develop at a different rate and so exist in various combinations of intensity, no relationship is stable, but rather will be always changing.

Love Satisfies Personal Needs

Human beings need recognition and affection, and a second quality of love is that it fills this basic need. Loving enables people to fulfill their needs for nurturance, creativity, and self-revelation.

It's all very well to state that a person's emotional needs can be fulfilled by love, but what kind of—and how many—needs can we expect to be satisfied? Psychologists stress that love cannot fulfill all needs, and they distinguish between legitimate and illegitimate needs.

Legitimate Needs Sometimes called "being needs," **legitimate needs** are those that arise in the present rather than out of deficits accumulated in the past (Crosby, 1976:41). Persons who have a healthy self-concept expect emotional support and understanding, companionship, and often sexual sharing from their partner. But they do not expect their partners to make them feel lovable or generally worthwhile; they already take those things for granted. Their need is to share themselves with loved ones to enrich their lives (Maslow, 1943).

Illegitimate Needs Sometimes called "deficiency needs," **illegitimate needs** arise from feelings of self-doubt, unworthiness, and inadequacy. People who feel deficient often count on others to convince them they are worthwhile (Crosby, 1976; Kernberg, 1978). "If you are not eternally showing me that you live for me," they seem to say, "then I feel like nothing" (Satir, 1972:136). They strive to borrow security from others.

To expect others to fill such needs is, of course, asking the impossible: No amount of loving will convince a person that he or she is worthwhile or lovable if that person doesn't already believe it. Hence, illegitimate needs for affection are virtually insatiable. Love does satisfy legitimate needs, however.

Love Involves Caring and Acceptance

A third important element of love is the acceptance of partners for themselves and "not for their ability to change themselves or to meet another's requirements to play a role" (Dahms, 1976:100). People are free to be themselves in a loving relationship, to expose their feelings, frailties, and strengths.

Related to this acceptance is caring: the concern a person has for the partner's growth. Psychoanalyst Rollo May defines this caring as a state "in which something does *matter*.... [It is] the source of eros, the source of human tenderness. It is a state composed of the recognition of another; a fellow human being like one's self; of identification of one's self with the pain or joy of the other" (1969:289). May's concept of caring contains elements of agape. Ideally, lovers support and encourage each other's personal growth. If a loved one wants to join a softball league or spend some evenings studying, for example, he or she is encouraged to do so. At the same time, partners respond to each other's needs for affection by recognizing budding feelings of insecurity or jealousy in each other and trying to be reassuring: "Just because I want to play softball doesn't mean I don't still love

■ Sharing a good time is an easy way to show affection, but the caring and sharing of love also include acceptance of and commitment to another person.

you," they explain; or "I love you, but I want to study now; let's get ice cream later."

Note also that experiencing feelings and expressing them may not be entirely the same thing. Cancian (1985) has observed that in our society women express feelings of love verbally more than men do (see also Critelli et al., 1986). Men's failings in this area have been noted by critics ranging from radical feminists (Firestone, 1970) to sociologists (Rubin, 1983) to authors of popular advice manuals (Scarf, 1987). Cancian maintains that men are equally loving, but that love is expressed in our society on feminine terms and women are the verbal sex. Nonverbal expressions of love such as men may make through doing favors, reducing their partners' burdens, and so on, are not credited.

BOX 3 · 2

A SELF-ESTEEM CHECKLIST

SOURCE:
Hamachek, 1971:248–51.

In this brief self-test you can broadly evaluate your own level of self-esteem. Do you

1. believe strongly in certain values and principles, so that you are willing to defend them?
2. act on your own best judgment, without regretting your actions if others disapprove?
3. avoid worrying about what is coming tomorrow or fussing over yesterday's or today's mistakes?
4. have confidence in your general ability to deal with problems, even in the face of failures and setbacks?
5. feel generally equal—neither inferior nor superior—to others?
6. take it more or less for granted that other people are interested in you and value you?

Cancian argues that a more balanced view of how love is to be expressed—one that includes masculine as well as feminine elements—would find men equally loving and emotionally profound. Less abstractly, a lover could consider the possibility that the partner expresses love differently and accept such differences, or else negotiate change openly.

Love and Intimacy: Commitment to Sharing

Intimacy is the capacity to share one's inner self with someone else and to commit oneself to that person despite some personal sacrifices. We can look more closely at two elements of that definition: first, the commitment involved in intimacy; and second, the dimensions of sharing.

Commitment In love, committing oneself to another person involves the determination to develop a relationship "where experiences cover many areas of personality; where problems are worked through; where conflict is expected and seen as a normal part of the growth process; and where there is an expectation that the relationship is basically viable and worthwhile" (Altman and Taylor, 1973:184–87).

Here we see the elements of storge. Committed lovers have fun together; they also share more tedious times. They express themselves freely and authentically. Committed partners do not see problems or disagreements as indications that their relationship is over. They view their relationship as worth keeping, and they work to maintain it in spite of difficulties. Commitment is characterized by this willingness to work through problems and conflicts as opposed to "calling it quits" when problems arise. In this view commitment need not include a vow to stay together exclusively for life or even for a certain period of time. But it does imply that love involves effort: Committed partners "regularly, routinely, and predictably attend to each other and their relationship no matter how they feel" (Peck, 1978:118).

Psychic and Sexual Intimacy Besides commitment, intimacy involves sharing. This sharing can take place on two often overlapping planes. At one level is sexual intimacy. In popular terminology people who have a sexual relationship are "intimate" with each other. At another level is psychic intimacy: people sharing their minds and feelings. This is the sense in which we use the term in this book. While sexual intimacy can either result from or lead to psychic intimacy, the two concepts are not synonymous. Strangers and people who like

7. accept praise without pretense of false modesty, and accept compliments without feeling guilty?

8. resist the efforts of others to dominate you, especially your peers?

9. accept the idea—and admit to others—-that you are capable of feeling a wide range of impulses and desires, ranging from anger to love, sadness to happiness, resentment to acceptance? (It does not follow, however, that you will act on all these feelings and desires.)

10. genuinely enjoy yourself in a wide range of activities, including work, play, creative self-expression, companionship, and just plain loafing?

11. sense and consider the needs of others?

If your answers to most of the questions above are "yes" or "usually," you probably have high self-esteem.

each other can enjoy sexual intimacy. Those who share with and accept each other experience psychic intimacy. They engage in the "work of attention": making the effort to set aside existing preoccupations in order to listen (Peck, 1978:120–121).

SELF-ESTEEM AS A PREREQUISITE TO LOVING

In this section we'll examine the idea that self-esteem is a prerequisite to loving. According to many psychologists, high self-esteem is one prerequisite for really loving others. **Self-esteem** is part of a person's self-concept; it involves feelings people have about their own worth. Social psychologist Stanley Coopersmith defines self-esteem as an evaluation a person makes and maintains of her- or himself. "It expresses an attitude of approval or disapproval, and indicates the extent to which the individual believes himself to be capable, significant, successful, and worthy" (Coopersmith, 1967:4–5).

Family therapist Virginia Satir suggests that people's self-esteem can be likened to pots, which

can be full, partly full, or nearly empty.[3] If you have high self-esteem, your pot is full. People with almost empty pots have low self-esteem (Satir, 1972). Probably most of us have pots that are neither as full as they could be nor completely empty; you can conduct a preliminary self-evaluation by answering the questions in Box 3•2, "A Self-Esteem Checklist."

People can also have a "pretty full pot" and then lose self-esteem through some incident (or set of

3. In her book *Peoplemaking,* Virginia Satir explains how she got the idea to liken people's selves to pots: "When I was a little girl, I lived on a farm in Wisconsin. On our back porch was a huge black iron pot.... My mother made her own soap, so for part of the year the pot was filled with soap. When threshing crews came through in the summer, we filled the pot with stew. At other times my father used it to store manure for my mother's flower beds. Whenever anyone wanted to use the pot, he was faced with two questions: What is the pot now full of, and how full is it? ... One day several years ago, a family was sitting in my office, and its members were trying to explain to one another how they felt about themselves. I remembered the black pot and told them the story. Soon the members of the family were talking about their own individual 'pots,' whether they contained feelings of worth or of guilt, shame, or uselessness" (1972:20–21). (This quotation is reprinted by permission of Virginia Satir, *Peoplemaking.* Palo Alto, Calif.: Science & Behavior Books, Inc., 1972).

SOURCE:
Hamachek, 1971.

BOX 3·3

LEARNING TO LOVE YOURSELF MORE

What can one do with feelings of inadequacy besides worry about them? People work in many ways to improve their self-esteem. For example, they may

1. pursue satisfying and useful occupations that realistically reflect their strengths and interests ("Young children make me nervous, but I'd like to teach, so I'll consider secondary or higher education");
2. work hard to develop the skills and interests they have rather than fret about those they don't;
3. work on being more honest and open with other people;
4. make efforts to appreciate the good things they have rather than focus on the more negative things in their lives;
5. avoid excessive daydreaming and fantasy living ("Boy, things would be different if only I were a little taller," or "If only I had not gotten married so young, things would be better");

---

incidents) that prompts them to question their worth. Doing poorly on an important exam, fighting with a roommate or teenage child, or going through a divorce are examples. Not only can people lose self-esteem, but they can also work to gain or regain it; Box 3·3, "Learning to Love Yourself More," contains some suggestions toward that end.

Self-Love Versus Selfishness

In defining self-esteem we should also explain a related concept (actually, a synonym in this book's context), that of *self-love*. People commonly confuse self-love with conceit—a self-centered, selfish outlook. But psychologists point out that self-love and selfishness are actually opposites. Self-love is the same as high self-esteem, and it enhances a person's capacity to love others. Selfishness, or narcissism, is a concern chiefly or only with oneself, without regard for the well-being of others. Selfishness results from low self-esteem (Kernberg, 1978). Disregarding others' needs results from preoccupation with one's own feelings of insecurity, together with the desire to compensate for such feelings.

Self-Esteem and Personal Relationships

Research indicates that self-esteem has a lot to do with the way people respond to others. On a broader social level persons with high self-esteem feel that they have less difficulty in making friends, are more apt to express their opinions, are less sensitive to criticism, and are generally less preoccupied with themselves (Coopersmith, 1967:48–71). In personal relationships people with very low self-esteem often experience a persistent and insatiable need for affection. As we saw in the discussion of illegitimate needs, that does not mean that they really love others. As Fromm puts it, "If I am attached to another person because I cannot stand on my own two feet, he or she may be a life saver, but the relationship is not one of love" (Fromm, 1956:112).[4]

---

4. Erich Fromm chastises Americans for their emphasis on wanting to *be loved* rather than on learning *to love*. Many of our ways to be loved or make ourselves lovable, he writes, "are the same as those used to make oneself successful, 'to win friends and influence people.' As a matter of fact, what most people in our culture mean by being lovable is essentially a mixture between being popular and having sex appeal" (Fromm, 1956:2).

6. continue their efforts even when they are discouraged ("Nothing works for me anyway");

7. reevaluate the standards by which they have learned to think of themselves as inadequate—they try to be satisfied to be smart *enough*, slender *enough*, or successful *enough* rather than continue to impose unrealistic standards on themselves;

8. decide to be their own good friends, complimenting themselves when they do things well enough and not criticizing themselves too harshly;

9. relax ("If I feel this way, it means this is a human way to feel, and everybody else has probably felt this way too at one time or another").

We will explore the difference between loving and dependency in the next section.

Self-esteem affects love relationships in some other ways. People with high self-esteem are more responsive to praise, whereas men and women with low self-esteem "are forever on the alert for criticism . . . and remember it long afterward" (Walster and Walster, 1978:54). People high in self-esteem are better at picking up signs of interest from other people and responding to them, whereas people low in self-esteem often miss such cues and, in general, are "set for rejection" (Walster and Walster, 1978:55).

Emotional Interdependence

Besides self-esteem, or self-love, a quality necessary for truly loving is the ability to be emotionally interdependent. Interdependence is different from both dependence and independence. **Dependence** involves general reliance on another or others for continual support or assurance, coupled with subordination—being easily influenced or controlled by those who are so greatly needed. **Independence,** on the other hand, involves self-reliance and self-sufficiency and may imply that the individual functions in isolation from others. It emphasizes separation from others.

Loving is different from both dependence and independence as we have defined them. It is **interdependence,** a relationship in which people with high-esteem make strong commitments to each other. John Crosby has distinguished between A-frame (dependent), H-frame (independent), and M-frame (interdependent) relationships. **A-frame relationships** are symbolized by the capital letter A: Partners have a strong couple identity but little individual self-esteem. They think of themselves as a unit rather than as separate individuals. Like the long lines in the letter A, they lean on one another. The relationship is structured so that "if one lets go, the other falls" (Crosby, 1976:49). And that is exactly what happens when one partner outgrows his or her dependency in a martyr-manipulator relationship.

H-frame relationships are structured like a capital H: Partners stand virtually alone, each self-sufficient and neither influenced much by the other. There is little or no couple identity and little emotionality: "If one lets go, the other hardly feels a thing" (Crosby, 1976:49). H-frame relationships are similar to liking rather than to loving.

George and I have been married 4½ years
we are an average couple, he is too Babyish
at times, some times our personalities Clash.
but most of the time we get along.
I FEEL LIKE I DEPEND ON GLORIA TO TAKE CARE OF ME
THAT MAKES ME VERY HAPPY.
George Brodzinski

■   What individual and social factors might help explain this couple's traditional views of love, their marriage, and their gender roles? Judging from George's comments, do they have an A-frame, M-frame, or H-frame relationship?

M-frame relationships rest on interdependence: Each partner has high self-esteem (unlike in the A-frame relationship), and partners experience loving as a deep emotion (unlike in the H-frame relationship). The relationship involves mutual influence and emotional support. M-frame relationships exhibit a meaningful couple identity: "If one lets go, the other feels a loss but recovers balance" (Crosby, 1976:49).

Acceptance of Self and Others

Loving partners need to have another quality besides self-love and interdependence, that of acceptance, or empathy. Each partner must try to understand and accept how the other perceives situations and people. If a loved one tells you he or she dislikes a friend of yours, for example, the accepting response is not "That's impossible!" but "Tell me why." Accepting relationships rest on unconditional positive regard. This doesn't mean that you, too, have to decide to dislike your friend. But even when loved ones do not share or condone specific attitudes and behavior, they accept each other as persons (Dahms, 1976:100–101). This, in fact, is the hallmark of a relationship that has survived to Stage III, described in Box 3•1, "Love in Three Stages."

Only people with relatively high self-esteem can accept others as persons. Because they accept their own feelings, anxieties, and frailties, they do not fear seeing these emotions in others. The more that persons can accept themselves, in other words, the more they can accept others.

Intimacy Versus the "Law of Self-Preservation"

Throughout this section we have touched on several variations of the same theme: the importance of self-esteem in loving relationships. One additional variation should be mentioned, and that is the role self-esteem plays in letting down barriers set up for "self-preservation."

Everyone has instincts for self-preservation, not just those people with low self-esteem. Rather than admit our ignorance, we may have pretended interest or changed the subject when others were discussing a topic we didn't know anything about. Another defensive measure is being unnecessarily critical of others to create an illusion of one's own competence. The law of self-preservation goes as follows: "Okay, I don't love me much and I know you won't. So I won't let you see me, and if you can't see the real me, you can't reject me and I am protected" (Vincent, 1976:137).

It takes a "pretty full pot" to be spontaneous and authentic, expressing feelings and thoughts honestly. In contrast to those with low self-esteem, people who love themselves are more able to let down barriers of self-preservation and to exhibit behavior "marked by simplicity and naturalness and by lack of artificiality or straining for effect" (Maslow, 1956:179). This ability is necessary in developing intimacy in a loving relationship.

For all, loving involves committing oneself to accepting others—something only those with sufficient self-esteem can do. We will now discuss how love happens.

LOVE AS A DISCOVERY

Love is discovered, not just found. The words *discover* and *find* have similar meanings. But to discover involves a process, while to find refers to a singular act. One definition of *discover*, for example, is to reveal or expose through exploration; *finding* more often means to attain or succeed in reaching. Loving is a process of discovery. It is something persons must do—and keep doing—rather than just a feeling they come upon. In psychologist Erich Fromm's words, love is "an activity, not a passive affect; it is a 'standing in,' not a 'falling for' " (1956:22).

Discovering Love

It's fine to say that love must be taken care of. But that doesn't answer the question of how love "happens." Don't people fall in love when least expecting it? Do they find they're in love after knowing each other awhile? Or do they work at learning to love each other? The answer to all these questions is "sometimes."

Some people know what kind of social characteristics they want in a partner before they even find one, as Chapter 6 explores further. He or she must be the right age, for example, and have the appropriate occupation, area of residence, or education. These people often find partners by joining organizations where they think it most likely to meet fitting mates (Lee, 1973:124–125).

Other people report that they "fell in love" on an accidental first meeting. Typically, their partners also fit well-defined images of those whom they could love; but these images emphasized physical attractiveness and potential for emotional and intellectual rapport (Lee, 1973:35–37).

Still others do not have any clear image or specific demands regarding potential love partners. Not actively "looking for love," they choose activities for their own sake rather than as a means to meet a partner. In these activities, however, they meet other people with the same interests (Lee, 1973:85, 75–80).

People can find love in any of these ways, and often in any combination. Psychologists warn, however, that romantically inclined individuals who insist on waiting for their "ideal" lover to come around the next corner may wait forever—and miss opportunities to love real persons. George Bach and Ronald Deutsch have counseled many single adults who hope to find love. Often, they report, clients ask where to meet potential partners. "Ironically, the questioner is [frequently] in the presence of some of the people he is looking for" (Bach and Deutsch, 1970:31). These psychologists point out, too, that waiting for accidental meetings to occur can be a barrier to finding love. A more realistic alternative is simply to introduce oneself to others who seem appealing.

Once a person meets the right partner, love can begin to develop. To describe this process of development, social scientist Ira Reiss has proposed what he calls the "wheel theory of love."

The Wheel of Love

According to Reiss's theory, there are four stages in the development of love, which he sees as a circular process—a **wheel of love**—capable of continuing indefinitely. The four stages—rapport, self-revelation, mutual dependence, and person-

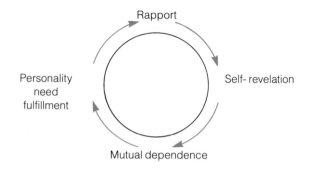

Figure 3·1

Reiss's wheel theory of the development of love. (Source: Reiss, 1960:143)

ality need fulfillment—are shown in Figure 3·1, and they describe the span from attraction to love.

Rapport Feelings of rapport rest on mutual trust and respect. People vary in their ability to gain rapport with others. Some feel at ease with a variety of people; others find it hard to relax with most people and have difficulty understanding others.

One factor that can make people more likely to establish rapport is similarity of background—social class, religion, and so forth, as Chapter 6 will discuss. But rapport can also be established between persons of different backgrounds, who may perceive one another as an interesting contrast to themselves or see qualities in one another that they admire (Reiss, 1976:94).

Social scientists are not certain which of these elements—similarity or difference—is more important. Similarity of *values* seems very important in the attraction not only of mates but also of friends (Byrne, 1971; Murstein, 1971). It is less clear whether similarity of *personality* is essential. One pair of social scientists hypothesized that a person would be attracted to someone who was different, since he or she would be able to fill the gaps in each other's emotional makeup. For example, a dominant and a submissive person might do well together. This theory of complementary needs (Winch, 1952) was supported by the research of Alan Kerchoff and Keith Davis (1962), but subsequent research has repeatedly failed to confirm it (Murstein, 1980). Whether initial attraction results

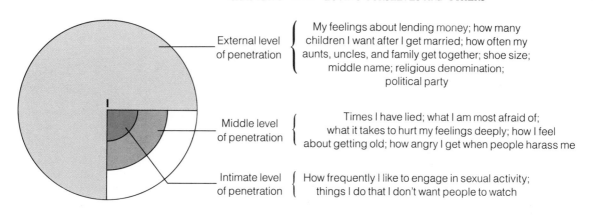

External level of penetration { My feelings about lending money; how many children I want after I get married; how often my aunts, uncles, and family get together; shoe size; middle name; religious denomination; political party

Middle level of penetration { Times I have lied; what I am most afraid of; what it takes to hurt my feelings deeply; how I feel about getting old; how angry I get when people harass me

Intimate level of penetration { How frequently I like to engage in sexual activity; things I do that I don't want people to watch

Figure 3·2
Social penetration. (Source: Adapted from Altman and Haythorn, 1965:411–26)

LINCOLN CHRISTIAN COLLEGE AND SEMINARY

from similarities or from differences, the rapport that two people establish often leads to a second phase in the wheel of love: self-revelation.

Self-Revelation Self-revelation, or **self-disclosure**, involves gradually sharing intimate information about oneself. People have internalized different views regarding how much self-revelation is proper. Men, for example, are socialized to be less self-disclosing than women (Rubin et al., 1980). And as we saw earlier in this chapter, people with low self-esteem will likely find it hard to share themselves fully.

Even for people with high self-esteem, however, loving produces anxiety. They fear their love won't be returned. They worry about being exploited. They are afraid of becoming too dependent or of being depended on too much.

One way of dealing with these anxieties is to deny them. This is a technique for self-preservation, and while it may seem easier at first, it can be harmful to a relationship in the long run. "Self-preservers" may come to view their partners as sources of stress rather than pleasure, for they can never relax around them (Jourard, 1964). No one is always successful or looks good all the time. None of us is consistently mild-mannered, and we're all boring sometimes. The gap between the real person and the image of oneself or one's partner—along with the pressure to maintain that image—creates even more anxiety.

The alternative to this kind of denial is self-disclosure—letting others see us as we really are and sharing our real motives, beliefs, and feelings. In their explanation of **social penetration**—the process through which persons gradually share intimate information about themselves—psychologists Irwin Altman and Dalmas Taylor (1973) describe how self-disclosure happens.

Altman and Taylor see the self as having penetrable layers (see Figure 3·2). People's "outer layers" are easily accessible to many others. We are willing to share information about our middle name, for example, or our religion with the general public. But the inner layers are progressively more private: These are revealed to fewer and fewer people and only after knowing them over time. As the figure shows, the self can be visualized as being opened in the shape of a wedge, gradually penetrating to the center. At the outer layers the symbolic wedge makes a wide space, allowing room for many others. As the wedge penetrates, the space gradually narrows, allowing increasingly fewer persons into the center.

In recent years social psychologists have done considerable research on self-disclosure. One of the strongest findings is that, in general, people reciprocate self-disclosure. If one person discloses personal information or feelings, the other is likely to respond on a similar level of intimacy (Chaikin and Derlega, 1976). Also, research on 212 college student couples revealed that patterns of self-disclosure are shifting from the traditional pattern of greater-female-than-male disclosure (Jourard, 1964;

■ Ethel remembers what first attracted her to Harry forty-seven years ago, and Harry still says his wife is "the smartest woman in town—because she married me." For some couples, love develops as an ongoing discovery, no matter how many years they've spent together.

Chaikin and Derlega, 1976) to an emerging norm of "full disclosure" by both partners in intimate, opposite-sex relationships (Rubin et al., 1980:305, 313).

As reciprocal self-revelation continues, an intimate relationship may develop while a couple progresses to the third stage in the wheel of love. Zick Rubin and colleagues, who developed scales to measure their concepts of "loving" and "liking" discussed earlier in this chapter, found high correlations between reports of self-disclosure and scores on the love scale (less so for the liking scale), "suggesting that many of our respondents may

have shared this view of intimate self-disclosure as a central element of love" (1980:314). This third stage is developing interdependence or mutual dependency.

Mutual Dependency In this stage of a relationship, the two people desire to spend more time together and thereby develop the kind of interdependence or, in Reiss's terminology, mutual dependency, described in the discussion of M-frame relationships. Partners develop habits that require the presence of both partners. Consequently, they begin to depend on or need each other. For example, a woman may begin to need her partner as an audience for her jokes. Or watching evening television may begin to seem lonely without the other person, because enjoyment now depends not only on the TV program but on sharing it with the other. Interdependency leads to the fourth stage: a degree of mutual personality need fulfillment.

Personality Need Fulfillment Every person has emotional needs: to love, to be loved, to confide, to be understood, to be supported and encouraged, and so forth. As their relationship develops, two people find they satisfy a majority of each other's emotional needs. As personality needs are satisfied, greater rapport is developed, which leads to deeper self-revelation, more mutually dependent habits, and still greater need satisfaction. Reiss uses the term *personality need fulfillment* to describe the stage of a relationship in which a stable pattern of emotional exchange and mutual support has developed. The relationship meets basic human needs. Reiss, as a sociologist, emphasizes needs associated with major adult social roles such as occupational and family roles. We would place as much emphasis on intimacy and emotional needs as on institutional roles in charting personality needs, which, furthermore, vary with the individual.

Reiss likens this four-stage process to a wheel (Figure 3·1). In a lasting, deep relationship the wheel turns indefinitely. Or the wheel may turn only a few times in a passing romance. Finally, the wheel can reverse itself and turn in the other direction. As Reiss explains: "If one reduced the amount of self-revelation through an argument, . . . that would affect the dependency and need-fulfillment processes, which would in turn weaken the rapport process, which would in turn lower the revelation level even further" (1960:143).

Keeping Love

The wheel theory suggests that once people fall in love, they may not necessarily stay in love. Relationships can "keep turning," or they may slow down or reverse themselves.

How do people stay in love? Keeping love requires continual discovery of both oneself and one's partner through mutual self-disclosure. As partners penetrate deeper toward the center of each other's personalities, they continually discover the remarkable and unique. Research involving a random sample of 120 Minneapolis working- and middle-class married couples supports the clinician's premise that the greater the self-disclosure, the greater the marital happiness reported (Jorgensen and Gaudy, 1980).

Love, then, is a continual process. Partners need to keep on sharing their thoughts, feelings, troubles, and joys with each other, an effort that will receive much more of our attention in Part Four of this text.

In a marriage relationship a vital dimension of this sharing is sexual intimacy. In Chapter 4 we'll turn to the physical expressions of love.

Summary

In an impersonal society love provides an important source of fulfillment and intimacy. Despite its importance, however, love is often misunderstood. It should not be confused with martyring or manipulating. There are many contemporary love styles that indicate the range of dimensions love-like relationships—not necessarily love—can take. John Lee lists six love styles: eros, or passionate love; storge, or familiar love; pragma, or pragmatic love; agape, or altruistic love; ludus, or love play; and mania, or possessive love.

Love may be different from love styles. It is defined as a deep and vital emotion resulting from significant need satisfaction, coupled with caring for and acceptance of the beloved, and resulting in an intimate relationship. Loving takes high self-esteem (self-love); the ability to be emotionally interdependent; an acceptance of oneself as well as a sense of empathy; and a willingness to let down barriers set up for self-preservation.

People discover love; they don't simply find it. The term *discovering* implies a process, and to develop and maintain a loving relationship requires self-disclosure. This mutual self-disclosure requires time and trust.

Key Terms

romanticizing *84*
martyring *85*
manipulating *88*
love styles *89*
eros *89*
storge *89*
pragma *89*
agape *89*
ludus *90*
mania *90*
love *91*
liking *91*
legitimate needs *92*
illegitimate needs *93*
self-esteem *95*
dependence *97*
independence *97*
interdependence *97*
A-frame relationship *97*
H-frame relationship *97*
M-frame relationship *99*
wheel of love *100*

Study Questions

1. Do you agree that loving is essential for emotional survival today? Why or why not?
2. What are some misconceptions of love? Why is each of them not really love?
3. Describe the six styles of love differentiated by Lee. Which styles do you think could be successfully combined in a single relationship? Which might be difficult?
4. What are the main components in the definition of love?
5. Explain the difference between liking and loving someone.
6. What kinds of needs can a love relationship satisfy? What needs can never be satisfied by a love relationship?
7. Discuss the characteristics necessary for a fully loving relationship.
8. What is the difference between self-love and selfishness? How is each related to a person's capacity to love others?
9. Describe A-frame, H-frame, and M-frame relationships.
10. Describe Reiss's wheel theory of love. Compare it with your ideas of how love develops.

Suggested Readings

Bellah, Robert N., et al.
1985 *Habits of the Heart: Individualism and Commitment in American Life.* Berkeley and Los Angeles: University of California Press.
A thoughtful examination of American society today by several renowned sociologists. A critical, yet hopeful, book, which concludes that "Perhaps enduring commitment to those we love and civic friendship toward our fellow citizens are preferable to restless competition and anxious self-defense" (295).

Berger, Peter, Brigitte Berger, and Hansfried Kellner
1973 *The Homeless Mind.* New York: Random House.
This theoretical work examines modern consciousness as it is shaped by an impersonal society in which people feel little sense of being rooted in communities.

Berne, Eric
1964 *Games People Play: The Psychology of Human Relationships.* Secaucus, N.J.: Castle.
This classic book examines how people tend to consistently play games in their relationships in order to avoid reality or genuine intimacy.

Fromm, Eric
1956 *The Art of Loving.* New York: Harper & Row.
A classic, this little book talks about love as an active choice to care for another person.

Goldstine, Daniel, Katherine Larner, Shirley Zuckerman, and Hilary Goldstine
1977 *The Dance-Away Lover and Other Roles We Play in Love, Sex, and Marriage.* New York: Morrow.
Excellent book about relationships that analyzes common roles and stages of a relationship in a fresh, realistic way.

Harris, Thomas A.
1967 *I'm OK—You're OK: A Practical Guide to Transactional Analysis.* New York: Harper & Row; Avon, 1973.
Another classic. Practicing psychiatrist Harris presents the basis of transactional analysis.

Peck, M. Scott
1978   *The Road Less Traveled: A New Psychology of
       Love, Traditional Values and Spiritual
       Growth.* New York: Simon & Schuster.
       More contemporary than *The Art of Loving*
       (Fromm), this popular work speaks of love as
       active, willful, disciplined, committed, and
       attentive.
Powell, John
1969   *Why Am I Afraid to Tell You Who I Am?* Niles,
       Ill.: Argus Communications.
       A paperback exploring why self-esteem is a pre-
       requisite for loving others intimately.
Walster, Elaine, and G. William Walster
1978   *A New Look at Love.* Reading, Mass.: Addison-
       Wesley.
       This paperback is oriented toward helping read-
       ers understand love in their own lives.

4 Our Sexual Selves

I have a fancy body.

MR. ROGERS, "Mr. Rogers' Neighborhood"

The real issue isn't making love; it's feeling loved.

WILLIAM H. MASTERS and VIRGINIA E. JOHNSON, *The Pleasure Bond*

From infancy to old age, people are sexual beings. Sexuality has a lot to do with both the way people think of themselves and the way they relate to others, especially in highly personal relationships. It plays a vital role in marriage and other long-term commitments.

Parents provide children with sexual information by the ways they relate to each other, by naming parts of the body, and by explaining the facts of life. But few modern children have had occasion to watch their parents or other relatives make love—the very idea of this seems startling. Yet discomfort about parents having sex in front of their children

is a problem created by the rising affluence and housing practices of the middle classes all over the world. In the past most families lived in one room and children learned what their parents did sexually by hearing the activity at night, seeing it in early evening or morning, observing activity in the city streets, parks, or in the countryside. In modern societies with a premium on privacy, children do not see their parents (or siblings or strangers) have sex together. The fact that they do not do so is neither good nor bad, it merely requires that they learn about it in other ways. [Gagnon, 1977:88] ■

Some of these other ways in which people learn about sex include peers and friends, sex manuals, the media, schools, and experimentation (Gagnon, 1977:85–95).

Despite these varied sources of sexual information—or perhaps because of them—sexuality is one of the most misunderstood parts of ourselves. In our society it is both exaggerated and repressed; rarely is it treated naturally. For this reason people's sexual selves are often sources of ambivalence and discomfort, and finding mutually satisfying ways of sharing sexual expression can be a challenge.

This chapter, along with Appendices A through F, discusses the sexual aspect of people's selves. We will describe the sexual anatomy and human sexual response. We will also look at some means of **sexual expression**: the way people act out or otherwise manifest the sexual aspects of themselves. We'll discuss sexual preference, one aspect of sexuality and sexual expression. We'll note social attitudes regarding sexuality and some ways these attitudes are changing, and we will examine the influence such attitudes can have on personal relationships. We'll look at conjugal sex and why it sometimes grows stale, and we'll outline some sexual dysfunctions. We will discuss sex as a "pleasure bond" that requires open, honest, and bonding communication. Finally, we will explore the impact of AIDS on sexual expression and relationships.

Before we begin, we wish to point out our society's tendency to reinforce the differences between women and men and to ignore the common feelings, problems, and joys that make us all human. The truth is, men and women aren't really so different. As Appendix A illustrates, many physiological parts of the male and female genital systems are either alike or directly analogous. Furthermore, the patterns of sexual response are very similar in men and women.

It is also true that physiological bases of human behavior cannot be isolated from their emotional, motivational, and social components. Such ordinary activities as eating, taking exercise, and even sleeping take on meaning according to why you're doing it, whether you're doing it alone or with someone, whether you like the person you're doing it with, and so forth. If it is hard to separate the physiology of such actions from their mental and emotional aspects, it is even more difficult to separate a person's sexual behavior from the rest of his or her person and relationships.

According to sociologist Ira Reiss, sexuality—comprised of physical pleasure and self-disclosure—is crucial to all important social relationships. Friendship and kinship relations entail physical pleasure in nonsexual embraces and self-disclosure.

What kind of close relationship would it be if there were no physical contact and no self-disclosure? Such pleasure and disclosure elements are the nucleus of almost all valued human relationships.... [S]exuality possesses, in pleasure and disclosure, the building blocks of human relationships.... Not all forms of sexuality are equally valued, but the relationship potential of sexual encounters is widely recognized [Reiss, 1986:235]. ■

Reiss sees self-disclosure (although by this he does not necessarily mean to imply affectionate ties) as characteristic of sexual expression. Experiencing orgasm "in front of another human being is an uncommon disclosure of oneself." More generally, the "basic self-disclosure of showing passion is a most common (though, of course, not guaranteed) outcome of sexual relationships" (1986:235). Human sexual response, then, inasmuch as it is pleasurable and self-disclosing, can be pivotal in building intimate relationships.

In the next section we discuss the physiology

of human sexual response. You may want to refer to Appendix A for explanation of anatomical references.

HUMAN SEXUAL RESPONSE

Our entire bodies respond to sexual stimulation. Blood pressure rises and pulse rate increases, breathing becomes deeper and faster, the genitals become engorged with blood, and when orgasm occurs, there is an almost explosive release of suspended physical tension.

Although these sensations are familiar to most adults, it is only in recent years that they have been scientifically observed and charted. Pioneers in this study were an internationally famous research team, William Masters and Virginia Johnson. Through carefully controlled laboratory observation over a period of eleven years, they recorded in detail the bodily changes that take place as a consequence of **sexual arousal**: the awakening, stirring up, or excitement of sexual desires and feelings in either ourselves or others.[1] Masters and Johnson describe four phases of human sexual response: excitement, plateau, orgasm, and resolution. These phases

---

1. William H. Masters, then an obstetrician at St. Louis's Washington University Medical School, and Virginia E. Johnson, who joined the project as a researcher, jointly published in 1966 a landmark study in human sexuality based on eleven years of research (Masters and Johnson, 1966). While Alfred Kinsey had pioneered the study of human sexuality by surveying men and women about their sexual behavior, Masters and Johnson were the first to study sexual behavior in the laboratory. Volunteers, both married and single, 382 women and 312 men, engaged in sexual activities, primarily intercourse and masturbation, in a laboratory setting in which their physiological responses were monitored by various recording devices including in some cases cameras that filmed internal changes in the vagina. Such physiological monitoring was supplemented by visual observation by the researchers and their assistants. Masters and Johnson have continued their research in human sexuality with development of a therapy program for sexual dysfunction (Masters and Johnson, 1970), publication of a popular volume intended to place the physiological aspects of sex into the context of human relationships (Masters and Johnson, 1976), and recent research on homosexuality (Masters and Johnson, 1979). Their research activities are now under the auspices of their nonprofit Reproductive Biology Research Foundation in St. Louis.

Masturbation

Psychologist Thomas Szasz defines masturbation as "taking things into one's own hands" (1976:21). More seriously, **masturbation** refers to providing sexual pleasure by means of self-stimulation, usually of the genitals. Some sexual partners find it arousing to watch each other masturbate.

Boys and girls begin to finger their genitals when they are babies, and they usually learn to masturbate at an early age.[4] This is particularly true for boys. About 94 percent of adult men and almost two-thirds of women report having masturbated at some time in their lives, and masturbation does not necessarily cease when a person enters a sexual relationship. About 70 percent of married men and women in their 20s and 30s masturbate—men about twenty-four times a year, and women about ten times (Hunt, 1974).

These figures may seem surprisingly high considering that in some religious groups there is a taboo against masturbation and that masturbation may seem a threat to relationship sex. But many counselors and therapists believe that masturbation can benefit a sexual relationship by helping people learn what will arouse them sexually—an understanding that can be communicated to a partner.

Kissing, Fondling, and Cuddling

Kissing, fondling, and sometimes cuddling are forms of **petting**: physical contact that is directed toward sexual arousal and does not involve intercourse (Saxton, 1977).

Kissing and fondling are highly effective stimulants, and techniques of arousal are virtually limitless, involving all areas of the body. Caressing and kissing often become more specific as arousal heightens. Direct stimulation of the partner's genital areas with one's hands and oral-genital stimulation can be either alternatives or preludes to

intercourse. **Cunnilingus** is the term for oral stimulation of a woman's genital area; **fellatio** is oral stimulation of the penis, scrotum, and perineum.

While embracing, fondling, and kissing may lead to intercourse, these activities themselves are forms of sexual expression. Montagu argues that among Americans the desire to be held and cuddled is considered childish and is acceptable only as a prelude to sexual intercourse. Because of this, men and women often "avoid embarrassment or shame" by engaging in intercourse when they really want to be held (Montagu, 1971:191). Alex Comfort, too, describes "real sex" as including many activities our culture often doesn't recognize: "Being together in a situation of pleasure or of danger or just of rest...; touching; old fashioned expedients like holding hands...; sleeping together even without, or especially after, intercourse" (Comfort, 1972:88–89).

Intercourse

Sexual intercourse, or **coitus**, involves the insertion of the penis into the vagina. In preparation for this, as we saw earlier in the discussion of sexual response, men and women usually experience some physiological changes. The sexually aroused man's penis becomes erect and rigid, and the walls of the woman's vagina become lubricated.

Partners can have coitus in numerous positions that are to some extent culturally influenced. In one of the most common positions in our culture, the woman lies on her back and the man lies on top of her, face to face. In other positions the woman is above and straddling the man; partners lie side by side and face to face; or the man inserts his penis into his partner's vagina from behind her. Counselors point out that no one position is "normal"; couples can experiment to find the positions that are most mutually satisfying.

A variation on coitus is anal intercourse, in which a man's penis is inserted into a woman's or another man's anus. About 50 percent of currently active male homosexuals practice anal intercourse. Although over one-half of the respondents to one survey did not agree that "anal intercourse between a man and a woman is wrong" (Hunt, 1974:23), most heterosexuals report that they "rarely" practice anal intercourse (Hunt, 1974:204). But some partners enjoy anal intercourse as an occasional

---

4. Some cultures encourage young children to masturbate and even to play at having intercourse. In these cultures sexual behavior is continuous from early childhood through adulthood. One anthropologist reported that, in a number of societies, sexual stimulation is used as a pacifier for infants and as an aid in weaning older babies from their mother's breast (Skolnick, 1978a:176).

or even as a regular means of sexual expression (Comfort, 1972:158).

Whole Body Stimulation

While lesbian partners may engage in activities that mimic intercourse, their lovemaking is more likely to be focused on whole body stimulation rather than on vaginal or anal entry. Heterosexual or male homosexual partners, too, may have more or less focus on vaginal or anal penetration, stimulating the rest of the body to produce excitation or orgasm. Space limits our ability to present much detail on the possibilities for sexual expression, but we want to point out that intercourse is not the only valued mode of sexual relating, particularly since sex therapists now emphasize the importance of whole body stimulation (Masters and Johnson, 1970).

We now turn to a discussion of sexual preference.

SEXUAL PREFERENCE

Sexual preference refers to whether an individual prefers a sexual partner of the same or opposite sex. **Heterosexuals** prefer sexual partners of the opposite sex, while **homosexuals** prefer same-sex partners. These terms do *not* designate general masculinity or femininity or other aspects of personality. It is a myth that homosexual males are necessarily effeminate, and lesbians (homosexual females) necessarily masculine (Beach, 1977a:312).

While homosexuality is more visible today than in the past, the percentage of homosexuals in our society has probably not increased. Perhaps 12 percent of males, 10 to 12 percent of single females, and 3 percent of married women have had some homosexual experience as adults (Hunt, 1974). A survey of over 4,000 college students revealed that 12 to 17 percent of males and 7 to 11 percent of females had had homosexual experiences (Hayes and Oziel, 1976). Conceptual problems—that is, deciding who is to be classified as homosexual (How much experience? How exclusively homosexual? How does one define him- or herself?)—preclude any accurate statement about estimates of homosexuality in our society (Mahoney, 1983).

We tend to think of sexual preference as a dichotomy: One is either homosexual or heterosexual. Actually, sexual preference may be a con-

tinuum. Kinsey, in fact, used a sevenfold rather than a twofold category system for classifying people in terms of partner preference (see Table 4•1). Freud and more contemporary psychologists and biologists (Beach, 1977b) maintain that humans are inherently bisexual. That is, although predominantly either hetero- or homosexual, humans may have the latent physiological and emotional structures necessary for responding sexually to either sex.[5] From one point of view these concepts themselves are social inventions. Before the end of the nineteenth century, sexual behavior was not examined scientifically (Weeks, 1985). Conceptual categories such as heterosexual, homosexual, or bisexual—or the ones describing human sexual response in the previous section—result from the development of "sexology"—the medical, psychological, and sociological scientification of sexual behavior.

In time, social pressures to view oneself as either homosexual or heterosexual may inhibit latent bisexuality (Gagnon, 1977). While at age 15 only 48.4 percent of males are "entirely heterosexual," by age 45 almost 90 percent are (see Table 4•1). In fact, from age 15 to 20, the percentage of males committed to heterosexuality increases from 48 percent to 69 percent. Some homosexual experience is fairly common during adolescence and does not predict adult sexual preference (McIntosh, 1968).

The pattern for females indicates less homosexual activity than for males. However, even though 27 percent of men and only 11 percent of women have had homosexual and bisexual experiences at age 20, by age 35 the proportion who are actively homosexual is the same for both men and women (3 percent). "Women seem to broaden their sexual experience as they get older whereas men become narrow and more specialized" (McIntosh, 1968:191–192). In any case there is probably more

---

5. A recent formulation of sexual preference presents a four-fold typology, based on the notions that persons may be more or less active along heterosexual/homosexual lines. That is, a person may be sexually active or not very active with same-sex or opposite-sex partners, or both. There are, then, (a) *bisexuals,* who are active with partners of both sexes, (b) *heterosexuals,* (c) *homosexuals,* and (d) *asexual* persons, who are not strongly identified or active (Storms, 1980). Development of sexual preference is probably strongly influenced by our tendency to think of preference as dichotomous: Individuals may sort themselves into the categories homosexual/heterosexual and to some extent behave accordingly.

TABLE 4·1 Heterosexual-Homosexual Rating: Active Incidence by Age[a]

Age	Percentage of Each Age Group of Male Population Having Each Rating[b]							
	X	0	1	2	3	4	5	6
15	23.6	48.4	3.6	6.0	4.7	3.7	2.6	7.4
20	3.3	69.3	4.4	7.4	4.4	2.9	3.4	4.9
25	1.0	79.2	3.9	5.1	3.2	2.4	2.3	2.9
30	0.5	83.1	4.0	3.4	2.1	3.0	1.3	2.6
35	0.4	86.7	2.4	3.4	1.9	1.7	0.9	2.6
40	1.3	86.8	3.0	3.6	2.0	0.7	0.3	2.3
45	2.7	88.8	2.3	2.0	1.3	0.9	0.2	1.8

SOURCE: McIntosh, 1968:190.
a. Based on Kinsey, 1948:652, Table 148.
b. X = unresponsive to either sex; 0 = entirely heterosexual; 1 = largely heterosexual but with incidental homosexual history; 2 = largely heterosexual but with a distinct homosexual history; 3 = equally heterosexual and homosexual; 4 = largely homosexual but with distinct heterosexual history; 5 = largely homosexual but with incidental heterosexual history; 6 = entirely homosexual.

experimentation with homosexuality and more potential for bisexuality among both women and men than has been realized. At the same time, there are fewer homosexuals or bisexuals than the attention given them would suggest.

The Development of Sexual Preference

We know little about how an individual's sexual preference develops. The origins of both heterosexuality and homosexuality remain a mystery. "There is no adequate theory of heterosexual development... [because] it is assumed that heterosexuality will flourish because it is 'natural'" (Gagnon, 1977:241).

Homosexuals do not appear to be distinct in their early family relationships and structures (Gagnon, 1977; Maddox, 1982; *Newsweek,* 1981). Homosexual parents produce heterosexual children (Maddox, 1982; Cohen, 1978). A study of 974 homosexuals and 477 heterosexuals by Kinsey Institute researchers Alan P. Bell, Martin S. Weinberg, and Sue Kiefer Hammersmith confirms earlier findings that unsatisfactory (or satisfactory)

relationships with one's parents have very little to do with one's sexual preference (Bell et al., 1981). In fact, "no particular phenomenon of family life can be singled out... as especially consequential for either homosexual or heterosexual development" (Alan Bell, quoted in the *Omaha World-Herald,* August 29, 1981, p. 5-A).

The existence of a roughly 10 percent homosexual population in virtually every society—in societies that treat homosexuality permissively as well as those that treat it harshly—suggests a biological imperative (Ford and Beach, 1971). Alan Bell, senior author of the recent Kinsey study, comments that "what we seem to have identified is a pattern of feelings and reactions within the child. Indeed, homosexuality may arise from a biological precursor that parents cannot control.... The researchers concluded that homosexuality is as deeply ingrained as heterosexuality" (in *Omaha World Herald,* August 29, 1981, p. 5-A). However, no clear genetic difference between homosexuals and heterosexuals has been established either (Gagnon, 1977; Masters and Johnson, 1979).

A sociological explanation would emphasize the socialization process and would assume a contemporary increase in homosexuality as society becomes more permissive and homosexual role models

we look like weatherbeaten survivors.
we try to understand each other. We can't always.
when we are young we think people will change, but
they will become only what they are.

now, we are at the end of our lives.
Growing old together eases the pain.

Paul W

grow more visible. But this does not appear to have happened. The vast majority of adults remain resolutely heterosexual. All this has led some researchers to conclude that studying how people get to be homosexual is probably useless. While it certainly is not clear whether homosexuality is genetically or socially determined, nonetheless one has to make choices about sexual preference and its expression.

Homosexualities

Because there is no one homosexual life-style, John Gagnon (cited throughout this chapter) prefers the term *homosexualities.* His point is that homosexuality may vary in its significance in people's lives and there "is a multiplicity of ways of organizing a homosexual preference into other ongoing life styles and commitments" (Gagnon, 1977:237). Some homosexuals marry heterosexuals, for example, then engage in homosexual affairs. (Discovery is likely to threaten the marriage if the partner had not known; some couples try very hard to make a go of such marriages, however; Dullea, 1987.) As homosexuals make choices throughout their lives, they may prefer a "body-centered sexuality" (in which sex takes place with little or no emotional interaction and with a variety of partners) or committed, person-centered relationships. As concern mounts regarding the AIDS virus, discussed later in this chapter and also in Appendix D, there is evidence that homosexual males are moving from a "body-centered" to a "person-centered" sexuality (*New York Times,* July 22, 1985, p. 15; Oct. 13). Much of what is said about sexual expression and relationships in a heterosexual context throughout this text is applicable to person-centered homosexual relationships.

Moreover, whatever one's sexual preference, the physiological processes that take place during sexual excitement and orgasm are the same.

SOCIETY AND SEX: CHANGING SCRIPTS AND MIXED MESSAGES

The sexual expressions described earlier in this chapter are learned, even though they are rooted in bodily responses. This learning process is not a simple one, for social attitudes have changed greatly

in the past few decades. People's views concerning sexuality and sexual expression are no exception.

In the next few pages we will focus on changing sexual attitudes and behaviors; then we will look at the mixed messages conveyed by two predominant sexual **scripts**—the traditional "patriarchal" view of sex and an emerging "expressive" view of sexuality—and the ambivalence created by their coexistence.

Changing Behaviors and Attitudes

We don't have to be told that both sexual behavior and social attitudes about sex change. There is evidence that people are engaging in sexual activity more often than they used to and in more varied ways.[6] During the 1960s, for example, the rate of nonmarital sex among college students increased dramatically (Bell and Chaskes, 1970; Christensen and Gregg, 1970), and this trend continued into the 1970s (King et al., 1977). Social historians estimated that by the mid-1970s the majority of unmarried adults had experienced intercourse. Some researchers claim that the rate of increase in permissiveness of behavior and attitudes has slowed since the mid-1970s and that there may even be a slight conservative trend (Walsh et al., 1983; Robinson and Jedlicka, 1982). But others see

6. Most of our information comes from extensive survey research (a technique described in the Prologue) conducted within the past few decades. The pioneer of these studies was the Kinsey reports on male and female sexuality (Kinsey, 1948; 1953). Several successive surveys, including the Hunt study (1974) written to compare with Kinsey, the *Redbook* survey (Tavris and Sadd, 1977), and the Hite report (1976), have helped to update our knowledge of sexual behavior in America. While the Hunt study is not a random sample (one in which persons are picked at random to be interviewed), it is probably more representative than the *Redbook* survey (limited to the magazine's readers) and the data produced by the haphazard methods of the *Hite Report.* The *Redbook* survey does provide data supportive of Hunt's conclusions. What is interesting about the *Hite Report* is the public's response, not the scientific validity of its data. Evidently, its themes of intense female interest in sex and criticism of male partners' willingness to collaborate in female satisfaction resonated with popular experience.

Conclusions based on survey research in sensitive areas such as sexuality must always be qualified by an awareness of their limitations: the possibility that respondents have minimized or exaggerated their sexuality and that people willing to answer a survey on sex are not representative of the public. Nevertheless, we must use these as the best data we have.

■ Communicating about sex—expressing what you want and when—is rarely as straightforward as a poster. Couples must deal with complex sexual scripts suggesting appropriate behaviors and attitudes. When partners are reading from different scripts, their mixed messages can create conflicts. How do posters like these aid and hinder communication?

a continuation of the trend toward permissiveness, finding that even in a relatively conservative group of college women, 83 percent of those over age 21 had had coitus (Bell and Coughey, 1980; Darling et al., 1984).

In 1986, as AIDS (see Appendix D) began to infect the heterosexual community—through sexual contact with partners who were bisexual or who had themselves had sexual contact with bisexual partners—discussion about the value of more conservative sexual behavior increased (*New York Times*, March 22, 1986). But since the data on sexual behavior reported in this chapter was collected *before* AIDS entered the scene, we do not know whether behavior has been modified from what we report here.

Studies of teenage women indicate that the minimum age of first intercourse has decreased

since the fifties (Zelnik and Kantner, 1977) and that many teenagers are experimenting with sex (this issue is addressed in Chapters 9 and 13). While there may not be any particular set of new societal norms explicitly *favoring* premarital sex, the sanctions *against* it have been greatly reduced. That is, the sanctions that could have discouraged sex in the past—fear of pregnancy, the concepts of sin and guilt, the value of virginity at marriage— have much less impact today (Bell and Coughey, 1980:357).

Postmarital intercourse (following the termination of a marriage) is also widespread (Gebhard, 1970). Research shows that almost 100 percent of divorced men and 90 percent of divorced women under age 55 are sexually active, with a median number of eight partners for men and four for women (within the year preceding the survey) (Hunt, 1974).

Other behaviors once considered taboo are becoming more widespread.[7] Persons surveyed about their sexuality report increased approval and practice of masturbation, either as a personal outlet for sexual tension or as preparation for orgasm during a sexual encounter (Hunt, 1974).

At least one social analyst suggests that the most significant change is in marital sexuality (Hunt, 1974). In comparison with the 1950s and 1960s, spouses are engaging in sexual activity more frequently and in more varied and experimental ways.[8] A study concerning sexual attitudes in the mid-1970s found that a majority of both men and women approve of oral or anal intercourse; over three-fourths of the men and women under age 45 approve of oral sex. More married women are experiencing orgasm, and they're doing so more often (Hunt, 1974).

Social scientists view these trends as evidence of changing social attitudes. There has been a shift toward viewing sexuality in terms of the needs and preferences of individuals. Even though people are free to make personal choices about sex, their choices are complicated by the mixed messages our changing society transmits.

Sexual Scripts

Two dominant sexual scripts coexist in our society. The traditional patriarchal script, described in Box 4•1, "Two Sexual Scripts," continues to influence our attitudes and behavior. At the same time, however, the emerging script of expressive sexuality (also described in the box) holds out conflicting beliefs and values.

The two scripts presented in the box are abstracted from reality. Real-life sexual behavior is more complex, falling somewhere in between or combining elements of the two types. Nevertheless, understanding typical patterns of behavior can give us some perspective on real-life modes of sexual behavior.

Sexual scripts, like social scripts, suggest appropriate behaviors and attitudes. Specifically, they tell us which partner should take the initiative in sexual expression, how long a sexual encounter should last, how important it is to experience orgasm, what positions are acceptable during intercourse, whether other forms of genital contact are permissible, and whether it is appropriate to masturbate. Sexual scripts specify legitimate and illegitimate reasons for sexual activity. And they say something about what sexual activity should mean to the participants. Depending on what script we follow, for example, a touch or an act of intercourse has different meanings for us.

Many attitudes dictated by the traditional patriarchal script are evident in our society. Some examples are the continuing disapproval of and distaste for masturbation, homosexuality, and the sexuality of older adults, and the feeling that sexual initiative should come from men. Another is the double standard, which continues to exist in some situations. A recent study of college students reveals a continuing double standard with regard to intercourse in the absence of feelings of affection. Eighty percent of the students surveyed approved of premarital sex for men in love, and 74 percent approved for women in love. But researchers found a great difference (45 percent for men, compared to only 16 percent for women) in approval of coitus when affection was not involved (Walsh et al., 1983:3).

Current attitudes and behavior also provide evidence of expressive sexuality. Social scientists note that men are becoming more interested in communicating intimately through sexual activity rather than viewing sex only as biological gratification (Pietropinto and Simenauer, 1977). At the same time, more women admit that they value physical sexual pleasure. It seems that men and women are moving closer together in their relative emphasis on both emotional ties and physical pleasure as reasons for sexual activity (Hunt, 1974).

From "His and Hers" to "Theirs"

The expectation for expressive sexuality marks a shift from the patriarchal, "his and her" attitudes about sex and gender roles that have traditionally dominated many people's thinking (see Chapter 2). A discrepancy may still exist, however, between men's and women's feelings and attitudes about sex, and this discrepancy is rooted in traditional life-style patterns and socialization.

---

7. However, over 70 percent of adult Americans believe that sexual relations between two adults of the same sex are always wrong (Davis, 1980, cited in Mahoney, 1983).

8. For a review of the quite complex changes in marital sexual frequency over time, see Mahoney, 1983, Chapter 8.

BOX 4 · 1

TWO
SEXUAL
SCRIPTS

PATRIARCHAL SEX

This script takes its name from the system of social organization called
patriarchy, in which descent, succession, and inheritance are traced through
the male genetic line, and the socioeconomic system tends to be male
dominated. This system is characterized by many beliefs, values, attitudes, and
behaviors developed to protect the male line of descent. Although many of the
traditional assumptions may sound old-fashioned, contemporary attitudes about
sex are still influenced by this script. Here are some of the basic assumptions of
the **patriarchal sexual script**:

1. Men own everything in the society, including women and women's sexuality.
   Exclusive sexual possession of a woman in monogamous marriage ensures
   that her children will be legitimately his.
2. Sex is a purely biological function whose only value is its procreative potential. Thus, coitus is the only appropriate sexual act. Other forms of genital
   contact, prolonged kissing and fondling, masturbation, homosexuality, sex
   between partners too old to have offspring, and even intercourse in varied
   positions are inappropriate.
3. Men are born with an urgent "sex drive" and women are sexually passive by
   nature. In some women sexuality can be "awakened" if the male is persistent
   enough—an idea that has been called the *sleeping beauty myth* (Gordon
   and Shankweiler, 1968).
4. Physical release of sexual tension through orgasm is necessary for males but
   not for females. When females do experience orgasm, two kinds are distinguished: "Clitoral orgasm" occurs through clitoral stimulation, and "vaginal
   orgasm" is caused through stimulation of the inner vaginal walls by the
   thrusting of the penis. A resulting myth is that vaginal orgasm is more
   mature.
5. Unmarried men and husbands whose wives do not meet their sexual needs
   can gratify those needs outside marriage. For women, however, sex outside
   marriage is not permissible; only "bad" women gratify men's sexual needs
   outside marriage or take an active role in initiating sexual activity.
6. Because women are dependent on men for economic support, they should
   keep their husbands happy. Even if unawakened, women should learn to tolerate sex in order to maintain a relationship with a man.

EXPRESSIVE SEXUALITY

A different sexual script is emerging as a result of several societal changes,
including the decreasing economic dependence of women, concern for

population control, and the availability of new methods of birth control. This **expressive sexual script** is based on the following:

1. Sexuality is basic to the humanness of both women and men. All individuals are free to express their sexual selves; there is no one-sided sense of "ownership."
2. For human beings, sexual activity is not purely a biological "drive" for the purposes of reproduction. It is an important means of enhancing personal communication and intimacy in an impersonal society (see Chapter 3), and all forms of sexual activity between consenting adults are acceptable.
3. The sexual needs and capacities of both women and men are considered to be basically the same. Women's capacity for sexual excitement and orgasm is comparable to men's.
4. Physical release of sexual tension through orgasm is important for females as well as for males. It is estimated that 90 percent of American women experience orgasm. The clitoris is involved in virtually all female orgasms, either through direct massage or through indirect stimulation (for instance, during body contact as the penis thrusts within the vagina). In other words, there is no such thing as a purely vaginal orgasm.
5. Sexual pleasure is a legitimate pursuit for all persons. Nonmarital sex is acceptable: It does not make women "bad," "loose," or "demanding." For both women and men, it can provide physical enjoyment and also strengthen emotional bonds between persons. Sex can create a "pleasure bond" between partners. Some people believe that sexual activity can be purely recreational, but psychotherapists caution that casual sexual encounters undermine human needs for intimacy (May, 1969).
6. Marital sex should be meaningful for both partners.

What contemporary attitudes can you think of that reflect patriarchal assumptions? Can you identify both patriarchal and expressive viewpoints in your own attitudes about sex? Have your views changed considerably over time? How does the concept of **marital rape,** where a husband forces his wife to engage in coitus with him against her will, fit into the expressive or the patriarchal script? (In 1978 a Michigan court acquitted a wife of murdering her husband while he was attempting to rape her. Could the same decision have been made thirty years ago?) To what extent do you think the definition of **nymphomaniac** reflects our society's sexual scripts?

Wives may feel lonely and emotionally separated from task-oriented, emotionally reserved husbands, while husbands feel that their wives ask too much emotionally. A startling number of current best-sellers (for example, Cowan and Kinder, 1987) deal with these issues, indicating their persistence despite changing gender roles. Furthermore, many adult women and men today have internalized vastly different messages about human sexuality. Husbands who have been trained from childhood not to express tender emotions may feel that sex is the one place where they are able to let their feelings out. Wives who receive the opposite training may find it difficult to be expressive about their sexual feelings (L. Rubin, 1976) (see Box 4·2—"Freeing Couples Up: Communicating About Sex"). Thus, husbands may complain that their wives are not sexually enthusiastic, while wives counter with "He's only really interested in me when we're in bed."

As more men come to value emotional intimacy in and out of the bedroom, and as more women come to value their sexuality, conjugal sex will cease to be "his and hers," and become "theirs." Evidence indicates that this is just what is happening. A majority of both husbands and wives today believe that husbands should listen to their mates, offer comfort and reassurance, and disclose confidences (Nye et al., 1976:111–29). Moreover, a fairly recent nationwide survey of men in all age, education, and occupational categories found that over one-third regarded love (not sex) as the most important thing in life. Another 30 percent said love made sex better or was essential for good sex (Pietropinto and Simenauer, 1977).

Meanwhile, a substantial and growing number of wives show increasing interest in the physical pleasure of sex (Hunt, 1974). And more and more, women feel equally responsible for initiating sex (Nye et al., 1976).

Making the Transition from Patriarchal to Expressive Sexuality

Today's changing sexual attitudes and behaviors may promise more satisfying sexual experiences, but they can also be sources of anxiety and ambivalence. Research shows that such ambivalence is more frequent among women, particularly among the wives of blue-collar workers. Family counselor Lillian Rubin explains: "Socialized from infancy to experience their sexuality as a negative force to be inhibited and repressed, women can't just switch 'on' as the changing culture or their husbands dictate" (1976:136). For wives, particularly older and working-class women, ambivalence may center around a husband's greater expectations. Rubin aptly describes a primary source of the difficulty: "For when, in the course of a single lifetime, the forbidden becomes commonplace, when the border between the conceivable and inconceivable suddenly disappears, people may *do* new things, but they don't necessarily *like* them" (L. Rubin, 1976:135).

Men are often more enthusiastic than their wives about having freer, more experimental sex, but this is not always the case. Sometimes when wives put aside their restraint and take the initiative, their husbands accuse them of being too aggressive or not feminine enough (Kaplan, 1974b:136). A primary reason for this is that their husbands, too, have ambivalent feelings about all the changes; they may not be used to experimenting and may feel anxious when their wives request changes (Kerr, 1977:37–39).

This ambivalence results mainly when spouses try to read from two contrasting sexual scripts—the patriarchal and the expressive—at the same time. In the patriarchal script the husband was the active instigator; his wife was only a passive receiver. Society is gradually recognizing women's sexuality, but it has continued to place sexual responsibility mainly on the male, who was supposed to be the one with natural expertise. Masters and Johnson summarize the results: "So the knowledgeable man who married in the 1950s and early 1960s, instead of doing something *to* his wife sexually, was prepared to do something *for* her sexually.... Unfortunately, in the role of doing *for* rather than just doing *to,* he had to assume even more sexual responsibility" (Masters and Johnson, 1976:6).

Then, too, as one writer noted, men in our society are put to the test more than women, for in almost every occasion of sexual expression, a man must "produce living, visible, upright evidence of [his] sexual potency" (Decter, 1976:386). There are no scientific data to substantiate the assumption that female assertiveness causes male impotence. But to the extent that men have accepted the patriarchal script, they may not appreciate women's sexual advances (Kerr, 1977). Where a man's sexual arousal and performance depend on a sense of power and control over women, female assertiveness and sexual demands could be sources of anxiety.

Masters and Johnson hold otherwise, arguing that changing gender roles will facilitate good sex. "The most effective sex is not something a man does to or for a woman but something a man and a woman do together *as equals*" (Masters and Johnson, 1976:88). From this point of view the female not only is free to initiate sex but also is equally responsible for her own arousal and eventual orgasm. The male is not required to "deliver pleasure on demand," but can openly express his spontaneous feelings.

In sharing sexual pleasure, partners realize that sex is something partners do *with* each other, not to or for each other. Each partner participates actively, as an equal in the sexual union. Further, each partner assumes **sexual responsibility**, that is, responsibility for his or her own sexual response. Masters and Johnson explain:

There is no way that a man can be responsible for a woman's sexual functioning, nor can she assume control over his sexual response patterns.... We can't breathe for the other person, we can't eat for the other person, and we can't respond sexually for the other person [1976:7]. ▪

When each partner takes responsibility for her or his own sexual response, the stage is set for conscious mutual cooperation. Both husbands and wives feel freer to express themselves sexually, and as they do, spouses often feel better about sex as their lives and marriages continue. The next section examines other elements that are important to good sexual relationships.

SEX AS A PLEASURE BOND

Masters and Johnson view sex as a **pleasure bond** by which mates commit themselves to expressing their natural sexual feelings together. Such expression may not be as easy as it seems, for it requires a high degree of self-esteem, the willingness to break

free of limiting stereotypes, and the ability to create and maintain an atmosphere of mutual cooperation. We'll look at each of these elements.

Sexual Pleasure and Self-Esteem

High self-esteem is important to pleasurable sex in several ways (Burchell, 1975). First, self-esteem allows a person the freedom to receive pleasure. People who become uncomfortable when offered a favor, a present, or praise typically have low self-esteem and have trouble believing that others think well of them. This problem is heightened when the "gift" is sexual pleasure. People with low self-esteem may "turn off" their erotic feelings because unconsciously they feel they don't deserve them.

Self-esteem also allows individuals to acknowledge and accept their own tastes and pleasures. This is vital in sexual relationships, because there is a great deal of individuality in sexual expression. An important part of sexual pleasure lies in doing what one wants to—not necessarily doing things the way others do them.

A third way in which self-esteem enhances sexual pleasure is by providing the freedom to search for new tastes and pleasures. As we've seen, some individuals let their sexual relationship grow stale because they do not accept or appreciate their own sexuality and their needs to experiment and explore with their partner.

Finally, high self-esteem will let one ask a partner to help satisfy one's tastes and pleasures. In contrast, low self-esteem can lead a person to be defensive about her or his sexuality and reluctant to express valid human needs. In fact, people with low self-esteem may actively discourage their partners from stimulating them effectively.

Sexual Pleasure and Gender-Role Stereotypes

A second important element in making sex a pleasure bond is the ability to see beyond gender-role stereotypes. Chapter 2 argued that when persons play traditional gender roles, they fail to develop the "other half" of themselves. For instance, a man may reject tender sexual advances and activities because he believes he has to be emotionally unfeeling, or "cool."

BOX 4 · 2

FREEING COUPLES UP: COMMUNICATING ABOUT SEX

"Historically, the whole scenario of the sexual encounter, from initiation and timing to positioning of the bodies, was expected to be initiated by men.... In contrast, the woman has been expected either to passively go along with men's sexual advances or to refuse to have sex...." (McCormick and Jessor, 1983:80). More often than not, the woman was taught to refuse, at least before marriage. And as a means to that end—making sure she refused—parents may have taught her "prohibitive attitudes about the body" (Gagnon, 1977:88).

But as cultural—and couple—sexual scripts move from patriarchal to expressive, both secular and religious sex therapists have zeroed in on couples' desire to enjoy sex more freely. Christian sex counselors Charlie and Martha Shedd, for example, conduct "Fun Marriage Forums" for evangelical couples. In their book *Celebration in the Bedroom*, they urge couples to prepare for lovemaking by reading the Song of Solomon (sample verse: "Your rounded thighs are like jewels") and other erotic biblical passages (Woodward, 1982:71).

Such shared reading may help partners overcome previously learned negative attitudes about their bodies.

If parts of the body are defined as bad or dirty or unclean or not to be shown to other people, then these attitudes must be revised when the time comes for sex. For some people the solution to the body problem is to turn out the lights, keep the touching to a minimum, and have sex with as little fuss as possible. It is entirely possible for some people to find this satisfactory, to have children and find happiness in marriage. However, if children have been taught that they should not look at other people's bodies, that certain body parts are bad, that touching parts of their own bodies and others' is wrong, then the sexual demands that they put on themselves and which others put on them will have to be negotiated differently later in life" (Gagnon, 1977:88).

Negotiation requires communicating about sex—a necessity for virtually all couples. But sex therapy expert Elizabeth Stanley, M.D., notes at least two cultural myths that continue to "blunt" couples' sexual communication and consequent satisfaction. Myth 1 relates to supposed male sexual omniscience.

The substance of this myth is that men are somehow born with instinct or telepathy which enables them to know precisely what to do to "turn a woman on." Consequently a woman may feel that she has no right to tell her partner what she likes and doesn't like. Moreover, if her partner's actions are unpleasurable, the woman thinks that she is at fault; since he apparently "knows" what to do, if she doesn't like it she believes that there must be something wrong with her. Another damaging aspect of this particular myth is that the man begins to feel that the success of their sexual relationship depends on him—an unnecessary and destructive burden for anyone to carry, which may contribute to other sexual problems [Stanley, 1977:23].

SOURCES:
Kerr, 1977; Gagnon, 1977;
McCormick and Jessor,
1983; Stanley, 1977;
Woodward, 1982.

Myth 2 is that good sex shouldn't be discussed. "On the contrary, good sex is a product of good communication" (Stanley, 1977:23). In the words of sex therapist Carmen Kerr,

Many women complain, "It's not romantic to talk during sex. It spoils it." They're right on one count—it's not old-fashioned romantic; and wrong on another—it doesn't spoil it. One of the biggest myths passed on to us is: The Golden Silence of Magical Sex. This has us believing that True Love and Romance is embodied in one classic love-making bout where we and our lover meet, unite perfectly, and have a simultaneous orgasm—all in five minutes flat. So how many times has that happened to you lately? [1977:90]).

But Kerr recognizes that "we all get tongue-tied and nervous when it comes to asking for what we want in sex" (1977:90), and so she offers some basic tips. While Kerr writes for women, much of her advice probably applies to men also.

Tip 1. "Rehearse ahead of time. In asking for what you want, begin by rehearsing it ahead of time. Do this either with your women's group (or with a good friend), or alone at home in front of a mirror, or both. Rehearsing enables you to smooth out all the kinks ahead of time. You can get as excited, melo-dramatic, shy, scared, or angry as you'd like before your mirror or group and thus refine this inchoate mass of emotions into the most sensible approach before confronting your partner.... It's difficult to overcome both female 'passivity' and the social injunction not to ask for needs. Practice makes perfect...."

Tip 2. "Don't ask in bed. The first time you ask for what you want, try not to do it in bed.... [People] have discovered that it is better to discuss major changes they'd like in love-making *before* getting involved in the sexual situation. Talk about such things when you're not sexually excited. When you're turned on, who has the patience for a complicated conversation?... One of my favorite ploys—because it's such a great tease—is to spend dinner discussing what you sexually enjoy.... Cue your lover ahead of time. It makes for a more sensual session later...."

Tip 3. "Ask your lover to do his (or her) fifty percent." Tell your partner that you need to know what he or she enjoys. "You need feedback—in sounds, words, or gestures. Be specific. 'I need to know when you come,' or 'I need to know if you like this caress.' By asking for what you want, you have set an example. You are opening love-making to change and to requests. When you take that romantic silence out of sex, you are giving your lover the freedom to ask, also...."

Tip 4. "Ask for one hundred percent of what you want. This is the final, and most important, part of asking for what you want. If you don't ask for every last bit of what you want, then you'll end up compromising before you've even begun to bargain.... Don't edit your copy beforehand. Don't assume that anything is impossible. Go for all of it, and you'll be surprised at how much you will get" (Kerr, 1977:96–100).

Likewise, women may have trouble in receiving or asking for pleasure because they feel uncomfortable or guilty about being assertive. Many women have been culturally conditioned to put their husband's needs first, and so they proceed to coitus before they are sufficiently aroused to reach climax. Such women are less likely to enjoy sex, which can detract from the experience for both partners.

Sex can be more effective as a pleasure bond when the relationship transcends restrictive gender-role stereotypes. To do this, partners must be equal and must communicate in bonding rather than alienating ways.

Communication and Cooperation

A third element in sharing sex as a pleasure bond is communication and cooperation. Partners can use conjugal sex as an arena for power struggles, or they can cooperate to enrich their sexual relationship and to nurture each other's sexual self-concepts. To create a cooperative sexual atmosphere, partners must be willing to clearly communicate their own sexual needs and to hear and respond to their partners' needs and tastes as well. When conflicts arise—and they do in any honest sexual relationship—they need to be constructively negotiated.

For example, one partner may desire to have sex more frequently than the other does, which could cause the other to feel pressured. The couple might agree that the partner who wants sex more often stops pressing, and the other partner promises to consider what external pressures such as workload might be lessening his or her sexual feelings.

Other couples might have conflicts over the use of four-letter words during coitus or whether to engage in oral-genital sex. It is important to communicate about such strong differences in taste. Sometimes a couple can work out a compromise; in other cases compromise may be difficult or impossible. The couple may reach a stalemate over oral-genital sex, for instance. Therapists generally agree that no one should be urged to do something he or she finds abhorrent. And labeling partners "perverted" or "prudish" obviously does not contribute to a cooperative atmosphere.

Open communication is important not only in resolving conflicts but also in sharing anxieties or doubts. Sex is a topic that is especially difficult for many people to talk about, yet misunderstandings about sex can cause genuine stress in a relationship.

Some Principles for Sexual Sharing

Some important principles can be distilled from the previous discussion to serve as guidelines for establishing and maintaining a nurturing, cooperative atmosphere even when a couple can't find a compromise that suits them both.

Partners should scrupulously avoid passing judgment on each other's sexual fantasies, needs, desires, or requests. Labeling a partner or communicating nonverbally that something is disgusting or wrong can lower a person's sexual self-esteem and destroy the trust in a relationship. Nor should partners presume to know what the other is thinking or feeling, or what would be good for the other sexually. In a cooperative relationship each mate accepts the other as the final authority on his or her own feelings, tastes, and preferences (Masters and Johnson, 1976).

Another principle is what Masters and Johnson call the "principle of mutuality." Mutuality implies that "all sexual messages between two people, whether conveyed by words or actions, by tone of voice or touch of fingertips, be exchanged in the spirit of having a common cause." Mutuality means "two people united in an effort to discover what is best for both" (Masters and Johnson, 1976:53).

An attitude of mutuality is important because it fills each partner's need to feel secure, to know that any sexual difficulties, failures, or misgivings will not be used against him or her. "Together they succeed or together they fail in the sexual encounter, sharing the responsibility for failure, whether it is reflected in his performance or hers" (Masters and Johnson, 1976:57, 89).

A final principle of sexual sharing is to maintain a **holistic view of sex**, that is, to see sex as an extension of the whole marital relationship rather than as a purely physical exchange, a single aspect of marriage. One woman described it this way:

I don't quite understand these references to the sex side of life. It *is* life. My husband and I are first of all a man and a woman—sexual creatures all through. That's where we get our real and central life satisfactions. If that's not right, nothing is [in Cuber and Harroff, 1965:136]. ■

Researchers John Cuber and Peggy Harroff found that, among the couples they interviewed, those who saw sex holistically were "remarkably free of the well-known sexual disabilities" (1965:136).

Recognizing its holistic emotional value is one way to keep marital sex pleasurable. Another is a commitment to discovering a partner's continuously changing fantasies and needs. For, as one writer put it, besides a mate's fairly predictable habits and character,

there is also a core of surprises hidden in us all that can become an inexhaustible source of freshness in life and love.

The Greek philosopher Heraclitus once said that it is impossible to step into the same river twice. By the same token, it is actually impossible to make love to the same person twice—if we let ourselves know it. . . .

Often it is enough simply to go to bed in a different, more attentive state of mind—giving and listening [Gottlieb, 1979:196]. ▪

Deepening the commitment to sharing and cooperation can make marital sex a growing and continuing pleasure bond. This does not mean that a couple regularly has great sex by some external standard. It means that each partner chooses to try—and keep on trying—to say and to hear more.

We turn now to a consideration of ways in which sexual expression may change over time.

SEXUALITY THROUGHOUT MARRIAGE

It used to be that describing sex over the course of a marriage would automatically be synonymous with discussing sex in marriages of long duration. Today this is not the case. Many couples marry or remarry later in life, so that at age 45, or even 70, one may be new to a marriage. Unfortunately, most current research focuses on marriages that were initiated by young people and continued throughout their lifetimes. Where we can comment specifically about length of marriage or age, we do so,

but for the most part we cannot. We will begin our discussion of sexuality with the premarital couple.

The Premarital Couple

Most newly married couples today begin their sexual relationship before marriage. As early as the 1950s (Kanin and Howard, 1958), studies reported that about 45 percent of couples had had premarital intercourse. Rates of premarital coitus have risen dramatically since then.

What is the impact of premarital sex on marital sexual adjustment? Research results are contradictory. Early studies (reported in Sievers et al., 1983) indicated that a permissive *attitude* toward sex before marriage was positively related to sexual adjustment. People who were less apt to feel guilty about sex in general seemed not to have guilt-related inhibitions after marriage and therefore experienced greater sexual adjustment.

Early studies also examined the effects of premarital sexual *behavior*. Engaging in intercourse before marriage apparently affected marital adjustment positively or negatively depending on the quality of the premarital experience. Positive experiences were associated with better marital adjustment, while negative experiences set up emotional blocks to subsequent satisfaction.

On the other hand, a recent, carefully done study of women married approximately five to eight years found no significant relationship between premarital behavioral permissiveness and the subsequent sexual adjustment of married females (Sievers et al., 1983). A recent exploratory study of thirty men and fifty women supports this conclusion as far as the frequency of sexual intercourse is concerned. This research found premarital sexual experience to be unrelated to sexual frequency—or to change in frequency—during the first five years of marriage (Greenblatt, 1983).[9] Despite the high frequency of premarital intercourse, research on its impact on marital sexuality is scanty; further study in this area is needed.

---

9. Greenblatt comments that "in some ways this is not surprising. Indeed, while the premarital sexual world is replete with proscriptions and prescriptions, there is little to guide the newlywed couple in how to develop a sexual pattern" (1983:294). Greenblatt argues that for both women and men the premarital sexual experience does not carry over to the newlywed experience.

■ When the honeymoon's over: After the first year of marriage, couples usually have sex less often. As with other aspects of married life, maintaining a satisfying sex life together does not happen automatically.

Early Years of Marriage

It is somewhat difficult to disentangle the experience of early marriage from characteristics associated with youth, since newly married couples—at least those studied—tend to be young. Little research has been done on the early marital experiences of remarried persons or persons who marry at an older-than-average age. Given the increased frequency of remarriage and of late marriage, we may soon have more such research.

Young spouses do engage in coitus more frequently than older partners; several factors account for this. Male sexual activity peaks at about age 18 in our society, for reasons that are at least partially biological (although there is some controversy over the relative contribution of biology and socialization). Other reasons are linked to differences in life-style. Young married partners, as a rule, have fewer distractions and worries, such as mortgage payments or small children. The high frequency of coitus in this age group may also reflect a self-fulfilling prophecy: These couples may have sex more often partly because society expects them to.

After the first year, however, couples can expect sexual frequency to decline (Greenblatt, 1983).[10] Table 4•2 shows frequency of coitus in early marriage by length of the marriage. As you can see from that table, frequency of coitus declines from an average of almost fifteen times per month during the first year of marriage to about six times per month during the sixth year. (Note, too, that

10. Greenblatt's sample of thirty men and fifty women was assembled by random digit-dialing in which persons married six years or less were identified and sent a questionnaire. The sample was diverse in ethnicity, religion, education, income, occupation, and parental status. Such variables as education, religion, remarriage, and age at marriage (as well as prior sexual experience) were *not* associated with first-year frequency. Nor were any variables other than first-year frequency strongly associated with later frequency.

TABLE 4·2 Frequency of Coitus in the First Six Years of Marriage

Years Married	N (Number of Respondents)	Frequency of Coitus per Month	
		Mean	Range
1	12	14.8	4–45
2	10	12.2	3–20
3	19	11.9	2–18
4	7	9.0	4–23
5	18	9.7	5–18
6	8	6.3	2–15

SOURCE: Greenblatt, 1983:292.

the averages reported in the table result from widely disparate responses, ranging from four to forty-five times per month for persons married under one year.)

Why does this decline occur? It seems that a frequency pattern is set the first year. And "from then on almost everything—children, jobs, commuting, housework, financial worries—that happens to a couple conspires to *reduce* the degree of sexual interaction while almost nothing leads to increasing it" (Greenblatt, 1983:294).

Despite declining coital frequency, respondents in the study emphasized the importance of sexuality. They pointed to the total marital relationship rather than just coitus, however—such aspects as "closeness, tenderness, love, companionship and affection" (Greenblatt, 1983:298), as well as other forms of physical closeness such as cuddling or lying in bed together. Nevertheless, the Greenblatt study concludes that, "to the extent that people do not *make time* for sex, do not maintain their early commitments to sex, we might well conclude that, in general, sex has decreasing importance after the first year of marriage" (Greenblatt, 1983:298). This research, while only exploratory and using a small sample, is insightful. It suggests that considerable effort is required of a couple who chooses to give priority to and enhance their sexual lives together. Marital sexuality does not maintain itself on sheer momentum for very long against the pressures of everyday life.

Maintaining a satisfying sex life in marriage, then, requires mutual commitment to that end, and also communication. In some respects young mates are

expected to know all there is to know about sex, especially since the "sexual revolution." An unfortunate side effect of this expectation is that partners may be reluctant to discuss their uncertainties with each other because they believe they ought to know everything.

But good sex is not something that just happens when two persons are in love. Forming a good sexual relationship is a process that necessarily involves partners in open verbal and nonverbal communication. To have satisfying sex, a wife needs to tell her husband what pleases her, and a husband needs to tell his wife what he enjoys.

Maintaining open communication about sex is important for couples of all ages, but it may be particularly important for young couples who are experiencing the transition from premarital sex to conjugal sex. As one young wife explained, "Married sex is different. Sometimes you get disappointed because it isn't as exciting as before marriage. Part of the thrill of premarital sex was that it was supposed to be wrong" (O'Brien, 1980:54).

This woman found that as she and her husband began to talk about each other's needs both in and out of bed, sex got better than ever. Many young husbands agree. "Sex has changed as I've become more involved in my partner's needs," said one. "This makes the experience more enjoyable for both" (Pietropinto and Simenauer, 1977).

Partners in Middle Age

With time, sex may become more broadly based in the couple's total relationship. During this period sexual relating may also become more sophisticated, as the partners become more experienced and secure. As one middle-aged husband said, "Sex used to interest me because of what I didn't know. Now it's because of what I know.... I'm less inhibited and more adventurous now" (in Pietropinto and Simenauer, 1977).

One reason middle-aged husbands often feel increasingly freer to be adventurous in bed is that their wives are feeling the same way. Women tend to feel more self-confident and more assertive—in sexual expression as well as in other areas—in the years following young adulthood. Yet while women's increased sexual involvement can promise greater enjoyment for both partners, middle age can be an uneasy period for partners sharing a sexual relationship, for several reasons.

■ While newlyweds often have more time and energy for sex before they have children, middle-aged couples may have more time for each other again when their children leave home.

One reason is imbalance of desire. In our society women and men peak in sexual desire and function at different ages. Males reach their sexual peak around age 18 or 19. Their sexual capacity remains high through most of their 20s, and while it never completely disappears in healthy males, it does diminish. Women, on the other hand, gradually increase in sexual desire and function until they peak sometime in their late 30s or early 40s.

The "emergence of strong sexual drives in women past thirty" (Stanley, 1977) is primarily attributed to our culture's repressive attitudes toward female sexuality.[11] By the time a woman is in her 30s or 40s, she has had time to overcome previously internalized barriers to sexual expression. Also by this time she has probably seen her last child off to school and therefore has more energy to channel into her marital relationship (Stanley, 1977:23). This peaking of women's sexual response after age 30 means that from early marriage up to this point, the partners' desire for intercourse tends to become increasingly similar. In early marriage men tend to want sex more frequently than do women. Since "the early disparity between their sexual desires may be a serious source of conflict, . . . the gradual enhancement of the wife's sexual response is usually beneficial to their relationship" (Stanley, 1977:26). It is possible that somewhere in midlife, however, women may experience greater sexual desire than their husbands, or that men may notice changes in their sexual capacity that, if not anticipated or recognized as normal, may create anxiety. By the time he reaches age 40 or 50, a man does not experience orgasm as often, as readily, or as

11. Although most experts see social-cultural factors as more salient, there are possibly some physiological factors at play in the sexual "peak" of women during their 30s and 40s. Increased pelvic vascularity (capacity for storing blood) following childbirth can increase sexual tension and response. Also, a positive effect of menopause may be the liberation associated with freedom from fear of pregnancy.

TABLE 4·3 Ability to Experience Orgasm: 611 Married Men with Available Partners

Age	Impotent (%)	Unsatisfactory Coitus (%)	Satisfactory Coitus (%)
65–69	16	11	73
70–74	30	11	59
75–92	43	9	48

SOURCE: I. Rubin, in Wiseman, 1976.

forcefully as before, and he will have a noticeably longer refractory period. These midlife changes can be a source of misunderstanding, frustration, and hurt feelings if couples are not aware of these patterns and do not discuss them openly.

Older Mates

During the past two decades beliefs about older persons' sexual capacity have swung like a pendulum between two views. Not too long ago public opinion viewed sex as unlikely and inappropriate for older people. Physical changes brought on by aging, the myth that sex is essentially procreative, and data on declining rates of sexual intercourse all appeared to support this conclusion.

With Masters and Johnson's more recent work indicating that many old people are sexually active, public opinion has swung the other way. The newer message is that biological changes are secondary to social and cultural factors and can therefore be transcended. But historian Thomas Cole cautions against the romantic view that "old people are (or should be) healthy, sexually active, engaged, productive, and self-reliant" and that biological aging can be abolished (1983:35, 39). Of course biological aging cannot be eradicated, and biological changes associated with aging do affect sexuality (Allgeier, 1983:140–41).

Several physiological factors affect sensation and sexual activity with aging. The phases of the sexual response cycle lengthen, especially after age 60. Manual stimulation may be needed to produce erection; pelvic thrusting and ejaculation diminish in intensity; orgasm contractions and the sensation of fluid emission may lessen. Postmenopausal women experience changes in vaginal texture; the bladder may more easily become irritated during intercourse; and lubrication may be lessened, although this is one function that seemingly can be maintained through regular sexual activity.

Health problems that may particularly affect sexual activity include prostate problems, diabetes and vascular illnesses, the need to take pain-killing drugs, and—contrary to the reassuring statements we sometimes read—hysterectomies. Sexual functioning may also be impaired by the body's withdrawal of energy from the sexual system in order to address life-threatening problems of other biological systems.

Table 4·3 provides a breakdown of sexual activity for married men over 65. As you can see from that table, the percentage experiencing satisfactory coitus declines with age. "Whatever scientists such as Masters and Johnson may have told us of the 'mythology' of declining biological potential, the evidence clearly indicates that the older people are, the lower their rates of marital intercourse" (Greenblatt, 1983:290).

On the other hand, sexuality, and even sexual intercourse, do not necessarily cease with age. As Table 4·2 also indicates, almost half of those between age 75 and 92 were experiencing satisfactory intercourse.

Variations among individuals, as in early marriage, are pronounced. Rates of activity in later life are associated with earlier rates; that is, those who were more active sexually earlier are also relatively more active than others during their older years. Retirement "creates the possibility for more erotic spontaneity, because leisure time increases. Patterns of sexuality, however, probably remain relatively unchanged after retirement" (Allgeier, 1983:146). Sexuality in old age is a continuation of many trends from midlife.

Where health problems do not interfere, both women's and men's emotional and psychological outlooks are as important as age in determining sexual functioning. Factors such as monotony, lack of an understanding partner, mental or physical fatigue, and overindulgence in food or drink can all have a profound effect on a person's capacity for sexual expression. Another important factor is regular sexual activity (Masters and Johnson, 1966).

Even though older spouses can and do remain sexually active, sexual factors play a lesser role in late-life unions than in young marriages. More important than sex to older couples are health concerns and companionship (Troll et al., 1979). That doesn't mean that sex is not present or vital for older couples, however.

Many people's expectations for sex in long marriages reflect the dichotomy mentioned earlier in this chapter. In our society images of sex tend so often to be associated with youth, beauty, and romance that to many young people it seems out of place in long marriages.

When satisfaction with sex severely declines over the course of a marriage, this is probably as much a result of choices the couple has made about their whole relationship as it is a function of their age or their familiarity. (In Chapters 9 and 10 we will look at other factors that affect the quality of sex besides the number of years a couple lives together.)

Therapists are quick to point out that just because spouses find they don't desire sex together much anymore—because they're bored, are engaged in power struggles, or have neglected to make time for intimacy—does not mean they no longer love each other. Nor do sexual dysfunctions necessarily mean that mates are no longer in love. Unfortunately, the myth that great sex follows naturally when a couple is "really in love" leads partners who are having problems to question whether they are well mated (Burchell, 1975). The next section discusses sexual dysfunctions and some suggestions therapists make for relieving them. (Appendices E and F address sexual dysfunctions and therapy, respectively.)

SEXUAL DYSFUNCTIONS

It is unrealistic to expect every sexual encounter to be timed perfectly, with both partners achieving orgasm together (or both consistently experiencing it at all). Research suggests that "self-reported sexual problems are relatively common for both males and females" (Mahoney, 1981:557). Yet if one or both individuals are unduly disappointed and anxious when they fail, their tension can be a source of future problems. They can feel unloved, for example, or unattractive, embarrassed, or depressed.

One problem that is often, though not always, associated with such anxiety is **sexual dysfunction**, the term used to describe any sexual inadequacy that inhibits orgasm, either alone or with one's partner.

Sexual dysfunction can result from physical problems such as poor general health, hormone imbalance, injury, or the excessive use of drugs or alcohol (McCary, 1979:217–18). Fatigue and stress are also sources of sexual dysfunction: A person who drives a taxi fourteen hours a day (Jacoby, 1975) or who has just lost his or her job may not be the best sex partner.

Sexual dysfunction is often caused by anxiety. We've seen that anxiety can result from the mixed messages characteristic of our society. Anxiety also results from excessive concern with "productivity" in sexual encounter in which too much emphasis is placed on goals. This kind of anxiety can lead to a vicious cycle, where one or two "failures" trigger a real problem. Regarding premature ejaculation, for example, McCary warns:

It is important to understand that at one time or another almost every man has ejaculated more quickly than he or his partner would have liked. The essential thing is that the man not become anxious over possible future failures. Otherwise what is a normal, situational occurrence may become a chronic problem [1979:215]. ▪

If the initial instances had not been perceived as failures, it is less likely that a real problem would have evolved.

Masters and Johnson, who initiated contemporary sex therapy, also point out that trying too hard can cause sexual problems. They use the term **spectatoring** to describe the practice of emotionally removing oneself from a sexual encounter in order to "watch" and judge one's productivity, and they state that this practice can inhibit orgasm. In their treatment of sexual dysfunction among men and women, Masters and Johnson encourage what they call "**pleasuring**": spontaneously doing what feels good at the moment and letting orgasm happen, rather than working to produce it (Masters and Johnson, 1976).

Masters and Johnson view any sexual dysfunction, no matter what it is, as a problem for *both* partners. Neither one is individually "to blame"; together they alter behavior so that both change. Along with the involvement of both partners in therapy, Masters and Johnson stress the expression of natural feelings, the importance of learning, and the creation of a nurturing, supportive couple relationship (Masters and Johnson, 1970).

Sexual dysfunctions, age and marriage length, and traditional and emerging sexual scripts are all strong influences on people's sexual attitudes and behavior, but they are not the only influences. As we will see in the next section, politics also influence individuals' choices about sex.

FROM PLATFORM AND PULPIT

People today are making decisions about sex in a climate characterized not only by tension between two conflicting scripts—and often between childhood socialization and adult preferences—but also by political conflict over sexual issues. "Ideologies have become more prominent and the ability to obtain a non-ideological view of human sexuality has accordingly decreased" (I. Reiss, 1981:282).

During the 1960s and 1970s it appeared that a synthesis of the two scripts (patriarchal and expressive) was taking place. Today, however, there may be more pressures to conform to one script over the other as sex has become a political issue, not merely a personal one. For example, injunctions for or against premarital sex reach us not only from peers and parents but also from various political-religious organizations and from politically active friends and relatives who may be more dogmatic about sexual issues than in the past. Society is perhaps more fragmented today than it was ten years ago.

Premarital and other nonmarital sex, homosexuality, abortion, contraception, and reproductive technology represent political issues as well as personal choices. In 1986, for example, the U.S. Supreme Court upheld a Georgia sodomy law, ruling, in effect, that consenting adults have no constitutional right to private homosexual conduct.[12] While the ruling was limited to homosexual sodomy, nothing in its sweeping language cast doubt on the constitutionality of state laws that also make heterosexual sodomy a crime, even when performed by married couples (*Bowers* v. *Hardwick*, 1986). Battles over sex education in many a school district may represent community conflict over the ac-

ceptability of sexual expression outside of marriage and of contraception and abortion.

Political polarization may simplify decisions for those who derive their sexual values from an overriding religious-political commitment, but many people still struggle with the ambivalence generated by a combination of scripts. Another very real influence on decisions about sex today—probably a factor that has grown in importance for many people in the last few years—is the threat of **AIDS** and other **sexually transmitted diseases.** In the next section we discuss sexually transmitted diseases generally; following that, we address AIDS specifically.

The Politics of Sexually Transmitted Disease

Sexually transmitted disease is more than a medical problem (medical aspects and treatment of sexually transmitted diseases are discussed in Appendix D). It is a condition imbued with social meanings and consequences. For different individuals and groups, STD means different things. For some, STD is primarily a pragmatic problem requiring pragmatic solutions. For others, it is evidence of God's judgment against "sinful" life-styles. And for many victims, having a sexually transmitted disease is a physical condition that requires some redefinition of oneself and one's relationships.

We have already described the ideological (political-religious) conflict over sexuality that seems to characterize the 1980s (I. Reiss, 1981). Research and treatment of STDs have been drawn into that conflict. Some who for religious reasons oppose nonmarital sexual relationships or homosexuality, for example, see AIDS as retribution for sin. "Nature Exacts Awful Penalty from Gays," runs one headline, "The Sexual Revolution Has Begun to Devour Its Children" (Buchanan, 1983:36). More liberal religious leaders, on the other hand, have publicly criticized this view. They argue that all human activities, even motherhood, result in some casualties and ask whether, for example, the fact that some women die in childbirth represents God's wrath against procreation.

Besides ideologies, aspects of social stratification have an impact on STDs. Syphilis, for example, is more likely to affect the poor and nonwhites. Therefore, its recent dramatic increase has attracted

---

12. *Sodomy* often refers to anal intercourse of one male with another. In many legal usages sodomy also refers to anal or oral intercourse with a member of the opposite sex. According to this latter usage, then, fellatio and cunnilingus (defined earlier in this chapter) are forms of sodomy and technically illegal in Georgia.

relatively little public attention. Herpes, meanwhile, tends to be a middle-class disease and "acquired a trendy air, mainly because its sufferers tend to be more affluent than those afflicted with other diseases" (Van Gelder, 1982:24).

Partly because herpes affects middle-class heterosexuals, continued commitment to its treatment and possible cure seems likely. Until recently, AIDS victims, on the other hand, expressed concern that society was not committed to help them because, as a group, they are primarily homosexual, or "deviant." The fact that AIDS has spread to the heterosexual population has undoubtedly increased government commitment of resources to combat AIDS, although gay activists remain convinced not enough is being done because of such discrimination. Dread of renewed discrimination can parallel fear of AIDS itself among homosexuals and others. Homosexuals are concerned that as an indirect result of the AIDS publicity, they might be excluded from employment, housing, public accommodations, and health services (Bayer, 1983:5).

The politics of STD, then, encompass the possibilities of discrimination against certain "deviant" or other minorities. This is compounded by an ideological debate over standards for sexual behavior generally. But STD affects many people on more personal levels than this.

Effects on One's Personal Life

Herpes, characterized by recurrences of energy-sapping symptoms, can be both debilitating and discouraging. Far more devastating is AIDS: Not only are the symptoms acute and frightening, but the disease is virtually always fatal.

Besides suffering physically, herpes victims often experience lowered self-esteem as a result of having an unappealing and stigmatized disease. "These are young, active people who've never really even been sick before.... Ultimately you learn to cope, but in the beginning there's a lot of 'Why me?'" (in Van Gelder, 1982:29). In a survey of 7,500 herpes patients, 35 percent reported impotence or diminished sex drive and 25 percent felt "destructive rage" (Van Gelder, 1982:29).

It follows that relationships become problematic. Eighteen percent of those in the Van Gelder study attributed the breakup of their marriage or long-term relationship to having herpes. Then, too,

having herpes may force the disclosure of a sexual relationship previously unknown to one's partner.

When established relationships break up, new ones may be difficult to begin. "I felt like I was out of the running for the rest of my life," said one herpes victim (in Clark, 1982:76). More than half of those surveyed gave up sex for a period of time. Because herpes and AIDS victims have an ethical obligation to tell prospective partners of their disease, the issue can intrude early in the relationship before trust has been established. (In fact, telling or not telling can have legal consequences: A Florida woman sued a sex partner who infected her after lying about his herpes [*Newsweek*, November 15, 1982, p. 77] and attempts have been made to treat intercourse by a person who knows he or she has AIDS as assault ["Court-martial of soldier," 1987].)

To provide social support for herpes victims who have lost emotionally supportive partners or who find it difficult to share the experience with friends, HELP groups have formed. Similar associations are developing among AIDS sufferers.

Whether it be due to having—or fear of contracting—a sexually transmitted disease or due to living in a society characterized by conflicting sexual scripts and mixed messages, anxiety can accompany the choice to develop a sexual relationship, and there is considerable potential for misunderstandings between partners. The next section addresses some principles of sexual responsibility that can serve as guidelines for sexual decision making.

SEXUAL RESPONSIBILITY

It's easy to see that while sexuality is a natural part of ourselves, it is more complex than just being a part of our physiological anatomy and functions. We will suggest a few guidelines that may help make sexual choices easier, despite the often confusing social context.

Nelson Foote, a social scientist, has observed that since sex is becoming increasingly dissociated from procreation, it is becoming more recreational, and less a form of "work" (Foote, 1954). Alex Comfort, in his book *The Joy of Sex,* calls it "the most important form of adult play" (Comfort, 1972:85).

If we use this terminology to describe sexual

expression, we should stress that it is adult play, not child play. People must take responsibility for the consequences of their behavior (Kirkendall, 1977:7–9). And so, certain rules and responsibilities are important.

One obvious responsibility concerns the possibility of pregnancy. Both partners should responsibly plan whether and when they will conceive children and use effective birth control methods accordingly. (Chapter 12 and Appendix C provide more information on this subject.)

A second responsibility has to do with the possibility of contracting sexually transmitted diseases (STDs) or communicating them to someone else.

Individuals should be aware of the threat and the facts concerning STDs. They need to assume responsibility for protecting themselves and their partners. They need to know how to recognize the symptoms of an STD and what to do if they get one (see Appendix D). Guidelines pertaining to AIDS are presented in the last section of this chapter.

A third responsibility has to do with communicating to partners or potential sexual partners. People should be honest with partners about their motives for wanting to have sexual relations with them. As we've seen in this chapter, sex can mean many different things to different people. A sexual encounter can mean love and intimacy to one partner and be a source of achievement or relaxation to the other. Honesty lessens the potential for misunderstanding and hurt between partners. People should treat each other as persons rather than things—as persons with needs and feelings. Sex should never consciously be used for exploitation or degradation.

A fourth responsibility is to oneself. In expressing sexuality today one must make decisions according to one's own values. A person may choose to follow values held as a result of religious training or put forth by ethicists or by psychologists or counselors. As we saw in Chapter 1, people's values change over the course of their lives, and what's right at one time may not be satisfying later. Despite the confusion caused both by internal changes as our personalities develop and by the social changes going on around us, it is important for individuals to make their own decisions about relating sexually.

AIDS: HOW IT AFFECTS RELATIONSHIPS, MARRIAGES, AND FAMILIES

Sociocultural conditions affect people's choices; in other words, people make decisions in social context. Nowhere is this more dramatically evident today than in examining how AIDS, a societal phenomenon, has changed and will continue to alter attitudes, options, the consequences of decisions, and thereby personal decision making or choices.

Biologist Stephen Jay Gould reminds us that "pandemics [that is, world-wide epidemics] have inexplicably arisen throughout human history and are a natural phenomenon" (1987:33). Still, people of our time and culture had come to view epidemics as something that happened in the past—say, the Middle Ages—or something that happens elsewhere in the world (in "less-developed" cultures) or perhaps something that could happen in the distant future, say, after a nuclear holocaust. Surely not now, not to us! So an expected result of the AIDS pandemic might be an erosion of the optimism that has been central to our culture, and, further, a perception that our sense of progress and mastery over nature has been founded on shaky ground.

AIDS is a viral disease that destroys the immune system, hence the name Acquired Immune Deficiency Syndrome. With a lowered resistance to disease, a person becomes vulnerable to infections and other diseases that other people easily fight off; the immediate cause of death is often a rare form of pneumonia or a cancer. (AIDS first appeared in the U.S. in the early eighties, when doctors began noticing a rare skin cancer [Kaposi's sarcoma] manifesting in some gay male patients.)

AIDS spread quickly in the United States. In 1981, the year AIDS was first identified, 261 cases were reported; in 1986, 11,414 cases were reported (see Figure 4·1). A total of over 36,000 cases have been recorded to date ("AIDS cases . . . ," 1987), and it is estimated that 270,000 cases will be identified by 1991 (Boffey, 1987; see also Figure 4·1). There have been 20,527 adult and 322 child deaths through mid-1987 from this usually fatal disease. ("AIDS cases . . . ," 1987). AIDS is now the leading cause of death for women aged 25–29 in New York City (Barron, 1987); by 1991 it will be second to accidents as the leading cause of premature death among American men ("AIDS called ...," 1987).

A person may be infected with the AIDS virus (HIV, or Human Immunodeficiency Virus) for a long period of time before developing the disease. Not everyone who has been infected with the HIV virus will develop full-blown AIDS, but the risk of developing the disease, once infected, seems to rise each year, as scientists are able to track the course of infection more closely (Altman, 1987b). Part of the public health problem is that a carrier of the virus can be unaware of its presence for perhaps as long as ten years ("Transfusions ...," 1987) and can infect others during this period if precautions are not taken. This problem creates concern about identifying AIDS carriers and finding ways to restrict the likelihood that they will infect others.

Clues to the transmission of the AIDS-producing virus come from epidemiological studies, that is, studies of the physical and social characteristics of the victims. Primary risk groups in the United States are homosexual and bisexual men (66 percent of the cases), who acquire AIDS through sexual contact, and intravenous drug users (17 percent), who get AIDS by sharing needles with infected people; an additional 8 percent of cases are those who are both homosexual and drug users.

Unprotected anal intercourse between men is ten times more likely to pass on the infection than unprotected vaginal intercourse, but 4 percent of American AIDS cases are the result of heterosexual contact. Most often the victims are women who had intercourse with drug users, or, less frequently, with bisexual men. Men got AIDS from coitus with infected women (Martz, 1987), but transmission from men to women is four times more likely than the reverse, for reasons as yet unknown (Richards, 1987). Still, the risk is only one in a thousand for a woman to become infected from a single contact with an infected man. Repeated encounters, however, resulted in about a third of the female sexual partners of infected men becoming infected themselves. Herpes victims are three times as likely as others to become infected from sexual relations with an infected partner, probably because the virus can enter through genital sores ("Study sees low AIDS risk ...," 1987).

Three percent of victims contracted AIDS from blood transfusions administered before the blood supply was screened (beginning in 1985), and two individuals have contracted AIDS from organ transplants (Martz, 1987; "Aids Cases ...," 1987).

■ A diagnosis of AIDS brings people together far more than it separates. After Chuck Solomon was diagnosed in 1985, his friends and family organized a huge party for his 40th birthday to celebrate his life. A network of people provided support for Solomon (shown here with his mother, Bette), alleviating the need for much government or private care. Support systems for people with AIDS have developed in many American cities; these volunteer groups will become increasingly important as the AIDS epidemic grows.

There were over 500 child victims of AIDS by 1987, mostly (79 percent) infants who contracted AIDS from their mother before or during birth or possibly through breast milk. Seventeen percent of children acquired AIDS from blood transfusions ("AIDS cases ...," 1987; Altman, 1987).

Black children are over thirteen times as likely to have AIDS as white children, and black adults are three times as likely to be victims of AIDS as whites ("Blacks face ...," 1987). Black women usually have been infected by partners who are intravenous drug users, whereas white women acquire AIDS from bisexual partners (Richards, 1987). Analysts estimate that there are 7 to 10 million bisexual men, twice as many as homosexuals (Nordheimer, 1987). Hispanics have two and a half times the risk of acquiring AIDS as whites, while Asian-American adults are less than half as likely to get AIDS. Differences between racial groups are largely, but not entirely, due to different rates of

Figure 4·1

AIDS cases diagnosed in the United States, shown in the graph, and computer projections. (Sources: U.S. Center for Disease Control; *Omaha World Herald*, June 4 and 17, 1987)

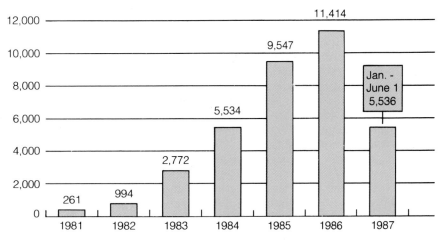

Projections on AIDs

- More than 270,000 people will be found to have AIDs by the end of 1991, of whom 179,000 will have died.

- About 74,000 cases will be diagnosed during that year. And of the 145,000 people expected to be treated for AIDS in 1991, about 75 percent would be among the estimated 1 million to 1.5 million who carry the virus now but probably do not know it.

- More than 70 percent of AIDS cases in 1991 will be diagnosed among homosexual or bisexual men, the highest risk group. About 25 percent of the cases wilkl be among drug addicts who use infected needles. Those two figures overlap, the agency said.

- About 9 percent of the cases will occur among heterosexual men and women, a figure estimated at nearly 7,000 cases and an increase from the current 7 percent level, reflecting a slow but steady spread of the disease outside the homosexual community.

drug use, but black drug users are more likely to get AIDS than white users ("Blacks face ...," 1987).

AIDS is hard to get—especially if precautions are taken when engaging in sexual intercourse or intravenous drug use. Studies indicate that "casual contact" and even intimate living (use of common towels, toothbrushes, bathing facilities, kissing, and so on) with AIDS patients carry no risk. Health personnel caring for AIDS patients are also at little risk if rubber gloves or other protective devices are

used to prevent blood from coming in contact with breaks in the skin (Altman, 1987d).

Information on how AIDS is transmitted—and who can get it—is crucial to personal and social planning. Part of the mystery of AIDS is that not all persons who have the HIV virus come down with AIDS; to date, approximately 1.5 million Americans are estimated to be infected with the HIV virus, far more than actually have AIDS. Estimates are that 20 to 30 percent of those who test positive will develop the disease within five years ("Court-martial...," 1987). Evidence indicates that genetic differences may be responsible for determining who is susceptible to AIDS; general health and resistance to disease may also be a factor. Doctors and researchers are seeking other cofactors that will determine whether or not AIDS develops in an infected person. Knowledge of conditions that inhibit or contribute to the development of AIDS has important implications for control of the disease.

Many people are frightened. Surveys indicate that in 1986 AIDS replaced cancer (48 percent to 47 percent) as the major health concern of the American public ("Poll showed...," 1987). Such concern is not unwarranted, given the geometric increase in the number of cases and deaths. Initial public reaction was conditioned by the association of AIDS with gay males, an already stigmatized group. Gay activist groups noted the discrimination implicit in the limited funds available for research, education, and treatment of AIDS prior to its spread into the heterosexual community. Many of the first treatment and education programs were developed by gay organizations responding to needs within their community. Many still believe not enough is being done ("Protesters pushing president...," 1987).

The progression of the disease into the heterosexual population, the increasing perception of AIDS as a pandemic not unlike the medieval plagues (Rosenthal, 1987), the keen interest of the medical establishment in a new disease, and the political activity of gays and other interested groups have focused media attention and public and private assistance on this problem. No one can predict when, or even if, a cure can be developed. One drug, AZT, has had some success in relieving symptoms in some cases; on the other hand, the discovery of an additional AIDS virus, HIV2 (Altman, 1987e), as well as some other similar viruses (Altman, 1987f), suggests that the development of effective vaccines and drug treatment will be a complex task (Begley, 1986).

Transmission of AIDS through heterosexual contact is so far infrequent in the United States. In Africa, however, about half of the AIDS patients are women, and AIDS seems to be spread largely through heterosexual contact. Is it only a matter of time before AIDS invades the American heterosexual world? Some experts anticipate the same geometric increase that occurred among homosexuals, as an increasing number of carriers infect others. While only 4 percent of current AIDS patients acquired AIDS through heterosexual contact, 26.5 percent of AIDS patients are heterosexuals capable of passing AIDS on to partners ("AIDS called...," 1987). Because the AIDS virus becomes more infectious over time, carriers become more and more likely to infect sexual partners (Altman, 1987a). In fact, the rate of transmission in the heterosexual population is twice as fast as in the homosexual population; AIDS cases increased by 131 percent from 1985 to 1986 (Richards, 1987; also "Heterosexual spread ...," 1987). U.S. Surgeon General Everett C. Koop has expressed fear of an "explosion" of AIDS in the heterosexual population ("Dr. Koop ...," 1987).

But other experts, who point to the small numbers (1,377) of heterosexually transmitted cases through mid-1987 ("AIDS cases ...," 1987), think that AIDS transmission in the United States will *not* replicate the African pattern because conditions in Africa are unique. They note that African men and women and American gay males have in common a prior history of infection that may have activated the immune system, making it less resistant to infection (Altman, 1987c). The chief AIDS epidemiologist at the U.S. Center for Disease Control emphasizes that there is no sign of a major spread of the AIDS virus among heterosexuals (Altman, 1987a). Expansion into the heterosexual community is likely to be a gradual one over a period of years.

The AIDS epidemic will have various social consequences.

Threat to Civil Liberties

AIDS poses a strong threat to concepts of personal privacy and civil liberties. With the exception of homosexuality (*Bowers* v. *Hardwick*, 1986), the courts have consistently defined private sexual behavior and reproductive choices as the province of individual choice. Americans are also constitutionally protected from unwarranted search and seizure.

Challenges to these new and old liberties arise with proposals for mandatory blood screening for AIDS and other suggestions for behavioral control. The blood tests for antibodies that are now available, indicating the presence of the HIV virus, are used to screen blood and organ donors to protect the recipients; of course donors are volunteers.

Individuals may volunteer to be tested so that they can make informed decisions about reproduction and sexual activity as well as health care. The military has had mandatory blood testing since 1985, and the federal prisons will soon begin screening prisoners upon entrance and exit from the prison; immigrants and illegal aliens will also be screened (Pear, 1987b). Proposals have also been made to test all hospital patients, couples applying for marriage licenses, and public employees.

Public health experts generally oppose mandatory or "routine" testing for the following reasons: (1) High-risk individuals may choose to avoid test situations and thus be less exposed to educational efforts that aim at encouraging behavior change; (2) there is no treatment or cure to offer identified victims; (3) tests are unreliable, producing as many as 28 percent false positives (indicating the presence of the AIDS virus when, in fact, the person is *not* infected); (4) massive testing is prohibitive in cost and overwhelming logistically—some cities already require waits of up to three months for voluntary testing; (5) some proposed testing programs are unlikely to reach the high-risk population. Gays are not as likely to marry, for example, and in many states and regions of the country, expensive and effortful programs of AIDS testing will identify few cases. Analysts estimate that testing the 4.8 million Americans who marry annually would identify only 1300 cases of AIDS, as well as falsely indicating that 528 uninfected persons have the virus.

Many experts argue that money is better spent on developing educational programs that urge people to change sexual behavior and voluntary testing that would include counseling. Testing and counseling efforts might be focused on high-risk groups (Pear, 1987a, b; Lambert, 1987; Goodman, 1987a). (On the other hand, some public health experts still support mandatory testing, especially for high-risk groups [(McDonald, 1986; Lambert, 1987]).

Civil libertarians argue that positive test results, which may or may not be accurate, will result in sharp curtailment of life choices in terms of jobs, education, and so on. Moreover, many HIV carriers will never develop AIDS, nor is AIDS transmissible through "casual" contacts, such as working together, attending school together, even living together. They argue that the public health threat is not severe enough to warrant such restrictions. Even the worst projections of the AIDS toll leaves it far short of

deaths that will result from heart disease and cancer. Presently deaths from AIDS are also rarer than deaths from cirrhosis, diabetes, atherosclerosis, influenza, pneumonia, motor vehicle accidents, homicide, suicide, and accidental falls in the home (Crewdson, 1987).

On the other hand, 61 percent of a national sample surveyed in 1987 supported mandatory testing ("Poll showed...," 1987); another poll found 77 percent supporting testing for those planning marriage and 33 percent for children entering school (Roper, 1987). Eighty-nine percent of a national sample expressed willingness to be tested themselves (Morganthau, 1986). Texas has passed a law subjecting people with AIDS to the quarantine provisions of the communicable disease law ("Texas bill...," 1987), and a soldier in Arizona is standing court-martial for aggravated assault because, though knowingly exposed to the AIDS virus, he had sexual relations with other military personnel ("Soldier to stand trial..., 1987").

AIDS and Homosexual Men

Life for gay men is becoming more difficult. Many in the gay male community are experiencing the frequent loss of friends and intimate partners. But living with loss and the burden of community or personal care for friends and lovers with AIDS is only part of the problem.

Many gay men and their families find the coming-out process more difficult, as knowledge of a gay male family member's sexual preference is also knowledge of his risk of illness and death (Robinson et al., 1987).

Moreover, a new wave of homophobia has resulted in increased hostility and violence toward gays; 20 percent of homosexual men report having experienced at least one assault at some point in their lives. The Gallup poll reports a rise in opposition to the legalization of consenting homosexual acts. Although only 39 percent of Americans favored criminalization of homosexuality in 1982, 55 percent did in 1986 (Johnson, 1987).

Wives of Gay Men At least 20 percent of male homosexuals marry at least once. Consequently, some heterosexual women may be regularly exposed to the virus themselves. Although some knowingly married gay men, 85 percent of a sample of wives in a support group were not aware of their husbands' homosexuality at the time of marriage.

Most of these women denied concern about infection, claiming that their husbands practiced safe sex or had only one partner. Counselors, however, are alarmed that an unknown but possibly large number of women are knowingly or unknowingly exposed to AIDS through marriage to men who have homosexual contacts. Revelation of husbands' homosexual activity through development of AIDS or through his protective revelation of risk is likely to change the dynamics of these marital relationships—and possibly end them (Dullea, 1987c).

AIDS and Sex

AIDS has and will continue to affect sexual attitudes and behavior. Sexual behavior of many gay males has already been modified (Kantrowitz, 1987); the declining rates of sexually transmitted diseases indicate that promiscuous sexual behavior has decreased ("Florida's top ranking . . .," 1987). Multiple, frequent, and anonymous sexual contacts were common elements of the life-style and sexual ideology for many gay males, but attitudes and behavior have changed dramatically.

Heterosexuals are also responding to the threat of AIDS with anxiety and changed behavior (Stevens, 1987; Davis, 1987; Dunning, 1986; Leishman, 1987; Kantrowitz, 1986): "Monogamy is definitely back" (Stevens, 1987:9). Singles who were sexually active in the past may now expect to have a longer period of acquaintance before initiating sexual contact, hoping to experience greater attraction, security, or commitment before deciding sex is "worth it." Some opt for periods of celibacy, with or without masturbation.

Many singles despair of the long-range chances of finding a mate in a social and sexual atmosphere frozen by fear. Others, regardless of the emotional state of affairs, decide to hang on to current partners or spouses whose sexual history is known and safe. Dating clubs whose members are required to be regularly tested for AIDS are developing in some larger cities (Geist, 1987).

Safe sex, a term gaining popularity in the heterosexual as well as the homosexual community, refers principally—but not exclusively—to the use of condoms. "Rubbers," or contraceptive sheaths that fit over the penis, reduce the likelihood that the AIDS virus will be transmitted to a sexual partner during genital or anal intercourse. Rubber dental dams or condoms can also be used for protection during oral sex.

"Safe sex" is a misnomer because condoms can be broken, and the AIDS virus can still be transmitted. Nevertheless, because condoms do substantially reduce the risk, much educational effort has been directed at encouraging their use (on the assumption that most individuals are not going to give up sex entirely).

A side issue of safe sex has become the placement of sexual responsibility, once again, on women (Barron, 1987). Forty percent of condom purchases are now made by women, who are encouraged to prevail upon their partners to use them. Requiring women to be sexually assertive is not always easy, especially because women have been encouraged to follow men's sexual lead in the past. Men may resist the use of condoms because folk wisdom holds that condoms cut down on sensation. But "If you say 'safe' and 'no' often enough, it will start to sink in," said a participant in a woman's AIDS workshop (Dunning, 1986).

To what extent various groups are using condoms, asking their partners' sexual histories, and being selective of sexual partners is uncertain. Although some college students have evinced more careful behavior in the form of safe sex and monogamous relationships, health educators are concerned that the reality of AIDS is not clear enough for the average college student because it usually strikes slightly older adults. Gay students have modified their behavior, but straight students have not been as responsive to warnings ("AIDS is felt . . .," 1987). In 1987, a survey conducted by a condom manufacturer at spring break in Daytona reported that only 50 percent used condoms; only 3 percent engaged in sex less often; and 28 percent were doing nothing at all to prevent AIDS. A Penn State survey found that 52 percent of gay men did not use condoms, and only 24 percent of women planned to—and these groups tended to be the most careful (Kantrowitz, 1987). "In the eyes of many students, AIDS is still Someone Else's problem. . . . Despite all the fearful talk, the action is pretty much the same (pp. 15, 17)."

Adults are not necessarily more responsible; only 32 percent report using condoms (of course, many may be in long-term, monogamous relationships or marriages). Fifty-eight percent do report "taking more care in the selection of a partner" (Morgan-thau, 1986).

Sex Education and Public Discussion Children are likely to be exposed to sex education at an earlier age. Surgeon General Koop, a fundamentalist Christian and political conservative, has been moved by public health concerns to propose explicit education about AIDS to children as young as 9, including the topics of homosexuality, anal as well as genital intercourse, and condoms.

Koop's position illustrates the complex effects AIDS is likely to create on the politics of sex. AIDS may have empowered conservative groups who would like to see sexual activity limited to heterosexual, monogamous, lifetime marriage. AIDS has been hailed by some as signaling the end of the sexual revolution and sexual liberation. Paradoxically, however, AIDS also forces extensive and explicit discussion of sex and reveals the existence of formerly hidden homosexual and extramarital sexual behavior. A married Republican congressman's (May, 1987) or a Catholic priest's death from AIDS raises questions about the degree to which conservative sexual norms are practiced by their advocates. Knowledge about the extent of premarital sex, nonmonogamous sex, gay sex, and sex on the part of those pledged to celibacy makes conservatives' insistence on traditional sexual norms less convincing. AIDS has carried the public discussion of sex to a new level.

How will all this influence people's personal decisions? Increasingly, people may choose to negotiate safe sex practices with new partners and/or forego new sexual opportunities. Sex may be limited to more serious relationships. Meanwhile, some campus health officials worry that a possible "overreaction . . . could lead to serious emotional problems. 'Right now, the emphasis is a fear-arousing emphasis . . . , sex-negative messages. What I'm concerned about is that the young people on college campuses simply not be left with fear about sexuality'" (Kantrowitz, 1987:17–18).

AIDS and Marriage

One in thirty men between the ages of 20 and 50 is already infected by the AIDS virus ("AIDS called . . . ," 1987). Chances of marriage for women, already limited by the low ratio of men to women, may be further restricted if men die prematurely or are ill or known to be infected. Even though gay men, a large part of the infected group, are infrequent candidates for marriage, some infected men may have been otherwise marriageable.

Although monogamy has definitely increased in appeal since the advent of AIDS, fear of the unknown—will AIDS appear in my spouse after a number of years?—may make a marital commitment seem emotionally risky for both men and women.

AIDS Means New Family Crises

Some families will face unprecedented crises because of AIDS. In one news story, a woman contracted the AIDS virus from a transfusion during a difficult birth and conceived another child before the disease became manifest; that child was infected. Mother and child died, leaving behind a young husband and 3-year-old daughter.

Then, too, we can imagine that some spouses may infect one another as the result of formerly secret extramarital affairs. Dealing with this kind of situation may prove exceptionally difficult.

But the burdens of AIDS will not all be emotional or involve physical care of victims; some will be financial. For example, we may see AIDS patients or those infected by the HIV virus dismissed from their jobs and refused health insurance. The Supreme Court did rule in favor of job protection for the handicapped (*Nassau County School Board v. Arline*, 1987) in a way that seems protective of AIDS patients, and other decisions have supported this protection ("First anti-AIDS bias suit . . . ," 1986). But no ruling exists to protect HIV carriers; furthermore, many job dismissals do not have to be explained, and the burden of proof of disability discrimination is on the complainant. Insurance companies have already begun to require a negative AIDS test to provide life insurance (Sullivan, 1987).

AIDS care is expensive; the AZT drug, for example, costs as much as $16,000 a year ("Desperate victims . . . ," 1987). Many gay males were financially secure and/or had health insurance, but more recent AIDS patients (and intravenous drug users, in particular) have fewer resources. Government regulations have restricted the ability of even dying AIDS patients to qualify for disability payments ("AIDS disability . . . ," 1987). Overall federal, state, and local responsibility for the health care of AIDS patients has not yet been determined, but most assuredly families with any financial resources will be expected to use them, leaving surviving family members hard-pressed financially and heavily in debt.

AIDS and Our Experience with Death

AIDS has meant the return of early, untimely death. We had grown unaccustomed to the death of young people in the twentieth century; life expectancy at birth was 74.6 in 1981 (U.S. Bureau of the Census, 1986b). More and more, obituaries report the deaths of people in their forties, thirties, and even twenties. In heavily hit areas, such as New York City's artistic community, friends may have attended ten funerals in a matter of months (Gerard, 1987). Provision of aid and dealing with the demoralization of such loss become compelling problems of the survivors.

Some Precautions

AIDS has changed sex, relationships, and life choices. Readers will want to keep updating their information; precautions that at present seem reasonable are:

1. Sexually active individuals who are not in long-term, securely monogamous relationships of at least six years' standing should use condoms (perhaps with spermicide) when having sex. Explicit information about protective practices is available in the Surgeon General's Report on AIDS (see Suggested Readings) and from other sources. Such guidelines should be followed.

   The Surgeon General's Report states: "Couples who maintain mutually faithful monogamous relationships (only one continuing sexual partner) are protected from AIDS through sexual transmission. If you have been faithful for at least five years and your partner has been faithful, too, neither of you is at risk. If you have not been faithful, then you and your partner are at risk. If your partner has not been faithful, then your partner is at risk, which also puts you at risk. This is true

for both heterosexual and homosexual couples. Unless it is possible to know with *absolute certainty* that neither you nor your sexual partner is carrying the virus of AIDS, you must use protective behavior. *Absolute certainty* means not only that you and your partner have maintained a mutually faithful monogamous sexual relationship, but it means that neither you nor your partner has used illegal intravenous drugs" (Koop, n.d.:16).

2. Inquiry about a potential sex partner's health, AIDS status, and previous partners is useful and may produce information on which to base a decision about having sex. It is entirely possible, however, that a prospective partner will not be honest. Moreover, antibodies to AIDS do not develop for several months after infection with the HIV virus, so an infected person who may appear virus-free in tests will report the possibly erroneous results in good faith.

   Communication about sex and disease is going to be necessary in a way that it never was before. Americans used to risk pregnancy without discussion; the stakes are higher now.

3. It would be prudent to confine sexual activity and relationships to those worth the risk. This can mean decisions about individuals or it can mean categorical decisions about multiple partners or sex with high-risk groups such as homosexuals, bisexuals, individuals who have multiple partners, intravenous drug users, or persons known to have AIDS or the HIV virus.

4. Decisions to take risks may involve others: your current or future sex partners, your children, and your family. A responsible sexually active individual will be voluntarily tested, and if the test is positive, will either refrain from sex or inform the partner beforehand and use condoms during sex. Informing partners about one's AIDS-risk status must include discussion of sexual history, that is, of past sexual activity with infected or high-risk individuals.

5. Women planning to become pregnant or not taking precautions against pregnancy should be sure that they are free of the HIV virus by being tested and perhaps retested over a six-month period of time. Sources of infection include not only sexual contacts but also

blood transfusions obtained between 1977 and 1985.

6. Health care workers should take the precautions recommended by guidelines for their occupation.

7. Citizens should support sex education designed to prevent the spread of AIDS. Appropriate AIDS education should be encouraged for children (because even young children can be exposed to AIDS through sexual abuse), teenagers, and adults. Surveys of adolescents, the next risk group, indicate that only 8 percent know that AIDS can be transmitted through sharing of drug needles and heterosexual intercourse ("Teen ignorance . . . ," 1987). Videotapes intended for home viewing are available from schools, libraries, public health departments, and commercial sources.

Keep informed yourself by consulting your local public health department, the American Red Cross, student services, gay activist groups, churches, and other sources, including newspapers, radio, and television. You can also write to the U.S. Centers for Disease Control, Center for Prevention Services, Division of Sexually Transmitted Diseases, Atlanta, Georgia 30333, or call the Public Health Service AIDS Hotlines (800-342-AIDS, or 800-342-2437).

In conclusion, private communication must rise to a new level, as potential sexual partners talk about sex and disease, precautions and risk, sexual history and sexual practices. If such communication in fact develops, it would be the realization of one of the few hopeful comments about AIDS— that "out of the peril of the plague could rise a strong new American ethic of sexual responsibility" (Rosenthal, 1987:A-23).

Summary

While our society in the past emphasized the differences in male and female sexual anatomy, many structures are either common to both sexes or directly analogous. Women and men also share the same physiological patterns of sexual response. Four phases of sexual arousal are distinguished: excitement, plateau, orgasm, and resolution.

People express themselves sexually in many ways. Some of these ways (for instance, masturbation) have traditionally been stigmatized; and others, such as cuddling and holding hands, have not been recognized as "sex."

We know little about how sexual orientation— that is, preference for a same-sex or opposite-sex partner—develops. It does not seem to result from family relationships or other socialization.

Social attitudes and values play an important role in the forms of sexual expression people find comfortable. Our society is going through a period of change, and the traditional sexual script of "patriarchal sex" is being replaced by one of "expressive sexuality." One result is greater opportunity for more open and satisfying sexual relationships. Especially in marriage, the movement toward more expressive sexuality has meant greater spontaneity, pleasure, and fulfillment for both spouses. But another result of living during this period of change in our society can be ambivalence and anxiety, particularly given the political conflict that developed around sexuality in the 1970s.

Conjugal sex changes throughout life. Young spouses tend to place greater emphasis on sex than do older mates. In these sexually liberated times young partners sometimes feel they ought to know everything about sex. Developing habits of open communication about sex helps a couple to meet their changing sex needs as they get older. In middle age partners face changes in their relationship. Wives often grow more assertive, and sometimes this is accompanied by a changing balance in the partners' relative sexual desire as the wife desires intercourse more frequently than her husband. Many men and women remain sexually active into old age.

Sexual dysfunctions exist in many American marriages. In general, treating the dysfunction includes both therapeutic counseling to improve the couple's relationship and sexual exercises that the couple carries out in private.

A factor to be considered when making decisions about sexual encounters is sexually transmitted disease. Older forms of sexually transmitted disease still exist, while newer STDs—herpes and AIDS—cause added concern. Some contemporary guidelines, then, for dealing with possible sexual relationships involve recognizing the responsibilities of sexual relating and being open and honest both with oneself and with one's partner.

Making sex a pleasure bond involves cooperation in a nurturing, caring relationship. To fully cooperate sexually, partners need to develop high self-esteem, to break free from restrictive gender-role stereotypes, and to communicate openly.

Key Terms

sexual expression *107*
sexual arousal *108*
excitement phase *109*
plateau phase *109*
orgasm *110*
orgasmic phase *110*
ejaculation *110*
multiorgasmic *110*
resolution phase *110*
refractory period *110*
sensuality *110*
erogenous zones *110*
masturbation *111*

petting *111*
sexual intercourse *111*
coitus 111
sexual preference *112*
heterosexuals *112*
homosexuals *112*
sexual responsibility *121*
holistic view of sex *124*
sexual dysfunction *130*
AIDS *131*
sexually transmitted diseases *131*

Study Questions

1. Describe the four phases of human sexual response outlined by Masters and Johnson.
2. Give some examples to illustrate changes in sexual behavior and social attitudes about sex. What do you think future attitudes and behavior will be? Why?
3. What are the two sexual scripts resulting in mixed messages in our society today? What is the effect of these mixed messages? How are the effects different for men and women? Give some examples of attitudes based on each script.
4. What are STDs, and what impact might they have on people's choices throughout their lives?
5. This book stresses that people must take responsibility for the consequences of their sexual behavior. What responsibilities does the book list? Do you agree with the list? What would you add or subtract?
6. How has the "sexual revolution" affected marital sex? Why?
7. Do you think that sex is changing from "his and hers" to "theirs"? What do you see as some difficulties in making this transition?
8. How do you account for the fact that younger spouses engage in coitus more frequently than older partners? Do you think this has to be the case?

9. Discuss the relative importance of biological factors and social factors in explaining married sexuality over the course of life.
10. Discuss the relationship between sexual pleasure and (a) self-esteem, (b) gender-role stereotypes, and (c) cooperation and communication.
11. Discuss the principles for sexual sharing that are suggested in this chapter. Are there any you would add?
12. How do you think AIDS will change sex and relationships? Do you anticipate that it will have a major impact on American family life or not?

Suggested Readings

Allgeier, E. R.
1983   "Sexuality and gender roles in the second half of life." Pp. 135–57 in Elizabeth Rice Allgeier and Naomi B. McCormick (eds.), *Changing Boundaries: Gender Roles and Sexual Behavior*. Palo Alto, Calif.: Mayfield.
Excellent discussion of aging and sex.

Barbach, Lonnie Garfield
1975   *For Yourself: The Fulfillment of Female Sexuality*. New York: Doubleday.
A guide for women who wish to increase their sexual pleasure and their orgasmic ability.

Beach, Frank A. (ed.)
1977   *Human Sexuality in Four Perspectives*. Baltimore: Johns Hopkins University Press.
Excellent source on the biology and physiology of sexuality.

Berne, Eric
1970   *Sex in Human Loving*. New York: Simon & Schuster.
Psychiatrist Eric Berne, originator of transactional analysis, writes on sex from a humanistic perspective. Worth reading even if you think you have read everything on this subject.

Boston Women's Health Book Collective
1985   *The New Our Bodies, Our Selves*. New York: Simon & Schuster.
Manual of women's health and sexuality that has enormous respect from the user public. Similar books have appeared for parents, gays, and men.

Comfort, Alex
1972   *The Joy of Sex*. New York: Crown.
A sex manual that tries to be "un-manual-like." It stresses the importance of spontaneity and

play in sexual expression and at the same time describes and illustrates various techniques and positions. Some readers find the numerous line drawings beautiful; others don't.

Gagnon, John H.
1977 *Human Sexualities*. Glenview, Ill.: Scott, Foresman.
       Readable short text on sexuality, sexual development, and sexual expression from a sociological perspective.

Harry, Joseph
1984 *Gay Couples*. New York: Praeger.
       New sociological study of gay relationships, with comparisons to straight relationships.

Harry, Joseph, and William B. DeVall
1978 *The Social Organization of Gay Males*. New York: Praeger. See also Thomas S. Weinberg, *Gay Men, Gay Selves: The Social Construction of Homosexual Identities*. New York: Irvington, 1983; and Martin P. Levin (ed.), *Gay Men: The Sociology of Male Homosexuality*. New York: Harper & Row, 1979.

Journal of Sex Research
       Academic periodical with interesting articles on new developments.

Kaplan, Helen Singer
1975 *The Illustrated Manual of Sex Therapy*. New York: Times Books.
       Readable self-help book by one of the top sex therapists. This is a popular version of Kaplan's professional manual, *The New Sex Therapy*.

Kerr, Carmen
1977 *Sex for Women Who Want to Have Fun and Loving Relationships with Equals*. New York: Grove.
       Sex and relationship manual written by a woman who is feminist and defines that to emphasize sharing cooperatively with men. Nitty-gritty physiological details are there, but the focus is on sexual scripts and on negotiating sex in the context of egalitarian relationships—including "what's in it for men to change."

Koop, C. Everett
n.d. *Surgeon General's Report On Acquired Immune Deficiency Syndrome*. Washington, D.C.: U.S. Department of Health and Human Services.
       A concise but comprehensive review of facts about AIDS, policy issues, and precautionary measures.

Leishman, Katie
1987 "Heterosexuals and AIDS: The second stage of the epidemic." *Atlantic Monthly* 259 (Feb.): 39–58.
       Thoughtful consideration of the implications of AIDS for heterosexuals.

Mahoney, E. R.
1983 *Human Sexuality*. New York: McGraw-Hill.

       Excellent textbook with information on all aspects of sexuality and thoughtful comments about the meaning of this information.

Masters, William H., and Virginia E. Johnson
1976 *The Pleasure Bond: A New Look at Sexuality and Commitment*. New York: Bantam.
       An easy-to-read book that applies Masters and Johnson's research findings.

Medical Aspects of Human Sexuality
       A periodical in a popular magazine format with plentiful illustrations and short articles; accurately reports the latest in sexual research and clinical comment by experts in medicine, psychology, sociology, counseling, and other relevant disciplines. Particular attention given to psychological and social factors in sexual dysfunction. Perfect way to spend an hour in the library.

Patton, Cindy
1986 *Sex and Germs: The Politics of AIDS*. Boston: South End.
       Discusses social and political issues of AIDS.

Ponse, Barbara
1978 *Identities in the Lesbian World: The Social Construction of Self*. Westport, Conn.: Greenwood Press.
       Excellent discussion of lesbian identity and lifestyles based on interviews and participant observation in gay organizations. Presents the complexity of sexual identity as we discuss it in this chapter. See also Deborah Wolf, *The Lesbian Community*. Berkeley: University of California Press, 1979.

Robinson, Bryan, Patsy Skeen, and Lynda Walters
1987 "The AIDS epidemic hits home." *Psychology Today* (Apr.):48–52.
       Describes the emotional issues for families of gays now that AIDS is epidemic. Based on a survey of 400 members of support groups for parents of gays.

Sisley, Emily L., and Bertha Harris
1978 *The Joy of Lesbian Sex*. St. Louis: Fireside.
       Sexual technique and relationship manual similar in style to Comfort's *The Joy of Sex*.

Slaff, James I., and John K. Brubaker
1985 *The AIDS Epidemic*. New York: Warner.
       Good basic explanation of AIDS. Fast-changing situation means no book can keep up, so must be supplemented by news and health services sources.

Zilbergeld, Bernie, and John Ullman
1973 *Male Sexuality: A Guide to Sexual Fulfillment*. Boston: Little, Brown.
       This book points out the influence of myths about male sexuality and focuses on helping men become aware of their real sexual feelings.

5 Being Single

> *Today marriage and parenthood are rarely viewed as necessary, and people who do not choose these roles are no longer considered social deviants.*
>
> ELIZABETH DOUVAN, 1979

> *Possibly, you thought that in this modern, enlightened age, women no longer mope about not getting married.*
>
> ROSE DEWOLF, 1982

In the past few decades a pronounced change has been taking place in American patterns of marriage. Throughout this century the trend had been for marriage to occur at an increasingly earlier age and for a larger part of the population. In the 1960s that trend reversed, and since then the trend has been for more and more American adults to be **single**: divorced, separated, widowed, or never married.[1] Being single has become a recognized way of life in our society.

In this chapter we will examine what social scientists know about singles. We'll look at some reasons more people are single today and discuss changing cultural attitudes about being single. (Despite the changes that have occurred, American society still considers marriage the "most correct" option.) We will explore four different standards, or moral proscriptions, for nonmarital sex, along with some important considerations and challenges that go along with being single. We also look at the variety of singles and of single life-styles. To begin, we'll examine some statistics on the increasing number of singles today.

---

1. We would probably classify singles who are "living together" differently—if we knew who they were and how permanent their relationship was likely to be. Since we don't know, it seems simpler to follow census terminology and treat singles as "not married."

SINGLES: THEIR INCREASING NUMBERS

The number of singles in the United States has risen strikingly over the last twenty-five years. Before about 1960, family sociologists described a rather standard pattern of marriage at about age 20 for women and 22 for men (Aldous, 1978). A first child came along within a few years, followed by at least several more. About 80 percent of these unions lasted until the children left home (Scanzoni, 1972).

Today, in contrast, we see an increasing number of never married young adults and of formerly married singles. As Figure 5•1 indicates, the number of singles has jumped from about 25 million at the turn of the century to over 65 million at present. Singles have increased in absolute numbers partly because the population as a whole has grown. But singles have also increased as a relative proportion of the population—from 32 percent of the total population in 1960 to 37 percent in 1984 (U.S. Bureau of the Census, 1986b). Figure 5•2 depicts the marital status of the American population over age 18 in 1984 and indicates the decrease from the 1960s to 1980s in the proportion of population married. As you can see from that figure, there are three demographic categories of singles: the never-married, the divorced, and the widowed.

The Never-Married

There is a growing tendency for young adults to postpone marriage until they are older. By 1985 the median age at first marriage for both men and women had risen to 23.3 for women and 25.5 for men (U.S. Bureau of the Census, 1986a), as high as any figures ever recorded. (See Figure 5•3.)

As a consequence, the number of singles in their twenties has risen dramatically (see Figure 5•4). In 1960, 28 percent of women age 20–24 were single; by 1984 that figure had risen to nearly 57 percent. While traditionally, larger numbers of men than women have remained single in their twenties, the ranks of single men age 20–24 have nevertheless increased from 53 percent in 1960 to almost 75 percent in 1984 (U.S. Bureau of the Census, 1979, 1986b). This increase is, in fact, especially striking when compared with the 1950s, but not so unusual in a broader time frame, that is, compared with the turn of the century (see Figure 5•5).

A theme of this text is that cultural values influence individual choices. Moreover, historical and demographic factors influence cultural values. A major historical event that affected people's decisions about marriage and families during the 1950s was the Great Depression of the 1930s.

With its extensive unemployment and poverty, the depression wreaked havoc on the traditional family pattern—breadwinner husband, homemaker wife, and moderate-to-large family size. One legacy of the Depression was a high cultural valuation of that threatened family form. Children born during the Depression, who came to maturity in the 1950s, appear to have acted on this high commitment to traditional family values: They married unusually early and began families soon after (Elder, 1974). Expanding economic opportunity characteristic of the 1950s facilitated such choices (Easterlin, 1987), since young men could get jobs easily and be relatively confident that real income would increase substantially. They were able to support stay-at-home wives and more children than their parents, and afford better housing.

We are accustomed to thinking of the fifties as typical of American marriage patterns, partly because of the images of family life presented by

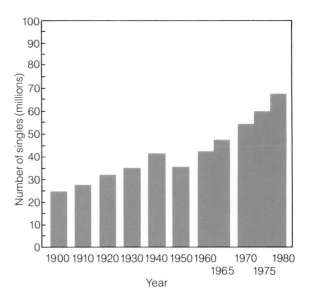

Figure 5•1

Number of singles, 1900–1980. (Adapted from Cargan and Melko, 1982:38; U.S. Bureau of the Census, 1981)

popular television shows during this period and partly because many adults can remember this era but not prior decades. The fifties were *not* typical, however, and the recent trend toward later marriage simply brings us back toward the pattern of the earlier part of this century. As Figure 5•5 indicates, the percentage of never married men and women age 20–24 today just approaches the proportions of young adults never married at the turn of the century.

Still, the increase in young singles over the last two decades does reverse a downward trend lasting from 1900 to 1960, and we need to ask why. At least three social factors may encourage young people today to postpone marriage. Increased job and career opportunities for women may make early marriage less attractive to females. In addition, improved contraception may contribute to the decision to delay getting married. With effective contraception fewer couples may find that they "have to" get married as a result of pregnancy (Cherlin, 1981).[2]

---

2. One can argue, however, that contraception could facilitate early marriage by offering the possibility of marriage without pregnancy.

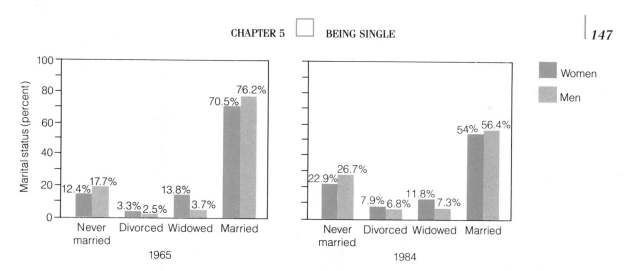

Figure 5·2

Marital status of the U.S. population, age 18 and over, 1965 and 1984. (Sources: U.S. Bureau of the Census, 1979:40; 1986b:38.

Figure 5·3

Median age at first marriage for men and women 1890–1984. (Source: U.S. Bureau of the Census, 1986a)

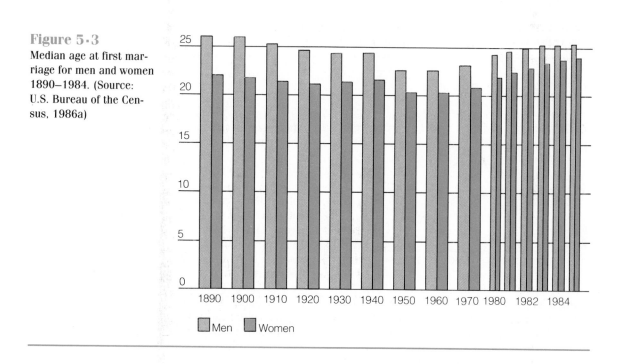

The Marriage Squeeze Another reason for the growing number of singles is demographics. After World War II the birthrate in America increased steadily. The resulting "baby boom" reached its peak in the mid-1950s and did not diminish significantly until after 1960. Because women tend to marry men who are two or three years older than they are, women born during the baby boom reached their average age for marriage two or three years before men born at the same time. Consequently, more women were looking for marriage partners among fewer men. The **marriage squeeze,** then, refers to the fact that there was an excess of young women of marriageable age before any significant

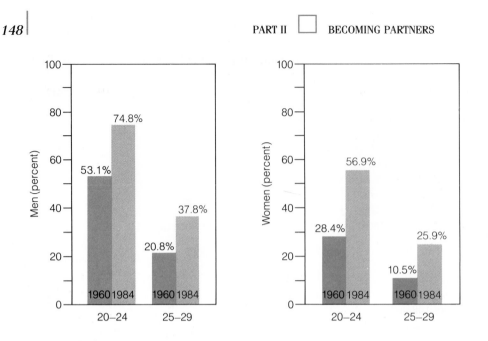

Figure 5·4
Change in the percentage of men and women age 20–29 remaining single,
1960–1984. (Source: U.S. Bureau of the Census, 1979:43; 1986b)

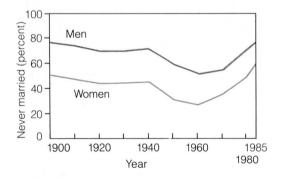

Figure 5·5
Percentage of never-married men and women age
20–24, 1890 to 1985. (Sources: U.S. Bureau of the
Census, 1975, pp. 20–21; 1981; 1986a)

increases occurred in numbers of marriageable
young men. The result was that a number of young
women postponed marriage or put it off entirely.[3]

The marriage squeeze for young people will
reverse in the 1980s because the smaller number
of women born each year after the baby boom will
have a larger pool of slightly older men to choose
from. However, in addition to these birth cohort
effects the sex ratio, the number of men per 100
women has declined over the long term. There have
been fewer men than women in our society since
World War II (see Chapter 6 for a fuller discussion),
a differential that is particularly pronounced among
blacks and in all age groups beyond young adulthood (Guttentag and Secord, 1983). No one is quite
sure how this trend will combine with birth cohort
differentials to affect chances of marriage in the
future.

---

3. Cherlin points out that "women tended to delay marriage
more than men did in the 1960s and 1970s" and notes research
findings that a larger proportion of women married in areas
of the country with a more favorable sex ratio (Cherlin,
1981:58–59).

The Divorced

There is a pronounced increase in the number of divorced or separated people today (see Figure 5•2). In 1984, 6.8 percent of men and 7.9 percent of women over 18 were divorced, a sharp increase from the mid-1960s. Because so many divorced persons do remarry, the proportion who have at some time been single due to divorce is three to four times the proportion currently single after divorce (Glick and Norton, 1979). The number of divorces almost tripled between 1962 and 1981 (U.S. National Center for Health Statistics, 1984a).

After a period of relative stability in the 1950s and early 1960s, the divorce rate doubled between 1966 and 1976, from 2.5 to 5.0 per 1,000 population. (Chapter 16 explains and discusses the meaning of divorce rates.) After 1976 it continued to rise, peaking in 1979 and 1981 at 5.3, but since then it has stabilized at around 5.0 (U.S. National Center for Health Statistics, 1982b, 1986a). The growing divorce rate has, of course, contributed to the increased number of singles. According to one analysis, 6 million of the 26.8 million rise in the number of singles between 1960 and 1979 was due to divorce (Cargan and Melko, 1982:42). While divorce rates are no longer increasing, the stable rate is high and the divorced will continue to be a substantial component of the single population (Norton and Moorman, 1987). (Divorce is discussed at length in Chapter 16.)

The Widowed

You may have noted in Figure 5•2 that, unlike the other singles categories, the proportion of widowed women declined during the 1960s and 1970s. Nevertheless, the overall percentage widowed is well within range of its historical tendency; in 1900, 7.6 percent of the total population was widowed, as opposed to 5.3 percent in 1979 (Cargan and Melko, 1982:43). Women are much more likely to be widowed than men. In 1975, for example, 15 percent of all those widowed were men, and 85 percent were women. This great difference is due to women's greater longevity and their lesser likelihood of remarrying after the death of a spouse. (Chapter 15 discusses widowhood more fully.)

The remainder of this chapter will focus on those two categories of singles that have increased in number: the divorced and the never married. Their marked increase over the past twenty years prompts us to examine whether American attitudes toward marriage itself are changing.

CHANGING ATTITUDES TOWARD MARRIAGE?

While the increase in never-married singles over the past twenty years totaled about 19 million, some 13 million of these, or 68 percent, can be accounted for by the increase in the population of youth due to the baby boom of the postwar period. There is simply a large number of young people today in the age bracket that is typically not married.

The status of the remaining 6 million singles represents a change in choice of life-style, temporary or permanent (Cargan and Melko, 1982). Whether these singles will eventually marry remains debatable. Some researchers view singlehood as a genuine lifetime alternative to marriage (Alwin et al., 1985). They see the increased number of singles as indicating that marriage is becoming a less attractive option when compared with the freedoms of singlehood. According to social scientist Peter Stein, "It is true that not everyone who wants to be married will be. But it is also true that many people—more every year—are freely choosing to be part of the never-married group" (1976:5). Stein includes as one of several reasons for the increase in singles "a shift in attitudes about the desirability of marriage among both college and noncollege youth." Stein goes on to cite other researchers who "suggest that people today are moving away from marriage and family norms as these norms conflict with the potentials for individual development and personal growth" (Stein, 1976:5, 6).

Other family sociologists disagree. Andrew Cherlin, for example, does not see changing attitudes about marriage as a reason for the increase in never-marrieds. He argues that first marriages today occur later in people's lives just as they did before World War II. "Consequently, there is no historical basis for claiming ... that the recent trend toward later marriage reflects widespread disenchantment with the institution of marriage" (Cherlin, 1981:45). Cherlin, then, tends to view "never married" as a temporary state, a postponement of

I WISH I COULD SEE MORE
SOFT NESS WITHIN MYSELF___
MOST OF THE TIME, AS THOUGH
IN LIMBO, I FEEL CAUGHT BETWEEN
AN ICEBERG AND A DESERT.

Elizabeth

■ Why might Elizabeth's comment about herself lead you to assume that she is single? How does she express—and contradict—a number of stereotypes about singles?

marriage until other goals are achieved.[4] The research reported in Box 5•1, "Singles: Myths and Realities," points to this same conclusion: A majority of singles plan to marry.

We have been discussing never married singles primarily. What about the divorced? Unlike the case with never married singles, "most of the increase in the divorced population is *not* attributable to population growth," but to "changes in life-style and outlook" (Cargan and Melko, 1982:42, 44), that is, in willingness to divorce.

This change in life-style and outlook, however, seems for most divorced people to represent a change in attitude about the permanence of marriage rather than the value of marriage as an institution. Moreover, it appears that this change in attitude toward divorce and marital permanence followed, rather than preceded, rising divorce rates (Cherlin, 1981). (Chapter 16 discusses in more detail the reasons for changes in divorce rates.)

It appears, then, that much of the increase in singlehood (1) is due to population increase in the appropriate age categories, (2) represents a continuation of long-term trends from which the rate of singlehood in the 1950s deviated, and (3) preceded rather than followed attitude change. The rise in singles is apparently *not* generally a result of changing values concerning marriage. Most people still want to marry. What has changed, however, are single people's attitudes toward being single.

Changing Attitudes Toward Being Single

Today society views being single as an optional rather than deviant life-style. During the 1950s both social scientists and people in general tended to characterize singles as neurotic, immoral, or unattractive (Yankelovich, 1981:95; Kuhn, 1955, cited in Stein, 1976:521). By the late 1970s that view had changed so that, in one public opinion poll, 75

percent considered it "normal" to be unmarried (Yankelovich, 1981:95).

Two researchers conducted a content analysis project on selected *Reader's Digest* articles from 1900 on. They found eight themes in articles about singles during the 1970s: (1) singlehood as a normal option, (2) the variety of singles, (3) image change of singles, (4) money, (5) loneliness, (6) freedom and responsibility, (7) attitudes toward singles, and (8) personal safety. Earlier articles, in contrast, asked such questions as "Why am I single?" and "How is my name to live on?" The researchers concluded that contemporary singles seem to take themselves for granted, experience an "explicit identity," and perceive themselves as normal (Cargan and Melko, 1982:61–65).

Family Values and Individualism

Viewing singlehood as normal rather than immoral or neurotic is indicative of a cultural shift in America since the 1950s (Ehrenreich, 1983). One theme of this text is that the cultural values of familism and individualism coexist in tension. Remember the trend we discussed in the Prologue, in which more Americans are recognizing the importance of their own self-fulfillment and welcoming the freedom to explore aspects of their identities apart from the roles of spouse or parent.

Compared with married people, singles hold more individualistic than familistic values. In one study interviewers asked singles and marrieds what was important to their happiness. Perhaps not surprisingly, marrieds tended to place a higher value on marriage, children, and love, while singles valued friends and personal growth more (Cargan and Melko, 1982:166–70). In the words of one divorced man, who had been single for five years and was finding he liked it, "I am having an experience I never had before. I was always answerable to someone—my family or wife. I never had the experience of being completely self-motivated, of not having to consider someone else's reaction to what I do— their approval or disapproval" (in Stein, 1976:77).

But is this man typical of singles? No, because there is not a "typical" single. We noted briefly that during the 1970s people began to recognize the variety of singles; the next section explores some aspects of that variety.

---

4. The United States has always been a highly married society, with over 90 percent of each cohort marrying at least once (Cherlin, 1981). This contrasts with a "European marriage pattern," in which larger numbers of adults never marry (Bernard, 1972).

BOX 5 · 1

SINGLES: MYTHS AND REALITIES

"There is a lot of mystification about single people" (Stein, 1976:3). Married people have distorted views about single people's lives, and singles themselves have distorted views about the lives of other singles, except those of their close friends. Singles are often stereotyped either as "beautiful," free people or—at the opposite extreme—as depressed and bitter.

In order to get some handle on the facts, Dayton, Ohio, social scientists Leonard Cargan and Matthew Melko polled some 400 systematically selected households in their city. Their sample consisted of 114 never married, 37 divorced, 205 married (first marriage), and 44 remarried persons. The sample, predominantly Protestant, was rather evenly distributed according to sex and age. The authors offer no information on the racial composition of the sample, and one must presume that it was all or mostly white.

Cargan and Melko supplemented their data with questionnaires administered to a local singles group and with some interviews with members of this group. The researchers also analyzed census data, along with some content analysis.

We must remember that the study is not a random sample and, strictly speaking, we cannot apply the results to areas beyond Dayton. Nevertheless, it is a thorough and interesting study in a newly emerging area of research.

In the book resulting from their study, Cargan and Melko examined, among other things, myths and realities about singles. We will look at some of these briefly here.

MYTHS

1. *Singles are tied to mother's apron strings.* "There is little difference between never-marrieds and marrieds in their perceptions of their relatives and parents. They do not differ in their perceptions of warmth or openness, nor are they much different about parental conflict" (193–94).
2. *Singles are selfish.* Singles indeed "were more likely to visit Club 99 than to visit Grandma (38 percent versus 16 percent) whereas for marrieds it was the other way around (19 percent versus 42 percent)." But singles "value friends more than [do] marrieds," and they are greater contributors than marrieds to community service (194–96).
3. *Singles are rich.* "More than 50 percent of all singles failed to make $10,000 annually" (196). The married people in the sample were better off economically than the singles.
4. *Singles are happier.* "Singles tend to think that marrieds are unhappier than singles, and marrieds tend to think that singles are unhappier than marrieds"

SOURCE:
Cargan and Melko,
1982:193–213.

(197). Singles are more likely to be less happy than marrieds, to feel depressed when alone, and to feel anxious.

5. *There are more singles now than ever.* "In a roomful of people, there were likely to be more singles in 1980 than there would have been in 1960, but not than there would have been in 1940 or 1920 or 1900" (199).

6. *Singles view being single as an acceptable lifetime option.* "In a supplementary questionnaire administered to singles groups, . . . the great majority saw themselves as being married in five years. Marriage is in their future" (200).

7. *There is something wrong with singles.* "By measures of happiness or loneliness, singles may not be as well off as marrieds, but there's nothing necessarily wrong with being lonely or sad some of the time, or more often than your neighbor. . . . No, there is nothing wrong with being single" (201–2).

REALITIES

1. *Singles do not readily fit into married society.* Married people feel that if they invite singles to their homes, they have to worry about whether to match them up with some "theoretically eligible person of the opposite sex" (204).

2. *Singles have more time.* "Singles are more likely than marrieds to be out on social activities twice a week and much more likely to be out three times a week. [It] appears that singles can make more choices and give more time to the leisure activities they choose" (205–6).

3. *Singles have more fun.* "It may seem something of a contradiction that while they are less happy, singles have more fun" (206–7). But they do go more often to dances, amusement parks, and nightclubs, and they have had more sex partners.

4. *Singles are lonely.* As a group, singles are more likely to be lonely. "This feeling [of loneliness] is far more pervasive for the divorced than for the never-married" (211).

5. *Life for singles is changing for the better.* Singles may still feel pressured to apologize for their status—and they may continue to advise one another on how to find a spouse—but things have improved for them. Housing situations have improved, for one thing, and employment opportunities for women have increased and expanded.

TABLE 5·1 Average Number of Years that White Males Lived in Specified Family Environments, by Age, 1960, 1970, 1980

Age interval	Not married			Married, childfree			Married, child(ren) under 6			Married, child(ren) 6–17 only			Total		
	1960	1970	1980	1960	1970	1980	1960	1970	1980	1960	1970	1980	1960	1970	1980
20–24	2.62	2.73	3.57	.82	1.03	.71	1.53	1.21	.70	.03	.03	.02	5	5	5
25–29	1.17	1.20	1.99	.64	.87	.99	3.07	2.72	1.82	.13	.21	.20	5	5	5
30–34	.68	.78	1.29	.39	.42	.66	3.17	2.79	2.08	.76	1.00	.97	5	5	5
35–39	.62	.64	.88	.44	.33	.44	2.35	1.99	1.45	1.59	2.05	2.73	5	5	5
40–44	.60	.63	.83	.73	.60	.69	1.43	1.05	.66	2.24	2.72	2.82	5	5	5
45–49	.59	.62	.78	1.31	1.32	1.43	.79	.51	.29	2.31	2.54	2.50	5	5	5
20–49	6.28	6.60	9.34	4.33	4.57	4.92	12.34	10.27	7.00	7.06	8.55	8.74	30	30	30

SOURCE: Eggebeen and Uhlenberg, 1985:253.

THE VARIETY OF SINGLES

We have already pointed out that singles vary according to whether they have never married or are divorced or widowed. Other factors such as age, sex, residence, religion, and economic status contribute to the diversity and complexity of single life. Twenty-year-old singles have no more in common with forty-year-old singles than newly married people have with middle-aged couples. Widows existing on social security payments and meager savings have vastly different life-styles from, for example, two single professionals living together in an urban area. Without much money it is difficult to translate singlehood's theoretical freedoms into reality. Single life in small towns differs greatly from that in large cities.

Besides these factors, race contributes to the diversity of singles' lives. Sociologist Robert Staples, who has specialized in research on black families, addresses singlehood among blacks.

Black Singles

Staples (1981a) notes the high value placed on marriage in the black community, despite popular perceptions to the contrary. At the same time, blacks

have shared in the recent trend toward greater singlehood. In fact, proportions of married blacks declined sharply, from 63 percent in 1960 to 47 percent in 1984 (U.S. Bureau of the Census, 1986b).[5]

Tables 5·1 and 5·2 list the average number of years that white and black males lived in "not married" environments in 1960, 1970 and 1980, determined from analysis of census data from 1960 and 1970 and *Current Population Survey* data from 1980 (Eggebeen and Uhlenberg, 1985). A substantial reorganization of both white and black men's lives occurred between 1960 and 1980. The most striking changes for whites are a 43 percent reduction in the amount of time spent in family environments where young children are present (from an average of 12.3 years in 1960 to 7.0 years in 1980), and a complementary 49 percent increase in the amount of time spent outside marriage (from 6.28 years in 1960 to 9.34 years in 1980). In both cases the bulk of the change occurred between 1970 and 1980.

While changes for black and white men are in the same direction, black men nevertheless "expe-

---

5. Because of the heavy incidence of desertion among blacks, Staples counts as "single" those who are legally married but separated. (Desertion has been called the "poor man's divorce" because it does not require money to pay attorneys' or court fees.)

TABLE 5·2 Average Number of Years that Black Males Age 20–50 Lived in Specified Family Environments, by Education and Residence, 1960, 1970, 1980

	Not married			Married, child-free			Married, child(ren) present			Total		
	1960	1970	1980	1960	1970	1980	1960	1970	1980	1960	1970	1980
Total:	10.3	10.7	15.1	4.7	3.7	3.3	15.1	15.6	11.6	30	30	30
(Education)												
H.S. or less	10.4	10.6	15.2	4.7	3.7	3.2	14.9	15.7	11.6	30	30	30
Some college +	8.8	11.2	14.4	4.7	3.6	3.5	16.6	15.2	12.2	30	30	30
(Residence)												
South	10.1	10.7	14.0	4.4	3.4	3.4	15.5	16.0	12.5	30	30	30
Nonsouth	10.5	10.7	16.1	5.1	4.1	3.2	14.4	15.3	10.8	30	30	30

SOURCE: Eggebeen and Uhlenberg, 1985:255.

rience a unique pattern of organization" (Eggebeen and Uhlenberg, 1985:255). A comparison of Tables 5·1 and 5·2 indicates some differences. For example,

the gap between blacks and whites in time spent outside of marriage widened from 1960 to 1980, with blacks spending an average of 5.8 more years than whites outside of marriage in 1980. The large increase in time spent outside of marriage by blacks reduced their time spent in marriages with no children, while for whites this time increased slightly. Furthermore, the differences between blacks and whites in average time spent in families with any children present increased from 3.3 years in 1970 to 4.1 years in 1980 [Eggebeen and Uhlenberg, 1985:255]. ∎

Staples explores demographic reasons for black singlehood. The fact that there are more women than men in this country was mentioned; the sex ratio imbalance is especially acute among blacks, for various reasons. Because young black men have relatively high mortality rates and are more likely to be imprisoned or to join the military,[6] there are

more young black women than men. The sex ratio is between 90 and 95 males per 100 females. In addition, the black homosexual rate exceeds the white, and more black men than black women have married partners of other races. When we recognize that many lower-class, never married black males are poorly educated and unemployed, and therefore unable to take on the support of a family,[7] it becomes apparent that choices are limited for black females wanting black men as marriage partners.

Staples' own research, conducted during the late 1970s, focused on 500 college-educated, middle-class blacks between ages 25 and 45. In this group men's marriage patterns differed from women's. Men with higher incomes were more likely to have married, whereas the more highly educated women were more likely not to have married or to be divorced. College-educated black women who desire to marry face a problem similar to that of their lower-class sisters: There are fewer college-educated black men than women, and fewer of these men are single because they may have married less-educated women. Thus, for black college-educated

6. Much could be said about the reasons for this, but ultimately, it points to the impact of discrimination. See Staples' work for a fuller discussion.

7. The male provider role would be part of many blacks' expectations of marriage in its ideal form, though often not realizable for lower-class black men for reasons with which we are familiar (Liebow, 1967).

women there is not an adequate pool of black partners. Furthermore, according to Staples, the uneven sex ratio means that "middle-class black men are able to screen out certain types of women"—perhaps those who are assertive—while women have fewer, if any, choices. The uneven sex ratio enables men to escape pressure to respond to changes that women are making in their lives and in their expectations of men, so that "women who want a sensitive, supportive, and affectionate mate find that men are socialized into emphasizing the values of success, leadership, and sexual performance" (Staples, 1981a:46). This impact of the sex ratio exists for white as well as black women (Doudna, 1981; Guttentag and Secord, 1983), but the sex ratio imbalance is more severe among blacks.

Various conclusions could be drawn from these facts about the sex ratio, depending on one's values and whether or not one agrees with Staples' characterization of black middle-class men. Staples, the dominant voice in black family sociology, is critical of black female singlehood, suggesting that middle-class black females "may be setting unrealistic standards in terms of the quantity and quality of the available pool [of black men]" (Staples, 1981a:27). He objects to middle-class black women's preference for "a troublesome singlehood . . . rather than compromise their standards for a mate" (Staples, 1981a:49). He gives priority to the social responsibility of black adults toward black children and the black community as a whole, which he defines as an obligation to marry and raise a family.

This pressure to place social responsibility ahead of personal fulfillment exists for all women because of the emphasis in female socialization on caring for others at the expense of self (Gilligan, 1982). But it is especially acute for black women because black cultural values emphasize the group over the individual (Richards-Ekeh, 1984).

It is difficult to determine representative black opinion on the subject, given the relatively limited sociological literature on the black family. Some people do not agree with Staples' emphasis on family at the expense of individual values. But at issue here, too, is the imposition of values from the dominant culture (Ladner, 1971), and we need to respect and acknowledge the black cultural commitment to collective values. Actually, the situation is complex, for most minority group members are socialized into both cultures. Overall, Staples' perspective is useful in clearly illustrating the tension between racial or ethnic concerns and individual

goals or gender-related interests that may make choices for blacks and other minorities especially difficult. The pervasive effects of oppression on the personal and family lives of minorities are also apparent in his analysis.

Staples' analysis also reminds us that singlehood may be freely chosen, imposed by a structural lack of options, self-imposed (by eliminating some of the alternatives [Richards-Ekeh, 1984], or a result of some combination of these. Again we see the theme that the social structure influences people's decisions, but that people do have choices to make. An individual black woman who faces the fact that there are fewer black men of marriageable age may choose to create a satisfying single life; to marry a black man who is not as "liberated" or "successful" as she would like; to share a black man with another black woman (Chapter 7 discusses polygamy); to marry a man of another race; or to establish a lesbian relationship.

Types of Singles

Staples has developed a typology of singles based largely on whether their status is freely chosen. He designates five singles types. While his discussion applies specifically to blacks, these types can be applied to other races and ethnic groups. The first type, and the most common one among blacks, is the "free floating," unattached single who dates randomly. The second type is a person in an "open-coupled relationship": "This person has a relatively steady partner but the relationship is open enough to encompass other individuals in a sexual or romantic relationship" (Staples, 1981a:44). Staples warns that "sometimes it is an open-coupled relationship in a unilateral sense, with one of the partners pursuing other people; this may be a matter of deception or merely rest on the failure of the couple to define the relationship explicitly" (1981a:44).

In the third type—the "closed-couple relationship"—on the other hand, partners look only to each other for their romantic and sexual needs. Fidelity is expected. The fourth type consists of committed singles living in the same household and either engaged or having an agreement to maintain a permanent relationship. The fifth type is an "accommodationist," one who either temporarily or permanently lives a solitary life, "except for friendships, refusing all dates and heterosexual

■ With health clubs becoming the singles bars of the eighties, the "happy hour" is no longer quite so happy, but it may be healthier.

contacts.... The permanent accommodationist will generally be in the older age group" (Staples, 1981a:45).

Staples' discussion here reminds us that singles' lives differ due to many factors, one of which, as we noted earlier, is age. Staples makes a further point: Singlehood may be temporary or permanent. Peter Stein has grouped "the heterogeneous populations of singles according to whether singlehood is voluntary or involuntary and stable or temporary" (Stein, 1981:10–12).

As you can see from Table 5•3, voluntary singles may be single either temporarily or permanently; the same is true for involuntary singles.

Voluntary temporary singles are younger never-marrieds and divorced persons who are postponing marriage or remarriage. They are open to the possibility of marriage, but searching for a mate has a lower priority than other activities such as career.

Voluntary stable singles are singles who are satisfied to have never married, divorced persons who do not want to remarry, cohabitants who do not intend to marry, and those whose life-styles preclude marriage, such as priests and nuns.

Involuntary temporary singles are singles who would like, and expect, to marry. These can be younger never-marrieds who do not want to be single and are actively seeking mates, as well as somewhat older people who had not previously been interested in marrying but are now seeking mates.

Involuntary stable singles are older divorced, widowed, and never married people who wanted to marry or to remarry, have not found a mate, and

---

TABLE 5·3 Typology of Singlehood

	Voluntary	Involuntary
Temporary	Never marrieds and former marrieds who are postponing marriage by not currently seeking mates, but who are not opposed to the idea of marriage	Those who have been actively seeking mates for shorter or longer periods of time but have not yet found them Those who were not interested in marriage or remarriage for some period of time but are now actively seeking mates
Stable	Those choosing to be single (never marrieds and former marrieds) Those who for various reasons oppose the idea of marriage Religionaries	Never marrieds and former marrieds who wanted to marry or remarry, have not found a mate, and have more or less accepted singlehood as a probable life state

SOURCE: Stein, 1981:11.

---

have come to accept being single as a probable life situation (Stein, 1981:10–11). (See Case Study 5·1, "Being Single: One Woman's Story.")

You may already have realized that throughout their lives people can move from one category to another. For example,

as younger never-marrieds who regarded singlehood as a temporary state become older, some marry. Others, unable to find an appropriate mate, remain single involuntarily and become increasingly concerned about the possibility that they will never find a mate. Others may enjoy their single state and begin to see it as a stable rather than a temporary condition. The same person can identify singlehood as a voluntary temporary status before marriage, then marry and divorce and become single again. This person may then be a voluntary stable, involuntary stable, or involuntary temporary single, depending on his or her experiences and preferences [Stein, 1981:11–12]. ▪

Then, too, singles may feel ambivalent about whether they would rather be married. Or they may see

benefits in both life-styles. Even involuntary singles may find much to enjoy in being unattached. In short, single individuals find that their experiences and feelings about being single, in addition to changing throughout their lives, may differ based on whether their status is voluntary and whether it is permanent, and on such factors as race, income, and age. These differences are reflected in singles' residential patterns.

RESIDENTIAL PATTERNS AND HOUSING

Singles' residential and housing patterns reflect factors such as age and economics. Census data indicate that most of the singles population is concentrated in specific areas of larger cities. This residential pattern reflects income and education to a certain degree.

Singles move from small towns to medium-sized cities and from medium-sized cities to larger metropolitan areas not only for employment but for other reasons. Often, they hope to avoid gossip and

TABLE 5·4 Young Adults Living with Their Parents, by Age, United States, 1940, 1970, 1984

Sex and year	Percentage living with their parents		
	18–19	20–24	25–29
Total			
1940	75	49	23
1970	77	37	9
1984	80	45	14
Men			
1940	83	58	27
1970	83	44	12
1984	85	53	17
Women			
1940	68	40	19
1970	72	31	7
1984	75	37	11

SOURCE: Glick and Lin, 1986a:108

other forms of small-town discrimination. As one woman put it, "What you value most as a single person is people minding their own business, and you only get that in a big city" (in Jacoby, 1975:121). They move, too, because they want to be near others who are like themselves. Gerda Wekerle's study of Carl Sandburg Village in Chicago concludes that this high-rise apartment complex attracted young singles because of the residents' similarities in age, income, interests, and, perhaps most important, their "different" status (Wekerle, 1975, cited in Stein, 1976:33–34). Finally, singles with money to spend on leisure activities migrate to larger cities because there is "more to do" there. As Susan Jacoby points out, "Singles are at a particular disadvantage in small cities with a sharply limited number of cultural activities, restaurants, and public places of entertainment" (1975:121).

The majority of singles live in apartments or other rental units, but the number of singles living at home is increasing. Table 5·4 lists the percentage of young adults living with their parents in 1940, 1970, and 1984. In 1940 the proportion of young adults living with their parents (43 percent) was higher, for the group as a whole, than it has

been since that time. Sociologists Paul Glick and Sung-Ling Lin suggest why:

The economic depression of the 1930s had made it difficult for young men and women to obtain employment on a regular basis, and this must have discouraged many of them from establishing new homes. Also, the birth rate had been low for several years; this means that fewer homes were crowded with numerous young children, and that left more space for young adult sons and daughters to occupy [1986a:108]. ■

Difficulty in finding adequate employment is also a factor in the proportion of young adults living at home in 1984. So, too, is marital delay: Never married young adults constituted "the preponderant majority" (92 percent) of persons between ages 18 and 29 who were living with parents in 1980 (Glick and Lin, 1986a:109). This group included college students as well as unmarried mothers. A large proportion of the remaining 8 percent consisted of the divorced and separated, most often separated and employed mothers with young children (Glick and Lin, 1986a).

Meanwhile, more singles are buying their own homes. In 1970, single people accounted for less than 1 percent of home purchases, but in 1980 they accounted for 24 percent, with home purchases more common for women than men ("Single People Are Buying More Homes," *Omaha World-Herald,* Apr. 27, 1981). Representing the "fastest growing segment" of the housing market, single women buyers tend to be young (40 percent are between 25 and 34), childless, and relatively affluent, with a median income of $24,000 (Mithers, 1986).

EMPLOYMENT, INCOME, AND DISCRIMINATION

Satisfaction with single living depends to some extent on income and employment, for financial hardships can impose heavy restrictions. A 29-year-old divorced mother told an interviewer:

I laugh when I read about how exciting the single life is, what wonderful changes there are for a girl alone today. "That Cosmopolitan Girl!" Wow! I'm a secretary to a man who owns a liquor store—the only other men I meet are married liquor dealers. If it hadn't been for my kids, I

CASE STUDY 5·1

BEING SINGLE: ONE WOMAN'S STORY

Mary, a pharmacy student, is 29, attractive, and never married. Having always viewed herself as temporarily single, she is beginning to see a possibility that she will never marry (that she may become an "involuntary stable single" [Stein, 1981:10–12]). Still wanting to parent a child, she talks here about artificial insemination.

Mary: The problem with somebody of my age is that most of the men that I meet have been married before and divorced and don't want to get married for a very long time or never want to be married again. Or they are confirmed bachelors. Or they are married and they want to have a fling with somebody my age. Meeting a man who is 29 years old, single, and wants to get married is the most difficult thing I have ever encountered. It is! It is rare!

So I have begun to consider artificial insemination. I have talked to my sister at length about it because she is older than I am. She is 30. She has already been married (and divorced) and doesn't want to get married again unless she really meets somebody that is really perfect for her. And the older I get, the more I think—and she agrees with me—that artificial insemination is ideal. I mean I don't want to be deprived of the joy of motherhood just because I don't have the proper mate, because I can't find somebody. And I don't want to be pushed into a marriage either. I think a lot of people do that. They get married because they are desperate so they compromise and fall into relationships that are not good for them because they want to have kids.

Interviewer: Would you want to raise a child by yourself?

would've moved to a bigger town... when my husband took off. But... my mother takes care of my two little girls while I'm working. With my education, I wouldn't make much better money in a big city, but a hunk of my check would go for day care. I just couldn't make it [in Jacoby, 1975:119]. ▪

This woman's situation illustrates a pervasive fact of life for many single women, especially those with children: They just do not make enough money. (The particular problems of single-parent families are addressed in Chapters 7 and 13.)

There is evidence that occupation and income are related to marital status. Married people are more likely to have white-collar jobs and higher incomes than singles, regardless of age and education. Cargan and Melko looked at income as part of their study described in Box 5·1:

On the whole we can say that a considerably higher percentage of singles perceive themselves to be poor, while a considerably higher percentage of marrieds perceive their income to be at least comfortable. Certainly these figures do not support the stereotype that singles, despite their preferences for movies, theaters, and nightclubs, can be called rich. By almost any comparison to marrieds, they appear to be relatively poor [1982:93]. ▪

An important cause of this difference in income is that today a number of married households operate on two incomes (Thurow, 1980). Another contributing factor, however, is probably employment discrimination (Cargan and Melko, 1982).

Job discrimination is often subtle, reflecting preconceptions more than direct policy. A survey in the mid-1970s of fifty major corporations found

Mary: Maybe it is naive, but I don't think it is. I will never consider artificial insemination until I am so financially stable that my child would not suffer economically. I am working on that now. So, I will wait until I am 35 years old. I feel, though, that I have so much love to give, because of the person that I am, that I don't think my child would ever suffer from lack of love from a father.

And I think that also what is important—what would be really helpful to my child by the time my child is old enough to understand that she or he does not have a father—is the fact that five years from now there are probably going to be more kids (born to single mothers) who were artificially inseminated. So my child will not be alone. I would feel worse by going out and dating somebody and getting pregnant and having a kid (out of wedlock). How do you explain that to your child? That would be more difficult to explain, I think, don't you? . . .

If I were to become artificially inseminated and my child came to me and said, "Mommie, why don't I have a dad?" I guess I would tell my child that I really tried to find the right person—a loving, warm, giving person—for a daddy but I wasn't able to do that. And I would say, "I wanted to have a special child like you, and I have love to give you."

■ How do you feel about Mary's plans for coping with being an "involuntary stable single"? You may want to read this box again when dealing with other subjects in this text. Artificial insemination, for example, is discussed in Chapter 12. Never married mothers are discussed further in Chapter 7.

---

that 80 percent asserted that marriage was not essential to job promotion. However, most of these corporations also indicated that only 2 percent of their executives, including junior management, were single. Over 60 percent reported that single executives tend to "make snap judgments," and 25 percent believed singles are "less stable" than married people (Jacoby, 1975:121).

Discrimination against singles may be lessening due to their growing numbers. Then, too, "because race, sex, ethnic origin, and religion are also bases for discrimination, discrimination against singles is often hard to isolate. Is a woman not promoted because she is a woman? Is a man kept back because he has never married or because his boss suspects he is gay? Whatever its cause, such discrimination victimizes many men and women who hope to get ahead in their work, or even just to get by" (Stein, 1981:236).

We might add that singles can face discrimination because of their presumed or actual attitudes and behavior concerning sex outside marriage. Sexual expression, then, is a third concern for most singles.

SEXUAL EXPRESSION

In the mid-1960s Helen Gurley Brown (the publisher of *Cosmopolitan* magazine) wrote *Sex and the Single Girl.* "Suddenly, single women not only could but should have sex lives" (Stein, 1976:49). Since the 1960s attitudes and behavior concerning nonmarital sex have changed dramatically.

This change has been documented by several studies. Morton Hunt's extensive 1972 survey of sexual attitudes and behavior found radical shifts toward greater permissiveness. While only 22 percent of adults previously surveyed (in 1959) indicated approval of premarital sex, Hunt's research indicated that over half of adults expressed approval (Hunt, 1974). With the possible exception of extramarital sex, Americans are changing their attitudes about sexual expression outside of marriage.

Behavior has also changed. In 1953 sex researcher Alfred Kinsey reported that one-third of the single women in his sample had experienced intercourse by age 25, whereas 70 percent of a 1972 sample of single women age 18–24 reported having had intercourse (Hunt, 1974). More recent surveys have found that two-thirds of married women age 15–44 interviewed in 1982 had had premarital intercourse (U.S. National Center for Health Statistics, 1985c), while 57 percent of today's teenagers have experienced intercourse by age 17 (Louis Harris poll, 1986).

After reviewing research conducted during the 1970s, one social scientist concluded that "there has been a unilinear trend toward more liberal attitudes about sex before marriage." The trend was uneven and varied by social category, however. For example, while upper-class persons showed little change from more conservative attitudes, more middle-class persons became "highly permissive," and lower-class persons showed some trend toward less restrictiveness (Mahoney, 1978).[8] The federal government, seeking to assess the implications of changing U.S. life-styles, in 1986 conducted its first survey of sexual behavior among single American women in their 20s. The survey found, among other things, that respondents had had sexual relations, on average, with 4.5 men, half of whom were partners in serious long-term relationships and half of whom were casual acquaintances ("Study," 1986).

Still, not all Americans condone sex outside marriage. Cultural standards about what's right and wrong vary. Social scientist Ira Reiss has developed a fourfold classification of standards for nonmarital sex. We should note that these are standards, or attitudes, *not* reports of what people actually do.

Four Standards of Nonmarital Sex

Reiss's (1976) four standards—abstinence, the double standard, permissiveness with affection, and

permissiveness without affection—were developed to apply to premarital sex. However, they have since been more generally applied to nonmarital sexual activities of divorced and separated persons as well. Throughout this discussion, both the terms *premarital sex* and *nonmarital sex* are used.

Abstinence The standard of **abstinence** maintains that regardless of the circumstances, nonmarital intercourse is wrong for both women and men. Traditionally, this standard has been supported by organized religion. Many contemporary religious groups, especially the more conservative or fundamentalist congregations, encourage abstinence. Another source of support for abstinence comes from older persons, who are more likely to object to out-of-wedlock sexual behavior than are younger adults. Adolescent children of unmarried (Cleveland, 1981)—or even married (Pocs et al., 1977)—parents may also object to parents' sexual life or deny its place in their parents' lives (Pocs and Godow, 1977).

Abstinence, or celibacy, receives some support from counselors and from feminists as a positive choice. These persons are not opposed to premarital sexual activity in principle, but are concerned about pressures on young persons to establish sexual activity before they're ready, or about pressures for men and women to engage in sexual relationships when they don't really want to. They maintain that celibacy, much devalued in the context of sexual liberalization, ought to remain a valid and respected choice in the absence of an emotionally meaningful relationship, following a divorce or other traumatic breakup of a relationship, or as a respite from a sometimes exploitative singles scene.

Despite the trend toward freer nonmarital sexuality, about 20 percent of college students surveyed in 1975 agreed that "premarital sex is immoral." One survey, in fact, reported that 56 percent of students agreed that premarital sex is sometimes or always wrong, though only 12 percent viewed premarital sex as always wrong ("Survey," 1986). There is also some suggestion from surveys of college students that an increasing number of them, particularly women, agree that "premarital coitus for both males and females is immoral and sinful" (Robinson and Jedlicka, 1982:240). At the same time, premarital sexual *behavior* is at higher levels. The researchers term this phenomenon "sexual contradiction" (Robinson and Jedlicka, 1982). This discussion is reminiscent of that in Chapter

---

8. For a review of trends in premarital sex prior to the 1970s, see Mahoney, 1983:204–9.

4, which addressed changing societal scripts and mixed messages debated by political-religious groups.

The Double Standard   You will probably recognize elements of the patriarchal script (described in Chapter 4) in this standard. According to the **double standard,** premarital intercourse is always more acceptable for males than for females. Some adherents to the double standard feel that unmarried women may have intercourse if they are in love or engaged. But the assumption still exists that a woman should have few partners, preferably only her (one) fiancé.

Ira Robinson and Davor Jedlicka (1982) report what they call a "new" double standard and note that the old double standard had "largely vanished" by 1975 (239). According to the "new double standard," both sexes feel more permissive about their own sex but expect more conservative behavior from the opposite sex. That is, "men expect stricter morality of women and women expect stricter morality of men" (240). Other social scientists, after reviewing thirty-five studies of college students' sexual behavior and attitudes conducted between 1903 and 1980, concluded that this country has witnessed "major shifts in the standards governing sexual behavior from the double standard to the single standard of permissiveness with affection" (Darling et al., 1984).

Permissiveness with Affection   The standard **permissiveness with affection** permits premarital intercourse for both men and women equally, provided they have a fairly stable, affectionate relationship. This standard arises from the expressive sexuality script, discussed in Chapter 4, and maintains that sexual expression, instead of being "wrong," enhances emotional attachment. Reiss concluded that this standard is probably the most widespread sexual norm among young, college and postcollege singles today. In a poll conducted by Daniel Yankelovich, 63 percent agreed that "if two people love each other, there's nothing wrong with having sexual relations" (1981:98).

Permissiveness Without Affection   Sometimes called the recreational sex standard, **permissiveness without affection** allows intercourse for women and men regardless of how much stability or affection there is in their relationship. Readers may recognize elements of ludus, described

in Chapter 3, in this standard. Casual sex—intercourse between partners only briefly acquainted—is permitted.

The recreational standard received much attention during the 1960s, but today there is evidence that only a small number of men and fewer women support this position (Reiss, 1976). Fear of AIDS may further this shift. In a 1986 survey conducted by the Gallup Organization for *Newsweek* magazine, 58 percent of those polled responded that in order to reduce their chances of contracting the disease, they were "taking more care in [their] choice of sex partners" (*Newsweek*, Nov. 24, 1986, pp. 32–33).

Morton Hunt found, for example, that there has been little change in number of premarital partners since Kinsey's time; over 50 percent of married men and women in Hunt's younger and older groups had only one premarital partner. Hunt concluded that for males there is no more casual sex today than a generation ago, and that while there may be an absolute increase for women (for whom this was relatively rare in the past),

the overall significance of our data is that while today almost any "nice girl" will do before marriage what only the daring girl would do a generation ago, today's "nice girl" is still guiding herself according to romantically and historically rooted values [Hunt, 1974:152]. ▪

In other words, her sexual activity is in the context of an exclusive and emotionally serious relationship.

Permissiveness without affection is most often a temporary standard, maintained between affectionate relationships, rather than a lifetime choice (Hunt, 1974). Older single persons have more partners, and so do those who are divorced or separated (a relatively small proportion of singles). The older singles tend to pass through a stage of experimenting and exploring their sexuality to "integrate their newly acquired or developed sexuality with their deeper emotional needs" (Hunt, 1974:252) and ultimately enter a relationship that becomes, or at least resembles, marriage.

Our changing society offers divergent sexual standards, from casual sex to abstinence. For many people, however, marriage is still "a rite of passage to legitimize sexual expression" (Libby, 1977:40). In such a climate parents may disagree with their single adult children about which standard is the right one.

Premarital Sex and Parents

Surveys indicate a generation gap in attitudes toward premarital sex. In general, parents tend to be more conservative about sex outside of marriage than are their adult children.

Seventy-three percent of the fathers and 83 percent of the mothers of the younger singles (college students) in Stein's sample disapproved either "strongly" or "somewhat" of premarital sex for their children. Meanwhile, 79 percent of the single adult sons and daughters approved of premarital sex, and about another 10 percent said they "didn't care" (Stein, 1976:57).

One effect of this generation gap can be that parents and their single adult children simply avoid communicating on this issue, steering clear of topics that might lead to the subject of sexual morality. In fact, noncommunication may be the best approach when value conflicts cannot be resolved, as it may also be in marriage (Udry, 1974; Broderick, 1978).

We do not know the future course of this "generation gap," as children of the sixties are now parents, raising children in the more conservative eighties. Some parents, particularly single parents, may experience a "reverse generation gap," finding themselves more liberal than their children on issues of sexual behavior.

Making Choices About Sex

While as a group married persons tend to have sex more frequently and to be more satisfied with their sex lives, singles tend to have more sexual partners (Cargan and Melko, 1982:101–11). As Figure 5·6 illustrates, 20 percent of singles report having had ten or more partners. But at the same time, about 36 percent report having had none or only one. Clearly, singles today face the necessity of making personal choices about sex.

As we have seen, there are various standards today concerning sex outside of marriage. While cultural attitudes are changing, they have not changed completely, and marital sex continues to be the only unanimously approved form of sexual behavior. Therefore, single adults who choose to satisfy their sexual desires must do so outside the traditional pattern.

Each unmarried adult has to determine what sexual standard he or she values, which is not always

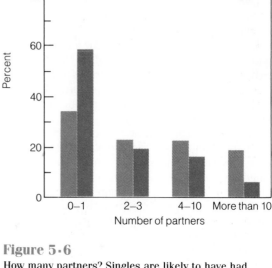

Figure 5·6

How many partners? Singles are likely to have had more sexual partners. (Source: Cargan and Melko, 1982:101)

easy. Because different groups and individuals adhere to various standards, and because attitudes toward sex are changing, today's adults may be exposed to several different standards throughout the course of their lives. Even when people feel they know which standard they value, decisions in particular situations can be difficult. If one believes in the standard of sexual permissiveness with affection, for example, then one must determine when a particular relationship is affectionate enough.

Making these choices and feeling comfortable with them requires recognizing and respecting one's own values, instead of just being influenced by others. Single adults who do not do this often may feel ambivalent and guilty (Luker, 1975; Goleman, 1985a). On the one hand, they try to convince their parents—and themselves—that they're being good. On the other hand, they may find themselves wondering whether they're prudes. In general, a healthy self-esteem and positive attitudes about sex are important for single people who choose to express themselves sexually.

■ There are three women for every man over age 60 because of differences in death rates. Besides demographics, social attitudes are a major reason many single, older women lack sexual partners.

Throughout this section we have been talking about cultural standards concerning sexual activities of singles. Besides young unmarried people, one other group of singles deserves special attention: older adults.

Sex and Older Single Adults: The Double Standard of Aging

Provided they are in good health, people are capable of sexual intercourse through their 80s (Kalish, 1975:45; Weiler, 1981). Decline in sexual abilities derives more from a lack of sexual activity and social discouragement than from physiological

incapacity, except in cases of severe physical deterioration. But older single women may have problems finding sexual partners. Because of differences in death rates, there are three women for every man over age 60. In a society that condemns homosexuality and encourages exclusive sexual relationships between one man and one woman, many older women are left without sexual partners.

Moreover, as they grow older, women are adversely affected by the **double standard of aging** (Sontag, 1976). That is, men aren't considered old or sexually ineligible as soon as women are. Being physically attractive is far more important for women than for men. Beauty, "identified, as it is for women, with youthfulness, does not stand up well to age" (Sontag, 1976:352). As a result, women in our society become sexually ineligible much earlier than men do.

The older woman is expected to be permanently out of circulation.... She can be a respectable married lady and a mother (or a widow), or even a grandmother, but she is not permitted to be a sexual person, both because she is beyond child-bearing and because no man admires her [Laws and Schwartz, 1977:70]. ■

An attractive man can remain eligible well into old age and is considered an acceptable mate for a younger woman. But for most women, even attractive ones, "aging means a humiliating process of gradual sexual disqualification" (Sontag, 1976:353).

For older single women this situation can exacerbate more general feelings of loneliness. But to some degree loneliness is an issue for most singles. The next section examines aloneness, loneliness, and mental health.

ALONENESS, LONELINESS, AND MENTAL HEALTH

The number of one-person households has increased dramatically over the past fifteen to twenty years—by nearly 69 percent between 1970 and 1980, and by another 12.6 percent from 1980 to 1985 (U.S. Bureau of the Census, 1986b). Over one-fifth of all U.S. households were occupied by one person in 1980 (see Figure 5•7). Some researchers are finding what some singles have felt all along: Living alone can be lonesome.

We need to remember, however, that "aloneness," that is, being by oneself, and "loneliness," a subjective sensation of distress, are different (Shahan, 1981). One can feel lonely in the presence of others, even a spouse, and happy alone. Moreover, living alone does not necessarily imply a lack of "social integration" or meaningful connections with others. In a 1978 national survey 3,692 respondents were asked how many neighbors they knew by name, the number of relatives and friends living close by, and how often they saw them. They were also asked the number of "good friends" that could be counted on in "any sort of trouble" and the

number of confidants—persons with whom they could discuss just about anything—they had. Those living alone had fewer relatives living close by and were less familiar with neighbors than did the married respondents, but they generally had greater amounts of contact with friends and confidants. The researchers concluded that

contrary to conventional wisdom, we find that many persons who live alone are not socially isolated relative to others. Indeed, under most (although not all) life circumstances, they seem to show signs of an active "compensation" phenomenon, so that they visibly exceed persons living with others in their magnitude of contact with persons outside the household [Alwin et al., 1985:327]. ■

Despite the "compensation phenomenon," however, singles report feeling lonely more often than do marrieds. In a 1981 national survey 27 percent of single women and 23 percent of single men reported feeling lonely. Corresponding figures for marrieds were 10 and 6 percent, respectively. While these percentages for singles hardly constitute a majority, the researcher concluded that "loneliness appears to be unusual among married men, somewhat more prevalent among married women, and quite prevalent among the unmarried of both sexes" (Weiss, 1981:161).

Earlier we pointed out that singles' lives vary based on social factors such as age and income. The survey just mentioned illustrates this: Poor and older singles were especially likely to be lonely, perhaps because the low incomes and ill health that tend to accompany old age make socializing very difficult (Weiss, 1981:162).

Besides age and income, whether one is single as a result of divorce apparently affects loneliness. The newly divorced tend to suffer from depression (Menaghan and Lieberman, 1986). One study found the divorced to be depressed by being alone about twice as often as other people (see Figure 5•8). The divorced were more likely to be unhappy living alone and more likely to feel lonely because they had no one to discuss or share things with. Divorced singles were also more likely to agree that "most people feel lonely." After expressing some surprise at these findings, the researchers explained that "what may be involved here are changes in perceptions over time. The never-married may not be lonely because they have not experienced mar-

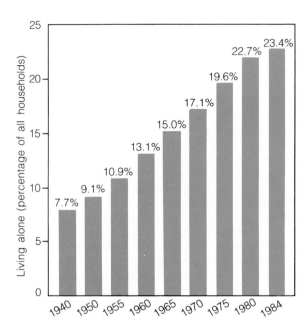

Figure 5-7
Percentage of U.S. households containing persons living alone, selected years, 1940–1984. (Source: U.S. Bureau of the Census, 1983a, 1986b; Alwin et al., 1985)

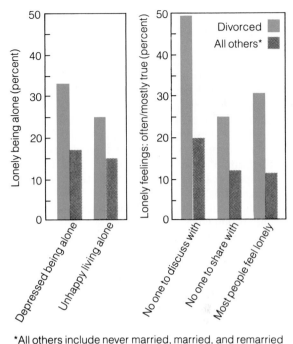

*All others include never married, married, and remarried people

Figure 5-8
Loneliness among divorced persons compared to never married, married, and remarried persons. Being alone may not mean loneliness, but it is more likely for the divorced. (Source: Cargan and Melko, 1982:128, 131)

riage, and therefore have not experienced the implications of loneliness. Two-thirds of them still live at home or with roommates of either sex. Others may be looking forward to breaking free" (Cargan and Melko, 1982:128). Moreover, as a group the never-married are younger, and we have already seen that among singles age is related to loneliness.

Looking more broadly at life satisfaction among American adults, researchers in a classic study found that single persons of both sexes are less likely to report that they are happy with their lives (Gurin et al., 1960:231–32); a resurvey in 1976 produced the same results (Veroff et al., 1981). In a national sample of over 2,000 married and single people, married people reported greater life satisfaction and more positive feelings about life in general than did singles (Campbell, 1975). Moreover, singles have

higher rates of both physical (Verbrugge, 1979) and mental illness (Gove and Tudor, 1973) than do marrieds.[9]

Although marrieds are better off than singles on indicators of overall health and well-being (Gove, 1979; Lynch, 1977; Pearlin and Johnson, 1981; Haring-Hidore et al., 1985), the stress involved in marriage and living with others does appear in many studies in response to certain questions, indicating that both statuses have their costs and benefits. For example, researchers have found that "those living alone are consistently better off than the

---

9. See Eaton, 1980:70–78, for a detailed discussion and interpretation of the research on marital status and mental illness.

married on the manifest irritation scale, in self-esteem among the widowed, in control over one's life among the never-married...." These authors point out that social scientists have tended to "focus on the benefits of social integration and ignore its costs" (Hughes and Gove, 1981:66). Other researchers have found marrieds to be worse off on some indicators of physical stress. Perhaps these findings "support our beliefs that marrieds may suffer more from feelings of mental stress than they admit" (Cargan and Melko, 1982:149); the complex pattern of results reported here would suggest this.

But what about gender differences in marriage and in singlehood? The next sections compare married and single women and men.

Single Women Compared with Married Women

About thirty years ago researchers became interested in comparing the mental health and happiness of single and married women. In the well-known Midtown Manhattan study conducted in the mid-1950s, social scientists interviewed 256 single and 437 married women between the ages of 20 and 50 (Srole et al., 1962). They discovered that married women between 30 and 39 showed more symptoms of psychological distress—nervous breakdowns, nervousness, inertia, insomnia, trembling hands, nightmares, headaches—than did singles. But their overall conclusion for women age 20–59 was that single females did not differ from married females in their mental health impairment (Srole and Fisher, 1978:245). However, more than ten years later the U.S. Public Health Service, after surveying over 7,000 adults, found fewer symptoms of distress (such as nervousness, insomnia, nightmares, headaches) in single women than in married women (Knox, 1975:88).

In her provocative book on marriage, sociologist Jessie Bernard (1982 [1972]) argues that there are two marriages—"his" and "hers." She means that because of traditionally different sex-role expectations (see Chapter 2), women's overall experience in marriage is substantially different from men's. Women have less power in the relationship, and because of their subordinate status, they make more accommodations. Noting that "the mental-health picture of wives shows up ... unfavorably

when compared with unmarried women," Bernard argues that "the psychological costs of marriage ... seem to be considerably greater for wives than for husbands and the benefits considerably fewer" (1972:30–32). "His" marriage is better for him than "hers" is for her.

Joseph Veroff and his colleagues (1981) find some support for Bernard's thesis of "his" and "her" marriages in their 1976 data and reanalysis of 1957 data: "There are many more indicators that marriage is good for men than that it is good for women" (403). Women are more likely (70 percent) to express resentment and irritation with husbands than vice versa (53 percent), and married women express more depression and worry. They interpret the pattern of results as indicating that women's life situations confront them with experiences that put them in a more vulnerable position than men, a position that engenders psychological difficulties (Veroff et al., 1981:374).

More recent work in this area has yielded contradictory results. A study of marital status and overall life satisfaction among black Americans found that married, widowed, and divorced women were more satisfied with their lives than were separated or never married singles. However, when the researchers controlled for—or took into account—age, health, income, and education, the differences were no longer statistically significant (Ball and Robbins, 1986). Two researchers in 1982 found that their data "do not support the notion that marriage is bad for women" and advise against "trying to develop a score sheet to establish, between the sexes, who has the best of marriage and the best of singlehood" (Cargan and Melko, 1982:65). Veroff and his colleagues claim that "being married makes a positive contribution to feelings of well-being for both sexes ... [and there is] no evidence in the data that marriage is bad for women" (403).

One reason for changing findings regarding wives' mental health may be that unhappily married women are more likely to divorce than they were in the 1950s and 1960s. Another reason may be that marriage itself is becoming more able to meet individuals' needs as partners increasingly choose to define their own marriage relationships.[10]

---

10. Changes in methodology and data analysis may also account for differences; Veroff, Douvan, and Kulka (1981) now concede that their 1957 data analysis did not take sufficient account of age differences among groups of single and married persons.

Her Singlehood Other explanations for the changing findings may be that singlehood, like marriage, has changed for women during the past twenty years. For one thing, never-married women in the 1960s and 1970s may have been more likely to be single by choice than those who are single today. Throughout the 1970s researchers pointed to expanding options for women, such as college education and career development, and women's changing attitudes toward marriage as reasons for increasing singlehood (as we ourselves did in the first edition of this text, Lamanna and Riedmann, 1981:131–32). While they recognized the "marriage squeeze" (defined earlier) as one reason for women remaining single, the overall emphasis was on choice.

For many women, however, the choice was for temporary, not permanent, singlehood. By the mid-1980s it had become clear that, due to the marriage squeeze, many single women who had planned on being married someday but had postponed it might not marry at all. This was particularly true for the highly educated and for blacks ("Too Late," 1986). Not marrying if one wants to marry is likely to significantly affect life satisfaction. Box 5·2, "Women's Chances of Marrying: Lessons from a Survey," discusses recent data and their implications.

The New Other Woman One response to women's declining chances to marry is represented by the emerging pattern of single women's affairs with married men. "The contemporary other woman is likely to be our neighbor, our sister, our daughter, our mother, ourselves: regular, normal, everyday single women. ... Demographically, there are simply not enough single men for all the single women" (Richardson, 1985:2). The "new other woman" sees the married man as her only real option. "Women who, in an earlier era, would have recoiled at the murmur of an entanglement with a married man [now] find a relationship with a married man acceptable" (p. 2). For the woman who would like to marry, but hasn't, or the woman who values independence and career over conventional domesticity, a partial, but often rather lengthy sexual and companionate relationship seems preferable to autonomous singlehood or a series of temporary relationships.

Laurel Richardson (1985) explored this increasingly common phenomenon in interviews with fifty-five women from varied social backgrounds: high school graduates and women with postgraduate degrees; skilled workers and professional and managerial women; traditional women and feminists. For the most part, the woman did not intend the affair; it developed inadvertently out of sustained work or social contact. Once begun, it seemed a rational solution to the woman's dilemma: how to meet her emotional, sexual, and companionship needs in the absence of marriage. Women whose work demanded a great deal of time and energy found the married man an appealing alternative. Furthermore, married men were perceived as more stable, attractive, and willing to express feelings than were unmarried men.

Women entered the relationship with a sense of personal efficacy born of the feminist movement. "Intimate relationships which may have appeared 'risky' to previous generations of women now appear 'safe,' because contemporary women see themselves as having control over the direction, intensity, and duration of the relationship" (7). Furthermore, "many [women] wonder, given the power imbalances between men and women and the differences in their socialization, whether a woman can maintain her identity as a separate self while in an intimate relationship with a man. And if she can, at what cost?" (7). Because of the distance and seeming independence built into the relationship, the affair with the married man seems one way of resolving the tension between identity and intimacy.

Various rationalizations protect the woman against empathy with the wife. But over time the affair often proved difficult and debilitating. Meetings and other contacts had to depend on the man's initiative. Emotional support was limited and certainly not available when needed. The classic limitation of an unsanctioned relationship, holidays spent alone, was more depressing than expected. Although some women were able to integrate their relationship with the rest of their lives, those who maintained secrecy felt cut off from family, friends, and work colleagues. The structure of the relationship gave most of the power to the man, and women felt this dependency and lack of control keenly.

Endings varied. Breakups might be initiated by the man in response to his wife's ultimatum, an out-of-town job, a new attraction. Women broke off when the relationship became too painful or, paradoxically, when the man came too close (for those whose motivation was distance). Some endings were sudden and unexpected; some dragged out; some

BOX 5 · 2

WOMEN'S CHANCES OF MARRYING: LESSONS FROM A SURVEY

As we write, a debate rages about women's chances of marriage. It began with the release of a study by sociologist Neil G. Bennett and economist David E. Bloom entitled "Marriage Patterns in the United States" (Bloom and Bennett, 1985). This study gave white, college-educated women born in the mid-1950s only a 20 percent chance of marrying if they had not done so by age 30, odds that dropped to 5 percent at age 35 and 2.6 percent at age 40. As they summarized it: "One out of every eight women born in the mid-1950s will never marry, compared to only one in 25 women in the preceding generation. Nearly one of five college-educated white women born in the 1950s will never marry. Among young black women, whether college-educated or not, almost three in 10 will never marry. Simply put, the extent to which young women today are not marrying is making modern demographic and social history" (Bennett and Bloom, 1986).

Some reactions reported by *Newsweek* include: "I never doubted I would marry, but I wasn't ready at 22. Now my time clock is striking midnight. That's a tough realization—that you may have waited too long"; and "All my friends are having kids. They tell me how glamorous my life is, but I just sit there and envy them their kids" ("A singular forecast," 1986, p. 61). One psychotherapist's client decided to marry a man she did not love after reading the study (Brooks, 1986).

Media reports of the research took a scolding tone, chiding women for pursuing careers and neglecting their ultimate interest—marriage and the family. They reported a rush to therapy. "If this is another single woman over 30 wanting to get married," [said one therapist to another], "don't even think about [referring her]" ("Difficulty in finding husbands," 1986, p. 8). Some feminists sharply criticized the study, reading as its message that women should (1) give highest priority to marriage, (2) be willing to compromise love, equality, career, and self-respect to do so, and (3) expect to be depressed should they not succeed.

The authors (Bennett and Bloom, 1986) and others (Brooks, 1986) quickly pointed out that the numbers themselves contained no such message and furthermore needed qualification and interpretation for a nonscientific audience. Psychologist Rita Cohen noted that people now tend to base important life decisions on social science research: " 'We tend to rely on experts because we don't have large extended families to turn to' " (quoted in Brooks, 1986), whereas "years ago . . . studies tended to be seen only by professionals in the relevant field who would view them in a more circumspect way." The study and the reaction to it became a lesson in the use of social science data on the family.

The authors also noted that the study did not include singles who had been divorced or widowed; it did include persons who were very likely not to marry for physical reasons. Most important, it did not include any information about whether or not the women were single by choice, or whether they preferred live-in or sequential relationships, gay relationships, or a truly single life. Bennett and

Bloom, in fact, read their study as indicating that "a woman's status no longer derives primarily from the man to whom she is married." They went on to note:

Some of the downturn in marriage is doubtless involuntary, resulting directly or indirectly from . . . discrepancies in numbers of available men and women, high unemployment rates, or out-of-wedlock childbearing. Sexism further narrows the options available to women. Although record numbers of women are active in the labor force, many husbands are unwilling to make the sacrifices that wives made in the past. Most men simply do not do their fair share of child care and housework. Further, husbands are often unwilling to move for the sake of their wives' careers. This lack of male cooperation confronts women with an obvious disincentive to marry. So, too, does the scarcity of programs designed to ease the burden on working couples.

But there has also been a voluntary shift in marriage patterns resulting from women's greater economic and social independence and their liberation from the assumption of motherhood. Unfortunately, this positive side of the study has had a difficult time finding its way into print. . . . In many respects, we are in the midst of a revolution that has given women greater latitude to exercise their own will. Rather than condemning women for taking advantage of the freedoms that men have always enjoyed, society should seek to formulate policies that better accommodate contemporary values and behavior" [1986].

Shortly after Bennett and Bloom wrote these comments, another study appeared that contradicted their results and illustrated the complexity of the interpretation and popular use of social science data. Jean Moorman of the Census Bureau reported from her analysis of the same 1980 census data that a single, college-educated woman, age 30, has a 66 percent chance of eventual marriage; 41 percent at age 35; 23 percent at age 40; and 11 percent at age 45. "'We have a disagreement' about whether young women are merely postponing marriage or deciding to forgo it entirely, Ms. Moorman said" ("Women given higher odds," 1986). Bennett and Bloom are convinced that their conclusions, which (unlike Moorman's) assume that marriage rates will continue to drop, are more valid.

Whether they are or not, psychologists cautioned against rash decision making and counseled careful evaluation of the study as well as one's life chances and choices. "It's a terrible thing," said one, "to let yourself go into a depression or a panic over something that may not even apply to you" (Dr. JoAnn Magdoff in Brooks, 1986).

were a carefully planned and respectful winding down. The latter, more purposeful endings left participants with good feelings and no regrets; other endings resulted in bitterness and a reluctance to enter new relationships.

Researcher Richardson is concerned about the power imbalance built into single women's affairs with married men. The current excess of women over men tends to place women in a position of dependence. The "new other woman's" affair with a married man sets up a contradiction between the autonomy and equality that are important goals for many women and the dependency and lack of initiative structured into the relationship. Richardson believes that in the long run the new other woman phenomenon supports male privileges while being a disadvantage to both lover and wife. Despite her criticism, Richardson's objective (rather than moralistic) analysis removes affairs with married men from the category of deviant behavior in order to treat this phenomenon as an alternative life-style.

Single Mothers   Another group whose single lives have some clear limitations are single women who are divorced mothers with children. These women head single-parent families rather than engaging in the mythical "singles" life-style characterized by personal freedom and consumerism. Many work two relatively low-paying jobs, one full-time and one part-time, then take care of their houses and children. For them "career advancement" means hoping for a small annual raise or just hanging onto a job in the face growing economic insecurity. Pursuing higher educational opportunities means rushing to class one evening a week after working all day and making dinner for the children. For reasons that we will examine in further detail throughout this book, many women's experiences as heads of single-parent households can be aptly described, in former Barnard social scientist Sylvia Hewlett's words, as "a lesser life" (1986).

Single Men Compared with Married Men

Studies that compare single men with married men were done mainly in the 1960s and 1970s and indicated that these two groups represent opposite extremes of mental health and happiness. Unmar-

ried men were about twice as likely to report low levels of happiness than were married men, and single males also reported more depression, feelings of loneliness, and anxiety than did married men (Knupfer et al., 1966; Knox, 1975:90–91). According to a current study of black Americans, however, married black men are significantly less satisfied than are divorced, separated, widowed, and never-married black men (Ball and Robbins, 1986).

His Singlehood   A classic explanation for the fact that, in general, single men are more depressed, lonely, and anxious than married men has been that single men in our society, as a result of the marriage gradient, are a rejected, "bottom of the barrel" group. Social scientist Jessie Bernard uses the concept of the **marriage gradient**—in which men marry down in educational and occupational status and women marry up—to explain some of the differences between unmarried men's and women's adjustment (Bernard, 1982).

According to Bernard, our society assigns the husband higher status, so it helps if he actually does have more of some characteristic. That is, marital matches may conform to this norm of higher status for males. Male partners are usually taller than female partners, for example, and they are generally older. Often, they have attained higher education, and they almost always have greater earning power. Traditionally, a woman wanted to be able to look up to her husband, and he wanted her to. And so men tend to marry women slightly below them in age, education, occupation, and in other characteristics. (Possible changes in this pattern are discussed in Chapter 6.)

In Bernard's view this marriage pattern leads to a process of selection whereby men who are harder to look up to—because of income, education, appearance, personality, and so forth—are the most likely to remain unmarried. At the same time, women who are superior in terms of the same criteria may have trouble finding mates they can look up to—and so they are more likely to remain single.

In Bernard's marriage gradient, then, single men as a group are more likely to have lesser self-concepts than are single women and their already low self-esteem is likely to be reinforced by rejection by women (Knox, 1975).

It is possible, however, that single men, if compared with their married counterparts today, would not fare so poorly on mental health indicators. For

■ Same-sex friendships evolve in different situations. Ready for their senior prom, Colin and Henry celebrate a friendship that developed in high school. War is another traditional source of comradeship for men. Less traditional is this support group of Vietnam veterans. As one members describes the group: "Our common experiences in war led to common experiences in our contemporary life. The group's purpose is to develop the individual. Sharing and mutual support are really the keys to what we are doing. Trust is another word we use a lot."

CASE STUDY 5·2

BEING SINGLE: ONE MAN'S STORY

Social-scientific research on unmarrieds is scanty, especially on working-class singles. The following is an edited interview with a 23-year-old, never married man named Rich. He works as an auto mechanic and trade school instructor. Throughout the interview, look for themes discussed in this chapter.

Rich: I've been here in the city about two or three years now. I moved in from my home town—it was real little. I live out on about 80th Street . . . in a basement. This older couple, they were looking for somebody to just be around and kind of keep an eye on the place and do odd jobs around the house. And when I moved to the big city, that was what I found. It was reasonable, provided you did odd jobs.

Interviewer: What kinds of things do you like to do?

Rich: Some buddies and I have a car we race. Weekends we take it to different towns around the circuit. We'll go to Kansas City around September, if we qualify.

Interviewer: Are you dating or anything like that?

Rich: Well, it's just one of those things. Racing takes up most the weekends. Friday night is getting ready, drive all day Saturday, figure out what isn't right with the car, work on it all Saturday night, and get in the elimination Sunday morning. Then put the car back up on the trailer and get back in time to go to work on Monday morning. . . .

I had a girlfriend. We used to make the circuit together. This was back in high school and probably a year beyond. We were planning to get married. But then one time I cracked up pretty bad, and she was there. She wanted me to quit after that. She kept saying, "You are going to get yourself killed."

Interviewer: Did you want to quit?

Rich: Well, I considered it. But freak accidents happen, it's just one of those things. And what's the chances of walking out on the street and getting hit by a city bus? Actually, it's safer inside a racing car than out driving the streets during rush hour.

Interviewer: So you and your girlfriend broke up because you didn't want to quit racing?

Rich: She couldn't take me for what I did or what I was. She had her things she wanted to do. I wanted to run my life the way I wanted. I suppose, looking back, I could have been a little more flexible.

Interviewer: How much would you be willing to compromise now?

Rich: There are times that I think I should have quit. But racing is the way it is, that's just the way it is. After the accident, my folks thought I was crazy to keep on driving. They recommended that I get psychiatric help.

Interviewer: How do you get along with your parents now?

Rich: Fine. I don't worry about their life, and they don't worry about mine. Now that's a wrong answer, because of course they worry, but they never say anything about it. . . .

When I was dating, the heat was on to get married, "Why don't you get married?" and this and that. I wasn't ready for it. Oh, we talked about it, but it was still a couple of years down the road. There were things I had to do. There were things she had to do. But they kept asking, "When are you going to get married?" Sometimes they asked, "When are we going to expect grandchildren?" I did find a way to shut that last one off.

Interviewer: How was that?

Rich: Just say, "In a few months now." They backed up and got off me about grandchildren after that.

Interviewer: How do you like being single?

Rich: Lots of things you do in the single life, it's just doing it and taking it for granted. If I don't like you and you don't like me, we go our separate ways. And it's rare to find any real companionship in a single life. Oh, Wednesday nights you maybe go out with the guys. You go to bars and drink, trade a couple or three rounds or something like that. But that only goes so far, and you've got several little gaps in your life. And they got to be filled. . . .

I think there could be a whole lot deeper kind of relationship, a lot more. I don't know what it's like being married—I can only assume and go from there—but what I feel is you get an occasional comforting hand or something like that.

Interviewer: Do you plan to get married then?

Rich: With the right gal, maybe. But any time you take two people, nobody has the same idea. And racing can get expensive. You can put $12,000 or $14,000 into a car plus expenses to buy your other equipment.

■ What does Rich share in common with other singles? How is he different from other unmarrieds? Where do his thinking and behavior reflect the traditional—and the changing—male sex role? Would you characterize him as "bottom of the barrel?" A "breadwinner revolt(er)"?

one thing, more men now may remain single by choice. We saw in the previous section that the "marriage squeeze" has limited women's marital options; conversely, men have more, not fewer, potential partners. For men, remaining single today may be more a result of choice than of not being chosen. (See Case Study 5·2, "Being Single: One Man's Story.")

Feminist social scientist Barbara Ehrenreich (1983) traces the historical development of what she calls the "breadwinner revolt" among men from the 1950s until now. She argues that through the 1940s men demonstrated their masculinity through family breadwinning, that is, by establishing and providing for a family. Beginning in the 1950s divergent cultural factors, from the *Playboy* mystique to the counterculture, have legitimated singlehood for men. As a result, men are choosing, in increasing numbers, to remain single.

Moreover, life for divorced men may be less painful than it was a decade or so ago. On average, men make one dollar for every sixty cents that women do, and as a group, divorced men tend not to live with and care for their children. They can thus avail themselves of the expanding consumer goods and social and leisure opportunities for singles.

Single Women Compared with Single Men

Nevertheless, at least one important and recent study shows that single men exhibit more signs of stress than do single women (Cargan and Melko, 1982). While single people in general evidence higher rates of mental illness than those who are married, single men have had mental health problems more commonly than women (Gove and Tudor, 1973; Gove, 1979; Srole et al., 1962). Results of a survey of over 2,000 American adults taken in the mid-1970s indicated that "women get along without men better than men get along without women.... Single women of all ages are happier and more satisfied with their lives than single men" (Campbell, 1975:38). This difference can be explained, at least partly, by the fact that women are more likely to maintain a network of close, intimate friendships.

Maintaining Supportive Social Networks

Perhaps the greatest challenge to unmarried individuals of both sexes is the development of strong social networks. Research shows that maintaining close relationships with parents, brothers and sisters, and friends is associated with positive adjustment and satisfaction among singles (Knox, 1975:91). Unmarried men may not cultivate intimate relationships, feeling they shouldn't bother others when they feel low (McGill, 1985). As one bachelor said, "When I feel lonely, I don't feel right about phoning someone and intruding on their life. I just get me a beer and watch TV" (Knox, 1975:90). Such isolation increases feelings of unhappiness, depression, and anxiety.

People's self-concepts depend greatly on other people's responses to them. People who have only secondary relationships know no one who understands them as a whole, unified person. Consequently, they may begin to feel fragmented. Moreover, human beings need others who can help confirm and clarify the meaning of situations and events. In marriage and other primary relationships, people discuss and agree on daily events and interpretations of those events. This process may be taken for granted, but it is an important source of stability for individuals (Berger and Kellner, 1970:5).

Social networks involve more than simply a series of dating partners or casual acquaintances to do things with. Social scientists stress that even singles who are in love and involved in an exclusive dating relationship need a supportive network of intimate friends. A single female, for example, must not make a relationship with a man the exclusive source of her emotional well-being or satisfaction (DeRosis and Pellegrino, 1976).

For both women and men, a crucial part of that network might be valued same-sex friendships. Sometimes these can be found in men's and women's support groups (Stein, 1976:90–91). Such groups are generally small, no more than about a dozen persons, and they may meet either formally or informally. A special quality of friendship often develops in such groups as women and men, both married and single, come to recognize the importance of having same-sex friends who share similar feelings and needs. Same-sex friendships may, of

■ Some friendships that start during schooldays continue. These two women posing before the Pacific have been friends for thirteen years. This quartet looks like an authentic female group, but they're masquerading as "The Saddle Bags" for a Halloween party. Kinship can provide another source of friends; these three sisters share more than a family resemblance.

course, develop spontaneously outside a support group, from work, neighborhood, parenting, leisure and community, and other contacts, or as a continuation of childhood or adolescent friendships or from kin ties. Other sources of support for singles involve opposite-sex friendships (either sexual or nonsexual) and group-living situations.

Although individuals may be single for many reasons, they cannot remain happy for long without support from people they are close to and who care about them. This support is necessary for feeling positive about and generally satisfied with being single. Feeling satisfied with being single, of course, probably also depends upon whether one is voluntarily single. At the same time, though, persons who find themselves involuntarily single may feel better about their status as they choose to develop supportive networks. Loneliness and isolation can "push" singles toward marriage when that option is available. Meanwhile, support structures may "pull" singles to remain in or return to singlehood. The next section explores these and other "pushes and pulls" toward marriage and singlehood.

PUSHES AND PULLS TOWARD MARRIAGE AND SINGLEHOOD

Earlier in this chapter we pointed to a theme of this text: that throughout their lives people make choices—choices influenced and limited by societal options. We saw that singles, particularly black women, may be involuntarily unmarried, presumably because of their inability to find appropriate partners. One pull toward singlehood, then, is demographic and does not involve choice. Meanwhile, social scientist Peter Stein, who emphasizes choice with regard to singlehood, summarizes "pushes and pulls" for individuals who do choose whether to be married or single (see Table 5•5).

Pushes toward singlehood (to leave permanent relationships) might also be labeled "reasons for divorce," and are addressed in Chapter 16. Pulls to stay single include career opportunities, availability of sexual experiences, an exciting and varied life-style, freedom, autonomy, and support structures or networks.

Pushes toward marriage include topics discussed in this chapter: loneliness, isolation, and discrimination. Another push toward marriage is parental pressure. We might add peer pressure.

Parental and Peer Pressures to Marry

Pressure to marry comes from parents and peers. These pressures can be felt keenly. Even without primary relationships, our society uses negative stereotyping to encourage people to conform. Parents and friends may begin to wonder whether their still-single child or peer is frigid, impotent, homosexual, selfish, or simply unable to get to know prospective partners well (Knox, 1975:87). These negative thoughts, subtly passed on to the single person in conversation, create strong social pressure to get married.

Most parents were themselves brought up to accept marriage as the only legitimate life-style, and they attempt to pass that value on to their children. Although parents generally don't want their daughter or son to marry "too early," with each successive year after college (or after high school among blue-collar families) "the intensity and depth of the question increases: 'Are you dating anyone?' 'Who are you going with?' 'When are you going to get married?' and 'What's wrong with you?' " (Knox, 1975:87).

Friends may also exert pressure when they marry and then ask a single person about his or her own plans. More subtle pressure comes from the shift in friendship patterns that often takes place as most of the members of a peer group marry and change their interests and social patterns. The person who remains single is likely to feel out of place, even with his or her closest friends.

This is why Stein lists approval of parents and example of peers as pulls toward marriage. Other pulls include love, the desire for children, and security. The next chapter further explores reasons for marrying.

Summary

Since the 1960s the number of singles has risen. Much of this increase is due simply to rising numbers of young adults who are typically single. Although there is a growing tendency for these young adults to postpone marriage until they are

TABLE 5·5 Pushes and Pulls Toward Marriage and Singlehood

Marriage	
Pushes (negatives in present situations)	Pulls (attractions in potential situations)
Pressure from parents Desire to leave home Fear of independence Loneliness and isolation No knowledge or perception of alternatives Cultural and social discrimination against singles	Approval of parents Desire for children and own family Example of peers Romanticization of marriage Physical attraction Love, emotional attachment Security, social status, social prestige Legitimization of sexual experiences Socialization Job availability, wage structure, and promotions Social policies favoring the married and the responses of social institutions

Singlehood	
Pushes (to leave permanent relationships)	Pulls (to remain single or return to singlehood)
Lack of friends, isolation, loneliness Restricted availability of new experiences Suffocating one-to-one relationship, feeling trapped Obstacles to self-development Boredom, unhappiness, and anger Poor communication with mate Sexual frustration	Career opportunities and development Availability of sexual experiences Exciting life-style, variety of experiences, freedom to change Psychological and social autonomy, self-sufficiency Support structures: sustaining friendships, women's and men's groups, political groups, therapeutic groups, collegial groups

SOURCE: Stein, 1976.

older, this is not a new trend but rather a return to a pattern typical early this century.

One reason people are postponing marriage today is that increased job opportunities for women may make marriage less attractive to them. Also, the "marriage squeeze" has caused a number of women to postpone marriage or put it off entirely. The number of divorced singles has also increased.

While attitudes toward marriage may not be changing, those toward singlehood are, so that now being single is viewed not so much as deviant but as a legitimate choice of life-style. Singles can be classified according to whether they freely choose this option (voluntary singles) or would prefer to marry but are single nevertheless (involuntary singles). Singles can also be classified according to whether they plan to remain single (stable singles) or marry someday (temporary singles).

Whatever category they fall into, maintaining supportive social networks is important for singles. Maintaining socially supportive networks, in fact, can be a pull toward deciding to remain single, just as parental and peer pressures often provide a push toward choosing marriage.

Key Terms

single *145*

marriage squeeze *147*

voluntary temporary singles *157*

voluntary stable singles *157*

involuntary temporary singles *157*

involuntary stable singles *157*

abstinence *162*

double standard *163*

permissiveness with affection *163*

permissiveness without affection *163*

marriage gradient *172*

Study Questions

1. What are some myths about singles? Some realities?

2. How do economics and income affect a single person's life?

3. Individual choices take place within a broader social spectrum, that is, within society. How do social factors influence an individual's decision about whether to marry or remain single?

4. What are the particular circumstances constraining black women who are single and would like to marry? Should black or white women compromise their expectations in order to find a marriage partner?

5. Explain the differences in Reiss's four standards of nonmarital sex. Are there any similarities?

6. What problems do older single adults face that are not faced by younger singles? How are these problems different for men and women?

7. Discuss Jessie Bernard's concept of the marriage gradient. Do you agree with it?

8. Research has shown that never married women tend to be better educated and have higher incomes and better jobs than women in other marital statuses. Why, do you think, is this so?

9. What are some components of a satisfying single life?

10. Do you consider an affair with a married man to be a satisfactory alternative to marriage for the single woman? Why or why not?

Suggested Readings

Bernard, Jessie
1982 *The Future of Marriage*. 2nd ed. New York: Bantam.
  In this scholarly yet readable book, Bernard, a sociologist, brings together a mass of research findings and draws out their implications for change in the marriage relationship.
Cargan, Leonard, and Matthew Melko
1982 *Singles: Myths and Realities*. Beverly Hills, Calif.: Sage.
  This is a report of a study of singles in Dayton, Ohio. The book explores singles' relations with parents, work, leisure, sexuality, friendship patterns, health, and happiness.
Guttentag, Marcia, and Paul Secord
1983 *Too Many Women: The Sex Ratio Question*. Beverly Hills, Calif.: Sage.
  Interesting analysis of the impact of the sex ratio, that is, the relative numbers of men and women, on singlehood, marital power, and feminism. Cross-cultural and historical data are analyzed.
Mahoney, E. R.
1983 *Human Sexuality*. New York: McGraw-Hill.
  Excellent, readable book on sexuality, with good material on sexual expression in a variety of contexts.
Moustakas, Clark E.
1961 *Loneliness*. Englewood Cliffs, N.J.: Prentice-Hall.
  This important book explores loneliness as essential (or existential) to the human condition. *Everyone* experiences periods of loneliness. According to Moustakas, loneliness causes not only pangs of terror, desolation, and despair but also deeper insights and renewed awareness of the world and the self.

1972 *Loneliness and Love.* Englewood Cliffs, N.J.: Prentice-Hall.

Here Moustakas describes how periods of loneliness and solitude can help a person move toward more authenticity, more honesty, and therefore toward more meaningful love relationships with his or her fellow human beings.

Richardson, Laurel

1985 *The New Other Woman: Contemporary Single Women in Affairs with Married Men.* New York: Free Press.

Richardson treats affairs sociologically, that is, nonjudgmentally. But she notes that the structure of the situation leaves women with little control over their lives.

Shahan, Lynn

1981 *Living Alone and Liking It: A Complete Guide to Living on Your Own.* New York: Warner.

Best-seller on how to handle single living.

Staples, Robert

1981 *The World of Black Singles: Changing Patterns of Male-Female Relationships.* Westport, Conn.: Greenwood.

Very detailed discussion of this subject by a respected social scientist.

Stein, Peter J. (ed.)

1981 *Single Life: Unmarried Adults in Social Context.* New York: St. Martin's Press.

Reader with many good articles on various types of singles and their lives.

Weiss, Robert

1974 *Loneliness: The Experience of Emotional and Social Isolation.* Cambridge, Mass.: MIT Press.

A readable discussion of loneliness based on qualitative research.

6 Choosing Each Other

"The Pasture"
I'm going out to clean
the pasture spring;
I'll only stop to rake the
leaves away
(And wait to watch the
water clear, I may):
I sha'n't be gone long.—
You come too.

I'm going out to fetch the
little calf
That's standing by the
mother. It's so young,
It totters when she licks
it with her tongue.
I sha'n't be gone long.—
You come too.
ROBERT FROST

People want to love and be loved. In our society this often means selecting someone, usually of the opposite sex, with whom to become both emotionally and sexually intimate. While people can maintain close relationships with several others, Americans value having one special relationship with a person they love best. In our culture this relationship is supposed to have a romantic quality. It may lead to marriage.

How well do our ideals of romance describe the kind of relationship people share in marriage? As we'll see, only recently in history have people even begun to equate the two concepts of love and marriage. While love is usually an important ingredient, "successful" marriages are also based on such qualities as the partners' common goals and needs, their maturity, and the soundness of their reasons for marrying.

You'll recall that Chapter 3 examines love—loving oneself and discovering a loving relationship with an intimate partner. In the following pages we'll examine some social variables that may influence choice of partners and marital stability. We'll also look at patterns by which individuals in our society develop commitments to each other.

LOVE AND MARRIAGE: HORSE AND CARRIAGE?

That marriages should involve romance and lead to personal satisfaction is a uniquely modern idea. According to an old song, love and marriage "go together like a horse and carriage." How did our notion of romantic love come about, and why is it assumed to be the basis of marriage in our society?

Courtly love (or romantic love) flourished during the Middle Ages. At the visible upper levels of society, most marriages during this period were based on pragmatic considerations involving property and family alliances (Stone, 1980). Tender emotions were expressed in nonmarital relationships in which a knight worshiped his lady, and ladies had their favorites. These relationships involved a great deal of idealization, were not necessarily sexually consummated, and certainly did not require the parties to live together. In time the ideology of romantic love was adapted to a situation for which it was probably much less suitable—marriage.

As urban economies developed and young people increasingly worked away from home, arranged marriages gave way to marriages in which individuals selected their own mates. Sentiment rather than property became the basis for unions (Shorter, 1975). The strong emotional and personal qualities of romantic love were in keeping with the individualism and introspection characteristic of the evolving Protestant capitalistic society of western Europe (Stone, 1980; Skolnick, 1978a).

In the absence of arranged marriages, love provided motivation for choosing mates and forming families and thereby served important social functions (Greenfield, 1969). This continues to be true. The connection between love and marriage serves to harness unpredictable feelings, to the service of society (Goode, 1959).

Romantic love, in the sense of a strong emotional attachment to the partner, is not necessarily bad, and the little research available does not support the assumption frequently expressed in textbooks that romantic love results in unhappy marriages (Spanier, 1972). Intense romantic feelings may serve to get the married couple through bad times (Udry, 1974); however, the idealization and unrealistic expectations implicit in the ideology of romantic love can cause problems. (Chapter 3 also addresses this issue.) Many Americans expect romance to continue not only through courtship, but in marriage, too. Combining the practical and economic elements of marriage with developing intimacy and love is a new goal historically.

But even during courtship romance is infused with the practical, particularly for women. Contrary to popular opinion, men tend to fall romantically in love sooner and to be more affected by breakups (Hill et al., 1976; Kanin et al., 1970), probably because men have traditionally taken the initiative in courtship and so have been able to pursue their romantic inclinations more freely (Walster and Walster, 1978:50–51). At the same time, because a woman's life-style and economic security have traditionally depended on the occupational success and reliability of her spouse, women, more than men, tend to assess and compare dates as potential mates, with some attention to practical considerations.

Falling in love, then, when we expect that it could lead to marriage, may be a more practical and rational process than we think. Social scientists use the analogy of the marketplace to describe how Americans choose marriage partners.

THE MARRIAGE MARKET

Imagine a large marketplace in which people come with goods to exchange for other items. In nonindustrialized societies a person may go to market with a few chickens to trade for some vegetables. In modern societies people attend hockey-equipment swaps, for example, trading outgrown skates for larger ones. Americans choose marriage partners in much the same way: They enter the **marriage market** armed with resources—their personal and social characteristics—and then bargain for the best buy they can get.

In many other cultures parents arrange their children's marriages through a bargaining process not unlike what takes place at a traditional village market. They make rationally calculated choices after determining the social status or position, health, temperament, and, sometimes, physical attractiveness of their prospective son- or daughter-in-law. In such societies the bargaining is obvious. Professional matchmakers often serve as investigators and go-betweens, just as we might engage an attorney or stockbroker in an important business deal. The exchange is accompanied by the **dowry,** a sum of money or property brought to the marriage by the female. A girl with a large dowry can expect to marry into a higher-ranking family than a girl with a small dowry, and dowries are often increased to make up for qualities considered undesirable (Kaplan, 1985:1–13). Parents in eighteenth-century England, for instance, increased the dowries of daughters who were pockmarked.

The difference between arranged marriages and modern freely selected marriages seems so great that we are inclined to overlook an important similarity: Both involve bargaining. What has changed in modern society is that the individuals, not the family, do the bargaining (Murstein, 1980).

Exchange Theory

The ideas of bargaining, market, and resources used to describe relationships such as marriage come to us from **exchange theory**. Exchange theory is a framework that family sociologists have begun to use relatively recently.

This theory was developed as a general theory of behavior independently by psychologists (Thibaut and Kelley, 1959) and sociologists (Homans, 1961; Blau, 1964). The basic idea is that whether or not relationships form or continue depends on the rewards and costs they provide to the partners. Individuals, it is presumed, want to maximize their rewards and avoid costs, so where there are choices, they will pick the relationship that is most rewarding or least costly. The analogy is to economics, but in romantic and marital relationships individ-

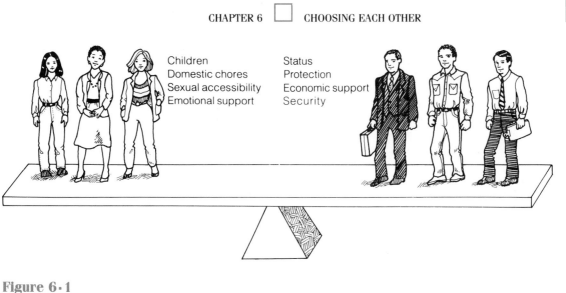

Children
Domestic chores
Sexual accessibility
Emotional support

Status
Protection
Economic support
Security

Figure 6·1
The traditional exchange.

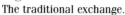

uals are thought to have other sorts of resources to bargain besides money: physical attractiveness, personality, family status, skills, emotional supportiveness, cooperativeness, intellect, originality, and so on. Individuals also have costly attributes: irritability, demandingness, ineptitude, low social status, geographic inaccessibility (a major consideration in modern society), and so on. If each individual adopts a strategy of maximizing outcomes, then stable relationships will tend to exist between people who have like amounts of resources, since they will strike a "fair" balance or bargain.

Theoretically, these bargains will last only until a better deal comes along. A weakness of exchange theory is that people who are married or with each other for a time find that considerable attachment and common identity develop, so that leaving becomes very difficult. Shared activities or a shared life leads the relationship to have a normative structure; that is, the patterns of everyday life become fixed in a way that deeply involves the partners. And community and interpersonal ties provide, even for unmarried persons, social support for the relationship and sanctions against breaking it off.

There is also the question of rationality. Are people actually so calculating about rewards and costs, even at an unconscious level? Further, in an exchange analysis, what is rewarding and what is costly? It varies with the individual.

Descriptions of exchange behavior are reminiscent of traditional arranged marriages. Nevertheless, we present an exchange perspective as a useful tool. In fact, the basic structures of American life have channeled men and women into different adult roles that have certain consequences for marital partnerships. (A careful look at economic and legal aspects of these partnerships as they interact with social roles can be found in Lenore Weitzman's *The Marriage Contract* [1981], discussed in Chapter 7.)

We need to be aware of the possibility of an underlying exchange structure to intimate relationships and marital ties. It is important for the individual in making choices. It is important in considering public policy: What form of social and economic organization provides the most encouraging setting for the intimate relationships we want?

That is a question of values. Let us look now at an exchange version of marital choice.

The Traditional Exchange

Individuals may bargain such characteristics as social class, age, physical attractiveness, and education, but the basic marital exchange is traditionally related to gender roles. Historically, women have traded their ability to bear and rear children and perform domestic duties, along with sexual accessibility and physical attractiveness, for masculine protection, status, and economic support (see Figure 6·1). While more and more women are gaining status by means of their own careers or professions, many of them continue to attain a higher status by marrying than they would have as single individuals supporting themselves. Being a doctor's wife may offer a higher status, for example, than being a teacher or nurse.[1]

Women have had some disadvantages in the traditional exchange. For one thing, men can bargain on their potential, taking their time to "shop" for a partner, while women lose an important advantage with time. A female's traditional bargaining assets of physical attractiveness and childbearing capacity are given less value as she ages. Men, meanwhile, can exchange promises of anticipated occupational success and power for marital security.

Sociologists point to a related bargaining advantage for males. Young men and women bargain for spouses with different degrees of available information. The male can more easily assess the female, observing whether she offers support and empathy as well as responding to her physical attractiveness. But the occupational abilities of many young men have generally not yet been tested. A woman must therefore base her appraisal on such cues as a young man's grades in school and his father's occupation (Glenn, et al., 1974; Marcus, 1977). This latter cue isn't always a good one, however; a majority of professionals' sons are in lower-ranked occupations than their fathers (Taylor and Glenn, 1976).[2] Older men and women may more easily evaluate prospective partners, since personal and economic characteristics are more established.

Bargaining in a Changing Society: The Optimistic View

As society changes, so does the basic exchange in marriage. Social scientists predict that, should true androgyny emerge, as was discussed in Chapter 2, exchange between partners will no longer depend greatly on practical or economic resources but will "instead entail expressive, affective, sexual-companionship resources" for both partners (Safilios-Rothschild, 1976:355–61). If women gain occupational and economic equality with men, the exchange should become more symmetrical, with women and men increasingly looking for similar characteristics in each other (Taylor and Glenn, 1976:497) (see Figure 6•2a).

Marriage based on both partners' contributing roughly equal economic and status resources should be more egalitarian, avoiding problems of power disparity (see Chapter 10). Current changes in men's roles toward greater emotional expressiveness may improve marriage, for research suggests that marriages in which both partners contribute expressively are happier (Laws, 1971). Furthermore, as gender roles change, even those exchanges that are complementary (that is, based on unlike resources) can be individualized. For example, an ambitious career woman might be comfortable bargaining for a nurturant, domestic husband, and vice versa. This is the bargaining we would anticipate in an egalitarian and androgynous society.

Bargaining in a Changing Society: The Pessimistic View

Another view would pay more attention to the substantial inequalities that remain, particularly women's marginal position in the economic system. While women have entered the labor market in large numbers, their jobs and incomes are still far inferior, on the average, to those of men. (Reasons for this disadvantage are many; for a careful analysis, see Huber and Spitze, 1983.)

Although social expectations may be moving toward androgyny, women are still at a disadvantage in the marriage market (Luker, 1975). Men continue to monopolize access to financial security and status. Meanwhile, many of the bargaining chips women have traditionally brought to the basic exchange—children, domestic services, sexual accessibility—have been devalued (see Figure 6•2b).

It may once have been true, for example, that "the way to a man's heart is through his stomach." Today, however, with fast-food chains and frozen dinners, cooking and other domestic skills and services are no longer monopolized by potential wives,

---

1. This brief comment does not do justice to the issue of women's social status and the wife's contribution to family income. For a discussion of this issue, see Max Haller's "Marriage, Women, and Social Stratification: A Theoretical Critique," *American Journal of Sociology* 86 (1981):766–95.

2. Some evidence suggests that there may be limits on the early assessment of personality characteristics of *either* sex. Recent books on change over the lifetime (see Chapter 1) point to considerable adult development and change. Several studies suggest "continuous change in . . . adult personalities" (Udry, 1974). One study found, in fact, that personality scores at engagement accounted for less than 25 percent of personality scores three or four years later (Burgess and Wallin, 1953).

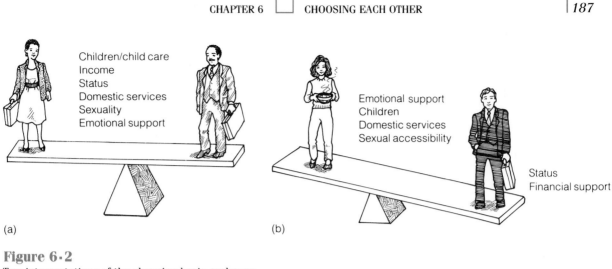

(a)   (b)

Figure 6·2
Two interpretations of the changing basic exchange.

and many men have discovered that they like to cook. Men can also have their shirts or uniforms commercially laundered and hire people to clean house for them. The increased acceptance of non-marital sex (however satisfying this may be to many women as well as men!) has weakened women's traditional bargaining position, decreasing the possibility of trading sexual accessibility for marriage. And finally, even the ability to have children may be less vital than in the past, as some people are questioning the value of having children (Luker, 1975). In this analysis the wife's primary resource in the marital exchange consists of the promise of lifelong affection and encouragement (Scanzoni, 1970).

Besides cultural expectations, there are demographic features of the current marriage market that negatively affect the bargaining position of women. Chapter 5 describes how the dual demographic phenomena of the marriage squeeze and the marriage gradient limit women's marital options and discusses how an unequal sex ratio limits choice of marriage partners.

Sex Ratio   The **sex ratio** is the ratio of men to women in a given society or subgroup of society.[3]

Historically, the United States had more men than women, mainly because more men than women migrated to this country, and, to a lesser extent, because a considerable number of young women died in childbirth. Today this situation is reversed due to changes in immigration patterns and greater improvement in women's than in men's health. Since World War II there have been more women than men (see Figure 6·3). In 1984, for example, there were under 95 men for every 100 women, while in 1910 there were nearly 106. Table 6·1 presents sex ratio data broken down by age category and marital status. As you can see, beginning at age 35, there are fewer unmarried men than women. If each of these people wished to marry, many women would be left out, increasingly so in the older age groups.[4]

Research suggests that older people, for whom the sex ratio is most imbalanced, may be exploring marital combinations other than the traditional ones. One study compared an Atlanta sample of 106 couples over age 65 with 192 younger couples from the same city, all of whom had married during 1978. In the older unions spouses were much less likely to be close in age. Moreover, the husband was much less likely to be the older partner (Dressel, 1980; see also Bytheway, 1981:925–27). One option, then, is for women to ignore the traditional marriage

3. The sex ratio is expressed in one number: the number of males for every 100 females. So a sex ratio of 105 means there are 105 men for every 100 women in a given population. More specialized sex ratios can be calculated, the sex ratio at various ages, for example, or of unmarried persons only.

4. Calculation of the availability of mates is complicated by the tendency of men to be two to three years older than the women they marry, as we discussed in Chapter 5 (see also Guttentag and Secord, 1983).

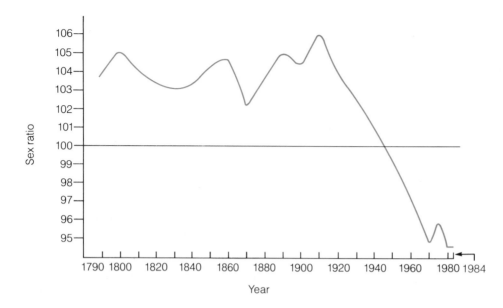

Figure 6·3
Sex ratios in the United States from 1790 to 1980. Since 100 represents a balanced sex ratio—an equal number of men and women—markers above the 100 line mean there are more men than women; markers below that line mean that there are more women than men. (Sources: U.S. Bureau of the Census, 1975 [cited in Guttentag and Secord, 1983:15], 1982, 1983b, 1986b)

gradient pattern and marry younger men. Recent popular literature and movies have presented this alternative as one that deserves wider consideration.

Some observers (e.g., Doudna, 1981) who note the dearth of male partners for women have proposed and predicted an increase in such alternative life-styles as permanent celibacy, lesbianism, single motherhood, polygamy, and communal living. (Chapter 7 addresses alternative family forms.)

An additional factor shaping marital choice is the tendency of people to marry others with whom they share certain social characteristics. Social scientists term this phenomenon *homogamy.*

HOMOGAMY: NARROWING THE POOL OF ELIGIBLES

Not everyone who enters the marriage market is equally available to everyone else. Americans, like many other peoples, tend to make marital choices in socially patterned ways, viewing only certain others as potentially suitable mates. The market analogy would be choosing only certain stores at which to shop. For each shopper there is an appropriate **pool of eligibles:** a group of individuals who, by virtue of background or birth, are considered most likely to make compatible marriage partners. From this pool Americans tend to choose partners who are like themselves in many ways. This situation is called **homogamy:** People tend to marry people of similar race, age, education, religious background, and social class. Traditionally, Protestant, Catholic, and Jewish religions, for example, have all encouraged **endogamy:** marrying within one's own social group. (The opposite of endogamy is **exogamy,** marrying outside one's group.)

The argument might be made that marriage has become less homogamous in recent years. The incidence of interfaith marriage is now quite considerable, for instance, and more children of blue-collar parents are marrying children from professional homes. By 1980 marriage across ethnic (e.g., Irish, Italian, Polish) lines had become so common

TABLE 6·1 Sex Ratio of Unmarried (Never Married, Divorced, and Widowed) Men to Women by Age, 1984

Age	Sex Ratio[a]
18–19	109
20–24	123
25–29	124
30–34	114
35–44	85
45–54	69
55–64	42
65–74	28
75 +	23

SOURCE: U.S. Bureau of the Census, 1986b. a. Numbers above 100 indicate more men than women. For example, at age 20–24 there are 123 unmarried men for every 100 unmarried women. Numbers below 100 indicate that there are fewer unmarried men than unmarried women. For example, at age 45–54 there are 69 unmarried men for every 100 unmarried women.

that only one in four American-born whites of non-Hispanic origin was married to someone with an identical ethnic heritage ("Sense of identity," 1985).

In spite of the trend toward less homogamy than in the past, homogamy is still a strong force. While partners may come from different economic backgrounds, for example, they have usually met in another homogamous group: college. College-educated women and men tend to marry each other; so do non-college-educated people. With regard to ethnic/racial intermarriage, nearly 99 percent of non-Hispanic whites marry other non-Hispanic whites, while 99 percent of black women and 97 percent of black men marry within their race. More than 72 percent of Asian Americans and 71 percent of Hispanics marry within their group. (However, nearly 54 percent of American Indians marry outside their race, mostly to whites.) ("Sense of identity," 1985).

Social scientists point out that while today people are marrying across small class distinctions, they still are not doing so across large ones. For instance, individuals of established wealth seldom marry the poor (Udry, 1974:152–68). All in all, an individual is most likely to marry someone who is similar in basic social characteristics. Let's look at a hypothetical case to see why this may be so.

Reasons for Homogamy

Susie is attracted to John (and vice versa) who is a college student (like herself), two years older, and single.... Susie's parents are upper middle class. They live in the expensive wooded section of her home town, have a full-time housekeeper, drink wine with their meals, and frequently have parties by their pool with a live band. John's parents are upper lower class. They are separated. His mother lives in a third-floor apartment, and works as a checker in the supermarket. The family usually drinks iced tea at mealtime, then watches TV on their 5-year-old portable black-and-white set [Knox, 1975:34]. ■

How likely is it that Susie and John will end up marrying? If they do marry, what sources of conflict might occur? We can help to answer these questions by exploring four related elements that influence both initial attraction and long-term happiness. These elements—propinquity, social pressure, feeling at home, and the fair exchange—are important reasons many people are homogamous.

Propinquity In our society propinquity (or geographical closeness) is a basic reason people tend to meet others much like themselves. Geographic segregation contributes to homogamous marriages (Peach, 1974; Morgan, 1981). Intermarriage patterns within the American Jewish community are an example. Until the 1880s the small size of this group and its geographic dispersal limited the availability of Jewish marriage partners and led to frequent marriages with non-Jews. The large Jewish migration from eastern Europe that began in the late nineteenth century changed this. Immigrants tended to settle together in Jewish neighborhoods; for this reason, among others, intermarriage rates dropped (William Petschek National Jewish Family Center, 1986b).

Propinquity also helps account for social class homogamy. Middle-class people live in neighborhoods with other middle-class people. They socialize together and send their children to the same schools; upper- and lower-class people do the same.

■ Two of a kind: For various reasons, people often choose partners who resemble themselves in many ways.

Parents conscious of the relationships between propinquity and homogamy often oppose interracial busing and school desegregation in general (Monahan, 1976:230) because they recognize the threat this poses to the homogamous marriages they evidently prefer. Unless they had met in a large, public university, it is unlikely that John and

Susie would have become acquainted at all.[5] The effort expended in associating with, or even meeting, people who are outside one's physical circle of friends encourages homogamy.

Social Pressure A second reason for homogamy is social pressure. Our cultural values encourage persons to marry others socially similar to themselves and discourage marrying anyone too different: Susie's parents, friends, and siblings are not likely to approve of John, because he doesn't exhibit the social skills and behavior of their social class. Meanwhile, John's mother and friends may say to him, "Susie thinks she is too good for us. Find a girl more like our own kind" (Knox, 1975:34). Sometimes, social pressure results from a group's concern for preserving its ethnic or cultural identity. When young Jews, particularly college students, began to intermarry more often in the 1960s, for example, Jewish leaders became concerned.

From pulpits across the country rabbis lamented the disintegrating Jewish family and the "demographic holocaust" that threatened the community. Federations rushed to form task forces on intermarriage; Hillel directors sought new ways to cement the group loyalties of Jewish college students so they would not intermarry; and a spate of "how-to-stop-an-intermarriage" books appeared [William Petschek National Jewish Family Center, 1986b:2]. ■

Feeling at Home People often feel more at home with others from similar backgrounds; and differences between persons in different social groups may make communication between them difficult

---

5. However, as Murstein (1976) points out, more and more people today choose spouses from open fields. An *open field* encounter refers to a situation in which the man and woman do not yet know each other well. A *closed field* encounter, on the other hand, is one in which partners are forced to interact by reason of their environment—in a small town, for example. Sociologist Judith Ericksen, in a survey of Philadelphia couples, found that 22 percent met their spouses at a "chance encounter"—not work, family, or usual social activities. She calls these meetings "marital pickups." But rather than occurring in singles bars, they happened on buses, in stores, on the street, or in elevators. Ericksen found, interestingly, that pairs who "grew up with their spouses," that is, knew them from school and the neighborhood, had lower divorce rates than "chance encounter" couples ("Cupid's arrows," 1981, p. 2-B).

and uncomfortable. With regard to social-class differences, John is likely to have different attitudes, mannerisms, and vocabulary from Susie. Susie won't know how to dress or behave in John's hang-outs and among his friends. Each may feel uncomfortable and out of place in the surroundings the other considers natural (Knox, 1975:34).

Striking a Fair Exchange As previously noted, exchange theory suggests that people tend to marry others whose social class, education, physical attractiveness, and even self-esteem are similar to their own—their social currency (Murstein, 1986).

The questions people ask on first meeting point up their concern with each other's exchange value. They want to know whether their dates are married or single, where they are employed, whether they attend college and where, what they plan to do upon graduation, where they live, and perhaps what kind of car they drive. If prospective partners are single, they will be asked whether they are divorced or still single and, especially in the case of women, whether they have children and how many.

If meeting in the marriage market can sound like a job interview, maybe that's because in at least one important way it is: The goal is to strike a fair exchange. And even without the benefit of interviews, people learn to discern the social class of others through mannerisms, language, dress, and a score of other cues.

We've discussed some reasons for homogamy, but, as we pointed out earlier in this chapter, all marriages are not homogamous. **Heterogamy** refers to marriage between those who are different in race, age, education, religious background, or social class. Race is considered the most differentiating social characteristic in our society. We will examine interracial marriage here.

Interracial Marriage: An Example of Heterogamy

In June 1967 (*Loving* v. *Virginia*) the United States Supreme Court declared that interracial marriages must be considered legally valid in all states. At about the same time, it became impossible to gather accurate statistics on interracial marriages. Many states no longer require race information on mar-

riage registration forms, so this source of information is incomplete at best (Monahan, 1976:224).

Available statistics show that the proportion of interracial to all marriages is very small, about 1.5 percent. However, the proportion of racially mixed unions among blacks increased 175 percent between 1970 and 1984, and the number of interracial marriages more than doubled between 1977 and 1984, from 310,000 to 762,000 (U.S. Bureau of the Census, 1986b).

Of all intermarriages in 1984, only 23 percent were black-white (0.3 percent of total U.S. marriages). The remainder, for the most part, were various combinations of whites or blacks with Asians, native Americans, and others (see Table 6•2). Four-fifths of black-white marriages involved black men married to white women (U.S. Bureau of the Census, 1982).[6]

Much attention has been devoted to why people marry interracially. Psychoanalytic and psychological hypotheses suggest that whites marry interracially because of rebellion and hostility, guilt, or low self-esteem. Such explanations smack of racism and are not supported by research. Another theory is **hypergamy:** marrying up socioeconomically on the part of the white woman who, in effect, trades her socially defined superior racial status for the economically superior status of a middle- or upper middle-class black partner. It is important to note that empirical research—by Monahan (1976) and Heer (1974)—provides no support for the theory of hypergamy.

One study of forty interracially married couples found, simply, that "with few exceptions, this group's motives for marriage do not appear to be any different from those of individuals marrying . . . within their own race" (Porterfield, 1982:23). As you can see from Table 6•3, many respondents in this study said that they married for love and compatibility.

---

6. Sociologist Kaylene Richards-Ekeh believes that white male/black female marriages are increasing and would increase even more except for the hesitancy of white males to express their interest and black females to respond to it. White male college students express concern about offending black women or being rejected by them because of the history in this country of white sexual exploitation of black females. Black females are wary for the same reason and because they fear criticism by other blacks for placing themselves in a situation perceived as vulnerable or exploitable (Richards-Ekeh, 1984).

TABLE 6·2 Interracial Married Couples in 1984

All black-white married couples	175,000
Husband black, wife white	111,000
Wife black, husband white	64,000
Other interracial married couples[a]	587,000
Husband white	340,000
Wife white	224,000
Husband black	17,000
Wife black	6,000
Total interracial married couples	762,000

SOURCE: U.S. Bureau of the Census, 1986b, p. 36, Table 47. a. Spouse is neither white nor black, but is Asian, native American, Aleut, Pacific islander, and so on.

TABLE 6·3 Number of Interracially Married Respondents Who Mentioned Specific Motives for Their Marriage

	Race and Sex of Spouse			
Motives	Black Male	Black Female	White Male	White Female
Nonrace-related motives				
Love	28	12	6	25
Compatibility	28	12	6	25
Pregnancy		1		1
Race-related motives				
Other race more appealing, interesting				2
Rebellion against society	3			
White female a "status symbol"	2			
White female less domineering	4			
Black female more independent, self-sufficient			1	
Marginality				
Desire for a husband of comparable educational-occupational status		2		
Ostracized from one's own racial group				1

SOURCE: Porterfield, 1982:23. Note: Although these categories are mutually exclusive, motives for marriage are not. Some of the respondents indicated a combination of reasons for marriage.

■ Trish and Nat describe themselves as a happy couple. They're also heterogamous and unusual—interracial marriage is still rare in America.

Heterogamy and Marital Stability

There are conflicting data on whether interracial marriages are more or less stable than intraracial unions. Monahan (1970) found in Iowa that black-white marriages were more stable than those between blacks and, furthermore, that couples in which a black man was married to a white woman had a lower divorce rate than did white couples. However, Heer (1974) found that intermarried couples (married in the 1950s and 1960s and surveyed in 1970) were less likely to remain married than homogamous couples of either race: These were the proportions still intact:

- black husband and white wife, 63 percent
- white husband and black wife, 47 percent
- both partners black, 78 percent
- both partners white, 90 percent (Heer, 1974)

Marital success can be measured in terms of stability—whether or how long the union lasts—and happiness of the partners. Marital stability is not synonymous with marital happiness, because in some instances unhappy spouses remain married, while less unhappy partners may choose to separate. In general, social scientists find that marriages that are homogamous in age, education, religion, and race are more stable (Burr, 1973), although some social scientists express reservations about the data for this conclusion (Udry, 1974; Dean and Gurak, 1978).

There are at least three explanations for this difference in marital stability. First, significant differences in values and interests between partners can create a lack of mutual understanding, resulting in emotional gaps. Second, such marriages are likely to create conflict between the partners and other groups, such as parents, relatives, and friends. Deprived of this social network of support, partners may find it more difficult to maintain their union in times of crisis. Finally, the higher divorce rate among heterogamous marriages may reflect the fact that these partners are likely to be less conventional in their values and behavior. Such unconventional persons may divorce more readily if things begin to go wrong, rather than remain unhappily, though stably, married (Udry, 1974).

Generally speaking, social scientists in the past have concluded that the greater the differences between partners, the more likely it is that their marriage will be conflicted (Udry, 1974). These conclusions have found their way into textbooks as subtle advocacy of homogamy. Recent data has begun to challenge these conclusions, perhaps because in the last twenty years society has grown more tolerant of diversity. One recent study found that age heterogamy (including husbands older than their wives by eleven years and wives older by four years) has no affect on marital satisfaction (Berardo, 1985). See Box 6•1, "Choosing an Interreligious or Interclass Marriage," for a discussion of research findings regarding these two options.

Heterogamy and Human Values

In any case, it is important to note the difference between scientific information and values. Social science can tell us that the stability of heterogamous marriages may be lower than that of homogamous marriages, but many people do not want to limit their social contacts—including potential marriage partners—to socially similar people. While many people may retain a warm attachment to their racial or ethnic community, social and political change has been in the direction of breaking down those barriers. Persons committed to an open society find intermarriage to be an important symbol, whether or not it is a personal choice, and do not wish to discourage this option.

From this perspective one can think of the negative data on heterogamy and marital stability not as a discouragement to marriage, but in terms of its utility in helping couples to be aware of possible problems. Intermarrying couples such as John and Susie may anticipate and talk through the differences in their life-styles (especially if they take a social science course!).

The data on heterogamy may also be interpreted to mean that it is common *values* and *life-styles* that contribute to stability. A heterogamous pair may have common values that transcend their differences in background. One study of friendship patterns, for instance, found that of the two variables, race and values, common values were more significant in maintaining friendships. Whites and blacks were more apt to be friendly with persons of the *different* race who shared their values than with those of the *same* race who did not (Rokeach and Mezei, 1966).

Furthermore, some problems of interracial (or other heterogamous) marriages have to do with social disapproval and lack of social support from either race. But individuals can choose to work to change the society into one in which heterogamous marriage will be more accepted and hence will pose fewer problems. Then, too, to the degree that racially, religious, or economically heterogamous marriages increase in number, they are less likely to be troubled by the reactions of society. Again we see that private troubles—or choices—are intertwined with public issues; social changes are needed to make heterogamous marriages work. Finally, "it seems untenable . . . to assume that heterogamy can lead only to negative consequences for the marital relationship" (Haller, 1981:786). If people are able to cross racial, class, or religious boundaries and at the same time share some important values, they may open doors to a varied and exciting relationship.

DEVELOPING THE RELATIONSHIP

We have seen how homogamy and the fair exchange help to narrow the field from which people choose marriage partners. This doesn't explain the whole process, however. If it did, people would inevitably marry according to very predictable patterns.

At First Meeting: Physical Attractiveness and Rapport

Why is it that we can be so drawn to one person and so indifferent to another? One reason that has only recently been taken seriously by social scientists is physical attractiveness. Deny it as we might, our evaluations of others, even in our early years, are influenced by their appearance. Research shows that cute children are perceived by adults as less naughty, as well as brighter, more popular, and more likely to attend college, than are less attractive children (Dion, 1972; Dion and Berscheid, 1972; Clifford and Walster, 1973). The same assumptions influence adults' perceptions of one another. Both women and men tend to see more socially desirable personality traits in people who are physically attractive than in those who are less attractive (Middlebrook, 1974).

To find out how important looks are in a situation where two people meet for the first time, several social psychologists planned an experimental college dance. Students who came to the dance were under the impression that a computer had selected their dates on the basis of similar interests. In fact, they were assigned at random. During the dance intermission the students were asked how they liked their dates. For both females and males, physical attractiveness seemed to determine whether these students were satisfied with their dates (Walster et al., 1966). Physical attractiveness is especially important in the early stages of a relationship (Levinger and Snoek, 1972; Murstein, 1971).

Physical appeal and other readily apparent characteristics serve to attract persons to each other, to spark an interest in getting acquainted, which leads to an initial contact. But whether this initial interest develops into a prolonged attachment depends on whether they can develop rapport: Do they feel at ease with each other? Are they free to talk spontaneously? Do they feel they can understand each other? When two people experience rapport, they may be ready to develop a loving relationship. Common values appear to play an important role here, though whether in early stages or only throughout courtship is not clear. Couples also seem to be matched on sex drive and interest in sex (Murstein, 1980), suggesting that this is an important sorting factor.

The wheel theory of love (discussed in Chapter 3) explained the role of rapport in the development of a relationship. It suggests that mutual disclosure, along with feelings of trust and understanding, are necessary first steps. Relationships leading to marriage do not always show these characteristics, however. For example, a person may marry someone because of status or other benefits expected from the marriage. Or, because it presents a challenge, a person may continue a relationship with someone who discloses very little about her- or himself.

Some social scientists have wondered to what extent our courtship process has encouraged such patterns and has failed to facilitate the development of deeper, more intimate relationships. In the next section we discuss American **courtship,** contrasting formal dating with the process whereby a couple develops a mutual commitment to marriage, "getting together," and cohabitation.

COURTSHIP: GETTING TO KNOW SOMEONE AND GAINING COMMITMENT

As romantic love has come to be associated with marriage and parents no longer arrange their children's unions, responsibility for finding marital partners has fallen to individuals themselves. The courtship pattern that has evolved has two apparent purposes: First, romantic partners try to get to know one another better; second, they attempt to gain each other's progressive commitment to marriage.

These two purposes can be at odds. On the one hand, courtship is supposed to lead to self-disclosure and intimacy. On the other hand, gaining a partner's commitment to marriage often involves marketing oneself in the best possible package. Before we look at the most frequent patterns of courtship in our society today, we will examine this potential contradiction.

Imaging Versus Intimacy

Whom shall I marry? That question seems obviously to be about my choice, about one of the most important controls I shall establish over my life. The more researchers probe that question, however, the more they find a secret question, more destructive, more insistent, that is asked as well: Am I the kind of person worthy of loving? This secret question is really about a person's dignity in the eyes of others, but it involves self-doubt of a peculiar kind [Sennett and Cobb, 1974:63]. ■

Many people fear not being worthy of love—a fear that is often associated with low self-esteem, as we saw in Chapter 3. As courtship progresses, these people may feel anxious, and in response they may avoid self-disclosure rather than develop it. They may "put their best foot forward," in a process called **imaging,** projecting and maintaining a façade as a way of holding the other person's interest. It is likely that everybody practices imaging to some degree.

BOX 6·1

CHOOSING AN INTER-RELIGIOUS OR INTERCLASS MARRIAGE

How does marrying someone from a different religion or social class affect a person's chances for a happy union? In answer to this, we will first examine interfaith marriages, then look at interclass partnerships.

INTERRELIGIOUS MARRIAGES

Interreligious, or interfaith, unions are increasing in number. Still, sociologist Norval Glenn estimates that about 80 to 85 percent of today's marriages are religiously homogamous. This leaves about 15 to 20 percent that are between spouses with different religious preferences, such as Protestant, Catholic, and Jewish (Glenn, 1982). (Glenn considers unions between partners of different Protestant denominations as homogamous.)

Marriages are less homogamous if one considers partners' religions before the wedding. Put another way, many partners who originally differed in religion switched for the purpose of making their religions the same as their partners' (Glenn, 1982).

Some of this "switching," no doubt, took place because partners agreed with the widely held belief that interreligious marriages tend not to be as successful as homogamous ones. Exploring this question by means of statistical analysis, Glenn found that religious heterogeneity lessened marital satisfaction for husbands but not for wives. The accompanying table presents data on various combinations of marriages. While almost 73 percent of Protestant, Catholic, and Jewish males in homogamous marriages reported themselves as very happy, only 64 percent of intermarried males did so. The corresponding figures for females were, however, about 68 percent under both sets of circumstances. These differences held even when social class, age, age at marriage, marital history, and frequency of church attendance were taken into consideration.

Glenn speculates that a husband's marital happiness might be more affected because religious heterogeneity is more likely to result in religious differences between father and children; "persons who are not disturbed by their spouse's being of a different religion frequently may be disturbed by their children's being of a different religion, if only because it may relegate them to a kind of outsider or minority status in their own family" (Glenn, 1982:564). If the spouses are traditional, the husband may see a wife's refusal to change her religion to match his as a threat to his authority, while the wife does not expect this concession. The sex role ideologies of the spouses were not investigated in this study, however.

Glenn concludes that

as interreligious marriages become more frequent and socially accepted, any negative effects that they have on marital quality are likely to diminish. For instance, some of the problems encountered by interreligious couples evidently have grown out of the disapproval of family and friends; and as such disap-

Percentages of Married White Respondents in Religiously Homogamous and Heterogamous Marriages Who Said Their Marriages Were "Very Happy"

	Percentage "Very Happy"			
	Percentage of Males	N (number in category)	Percentage of Females	N (number in category)
Homogamous marriages				
A. All Protestants, Catholics, and Jews in homogamous marriages	72.5%	(2,106)	67.8%	(2,303)
1. Protestants married to Protestants	72.2%	(1,513)	68.3%	(1,627)
2. Catholics married to Catholics	73.0%	(548)	65.7%	(603)
3. Jews married to Jews	77.8%	(45)	74.0%	(73)
B. Persons with no religion married to persons with no religion	62.0%	(50)	59.4%	(64)
Heterogamous marriages				
A. All Protestants, Catholics, and Jews intermarried within the three major religious categories	64.3%	(241)	68.4%	(291)
B. 1. Protestants, Catholics, or Jews married to persons with no religion	58.6%	(29)	54.9%	(142)
2. Persons with no religion married to Protestants, Catholics, and Jews	61.4%	(132)	60.5%	(43)

SOURCE: Glenn, 1982:562, based on pooled data from six U.S. national surveys (General Social Survey) conducted in 1973–78 by the National Opinion Research Center.

proval diminishes, so should some of the disruptive influences on interreligious marriages [1982:564].

This is also true, as is pointed out elsewhere in this chapter, for interracial marriages.

(continued)

BOX 6 · 1
Continued

INTERCLASS MARRIAGES

Our society is stratified according to income and education, among other things. Such stratification influences mate selection because childhood experiences, shaped by parents and by educational and occupational experiences, affect both one's identity and one's expectations about love and marriage (Haller, 1981; Glenn et al., 1974). But there *are* interclass unions today. What about the marital satisfaction of the partners?

An often-cited study of marriage in urban Chicago (Pearlin, 1975) found that partners experienced more stress in these class-heterogamous unions. Moreover, the spouse who had married down was more stressed than the one who had married up.

It is important to note, however, that the relationship between stress and marrying down existed only when status-striving was important to the individual. Those persons for whom status was important and who had married down perceived their marriages more negatively, as less reciprocal, less affectionate, less emotionally supportive, and with less value consensus than those who had married up. In an exchange framework the partner who had married down had not struck a good bargain in an important area. For persons for whom status was *not* important, however, neither marrying up nor down produced any difference in their evaluation of their marriages.

Although this research does support earlier work suggesting marital difficulty among couples with status differences, it also contradicts the often-repeated assumption that differences in cultural background necessarily produce stress and conflict. While persons marrying up and persons marrying down encounter the same cultural differences, only those marrying down for whom social status is important experience related stress. Status inequality and heterogeneity in and of themselves do not create problems.

We need to add a note of caution here. Chapter 3, you may recall, addresses the need to know and accept oneself as a prerequisite to forming an intimate relationship with another person. Status-striving might sound like a negative characteristic and so be denied as a part of oneself, without much introspection. "Not me; I'm not into keeping up with the Joneses," one easily says. This may not be so true.

Psychotherapists George Bach and Ronald Deutsch illustrate how this happens, using conversations between "Susan" and "Paul" (who have dated twice in the last two weeks). Here they are making themselves comfortable in Susan's apartment:

PAUL: Say, this is neat. (He looks around.) And I like that Van Gogh print. He's one of my favorite artists.
SUSAN: Is he? Mine too. I don't know just what it is. The color and vitality, I guess.
PAUL: Yes, that's what it is.

SUSAN: (She starts to put records on her stereo.) What do you like, Paul? . . .

PAUL: Either one. (The music begins.) Why, I have that *same* album! (He beams with the discovery.)

SUSAN: Really? Mine is almost worn out. The first two bands, anyway. They really turn me on. . . .

PAUL: Right. It's the first two bands that made me buy the album. (Bach and Deutsch, 1970:43–44)

Clearly, Paul and Susan are intent on selling themselves. Both are imaging, but neither seems to realize that the other is doing so. "To both, the constantly appearing bits of likeness seem amazing" (Bach and Deutsch, 1970:44). When they do discover important differences, the way they handle them is worth noting:

SUSAN: Well, I don't think I want any [children]. You know, with all the overpopulation and that. . . .

PAUL: No children at all? . . .

SUSAN: Well, I saw what it did to my mother, how dependent it made her, how—helpless, and I don't know. . . .

PAUL: The right man wouldn't let that happen. . . .

SUSAN: I guess it really is an experience any woman would want to have. After all, one child, when she was in her thirties and she'd had time to do things. (Bach and Deutsch, 1970:46–47)

Here a basic difference in values and a source of potential marital conflict have been smoothed over in a matter of minutes, in order that courting (which is intended to uncover such differences!) can proceed.

People are tempted to image in any courtship process. Social scientists agree, however, that some courting practices encourage more imaging than others. In the next few sections, we will contrast three styles of courtship that are familiar to Americans today: the traditional ritual of dating, "getting together," and cohabitation.

Dating

The dating system emerged in our society at the beginning of the twentieth century, prevailed through the 1950s and early 1960s, became less popular in the late 1960s and early 1970s, and appears to have become popular again in the 1980s. At least into the 1960s, dating was to lead to marriage. Since everyone was expected to marry, the freedom of Americans to choose their own marital partners was accompanied by "demanded dating" (Mead, 1949:284).

Dating consists of an exclusive relationship developed between two persons through a formal series of appointed meetings. Dating relationships develop into marriage through a carefully orchestrated series of stages: going steady, informal engagement, formal engagement. Evolving, progressive commitment is expected, along with greater emphasis on sexual exclusivity (Libby, 1976:172).

A complex set of rules defines traditional dating. Males telephone females to ask them out. Once a female has dated a male a certain number of times, she often finds herself going steady by default. Other males respect her partner's territory and don't ask her out. If the couple gets along well, the relationship proceeds to engagement and marriage.

The traditional date is a fairly stylized process. The male picks up the female at her home at a certain time and drives to a movie, party, drive-in, or out to dinner, where he pays. He might make sexual advances, which the female may rebuff.

A recent study of college students at Appalachian State University in Boone, North Carolina, found that this pattern still exists. While we caution against overgeneralizing from this study, the results were nevertheless interesting. Responses by 130 male and female freshmen and sophomores indicated that male and female college students follow traditional gender roles in dating—the male is often expected to "pay," which he does with some resentment, and the female to "put out." These perceptions were reported for first dates, which seemed to be characterized by mistrust and uncertainty, with males and females falling back on traditional "games," but not very happy about it. The authors speculate that role-playing, exploitation, and mistrust fade as dating (with the same person) continues. They also think some degree of traditional strategizing remains (Milano and Hall, 1986).

There is evidence of change as well. Fifty-five percent of a sample of 400 college women reported paying for dates at least sometimes (Korman and Leslie, 1982). A study comparing feminist and nonfeminist women found that the former, as expected,

■ Getting to know you: On a first date, people are on their best behavior; subsequent dates are less aritifical. Did any of these three couples go on to marry each other? Yes, no, and maybe.

were more likely to share expenses on dates in both high school and college. But both sets of women perceived male sexual expectations in the same way: 62 percent of the feminists and 58 percent of the nonfeminists believed that men expected women "to engage in more sexual activity on dates than the women really desired when the men paid" (Korman, 1983:579). Only 23 percent of each group reported fulfilling these expectations.

While dating continues, the feminist movement and other social changes have transformed dating into a somewhat more egalitarian experience with some features of the pattern we have called "getting together." They also indicate considerable confusion, mistrust, and uncertainty about what rules and preferences are operating in a given situation. Such misunderstanding may contribute to "date rape" (although that can be a straightforward aggressive and exploitative act). Colleges and other groups are beginning to deal with this hazard of dating (see Box 6•2, "Date Rape").

In 1949 anthropologist Margaret Mead severely criticized the dating pattern that had emerged in the United States. She perceived the process not as one in which two persons genuinely try to get to know each other, but as a competitive game in which Americans, preoccupied with success, try to be the most popular and have the most dates. (Sociologist Willard Waller [1937] had termed this "rating and dating.")

Mead saw at least two major problems in dating. First, it encourages men and women to define heterosexual relationships as "situational," rather than ongoing. "You 'have a date,' you 'go out with a date,' you groan because 'there isn't a decent date in town'" (Mead, 1949:276). Because dating is formalized, women and men—even as they approach marriage—see each other only at appointed times and places. Partners look and behave their best during a date; they seldom share their "backstage behavior."[7]

Second, sex becomes depersonalized and genitally oriented, rather than oriented to the whole person. That is, the salient question becomes whether a couple "went all the way"—or whether the male is "getting any"—rather than how much emotional and sensual rapport partners share.

The ways in which men and women get to know each other have changed somewhat in the thirty years since Mead's insightful criticism. For one thing, an alternative script, which Libby (1976) terms "getting together," has emerged.

Getting Together

Getting together can be a courtship process in which, unlike dating, groups of women and men congregate at a party or share an activity. Getting together does not emphasize relating to one member of the opposite sex. From childhood individuals are encouraged to develop their own interests and to share them with others, regardless of gender. These expectations continue through junior high, high school, and after. Multiple relationships are encouraged without emphasizing the dichotomy between sexual and nonsexual relationships. In getting together, females play a similar role to males, initiating relationships and suggesting activities. Women may pay; they may also either meet men at a mutually convenient spot or pick them up (Libby, 1976). Meetings are often less formal than in the traditional date.

These changes in how women and men relate to each other are associated with changing attitudes toward marriage itself. In one significant change the pattern of getting together is not as closely oriented to marriage as dating was in the 1950s. Remaining single, at least for a good part of one's 20s, is a more attractive alternative for many people today. As a result people who are freed somewhat from the pressure to date and to marry can be more casual and spontaneous with each other. They are less likely to focus so intensely on their physical appearance and more likely to see each other in a variety of settings and moods (Murstein, 1986:67).

As a courtship process, getting together places less emphasis on the end result, marriage, than dating does. Ironically, this de-emphasis may be effective, as it allows persons to choose partners whom they really know and could be happily married to. A third process, which often allows partners to get to know each other even better, is **cohabitation:** living together without being married.

Cohabitation

We saw earlier that Margaret Mead was critical of the American tradition of dating. In 1966 she suggested an alternative that is worth describing here, for it shares many features with the popular pattern of cohabitation.

Mead's idea was what she called the **two-stage marriage.** As the name suggests, it consisted of two sequential types of marriage, each with a different license, different ceremonies, and different responsibilities. The first stage, called *individual marriage,* involved "serious commitment... in

---

7. Sociologist Erving Goffman (1959), in *The Presentation of Self in Everyday Life,* differentiates between people's front- and backstage behavior. Frontstage behavior is what we show the public; backstage behavior is more private. We can think of individuals' grooming rituals—shaving, doing their hair, applying makeup—as taking place backstage. They are preliminary preparations for meeting one's audience. Developing intimacy involves gradually allowing another person to see more of one's backstage behavior.

BOX 6 · 2

DATE
RAPE

At its 1985 national convention members of the national Pi Kappa Phi Fraternity unanimously adopted the following resolution:

STATEMENT OF POSITION ON SEXUAL ABUSE

WHEREAS we, the members of Pi Kappa Phi Fraternity, believe that the attitudes and behavior exhibited by members of the collegiate population have direct bearing on the quality of their present and future lives, and

WHEREAS there is an increased consciousness of sexual exploitation and violence and incidences thereof not just on the nation's college campuses but in society, and

WHEREAS the Greek community has stated its responsibility in leadership, scholarship, community service, human dignity and respect, and

WHEREAS Pi Kappa Phi is committed to excellence in the Greek community, and this requires us to identify and solve serious problems that prevent the growth and development of our brothers, and

WHEREAS Pi Kappa Phi strives to foster an atmosphere of healthy and proper attitudes and behavior towards sex and the sex roles, and wishes that the incidences of sexual abuse (mental and physical abuse—coercion, manipulation, harassment) between the men and women of the collegiate community be halted,

THEREFORE

BE IT RESOLVED that Pi Kappa Phi Fraternity will not tolerate or condone any form of sexually-abusive behavior (either physically, mentally or emotionally) on the part of any of its members, and

BE IT FURTHER RESOLVED that the Pi Kappa Phi Fraternity encourages educational programming involving social and communication skills, interpersonal relationships, social problem awareness, etiquette and sex-role expectations; and will develop a reward system to recognize chapters and individuals that lead in fostering a healthy attitude towards the opposite sex. ■

In addition to the resolution, the fraternity produced the poster pictured here and distributed it to chapters across the country. The illustration is a detail from the print "The Rape of the Sabine Women." Beneath the large message a smaller one reads: "Just a reminder from Pi Kappa Phi. Against her will is against the law."

"We focused on the problem of date rape because it is a problem which needs a greater awareness among both males and females," the fraternity's executive director explained.

Date rape or **acquaintance rape**—being invoved in a coercive sexual encounter—has emerged as an issue on college campuses over the past several years. Psychologists who deal with the problem agree that, while we are only

SOURCES:
Pi Kappa Phi Fraternity; Meyer, 1984:1, 12; *The Chronicle of Higher Education*, 1986.

(continued)

BOX 6 · 2

Continued

now acknowledging it, the phenomenon has plagued the dating scene for a long time—probably decades.

Available estimates suggest that more than 20 percent of college women are victims of rape or attempted rape. Most victims know their rapists. According to a survey at one large midwestern university, conducted by Kent State psychology professor Mary Koss, of those male students who said they had forced sex on a woman, 100 percent knew the victim.

According to Barry Burkhart, psychology professor at Auburn University, the phenomenon is prevalent because of "hidden norms" in society that condone sexual violence. That is, people have internalized gender roles according to which male aggression is acceptable. While rapists have typically been thought of as psychotics or criminals, Burkhart argues that research on acquaintance rape demonstrates that "normal" men are capable of rape. Other experts agree that date rape exposes commonly held attitudes among male students toward women, not aberrant behavior.

Findings about acquaintance rape point to the need to revamp many campus rape-prevention plans. Most campus intervention has focused on the much less frequent "stranger rape." While colleges have improved campus lighting and installed additional locks on dormitory doors to prevent rape by strangers, experts insist officials should also conduct seminars and discussions to educate students about acquaintance rape.

■ *What does the idea that "normal" men are capable of date rape or acquaintance rape say about gender roles today and whether, how, and how much they are changing? What does the response of the Pi Kappa Phi Fraternity to the date rape issue say about men? About gender roles today? How do you define rape? Chapter 7 addresses the issue of marital rape. How are marital and date rape alike, do you think? How are they different?*

which each partner would have a deep and continuing concern for the happiness of the other" (Mead, 1966:50). It limited responsibilities, however, for the couple agreed not to have children during this time. The second stage, *parental marriage,* would follow only if a couple decided that they wanted to continue their relationship and to share the responsibility of children.

Mead's proposal is very much like what has come to be known as *trial marriage,* a form of courtship in which couples live together to test and further develop their relationship before marrying.

Some Patterns of Cohabitation While some unmarried couples have chosen to live together in the past, growing acceptance of cohabitation is a recent development among the working and middle classes in our society (Newcomb, 1979). In April 1968, Linda LeClair, a Barnard College sophomore, made national headlines when she announced she had been living with a man off campus in violation of school regulations. Studies indicate that today as many as 80 percent of college students approve of cohabitation and would choose to live unmarried with someone of the opposite sex, given the

Figure 6·4

Unmarried couples living together in the United States, 1960–1986. (Sources: Glick and Norton, 1979, courtesy of the Population Reference Bureau, Washington, D.C.; U.S. Bureau of the Census, 1985b; 1986c)

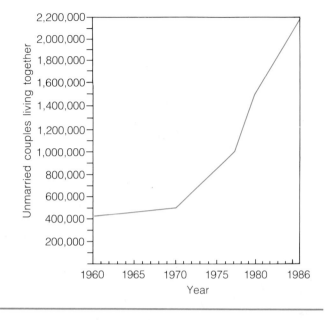

opportunity and the right partner (Macklin, 1983). Cohabitation has increased dramatically since 1960, slowing more recently, but reaching an all-time high in 1986 (see Figure 6·4). "There have been few developments relating to marriage and family life which have been as dramatic as the rapid increase in unmarried cohabitation" (Glick and Spanier, 1980).

The practice of cohabiting, however, is not nearly as widespread as the attitudes of college students or its relative increase might indicate. The Census Bureau estimates that in 1986 about 4 percent of all couples were living together unmarried (U.S. Bureau of the Census, 1986a). A nationwide sample of men age 20–30, drawn from Selective Service records, indicates that 82 percent of them have never cohabited for six months or longer. Blacks are three times as likely to cohabit as whites (Macklin, 1983).

Living together is also a more frequent occurrence in large cities, in the northeastern and western regions of the country, and among persons who are liberal in other respects (Clayton and Voss, 1977; Glick and Spanier, 1980). Cohabitants are less likely to attend church regularly (Macklin, 1983). They tend to be younger than married persons on the average; in one study 60 percent of cohabitants but only 30 percent of married persons were under age 30 (Yllo, 1978; Macklin, 1983) (see Table 6·4).

TABLE 6·4 Age of Cohabitants, 1984

Age	Women (%)	Men (%)
Under 25	26.6	18.8
25–34	44.2	46.2
35–44	11.4	17.8
45–64	9.3	13.2
65	8.3	4.0
Total	100.0%[a]	100.0%[a]
	N = 770,000[b]	N = 1,216,000[b]

SOURCE: U.S. Bureau of the Census, 1985b, Table 7, pp. 47–48. a. Percentages do not total 100.0% exactly, due to rounding error. b. N refers to the "householders" on which the percentages are based, for example, 770,000 women who have unrelated males living with them. The presumption is that unrelated adults of the opposite sex are living as couples, but the totals may also include some roommate or boarder situations.

TABLE 6·5 Nature of Relationship When Couple First Started Living Together for at Least Four Nights per Week, as Reported for Thirty-Five Cohabitation Relationships

Nature of Relationship	Number of Relationships
1. Formally engaged	1
2. Tentatively engaged (contemplating marriage)	3
3. Strong, affectionate relationship; not dating others ("going steady")	17
4. Strong, affectionate relationship, open to other dating relationships	12
5. Friends	1
6. Other ("met and immediately started living together")	1
Total	35

SOURCE: Macklin, 1972.

Despite its popular association with college life, cohabitation actually appears to be more common among young people who are not attending college (Clayton and Voss, 1977; Glick and Norton, 1979). But because so little research has been published on cohabitation, much of our information comes from intensive studies of small samples of college cohabitants.

In one of the first studies of this emerging phenomenon, social scientist Eleanor Macklin interviewed forty-four cohabitants at Cornell University during 1971. Macklin defined cohabitation as sharing a bedroom with someone of the opposite sex for at least four nights a week for at least three consecutive months. She found that women tend to move into men's apartments, although most women also maintained their own residence for several reasons. It was a place to return to if the relationship did not work out; it helped them maintain contact with their female friends; and it served as a convenient place to study and store things. (It also helped them avoid explaining their situation to parents.)

Reasons for Cohabiting Macklin's study also provided some information about why students live together. Most of them gave as a reason their desire for meaningful relations and their rejection of what they saw as the superficiality of dating. They pointed out that intimacy provided emotional satisfaction in the loneliness of a large university. Many were uncertain about marriage and wanted to try out a relationship before there was any question of permanency. As Table 6·5 shows, about half indicated that they had a strong and exclusive affectionate relationship. (Another third indicated they had a strong, affectionate relationship, but that they were also open to other relationships; a few couples indicated tentative engagement.)

Macklin's subjects perceived several benefits from their living together. They expressed a deeper understanding of themselves—their needs, expectations, and inadequacies—along with increased knowledge of what is involved in a relationship. Some believed that they had begun to clarify what they eventually wanted in marriage. They felt increased emotional maturity and self-confidence, and they also felt more able to understand and relate to others. The most obvious current benefit was companionship. Macklin concludes that "the pattern which is currently evolving appears to be primarily concerned with total relationships and only incidentally with sexual aspects" (1972).

In that sense it is an extension of getting together and a rejection of dating. In another study cohabitants also seemed to be motivated by the financial benefits of two living as cheaply as one. We have no way of noting the relative importance of this motive. It is apparent that cohabitants are financially less well off than the general population (Glick and Spanier, 1980).

Although cohabitation helps partners avoid the superficiality of dating, it does not alleviate all the problems of courting. When two researchers asked students their reasons for living together, they found that men's and women's goals continued to differ. Men were more likely to indicate sexual gratification as their reason, while women more often hoped cohabitation would lead to marriage (Arafat and Yorburg, 1973). Furthermore, it seems clear from Macklin's study as well as others that cohabitation is very often *not* trial marriage. (In another college campus study it was found that the cohabiting experience lasted less than three months for 82 percent of the men and 75 percent of the women [Peterman et al., 1974]). Viewed as courtship it may not be a very efficient means of gaining a partner's commitment to marriage. Estimates are that only about one-third of cohabitants eventually marry each other (Clayton and Voss, 1977). Engagement is a less reversible step toward marriage than is living together (Schulz and Rodgers, 1975).

Moreover, cohabiting does not always result from a well-considered choice. Like some of the decisions discussed in Chapter 1, it can also happen by default. As one college student explained, "It just got to be too much bother to go home every morning." When partners move in together without understanding each other's motives first, the result can be the "burden of misunderstood intentions, bitter recriminations, and self-destructive guilt" that Margaret Mead hoped to avoid.

Carl Ridley and his colleagues (1978) stress the importance of clarifying motivations and goals for cohabiting before the step is taken. They state that cohabitation can be an experience of some value as a preparation to marriage, either to test a particular relationship or to help the individual mature and become better able to sustain intimate relationships. On the other hand, cohabitation for the wrong reasons or for individuals who are not prepared can lead to "misunderstanding, frustration, and resentment" (Ridley et al., 1978:129). Box 6▪3, "Four Common Patterns of Cohabitation," describes a range of cohabiting motives and experiences. To some extent, "it's not whether you won or lost, but how you played the game" that counts in the success of a cohabitation arrangement.

Ridley and his associates also stress the importance of individuals being relatively independent before they decide to cohabit, having clear goals and expectations, and being sensitive to the needs of their partners. Experience in dating is essential, for it provides a prior relationship of some depth, though it does not involve cohabitation. Table 6▪6 presents some "concern" signs that, although directed to counselors, can serve as guidelines for individual decision making.

Cohabitation and Marriage

Cohabitation does not necessarily lead to marriage, of course, and some couples live together as an alternative to marrying, as we discuss in Chapter 7. If a cohabiting couple does decide to wed, however, how does having lived together affect their subsequent marriage? First, it does not appear that a couple's courtship is prolonged because the future marrieds choose to live together before their wed-

ding. Studies comparing couples who cohabited with those who did not indicate that about the same length of time elapsed between their first date and marriage. On the whole, moreover, research has found little difference in the marriages of those who cohabited before marrying and those who did not in terms of emotional closeness, satisfaction, conflict, equality, self-disclosure, commitment, marital satisfaction, and intimacy (Macklin, 1983).

Because different studies yield different, and sometimes contradictory, results, we can only conclude that the evidence thus far is equivocal as to whether cohabitation contributes to an ultimately happy marriage. It does not appear to operate as an effective screening device in partner selection. Nor does it appear to modify traditional gender roles (Newcomb, 1979). Its relative contribution as a general preparation for marriage is still an open question, not yet substantiated by research.

We have looked at dating, getting together, and cohabiting as courtship processes. Of course, in many real-life instances there are likely to be elements of each. A couple's courtship experience and their reasons for marrying do make a difference in their long-term happiness. For this reason, when couples find themselves drifting into a default decision to marry—through dating, cohabiting, or any other form of formal or informal courtship—they are wise if they stop, reconsider, and weigh the pros and cons. Box 6▪4, "How to Tell When He or She Is Wrong for You," provides some guidelines. Making a conscious decision about marrying increases the chances of *not* marrying, however, and of letting go of a special relationship, and that can be a painful experience. Before evaluating qualities that make for a happy marriage, we'll look briefly at the experience of ending courtship by breaking up.

Breaking Up

The popular songs "Breaking Up Is Hard to Do" and "Fifty Ways to Leave Your Lover" tell us how difficult it is to break off a romantic relationship. While breaking up is hard to do any time, breakups before marriage are generally less stressful than divorce. That was the conclusion of one study of breakups before marriage, in which social scientists queried a sample of college students in the Boston area. They found that about half of those who were dating someone exclusively in 1972 had broken up by 1975. Breakups were shown to occur

BOX 6 · 3

FOUR COMMON PATTERNS OF COHABITATION

In their review of research and clinical observation, Carl Ridley and his colleagues (1978) detected four common patterns of cohabitation: "Linus blanket," emancipation, convenience, and testing, which vary in their utility as training grounds for marriage.

LINUS BLANKET

This type of cohabiting relationship develops out of the dependence or insecurity of one of the partners, who prefers a relationship with *anyone* to being alone. This same insecurity, however, inhibits a mutual give-and-take and the open communication needed to resolve conflicts. The relationship often breaks down through the resentments built up in the stronger partner, who shoulders the planning and decision-making burden but feels constrained from criticizing his or her (usually his) fragile partner. Eventually, the strong partner explodes with resentment or buckles under the burden of the partner's inordinate need for reassurance. This relationship usually ends with the insecure partner worse off in terms of self-esteem, while the other is also unlikely to have had a constructive cohabiting experience.

EMANCIPATION

A series of short-term, repeated cohabiting relationships tends to be characteristic of those using cohabitation to gain independence from parental values and influence. Such persons are often Catholic females, seeking to be more emancipated sexually than is permitted by their parents or their faith, but who become overwhelmed with guilt and break off the relationship. They continue to repeat this pattern, which has little value as a relationship experience, since the unfinished business of gaining personal autonomy and clarifying sexual values interferes with the potential utility of the cohabiting experience. As we suggested in Chapters 2 and 3, needs for individual development and self-esteem must be met before successful relationships with others can be maintained.

more often between partners who were not equally involved in the relationship. Few breakups were mutual: Most were initiated by the person less involved, often at the beginning or end of a school year.

According to Hill and his associates, men tend to fall in love more readily than women, but women tend to fall out of love more readily than men (Hill et al., 1976). Women initiated 51 percent of the breakups, and men 42 percent. (Chances are far better for couples to remain friends when the man precipitates the breakup.) The social scientists suggest two explanations for women initiating breakups more often. First, a married woman's income and status are far more dependent on her husband than his are on her. Consequently, women must be especially discriminating, while men can afford to be more romantic. Second, women are

CONVENIENCE

The convenience relationship involves a man who is in a relationship primarily for sex and domestic maintenance and a woman who supplies loving care and who hopes, but dares not ask, for matrimony. This form of cohabitation can be easily dismissed as exploitive, hence destructive, but Ridley and his associates claim that it can be a useful experience. (The authors of this text are not quite convinced.) Their argument is that the male gains in terms of preparation for marriage, not only learning something about domestic living but also increasing his interpersonal skills.

What does the female gain? She learns "the idea of reciprocity—mutual giving and getting in a relationship. She can learn that unconditional giving can have limited long-range payoff and that assessments of what one is giving and getting are important in certain contexts" (Ridley et al., 1978:132). This is a useful lesson, since relationships may not continue if they are inequitable. Lack of assertiveness accompanied by pent-up resentment is, in the long run, as poor a strategy in a relationship as is the more obvious maximization of gain of the male. The partners are likely to part, older and wiser.

TESTING

This mode of cohabitation is what we think of when we view cohabitation as trial marriage. Two partners, relatively mature and with a clear commitment to test their already satisfying intimate relationship in a situation more closely resembling the marriage they tentatively anticipate, move in together. If all goes well, they get married. If all doesn't go well, they separate, but because of their preparation and skills in communication they are able to understand and assimilate the experience. It becomes a beneficial experience in their development and contributes to the success of the marriage they ultimately formalize.

Thus, Ridley and his associates see a variety of motives and relationships in cohabitation, some of which are useful preparation for marriage, and some of which provide little or no gain and some erosion of self-esteem.

more sensitive than men to the quality of interpersonal relationships. Hence, their criteria for developing love may be higher than men's. A woman may experience lack of rapport or self-revelation in a relationship, for example, while a man does not. As a result, women may evaluate and reevaluate their relationships more carefully.

Whatever the end results may be, the act of breaking up can be an ordeal; Box 6•5, "Breaking Up: Some Guidelines," can help minimize awkwardness and ill feelings.

To this point in the chapter, we have been discussing some of the events and motivations that bring a couple to marry or not to marry. The final section of this chapter will lay some of the groundwork for Parts III and IV of this text by looking ahead to see how these factors influence the long-term happiness and stability of marriage.

TABLE 6·6   *Should You Live Together?*

Counselor Questions	"Good" Signs and "Concern" Signs
1. Could you talk a little bit about how each of you came to the decision to live together?	*Good signs*: Each partner has given considerable thought to the decision, including the advantages and disadvantages of living together. *Concern signs*: One or both partners have given little thought to the advantages and disadvantages of living together.
2. Perhaps each of you could discuss for a minute what you think you will get out of living together?	*Good signs*: Each individual is concerned about learning more about self and partner through intimate daily living. Both wish to obtain further information about each other's commitment to the relationship. *Concern signs*: One or both partners desire to live together for convenience only. They want to live together to show independence from parents or peers.
3. Could each of you discuss what you see as your role and your partner's role in the relationship (e.g., responsibilities, expectations)?	*Good signs*: Each individual's expectations of self and partner are compatible with those of partner. *Concern signs*: One or both individuals have given little thought to the roles or expectations of self and/or partner. Individuals disagree in terms of their expectations.
4. Could each of you identify your partner's primary physical and emotional needs and the degree to which you believe that you are able to fulfill them?	*Good signs*: Each individual has a clear understanding of partner's needs and is motivated and able to meet most of them. *Concern signs*: One or both individuals are not fully aware of partner's needs. Individuals are not motivated or able to meet needs of partner.
5. Would each of you identify your primary physical and emotional needs in your relationship with your partner? To what degree have these needs been met in the past? To what extent are these needs likely to be met if the two of you were to live together?	*Good signs*: Each partner clearly understands his or her needs. Most of these needs are presently being met and are likely to continue to be met in a cohabiting relationship. *Concern signs*: One or both partners are not fully aware of their needs. Needs are not being met in the present relationship and are not likely to be met if the individuals live together.
6. Could each of you discuss what makes this relationship important to you? What are your feelings toward your partner?	*Good signs*: Partners care deeply for each other and view the relationship as a highly significant one. *Concern signs*: One or both individuals do not care deeply for their partner or do not view the relationship as a highly significant one. Partners have an emotional imbalance with one partner more involved in the relationship than the other.

Counselor Questions	"Good" Signs and "Concern" Signs
7. Could each of you explore briefly your previous dating experiences and what you have learned from them?	*Good signs*: Both individuals have had a rich dating history. Individuals have positive perceptions of self and opposite sex and are aware of what they learned from previous relationships. *Concern signs*: One or both partners have had minimal dating experience. Individuals have negative perceptions of self and/or of the opposite sex and do not seem aware of having learned from their prior relationships.
8. Perhaps each of you could talk for a minute about how your family and friends might react to the two of you living together?	*Good signs*: Each individual is aware of the potential repercussions of family and friends should they learn of the cohabiting relationship. Family and friends are supportive of the cohabiting relationship, or couple has considered how they will deal with opposition. *Concern signs*: One or both individuals are not fully aware of possible family and friends' reactions to their living together. Family and friends are not supportive of the cohabiting relationship.
9. Could each of you discuss your ability to openly and honestly share your feelings with your partner?	*Good signs*: Each individual is usually able to express feelings to partner without difficulty. *Concern signs*: One or both individuals have difficulty expressing feelings to partner or do not believe expressing feelings is important.
10. Could each of you discuss your partner's strengths and weaknesses? To what extent would you like to change your partner, relative to his or her strengths or weaknesses?	*Good signs*: Each individual is usually able to accept feelings of partner. Individuals are able to accept partner's strengths and weaknesses. *Concern signs*: One or both individuals are not able to understand and accept partner. Individuals have difficulty accepting partner's strengths and weaknesses.
11. How does each of you handle relationship problems when they occur? Can you give some examples of difficult problems you have had and how you have dealt with them?	*Good signs*: Both individuals express feelings openly and are able to understand and accept partner's point of view. Individuals are able to mutually solve problems. *Concern signs*: One or both partners have difficulty expressing feelings openly or accepting partner's point of view. Couple frequently avoids problems or fails to solve them mutually.

SOURCE: Ridley et al., 1978:135–36.

BOX 6·4

**HOW
TO TELL
WHEN HE
OR SHE
IS WRONG
FOR YOU**

SOURCE:
"J" (Joan Garrity), 1977.

Sometimes, people pretend to themselves that sexual desire, the fear of being alone, or the hope for financial and other social advantages can be turned into feelings of love. Before marrying, persons need to ask themselves the following questions about their partners:

1. *Does he or she have several close friends?* A person who has learned to enjoy and foster intimate friendships can put this talent to work in a marriage relationship. But if no one likes him or her well enough to be a close friend, shouldn't you wonder why *you* like him or her?
2. *Do you keep putting off introducing him or her to your friends and relatives? Does he or she put off introducing you to his or her friends and relatives?* Why? A hesitancy to show off a partner to those people who are most important to you may be a sign of uncertainty: Will the family and friends think it is a mistake?
3. *If the love relationship folded, would you still want to keep each other as friends?* For some lovers, this seems impossible. But the question here is whether the two people share enough respect and interests to want to be together even if no longer sexually intimate. Marriage involves companionship as well as sexual attraction.
4. *Do you spend most of your time trying to stay out of his or her bed?* A yes to this question can point up one of two problems: Either the "chemistry" just isn't there for you—and probably never will be—or your partner's emphasis on the importance of sex in an intimate relationship is considerably different from yours.

MARRIAGE: WHEN AND WHY

A couple's happiness in marriage frequently depends on when and why they married. In this section we will look first at the relationship between marital stability and age at marriage. Later we will discuss some reasons for marrying that are less likely than others to lead to happiness.

The Stability of Early and Late Marriages

In 1985 the median age for men at first marriage was 25.5; for women, 23.0 (U.S. Bureau of the Census, 1986a). Statistics show that marriages are more likely to be stable when partners are in their 20s or older. Marriages that occur when the woman is over 30 may be slightly more stable than those that take place in the 20s, but the really important distinction is between teenage and all other marriages (Norton and Moorman, 1987).

Teenage marriages are twice as likely to end in divorce as marriages of those in their 20s (Norton and Moorman, 1987). Social scientists generally maintain that people who marry young are less apt to be emotionally or psychologically prepared to select a mate or to perform marital roles (Lee, 1977:494). Low socioeconomic origins, coupled with school failure or lack of interest, are associated with early marriages (Elder and Rockwell, 1976:35). Higher fertility and economic deprivation are also associated with early marriages (Otto, 1979:117–18).

Age itself is probably not the key variable in

5. *Are you happy with the way he or she treats other people?* If he or she is condescending or rude—even physically violent—to others, you'll get the same treatment eventually. Watch how he or she deals with employees, waitresses, maids, salesclerks, parking-lot attendants, telephone operators, and so forth. Also, study his or her behavior with family members and close friends. If he or she doesn't treat them the way you want him or her to treat you, he or she is wrong for you. You may be an exception now, during courtship, but you won't be later.

6. *Do you know what he or she is like sexually?*

7. *Was your life stimulating and satisfying before you met her or him?* "Never, *never* bind yourself to someone because you need him or her to transform your unsatisfactory life into a super one."

8. *Do you often feel apprehensive about your future happiness together?* Little panics are normal, but they should be few and far between. If you are apprehensive more often than optimistic, this should serve as a warning signal.

9. *Are there taboo topics that you cannot discuss with each other?* Good relationships are built on trust, respect, spontaneity, and lack of stress. People are free to talk about almost anything. Even though they may hold very different views, not many subjects are taboo. Topics that have a bearing on the relationship are *never* taboo.

determining the likelihood of a marriage succeeding (Knox, 1975; Otto, 1979). Rather, it seems likely that one's age at marriage is associated with other elements contributing to marital instability, such as "parental dissatisfactions accompanying precocious marriage, social and economic handicaps, premarital pregnancy or the female's attitude toward the pregnancy condition, courtship histories including length of acquaintance and engagement, personality characteristics, and the rapid onset of parental responsibilities" (Otto, 1979:119; references deleted). According to one recent study, however, marrying before age 20 remained a significant predictor of divorce even after all these factors were statistically controlled for or taken into consideration. Respondents often mentioned sexual infidelity as reason for conflict. As a result, the researchers hypothesized that teens who marry

do so when their unmarried peers are experimenting sexually with more than one partner and before they are emotionally ready or willing to relinquish this behavior. In the words of the researchers,

[I]t is striking that the role performance variable which best accounts for instability has to do with a lack of sexual exclusiveness. What is intriguing is that this perceived problem coincides with the peak in sexual interest, especially among males, hinting at the possibility that part of the instability experienced may have a biosocial origin. Perhaps individuals constrained to limit their sexual activity to a single individual at a time in their life when variety is important develop a pattern of acting out their impulses throughout much of their life [Booth and Edwards, 1985:73]. ■

BOX 6 · 5

BREAKING UP: SOME GUIDELINES

Sociologist David Knox, Jr., author of *Marriage: Who? When? Why?* (1975), offers the following guidelines for ending a relationship:

1. Decide that terminating the relationship is what you really want to do. "This necessitates careful thought, and implies that the alternative to breaking up is to improve your relationship."
2. Assuming you have definitely determined to break up, prepare yourself for the "phone-booth response." Knox explains from his own experience:

After having been formally engaged to a girl for nine months, I decided to terminate the relationship. The day after I had told her that it would be best that we not continue the relationship (translate, I wanted out), I became extremely anxious and upset. . . . To alleviate my misery, I walked to a phone booth near my apartment, placed a dime in the appropriate slot, and called my ex-girlfriend with the hope of reestablishing the relationship. I received a busy signal. I took this busy signal to be a "message from the gods" that I was to get out of the phone booth and try to calm myself so as not to call her again.

This phone-booth response is typical of the reaction which occurs after a relationship is terminated. Immediately following the termination of a reinforcer (girlfriend or boyfriend), misery, unhappiness, and a frustrated feeling of loneliness occur. One way to reduce temporarily the unpleasant feeling is to reestablish the relationship. . . . After the exciting make-up period is over, [how-

SOURCE:
Knox, 1975:143–45.

Although one's age at marriage in only one factor contributing to marital stability or instability, age still is associated with maturity, and Knox isolates four elements of maturity that he does consider to be critical: emotional, economic, relationship, and value maturity (Knox, 1975).

Emotional Maturity The emotionally mature person has high self-esteem, which permits a greater degree of intimacy and interdependence in a relationship, as we saw in Chapter 3. Emotional maturity allows people to respond appropriately to situations. When conflict arises, emotionally mature people aim to resolve it, rather than becoming defensive or threatening to end the relationship.

Economic Maturity Economic maturity implies the ability to support oneself and a partner if necessary. Especially for teenagers who have had little formal training or other job preparation, economic problems can put heavy strains on a marriage. Without a decent wage people's physical and emo-

tional energy can be drained as they try to scrape together enough to live on. Developing a loving relationship under these conditions is extremely difficult.

Relationship Maturity Relationship maturity involves the skill of communicating with a partner. People with this kind of maturity are able to (1) understand their partner's point of view, (2) make decisions about changing behavior a partner doesn't like, (3) explain their own points of view to their partner, and (4) ask for changes in their partner's behavior when they believe this is appropriate. Without the willingness and skills to understand each other and to make themselves understood, it is difficult or impossible for a couple to maintain intimacy.

Value Maturity Value maturity allows people to recognize and feel confident about their own personal values. By their mid-20s most people have developed a sense of their own values. A high school

ever,] the likelihood of reexperiencing the same unhappy relationship is great. This is because issues which led to the breakup of the relationship usually are not resolved during the makeup period [143–44].

3. A third guideline is to plan the discussion at a location from which you can readily withdraw. Knox points out, for instance, that the drive-in theater is a poor choice—the ride home is "unbearable."

4. Explain your reasons for breaking up in terms of your own values. For example, a senior woman majoring in religion told her boyfriend that she wanted to marry a practicing Christian, "which her pot-smoking, agnostic [boyfriend] was not" (Knox, 1975:145). Rather than tell him she didn't love him any more, she told him their values were different.

5. Make the break final. While research (Hill et al., 1976) shows that couples can break up and remain friends, Knox suggests that hoping for a "let's be friends" type of relationship can be problematic. It's too easy for one or both partners to expect too much from the continued contact.

6. Seek out new relationships.

Numbers 5 and 6 are also good advice for those who've recently been broken up with.

---

senior or a first-year college student, however, may still have a number of years of testing and experiencing before he or she reaches value maturity. (As we saw in Chapter 3, however, these values may change considerably in adulthood.)

Age, then, is an important variable in determining a relationship's potential for success. We can measure both age and homogamy objectively; that is, statistics can tell us how the factors of race, religion, age, and so forth relate to marital stability. Other factors are more subjective, for they relate to the explanations people give for marrying a certain person, but these reasons are also associated with the success of a relationship.

Reasons for Marrying

The reasons people give for marrying are far more complex than "because we were in love." It is a combination of many complicated situations and needs that motivates people to marry. We'll look at several common reasons—first, those that are less likely to lead to a stable marriage; and second, more positive reasons—and see how each relates to the probability of a marriage's success (Knox, 1975: 134–48).

Premarital Pregnancy One problematic reason for marriage is premarital pregnancy. Research indicates a consistent relationship between premarital pregnancy and unhappiness in marriage (for example, Norton and Moorman, 1987). Ironically, as one study shows, teenage women who married to avoid single parenthood often found themselves to be single parents after all, as 60 percent of the marriages had broken up after six years (Furstenberg, 1976). Research indicates that for both black and white couples, a premarital birth is most associated with subsequent marital breakup, followed by premarital pregnancy and no premarital pregnancy, in that order (Glick and Norton, 1979; Teachman, 1983).

There are several reasons for such unhappiness

or failure. First, the marriage is forced to occur at a time not planned. Often, pregnant brides are teenagers. At least two-thirds of all first births to teenagers were conceived out of wedlock. About 25 percent of teenage first births are legitimated by marriage prior to birth (U.S. Bureau of the Census, 1986b). Second, babies are expensive, and a couple not financially prepared for the costs can be overwhelmed. Third, "babies shatter goals": Teenage parents, for example, are less likely to attain educational goals, whether high school or beyond; and they are more likely to have lower incomes and occupational status, to have more children than they would like, and to go on welfare (Furstenberg, 1976; Alan Guttmacher Institute, 1976; Moore, 1978; Card and Wise, 1978). Fourth, the in-law relationship may be marred if parents resent their child's marital partner for having brought about a marriage they did not want or viewed as too early (Knox, 1975). Finally, the couple may not ever have decided they were compatible enough for marriage and may resent each other, either overtly or subconsciously, during the marriage. Of course, other options—abortion, giving the child up for adoption, or raising the child as a single parent—also have an impact on the lives of the young couple. And values and emotions may vary widely among individuals. Still, it is difficult to be encouraging about young, pregnancy-inspired marriages, and some churches have been reluctant to sanction them unless the young couple is unusually mature.

There are certainly exceptions to this scenario. Factors that reduce the damaging effects of pregnancy-inspired or teenage marriage include having a supportive family (giving both financial and emotional support), being able to remain in school and then become steadily employed, controlling further fertility, and being older when the pregnancy occurs (Furstenberg and Crawford, 1978; Presser, 1978). One study (Freedman and Thornton, 1979) found that families that had begun with a pregnancy had caught up in most respects after fifteen years. But this recoupment took place in a period of financial expansion, and the study was limited to whites, many older than teenagers, who married before the birth—so it cannot be generalized regarding many of today's premaritally pregnant young people.

Rebound Marriage on the rebound occurs when a person marries very shortly after breaking up another relationship. To marry on the rebound is undesirable because the wedding occurs as a reaction to one's previous partner, rather than being based on real love for the partner.[8]

Rebellion Marriage for the sake of rebellion occurs when young people marry primarily because their parents disapprove. Social-psychological theory and research show that parental interference can increase feelings of romantic attraction between partners (Brehm, 1966; Driscoll et al., 1972); this has been called the *Romeo and Juliet effect*. As with marriage on the rebound, the wedding is a response to someone else (one's parents) rather than to one's partner.

Escape Some people marry to escape an unhappy home situation. The working-class male who hasn't gone to college, for instance, may reason that getting married is the one way he can keep for himself any money he makes instead of handing it over to his parents. Or, denied the opportunity to go away to college, working-class youth often use marriage as an escape from parental authority (L. Rubin, 1976:57).

Physical Appearance Marrying solely because of the physical attractiveness of one's partner seldom leads to lifelong happiness. For one thing, beauty is "in the eye of the beholder," and if the beholder finds he or she really doesn't like the partner, that beauty is certain to diminish. Second, the physical beauty of youth changes as partners age. The person who married for beauty often feels she or he has been cheated. After a time, there is little left to be attracted to and love (Berscheid and Walster, 1969).

Loneliness Sometimes people, especially older adults, marry because they don't want to grow old alone. Marrying is not always the solution, for people can be lonely within marriage if the relationship isn't a strong one. In other words it is the relationship rather than the institution that banishes loneliness.

Pity and Obligation Some partners marry because one of them feels guilty about terminating

---

8. Actually, people may tend to fall in love more easily when they're on the rebound. Sociologist Elaine Walster (1965) experimented with the concept of love on the rebound. She concluded that when people have low self-esteem, due to having been broken up with, they may be less discriminating in choosing love partners and may fall in love more easily.

I keep thinking where we went wrong. We have no one to talk to now, however, I will not allow this loneliness to destroy me,— I STILL HAVE MY DREAMS. I would like an elegant home, a loving husband and the wealth I am used to.

Countess Vivianna de Blonville.

■ The Countess looked at this picture and thought only about her choices—where she went wrong. Is it just the loving husband she hasn't had?

a relationship: A sense of pity or obligation substitutes for love. Sometimes this pity or obligation takes the form of marrying in order to help or to change a partner, as when a woman marries a man because she believes that her loyal devotion and encouragement will help him quit drinking and "live up to his potential." Such marriages don't often work: The helper finds that his or her partner won't

change so easily, and the pitied partner comes to resent being the object of a crusade.

Social Pressure As Chapter 5 points out, parents, peers, and society in general all put pressure on singles to marry. The expectations built up during courtship exert a great deal of social pressure to go through with the marriage. As engagements are announced or as people become increasingly identified as a couple by friends and family, it becomes more difficult to back out. Still, breaking an engagement or a less formal commitment is probably less stressful than divorcing later or living together unhappily.

Economic Advancement Marrying for economic advancement occurs in all social classes. Young divorced mothers may consider remarriage primarily because they are exhausted from the struggle of supporting and caring for their small children; and working single women often associate marrying with the freedom to stay home at least part of the time. Men, too, can marry for reasons of economic advancement. This can be especially true in some professions where social connections provide important business ties. In the words of one executive, marrying the right woman "open[s] up doors in the same way as going to the right college" (in Cuber and Harroff, 1965:82–83).

Is marrying for economic advancement the right reason? The answer depends on the individuals. After a few years some spouses reevaluate their utilitarian reasons for marrying and wish they had emphasized the quality of their relationship. Other couples remain satisfied with their marriages and the partners they chose. A person going into a marriage mainly for economic reasons should be very honest with her or his partner, so that both know what the marriage means to the other.

More Positive Reasons for Marrying We have seen that rebounding, rebellion, escape, physical appearance, loneliness, obligation, and social pressure are all unlikely bases for a happy marriage. What are some positive reasons? Knox (1975) lists three: companionship, emotional security, and a desire to parent and raise children.

Marriage is a socially approved union for developing closeness with another human being. In this environment, legitimate needs for companionship—to love and to be loved by someone else—can be satisfied. Marrying for emotional security implies that a person seeks the stable structure of marrying to help ensure the maintenance of a close interpersonal relationship over time. Although most people do not marry only to have children (and this alone may *not* be a positive reason for marrying), many regard children as a valuable part of married life. "The benefits of love, sex, companionship, emotional security, and children can be enjoyed

without marriage. But marriage provides the social approval and structure for experiencing these phenomena with the same person over time" (Knox, 1975:143).

In Chapters 7 and 8 we will examine the influence of marriage as an institution on intimate relationships. It seems to us, however, that the most positive motivation toward marriage involves the goal of making permanent the relationships of love and intimacy, as was discussed in Chapter 3. This theme will be repeated throughout Part Three, "Defining Your Marriage and Family."

Summary

Americans have been used to thinking of love and marriage as going together like a "horse and carriage," but this association is virtually unique to our modern culture. Historically, marriages were often arranged in the marriage market, as business deals. Many elements of the basic exchange (a man's providing financial support in exchange for the woman's child-rearing capabilities, domestic services, and sexual availability) remain, although women may be losing some of their "currency" as society changes.

What attracts people to each other? Two important factors are homogamy and physical attractiveness. Some elements of homogamy are propinquity, social pressure, feeling at home with each other, and the fair exchange. Three patterns of courtship familiar in our society are dating, getting together, and cohabitation.

Besides homogamy and the degree of intimacy developed during courtship, two other factors related to the success of a marriage are a couple's age at marriage and their reasons for marrying. People who marry too young are less likely to stay married; and there are several negative reasons for marrying that can lead to unhappiness or divorce.

If potential marriage unhappiness can be anticipated, breaking up before marriage is by far the best course of action, however difficult it seems at the time. A certain number of courting relationships will end in this fashion.

But many couples will go on to marry. Part Three describes which form the marriage is likely to take and some choices the couple makes in setting up their marriage. Part Four discusses some of the basic dimensions of marriage.

Key Terms

courtly love *183*	exogamy *188*
dowry *184*	heterogamy *191*
exchange theory *184*	hypergamy *191*
pool of eligibles *188*	dating *199*
homogamy *188*	getting together *201*
endogamy *188*	cohabitation *201*

Study Questions

1. Explain how our notion of romantic love came about.
2. How are modern marriages similar to arranged marriages? How are they different?
3. Compare the way we choose marriage partners with the process at a marketplace. Why do women in the marriage market tend to be more serious shoppers than men?
4. Give four reasons people are likely to be homogamous. What difficulties are people in heterogamous relationships likely to face?
5. Why, do you think, are homogamous marriages more stable than heterogamous marriages? Does this necessarily mean that homogamous marriages are more successful? Why or why not?
6. Explain why the two aspects of courtship—getting to know each other better and gaining commitment to marriage—are a potential contradiction.
7. Why did Margaret Mead (1949) criticize the dating pattern that had emerged in the United States? What problems did she think were caused by dating? Do we still face these problems today?
8. Differentiate the four common patterns of cohabitation put forth by Ridley and his associates. Which are more useful as training grounds for marriage? Why?
9. Do you agree with Knox's idea that age itself is not the key variable in determining a marriage's likelihood of succeeding? Describe what Knox considers to be critical.
10. Do you agree with Booth and Edwards that age itself *may* be a key variable in determining marital stability, due to a biosocial understanding of sexuality?
11. Discuss some problematic and more positive reasons for marrying, and how each relates to the probability of a marriage's success.

Suggested Readings

Bach, George R., and Ronald M. Deutsch
1970 *Pairing.* New York: Avon.
   Psychoanalyst Bach founded the Institute of Group Psychotherapy in Beverly Hills, California. This interesting and readable paperback tells something of his work there and explores intimate "pairing" as an alternative to traditional courtship, in which partners always "put their best foot forward" in an effort to "sell themselves."

Kaplan, Marion A.
1985 *The Marriage Bargain: Women and Dowries in European History.* New York: Harrington Park Press.
   This collection of five essays by social and family historians explores the relationships between dowries and economic conditions, and between dowries and women's rights and position in society. It offers significant insights into the historical functions of marriage.

Knox, David
1975 *Marriage: Who? When? Why?* Englewood Cliffs, N.J.: Prentice-Hall.
   This practical text is written particularly for young-adult, unmarried college students. It uses social-scientific research findings to answer the questions in the title.

Luker, Kristin
1975 *Taking Chances: Abortion and the Decision Not to Contracept.* Berkeley and Los Angeles: University of California Press.
   This book examines reasons for women's willingness to take contraceptive risks. Among other things, it explores the perceived benefits of pregnancy and sees women's willingness to chance pregnancy outside marriage as one result of their diminishing currency in today's marriage market.

Murstein, Bernard
1986 *Paths to Marriage.* Beverly Hills, Calif.: Sage.
   Well-written social science on dating, courtship development, love, and theories of marital choice.

Nye, F. Ivan
1979 "Choice, exchange, and the family." In Wesley Burr et al., *Contemporary Theories About the Family.* New York: Free Press.
   Article summarizing research in an exchange framework and developing an exchange theory of the family.

Staples, Robert
1978 "The black dating game." In Robert Staples (ed.), *The Black Family: Essays and Studies,* 2d ed. Belmont, Calif.: Wadsworth.
   In this essay Staples, a black social scientist, discusses courtship as it applies to black Americans.

III Defining Your Marriage and Family

Nursery rhymes typically end with the hero's choosing a spouse. As children, we probably assumed there wasn't much to tell after that. But people now recognize that even after the wedding ceremony partners continue to make choices about their marriage and family.

Defining one's own marriage and family involves choosing what family will take: Will it be (for example) dual-career, communal, extended, or nuclear? Besides creating their own family form or structure, partners choose, either consciously or by default, what kind of marital relationship they will have.

Chapter 7 examines the family as combining the traditional and the new. We'll see that originally families filled physical needs by providing food, clothing, and shelter. Families continue to help provide these basic necessities, but people are no longer as dependent on families for their livelihood. One result is that they feel freer to experiment with family structure, and the family becomes more flexible. The family today shows flexibility in its transition from a basically patriarchal institution to a more democratic one. Chapter 7, along with much of Part Four, addresses this area of change.

Just as deciding on a satisfying family form requires making choices, so does creating a mutually satisfying marital relationship. Chapter 8 explores some aspects of making knowledgeable choices about one's marriage relationship. As we have seen, a marriage today is made up of two continually changing individuals, each hoping to get most of his or her emotional needs met. In Chapter 8 you'll see that one creative way to meet this challenge is for couples to take time to discuss and then write a "personal marriage contract." We talk about how to begin such a process, and what kinds of issues to consider.

A recurring theme in many of these chapters is communication. Chapter 9 discusses communicating about conflicts and notes that partners can ignore conflicts, fight in alienating, hurtful ways, or try to fight fairly. Being able to fight openly and fairly requires that the husband and wife have a fairly equal amount of power in their relationship, a topic much discussed since the revival of the women's movement in the 1960s. Chapter 10 explores the role of power in marriage.

7 The Family: A Flexible Institution

Life does not give itself to one who tries to keep all its advantages at once. I have often thought morality may perhaps consist solely in the courage of making a choice.

LEON BLUM, *On Marriage*

I n the past, Judeo-Christian tradition, the law, and general cultural attitudes converged in a fairly common expectation about what form the American family should take. The "natural" family was considered to be nuclear in form and to consist of two monogamous heterosexual parents and their children. Husbands were breadwinners; wives, homemakers.

In the past two decades, however, this pattern has become less rigid. The family remains a social institution that fulfills essential group needs in all cultures. But the family in the United States today has become a more flexible institution.

This chapter examines the contemporary fam-iliy's flexibility in two respects: First, the family is moving from a traditional patriarchal institution toward a democratic one; second, the forms that families take today are more diverse. The chapter ends with a discussion of "living together" as an alternative family form. To begin, we will look at the family as a social institution.

THE FAMILY AS A SOCIAL INSTITUTION

Social scientists use the term *institution* differently than do people in ordinary conversation. In everyday language an institution might be a uni-versity or a prison or a hospital, but in the social sciences the term *institution* has broader connotations. **Social institutions** are patterned and predictable ways of thinking and behaving—beliefs, values, attitudes, and norms—concerning important aspects of our lives. They are organized around vital aspects of group living and serve essential functions in society. The major social institutions are religion, economics, government, education, and the family. In all cultures, and in dramatically different ways, the institution of the family performs critical functions.

Structure-Functional Theory[1]

This approach—emphasizing functions in society—to the study of the family is called *structure-functionalism*. Here we look at the family from the point of view of society. What does it take for a society to exist? What needs must be met for societal survival? How does society—and, from our point of view, the family—meet these needs?

These needs, called *functional requisites*, include providing new members for the society,

---

1. We use the term *theory* loosely in this text, to indicate conceptual analysis of the family. Strictly speaking, most conceptual frameworks for the study of the family do not meet the criteria of a scientific theory (Broderick, 1971).

■ Portraits of the family: There are exceptions to any generalization, but "all family portraits depict happy families" is true more often than not. Marion and Bernie Kaminski vacation with their three children at the family cabin in 1968. (Marion is the daughter of the bride in the Prologue's wedding portrait.) Lynda and Joe lived together for twelve years before marrying and having children. On his wedding day, the oldest son in the Roberts family is joined by his brothers and sisters and their children. In 1935, the children of Agnes and Michael Gaspar arranged a celebration of their parents' twenty-fifth wedding anniversary. Matthew and Lucy Anderson and their children are a picture of middle-class prosperity at the turn of the century.

Frances B. Johnston, *A Hampton Graduate at Home*, 1899–1900.
Platinum print, 7½ × 9½″.
Collection, The Museum of Modern Art, New York. Gift of Lincoln Kirstein.

training them to become useful and loyal members of the society, providing a material base for the society, and so on (see Suggested Readings for sources of more information about this theory). Various institutions of a society meet these needs.

One of the features of structure-functional theory is that it tends to abstract a particular family structure as *the* pattern in the society, obscuring the real variation that exists. Many families in our society depart from the nuclear family pattern. When half of the families in a society contain no children under 18, and almost one-fourth of families with children contain only one parent, one has

to wonder to what extent structure-functional analysis is useful when it depicts the American family as nuclear (Parsons and Bales, 1955; Goode, 1963).

There is also a tendency in structure-functional analysis to take the dominant family pattern as normative, that is, as "good," or "functional," for society. By implication, other family structures are deviant or harmful to society. Critics of structure-functional theory have pointed out these limitations, and social scientists, policymakers, and textbook authors are now quite aware of possible bias. In this text our intention is to treat alternative forms as viable choices rather than oddities or departures from the "normal."

If one is aware of these biases, structure-functional theory can be quite a useful tool when examining the variety of family forms in various cultures or groups and when analyzing the functions performed by the family.

The Functions of the Family

Social scientists have compiled several slightly different lists of family functions, depending on the societies they are studying and on their own interpretations. We will examine the most basic functions in an advanced industrial society such as ours. These include primary responsibility for bearing and rearing children, providing economic security and a domicile for members, and giving members emotional security.

Responsible Reproduction A primary function of the family is to provide "social control of reproduction and child rearing" (Cherlin, 1978:634). To perform this function of caring for children, it has been assumed that two parents are better than one. To our knowledge, no known society has yet encouraged reproduction outside the family setting,[2] and this holds true in our society as well. While almost one-quarter of American births today are to single women, the universally approved locus of reproduction remains the family.

Parents, whether single, divorced, or married, are expected not only to care for their children but also to be responsible for their children's moral and intellectual development. The family, in other words, is primarily responsible for children's socialization.

This does not mean that the family is the *only* socializer. In contemporary American society schools, churches, and recreational agencies or clubs such as Girl or Boy Scouts participate in this socialization. Schools depend on parents, for example, to motivate and support the learning that takes place in the classroom. (Guiding children's devel-

opment remains a central function of the family, as is discussed in detail in Chapter 13.)

Economic Support A second universal family function is economic support. For much of history the family was primarily an economic unit rather than an emotional one (Shorter, 1975; Stone, 1980). Even today almost every family engages in activities aimed at providing for such practical needs as eating, acquiring clothes, and finding shelter. By assisting one another in these functions, family members create some sense of physical security. Marriage has, in fact, been defined as "primarily an economic matter, an arrangement of cooperation in the service of self-maintenance" (Sumner, in Winch, 1952:55).

Historically, the family has often come close to being a **self-sufficient economic unit**, in which family members cooperatively produce what they consume. The typical American rural family of the eighteenth century, for example, produced far more of its own food, clothing, and housing than does the modern family.

The relatively high degree of self-sufficiency in the early rural family depended on cooperation. Likewise, in the crafts and shops of the growing cities and in the early home- and factory-based industries, family members worked together as a productively interdependent unit (Tilly and Scott, 1978). This interdependency was reflected in mate selection: Choosing a mate meant choosing a business partner. Health, energy, abilities, and industry were all important—and highly practical—qualities. Even among the wealthy classes of Europe and America, choosing a mate was more pragmatic than romantic. Marriage was a means of furthering one's economic, political, or social positions (Stone, 1980).

Family living has become less an economic necessity in modern America, as the 85 percent increase in single-person households between 1970 and 1981 indicates (23 percent of households today are single-person ones). But today, too, families have economic implications; the family economy of shared income and expenses helps one achieve financial security. With the rise in both unemployment and underemployment, along with the higher cost of living and the greater number of working women, a more recent kind of **economic interdependence** has become apparent. Today more than half of all married women are employed outside their homes. By pooling their earning power,

---

2. This doesn't mean that all (or even most) societies condemn premarital intercourse or conception. Frequently, in fact, a couple doesn't marry or isn't formally considered to be married until after the woman becomes pregnant (Malinowski, [1930] 1974).

wives and husbands maintain a standard of living that neither could achieve alone. Conversely, many single-parent households supported by a female breadwinner are slipping into poverty (see Chapter 16).

Furthermore, contemporary spouses can provide unemployment insurance for each other, mutually assuring that if one is unable to work—because of long illness, the desire to change jobs or careers, or the desire to stay home with children—the other will support both of them.[3] And family living helps ensure economic support for older wives, often untrained and lacking sufficient work experience to compete for good-paying jobs outside the home. (The growing problem of displaced homemakers––housewives who lose their means of economic support––is addressed in Chapter 16).

The functions of reproduction and economic survival have changed with modernization. Then, too, modernization has caused a third family function to become important. In the impersonal world we live in, the family has grown more important as a source of emotional security.

Emotional Security   People today are not closely tied to a small village or urban neighborhood as they might have been in the past. They may move around, sometimes quite far. Work takes place away from the household, in a relatively impersonal setting, and many of the contacts in everyday life are likewise quite impersonal. Private life in the family becomes very important in meeting needs for human contact and emotional involvement (Berger et al., 1973).

The family acts to provide emotional security by countering family members' feelings of isolation and giving them a sense of belonging. In one writer's words families are now expected to create a "protective blanket of care and concern for their members" (Kapel, 1978). This is not to say that families can solve all our longings for affection, companionship, and intimacy, for they cannot. (Frequently, the family situation itself is a source of competition, as we'll discuss at greater length in Chapters 9 and 10). Nor is it true that spouses

never experience loneliness, or that they can possibly fill all of each other's emotional needs.

Realistically, marriage and the family can't fulfill all emotional needs, but they can offer members some degree of emotional security. "I don't care what anybody says," said a wife and mother, married eighteen years and now partner in business with her husband. "I think marriage is the way to go. It's having a place where you can be yourself, even sometimes your worst self, and still belong."

This woman speaks specifically of marriage, but her words also apply to the family. And while we have been accustomed to thinking of ourselves as a society of nuclear families, her description also applies to many extended families. The broader family network—grandparents, grown sisters and brothers, aunts and uncles—is often an important source of emotional support. This is especially true in times of crisis, as we'll see in Chapter 15, but it is also important from day to day. In a society where people rarely stay in the same neighborhood all their lives (and even if they do, the neighborhood is sure to change), families may take on growing importance as the one place where an individual will always "belong."

While providing emotional security grows more important as a family function, changes in family roles and forms are also taking place. We'll look at these two important dimensions of change throughout the rest of this chapter.

CHANGING ROLES: FROM PATRIARCHY TO DEMOCRACY

We looked at some aspects of patriarchy in Chapter 2 and saw that its basic focus is on the concept of male dominance and the male line of descent.[4] The

---

3. Family members care for one another in other practical ways, too. Families engage in preliminary diagnosis of illness, for example, and nurse and medicate their members. How families today go about the practical aspects of everyday living is explored in Chapters 11 and 14.

4. The term *patriarchal* describes the authority (including the right to respect from others and the right to make decisions) that is vested in males, particularly older males, in a family and society. Although we are not placing great emphasis on kinship terminology in this text, we want to distinguish the term *patriarchal* from the associated terms *patrilineal* (which refers to inheritance and tracing kinship ties through the male line) and *patrilocal* (a term indicating residence with the male's family or village). Corresponding terms indicating female authority, descent, and residence are *matriarchal, matrilineal,* and *matrilocal.* The matter is actually more complex than that, for one may trace descent through both father's and mother's lines *(bilateral descent),* as we

development of patriarchy is associated with the agricultural revolution. People's livelihood depended on their plot of land, and the male line of descent provided a way of keeping land in the family after the owner's death.

Historically, the tradition of patriarchy has been embellished by **deference customs**, whereby both children and wives were expected to show their subordination to the head of the household in many ways: kneeling or bowing when addressing him, for instance, or giving him the seat of honor at the table.

More basic than this, of course, are many of the legal and practical holdovers in wives' and husbands' family roles and relationships. Here continuity is mixed with some degree of change. A review of family law conveys this mix: Traditional definitions coexist with some change.

Husbands: Heads of Households and Breadwinners

The husband's patriarchal authority as **head of household** is still highly evident and is upheld by law in a number of ways. For instance, the legal assumption still exists in many states that the husband may choose any reasonable place or mode of living and that the wife must conform to his choice.

In some states a woman's refusal to accept her husband's choice of domicile (by not moving with him to another city, for example) can be grounds for ruling that she has legally deserted him (Weitzman, 1981).

Patriarchal attitudes are also evident in the assumption that husbands should be the primary breadwinners. In most states today the husband has a legal obligation to support his wife and children; the rest of the states presume this, based on common law (Weitzman, 1977:292). In contrast, wives are held legally responsible for support only when their husbands are unable or unwilling. The husband's legal duty to support his wife formed the basis for traditional husband-to-wife alimony laws. Today, though the Supreme Court has ruled that alimony laws may not automatically exclude husbands (*Orr v. Orr,* in *Newsweek,* March 19, 1979) and alimony is occasionally awarded to a man, "an award to a husband is considered extraordinary" (Heyman, 1976:303).

Along with his obligation to support his family, the husband is often given the sole right to determine what, beyond basic minimum requirements, constitutes adequate provision.

This is not to say that there have been no areas of change. One long-standing holdover from British common law, the assumption that two spouses are one legal person (the husband), was judicially altered in our country in 1960.

Another change has been the recognition of the right of wives to hold property and to borrow money. The Married Women's Property Acts, passed in most states during the nineteenth century, had recognized wives' right to hold property, but consumer credit procedures generally considered a married couple's credit rating as belonging only to the husband. Divorced or widowed women thus often found themselves without an established credit record and virtually unable to borrow money or open charge accounts.[5] The **Equal Credit Opportunity Act** of 1975 allows a married woman's good credit rating to continue to belong to her after divorce or widowhood or if she wants to establish credit in her name only. The law also forbids discrimination on the basis of sex or marital status in any legal transaction, and a number of procedures and regulations have since been established to implement the intent of that law.

---

do in the United States. In the United States we also typically have *neolocal residence:* The young couple does not reside with either family, but moves to a new location. We think of our authority structure in this country as *egalitarian,* that is, not favoring either males or females, but considering them equally. In fact, we have mixed elements of patriarchal and egalitarian authority.

The dominant form, historically and cross-culturally, has been patriarchal authority, patrilineal descent, and patrilocal residence. As we have come to theorize about and oppose male dominance in our society, we use the term *patriarchy* as a global term for this generalized male dominance, which contains elements of male preference in authority, descent, residence, and other aspects of the society. Patriarchy, then, moves from its place as a neutral descriptive term in the analysis of kinship systems to become an ideological concept in a feminist or conflict theory. Patriarchy is defined as oppressive, and social change to more egalitarian roles is advocated. From this perspective conflict is expected between oppressor (patriarchal) and resistant (feminist, egalitarian) elements of the society, which both mobilize what power they can including the power of ideology. Our discussion in this chapter does have overtones of conflict theory; our values are egalitarian and patriarchy is given a negative cast. We discuss conflict theory in Chapter 11.

---

5. Single women also found it difficult to get credit before the passage of the Equal Credit Opportunity Act.

Wives: Child Care, House Care, and Husband Care

The woman's role in patriarchal families offers a sharp contrast to the traditional male role. The law has assumed that the wife is responsible for child care both during and after marriage. While most revised divorce statutes are written in sex-neutral terms, in many jurisdictions courts continue to give women preference in custody disputes.

In the past the wife's house care responsibilities have been legally binding. One 1962 ruling, for example, maintained that a wife "must perform her household and domestic duties.... A husband is entitled to the benefit of his wife's industry and economy" (*Rucci* v. *Rucci*, 1962, cited in Weitzman, 1977:296–97). Although such a provision was unenforceable, it had important contemporary implications. A wife's work on a family farm or in a business was included as part of her marital role, which meant the wife earned no credit toward a share of such property. Farm widows, who labored for years alongside their husbands, had to pay heavy taxes on their share of "his" estate, since they were not presumed to be joint proprietors (Tevis, 1979). In recent years some states have made changes in these laws and have begun to define farm wives as partners rather than heirs; women working in other businesses with their husbands are still vulnerable legally (Weitzman, 1981).

In addition, the wife has also had a duty "to be [her husband's] helpmate, to love and care for him in such a role, to afford him her society and her person, to protect and care for him in sickness" (*Rucci* v. *Rucci*, 1962, in Weitzman, 1977:296–97). This presumes that she is his willing sex partner. This cultural expectation has recently been brought into focus by the emerging issue of marital rape, defined by a Michigan judge in November 1974 as "a married woman ... [being] compelled to submit against her will, to sexual contact with her husband which she finds offensive" (*Equal Rights Monitor*, Oct. 1976, p.17). Rape laws have been revised in many states in the last few years. For a husband to rape a wife, even while the two are living together, is now a crime in twenty-five states (Barden, 1987). Some states have gone in the other direction by extending spousal immunity to a rape charge to unmarried partners, thereby reducing the legal difference between married partners and cohabitants (Jeffords and Dull, 1983).

Those who argue that there is no such thing as marital rape are presuming that sex is a wife's duty. Statutes have stipulated, for instance, that "a person does not commit sexual assault under this act if the victim is his or her legal spouse, unless the couple are living apart and one of them has filed for separate maintenance or divorce" (Revised Statutes of Michigan, 1975, cited in *Equal Rights Monitor*, Oct. 1976, p. 17).

Although it was stated in sex-neutral language, the law just cited had the effect of enforcing the wife's sexual obligations more than her husband's. One social scientist studying family violence concluded that "a number of women are forced into having sexual relations with their husbands through intimidation or physical force" (Gelles, 1977:346). The same researcher also notes that while marital rape may not yet be legally recognized in many areas, it is now being talked about and reported. (The issue of wife abuse will be discussed more in Chapter 10.)

A wife's traditional obligations to perform domestic services, care for children, and comply sexually all reflect the husband's position as patriarchal authority. But in everyday family living this is changing.

Toward Democratic Families

In some important ways today's family relationships are more similar to those that existed before the agricultural revolution than to those in the period of patriarchal families that followed. In primitive hunting-and-gathering societies women produced 80 percent of the food supply through their gathering activities. Men's dependence on women for much of their food (women depended on men for animal protein) gave women more freedom and power in group and family decisions (Boulding, 1976). Moreover, since meat could not be preserved and families were constantly moving around in search of game and new foraging areas, there was no accumulation of surplus wealth that might be inherited. Consequently, legitimacy was not a concern. Our society, like hunting-and-gathering societies, encourages individualism and equality. Both kinds of cultures have less need for cooperative family labor; both also offer more individual geographic mobility (Nimkoff and Middleton, 1960).

Social scientists recognize the changes that differentiate our society from the patriarchal system

■ A new family recipe: Traditional patriarchal attitudes assume that the father should be the breadwinner. With the less strict separation of roles in a modern democratic family, Dad may bring home the bacon—and cook and serve it, too.

and have different names for these systems. They refer to agricultural-patriarchal societies as *traditional* and call advanced industrial societies *modern*, meaning that they encourage individualism, social and personal change, and flexibility. Table 7·1 outlines how these differences translate to family beliefs, values, and behavior.

Reasons for the Shift There are numerous reasons why the traditional family no longer satisfies many people's needs; two are particularly relevant. But since they have been discussed elsewhere in this book, we will look only briefly at them here.

One reason people have developed more democratic families is that, increasingly, they want emotional support, companionship, and intimacy from family living.[6] A **democratic family** is one

6. For information on the historical change toward affectionate relationships in family life, see the works of Stone, Shorter, and Lasch listed in the References.

that emphasizes egalitarian decision making and individual development of family members. Strict separation of husband-wife roles, along with wives' and children's unquestioning respect for patriarchal authority, diminishes opportunities for spontaneity and intimacy. In cultures where deference roles play an important part in family living, "extreme power inequality seems to generate stiff, formal behavior from everyone in the family, and may even result in family members avoiding each other" (Skolnick, 1978a:101). One writer bemoans the fact that as women and men are given separate "places" in traditional marriages, they also experience "mental separations." He argues that "even sexual interest heightens in an unstereotyped relationship" (Farrell, 1974:164).

A second reason for the decline of patriarchal values is our attitude toward authority. As American family members come to value friendship and recognition more, there is less emphasis on patriarchal authority. While some patriarchal attitudes and behaviors still remain in most families

TABLE 7·1 Traditional Versus Democratic Family Beliefs, Values, and Behavior

Patriarchal Traditionalism	Democratic Modernism
1. Almost everything a person does is done as a member of a family.	The family is differentiated from economic, political, and social life; recruitment to jobs is independent of one's relatives.
2. Most adults work at home; the family is a self-sufficient economic unit: school, hospital, and old-age home as well as workshop.	Separation of home from work; household consumes as well as produces. Hospitals, public schools, Social Security, and other institutions help care for dependent individuals.
3. Sons inherit fathers' land, property, or business.	Sons can get jobs or choose careers independently.
4. Wives and daughters engage in homemaking.	More jobs and career opportunities are open to women.
5. Primary functions of the family are to provide for responsible childbearing and economic support of members.	Primary functions of the family are to provide emotional support and security through companionship and intimacy.
6. Little emphasis on emotional involvement among family members, particularly between spouses; marriage not based on love.	Relatively intense emotional involvement expected between spouses; hopes for marital happiness; marriage based on love.
7. Men are dominant over women, children.	Relationships are relatively egalitarian.
8. The extended family may be the basic unit of residence and domestic functions, for example, meals and child care.	The extended family is not so prevalent; more individualistic and numerous family forms, such as dual-earner, single-parent, homosexual, and group marriages.
9. People value tradition, duty, personal sacrifice for the common good, individual submission to authority, God, and to fate.	People value personal advancement, individual rights, equality, freedom, and personal growth.

SOURCE: Adapted from Skolnick, 1978a:109.

today, few fathers exercise the authority that their own fathers did (LeMasters, 1977), and fathers may have become emotionally closer to their children as a consequence.

Wives and husbands are also experiencing more **egalitarian,** or **equalitarian, relationships** as couples share both practical responsibilities and decision making. (Chapter 10 addresses the ideology and the reality of egalitarian relationships in contemporary America.)

Assessing Actual Change Families are becoming more democratic, but are marriages changing? Studies of specific aspects of marital roles in contemporary marriages consistently find that while patriarchal attitudes persist, expectations of marriage *are* changing (Nye et al., 1976; Pleck, 1985; Hiller and Philliber, 1986).

Sociologists Dana Hiller and William Philliber (1986) examined marital-role expectations and behavior in a 1983 sample of 489 married couples in Cincinnati, Ohio, in which they conducted personal interviews in dual-earner, husband-only-earner, and wife-only-earner households. Participants were selected by randomly dialing households and securing appointments for simultaneous interviews with husbands and wives. (In comparing their sample with 1980 census data, the researchers found that their subjects were probably of somewhat higher socioeconomic status than the general American population.) Among other things, Hiller and Philliber investigated the degree of agreement between spouses about what marital duties each partner was expected to perform. They also looked at the difference between these expectations and actual behavior.

Hiller and Philliber concluded that while marital-role expectations and behaviors are changing, "marriage partners are still emotionally attached to their own traditional sex roles even though they are willing to participate in the traditional roles of the opposite sex" (1). Partners were asked, "How important is it to be better than your spouse" at various tasks. Results suggest that husbands remain attached to the breadwinning role and wives to child care. Among husbands, 58 percent considered it important to be better than their wives at earning income. Among wives, 43 percent considered it important to be better than their husbands at child care, and 38 percent felt that way about housekeeping (7).

In looking at differences in expectations, what is most striking is the consistent trend for wives to be more traditional with respect to traditional female roles and husbands to be the more traditional with respect to the traditional male roles. Spouses are interested in and willing to participate in the roles of the opposite sex, but they are not eager to give up their preeminence in their traditional roles [12]. ■

Table 7·2 lists spouses' expectations about who should perform various marital roles. As you can see, 84 percent of the couples agreed that child care should be shared, and 69 percent agreed that money management should be shared. This is evidence of changing role expectations. Meanwhile, only 38 percent agreed that housework should be shared; only 24 percent agreed that income earning should be shared. Forty-three percent of these couples agreed that income earning is the husband's job, while almost one-third (30 percent) believe housework is the wife's job.

The researchers found that if the wife is employed, the husband is more likely to share in child care (but not necessarily in housework) than if the wife stays at home. With regard to housework sharing, "the husband's attitude appears to be more important than the wife's" (9).

While patriarchal attitudes and behaviors persist in marriages, there are also signs of change toward more flexible role bargains.

Nearly all couples believe childrearing is a two-parent job, over a third believe housework should be shared, and over two-thirds of the husbands like or would like their wives being employed, and another 15 percent say they do not care.... These results all attest to change in sex-role attitudes that may have taken place in recent years. While tradition still dictates much about the actual role bargains of married couples, many people are at least perceiving the possibility of new arrangements [13]. ■

The picture of the traditional patriarchal family is becoming gradually less accurate as individuals' needs, attitudes, and expectations change. A more obvious change, though, may be the great diversity of forms taken by man-woman and parent-child relationships. For many, "needs ... can be met in a conventional family setting, but for others the availability or desirability of this path is limited" (Kornfein et al., 1979:260). A result is alternative family forms in the United States today.

THE FAMILY'S MANY FORMS

In societies throughout history the family has taken many forms besides the nuclear one described in the Prologue. Increasingly in our society, adults are moving from one family form to another, and perhaps to a third or fourth. A person may begin a child-free, dual-earner family, for example, then later

TABLE 7·2 Spouses' Expectations About Who Should Perform Marital Roles

	Wife's Traditional Roles	
	Child Care (N = 483)	Housework (N = 488)
Agree it is wife's job	2%	30%
Husband thinks it's wife's job / Wife thinks they should share	7	13
Husband thinks they should share / Wife thinks it's wife's job	8	20
Agree job should be shared	84	38

	Husband's Traditional Roles	
	Money Management (N = 487)	Income Earning (N = 484)
Agree it is husband's job	9%	43%
Wife thinks it's husband's job / Husband thinks they should share	5	9
Wife thinks they should share / Husband thinks it's husband's job	17	25
Agree job should be shared	69	24

SOURCE: Hiller and Philliber, 1986.

have children, and still later become a member of a stepfamily or a single parent.

These alternatives may be freely chosen or may be a response to circumstances. One's partner, not oneself, may decide to divorce, for example, and as Chapter 5 pointed out, being single may result in part from demographic conditions.

The Social Context of Alternative Families

Personal decisions are influenced and limited by social context. For example, the unbalanced sex ratio among older people (see Chapter 6) has led some observers to suggest that people create group marriages (Kassel, 1966) and lesbian relationships (Doudna, 1981).

Not only demographic but also economic conditions affect family forms. Sociologists Marie Peters and Harriette McAdoo wryly observe that the idea of family "alternatives" is a white, middle-class discovery of what has existed in the black community all along. Strong extended families, two-worker families, single-parent families, and "augmented families" (with nonrelatives living in a quasi-extended family), along with cohabitation, have always been present among blacks. This has been due not only to the Afro-American cultural heritage, but also to an adaptation to an imbalanced sex ratio and to economic deprivation (Peters and McAdoo, 1983). In fact, strong extended families have been common among working-class whites as well, because of economic deprivation or ethnic heritage.

Recent economic pressures may affect middle-class families as well. Hard times can cause the divorce rate to fall because couples cannot afford to separate. Dual-paycheck families have become a necessity for most families who want to own their own homes. A 1983 Louis Harris poll reported that some 90 percent of couples who want to own a house anticipate that both partners will have to work to pay for it. Moreover, a depressed economy may encourage extended families, communal living, and shared households for dating partners who might not have moved in together otherwise (Wiseman, 1981:264). For others, such constraints are less important than the positive desire to choose a way of life that will be rewarding to family members, fostering intimacy, responsibility, or whatever values are considered important in family life.

Indeed, these people may need to be not only resourceful but also resilient, because forming nontraditional families may entail certain problems.

Some Problems Associated with Alternative Family Forms

Membership in a nontraditional family means being out of the mainstream, with some consequent problems or concerns. First, few norms or mutually understood rules for behavior exist, making it necessary for family members to negotiate even minor issues. Not only norms but also family rituals need to be invented (Bossard and Boll, 1943). All this requires considerable creativity, time, effort, and commitment. A successful effort may be rewarding, however.

Introducing children into an experimental family form may prove more difficult than rearing them traditionally. For example, gay parents may encounter legal custody battles involving either adoption or rearing their natural offspring. Then, too, children may feel embarrassed that their family is other than typical. As one social scientist observes:

If history repeats itself cyclically, the children of hippie parents or parents who cohabited without getting married will be very traditional in their own approach to sex and marriage. Thus, we may have a situation opposite to that of the sixties—embarrassed children trying to decide how to explain their parents' lifestyle to their [teachers, scout leaders, and] friends [Wiseman, 1981:265]. ∎

Data from a longitudinal study of conventional and alternative families suggest, however, that child mental and motor development—and also parent-child interaction—proceeds as well in the latter as in the former. This UCLA Lifestyles Project, begun in 1973, has followed 200 families: 50 legally married couples, 50 cohabitants, 50 communal families, and 50 single-mother families. The project was interdisciplinary (psychology, sociology, and anthropology) and also investigated 50 children belonging to these different family forms. Subjects were caucasian, middle-class, college-educated mothers, with 50 percent from the Los Angeles area, 30 percent from northern California, and 20 percent from San Diego. The study addressed problems of resources, task organization, child nurturance, social support, and the mother's relationship with the father or other men. Mothers were followed from their third trimester of pregnancy, and data have now been reported from extensive research during the first year and at three years (Eiduson et al., 1982). The researchers concluded: "Social, intellectual, and emotional competence scores summarizing the child's performance on all 3 year tests revealed no differences by life-style. . . . The life-style of the family in which the children were being raised had no systematic effect on the children's development. Stated differently, the children appeared to be developing normally" (Eiduson et al., 1982:344). Those who want to choose one of these family forms will find these data reassuring. On the other hand, they suggest there is no particular developmental advantage to the alternative forms.

Besides difficulties posed by lack of norms and rituals and concern about raising children, alternative families can encounter problems with the law or public policy, which favor traditional forms. State laws may proscribe gay sexual activity or cohabitant living, for example, and cohabiting couples lose tax advantages reserved for the married. Also, they may not be considered next-of-kin in medical emergencies, and a person who would be allowed to leave work in order to care for an ailing spouse may be denied the privilege when the loved one is not a legal mate. Difficulties such as these may lead to a perceived need for secrecy—from employers, the children's schools, and even from parents—which can be isolating and stressful.

Despite such problems, however, pollster Daniel Yankelovich argues that the change evident in the sixties toward values of individualism and self-fulfillment remains intact (1981). While American society and the family seem to have stabilized following a period of upheaval (Cherlin, 1981), this does not mean that the clock has been turned back on alternative family forms. We'll look now at a sampling of the variety of family forms that exist in America today.

Extended Families

Extended families, you'll recall from the Prologue, consist of parents and their children who live in the same household with other relatives, such as the parents or a brother or sister of one of the spouses.

Extended families were prominent in traditional agricultural societies, for they provided a network of property ownership and support that contributed to the family's self-sufficiency. In those societies the extended family most often resulted when a young married couple moved into the home of one spouse's parents. The spouse's parents continued to own the family property until they died, and all members of the household participated in the family business or farming. Not only did these families tend to be patriarchal, but obedience to familial authority was valued more than individual advancement and growth. Furthermore, loyalty to the ties of blood kinship typically was valued more highly than intimacy between spouses.

Today's extended families may also experience tension between family loyalty and individual advancement or couple intimacy. In some of the black families studied by anthropologist Carol Stack, for example, some extended families attempted to prevent or break up marriages that competed for scarce resources with the needs of kin (Stack, 1974).

Today just under 4 percent of American family households are extended-family households (U.S. Bureau of the Census, 1986b). Households where grandchildren live with grandparents are more common among blacks and American Indians than among other racial and ethnic groups, and they are especially likely to occur when one or both of the parents is not residing in the household (Hernandez, 1986).

■ "And then Little Red Riding Hood said to the wolf . . .": In an extended family, formed by choice or necessity, relatives often share in child care.

Other data (Hofferth, 1984), as well as community studies (Stack, 1974), suggest that blacks are more likely than whites to live in extended-family households. This racial difference in extended families seems to be a result of the greater proportion of female-headed households among blacks; a greater proportion of such households are headed by never-married women, who are especially likely to live with extended kin. Black married couples are no more likely than white married couples to live with extended kin (Hofferth, 1984).

These modern extended families are usually somewhat different from the traditional ones in both function and form. In white middle-class circles extended families today usually result either when spouses take in an aging parent or when recently divorced or never married single parents return to live in their parents' home while they find jobs or pursue further education. Certain ethnic groups, Asians and Italians, for example, may continue the extended family groupings of their homelands, with young couples residing near or with parents and aging parents living in the homes of adult children. Lower-class black communities may operate primarily as extended families, with shifting combinations of kin residing together and sharing economic resources, child-rearing responsibilities, and so forth. White working-class families have commonly had such mutual support patterns also.

Mutual aid (material aid and such services as repairs and child care) is an important function of most extended families. Few contemporary families, however, have the shared economy characteristic of traditional families, in which property—land or a shop or craft workshop—is jointly owned and worked by extended-family members. Important contemporary exceptions are farm families, families with "mom-and-pop" stores or restaurants, and upper-class families with extensive wealth and property, or a major family-dominated business. Such families, however, are not very numerous. For most extended families, work takes place outside the family, though economic and other sorts of resources may be shared and family members may pass along information about jobs or attempt to get jobs for family members.

Earlier we noted that 4 percent of American households are extended-family households. Actually, this figure represents only three-generation households, that is, extended families in which three generations (parent, child, and grandchild) live together. But other combinations of kin may live together; a 1977 Supreme Court decision (Moore v. City of East Cleveland) defined the right of extended families to live together as an important privacy right that extends to aunts, uncles, cousins, and perhaps other relatives. This principle has not, however, been extended to households of nonrelatives who would like to consider themselves "family."

According to Carol Stack (1974), even families who do not live together regularly may be organized around exchanges of goods and services among extended kin. This finding has been supported by more recent research (e.g., Taylor, 1986). Stack's methodology was participant observation. She lived in a black community in Illinois for three years. Although she is white, she participated in the everyday life of the community and was herself sometimes drawn into family exchange networks as a "fictive kin," a person who occupies the status of a relative though not actually a relative. Her study focused on the many members of two extended-kin families and their friends and was supplemented by quantitative data from 188 AFDC (welfare) case records involving 951 children and 373 adults. Stack observed that parents, adult siblings, aunts, uncles, cousins, neighbors, and family friends may share housing, meals, clothing, money, cars, and services. The following is from Stack's field notes:

Cecil (35) lives in The Flats with his mother Willie Mae, his oldest sister and her two children, and his younger brother. Cecil's younger sister Lily lives with their mother's sister Bessie. Bessie has three children and Lily has two. Cecil and his mother have part-time jobs in a café and Lily's children are on aid. In July of 1970 Cecil and his mother had just put together enough money to cover their rent. Lily paid her utilities, but she did not have enough money to buy food stamps for herself and her children. Cecil and Willie Mae knew that after they paid their rent they would not have any money for food for the family. They helped out Lily by buying her food stamps, and then the two households shared meals together until Willie Mae was paid two weeks later. A week later Lily received her second ADC check and Bessie got some spending money from her boyfriend. They gave some of this money to Cecil and Willie Mae to pay their rent, and gave Willie Mae money to cover her insurance and pay a small sum on a living room suite at the local furniture store. Willie Mae reciprocated later on by buying dresses for Bessie and Lily's daughters and by caring for all the children when Bessie got a temporary job [1974:37]. ■

Kin, then, provide an assistance network in which "swapping" reinforces affective ties. Not only material goods and services but also children are swapped—overnight or for extended periods—both to assist beleaguered parents (a single mother who is ill or beginning a new relationship, for example, or who is too young to properly care for a child) and to cement personal ties by sharing one's most precious possession. Children are highly valued and have a wide variety of affectionate, significant caretakers. Native American families function in much the same way (Staples and Mirande, 1980). And

Jaime Sena-Rivera (1979) argues that the Chicano is similarly a shared-aid extended family, although it is not typically co-resident.

Stack sees this family form as very effective in coping with poverty because resources are shared and individuals are thereby cushioned from absolute disaster. But on the other hand, she concedes, an individual or couple can seldom "get ahead" by saving for a home, for example, or for a child's college education. The following excerpt explains why:

In 1971 Magnolia's uncle died in Mississippi and left an unexpected inheritance of $1,500 to Magnolia and Calvin Waters. The cash came from a small run-down farm which Magnolia's uncle sold shortly before he died. It was the first time in their lives that Magnolia or Calvin ever had a cash reserve. Their first hope was to buy a home and use the money as a down payment....

Three days after they received the check, news of its arrival spread throughout their domestic network. One niece borrowed $25 from Magnolia so that her phone would not be turned off....

During the weeks following the arrival of the money, Magnolia and Calvin's obligations to the needs of kin remained the same, but their ability to meet these needs had temporarily increased. When another uncle became very ill in the South, Magnolia and her older sister, Augusta, were called to sit by his side. Magnolia bought round-trip train tickets for both of them and for her three youngest children....

Winter was cold and Magnolia's children and grandchildren began staying home from school because they did not have warm winter coats and adequate shoes or boots. Magnolia and Calvin decided to buy coats, hats, and shoes for all of the children (at least fifteen)....

Within a month and a half, all of the money was gone. The money was channeled into the hands of the same individuals who ordinarily participate in daily domestic exchanges, but the premiums were temporarily higher. All of the money was quickly spent for necessary, compelling reasons [Stack, 1974:105–7]. ■

Such a potent kin system, then, tends to direct resources away from individual achievement. Despite this, we foresee a possible increase in this family form among middle- and lower middle-class whites. With today's high divorce rate and difficult economic circumstances, adults may increasingly

find that their more permanent kin ties are with their families of origin rather than with their mates. Consequently, they may rely more on kin for emotional support, financial assistance, and exchange of services. Put another way, we may increasingly see a "vertical family" (attachment to parents and family of origin) as opposed to the "horizontal family" (stressing priority and permanence of the marital bond, which has characterized American society from its beginning). While extended families as residential groupings represent a small proportion of family households, kin ties—contrary to myth—remain salient and may become more so.

Families Without Children

We use the term **child-free family** for married adults who choose not to have children but nevertheless think of themselves as a family. Because of the increasing cost of bearing and rearing children, the increase in knowledge and availability of contraception, the decline in the social demand to have children, and the appeal of competing arenas of self-fulfillment (such as careers for women), it is likely that more married couples will at least consider remaining child-free. (This option is discussed thoroughly in Chapter 12, so we will not develop it here.) All marriages, of course, eventually become childless when the children leave home. About half of American families do not have children under age 18 in the household (U.S. Bureau of the Census, 1986b).

Dual-Earner Families

The family form that includes two adults, each with a full-time job and each contributing to the household in terms of money and tasks, is a **dual-earner family**. Dual-earner families may or may not have children. Couples often choose this family form after their children are grown or have reached a certain age, but increasingly, families with preschool children have two wage earners.

A distinction should be made between dual-earner (or two-paycheck) and dual-career families. In the **dual-career family** both partners have a strong commitment to the lifetime development of careers; in the dual-earner family the wife (and perhaps husband) has less psychological involvement in her work, which may be viewed as temporary or supplemental to her "real" job in the home. In the dual-career family both partners are strongly committed in terms of identity, time, and resources to self-actualization through an unfolding career. The dual-career family, although only a small minority in our society, probably represents a growing trend. It tends to involve a commitment to more equally shared household responsibilities, even though this commitment is not always carried out in practice. In any case a wife's working, whether at a "job" or a "career," tends to involve a shift toward a more egalitarian marriage in terms of decision making (Dual-earner and dual-career marriages are explored in detail in Part Four of this text, particularly in Chapter 11.)

Single-Parent Families

The **single-parent family** consists of a widowed, divorced, or never married parent and biological or adopted children. In 1984, 23 percent of all families with children had only one parent (U.S. Bureau of the Census, 1986b). Their number more than doubled between 1970 and 1984 (U.S. Bureau of the Census, 1986), due mainly to the high divorce rate.

Historically, one-parent families most often resulted from death, but today divorce has become a more common cause. Some divorced single parents have actively chosen this family form by their decision to divorce and take custody of their children. Other divorced parents find themselves living in single-parent families against their personal preferences. (Sometimes the absent parent continues to play an important role in the family. See, for example, Case Study 7•1, "The Family as a Child-Rearing Institution.") (The single-parent family that results from divorce is discussed in Chapter 16.)

Some single-parent families are not the products of divorce, death, or "accidental" pregnancy at all; they result from choice. Unmarried men or women may adopt children; unmarried women may purposefully give birth, an option discussed in current literature (e.g., Renvoize, 1985).

Another trend is for never married women who give birth to keep their infants even when the pregnancy was not intended. Traditionally, this happened more frequently among black than among white unwed women, the latter being more likely to give their babies up for adoption. White women are now very likely to keep their babies. We do not know the exact proportion of unwed mothers in older age groups who kept their babies, but in 1976 over 90 percent of black teenage (age 15–19) mothers and over 87 percent of white teenage mothers kept their babies (Zelnick and Kantner, 1978b).[7]

As opportunities grow for women to support themselves, and as the permanence of marriage becomes less certain, the principle of legitimacy becomes less important economically (White, 1979). That is, there is less motivation for a woman to avoid giving birth out-of-wedlock, since she cannot count on lifetime male support for the child even if she is married. Furthermore, the stigma accompanying and discrimination against unwed mothers have somewhat lessened, and the distinction in legal terms between legitimate and illegitimate children has been virtually eliminated (Weitzman, 1981). Nevertheless, the burden of sole responsibility for support and care of the child remains on the mother.

The UCLA Family Lifestyles Project investigated single motherhood in cases where the mother was not married when her child was born. The researchers (Kornfein et al., 1979) described these mothers by using three categories: nestbuilders, post hoc adaptors, and unwed mothers. About one-third of the women were nestbuilders. Often older and vocationally established, these women had made a conscious choice to become parents. Viewing single motherhood as desirable, some rejected marriage on ideological grounds; others simply were not in relationships with the potential for marriage. Generally, these women sought out men perceived as good biological fathers and expected little or no continued involvement. Nestbuilders were information seekers, reading and consulting experts on

---

7. Women age 18–24 have the highest rates of out-of-wedlock births of any age group (U.S. National Center for Health Statistics, 1987b). While the number of teen premarital pregnancies increased with increasing teen sexual activity in the 1970s and early 1980s (teen pregnancy rates declined, but more young women were at risk of pregnancy [Hofferth et al., 1987]), abortion has reduced the proportion of pregnant teens giving birth. Forty-three percent of white teen pregnancies (women age 15–19) and 20 percent of black teen pregnancies are ended by abortion. Fewer than 1 percent of teen women who give birth relinquish the child for adoption (Zelnick and Kantner, 1980). Blacks have higher rates of births to unmarried mothers than do whites, but black rates are falling, whereas white rates are rising. The overall illegitimacy rate reached an all-time high in 1985 (U.S. National Center for Health Statistics, 1987b).

■ When Dad's out of the picture, sometimes it's because he has the camera. But today, single-parent families make up one out of four American families with children. Although this single mother may be a widow or may never have married, chances are she is divorced.

child development. They consciously established social networks and carefully planned child care.

Unlike this first category, the other two groups—post hoc adaptors and unwed mothers—did not plan to become parents; for them, pregnancy was "a problem, not a solution" (Kornfein et al., 1979:266). These women were younger and less well educated and sometimes relied for support on government assistance (Aid to Families with Dependent Children). For many, becoming a mother meant interrupting education or career goals. Arrangements for child care and social support tended to be "ad hoc," that is, to derive from whatever resources were available at that time. Grandparents or other women in similar circumstances might help. So, temporarily, might roommates. Most of the women in these two categories would have preferred to be married. Since they were not, however, many—at least the post hoc adaptors—found collective living attractive.

Unwed mothers differed from post hoc adaptors

in that the former felt victimized by their pregnancies. As a group these women were the youngest, often about 18, and the least established. Rather than considering alternatives, they tended to see marriage to the father as the only desirable solution and to put considerable effort into achieving that end. When the wedding did not occur, they often returned to their parents' household, where the grandmother assumed a parental role toward her grandchild.

In this study, then, single mothers differed in their conscious choosing of this life-style and, accordingly, in their adaptation and coping with it.

Stepfamilies

A **stepfamily** contains a man and a woman, at least one of whom has been married before, and one or more children from the previous marriage of either or both spouses. (Remarried couples

CASE STUDY 7·1

THE FAMILY AS A CHILD-REARING INSTITUTION

Jo Ann is 38 and has been divorced for six years. She has five children. Gary, 19 and her oldest, lives with his father, Richard. At the time of this interview, Jo Ann and Richard and their children had recently begun family counseling. The purpose, Jo Ann explained, was to create for their children a more cooperative and supportive atmosphere. Jo Ann and Richard do not want to renew an intimate relationship, but they and their children are still in many ways a family filling traditional family functions.

We've been going to family counseling about twice a month now. The whole family goes—all five kids, Richard, and me. The counselor wants to have a videotaping session. He says it would help us to gain insights into how we act together. The two older girls didn't want any part of it, but the rest of us decided it might be really good for Joey to see how he acts.

[Joey's] the reason we're going in the first place. At the first counseling sessions, he sat with his coat over his head....

Joey's always been a problem. He's used to getting his own way. Some people want all the attention. They will do anything to get it. I guess I never knew how to deal with this.... He drives us nuts at home. He calls me and the girls names.... He was disrupting class and yelling at the teacher. And finally they expelled him.... Joey gets anger and frustration built up in him....

So I took him to a psychologist, and the psychologist said he'd like the whole family to come in, including Richard. Well, Richard still lives in this city and sees all the kids, so I asked him about it. And he said okay....

In between sessions, the counselor wants us to have family conferences with the seven of us together. One day I called Richard and asked him over for

without previous children are structurally similar to couples in their first marriage [Cherlin, 1978].) Stepfamilies are becoming more common in our society because of rising rates of divorce and remarriage. In 1982, 45 percent of all marriages were remarriages for one or both partners, compared to 33 percent in 1972 (U.S. National Center for Health Statistics, 1985a). (Stepfamilies are examined in detail in Chapter 17, and so are not discussed here.)

Communal Living

Groups of adults and children who live together, sharing aspects of their lives in common, are known as **communes**. In some communes, such as the Israeli kibbutz (Spiro, 1956) or some nineteenth-century American groups such as the Shakers and the Oneida colony (Kephart, 1971; Kern, 1981), all economic resources are shared. Work is organized by the commune, and commune members are fed, housed, and clothed by the community. Other communes may have some private property; even some Israeli farming cooperatives that superficially resemble kibbutzes have private land plots, although members share a communal life (Schwartz, 1954).

There is also variation in sexual arrangements among communes, ranging from monogamous couples (the kibbutz, and some communes in this country) to the open sexual sharing found in the Oneida colony, as well as some modern American groups. Couples may maintain a separate household or may have a room in a group home.

supper. In the back of my mind I thought maybe we could get this family conferencing started.

Well, after dinner Joey, our 11-year-old, started acting up. So I went for a walk with him. We must have walked a mile and a half, and Joey was angry the whole time. He told me I never listen to him; I never spent time with him. Then he started telling me about how he was mad at his dad because his dad won't listen to him.

He said his dad tells all these dumb jokes that are just so old, but he just keeps telling them and telling them. So when we got home, I saw Richard was still there, and I asked Joey, "Would you like to have a family conference? Maybe tell your dad some of the things that are bothering you?" And he said, "Could we?" . . .

[During the conference] Joey talked first. Then everybody had a turn to say something. There was one time I was afraid it was going to get out of hand. Everybody was interrupting everybody else. But the counselor had told me you have to set up ground rules. This is where we learned that we've got some neat kids because when I said "Let somebody else talk," everybody did! So it went real well. . . . And then finally Richard said, "I think it's time for us to come to a conclusion." I said, "Well, you're right."

- In what ways are divorced families still families? In what ways are they not? Even though Jo Ann and Richard's family is no longer intact, what functions does it continue to perform for its members? For society? What roles do you think Richard plays?

Finally, children may be under the control and supervision of their parents, or they may be communally reared, with a de-emphasis on biological relationships and responsibility for discipline and care vested in the entire community. The UCLA study found vast differences in how various communes define parent-child responsibilities. In some, nuclear families were clearly demarcated. In others, children were community responsibilities, with professional or designated caretakers. In still others, child care was assigned to whoever happened to be present. Even in communes with collective child rearing, such as the kibbutz, relationships with biological parents may be deeply significant emotionally (Spiro, 1958; Shipler, 1984.).

Communal living may be one way to cope with some of the problems of aging. For example, one group of four midwestern married couples who were long-term friends bought a building with living quarters for four families. They saved money by having common laundry and maintenance facilities. More important, they expected to provide emotional support, companionship, and practical support for each other as illness and death began to play a part in the life of the group.

Likewise, communes may offer a way of coping with singleness or with single parenthood. One study of sixty urban communes found that the majority were formed to provide social support for individuals or single parents (Zablocki, 1977). As with any family form, of course, there are positives and negatives here. Single mothers may get help, but they also relinquish some parental control. One mother, for example, left a commune because she was opposed to the commune's commitment to corporal punishment of children (Kornfein et al., 1979). Still, communal living represents an attempt to provide members with greater opportunities for social support, family companionship, and personal growth.

Polygamy

Polygamy is a kinship term referring to a family system with multiple partners for at least one of the spouses; it is also known as **group marriage**. In our society the term *polygamy* has negative overtones because our legal system and social norms endorse monogamy. But because in this section we discuss some patterns that really are not group marriages, in the sense that all the parties are equally involved, we use the anthropological term *polygamy* for our discussion.[8]

Historically, polygamy was quite common (remember the Old Testament patriarchs), but it has been illegal in the United States since 1878, when the Supreme Court ruled that freedom to practice the Mormon religion did not extend to multiple wives (*Reynolds* v. *United States*, 1878). Courts today still take the bigamy laws quite seriously.

Though polygamy may seem to be an esoteric topic, we include it because there are, in fact, contemporary alternative family forms that are polygamous. To begin with, although the mainstream Mormon church no longer permits polygamy, there are a number of Mormons who follow the traditional teachings and take multiple wives. Members of these families have appeared anonymously on television to explain and advocate their life-style.

The courts have been vigilant in the pursuit and prosecution of these families.

Sociologist Joseph Scott (1980a) has studied what he terms polygamy among American blacks. In the **black polygamous family**[9] two (or more) women maintain separate households and are independently "pair-bonded to a man whom they share and who moves between . . . households as a husband to both women" (Scott, 1980a:43). In view of the particularly unbalanced sex ratio among blacks (see Chapter 5), Scott suggests "the only way many black women may have men permanently in their lives would be to share them with women who already have them as husbands or friends" (1980a:48).

Scott interviewed twenty-two black women who either were or had been in a polygamous relationship. Half the women were single (consensual wives), and half were married (legal wives). Their relationships varied in length from two to twelve years. These women tended to be relatively young, of low socioeconomic status, and to have experienced premarital pregnancies for which they were ill prepared (Scott, 1980a:57). They believed men to be polygamous by nature and resigned themselves to sharing. Consensual wives saw the single black men available to them as relatively unreliable compared to those already married. "Married men, the women say, were generally more emotionally stable, more knowledgeable about family life, and very importantly, more financially able to assist them" (Scott, 1980a:53). Most of the legal wives became involved in polygamy because their husbands had other close female companions before marriage and kept them. Generally, they accepted their situations as inevitable, "given the scarcity of what they call 'good men'. . . . They all shared the view that if their husbands maintained their economic priorities to their legal families, this was evidence of their giving priority to the legal marriages themselves" (Scott, 1980a:60). According to Scott, the polygamous family is "perhaps the most neglected [by social scientists] type of comarital relation" in existence. His hope is that his research "will begin to foster an understanding of these relationships in contemporary American society" (Scott, 1980a:60–61).

---

8. The term *polygamy* means more than one spouse at a time for a partner of either sex. *Polygyny* refers to multiple wives for a man, and *polyandry* to multiple husbands for one wife. *Group marriage* in this framework indicates a marriage of more than one woman to more than one man. Polygyny has been very common throughout history as a permissible pattern in many cultures. Where permitted, though, it is not always that frequent, for many men cannot afford multiple wives. Polyandry is rare and tends to exist in very poor societies in which female infanticide is practiced to reduce the number of mouths to feed, with the result that there are not enough women to go around for marriage in adulthood. It is also practiced where brothers share a wife, again, often because of economic constraints. Group marriage is still rarer because of the obvious difficulties in balancing rights and duties, and working out conflicts and loyalties in this system (Stephens, 1963).

---

9. Scott initiated this research because he was interested in the phenomenon of polygamy among blacks. We have little notion whether a similar phenomenon exists among whites (or Asians) since no interested researcher that we know of has pursued the matter to any degree.

Scott's interpretation of his research as demonstrating the existence of a polygamous family form among blacks has been criticized. Critics question whether polygamy is a socially legitimate form in the black community. They also question whether it is a family alternative in the sense of a freely chosen family life-style; rather, it seems imposed on the women by circumstance and the men's behavior (Staples, 1985). Black polygamy could be viewed as one more instance of the effects of poverty and discrimination on minority peoples, rather than as a structural adaptation to unfavorable conditions (a neutral evaluation) or as a positive and innovative choice (Allen and Agbasegbe, 1980; McAdoo, 1981). Scott (1980b) replies to the critics that, in fact, the polygamy is consensual (that is, agreed to by the women) and that these unions are socially recognized as legitimate family constellations in the black community.

Peters and McAdoo (1983) present an interesting comment on what they call "perhaps the only newly developing life-style in the Black community that fits the popular conception of alternative life-styles" (301). They link black polygamous family formation to deficits in the (individual) development of these women, who "had most of their life choices determined for them" (302). They go on to comment:

Scott's contention that polygamy is a functional answer to imbalanced sex ratios and single-mother parenting among Blacks has been widely commented upon by social science researchers. Although this research has encountered considerable criticism for a number of reasons, including the fact that only women were interviewed, it is interesting to note that Black male researchers seem unanimous in their fascination with this alternative, while female researchers are almost equally unanimous in their opposition to this as a viable family alternative. While demographically it may be a logical solution to the lack of adult Black males in urban settings, many are concerned about the vulnerability of the mother/child units in "man sharing" and see the pattern as one more instance of the exploitation of poor women [Peters and McAdoo, 1983:302–3]. ▪

Polygamy in any form has one significant social fact in common with homosexual families, the next alternative family form we will discuss. Both have been the subject of litigation in which the Supreme Court has ruled that they are not acceptable alternatives within the framework of American law.

(Rulings with regard to cohabitation have been mixed; courts are much less ready to restrict cohabitation, though it may have secondary status and fewer privileges than marriage.)

Homosexual Families

State courts have ruled (e.g., *Singer* v. *Hare*, 1974) that homosexual unions cannot be legal marriages. Nevertheless, like heterosexual cohabitation, homosexual pair-bonding falls well within the scope of a social-psychological definition of the family.

In **homosexual families**, members of the same sex live together and share sexual and emotional commitment. They may consider themselves married as a result of personal ceremonies in which they exchange vows or rings, or both. Or they may form more public unions, religiously recognized by the Metropolitan Community Church (the national gay church). There may also be children living with the partners, either children from a marriage or planned children born to lesbian mothers by artificial insemination (or intercourse) who are treated as children of the gay couple.

Morton Hunt's survey research on the sexual behavior of a nonrandom sample of respondents in the early seventies (Hunt, 1974) found no increase in homosexuality over the Kinsey surveys published in 1949 and 1953. But homosexuals have become more visible in society. One result may be that the homosexual family form, though not necessarily homosexuality itself, becomes more widespread. (Such a family form will not necessarily be transmitted from generation to generation, since children of gays tend to be heterosexual.)

About 20 percent of gay men and about 33 percent of lesbians are or have been heterosexually married.[10] Approximately half the gay men's marriages resulted in children (Harry, 1983), and that figure may be higher for lesbians. Should they divorce, few gay men retain custody of their children, and visiting rights are often an issue. While about 56 percent of lesbian couples have children

---

10. Gay men may marry heterosexually because they are unaware of their homosexuality, believe it is peripheral, or hope that marriage will change them. A minority (about one-third) of their wives are aware of the homosexuality at the time of marriage but assume it is peripheral. Such unions are problematic. They tend to foster resentment over infrequency of sexual relations, nonexclusivity of the husband as he searches for partners, and often deception (Harry, 1983, citing Ross, 1971).

■ Homosexual families may become more common as homosexuals become more visible and vocal in society. These men, shown in San Francisco in 1979, are the first gay male couple to legally adopt a child. Now, because of AIDS, we might expect renewed controversy about whether gay men should adopt children.

living with them, custody may be an issue (Harry, 1983). The courts have increasingly taken the position that sexual preference is not an issue if the children are well cared for and well adjusted (Gutis, 1986). However, a recent decision of the Supreme Court (*Bowers* v. *Hardwick*, 1986) has made the legal situation of gays more problematic. The Court's ruling let stand state laws that prohibit homosexual conduct, so that the legal options and resources of gay couples vary considerably from state to state.

In other respects intimate homosexual relationships are similar to heterosexual ones. A major study by Letitia Peplau (1981) based on questionnaires administered to 218 gay men, 127 lesbians, and 130 unmarried heterosexual women and men found that both hetero- and homosexuals struggle to balance "the value placed on having an emotionally close and secure relationship" with that of "having major interests of . . . [one's] own outside the relationship [and] a supportive group of friends as well as . . . [one's] romantic sexual partner" (Peplau, 1981:33). Peplau and colleagues recruited respondents through homosexual organizations, advertisements, and informal social networks. As volunteers, the respondents were not necessarily rep-

resentative of all gays. For lesbians, ages ranged from 18 to 59, with a median age of 26. Half were employed full-time, and half were students. About 38 percent were Protestant, 35 percent Catholic, and 17 percent Jewish. Few were very religious. Gay men ranged in age from 18 to 65, with a median age of 25. Half were students. About 33 percent were Protestant, 39 percent Catholic, and 16 percent Jewish. As with the lesbian sample, few were very religious.

The men's first same-sex relationship began at a median age of 20, with a range of 12 to 38. For the lesbians, that figure was just past 20, with a range of age from 13 to 47.

For comparisons on attitudes and values, matched groups of 50 gay men, 59 heterosexual men, 50 lesbians, and 59 heterosexual women were selected. All were white students, matched for age, educational level, and length of current romantic relationship.

Regarding gays' similarities with—or differences from—heterosexuals, Peplau concluded:

We found little evidence for a distinctive homosexual "ethos" or orientation toward love relationships. There are many commonalities in the values most people bring to intimate relationships. Individual differences in values are more closely linked to gender and to background characteristics than to sexual orientation [1981:22]. ■

Blumstein and Schwartz's study (1983) of married heterosexual couples, unmarried heterosexual cohabitants, gay male couples, and lesbian couples reached a similar conclusion: that gender is a more important determinant of the nature of couple relationships than sexual preference is.

But while there may be no distinct homosexual "ethos," gay relationships do differ from others in two important ways. First, homosexuals are much less likely to adopt traditional masculine and feminine roles in their relationships. Instead, couples assume a "best friends" or "roommates" pattern (Harry, 1983:217; Peplau, 1981). One reason many gay relationships are relatively egalitarian is that pairings of two men or two women generally provide members of the couple with similar incomes, whereas a heterosexual couple tends to be characterized by higher income, and therefore more power, for males (Harry, 1983). (Chapter 10 addresses the association of income equality with egalitarian decision making.) Research among gay couples reinforces the conclusion that income disparities rather than biological differences produce power inequities in heterosexual relationships (Harry, 1983; Peplau and Cochran, 1981; Blumstein and Schwartz, 1983).

Besides their more egalitarian roles, homosexual relationships differ from others in that they are not as likely to be exclusive. On average, relationships for both gay men and women last two to three years, and a pattern of serial monogamy exists (Harry, 1983). This results partly because gay unions are not reinforced by societal expectations of permanence (see Chapter 8). For lesbians, nonexclusivity may be tied to "feminist critiques of monogamy"; for gay men, nonexclusivity may result from "traditional male gender role expression" (Peplau, 1981:33).

While male homosexual and lesbian relationships have much in common, they also differ as a result of divergent gender socialization. The fact that lesbian couples consist of two *women* and gay male couples of two *men* is significant (Blumstein and Schwartz, 1983). Lesbians are more likely to live together (about three-fourths of coupled women compared to slightly over half of coupled men) and place a higher value on emotional expressiveness,

such as sharing feelings and laughing together (Peplau, 1981; Peplau and Gordon, 1983). According to two major studies (Harry, 1983; Bell, Weinberg, and Hammersmith, 1981),[11] about 40 to 50 percent of gay men are partners in stable relations at any one time, as compared to about 75 percent for lesbians. Likewise, lesbians find a new partner more quickly after a breakup, while gay men tend to go through long transition periods of nonexclusive sexual activity (Harry, 1983). (Bell, Weinberg, and Hammersmith [1981] found that, on average, gay men had had sex with hundreds of others, and 40 percent had had more than 500 sex partners.) Moreover, lesbian couples are likely to have met through friendship networks, with less reliance on the gay bar. And "among lesbians a sexual relationship usually arises out of a developing affectional relationship while among gay men affection may develop out of a sexual relationship" (Harry, 1983:227). Such differences remind us of our discussion of gender socialization in Chapter 2: "Males are socialized to engage in sexual behaviors both with and without affection while women are more expected to combine the two. As a result when two men enter a partnership, nonexclusiveness can be expected, while when two women enter a partnership, exclusiveness could be expected" (Harry, 1983:226).

Living Together

The family form cohabitation, or "living together," has gained increasing popularity and widespread attention in recent years. Between 1970 and 1977 the number of unmarried people of opposite sex sharing a household doubled, and almost doubled again during the next five years (Thornton and Freedman, 1983). Underreporting of cohabitation is likely also. Then, too, there are many persons who have cohabited and who are not currently cohabiting and therefore are not counted. It is likely that the proportion of people affected by cohabitation is somewhat higher than the census estimate that just over 4 percent of all couples are

---

11. Joseph Harry and colleagues analyzed completed questionnaires from 1,556 respondents, all homosexual males solicited from gay bars, networks, and organizations.

A second important study took place at Kinsey's Institute for Sex Research at Indiana University (Bell, Weinberg, and Hammersmith, 1981). In this project 979 female and male homosexuals and 477 heterosexuals living in San Francisco were interviewed.

CASE STUDY 7·2

WE'RE "PARTNERS"— NOT HUSBAND AND WIFE

By Mary Jo Deegan and Michael Hill

Mary Jo Deegan is a professor of sociology at the University of Nebraska, where she met her "life-partner," Michael Hill. Hill holds a Ph.D. in geography and is pursuing another in sociology.

On May 1, 1982—International Workers' Day—we celebrated and consecrated our relationship with friends and family. Our partnership ceremony included blessings by a Presbyterian minister, piano music played by a close friend, and readings by Frederick Engels on marriage as slavery for women and by Jane Addams on the right of all people to live in societies they created. We did not obtain a marriage license, we did not exchange "marriage vows," and we specifically chose to *not be married*. Our celebration cake was covered with white frosting and in red letters the slogan "Workers Should Unite—Not Marry" merrily conveyed our happy tidings.

The choice to be partners, or, as we sometimes say, "life-partners," has dramatically structured our relationship to others. Since we both had been married to other people, we had experienced traditional relationships being imposed on our nontraditional selves. Our present experiences are very different from these prior ones. People inevitably pause after we introduce ourselves as partners. Often they ask us what that means, and we explain our commitment to each other and our opposition to state control over it. One dramatic difference for a woman is the immediate use of her full name. Although "Mary Jo Deegan" is a name I have used throughout my life, when I was married a large number of people told me they "couldn't remember it!" They would inevitably address me and introduce me using my husband's last name. My name causes no lapse of memory in a partnership.

---

living together (U.S. Bureau of the Census, 1986a).[12]

The majority of cohabiting relationships are relatively short term; 63 percent had shared the same household for less than two years. Of course, some cohabitants, perhaps one-third, will marry, thus removing themselves from statistics (Glick and Spanier, 1980).

Living together is a way of life that more and more people are choosing, for many reasons. People from all social, educational, and age groups have at least experimented with this family form (Clayton and Voss, 1977). Although 82 percent of cohabitants are under age 45, older retired couples have also found that living together without being legally married can be economically advantageous, as financial benefits contingent on not marrying are retained. Six percent of cohabitants are over age 65 (U.S. Bureau of the Census, 1986b).

Living together is almost equally frequent among formerly married persons and those who have not been married. Among couples living together, 47 percent of men and 48 percent of women were previously married (U.S. Bureau of the Census, 1986b). For this group, living together may provide a respite from the singles scene and a return to the domestic life-style they are accustomed to; or it may be, as for the never-married, a way station on the way to marriage. While 85 percent of the never married cohabitants are under 35, cohabitation among the formerly married touches all age groups: Almost two-thirds are over 35, and one-third are over 55 (Glick and Spanier, 1980).

Cohabitants are likely to be less actively religious, more politically liberal, more likely to be liv-

---

12. The Census Bureau does not differentiate between types of "persons living with an unrelated person of the opposite sex." Consequently, the numbers may include roommates who are not sexually involved with one another.

As nontraditional individuals in a traditional marital status, we both experienced a large number of interactions where others assumed we shared their traditional ideas on home, children, and marriage. We had few options in these situations. We could endure them in silence, argue, or present our views and be greeted by silence. Now, no one assumes that we think traditionally and we are accepted from the start as different from the traditional "husband and wife."

We also share the marvelous experience of supportive nontraditional people. Many individuals are searching for new ways to express their commitments, but they find traditional marriage ceremonies, promises, and relationships are empty and restrictive. Living without ceremonies to celebrate their joint lives is a common, but often unsatisfactory, solution. They often want to share their religious feelings and promises, however, and they are surprised to learn that it is possible to have a religious ceremony without a formal marriage. Thus we find ourselves explaining our commitment, ceremony, relatives' responses, and experiences to a number of people.

Surprisingly, many traditional people find our choices to be quite logical and acceptable. Nontraditional people are often delighted. We hope you will share in our joy and explore the ways you can commit yourself to others without losing an essential part of your own humanity.

■ How might some individuals find traditional marriage ceremonies, promises, and relationships empty and restrictive? How is Deegan and Hill's partnership different from marriage? How is it similar?

ing in large urban areas in the Northeast and West, and more likely to have more liberal attitudes. (If cohabitation increases, differences between cohabitants and others will probably lessen, since living together outside marriage will be more generally accepted and less often perceived as deviant [Macklin, 1983].)

Blacks have cohabitation rates three times those of whites. Moreover, unmarried couples are more likely than married couples to be interracial. Nine percent of unmarried couples and 1.5 percent of married couples are interracial: "A reasonable speculation is that interracial couples violate strongly held social norms; and, therefore, some of them may be reluctant to formalize their relationship by marriage" (Glick and Spanier, 1980:26). They may also receive more social support for their relationship if it is not formalized.

Most cohabiting households include only the couple; only 31 percent contain children under age 15. This proportion changed little between 1970 and 1984 (U.S. Bureau of the Census, 1986b). Although many cohabitants consider this life-style a means of courtship, as was noted in Chapter 6,[13] and most say they would plan to marry before deciding to have children, unmarried marriage is an alternative to legal wedlock. People's reasons for living together outside of legal marriage include the wish not to make the strong commitment that marriage requires, along with the belief that legal marriage can stifle communication and equality between partners. Some express fear of falling into traditional husband-wife roles. Case Study 7·2,

---

13. Observers (Risman et al., 1981; Macklin, 1983) agree that cohabitation in the United States—as opposed to Scandinavia, for instance—remains more or less a courtship stage and temporary rather than a deinstitutionalization of and replacement for marriage.

BOX 7 · 1

THE LEGAL SIDE OF LIVING TOGETHER: SOME CAUTIONARY ADVICE

When unmarried lovers decide to move in together, they can encounter regulations, customs, and laws that cause them problems, especially if they're not prepared for them. There are no firm legal guidelines to follow. State laws vary, and new court decisions can effect changes. But a look at some of the potential trouble spots can help.

SEX LAWS

Many state laws still forbid—under threat of fine or jail—sex between persons not married to each other. While such laws are seldom enforced these days, occasionally they are, particularly if someone makes a complaint.

A LEASE

When renting an apartment or house, renters usually must sign a lease. This is a legal contract, and failure to abide by it can mean eviction. Many leases specify how many people will live in the rental unit. For a single person who later decides to take in a friend, an objecting landlord proves troublesome.

When two or more unmarried people are looking for a place, landlords may ask each of them to sign the lease so that everyone involved is held individually responsible for its terms, including the total rent. This may also be true for utilities.

BANK ACCOUNTS

There are no legal restrictions against an unmarried couple's opening a joint bank account. It's important to realize, though, that one of the couple may then withdraw some or all of the money without the other's approval. Separate personal accounts could well be more sensible.

CREDIT CARDS AND CHARGE ACCOUNTS

Unmarried couples generally find it difficult to open joint charge accounts. Creditors view the relationship as unstable and fear that, as a result, bills may not be paid. A recent court decision, however, may lead to changes in this policy (see Weitzman, 1981:371).

If a store or utility company does issue a two-name account, both partners are legally responsible for all charges made by either of them, even if the relationship has ended. And creditors generally will not remove one person's

SOURCE:
Changing Times, May 1976; Weitzman, 1981.

name from an account until it is paid in full. Separate charge accounts are probably more advisable.

TAXES

It is illegal for unmarrieds to file a joint income tax return.

PROPERTY

When unmarrieds purchase a house or other property such as home furnishings together, it is a good idea to have a written agreement about what happens to the purchase should one partner die or the couple break up. If the property is held in "joint tenancy with the right of survivorship" and one dies, the other would take ownership without probate. If partners don't want one partner's share of the property to go to the other person, it can be held as "tenants in common," which means that it would go into the estate, to be distributed according to a will. In either case, if a partner decides to sell, a buyer will want both names on the deed. (The same would hold true for a jointly owned car; any buyer would want both names on the title.)

Surviving partners who do not have legal title to the couple's possessions or property have to establish a legal right to ownership in order to keep the property (Weitzman, 1981). On the other hand, it may be wise not to mingle property through joint title ownership because creditors could take one partner's property if the other partner gets into problems with debts.

INSURANCE

Anyone can buy life insurance and name anyone as the beneficiary. However, insurance companies sometimes require an "insurable interest," generally interpreted to mean a conventional family tie. Moreover, the routine extension of auto and home insurance policies to "residents of the household" cannot be presumed to include nonrelatives; one should check with the company about the terms of the policy (Weitzman, 1981:371).

WILLS

Nearly everyone has some property. Therefore, it's good planning for each partner to have a properly drawn up will. Telling relatives or friends what to do in case of death often doesn't work out. Since handwritten wills are not

(continued)

BOX 7 · 1

Continued

recognized in a majority of states and could cause more problems than they solve, it's better to have a lawyer's assistance.

CHILDREN

Children born to unmarried couples bring new legal issues. In some states the birth certificate indicates whether a child is legitimate. In many others it does not, listing only the mother's maiden name. Most states provide that children become legitimized if the natural parents marry or if the father accepts the child into his home or acknowledges the child as his, even though he doesn't marry the mother. While the question of legitimacy no longer has the significance it once did, cohabiting parents would be wise to formally acknowledge paternity in conformity with the laws of the state (Weitzman, 1981).

Recognition of an unmarried father's interest in custody or visitation of children was established in 1972 in the case of *Stanley* v. *Illinois* (405 U.S. 645), so that the unwed mother is no longer entitled to sole disposition of the child (Weitzman, 1981). Although the courts have placement discretion, couples should stipulate in writing that custody is to go to the father (if so desired) should the mother die.

BREAKING UP

One advantage people sometimes see in cohabiting is avoiding legal hassles in the event of a breakup. But if couples do not take care to stipulate in writing— and preferably before an attorney—paternity, property, and other agreements, legal hassles *can* result. An example is the much publicized Marvin case in which Michelle Triola asked for support from actor Lee Marvin after having lived with him for years and breaking up (*Marvin* v. *Marvin,* 18 Calif. 3rd 660, 1976).

Individuals have to decide how they want to live, based on their needs, values, and goals. In so doing, they will do well to be aware of the laws of their state. At the present time there are discrepancies between how people live (social reality) and the law (Weitzman, 1981). People may make choices that seem reasonable to them and that conform to their values, only to find they are not protected as they thought they were (in insurance or property rights while cohabiting, for example, or in a relationship to a stepchild whose biological parent dies). The law is slowly catching up to changes in gender roles and family life-styles. In the meantime the burden is on individuals and couples to keep informed.

"We're "Partners"—Not Husband and Wife," illustrates this view. Research based on census data suggests that cohabitation has a special appeal for young college and career women. The "evidence suggests that cohabitation is seen as an alternative or precursor to marriage for less traditional women interested in higher education and career.... Cohabitation can provide the emotional security of an intimate relationship without the legal and economic ties of marriage" (Bianchi and Spain, 1986:19–20).

Legal marriage does tend to impose expectations about what is appropriate husband-wife role behavior. Couples may live together with the expectation of expanding their choices in marriage; that is, they may expect to create their roles and allocate household tasks more freely than in traditional marriages. Thus far, however, this egalitarianism has been almost as elusive as it is in a legal marriage. One study that compared married with cohabiting women and men (childless college students) found that both married and unmarried couples tend to accept a very traditional division of labor by gender roles. This division is apparent in both the responsibility they see as their own and their actual performance. While cohabitants were somewhat less traditional in allocation and performance of household tasks, "cohabitation is apparently not the cure-all for traditional sex role ideology" (Stafford et al., 1977:54). Cohabiting men are more apt to do dishes and laundry, and women to engage in lawn mowing and home repairs, but there is little actual difference in roles between these young people and their parents. What seems to be preventing change is the carry-over of traditional socialization on the women's part and the reluctance of the less committed men to share housework (Stafford et al., 1977). The UCLA Lifestyles Project, however, researched fifty "social contract," or cohabiting, couples and found them less likely to have a traditional division of labor in domestic and financial tasks than marrieds. For those living together outside marriage, "tasks tended to be unplanned and shared in a flexible, variable manner" (Kornfein et al., 1979:271). Although the mother was the primary caregiver and child care was not equally divided, it was more so than with the legally married couples, where the mother was usually the sole caregiver. One facilitating factor was that—as a consequence of other aspects of their value systems—fewer fathers had regular jobs and hence were more available for child care.

A further concern of couples who seek to maximize personal choice by living together rather than marrying is that they may still be very much affected by legal regulation of their relationship. As people choose cohabitation, the legal aspects of living together outside of marriage are coming into focus and also changing. In 1984, for example, Berkeley, California, became the nation's first city to extend health and welfare benefits to live-in partners of its unmarried employees ("Berkeley Makes Unwed Partners Eligible," *Omaha World-Herald*, Dec. 16, 1984). Box 7•1, "The Legal Side of Living Together," outlines some important considerations for cohabitants *and* for married couples.

Alternatives: A Real Choice?

While the law, as well as one's socialization, may constrain choices, there are increasing options today for family living. The contemporary family's flexibility allows it to fill both practical day-to-day needs and emotional needs, as we've seen in this chapter. There are a variety of family forms from which to choose, and within those forms roles and life-styles may be negotiated.

But this flexibility requires individuals to make conscious decisions. People have to choose the family form that they are most comfortable with—a decision that is made initially and then perhaps remade later in one's life.

Summary

The family is a social institution that performs three critical functions in all cultures: reproduction and child rearing (with the father playing a basic role), economic support, and emotional security. The third function, emotional support, has become more and more important in recent years.

Families have changed both in the role structure within the family and in the family form itself. In traditional patriarchal societies the husband held the position of authority as the breadwinner of the family, while the wife and children deferred to his needs or wishes. Families have become more democratic, reflecting a shift to modern values, expectations, and attitudes. However, there are many holdovers from patriarchal customs.

Shifting needs and expectations have also caused family forms to change. A diversity of family forms exists today: the extended family, child-free families, dual-earner families, single-parent families, stepfamilies, communal families, homosexual families, and cohabiting partners. Since the last three forms may not be legally regarded as families, people who choose these life-styles may need to consider the legal implications of their choice.

Families must make decisions about what form they want their own family to take and also about how democratic they want it to be. The next chapter looks closely at some different kinds of relationships in marriages. We'll see, for example, that some couples focus on the practical functions and benefits of family living, while others emphasize their need for an emotionally supportive and intimate relationship.

Key Terms

social institution *223*

self-sufficient economic unit *226*

economic interdependence *226*

Equal Credit Opportunity Act *228*

democratic family *230*

egalitarian marriage *231*

child-free family *237*

dual-earner family *237*

dual-career marriage *237*

single-parent family *238*

stepfamily *239*

homosexual family *243*

Study Questions

1. Discuss the family as a social institution. Include a definition of social institutions and describe how the family fits that definition.
2. What, in detail, are the three most basic family functions in an advanced industrial society such as ours?
3. Is each of the three most basic family functions becoming more or less important as society becomes more complex? Why?
4. Discuss the notion of patriarchy as a family form. What are some examples of patriarchy in our society today?
5. Is patriarchy as strong in America as it used to be? Why or why not?
6. How do a wife's traditional obligations to her husband and family reflect the husband's position as patriarchal authority?
7. Some scientists believe that our society is shifting from a traditional to a modern family form. What differentiates these two types of systems? What might be some of the reasons for the shift?
8. What can research on homosexual relationships teach us about heterosexual relationships? About gender roles?
9. Differentiate among the many family forms that exist in our society. What do you see as advantages and disadvantages of each form?
10. Discuss your own notions of the ideal family.
11. Examine the effect that different family forms have on the child care provided in those families. How do these differences compare with your expectations of the kind of child care you would like to provide any children you may choose to parent?

Suggested Readings

Blumstein, Philip, and Pepper Schwartz
1983 *American Couples: Money, Work, Sex.* New York: Morrow.
   A new study of married couples and gay male, lesbian, and heterosexual cohabiting couples.

Lamb, Michael E. (ed.)
1982 *Nontraditional Families: Parenting and Child Development.* Hillsdale, N.J.: Lawrence Erlbaum.
   Important information for parents interested or involved in alternate family forms.

Lindsey, Karen
1982 *Friends as Family.* Boston: Beacon.
   Describes, advocates, and advises on development of friendship relationships into what are, functionally, kin relations.

Macklin, Eleanor D., and Roger H. Rubin (eds.)
1983 *Contemporary Families and Alternative Lifestyles: Handbook on Research and Theory.* Beverly Hills, Calif.: Sage.
   Up-to-date, well-researched articles on alternative life-styles.

Nye, F. Ivan, and Felix M. Berardo
1981 *Emerging Conceptual Frameworks in Family Analysis* (rev. ed. of Nye and Berardo, 1966). New York: Praeger.
   This volume contains definitive articles on theories of the family, including the structure-functional conceptual framework.

Peters, Marie F., and Harriette P. McAdoo
1983 "The present and future of alternative lifestyles
      in ethnic American cultures." Pp. 288–307 in
      Eleanor D. Macklin and Roger H. Rubin (eds.),
      *Contemporary Families and Alternative Life-
      styles: Handbook on Research and Theory.*
      Beverly Hills, Calif.: Sage.
      Review of research on alternative family forms
      among minority racial and ethnic groups.
Queen, Stuart A., Robert W. Habenstein, and Jill S.
      Guadogno (eds.)
1985 *The Family in Various Cultures,* 5th ed. New
      York: Harper & Row.
      This book stresses variations in family structure.
Renvoize, Jean
1985 *Going Solo: Single Mothers by Choice.* Boston:
      Routledge & Kegan Paul.
      This potentially controversial book explores
      issues surrounding women deliberately choos-
      ing to have children outside a permanent rela-
      tionship. The author analyzes the position of
      both the children of these single families and
      their mothers. She looks at men's feelings about
      being used as a "stud" and uncovers the desire
      of some men to father children without being
      financially and/or emotionally involved with a
      long-term partner.
Shorter, Edward
1975 *The Making of the Modern Family.* New York:
      Basic Books.
      Readable history of the change from practical to
      sentimental family relationships.
Spiro, Melford
1956 *Kibbutz: Venture in Utopia.* Cambridge, Mass.:
      Harvard University Press.
1958 *Children of the Kibbutz.* Cambridge, Mass.:
      Harvard University Press.
1979 *Gender and Culture: Kibbutz Women Revis-
      ited.* Durham, N.C.: Duke University Press.
      An interesting and analytical account of this
      successful venture.
Stack, Carol
1974 *All Our Kin: Strategies for Survival.* New
      York: Harper & Row.
      A contemporary urban anthropological study of
      black subculture, particularly the black family.

8

Marriage: A Flexible Relationship

Marriage is not an answer, but a search, a process, a search for life, just as dialogue is a search for truth.
SIDNEY JOURARD

As the three following statements suggest, married couples can have vastly different relationships. Despite the wide variations, all marriages have an important element in common: the commitment that partners have made to each other through the act of marrying.

I wish [marriage] would be more exciting, but I should have known it couldn't last. In a way, it's calm and quiet and reassuring this way, but there are times when I get very ill at ease—sometimes downright mad. Does it *have* to be like this? [in Cuber and Harroff, 1965:54–55].

We've been married for over twenty years and the most enjoyable thing either of us does—well, outside of the intimate things—is to sit and talk by the hour [in Cuber and Harroff, 1965:57].

I don't know how many marriages I have had by now, but I am married at the present time to a different woman of the same name in ways that are suited to our present stage of growth as human beings [Jourard, in Williams and Crosby, 1979:233]. ■

Marriage—both the common element of commitment and the ways in which (and reasons why) marriages vary—is the subject of this chapter. In the discussions that follow, we'll look especially at how marriage relationships reflect personal choices, either active or by default, for the kind of relationship a couple shares is a product of the values, expectations, and efforts they invest in it. We'll also propose our own views about ways a couple can plan or alter their marriage relationship to better meet their needs. Guidelines for one way of doing this, through a personal marriage contract, appear toward the end of the chapter. Finally, we will explore preparation for and the first years of marriage. To begin with, we'll examine the common beliefs, values, and expectations inherent in the *marriage premise.*

THE MARRIAGE PREMISE

In March 1979 the following letter appeared in Ann Landers' column:

Dear Ann:
   Al and I are college seniors. We met during our freshman year. The attraction was instant and mutual....
   We talked about getting married after graduation. I thought we had an understanding so I let him move in with me.
   Last night I started to talk about the kind of wedding I wanted. He looked very uncomfortable.

■ When they were married fifty-eight years ago, Arthur and Ida assumed they would spend the rest of their lives together. Even with today's high divorce rate, couples continue to accept the two main tenets of the marriage premise: permanence and primariness.

Finally he blurted out, "Don't let's spoil everything by getting married." . . .

His message was clear—two people should stay together and remain faithful because they want to, not because they are bound together by law.

I am shattered and heartsick. Now I am asking myself, why should he marry me? He has all the advantages of marriage and none of the responsibilities. ■

The letter dramatizes three important points. First, marriage is different from cohabiting—the letter writer and her partner agree on that. Second, marriage, like cohabiting, can offer people advantages, such as companionship, psychic and sexual intimacy, and emotional support. Third, marriage involves more responsibilities than cohabiting. By getting married, partners accept the responsibility to keep each other primary in their lives and to work hard to ensure that their relationship continues. Essentially, this is the **marriage premise**. We can look more closely at the two important elements of this definition: permanence and primariness.

Expectations of Permanence

A wedding is a community event marking a bride and groom's passage into adult family roles. Whether spouses loved each other was only recently considered important, as we saw in Chapter 6. And with few exceptions, marriages were always thought of as permanent, lifelong commitments.

Although it is statistically less permanent now than it has ever been in our society, marriage is still pretty much "for keeps." The marriage contract remains the one legal contract between two persons that cannot be broken without permission of society or the state. Many religions also urge permanence in marriage. In our society couples usually vow publicly to stay together "until death do us part," or "so long as we both shall live." Marriage, more than any other relationship, holds the hope for permanence. People enter marriage expecting—hoping—that mutual affection will be lasting.

Expectations for permanence derive from the fact that, historically, marriage has been a practical social institution. Economic security and responsible child rearing required marriages to be permanent, and even at the turn of the century, parents only occasionally outlived the departure of their last child from home.

Today, as we've seen in earlier chapters, marriage is somewhat less important for economic security. However, another function has become more important for most people: They expect marriage to provide emotional support and love. It might be said that we are coming closer to realizing a prediction made by social theorist Herbert Spencer in 1876, that someday "union by law" would no longer be the essential part of marriage. Rather, "union by affection will be held of primary moment" (Spencer, 1876, cited in Burgess and Locke, 1953:29).

Today even intimate marriages are usually held together by more than mutual affection, and that is why marriages remain more permanent than other intimate relationships. If there were no legal contract, marriage would be no different from living together. Today's marriages continue to be bolstered by mores (that is, by strongly held social norms), public opinion, and the law, although less so than in the past. Tradition, religious beliefs, and social pressure from family and friends all encourage couples to spend considerable time and energy working to improve their relationship before they contemplate divorce. As a result, marriages, more than other intimate relationships today, last for life.

As far back as 1949, Margaret Mead pointed out that "all the phraseology, the expectation of marriage that would last, 'until death do us part,' has survived long after most states have adopted laws permitting cheap and quick divorces" (1949:334). The result is "great contradictoriness" in American culture. People "are still encouraged to marry as if they could count on marriage's being for life, and at the same time they are absorbing a knowledge of the great frequency of divorce" (Mead, 1949:335). The recognition of this cultural contradiction is a step toward self-understanding and a help in making personal choices about permanence in marriage. Today "marriage *may* be for life, *can* be for life, but also may not be" (Mead, 1949:338).

Marital relationships can be permanently satisfying, counselors advise, only if spouses give up the romantic myth of the effortless, conflict-free, and "happy" relationship. Loving, but not romanticizing, can grow with time, knowledge, intimacy, and shared experience. Spouses who want to stay together must learn to care for the "unvarnished" other, not a "splendid image" (van den Haag, 1974:142). In this regard psychoanalyst Sidney Jourard addressed an audience about his own marriage of twenty-six years. Here is part of what he said:

Marriage is not for happiness, I have concluded after 26½ years. It's a many splendored thing, a place to learn how to live with human beings who differ from oneself in age, sex, values, and perspectives. It's a place to learn how to hate and

to control hate. It's a place to learn laughter and love and dialogue [Jourard, 1979:234]. ■

Getting married, then, can encourage partners to continue to commit themselves to learning how to live with each other, to developing, through the course of their individual life cycles, an ongoing love relationship.

Expectations of Primariness

You can see that people's expectations for marriage are more flexible than they were in the past. Just as some people are recognizing that marriages are not necessarily for life, people are marrying for different reasons than they once did. Especially among middle-class Americans, marriage involves the expectations of **primariness**: the commitment of both partners to keeping each other the most important persons in their lives. This commitment can be interpreted in two ways, either strictly or more broadly.

Primariness as Sexual Exclusivity   Often, but not always, couples agree that primariness will include expectations of **sexual exclusivity**, sometimes referred to by social scientists as monogamy or **strict monogamy**, in which partners promise to have sexual relations only with each other. Strict sexual exclusivity emerged as a cultural value in traditional society to maintain the patriarchal line of descent; the wedding ring placed on the bride's finger by the groom symbolized this expectation of sexual exclusivity on her part. The Judeo-Christian tradition extended expectations of sexual exclusivity to include both husbands and wives. For example, the Book of Common Prayer asks both partners to "forsake all others." Today brides and grooms often exchange wedding rings, and the majority of husbands and wives feel that extramarital sex for either partner is wrong (Hunt, 1974).

How closely do the actions of married couples support these beliefs? One writer points out that while monogamy remains the cultural ideal, it is not as widespread in practice as people think. The available data, according to one social scientist, "support the notion that we pay lip service to the monogamous ideal but in fact do maintain a significant variety of other sexual lifestyles" (Whitehurst, 1977:17).

Social scientists and marriage counselors may argue as to whether strict monogamy enhances a marital relationship; they do agree, however, that it does not do so automatically. One writer argues that monogamy remains "simply a form of private property" and promotes jealousy and undue worry about whether a partner will "cheat." Should a spouse be "caught," the result is resentment, antagonism, guilt, and loss of self-worth for both partners. The divorce that can result may be unnecessary (McMurtry, 1977:5–8).

Extramarital Sex

Taboos against extramarital sex are widespread among the world's cultures, but the proscription against extramarital sex is stronger in the United States than in most other parts of the world. In 1980, 70 percent of Americans believed that extramarital sex was "always wrong"; and only 4 percent felt that it is never wrong (Davis, 1980).

While a large majority of Americans publicly disapprove of extramarital sex, in practice the picture is somewhat different. Alfred Kinsey's 1953 study of American sexuality showed that 26 percent of wives and 50 percent of husbands said they had had at least one affair by the time they were 40 years old (Kinsey et al., 1953). Statistics on extramarital sex are probably less than totally accurate because they are based on what people report—some spouses hesitate to admit an affair; others boast about affairs that didn't really happen. Nevertheless, widely accepted figures do suggest that more than half of all American husbands and 30 to 50 percent of wives have been unfaithful at least once. While the sexual revolution of the 1960s did not seem to immediately increase the incidence of extramarital sex, research done in the 1970s and 1980s found that the percentages were somewhat higher for spouses under 30, especially wives (Hall, 1987; Hunt, 1974; Levin, 1975; Tavris and Sadd, 1977). The fact is that today, as in the past, many spouses are torn between lifelong commitment to a sexually exclusive relationship and the desire for outside sexual relationships.

Reasons for Extramarital Affairs Many affairs are prompted neither by deep emotional dissat-

isfaction with one's spouse nor by the desire to find a new one. Social scientist Robert Bell (1966) lists eight reasons why people engage in extramarital sex:

1. They are seeking variety.
2. They are retaliating against a real or imagined infidelity on the part of their mate, or they are seeking revenge for some hurt inflicted by their partner.
3. They are rebelling against the norm of monogamy.
4. They are seeking emotional satisfaction.
5. They have friendly relations with the outside partner that have developed into a sexual relationship.
6. The husband or wife encouraged the affair.
7. They are proving that they are still young and attractive.
8. They are engaging in extramarital relations for pure pleasure.

Actually, reasons for affairs are seldom clear-cut or easy to explain. A person may be motivated by a combination of reasons. Many affairs are prompted by curiosity or a desire for variety, and the opportunity presents itself at the "right" time (Bernard, 1982). Sociologists Stanford Lyman and Marvin Scott argue that extramarital affairs are one of the few areas of "adventure" available in modern society (Lyman and Scott, 1975). Studies have found that people with liberated attitudes toward premarital sex are also likely to have fairly permissive attitudes toward extramarital sex (Tavris and Sadd, 1977; Singh et al., 1976; Bukstel et al., 1978).

Affairs may also result from an identity crisis during a period of transition in one's life (Lasswell and Lobsenz, 1977). When he feels the first pangs of aging, for example, a husband may feel the need to reaffirm his attractiveness and virility with women. A wife may decide, "This is my last chance to have a fling before I lose my looks" (Sheehy, 1974).

Some extramarital affairs are casual and unemotional; others are more enduring—the person may feel that she or he is really in love. Falling in love may occur because the partner feels that his or her emotional needs are not being met at home. One study found that extramarital affairs may fulfill needs that are associated with a person's age and sex. For older wives and younger husbands, these relationships were likely to fill an emotional void or to compensate for marital unhappiness. For younger wives and older husbands, affairs developed not out of marital dissatisfaction but from the desire for sexual variety and adventure (Glass and Wright, 1977).

Effects of Extramarital Affairs For many spouses, concern about AIDS possibly contracted by means of extramarital sex—particularly the casual "one-night stand"—may increase anger, distrust, and turmoil over affairs. Still, the effect an extramarital affair has on a marriage is not always adverse. The result depends on a number of factors, including partners' reasons for entering affairs, their honesty with each other, and their expectations for each other. Generally, the effect of an extramarital affair depends on how each partner balances appropriate individual and family needs.

In 1972 several social scientists were asked how an affair affects a marriage. James Framo, chief of the family therapy training unit at a Philadelphia mental health center, replied, "It is rare for the affair itself to break up the marriage. In some cases the affair turns out to have a therapeutic effect by revitalizing a depleted relationship. In others, the basic trust never gets reestablished and the heightened suspicion gets incorporated into other problems the couple might have" (Framo, in Duberman, 1977:67).

Whether the basic trust is reestablished depends on several factors. One is how much trust there was in the first place, and that is difficult to determine. Survey data consistently link extramarital sex to marital unhappiness and divorce. Whether extramarital sex causes marital strain, which in turn leads to divorce, or whether extramarital sex results from marital dissatisfaction is an open question. Probably both are true. Two social scientists suggest the following sequence of events: The more severe the marital strain, the lower the frequency of marital coitus; as the latter becomes less frequent, extramarital sex is more likely to occur (Edwards and Booth, 1976).

We saw that older men who are involved in affairs are not particularly dissatisfied with their marriages, but they do have a higher divorce rate than older women who become involved in affairs. These women may remain married for pragmatic reasons and may continue to meet their emotional needs through extramarital sex. Older husbands may divorce more often, either because those who

divorce have unexpectedly become caught up emotionally with the extramarital partner and can financially afford to leave the marriage, or because their wives divorced them when they discovered the affair (Glass and Wright, 1977).

There is potential for harm to a primary relationship, or at the least, competition for time and emotional energy between a primary relationship and an outside sexual relationship. Jealousy is a real issue to be dealt with in marriages and other intimate relationships (see Box 8·1, "Jealousy"). But some people may regard extramarital sex as an activity quite segregated from the marriage or as an openly acknowledged freedom of the parties within the marriage.

Given that a significant amount of extramarital sex does occur, there will also be many who rethink the issue when they discover that a partner has engaged in extramarital sex without their consent. They will need to consider how important that is to them vis-à-vis the marital or primary relationship as a whole.

Marriage and Opposite-Sex Friends As a society publicly dedicated to strict monogamy, Americans are wary of opposite-sex friendships because of their potential for sexual involvement (Bell, 1975; Booth and Hess, 1974). Thus, there is no widely accepted role for cross-sex friendships or cross-sex colleagueships at work (Safilios-Rothschild, 1983). Perhaps the nearest role that society knows and understands is that of a lover, says Philip Lampe, and this can create a self-fulfilling prophecy:

Individuals involved in such a normless role as friends-of-the-opposite-sex to a married person may ultimately be driven by the forces of the self-fulfilling prophecy, or they may simply find it easier to gravitate in the clearer, more defined and "accepted" role of lovers [1976:14]. ■

An exception occurs when a wife develops a friendship with one of her husband's male friends (Booth and Hess, 1974). Here, respect for the husband's patriarchal claim prompts all three to define the friendship as inherently platonic.

At least into the 1970s, research indicates that more husbands (about one-third) than wives (about one-fourth) have formed opposite-sex friendships (Booth and Hess, 1974). Much of this difference was due to the fact that until recently, married

BOX 8 · 1

JEALOUSY

It has sometimes been assumed that as American spouses, we do not—or should not—feel jealous. Indeed, in some circles the partner who is jealous feels guiltier than the partner with an extramarital involvement (Kafka and Ryder, 1974). Until fairly recently, the topic of jealousy has been neglected by researchers. They apparently assumed that this emotion was not a serious concern in contemporary American marriages (see Bernard, 1977). Today, however, we're realizing that jealousy is widespread and perhaps even inevitable. In one study 96 percent of the respondents reported feeling jealous at some time (Bryson, in Adams, 1980).

One reason jealousy is so prevalent is that America is a paired, family-oriented society that emphasizes ownership and private property. "It is characterized by competition and a strong desire to have a perfect relationship. All these aspects of contemporary American society tend to aggravate the feeling and expression of jealousy" (Aronson and Pines, in Adams, 1980:107). Moreover, jealousy may be inherent in love and intimacy: "It may be that precisely what we most value about certain relationships is what also makes them essentially non-replicable and nonshareable and hence leaves a place for jealousy" (Aronson and Pines, in Adams, 1980:107).

While we tend to equate feeling jealous with sexual threats to a relationship, other threats also evoke jealousy. Friends, colleagues, work, education or leisure commitments, and even a couple's children can be perceived, in the words of sociologists Gerald McDonald and Marie Osmond, as "trespassers" (1980:4). McDonald and Osmond note Ronald Mazur's (1977) separation of different types of *perceived threat:* (1) "possessive jealousy," in which the "spouse is seen only as an extension of the self"; (2) "exclusion jealousy," where the spouse is fearful of being left out of the partner's enjoyable experiences; (3) "competition jealousy," where one partner compares him- or herself to the other and is concerned about relative achievement and recognition; (4) "egotism jealousy," where one

women were primarily full-time homemakers and had relatively little opportunity to meet and form friendships with men. But the difference also stems from the belief that opposite-sex friendships "naturally" lead to adultery, along with the fact that patriarchal societies are more concerned about wives' adultery than about husbands'.

Observers point out that pressures against opposite-sex friendships in our society are restrictive. In most cases these pressures mean that once we become adults, we must eliminate the possibility of friendship with half the members of society (Bell, 1975:155). An alternative is for partners to adopt a more flexible attitude and allow each

other to have opposite-sex friendships. Partners will need to negotiate this agreement carefully, however, and explicitly define whether these outside friendships will include sex.

Flexible Monogamy Some counselors emphasize that monogamy is very meaningful in today's relationships, but the definition may be changing. Rather than defining primariness only as the banning of extramarital intercourse specifically, some spouses are shifting to a more positive definition, "one that is based on a broader commitment to a partner and to a relationship, a commitment that may or may not emphasize sexual exclusivity as its

partner is expected by the other to conform to role stereotypes; and (5) "fear jealousy," associated with low self-esteem and fear of rejection by the partner. Again referring to Mazur's work, McDonald and Osmond (1980) note that different types of jealousy may evoke different emotions, such as rage or depression.

Several research projects—one a survey of 150 "romantically involved" heterosexual couples, mostly UCLA students; another a laboratory observation of emotional responses to a videotape of a woman meeting her partner's old flame—conclude that the more dependent, or the more involved, partner is more likely to be jealous (Horn, 1978; Adams, 1980). Those who feel insecure or have poor self-images are more inclined toward jealousy. Moreover, "the men and women with the greatest overall dissatisfaction with their lives were those who felt jealous most often" (Adams, 1980:41).

While both women and men experience jealousy, research has found differences in how each reacts to it. Women, being more likely to monitor relationships, are more apt to try to change to please their partners so as to avoid the threat of another relationship. Men, meanwhile, are more apt to seek solace or retribution in alternative relationships. Furthermore, a woman is more likely to test a relationship by deliberate attempts to make her partner jealous. (Chapter 10 addresses power in heterosexual relationships.) "For women, especially for those who feel more involved than their mates, provoking jealousy may be a way of trying to gain control and of redressing the balance of power" (Adams, 1980:105).

While marital jealousy can probably never be completely eliminated, mutually supportive encouragement may lessen feelings of insecurity and jealousy. Finally, nurturing one's self-esteem and trust can allay jealousy. Jealousy, like pain, may need to be viewed as a warning signal. It may mean that one or both partners' interests in outside activities need to be functionally balanced with activities within the relationship.

sole or most important ingredient" (Lasswell and Lobsenz, 1979:60).

Those who advocate this interpretation of primariness as **flexible monogamy**, in which a couple allows each other some sexual freedom, insist that the marital relationship should remain the primary one. In a primary relationship, as distinct from a necessarily exclusive relationship, two persons give their first loyalty to each other rather than to society's traditional expectations.

If we interpret fidelity to mean a primary commitment to one's partner and the relationship, then maintaining emotional intimacy becomes essential to being faithful. Without continued intimacy and self-disclosure, partners may not remain in love or keep a central place in each other's lives. Emotional commitment, in this view, is the essential element of primariness.

This new focus on the more flexible values of primariness can make marriage relationships more satisfying. It can also make marriage more difficult to maintain, for it emphasizes the quality of the relationship rather than a couple's responsibility to society.

We've just seen that marriage implies both permanence and primariness, and that different individuals interpret these two values in very different ways. While the marriage premise is a foundation on which all marriages rest, it is also a flexible base that allows partners a great deal of leeway.

The quality of flexibility is one of the most notable aspects in marriage, and in the next two sections we'll look at two dimensions of this flexibility. The first is the ways partners have of relating to each other, and the kinds of needs their relationships fill (or don't fill); the second is the degree of flexibility in a long-term relationship: how capable it is of changing over time as individual partners change. We'll look at the variety of types of marriages first, starting with two relationships that lie at opposite ends of the marriage spectrum—utilitarian and intrinsic.

TYPES OF MARRIAGES

Depending on individual preferences and socioeconomic backgrounds, American spouses choose to emphasize either practical or emotional benefits of marriage. The more practical style can be called *utilitarian marriage;* the more emotional, *intrinsic.* In utilitarian marriages the emphasis is on marriage as a means to other ends; in intrinsic marriages the relationship is an end in itself. Our discussion of these and other relationships is drawn from the categories outlined by John Cuber and Peggy Harroff (1965), who examined marital relationships by conducting extensive interviews with upper middle-class couples.

Utilitarian Marriages

Utilitarian marriage is a union begun or maintained for primarily practical purposes. Sometimes referred to as marriages of convenience, utilitarian unions do not focus on intimacy between partners. Single parents may enter or reenter marriage, for example, primarily to gain a spouse's help with child rearing. There are several reasons people may enter utilitarian marriages.

Reasons for Entering Utilitarian Marriages
For some people, utilitarian marriage may provide material luxuries or career advancement or simply basic economic security. Studies suggest that some groups are more likely to marry for economic security than are other groups—for example, divorced women with children to support (White, 1979). But utilitarian marriages exist in all social classes.

For many Americans, reasons for marrying reflect the basic exchange described in Chapter 6, in which women offer homemaking abilities, child care, and sexual availability in return for economic security. As one blue-collar husband explained, "A man, sooner or later, likes to have a home of his own, and some kids, and to have that you have to get married. There's no way out of it—they got you hooked" (LeMasters, 1975:37).

Economic reasons and the basic exchange are not the only motivations for utilitarian marriages. These relationships are often held together by a sense of duty and obligation. Wealthier spouses often express pride in doing what they "ought" to do: maintaining a "good family" in good taste, achieving occupational prestige, contributing to the community, and providing their children with opportunities for high educational achievement (Cuber and Harroff, 1965:111–15).

Duty motivates blue-collar couples as well. Sociologist E. E. LeMasters participated in the social life at a blue-collar neighborhood tavern, listening to patrons and observing their behavior. He observed:

In a very real sense, these couples ... are traditionalists when it comes to marriage: they literally took an oath "for better or worse" and have abided by the agreement. One wife said: "Nobody told me how bad 'worse' could be but then I never asked. I was too anxious to get married to ask any questions" [LeMasters, 1975:48]. ▪

While duty can have negative implications, spouses may still be highly appreciative of and affectionate toward each other. Utilitarian spouses often tell of the positive side of their partners in pragmatic terms, such as their value as homemakers or economic providers, or their supportiveness for careers. Their reasons for staying married are also pragmatic or "institutional," motivated by benefits traditionally associated with the family as an institution. Put another way, the forces holding utilitarian marriages together are other than the desire to continue intimacy through time (Cuber and Harroff, 1965:110).

Characteristic Relationship Patterns Utilitarian spouses characteristically have segregated roles and interests. Sociologist Jessie Bernard noted what she called a **parallel relationship** pattern among spouses in the working class, and she distinguised this pattern from the **interactional marriage pattern** that exists in an intrinsic marriage (described later).

If the man is a good provider, not excessive in his sexual demands, sober most of the time, and good to the children, this is about all a woman can reasonably ask. Similarly, if the woman is a good housekeeper and cook, not too nagging, a willing sex partner, and a good mother, this is all a man can really expect. Each lives his or her own life primarily in a male or female world.... Companionship in the sense of exchange of ideas or opinions or the enhancement of personality by verbal play or conversation is not considered a basic component in this pattern [Bernard, 1964:687]. ■

This parallel relationship pattern contrasts with an interactional relationship pattern in which the partners' lives are entwined and they are more emotionally involved with each other. According to sociologist Lee Rainwater's classification, couples fall into three types, which are closely related to economic classes. In **joint conjugal relationships** couples carry out most of their activities jointly. They share their leisure time and are highly involved emotionally with each other. In contrast, other couples, particularly those in the lower class or the lower ranks of the working class, have **segregated conjugal relationships** in which each partner has separate leisure pursuits and friends. The husband has his buddies, the wife her female neighbors and relatives (Rainwater, 1968; Bott, 1957). The wife's freedom to go out (although not the husband's) is usually curtailed, however, and this may be true also in higher-level working-class families (Komarovsky, 1962; Marciano, 1977).

Between joint and segregated relationships are **intermediate conjugal relationships**, characteristic of some working-class and most lower middle-class families, in which the middle-class value of couple togetherness and intimacy limits separate leisure pursuits. Rainwater points out that active sharing is not emphasized strongly in these relationships. Although couples might be together, watching TV or reading magazines, they "amuse themselves alone, do not talk with each other about what they see or read, but still feel that such activ-

ities reflect their 'togetherness'" (Rainwater, 1965:277).

In the 1960s social scientist Herbert Gans studied blue-collar Italian-Americans in Boston. Their marriage relationships at that time, he concluded, tended to be "qualitatively different" from the middle-class ideal, with less communication and little emotional gratification. There existed a "sexual barrier": When one partner had troubles, that person was most likely to seek support from his or her same-sex friends or siblings, not from the other partner (Gans, 1962).

There is a clear segregation of roles in affluent utilitarian marriages, too. A husband who had married to secure a promotion explained that his bride had been "ready for maternity wards and rose gardens." "We stay out of each other's lives all we can," he added, "but we cooperate in every way with what the other one wants" (Cuber and Harroff, 1965:108–9). As was noted above, however, there may also be affectionate ties between utilitarian couples: Not all partners "Stay out of each other's lives" so completely.

Intrinsic Marriages

Although a number of people marry for utilitarian reasons, most middle-class Americans value intrinsic marriages as a cultural ideal and personal goal. The basic quality of **intrinsic marriage** is "the intensity of feelings about each other and the centrality of the spouse's welfare in each mate's scale of values" (Cuber and Harroff, 1965:144).

Intrinsic marriages rest on intimacy and mutual affection between partners. While utilitarian marriages offer *community rewards*, such as financial security, extended kin and other social approval, and acceptance, intrinsic marriages offer *personal rewards*. Partners work to fill as much as possible each other's personal needs for sexual expession, companionship, and affection. One study of 301 married individuals in Dane County, Wisconsin, investigated spouses' "relational commitment." The researchers found that a high level of emotional interdependence between spouses—coupled with their perception that the relationship was equitable (in other words, that, all things considered, the outcomes they derived from their relationships were proportionate to their investments)—more strongly predicted marital commitment than did utilitarian reasons for staying together (Sabatelli and Cecil-Pigo, 1985).

Jessie Bernard contrasted the parallel marriage pattern, common to utilitarian unions, with the interactional marriage pattern, which demands a great deal more personal empathic involvement. Partners emphasize companionship and expressions of love, and uniqueness of personality is cherished more than role performance (Bernard, 1964:688). Intrinsic partners genuinely enjoy being with each other and their recreational activities together are often "much less standardized, less conventional, less formal" than among utilitarian couples (Cuber and Harroff, 1965:137).

Despite the closeness with which they merge their lives, intrinsic partners do experience separateness, conflict, and even loneliness. Couples can work at sharing most things, but they cannot share everything. And as we saw in the discussion in Chapter 3 of legitimate and illegitimate needs, no two people can completely fulfill each other. The failure of many people to accept this fact is a major reason social scientists give for our increasing divorce rate.

In fact, intrinsic marriages are more vulnerable to divorce than are utilitarian marriages. People's high expectations about intrinsic relationships are often unrealistic. Unlike utilitarian marriages, intrinsic ones are held together primarily by mutual affection and intimacy; and despite partners' closeness and empathy, there can be no guarantee that the intimacy will continue indefinitely. Partners are less likely to stay together for economic and practical benefits, or from a sense of duty and obligation. As one man reported, "When something came up which destroyed the closeness, the relationship quickly disintegrated" (Cuber and Harroff, 1965:144).

In real life very few marriages are either completely utilitarian or completely intrinsic. Rather, these two types represent opposite ends or poles of an imaginary line or continuum. Real-life marriages fall somewhere on the continuum to varying degrees, combining elements of pragmatism and emotional sharing. Between the two extremes is an almost limitless variety of types of marriage relationships.

We can't look at every possible kind of relationship here, but we can look at a few representative types based on the research of social scientists John Cuber and Peggy Harroff, who conducted extensive interviews with upper middle-class cou-ples. From their research Cuber and Harroff classified five kinds of marital relationships that act as useful prototypes.[1] Two are utilitarian, two are intrinsic, and one (conflict-habituated) is difficult to define as either utilitarian or intrinsic.

Five Marriage Relationships

Based on their interviews with 107 men and 104 women, Cuber and Harroff classified marital relationships as follows: conflict-habituated, devitalized, passive-congenial, vital, and total. They emphasized that their findings represented "different kinds of adjustment and conceptions of marriage, rather than degrees of marital happiness" (Cuber and Harroff, 1965:61). In other words couples living in any of these relationships might or might not be satisfied with them. The relationships differ according to how spouses feel about their marriages. Other researchers also have found these five relationship types among cohabitants (Clatworthy, 1975:77ff.).

Conflict-Habituated Couples with a **conflict-habituated marriage** experience considerable tension and unresolved conflict. Spouses habitually quarrel, nag, and bring up the past. As a rule, both spouses acknowledge their incompatibility and recognize the atmosphere of tension as normal.

Conflict-habituated relationships differ from those in which conflicts arise over specific issues. In conflict-habituated relationships the subject of the argument hardly seems important, and partners generally do not resolve, or expect to resolve, their differences. "Of course we don't settle any of the issues," said a veteran of twenty-five years of this type of marriage. "It's sort of a matter of principle *not* to. Because somebody would have to give in then and lose face for the next encounter" (Cuber and Harroff, 1965:45).

---

1. In a smaller study psychoanalytic therapist George Bach selected and interviewed fifty "normally happy" couples. While he concluded that three, rather than five, groups emerged, his findings generally support Cuber and Harroff's. The largest group, Bach reported, "were held together largely by the partners' . . . concern for appearances, social success, status, and 'respectability'" (Bach and Wyden, 1970:47). Partners in a second, smaller group were "somewhat more intimate" but generally devitalized; and the third group—"natural geniuses at maintaining realistic intimacy"—consisted of only two couples.

I wish that Stanley and I could like each other when we are together - But we don't.

Patty Brann

These relationships do not necessarily end with divorce. In fact, it has been suggested by some psychiatrists that for some partners this kind of marriage fulfills a need for conflict. In this sense conflict-habituated relationships are intrinsic relationships, for they fill partners' emotional needs. The relationships cannot be called intimate, however, for they are not based on mutual acceptance and support or on honest self-disclosure.

Devitalized Partners in a **devitalized marriage** have typically been married several years, and over the course of this time, the relationship has lost its original zest, intimacy, and meaning. Once deeply in love, they recall spending a great deal of time together, enjoying sex, and having a close emotional relationship. Their present situation is in sharp contrast: They spend little time together, enjoy sex less, and no longer share many interests and activities. Most of their time together is "duty time" spent entertaining, planning and sharing activities with their children, and participating in community responsibilities and functions. Once an intrinsic union, the marriage has become utilitarian.

Cuber and Haroff found devitalized marriages

exceedingly common among their respondents. They also found several reactions among devitalized partners. Some were accepting and tried to be "mature about it." As one wife explained, "There's a cycle to life. There are things you do in high school. And different things you do in college. Then you're a young adult. And then you're middle-aged. That's where we are now" (in Cuber and Harroff, 1965:47–48). Others were resentful and bitter; and still others were ambivalent. From his study of a group of fifty marriages, psychoanalyst George Bach provides a description:

Essentially they had resigned themselves to . . . ritualized routines. . . . They were mutual protective associations who looked on their marriage as pretty much of a lost cause but felt it would be disloyal and ill-mannered to complain about it, especially since the loneliness of being unmarried would probably be worse [Bach and Wyden, 1970:47–48]. ■

Emotional emptiness does not necessarily threaten the stability of a marriage. Many people, like the accepting wife just quoted, believe that the devitalized mode is appropriate for spouses who have been married several years. Devitalized partners frequently compare their relationship with others who have similar relationships, concluding that "marriage is like this—except for a few oddballs or pretenders who claim otherwise" (Cuber and Harroff, 1965:50).

Passive-Congenial   Partners in a **passive-congenial marriage** (utilitarian), like devitalized partners, accent qualities other than emotional closeness. These qualities may be different for different groups. Upper middle-class couples tend to emphasize civic and professional responsibilities and the importance of property, children, and reputation; working-class people focus on their need for economic security, the benefits of the basic exchange, and their hopes for their children. (See Box 8-2, "Working-Class Marriages" for a discussion of difficulties working-class partners experience in their unions.)

Unlike the devitalized marriage, passive-congenial partners never expected marriage to encompass emotional intensity. Instead, they stress the "sensibility" of their decision to marry. There is little conflict, but that does not mean there are no unspoken frustrations. And while there is little intimacy, these unions fill partners' needs for more casual companionships.

Passive-congenial marriages are less likely to end in divorce than unions in which partners have unrealistic expectations of emotional intensity. Partners may decide to terminate passive-congenial unions, however, if they feel the marriage is not adequately filling their more practical needs, such as for economic support or professional advancement. Or one partner may discover that he or she wants greater intimacy from a relationship or may inadvertently fall in love with someone else.

Vital   The vital relationship offers an extreme contrast to the three foregoing kinds of marriage. In a **vital marriage**, a type of intrinsic marriage, being together and sharing are intensely enjoyable and important. One husband said:

The things we do together aren't fun intrinsically—the ecstasy comes from being *together in the doing.* Take her out of the picture and I wouldn't give a damn for the boat, the lake, or any of the fun that goes on out there [in Cuber and Harroff, 1965:55]. ■

This statement should not lead you to believe that vital partners lose their separate identities, nor that conflict does not occur in vital marriages. There is conflict, but it is more apt to center on real issues rather than the "who said what first and when" and "I can't forget when you . . ." that characterize conflict-habituated marriages. And vital partners try to settle disagreements quickly so they can resume the relationship that means so much to both.

Because partners settle differences as they arise, few areas of tension remain in vital marriages of long duration. (Facing and resolving conflict in marriage are addressed in Chapter 9.)

Typically, vital partners consider sex important and pleasurable. "It seems to be getting *better* all the time," said one spouse, age 55. Instead of being dutifully performed as a ritual, sexuality pervaded vital partners' whole lives. A grandmother spoke about it this way:

You can't draw the line between being in bed together and just being alive together. You can touch tenderly when you pass; you wait for the

■ "His and hers" means "ours" in a total marriage, a partnership of friends and lovers. Learning and growing together, such couples act as a team, sharing work, friends, and hobbies in addition to their home life.

intimate touch in the morning. Even the scents you make in bed together are cherished [in Cuber and Harroff, 1965:135–36]. ■

Vital marriages are a minority, and most vital partners know it. Those in Cuber and Harroff's research often reported feeling that their life-styles were neither experienced nor understood by their associates. Even more rare are total marriages.

Total **Total marriages** are also intrinsic. They are like vital marriages, only more multifaceted. "The points of vital meshing are more numerous—

in some cases all of the important life foci are vitally shared" (Cuber and Harroff, 1965:58).

Spouses may share work life (similar jobs, same employer, or projects such as writing a book, making a film, or running a family business) and friends and leisure activities, as well as home life. They may organize their lives to make it possible to be alone together for long periods. Both vital and total marriages are emotionally intense, but the total marriage is more all-encompassing, while the vital marriage leaves areas of individual activity to each partner. Total marriages are rare, but they do exist and can endure.

BOX 8 · 2

WORKING-CLASS MARRIAGES

Cuber and Harroff studied upper middle-class marriages and found a diversity of marital types within that social stratum. Some marriages that correspond to these types may be found at other class levels; however, generally speaking, marriages in the working class are not likely to fit neatly into the Cuber and Harroff categories. Family counselor Lillian Rubin interviewed fifty white working-class families and compared them with twenty-five middle-class professional families. Her book, entitled *Worlds of Pain* (1976), details the difficulties faced by many of these couples, whose lives are very much shaped by the struggle to survive economically and maintain stability.

The marriages of working-class couples cannot usually be seen as either intrinsic or utilitarian, because neither of the related goals, an economically successful life-style or an intimate personal relationship, can be realistically anticipated. "'He's a steady worker; he doesn't drink; he doesn't hit me'" (L. Rubin, 1976:93) are the qualities of a good working husband; none of those traits was mentioned by professional women, who take them for granted. Many working-class couples lack the psychic and economic security of the "passive-congenial" marriage, nor can they be classified as "devitalized," for there is no period of personal closeness for them to look back on. As Rubin reports, marital difficulties begin early with immaturity, uncertain employment, early parenthood, past experiences of emotional and economic deprivation, and continued dependence on the parents most young people had married in part to escape:

"Unfortunately, Ellen was pregnant when we got married and five months after, our first kid was born. That was when things really sort of collapsed around me. I was filled with resentment of him because then I didn't have someone who just cared about me anymore. There I was, just a kid myself and I finally had someone to take care of me. Then suddenly, I had to take care of a kid, and she was too busy with him to take care of me. The whole thing didn't make sense" [84].

"Then he'd get mad because he didn't always have the money for the things I needed, and he'd get mad because he felt bad about that. But how was I supposed to know that then? I was only a kid myself, and I was stuck with a bawling baby, and not enough money, and having to depend on a husband who didn't even go to work all the time" [81].

Some eventually establish what could be classified as a passive-congenial style and are quite content:

"I like being married now. I don't even feel tied down anymore. I'm out all day, and, if I want to have a drink with the boys after work, I just call her up and tell her I'll be home later. When I get home, there's a meal—she's a real good cook—and I can just relax and take it easy. The kids—they're the apples of my eyes—they're taken care of; she brings them up right, keeps them clean, teaches them respect. I can't ask for any more. It's a good life" [95].

Economic reality precludes complete satisfaction along utilitarian lines, and working-class couples have few models to use in striving for and developing intrinsic marriages. Still, the sense that more is possible is often there:

"I don't know what's the matter with me that I don't appreciate what I've got. I feel guilty all the time, and I worry about it a lot. Other women, they seem to be happy with being married and having a house and kids. What's the matter with me?" [115].

The wives in particular would like more emotional closeness:

"It sounds silly, I know, but here I am in a house with three kids and my husband, and lots of times I feel I might just as well be living alone" [114].

He may not understand:

"I just don't know what she wants" [114].
"It makes me feel like I'm doing something wrong, like I'm not a very good husband or something" [115].

And he may find it difficult to meet his wife's need for "communication":

"When she comes after me like that, yapping like that, she might as well be hitting me with a bat" [113].

Even the conflicts in working-class marriages do not fit neatly into the Cuber and Harroff conflict-habituated marital style. Conflicts are not always verbalized and may reflect and extend the emotional distance characteristic of these couples:

"I just got mad and I'd take off—go out with the guys and have a few beers or something. When I'd get back, things would be even worse" [77].

"The more I screamed, the more he'd withdraw, until finally I'd go kind of crazy. Then he'd leave and not come back until two or three in the morning sometimes" [79].

And the inarticulated dream of openness, companionship, and communication in marriage remains but is unrealized owing to economic pressures and pressures of early parenthood and to the limited expectations of marriage and the difficult childhood experienced in the parental home:

"I don't think we ever had a good concept of what marriage was about. His family was the opposite of mine. They didn't drink like mine did, and they were more stable. Yet he feels they didn't give him a good concept either. There

(continued)

BOX 8 · 2

Continued

wasn't any drinking and fighting and carrying on, but there wasn't any caring either" [122].

Working-class marital relationships seem less free to develop according to the personalities and life-style choices of the participants. They seem channeled by restricted childhoods and current economic pressures into a preoccupation with day-to-day survival and with attaining a minimum of order and stability, and handicapped by the spiral of alienation likely to develop out of the early struggles. Many working-class couples have the desire but not the skills, models, or freedom from worry to sustain an intimate relationship.

On the negative side, total marriages are vulnerable to rapid disintegration if marital quality changes. They foster a mutual dependency that makes it hard for the remaining partner to adjust in case of death or divorce. On the positive side, they provide a wide range of fulfillment focused on the couple as a unit.

A Matter of Choice

Whether spouses develop intrinsic relationships depends on choices they make. People choose utilitarian relationships either intentionally or by default. For example, a passive-congenial marriage can be a deliberate arrangement for partners who want to direct their creative energies outside of their relationship—into careers, for example, or raising children. Or it can be a taken-for-granted marital style that is never questioned. We are emphasizing the difference between intentional and default choices here, but as Box 8·2 indicates, economic and other pressures may constrain those choices by limiting the options available.

Cuber and Harroff point out that for traditional upper middle-class husbands, the utilitarian marriage can be "tailor-made." Careers are physically and psychologically demanding, yet traditionally, the career man wants also to be a family man. The utilitarian marriage is made to order: It allows him freedom to travel and work long hours, yet it also provides him the comforts of home—and family life can provide an image helpful to career success.

For such reasons, utilitarian marriages have represented, especially to achievement-oriented men, a reasonable and often attractive option.

Women have traditionally chosen utilitarian marriages to gain economic support from bread-winning husbands and to be able to raise children. Partners often combine these practical goals with the need for casual but dependable companionship offered in marriage.

Utilitarian unions, however, can be chosen mainly by default. Couples allow themselves to drift, ignoring their initial commitment to keep each other primary in their lives. Increased emphasis on other things, such as career advancement or children, results in slow emotional erosion. Among Cuber and Harroff's devitalized couples, promoted husbands grew busier, came home later, and brought with them "bulging briefcases." Wives busied themselves with children and community organizations. Today both partners may be concentrating on careers rather than building intimacy.

While many utilitarian marriages are chosen by default, successful intrinsic couples often shape their relationship "deliberately, consciously, sometimes even ruthlessly" (Cuber and Harroff, 1965:134). They are willing to turn down economic or career opportunities that may threaten their relationship. In one instance reported in this study, a husband married for twenty-two years had passed up two promotions because one would have required some traveling and the other would have taken evening and weekend time away from his wife (Cuber and Harroff, 1965:56).

Keeping one's marriage vital requires partners to consciously and continuously strive to maintain primariness and intimacy, which can entail personal sacrifice in career goals or other areas of life. As a result, intrinsic partners see their relationship as the product of an enormous investment: in time, effort, and priorities. In other words an emotionally meaningful relationship does not often develop "by drift or default" (Cuber and Harroff, 1965:142–45).

Clearly, the nature and quality of a marital relationship has a great deal to do with choices partners make. They risk disillusionment less when they make their choices consciously and knowledgeably. People are freer today to design their own unions, both the form their marriages and families will take and the kind of relationship they will develop. Partners, therefore, need to be as honest as they can be with each other (and with themselves) about their expectations and goals, both before and throughout a marriage. We saw in Chapter 1 that as people change throughout life, the kind of relationship they need also changes. Thus, marriages need to be flexible if they are to continue to be satisfying to changing partners. In the next section we'll see what this flexibility entails.

STATIC VERSUS FLEXIBLE MARRIAGES

For years, writes Sidney Jourard,

spouses go to sleep night after night, with their relationship patterned one way, a way that perhaps satisfies neither—too close, too distant, boring or suffocating—and on awakening the next morning, they reinvent their relationship *in the same way* [1976:231]. ■

Spouses who choose to behave in this way are shaping **static**, or **closed, marriages** (O'Neill and O'Neill, 1972). Partners in static marriages rely on their formal, legal bond to enforce permanence, strict monogamy, and rigid husband-wife role behavior. Spouses who rely on formal rules to maintain their feelings of intimacy, however, have unrealistic expectations about marriage. They may expect, for example, that their loving relationship will (in spite of the rising divorce rate) last forever. They may falsely believe that marriage guarantees

their own and their partner's total commitment. Often they begin to think that their mate belongs to them.

Unrealistic expectations about marriage relationships usually derive from hopes for security and permanence. Poeple assume that marriage has a self-sustaining quality. As John Crosby writes, "When it comes to love we are motivated by a desire for reassurance. We want the security of knowing that we will feel the same about each other in ten or thirty years as we feel right now." People often hope to "freeze the moment so that it will last and endure forever" (Crosby, 1976:177). By entering into a closed marriage contract, they promise, in effect, not to change, and they ask their partners never to change. Viewed this way, marriage is a static state, and partners are locked into a pattern that, once established, will supposedly provide unchanging and continued fulfillment of all expectations (O'Neill and O'Neill, 1972:83).

People do change, however, and promises will not prevent change. Partners who vowed never to change may try to hide their personal growth from each other, with the result, of course, that intimacy diminishes. They may be left with a permanent, but stale, relationship.

An option is to actively pursue a **flexible marriage**, one that allows and encourages partners to grow and change. In a flexible marriage spouses' roles may be renegotiated as the needs of each change.

Flexible marriages are more likely to be intrinsic, as partners are freer to reveal their changing selves and the parts of themselves that no longer fit into their established pattern. They can continue to be in touch at a deep emotional level while they alter the outer framework of their lives. Utilitarian marriages are also likely to benefit from flexibility, as utilitarian needs are likely to change over time.

How can marriages remain or become flexible? Some people may have an intuitive knack for achieving this kind of marriage. Others are able to act and react creatively on realizing the need for flexibility, without following any particular pattern. Some partners may object in principle to the idea of consciously and formally considering their marriage arrangements in order to make the marriage more flexible. But again, we want to stress the way in which decisions, in the absence of conscious reflection, often are made by default, and we suggest negotiating a personal marriage contract. Even for those who do not wish to exercise this option, the following section outlines some of the issues likely to arise in a flexible marriage.

WRITING YOUR OWN MARRIAGE CONTRACT

How do people design flexible marriages? Many begin by consciously negotiating personal marriage contracts.

When partners marry, they agree to two contracts: a legal-social one between the couple and the state or society and a personal one between the partners themselves. "The legally married nuclear family has access to this ready-made blueprint for building a family: familiar models, designated roles, and socially approved patterns of behavior" (Kornfein et al., 1979:284–85). But at the same time, the legal-social contract is "hidden," or generally outside people's conscious awareness; it is seldom verbalized or evaluated. "It is in many ways an unconscious contract, agreed to by default in the sense that it is unwitting" (O'Neill and O'Neill, 1972:51). But that does not make the contract any less binding on how partners think, feel, and behave toward each other. Indeed, the power of the hidden legal-social contract to constrict spouses' relationships is tremendous. Cohabitants refer to this power when they explain that they will not marry because they prefer to keep thinking of each other as *persons* rather than as property or in roles, such as wage earner, cook, or housekeeper.

But static relationships can be found among cohabitants, too (O'Neill and O'Neill, 1972:43–50; Clatworthy, 1975:82). One way for couples to develop flexible marriages is to write **personal marriage contracts**, which involve articulating, negotiating, and coming to some agreement on expectations about how you and your partner will behave.

To develop flexible marriages, partners need to renegotiate their contracts often, to keep the relationship pliable enough to accommodate the changes in two persons over time. Static marriage contracts too often lead to disillusionment (Crosby, 1976). When the rules begin to seem too rigid or it becomes clear that unrealistic expectations will not be met, closed contracts leave only two alternatives: divorce or a devitalized relationship.

In drawing up a personal marriage contract, people begin by separately writing down their expectations about their relationship. Even if they are single and not seriously involved in a relationship, thinking about and writing down their expectations about intimate relationships is important for self-understanding. Later they can compare and negotiate the differences in their expectations. The result is a contract—a working marital agreement.

The goal of personal marriage contracts is not legal enforcement, but to help partners actively define their relationship. Because unmarried partners can also benefit from this process, such personal contracts could also be termed **relationship agreements**. To those who like to be romantic about intimate relationships, writing a contract or agreement may seem rational and cold. Or it may seem to define a commitment that is limited, like a business contract, not one that is open ended and at least intended to last "forever," like marriage. But there are important reasons for defining a marriage with some degree of consciousness and awareness.[2]

Reasons for a Marriage Contract

One important reason for writing a marriage contract is that it helps partners to be aware of and avoid choosing closed marriage by default. There are other reasons a contract can be helpful.

First, partners need to articulate the primary focus of their marriage. Will their union be—or is it—mainly utilitarian or intrinsic? The middle-class emphasis on intimacy in marriage can foster guilt or ambivalence among persons who prefer utilitarian marriages. Spelling out pragmatic marital goals helps people identify and accept these. At the same time, being honest with your partner about the practical advantages motivating you to marry can prevent misunderstanding later.

Partners who want intrinsic unions need to articulate that, too, or they may unwittingly allow occupational, household, educational, or other responsibilities to drain their energies. When this happens, they may have little time and emotional energy for their relationship. Developing and maintaining an intimate relationship takes conscious

---

2. Sociologist Lenore Weitzman (1981) points out that although a marriage contract will not be directly enforceable, it may have some legal force as an indication of partners' intentions and understandings. This is particularly true of provisions relating to property, support, and child custody.

effort and adequate amounts of time together. Writing a marriage contract helps spouses be aware of that.

Second, writing a personal agreement can allow partners to understand each other's role expectations. For example, rigidly segregated roles can be satisfying if both partners accept the arrangement. Spouses who wish to develop more egalitarian relationships, however, must battle remnants of patriarchal tradition, both in society and in their own previously internalized attitudes. Women who are willing to share the provider role may still expect a husband to do all the small household repairs and plan the long-term finances. They may resent working if the husband becomes unemployed or ill, in spite of their egalitarian values or practical necessity. Men who in many ways truly appreciate their wives' achievements may wish they didn't have to worry about the wife's schedule or her need to travel, or they may wish she were more available to play hostess, or run to the cleaners, or deal with the children.

Sociologist Sy Miller describes his marriage to a practicing physician. Though priding himself on his early commitment to the liberation and equality of women, he describes his "limited" participation: "[I did not] object in principle to housekeeping and child-rearing. I don't find such work demeaning or unmasculine—just a drain of my time. ... My energies are poised to help me work on my professional-political concerns [so that] my wife does not expect much of me" (Miller, 1977:247). In retrospect, Miller finds that "the years have been less happy than they would have been if I had been more involved. ... What are the lessons of this saga of a well-meaning male? One is that ... backsliding and accommodation [to conventional roles] are likely to occur unless there is, at least occasionally, effort to bring about true commonality rather than peaceful adjustment" (Miller, 1977:247). Developing a personally comfortable degree of role flexibility requires conscious and continual effort. Writing a marriage contract can help.

Third, partners may have different ideas of what marriage means and different expectations about how they will behave in marriage (see Weitzman, 1981:422). For example, one partner may expect to continue going out alone with his or her separate friends; the other may expect to build a joint social network. Or one partner may assume they share a desire to buy a house and to sacrifice small pleasures to build up a nest egg, while the other placed more emphasis on the day-to-day sharing of movies, dinners out, small gifts, and travel experiences.

Discussing and negotiating these differences is important. Writing a contract before marrying can point up differences, many of which can be worked out. If partners uncover basic value differences and cannot work them out—for example, about whether or not to have children—it would probably be better to end their relationship before marriage than to commit themselves to a union that cannot satisfy either of them. Writing a contract after having been married for some time can point up previously unrecognized disagreements. Facing these squarely is important in maintaining a mutually supportive relationship. A recent study of marital openness based on the marriage contracts of twenty-six university students and their spouses found, among other things, that at least for women, "agreement with their spouses on the nature of the marital contract is significantly related to marital adjustment" (Wachowiak and Bragg, 1980:62). (Chapter 9 discusses how to negotiate differences constructively.[3])

Fourth, love before and during the early years of marriage is often "blind." As we saw in Chapter 3, courting partners often romanticize each other, creating images and refusing to see anything that contradicts those images. Negotiating personal contracts helps cut through this tendency to romanticize, for the process involves asking questions about daily living together. These questions are important, and great care should be taken in designing them.

Finally, in areas such as property ownership and distribution, a personal contract clarifies the intent of the married couple. This can be particularly important in separate-property states (states where property is held to belong to the spouse who has title or who earned the money that purchased the property; community-property states consider all property acquired during the marriage to be jointly owned [see Weitzman, 1981]). The following paragraphs provide an overview of some of the most critical subjects of negotiation.

---

3. Research indicates that the need to resolve such issues as sexual exclusivity, division of labor, and power and decision making is not much different in gay male or lesbian pairings than in heterosexual pairings or marriage (Harry, 1983; Peplau, 1981).

Some Questions to Ask

An initial marriage contract can be short or long, general or detailed. Weitzman's book *The Marriage Contract* (1981) contains examples. Some contracts include such fine points as exactly how spouses will allocate money and household chores. Others are more general, emphasizing marital goals, values, and atittudes. (A general contract may become more specific in the course of renegotiations or further development.) However it evolves, the contract should consider the following basic questions, along with any others that are important to particular couples (Crosby, 1976:278–79):

1. *Preliminary statement of marital goals.* Will you aim primarily at developing intimacy? Or do you want to emphasize more practical advantages from marriage, such as economic security or escape from your parents' home, for example? What kind of relationship do you and your partner realistically anticipate: conflict-habituated? passive-congenial? vital? total? How do you feel about devitalized relationships? Should partners learn to accept these gracefully, work toward changing them, or divorce?

2. *Provisions for revision and renewal of contract.* Because spouses change, marriage agreements need to be rewritten often. Couples can plan to discuss and revise their contract periodically—every six months, for example. Ideally, they agree that their contract is a "living" document, to be renegotiated and changed any time one partner feels the need. Is there any part of this contract that you think now you would never, under any circumstances, consider changing?

3. *Provisions for dissolution of the legal marriage.* When should a marriage be dissolved and under what conditions? How long and in what ways would you work on an unsatisfactory relationship before dissolving it?

4. *Decision making and division of labor.* Will decisions be made equally? Will there be a principal breadwinner? Or will partners equally share responsibility for earning money? How will funds be allocated? Will there be "his," "her," and "our" money? Or will all money be pooled? Who is owner of family property, such as family business(es), farms, or other partnerships? Will there be a principal homemaker? Or will domestic chores be shared?

5. *Religious beliefs and practices and educational goals.* What are your religious values? Do you expect your partner to share them? Will you attend church services together? How often? If you are of a different religion from your mate, whose church will you attend on special religious holidays? What about the children's religion?

   What are your educational goals? What educational goals do you expect your partner to have? Under what circumstances could you or your partner put aside wage-earning or housekeeping responsibilities to pursue advanced education?

6. *Relationships with other relatives.* How will you relate to your own and to your spouse's relatives? How do you expect your partner to relate to them? Will you expect to share many or most activities with relatives? Or do you prefer more couple-togetherness, discouraging activities with relatives?

7. *Children.* Whose responsibility is birth control and what kind of contraception will you use? What is your attitude toward unwanted pregnancy: abortion? adoption? keeping and rearing the child? Do you want children? If so, how many and how would you like to space them? How will you allocate child responsibilities and tasks? Will either spouse be primarily responsible for discipline? What are some of your values about raising children?

8. *Expectations for sexual relations.* Can you discuss your sexual needs and desires openly with your partner? Are there sexual activities which you consider distasteful and would prefer not to engage in? How would you expect to deal with either your own or your partner's sexual dysfunction if that occurs?

9. *Extramarital friendships, psychic and sexual.* How much time and how much intimate information will you share with friends other than your partner? What is your attitude toward friendships with persons of the opposite sex? Would you ever consider having sex with someone other than your mate? If so, under what circumstances? How would

you react if your partner were to have sex with another person?

10. *Privacy expectations.* How much time alone do you need? How much are you willing to allow your partner?

11. *Communication expectations.* Will you purposely set aside time to talk with each other? What topics do you like to talk about? What topics do you dislike? Are you willing to try to become more comfortable about discussing these? If communication becomes difficult, will you go to a marriage counselor? What percentage of your income would you be willing to pay for marriage counseling?

12. *Vacations.* What kinds of vacations will you take? Will you take couple-only vacations? Will you take separate vacations? If so, how often and what kind?

13. *Definition of terms.* What are your own and your partner's personal definitions of *primariness, intimacy, commitment,* and *responsibility?*

Addressing these questions and others like them is important to keeping a marriage relationship vital. In negotiating with each other, people must try to keep an open mind and use their creativity. Jourard comments on this:

As a psychotherapist, I have often been called upon to do "marriage counseling," and I have been struck by the incredible lack of artistry and creativity in marriage partners. Either person may be imaginative in making money or decorating a house, but when it comes to altering the design of their relationship, it is as if both imaginations had burnt out [in Powers and Lees, 1976:231]. ■

Creatively negotiating not only a contract but a working relationship is difficult, if only because two persons, two imaginations, and two sets of needs are involved. Differences *will* arise because no two individuals have exactly the same points of view. (Some methods for reconciling these differences, and other conflicts, are discussed in Chapter 9).

Marriage contracts, of course, can be negotiated—and renegotiated—at any time during or before marriage. They are, in fact, good preparation for marriage. The next section explores preparation for marriage and the first years of marriage.

BEGINNING A MARRIAGE

Our theme of making choices throughout life surely applies both to early years of marriage and to a couple's preparing for marriage. Unfortunately, however, there are surprisingly little data on either of these topics. The definitive study of engagement was published in 1953 (Burgess and Wallin, 1953), and some studies on engagement and honeymoons appeared in the early sixties (Rapoport, 1962; Rapoport and Rapoport, 1964; Cutler and Dyer, 1965), but there has been virtually no research on these topics since. Marriages and families have changed so much in the meantime—for example, couples today are more likely to have established a sexual relationship before marriage, many couples live together before marriage, and young people are marrying at older ages—that we probably cannot infer much from those early studies. Still, we have a few things to say based on our own ideas, those of other family sociologists, the information available in the media, and the limited research available.

Preparation for Marriage

Given today's high divorce rate, clergy, teachers, parents, policymakers, and others have grown increasingly concerned that individuals be better prepared for a marital relationship. Family life education courses, which take place in high school and college classrooms, are designed to prepare individuals rather than intimate couples for marriage (see Moss and Brasher, 1981). Premarital counseling, which generally takes place at churches or with private counselors, is specifically oriented to couples who plan to be married. Many Catholic dioceses, for example, require premarital counseling before a couple may be married by a priest. Such programs are designed and generally conducted by professionally trained persons and have spread to other churches. Other couples may seek premarital counseling on their own initiative.

Premarital counseling has two goals: first, to evaluate the relationship with the possibility of deciding against marriage; second, to sensitize partners to potential problems, and to teach positive ways of communicating about and resolving conflicts. While common sense suggests that these kinds of programs help, they have not been in existence long enough that we can scientifically evaluate their impact on subsequent marriages (Bagarozzi and Rauen, 1983:594).

Besides education and counseling, living together has been viewed as an option in preparing for marriage. The great increase in cohabitation rates during the 1970s was partly due to the belief that couples could test their relationship before marrying. As a result of this testing, partners might either break up without marrying or enjoy an improved relationship after marriage. In fact, however, there is little evidence that couples who have lived together have better marriages. Indeed, in one study (Watson, 1983) of fifty-four couples married one year, those who had not lived together actually had higher overall adjustment scores than those who had. One explanation offered by the researcher reminds us of our earlier discussion of the "hidden" marriage contract:

The act of becoming formally married may have deep and quite different meanings for those who marry after cohabiting or after traditional courtship. To the latter, marriage is a liberating ritual through which new possibilities, notably, the public establishment of a common household, are opened to a couple and are celebrated. Cohabitors have already established common residence and have had to define their roles. . . . To them, the aspect of marriage which is emphasized is not the freedom it brings, but the assumption of new responsibilities [Watson, 1983:146]. ■

This view assumes the symbolic importance of the wedding ceremony.

The Wedding Ceremony

Weddings tend to reflect the prevailing sociopolitical ideology of the time. Traditional weddings of the 1950s, for example, gave way to "do-it-yourself" ceremonies of the 1960s and 1970s, in which couples wrote their own vows and were married in locations other than churches. This change in ceremony reflected the shift in marriage from an institution to a relationship, one theme of this text. Recent popular articles indicate that traditionalism is back in weddings (e.g., "1984 Brides Spend More," UPI, in *Omaha World Herald*, March 11, 1984). At the same time, couples continue to per-

sonalize the event just as they attempt to individualize their marital relationships. Another change in marriage ceremonies reflects changing gender roles, as grooms are now sometimes included in events formerly reserved for the bride, such as showers (Berardo and Vera, 1981).

Besides reflecting conditions in the larger society, wedding ceremonies symbolize, and indeed help create, the marriage premise, explored at the beginning of this chapter. Weddings are public ceremonies, designed to announce a couple's new status and their intent to maintain that status permanently. Internalizing their new status, in fact, is a couple's primary task in the early years of marriage.

The Early Stages of Marriage

In the 1950s marriage and family texts characteristically referred to the first months and years of marriage as a "period of adjustment," after which, presumably, spouses had learned to play traditional marital roles. Today we view early marriage more as a time of role *making* than of role *taking.* Moreover, the time of role making is not a clearly demarcated period (Udry, 1974), but continues, as we have suggested earlier, throughout marriage.

Even though the early stages of marriage are not a distinct period, sociologists continue to speak and write about them as such. One thing we know is that this period tends to be the happiest, with gradual declines in marital satisfaction afterward (Spanier et al., 1975). (Perhaps this is where we get the popular expression, "The honeymoon's over.") Why this is we don't know for sure because, unfortunately, we have little or no data on the actual processes of the early marital relationship.

We do know something about the structural advantages of early marriage, and it is likely that these contribute to high levels of satisfaction (Aldous, 1978:149–51). For one thing, partners' roles are relatively similar or unsegregated in early marriage. Spouses tend to share household tasks and, because of similar experiences, are better able to empathize with each other. Early marriage may also be less vulnerable to stress arising from dissatisfaction with finances. Typically, both partners are employed, and though their salaries may be relatively low, so are their expenses. And there is often the belief that any economic hardships are temporary.

But early marriage is not characterized only by

■ *Wedlock* comes from an Old English word meaning "to make a pledge." The rituals symbolizing matrimony vary, but their intent is the same: Wedding ceremonies publicly proclaim a couple's new status.

happiness. Couples must also accomplish certain tasks during this period. First, they have to negotiate some division of labor (Aldous, 1978). Then, too, "the solidarity of the new couple relation must be established and competing interpersonal ties modified" (Aldous, 1978:141). Friendship networks, for example, may need to be transformed. What happens in this instance

very simply is a slow process in which the husband's image of his friend is tranformed as he keeps talking about this friend with his wife . . . into a "joint image." . . . The old friend is . . . likely to fade out of the picture by slow degrees, as new kinds of friends take his place. . . . The couple is pushed toward groups that strengthen their new definition of themselves and the world, and avoids those that weaken this definition [Berger and Kellner, 1970:59–60]. ■

The couple constructs relationships and interprets events in a way that reinforces their sense of themselves as a couple. What occurs during the early stages of marriage, through changing friendships, perhaps, among other things, is that the couple develops a sense of couple identity. Put another way, "Marriage in our society is a *dramatic* act in which two strangers come together and redefine themselves" (Berger and Kellner, 1970:33).

Summary

Although marriage is less permanent and more flexible than it has ever been, it is still set apart from other human relationships. The marriage premise includes expectations of permanence and primariness. As both of these expectations come to depend less on legal definitions and social conventions (such as strict monogamy), partners need to invest more effort in sustaining a marriage.

Two opposite poles on a continuum of marriage are the utilitarian and the intrinsic marriage. Most real marriages fall somewhere in between. Some frequently occurring marital types are the conflict-habituated, the devitalized, the passive-congenial, the vital, and the total marriage.

While little data are available on the period just prior to marriage, there is much concern about preparation for marriage—is it adequate in today's society? Premarital counseling and family life education in the schools are two approaches that have been developed, but there are little data on their effectiveness. Living together as a preparation for marriage does not seem to prevent problems or to screen out incompatible couples as hoped. We need to learn more about the transition into marriage, although it appears that the early years of marriage tend to be a happy time.

Partners change over the course of a marriage, so a relationship needs to be flexible if it is to continue to be intrinsically satisfying. Static marriages are usually devitalized. Marriage contracts, which can be renegotiated as the need arises, are one useful way of coming to mutual agreement. Working on a marriage contract together can help partners develop a "couple identity"—one of the tasks of early marriage.

Key Terms

marriage premise *256*
primariness *257*
strict monogamy *257*
flexible monogamy *261*
utilitarian marriage *262*
joint conjugal
    relationship *263*
segregated conjugal
    relationship *263*
intermediate conjugal
    relationship *263*
intrinsic marriage *263*
conflict-habituated
    marriage *264*

devitalized marriage
    265
passive-congenial
    marriage *266*
vital marriage *266*
total marriage *267*
static (closed) marriage
    271
flexible marriage *271*
personal marriage
    contract *272*

Study Questions

1. Discuss the expectation of permanence in a marital relationship. How does it affect a relationship?
2. Partners' expectations of primariness in marriage may be interpreted strictly or broadly. How do these two interpretations differ? Which do you agree with? Why?
3. Give some reasons people enter utilitarian marriages. How do these differ from reasons for entering intrinsic marriages?
4. Why are intrinsic marriages more vulnerable to divorce than utilitarian marriages?
5. Describe the five kinds of marital relationships classified by Cuber and Harroff. Which kinds are utilitarian and which are intrinsic? Explain your reasoning.
6. Why do you think that vital marriages and total marriages are so rare?
7. What are some intentional choices people make that lead to utilitarian relationships? How do these differ from choices by default?
8. Do you think it is easier to develop a utilitarian or an intrinsic relationship by default? Why?
9. Differentiate static and flexible marriages and discuss the reasons a marriage contract can be helpful.
10. This chapter lists thirteen questions that the authors think are important to consider in any marriage contract. Which do you think are the most important? Which do you think are the least important? Why?
11. Design your own marriage contract. What does it tell you about your ideas on marriage?
12. What do you think young couples should do before marriage to improve their chances of having a happy and stable marriage?
13. What do you think are likely to be the most important issues in the early years of marriage?

Suggested Readings

Cuber, John, and Peggy Harroff
1965   *The Significant Americans.* New York: Appleton-Century-Crofts. (Published also as *Sex and the Significant American.* Baltimore: Penguin, 1965.)
    Classic study of "five types of marriage."
Greenblatt, Cathy, and Thomas Cottle
1980   *Getting Married.* New York: McGraw-Hill. Research on the transition to married life and the early years of marriage.
Hall, Francine S., and Douglas T. Hall
1979   *The Two-Career Couple.* Reading, Mass.: Addison-Wesley.

Sociological discussion of flexible marriage in the context of two careers. Good advice.

O'Neill, Nena
1977 *The Marriage Premise.* New York: M. Evans.

O'Neill, Nena, and George O'Neill
1972 *Open Marriage.* New York: M. Evans. *The Marriage Premise,* written five years after *Open Marriage,* is a reconsideration of the values of traditional marriage.

Weitzman, Lenore
1981 *The Marriage Contract: Spouses, Lovers, and the Law.* New York: Free Press.
Up-to-date information on the law, with advice and examples of contracts.

9

Communication in Marriages and Families

I know you believe you understand what you think I said, but I am not sure you realize that what you heard is not what I meant.
ANONYMOUS, from a poster

When two people always agree, there's no need for one of them anyway.
BEN BROWN, 54, married thirty-one years

One important effect of loving is that it provides individuals with a sense of being personally and specially cared for in an impersonal society. As we saw in Chapter 7, providing emotional security and feelings of belonging is an important function of the family today.

Families today are powerful environments. Nowhere else in our society is there such power to support, hurt, comfort, denigrate, reassure, ridicule, love, and hate. For most Americans, belonging to a family probably yields both positive and negative feelings. At one moment a person feels supported and reassured; at another, unappreciated and misunderstood. For virtually all members, family living involves striking a delicate balance between belonging and feeling constrained. Striking such a balance involves effective communication, among other things.

Today countless books and articles offer advice to help spouses learn how to relate to and behave toward each other. Family-life courses in high schools and colleges teach future spouses how to communicate. Marriage counseling is a growing profession. Marriage enrichment programs assist couples who have no serious conflict but who want to enhance their relationship. And social scientists and counselors are finding that improving and enriching an intimate relationship often centers around learning to communicate effectively.

Research on couple communication has found that unhappily married couples are distinguished by their failure to manage conflict; they do not differ from other couples in terms of positive communication. The inability of some couples to manage conflict leads to negative exchanges that put their marriages on a downward spiral (Gottman, 1979). It is very important, then, to learn to fight, that is, to communicate about conflict.

In this chapter we'll see that the sulking that characterizes unhappiness and boredom in marriage often results from spouses' attempts to deny or ignore conflict, and we'll examine several other outcomes of refusing to deal openly with conflict. We will also explore some alienating practices that should be avoided when fighting. Finally, we will discuss some healthy attitudes and propose some guidelines for communicating constructively. To begin, we will address the idea of families as powerful environments.

FAMILIES AS POWERFUL ENVIRONMENTS

Charles Horton Cooley (1902) used the term **looking-glass self** to describe the process by which people adopt as their own, and gradually come to accept, the evaluation, definitions, and judgments

Figure 9·1

The looking-glass self. People accept and believe the evaluations of themselves that they get from other people, especially family members.

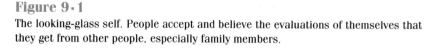

of themselves they see reflected in the faces, words, and gestures of those around them (see Figure 9·1).

Cooley's description has broad applicability in social environments, but perhaps nowhere is it more evident than in the family, for two reasons. First, people reveal more of themselves in families than they do in superficial relationships; thus, they are more vulnerable to evaluation, encouragement, and criticism. And second, the opinions of family members have a significant influence on the way people perceive themselves. Family members are **significant others:** persons whose opinions about each other are very important to each individual's self-esteem.

Symbolic Interaction Theory

Significant other and *looking-glass self* are terms from symbolic interaction theory. As the name implies, this theory focuses on *interaction*, the face-to-face encounters and relationships of individuals who act in awareness of one another. The family thus becomes a "unity of interaction per-

sonalities" (Burgess and Locke, 1953), with the emphasis on the impact family members have on one another.

A major concept in symbolic interaction theory is the *self-concept*, an individual's idea about what sort of person she or he is. The self is developed initially in a family setting. Parents, especially, and siblings and other relatives are the most influential or significant figures in a young child's life. The response of these other persons channels the development of the child's self-concept. For example, a child who is loved and warmly hugged comes to think he or she is a valuable, lovable person. A child who is given some tasks and encouraged to do things comes to think of him- or herself as competent. We can imagine negative family feedback and the effects it might have.

Self-concept is not only a question of general esteem and confidence, but involves the development of specific traits. For example, a child who drew back when adults said, "And how are you?" consistently heard them say to her mother, "She's shy, isn't she?" Soon the child was announcing right off, "I'm shy." That had become part of her self-concept. The incorporation of the responses of others into one's self-concept is termed *internalization.*

As the child grows older, interaction takes place with persons outside the immediate family, especially peers, teachers, more distant relatives, and various activity leaders such as scoutmasters and little league coaches. A wider variety of others now influences the self and behavior, and the individual must manage many relationships at the same time (Mead, 1934).

Selves and interaction have much to do with *roles,* or positions in the social structure that have associated behavioral expectations. Even young children associate different behavior with the different roles of mother, father, teacher, police officer, and so on, and much of their play consists of imitation of these visible roles. *Role taking,* or playing out the expected behavior associated with a social position, is how children learn behavior appropriate to the roles they may play in adult life. When as adults they assume specific occupational or other roles—college professor, for example—they learn appropriate behavior by interacting with others. That behavior is incorporated into the self-concept.

In family sociology we are particularly interested in family roles. In looking at the roles of husband and wife (and child) from a symbolic interaction perspective, we look not only at the social prescriptions for these roles, but at the way in which husbands and wives actually enact their roles. How much will individuals depart from social prescriptions to act out their individually created versions of what a husband or wife should do?

Remember that interaction consists not only of acting out one's own part or role, but doing so in awareness of the personalities and actions of others as well as oneself. How do family members see themselves? What perceptions do they have of the roles that are being played by others in the family? What expectations do they have for others' behavior?

In using a symbolic interaction perspective, we look not only at what family members do or say out loud, but at what they think about each other. We are interested in meanings: What does the actor (the husband, wife, or child on whom we are focusing) intend by his or her action? How is it interpreted by other family members? The term *symbolic* refers to meanings assigned to actions, to the interpretations of actions. For example, what does it *mean* to a husband when his wife changes her role in midlife? Does it symbolize lack of love? Does

it symbolize creativity and energy? Does it symbolize economic need?

Symbolic interaction theory is hard to specify with precision, since it implies that each family is a little different and that behavior does not have a single meaning, but can be variously interpreted by the individuals involved. This can be very difficult to get at in research. Nevertheless, much of the research in family sociology over the years has used this framework and has certainly focused on the interior of the family, that is, the interaction and relationships of husbands, wives, and children. Generally, family members have been asked about their thoughts and behavior, rather than being observed, although the method of participant observation is most commonly associated with symbolic interactionism.[1]

Attributions

A central theme of symbolic interaction theory is the influence of the family on self-concept and behavior. So powerful is the family in shaping people's self-images that psychoanalyst R. D. Laing compares the process to hypnotism. In hypnosis one person gets another not only to *do* but also to *be* what the first person wants. Family members exercise hypnotic power over one another by implying that a member *is* a kind of person—selfish, kind, competent, lazy, and so on. This is accomplished through the process of **attribution:** ascribing certain character traits to persons. For example, a person is told she or he *is* intelligent, not directly instructed to *act* intelligently. In fact, attributions can be considered part of a family's archives. Anecdotes reinforce a particular member's identity as reckless, helpful, or unlucky (Weigert and Hastings, 1977).

Attributions are often more powerful in a primary group of more than two: One person says or

---

1. Fred Davis's *Passage Through Crisis,* in the Suggested Readings for Chapter 15, is a classic symbolic interaction piece. More than any other theory we present, symbolic interactionism is a unique and separate perspective. It has its adherents, who use the separate vocabulary and approach of this theory exclusively, and its critics, who consider it "fuzzy." It is generally found to be interesting and thought provoking by neutral observers, once it moves from the abstract definition of terms to the concrete analysis of families or other environments.

implies something about a second person to a third person in front of the second. For example, a mother might tell her children in front of their father that he is a skilled handyman. With repetition, the father may soon have a family reputation, which even he believes, of being able to fix anything—even if he can't.

As the process of attribution occurs again and again, family members unconsciously begin to behave according to their reputations. In a sense family interaction can be viewed as a play in which the same theme is repeated in scenario after scenario, such as being late for work "again" or becoming flustered before guests arrive. Each member, without thinking, plays out the part attributed to him or her (Laing, 1971:78–80).

Consensual Validation

Family members' definitions of the world around them are also influenced by their families. People see things differently from one another, and as a result, they define reality in many different ways. They also depend on others, especially significant others, to help them affirm their definitions. This process is called **consensual validation,** and it is an important dimension of family functioning (Reiss, 1971a, 1981). Through conversation, members can help one another feel comfortable about how each perceives the world. For example, husbands and wives may feel stronger in their political convictions—or their views on social issues such as the energy crisis or the death penalty—if their spouse agrees; or a teenager may feel more comfortable when she refuses to drink with her friends if she has a sibling who thinks she's doing the right thing.

Consensual validation also takes place in a much broader sense. In Berger and Kellner's words, family interaction

validates over and over again the fundamental definitions of reality once entered into, not, of course, so much by explicit articulation, but precisely by taking the definitions silently for granted and conversing about all conceivable matters on this taken-for-granted basis [1970:52–53]. ■

One of the alarming aspects of marital breakup is that the taken-for-granted world is no longer validated by the partner (Vaughan, 1986).

Family Cohesion

A goal that family members strive for, and that some succeed in creating, is **family cohesion:** the emotional bonding of family members (Olson et al., 1983). Case Study 9•1, "Making a Marriage Encounter Weekend," describes how one couple improved family cohesion through "Marriage Encounter." More generally, how do people create family cohesion?

In an effort to find out what makes families strong and cohesive, social scientist Nick Stinnett researched 130 "strong families" in rural and urban areas throughout Oklahoma (Stinnett, 1978).[2] Six qualities stood out.

First and most important, members often communicated *appreciation for one another.* They "built each other up psychologically." In Stinnett's assessment, "people like to be with others who make them feel good about themselves"; thus, the family liked being together.

Stinnett suggests an exercise to help family members express appreciation for each other. Family members sit in a circle. Taking turns, each tells something he or she likes about the person to her or his left. When they have gone around the circle once or twice, each member then shares something he or she likes about himself or herself. After that, the direction is reversed, and members say something they like about the person to their right. The exercise needn't take long, and even when all members are not present, it helps build a sense of family togetherness and appreciation for one another. Studies show that families maintain more supportive interaction patterns for a time after the experience. To create togetherness, then, families might use this technique periodically.

Second, Stinnett found that members of strong families *arranged their personal schedules* so that they could do things, or simply be, together. The members of some families agreed to save Sundays for one another. Or members could agree to reserve every other weekend strictly for family activities. What families do together at home doesn't

---

2. Stinnett's families were selected with help from home economics extension agents. We need to remember that this area may not be typical of the entire U.S. population, nor are the families necessarily typical of the area. Nor will we all agree on what constitutes a "strong" family. Nevertheless, this study represents an attempt to distinguish qualities that facilitate what seems to be a satisfying family life.

■ Sometimes the arrival of a second child is a source of friction and stress, but Belinda seems to enjoy having a little sister. Adjusting to a new family member is part of developing family cohesion, which involves more than just getting along together.

have to be routine, habitual, or boring: They might have a winter picnic in front of the fireplace, for example (Dyer, 1977:88).

A third characteristic Stinnett found was *positive communication* patterns such as those described later in this chapter. Family members took time to talk with and listen to each other, conveying respect and interest. They also argued, but they did so openly, sharing their feelings and talking over alternative solutions to their problems.

Fourth, members of strong families had a *high degree of commitment* to promoting one another's happiness and welfare and to the family group as a whole. And they "put their money where their mouths were," investing time and energy in the family group. When life got so hectic that members didn't have enough time for their families, they listed the activities they were involved in, found those that weren't worth their time, and scratched them off their lists, leaving more free time for their families. Stinnett comments on the element of knowledgeable decision making in that action:

That sounds like a very simple thing, but how many of us do that? We too often get involved and overinvolved, and it's not because we want to be. We could change that. We act so often as though we cannot. But we can; we have that choice [Stinnett, 1978]. ■

A fifth characteristic of the families Stinnett studied was *spiritual orientation.* Although they were not necessarily members of an organized religion, they had a sense of some power and purpose greater than themselves.

And sixth, Stinnett found that strong families were able to *deal positively with crises.* Members were able to see something good in a bad situation, even if just gratitude that they had each other and were able to face the crisis together, supporting one another. (Chapter 15 discusses dealing creatively with crises.)

In general, Stinnett's families took the initiative in structuring their life-styles to enhance family relationships. Instead of drifting into a family rela-

CASE STUDY 9·1

MAKING A MARRIAGE ENCOUNTER WEEKEND

According to its promotional literature, Marriage Encounter is a weekend for couples "who have a good thing going for them, and who want to make it better." Worldwide Marriage Encounter is a movement devoted to the renewal of the sacrament of matrimony in and for the Catholic Church. However, at least ten other faiths offer similar weekends. The movement began in the New York area in 1968. Since then, more than one million couples throughout the United States have made the weekend, and the movement has spread into fifty-five foreign countries. Here, a woman tells about her Marriage Encounter Weekend.

We were going along fine. But I think we both had begun to feel we were maybe taking each other pretty much for granted. So we signed up for a Marriage Encounter weekend. Believe me, it was a big step: finding a babysitter and everything just to go *talk*!

Marriage Encounter is an intensive forty-four hours of uninterrupted togetherness. You do nothing else but eat, sleep, and share with each other. There's virtually no socializing with the other couples. It's just the two of you.

You write letters to one another. You write them alone, privately, and then you exchange them. You aren't using your body language while you're writing this, of course, or being interrupted or interrupting the other person. You have a train of thought. With just trying to talk sometimes, you know, the other person jumps in or tells you what you're saying is positive or negative, and you've gotten off the track. So we would write for ten minutes, picking a topic like, "How do I feel about sex?" Or, "How do I feel about anything really?" And both write.

Then you exchange notebooks and you each read it through twice—once with the heart and once with the head, as they say. And then you what they call dialogue on it for ten minutes. It really leads into neat areas....

I was amazed at how little I had been into feelings, and how much I was into thoughts. And the same for Jerry. It was just really weird how we both

---

tionship by default, they played an active part in carrying out their family commitments. Later in this chapter, we'll examine some practical strategies for doing this.

Making Time for Intimacy

Just as it is important for families to arrange their schedules so that they can spend time together, it's also important for couples to plan time to be alone and intimate.

One element that often contributes to the ero-

sion of sexual communicating, for example, is carried over from the work ethic: the principle that being productive is always more important than being pleasured (Masters and Johnson, 1976:97). In nineteenth-century America people thought intercourse drained vital energy and productive power from men (Barker-Benfield, 1975). Few people consciously hold that belief today, yet many continue to give low priority to sex and intimacy. As two professional therapists put it, sex for marrieds is not always honored as an activity that is planned for, or counted on, for which time is set aside, or that even takes place at times when both thought we were expressing our feelings before the encounter. But we weren't. Not completely anyway. We thought we'd been letting it all hang out, but we weren't. We were expressing our thoughts and our grudges and our hang-ups. But not our true—not all our true—feelings. . . .

I prayed too. I don't want to leave that out. I don't want to minimize that. I want to have the courage to emphasize that I prayed; I prayed hard that weekend, partly because when I went into the room where I was going to write down my feelings about something, I sometimes found myself surprisingly afraid.

And then when we'd start writing, I'd say to myself, "Do I feel like *this*?" I would be surprised at how I felt, and I'd be surprised at how he felt too. It's such a revelation—almost as exciting for you alone as it is for your relationship, because you find out a lot of stuff about yourself that you had no idea about. Anyway I did. And Jerry did too.

When we left that weekend, they gave us a list of ninety topics, suggestions for continuing the dialogue. Things like sex, kids, finances. You can think up anything you want to dialogue about, but we've been more or less going by this list. We recognized, though, that for a while we were skipping around on the list. And then we realized that we were avoiding subjects that we were afraid to talk about. So we've decided—and this took courage, believe me—to go just straight down the list and take the topics as they come. . . .

It's really been a revelation. But maybe the very best thing about it is just that we're making the time to do it.

■ How might weekend encounters such as this one enhance family commitment? What might be some drawbacks or problems with a marriage encounter weekend? In what ways does intimacy (described in Chapter 3) affect family cohesion, do you think? Why?

partners are relaxed and rested. Instead, it seems for many to be relegated to a time when there is nothing else to do (Zussman and Zussman, 1979:75).

This attitude explains why some couples "rediscover" sex when they are off alone together on vacation. They aren't distracted by business, household, or child-care responsibilities. But they resign themselves to the fact that when they return home, the distractions and obligations will resume and take their inevitable toll on sexual pleasure (Masters and Johnson, 1976:97). This may be particularly true in two-career marriages, where both mates have outside job pressures and may bring

work home to do in the evenings—on top of household chores (Johnson et al., 1979).

Sex therapists are unanimous in insisting that married couples need to plan time for intimacy. This kind of planning involves making conscious choices. Partners can decide to move the TV from their bedroom, for example. They can choose to set aside at least one night a week for themselves alone, without work, movies, television, the VCR, the computer, another couple's company, or the children. They do not have to have intercourse during these times: They should do only what they feel like doing. But scheduling time alone together does mean mutually agreeing to exclude other preoccupations and devote full attention to each other (Zussman and Zussman, 1979:75). Some therapists advise couples to reserve at least twenty-five minutes each night for a quiet talk, "with clothes off and defenses down" (Koch and Koch, 1976a:35).[3]

Boredom with sex in long marriages may seem at least partly the consequence of a decision by default. Therapists suggest that couples can avoid this situation, perhaps by creating romantic settings—a candlelit dinner or a night away from the family at a motel—by opening themselves to new experiences, such as describing their sexual fantasies to each other, reading sex manuals together, or even renting an erotic movie. (The important thing, they stress, is that partners don't lose touch with either their sexuality or their ability to share it with each other.)

Negative Family Power

Family interaction does not always validate members' perceptions of situations and events. Significant others in a family have power, if they choose to use it, to make one member feel "out of step." One way families do this is by a process Bach and Wyden (1970) call *gaslighting*. The term comes from the old movie *Gaslight*, in which a husband attempts to drive his wife insane so she can be put in an asylum. He gradually turns down their gaslight over a period of time but tells his wife she's wrong when she perceives that their home is becoming dimmer.

In **gaslighting,** one partner chips away at the spouse's perception of him- or herself and at the other's definitions of reality. Typically, this occurs through destructive snipes at a partner, sometimes faintly camouflaged as humor. Often the gaslighter uses mixed messages or sarcasm. When a spouse protests or questions, the gaslighter denies everything and insists that the spouse must be crazy. In the movie the husband *wanted* to drive his wife insane; in real families members can accomplish the same results without intending to. Laing, who views family living as a kind of hypnotic trance, suggests that attempts to "wake up"—that is, to disagree with other family members or to pursue individuality—may be punished by "those who love us most." Family members "think anyone who wakes up, or who, still asleep, realizes what is taken to be real is a 'dream' is going crazy." Meanwhile, individuals who realize that "this is all a nightmare" are often afraid they are "going crazy" (Laing, 1971:82). A related destructive family behavior is **scapegoating:** consistently blaming one particular member for virtually everything that goes wrong in the family (Vogel and Bell, 1960; Laing, 1971).

The power of the family over its members is attributed partly to the perception of the private family as sanctuary and retreat (Laslett, 1973; Shorter, 1975:244). Ironically, the family's tendency to create boundaries not only gives members a "place to belong" but also increases their power to undermine one another's self-esteem.[4]

Systems theory, which we will explore next, represents one way of explaining how this occurs.

---

3. This last suggestion may be easier for parents with young children who are put to bed fairly early. A common complaint from parents of older children is that the children stay up later, and that by the time they are teenagers, the parents no longer have any private evening time together even with their clothes *on.* One woman, after attending an education course for parents, found a solution. She explains:

> Our house shuts down at 9:30 now. That doesn't mean we say "It's your bedtime, kids. You're tired and you need your sleep." It means we say, "Your dad (or your mom) and I need some time alone." The children go to their rooms at 9:30. Help with homework, lunch money, decisions about what they'll wear tomorrow— all those things get taken care of by 9:30 or they don't get taken care of. We allow interruptions only in emergencies—and I'm redefining what an "emergency" is too [personal interview]. ▪

---

4. Social scientists vary in their conclusions about whether there are essentially different interaction patterns in "normal" or generally functional families and dysfunctional families. Looking for causes of schizophrenia, scientists observed interaction in families of schizophrenics, usually in a laboratory setting. They found distinct and different interaction patterns among families of "normals," schizophrenics, and delinquents (Walsh, 1982; Stabenau et al., 1968; Reiss, 1971b). But other researchers assert that unhealthy behaviors were common to both "pathological" and "normal" families (see, for example, Henry, 1971; Lennard and Bernstein, 1969), although the frequency of these behaviors might vary (Mishler and Waxler, 1968b). Research reviews conclude that "family interactions studies . . . have not yet isolated family patterns that reliably differentiate disturbed from normal groups" (Jacob, 1975:56, cited in Rausch et al., 1979, who reached the same conclusion). Much of the criticism of family interaction research raises questions about research procedures, which can be remedied by further work. Clinicians, meanwhile, tend to continue with the common-sense assumption that families do in fact influence their members' perceptions and actions. In other words, families exercise subtle but salient power over members.

Systems Theory

Systems theory is based on the idea that the family is a system. Some people wonder if there is anything left to say after that. In fact, systems theory includes a whole body of interesting analysis of family interaction.

Systems theory, in other forms, is an old idea in sociology. Social scientists over the centuries have tended to fall back on the biological analogy of comparing a society or a family to an organism such as the human body, which has (1) identifiable boundaries between the system (the body) and the environment; (2) identifiable parts (the organs), which perform different functions; and (3) stable relationships among the parts, which are organized as a totality to maintain the system in operation (our heart, lungs, brain, kidneys, and so on work in coordination to keep us alive).

Similarly, the family has identifiable boundaries (some people are in, some are not) and identifiable parts (the individuals in the family, who usually do engage in different activities). The family operates as a system in that each member's activities, both behavioral and psychological (thought processes and emotions), take place with reference to the other family members and the family system.

A basic idea in systems is that of feedback. Organic systems, like the human body, regulate themselves and maintain an equilibrium or balance of the activities of the system. If we are exposed to too much heat, our body sweats to cool the body temperature. Analogous processes take place in the family. If one person is upset, other family members will listen, sympathize, offer some distracting activities, help with tasks, and so on, to restore the equilibrium, the harmony, and the competence of the system.

The concept of system is neutral, yet, as with the human body, we tend to think of systems as healthy or unhealthy. Clearly, this was so in our discussion of normal and pathological family interaction. Systems theory, in fact, is very much associated with certain schools of family therapy.

Pursuing the body analogy, we can think of family systems that may continue to work, but at the cost of a heavy burden on one part of the system. Sometimes, parents mask their marital conflict by displacing it onto a child (Vogel and Bell, 1960), for example. Therapists often find, when asked to deal with an individual whose behavior is problematic, that the individual's problems are rooted in the family system. The presenting individual (the one sent for therapy) may not be the major source of the family's problems (Laing and Esterson, 1964). Moreover, a conflict-habituated marriage or an overly close family might be viewed as needing therapy even if no one in the family complained.

Systems theory is closely associated with the practice of therapy. It implies that a whole family must be treated, because the problem is in the system. If one treats an alcoholic, for example, one must also work with the spouse and children, because the problem is likely to have become entrenched in the family system. Family members may play rescuer or other complementary roles. A wife of an alcoholic husband may be fearful of relinquishing the responsibilities she has taken on to adapt to the husband's alcoholism. A cure for the alcoholic without family therapy will disrupt the family system.

Systems theory can have implications that therapists or activists interested in certain problems may not accept. In treating incest, for example, does one assume that the problem is in the system, so that all family members are implicated in some way? Does one advise family therapy to work things out within the family system or does one prosecute (Stewart, 1984)?

A major criticism of systems theory is its vagueness. "It has been a source of disappointment to some that . . . efforts have not yet resulted in a body of specific, testable theoretical assertions that can be clearly applied to the family" (Broderick and Smith, 1979). On the positive side, it has generated some excellent research on the family, most notably David Kantor and William Lehr's analysis of boundaries and distance in family relationships (1975), and it *has* proved enormously useful in therapy.

Systems theory implies that emotionally destructive behavior in families can be changed only by modifying the family system. This can be done by gaining support outside the system for change within it.

Antidotes to Destructive Behavior

An antidote to destructive behavior such as gaslighting or scapegoating (discussed earlier) in families is for a victim to begin thinking more independently and challenging negative attributions. People do this more readily when they have sources for building self-esteem outside their families. Among adolescents, for example, the peer group is a common resource (Thomas et al., 1974). Other sources are grandparents and other relatives, teachers, work colleagues, or therapists (Laing and Esherson, 1964). With such help from the outside, people can more easily resist the temptation to let destructive significant others define their identities (Bach and Wyden, 1970:156).

A second antidote is to begin to foster a family atmosphere of encouragement rather than criticism. This does *not* mean that families are or should be centers of solidarity, consensus, and harmony—and never of conflict, anger, or fighting. But according to an idealized image, as we will see in the next section, this is what many people expect the family to be.

THE MYTH OF CONFLICT-FREE LOVE

Our society holds out a **conflict taboo** that considers conflict and anger morally wrong, and it discourages these emotions even (or especially) within the family. The assumption that conflict and anger don't belong in healthy relationships is based partly on the idea that love is the polar opposite of hate (Crosby, 1976:128–29). But the line between love and hate is really very thin. Emotional intimacy necessarily involves feelings of both love and hate; of wanting to be close and needing to be separate; of agreeing and disagreeing.

Marital anger and conflict are necessary forces and a challenge to be met rather than avoided. This is especially true in the early years of marriage, when individuals are often still engaged in the process of getting to know each other. (At this point, a complete lack of conflict might even be cause for concern!) It is also true at points throughout a good relationship. As we saw in Chapter 1, partners do not necessarily undergo the same changes at the same time. In one observer's words, "for a marriage to be reasonably productive, a couple needs to arrive at a balance of love *and* hate, honor *and* dishonor, obedience *and* disobedience," with partners acting not only as each other's companions and lovers but also as each other's critics (Charny, 1974:55). As we will see, partners who refuse to accept conflict openly not only miss opportunities to creatively challenge and be challenged by each other but also risk more negative consequences.

DENYING CONFLICT: SOME RESULTS

Many married couples are reluctant to fight. This reluctance can have destructive effects on the partners as individuals and on their relationship. In the following paragraphs we'll look at several of these negative side effects, first those that relate to the individual, then those that affect the marriage relationship.

Anger "Insteads"

Most people know when they are angry, but they feel uncomfortable about expressing anger directly. Through years of being socialized into the conflict taboo, people learn not to raise their voices and not to "make an issue of things." One result is that many people resort to anger substitutes, or **anger "insteads"** (Kassorla, 1973), rather than dealing directly with their emotions.

Figure 9•2 depicts "insteads"—such as overeating, boredom, depression, physical illness, and gossip (Kassorla, 1973)—that are probably familiar to most readers. While these "insteads" may be more socially acceptable than the direct expression of anger, they can be self-destructive. Because of this, they are costly, both to the individual who uses them and to any intimate relationship of the individuals. For example, sex therapists report that one of the commonest complaints they hear from married couples these days is that "we're just not interested in making love anymore" (Gottlieb, 1979; Kaplan, in Switzer, 1977). Repressing one's anger can contribute to this sexual boredom.[5]

---

5. Sexual boredom is not inevitable in marriage. Some longitudinal data on sex in marriage (the only such data available today) compares 161 couples' feelings about sex shortly after they married in the late 1930s with their feelings twenty years later, in 1955. Only 5 percent of the husbands and 10 percent of the wives were indifferent or negative about sex. (Three percent of husbands and 13 percent of wives reported feeling indifferent or negative about sex at the time of marriage.) Although their sexual activity had decreased over the years (from nine times a month or more in the first three years to six times a month in the middle period and three times a month in the three years preceding the study), for most of the couples sex continued to be an important and enjoyable aspect of their union. After analyzing the data, the author concluded that "familiarity did not breed contempt, for these couples, and novelty of partner was not necessary for continuing sexual satisfaction" (Ard, 1977:284).

| Overeating | Boredom | Depression | Physical illness | Gossip |

Figure 9·2
Some anger "insteads." (Source: Based on Kassorla, 1973:65–76)

Passive-Aggression

The anger "insteads" can be subtle forms of what psychologists call **passive-aggression.** When a person expresses anger at someone but does so indirectly rather than directly, that behavior is passive-aggression. People use passive-aggression for the same reason they use anger substitutes—they are afraid of direct conflict.

Chronic criticism, nagging, nitpicking, and sarcasm are all forms of passive-aggression; like overeating, these actions momentarily relieve anxiety. In intimate relationships, however, they create unnecessary distance and pain. Most people use sarcasm unthinkingly, for instance, and they often aren't aware of its effect on a partner. But being the target of a sarcastic remark can be painful; it also can result in partners' feeling alienated from each other (Kassorla, 1973:165).

Sex becomes an arena for ongoing conflict when mates habitually withhold it or use it as passive-aggressive behavior (Feldman, 1975). For example, a partner is late for dinner or makes a disparaging comment in front of company. The hurt spouse says nothing at the time but rejects the other's sexual advances later that night because "I'm just too tired." It is much better to express anger at the time an incident occurs. Otherwise the anger festers and contaminates other areas of the relationship.

While it is not always true, anger may often be the issue when one partner or the other is just "not in the mood" for sex. For example, an otherwise submissive wife may avoid sex in order to feel that in one element of the relationship she has the upper hand. As one woman explained, "He controls

■ Smoking, drinking, and eating too much are sometimes indirect expressions of anger. Such behavior can be self-destructive, and long-term avoidance of conflict can create a depression throughout a family.

everything else around here; the least I can do is control the bedroom" (Halleck, 1969:13–14). It is not difficult to see how a devitalized sexual relationship can result from spouses' failure to resolve conflicts in bonding and constructive ways.

Other forms of passive-aggression are sabotage and displacement. In **sabotage** one partner attempts to spoil or undermine some activity the other has planned. The husband who is angry because his wife invited friends over when he wanted to relax may sabotage her evening, for example, by acting bored. In **displacement** a person directs anger at people or things the other cherishes. A wife who is angry with her husband for spending too much time and energy on his career may hate his expensive car, or a husband who feels angry and threatened because his wife returned to school may express disgust for her books and "clutter." Often, child abuse can be related to displaced aggression felt by a parent, as is discussed further in Chapter 13.

Devitalized Marriages

Another possible consequence of suppression of anger, the devitalized marriage, was discussed in Chapter 8. As we saw there and in Chapter 3, it is impossible to suppress some emotions and not others. What is the result of suppressing anger over a long period of time? George Bach and Peter Wyden provide the scenario of a typical evening in the home of nonfighting "pseudo-intimates" who have been suppressing anger for years:

He: (*yawning*) How was your day, dear?
She: (*pleasantly*) OK, how was yours?
He: Oh, you know, the usual....
She: Anything special you want to do later?
He: Oh, I don't know....

In this home, the authors conclude, "Nothing more meaningful may be exchanged for the rest of the evening." Because these partners refuse to recognize or express any anger toward each other, their penalty is the "emotional divorce" of a devitalized marriage (Bach and Wyden, 1970:21).

This kind of gradual erosion takes place not only within marital relationships. Unmarried lovers who feel progressively less enthusiastic about their partners may be refusing to accept and voice anger, too. Little irritations build up until finally one decides, "I'm tired of his (or her) always doing —

—." If the irritations had been brought into the open, the offending lover could have chosen to change, and the relationship might have continued.

While the suppression of anger can be a source of boredom and devitalization, partners can go too far in the opposite direction and habitually or violently hurt each other in angry outbursts. We'll look briefly at family violence. (Chapter 10 addresses spouse abuse specifically.)

Family Violence

Unresolved family conflict can escalate into violence. Often we assume that violent crimes are typically committed by strangers. But according to a U.S. Census Bureau survey of 58,000 households, less than half of all robberies, rapes, and assaults between 1982 and 1984 were committed by people unknown to the victims. (Box 6•2, "Date Rape," reports similar findings.) In this survey 39 percent of violent crimes involved victims' friends, relatives, or acquaintances. Friends accounted for 17 percent, while more casual acquaintances accounted for 14 percent and relatives for 8 percent of 1.5 million criminally reported acts of violence. According to the report, the number of crimes committed by family members may be underestimated because "individuals victimized by relatives may be reluctant to discuss the event ... for fear of reprisal or out of shame or embarrassment. Further, some victims of domestic violence may not perceive these acts as criminal."

Of the crimes in which a relative was the offender, 77 percent of the victims were women. More than half of the crimes by relatives against women were reported by those who were divorced. Spouses or ex-spouses committed more than half of all crimes by relatives and about two-thirds of all crimes by relatives against women ("Many Victims", 1987, p. 18).

Social scientists Raymond McLain and Andrew Weigert (1979) view the family as paradoxical in many ways. For one thing, the intense attachment family members feel toward one another can generate extremes of anger and hate. According to the editors of an anthology on family violence, to see the family as the center of harmony and consensus is to adopt a myth.

We tend to see the family... as a center of solidarity and love rather than of conflict and violence. Of course, everyone knows about the relatively few but horrible cases of wife or husband, child or parent murder. We also know about drunken brawls and occasional loss of control. But the tendency is to consider all of these cases as abnormalities—as exceptions to the usual state of affairs.

A more accurate view is that these sensational events are just the tip of the iceberg. Underneath the surface is a vast amount of conflict and violence—including the punishment of children, pokes and slaps of husbands and wives, and not altogether rare pitched battles between family members [Steinmetz and Straus, 1974:6]. ▪

Reasons for Family Violence There are a number of reasons for widespread family violence. One is that American society encourages violence in many ways. A national survey in the late 1960s for the federal Commission on the Causes and Prevention of Violence concluded that, despite our cultural conflict taboo, and although familial norms forbid violence within the family, "the larger value system of American society is hardly non-violent" (Steinmetz and Straus, 1974:15). An interview with some New York feminist mothers found that many of them considered it part of their duty to train sons to be "tough" (Van Gelder and Carmichael, 1975). Then, too, American television and movies often depict violence as acceptable and even glamorous.

A second reason for widespread family violence is that, ironically, the conflict taboos may actually precipitate rather than discourage violent outbursts. This is because familial violence may occur as a climax to repressed conflict (Steinmetz and Straus, 1974:5–6). Social theorist Lewis Coser has pointed out that groups usually consider conflict and tension among members dangerous to their survival and consequently try to avoid them. Perceived wrongs are suffered in silence, but this only leads to accumulated and intensified feelings of hostility, which eventually "reach uncontrollable proportions" (Steinmetz and Straus, 1974:5–6).

This line of reasoning leads logically to the conclusion that families can avoid violence if they find ways of releasing tension or "letting off steam." While this is true, it should be stressed that there are both right ways and wrong ways of doing this. One wrong way, catharsis, deserves special note here.

The Catharsis Myth According to the **catharsis myth,** family members can release tension by

regularly or routinely expressing verbal or mild physical aggression toward one another. Occasional low-level aggression, in other words, reduces the likelihood of severe outbursts of violence. The flaw in this reasoning lies in its failure to distinguish between aggressiveness and assertiveness (Steinmetz, 1977).

In **assertive action** a person expresses positively, affirms, defends, or maintains his or her opinions or feelings about an issue. To assert is to state one's position boldly enough that it is taken seriously by others. Recall that in **aggressive behavior** a person acts in a hostile fashion, launching a verbal or physical attack on another. Aggression seeks not only to state one's own position but also to attack the other's point of view. While assertive behavior does not include the need to compete or win, aggressive behavior does.

Social scientist Murray Straus points out that attacking others can actually heighten patterns of aggression rather than diminish them (Straus, 1974; Steinmetz and Straus, 1974). For example, experiments in which some children are given the opportunity to express violence and aggression show that those children are more likely to continue to express aggression than are children who haven't had that opportunity (Kenny, 1952). Even the vicarious experience of viewing unpunished aggressive acts increases rather than decreases children's aggression, as Figure 9·3 indicates. All this suggests that aggression within the family is "catching"; that is, it may influence other members of the family to become more rather than less aggressive.

Violence and aggression are not found in every family situation. But conflict is a part of marriage and family life, and learning to resolve it productively is an important part of an individual's commitment to the family. Now we will focus on ways to handle conflict. We'll look first at a few don'ts—mistakes people often make in fighting with each other. Then we'll provide some suggestions and tentative guidelines for handling conflict in a positive way.

SOME ALIENATING PRACTICES

Alienating fight tactics are those that tend to create distance between intimates. They don't resolve tension or conflict; they increase it. Many

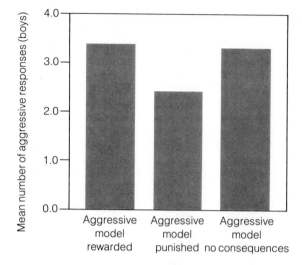

Figure 9·3

Aggression is catching. Experiments show that children who have seen people on TV being violent and aggressive without being punished act more aggressively later than children without this experience. In a study of thirty-three nursery school children, age 42–71 months, psychologist Albert Bandura had each child watch a five-minute movie on a TV screen in which a man beat an adult-sized rubber doll that was in his path. The movie had one of three endings: In one ending, the man (the adult model) was rewarded by another adult by being called a "strong champion" and given soda pop and candy; in another ending the man was called a "big bully" by another adult and spanked with a magazine; and in the third version the movie ended after the first scene, with no positive or negative consequences for the aggressive model. Children were then placed in a room with a number of toys, including a rubber doll similar to the doll in the movie, and were observed to see if they would imitate the aggression or perform other aggressive acts. Bars indicate the differences in average number of aggressive responses for boys who saw the three different versions of the movie. As you can see, boys who saw the aggressive model rewarded or unpunished were more apt to be aggressive themselves. Responses for girls showed a similar pattern, although girls were less aggressive overall. (Source: Bandura, 1965)

of the tactics discussed below are prevalent among conflict-habituated couples (although almost everyone has probably had firsthand experience with some of them).

Fight Evading

Chronic fight evaders fear conflict and hesitate to accept their own and others' hostile or angry emotions.

Fight evaders employ several tactics to avoid fighting, such as

1. leaving the house or the scene when a fight threatens;
2. turning sullen and refusing to argue or talk;
3. derailing potential arguments by saying, "I can't take it when you yell at me";
4. flatly stating, "I can't take you seriously when you act this way";
5. employing the "hit and run" tactic of filing a complaint, then leaving no time for an answer or for a resolution (Bach and Wyden, 1970).

Fight evaders often argue that they avoid conflicts because they don't want to hurt their partners. Often, however, the one they are really trying to protect is themselves. (Case Study 9·2, "Sharing a Grievance," illustrates the anxiety that can accompany sharing a grievance.) "A great deal of dishonesty that ostensibly occurs in an effort to prevent pain actually occurs as we try to protect and shield ourselves from the agony of feeling our own pain, fear, fright, shame, or embarrassment" (Crosby, 1976:157–58). Moreover, evading fights can make partners who want and need to fight feel worse, not better, as we saw earlier.

Gunnysacking and "Kitchen-Sink" Fights

Fight evading encourages **gunnysacking:** keeping one's grievances secret while tossing them into an imaginary gunnysack that grows heavier and heavier over time. Martyring (see Chapter 3) is typically accompanied by gunnysacking. When marital complaints are toted and nursed along quietly in a gunnysack for any length of time, they "make a dreadful mess when they burst" (Bach and Wyden, 1970:19).

Gunnysacking and the collecting of grievances have been thought to be predominantly feminine tactics, but Bach and Wyden's research found them to be common among men as well.

A typical result is a destructive and ineffective kind of fighting that Bach and Wyden call the **kitchen-sink fight,** in which partners don't focus on resolving specific issues. Instead, "the kitchen plumbing is about all that isn't thrown in such a battle." The following is an illustration of a kitchen-sink fight by a married couple who meets for a dinner date. The wife is twenty minutes late.

He: Why were you late?
She: I tried my best.
He: Yeah? You and who else? Your mother is never on time either.
She: That's got nothing to do with it.
He: The hell it doesn't. You're just as sloppy as she is.
She: (*getting louder*) You don't say! Who's picking whose dirty underwear off the floor every morning?
He: (*sarcastic but controlled*) I happen to go to work. What have *you* got to do all day?
She: (*shouting*) I'm trying to get along on the money you don't make, that's what.
He: (*turning away from her*) Why should I knock myself out for an ungrateful bitch like you? [Bach and Wyden, 1970:18–19].

These fighters reached into their gunnysacks to drag totally irrelevant and past occurrences into their argument. The immediate issue—her being late—is not resolved. In fact, it seems to have been temporarily forgotten (or itself gunnysacked to be used as future ammunition!). Obviously, this fight did not make the partners feel better about themselves as individuals or about their relationship. Bach and Wyden suggest that gunnysacking couples try to focus their arguments and keep up to date on their grievances as a way of discouraging this habit.

Mixed, or Double, Messages

A third alienating tactic is the use of **mixed,** or double, **messages:** simultaneous messages that contradict each other. Contradictory messages can be verbal, or one can be verbal and one nonverbal. For example, a spouse agrees to go out to eat with a partner but at the same time yawns and says that he or she is tired and had a hard day at work. Or a partner insists "Of course I love you" while picking an invisible speck from her or his sleeve in a gesture of indifference.

Senders of mixed messages may not be aware of what they are doing, and mixed messages can be very subtle. They usually result from simultaneously wanting to recognize and to deny conflict or tension. Mixed messages allow senders to let other persons know they are angry at them and at the same time to deny that they are. A classic example is the "silent treatment." A spouse becomes aware that she or he has said or done something and asks what's wrong. "Oh, nothing," the partner replies, without much feeling, but everything about the partner's face, body, attitude, and posture suggests that something is indeed wrong.

Besides the "silent treatment," other ways to indicate that something is wrong while denying it include making a partner the butt of jokes, using subtle innuendos rather than direct communication, and being sarcastic (also defended as "just a joke" by mixed-message senders).

Sarcasm and other mixed messages create distance and cause pain and confusion, for they prevent honest communication from taking place. Expressing anger is a far better tactic, for it opens the way for solutions. The next section presents guidelines for fighting more constructively.

GUIDELINES FOR BONDING FIGHTS

The tactics described previously are likely to alienate partners, but some goals and strategies can help make fighting productive rather than destructive. This kind of fighting, which brings people closer rather than pushing them apart, is called **bonding fighting.**

The key to creating a bonding fight is for partners to try to build up, not tear down, each other's self-esteem while fighting. In one way or another, the following guidelines all have this goal.[6]

---

6. These guidelines are taken from Bach and Wyden's *The Intimate Enemy* (1970) and Crosby's *Illusion and Disillusion: The Self in Love and Marriage* (1976).

CASE STUDY 9·2

SHARING A GRIEVANCE

Janet, 28, is married to Joe, who is divorced and has two sons. Here Janet talks about her need to share a grievance with Joe and the anxiety that taking such a risk can cause.

Joe's sons live with their mother in Colorado. They come to stay with us Christmas, spring break, and summers. Last summer when they were here, I was a wreck. I was jealous of Joe's relationship with the boys. He did so much with them, it seemed, and I was feeling left out. I was so upset, I was feeling sick.

I went to a physician, trying to figure out whether I really was physically ill or whether it was my head. He said, "Just take some time out and think about where you stand. And as time goes by and you feel the time is right, certainly discuss these feelings with your husband." Which is exactly what I did!

It was really kind of tricky though. Joe wanted so desperately for everybody to be happy, for us to have the one great big happy family. It was tricky because I had to find the right moment, the right atmosphere to speak what was on my mind. But I did. And it worked!

I remember so vividly reaching the point where I knew that I had to say something real soon or else it was gonna be bad for everybody. I knew Joe and I had to be away from the boys when we talked. And Joe had to be away from the phone.

So one Saturday afternoon he had to go to his office to pick something up, and I volunteered to go with him. But the atmosphere wasn't right in the car. I

Level with Each Other

Partners need to be as candid as possible; counselors call this *leveling*. **Leveling** means being transparent, authentic, and explicit about how one feels, "especially concerning the more conflictive or hurtful aspects" of an intimate relationship (Bach and Wyden, 1970:368). Leveling is self-disclosure in action.

Various studies indicate that because of boredom (an anger "instead"), indifference, or the mistaken impression that the partner already knows how the other feels, spouses often overestimate how accurately their partner understands them. Underlying conflicts go unresolved because partners fail to voice their feelings, irritations, and preferences— and neither is aware that the other is holding back. The solution to this problem is to air grievances— to candidly explain where one stands and how one feels about a specific situation.

Being candid does not mean the same thing as being tactless. Leveling, in fact, is never intentionally hurtful and is consistent with the next guideline.

Use I-Statements to Avoid Attacks

Attacks are assaults on a partner's character or self-esteem. A rule in avoiding attack is to use *I* rather than *you* or *why*. The receiver usually perceives I-statements as an attempt to recognize and communicate feelings, but you- and why-statements are more likely to be perceived as attacks— whether or not they are intended as such. For example, instead of asking "Why are *you* late?" a statement such as "*I* was worried because you hadn't arrived" may allow more communication.

I-statements are most effective if they are communicated in a positive way. A partner should

didn't say anything. I thought, "Well, as soon as—when we get to the office—I'll just sit down and kind of open up then."

Well, the janitor that opened up the outside door also had to open the door to Joe's office. He kept standing there, so I couldn't open up. I can remember the anxiety. My hands were sweating.

Finally, back in the car, before we got home, I said, "We have to stop for a drink because there's something on my mind and I really have to talk to you about it." We did. I think I opened the conversation by saying, "You know, I finally realize what it feels like to be a father when there is a newborn in the house." Because there was this bonding between him and the boys, and you hear all the time about the father's feeling left out with a newborn. And that was just exactly how I felt.

He said, "Well, let's see. How shall we approach this?" He was very open. And I, I laugh now at all my anxiety because there was a tremendous effort on his part to really understand what my feelings were.

■ Why do you think Janet felt anxiety about sharing her feelings with Joe? What risk did she take in being honest? What did she gain? What did Joe gain?

Suppose Joe had been hostile rather than supportive. In your opinion, would the risk still have been worth it for Janet? What do you believe might have happened in the long run had Janet not risked initiating a fight?

express his or her anger directly, but it will seem less threatening if he or she conveys positive feelings at the same time negative emotions are voiced. The message comes across, but it's not as bitter as when only angry feelings are expressed.

Give Feedback

Partners must also ensure that complaints and other messages are properly understood. Communication consists of a sender, a receiver, and a message. A message is sent not only through the content and emotional tone of words but through facial expressions, gestures, "body language," and voice quality as well. In fact, the actual words of an emotional message have far less effect than do the speaker's facial expression or tone of voice. A study by Albert Mehrabian (1972) revealed that a speaker's facial expression and tone of voice had a far greater share of the total impact on the receiver (55 and 38 percent, respectively) than did the actual words (only 7 percent). The receiver has to evaluate all the components of the message and then make some judgment about what the message means. Obviously, there is much room for error in interpreting a message, because words and nonverbal cues alike can have different meanings in different contexts.

Partners can ensure that they receive messages accurately by giving **feedback:** They repeat in their own words what the other has said or revealed. For example, a husband says, "I don't like it when you talk on the phone in the evenings when I'm home." To give feedback, his wife would respond with something like, "I realize it irritates you when I'm on the phone in the evenings instead of visiting with you." Giving feedback requires self-esteem because it involves facing and dealing with an issue rather than becoming defensive or avoiding it.

■ A candid couple: Cheryll and Jonathan have mastered the fine art of fighting effectively. Because they are both direct about voicing their own needs and respectful of each other as individuals, their conflicts are constructive instead of destructive.

Checking-It-Out Since studies consistently show that partners seldom understand each other as well as they think they do, a good habit is to ask for feedback, by a process of **checking-it-out:** asking the other person whether your perception of her or his feelings or of the present situation is accurate. Checking-it-out often helps avoid unnecessarily hurt feelings. As the following example shows, the procedure can also help partners avoid imagining trouble that may not be there:

She: I sense you're angry about something. (*checking-it-out*) Is it because it's my class night and I haven't made dinner?
He: No, that's not why, but I am angry. I'm angry because I was tied up in traffic an extra half hour on my way home.

Bach and Wyden propose a fight plan in which partners take turns airing grievances, checking things out, and giving feedback. First, the complainant states a grievance. Without interrupting or becoming defensive, the recipient listens, then asks questions for clarification if necessary and gives feedback. When both are satisfied that they understand each other, the recipient begins to level, responding to the complainant's grievance. Now the complainant listens quietly, then offers feedback. Partners take turns leveling, listening, checking things out, and giving feedback until both positions are clearly understood. (Box 9•1, "Listening," lists some of the advantages to be gained from learning to listen well.

Choose the Time and Place Carefully

Fights can be nonconstructive if the complainant raises grievances at the wrong time. One partner may be ready to fight when the other is almost asleep or is working on an important assignment, for instance. At times like these, the person who picked the fight may get more than he or she bargained for.

Partners should try to negotiate "gripe hours" by pinning down a time and place for a fight. Fighting by appointment may sound silly and may be difficult to arrange, but it has two important advantages. First, complainants can organize their thoughts and feelings more calmly and deliberately, increasing the likelihood that their arguments will be persuasive. Second, recipients of complaints have time before the fight to prepare themselves for some criticism.

Focus Anger Only on Specific Issues

Constructive fighting aims at resolving specific problems that are happening *now*—not at gunnysacking. To maintain their self-esteem, recipients of complaints need to feel that they can do something specific to help resolve the problem raised. This will be more difficult if they feel overwhelmed.

Know What the Fight Is About

Fighting over petty annoyances, such as who should have put gas in the car, is healthy and can even be "fun" as an essentially harmless way to release tension. But partners sometimes unconsciously allow trivial issues to become decoys, so that they evade the real area of conflict and leave it unsolved. An irate husband, for example, who complains about how his wife treats their children may really be fighting about his feelings of rejection because he feels that his wife isn't giving him enough attention. Before partners bring up a grievance, they need to ask themselves what they are really fighting about.

Ask for a Specific Change, but Be Open to Compromise

Initially, complainants should be ready to propose at least one solution to the problem. Recipients, too, need to be willing to come up with possible solutions. If they are careful to keep proposed solutions pertinent to the issue at hand, partners can then negotiate alternatives.

Resolving specific issues involves bargaining and negotiation. Partners need to recognize that there are probably several ways to solve a particular problem, and backing each other into corners with ultimatums and counter-ultimatums is not negotiation but attack. John Gottman found that happily married couples reach agreement rather quickly. Either one partner gives into the other without resentment or the two compromise. Unhappily married couples tend to continue in a cycle of conflict (Gottman, 1979).[7]

Be Willing to Change Yourself

Communication, of course, needs to be accompanied by action. The romantic belief that couples should accept each other completely as they are is often merged with the individualistic view that people should be exactly what they choose to be. The result is an erroneous assumption that if a partner loves you, he or she will accept you just as you are and not ask for even minor changes. On the contrary, partners need to be willing to change themselves, to be changed by others, and to be influenced by "reasonable argument, admonitions, exhortations, and the appeal to the emotions" (Kubie, in Bach and Wyden, 1970:56–57). Every intimate relationship involves negotiation and mutual compromise; partners who refuse to change, or who insist they cannot, are in effect refusing to engage in an intimate relationship.

---

7. Gottman and colleagues conducted a very complex research study on couple communication. They used a sample of twenty-eight couples, half of whom were seeking marriage counseling and half of whom answered an ad addressed to couples who described their marriages as "mutually satisfying." The researchers gave all the couples the Locke-Williamson Marital Relationship Inventory and selected the extremes from their sample. They termed the five clinic couples scoring the lowest on the MIR "distressed" and the five nonclinic couples scoring highest on the MRI "nondistressed."

Couples were presented three problems to discuss and were asked to reach agreement on a solution to one of them. Their conversations were videotaped and systematically analyzed in terms of verbal and nonverbal communication characteristics. There were some subsidiary studies involving an additional sixty couples. These are too complicated to present here in detail but the Gottman study is undoubtedly one of the most extensive studies of marital communication ever undertaken. We report some specific findings throughout the chapter and find much in common between this research and the recommendations, based on clinical experience rather than research, of psychologist George Bach and colleagues. Gottman's research is carefully done but based on a relatively small sample. Systematic research on marital communications is relatively recent, but it is growing rapidly.

BOX 9 · 1

LISTENING

SOURCE:
Broderick, 1979a:40–41.

Listening is so basic we often assume we're doing it effectively. But in couple conflict, listening may be forgotten as both partners strive to put forward their points of view. Thinking a bit about what listening does may help one listen as well as talk.

Good listening has some important results, according to sociologist/counselor Carlfred Broderick:

1. The attitude of listening itself shows love, concern, and respect.... Any act that expresses a positive attitude is likely to trigger a sequence of positive responses back and forth....
2. The avoidance of interrupting and criticism prevents the sending of negative messages such as "I don't care how you feel or what you think." "You're not worth listening to." ...

Don't Try to Win

Finally, partners must not compete in fights. American society encourages people to see almost everything they do in terms of winning or losing. However, bonding fights, like dancing, can't involve a winner and a loser. If one partner must win, then the other obviously must lose. But losing lessens a person's self-esteem and increases resentment and strain on the relationship. This is why in intimate fighting there can never be one winner and one loser—only two losers. Both partners lose if they engage in destructive conflict. Both win if they become closer and settle, or at least understand, their differences.

If a couple cannot designate a winner and a loser, they can be at a loss to know how to end a fight. Ideally, a fight ends when there has been a mutually satisfactory airing of each partner's views. Bach suggests that partners question each other to make sure that they've said all they need to say.

Sometimes, when partners are too hurt or frightened to continue, they need to stop fighting before they reach a resolution. Women often cry as a signal that they've been hit below the "beltline" (the beltline being Bach's image for a person's tolerance limit) or that they feel too frustrated or hurt to go on fighting. Men experience the same feelings, but they have learned from childhood not

to cry. Hence, they may hide their emotions, or they may erupt angrily. In either case it is necessary to bargain about whether the fight should continue. The partner who is not feeling so hurt or frightened might ask, "Do you want to stop now or to go on with this?" If the answer is, "I want to stop," the fight should be either terminated or interrupted for a time.

CHANGING FIGHTING HABITS

Social scientist Suzanne Steinmetz traced the patterns of how families resolve conflict in fifty-seven intact urban and suburban families. Her research shows not only that individual families assume consistent patterns or habits for facing conflict but also that these patterns are passed from one generation to the next. Parents who resort to physical abuse teach their children, in effect, that such abuse is an acceptable outlet for tension. In this way the "cycle of violence" is perpetuated (Steinmetz, 1977). Kassorla points out that a similar process takes place as people learn anger "insteads" from their parents (Kassorla, 1973).

There are some training programs in communication, conducted by psychologists, that have

3. You discover how things actually look from your spouse's or partner's point of view. There's a risk, because what you hear may be surprising and even unsettling. But it is nearly always worth it. In fact, it's hard to imagine how any couple can become close without achieving insight into each other's feelings.

4. You lose your status as chief expert on what your spouse really thinks, wants, fears, and feels. Instead, your spouse takes over as the final authority on his or her own feelings.... [Furthermore] if you listen sympathetically to your spouse, he or she is able to develop greater clarity in areas that may have been confused and confusing....

5. You set an example for your spouse to follow in listening to your ... feelings.

proven quite effective in helping people to change these behaviors. One such program, which is based on Gottman's research, is a program for engaged couples at the University of Denver. Thirty-five couples who received training in expression of feelings, constructive conflict, and communication skills were reported to be happier one year later than couples who received no training (Brandt, 1982). The following steps are given to help people work for change on their own.

The first step in changing destructive fighting habits is to adopt the attitudes described by Israel Charny in Box 9-2, "Some Attitudes for Marital Fighting." Feeling that conflict is "wrong" or that it should be "kept out of the children's sight," for example, can cause dangerous buildups of tension.

A second, related step is to begin to use the guidelines for bonding fighting we have described. But changing can be a confusing and frightening process. For example, partners who have been hardened fight evaders may suddenly need to argue over just about *everything.* Afraid that they won't like themselves this way, that their family and friends "won't even know me," or that their partners won't understand or cooperate, these spouses will be tempted to return to their old and familiar ways. They need to realize two important things.

First, the feeling that one wants to fight "over everything" is largely a short-term result of releas- ing long-harbored resentments. The best way to counteract this tendency is to concentrate on keeping arguments focused only on current and specific issues. Recognizing old resentments is an indication of growth and well-being, but fighting about them isn't necessary.

Second, as partners grow more accustomed to voicing grievances regularly, their fights may hardly seem like fights at all: Partners will gradually learn to incorporate many irritations and requests into their normal conversations. Partners adept at constructive fighting often argue in normal tones of voice and even with humor. In a very real sense their disagreements are essential to their intimacy.

When partners are just learning to fight, however, they are often frightened and insecure. One way to begin is by writing letters or using a tape recorder. In this way the complainant is not inhibited or stopped by a mate's interruption or hostile nonverbal cues. The the mate can read or listen to the other's complaints in privacy when she or he is ready to listen. Letters and tape recorders are no substitute for face-to-face communication, but they don't intimidate either. Once partners become more comfortable with their differences, they can begin to fight face to face.

Another option is to record a fight and play it back later. This exercise can help spouses look at themselves objectively. They can ask themselves

BOX 9·2

SOME ATTITUDES FOR MARITAL FIGHTING

In an article called "Marital love and hate," Israel Charny suggests some helpful attitudes toward marital fighting.

1. *"It is natural and right to feel anger."* Contrary to the myth of conflict-free love, angry and hostile feelings are an integral part of being human. However, nearly everyone has internalized the conflict taboo to some extent.

2. A second helpful attitude proposed by Charny is to recognize that *"there is much to be gained from learning how to fight with one's spouse openly, saying what we feel but not promiscuously, sharing our angers, but not overwhelming one another."* Family therapists point out one reason it can be more threatening to fight with family members: In intimate relationships where people reveal more of themselves, they are most vulnerable to ridicule, attack, and "overwhelming" criticism. Studies show that people who are unhappily married attack the self-concept and esteem of their mates more than do couples who report being happily married (Mathews and Mihanovich, 1963). Learning to express one's feelings assertively, then, but not "promiscuously" or abusively is advantageous to partners.

3. *"It is very much wrong to hurt another person, overtly, in acts (words or physical attacks) against the other person, but to feel like hurting another is a natural expression of anger."* As Crosby writes, "feelings are neither right nor wrong—they simply are" (Crosby, 1976:131). They need to be recognized and accepted as natural. Feelings are not the same as actions. Abusive *acts* are wrong.

4. The fourth attitude Charny suggests is that *"husbands and wives are far better off when they learn that in the course of marital fighting a good deal of unfairness, exaggeration, and extremes is natural."* Partners can benefit from using rules and fighting fair, but even the fairest fighters probably break some of the rules some of the time. Learning not to be inordinately offended by one's own or a partner's unfairness or exaggeration is part of learning to fight intimately.

SOURCE:
Charny, in Steinmetz and Straus, 1974.

---

whether and where they really listened, offered feedback, and stuck to specifics or resorted to hurtful, alienating tactics (O'Neill and O'Neill, 1972:131).

Although the suggestions made in the text and in the boxes may all help, learning to "fight fair" is not easy. A good number of fights are even about fighting itself. Sometimes one or both partners feel that they need outside help with their fighting, and they may decide to have a marriage counselor serve as referee. Box 9·3, "Hiring a Referee: Marriage Counseling," discusses this alternative.

THE MYTH OF CONFLICT-FREE CONFLICT

By now, so much attention has been devoted to the bonding capacity of intimate fighting that it may seem as if conflict itself can be free of conflict. It can't. Even the fairest fighters hit below the belt once in a while, and it's probably safe to say that all fighting involves some degree of frustration and hurt feelings. Anger, after all, is anger, hostility is

5. A fifth attitude Charny suggests that partners adopt is that *"even when we hate we love."* Even moments filled with the bitterest hate can contain love at the same time. "An excellent emotional exercise in the heat of marital battle is to conjure up . . . just how much one cares for one's now quite-hated spouse, so as to experience one's hate and love as coexisting streams of feeling" (Charny, 1974:212).

6. Charny asserts that *"it is all to one's good to be committed increasingly to stay with one's marriage if at all possible—to work hard at reducing undue pain and at gaining the best this union can grow to create."* Such commitment, Charny writes, is good for oneself, one's spouse, and one's children because it "offers a sense of security and meaning to oneself and to one's family, especially when the going gets rough, as it always does" (Charny, 1974:211).

7. A final attitude discussed by Charny concerns marital fighting in front of their children. Although the conflict taboo causes many partners to hide their fighting from their children, Charny encourages partners to *"fight fairly often in front of the children, but fight wisely and well."* Parents are encouraged not to avoid or "put anger away" but to offer their children examples of how to deal with hostile feelings fairly and without inflicting unnecessary injury (Charny, 1974:212).

When partners adopt these positive attitudes toward conflict, the result can be healthy, more supportive relationships. The goal of intimate fighting should be to resolve conflicts and at the same time to make both partners feel better, not worse, about themselves.

Since Charny encourages couples to fight, why are his suggestions unlikely to lead to conflict-habituated relationships such as those described in Chapter 8? In light of Charny's suggestions, when do you think it might not be all to one's good to stay married?

hostility, and hate is hate—even between partners who are very close to each other.

Moreover, some spouses are married to mates who don't want to learn to fight more positively. As we saw in Chapter 8, partners can indeed be satisfied with passive-congenial, devitalized, or even conflict-habituated unions. In marriages where one partner wants to change and the other doesn't, sometimes much can be gained if just one partner begins to communicate more positively. Other times, however, positive changes in one spouse do not spur growth in the other. Situations like this often end in divorce.

Even when both partners develop constructive habits, all their problems will not necessarily be resolved, and their marriage might not last. One social scientist who interviewed couples about to marry discovered a contemporary version of romantic mythology: They believed their marriages would surely, almost magically, last "because we can discuss our problems together" (Hilsdale, 1962:142).

BOX 9 · 3

**HIRING A
REFEREE:
MARRIAGE
COUNSELING**

Marcia Lasswell is a marriage counselor who coauthored the book *No-Fault Marriage* (1976). She suggests that couples should visit a marriage counselor:

1. When conflict goes unresolved so long that it hardens into rigid confrontation with neither spouse feeling able or willing to budge from an inflexible position;
2. when a couple cannot figure out how to solve their difficulties themselves;
3. when partners' communication is incessantly hostile and they are unable to reach out to each other in understanding;
4. when a relationship has deteriorated to the point at which a spouse feels she or he must resort to some dramatic, climactic gesture, such as leaving home, becoming physically violent, or attempting suicide;
5. when a problem in the relationship appears to be linked to a personality disorder in one or both partners, such as chronic drinking, severe depression, acute nervousness, or deep feelings of insecurity and inadequacy (Lasswell and Lobsenz, 1976:259).

Even when individual personality problems are not involved, marriage counselors can help by acting as objective, neutral referees. They can give partners feedback and help each to level. Counselors can also help fighting intimates to negotiate solutions to their difficulties with fairness. Another benefit of marriage counseling is that fighters have a tendency to "gang up" on a referee, a phenomenon that can draw combating partners together (Bach and Wyden, 1970:72).

QUALIFICATIONS OF COUNSELORS

The qualifications of marriage counselors vary. A counselor who is a member of the American Association of Marriage and Family Therapists (AAMFT) has a graduate degree (in either medicine, law, social work, psychiatry, psychology, or the ministry) in addition to special training in marriage or family therapy or both and at least three years of clinical training and experience under a senior counselor's supervision.

Not all those who practice counseling are so well qualified, however, and some have, in fact, taken on the responsibility of training themseves. A few states

One study of young married couples concluded that "contrary to what might be expected, an open talking about the violation of expectations does not always lead to an adjustment" (Cutler and Dyer, 1965:201). While a complainant may feel that he or she is being fair in bringing up a grievance and discussing it openly and calmly, the recipient may view the complaint as critical and punitive, and it may be a blow to that partner's self-esteem. The recipient may not feel that the time is right for fighting or may not want to bargain about the issue. Finally, sharing anger and hostilities may violate what the other partner expects of the relationship.

Another study compared mutually satisfied

license marriage counselors, requiring that they pass oral and written tests in order to practice. Most states, however, require no license at all. The safest way to choose a counselor is to select one who belongs to the AAMFT. Personal references from friends may also be helpful.

It is important to have a counselor you like, trust, and feel is sympathetic to you. It is also important that the counselor respect your religious and personal values. If after three or four sessions you do not feel comfortable with the counselor or don't believe she or he is effective, it might be a good idea to try someone else. Careful shopping is at least as important in selecting a therapist as it is in buying a new car (Broderick, 1979a).

MARRIAGE COUNSELING APPROACHES

Marriage counseling can be either a short- or a long-term arrangement. A difficulty might be cleared up in a few weekly sessions. In other cases counseling might last a year or more. Or a couple might work through a problem in a few visits, then quit with the understanding that they'll return if conflicts once more begin to go unresolved. In all cases counseling should have definite goals and should aim at termination instead of becoming an indefinite program.

Qualified marriage counselors have widely varying approaches to their work, and couples do well to inquire about this before engaging a counselor. For example, counselors whose primary training is in psychiatry or psychoanalysis may view problems in relationships as the results of one or both partners' personal neuroses. Such counselors would believe that restoring each partner to emotional health is the first and most important step in improving the marriage and so would probably suggest seeing each partner individually.

Another approach to marriage counseling is **conjoint marital counseling,** or family therapy. Instead of counseling one partner at a time, the counselor sees husband and wife together. In such an approach counselors help partners learn to interact more constructively.

All we've said about marriage counseling and a couple's learning to fight fair is based on the presumption that both partners are willing to cooperate. It is entirely possible, however, that one's spouse may not be willing. Something no marriage counselor can or will attempt to accomplish is changing a spouse to a partner's liking without the spouse's active cooperation.

couples with those experiencing marital difficulties and found that when couples are having trouble getting along or are under "stressed" conditions, they tend to interpret each other's messages and behavior more negatively. Satisfied partners did not differ from distressed ones in how they intended their behavior to be received by mates. But distressed partners actually interpreted their spouses' words and behavior as being more harsh and hurtful than was intended (Gottman, Notarius, Gonso, and Markman, 1976; Gottman et al., 1977).

Moreover, not every conflict can be resolved, even between the fairest and most mature fighters. If an unresolved conflict is not crucial to either partner, then they have reached a stalemate. The two may simply have to accept their inability to resolve that particular issue. However, when they reach a stalemate over an issue of vital importance to both of them, living together may no longer be feasible, and divorce may be their only alternative (Crosby, 1976:160).

Finally, Bach, who founded and directs an institute to teach "constructive aggression," warns that "fight training does not always end 'happily'." In one instance a couple attending Bach's fight training sessions realized through their better communication that the husband felt he should not have married at all. He believed he was "not the marrying type." His former passive-aggressive behavior had been a signal that he wanted to leave his wife. When this was exposed in fight training, the couple decided on a trial separation and eventually got a divorce (Bach and Wyden, 1970:107). Like love, fair fighting doesn't conquer all. But it can certainly help partners who are reasonably well matched and who want to stay together. Success in marriage has much to do with a couple's skills in relating to one another—perhaps much more than the social similarity, financial stress, and age at marriage often emphasized by social scientists in earlier studies of marital adjustment (Gottman, 1979). The next section addresses an issue that requires positive communication skills in virtually all intimate relationships.

SELF-ACTUALIZATION WITHIN THE FAMILY: NEGOTIATING FOR FREEDOM AND TOGETHERNESS

In a modern society like ours, we expect to combine our family commitments with continued development as an individual, a process termed self-actualization. **Self-actualization** entails the pursuit of activities, interests, and relationships that bring us pleasure and enrich our personalities. Although there has been much questioning of the "me-generation" and we now no longer so frequently hear terms like *self-actualization,* few people in fact marry or enter other relationships without expecting to continue their pursuit of individual interests and goals. But the tension between self-actualization and responsibilities to others—indeed, the pleasure of sharing life intimately with

others—is an inevitable part of the existence of these two desires. Psychologist Catherine Chilman summarizes the need for balance between self-actualization and responsibility to others. "The opposing drives for autonomy and belonging forever create a conflict between 'me' and 'us.' . . . When life is all 'me' there is loneliness and dread. When life is all 'us' there is a sense of entrapment" (Chilman, 1978a).[8]

An attempt to synchronize members' differing needs for freedom and togetherness can bring conflict, and the conflict may be intense. Social theorist Lewis Coser has pointed out that hostilities are likely to be the most intense within groups characterized by close emotional ties among the members:

If they witness the breaking away of one with whom they have shared cares and responsibilities of group life, they are likely to react in a more violent way against such "disloyalty" than less involved members [1956:68]. ■

Keeping Conflict in Perspective

In trying to see in conflicts a potential for growth, it may be helpful to remember a few points. First, the issue of privacy and freedom exists in virtually all households. One study of communes (formed mainly so that members could have greater social support) found that the most frequently mentioned complaints were the lack of privacy and the interpersonal conflict. Noting the irony in this, the authors concluded:

Although social support was the single most important advantage of communes, it is not without attendant disadvantages. The time and energy required to maintain good interpersonal relationships with a variety of other adults was mentioned as a disadvantage by . . . respondents [Stein et al., 1975:185]. ■

---

8. Theoretical work and research by Olson and associates from the family systems theory perspective supports Chilman's statement. These scientists find that intermediate levels of family cohesion are "most viable for family functioning because individuals are able to *experience* and *balance* being independent from, as well as connected to, their families" (Olson et al., 1980:975; also Minuchin, 1974).

■ Mealtime is usually family time—and often fight time, too. How a family handles its conflicts and resolves fights affects everyone in the household.

The writers go on to point out that the two sources of conflict most often mentioned were inconsideration and lack of communication; both were behaviors that contradicted the group's avowed function of social support. This is also true, of course, for more traditional family forms.

A second point to remember is that everyone needs space and time alone, and that some people need more than others. Separate vacations, periodic "days off" from the relationship, and even longer temporary separations can be crucial in fulfilling one partner's need to recover a sense of self. Such requests don't necessarily mean that love has ended or that the family member is rejecting a partner or the family group (Jourard, 1979).

A third important point is that the feeling of having enough freedom lets family members be more open with each other. Also, family members are more likely to give each other privacy if they feel they are getting enough attention. A key to solving the conflict between separateness and togetherness, then, is to try to develop intimacy, not to focus just on physical togetherness. As we have seen, intimacy results from positive communication patterns and fair fighting.

Compromise and Commitment

Often, the solution involves compromise. When both spouses (or more than one family member) are heavily involved in outside activities, for instance, a trade can be negotiated: "I'll take only one evening course next semester if you'll stop playing tennis on Saturday mornings." Regarding negotiating between "night persons" married to "day persons," sociologist and marriage counselor Carlfred Broderick makes a similar suggestion:

Synchronizing in such cases may involve the early bird's coming home and taking a nap in the early evening so as to be "up" for a late evening activity with his or her late-blooming spouse. On other occasions, the night person may agree to "go to bed" early with the spouse for purposes of affection and sex and then get up again afterward to continue other activities while the mate sleeps [1979b:253]. ■

Compromise means giving something up, of course, but as Crosby points out, it's necessary. "There simply is no way that a relationship can be nurtured if both partners covet total independence and autonomy" (Crosby, 1976:264). Willingness to compromise stems from a "triple commitment" to the self, the mate, and the relationship—not just to external or culturally imposed vows. One must simultaneously recognize two things: first, that neglecting one's self is destructive to both the self and the other; and second, that "independence carried to the furthest extreme is just loneliness. . . . There is no growth in it" (Shain, 1978:14). The lesson that we saw in Chapter 3 of this text, then, is carried through in our examination of the individual in the family. Self-love is important for sharing; and sharing is essential for personal development.

Summary

Families are powerful sources of support for individuals, and they reinforce members' sense of identity. Because the family is powerful, however, it can cause individuals to feel constrained. Tactics such as gaslighting, scapegoating, or negative use of the "looking glass" can all be stressful or denigrating to an individual.

According to Stinnett, six characteristics that help make families strong and cohesive are expressing appreciation for each other, doing things together, having positive communication patterns, being committed to the group, having some spiritual orientation, and being able to deal creatively with crises.

Developing positive communication patterns involves, among other things, personally discarding the "conflict taboo." Americans are socialized to respect the conflict taboo, but both sociologists and counselors are recognizing that conflict and tension should be expressed, not repressed. Denying conflict can be destructive to both individuals and relationships.

While fighting is a normal part of the most loving relationships, there are "right" and "wrong" ways of fighting. Alienating practices should be avoided: They hurt a relationship because they lower partners' self-esteem. Bonding fights, in contrast, can often resolve issues and also bring partners closer together by improving communication. Three important bonding techniques are leveling, using I-statements, and giving feedback. In bonding fights both partners win.

Family members have strong individual needs; they must also make strong family commitments. It is not easy to balance personal goals and family needs. To negotiate for both freedom and intimacy within the family, individuals need to make a "triple commitment"; to themselves, to their partner, and to their relationship.

Key Terms

looking-glass self *281*	aggressive behavior *293*
significant others *282*	alienating fight tactics *293*
attribution *283*	
consensual validation *284*	gunnysacking *294*
family cohesion *284*	kitchen-sink fight *295*
gaslighting *288*	mixed, or double, message *295*
conflict taboo *290*	bonding fighting *295*
anger "insteads" *290*	leveling *296*
passive-aggression *291*	feedback *297*
sabotage *292*	checking-it-out *298*
displacement *292*	conjoint marital counseling *305*
the catharsis myth *293*	
assertive action *293*	

Study Questions

1. Explain why families are powerful environments. What are the advantages and disadvantages of such power in family interaction?

2. Do you agree that marital anger and conflict are necessary to a vital, intimate relationship? Why or why not?

3. Discuss the possible negative side effects of denying conflict in a marriage relationship. Include the effects on the individuals and on their relationship.

4. Define passive-aggression and give examples of behavior that could be passive-aggressive.

5. How is passive-aggression different from self-destructive anger "insteads" and from behavior in marriages that are devitalized as a result of suppressed anger?

6. Discuss the relationship of marital violence to suppressed anger. What do you think society should do about marital violence?

7. Explain the difference between assertiveness and aggression, and describe how each functions in a conflict.

8. Describe some alienating fight tactics. If someone you care for used such methods in a disagreement with you, how would you feel? What might you say in response?

9. Discuss your reactions to each of the guidelines proposed in this chapter for bonding fights. What would you add?

10. Why might it be difficult for people to change their fighting habits? What do you think is necessary for change to occur?

11. In your opinion, when should couples visit a marriage counselor? Explain your reasoning.

Suggested Readings

Bach, George, and Peter Wyden
1970   *The Intimate Enemy: How to Fight Fair in Love and Marriage.* New York: Avon.
        Much of this chapter is based on *The Intimate Enemy,* which has become a classic.
Broderick, Carlfred
1979   *Couples: How to Confront Problems and Maintain Loving Relationships.* New York: Simon & Schuster.
        Sensible advice from a sociologist/counselor.
Broderick, Carlfred, and James Smith
1979   "The General Systems approach to the family." Pp. 112–29 in Wesley Burr et al., *Contemporary Theories About the Family.* V. 2. New York: Free Press.
        Overview of systems theory and the family in a major review volume on family theory.

Bry, Adelaide
1976   *How to Get Angry Without Feeling Guilty.* New York: New American Library, Signet.
        Bry is a psychoanalyst who sees anger as essential to being human and explores constructive ways to vent one's anger.
Burr, Wesley R., Geoffrey K. Leigh, Randall D. Day, and John Constantine.
1979   "Symbolic interaction and the family." Pp. 42–111 in Wesley Burr et al., *Contemporary Theories About the Family.* v. 2. New York: Free Press.
        Overview of symbolic interaction theory and the family in a major review volume.
Gottman, John M.
1979   *Marital Interaction: Experimental Investigations.* New York: Academic Press.
        Important research investigation that views relationships as information systems.
Kantor, David, and William Lehr
1975   *Inside the Family: Toward a Theory of Family Process.* San Francisco: Jossey-Bass.
        Theoretical treatment of family interaction based on observation of families. Good for those who would like a thorough academic treatment of family interaction, heavy going for others.
Laing, Ronald D.
1971   *The Politics of the Family.* New York: Random House.
        Psychiatrist analyzes family interaction, particularly the power of the family to shape identity and definitions of the situation.
Minuchin, Salvatore
1974   *Families and Family Therapy.* Cambridge, Mass: Harvard University Press.
        Pioneering work in family therapy based on family systems concepts.
Powell, John, S.J.
1969   *Why Am I Afraid to Tell You Who I Am?* Niles, Ill.: Argus.
        A book about self-understanding and the development of intimacy.
Vaughan, Diane
1986   *Uncoupling: Turning Points in Intimate Relationships.* New York: Oxford University Press.
        Looks at changing relationships as they are deconstructed. That is, how do relationships look to people who no longer believe in them? This perspective enables us to understand the way in which an ongoing relationship functions because of the partners' shared belief in it.

10 Power In Marriage

*To the extent that power
is the prevailing force in
a relationship—whether
between husband and
wife or parent and child,
between friends or
between colleagues—to
that extent love is
diminished.*

RONALD V. SAMPSON,
The Psychology of Power

People associate power with military force, multinational corporations, and high political positions. According to romantic myth, love is exempt from power struggles; but in reality couples often encounter power issues. Some people have internalized the cultural need to compete and win. They don't turn off this need just because they are at home or interacting with each other. Also, most people would prefer to have things their way, and they may use various forms of power to realize their preferences. Perhaps, "the uncertainty of life is the basis of the human need for power and control. Because the future is unforeseeable, we experience a sense of . . . helplessness and anxiety. Neither our fortune nor our fate is ultimately within our control. . . . We respond by seeking ways to relieve this sense of helplessness and anxiety, this feeling of not being in control" (Lipmen-Blumen, 1984:7). Case Study 10•1, "An Ice-Skating Homemaker in a Me-or-Him Bind," illustrates a spouse's attempt to assert power over a partner he perceives as becoming too independent.

This chapter examines power in relationships, particularly marriage. We will discuss some classic studies of decision making in marriage. We'll look at what contemporary social scientists say about conjugal power. Finally, we will discuss why playing power politics is harmful to intimacy and explore an alternative. We will begin by defining power.

WHAT IS POWER?

Power can be defined as the ability to exercise one's will. There are many kinds of power.[1] Power exercised over oneself is **personal power,** or autonomy. As Chapter 2 points out, having a comfortable degree of personal power is important to self-development. **Social power** is the ability of persons to exercise their wills over the wills of others. Social power can be exerted in different realms, even within the family. Parental power, for instance, operates between children and parents. In this chapter our discussion of power in families will focus on power between married partners, or **conjugal power.** What are the sources of conjugal power? We'll seek to answer that question in this chapter.

CONJUGAL POWER AND DECISION MAKING

Research on marital power began well before the feminist movement, the development of family

1. The three overlapping realms of power we distinguish here are drawn from sociologist Richard Clayton's classification (Clayton, 1979).

CASE STUDY 10·1

AN ICE-SKATING HOMEMAKER IN A ME-OR-HIM BIND

Joan is an attractive, full-time homemaker. She has been married nineteen years. Recently she began taking courses at a local university and also became involved in learning to figure-skate.

Interviewer: When did you begin ice-skating?

Joan: Well, I took one year when I was a kid, but I had to ride the bus and the streetcar and all that.... And then I didn't skate again until last year. I've been skating for two years now and I just love it. I'm getting better. I can do three turns real well and three of the very basic dances....

I try to skate twice a week. But it's created a problem with Chuck. Last year he was working days during the skating season. But now he works midnight to eight and he just hates for me to go there during the day.... I don't know whether it's because I like it real well or what. There's nothing there to be jealous of because I skate with the housewives.... I don't know whether it's that I enjoy something he can't do well or what it is. But he doesn't like it. When he works midnight to eight, he knows every time I go. When he was working days and I went, as long as my work was done and I had dinner on the table, there was no problem when he came home from work.

Now he knows every time I leave this house. Every place I go he knows. Every time the garage door opens, it wakes him up. It's almost like being in prison without the doors being locked....

One time I stayed too late. I got home at five thirty. My brother was there—I got home at five thirty and no dinner or nothing. He told me, he said, "If you ever do this again—there's no dinner—if you ever do this again, I'm going to cut your skates." Oh boy! So I try to avoid doing that. I come home about four o'clock, so I can get dinner on okay. But the trouble [with the ice skating] is I can go there and it's almost like on that ice nothing—I just get totally absorbed in it and I forget I'm a mother, forget I'm a wife, I forget everything, I'm just there. I felt that way about golf and water-skiing too, but those things didn't bother Chuck because I was doing them with him I think. Skating excludes him....

therapy, and the identification of family violence as a social problem invited closer attention to the inner workings of the family. Social scientists Robert Blood and Donald Wolfe simply had an academic interest in conjugal decision making. Their book *Husbands and Wives: The Dynamics of Married Living* (1960) was based on interviews with wives only. Nevertheless, it was a significant piece of research and shaped thinking on marital power for many years.

Egalitarian Power and the Resource Hypothesis

The Resource Hypothesis Blood and Wolfe began with the assumption that although the American family's forebears were patriarchal, "the predominance of the male has been so thoroughly undermined that we no longer live in a patriarchal system" (Blood and Wolfe, 1960:18–19). On this

At first I thought it was jealousy. No, it's not jealousy. It's possessiveness. He wants to control what I do. We got married before women's lib, which nobody even talked about. There was no such thing. So when a lot of men got married in those days, it was like owning something. "This is a possession now; I own this person; I can control her mind and her body."

My daughter's starting to want to skate now too. The rink is open for the public this summer and I'm not going to be skating very much because I'd have to go in the evenings and that's just not going to work out with our schedule. But I'll try to go. Like this weekend Chuck will be out of town, so I'm going to go then. Anyway, my daughter's going to go with me when she's out of school. She's getting so she can skate pretty well and she's starting to like it. So she wants a pair of skates. Now he won't buy her the skates. He says, "No, we're not going to spend the money on something like that." Now I think that's terrible. . . .

I could just go buy them because I definitely bought my own skates. I just went out and bought them. And then at first I lied to him—this is awful—I told him, "Oh, these are just my sister-in-law's skates. . . ." Then finally once I told him they were my own. He said, "Oh! You can afford those skates and I can't afford a jacket." I said, "You can afford a jacket. Go buy one if you want. . . ."

A lot of times he'll say, "What are you going to do today?" And I say, "Well, it's Tuesday and I skate on Tuesday." He's known that all year, but every time he wants to take me to lunch or go somewhere, it is always on Tuesday. . . . One time I said, "Why can't we do it on Monday or Wednesday?" He said, "Oh, I never thought about that. . . ."

He gets mad about everything I really like. Like when I started bowling and I really liked that, he gave me a hard time. It's really not just the skating. If he took the ice skating away, and I replaced it with something else I liked equally well, that would be the thing he'd be against.

- Whether a spouse is free to spend time in self-actualizing pursuits, how much time is allowed, and which pursuits are allowed depend largely on conjugal power.

basis they developed their major hypothesis about what had replaced the system of patriarchy.

They reasoned, in their **resource hypothesis,** that the relative power between wives and husbands results from their relative "resources" as individuals: The spouse with more resources has more power in marriage. These resources, according to Blood and Wolfe, include education and occupational training. Within marriage a spouse's most valuable resource would be the ability to pro-

vide money to the union. Another resource would be good judgment, probably enhanced by education and experience. (Recall the discussion of exchange theory in Chapter 6, and note that the resource hypothesis is a variation on exchange theory.)

To test their resource hypothesis, the researchers interviewed about 900 wives in greater Detroit and asked who made the final decision in eight areas; such as what job the husband should take,

■ Father knows best: Many women today would consider the patriarchal system that once ruled American families as outmoded as the horse and buggy. But can we accurately claim that modern marriages are egalitarian? Who is really in the driver's seat?

what car to get, whether the wife should go to work (or quit work), and how much money the family could afford to spend per week on food. Blood and Wolfe chose these eight areas because all affected the family as a whole, and they ranged from typically "masculine" to typically "feminine" decisions. Each decision was given equal weight.

The Findings From their interviews Blood and Wolfe drew the conclusion that most families had a "relatively equalitarian" decision-making structure (72 percent), although there were more families in which the husband made the most decisions (25 percent) than there were wife-dominated families (3 percent). Besides the conclusion that most families shared in decision making, Blood and Wolfe also found that conjugal power was allocated differently according to the issue being decided.

These findings supported the resource hypoth-

esis in two ways. First, researchers found that the higher the education and occupational status of husbands, the greater their conjugal power. White-collar husbands made more final decisions than did blue-collar husbands.

The second area of support for the resource hypothesis was the finding that the relative resources of wives and husbands were important in determining which partner made more decisions. Older spouses and those with more education made more decisions. Blood and Wolfe also found the relative power of a wife to be greater after she no longer had small children or when she worked outside the home and thereby gained the wage-earning resource for herself. They reported little on black families, except to say that black husbands, when compared with whites, had unusually low decision-making power in comparison to their wives.

Criticism of the Resource Hypothesis In all, Blood and Wolfe's study had the important effect of encouraging people to see conjugal power as shared rather than patriarchal. The power of individual partners was seen as resting on their own attributes or resources rather than on social roles or expectations, a perspective that changed the thinking of social scientists. But Blood and Wolfe's study has also been strongly criticized.

One criticism concerns Blood and Wolfe's criteria for conjugal power. Critics stated that power between spouses involves far more than which partner makes the most final decisions; it also implies the relative autonomy of wives and husbands, along with questions about division of labor in marriages (Safilios-Rothschild, 1970). (Spouses' relative autonomy is explored later in this chapter; Chapter 11 discusses conjugal division of labor.)

A second criticism has to do with the resource hypothesis, which focused narrowly on partners' background characteristics and abilities, but not on their individual personalities and the way they interacted.

A third criticism was that Blood and Wolfe should not have given equal weight to each of the eight decision-making areas. Furthermore, some important decisions are not included in Blood and Wolfe's list: When to have sex, how many children to have, how often to see relatives, and how much freedom a partner has for separate same-sex or opposite-sex friendships are but a few examples.

A fourth criticism concerned the fact that Blood and Wolfe interviewed only wives and not husbands. Yet a subsequent study found that almost a quarter of the couples studied "would have been substantially misrepresented had only one spouse reported on the decision-making process" (Monroe et al., 1985:733).

Finally, Blood and Wolfe have come under heavy fire for their assumption that the patriarchal power structure has been replaced by egalitarian marriages.

Resources and Gender

Feminist Dair Gillespie (1971) pointed out that power-giving resources tend to be unevenly distributed between the sexes. Husbands usually earn more money even when wives work, and so husbands control more economic resources. Husbands also usually are older and better educated than their wives are (the "marriage gradient" discussed in Chapter 5), so husbands are likely to have more status and they may be more knowledgeable, or seem so. Even their greater physical strength may be a powerful resource, although an emotionally destructive one, as we will see later in this chapter.

Moreover, women are likely to have few alternatives to the marriage if they cannot support themselves or are responsible for the care of young children. Divorce often makes it clear that "women's social status as well as their access to various systems of resources are determined largely by their relationships with men through marriage" (Kalmuss and Straus, 1982:277; see also Weitzman, 1985).

Consequently, according to Gillespie, marriages are not egalitarian but "still a caste/class system." The resource hypothesis, which presents resources as neutral and power as gender-free, is simply "rationalizing the preponderance of the male sex." Furthermore, women are socialized differently from men so that by the time they marry, women have already been "systematically trained to accept second best," and marriage is hardly a "free contract between equals" (1971:449).

Research tends to support Gillespie's insight that American marriages continue to be inegalitarian even though they are no longer traditional. True, resources make a difference, and an important factor in marital decision making is whether or not a wife is working. Wage-earning wives have more to say in important decisions such as family size and how to use family money (Blood, 1969). As one wife put it: "I think we share in the decision-making. I make decisions at the office from nine to five and I think it would be a little strange if I came home and was treated like a pussycat" (Blumstein and Schwartz, 1983:141).

Community involvement, as well as working outside the home, increases a woman's participation in important decisions. One researcher explained power shifts in blue-collar marriages: "When a wife comes home after testifying at a City Council hearing, from a meeting of the local school or hospital board, or from helping to out-maneuver a local politician or win a vote for day care in her union, she is changing the balance of power in her marriage in the most fundamental way, often without realizing it" (Seifer, 1973:45).

But resources are gender determined, and one way in which women come to have fewer resources is through their reproductive roles and resulting economic dependence. Wives who do not earn wages, especially mothers of small children, have considerably less power than do women who earn an income. Relationships tend to become less egalitarian with the first pregnancy (LaRossa, 1977) and birth (Aldous, 1978). Just after marriage the relationship is apt to be relatively egalitarian, with the husband only moderately more powerful than the wife—if at all. Often at this point the wife has considerable economic power in relationship to her husband. That is, she is working for wages and may even have established herself in a high-paying career. She may be financing her husband's education.

But during the childbearing years of the marriage, the practical need to marry and remain married is felt especially strongly. Divorce is likely to mean that the woman must parent and support small children alone. LaRossa found from his in-depth research with sixteen couples who were expecting their first child that expectant mothers lose not only economic power but also "sexual attractiveness" power. Moreover, they have fewer alternatives and less energy or physical strength to resist dominance attempts, and they may be vulnerable to the manipulative offer or withdrawal of the husband's help with child care. (As one exception, LaRossa points to a wife who, following the birth of her baby, exerted power over her husband by threatening to leave, taking the infant with her.)

Working, then, contributes to marital power, but in some areas of decision making, such as how to discipline children or how to use leisure time, whether wives work for wages may make no difference in their relative power (Safilios-Rothschild, 1969). Moreover, while the working wife is less obliged to defer to her husband and has greater authority in making family decisions, she still does not participate equally in decision making and is unequally burdened with housekeeping, child rearing, and caring for her partner. In a recent study, Hiller and Philliber (1986) found that the husband's expectations continue to determine how and whether housekeeping roles will be shared. Even if she is employed, a wife does more housework if her husband believes she should than if her husband thinks he too should be involved. Working does not necessarily give a wife full status as an equal partner (Pleck, 1985; Scanzoni, 1972; Huber

and Spitze, 1983). There are a variety of explanations for this continuation of male dominance in a society that, on the whole, articulates an ideology of marital equality.

Resources in Cultural Context

The cultural context may determine whether or not a resource theory explains marital power. Studies comparing traditional societies, such as Greece, with more modern ones, such as France, suggest that in a traditional society norms of patriarchal authority may be so strong that they override personal resources to give considerable power to all husbands (Rodman, 1970; Safilios-Rothschild, 1967). Even in the United States, we must recognize the continuing salience of tradition and the assumption that it is legitimate for husbands to wield authority in the family. A study of Japanese-American couples in Honolulu, for instance, found that even though wives actively participated in making countless decisions, they did so by virtue of delegation of power from their husbands (Johnson, 1975). The continued importance of traditional legitimations of husbands' authority is apparent in certain religious groups (D'Antonio and Aldous, 1983), such as fundamentalist Protestants, charismatic Catholics, and Mormons. The new religious right is committed to the restoration of traditional family norms and roles (Hess, 1984).

Male dominance is also strong in ethnic groups that have recently immigrated to the United States. A study of Puerto Rican families (Cooney et al., 1982), for example, found that the norms of the parent generation born in Puerto Rico were patriarchal. "[These] norms emphasize the generally superior authority of the man within the family" (Cooney et al., 1982:622). The specific socioeconomic and personal resources of the husband are irrelevant: He has the power. However, the generation born in the United States had moved to a "transitional egalitarian society" typical of the rest of the United States. That is, "husband-wife relationships are more flexible and negotiated . . . [and] socioeconomic achievements become the basis for negotiation within the family" (1982:622).

Since immigration has taken a recent upturn, and new immigrants may be increasing as a proportion of our population (Weeks, 1986), we may expect a momentary increase in traditional patriarchal families. Subsequent generations, however, can be expected to adopt the more common American pattern, in which husbands wield greater power by virtue of their greater access to resources.

We must note another way in which cultural context conditions the resource theory; it explains marital power only in the absence of an overriding egalitarian norm as well as a traditional one. That is, if traditional norms of male authority are strong, husbands will almost inevitably dominate, regardless of personal resources. Similarly, if an egalitarian norm of marriage were completely accepted, then a husband's superior economic achievements would be irrelevant to his decision-making power because both spouses would have equal power (Cooney et al., 1982). It is only in the present situation, in which neither patriarchal nor egalitarian norms are firmly entrenched, that marital power is "negotiated" by individual couples and the power of husbands and wives may be a consequence of their resources. Since husbands tend to have more resources, they are more likely to dominate.

Our comments about marital power have for the most part been very general. Box 10•1, "Power in Courtship," takes a look at traditional and egalitarian models in courtship. We need also to look at some social class and racial/ethnic variations in conjugal power.

Social Class, Minorities, and Conjugal Power

The finding by Blood and Wolfe that white-collar husbands were able to make more important decisions than blue-collar husbands has not been seriously challenged, even though middle-class husbands espouse a more egalitarian ideology than do working-class husbands (Gillespie, 1971:134). The reason for this was mentioned in the discussion of different types of power bases early in this chapter: White-collar husbands can adhere to an egalitarian ideology but exert power as "experts" (L. Rubin, 1976:99). As William Goode summarizes, the white-collar husband "takes preference as a professional, not as a family head or as a male; nevertheless the precedence is his" (1963:21). By contrast, "lower-class men demand deference as *men*, as heads of families" (Goode, 1963:21). Blue-collar husbands rely more heavily on tradition to support their patriarchal authority.

Although blue-collar men may claim more relative power than their wives, studies show that their wives make more decisions than do middle-class wives. An explanation for this is that proportionally more blue-collar than white-collar wives work outside their homes, and those who do work make a proportionally greater contribution to the family income (Gillespie, 1971).

While white-collar husbands tend to exercise more marital power than blue-collar husbands, the relationship of income and status to conjugal power is not clear-cut. Research has supported Blood and Wolfe's early finding that lower-status blue-collar husbands have more marital power than do high-status blue-collar husbands. Mirra Komarovsky suggested a possible explanation: Because of their relatively high earnings, skilled workers may be able to marry women with as much or more education than they have. By marrying upward in this sense, skilled blue-collar husbands may lose a degree of power that the semiskilled worker exerts over his less well educated wife (Komarovsky, 1962).

Social-class patterns among blacks and Mexican-Americans are similar to those among whites. During the 1950s and 1960s social scientists believed that black marriages were characterized by a matriarchal power structure in which wives and mothers were dominant; however, recent research suggests otherwise. Black marriages tend to be more egalitarian than whites', but talk about "black matriarchy" was an exaggeration (McDonald, 1980; Gray-Little, 1982). One reason black marriages are more egalitarian than whites' is that proportionally more black than white wives are wage earners (Willie and Greenblatt, 1978).

Just as black matriarchy is a myth, so may be the belief that Mexican-Americans behave according to patriarchal standards. One study of seventy-six Mexican and Mexican-American migrant farm workers in California found that wives and husbands believed they made most decisions jointly. The one area decided more often by the husband alone was where the family would live. The authors concluded that "dominance-submission are much less universal than previously assumed. Either they never existed but were an ideal or they are undergoing radical change" (Hawkes and Taylor, 1975:807).

Recent research indicates that differences between minority groups, such as blacks and Mexican-Americans, and Anglo-Saxons are not more pronounced than social-class differences *within* these groups themselves (Cromwell and Cromwell, 1978).

BOX 10 · 1

POWER

IN

COURTSHIP

Chapter 3 addresses falling and staying in love, while Chapter 6 discusses social factors affecting courtship. Here we will look briefly at power issues in courtship. Sociologists McCormick and Jessor (1983) comment in an essay that

students sometimes balk when we suggest that nice people, not just sadists, use power during courtship. . . . [But] not everyone sees dating and mating in the same romantic light as these . . . students. . . . Power, the potential to influence another person's attitudes or behavior, may be an essential component of any romantic attraction or sexual relationship [McCormick and Jessor, 1983:66–67].

McCormick and Jessor point out that "the development of skills and knowledge, being perceived as attractive and likeable, and even acting helpless or 'needed' can all be used to influence someone else" (McCormick and Jessor, 1983:67).

These same sociologists researched, among other things, whether the rules for courtship have changed in recent years. What they conclude has some bearing on discussions of both sex roles and power. According to their research findings, the courtship game has changed in three ways.

First, thanks to the weakening of the double standard and encouragement from feminists, women are freer to make the first move in a flirtation and to have premarital sex than in the past. Second, men seem to be encouraging women to be more assertive in intiating sexual relationships. Third, given the opportunity, men would reject sex and women would try to have sex with the same strategies that are characteristically used by the other gender.

Despite these changes, the courtship game continues to follow gender-role stereotypes. Men ask women out more than vice versa. Men are more likely to influence a date to have sex; women are more likely to refuse sex. The persistence of gender role playing is associated with a number of factors, such as women's more conservative attitudes toward sexuality. Another factor that contributes to the courtship game is that North American society views people who behave "out of role" (that is, passive men and assertive women) as less well adjusted and popular. . . .

As the women's liberation movement gains increasing acceptance, the courtship game will probably become less rigid. For instance, although women prefer masculine over feminine men, male college students are *not* more attracted to feminine women than they are to masculine women. . . . Even more indicative of social change, recent research contradicts earlier reports . . . that men are turned off by profeminist women. . . . As attitudes toward feminist women become more liberal, people may try out more egalitarian ways of dealing with courtship. However, such experimentation is likely to be minimal at first because out-of-role behavior is especially risky within sexual encounters where people already feel emotionally vulnerable [McCormick and Jessor, 1983:85].

Although experimenting with egalitarian courtship practices is likely to be "minimal at first," some research on how flirtations and sexual encounters proceed suggests that, at least with beginning flirtations, "both genders have equal power." That is, "each person takes a turn at influencing the partner and at signaling that the other's influence attempts are welcome" (McCormick and Jessor, 1983:76).

But such "equal power" may not last as courtship continues. In fact, popular magazines for young people, along with college counselors and others, have just begun to recognize that power struggles play a part in dating and courtship—sometimes to the point of violence.

COURTSHIP VIOLENCE

Box 6•2 discusses date rape. According to one sociologist, "it appears that violence is a common, albeit neglected, aspect of premarital heterosexual interaction" (Makepeace, 1981:100–101). In a study of 202 male and female freshman and sophomore college students at a single college (these students were primarily from middle-income families in small towns and rural areas; hence the study sample is not necessarily representative of all youth or even of all college youth), 20 percent reported personal involvement in an incident of courtship violence. Some of these incidents were pushes, shoves, and threats, while 4 percent were assaults with clenched fists. One percent of the incidents involved assault with a weapon and 1.5 percent involved choking. Incidents tended to occur over jealousy (27 percent) or with sexual denial or disagreement over drinking behavior. These self-reports fit traditional sex-role stereotypes discussed in Chapter 2. That is, women were more apt to report themselves as victims (91.7 percent), while 69.2 percent of the men saw themselves as the aggressors. The researcher found it surprising that about half of these relationships continued after the violence rather than being broken off. Given that the economic and social constraints of marriage are not usually applicable to courtship relationships, the author wondered about the reasons for continuing these relationships (Makepeace, 1981). Perhaps the study described below suggests some answers.

TRADITIONAL AND EGALITARIAN COURTSHIP PATTERNS

Actually, two models of power coexist in dating relationships: the traditional and the egalitarian. Peplau surveyed 231 college-age dating couples about their courtship behavior and attitudes. These students, who were a random sample of students at four colleges and universities in the Boston area, were asked about

(continued)

BOX 10 · 1

Continued

power both in general and in specific areas, such as recreation, conversation, sexual activity, amount of time spent together, and activities with other people. Most of those questioned had *attitudes* favoring equality. Ninety-five percent of the women and 87 percent of the men agreed that "dating partners should have 'exactly equal say' " (Peplau, 1979:108). But only 59 percent of the women and 42 percent of the men reported actually having equal power. (Forty-five percent of the men and 35 percent of the women reported more male power; 13 percent of the men and 17 percent of the women reported more female power.)

Many students pointed out that a simple "his power or her power" dichotomy did not reflect their real decision-making process and reported other modes of compromise similar to the no-power concept described in this chapter. That is, they told of taking turns, being sensitive to a partner's moods, or making concessions freely. Still, fewer than half the couples believed they had an equal power relationship, although most wanted to. Reasons for that, according to Peplau, appear to be, first, that many still have traditional sex-role attitudes. Moreover, the "principle of least interest," discussed in this chapter, is operating. That is, the partner least involved wields more power. Those who said they had alternatives to the relationship had greater power than their partners. Women with higher educational levels or career plans had greater power. Finally, and perhaps at the root of these students' failure to establish egalitarian relationships, according to Peplau, is the fact that few of them had egalitarian parental relationships after which to model.

Some of these same dynamics probably operate to influence battered partners to maintain violent courtship relationships. Moreover, it may be true that at least some individuals in our society believe it is better to have a mate or a relationship, even a violent or unhappy one, than to have none at all.

Love, Need, and Power

Some have argued that a primarily economic analysis does not do justice to the complexities of marital power. Perhaps wives have considerable power through their husband's love for them:

The relative degree to which the one spouse loves and needs the other may be the most crucial variable in explaining total power structure. The spouse who has relatively less feeling for the other may be the one in the best position to control and manipulate all the "resources" that he [sic] has in his command in order to effectively influence the outcome of decisions, if not also to dominate the decision-making. Thus, a 'relative

love and need' theory may be . . . basic in explaining power structure [Safilios-Rothschild, 1970:548–49]. ■

This theory is congruent with what sociologist Willard Waller termed the **principle of least interest.** The partner with the least interest in the relationship is the one who is more apt to exploit the other. The spouse who is more willing to break up the marriage or to shatter rapport and refuse to be the first to make up can maintain dominance (Waller 1951:190–92; Heer, 1963). Dependence on the relationship can be practical and economic as well as emotional. Women with small children are often financially dependent, for example. Aging women have less probability of remarriage after

■ The variables influencing power within a marriage include income and status. Perhaps the key factor influencing decision making within a family is whether the wife works outside the home and how much she earns.

divorce or of significant employment (if they have not already established a career), so they may be reluctant to leave a marriage.

Like resource theory, the **relative love and need theory** is a variation of exchange theory. (See Chapter 6.) Each partner brings resources to the marriage and receives rewards from the other partner. These may not balance precisely, and one partner may be gaining more from the marriage than the other partner, emotionally or otherwise. This partner is most dependent on the marriage and thus is most likely to comply with the other's preferences.

The relative love and need theory does not predict whether husbands or wives will generally be more powerful. In other words, it assumes that

women are as likely to have power as men are: "The man who desires or values the woman as a mate more than she desires or values him will be in the position of wanting to please her. Her enchantment in his eyes may be physical attractiveness, pleasing personality, his perception of her as a 'perfect' wife and mother" (Hallenbeck, 1966:201).

Generally, however, the wife holds the less powerful position. How does the relative love and need theory account for this? One explanation offered is that "love has been a feminine specialty" (Cancian, 1985:253). As we saw in Chapter 2, women are more socialized to love and need their husbands than the reverse (Firestone, 1970). They also tend to be more relationship-oriented than men are (Gilligan, 1982). According to the principle of least interest, this puts women at a power disadvantage (Cancian, 1985). Women "come to have a vested interest in the social unit that at the same time imposes inequalities on them" (Goode, 1982:138).

Moreover, Americans *believe* that women are more dependent on the marital relationship than men are. "If most people believe that women need heterosexual love more than men, then women will be at a power disadvantage" (Cancian, 1985:257). In our society women are encouraged to express their feelings, men to repress them. Men are less likely, therefore, to articulate their feelings for their wives and "men's dependence on close relationships remains covert and repressed, whereas women's dependence is overt and exaggerated" (258). Overt dependency affects power: "A woman gains power over her husband if he clearly places a high value on her company or if he expresses a high demand or need for what she supplies.... If his need for her and high evaluation of her remain covert and unexpressed, her power will be low" (258).

Micropolitics: The Private Sphere

In sum, according to Cancian, "men dominate women in close relationships [and]... husbands tend to have more power in making decisions, a situation that has not changed in recent decades" (1985:259). But, argue several social scientists, men are far less powerful in the private, intimate sphere than they are in the public world. Therapists and mass media, and to an increasing degree the public, support women's desire for more expression of feeling, reducing men's ability to minimize the

My wife is ACCEPTABLE.
Our relationship is satisfactory.
                    Edgar G.

Edgar looks splendid here. His power and strength of character come through. He is a very private person who is not demonstrative of his affection; that has never made me unhappy. I accept him as he is.

We are totally devoted to each other.

                    Regina Goldstine

Dear Jim:
        May you be as lucky in marriage!

■ Does this couple really have such different feelings about their marriage as their comments seem to indicate? How might the concept of gender roles explain the apparent disparity—and the fact that Regina feels she is lucky in her marriage?

emotional sphere where women are deemed more competent. Men's ability to get what they want may also be limited by the very "avoidance of dependence" built into the male role. "He may not even know what he wants or needs from her, and therefore, may be unable to try to get it" (Cancian, 1985:259). Men are as likely to feel controlled by women as women believe they are controlled by men:

Insofar as love is defined as the woman's "turf," an area where she sets the rules and expectations, a man is likely to feel threatened and controlled when she seeks more intimacy. Talking about the relationship, like she wants, feels like taking a test that she made up and he will fail. The husband is likely to react with withdrawal and passive aggression. He is blocked from straightforward counterattack insofar as he believes that intimacy is good [260]. ▪

Cancian's view of this dilemma is presented with much empathy for men. L. Rubin's work on men and women in intimate relationships (1976; 1983) looks at these differences between men's and women's styles of expressing love neutrally, in terms of the problems they produce for couples. A more acid view is presented by Lipmen-Blumen (1984) as she discusses women's greater relationship skills from the perspective of conflict theory. (Conflict theory is presented in Chapter 11.) In her view, women are oppressed by men and respond with "micromanipulation," that is, manipulation of interpersonal power in the micro, or private, sphere.

Lipmen-Blumen concedes that men dominate the public sphere of work and political leadership, while women "remain locked in" the private sphere. If men dominate public policy, then women:

through their long history as the subordinate group . . . have learned how to survive . . . [by] the use of interpersonal behaviors and practices to influence, if not control, the power balance. . . . Women, as well as other powerless groups, become well versed in interpreting the unspoken intentions, even the body language, of the powerful. They learn to anticipate their governors' behavior, to evoke as well as smother pleasure, anger, joy, and bafflement in their rulers, to charm, to outsmart, even to dangle the powerful over the abyss of desire and anguish. By the various interpersonal strategies of micromanipulation, women have learned to sway and change, circumvent, and subvert the decisions of the

powerful to which they seem to have agreed. They know when to observe the rules the dominant group has created. Women have also mastered how to "obey without obeying" those rules they find overly repressive. When necessary, they cooperate with men to maintain the mirage of male control. True, a growing minority of women have also consciously rejected the tools of micromanipulation in favor of a more direct assault [by becoming involved in the public arena of work and politics]. The majority, however, continue to operate primarily at the interpersonal level [30–31]. ▪

With Lipmen-Blumen's analysis, we have come full circle, for in her view power depends on position and resources in the larger society, the public world of work and politics. If women have relied on micromanipulation, it is primarily because, as we noted in Chapter 2, they are not yet integrated into the higher levels of the occupational structure or political leadership.

Lipmen-Blumen's description reinforces our initial premise: Power disparities discourage an intimacy based on honesty, sharing, and mutual respect. Realization of the American ideal of equality in marriage, on the other hand, would seem to enhance the possibility of developing intimacy in relationships.

The Future of Marital Power

Equalization of the marital power of men and women can occur in a number of ways. First, women can attain equal status in the public world and develop resources that are truly similar to men's. The trend of the times is in this direction, as more and more women have entered the higher professions and the executive track. Occupational segregation persists, but recent court decisions (*Johnson* v. *Transportation Agency of Santa Clara County, California*, 1987) have endorsed affirmative action programs, and the attention being given to maternity leave should result in some action to facilitate combining work and motherhood.

Second, society can come to value more highly women's resources of caring and emotional expression. This may also be happening. Although the counterculture and human potential movements of the sixties that sought to implement less instrumental and more "feminine" values (Hargrove, 1983) have come and gone, some argue that a powerful legacy remains (Yankelovich, 1981). Others point to the impact of feminism itself on American culture, the way women's values are changing public and private lives (Lenz and Myerhoff, 1985). Men's liberation movements also articulate expressive values (e.g., Farrell, 1974; David and Brannon, 1974), contributing to a cultural climate in which women's traditional assets are increased in worth.

And finally, norms of equality can come to be so strong that men and women will have equal power in marriage regardless of resources. Equality is an important value in American culture (Williams, 1951), and our history on the whole illustrates movement toward greater equality. Social movements such as the civil rights movement strengthened our commitment to the value of equality. Our society could come to legitimate norms of equality in marriage as strongly as it endorsed patriarchal authority in the past.

SOME AMERICAN COUPLES

Having looked at theories and research on conjugal power, we might look more closely now at a recent study of American couples to observe the workings of power in the everyday lives of some contemporary couples.

Sociologists Philip Blumstein and Pepper Schwartz (1983) undertook a comparison of four types of couples: heterosexual married couples (3,656); cohabiting heterosexual couples (653), gay male couples (1,938) and lesbian couples (1,576). Twenty-two thousand questionnaires were sent to couples who responded to media advertisements for participants or to the researchers' solicitation for participants at various events and meetings. Over 12,000 questionnaires were returned and some 300 couples were interviewed; data were used only if both parties participated.

The results confirm some of our ideas about power. Gender was by far the most significant determinant of the pattern of power. Composed, by definition, of a male and a female, marital and cohabiting couples tended to be the least egalitarian. As the resource theory suggests, money was a major determinant of power, and two men or two women were far more likely to have similar incomes. But money strongly affected power even in a same-sex couple. High-earning individuals (or the employed partner with an unemployed companion) tended to be excused from tiresome household chores and got to pick leisure time activities. The more powerful position of a successful partner, the way in which success in the wider world serves as a basis for claiming relationship benefits, is illustrated by the reaction of a gay male partner:

> Our biggest arguments are about what I haven't done lately. He'll rave and rant, or just pout, about the things I promised to do around the house that haven't got done.... I am willing to help out when I can, but my career is not just nine to five and usually I either don't have the time or I'm so tired when I come home that the last thing I'm going to do is clean the kitchen floor.... We had this one discussion where he suggested I get up earlier in the morning to help clean up if I'm too tired at night. I blew up and told him that I was the one with the career here and it was my prospects and my salary that gave us his vacations and you just can't be a housewife and a success all at the same time.... He was hurt and I felt bad but it is true.... He doesn't understand because he hasn't decided on anything yet and I am in the middle of my climb. [Blumstein and Schwartz, 1983:152–53]. ■

The impact of gender was apparent in a comparison of gay male and lesbian couples. Two men tended to be extremely competitive, very aware of each other's earning power and other signs of status in the public world. Lesbians, on the other hand, with "feminine" values of cooperation and pleasing others, worked very hard at their relationship and often deferred to each other. In fact, nonassertiveness sometimes became a problem—neither partner liked to initiate sex.

Lesbian couples illustrate another principle of conjugal power: the importance of norms and the cultural context. Committed to egalitarianism and cooperative decision making, these couples were the only ones to transcend the principle that economic resources determine decision-making power. Norms of equality were simply so strong that lesbians made strenuous efforts not to let differential earning power or unemployment affect control over the relationship.

Finally, this study tells us that commitment influences power. In marriages, representing the highest level of commitment, low-resource partners (usually the women) felt much freer to spend money earned by the partner than did individuals in a cohabiting relationship. They were likely to view resources as joint ones. The formal commitment represented a barrier to separation that limited the principle of least interest. Since both partners would have found it hard to leave the relationship, both felt secure in the relationship. They were less apt to believe that money or other resources were divided into "yours" and "mine." As the other couples intensified their less formal commitment over time, the partner with fewer resources also gained in power (Blumstein and Schwartz, 1983).

Perhaps because of their greater sense of separate identity and need to be economically independent if necessary, maintaining equality was very important to individuals in gay male, lesbian, and cohabiting couples. "Only married couples do not rely on equality to hold them together" (1983:317). Resources, rather than a commitment bond, ensured their security and power within the relationship. Married couples took a longer view of the rewards obtained from marriage, which perhaps explains why another study (Schafer and Keith, 1981) found that the power inequity perceived by wives diminished over time. Regardless of actual power in the marriage, it seems that as the years pass, spouses develop an increased sense of identity with each other and so are more apt to view marital decisions as joint ones. They also believe, despite periods of inequality, that relative commitment, energy, and marital rewards even out over time.

Blumstein and Schwartz emerged from their project impressed by the advantages of marriage. The stability of a formal commitment enabled couples to survive difficulties and required a sharing and negotiation of conflict that in the long run strengthened the relationship. Still, they noted an important drawback:

The institution of marriage, at least until now, has been organized around inequality, and attempts to change this framework have not been very successful. The traditional married couples in our study often laid their solid foundation on rules that stabilized the relationship but gave the women some of the less pleasant responsibilities such as housework.... If tasks were allotted on the basis of efficiency or affinity, we would expect that married couples could reassign household chores and have the institution remain as durable as ever. We have found, however, that when roles are reversed, with men doing housework and women taking over as provider, couples become dreadfully unhappy [324]. ■

Here's one husband:

We have a very traditional labor pattern. Very traditional. She does all of the household chores—at least up to a short time ago. Then all I did was take out the garbage.... Now she's at work and I have to help out more, but I resist doing things I'm not supposed to do. I'll do the outside work, but the inside work has always been her territory and I don't think I should have to learn things that she has spent twenty years perfecting.... So we have got me in this mode of helper—which I don't like very much—but it is more necessary right now if the house is going to be well kept.... I am willing to make her life a little easier but I can't say I enjoy any of it. ■

Another husband had an even more negative reaction to his wife's suggestion that he help with the housework:

Our biggest arguments are about her being such a slob. I can't believe the things she will let go. She thinks I'm making a big deal out of nothing, but ... I can't get used to her hair in the bathtub or no toilet paper when I go to the toilet or her clothes in a pile next to the shower.... We have screaming fights about it and she says if I want things different so bad, I should do them myself. Yeah, I'll do them myself over my dead body. She is going to have to shape up because I am not going to live like this and I don't think our kid should live like this. She is going to have to grow up [Blumstein and Schwartz, 1983:146]. ■

According to Blumstein and Schwartz, "Even couples who willingly try to change traditional male and female behavior have difficulty doing so. They must not only go against everything they have learned and develop new skills, but they have to resist the negative reaction of society" [1983:324].

We will now discuss the process of changing power relationships in marriage.

POWER POLITICS VERSUS NO-POWER

Sociologists have investigated the effects of male-dominated, egalitarian, and female-dominated relationships on courtship and marital satisfaction. Generally, they have found male, or husband, dominance to be associated with higher satisfaction for

■ "No-power" describes a sharing of equal power, not the absence of power. Although such sharing may seem ideal for mutual marital satisfaction, the norm in our culture has been dominance by the husband—and couples may encounter problems in deviating from that norm.

both spouses, while female-dominant relationships have lower satisfaction (McDonald, 1980; Peplau, 1979). A recent study of black couples found that husband-led couples were highest on marital quality or satisfaction, though not significantly higher than wife-led couples, while egalitarian relationships were lowest in satisfaction (Osmond and Martin, 1978:328). Regarding their own study, Osmond and Martin conclude that there is "very little consistent evidence that egalitarian couples are more satisfied with their marriages than husband dominant couples" (Gray-Little, 1982:634). But evidence from social psychological studies (Walster, Walster and Berscheid, 1978) does indicate that equitable relationships are generally more apt to be stable and satisfying, as we argue throughout this chapter.

Marital satisfaction in various power patterns may depend on the cultural context—and in our society at least some husband dominance has been normative. Deviating from the norm may cause tensions that lead to less satisfying relationships for egalitarian and, especially, wife-led couples. "This

argument would suggest that if cultural norms become sufficiently flexible to acknowledge the validity of a wider variety of spousal and family norms, couples will develop relationships best suited to their individual needs and assets" (Gray-Little, 1982:643). With a goal for couples of developing relationships best suited to partners' individual needs and assets, marriage counselors today are virtually unanimous in asserting that intimacy takes place only insofar as partners are equal. Social scientist Peter Blau terms this situation *no-power*. **No-power** does not mean that one partner exerts little or no power; it means that both partners wield about equal power. They have the ability to mutually and reciprocally influence and be influenced by each other.[2] They are able to avoid **power politics,**

---

2. As we use the term, *no-power* also implies partners' unconcern about exercising their relative power over each other. No-power partners seek to negotiate and compromise, not to "win" (see Chapter 9). In French and Raven's classification, they influence each other with informational or referent power.

a term that relates broadly to the power bases and tactics discussed in this chapter (see Box 10·2, "Disengaging from Power Struggles").

Power Politics in Marriage

Unequal relationships discourage closeness between partners: Exchange of confidence between unequals may be difficult, especially when the husband thinks self-disclosure will undermine his authority (Glazer-Malbin, 1975:58–59). Wives, feeling less powerful and more vulnerable, may resort to pretense and withholding of sexual and emotional response (Halleck, 1969).

Unequal power relationships in marriage are said to encourage power politics: partners' struggles to gain or keep power over each other. This may also be true of relatively egalitarian unions. As gender norms move from traditional to egalitarian, all family members' interests and preferences gain legitimacy, not only or primarily those of the husband or husband-father. The man's occupation, for example, is no longer the sole determining factor in where the family will live or how the wife will spend her time. Thus, decisions formerly made automatically, or by "spontaneous consensus," must now be consciously negotiated (Scanzoni, 1979:306). A possible outcome of such conscious negotiating, of course, is greater intimacy; another is locking into power politics. If the essential source of conjugal power is (as the relative love and need theory suggests) "the greater power to go away," then "politics in marriage has to do with suggesting the use of that power to leave the marriage." A spouse plays power politics in marriage by saying, in effect,

"This is how it would be if I were not here." A wife suggests—not, of course, openly, unless the marriage is far, far gone—that there would be no sex, no food, no children, no warmth, no clean clothes, no smiles if she were not there. A husband suggests, ever so subtly, that there would be no money, no protection, no sex, no status in the community, no one to put up the storm windows [Cadden, 1973:300–301]. ■

One study of forty-two married college students tested the results of engaging in power politics in marriage. Scientists found that "exchange-oriented" spouses—those who calculated which partner did more for the other—were least happily married (Murstein et al., 1977).

Both equal and unequal partners may engage in a cycle of devitalizing power politics. Partners come to know where their own power lies, along with the particular weaknesses of the other. Often they alternate in acting sulky, sloppy, critical, or distant. The sulking partner carries on this behavior until she or he fears the mate will "stop dancing" if it goes on much longer; then it's the other partner's turn (Cadden, 1973:300–301). This kind of seesawing may continue indefinitely, with partners taking turns manipulating each other. The cumulative effect of such power politics, however, is to create distance and loneliness for both spouses.

Few couples knowingly choose power politics, but this is an area of marriage in which "choosing" by default may occur. Our discussion of power in marriage is designed to help partners become sensitive to these issues so that they can avoid such a power spiral, or reverse one if it has already started.

Alternatives to Power Politics

There are alternatives to this kind of power struggle. Robert Blood and Donald Wolfe proposed one in which partners grow increasingly separate in their decision making, that is, they take charge of separate domains, one buying the car, perhaps the other in charge of disciplining children. This alternative is a poor one for partners who seek intimacy, however, for it enforces the separateness associated with devitalized marriage.

The Neutralization of Power A second, more viable alternative to perpetuating an endless cycle of power politics is for the subordinate spouse to neutralize the dominant partner's power. In **neutralizing power** a subordinate weakens the powerful person's control by refusing to cooperate in that power. Neutralizing power is different from playing power politics. Mates involved in power politics seek to wield power over each other, usually by combining coercive and reward tactics. A subordinate partner who seeks only to neutralize power does not work to gain dominion or control but tries to move toward an equal position.

One way to neutralize conjugal power is for the less powerful spouse to obtain needed services from some other source. For example, the wife who is compliant and deferent because she needs her husband's financial support can neutralize this situation by becoming employed—a process that enhances her relative power in the marriage, as we have seen. A second neutralizing technique is to accept the services from the powerful one but—

BOX 10 · 2

DISENGAGING FROM POWER STRUGGLES

Carlfred Broderick, sociologist and marriage counselor, offers the following exercise to help people disengage from power struggles. He begins by pointing out that almost nothing is more frustrating and resentment-inducing than an elaborate, unilaterally developed plan for yourself, your spouse, your children, and your friends. It is frustrating because when you try to live by such a script, or set of rules, you are condemned to seeing yourself as a failure (since neither you nor your children ever measure up) and to feeling rejected (because your spouse and friends never come through). Moreover, you are likely to imagine that you are surrounded by lazy, selfish, unfeeling, stubborn, underachieving, low-quality people.

The object of this exercise is to get you out of the business of monitoring everyone else's behavior and so free you from the unrewarding power struggles resulting from that assignment. Here is the exercise:

1. Think of as many things as you can that your spouse or children *should do*, *ought to do*, and *would do if they really cared*, but *don't do* (or do only grudgingly because you are always after them). Write them down in a list.
2. From your list choose three or four items that are especially troublesome right now. Place each one at the head of a sheet of blank paper. These are the issues that you, considerably more than your spouse, want to resolve (even though he or she, by rights, should be the one to see the need for resolution). Right now you are locked in a power struggle over each one, leading to more resentment and less satisfaction all around.
3. In this step you'll consider, one by one, optional ways of dealing with these issues without provoking a power struggle. Place an A, B, C, and D on each page of your paper at appropriate intervals. Listed below are these four options. Depending on the nature of the issue, some of these options will work better than others, but for a start, write a sentence or paragraph indicating how each one might be applied in your case. Even if you feel like rejecting a particular approach out of hand, be sure to write something as positive as possible about it.

Example: Let's say you can't get your partner to pay the bills in his or her business without continual nagging. Dark fantasy: If you quit nagging, your partner won't pay the bills and the business will fail. Now for the options:

OPTION A: RESIGN THE CROWN

Principle: Swallow your pride and cut your losses by delegating to the other person full control and responsibility for his or her own life in this area. Let your partner reap his or her own harvest, whatever it is. In many cases your partner will rise to the occasion, but if this doesn't happen, resign yourself to suffering the consequences.

Application: The nagging spouse will turn all the bills over to the responsible partner, explaining why. Then the former nagger will forget the whole thing and let the bill collectors remind the partner if necessary. This will relieve tension and redistribute worry in a wholesome way.

SOURCE:
Broderick, 1979a:117–23.

Observation: Most people who are locked into power struggles will reject this solution, even though it is often the most effective. Their dark fantasies are simply too dark and too real. At this point they nearly always ask, "So what are the other three choices?"

OPTION B: DO IT YOURSELF

Principle: There's an old saying, "If you want something done right, do it yourself." Accordingly, if you want something done, and if the person you feel should do it doesn't want to, it makes sense to do it yourself the way you'd like to have it done. After all, who ever said someone should do something he or she doesn't want to do just because you want him or her to do it?

Application: The nagging partner will do the bills. It takes less energy than getting the spouse to do them. The trick, of course, is to avoid saying to yourself, "Why should I have to do my work and my mate's too?" The right attitude is, "Boy, am I glad to be getting these done on time!"

Observation: The virtue of this option, like Option A, is that it gets you out of a destructive power struggle. You may not feel Option B is fair to you, however, and want to consider Option C.

OPTION C: MAKE AN OFFER YOUR PARTNER CAN'T REFUSE

Principle: Too many interpret this, at first, as including threats of what will happen if the partner doesn't shape up. The real point, however, if you select this approach, is to find out what your partner would really like and then offer it in exchange for what you want him or her to do. After all, it's your want, not your spouse's, that is involved. Why shouldn't you take the responsibility for making it worth your spouse's while?

Application: This will be unique, depending on what the partner wants in exchange for paying the bills on time.

Observation: Someone always complains that this is nothing more or less than bribery. Quite so. But reinforcement is a fundamental element in all learning, and one of the most effective ways to teach is to make it rewarding for the learner to learn. The next option is an even better example of this.

OPTION D: JOIN WITH JOY

Principle: Often the most resisted task can become pleasant if one's partner shares in it, especially if an atmosphere of play or warmth can be established. This calls for imagination and goodwill, but it can be effective in putting an end to established power struggles.

Application: Pop some corn and do the bills together.

Observation: When this alternative can be applied, it is the most satisfying of them all.

realizing there is an element of voluntarism in power—to refuse to feel reciprocally obligated, deferent, or compliant. For example, a husband who needs his wife's cooperation in entertaining business associates can accept her services but refuse to feel consequently obliged to paint the house. The less powerful partner can also resign him- or herself to doing without the service or can perhaps find a substitute for it. If one spouse wields power because the other finds it difficult to handle social situations and depends on the spouse to arrange social activities, the socially dependent spouse may work toward improving his or her social skills and self-esteem to the point that he or she can create some rewarding social contacts on his or her own (Emerson, 1962; Clayton, 1979:407–8).

The Importance of Communication Techniques of power neutralizing often bring the risk of devitalizing a relationship, depending on how spouses undertake them. Subordinate mates who go about neutralizing their situation without explaining what they are doing and why risk estrangement. The reason is that dominant partners may mistake a subordinate mate's acts of deference and compliance as evidence of love rather than fear. If signs of deference are withdrawn, a dominant partner can conclude that "she (or he) doesn't love me anymore." The harder the subordinate partner works to neutralize power, the more effort will the dominant one invest in regaining control. The result is estrangement (Bird, 1978). Case Study 10•1, "An Ice-Skating Homemaker in a Me-or-Him Bind," illustrates this pattern.

One wife reported that she had lived ten years in a husband-dominated marriage before she returned to school, and when she did return, their power relationship changed. Receiving substitute nourishment for her self-esteem in good grades and new friends, she no longer relied totally on her husband's signs of affection. In subtle ways she showed decreasing deference and felt herself growing toward equality in the marriage. But the couple did not discuss these changes. Meanwhile, her husband had began to drink heavily. The wife remained convinced he would "come along." Four years later, the couple were hardly speaking to each other and began marriage counseling. "I thought she didn't love me anymore," her husband said. "After she went back to school, she stopped doing things for me."

This couple might have avoided estrangement through mutual self-disclosure. The husband could have shared his anxiety. The wife could have explained that, from her point of view, signs of deference—"doing things" for him—did not show love. Perhaps the couple could have negotiated an agreement whereby he continued to feel loved while she proceeded to gain equality. As couples assert their interests and bargain in marriage (Scanzoni, 1979), communication is especially important in establishing and maintaining trust.

The Change to a No-Power Relationship Even when couples discuss power changes, living through them can be difficult. Case Study 10•2, "Living Through Power Changes," provides a firsthand illustration.

Changing conjugal power patterns can be difficult, even for couples who talk about it, because these patterns usually have been established from the earliest days of the relationship. While spouses may not have discussed them directly, they set up unconscious agreements by sending countless verbal and nonverbal cues. As partners experience recurring subtle messages, they build up predictable behavior patterns (Lederer and Jackson, 1968:177). Certain behaviors not only come to be expected but also to have symbolic meaning. For many couples, initiating or responding to sexual overtones, spending holidays in a certain way, or buying favorite foods or other treats symbolizes not just who has how much power but love itself. Sociologist William Goode (1982) believes that the most important change in men's position, as they themselves see it, is a "loss of centrality," a decline in the extent to which they are the center of women's attention. According to Goode:

Boys and grown men have always taken for granted that what they were doing was more important than what the other sex was doing, that where they were, was where the action was. Their women accepted that definition. Men occupied the center of the stage, and women's attention was focused on them. Although that position is at times perilous, open to failure, it is also desirable.

Men are still there of course, and will be there throughout our lifetime. Nevertheless, some changes are perceptible. The center of attention shifts to women more now than in the past. I believe that this shift troubles men far more, and creates more of their resistance, than the women's demand for equal opportunity and pay in employment [1982:140]. ■

It is likely that spouses have never experienced a no-power man-woman relationship. By experience each knows either the dominant or the submissive role; vicariously, each knows how to play the other's role. When undergoing changes in power, they may be more inclined to reverse roles, moving to behavior they know vicariously, rather than creating new egalitarian roles.

Husbands may respond to wives' power challenges by abdicating interest in decision making, assuming a submissive rather than an equal stance (Dyer, 1977). Their reaction is "It's up to you" or "Whatever you want. I don't have anything to say around here anymore anyway." They relinquish, along with husbandly authority, their willingness to influence the relationship. Much of this is probably passive-aggressive behavior. Blood and Wolfe (1960) found that wives whose husbands had abdicated their influence were the most unhappy.

The best way to work through power changes is to openly discuss power and to fight about it fairly, using techniques described in Chapter 9. The partner who feels more uncomfortable can bring up the subject, sharing his or her anger and desire for change but also stressing that he or she still loves the other. Meanwhile, partners need to remember that this is easier said than done. Attempts at communication—and open communication itself—do not solve all marital problems. Changing a power relationship is a challenge to any marriage and painful for both partners. One option is to seek the help of a qualified marriage counselor. (Box 9•3, "Hiring a Referee: Marriage Counseling," discusses this option.)

The Role Marriage Counselors Can Play

Today many marriage counselors are consciously committed to viewing couples as two human beings who need to relate to each other as equals. In other words they are committed to helping couples develop no-power relationships. They realize that once *both* spouses admit—to themselves and to each other—that they do in fact love and need each other, the basis for power politics is gone. On this assumption counselors help spouses learn to respect each other as persons, not to fear each other's coercive withdrawal.

Couples need to be aware that, like everybody in society, marriage counselors have internalized masculine and feminine biases. Also, they have personal reactions to and feelings about women's emerging rights. Some counselors are angry about past injustices. They may be more committed to urging a wife's separate autonomy through divorce, if necessary, than to helping her reach a no-power marital relationship. In the first session, or before if possible, clients should ask prospective counselors about their feelings on this issue. One counselor may assume, for example, that whenever marriage seriously threatens personal growth, it should be dissolved. Another may assume that partners need to learn to communicate and, only after that, to determine whether they want to stay married or to divorce.

Choosing an appropriate marriage counselor can be difficult for reasons other than their varying personal assumptions. A dominant husband, fearful that "it's going to be two against one," may feel threatened by a female counselor. On the other hand, a wife may fear that a male counselor will be too traditional or unable to relate to her. In this situation counselors sometimes work as a team, woman and man.

It is important that both partners feel comfortable with a counselor from the beginning, for two reasons. First, clients will hesitate to be frank with counselors they don't like or mistrust. Without honesty and openness, marriage counseling is only an expensive hour away from work or home. Second, as counselors gradually probe deeper into the couple's problems, one or both spouses may begin to feel threatened. Problems they had never recognized emerge into consciousness. As one counselor put it, "Things get worse before they get better." A common reaction is to dismiss the counselor's insight as all wrong, "sexist," or "just more women's lib talk." If couples quit at this point, they may find themselves more estranged than before they began. Understanding and accepting a counselor's assumptions from the beginning help to avoid failure.

Marriage counseling does not keep all marriages intact. One wife explains how power shifts in her marriage led to divorce even after attempts at marriage counseling:

The more involved I got in the job or community, the more it threatened [my husband]. . . . He wanted a life and I was supposed to contribute to it, but not have a life of my own.

When I won a citizen award it was a real reversal. I gave the speech and he was the spouse sitting in the audience. He just couldn't handle it. . . .

**CASE STUDY
10·2**

**LIVING
THROUGH
POWER
CHANGES**

Mike, 41 and married eighteen years, is the father of three teenagers. In the case study "An Inside View of Adult Change" in Chapter 1, he described personal changes he has experienced in his life. Here he talks about his ambivalent reactions to his wife's growing assertiveness as she changes.

Mike: I feel I started changing about six years ago. My wife started going through some changes at about that same time. In fact (*laughs*), the changes all started happening about the time the book *Passages* came out. I read that and said, "Boy, I really fit in there," because at the time I was just about 40 and I was looking at what I had done with my life, and I just laughed—I was right in the middle. I had to make changes, and I am making them. At least I'm going in the direction that is progressing. But the changes that my wife started to go through were in a different direction. She was growing also, but I think in a little different way. She was involved more in the women's liberation—with the women's movement.

She got involved in a consciousness raising group. I don't mean to make "involved" sound like a dirty word, although there were times when I've been very, very bitter because—

She began looking at her own self as being unfulfilled in her position and looking at the marriage role that she was in where she had the responsibility of the children, and all of these things, and felt really kind of cheated. She felt that really she needed some kind of assertiveness training or consciousness raising—that kind of thing.

Interviewer: Did that worry you?

Mike: Yeah. It caused a lot of conflict. But, and I think she's grown a lot through this. She's been involved a year and a half or two years now. . . . It's caused a lot of problems in our relationship. . . . I haven't accepted the new person that she is.

My definition of marriage was very, very rigid and very much patterned after the way I grew up. My observations of my parents were that the man is the authority of the family. He established the rules and the rest of the family—the wife and the children—obeyed the rules. Nobody questioned the rules. Once he spoke, you know, it didn't even have to make sense—but once he spoke, it was the rule.

Through this new awareness that she has been through, all of a sudden everything was questioned. And I wasn't used to that. It was extremely difficult for me and it still is. . . .

I still make arbitrary rules that don't make sense. Rules like, "You don't ever read at the table," or "You don't sleep in on Saturday mornings." All of these things that I was brought up with were my rules, and I had never challenged them. My kids, now, they follow their mother's lead and they challenge me. "Why is that a rule, Dad?" And it's well that they challenge me, I'm very pleased when they do. Before they were always afraid. And they would lots of times not [obey] and [then] avoid me. So I'm breaking out of the mold: I'm breaking out into the real world.

But I was really going through a difficult time. I didn't know what was right or what was wrong. I wound up about that time [that all this began] challenging my wife that she get out of that terrible group. I saw that as the source of all our problems. She wasn't about to drop out. I didn't know what to do. I threatened divorce. But it didn't work, and I thought I was going insane. And I think some of the things that I said, they sounded insane. . . . I wound up having a nervous breakdown. . . . I started working with a psychiatrist, and he felt that, well, I wasn't so crazy after all—that maybe what I really needed—that what *we* needed was some counseling help. And so we've been, the last eight months, involved with him in marriage counseling about once every week or week and a half—something like that.

Interviewer: He counsels you and your wife together?

Mike: Together, right. He won't see us apart. [He says] it's not a contest and he doesn't want to choose the best of us. . . . We've really worked out a lot of problems. Some of the sessions are pretty rough. It's the kind of thing that you look forward to and yet you know it's going to get painful and you try to back off. . . .

I think I had a more rigid stand on most everything, so I think it's necessary that I become more flexible. When you go into marriage, you don't realize how unbalanced the sex roles are. And now—now it's like there's a conspiracy to get the married male (*laughs*)! She's still in the group; I have tolerated the group.

[But] she's sharing a part of herself with other people and I—and in a traditional sense, I should be getting that part too. The Ideal Mate—this one person who can give us all—I have that expectation of her. And she says, "There's no way that I can do that for you. You'd better find someone else who can fulfill part of it because I don't have that much to give." Uh, that's a hard thing for someone coming from where I came from to accept. . . . Things [like that] make sense to your head, but you feel rejected.

I really get frustrated and angry. It's really a conflict—wanting her to grow and yet . . . growth is painful because we're throwing away old ways of doing things that were really part of us.

■ Do you think this husband's reactions are representative of many husbands? Would younger husbands react differently or feel similarly? What are some indications from Mike's conversation that exerting patriarchal authority diminishes intimacy? At this point, does Mike view conflict in his marriage as bonding or alienating? Or is he caught in the middle?

I was at a point where I had tried to go to marriage counselors, and when he was confronted with ways he could change, he would just quit. He wouldn't change. So divorce was the only way I could see to meet my needs [in Hall and Hall, 1979:219]. ▪

No marriage, indeed no relationship of any kind, is entirely free of power politics. But together partners can choose to emphasize the "politics of love" or no-power over the politics of power (Cadden, 1973). One spouse can't do it alone, however. No-power involves both spouses' conscious refusal to be exchange-oriented or to engage in psychological bookkeeping. No-power involves honest self-disclosure and negotiation rather than passive-aggressive maneuvering. As Chapter 9 points out, the politics of love requires fighting so that both partners win. Case Study 10•2, "Living Through Power Changes," describes just that. In contrast, in situations of marital violence, both partners generally lose.

MARITAL VIOLENCE/SPOUSE ABUSE

The use of physical violence to gain dominance in a marriage has occurred throughout history, but only recently has spouse abuse been clearly labeled a social problem. The discovery of child abuse in the 1960s was followed in the 1970s by attention to spouse abuse as a widespread problem with roots in assumptions about marital power.

The National Crime Survey by the Justice Department estimates that 450,000 cases of family abuse occur each year, of which 57 percent represent violence between spouses or former spouses. Most of this violence—about three-fourths—is between ex-spouses ("Official says," 1984). Such statistics, however, are not very accurate because of the reluctance of spouses to report such incidents, as well as other problems with data (Straus, Gelles, and Steinmetz, 1980; Straus and Gelles, 1986). Until recently, the best estimate of the extent of marital violence was provided by a 1975 survey (Straus et al., 1980) of a national probability sample of 2,143 husbands, wives, and cohabiting individuals. The study found that in 16 percent of the couples, at least one of the partners had engaged

in a violent act during the year prior to the 1975 study. In other words, every year in about one out of every six couples in the United States, an individual commits at least one violent act against his or her partner. And if the period considered is the entire length of the marriage rather than just the previous year, in 28 percent, or between one out of four and one out of three couples, a violent act is committed. In short, if you are married, the chances are almost one out of three that your husband or wife will hit you (Straus et al., 1980).

More recently, the 1985 National Family Violence Re-Survey gathered comparable data from a national probability sample of 6,002 married and living-together households (Straus and Gelles, 1986); Table 10•1 compares marital violence rates from the two surveys. Straus and Gelles (1986) admit they cannot be sure just how to interpret these findings. Although it is unlikely, the slight decline in marital violence between 1975 and 1985 may be due to methodological differences in the two surveys (the first survey used face-to-face interviews, whereas the second was conducted by telephone). Then, too, the decline may reflect people's increased reluctance to admit to marital violence due to heightened negative public attention to the problem. It is also possible that the data accurately reflect a real decline since the mid-1970s. We'll look at reasons why this might be so later in this section.

Marital violence exists in all social classes. There is some statistical evidence that it occurs more often in blue-collar and lower-class families (Steinmetz and Straus, 1974:5), a finding partly attributable to the fact that middle-class families have greater privacy than lower-class families and hence are better able to conceal beatings (Straus et al., 1980). Also, middle-class spouses have recourse to friends and professional counselors to help deal with their violence; consequently, their altercations are less likely to become matters for the police.

Both wives and husbands resort to violence. In fact, wives are about as likely to engage in violence against husbands as vice versa (Straus et al., 1980.) Figure 10•1 shows the percentage of both spouses who admitted to an act of violence in a one-year period. One study based on a national sample of 960 men and 1,183 women (not married to each other) found that one in eight husbands and about the same number of wives (11.6 percent of husbands, 12.1 percent of wives) had committed at least one violent act during the year in which the research was conducted. In 49 percent of the vio-

TABLE 10·1 Marital Violence Indexes, 1975 and 1985

Violence index	Rate per 1,000 couples	
	1975	1985
Husband-to-Wife		
Overall violence	121	113
Severe violence	38	30
("wife beating")		
Wife-to-husband		
Overall violence	116	121
Severe violence	46	44
Couple		
Overall violence	160	158
Severe violence	61	58
Number of cases	2,143	3,520

SOURCE: Adapted from Straus and Gelles, 1986:470.

lent situations, both partners engaged in some form of physical abuse. Often, then, the pattern was one of mutual violence. In the remaining situations about an equal number of husbands and wives were violent while their partner was not (Straus et al., 1980).

Wife Abuse

Wife abuse is a serious and significant problem whose most visible manifestation is in wife beating. **Wife beating** can be defined as "a blow with a clenched fist (not a slap)" that a husband delivers to his wife repeatedly over time (Newman, 1976:22). Other forms of violence, such as kicking, pushing down stairs, and hitting with an object, are also considered wife abuse.[3] In a survey of 100 battered wives in England, almost half said they had been assaulted with weapons, including belt buckles,

knives, razors, and broken bottles. Thirty percent had had one or more bones broken (Gayford, 1975).

The Three-Phase Cycle of Domestic Violence Experts are finding that the initial violent episode usually comes as a shock to the wife, who treats her mate's violence as an exceptional, isolated outburst. He promises it will not happen again; she believes him. She also tries to figure out what she did to cause his reaction so there will be no reason for it to happen again. The likelihood is that it will, however, because of what counselors call the *three-phase cycle of violence*. First, tension resulting from some minor altercations builds over a period of time. Second, the situation escalates, eventually exploding in another violent episode. Third, the husband becomes genuinely contrite, threatening his wife lovingly. She wants to believe that this change in him will be permanent. This cycle repeats itself, usually with the violence worsening, if something is not done to change things (Sonkin et al., 1985:11).

Two questions come to mind: Why do husbands beat their wives? And why do wives tolerate it? Both questions can be answered by the relative love and need theory.

Why Do Husbands Do It? Studies indicate that husbands who beat their wives are attempting to

_____

3. It is difficult to define *wife abuse* so that it includes other acts of physical violence and excludes verbal abuse and a less severe physical act such as a slap. While the latter are of great psychological importance, it is *physically injurious* and *repetitive* acts that we include in our discussion of wife abuse.

Other kinds of family violence are child abuse, incest, and marital rape. Marital rape was briefly discussed in Chapter 4. Child abuse will be addressed in Chapter 13.

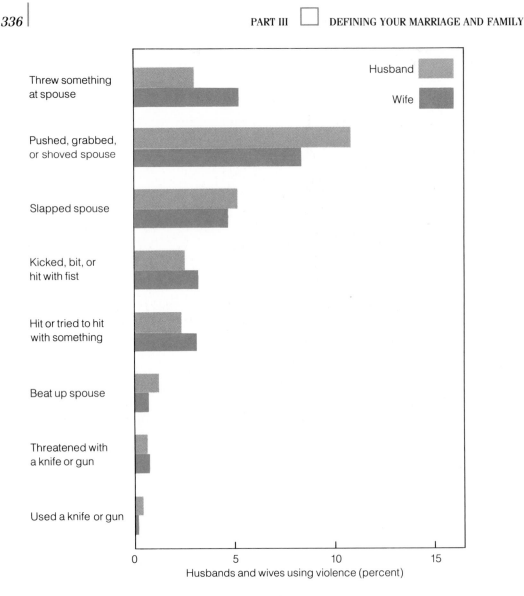

FIGURE 10·1
Percentage of husbands and wives who reported committing certain violent acts during the preceding year (adapted from Straus et al., 1980:37).

compensate for general feelings of powerlessness or inadequacy—on their jobs, in their marriages, or both. As Chapter 2 indicates, our cultural images and the socialization process encourage men to be "strong" and self-sufficient. Husbands may use physical expressions of male supremacy to compensate for their lack of occupational success, prestige, or satisfaction. Husbands' feelings of pow-

erlessness may also stem from an inability to earn a salary that keeps up with inflation and the family's standard of living or the stress of a high-pressure occupation.

One study compared husbands who beat their wives with husbands who did not. The men who exhibited violent behavior were more often seriously dissatisfied with their jobs, were dropouts

■ The cycle of violence in domestic abuse—when one spouse beats the other—creates a climate of fear. Because violence is frighteningly routine in this family, this boy is ironically, and tragically, being "trained" to be a future wife-beater.

from either high school or college, or brought home earnings that were a source of serious or constant conflict (O'Brien, 1971). Other studies have shown that wife beating occurs more often in marriages in which the wife can express herself better than her husband or has more education than he has (Gelles, 1979; O'Brien, 1971). One woman, an educational administrator who was often beaten by her husband, analyzed her situation:

I remember receiving exasperated punches after he'd felt humiliated at work, being kicked (in the bathroom) when friends (in the living room) wouldn't agree with him, being hit against the wall hard when he couldn't make me "act right" [in Bedard, 1978:86]. ■

Wife beating apparently is a resource a husband can draw on to maintain dominance, especially in the absence of other, more "legitimate" resources such as economic or intellectual superiority (Goode, 1971; Frieze et al., 1978:316). A study of blue-collar families found exactly that: Husbands who did not possess superior resources were more likely to fall back on violence to maintain their superiority (Allen and Straus, 1980).

Why Do Wives Put Up with It? Women do not like to get beaten up. They do not cooperate in their own beatings, and they often try to get away. They do, however, stay married to husbands who beat them repeatedly. For the most part, battered wives seek divorce only after a long history of severe violence and repeated conciliation (Bell, 1977:22).[4] There are several reasons for this, and they all point to these women's lack of personal resources with which to take control of their own lives.

Battered wives' lack of personal power begins with fear. "First of all," reports social scientist Richard Gelles, "the wife figures if she calls police or files for divorce, her husband will kill her—literally" (Gelles, in C. Booth, 1977:7). This fear may not be unfounded. Homicides within families are more common than any other kind, and statistics show that husbands kill wives about four times as often as wives kill husbands (Gelles, in C. Booth, 1977:4, 7).

Furthermore, our cultural tradition historically has encouraged women to put up with abuse. English common law, the basis of the American legal structure, asserted that a husband had the right to physically chastise an errant wife, provided the stick was not bigger than his thumb (a legal norm still prevalent in the nineteenth century) (Straus and Gelles, 1986).

While the legal right to physically abuse women has long since disappeared, our cultural heritage continues to influence our attitudes. A survey conducted in 1978 by Louis Harris for the National Commission for the Causes and Prevention of Violence found that one-fifth of all American husbands could approve of slapping a wife's face (Steinmetz and Straus, 1974:6).

Legally, there has been little protection for battered women until recently. Studies show that in the past police typically avoided making arrests for assault that would be automatic if the man and woman involved were not married ("All-American," 1976). The laws themselves contributed to police reluctance. Statutes might require a policeman to witness the act to make an arrest at the scene, or more severe injury before prosecution for battery. Over the last ten years, however, laws have been changed to make arrests for domestic violence more feasible.

Some information has emerged on the effectiveness of police arrest in deterring future violent incidents. The Minneapolis Spouse Abuse Experiment (Sherman and Berk, 1984) used a sample of 314 misdemeanor spouse assault (mainly wife-battery) cases in that city. Police randomly responded in one of three ways: arrested the offender, ordered the offender from the premises for eight hours, or offered "advice." Using follow-up data from police records and victim interviews, researchers concluded that arrest was most effective in reducing new violent incidents. A year later, two University of California sociologists replicated the Minneapolis study (Berk and Newton, 1985). Using longitudinal data from the criminal justice system on 783 wife-battery incidents in Southern California, they obtained similar results: On the average, police arrests deterred new assaults. Moreover, the courts now permit civil suits against police failure to protect (Gundle, 1986). More research is needed, but meanwhile, "perhaps presumptory arrest should be the operational policy until strong evidence is presented showing that other forms of police intervention are more effective" (Berk and Newton, 1985:262).

Wives may also tolerate abuse, not because they enjoy being battered, but because they love their husbands, depend on their economic resources, and hope they will reform. Battered wives who stay with their husbands fear the economic hardship or uncertainty that will result if they leave. They hesitate to summon police or to press charges because of the loss of income or damage to a husband's professional reputation that could result from his incarceration. One study found that a battered wife is less likely to leave when she has not finished high school or is unemployed (see Table 10•2). This economic hardship is heightened when children are involved.

Another frequent factor in women's tolerance of abuse is childhood experience. Gelles speculates that persons who experienced violence in their parents' home while growing up may have an increased tolerance for violence and regard beatings as "all part of married life" (Gelles, in C. Booth, 1977:7). The study cited earlier of battered women in England found that 23 percent said violence was a "regular feature" in the family of orientation, and 41 percent said their fathers were chronically aggressive. The brutalized women reported that over half the husbands had also come from homes

---

4. The average woman entering Rainbow Retreat, a shelter for battered women in Phoenix, is 36 years old, has been married seventeen years, and has four children. She also has no job experience. According to director Joanne Rhoads, "She has systematically extinguished her various alternatives through fear and mistrust of her own decisions" (Bell, 1977:18–19).

TABLE 10·2 The Ways in Which Forty-One Wives Dealt with Marital Abuse (Compared by Level of Education, Occupation, Number of Children, and Age of Oldest Child)

	Mean Education	Percentage Completed High School	Percentage Employed	Mean Number of Children	Mean Age of Oldest Child
No intervention (N = 11)	11.9	63%	25%	2.5	9.3
Divorced or separated (N = 9)	11.7	66%	44%[a]	3.3	9.3
Called police (N = 13)	11.0	69%	38%	3.0	13.0
Went to agency (N = 8)	11.1	62%	75%	2.6	13.7
Any intervention	11.3	67%	50%	3.0	12.0

SOURCE: Gelles, 1976:664.

a. For those wives who are divorced or separated, some may have found employment *after* the divorce or separation. The data did not allow us to determine *when* the wife found employment.

where they saw their fathers beat their mothers (Gayford, 1975).

Another factor that helps perpetuate wife abuse is that women accept the cultural mandate that it is primarily their responsibility to keep their marriage from "failing" through divorce. "Women are trained to stay. They are responsible for the marriage. If they leave, it's their fault" (Gelles, in C. Booth, 1977:7). Believing this, wives are often convinced that their husbands will change and that their support can lead husbands to reform. Thus, wives often return to violent mates after leaving them.

Finally, unusually low self-esteem causes battered women to confuse love and need. They are convinced "that their self-worth hinges on having a man: and they're willing to pay any price, because the concept of being alone equals worthlessness and abandonment" (Lang, in Bell, 1977:22). At the same time, they feel that the outside world is hostile. As one woman in her mid-30s expressed it:

These men we live with are the people who are supposed to love us and the people we are supposed to love. And if the person who loves you treats you like that, what is the rest of the world going to do to you? [Lang, in Bell, 1977:22]. ■

A Way Out A woman in such a position needs to redefine her situation before she can deal with her problem, and she needs to forge some links with the outside world to alter her relationship.

One source of support for women has developed in recent years: a network of shelters for battered wives. Such shelters provide a woman and her children with temporary housing, food, and clothing to solve the problems of economic dependency, and physical safety. These organizations also provide counseling to encourage a stronger self-concept so that the woman can view herself as worthy of better treatment and capable of making her way in the outside world if need be. Finally, shelters provide guidance in obtaining employment, legal assistance, family counseling, or whatever practical assistance is required for a more permanent solution.

This last service provided by shelters—obtaining help toward more long-range solutions—is important, research shows. Face-to-face interviews with the same 155 wife-battery victims were conducted twice (a "two-wave panel study") within eighteen months during 1982 and 1983 in Santa Barbara, California. Each of the women interviewed had sought refuge in a shelter. Findings showed that victims who were also taking other measures (for example, calling the police, trying to get a restraining order, seeking personal counseling or legal help) were more likely to benefit from their shelter experience. "Otherwise, shelters may have no impact or perhaps even trigger retaliation (from husbands) for disobedience" (Berk et al., 1986:488). The researchers conclude:

The possibility of perverse shelter effects for certain kinds of women poses a troubling policy dilemma. On the one hand, it is difficult to be enthusiastic about an intervention that places battered victims at further risk. On the other hand, a shelter stay may for many women be one important step in a lengthy process toward freedom, even though there may also be genuine short-run dangers. Perhaps solutions can be found in strategies that link together several different kinds of interventions [Berk et al., 1986:488]. ■

Violence and Women's Liberation   What effect will societal changes, inspired by the women's movement, toward greater economic and psychological independence of women have on wife abuse? Some studies associate marital *dependence*—that is, the wife's tendency to be practically and emotionally dependent on the marriage—with tolerance for abuse. Other studies associate wives' *independence,* or her relatively higher status and resources compared to her husband, with increased husband violence.

Contradiction in the effects of women's liberation on family violence can be explained by noting that some effects are short-term and some long-term. Social scientists Debra Kalmuss and Murray Straus believe that as women gain equality for themselves, wife abuse will decline over the long run. Wife abusers' "perceived right to abuse their wives" will decrease, women will have greater access to alternatives to the victim's role, and social institutions will become more responsive to the problem of wife abuse. However, in the meantime we may see more violence because wife abusers find it difficult to give up their dominant role. "Husbands, in fact, may resort to violence if the struggle for sexual equality increases their wives' resource base and encourages women to question the power relationships" (Kalmuss and Straus, 1982:278).

Kalmuss and Straus explored marital dependency and violence in detail and came up with results that have some important implications for public policy. In a national sample they found that "severe violence" was associated with "objective dependence"—that is, economic dependence as measured by employment status, presence of young children, and whether or not the husband earned 75 percent or more of the family income. Severe violence was not found to be related to subjective marital dependency or the extent of the wife's emotional attachment to her mate. Kalmuss and Straus conclude that therapeutic, educational, and support services developed to deal with wife abuse are not enough. The conditions that bind women to marriage must also be changed. "This may be partially accomplished by fundamental changes such as universal child care services, reduced occupational discrimination against women, and an end to sex-based wage differentials" (Kalmuss and Straus, 1982:285). Once again we see a major theme of this text: Personal, individual problems and decisions are interrelated with public issues.

Husband Abuse

Straus and Gelles find it "distressing" that, "in marked contrast to the behavior of women outside the family, women are about as violent within the family as men" (1986:470). They note the lack of public concern about husband abuse: "There has been no publicity, and no funds have been invested in ameliorating this problem because it has not been defined as a problem" (472). Yet some might argue it is even more serious than wife abuse because of the humiliation accruing to a male in our society who is a victim of attacks from women.

Others argue that "it would be a great mistake if our new awareness of husband abuse were to deflect attention from wives *as victims.*" This is so for the following reasons, all based on the research:

1. Husbands have higher rates of the most dangerous and injurious forms of violence, such as severe beatings.
2. Violence by husbands does more damage, even it if is an exchange of slaps or punches, because of the man's generally greater physical strength; the woman, therefore, is more likely to be seriously injured.

3. Violent acts by the husband tend to be repeated over time, whereas those by wives do not. (Statistics showing about equal incidences of husband and wife violence are in response to a research question about "at least one" incident.)

4. Many wives are attacked while pregnant, thus endangering another life.

5. Much of wives' violence appears to be in self-defense. "One of the most fundamental reasons why some women are violent within the family, but not outside the family, is that the risk of assault for a typical American woman is greatest in her own home" (Straus and Gelles, 1986:471).

6. Husbands are more apt to leave the relationship within a short time. Having more resources, men rarely face the choice women do of choosing between poverty (for their children as well as themselves) and violence (Straus et al., 1980).

For this reason women are quite rightly concerned about losing public attention and resources to what is perceived as a less drastic need. Yet it would be a shame to deny the need for some public support including programmatic support for male victims of spouse abuse. Both needs must be met.

The Abusing Husband

The interests of men and women in curbing spousal violence converge when we consider the issue of male victims of spousal homicides. *The Burning Bed* depicted Francine Hughes's killing of her ex-husband (McNulty, 1981). It is clear that Hughes was incredibly victimized and brutalized by her husband. While few would endorse murder as the solution of choice, lawyers have recently been convincing the courts that women may rationally conclude that there are no alternatives in some cases to this form of self-defense (Schneider, 1986; see also Browne, 1987).

Police protection and arrest of wife abusers does now offer an alternative that may be in the long-run interests of the abuser as well as the abused. If a wife has an effective means of coping with violence, she will not be forced into violent self-protective acts.

More direct assistance to receptive wife abusers has recently begun to be offered. Counseling and group therapy, thought to be ineffective with male abusers, has now been tried with some success. Here we mean not conventional marital therapy but group therapy for abusive men who wish to stop. Many abused husbands have difficulty controlling their response to anger and frustration, dealing with problems, or handling intimacy. While many abusers are not reachable, others have a sincere desire to stop. The "contrite, loving" stage of the cycle of violence occurs in part because many husbands do have feelings of love for their wives. Group therapy reduces stigma and provides a setting in which abusive husbands can learn more constructive ways of coping with anger and how to balance autonomy and intimacy, often another area of difficulty (Shoehigh, 1985).

Summary

Power is the ability to exercise one's will and may rest on cultural authority, economic and personal resources that are gender based, love and emotional dependence, interpersonal manipulation, or physical violence.

The relative power of a husband and wife in a marriage varies by national background and race, religion, and class. It varies by whether or not the wife works and the presence and age of children. American marriage experiences a tension between male dominance and egalitarianism. Studies of married couples, cohabiting couples, and gay male and lesbian couples illustrate the significance of economic-based power, as well as the possibility for couples to consciously work toward more egalitarian relationships.

Physical violence is most commonly used in the absence of other resources. While men and women are equally likely to abuse their spouses, for various reasons wife abuse is a more crucial social problem and has received the most programmatic attention. Recently programs have been developed for male abusers, but less attention has been paid to male victims. Experiments indicating that arrest is an important deterrent to further wife abuse illustrate the importance of public policies that meet family needs. Couples themselves may develop more egalitarian relationships by conscious effort. Some strategies are offered for working toward a "no-power" relationship.

Key Terms

Study Questions

1. Differentiate social power and conjugal power.
2. What is Blood and Wolfe's *resource hypothesis* of conjugal power? Do you agree with this hypothesis? What are your specific agreements and criticisms?
3. How does the more recent research on conjugal power either confirm or refute the ideas and findings of Blood and Wolfe? Include specific examples of more recent research.
4. What is the *principle of least interest?* How does it fit into the relative love and need theory? Do you agree with this theory more or less than you agree with the resource hypothesis? Why?
5. How is gender related to power in marriage? How do you think recent social change will affect power in marriage?
6. What does Blumstein and Schwartz's study of four types of couples tell us about power in relationships?
7. How does the relative love and need theory explain wife-beating and wives' reactions to the beatings? Do you think that battered wives' shelters provide an adequate "way out" for these women? Why or why not? What about arrest?

8. How likely do you think it is for a couple to develop a no-power relationship? What are some of the difficulties that you see in trying to develop such a relationship?

Suggested Readings

Blumstein, Philip, and Pepper Schwartz
1983   *American Couples: Money, Work, and Sex.* New York: Morrow.
   Power should have been in the title because the book is about the dynamics of power in four types of relationships: married heterosexual couples, cohabiting heterosexual couples, gay male couples, and lesbian couples. Money, work, and sex, of course, have a lot to do with power. Only lesbian couples succeed in having no-power relationships, but their strategies could be employed by any couple.

Cheek, Donald K.
1976   *Assertive Black... Puzzled White: A Black Perspective on Assertive Behavior.* San Luis Obispo, Calif.: Impact.
   Presents the view that assertiveness training for blacks needs to take into account the realistic environmental constraints blacks have experienced.

Gelles, Richard J., and Claire Pedrich Cornell
1985   *Intimate Violence in Families.* Beverly Hills, Calif.: Sage.
   New work by important family violence researchers.

Goode, William J.
1986   "Why men resist." Pp. 131–147 in Barrie Thorne and Marilyn Yalom (eds.), *Rethinking the Family: Some Feminist Questions.* New York: Longmans.
   A well-written and thoughtful essay by a highly respected sociologist about why men resist women's (and their own) changing gender roles.

LaRossa, Ralph
1977   *Conflict and Power in Marriages: Expecting the First Child.* Beverly Hills, Calif.: Sage.
   Analysis of case studies.

Lipmen-Blumen, Jean
1984   *Gender Roles and Power.* Englewood Cliffs, N.J.: Prentice-Hall.
   Looks at our system of gender roles as a major determinant of social power inside and outside the family.

Phelps, S., and N. Austin
1975   *The Assertive Woman.* San Luis Obispo, Calif.: Impact.
   Shows how assertiveness training for women may help achieve more egalitarian and satisfying relationships with men (and children).

Schneider, Elizabeth
1986 "Describing and Changing: Women's Self-Defense Work and the Problem of Expert Testimony on Battering." *Women's Rights Law Reporter* 9 (3, 4):195–222.
Excellent resource on homicide provoked by wife abuse as a legal, ethical, and feminist issue.
Straus, Murray A., Richard J. Gelles, and Suzanne K. Steinmetz
1980 *Behind Closed Doors: Violence in the American Family.* New York: Doubleday.
Major study by the foremost authorities on family violence.

IV Experiencing Family Commitment

ever married adults sometimes ask married people what marriage is "really" like. Spouses sometimes wonder in what ways other couples' unions are like their own. While every person's marriage is in some ways unique, the four chapters in this section explore some common aspects of American marriages today.

Chapter 11 explores how work—both inside and outside the home—affects marital relationships.

One of the most vital issues that couples face is the decision whether to have children. Chapter 12 explores the pros and cons of parenting. We will look at the value of children to parents, along with some of the costs they can impose on the marital relationship. And we will discuss some choices couples are making about having children, such as postponing pregnancy until they are in their 30s and having an only child.

Chapter 13 discusses parenting. Here the emphasis is not so much on the dos and don'ts of good parenting as on building a supportive relationship between parents and children.

Finally, Chapter 14 explores managing resources: money, housing, and health. This practical chapter has guidelines for drawing up a family budget, obtaining quality health care, and so forth.

The theme that marriage relationships change over the years runs through all these chapters. Situations change: Children grow older; living with a toddler is different from living with a teenager; and both of these are different from developing a relationship with a young-adult child or from being a grandparent. Furthermore, partners' attitudes about themselves and their marriages change. For instance, a couple may arrange their work roles inside and outside the home one way during one phase of their marriage and prefer to do things differently at another time. Making these changes (as Chapter 8 points out) requires that each partner be willing to change his or her attitudes about what to expect in the marriage and how things should be done.

11

Work and Family

*I look out cross the yard.
I see Sofia dragging a
ladder and then lean it
up gainst the house. . . .
Got her head tied up in
a headrag. She clam up
the ladder to the roof,
begin to hammer in
nails. Sound echo cross
the yard like shots.*
ALICE WALKER, *The Color
Purple*

“**D**o you work?” and “Where?” are new questions in human history. Spouses have always worked: Until recently, cooperative labor for survival was the primary purpose of marriage (Tilly and Scott, 1978). But only since the industrial revolution has working been considered separate from family living, and only since then have the concepts *employed* and *unemployed* emerged. For those who stayed home (usually wives and mothers), working in the public sphere was beyond their experience and took on an aura of mystery. For those who labored outside the home and earned money (mainly husbands), partners who stayed at home seemed unproductive; they were not “employed.”

This different work status is one aspect of what Jessie Bernard called the “his” and “her” marriage: a married life-style that is different for each sex. “His” work has been in the public sphere, for money; “her” work has taken place in the private sphere of the household, for free. Spouses’ work roles have been sexually segregated, with neither spouse understanding how it felt to do the work of the other.

Today, although sexual segregation and discrimination in employment persist, the trend is clearly away from distinguishing work based on sex. Couples can more freely allocate wage-earning and housekeeping responsibilities because many women work outside the home.

Many chapters in this book discuss social changes and the resulting changes in people's life-styles, attitudes, and family life. This chapter looks at one more aspect of modern living that is profoundly affecting marriages and families. We'll explore traditional employment patterns that have characterized our society as we know it, then look at emerging patterns and the interrelationship of work and family roles for both women and men. We'll see that, as with other changes, the trend toward women's working outside the home is a source of ambivalent feelings and requires both women and men to make many personal adjustments. To begin, we will examine the concept of “labor force” as a social invention.

THE “LABOR FORCE”—A SOCIAL INVENTION

While human beings have always worked, it was not until the industrialization of the workplace in the nineteenth century that people characteristically became wage earners, hiring out their labor to someone else and joining a “labor force.” The concept *labor force*, then, is a social invention.

Social scientists from Karl Marx to Sigmund Freud have agreed that working is inherently self-actualizing. To be so, however, working must be meaningful to the worker; that is, it must be characterized by some appreciable degree of creativity. But with industrialization capitalists (those who owned factories and/or other means of production) organized the labor force in order to enhance profit margins. "Individuals became organized in accordance with the requirements of technological production" (Berger et al., 1973:32). Efficiency, not worker creativity or self-direction, became an overriding principle.

The Labor Force in Postindustrial Society

Gradually throughout this century, our society has moved from an industrial one that manufactured products to a postindustrial one that transmits information and offers other services. In such a "service society" production is transferred to the office. Synchronized clerical workers, administrators, and other bureaucrats, working according to a "job description," perform one step in a sequence of activity. As a clerical worker told an interviewer, "When they say you've got to think for yourself, that means you've got to figure out whether to use a capital or a small key" (Burris, 1983:99).

Furthermore, employees are increasingly aware that they are replaceable, if not dispensable. In 1987 the catch phrase in the workplace became "lean and mean." Partly in order to compete with foreign markets and partly to maintain corporate profits in a generally constricting economy, employers dedicated themselves to reducing costs by streamlining their operations. One way they would do that, many announced publicly, was to let some workers go. Job security became an issue even for highly educated managerial employees.

Moreover, a great proportion of the new jobs created by the service economy pay less than did industrial work. Many are part-time and offer no employee benefits such as contributions to retirement or health care. (Part-time jobs increased 58 percent from 1970 to 1982 [Beck, 1984]). Though other factors are involved, Americans workers' average hourly wages, when adjusted for inflation, declined by 6 percent over the past ten years (Fuller, 1984). (Chapter 14 discusses managing family resources in a constricting economy.) One way families have adapted to this decline in real income

is for both wives and husbands to become employed. By 1986, 54.9 percent of all married couples in the United States had both spouses in the labor force (U.S. Bureau of Labor Statistics, 1986b).

Many Americans find their positions or "careers" challenging and satisfying. But a significant, and growing, proportion of workers have difficulty finding meaning, security, or personal satisfaction in their jobs; nor do their wages keep up with inflation. It is in this context that we explore the relationship between work and family. We will look next at what has traditionally been husbands' work.

WORKING AND HUSBANDS

"What do you want to be when you grow up?" In this century people have asked little boys this question more often than girls. Boys have been expected to want to "be something." Competing for success in a chosen occupation has been essential to the traditional masculine gender role. (Chapter 7 points out that a husband has been culturally and even legally expected to be his family's principal breadwinner.) But as we'll see in this section, traditional work roles for men are changing: Men are no longer culturally bound to the good-provider role.

The "Good Provider" Role: Have Men Tired of It?

What sociologist Jessie Bernard (1986) terms the **"good provider" role** for men emerged in this country during the 1830s. Before then a man was expected to be "a good steady worker," but "the idea that he was *the* provider would hardly ring true" (Bernard, 1986:126). The good-provider role lasted into the late 1970s. Its end, again according to Bernard, was officially marked when the 1980 Census declared that a male was no longer automatically assumed to be head of the household.

Rewards and Costs The good-provider role entailed both reward and costs for men. Rewards included social status and reinforcement of the husband's patriarchal authority in the family (see Chapter 10). Moreover, the "basic exchange,"

■ Mining, more than most occupations, remains almost exclusively a man's job. These Kentucky coal miners have just completed their shift. Regardless of whether their work is as physically demanding and dangerous as mining, men take satisfaction in a job well done and in their role of being the "good provider" for their families.

described in Chapters 6 and 7, meant that the male exchanged breadwinning for the female's home-making, child rearing, and sexual availability.

A serious cost was that the good-provider role encouraged a man to put all his "gender-identifying eggs into one psychic basket." That is,

success in the good-provider role came in time to define masculinity itself. The good provider... was a bread*winner*.... Men were judged as men by the level of living they provided.... The good provider became a player in the male competitive macho game. What one man provided for his

family in the way of luxury and display had to be equaled or topped by what another could provide [Bernard, 1986:130] ■

Consequently, failure, or even mediocre performance, in the role meant one had failed *as a man*, indeed *as a* (male) *person*. Other costs involved being expected to work steadily, perhaps at an unsatisfying job, for most of one's lifetime, generally without the option of quitting or even changing jobs. Despite this, the benefits of the good-provider role apparently outweighed the costs for most men (Bernard, 1986).

New Expectations/New Alternatives Over the past several decades the good-provider role has taken on new meaning. Family life for males now includes the additional expectation of emotional expressivity, together with the sharing of household responsibilities. In the past this was not the case. Thus, "the role has become even more burdensome" (Bernard, 1986:137). It is hardly surprising, then, according to Bernard, that surveys comparing men's attitudes in 1957 with those in 1976 found that the proportion of working men who considered marriage "burdensome and restrictive" had more than doubled, from 25 percent to 56 percent. "Although some of these changes reflected greater willingness in 1976 than in 1957 to admit negative attitudes toward marriage and parenthood—itself significant—profound changes were clearly in process" (137).

Historically, a small minority of men have resented "the burdens the (good provider) role has forced them to bear" and have found ways to avoid it; hobos are one example (Bernard, 1986:131). But today it appears that men's complaints "have become serious, bone-deep" (137). Why?

For one thing, work itself, increasingly bureaucratized, may be less satisfying for men than it used to be. For another, the family that men "have been providing for is not the same family it was in the past" (137). Increasingly, wives are employed, and they are not as deferential to husbands as they were. Furthermore, as the Prologue points out, the rising divorce rate has lessened the conviction that one's marriage will last. As a result, men may have become more reluctant to invest their earnings in a family. Then, too, beginning in about the 1950s men were offered alternative roles (such as "playboy") as avenues to prove their masculinity (Ehrenreich, 1983).

The growing proportion of never married men, combined with the increasing number of divorced men who appear to have relinquished the provider role, has led observers to suggest that the role may be losing its validity. Men will continue to derive satisfaction from marriage, "but this does not necessarily mean they are willing to pay for the benefit" (Bernard, 1986:137). Meanwhile, more and more women may be relinquishing the childbearing role. (Women's decision whether to have children is discussed in Chapter 12.)

Nevertheless, the majority of husbands today continue to believe that they should be breadwinners, if not *sole* breadwinners or "good providers." The next section examines the relationship between the husband's breadwinner role and family satisfaction.

The Breadwinner Role and Family Satisfaction

Although the role of family breadwinner is no longer reserved for husbands, many Americans—more than one-third in 1983, according to one national survey (Booth et al., 1984)—still believe that the man should be the principal provider for his family. Traditionally, people assumed that the more success a husband has in his occupation, the more satisfied the wife will be and the better their marriage will be. This assumption incorporates the instrumental-expressive dichotomy discussed in Chapter 2. As the husband fulfills his instrumental obligations as provider, the wife is motivated to fulfill her role as the expressive or supportive agent of the family. According to this view, the process of exchange—breadwinning for husband care—continues only so long as the husband carries out his role as provider (Scanzoni, 1970).

Research has discredited the idea that high income necessarily produces a happy marriage. In one study of middle-aged, middle-class couples, those who were most likely to report a decrease in happiness over the years were couples in which the husband had increased his income greatly and had risen to the top of his profession. This was especially true when he had also increased his involvement in community organizations (Udry, 1974). Another study found that the highest percentage of "very happy" relationships were in marriages where both husband and wife placed primary emphasis on family instead of on career roles (Bailyn, 1970). Husbands who devote their energies to occupational success and neglect their wives may end up with unhappy, not happier, marriages.

There is evidence, however, that husbands' provision of *adequate* financial support is important to their own and their wives' marital satisfaction. Satisfaction with economic support is closely related to prior expectations and ambitions. A study of 120 couples, for example, found that wives who expected to gain status from marriage thought their husbands should be the ones to provide increasing income. When these wives married into a lower social class, they generally perceived their marriages as conflict-habituated; those who married up reported less conflict (Jorgensen, 1977). In general, because men and women are still committed to the male provider role (recall Chapter 2), adequate economic support by husbands is important to marital satisfaction in all social classes. The importance of an adequate income is more apparent, however, in lower- and working-class marriages, where economic support is less taken for granted.

About half of all American men work in blue-collar occupations, and although they receive what appear to be high hourly wages, most of them do not earn sufficient income to meet modest budget requirements, let alone to accumulate savings. Liable to sudden layoffs, they are also likely to have few retirement benefits. In recent years plant closings and contract "give-backs" (cuts in pay and fringe benefits such as health insurance coverage) have further eroded the blue-collar family economy. The greatest source of strain in working-class marriages usually lies in economic difficulties. For this reason, the husband's role as primary breadwinner is psychologically reinforced. If a blue-collar wife has a husband who is a steady worker, doesn't drink, and doesn't hit her (writes one family counselor), she probably feels she "can't complain" (L. Rubin, 1976:93).

This observation about the importance of the breadwinner role in a marriage has been supported by some research on lower-class men. When anthropologist Elliot Liebow lived among and studied a group of black men in Washington, D.C., he found that a husband's ability to provide money was clearly important to a wife's expectations. "To pay the rent, buy the groceries, and provide for the other necessary goods and services is the *sine qua non* (absolutely essential quality) of a good husband" (Liebow, 1967:129). While there might be alternative sources of financial support, including the wife's wages, the responsibility was the husband's, no one else's. This does not mean that black wives did not expect to work for wages; but they assigned the role of *principal* breadwinner to the "good" husband.

The blue-collar husband's inherent lack of satisfaction with and achievement in his job also has an effect on the family. Although the working man accepts the ideology that ability grants a person the right to ascend the class ladder, in fact he usually does not progress. He is caught in a limited-opportunity structure: No matter how hard or how well he works, he will probably be working in the same position years later. Denied advancement in the world of work, he views family life as "real life" and finds meaning in his labor only insofar as it represents sacrifice for the benefit of his family (Seifer, 1973; Yankelovich, 1974:44–45). Through such sacrifice husbands confirm their masculinity.

Sociologist Helena Lopata (1971) notes the importance placed on the husband's provider role by *middle-class* housewives, as well as by those in the working and lower classes. The breadwinner role has been seen as a husband's most important contribution—a contribution that is seldom nullified even by negative behavior.

We have discussed some interrelationships in men's occupational and family lives. However, social scientist Joseph Pleck has argued that "the most obvious and direct effect" of the male's breadwinning role—"the restricting effect of the male occupational role on men's family role"—has received relatively little attention (1977:420). Society has encouraged men to give primacy to their work and to let their family relationships come second.

This situation has many effects. It creates absentee fathers—fathers who are away from home for extended periods of time and who seldom see their children, especially when the children are young. It also encourages "workaholism," discussed later in the chapter, which can lead to devitalized marriages.

New Options for Men

Some husbands today are rejecting the idea that dedication to one's job or occupational achievement is the ultimate indicator of success. Some men are choosing less competitive careers and are spending more time with their families. Such men place the needs of their families and their own desire for time with their families ahead of career success.

Husbands who want to share household work and child care will not find it easy. "The male feels not just conflicts, but intense pressures," said a Los Angeles lawyer and father in a recent *New York Times Magazine* article. "Society hasn't lowered its level of job performance, but it has raised its expectations of our roles in our children's lives"

(Gregg, 1986:48). As Pleck points out, in the present occupational system, the "diversion of their energy from work into the family will indeed penalize them in the competition for job advancement" (1977:424). For this reason, partners who want to create new options for themselves need to work for changes in the public sphere. An example would be paternity leave, so that fathers as well as mothers can be home with their infants or small children. This request for paternity leave "is perhaps the first indication of the kind of workplace practices needed to legitimate a shift of husbands' energies from work to the family" (Pleck, 1977:424). Some corporations or institutions have instituted such leave. But one New York–based research organization found that, of the 119 major corporations surveyed that offered paternity leave, 41 percent responded that "no time" was the appropriate amount of time for a man to take off at the birth of his child (Gregg, 1986:50).

Unfortunately, the generally constricted economy diminishes workers' power to obtain family-oriented benefits from employers. In contrast, Sweden has a national policy of paternity leave, making dual-parenting much more feasible. Sweden's experience does suggest the importance of changes in attitudes as well as in organizational policy; few fathers take advantage of the paternity leave program, perhaps for fear of handicapping their careers (Lamb and Levine, 1983). Still, the Swedish policy presents a model of the kind of changes in policy needed to make dual-parenting and dual careers realizable.

House Husbands While some husbands persist in fighting to decrease the demands of the workplace in order to participate more at home, a very small minority are relinquishing breadwinning completely to become **house husbands:** husbands who stay home to care for the house and family while their wives work. This option, however, is restricted to relatively few husbands because of the generally limited earning power of women (Gregg, 1986:50), the financial effects of which are exacerbated by today's constricting economy.

Reasons younger house husbands give for staying home include unemployment, poor health, disillusionment or dissatisfaction with the competitive grind, the desire to spend more time with their children, and their wives' desire to pursue full-time careers. As Letty Pogrebin (1977) points out, these situations are still considered "role reversal" rather than normal family situations. But acceptance is growing. One house husband is a native American whose wife is a legislative aide for the Native American Rights Fund. He believes that his wife's work is of such significance that it deserves priority, so he looks after their 5-year-old son as well as the house. He claims, "I get kidded, but I think people pretty much respect me for it." He plans to take a regular job when his son enters kindergarten.

Another house husband, whose wife worked for a year so he could write a book, recommends it only for short stretches but believes the experience increased his children's respect for women. House husbands also cite closeness to children as a plus (Beer, 1983:78–79). Interruptions to work, financial dependency, and the essential tedium of housework are some negative elements they report (*Omaha World Herald,* July 18, 1978).[1]

If women eventually earn wages comparable to men's, and as people liberate themselves from traditional stereotypes, the number of house husbands may grow. However, while both spouses increasingly are in the labor force, the more acceptable pattern is still for the wife to stay home if either spouse does. The next section examines wives' traditional work role, along with some ways that contemporary homemakers are changing that role.

WORKING AND WIVES

Historically, the "housewife"—the married woman who remains in the home to do housework and rear children—is a relatively modern role. Prior to industrialization, women produced goods and

---

1. Meanwhile, the proportion of older men leaving the labor force is increasing. Just 19 percent of husbands over 65 were employed in 1982; this compares with 48 percent thirty years ago (Waldman, 1983). Older husbands don't necessarily retire in order to help out at home, of course. In fact, professional and managerial workers who retire voluntarily because of good pension plans often drift back into the labor force either to cope with inflation or to overcome boredom (Sproat, 1983). Other men retire involuntarily because of poor health, mandatory retirement plans, or unemployment. "Retirement is, perhaps, a mechanism for dealing with long-term chronic unemployment . . . a way of managing spoiled identity that long-term unemployment can produce" (Bould, 1980; Sproat, 1983:41). (Retirement is explored further in Chapters 14 and 15.)

income by working on the family farm or, for example, by taking in boarders. As the industrial revolution removed employment from the household, women could less easily "combine employment with care of the home. At the same time, the increase in real income made it feasible for most wives to devote their time solely to housekeeping. As a result, even as recently as 1940, only . . . 14 percent of married women were in the labor force" (Thornton and Freedman, 1983:24). By 1986, 55 percent of married women were employed, including over half of mothers with children under age 3 (U.S. Bureau of Labor Statistics, 1986c).

Job Description

While the trend has been for wives to join the labor force, currently, between one-third and one-half of wives are full-time homemakers. Although legal and traditional assumptions minimize the value and importance of housework, these tasks consume more hours than full-time "real" jobs. Calculated from five different studies, the average housewife spends between 3,000 and 4,000 hours a year, or between 55 and 75 hours a week, on housework (Oakley, 1974:6).

The economic benefits of a full-time homemaker to her family have been evaluated in many ways.[2] One is to figure the value of her projected earnings were she to join the labor force. Another is to calculate the replacement cost of the homemaker's services. For example, if the average wage for household work is $6 per hour and if a housewife spends 50 hours per week on producing household services, she has an economic, or replacement cost, of $300 per week. A related method takes into consideration the relative value of different family services, such as at-home "early childhood education" for one's own preschoolers. In some situations economists conclude that a full-time housewife with at least one child under age 6 contributes household services equal to more than 100 percent of family money income.

Even these calculations ignore important economic benefits to society provided by homemakers. For example, older wives often provide nursing services for their husbands. "Without such care, medical costs to society would spiral. [But the] personal costs to the wives are not usually recognized" (Troll and Parron, 1981:127).

Moreover, women have traditionally been socialized not to expect monetary rewards for their services. For example, according to a 1957 booklet entitled *A Mother's Wages:*

When the Egyptian princess turned the baby Moses over to his mother, she said, "Take this child . . . and nurse it for me, and I will give thee thy wages" (Exodus 2:9).

In a real sense God says the same thing to every mother when He gives her her baby. And a good mother probably is the highest paid person in the universe [Strachan, 1957:9]. ∎

Homemakers are not direct producers; they serve others (husbands) who participate directly in the economic and political world by meeting their needs for everyday maintenance (food, clothing, and so on) and emotional support. As Joan Huber and Glenna Spitze (1983) note, work that is directly productive is more highly valued and rewarded in most modern, industrialized societies. It is therefore not surprising to find that the "job" of homemaker has low status and low economic rewards.

Social scientist Jessie Bernard has suggested that housewives be paid for their job of keeping the work force motivated and in good condition (Bernard, 1972). But homemaking is not formal employment that brings money or prestige. No financial compensation is associated with this position.

One study investigated the hypothesis that the homemaker role is particularly stressful in modern American society—which emphasizes individual achievement—but that this may not be so in more traditional, familistic societies where the homemaker role is more highly valued (Ross et al., 1983). Mexican culture, for example, places more importance on the family than on work for both sexes. And "the Mexican female, as the center of the family, is accorded honor and prestige that is not available to her American counterpart." It is therefore not surprising that data from a survey of 330 married persons conducted in El Paso, Texas, and Juarez, Mexico, suggested that women of Mexican ethnic identity were somewhat less psychologically distressed by the homemaker role than were Anglo women. In both cultures, however, employed

---

2. Economists have interested themselves in this issue, often as a service to insurance companies or personal injury trial attorneys who want to establish the projected value of a disabled homemaker's loss of services.

women were found to be less distressed than homemakers, a pattern found in other studies as well (e.g., Gore and Mangione, 1983).

The Two-Person Career

A variation on the traditional homemaker role is the two-person career, in which the woman actively participates in her husband's career. Particularly among middle-class and professional families, wives are expected to help their husbands professionally by cultivating appropriate acquaintances and by being charming hostesses and companions. Many large corporations do not hire a middle or top executive without first meeting and evaluating the candidate's wife (L. Rubin, 1976:98). An article on automobile executives' wives claims that "they don't marry men, they marry companies" (Warbelow, 1979). Similarly, in universities, where the majority of professors are still men, the typical faculty wife works at her husband's career in a myriad of ways, including entertaining, typing and editing manuscripts, collaborating in the laboratory, taking notes in classes and meetings, participating in fieldwork, and helping write his books (Hochschild, 1975:67; Papanek, 1973:98).

Social scientist Hanna Papanek called the situation in which one spouse, usually the wife, encourages and participates in the other partner's career without direct recognition or personal remuneration the **two-person single career.** Here the employer gets two workers for the price of one. Not only corporations and universities benefit from the two-person single career; large private foundations and the United States armed forces and foreign services benefit also. In some cases the wife's participation is publicly taken for granted: the ambassador's wife, the mayor's wife, and so on (Papanek, 1973).

Among other things the partner in a two-person career may provide food, clothing, and shelter so that the "First Person" does not need to worry about such practicalities; be willing to move for the benefit of the other's career; provide emotional support; and provide practical assistance such as secretarial help, research, and entertainment of business associates (Bird, 1978:233–38).

The wife may participate in her husband's career to improve his competitive advantage, because she finds the work intrinsically satisfying, or because she identifies with her husband and enjoys helping

him. But the work of these wives is largely invisible and unrecognized by the employers who benefit from it. Their principal status in the community is that of "his wife." While middle-class housewives are proud of their husbands' above-average incomes and may derive satisfaction from their contribution, studies indicate that they do not always vicariously experience their husbands' feelings of success. As they compare their own competence in the world with that of their husbands, silent partners in two-person single careers often feel less competent. A result is lowered self-esteem (Macke et al., 1979).

Furthermore, in the United States today only a small minority of states have "community property" laws in which all the couple's property is considered to be owned equally and in common (whatever the actual work, earnings, or contribution of homemaking activities or support services). In the remaining states wives, even those who participate in their husband's career, are not legally entitled to the resulting economic rewards either during the marriage or after divorce or the husband's death. Couples in which the wife participates in the family craft, business, or profession imagine that their marriage is an economic partnership, but the law has not moved as far in this direction as one might think (Weitzman, 1981). Consequently, with the rising divorce rate many women who thought they had a two-person career find themselves stranded in midlife with few marketable job skills, no employment record, and no benefits.

Steps may be taken to address these inequities. Changes in the Social Security System favorable to homemakers have been proposed but not enacted. Politically active groups have proposed that Congress pass a "Homemaker Bill of Rights," granting—among other things—legal recognition of homemakers as equal economic partners in marriage, salaries for homemakers, revision of discriminatory Social Security provisions so that a homemaker can be covered in her own name in and out of marriage and the labor force, eligibility for unemployment compensation, and inclusion in the gross national product of the value of the goods and services homemakers produce (*National NOW Times,* July, 1979, p. 12).

While some of these goals are probably unrealistic in today's political and economic climate, legal changes regarding inheritance and property rights are gradually effecting a move toward an economic-partnership concept of matrimony (Weitz-

■ They used to be called *housewives*, a term suggesting wedlock to a dwelling place. *Homemaker* more positively suggests creative activity. But less important than terminology is how women feel about their home responsibilities. The happiest full-time homemakers are those who *choose* to work at home.

man, 1981). For example, guidelines have changed so that full-time homemakers are permitted to set up individual retirement accounts (IRAs). In 1984 Congress passed the Retirement Equity Act (REACT), which acknowledged "marriage as an economic partnership, and the substantial contribution to that partnership of spouses who work both in and outside the home." In general, REACT better protects the spouse of an employed participant in private retirement plans. For example, some retirement plans offer the participant a choice of whether to include lifetime survivor income, similar to life insurance benefits. REACT provides that a married participant can waive the survivor benefit—thus taking more in retirement income while living—but only with the written consent of the spouse. Moreover, REACT supports the existing power of state courts to split pension benefits

between divorced and separated partners ("Two More Laws," 1985). Nevertheless, more changes are required—both legally and socially—before women can claim equal rights in marriage.

Homemakers by Choice

A *New York Times* poll conducted in late 1983 asked 1,309 full-time homemakers and women in the labor force about their attitudes toward work and family (see Table 11·1). Of the nonemployed women, 62 percent said they preferred staying home. While 58 percent of employed women said they preferred their job to home responsibilities, one-third told pollsters they would prefer to stay home. Of employed women with children, about 60

TABLE 11·1 Working or Staying at Home: A Comparison[a]

	Prefer a Job	Prefer to Stay Home
Total	58%	35%
All men	72	21
All women	45	47
Working women	58	33
Working men	72	21
Nonworking women	31	62
Nonworking men	73	21
Working women with children	50	40
Working men with children	70	23
Working women without children	69	24
Working men without children	74	19
Women by age		
18–29	56	37
30–44	47	44
45–64	39	51
65 and older	32	63
White women	42	50
Black women	61	30
Liberal women	55	39
Moderate women	52	41
Conservative women	35	58
Professional and managerial women	63	27
Professional and managerial men	70	21
Blue-collar women	43	49
Blue-collar men	70	22
Women teachers or nurses	60	32
Other white-collar women	65	26
Women making below $10,000	53	36
Women making $10,000–20,000	62	32
Men making below $20,000	68	24
Women making over $20,000	62	28
Men making over $20,000	77	17

SOURCE: *New York Times,* Dec. 4, 1983, p. 67.

a. Respondents were asked: "If you were free to do either, would you prefer to have a job outside the home or would you prefer to stay home and take care of your house and family?"

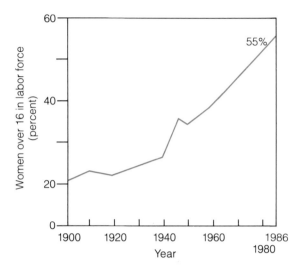

FIGURE 11·1

The participation of women over age 16 in the labor force, 1900–86. (Source: U.S. Bureau of Labor Statistics, 1986a; Thornton and Freedman, 1983)

percent said they preferred the job, while 40 percent said they would prefer to stay home (*New York Times*, Dec. 4, 1983; Littrell, 1986a). In a study of 317 mothers of infants, researchers interviewed the mothers whose babies had just been born and had them complete questionnaires three months later. The majority of new mothers sampled believed that they alone could best meet their children's needs. At the first interview almost 70 percent of the mothers said they would rather stay home with the baby than seek outside employment; after three months this proportion had risen to 75 percent (Hock et al., 1984).

Clearly, a significant proportion of homemakers enjoy their work. And a number of employed women would rather be full-time homemakers but, presumably because of financial constraints, do not have this option. When social scientist James Wright analyzed the results of six national surveys conducted during the 1970s, he found little evidence of dislike for housework, and some homemakers expressed an unqualified liking for their role (Wright, 1978). The critical difference between full-time homemakers who enjoy their work and those who don't is choice. Satisfied homemakers are women who don't want to work for wages (Fidell

and Prather, 1976) and who are exercising their preference to work in the home.

The social status of homemaker is ambiguous at present. On the one hand, the high proportion of women in the labor force, along with the prevailing image of the successful woman as professionally employed, has made the homemaker choice seem atypical and in need of defense. On the other hand, many women—including feminists—make valid claims for the social worth of homemaking. Creating a loving, supportive environment for people is of greater intrinsic value, they argue, than most paid jobs. What is demoralizing about being a homemaker is primarily that society defines it as unimportant. Still, many women are leaving this role. In the next section we'll look at working women and their effect on marriage.

The Employed Wife

Figure 11·1 depicts twentieth-century women's participation in the labor force as paid employees. It is important to remember, however, that not only throughout this century but prior to it, women engaged in productive work other than paid employment. As farm wives, for example, they raised and sold produce and dairy products. Women were the "moms" in "mom and pop" stores. They did piecework at home, took in sewing and laundry, and managed boardinghouses. This section, however, deals primarily with the wife who is employed outside her home.

As Figure 11·1 shows, women's participation in the labor force has increased greatly since the turn of the century. This trend accelerated during the war years and the Great Depression, then slowed following World War II. As soldiers came home to jobs, the government encouraged women to return to their kitchens. As part of this process, the full-time homemaker and mother was idealized in movies and magazines. The number of wage-earning women continued to rise during the 1940s and 1950s, but the growth was not as dramatic. However, beginning in about 1960, the number of employed women began to increase rapidly. That trend continued through 1979, when for the first time a majority of women were employed outside the home (U.S. Bureau of the Census, 1979). In 1986, 55 percent of women over 16 were employed or looking for work (U.S. Bureau of Labor Statistics, 1986a).

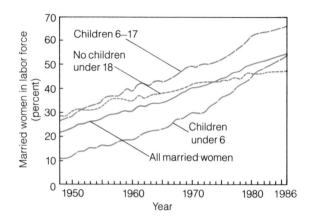

FIGURE 11·2

Participation in the labor force on the part of married women, 1948–86. (Source: Thornton and Freedman, 1983; U.S. Bureau of Labor Statistics, 1986c)

Throughout most of this period the largest group of wage-earning women were young (age 20–24), and relatively few women worked during child-rearing years. The picture has changed in the decades since 1950, however; there has been a dramatic increase in wage earning for women age 35–54 (Frieze et al., 1978:152). In 1982 almost 60 percent of women age 45–54 earned wages, compared with 32 percent in 1950 (Waite, 1981). While women were still leaving their jobs to rear young children, they were now returning by about age 35. Figure 11·2 shows that by 1986, 68 percent of wives with children between 6 and 17 earned wages.[3]

Although this trend is generally true for all women, the rate of increase has been greater for white than for nonwhite older women workers. Black women, the largest group of nonwhite women in the United States, have historically been more likely to work for wages than have white women (Spitze, 1984). These differential increases for the two groups mean that caucasian women are now beginning to catch up with black women (Gump, 1975).

3. The fact that this figure surpasses the number of married working women with no children younger than 18 reflects the older age of that group, on the average, which signifies a difference both in employability and in attitudes about being employed.

The last women to move into employment outside the home, mothers of small children, have been entering the labor force in increasing numbers. As Figure 11·2 illustrates, a slight majority of wives with children under age 6 in 1986 were paid employees (U.S. Bureau of Labor Statistics, 1986b). By 1986 almost 51 percent of married mothers with children under age 3 had joined the labor force. A little less than half (49.4 percent) with children less than a year old had done so (U.S. Bureau of Labor Statistics, 1986c). Formerly, mothers of small children were likely to work only in situations of economic hardship, but the recent trend toward working for pay has extended to women whose husbands are in the highest income quartile. (Since 1960, in fact, the largest increase in participation in the labor force has been among wives of high-income husbands.) The number of working mothers of preschool children in this group increased 168 percent between 1960 and 1977 (Chapters 12, 13, and 16 also address issues concerning mothers in the labor force. Issues related to day care and employed parents are addressed in Chapter 13.)

Pink-Collar Work Although more and more women are working, most of them earn low wages at "pink-collar" jobs. Figure 11·3 depicts the percentages of women workers in ten occupational categories. Over one-third of all employed women are clerical workers, and service workers (including workers in private households) make up another 19.8 percent of the female labor force. Only about 7 percent of employed women are in managerial or administrative positions. Almost two-thirds of all working women are clerks, saleswomen, waitresses, or hairdressers. Moreover, jobs are sexually segregated even within occupational categories. For example, of the professional and technical workers in 1985, about 73 percent of the non-college teachers were female, while 93 percent of engineers were male. Likewise, two-thirds of commissioned sales workers were men, while about the same proportion of the generally lower-paid retail sales positions were held by women (U.S. Bureau of the Census, 1987, Table 657, p. 385). In short, "Occupational segregation by sex is as widespread now as it was at the turn of the century" (Waite, 1981:26).

Women workers are concentrated in low-paying occupations. And despite demands of the women's movement for equal pay for equal work, the discrepancy in pay for employed men and women per-

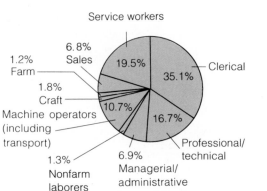

FIGURE 11·3

The jobs women hold, 1980. (Source: U.S. Department of Labor, Bureau of Labor Statistics, 1980; Hacker, 1983, Tables 4 and 5, p. 131)

sists, primarily due to job segregation (see Hacker, 1986). Women who worked full-time in 1986 earned about sixty-nine cents for every dollar earned by men (U.S. Bureau of Labor Statistics, 1986b). Because black men are relatively disadvantaged, the gap between black women's and men's earnings is less than the earnings gap between white men and women. Black women earn 80 percent of the amount earned by black men, while white women earn only 66 percent of what more privileged white men earn (U.S. Bureau of the Census, 1986b; 1984 data). Bureau of Labor Statistics demographer Nancy Rytinn concludes that "a substantial chunk of the wage gap is... due to discrimination" (in Quinn, 1983:80). Because of the differential between women's and men's jobs and pay, employed wives on the average contribute only 25–40 percent of the family income. This proportion has been fairly constant since 1970 (Johnson, 1980).[4]

The segregation of "women's work" into low-status, poorly paid jobs in both the public and private spheres points up an important fact: The unpaid homemaker's and the low-paid female employee's plights are interrelated. In the words of Juanita Kreps, former U.S. secretary of commerce:

The low value imputed to women's domestic work may help to explain the similarly low appraisal of the work she does for pay. From the "free" services offered in the home, low-priced services in the labor market called for only a comfortably short step [Kreps and Leaper, 1977:56]. ■

The interrelationship of low-status "women's work" in the public and private spheres is further explained when we look closely at the nature of the services employed women perform. For the most part, women's public jobs consist of teaching children, nursing, and being clerical and professional helpmates to "more important" employees—work analogous to the traditional woman's role in the home. Put another way, women tend to be employed in female-dominated occupations. Eighty percent of women employees work in only 25 of the 420 jobs listed by the Department of Labor (U.S. Congress Subcommittee on Human Resources, Civil Service Compensation, and Employee Benefits, 1983).

Researchers disagree on why females remain segregated in a limited number of occupations. One explanation, of course, is discrimination on the part of employers. On the other hand, women may aspire to traditionally female occupations because they believe these are the only ones open to them. Still another view holds that women tend to put wife and mother roles first and thus consciously trade off higher wages and advancement for the reduced demands that traditional female occupations sometimes make. Even women who show a lifetime commitment to work "are not in occupations that are substantially less segregated than those of women with intermittent work patterns, nor do they earn substantially higher wages" (Waite, 1981:28).

Whatever the reason for women's concentration in female-dominated, low-paying occupations, the disparity in status and pay between most men's and women's employment affects husbands' and

---

4. Interestingly, there is a tendency for higher-income men to be married to higher-income women, and one of the effects of the trend toward dual-earner families is increasing inequality between families with two high-status, high-pay "careers" and those with two poorly paid jobs (Carol, 1983). Families depending on one woman's income fare worse economically, a problem addressed in Chapter 16.

■   While women—including mothers of small children—increasingly join the labor force, most of them are employed in low-paying clerical and service work. This woman is not a secretary, however; she's an attorney and executive director of the Mexican-American legal defense fund.

wives' power within the family.[5] Later in this chapter we'll look at other reasons why serious pursuit of a career is more difficult for wives than for husbands.

Why Wives Work   If women's work in the public sphere resembles the homemaker's role in status and expectations, why do wives work? There are a number of explanations.

Many wives work because they need to, not because they want to. Table 11·2 lists employed women's responses to a 1986 *Newsweek* poll that asked why they worked. Over half—56 percent—of the women said they worked "for the money" rather than "for other reasons, such as strong interest in what you do or because a job gives you a sense of identity" (*Newsweek*, March 31, 1986, p. 51). Among women with no college education, 65 percent said they were working "for the money"; for clerical and sales workers, that proportion was 68 percent. With a constricting economy, some women who would like to stay home can't rely on their husband's wage-earning ability and must help support their families.

As an economic analyst notes, "Without the enormous influx of women into the job market, the impact of inflation on our living standards would be far more severe"; working spouses are "unemployment insurance" (Malabre, 1978). For example, wives' paychecks make it possible for families who otherwise could not qualify for a loan to buy homes (Fuller, 1984). A growing number of people believe that both spouses should earn wages. "Some Americans now expect rather than discourage outside employment for wives" (Thornton and Freedman, 1983:25).

5. Never married and divorced and separated women work too, of course, and many of them—particularly divorced women—are combining work and family. This is discussed in Chapter 16.

TABLE 11·2 Why Women Work[a]

Do you work more for the money or for other reasons, such as a strong interest in what you do or because a job gives you a sense of identity?

	Money	Other
Total working women	56%	41%
College grads	36	59
No college	65	33
By occupations:		
Blue collar	60	37
Clerical and sales	68	29
Professional and business	40	57

SOURCE: *Newsweek*, March 31, 1986, p. 51.

a. The Gallup Organization interviewed 1,009 women 18 years and older by telephone in February 1986. Some "Don't know" answers are omitted. The margin of sampling error is plus or minus 4 percent. The Newsweek Poll © 1986 by Newsweek, Inc.

Other reasons wives become employed are that they do not like housekeeping and that they feel they can put their talents and abilities into more profitable use. Women who earned wages before having children are more likely to reenter the labor force than wives and mothers who did not (Scanzoni, 1976; Gordon and Kammeyer, 1980). This is also true of women who can get higher-prestige jobs (Hiller and Philliber, 1980). Although women in lower-income families are more apt to work than women in higher-income families, wives who can get higher-status jobs are more attracted to the labor force. As Table 11·2 shows, 59 percent of college-graduated women told *Newsweek* they worked outside their homes for reasons other than money.

Still another reason that a wife may join the labor force is related to the discussion of conjugal power in Chapter 10. Research shows that wage earning enhances a wife's self-esteem, power, and influence on the couple's decisions. Some wives say they work for the feeling of independence and autonomy that wage earning brings. Those who took a job over a husband's opposition often believe it was "worth the risk" (Ferree, 1976). Freedom of choice is, of course, a key element, but if a wife works because she wants to, she is better satisfied

with her marriage than either homemakers or employed wives who wish they were not working (Safilios-Rothschild, 1970).[6]

An additional factor contributing to the rising number of wives taking jobs is that couples are having fewer children. Thus, one of the major and most satisfying aspects of the homemaking role—child care—occupies fewer years, and many wives find the decreasing homemaker role less fulfilling as they grow older (Bart, 1972). Related to this is the fact that people are living longer. As one homemaker who had recently taken a cashier's job explained:

One day it just dawned on me: When my kids are gone, I'm going to be one of *those* mothers—the ones who just sit around with nothing to do. For so many years, it seemed as if every day was spent getting ready for something that involved one of the kids, and I realized that they were not only spreading out, one of these days they really will be gone and I'll have nothing because I have done very little for myself [in Garrett, 1978:60]. ■

TWO-PAYCHECK COUPLES

Not only do people believe that both spouses should earn wages, but their life-styles reflect this expectation. In 1986 55 percent of all marriages were **two-paycheck marriages**; in only 20 percent of marriages did the husband alone earn wages. (In the remaining marriages there were either no wage earners (13 percent), due perhaps to retirement

6. Even employed wives, however, may experience a marriage based on traditional family work roles. According to one study, employed wives are more likely than husbands "to characterize their relationship as being like two separate people rather than like a couple. They express considerably more dissatisfaction and frustration with the relationship than do men. In comparison to husbands, [employed] wives feel more inadequate in their parenting, experience more infrequent marital interaction—whether conversational or physical, and are more upset by marital conflict. They are also more likely to feel irritated by their spouses' behavior, to feel misunderstood and to feel their spouses should express more of their thoughts and feelings.... The fact that these effects occur regardless of whether or not the wife works suggests that the assumption that employment in and of itself is a solution to features of married life that are problematic for women is erroneous" (Locksley, 1980:345).

or unemployment; or the husband did not earn wages while a second family member did (5 percent); or the husband and another family member worked but not the wife (7 percent) (U.S. Bureau of Labor Statistics, 1986c.) Even as far back as 1968, there were equal percentages (45 percent) of dual-earner and traditional-earner couples (Hayghe, 1982). This pattern, then, is no longer unusual; it is the statistical norm.

This is not to say, however, that two-paycheck unions present no problems for couples. For one thing, not all employed wives feel the same way about working outside their homes. Among some couples the wife and husband both wish the wife didn't have to work. Other wives would like to quit working but their husbands encourage them to keep their jobs. For still other wives, working is what both they and their husbands want. And finally, some wives are working because they want to, even though their husbands don't like it (Bird, 1979c:35–37).

In *Worlds of Pain* marriage and family counselor Lillian Rubin describes the resistance of many working-class husbands to their wives' working or going to school. One husband said:

I think our biggest problem is her working. She started working and she started getting too independent. I never did want her to go to work, but she did anyway. I don't think I had the say-so I should have [1976:177]. ▪

"Especially among working-class couples in which the wife works out of economic necessity" (Rubin, 1983: 71–72), the husband may see his wife's "having to work" as indication of his personal inadequacy; that is, he feels he has failed to be a "good provider" (Bernard, 1986).

While working-class husbands who disapprove of their wives' working are often more straightforward about it, middle-class and professional husbands sometimes feel the same way. They accept the situation reluctantly, "out of a sense of fair play, of wanting to see the wife happy, or out of resignation to the inevitable" (Burke and Weir, 1976:285). But as we saw in Chapter 10, husbands' authority decreases when their wives go to work. "The husband may have to deal with a diminished sense of self-worth . . . whereas the wife's sense of self-worth is likely to be enhanced" (Burke and Weir, 1976:285).

On the other hand, the mainly positive reactions that may occur if a wife returns to work or school are illustrated by several studies. One study of 361 relatively affluent suburban homemakers who had returned to school (two-thirds of them had been full-time homemakers) found that the wives perceived their husbands to be emotionally supportive but not likely to help with household responsibilities (Berkove, 1979). Another study, of twenty-four husbands of women who had returned to school, found that "men's self-esteem was either somewhat improved or unaffected by their wives assuming the student role" and "not one man said he felt worse" (Hooper, 1979:460). The husbands also reported enhanced self-esteem on the part of their wives. While the men denied that they worried about their relationship with their wives, responses to open-ended questions did indicate some concerns:

"She's so involved. She studies like crazy. We have to do more around here, and she's got some weird ideas," said one husband of a graduate student. Another commented that "there's been quite a change in that we don't do as many things together as we used to. I'm kind of jealous of the time I have at home, and school has taken that away." One man wondered, "If she gets a job, who moves where?" [Hooper, 1979:460]. ▪

Some evidence suggests that younger husbands are less inclined to experience jealousy over wives' involvement outside the home. In one longitudinal study (Spitze and Waite, 1981) 1,069 wives age 14–24 in 1968 were interviewed yearly, with attitude and behavior measures, from 1968 to 1972. (Eighty-eight percent of them were mothers.) The researchers concluded that during the early years of marriage, husbands revise their attitudes toward whether their wives should work. They revise these attitudes "to conform to their wives' attitudes and preferences" (123), so that husbands who might initially have opposed their wives' working when the children were small change their minds. In the words of the authors, "husbands seem to have little to lose and much to gain through their wives' employment. Bringing their wives' employment into line with their own preferences could be costly, but a change in attitudes is cheap" (123). Contradictory evidence about husbands' satisfaction in sharing the breadwinner role tends, however, to be more heavily weighted in the positive direction. In one study husbands of working wives reported more mutual give-and-take in disagreements, but less

■ But does he do windows? Although some husbands help out with some household chores, women continue to do most housework, even when both spouses are employed. Who does what depends not as much on ability as on a willingness to take time for chores. To many men, vacuuming—which relies on a machine—is a more acceptable task than scrubbing the bathroom.

happiness with their marriages and poorer mental and physical health (Burke and Weir, 1976). But a study conducted by Alan Booth (1977), who criticized the methodology of the Burke and Weir study, found that husbands and wives are adapting well, with few differences between husbands of working and nonworking wives. Where differences existed, they favored the husbands of working wives, who were more apt to report that the spouse is "just as loving" and "not more critical," who were less likely to have an infectious disease, and who received more favorable mental health ratings. Booth's conclusion:

Conservatively, we may conclude that wife's employment does not contribute to the marital discord or stress experienced by the husband. From a less conservative point of view, we may conclude that wife's employment has beneficial effects on the husband. While there is no doubt that wives, and probably husbands, go through a period of adjustment that is stressful when the woman first joins the labor force, our evidence suggests that it is short-lived. The added income

and the greater personal fulfillment the wife and *probably* the husband eventually enjoy far outweigh the short-term disadvantages which female employment may bring to the couple [1977:649]. ■

Similarly, a more recent report of research based on national survey data found "no evidence . . . for any effect of wives' employment or degree of interest in their work activity on marital adjustment and companionship whether determined on the basis of husbands' or wives' responses" (Locksley, 1980:345).

Wives' Employment and Sharing Homemaking

Wives' employment sometimes modifies both spouses' ideas about housekeeping responsibilities but not their actual behavior. Studies of time budgets indicate that husbands contribute about the same time to family tasks whether their wives are

BOX 11 · 1

CONFLICT THEORY: WHY WIVES DO THE HOUSEWORK

Conflict theory involves the idea that various individuals and groups in a society have different interests, and these may be in conflict. This may seem obvious, but in fact, social scientists tended in the past to see only the harmony in society. They emphasized the way in which the established social order functioned efficiently to ensure societal survival. They overlooked the way in which social patterns that benefited some disadvantaged others, generally the less powerful. In most societies life is more pleasant for powerful people than for others.

Conflict theory applied to the family challenges our image of the family as a harmonious group. It questions the assumption that what is good for "the family" is good for everyone in it. In particular, it makes us aware that the family may be structured to benefit men more than women.

Power is an important concept in conflict theory. More powerful groups or interests dominate less powerful ones. In particular, men dominate women, and adults dominate children. (The application of conflict theory to adult-child or parent-child relations is complex, however, because some parents are women and thus have less power. Also, the "power of the weak," infants, for example, to compel action from caretakers is well known.)

Physical force compels the subordination of men to women in some cases, and family violence (see Chapter 10) is a topic that clearly lends itself to analysis in a conflict framework. In most cases socialization and cultural pressures from the media (Richardson, 1981) or psychiatry (Chesler, 1972), not to mention friends and family, are sufficient to maintain this subordination.

Conflict theory goes beyond intellectual analysis to generate action, and subordinate groups are urged to mobilize power on their own behalf. To do this, the group's consciousness of its exploitation must be revised, hence the consciousness-raising groups of early feminism (Richardson, 1981). Conflict

---

employed or not (Walker, 1970; Meissner et al., 1975; Robinson et al., 1976; Pogrebin, 1983; Schooler et al., 1984; Pleck, 1985). Box 11·1, "Conflict Theory: Why Wives Do the Housework," discusses some reasons for this. Precise figures are of interest here. Unemployed wives spend an average of 8.1 hours a day in family work, their husbands 1.6 hours. Employed wives spend an average of 4.8 hours a day in family work, their husbands 1.6 hours (Walker and Woods, 1976; Pogrebin, 1983). Partly because husbands have tended not to increase their help with housekeeping chores in proportion to their wives' employment, newspapers and women's magazines abound with such articles as "How Do You Get a Husband to Help with Housework?"

Meanwhile, high-income, dual-earner families allocate more of their income to goods and services designed to assist the wife by reducing time spent on food preparation, laundry, and child care (Strober, 1977, in Hayghe, 1982a). It is worth noting that such families often hire other women at low wages to do such chores. Rather than equally sharing domestic tasks with her spouse, as we often assume the working career wife will do, she "has instead managed to perform two roles through the skillful allocation of her own time and energies and effective utilization of the labor of other women" (Hunt and Hunt, 1982:44).

Wives who work part-time usually have a somewhat easier time combining their two roles. Because

theory, by the way, is a very loose umbrella term. Marxism and many feminist theories would be considered conflict theories.

While we might have introduced conflict theory in Chapter 10 on power, we prefer to insert it here because the issue of who does the housework so clearly indicates the conflict of interest of men and women within the family. Both, presumably, want a clean house. Both may also want to work outside the home; the husband may very well want his wife to work for the money or for her fulfillment. But given the drudgery of most housework (an assumption of most analyses of this problem), neither wants to do it. Nevertheless, most women end up doing it even though responsibility for housework has been demonstrated to be a handicap for women's careers (Huber and Spitze, 1983).

Why? Because, according to this analysis, men have more power and they don't want to do housework. Even though a majority of wives work and a large proportion of men and women believe in shared marital tasks in principle, many women continue to bear the burden of housework.

Users of conflict theory usually move beyond the family to look for explanations of differential power in the larger society. Men, of course, are more likely to have high-status, high-paying jobs and therefore tend to have more power in the family (there is some overlap here with exchange theory). Whether "capitalism" "patriarchy," or some other force bears the responsibility for this situation is open to debate (Richardson, 1981).

Conflict theory may be used to analyze other relationships within the family or other family-related issues. For example, the need of career women for inexpensive household help creates an interest in maintaining a subordinate class of women who will do this work. The subordinate position of blue-collar or lower-class men in our society makes it difficult for these men to support families and creates pressures that contribute to marital tensions.

---

of this, part-time workers were more satisfied with their lives and marriages than full-time workers (Ferree, 1976). Wives employed full-time sleep less well and also have less free time than their husbands (Robinson, 1977). Furthermore, many husbands are not motivated to change, because they view their work not as self-realization or a separate activity but as their primary contribution to the family (Lein, 1979). And wives are not always comfortable with requesting, demanding, or even receiving unsolicited help, regardless of their task load:

I am the type of person that felt laundry, chores, etc.... were my responsibility and I would get frustrated a lot because I never had any free time for myself. My family was willing to help if I asked, but I didn't feel I had the right to ask [Berkove, 1979:455]. ■

At this point we have a somewhat discouraging picture of the working wife's life and a rather negative portrayal of husbands. But one social scientist doing research in this area views such a state of affairs as temporary and predicts that the man's family role is now (beginning in the late 1970s and early 1980s) expanding in response to changes in the woman's role. A 1977 study found for the first time that husbands of working women *are* spending more time in child care than husbands of nonworking women, leading the author to an optimistic conclusion:

Men are beginning at last to increase their family work when their wives are employed. There is no question, of course, that wives continue to hold the primary responsibility for family work. But even as this reality is acknowledged, it is important to recognize that men's behavior is changing on important social indicators. The pace of change may seem slow. Yet it should not be dismissed or taken-for-granted [Pleck, 1979:487]. ■

In a subsequent book Joseph Pleck (1985)—still seeing the pace of change as slow—remained optimistic. (Case Study 11·1, "The Changing American Family: From Patriarchy to Democracy," illustrates some of these changes.) Socialization of a new generation should consolidate whatever change occurs.

According to research comparing 1965 with 1975, women in paid employment now have approximately the same amount of leisure as do men. Wives have gained this leisure partly by spending less time on house and child care, and this is partly because most households now contain fewer children. However, women still spend six times as much time on housework and child care as do men (Stafford, 1980).

Here, as elsewhere, choice seems significant. A recent study of husbands who were sharing the household work in two-career families found varied reactions. Those who were helping because of pressure from their wives had marriages that were significantly less happy than those with less role sharing. But those husbands who were committed to the idea of shared roles did not sacrifice marital happiness when they participated substantially in the housework.

At the same time, women who expect their husbands to share housework may react negatively when husbands do not. In a national telephone survey of married couples, sociologists Joan Huber and Glenna Spitze asked women if they had ever considered divorce. They found that those wives who believed housework should be equally shared were more likely to have considered divorce than wives with more traditional views. But the likelihood of a woman's thinking of divorce decreased with each additional task her husband performed at least half the time (Huber and Spitze, 1980).

All in all, the evidence suggests that wives do not go to work to free themselves from housekeeping and child care; they continue to perform these tasks. Rather, wives work for money and for certain intrinsic gratifications. This is true for women in pink-collar jobs and also for career women, who rely on inherent satisfaction of their work to help nourish their self-esteem.

THE TWO-CAREER COUPLE

Careers differ from *jobs* in that they hold the promise of advancement, are considered important in themselves and not just a source of money, and demand a high degree of commitment (Rapoport and Rapoport, 1971:3). While the majority of women work in "early-ceilinged" jobs (Hall and Hall, 1979), career women hope to climb the occupational ladder. Career women work in occupations such as medicine, law, politics, banking, and company management that usually require education beyond the bachelor's degree.

The vast majority of two-paycheck marriages can hardly be classified as dual-career. Indeed, "the most significant occupational developments in the post–World War Two period in the U.S.A. have been the growth of adult women's employment in clerical, lower level professional and service jobs" (Benenson, 1984:30). Nevertheless, today's college students apparently view the **two-career marriage** as an available and workable option. A 1984 Carnegie Foundation national survey of undergraduates found that almost 96 percent of the women saw both "career success" and "a good marriage" as important. Among the men, 98.4 percent and 94 percent, respectively, saw career success and a good marriage as important. Eighty-six percent of college women and 85 percent of the men viewed raising children as important ("College Students" 1986:27–31). Increasingly, however, experts are pointing out—both from research and from personal experience—that expecting to "have it all" in a two-career marriage, particularly one with children, may be unrealistic (Hunt and Hunt, 1986; Hewlett, 1986).

The Two-Career Family in a One-Career World

The earlier discussion of the two-person single career suggests that a career is not an individual phenomenon. Rather, it is a life-style that largely

■ The phrase *two-career family* suggests that a wife and husband are equal partners in terms of employment. While they may share child care and chores—or hire others to help—such couples rarely give equal weight to their work. The husband's career tends to take precedence.

depends for its success on the active assistance of one's spouse (Hunt and Hunt, 1977). Research on couples in which one or both held a doctorate degree found that, for both husbands and wives, marriage to a similarly educated (and career-oriented) spouse had some negative effects on career advancement. Wives with Ph.D.'s whose husbands also had doctorates participated less in the labor force than did other women who held Ph.D.'s. Doctorate-holding husbands whose wives also had Ph.D.'s held fewer offices and published fewer articles than husbands whose wives did not have doctorates (Ferber and Huber, 1979).

These findings suggest that careers rest on the "assumption that there will be only one career in the family and that interests of other family members will be subordinated to it" (Holmstrom, 1972:29). To the extent that a man's family

(1) does not positively help him in his work or (2) makes demands on his time and psychic energy that compete with those devoted to his job, they lower his chances for survival. This is true insofar as he is competing with other men whose wives either aid them or do not interfere with their work [Hochschild, 1975:67]. ■

The two-career marriage is hectic and often tense as partners juggle schedules, chores, and child care. "Career and family involvement have never been

CASE STUDY 11·1

THE CHANGING AMERICAN FAMILY: FROM PATRIARCHY TO DEMOCRACY

Marilyn, age 36, has been married sixteen years and has two children, Todd, 14, and Tracy, 11. In 1977 she began a T-shirt printing business, which has become very successful. Her husband, Don, is a stockbroker. Here Marilyn talks about some of the changes she and Don have experienced in moving from a traditional to a dual-career family. She begins by talking about her business.

Marilyn: We're getting progressively bigger! I have increased my office and printing space. Everything is growing. I have to get more equipment. Any time you do that, it's scary. But I'm getting more and more confident and at home with [the business]. It's part of my life now. I honestly don't know what I'd do without it. . . .

Don does a lot with the business too. He makes all the silk-screens and helps with the ordering and the mailings. He does a little bit of everything, so we really do it together—although I probably get more out of it. I get the ego trip!

One of the positive things [Don gets] is that he no longer has full responsibility for the family finances. In fact, he's beginning to talk about doing some things that he would not be able to do if it weren't for this: making some changes with his career—maybe having some kind of retail shop of his own. He doesn't want anything big; he just wants to be more his own boss.

Interviewer: Have you and Don made changes in your household work routines?

Marilyn: (*smiling broadly*) One time we went out and tried to discuss this rationally. We drank a lot of sherry, but basically it worked out that Don is never going to really share responsibility for the housework with me. He says he's not opposed to helping. But he's so inept—purposely—that it's easier if he doesn't do it. So he does other things.

He's a [fifth grade] room parent this year. They had always been called room *mothers*, but Don had them change that.

Interviewer: What made Don decide to be a room parent?

Marilyn: He just felt he was missing something by not.

Interviewer: Did you convince him of that?

Marilyn: No, I don't think so. One day he said, "Well, you did it, so I'll do it."

Now the trouble *I* have is with the other room mothers: They call *me*. One mother called me at my office about a [classroom] Halloween party. I said, "Call *Don* at *his* office." "Oh, no," she said, "I couldn't do that!" Well, she finally did call him and put him in charge of games. That was fine with him— he loves games. But then she called *me* again and asked me to bake cupcakes.

Don is really great with the kids. He coaches basketball and soccer. And he runs a lot of the errands, because I hate to do that. He does all that. He took the dog to the vet the last time. He cleaned the refrigerator last week because it bugged him, but it wasn't bugging me yet. So it gets down to this maybe: The things that bug each of us the most when they're dirty, we clean. He was doing the wash for a while, but not any more. He realized it was as much of a problem as I'd said it was. Well, just the knowledge of that helps. Now if it doesn't get done, I don't hear a lot about it. . . .

I still have the lion's share of [the housework], but I also get in a bad mood about it and he understands that a bit more than he used to. Things change little by little, you know. . . .

Things were very traditional in the beginning. He was the breadwinner, although I had a job and mine paid more than his did in the very beginning. But mine was always considered to be temporary. I had a college degree, but I didn't do anything with it. I did whatever I could to make the most money at the time, so I was a secretary.

I could have done something in my field, except the one job available to me—it involved traveling, being gone more than one day at a time. I didn't even consider it, because I felt that if I was getting married, I couldn't do that—whereas now that wouldn't stop me. So there's a change. . . .

Those first years were tough. I had Todd a year after we were married. I quit working then, except for Saturday mornings, and I was home the majority of the time. . . .

Well, that's the time when Don was very much involved with his career—almost totally concerned with it. He spent a lot of evenings away from home, engrossed in his job. As I look back on it now, I can almost understand it. Having a career myself helps me to understand it. You reach a certain high in your day—things click and people click and there's a certain level of activity that you reach—it's feeling that things are moving, and that you're moving with them. And it would be very hard to come home to a wife and a baby who had done nothing more interesting than scrub a floor.

I can see that now, but at the time what I wanted more than anything was to nurture that whole feeling of home. I was into decorating the house and being the mother of a preschooler and all of that. I wanted Don to come home and share that with me. He probably wanted me to come out and share what he was doing with him. We were in different places—there was a lot of unhappiness during that time. We were separate about how we felt about things. I think it is hard for a relationship to continue that way. . . .

■ How is this relationship becoming more democratic? How is it still traditional or patriarchal? Do you think Marilyn and Don are happier now than when they were first married? Why? How do other social institutions—in this case, schools—reinforce people's attitudes and behaviors in their families? What are some big and little choices Marilyn and Don have apparently made over the years about their marriage and family? How are Don and Marilyn changing attitudes in the larger society, that is, in their community?

combined easily in the same person" (Hunt and Hunt, 1986:280). Research shows that wives bear the brunt of this overload, yet husbands also feel taxed with housekeeping responsibilities (Miller, 1977). In one assessment "this may explain why power-motivated men do not live in [two-career marriages]" (Winter et al., 1977). The public nature of careers—the requirement to entertain, for example, or to be available as a couple to attend career-related events—disadvantages the man whose wife pursues a career of her own.

At the same time, because society encourages a couple to have one career—the husband's—career wives are more disadvantaged than husbands. Career women often find themselves in a catch-22 situation. The career world tends to view the person who splits time between work and family as being less than professional (Holmstrom, 1972), yet society encourages working women to do exactly this: "When there is a crisis for a child at school, it is the child's working mother rather than working father who will be called to take responsibility" (Pleck, 1977:423).

A negative cycle emerges: The woman's work role is expected to be more vulnerable to family demands than the man's work role. This gives employers reason to pay women less than men. This lower pay, coupled with society's devaluation of family in favor of job demands, encourages husbands to see their wives' work as less important than their own—and to conclude that they really shouldn't be asked to take responsibility for home-making. And even though research consistently shows that the husbands of successful career women tend to be supportive, the woman's career often takes second place.

Career Marriages: Equal Partnerships?

In 1970 social scientists interviewed fifty-three couples in which the wife was an attorney, a medical doctor, or a college professor. Their findings, and subsequent ones, provide an interesting profile of the career couple. More recent reviews (Hicks et al., 1983) find that little has changed: "Research [from] ... the 1970s ... served to substantiate earlier findings, pointing to the ... potential for stress [see also Rapoport and Rapoport, 1978] and noting

that by and large the husband's career still takes priority over the wife's" (Hicks et al., 1983:168).

In general, the career wives in the study of professional couples played down the importance of their careers relative to their husbands'. Couples considered the wife's career to be interesting and important for her self-satisfaction, but her career did not significantly influence decisions such as whether to move to another city. (In fact, none of the couples expected the husband to move to accommodate the wife's career.) The women spent less time in professional activities than did their husbands (eighteen of the women worked part-time); and only ten considered their careers to be equal in importance to their husbands'. Most turned down opportunities for advancement and saw a happy home situation as more important (Poloma and Garland, 1971a, b, c). They also tended to overestimate the minimal support they actually received from their husbands for their career and home-making tasks. The researchers concluded that this misperception on the part of wives masked considerable deviation from the ideology of equality that many said they believed in.

Another study contrasted twenty "professional" couples (in which both spouses pursued careers) with seven "traditional" couples (in which the wife held an advanced degree but had limited her career significantly) (Holmstrom, 1972). The "professional" husbands helped more with household tasks and child rearing than did "traditional" husbands (the professional group was also more likely to hire housekeeping help); and in twelve of the fifteen cases where the issue of relocation had arisen, the husband's decision was influenced by his wife's career.

There were also some similarities between the two groups. Even among the "professional" couples, in only one-third of the marriages did the husbands help regularly with household tasks; slightly more than two-thirds of the husbands helped regularly with child rearing. If one parent officially modified his or her work schedule to accommodate children, it was typically the wife. And it was still the wives who "made the greater career sacrifices when deciding where to live" (Holmstrom, 1972:38). A subsequent study on a national sample of young, white, female college graduates and their spouses found that the best predictor of whether and where a couple would move was the husband's occupational prestige and opportunities for advancement. The wife's occupational prestige, potential income, and opportunities for advancement did not affect migration decisions of two-career couples (Duncan and Perrucci, 1976).

The Geography of Two Careers

Career advancement often requires geographic mobility. For example, in order to advance and broaden their experience, banking executives in midsize cities may need to relocate to larger banks in larger cities. Attempts to juggle two such careers can prove difficult for couples.

One study (Berger et al., 1978), based on questionnaires of 160 two-career couples holding advanced degrees, along with fifteen supplementary interviews, explored job-seeking strategies. The researchers classified slightly over half the couples as starting out with a strong commitment to egalitarian decision making about job choices and career and geographical mobility. That is, they believed that both partners' interests should and would be considered. But they found that the man had an easier time finding a job—and a better job at that. Consequently, the couple's initial move, and perhaps subsequent moves, favored the husband's career. Moreover, employers, observing that wives tend to follow their husbands, then justify their non- or underemployment of married women "on the grounds that ... women are not as devoted to their own careers as men and will sacrifice them to follow their husbands" (Berger et al., 1978:26–27). Sociologist Glenna Spitze (1984) analyzed national survey data (National Longitudinal Surveys of Young and Mature Women) collected by the Census Bureau to see how moving affected black wives' employment. Not surprisingly, she found that white women's husbands are substantially more likely to be transferred than are black women's husbands. Moreover, black and white wives are equally unlikely to have new jobs lined up at the time of their move. It appears, however, that after moving, black women are more likely to become employed in jobs similar to those they had previously held. In Spitze's opinion:

This may mean that black women, while at a disadvantage in the labor market relative to men and whites, are less likely to be specifically disadvantaged by long-distance family moves than are white women....

However, this also may imply that, as black men become further assimilated into professional and corporate job ladders that tend to involve geographic mobility as an expected component of promotions, black women will increasingly face the problem of tied movement [788]. ■

Besides the options considered by the research just described, still another choice exists for two-career couples—living apart. Sociologists have called marriages in which couples live apart **commuter marriages** or **two-location families.**

Commuter Marriages   Since research began on commuter marriages in the early 1970s, scientists have drawn different conclusions. Some studies suggest that the benefits of such marriages—greater economic and emotional equality between spouses and the potential for better communication—counter its drawbacks. Subsequent research suggests a different view, however, focusing on difficulties in managing the life-style. Case Study 11•2, "Carol and Dean: Two Careers and the Possibility of a Two-Location Family," depicts one couple's battle to avoid work-related separation. However one looks at it, commuter marriages probably work better in the absence of dependent children (Gerstel, 1977).

In one study Harriet Gross (1980) interviewed forty-three spouses, representing twenty-eight unions. The respondents were legally married but lived separately at least four days at a time over a period of at least three months. Relatively affluent, they had been married an average of twelve to thirteen years; about half were in academia either as graduate students or faculty. One of two situations prompted their setting up this life-style: Either they expected to see one another often enough to make the separation tolerable or they saw the separation as necessary, as in the case of one wife who was accepted at only one medical school, which was 1,000 miles from where her husband worked. Gross found that couples who choose to live apart would rather not do so but endure the separation for the sake of career or other goals (1980:570–71). More recent research supports this conclusion (Rhodes and Rhodes, 1984).

Couples who have been married for shorter periods of time seem to have more difficulties with commuter marriages. Younger couples who are simultaneously beginning their careers and their relationship often lack not only experience but also

CASE STUDY 11·2

CAROL AND DEAN: TWO CAREERS AND THE POSSIBILITY OF A TWO-LOCATION FAMILY

Carol, 31, and Dean, 30, are an Air Force couple, married 9 years. Each has been in the military for 13 years and looks forward to retirement on half-salary in another 7 years. They have two daughters: Courtney, 8, and Lindsey, 20 months. They were interviewed together while stationed at Strategic Air Command, Offutt Air Force Base, Bellevue, Nebraska. Here they discuss their reactions to the possibility of being stationed apart.

Carol: One day a few months ago I got a phone call. Your orders come down through a computer system. I had been selected for an assignment in Germany.

When we first got married, there were no problems getting stationed together. In fact, during the mid-seventies the Air Force started a computer program to code married military so that their assignments would automatically come down together. But now there are so many military marrying military that they say it's impossible to match assignments. The Air Force, you know, it's a good job—but they have the philosophy that the job comes first and the marriage and family go second. There's an old joke that if the military wanted you to have a family, they would have issued you one.

We ran into problems with the Germany assignment because they didn't need Dean over there, and it was a very scary feeling when they told me that. . . .

Dean: I think she had mixed emotions. Everyone knows that that area offers so much in traveling and all. That's kind of exciting as long as your whole family can go.

Carol: I went back and forth about taking the children. I decided I had to take Lindsey, then I'd think maybe I shouldn't or couldn't. But I would be leaving on her second birthday and not seeing her again—and *her* not seeing *me* again—until her fourth birthday. She wouldn't know me!

Dean: I thought it would be a good opportunity for the whole family. But just for her to go, no I didn't like that. I think the mother should be near her kids and her husband regardless of whether she works, unless she is forced not to be.

Carol: We have a slight conflict at times with our careers because he grew up with the philosophy that the mother stays home and her job is the home and the children.

Dean: But I'm wise enough to know that that's impossible to do these days.

Carol: And I wouldn't be happy as a housewife. That is not my nature. I worked when I was growing up. I left home to join the Air Force and I have just always worked and the kids have just kinda come along and fallen into the situation. . . .

But, anyway, you know, I finally got out of this assignment. So at this point none of us is going to Germany.

Interviewer: Was there a feeling that Carol should have given up her career rather than take this assignment?

Dean: She couldn't. She can't get out now.

Carol: See, I just reenlisted, so I don't have a choice.

Dean: She signed for four more years. Between now and then they have her. . . . I knew that something like this would happen—and it is going to happen again too. And I felt like since she had gone back to school and gotten a degree, she could get out of the service and still work and make good money. So, no, I didn't want her to reenlist. I think she knew it too.

Carol: Oh, you *think*! He flat out told me! He was pretty open about it. We've always been pretty open with each other, and he told me that he was not happy about [my reenlisting]. But he also said that it was my decision to make. Well, I was in my twelfth year and, you know, if I can stick it out to twenty, we'll have two pensions. With both of us retiring, we'll have the income that a lot of families are living on. We will still have the opportunity to do what we want. . . .

But [over the assignment to Germany] we went through turmoil for a month and a half. Every other day it was a different story. I was in contact with the people who do assignments, and they were trying very hard to get Dean an assignment in Germany too. One day it looked good and we'd feel great, and then I would call back down to check on it, and it wouldn't look good.

Dean: I wanted to say, "I told you not to reenlist. Look what happened."

Carol: I have to give him credit. He never did say it. I was waiting for it, but he never did say it.

■ Most of the research cited in this text is on dual-career couples either in the professions or in academia. How do Carol and Dean differ from two-career academic couples? How are they similar? Is Carol and Dean's an egalitarian marriage or a traditional one? Whose career comes first in your opinion, or are both careers considered equal in importance? What feelings do you get about Dean and Carol's relationship; that is, how do you feel they get along, and why?

information about managing a two-career marriage. Their problem-solving skills may be limited, and conflict at home can be compounded by what Hall and Hall (1979) call "fear of the organization." That is, "many couples are afraid to discuss their problems with a boss or superior in the firm for fear it will reflect negatively on their career commitment. They tend to see company policies as rigid (whether they actually are or not) and to accept corporate alternatives as 'givens' without testing their assumptions" (Hall and Hall, 1979:44).

Perhaps because of their history of shared time, more "established" couples in commuter marriages have a greater "commitment to the unit." While they may have conflicts over child care—especially when the children reside with their father—their feelings of resentment and guilt are less significant. This may be partly because these couples sense that the wives "are correcting an imbalance in the marital relationship" (Gross, 1980:573). The man's career probably did come first once, after all. And now, later in the marriage, it is her turn.

Among other things, this study by Gross points once again to a theme of this text: that those choosing new family patterns should be aware of the influence of cultural expectations on individuals' choices, as well as their feelings about those choices. As the author concludes, "Two-residence living may be an inevitable outcome of women's currently more realizable professional aspirations. But it may not be an effortless response until our ideas about sex, marital and occupational roles catch up with the changes propelling women into careers" (Gross, 1980:575). That our attitudes and behavior need to catch up with wives' entry into careers is also apparent when we explore two-career marriages throughout life.

Two-Career Marriages Throughout Life

Sociology, in keeping with the larger society, has tended to see a husband's career pattern as given: Once a husband enters the labor force, he will remain there full-time until retirement. While there is some discussion of house husbands in the social science literature, that role for men continues to be viewed as an exception rather than the rule in a two-career marriage. Consequently, the literature available today on two-career unions over the

course of life focuses on married professional women.

One source (Poloma et al., 1982) identifies four major career lines among women: *regular, interrupted, second,* and *modified-second.* In a regular career a woman pursues professional training upon finishing high school or college and subsequently begins and continues to work. Regular careers usually involve full-time employment, although part-time regular careers "are also frequent among physicians and attorneys who have the freedom to set up, limit, and build private practices" (Poloma et al., 1982:183). An interrupted career begins as a regular career but is halted for several years, usually for child rearing. Second careers are those in which training for a profession occurs only after or near the time the children are grown and about to leave, or after a divorce. A modified-second career begins earlier; professional training and subsequent career involvement may occur after the last of the children is deemed old enough not to need full-time mothering, usually between the ages of 3 and 7 (Poloma et al., 1982).

While the career pattern of professional wives in the first (regular) category most closely approximates what we might expect of males in the same professions,

almost without exception married professional women with children found it necessary to compromise some of the "extras" of professional demands because of the family. Lectures, evening work, travel, and annual meetings often could not be integrated into their hectic schedules. They found their professional involvement greatly curtailed when their children were younger, gradually increasing as they got older, and leading to greater involvement—with the rewards of professional honors—only after the children had been launched [Poloma et al., 1982:184]. ■

Professional women with interrupted careers choose to limit their work experience for childbearing and rearing. Some are (and see themselves as) temporarily unemployed, while others opt to be professionally involved part-time. Second careers begin later in life but usually with considerable momentum due to the children's older ages; modified-second careers appear to start slowly to accommodate family demands that are still present, then increase in momentum as the children get older (Poloma et al., 1982:184–86).

Whatever her career pattern, the professionally employed wife enters the height of her career after at least her first child has left home. All in all, "marriage does not affect a woman's career line as seriously as having a family" (Poloma et al., 1982:184–86). We can conclude that the biggest differences between two-career and more traditional families are probably *not* qualitative differences in role expectations. Traditional role expectations usually remain in two-career marriages, although often to a modified degree; career wives resign themselves to juggling roles and receiving some help from husbands instead of demanding that homemaking responsibilities be reallocated.

Partly because of this, perhaps, two-career unions are likely to be more compatible when the two jobs allow autonomy and flexibility. Then too, "Two careers are more likely to be compatible if the partners are mutually supportive, skilled at problem solving, and committed to each other's career" (Hall and Hall, 1979:53). The next section explores more of the problems of two-paycheck and two-career marriages and offers some suggestions for dealing with these problems.

ADJUSTING TO THE TWO-PAYCHECK OR TWO-CAREER MARRIAGE

Throughout this chapter we discuss problems associated with two-paycheck or two-career marriages—marriages in which both partners work for wages. But research also points to the heightened satisfaction, excitement, and vitality that such couples can experience, as individuals and in their relationship. Marriages in which both partners work outside the home provide companionship and a sharing of lives facilitated by similar roles. A survey of 842 women and 691 men by the National Opinion Research Center found that wives who were educated to and capable of holding high-status occupations were more frustrated and unhappy with their lives and marriages when they were not employed than were those who were working (Richardson, 1979). In contrast, the study also found that women who had remained in careers and "presumably experienced" both income increases and promotions also experienced increased marital happiness. Furthermore, the data showed no relationship between marital happiness and the couple's perception of which partner had achieved greater occupational prestige (Richardson, 1979). In short, the potential rewards from such marriages make them worthwhile for many couples (Rapoport and Rapoport, 1971).

The two-paycheck or two-career marriage is a choice more and more couples are making. How, then, can they run their lives to provide as much satisfaction as possible within that option? We'll look at two issues: workaholism and overload. Although workaholics may be found in single-career partnerships, we discuss them here because they can be either women or men. Then we will look at some practical adjustments couples are making and offer some suggestions to facilitate that process.

Career Success and the Workaholic

Some people truly love their work and find inherent satisfaction in it, and social scientists generally hold that a satisfying career will probably enhance a relationship, and vice versa. However, devoting time and energy to career success can mean neglecting family relationships. Work can become addictive, as Francine and Douglas Hall conclude, "and over-involvement can destroy a marriage. Many people have discovered painfully that... success was not all it was cracked up to be and being married to the job killed their marriage" (Hall and Hall, 1979:172).

People whose work has become addictive are **workaholics.** For the workaholic, the work life takes over such a large portion of his or her identity and time that it interferes with physical health, personal happiness, interpersonal relationships, and often effective work performance itself (Hall and Hall, 1979:179).

One side effect of workaholism is a malady that at least one psychologist calls **leisure phobia.** People with leisure phobia have trouble enjoying free time. They feel guilty because they aren't "doing" or accomplishing something—which, of course, means doing productive work (Hall and Hall, 1979:182). Furthermore, because developing a loving relationship demands a considerable amount of time, workaholics limit their capacities for intimacy.

Many workaholics may not recognize their condition. An *Esquire* survey found that young professional men in their 20s and early 30s verbally reject the work ethic and profess that "being loving" is more important to them than either "being ambitious" or "being able to lead effectively." Yet these same men were, in fact, working up to twelve hours a day in an effort to make it to the top (Sheehy, 1979). As career advancement becomes more available to women, one can expect that husbands, too, will complain about being ignored by workaholic, leisure-phobic spouses. One study, conducted as a master's thesis in the University of Texas School of Business, analyzed data from 1,500 respondents—88 percent of whom were male—who had received M.B.A.'s from Texas University between 1911 and 1980. Workaholics were operationally defined as those who worked at least 50 hours a week. Compared with 16 percent for male workaholics, 51 percent of female workaholics had never married. In the words of the researcher, the finding "points up again that society has a lot of things to resolve in terms of women working. Definitely it's cutting against the woman and not against the man" ("Study: Success Costlier," 1984).

Some partners use the demands of their work to shield themselves from intimacy because they find self-disclosure and possible rejection too threatening. They may commit themselves to their careers because they don't want to work on a relationship. As one man said,

It's easier to succeed at a career than at a relationship. You get all the rewards and you don't have to give the same things of yourself that you do in a relationship. When push comes to shove, it may be easier to go with a career [in Hall and Hall, 1979:223]. ■

Other people become workaholics by default. Some of these people pay undue attention to external signs of success, such as the admiration of fellow workers or peers, salary, title, and so forth (Hall and Hall, 1979:172; Marks, 1977:931). Others simply love their work.

Another explanation for workaholism may be a real economic need. In today's contracting economy, with more people competing for jobs, some workers, such as university faculty members, find that they have to work harder and produce more just to keep their positions (Easterlin, 1978; Collins, 1979).

Finding a Balance   If obsession with a job keeps one partner from the family, intimacy will be threatened. Hall and Hall suggest that partners who desire both job fulfillment and intrinsic relation-

ships need to consciously make choices about their life-styles. Couples who choose their life-styles by default may find themselves unnecessarily directed by career demands and needs. The organization for which the husband (and increasingly, the wife) works takes charge of their lives. Without thinking about it, the couple values advancement and admiration from colleagues over intimacy.

An alternative is for couples to direct themselves rather than being controlled "by any external force, be it employer, community norms, stereotyped sex roles, or traditional definitions of 'marriage' and 'family'" (Hall and Hall, 1979:17). As Chapter 8 argues, couples who want vital or intrinsic relationships have to choose them deliberately. Such choice diminishes the likelihood that career demands will devitalize the relationship by default. Still, as the next section suggests, overload can be a problem even where workaholism does not exist.

Overload

Working couples often experience stress from role conflict or overload. **Overload** results from having to juggle too many roles and too many demands simultaneously (Hall and Hall, 1979:96). Aspects of work that affect role overload include what demands one's job makes and how much control one has over one's time (Katz and Piotrowsky, 1983). When homemaking and child-care responsibilities conflict with work obligations, the result is often a no-win situation. Whichever obligation the person chooses to meet, he or she may feel anxiety, stress, and guilt about omitting the other, equally important, obligation.

Table 11·3 lists some common overload reactions of employed wives and mothers.[7] These are all immediate responses; the long-term effects can be more serious. Irene Frieze and her coauthors point out that "sustained overload can lead to demoralization and fatigue" and that individuals who allow overload to continue while using the means of coping described in this table are not solving their problem (Frieze et al., 1978:161).

---

7. The concept *role overload* was originally perceived as a woman's problem and, indeed, one message of this chapter is that women continue to bear a heavier burden in duties and sacrifice than do men in two-paycheck marriages. Yet many couples today who are struggling to share family responsibilities while they both work or develop careers will find both husband and wife experiencing these stresses.

TABLE 11·3 Role Overload and Women's Role Performance

Overload Reaction	Wife-Mother's Response
1. Omission: temporarily omitting certain demands	1. Forgetting to pick up the cleaning; not hearing a child's request while talking on the phone
2. Queuing: delaying response during high overload period	2. Promising a child that Mother will talk about his or her problem after dinner; telling someone to call back after the children are asleep
3. Filtering: neglecting to process certain types of information while processing others	3. Neglecting household tasks or elaborate food preparation to take care of children's needs
4. Being less discriminating: responding in a general way to a number of demands	4. Preparing common meals that disregard the food preferences of different family members; having a common bedtime hour for children of different ages; not responding to the unique needs of each child
5. Employing multiple channels: processing information through two or more parallel channels at the same time	5. Talking to children or husband while cooking or ironing; changing a diaper while talking on the phone
6. Errors: processing demands incorrectly	6. Confusing the date of a meeting or social engagement; burning the dinner; yelling at a child for something that she or he had gotten permission to do
7. Escape	7. Going to a movie; falling asleep; leaving home

SOURCE: Frieze et al., 1978:161.

Overload can also sap couples' energy and desire for sex (Johnson et al., 1979; Findlay, 1985).

Instead of juggling too many roles at once, a better solution is to reallocate roles—redefine tasks so that more members of the family can share the workload. There is a difference between helping a spouse perform his or her expected role and reallocating family work responsibilities. Yet, although some families are beginning to reallocate roles, role reallocation is still unusual.

Interestingly, however, family role reallocation is hardly a couple's most radical option. A couple can look for ways to restructure their jobs so that their family and work lives won't be so much at odds. Other possibilities are to remain childless or to emphasize success and performance less in favor of family life. Another solution might come from support given by groups, organizations, or the government itself (Handy, 1978:45).

This last suggestion places marital and family interaction in political context. Indeed, Janet and Larry Hunt, a sociologist dual-career couple, argue (1982, 1986) that in the United States today there is a "differentiation of lifestyles" between those who value more traditional family living and those who give priority to careers. The needs for societal benefits and services, along with the expenses and consumptive patterns, of these two life-styles are different. This situation will "create distinct interest groups that will begin to compete for resources and contend over public policy" (53). A resulting possibility is that

under these conditions, those with families, particularly, will be vulnerable. Their added workload and financial obligations will be treated as lifestyle choices freely made and for which they are individually responsible. While their earning power will be limited by family commitments, they will be expected to absorb personally most of the growing costs of families and/or trade important benefits, such as retirement pensions, for child care or family health insurance [Hunt and Hunt, 1982:53]. ■

But just as cultural definitions and social policy affect family living, so, too, family members can organize to influence social policy through community and political action.

Making Positive Adjustments: Some Suggestions

The first suggestion for adjusting to a two-paycheck marriage is for husband and wife to recognize that each will have both positive and negative feelings. It is never easy to adjust to new roles, and men especially may feel they have a lot to lose. If a man expects to be dominant, he may feel threatened by his wife's move toward equality. A husband may also worry that "if she doesn't need my paycheck, she won't need me"—and if she doesn't need him, she won't love him.

Wives may also be ambivalent. Many women have learned from early childhood to offer acts of submission and unilateral nurturance as proof of their love for a man. As their self-esteem and autonomy increase, they begin to change this view. Typically, conflicting feelings become evident: Wives want their husbands to be happy; they want their husbands to help and support them; they feel angry about past inequalities; and they feel guilty about their decreasing tolerance for submissiveness and declining interest in housekeeping and husband care.

Once partners recognize their ambivalent feelings, the next step is to be open about them (see Chapter 9). Intimate sharing between partners is important, and family meetings and group discussion with several couples can also be beneficial (Hopkins and White, 1978:258). When husbands feel anxious but don't share their anxiety, they tend to resort instead to increased displays of dominance, as if they could *demand* a wife's love. If a husband is honest about his fears, his wife has the opportunity to empathize and to reassure him. Similarly, when wives are not open about their anger and guilt, they may confuse husbands by first angrily demanding that housekeeping responsibilities be reallocated, only later to reassume those responsibilities guiltily. Also, wives may be reluctant to surrender control of their traditional area of dominance—the home (Waite, 1981).

Once partners begin to share their feelings about changing roles, the next step is to empathize. This can be difficult. The changing of roles is impeded not only by husbands' reluctance to relinquish dominance but also by wives' tendency to retaliate for past injustices and hurts. Partners who retaliate rather than empathize are trying to win or "show" the other. But if couples are to maintain intimacy, they must make sure *both* partners win.

After partners commit themselves to empathy, they must create substitute ways for letting each know the other is loved. Traditional role expectations were rigid and limiting, but they sometimes let spouses know they were cared for. For example, when a husband saw to it that the oil was changed in his wife's car, she felt cared about. Conversely, when a wife sewed buttons on her husband's shirt, he felt cared about. As partners relinquish some of these traditional attitudes and behaviors, they need to create new ways of letting each other know they still care.

Getting comfortable with changing roles in marriage is not a quick and easy process. It can take years. Transition characterized by power politics leads to divorce or conflict-habituated marriages. If the transition proceeds from a mutual commitment to the achievement of an equitable, no-power relationship, however, the result can be greater intimacy (Rapoport and Rapoport, 1975).

Summary

The labor force is a social invention. Traditionally, marriage has been different for men and women: The husband's job has been as breadwinner, the wife's as homemaker. These roles are changing as more and more women enter the work force, a trend that has accelerated in the last few decades.

Working wives still usually earn less, often in pink-collar jobs. There are a growing number of two-career marriages, however, where wives and husbands both earn high wages and work for intrinsic rewards. Even in such marriages, the husband's career usually has priority, partly because opportunities for women are still restricted, a public problem that affects private decisions.

We have emphasized that both cultural expectations or definitions and public policy affect people's options. As individuals come to realize this, we can expect increased competition between career-oriented and family-oriented marriages for social resources (Hunt and Hunt, 1982, 1986).

On a more personal level, we are reminded that

the "process of adapting marriage patterns to the requirements and circumstances of our life cycles can be helped along by conscious thought and understanding. We are not totally the creatures of circumstance. Roles and organizations do shape attitudes and behavior but the reverse is also true" (Handy, 1978:44).

People may have ambivalent feelings about changing roles, and the two-paycheck or two-career marriage requires adjustments for both spouses. Role overload and insecurity in the relationship are common. Recognition of both positive and negative feelings and open communication between partners can ease this adjustment.

Key Terms

good-provider role *348*
house husband *352*
two-person single career *354*
two-paycheck marriage *361*

two-career marriage *366*
commuter marriage *371*
overload *376*

Study Questions

1. Discuss the idea that distinctions between husbands' and wives' work are disappearing.
2. Discuss the breadwinner role as it is performed by professional and blue-collar husbands.
3. What happens when men give primacy to work and let their family relationships come second? When women give primacy to work?
4. What do you see as the advantages and disadvantages of men's being house husbands? Discuss this from the points of view of both men and women.
5. How might a two-person single career result in lowered self-esteem for the wife? Can you think of circumstances in which this would be less likely to occur?
6. Discuss the similarities between "women's work" in the public sphere and women's work in the private sphere. If they are so similar, why do women work?
7. What are the critical differences between career wives and husbands and other categories of wives and husbands?
8. Discuss the problems inherent in two-paycheck or two-career families. What influence does the social environment have on these families?

Suggested Readings

Beer, William R.
1982 *House Husbands: Men and Housework in American Families.* New York: Praeger.
One of the few systematic sources of information on house husbands. Includes many insightful quotes from house husbands.

Cardozo, Arlene Rossen
1976 *Woman at Home: A Sourcebook for the Modern Woman Who Chooses to Explore the Potentials of Life at Home.* New York: Doubleday.
How to have a meaningful and productive life as a housewife.

Ehrenreich, Barbara
1983 *The Hearts of Men: American Dreams and the Flight from Commitment.* Garden City, N.Y.: Anchor Press/Doubleday.
A readable and perhaps controversial book tracing the history of men's rejection of the "good provider" role, beginning with *Playboy* magazine in the 1950s.

Gerson, Kathleen
1985 *Hard Choices: How Women Decide About Work, Career, and Motherhood.* Berkeley: University of California Press.
Interesting research on women's work and family choices.

Greenleaf, Barbara F., with Lewis A. Schaffer
1979 *Help: A Handbook for Working Mothers.* New York: Crowell.
Thoughtful, helpful book about practical arrangements and decision making in this area.

Hall, Francine S., and Douglas T. Hall
1979 *The Two-Career Couple.* Reading, Mass.: Addison-Wesley.
How to handle a two-career marriage.

Ogden, Annegret S.
1986 *The Great American Housewife: From Helpmate to Wage Earner, 1776–1986.* Westport, Conn.: Greenwood Press.
A well-written, well-documented historical survey, tracing the history of the housewife role from 1776 to 1986.

Richardson, Laurel Walum
1983 *The Sociology of Sex and Gender.* 3d ed. New York: Houghton-Mifflin.
Excellent chapter on work from a conflict perspective.

Tilly, Louise, and Joan Scott
1978 *Women, Work, and Family.* New York: Holt, Rinehart & Winston.
History of women's work and the relationship of family to work.

12 To Parent or Not to Parent

And now I want a child.
And I want that child to
carry me in his head
forever, and to love me
forever. . . .
Is that a sentence of life
imprisonment?
A lifetime of love?
The way the world is
structured?

JOYCE CAROL OATES, *Do with*
Me What You Will

A remarkable change has taken place in American family patterns. From an all-time high in 1957 the total fertility rate in the United States has reversed itself sharply, and by 1976 it was the lowest ever recorded.[1] It has remained low, fluctuating between 1.7 and 1.9 through 1985. This figure is lower than the previous all-time low (2.1) of the depression years and substantially lower than the peak of 3.6 in 1957 (U.S. Center for Health Statistics, 1987b; Thornton and Freedman, 1983).

This change is related to the fact that married women are waiting longer to have their first baby, allowing more time between births, and choosing to have smaller families than did women in previous decades. In 1982, for example, 63 percent of women age 20–24 were still childless, compared with 50 percent of women in the previous generation. Even more remarkable is the comparison of 37 percent of women age 25–29 who were childless in 1982 and 19 percent for their counterparts in the fifties (Thornton and Freedman, 1983). By 1984, 24 percent of women age 30–34 had not had any children, compared with just 12 percent in 1970 (U.S. National Center for Health Statistics, 1985b).

Beginning in the late fifties, cultural attitudes about ideal family size changed, and couples began to favor families of two children (Blake, 1974). Moreover, cultural attitudes about whether to have children at all have changed in recent years, so that choosing not to parent is more acceptable today.

---

1. Explanation is in order here about birth and fertility rates. The *birthrate,* or **crude birthrate**, as it is technically termed, is the number of births per thousand population. The total number of births and the birthrate depend not only on how many births each woman has but also on how many women of childbearing age there are in the population. For example, in the United States today, the crude birthrate is very low, but there are many women of childbearing age now because the large baby-boom cohort (babies born during the post–World War II baby boom) has reached childbearing age. As a result, the total number of births has risen in recent years, even though the rate of childbearing by individual women has declined drastically.

A more specific measure is the *general fertility rate*, which is the number of births per thousand women in their childbearing years (age 15–44). However, even this statistic does not tell us much about family size.

The **total fertility rate** for a given year—the rate to which we will refer most often in this text—is the number of births that women would have over their reproductive lifetimes if all women at each age had babies at the rate for each age group that year. In reality, this is an artificial figure: the family size that the average woman would have at average childbearing rates provided those rates continued.

A final measure is *completed fertility*; that is, the number of babies per woman of a given cohort (women born in a given year, such as 1946, for example). However, to actually ascertain completed family size, we need to wait until the cohort is 45 or 50 to know what these women's completed fertility is. So, while completed fertility rates might be more accurate, they are long in coming; and the figure most often used to grasp family size is the total fertility rate.

Although the decline in the birthrate actually began before widespread distribution of "the Pill," newer methods of contraception have allowed people to translate their preferences into reality. Being able to make knowledgeable choices makes a great difference is people's attitudes about marriage and, often, in their degree of satisfaction with family life. Throughout this chapter we'll be looking at the choice individuals and couples are making about whether to have children, the pressures and responsibilities that accompany this choice, and the methods available to help people control family size. Among other things we'll see that modern scientific and technological advances have both increased people's options and added new concerns to their decision making. (We'll see, too, that technological progress does not mean that people can or do exercise complete control over their fertility. Options have increased, but some things remain beyond the individual's or couple's control.) To begin, we'll review some United States fertility trends. Then we'll examine the decision whether to parent.

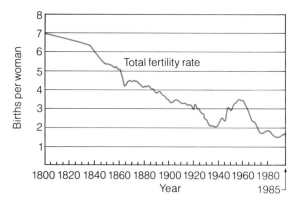

Figure 12·1

Annual total fertility rate, white women (1800–1985). The rate has been declining for over 100 years except for the baby-boom period of the 1940s and 1950s. (Source: Thornton and Freedman, 1983:13; U.S. Bureau of the Census, 1986b; U.S. National Center for Health Statistics, 1985b; 1987b)

FERTILITY TRENDS IN THE UNITED STATES

Declining American fertility appears to be a sudden change when we compare current birthrates to those of the 1950s. But, as Figure 12·1 indicates, the trend is actually a continuation of a long-term pattern dating back to about 1800. Causes of this long-term trend include the fact that alternatives to the motherhood role began to open up with the industrial revolution and the resulting creation of a "labor force" (see Chapter 11). Women could combine productive work and motherhood in a preindustrial economy, but when that work moved from home to factory, the roles of worker and mother were not so compatible (Tilly and Scott, 1978). Consequently, as women's employment increased, fertility declined. Since the 1940s women have entered the labor force in growing proportions, partly in response to an expanding postindustrial economy that required more clerical and service workers. A second cause was declining infant mortality, a result of improved health and living conditions. Gradually, it became unnecessary to bear many children to ensure the survival of a few. Changes in values accompanying these transformations in American society (and in other indus-

trialized societies) made large numbers of children more costly economically and less satisfying to parents (Easterlin and Crimmins, 1985). We will explore this more thoroughly later in this chapter.

In the face of this long-term decline, the rapid surge in fertility in the late 1940s and 1950s requires explanation. It appears that parents who had grown up during the Great Depression, when family goals were limited by economic factors, found themselves as adults in an affluent economy—one that promised support for their own children. Thus, they were able to fulfill childhood dreams of happy and abundant family life to compensate for deprivations previously suffered as children (Easterlin, 1987). The family was so highly valued during this period that marriage and motherhood became primary cultural goals for American women. Men also concentrated their attention on family life.

Family Size

As Figure 12·2 illustrates, women born during the depression years of the 1930s favored larger families. Compared with prior cohorts, many more had "three or four" or "five or six" children. Before this time the trend had been toward smaller families. The percentage of families with five or more children dropped from about 35 percent in the cohort of women born in 1870 to 12 percent for the women

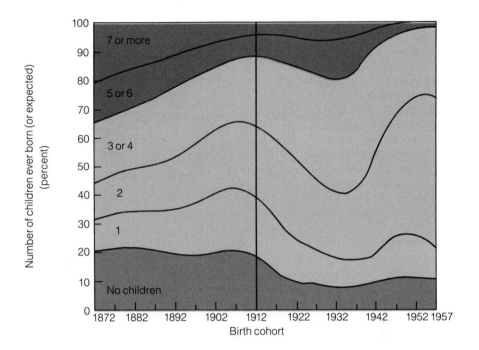

Figure 12·2

Percentage distribution of number of children ever born (or expected), cohorts of white women: 1872–1957. To read the graph for a given year, draw a vertical line above the year, as we have done for the year 1912. Then read the percentages at the curves separating the number of children. So, for all the women born in 1912 (the 1912 cohort), 18 percent of them had no children, 20 percent had one child (38–18 percent), 25 percent had two children (63–38 percent), 25 percent had three or four children (88–63 percent), 7 percent had five or six children (95–88 percent), and 5 percent had seven or more children (100–95 percent). (Source: Thornton and Freedman, 1983:14)

born in 1910. The percentage of one- to three-child families increased from 35 to 60 percent (Thornton and Freedman, 1983:14); this latter figure is not determinable from Figure 12·2.

Today, the growing preference is for two-child families. In fact, this is the principal reason for the current decline in our fertility rate. (The lower fertility rate is due to a drop in married, not unmarried, births. The birthrate for unmarried women has risen, a phenomenon explored later in this chapter.) In response to questions about family size expectations, the majority of women, of all ages, specified two (U.S. Bureau of the Census, 1986b:64).[2] In America today two-child families are

favored, while families of three to four children are tolerated, and larger families tend to be viewed as socially irresponsible (Griffith, 1973). But this general pattern varies according to social class and ethnicity.

Differential Fertility Rates

Fertility rates and decisions whether to parent have both cultural and economic origins. In general, the more highly educated and well-off families have fewer children. They have more money, and they value spending more on their youngsters. They also expect to send their children to college. Moreover, persons with high education or income have other options besides parenting. For example, they may

2. Every June the Census Bureau surveys a national sample of women about their fertility and their birth expectations.

■ At least partly because of prohibitions against birth control, Catholics have tended to have more children, as these two families illustrate. During the baby boom of the 1950s, the Paziks of Pennsylvania had their own baby boom; here they are in 1968, vacationing in the Poconos. Early in this century, the Nerneys, an Irish family from Lowell, Massachusetts, had more children than average. Today, large families are increasingly rare.

be involved in demanding careers or enjoy travel, activities they weigh against the greater investment required in parenthood (Weller and Bouvier, 1983). This tendency for the more highly educated and wealthier to have fewer offspring is characteristic of all racial groups in the United States. Fertility rates for college-educated black women, for example, are even lower than those of college-educated white women (Reid, 1982).

Fertility Rates Among Black Americans At the end of the eighteenth century in this country, white and black women appear to have borne children at approximately the same rates. At about this time, the white population began to reduce its fertility, so that by the end of the nineteenth century, childbearing among whites had declined significantly. The birthrate among blacks, meanwhile, did not decline significantly until after 1880, when

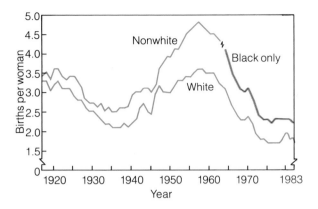

Figure 12·3

Total fertility rates for nonwhite and white women: 1917–83. (The Census Bureau used the category "nonwhite" until 1964, so that black births were combined with Asian, native American, and other nonwhite births. Blacks, however, made up 90 percent of this category, so nonwhite rates can be used as a fairly accurate indicator of black rates. Beginning in 1964, black births were counted separately.) (Source: Reid, 1982; U.S. National Center for Health Statistics, 1985c: 17–18).

it began to drop rapidly; by the 1930s it was close to that of whites (see Figure 12·3). Since then, black fertility has generally paralleled white childbearing patterns, increasing during the post–World War II baby boom and decreasing after the late 1950s (Wells, 1985:47–48). Generally, however, blacks have had higher fertility rates than whites. While the fertility rate of blacks has risen and declined along with that of the white majority, a considerable difference between the two groups remains (Reid, 1982). The total fertility rate for blacks has declined to less than 2.3 and remained there since 1973. This compares to a total fertility rate of about 1.8 for the general population (U.S. National Center for Health Statistics, 1985c). A substantial proportion of births among blacks today are to unmarried teenagers, an issue explored more fully later in this chapter.

We suggested earlier that since about 1800 expanding opportunities and changing values have made large numbers of children less economically rewarding and less personally satisfying to individuals. The differing decline in fertility rates between white and black populations in this country suggests that while education and other opportunities opened up for whites with the industrial revolution earlier in the nineteenth century, they did not do so for blacks until well after the Civil War. "Beginning about 1880 black Americans began to be better educated, more highly urbanized, and began to earn better wages, all phenomena that have been associated with the control of fertility among white Americans" (Wells, 1985:47–50). In other words, it is only when individuals have satisfying options other than parenthood that they choose to limit their childbearing.

With regard to the present higher fertility rate among black Americans, the same explanation holds true (Moore et al., 1986). There is some evidence that, at least into the late 1970s, blacks held more sexually permissive attitudes than did whites. But even this finding can be linked to a relatively limited opportunity structure. "Since blacks have a low status in society and their mobility is impeded by racial barriers, they are less inclined to adhere to American mores because they have less to lose in the form of social status" (Staples, 1978:740). Due to advances in birth control techniques, of course, sexual permissiveness need not result in high fertility rates, but individuals must be motivated to use the available contraception. What does cause high fertility is lack of opportunity—the absence of viable and desirable alternatives to childbearing (Hogan and Kitigawa, 1985).

Fertility Rates Among Hispanics Hispanics have the highest fertility rate of any racial-ethnic minority. Their 1984 fertility rate was 42 percent above that of non-Hispanic women. Rates for Mexican-American women are highest among Hispanics. Puerto Ricans and Cubans have relatively lower rates (Ventura, 1984). It has been predicted that, due to high fertility rates coupled with continuing immigration, Hispanics could become our nation's largest minority group (surpassing blacks) within about thirty-five years (Stern, 1985).

Reasons for their relatively high birthrate include the fact that Hispanics immigrate from nations with high birthrates and traditions that value large families. Then, too, among poor minorities large families may serve important functions. In one study (Sharff, 1981) of Hispanics on New York's Lower East Side, children provided valuable services for parents. A child might be an insurance policy against a parent's old age, for example. Once educated and earning a steady income, children can—and will be expected to—contribute to the support of their parents. (This is a phenomenon common to less industrialized societies without bureaucratized welfare systems such as Social Security.) Even while growing up, children's wages were an important part of the family income; children worked, for example, as translators and representatives to bureaucratic agencies. Also, children—particularly adolescent and young adult males—might serve as physical protection for their mothers and for other older family members.

All in all, differential birthrates imply, among other things, that individuals in various social settings are faced with different options on which to base their choices about having children. The next section explores these choices.

THE DECISION TO PARENT OR NOT TO PARENT

In traditional society couples didn't "decide" to have children. Children just came, and preferring not to have any at all was unthinkable. Earlier in this century, family-planning efforts still focused on the timing of children and family size rather than on whether to have them. Now choices include "if" (that is, whether to have children) as well as "when" and "how many."

While social change and technology provide more choices, they also present dilemmas. It is not always easy to choose whether to have children, how many to have, and when to have them. In the following pages we'll look more closely at some of the factors involved in deciding about children: first, the social pressures; then, the personal pros and cons.

Social Pressures

We saw in Chapter 5 that single people in our society often feel strong pressures to conform by marrying. The same kinds of pressures exist for married people who don't want to have children.

Although these pressures are less so than in the past, our society may still have a **pronatalist bias:** Having children is taken for granted, while not having children must be justified. Some of the strongest pressures can come from the couple's parents, who often have difficulty accepting and respecting

their children's choices about whether to have children, let alone when and how many. As one husband (who chose *not* to have children) said, "The biggest sadness of not having children will be the effect it has on my mother" (Nason and Poloma, 1976:31). Hopeful prospective grandparents are not always subtle: One gave his wife a "grandmother photo album" for Christmas, although his childless daughter and her husband were not aware of any grandchildren on the way!

Although socialization still inclines persons toward parenthood (Blake, 1979; Straits, 1985), the expectation for married couples to have children is becoming less pronounced. For example, the term *child-free* is often used now instead of the more negative-sounding term *childless*.[3] Sociologist Joan Huber, in fact, argues that public opinion has virtually shifted to an antinatalist—that is, against having children—position (Huber, 1980:481).

Is American Society Becoming Antinatalist? Some observers have suggested that the social pressures *not* to have children are becoming too strong, especially for some young, highly educated women. Betty Friedan expresses concern that the element of choice is being taken away, and sees little hope for improvement if some women today "have to give up motherhood to keep on in jobs or professions as my generation gave up jobs or professions to make a career of motherhood" (Friedan, 1978:196, 208).

In the ten years or so since Friedan voiced these worries, many observers have raised similar—and broader—concerns. They warn that American society is characterized by **structural antinatalism** inasmuch as "parenting couples are disadvantaged in comparison to nonparenting ones" (Huber, 1980:485, 489). Barbara Ehrenreich (1983) points out that the tradition of the "family wage"—the moral, social responsibility to pay a wage adequate for supporting families with children—has been all but abandoned by employers. Sociologists Janet and Larry Hunt, who in the 1970s optimistically investigated dual-career families, now warn that corporate institutions are "committed to 'masculine' values." Their "primary goals are power and profit . . . over family well-being" (1986:281). Should American values not change, the Hunts predict

---

3. Each term conveys an inherent bias. For that reason and because there are no easy-to-use substitute terms we make equal use of both *childless* and *child-free* in this text.

not only a sense of exclusion on the part of those with families, but a widening gap in the standard of living between parents and non-parents.... Those with children will tend to have lower incomes, in addition to absorbing the expenses of children, and will fall further and further behind their child-free counterparts [1986:283]. ▪

How, exactly, might those with children come to be excluded? One example comes from the National Advocacy Project on Family Day Care. According to officials, controversy over home-based day-care facilities is dividing communities throughout the country. Neighbors' opposition to child-care homes center on noise and added commotion, increased traffic as parents deliver and pick up their children, and the fact that a residentially zoned house is being used as a business (Brooks, 1984a, p. C8).

A second example involves work leave for parents, an issue touched on in Chapter 11. In January 1987 the U.S. Supreme Court upheld a California law requiring employers to grant leave to women who are physically unable to work because of pregnancy. The same month, the Court ruled that a Kansas City employee who was not reinstated after a pregnancy leave had no claim to employment benefits. "Those seemingly contradictory rulings stem from the judges' conviction that Congress has forbidden discrimination against pregnant workers but has not mandated special treatment for them" ("Pregnant question," 1987). In early 1987 a bill that would require employers to give new parents an eighteen-week *unpaid* leave was under attack from various business organizations, including the Chamber of Commerce. But "it's time," wrote the editor of *The Nation,* that "this country... acknowledged that children are society's responsibility, not just their mothers' " ("Pregnant question," 1987). Proposed legislation on work leave for parents is discussed in Chapter 14.

Other observers point out that as a nation we have increased military spending while cutting programs directly affecting the welfare of our children. Between 1981 and 1983, for example, military spending increased by $55 billion, while $10 billion was cut from federal programs that provided health care, nutrition, and education to our youth.

Some of the programs that have suffered severe reductions in their budgets and changes in regulations and eligibility requirements are as follows:

Head Start; Chapter I (Title I of the Education and Secondary Education Act); Education for All Handicapped Children; Special Supplemental Food Program for Women, Infants, and Children (WIC); Title V Maternal and Child Health and Crippled Children's Program; Medicaid; Aid to the Families with Dependent Children (AFDC); Child Abuse Prevention and Treatment Act; Title XX Social Services Program; Adoption Assistance and Child Welfare Act; School Lunch Program; Summer Food Service Program; Child Care Food Program; Food Stamps; and the Job Training Partnership Act (replacement of CETA) [Edelman, 1985:80]. ▪

By 1984, partly as a result of such cuts—and of the absence of national support for a family wage—children, "who represented less than 27 percent of the overall population, comprised 40 percent of the poor. Children were the only age group over represented in the poverty population" (Moynihan, 1986:112).

Antinatalism has other, potentially detrimental, consequences as well. Psychoanalyst Erik Erikson, who has focused on adult development in his work, expresses concern that as the birthrate continues to fall (in response to perceived antinatalism or for other reasons) some couples will become self-absorbed and will neglect other outlets that exist to help them take some responsibility for the generations to come. To avoid what he calls stagnation, Erikson advises people who choose not to have children to channel their procreativity "in active pursuits which universally improve the condition of every child chosen to be born" (Erikson, 1979). Similarly, sociologist Christopher Lasch argues that Americans' pervasive feelings of "emptiness and insignificance" arise essentially from "the erosion of any strong concern for posterity.... We are fast losing the sense of historical continuity, the sense of belonging to a succession of generations originating in the past and stretching into the future" (Lasch, 1980:5).

There are social pressures in our society to have children and not to have children. Either kind of pressure can influence a person's choice and act as a source of guilt or self-doubt. The decisions people make should reflect not only external social pressures but also their own needs, values, and attitudes about becoming parents. In the next section we will look at some of the advantages and disadvantages associated with parenthood.

Children's Value to Parents

Children can be fun. One study found that the single most important satisfaction reported by parents was the excitement of having children around (Lamanna, 1977). Children can add considerable liveliness to a household, and they have fresh and novel responses to the joys and vexations of life. Children provide a sense that something new and different is happening, which may help to relieve the tedium of everyday life. Playing with them can give parents the feeling of reliving their own childhoods:

I think a lot of what I get in seeing my kids kind of brings back memories of when I was little. They were happy memories, especially the two fishing, and I get a kick out of watching them fish, it brings back memories. And it keeps you young. [My little girl] brings a lot of joy [personal interview, Lamanna, 1977]. ▪

In a study of 200 white working-class and middle-class biological and adoptive parents in the Midwest, coauthor Mary Ann Lamanna found parents reporting a variety of satisfactions from having children. Many stated that children gave their lives meaning and purpose, a sense of destiny. Children provide a sense of continuity of self—as one parent put it, "the advantage of seeing something of yourself passed on to your children" (although this can be a mixed blessing: "Sometimes you see some bad things in yourself that have been passed on to your children").

Others report that their satisfaction is in belonging to a close family unit, which they associate with having children, not just with being married:

I think it brings the husband and wife a lot closer. You can't just go your separate ways; there has to be some kind of unity.... I think love is more or less having a family, children, having a relationship with your wife and togetherness and it brings you a lot closer. Makes a foundation for the home; you have to have the roots to start off with. I think when you have children you form that root, of course; you're adding on generation to generation.... It makes, to me, a lot happier home as far as the parents are concerned. If there's love it will grow stronger... especially if you have both parents working with the children... not just the mother [personal interview, Lamanna, 1977]. ▪

Another comments that "it gives us one more thing to talk about all the time together.... Since the daughter, we all do things together more than we used to—the zoo, picnics, and things like that."

Many enjoyed the satisfaction of nurturing the emotional and physical growth of their children. The challenge involved in child rearing can help fill needs for creativity, achievement, and competence:

What I like best of being a parent is that my wife and I have an opportunity to share our lives with someone other than ourselves and to be able to do things for someone directly associated with us other than the two of us.... I think that's the best part, is the sharing. I think we all have our own ideas on how children should be raised. It's interesting to see our children reacting to us and our ideas and their response to the way we treat them; it's a challenge [personal interview, Lamanna, 1977]. ▪

Others spoke of the joy of loving and being loved by their children. "I think just love primarily, having someone to love and having someone love you so much." One parent sums up:

I think it's a unique warmth, the way they address you and the way they treat you. They make you feel bigger than if you didn't [have them]. They are fun to come home to. Watching them grow and develop, seeing their bodies and minds develop. It's interesting [personal interview, Lamanna, 1977]. ▪

Children provide several other satisfactions: They may represent (though to an ever-lessening degree) a potential means of support and security for parents once parents are no longer able to provide for themselves. As we have seen, this was and is still extremely important in a less modern society where government programs of old-age support do not exist (Hoffman and Hoffman, 1973). However, the parents in our American study thought this was *not* a good reason for having children. Also, even more than completing school, taking a first job, or getting married, having children is tangible evidence that one has reached adulthood. A recent study found that 40.2 percent of white women, 31.6 percent of white men, and 34.8 percent of black women (though only 11.5 percent of black men) with children reported that parenthood was the event that gave them a sense of feeling like an adult (Hoffman and Manis, 1979). In addition, children give parents a chance to influence the course of others' lives and to feel looked up to; they can be symbols of accomplishment, prestige, or wealth; and they attest to the parents' sexuality (Hoffman and Manis, 1979).

Lower-income parents may perceive rewards in having children that they may not get any other way (Rainwater, 1965:181). As we saw in Chapter 11, women with lower incomes often do not have satisfying jobs or careers. For them, motherhood provides meaning. As Chapters 10 and 11 point out, fatherhood provides special satisfactions for the lower-income man. If often he cannot take as much pride in his work as does a middle-income man, he can take pride in his family. Family life also offers an opportunity to exercise a kind of authority and influence that he does not have at his job (Blau and Duncan, 1967:428). Some ethnic groups particularly value children, even when they strain the family's resources and energy.

Costs of Having Children

While the values of having children can be immeasurable, the experience can also be costly (Huber, 1980). This is especially true for people who choose parenthood by default; but it is true even for those who want children.

Costs can be measured in several ways. On a purely financial basis they decrease a couple's level of living considerably. And costs are increasing rapidly. One estimate of the cost of maintaining a child in the United States and sending him or her to a state university in 1985 was $232,000 (Belkin, 1985).

Added to the direct costs of parenting are **opportunity costs:** the economic opportunities for wage earning and investments that parents forego when rearing children. These costs are felt most by mothers (Haggstrom et al., 1985). 1977 estimates were that the opportunity cost over a lifetime of having the first child was about $75,000 for well-educated women, and up to $155,000 for women with a postgraduate education, with an average for all women of about $100,000 (Espenshade, 1977:26–27).

Financial costs are measurable, but emotional costs are harder to quantify. These costs may also take the form of opportunity costs—a woman's giving up the satisfactions of a career to become a mother, for instance. Conversely, the loss of free time is one important cost of trying to lead "two lives" as a mother and as a career person.

One of the authors analyzed the emotional-psychological costs of parenting among 200 biological and adoptive parents (Lamanna, 1977). Both groups said children added tension to the household and restricted parents' outside activities. Children made for substantial additional work—not only physical care but also the "work of parenting": socialization and guiding the child's emotional growth. Especially for mothers there were ever-present worries about children's safety and development. This preoccupation, which can disrupt spouses' relationships, may even increase as children become adolescents.

Besides these costs, having children usually requires some household reorganization. Children may crowd the house, for example, or restrict decorating efforts. Children require a more efficiently organized residence and a daily routine, which limits the parents' spontaneity (Lamanna, 1977). This may mean serving lunch or planning naps at about the same time daily or staying home Saturday nights to make sure that the teenager comes home when she or he is supposed to. Adding to these emotional costs is the parent's recognition that, once assumed, the parent role is one that a person cannot easily escape (LeMasters, 1977; Rossi, 1968; Lamanna, 1977).

How Children Affect Marital Happiness

Another common cost of having children may be marital strain. Statistical evidence shows that children—especially when there are many or they are of preschool age—stabilize marriages (Thornton, 1977; Cherlin, 1978; Haggstrom et al., 1985); that is, such couples are less likely to divorce.[4] But as Chapter 8 points out, a stable marriage is not necessarily the same as a happy and satisfying one.

Many couples report that the happiest time in marriage was before the arrival of the first child and after the departure of the last (Spanier et al.,

---

4. At least one analysis, in fact, concludes that most of the difference in marital happiness between parents and nonparents is not due to a decline in marital happiness after children are born but to the fact that unhappy parents tend to stay married while unhappy nonparents more often divorce. Therefore, when parents and nonparents are compared in cross-sample studies, still-married nonparents show up happier as a group (White and Booth, 1985a).

■ Although comparisons of marriages with and without children indicate that those without children are happier, most couples choose to be parents and are satisfied with that decision.

1975; Campbell et al., 1976; Nock, 1979). Anthropologist Paul Bohannan has observed that middle-class Americans establish a kind of antithesis between parenting and spousing (reported in Troll et al., 1979). The arrival of the first child often marks "the end of the honeymoon" and has a significantly negative effect on the marital relationship (Aldous, 1978). Even when partners believe in parenting and greatly appreciate their children, they report that their children have a disruptive influence.

Marital satisfaction sometimes decreases with the first pregnancy when the hidden marriage contract, discussed in Chapter 8, comes into play. When they become parents, spouses may find that they begin responding to each other more in terms of role obligations. By assuming the traditional mother and father roles spouses may become sexually segregated. Now, more than before, the husband is responsible for breadwinning and the wife for house and child care (Aldous, 1978; White et al., 1986). Spouses who, as parents, are not only busier but also sexually segregated begin to do fewer things together and to share decision making less (White et al., 1986). In one study couples with young children reported a dramatic drop in companionable activities (Renne, 1970). In a sample of Mexican-Americans, husbands and wives were more satisfied with the affectionate side of their marriage when there were fewer children present and when the husband-wife relationship was more egalitarian (Bean et al., 1977). Children and the hidden marriage contract of segregated roles seem to go together.

Studies comparing marriages with and without children consistently report marital happiness to be higher in child-free unions (Glenn and McLanahan, 1982). In Norval Glenn and Sara McLanahan's analysis of gender, religious, racial, educational, and employment status subgroups, the only group who reported that having children in the home is more positive than negative are those white persons who feel that four or more is the ideal number of children for a family; yet even in this group "there is no convincing evidence for distinctly positive mean effects" (Glenn and McLanahan, 1982:69). Moreover, "effects continue to be on balance negative" even after the offspring leave home (Glenn and McLanahan, 1982:71). Effects of children on personal happiness are also generally negative (Glenn and Weaver, 1979), even in the later years of life (Glenn and McLanahan, 1981). In view of all this, "it is ironic that most Americans want to have children and do have children" (Glenn and McLanahan, 1982:71).

Despite the costs, most couples choose parenthood. Polls regularly show 80 percent of couples reporting satisfaction with their decision to become parents (Chilman, 1978a). And while the addition of a child necessarily influences a household, the arrival of a child is less disruptive when the parents get along well and have a strong commitment to parenting. In addition, good maternal health and an "easy" baby greatly reduce disruption (Russell, 1974). (Chapter 13 looks more closely at the relationship between parents and their children.) Of course, choosing to have a child or children is but one of several options facing couples, as the next section will discuss.

THREE EMERGING OPTIONS

We have been discussing several factors that influence the choice to have or not to have children. In this section we will look at three emerging options: choosing to remain childless, postponing parenthood, and having a one-child family.

Remaining Child-Free

Despite many people's beliefs, individuals who choose to remain childless are usually neither frustrated nor unhappy. Voluntarily childless couples typically have vital or total relationships (see Chapter 8). Often, they believe that adding a third member to their family would change the character of their intense personal relationship.

Child-free women tend to be attached to a satisfying career. Childless couples value their relative freedom to change jobs or careers, move around the country, and pursue any endeavor they might find interesting (Nason and Poloma, 1976; Veevers, 1974). A study comparing parents with childless couples in a 1979 national Canadian sample of 338 elderly persons concluded that "today's childless elderly have levels of well-being that match and sometimes exceed those of parent elderly" (Rempel, 1985).

Remaining Childless: Differences in Commitment Not all couples are equally committed to remaining child-free. In one study of thirty voluntarily childless couples, it was apparent that the degree of resolve varied among the respondents (Nason and Poloma, 1976). Some—those who had been sterilized—were irrevocably committed. Others were "strongly committed." They used effective contraception, discussed sterilization, and agreed that if contraception failed, the wife would have an abortion. As a couple they showed no signs of ambivalence about not having children, but they did not entirely rule out the possibility of parenting if their current relationship ended.

The "reasonably committed" expressed some minor doubts about the permanence of their decision, but used contraceptives regularly and effectively and said they would probably have an abortion if contraception failed. Some couples were "committed with reservations." They used contraceptives effectively but expressed some doubt about their decision and stated flatly that they would not consider an abortion in the event of unwanted pregnancy.

It is easier to feel strongly committed to remaining childless when in one's 20s; as a 31-year-old wife and law professor put it, when you're young "there's an unreality to it. I had my mind made up then. Now I'm more flexible" (in *Newsweek*, Jan. 14, 1980, p. 96). Because people often change their minds, sterilization may not be a wise choice before the age of 30.

Women's and Men's Reasons From a number of recent studies of couples who decide not to have children, we can draw the following conclusions:

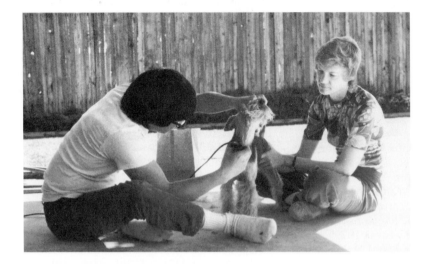

■ Couples who choose not to have children, or who have not yet started a family, may focus their attention on a dog or cat—as with this Welsh terrier, Millie, and her owners, David and Jerilyn.

1. It is more often the woman who first takes the child-free position (Nason and Poloma, 1976). Often, she is an achievement-oriented only child or a first-born child who had to help raise younger brothers or sisters.

2. Husbands who want to remain childless tend to be more confident about their decision than do women, who express more ambivalence. Husbands like to have freedom and privacy to enjoy life, and they like to have more money. Men in egalitarian marriages prefer having fewer or no children over sharing the work of raising them (Scanzoni, 1976).

3. When a husband and wife disagree about having children, the wife usually accedes to her husband's position (Marciano, 1979).

4. Substantial marital conflict and tension may occur around this issue before it is resolved (Marciano, 1979). It is, of course, possible that it cannot be resolved. A difference in the desire for children is such a serious matter that it ought to be talked out before marriage. However, it is difficult to anticipate how one will feel about it when the time comes.

The Decision Not to Parent: Deliberate or by Default Until recently, most child-free couples decided after they married not to have children. In some cases the couple did not consider the subject before marriage, but shortly after marrying they began to discuss the possibility of staying child-free. The greatest number of these couples probably made their decision after several years of marriage, as a result of continued postponement. Initially, they took parenthood for granted but put it off until the idea faded in favor of childlessness (Nason and Poloma, 1976). This kind of decision by default often results when the wife wants to devote the first several years of marriage to her career. By her 30s or early 40s, she may be so involved in her career that she does not want to take time for children, or she may worry about her own health and the effect of her age on the fetus. Also, as we'll see later in this chapter, fertility tends to diminish slowly, but gradually, after about the mid-20s, and it may be more difficult for couples to conceive. The couple may be concerned about adapting their relationship to the presence of children. Sometimes, partners use prolonged postponement to avoid confronting the issue of permanent childlessness, although they eventually realize that they will not have children.

The main disadvantage of not having children at the typical age is that a couple may not make any decision or may make a decision they will regret when they grow old. Many couples, however, change their minds and have children before it is "too late." Recent evidence shows "a clear trend of substantial increase in first order births for women in their thirties in recent years" (U.S. National Center for Health Statistics, 1982a:4). The rates of first births for women both in their early 30s (30–34) and in their late 20s more than doubled between 1972 and 1983 (U.S. National Center for Health Statistics, 1985c:3). First births to women in their 30s, including the late 30s, continued to increase in the mid-1980s (U.S. National Center for Health Statistics, 1987b). Delayed parenthood is a second option available to couples.

Postponing Parenthood

The desire of many women to complete their education and become established in a career appears to be an important factor in the high levels of postponed childbearing. In 1979 nearly half of the first-time mothers age 30–34 years had completed four years of college, compared with just 28 percent in 1970 (Ventura, 1982:1). These figures may reflect, at least in part, the attitudes of young men today.

Journalist Gail Sheehy dubbed highly educated young men the "postponing generation" (Sheehy, 1979). Many are more interested in "temporary self-indulgence" than in marrying or having children. As one young married man explained, "Right now, neither of us wants to have to give anything up to stay home and raise a child." At the same time, a large majority of the child-free couples want children "someday." But according to Sheehy, "the trick for these young men seems to be having children *at the right time*. The most satisfied among them are fathers who have postponed having children until their careers are well-set" (Sheehy, 1979:29). With better contraception, with abortion, and with the trend toward having only two children, couples can now "locate" their parenthood early or late in their adult lives.

Many couples are postponing parenthood not just for a year or two after marriage but for five, eight, or ten years—"as long as it takes to accomplish intricate 'preparental' agendas of personal,

marital, and career development" (Daniels and Weingarten, 1980).

Postponing Parenthood: By Default or Programmatic   To assess the arguments for and against late first-time parenthood, Pamela Daniels and Kathy Weingarten interviewed seventy-two couples, half of whom had their first child in their late 20s or later.

They found that more than half of the thirty-six couples who postponed parenthood did not deliberately choose late parenthood but spent years "suspended and waiting." For them, the value of their early child-free time became apparent only in retrospect. "If I had been more thoughtful about that time I was fooling around not having a baby," said a 40-year-old mother of three young children, "I might have done something more constructive with that time" (Daniels and Weingarten, 1980).

The remaining number of late first-time parents were **programmatic postponers;** that is, they arrived at late first-time parenthood by a deliberate, self-conscious process of mutual intention, negotiation, and planning. They knew beforehand exactly why they were putting off having their first baby, and their reasons amounted to a catalogue of the advantages: the need for psychological readiness and a time to be free to explore and experiment; the desire to find the right partner and create a strong marriage first; and the desire to prolong a career (especially for wives)—all were frequently mentioned.

A "Two-Sided Coin"   But programmatic late parenthood, the researchers concluded, is a two-sided coin—"one side clear and visible at the start, the 'other side' emerging only as daily parenting unfolds, creating an experience these late parents found unexpectedly dense and complex" (Daniels and Weingarten, 1980). For one thing, programmatic postponers had unusually high expectations of themselves as spouses, workers, and parents and of their abilities to combine these roles. Said one 42-year-old woman who had her first baby at age 33, "The irony is that you think you know more than you do." For programmatic postponers, the arrival of the first baby causes just as much disruption as it does for other parents.

Whereas early first-time parents in the study "couldn't remember a time when they weren't parents," programmatic postponers reported a sharp sense of "before" and "after." While they were not sorry they had children, they missed the child-free life-style. Moreover, the mothers in this study found that combining established careers with parenting created unforeseen problems. Those who set their careers temporarily aside to be full-time mothers met with criticism from their work colleagues and peers. Those who continued to work, even though they reduced their hours, felt they missed important time with their children or were generally overloaded. One special difficulty with choosing late parenthood is that career commitments may ripen just at the peak of parental responsibilities. As a successful 50-year-old professional woman and mother of three adolescents put it:

To have a child in your 30s, when part of the reason was to get established in your work in your 20s, means that you will have young children at a point in your career cycle when professional demands are beginning to be made on you outside your home base [Daniels and Weingarten, 1980]. ■

Researchers found another element to the two-sided-coin aspect of postponing parenthood. Late parents reported their impatience for the "empty nest" stage of life, when they could return to the personal privacy and freedom from responsibility they enjoyed before their children were born. Early first-time parents, on the other hand, felt they reaped definite pluses later on. One woman, who had been a first-time mother in her early 20s and was now older and a systems analyst, said,

I like the fact that my children are as old as they are, and that I'm as young as I am and my career is so open ahead of me. I'd hate to be in my career position, wanting to have children and not knowing when to make the break [Daniels and Weingarten, 1979]. ■

In this respect postponing parenthood means making a trade-off: More free time before having children means less time after the children are grown. An awareness of this fact—plus an understanding that having children, while rewarding, can cause logistic and emotional complications—is important for people who consciously decide to postpone being parents.

Throughout this discussion we've been talking about the choice between having or not having children, or waiting to have children. We have used the plural, reflecting a common assumption in our society that when a couple become parents, they will have at least two children. While it is essentially true that there's no such thing as "halfway" parents, it is also true that there are some differences in degree between having one child and having several children. We'll consider the one-child family as a third option available to couples.

The One-Child Family

According to one expert's estimate, 22 percent of families with children now have only one child (Collins, 1984). The proportion of one-child families in America appears to be growing because of a constricting economy, the high and rising cost of raising a child through college, and some women's increasing career opportunities and aspirations. As a mother with a second new baby put it, "I underestimated the immensity and constancy of the responsibility of *one* child.... And two children *are* more than one. More work, more time, more patience, more money" (Campbell, 1984:140). Still, Judith Blake (1979) argues that the one-child family does not have popular support. Maya Pines observes that "probably many more American couples would choose to have just one child were it not for the persistence of unfavorable stereotypes of such children" (Pines, 1981:15). Negative stereotypes present only children as spoiled, lonely, dependent, and selfish. To find out whether there is any basis for this image, psychologists have produced a staggering number of studies in recent years. "The overall conclusion: There are no major differences between only children and others; *no* negative effects of being an only child can be found" (Pines, 1981:15). One study interviewed adults between ages 17 and 62 who had been only children and concluded that despite many people's beliefs, only children turn out to be no more selfish, lonely, or less well adjusted than those with siblings (Falbo, 1976).

Another study (Hawke and Knox, 1978) compared the positive and negative aspects of having an only child by interviewing 102 parents of only children and 105 only children. These only children had better verbal skills and higher I.Q.'s than children in any other size family, whether eldest, youngest, or whatever. Their grades were as good or better. They displayed more self-reliance and self-confidence than other children and were often the most popular among elementary school stu-

■ Only one: These parents will select a puppy from this litter for their son, an only child. Perhaps as one-child families become more common in America, "an only child" will sound less negative. The phrase suggests a forlorn youth disavantaged by the absence of sisters and brothers, but studies do not support this notion.

dents. They were as likely to have successful college experiences and careers, happy marriages, and good parenting experiences as children with brothers and sisters.

Parents with only one child found that they could enjoy parenthood without being overwhelmed and tied down. They had more free time and were better off financially than they would have been with more children. The researchers found that family members shared decisions more equally and could afford to do more things together (Hawke and Knox, 1978).

Another study asked parents with two children about the differences between having one and two children. While parents' adjustment to the second child was easier, parents found that the second child created more work than they had anticipated. Marital satisfaction declined slightly more after having the second child than after having the first (Knox and Wilson, 1978).

There were disadvantages, too, in a one-child family. For the children, these included the obvious lack of opportunity to experience sibling relationships and the extra pressure from parents to succeed. They were sometimes under an uncomfortable amount of parental scrutiny, and as adults they had no help in caring for their aging parents. Disadvantages for parents included the constant fear that the only child might be seriously hurt or die and the feeling, in some cases, that they had only one chance to prove themselves "good" parents.

To this point in the chapter, we have taken for granted a very important factor: the element of choice in having or not having children. Indeed, the extent to which we have this choice is itself remarkable. Until a few decades ago (in some cases a very few years ago), most of the technology on which this ability to choose depends simply didn't exist. The next sections explore some personal and relationship ramifications of fertility technology. We'll look first at some issues surrounding contraception. (Details on contraceptive techniques can be found in Appendix C.)

PREVENTING PREGNANCY: HISTORY AND ISSUES

During the 1830s two books describing birth control techniques were published in the United States. Twenty years later, newspaper advertisements offered various mechanical and chemical birth control devices. Of course, a majority of these were relatively ineffective and/or dangerous. Although the diaphragm was relatively safe and effective, it was not until the 1960s, with the development of the Pill, that a significant technological breakthrough in controlling births was achieved.

Prior to the Pill, many of women's abortive or contraceptive efforts were no doubt made privately and in secret. Nineteenth-century America was obviously a more patriarchal society (see Chapter 2) than we live in today. Indeed, men were only beginning to recognize a woman's right to have a say in how many children she bore. "Edward Foote's advocacy of the cervical diaphragm in 1864 because it, 'places conception entirely under the control of the wife, to whom it actually belongs,' is a rare early instance of male support for women controlling reproduction for their own reasons" (Wells, 1985:53). Women's gaining some control over fertility decisions, then, represented a move away from absolute patriarchy and toward sexual equality.

While heavy reliance in the twentieth century on the condom as well as the diaphragm implied male as well as female responsibility for contraception, since the advent of the Pill in the sixties, contraception has been viewed as entirely—or at least mostly—the female's responsibility. Writing in *The New Our Bodies, Ourselves*, the Boston Women's Health Book Collective advises:

Placing *total* responsibility for birth control on women is unfair. It means that we must make arrangements to see a practitioner for an exam and a prescription, go to the drugstore, usually pay for supplies and make sure they don't run out. With the Pill (or other contraceptives designed for the female), we feel the effects and, more seriously, take whatever risks are involved....

Many of us do not talk much about birth control with our partners. Yet a man can share the responsibility of birth control in several ways. When no good method is available at the moment, a supportive partner will join us in exploring ways of lovemaking without intercourse. He can use condoms, and not just when we remind him to; help pay the doctor and drugstore bills; share in putting in the diaphragm or inserting the foam; check to see if supplies are running low. He can, if it is a long-term relationship where no children or no more are wanted, have a vasectomy [1984:221]. ■

The authors add that women may choose not to use birth control for many reasons, among them their hesitation to "inconvenience" a partner. But this "fear of displeasing him is a measure of inequality in our relationship" (222).

This, of course, is the traditional double standard, which assigns women the responsibility for controlling sex. The double standard may be in effect here because men can more readily escape the consequences of an unwanted pregnancy. And the physical and opportunity costs of children tend to be higher for women than for men. Furthermore, it is women who physically experience abortion or carry and bear children and who more often relinquish careers and education for parenthood (The Boston Women's Health Book Collective, 1984).

Feminists note that not only do couples assign contraceptive responsibility to the woman but also that researchers and manufacturers tend to focus on female rather than male contraceptives, even though systemic contraceptives such as the Pill may entail substantial health risks for women. Recently, there has been more interest in male contraceptives, with testing beginning on a male hormonal contraceptive ("Researchers test," 1987) and a strong resurgence of interest in condoms because of the protection they provide against AIDS and other venereal diseases.

We have seen that people take many factors into consideration in their decision to have or not to have children; we know that several methods are available both for contraception and for attempting to increase fertility. Clearly, people today are more able to make decisions about parenthood than they have ever been. However, as with other kinds of personal choices we have considered throughout this text, people don't always choose knowledge-ably about having children. Default decisions are one (but not the only) reason pregnancy and par-enthood can profoundly disrupt people's lives. Society has a considerable stake in the next gen-eration, and issues related to procreation tend to be central. Pregnancy outside of marriage and abortion are two reproductive issues that are social as well as personal concerns.

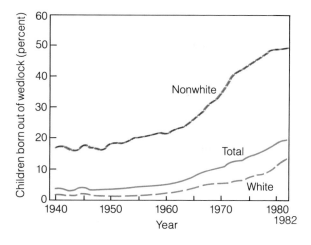

Figure 12·4

Percent of children born out of wedlock: 1940–82. (Source: Thornton and Freedman, 1983:22; U.S. National Center for Health Statistics, 1984c)

PREGNANCY OUTSIDE OF MARRIAGE

There is a slight trend today for single, well-edu-cated career women to bear and rear one or more children outside marriage. This type of single-par-ent family is described in Chapter 7. Here we will address unwed motherhood among teenagers and young women in their early twenties. Premarital sex among teenagers increased during the 1970s as one element of the so-called sexual revolution. But in that decade only about one-fifth of never married, sexually experienced teenagers used effective contraception (Zelnik and Kantner, 1978b). The fact that many premarital pregnancies occurred among teenagers and that this propor-tion was growing prompted then–Secretary of Health, Education, and Welfare Joseph Califano to call premarital pregnancy an epidemic and one of the most serious and complex challenges facing the nation in 1979 (Macdonald, 1979).

Figure 12·4 shows the percentage of children born out of wedlock between 1940 and 1982. The total percentage has continued to increase; by 1985, 22 percent of all births occurred among unmarried mothers (U.S. National Center for Health Statistics,

1987b). This situation represents a profound change in our society over the last fifty years. As recently as 1940, fewer than 5 percent of all live births were to unmarried mothers.

The illegitimacy rate began to decline among blacks[5] toward the end of the 1970s and has risen among whites. The racial differential continues to narrow and, according to National Center for Health Statistics investigators, "has been sharply reduced" (U.S. National Center for Health Statistics, 1984c). Still, 60 percent of black births (compared with 15 percent of white births) took place outside of mar-riage in 1985 (U.S. National Center for Health Sta-tistics, 1987b). For black women, who have lower marriage and higher illegitimacy rates, marriage and parenthood are separate experiences, the for-mer usually following the latter (Cherlin, 1981).

The "epidemic"[6] in unwed motherhood has been largely a function of the large number of children born during the baby boom. As these females reach

---

5. Note that blacks make up 90 percent of the nonwhite rate; therefore, the nonwhite rates used in Figure 12·4 can be used as a fairly accurate indicator of black rates.

6. Actually, some demographers question the concept of epi-demic, arguing that the increase in the proportion of births to unmarried women is partly a result of the steep decline in married fertility, discussed earlier.

childbearing age, there are more of them who may bear illegitimate children. In recent years, as the baby-boom cohort grows older, women over 20 have accounted for a larger share (55 percent) of the out-of-wedlock births. There are now fewer teenagers and more women in their 20s in the population; age at marriage has risen, so a larger proportion of women in this age group are unmarried; and women in their 20s now have higher rates of unwed childbearing than do teens (U.S. National Center for Health Statistics, 1987b).

There are several serious side effects of this "epidemic." For one, because there is less social stigma attached to premarital pregnancy today, about 90 percent of black and white unmarried teenage mothers keep their babies (Zelnik and Kantner, 1978b). Doing so can mean an earlier marriage, with less than an even chance of its lasting more than four years (Furstenberg, 1976).

Besides limiting one's chance for a stable marriage, early premarital pregnancy presents serious health hazards for the mother and child: Complications of pregnancy, miscarriage and stillbirth, prematurity, and birth defects and neurological handicaps are more likely with teenage mothers than mothers in their 20s and early 30s (Alan Guttmacher Institute, 1976). Teenage parents usually face a bleak educational future, a stunted career, and a very good chance of living in poverty, compared with peers who do not become parents as teenagers (Furstenberg, 1976; Alan Guttmacher Institute, 1976). In fact, for *both* sexes, teenage parenthood has a greater negative effect on future educational and occupational attainment than do factors such as race, social or economic family status, academic aptitude, or early ambition (Card and Wise, 1978). Moreover, these negative consequences tend to be passed on to the next generation. Long-term prospects for children of teenage parents include lower academic achievement and a tendency to repeat the cycle of early, unmarried pregnancy (Card, 1981).

Social scientists and others have pointed to the need for support programs to help young parents, and to help their families help them. Such programs might include health centers, family planning clinics, nutritional services, primary and preventive health care, vocational counseling, and legal and educational services and parental training courses in the public schools. Public schools should make allowances in policy and scheduling so that pregnant girls can either stay in school or be edu-

cated in some other way through the public school system (Colletta and Gregg, 1979). Many social workers and policy makers point to the need for including the unwed father in programs and services (Leashore, 1979). In 1986, for example, New York City launched a "Young Fathers Program" for fathers of illegitimate children. The program offers birth control information, helps young men to find jobs in order to help support their offspring, and generally encourages "accepting the consequences of one's actions" (Freedman, 1986).

One solution to the rising incidence of premarital pregnancy is to give teenagers more information about contraceptives and increase their availability. Some parents have disapproved of this, fearing that more information about contraceptives, plus greater availability, will encourage sexual promiscuity. But studies show that the number of sex partners a teenager has does not increase by making contraception available to him or her (Reicheit, 1978), nor is sexual activity likely to occur earlier if parents discuss this issue with their teenagers (Inazu and Fox, 1980). On the contrary, teenagers usually initiate sexual activity well before they begin to use effective contraception (Zelnik and Kantner, 1978a).

Sex education programs have some effect in preventing teenage pregnancy. Young women who have had sex education in school are no more likely than others to be sexually active. But if active, they are less likely to become pregnant (Zelnik and Kim, 1982). Some high schools have experimented with coordinated health clinics, which offer pregnancy prevention and contraception in a context of general health care. A Minnesota program that taught teenagers about contraceptives and made them available reduced teen pregnancies by 40 percent ("St. Paul maternal," 1982; Dryfoos, 1984).

Reasons for the Rise in Premarital Pregnancy

Figures from a 1982 national sample show that, of never married women age 15–19 who "had been exposed to the risk of unintended pregnancy" within three months prior to their being questioned, about two-thirds were using some form of birth control. Among whites, this figure was 69 percent, while among blacks it was 64 percent. Sixty percent of women age 15–17 were using some method of birth control—60.2 percent of whites and 58.7 percent

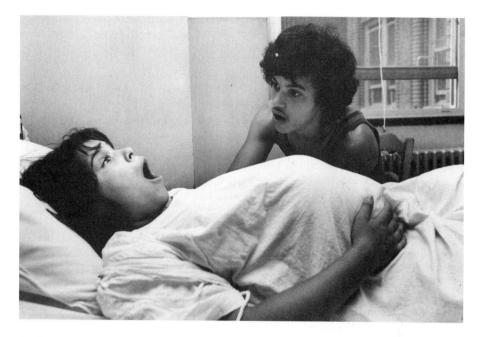

■ Children having children: Jeanette is 15, and Victor is 14. With nearly one out of three American babies born to unwed mothers today, there is less social stigma attached to premarital pregnancy. As with the majority of teenage mothers, Jeanette will keep her baby; less certain is marriage—most teen marriages fail within a few years.

of blacks. Among women age 20–24 almost 82 percent of whites and 77 percent of blacks reported using birth control (Bachrach and Mosher, 1984:5). While the proportion of sexually active young women who report using birth control methods is up from late 1970s estimates, nearly one-third of sexually active teenage women and 20 percent of those in their early twenties do not use birth control. Moreover, the 1982 survey included—along with other methods—periodic abstinence, withdrawal, and douches as "birth control" techniques; as Appendix C points out, these are relatively ineffective means for preventing pregnancy.

It is ironic that at a time when so many contraceptive devices are available, the rates of premarital pregnancy are increasing. A number of researchers have tried to explain this contradiction. They found that males may often believe, according to the sexual double standard, that the "real" parent and the one responsible for contraception is the female. And teen women may be reluctant to antagonize a partner who is unenthu-

siastic about, say, condoms. Teen women in regular relationships where the male is somewhat committed are more likely to use contraceptives and less likely to get pregnant (Fisher et al., 1979). But much teen sex is sporadic.

Some explanations for the female partner's failure to use contraceptives are provided by a study of 18–19-year-old undergraduate women at Indiana University (Byrne, 1977). The term **paradoxical pregnancy** was used to summarize the finding that the more guilty and disapproving these women were about premarital sex, the less likely they were to use contraceptives regularly, if at all. Such paradoxical pregnancies resulted because personal disapproval of premarital sex was often not strong enough to inhibit sexual behavior, but it did inhibit the use of contraceptives.

The researchers had four explanations of why such pregnancies happen. First, the sexually negative individual avoids the expectation that intercourse will occur. Because sex becomes a spontaneous event, he or she is unprepared. A second reason has to do with embarrassment or reluctance to let others know about one's sexual activity. Procuring birth control devices means going to a doctor or a drugstore and asking for them. To some individuals, this is like giving public notice of their private affairs.

A third element of paradoxical pregnancy is a lack of communication. Sexual partners need to talk to each other about contraception to make sure somebody has done something. Yet partners who disapprove of premarital sex are less likely to talk to each other about either sex or contraception. A fourth reason, the researchers found, has to do with using contraceptive devices. The Pill requires an individual to think about sex at least once daily and mechanical devices require some direct contact with the genitals. Persons who disapprove of premarital sex may shy away from this.

Besides these reasons, a woman may fear she will be considered "too active" if she prepares herself for sex beforehand. So she needs to pretend that intercourse "just happened." For this reason, many women have "relationship-specific" contraceptive partners: They use contraception effectively with one male friend or husband but discontinue contraception when the relationship ends (Zimmerman, 1977).

Although it usually happens by default, some observers point out that pregnancy is sometimes used by women as an inducement to marriage and to test a partner's commitment. We have seen that society encourages men and women to have different goals regarding courtship and marriage and that women's bargaining power in the marriage market has been reduced. A woman may choose to risk pregnancy because it provides a situation in which her sexual partner must define his commitment to her (Luker, 1975). In some cases pregnancy gains a partner's commitment to marriage.

A recently published longitudinal study first interviewed seventh-graders in a randomly selected half of the Houston Independent School District junior high schools in 1971. In the late 1980s researchers began follow-up tracing of these respondents and were able to report results on over 2,000 of them. Predictors of (or factors found in the seventh-graders that later correlated with) adolescent pregnancy included school difficulties and low socioeconomic status for both males and females. For females, other factors included father absence, a relatively large number of siblings, and family stress (Robbins et al., 1985).

Contraception provides a solution to the prob-

lems associated with pregnancy outside of marriage. In general, the more committed the unmarried partners and the higher their self-esteem and acceptance of their own sexuality, the more likely they are to use contraceptives (Reiss, 1975:628; Hornick et al., 1979). When contraception isn't used, however, many women who don't want to remain pregnant decide to have an abortion. We will look next at this option, which is itself a controversial social issue.

ABORTION

Abortion is the expulsion of the fetus or embryo from the uterus either naturally (spontaneous abortion or miscarriage) or medically (induced abortion). This section addresses the phenomenon of induced abortion. From earliest history, abortion has been a way of preventing birth. The practice was not legally prohibited in the United States until the mid-nineteenth century. At that time it was outlawed because of its mortality risk; because of its performance by women medical entrepreneurs at a time when physicians sought to establish their professional respect and control; because many physicians were convinced that fetal development was a continuous process and that human life should be protected from the time of fertilization; and because of fears that decreased childbearing among native Protestant white women would permit the overwhelming of American society by newly emigrated ethnic groups with high birthrates (Mohr, 1978).

Laws prohibiting abortion established during the nineteenth century stood relatively unchallenged until the 1960s, when an abortion reform movement directed toward legislative change resulted in modification of some state laws and court challenges. Litigation at the federal level culminated in the 1973 *Roe* v. *Wade* decision that legalized abortion. Abortion can be obtained without question in the first trimester of pregnancy but is subject to regulation of providers and procedure in the second trimester. A 1976 ruling in *Danforth* v. *Planned Parenthood of Central Missouri* struck down requirements of spousal consent or consent of parents of minors. Recent successful litigation has restricted federal funding for abortion (the Hyde amendment) and permitted states to require notification of minors' parents, but has not permitted states or cities to require waiting periods, "informed consent" procedures, or performance of the abortion in a hospital.

The Safety of Abortions

Before abortion was legalized in 1973, illegal and self-induced abortions were accompanied by very high rates of death and serious injury. But death rates for legal abortions properly performed are lower than those for normal childbirth. In 1985 just under 1.6 million legal abortions were performed in the United States (Henshaw, Forrest, and Van Veld, 1987). More than four-fifths of abortions are obtained by unmarried women. Over 90 percent of all abortions are performed in the first twelve weeks of pregnancy (Henshaw, 1987; 1983 data.). Abortion is now one of the safest medical procedures when it is performed in a hospital or a clinic in the first trimester. Abortions in the second trimester— months four, five, and six—are about ten times more dangerous than those performed in the first three months. But fewer than 10 percent of all abortions are performed during the second trimester. When we compare abortion deaths with deaths during delivery of full-term live babies, we find that 0.5 deaths occurred per 100,000 abortions in the United States in 1978, while 8.0 deaths occurred for every 100,000 live births ("Researchers confirm," 1982).

During the first trimester of pregnancy, the fetus is removed by suction (vacuum aspiration) or in a surgical process in which the cervix is dilated and the contents of the uterus scraped out with a sharp instrument (dilatation and curettage, or D & C). In the second trimester a small amount of amniotic fluid is replaced by a salt solution, or a woman is injected with a powerful drug called prostaglandin. Both procedures induce contractions of the uterus, causing the fetus to be expelled. Another method used in the second trimester is *hysterotomy* (not to be confused with hysterectomy), in which the woman's abdomen is opened and the fetus and placenta are removed, much as in a caesarean section delivery.

The effects of abortion on reproduction were hotly debated, with strong research studies initially appearing in the *Journal of the American Medical Society* and the *New England Journal of Medicine* to support both sides (Hogue, 1977; Levin et al., 1978; Harlap et al., 1979). Some see a greater risk in future pregnancis of low birth-weight babies, premature deliveries, or spontaneous abortions; others do not. The most recent review concluded that there is no risk to future child-bearing from a first trimester vacuum aspiration abortion of first pregnancy. The preponderance of the evidence regarding D & Cs suggests that there is no risk (Hogue et al., 1983). Finally, recent research suggests that techniques used since 1973 have averted the risk of miscarriage initially found to be associated with multiple abortions (Kline et al., 1986).

According to recent and compelling evidence, abortion has no impact on the ability to become pregnant; sterility following abortion is very uncommon. Boston researchers compared 1,235 women who had had abortions to women in similar circumstances who had not and found no difference in pregnancy rates (Stubblefield et al., 1984).

But it is questions of social acceptance and psychological distress that are most often raised when abortion is considered as a solution to unwanted pregnancy.

Social Attitudes About Abortion Polls show that a substantial majority of Americans believe that abortion should be legal; 69 percent oppose a constitutional amendment to ban all or most abortions (*New York Times*/CBS News Poll, Sept. 19, 1984, p. 89).

Table 12·1, which lists the results of another national poll, shows that the particular circumstances influence people's attitudes about abortion. There is most support for the so-called "hard reasons" of health, genetic defect, and pregnancy resulting from rape, and less support for the "soft" reasons of low income, not being married, or simply not wanting more children in the family. Thirty-nine percent support abortion "for any reason" ("Most Americans remain opposed," 1984).

Attitudes vary according to the stage of pregnancy as well. Seventy-one percent believe "a woman who is three or fewer months pregnant should have the right to decide, with her doctor's advice, whether or not she wants to have an abortion" ("Little or no change," 1985; comment on Louis Harris poll, 1985). However, majority opinion favors abortion in the second and third trimesters only when the woman's life is endangered, although roughly 25 percent would still allow abortion in the case of a threat to health, genetic defect, or rape/incest pregnancy (Gallup, 1978).

Second-trimester abortions create greater moral

TABLE 12·1 Percentage of U.S. Adults Approving of Legal Abortions Under Certain Circumstances, 1984

If the woman's health is seriously endangered by the pregnancy	90%
If there is a strong chance of a serious defect in the baby	80
If the woman became pregnant as a result of rape	80
If the family has a very low income and cannot afford any more children	46
If the woman is not married and does not want to marry the man	44
If the woman is married and does not want any more children	43
For any reason	39
Average approval for all seven reasons	69

SOURCE: "Most Americans remain opposed," 1984: 233; based on National Opinion Research Center General Social Survey, 1984.

problems for many people because they interrupt the fetus's development at a later, "more human," stage. But only during this period can doctors check for diseased or defective fetuses by taking samples of amniotic fluid. Other second-trimester abortions are obtained by women who may not have realized they were pregnant or who could not make arrangements for a first-trimester abortion.

Although the American public generally takes a centrist position that favors abortion only under certain circumstances, legislation and other public policy in this area have been shaped by the conflict of those holding polar positions. The text section "From Platform and Pulpit" in Chapter 4 discusses the recent trend for moral and political issues to fuse. In the abortion arena the politico-religious prolife movement has helped elect sympathetic members of Congress and maintained the Hyde amendment that forbids federal funding for abortions for poor women. Meanwhile, the prochoice supporters have succeeded in repelling restrictive legislation on abortions at federal and state levels. What all this means for individuals is that women making decisions about abortion today do so in a far more political climate than before. In fact, even assumptions and conclusions about the emotional response to abortion have been heavily colored by political positions.

Still, it's safe to say that for most women (and for many of their male partners) abortion is an emotionally upsetting experience (Freeman, 1978; Shostak, 1979, 1984). The decision to abort is serious. In one study pregnant young women who chose to abort instead of bearing the child were more likely to report that their decision was very difficult and that they regretted having made it (Bracken et al., 1978), "although studies also report feelings of relief" (Freeman, 1978). Factors representing the other side of the coin are the ultimately stronger educational and occupational position of women who abort rather than have their infants and the fact that the emotional turmoil of the women does not normally lead to severe or long-lasting psychological problems.

In one study (Zimmerman, 1977) forty women were interviewed six to ten weeks after they had had abortions. About half were troubled and half were untroubled by the experience. Before their own abortions, about 70 percent had disapproved of abortion to some degree, and 80 percent had believed that a majority in their community disapproved. These women not only recognized but had internalized disapproving social attitudes about abortion. The researcher found that the women in this study coped with their decision to abort, not by changing their feelings about its morality, but by refusing to take responsibility for the decision: They rationalized that they had "no other choice."

On the one hand, abortion may be an emotionally difficult solution. On the other hand, abortion has had an important effect on teenage fertility rates. One study indicates that women obtaining abortions were less disadvantaged than women giving birth, in terms of education, work, welfare dependency, and marriage (Athanasiou et al., 1973). Regardless of predicted outcomes, women (and men) making decisions about abortions are most likely to make them in the context of their values, and a detailed review of the ethical and social issues involved is outside the scope of this text.

We have discussed abortion primarily within the context of unmarried, accidental pregnancy. Abortion is also an issue, however, for married couples—particularly older ones—because of new technology that allows detection of a defective fetus. Box 12·1, "High-Tech Pregnancy: Ultrasound and Amniocentesis," describes this development. Appendix B outlines the physiological aspects of conception, pregnancy, and childbirth.

While society currently focuses most of its attention on birth control and the prevention of conception, a growing minority of individuals or couples face a different problem. They want to have a child, but either they cannot conceive or they cannot sustain a full-term pregnancy.

INVOLUNTARY INFERTILITY

Involuntary infertility is the condition of wanting to conceive and bear a child but being physically unable to do so. Several factors can contribute to involuntary infertility: A man may have relatively few sperm in his semen (low sperm count), or a woman may have a blockage in her fallopian tubes. There are some cases where each partner might be capable of conceiving with another individual. When both partners have a small problem, however, their chances of conceiving together are lowered.

Through advances in medicine, the incidence of involuntary infertility declined for over eighty years (Glick, 1977:9). But recently, it has increased somewhat. It is estimated that one in five couples in this country have some kind of infertility problem (Berg, 1984). One reason is that both women and men are maximally fertile in their mid-20s and

earlier. The present tendency to postpone child-bearing into one's 30s and 40s contributes to the increase in infertility problems. So does smoking and excessive exercise ("Fertility study," 1985; "Researchers," 1985).

Another factor contributing to recent increases in infertility is the rising incidence of venereal disease, which can scar the reproductive systems of both women and men; another is the increased use of some contraceptive methods (such as the IUD) that can cause uterine infection and scar the fallopian tubes. Exposure to various drugs, chemicals, and radiation can also cause infertility. However, while earlier studies suggested that repeated abortions could damage the cervix, resulting in the inability to carry a subsequent pregnancy to term, later studies indicate that abortion—using methods common since 1973—has no negative effect on fertility (Hogue et al., 1983; Kline et al., 1986).

Difficulty conceiving or carrying a pregnancy to term is highly frustrating.[7] When faced with involuntary infertility, an individual or a couple experiences a loss of control over life plans and feels helpless, damaged or defective, angry, and often guilty (Kirk, 1964). According to one counselor, the psychological burden of infertility may fall more heavily on professional, goal-oriented individuals. These are people "who have learned to focus all their energies on a particular goal. When that goal becomes a pregnancy that they cannot achieve they see themselves as failures in a global sense" (Berg, 1984:164). Besides having an effect on each partner's self-esteem, the situation can hurt their relationship and can create a marital crisis. According to sociologists Ralph and Anne Matthews, for many couples, involuntary infertility not only calls the procreative function of marriage into question but also "directly challenges the social function of marriage as providing some control over a private world." Slowly, the partners become aware that they confront a situation "of which they can make no sense." Moreover, this creeping awareness often arises at about the time when other couples they know are publicly planning their pregnancies without apparent difficulty. "It is under these social conditions that most couples embark on the quest for a medical solution to their problem" (1986:643).

For many couples, the first step in treatment is

---

7. A national organization called Resolve provides support groups, counseling, and referral services to infertile persons.

BOX 12 · 1

HIGH-TECH
PREGNANCY:
ULTRASOUND
AND
AMNIOCENTESIS

High tech has come to pregnancy. Recent years have seen extraordinary scientific advances in fetal technology. Here we look at two such advances: ultrasound and amniocentesis.

ULTRASOUND

In ultrasound sound waves are bounced off the abdomen of the pregnant woman to determine the shape and position of the fetus. Some obstetricians already use it in every pregnancy; others prefer to use it only where clearly indicated while waiting for long-term studies. Doctors who use it at about the fifth month say that it helps to predict the date of birth within two weeks, that it can detect twins 90 percent of the time, and that it shows whether the fetus is maturing as it should. Ultrasound can also reveal several different kinds of birth defects—especially malformations of the skeleton—early enough for a legal abortion if parents choose to have one.

The use of ultrasound has implications beyond diagnosis, however. The fact that sonograms permit prospective parents to do something they have never been able to do before—observe the fetus—is pushing back parental bonds to before birth (Powledge, 1983:38). Patients often ask for copies of the Polaroid fetal snapshots. As one genetic counselor said, "It seems that with sonography there's really that *connection*, especially if the fetus happens to move. . . . I guess seeing that image creates a stronger bond" (in Powledge, 1983:38). Ultrasound imaging may be the most common technique for prenatal diagnosis, but amniocentesis is probably the best known.

AMNIOCENTESIS

In amniocentesis a physician inserts a sharp syringe through the abdominal wall into the uterus, withdrawing a small amount of amniotic fluid. Cells and other substances that the fetus has cast off float in this fluid, which technicians can examine for clues to fetal health. Among other things, the cells in the sampling are cultivated and checked for evidence of possible birth defects, particularly Down's syndrome. When doctors suspect that a woman might give birth to a child with a particular disorder—often because she carries a recessive gene for this disorder or because she has already given birth to a child with the disorder—scientists can examine the fluid for other conditions as well, including

SOURCES:
Powledge, 1983:37–42;
Cooke and Dworkin,
1981:15; *Newsweek*, May
18, 1981, pp. 120–24.

to go to a doctor. After an examination the doctor often recommends that they "relax" for another six months or so and also try to have sexual relations at scheduled times, when the wife is most likely to be ovulating. This often involves keeping accurate temperature charts, for a woman's body temperature rises after ovulation. Unfortunately, scheduling sexual relations in this way is not likely to help a couple relax as they were advised to do.

If after a period of time conception has still not occurred, further medical treatment may be sought. This might include various drugs (to induce ovu-

nearly 100 rare genetic diseases. As women postpone childbearing to older ages, they have more concern about the risk of such birth defects as Down's syndrome; the risk increases with age.

Experts on prenatal diagnosis also note that an increasing number of women under 35 are asking for chromosome tests, although their risk of having an abnormal child is lower than the risk associated with amniocentesis. The eager test-takers are frequently women whose careers are paramount, and who feel that they could not give a handicapped child the necessary time and attention. For them, prenatal diagnosis is simply a logical extension of family planning [Powledge, 1983:42].

In experienced hands amniocentesis appears reasonably safe, but the technique is not without hazards. Such hazards include spontaneous abortion, presumably as an indirect result; needle punctures to the fetus; and risk of premature birth. As a result, amniocentesis is used sparingly.

Accompanying this new technology is a growing number of a new kind of counselor, the genetic counselor. Genetic counselors advise couples who have undergone amniocentesis and obtained the results on the risks of delivering a baby with birth defects.

But the technology that has made genetic screening and genetic counseling possible has also made this field one of the most controversial in medicine. Detection of an abnormal fetus gives prospective parents the chance to knowledgeably choose abortion. For this reason, right-to-life groups have objected strenuously to screening and genetic counseling. The fact is that fewer than 3 percent of women who undergo amniocentesis later have abortions (*Newsweek*, May 18, 1981, p. 122). For those faced with evidence of a defective fetus, however, abortion is not an easy answer. "Patients and genetic counselors alike report that mourning a pregnancy ended because of an abnormality is almost identical to mourning the death of a newborn infant" (Powledge, 1983:40).

At present, all prenatal diagnosis must take place during the second trimester when sufficient amniotic fluid is present. This timing is a major drawback. It probably contributes to the emotional intensity surrounding prenatal diagnosis, and certainly heightens the risk to the woman who faces abortion. Tests in the initial twelve weeks, or first trimester, would be a remarkable advance, and such early tests may be on the way.

lation, for example) or minor surgery (to repair blocked fallopian tubes in the female, for instance, or to repair a blockage in the testicles in the male). Other medical procedures are becoming more available today. These include artificial insemination, in vitro fertilization, embryo transplants, surrogate motherhood, embryo freezing, and other related techniques. As we'll see, these procedures can be successful, but they all raise the question of whether and to what extent technology should be involved in human creation. Adoption is a fifth option discussed here.

Artificial Insemination

This procedure may be indicated when a wife is presumably fertile but her husband is not. In **artificial insemination** a physician injects live male sperm into a woman's vagina when she is ovulating. In cases where the husband's sperm count is low, the physician may accumulate several of the husband's ejaculations (which are preserved by refrigeration) so that the greater quantity of semen introduced into the vagina overcomes the low sperm count. Should this fail, sperm from a donor other than the husband can be obtained and either mixed with the husband's sperm or used alone. (When a donor's sperm is used, the physician may attempt to match physical characteristics with the husband's.) The practice of mixing the donor's and the husband's sperm increases the possibility of fertilization by the husband's sperm—a possibility that can be extremely important to the couple psychologically.

Although it is not publicized, couples choose artificial insemination far more often than people may realize. The procedure is still very complicated, both emotionally and legally. The legal status of both the procedure and the child conceived varies from state to state (Mazor, 1979). Since some states may technically regard the practice as adultery and the child as illegitimate, it is important to get legal advice if this choice is made. The emotional issues are also complex: A husband may feel increased loss of manhood after the procedure, for example, along with jealousy of both the donor's and the wife's fertility.

In Vitro Fertilization

With **in vitro fertilization** a baby is conceived outside the woman's body (in a laboratory dish or jar) but develops within a woman's uterus. The process can be used when a woman with diseased or blocked fallopian tubes wants to give birth. An egg is removed from her surgically, fertilized in the laboratory with sperm from her husband (or, if her husband is infertile, from another donor), and reimplanted in her uterus within a few days. Pregnancy and childbirth follow the natural pattern described above.

The first in vitro baby, Louise Brown, was born in England in 1978. Since then, in vitro fertilization has "improved dramatically and become one of medicine's most glamorous fields" (Locke, 1982).

As of September 1983, there were twenty-five in vitro clinics in the United States, and it was predicted that there could be as many as fifty by that year's end. New centers were opening up so fast, in fact, that the method's pioneers were urging caution. In vitro fertilization, they warned, should remain a last resort, to be used only when all conventional therapy has been exhausted.

Modern technology continues to effect new fertilization techniques. In 1985 a process known as gamete intra-fallopian transfer (GIFT) was developed. In this procedure eggs are collected from the ovaries and mixed with sperm. The eggs and sperm are placed immediately in the woman's fallopian tubes, and the fertilized egg then travels to the uterus, as is the case in a normal pregnancy ("New fertilization technique," 1985). Another relatively new technique is for embryos, after being fertilized in vitro, to be frozen and implanted in a woman's uterus days or months later ("Embryo freezing," 1984).

In spite of obvious benefits to infertile married couples, artificial insemination and in vitro fertilization raise serious ethical questions for some people and have tremendous social implications. For example, with either the in vitro procedure or artificial insemination, a single woman could conceive and bear a child without ever developing any relationship, sexual or otherwise, with a man. Or a child could be born who is socially parentless. For example, future parents of a frozen and not-yet-implanted fertilized egg might be killed in an accident, as happened in Australia, leaving others to address the moral implications of what to do with the embryo ("Embryo freezing," 1984). Concern has been expressed about the destruction of partially developed fetuses or even fully developed infants who have no social sponsors (that is, parents), about "baby farms," and about selectivity—generating a number of babies from whom only the best are to survive. Experience suggests that family relationships persist in the face of technological change, so it seems possible that the potential for good in this method—reducing involuntary infertility—can be retained without the horrifying developments that are sometimes prophesied.

Surrogate Mothers

When a woman cannot carry a child to term and her husband is fertile and wants a child biologically his own, they can turn to a **surrogate mother**.

Here a husband fathers a child with another woman by artificial insemination; the woman, or surrogate mother, carries the child to term, then turns the baby over to the couple.

Surrogate motherhood, although not widespread, is increasing. In 1986 it was estimated that 500 children have been born to surrogate mothers since 1976 (Lawson, 1986). Like other methods described here, surrogate motherhood can be emotionally complex, involving jealousy on the part of the wife, possessiveness on the part of the surrogate mother, and the couple's feeling that the child is not completely theirs.

Moreover, the procedure worries attorneys who note that it exists in "legal limbo." Who is legally responsible for the baby should it be born deformed, for example, and should neither mother want it? In 1987 the case of "Baby M" made it clear that such fears are not unwarranted. Mary Beth Whitehead had contracted to bear a baby through artificial insemination for William and Elizabeth Stern. Stern's sperm was used to inseminate Whitehead, and she was to be paid $10,000 for her services. But later she turned down the money, preferring to keep the baby. The trial that followed raised several issues. The most central, of course, was whether a birth-mother has a natural right to her baby that supersedes legal contracts. Moreover, at least one observer pointed out that paid surrogates raise issues about social class and inequality in this country:

In the Baby M trial, M stands for money. . . . In the beginning both the Whiteheads and the Sterns chose to believe that Mary Beth wanted to carry this child for altruistic reasons. . . . But in real life the wealthy don't become surrogates and the poor do not buy surrogates and the hired matchmakers do not work for love [Goodman, 1987b]. ▪

Several states have considered laws to regulate surrogate motherhood. But such laws are sometimes met with opposition, largely from those who oppose surrogate motherhood as psychologically or morally wrong.

Then, too, setting a precedent for legal control over childbearing raises other troublesome issues. In 1987 San Diego County prosecutors brought a woman to criminal trial for contributing to her own baby's death by disobeying doctor's orders during her pregnancy. While a judge dismissed the charges, he did say that the California legislature "could, under certain narrowly defined circumstances, restrict the actions of pregnant women" to protect the health of fetuses. Most heralded the judge's dismissal as a victory for personal privacy and integrity ("Judge," 1987). Meanwhile, the case serves as a warning that high-tech procedures for having children may have inadvertently opened the door wider than many would prefer for legal control of conception and pregnancy. A fourth procedure, which we'll look at now, is the embryo transplant.

Embryo Transplants

In early 1984, a baby boy was born after being conceived through an **ovum transplant**, or **embryo transplant**, in which a fertilized egg is implanted into an infertile woman. The recipient of the embryo was an infertile woman in her 30s. The donor was a fertile woman with similar blood type and hair and eye color who was inseminated with sperm from the infertile woman's husband. Researchers extracted the embryo from the donor five days after fertilization and implanted it into the infertile woman.

Professor John E. Buster, who headed the project at the UCLA Medical School, said the procedure could be used in women who lack ovaries, as well as women with genetic disorders, such as cystic fibrosis, who want to give birth "without the worry of producing children with the same genetic problems" (quoted in "First 'ovum transfer' baby born," 1984:7).

Meanwhile, author Jeremy Rifkin, president of the Foundation on Economic Trends, located in Washington, D.C., and an opponent of genetic engineering, said he would take legal action to challenge plans to patent the process.

These plans reduce the process of human reproduction to a commercialized product to be bought and sold in the marketplace. We are starting on a journey here in which human life is being transformed into a consumer product to be packaged, marketed, and sold like every other [quoted in "First 'ovum transfer,'" 1984:9]. ▪

The private research firm that financed the research for the embryo transplant said it plans to set up clinics across the country where infertile women can pay from $4000 to $7000 to receive a fertilized egg from a donor. The firm has applied for patents on the process and the equipment used in the transfer, and for a copyright on the computer programs that match the donor with the infertile woman who will bear the child.

New high-tech processes such as these increase people's options. At the same time, they raise previously unimagined ethical questions. Another method of having children when conception is difficult or impossible is more traditional and differs from those we've already considered here. In **adoption**, individuals or couples become the legal parents of a child not biologically theirs.

ADOPTION

About 4 percent of American women will eventually adopt a child. More highly educated women, those not working full time, and those enjoying higher incomes are more likely to adopt. In each category black and white women are equally likely to adopt. The total number of adoptions increased steadily over recent decades and reached a peak in 1970 of about 175,000 children, but the number steadily declined since then. There is some national survey evidence that the downward trend in the annual number of adoptions has leveled off (Bachrach, 1986). Currently, there are fewer infants available for adoption because of increasingly effective contraception, legalized abortion, and the growing trend for women to keep babies they might bear out of wedlock (Bonham, 1977).[8] Would-be parents (including parents who already have chil-

dren) may adopt so-called "hard-to-place children"—those who are not white infants, but are older; black, Asian, or Hispanic; or handicapped. But transracial adoption, which was a developing pattern in the 1960s and early 1970s, has been much curtailed due to the objections of black community and professional groups. Black adopting parents, who are more apt to both be working, tend to prefer older children from age 2 to 6, who can be more easily taken care of in a dual-earner family. Consequently, black infants must wait three to six months to be adopted, while there are ten to forty agency applications for every white infant.

Parents seeking babies have turned to foreign adoptions and to independent adoptions; the latter are arranged directly with the mother or her agent (usually a lawyer) rather than through an adoption agency. The ratio of independent to agency adoptions is now 50:50 where a decade ago it was 30:70. Independent adoptions are criticized as rendering both the biological mother and the adopting parents vulnerable to exploitation, as well as being expensive. Agencies carefully screen prospective parents and ensure that the mother genuinely consents before the adoption. Agencies, however, are criticized for cumbersome bureaucratic procedures and a reluctance, according to some observers, to place children and relinquish control over them (Rule, 1984).

Until fairly recently, the adoption process was virtually always shrouded in secrecy. Natural parents did not know who adopted their children, and neither adoptive parents nor adopted children knew the natural parents. Today some of this is changing. Box 12-2 explores the recent trend toward making the adoption process less secretive.

While adoption is one solution to the problem of involuntary infertility, adoption takes place under other circumstances also. For example, single parents, female or male, may have adopted their child. A stepfather may adopt his wife's children by a former spouse; approximately 65 percent of adoptions involve related persons, often stepchildren (this proportion has increased as the number of infants or other [unrelated] children available for adoption has decreased [Bonham, 1977]). Or, in order to enrich their families, and acting out of a sense of social responsibility, couples may adopt hard-to-place children: older children, those of mixed races, the physically or mentally handicapped, and so forth. Couples may adopt some or all of their children out of concern for the problem of overpopulation.

---

8. It is interesting to note that much data on childbearing and other ways of becoming parents are reported as data on women, as though men had nothing to do with becoming parents. This tends to occur for two reasons: One is the traditional mode of thinking that associates children and women. The other has to do with methodological strategies. Women are thought to be more reliable sources of data on fertility, contraception, abortion, and so on. Men, even husbands, may not be fully informed about the woman partner's pregnancy history or use of contraception; women, of course, may become pregnant when not in a regular relationship with a man. In the past women were also more easily interviewed, as they were at home more often. If it was more efficient to interview only one member of the couple, the wife was chosen (Safilios-Rothschild, 1969).

We have recently become more sensitive to the quite different perspectives that husbands and wives may have about the same events. Many studies now interview both husbands and wives and compare their responses. We have also become less neglectful of the male's role in reproduction. Arthur Shostak's recent book on men in abortion (Shostak and McLouth, 1984) draws attention to the social and psychological consequences of excluding men from various aspects of the reproductive process and from research on this process.

While adoption rates are higher for infertile couples, over half of all women who have adopted have also given birth to a child (Bonham, 1977). It should be noted, however, that adoption is not a cure for infertility: Couples who have adopted a child conceive at about the same rate as those who have not adopted (Mazor, 1979:112). Moreover, statistically it is more likely that adopting follows giving birth than the other way around (Bonham, 1977).

Summary

Today, individuals have more choice than ever about whether, when, and how many children to have. Although parenthood has become more of an option, there is no evidence of an embracement of childlessness. The majority of Americans continue to value parenthood, believe that childbearing should accompany marriage, and feel social pressure to have children. Only a very small percentage view childlessness as an advantage, regard the decision not to have children as positive, believe that the ideal family is one without children, or expect to be childless by choice (Thornton and Freedman, 1983:16). Chapter 13 discusses living with children.

Nevertheless, it is likely that changing values concerning parenthood, the weakening of social norms prescribing marriage and parenthood, a wider range of alternatives for women, the desire to postpone marriage and childbearing, and the availability of modern contraceptives and legal abortion will result in a higher proportion of Americans remaining childless (Thornton and Freedman, 1983:16). In fact, some observers have begun to worry that American society may be drifting into a period of structural antinatalism.

Children can add a fulfilling and highly rewarding experience to people's lives, but they also impose complications and stresses, both financial and emotional. Couples today are faced with three options other than the traditional family of two or more children: remaining childless, postponing parenthood until they are ready, and having only one child. Often, people's decisions concerning having a family are made by default.

Birthrates in general are declining for married women and for older unmarried women. Women are waiting longer to have their first child and are having, on the average, two children. Pregnancy outside of marriage has increased, particularly for women in their teens and early 20s. This experience can be emotionally costly, and the odds are against success in marriages that take place to legitimize a baby. It is difficult to be a single teen parent, and there are lifetime economic and educational disadvantages. Many unmarried women choose abortion, which permits the woman to continue her original life plan, but which may be emotionally distressing to both the woman and her partner.

Several methods of contraception are available and these are discussed in Appendix C. The anatomy and physiology of pregnancy and childbirth are presented in Appendix B. For couples who have difficulty in conceiving, there are several alternatives. These include artificial insemination, in vitro fertilization, embryo transplant, and use of a surrogate mother. Adoption is a way of becoming parents without conceiving; many families have both adopted and biological children.

Key Terms

crude birthrate *381*	involuntary infertility *403*
total fertility rate *381*	artificial insemination *406*
pronatalist bias *386*	in vitro fertilization *406*
structural antinatalism *386*	surrogate mother *406*
opportunity costs *389*	embryo or ovum transplant *407*
programmatic postponers *393*	adoption *408*
paradoxical pregnancy *399*	
abortion *400*	

Study Questions

1. Discuss reasons why there aren't as many large families as there used to be.
2. How is a pronatalist bias shown in our society? What effect does such a bias have on people who are trying to decide whether to have children?
3. Discuss the advantages and disadvantages of having children. Which do you think are the strongest reasons for having children? Which do you think are the strongest reasons for not having children?
4. What do you see as the major differences among couples choosing to have children

BOX 12·2

"SHARING"

OPENS

·WINDOW

ON SECRETS

OF ADOPTION

The desire of many adopted persons to contact their birth parents have developed into a movement to change state laws to permit the opening of adoption records. Many states now have laws permitting the adoptee access to records at a certain age or under certain conditions. Advocacy groups of adoptees have formed to support these legal changes; other groups of adoptive parents have opposed change in some cases, while social workers and other professionals have taken varying positions. The outcome of this political process has varied; some laws have been changed, and others have not.

In the excerpt below, another approach is presented concerning the adopted child's desire to know about his or her parents. In open (or semi-open) adoption biological and adoptive parents may agree to exchange information. This will not necessarily lead to contact between the adopted child and his or her biological parents in adulthood but does have some advantages for both, while permitting the adoptive parents to exercise some control also.

Kathy, a 17-year-old high school senior, has received 10 pictures of her infant son since she gave him up for adoption last spring. She knows what Shawn looks like, when the 7-month-old got his first teeth, how much he weighs, and when he was able to hold up his head by himself.

His adoptive parents began sharing pictures and developmental information about Shawn soon after the baby joined their family.

The three Omahans are taking part in a relatively new, and more open, approach to adoption....

"Adoption is increasingly recognized as a dynamic, ongoing, lifelong process for all parties involved," [Carol J. Sorich, a Louisiana adoption specialist] said. "Birth parents' pain and guilt may be lessened, adoptive parents' fears and questions may be diminished, and the adopted person's need for continuity and genetic information may be attained more realistically and accurately with the use of alternatives."

FIRST NAMES ONLY

Art and Pat, Shawn's adoptive parents, and Kathy know each other only by their first names. They have agreed to a semi-open adoption, which means that the birth parent meets the adoptive parents, but identities are not revealed.

At the meeting, which usually takes place at the agency handling the adoption, both parties exchange personal information. Generally, this occurs after the birth parent has signed relinquishments but prior to the actual placement of the child.

Later, if a sharing agreement has been made, an exchange of information and photographs is monitored by the agency, which in this case is the Child Saving Institute in Omaha....

Choices in the approach offered at CSI include: sharing the child's pictures and developmental information with the birth parent without meeting; semi-

SOURCE:
Brown, 1982; p. 16-E.

open adoption with a meeting and partial identification; and open adoption, in which the adoptive parents and birth parents are fully identified.

By providing these options in varying degrees, CSI is opening the adoption process for all parties involved, [said Donna Heger of CSI].

But the options are only for those who want them. "We don't pressure anyone into doing something they won't be comfortable with," she said. "It should be stressed that not all birth parents or adoptive parents will desire a more open approach." . . .

"FEELINGS OF LOSS"

Relinquishing a baby is similar to the grief process a person goes through when a loved one dies, Ms. Heger said. "A natural mother just doesn't relinquish her baby and shut the door. She grieves over her loss."

And because "the concern of the birth parent for the child does not end with the signing of the relinquishment, and her feelings of loss and need to complete the grieving process are, in fact, hampered by the closed system," adoption agencies are beginning to open up, Ms. Sorich said. . . .

"In follow-up contacts, social workers could observe how viewing the pictures gave peace of mind, reassurance and comfort to the birth parents as they worked through the grieving process. . . . The girls are dealing with the fact that they are the biological parent but the adoptive parents are their baby's 'real' parents."

Kathy said she has no difficulty in accepting Art and Pat as Shawn's "real parents."

"I realize that they will be the ones who dry his tears and marvel at his accomplishments." . . .

Under the agreement between Shawn's parents and Kathy, Kathy will receive pictures of Shawn once every three months for two years and once a year thereafter, indefinitely.

In turn, Pat said she has asked Kathy for a picture of her and the baby's natural father so Shawn will know what his parents looked like.

WHAT THEY LEARNED

When Kathy, her mother and Art and Pat met with a social worker at CSI, the group stayed for 3½ hours.

"We kept wanting to talk and talk," Pat said.

Kathy said meeting Shawn's adoptive parents made her feel better about giving up her son.

"It was important for me to be able to envision the kind of people he would call Mom and Dad. I could tell by listening to them talk and watching them listen to each other talk, that they were the kind of people I would want the baby to spend the rest of his life with."

(continued)

BOX 12·2

continued

And Pat said she and Art learned that their son's mother was "a delightful person . . . very intelligent, with a lot of ambition." She said she will now be able to answer questions the boy might ask someday about his natural mother. "If he asks, 'What was she like?' I can say, "Well, I talked to her and she said. . . .

Kathy said her parents were apprehensive about meeting the adoptive parents three days after she had relinquished her baby. "They were afraid of what I would do if I didn't like them—that I would have no peace." But the meeting went well.

On the day in April when Shawn first met his new parents, he was wearing a nightie, cap and quilt made by his natural grandmother. Pinned to his undershirt was a locket that belonged to his grandmother's mother.

"I put that away for him," Pat said.

A LETTER FOR SHAWN

There is also a letter for Shawn from Kathy. Art and Pat placed it in a safe deposit box to be given to the boy "when he is old enough to handle what is in it," Pat said.

Kathy said she hopes that when Shawn reads the letter, he will better understand why she did what she did.

"I told him that I want him to know he wasn't unloved or unwanted, just unplanned . . . that I wasn't prepared to take care of him the way he deserved to be taken care of."

---

soon after marriage, those choosing to remain childless, those postponing parenthood, and those choosing to have only one child?

5. What can cause involuntary infertility? What might account for the recent increase in its frequency?

6. Rate artificial insemination, conception outside the body, and enlisting a surrogate mother as methods of conception. Discuss emotional, physical, and legal difficulties associated with each method.

7. What are some important issues surrounding abortion? How does a social scientific perspective on abortion differ from that of either prolife or prochoice?

8. Do we live in an antinatalist society? Why or why not?

Suggested Readings

"After contraception: Dispelling rumors about later childbearing." *Population Reports*, Series J (28) (Sept.–Oct. 1984). Population Information Program, Johns Hopkins University, Hampton House, 624 North Broadway, Baltimore, Md., 21205.
    A readable publication in pamphlet or magazine format, giving details on various contraceptives and their effect on fertility. Write Johns Hopkins for it, or ask your librarian.

Arditti, Rita, Renate Duelli Klein, and Shelley Minden (eds.)

1984   *Test-Tube Women: What Future for Motherhood?* London: Routledge and Kegan Paul (Pandora).

Fascinating set of readable articles, from a feminist perspective, on all aspects of reproduction technologies, including surrogate parenting and artificial insemination. Also includes readings on issues of disability.

Bean, Philip (ed.)
1984 *Adoption: Essays in Social Policy, Law, and Sociology.* London and New York: Tavistock Publications.
A collection of scholarly essays by experts in all areas of adoption. Topics include, among others, the role of voluntary societies in adoption, adopting older children, and stepparent adoption.

The Boston Women's Health Book Collective
1984 *The New Our Bodies, Ourselves: A Book by and for Women.* New York: Simon & Schuster.
A book worth having, whether you're male or female. Gives detailed, realistically and respectfully presented information on women's anatomy and physiology, on "taking care of ourselves," on relationships and sexuality, fertility control, childbearing, and growing older, and on "the politics of women and medical care."

Daniels, Pamela, and Kathy Weingarten
1982 *The Timing of Parenthood in Adult Lives.* New York: Norton.
An intensive research study of some seventy couples.

Fabe, Marilyn, and Norma Wikler
1979 *Up Against the Clock: Career Women Speak on the Choice to Have Children.* New York: Random House.
Review of the options on childbearing for career women growing out of the authors' own experiences. Includes illustrative case studies.

Furstenberg, Frank F., Jr., Richard Lincoln, and June Menten
1981 *Teenage Sexuality, Pregnancy, and Childbearing.* Philadelphia: University of Pennsylvania Press.
Comprehensive set of articles on this important social problem.

Luker, Kristin
1975 *Taking Chances: Abortion and the Decision Not to Contracept.* Berkeley and Los Angeles: University of California Press.
Research study based on interviews with women obtaining abortions, but really about how contraceptive use is influenced by relationship pressures, desire for spontaneity and "romance," and attitudes toward self and sexuality.

Macfarlane, Aidan
1977 *The Psychology of Childbirth.* Cambridge, Mass.: Harvard University Press.
Discusses social and psychological factors in childbirth. Goes through the birth process step-by-step, including the mother-infant relationship after birth.

Peck, Ellen
1971 *The Baby Trap.* New York: Bernard Geis.
Argument for a child-free life-style.
1977 *The Joy of the Only Child.* New York: Delacorte.
Argument for the only child.

Rothman, Barbara K.
1985 *The Tentative Pregnancy: Prenatal Diagnosis and the Future of Motherhood.*
Examines the new birth technology, especially amniocentesis.

Shostak, Arthur
1984 *Men in Abortion: Losses, Lessons, and Love.* New York: Praeger.
Essays and research reports on men's attitudes, feelings, and roles in abortion.

Tanzer, Deborah, and Jean L. Block
1972 *Why Natural Childbirth? A Psychologist's Report on the Benefits to Mothers, Fathers, and Babies.* New York: Schocken.
Study of women experiencing natural compared with standard childbirth indicates that natural childbirth facilitates not only mother-child bonding but also the husband-wife relationship.

Walter, Carolyn Ambler
1986 *The Timing of Motherhood.* Lexington, Mass.: Heath.
A readable book, based on scholarly research, investigating the effect of timing on motherhood. The book looks at women's perception of the mother role, satisfaction with parenthood, relationships and family patterns, balancing the dual roles of motherhood and employment, and "energy of youth versus perspective of maturity."

Zimmerman, Mary K.
1977 *Passage Through Abortion: The Personal and Social Reality of Women's Experiences.* New York: Praeger.
Sociological research study of women in abortion, distinguishing women who have a "difficult passage" through abortion from women who have a "smooth passage" through abortion because they have social support.

13 Rearing Children

*It's difficult to have faith
in the miracle of growth
when so much is at
stake.*
EDA LE SHAN

In being a parent one engages in personal relationships with one's children. The parent-child
relationship, like other intimate relationships, is
characterized by love and hate, warmth and anger,
satisfaction and frustration. These sometimes contradictory feelings often take parents by surprise,
for our society prepares people to expect the
rewards of parenthood but not the frustrations.

In this chapter we will discuss a limited range
of parenting issues. We'll begin by looking at parenting roles and how they vary according to family
makeup and individual parenting styles. We will
then look at parenting over the course of life. We'll
discuss some common parenting issues as well as
the more extreme problem of child maltreatment
in the United States today. Finally, we'll examine
how parents can make relationships with their children more satisfying.

PARENTS AS CAREGIVERS

For most of human history, adults reared children
simply by living with them. From a very early age
children shared the everyday world of adults,
working beside them, dressing like them, sleeping
near them. The concept of childhood as different
from adulthood did not emerge until about the sev-
enteenth century (Ariès, 1962). Children were
increasingly assigned the role of student and were
gradually drawn away or segregated from the adult
world. While children may continue to do household chores, especially in rural areas, the move to
school has been a move away from participation in
the everyday lives of adults. One result is that people today regard children as persons who need *child
care*—special training, guidance, and care
(DeMause, 1975). This section explores the part
mothers and fathers play in modern child rearing.

The Mother's Role

Our cultural tradition stipulates that mothers
assume primary responsibility for child rearing, as
Chapter 7 points out. While this is changing, child
care in the United States is still regarded as the
personal responsibility of the mother; and it is the
mother who is expected to be the child's primary
psychological parent, assuming the major emotional responsibility for the safety and upbringing
of her children.

Mothers: Myth Versus Reality Our society not
only expects mothers to be the primary parent, it
often puts forth a romanticized, unrealistic image
of motherhood and the "maternal instinct" as well
(Wortis, 1974). For example, an essay entitled

"What's a Mother?" in the *Farmer's Almanac* gives this definition:

A mother is a woman who can bake a cake with six other hands helping her, and still have it turn out fine....

A mother is different. She likes chicken wings and backs—things that kids and Daddy don't care for. She never takes the last chop on the plate, and she always saves the candy from her tray at the club to bring home to the children....

When a mother dies, she must face Him with her record of accomplishments. If she's done a good job of caring for her children, she'll get the most sought-after position in heaven, that of rocking baby angels on soft white clouds, and wiping their celestial tears with the corner of her apron. ∎

Essential to the romanticizing of mothers is the assumption that children's mothers are *best* able to fill their physical and emotional needs. A related assumption is that dire consequences will follow from *maternal deprivation:* regular or prolonged separation of children, especially infants and pre-schoolers, from their mothers. Social scientists point out that romanticizing motherhood and focusing on the dangers of maternal deprivation lead people to overlook the stressful realities of mother-child relationships (Wortis, 1974).

Social scientists have examined the assumption that mothers should be children's primary and full-time caretakers. They have found, for one thing, that the roles of full-time homemaker and mother "do not necessarily go neatly together." Being a good homemaker may interfere with quality time for children (Oakley, 1974b). One study found that, on the average, full-time homemakers spent only about seventy-five minutes a day directly interacting with their children (Robinson, 1977). Then, too, as Chapter 11 explores, full-time homemaker-mothers, especially those with young children, often find themselves segregated from the outside world. Modern American society is unusual in placing the burden of child rearing squarely on the mother. When mothers feel isolated as a result, their relationships with their children are not likely to be satisfying.

The late Margaret Mead interviewed mothers who were happy with their role. Important to their satisfaction, she found, was the fact that they had "arranged for some personal freedom from child care." Mead found these women's attitudes to be different from those of young mothers she had talked with ten years before, who often felt harassed but were "far less willing" to leave their children with other caregivers (Mead and Metraux, 1979:79–80). How does this change affect children? Research into employed mothers with children provides some answers.

Employed Mothers as Caregivers Research indicates that mothers' employment, in and of itself, is not harmful to children. In some respects, in fact, it has positive effects. For example, girls generally admire their mothers more if the mothers are employed. Mothers in professional occupations tend to have high-achieving children (Etaugh, 1974:74).

Of course, such positive effects may not be automatic. The two important elements are how much interaction takes place between the working mother and her children and the quality of that interaction. Children can form as strong an attachment to a working parent as to a nonworking one, provided they interact frequently when they are together (Etaugh, 1974).

The quality of the interaction is related to several factors besides the individual personalities of mother and child. There is evidence that the presence of an emotionally supportive father positively affects "maternal competence" (Parke, 1986:61). An overloaded mother experiencing role conflict and stress is less likely to feel relaxed with her children. Single mothers, particularly those who may be working *more* than full-time, don't have much occasion for relaxed time with their children. Whether employed full- or part-time, some mothers respond by feeling short-tempered and guilty; they may overcompensate by trying to accommodate their children's every request. But if a woman and her family can deal creatively with overload problems, which were discussed in Chapter 11, employment can have positive effects on the mother-child relationship, especially if the mother is happy in her employment. The quality of child-care help that dual-breadwinner families receive is another important factor, as we'll see at the end of this chapter.

The parenting role of a mother with a full-time job is growing more similar to the role fathers have traditionally played. What elements does the father's role have in common with, and how does it differ from, the mother's role?

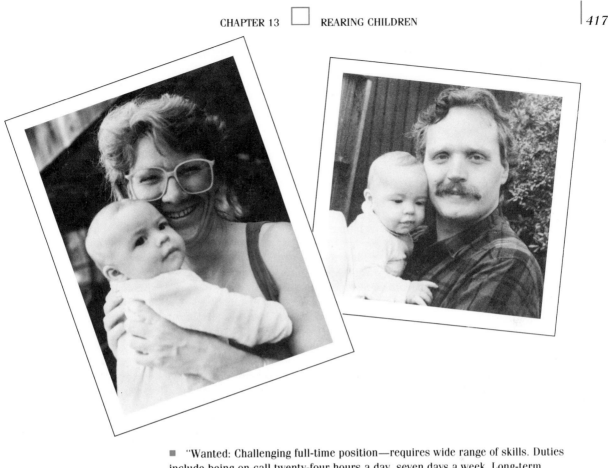

■ "Wanted: Challenging full-time position—requires wide range of skills. Duties include being on-call twenty-four hours a day, seven days a week. Long-term commitment required. Must be able to handle stress and be willing to change diapers. Stamina and flexibility are a plus. No previous experience required." What qualities would you add to this job description for parents?

The Father's Role

Just as the myth of motherhood leads people to expect mothers to be better equipped for parenting than fathers, a myth of fatherhood implies that fathers just aren't "cut out" for the role.

According to Michael Lamb, social scientists themselves have contributed to this myth:

There is a peculiar tendency to infer sequentially that, because mothers are the primary caretakers, they are more important than fathers, and thus that they alone deserve investigation. This rapidly becomes translated into a belief that mothers are uniquely important (1976:29). ■

The Importance of Fathering Social scientists have tested these theories, with interesting findings. In one study of the popular assumption that fathers are less competent than mothers to care for newborns, researchers found that while mothers spent more time in caretaking activities, fathers were no less sensitive to feeding cues from the infant (Parke and Swain, 1976). As Case Study 13·1, "A Full-Time Father's Story," illustrates, fathers who care for older children may display nurturant behavior in the same way mothers do.

Another study compared mothers' and fathers' attitudes about the division of labor in parenting (Nye et al., 1976). In this survey conducted in the early seventies, a substantial majority of fathers

CASE STUDY
13·1

A FULL-TIME
FATHER'S
STORY

Bob is 31, comes from a working-class background, and has been married seven years. At the time of this interview, he had just gotten out of the Air Force and was collecting unemployment benefits. His wife is a clerical worker. His future goal, he said, is to be a child psychologist. He has two children—Tim, 6, and a daughter, Nicole, 18 months. His father deserted the family when Bob was a baby, and he feels he suffered greatly as a result. Here he describes what it's like for him to be a temporary house husband and full-time father.

Today I took a bunch of kids from my son's school to the zoo. Kindergartners. You know I like kids (*laughs*).... It was something hectic. The kids, they all want to run six different ways. They were climbing over the fences and through the fences to the elephants....

I think fathers should be more involved with their kids when it is possible. In fact, a couple of mothers commented [at the zoo] that they were happy to see a father along for a change. I never had a father.... I'm determined that my son and I should have time together—which is tough when I'm working.... [But for a while now] I've got the two kids. I fix them lunch and all that. You fix a can of soup, you give her half, you give him half. Hers you don't have any soup in it—just noodles and stuff because she eats with her fingers and you don't want any soup in there. And while they're eating I usually get dressed to take them out. And after they're done eating, I dress them.

I change her diaper and dress her and I dress my kid for school and take him to school. And while the kid's at school, we go somewhere like the park— me and the baby.... There aren't too many dads in the park, I'll tell you. Most of them are out working. I get some strange looks once in a while, but it doesn't bother me. I really doesn't. Besides, if some fox comes by, I'll just tell her my wife and I were divorced and I got the kids, right? (*laughs*).... Then

thought that parents should share child care equally. In fact, considerably more fathers (62 percent) than mothers (44 percent) felt this way. This research also showed that 51 percent of mothers (and only 27 percent of fathers) thought mothers should spend the most time in child care. There was more agreement that both parents should share in children's socialization. In most aspects of socialization—for instance, teaching the child to get along with others—the majority of mothers and fathers concurred. Ninety percent of mothers and 93 percent of fathers thought parents should share equally in teaching children right from wrong.

In practice, fathers participated less in child care (physical care and nurturance) than did mothers. However, fathers did contribute fairly equally in socialization (values training), especially in tasks dealing with moral and social development (Nye et al., 1976).

The Nye study is based on a sample from Yakima County, Washington, an area with more farm population and lower income than the U.S. population as a whole (for 1970). A more recent national poll with a wide range of respondents (not all were parents) found a slightly lower percentage of support for the notion that "both sexes have the responsibility to care for small children," but a majority (56 percent) supported this point of view

about two thirty, quarter to three, I drive over to the school from the park, and it's time for him to get out. Not the stereotype you'd think, huh?

Sometimes it's a pain, you know. I can't get anything done. And there's a lot of things I could do, but it's really a chore to keep track of the baby. She's at the age now where she wants outside all the time, and it's really a hassle. I mean I'll bring her in the back door, and while you're locking the back door, she goes out the front. She's one door to the other, and she's out again. Yesterday our son came in, yelling, "She's out walking down the sidewalk!" She was having herself a good old time. . . .

I would do it [though] anytime I was off work because, well, I look at the economical aspects. I can't afford to pay for child care when I'm at home. It's much, much cheaper for me to go ahead and do it myself, and it's not really that much of a hassle . . . unless you've gotta go to the library or something like that. You can't drag them with you because—I took them to the library to get some books and I about went nuts chasing the little one around the shelves. She's really too young to understand "Now you stay there!" And she smiles and she's gone by the time you can turn around. . . .

I'm going to keep doing this until my twenty-six weeks is up or I find a job. I'm not saying I'm not looking for a job now, but I am saying I'll probably keep doing this all the twenty-six weeks. . . . I love those kids to pieces. I can just sit there and just look at them, and just smile inwardly at what they do, you know. I don't know if it detracts from my image or anything. . . .

■ In what ways might Bob and his wife's arrangement be better than day care, do you think? Not as good as day care? As a parent, what would you do differently from Bob? What do you like about Bob's style of fathering? Do you think Bob is a house husband and full-time father now only because of economics? What else motivates him?

in 1980. The trend in the 1980 poll was toward greater support for the involvement of both parents than in 1970 (when it was 33 percent) (Yankelovich, 1981), a trend reflected in the greater involvement of fathers in the birthing process.

Fathers and Birthing It is now common for fathers to be allowed into delivery rooms; this practice was considered dangerous and inappropriate just two decades ago. The involvement of fathers, who may be active participants in delivery as "coaches," timing contractions, encouraging proper breathing, and providing emotional support, indicates the extent to which we have redefined parenting roles. The father is to be an active parent not only after birth but throughout the pregnancy and birthing process.

A study of 218 married women giving birth (Black et al., 1981) indicates, however, that this practice is very much limited to the urban, white, upper middle class. The authors advocate wider participation in prenatal classes and labor for fathers, finding from their study that reduced pain and enhanced enjoyment of the delivery process were associated with the active participation of the father in prenatal classes and labor. Women often did not attend such classes, in fact, if their husbands did not approve or were not interested enough to go.

Observations of Fathers Recent research has focused on fathering, the actual behavior of fathers and its impact on children (e.g., Robinson and Barret, 1986). (Parenting studies in the past, especially studies of infants, more often focused on mothers, and when fathers were the subject of investigation, the data were usually obtained from mothers rather than by direct observation or interviews of fathers [Lamb, 1978].)

Naturalistic observation in home settings with both parents present shows that infants attach to both parents equally strongly. "There was no indication that either parent could be described as a primary or preferred attachment figure" during the first year (Lamb, 1978:91). By age 2 the overall attachment preference was for fathers. This result was an outcome of the boys' consistent preference for fathers, while girls were less consistent—some preferring father, some mother, some neither. Infants in the second year of life did, however, prefer mothers when under stress.

Fathers and mothers, according to Lamb's research on infants, give their children different experiences. Fathers provided physically stimulating play and unpredictable games; mothers, toy-mediated play and conventional games. Mothers are more apt to pick up the baby to care for it or to move the child away from forbidden areas or objects; fathers held infants in play or in response to infants wanting to be held (Lamb, 1978).

In Sweden, where fathers are less apt to engage in play with infants, the infants have less attachment to them, clearly preferring mothers, unlike American infants. Except for the difference in play behavior, Swedish fathers, like American fathers, were distinctly different from mothers in their behavior with children. Mothers were more apt to talk to, give attention to, touch and hold, and be affectionate toward infants. The behavior of nontraditional Swedish fathers, those who had taken at least three months' paternity leave to be the child's primary parent during this period, did not differ from the behavior of traditional fathers (Lamb et al., 1983).

Other research shows that fathers play a significant role in influencing both their daughters' and their sons' gender-role identification and adoption of general cultural values (Heilbrun, 1976; Lamb and Lamb, 1976). Research on ninety boys age 8–11 found that a son's personality development was related to his father's nurturance and participation in the son's care (Lynn, 1976).

Lamb believes that "fathers may be playing an especially important role in the personality development of their children from early in the first years of their children's lives" (Lamb, 1978:92), particularly with regard to gender identity. The influence of fathers on gender-role identification may be due to their greater interactive efforts with sons (compared to their efforts with daughters and compared to mothers' efforts with sons). In research on children under age 2, "it seemed that the parents were behaving in such a way as to maximize the salience of the same-sex parent in the infant's life, and . . . the sex differentiating behavior of the fathers was most significant" (Lamb, 1978:92).

Some professionals view the father's relationship with the child as an indirect one mediated by the mother-child bond (Clarke-Stewart, 1977). But Lamb sees the father's relationship with the infant as an independent one. He maintains that the father has a direct effect on the child, rather than an indirect influence through the father's relationship to the mother. Since each parent-infant relationship is "qualitatively different . . . [and] may make independent and important contributions to the personality development of the child," encouragement of father-child relationships is desirable (Lamb, 1978:102). Lamb does not go so far as to conclude that single-parent families have damaging effects—in fact, he cites research to the contrary, which suggests that it is the economic impact of the father's absence that may account for many differences that exist. Nevertheless, his research suggests that where it is possible, arranging matters so that fathers can spend significant amounts of time with children is important. (Chapter 2 includes a discussion of Nancy Chodorow's theory of gender-role socialization, which posits certain effects of imbalanced parenting roles.)

Employment and the Father's Role Today, many fathers are more motivated than their own fathers were to meet the emotional needs of their children (Franklin, 1984:114–15). Fathers are "less authoritarian and arbitrary, and are much less austere and unapproachable than fathers of the recent past" (Lynn, 1977:384). Nevertheless, "Despite the highly publicized rhetoric of the 'new fatherhood,' the tradition of the absent, distant, silent father is still very much with us" (Shapiro, 1984:68). As we've seen throughout the text, the parenting role of fathers is undermined by social expectations (Stein, 1984). These expectations include more than the popular attitude that father's aren't "cut out" for a nurturant role; work demands are also involved (Pleck, 1986).

As Chapter 11 discussed, tradition keeps fathers out of the house for long hours. Ironically, the executive-professional man's working hours have been increasing in recent years (Lynn, 1977), and more and more workingmen are taking second jobs to keep up with inflation. The heavy economic demands of childbearing and child rearing (Oppenheimer, 1974) tend to remove the husband from the home just when he is most needed by his children. At least one national study found that, while women entered the labor force in large numbers between 1965–1975, men's involvement in housework or childcare increased very little (Coverman and Sheley, 1986). In David Lynn's words, "In our society the absence of the father through death or divorce can be considered simply an extreme on the prevailing continuum of father absence" (Lynn, 1977:39). Research also shows that a father's authority at home is undermined as a result of his absence (Cohen, 1977).

At the other end of the continuum, recent research by child psychologist Kyle Pruett on seventeen stay-at-home fathers (with breadwinner wives) found those infants, age 2–22 months, scored "way above the norms" on development measures, which Pruett attributes to love and attention from *both* parents. The working mothers continued to be very involved with their babies, often breastfeeding, while fathers and babies formed "deep attachments." According to Pruett, the babies thrived "because instead of having one and a quarter or one and a half parents, they have two real parents" (Carro, 1983:71). A two-year follow-up indicated continued high rates of development, even when some of the fathers eventually returned to work and placed the children in day care.

Modern Parenting: Sometimes a Frustrating Experience

The incompatibility of the parenting role with the working role is but one source of frustration for fathers and mothers trying to raise their children. Parenting is characterized by frustration, especially today. We can identify at least five reasons why this is so.

First, as we have noted previously, parenting today requires one to learn attitudes and techniques that are different from those of one's parents. Second, parents today rear their children in a pluralist society, characterized by diverse and conflicting values. Parents are only one of several influences on children. Others are schools, peers, television, movies, music, books, and travel. While parents want to pass their own ideas and attitudes on, their children may reject these for other, quite different points of view. Third, as we'll see in the discussion of parenting styles, the recent emphasis on the malleability of children tends to make parents feel anxious and guilty about their performance. Psychologists have popularized the fact that parents influence their children's I.Q.'s and self-esteem. As a result, writes social scientist Arlene Skolnick, "popular and professional knowledge does not seem to have made parenting easier" (1978b:56).

This is complicated by a fourth fact—that child-rearing experts disagree among themselves. Over the years they have shifted their emphasis from one child-rearing goal to another, from one "best" technique to another. Fifty years ago, notes psychologist Jerome Kagan, parenting was much easier because parents felt they knew what to do when their children got into trouble at school. In contrast, "There is no consensus in America today as to what a child should be like when he is a young adult—or about how you get him there" (*Newsweek*, Sept. 22, 1975, p. 48).

A fifth reason why being a parent can be particularly frustrating today is that our society does not offer parents much psychological or social support. Many people consider child rearing a low-status endeavor, and as Urie Bronfenbrenner points out, society is generally indifferent to the needs of parents. When compared with occupational success and individual actualization for adults, "the family takes a low priority" (Bronfenbrenner, 1977:41). (Chapter 12 discusses whether American society is becoming structurally antinatalistic.)

FIVE PARENTING STYLES

Considering the lack of consensus about how to raise children today, it may seem difficult to single out styles of parenting. From one point of view there are as many parenting styles as there are parents (Laws, 1978). Yet certain elements in relating to children can be broadly classified. One helpful grouping is provided in E. E. LeMasters's listing of five parenting styles: the martyr, the pal, the police officer, the teacher-counselor, and the athletic coach (LeMasters, 1977).[1] Individual parents probably combine elements of two or more of these styles in their own personal parenting styles. We will discuss each of these.

The Parent as Martyr

Martyring parents believe "I would do anything for my child." (Remember the "What's a Mother?" excerpt near the beginning of this chapter?) Some common examples of martyring are parents who habitually wait on their children or pick up after them, parents who nag children rather than letting them remember things for themselves, parents who buy virtually anything the child asks for, and parents who always do what the children want to do.

This parenting style presents some problems. First, the goals the martyring parents set are impossible to carry out, and so the parent must always feel guilty. Second, as Chapter 3 pointed out, martyring tends to generate manipulative behavior. Finally, it is useful to ask if persons who consistently deny their own needs can enjoy the role of parenting and if closeness between parent and child is possible under these conditions.

The Parent as Pal

Some modern parents, mainly those of older children and adolescents, feel that they should be pals to their children. They adopt a **laissez-faire discipline** policy, letting their children set their own goals, rules, and limits, with little or no guidance from parents (Jurich, 1978:21–22). According to LeMasters, "pal" parents apparently believe that they can avoid the conflict caused by the generation gap in this way.

Pal parenting is unrealistic. For one thing, parents in our society *are* responsible for guiding their

children's development. Children deserve to benefit from the greater knowledge and experience of their parents, and at all ages they need some rules and limits, although these change as children grow older. Much research relates laissez-faire parenting to juvenile delinquency, heavy drug use, and runaway behavior in children (Jurich, 1978:21–22).

LeMasters points out that there are also relationship risks in the pal-parent model. If things don't go well, parents may want to retreat to a more formal, authoritarian style of parenting. But once they've established a buddy relationship, it is difficult to regain authority (LeMasters, 1977).

The Parent as Police Officer

The police officer (or drill sergeant) model is just the opposite of the pal. These parents make sure the child obeys all the rules at all times, and they punish their children for even minor offenses. Being a police officer doesn't work very well today, however, and **autocratic discipline**, which places the entire power of determining rules and limits in the parents' hands, has been associated—like laissez-faire parenting—with juvenile delinquency, drug use, and runaway teenagers (Jurich 1978).

There are several reasons why the police officer role doesn't work today. First, Americans have tended to resist anything resembling tyranny ever since the days of the Boston Tea Party. Hence, children are socialized to demand a share of independence at an early age.

Second, rapid social change gives old and young people different values and points of view and even different knowledge. In our complex culture youth learn attitudes from specialized professionals, such as teachers and school counselors, who often "widen the intellectual gap between parent and child" (Davis, 1974:455).

Third, children, who find support from their adolescent peers, will eventually confront and challenge their parents. LeMasters points out that the adolescent peer group is "a formidable opponent" to any autocratic parent who insists on strict allegiance to authority (LeMasters, 1977:195).

Finally, as one study of 451 college freshmen and sophomores at a large western university indicated, adolescents are far more likely to be influenced by their parents' knowledge and expertise or a wish to identify with parents' values than by the parents' authority. The key is respect and a

---

1. There are some similarities between the police officer, the coach, the pal, and Baumrind's authoritarian, laissez-faire, and authoritative parenting styles (Baumrind, 1971:1–102). The reader who would like a more scholarly presentation of modes of parental control should pursue Baumrind's article and related psychological research. See also Cromwell and Olson, 1975; Thomas et al., 1974; Straus, 1974; Broderick, 1978:321–23; Bronfenbrenner, 1958:61; and Kagan et al., 1978.

■ "My dad knows everything": For children facing a world full of such peculiar elements as the internal combustion engine, parents can provide "how-to" expertise that serves as a model for development. But as parents soon learn, some answers do not satisfy children's favorite question, "Why?"

close relationship; habitual punishment and the "policing" of adolescents are far less effective modes of socialization (McDonald, 1977).

The Parent as Teacher-Counselor

The parent as teacher-counselor acts in accord with the **developmental model of child rearing,** in which the child is viewed as an extremely plastic organism with virtually unlimited potential for growth and development. The only limitations on this rich potential are in the inability of the parent to tap and encourage it (LeMasters, 1977:453). This model conceptualizes the parent(s) as almost omnipotent in guiding children's development (Skolnick, 1978b:56). If they do the right things at the right time, their children will more than likely be happy, intelligent, and successful.

Particularly during the 1960s and 1970s, authorities have stressed the ability of parents to influence their children's intellectual growth. Psychologist J. McVicker Hunt, for example, stated that he believes "you could raise a middle-class child's I.Q. by 20 points with what we know about child-rearing" (in Pines, 1979:67).

The teacher-counselor approach has many fine features, and children do benefit from environmental stimulation. Yet this parenting style also poses problems. For one thing, it puts the needs of the child above the parents' needs. It may be unrealistic for most parents to always be there, ready to stimulate the child's intellect or to act as a sounding board. Also, parents who respond as if each of their child's discoveries is wonderful may give the child the mistaken impression that he or she is the center of everyone's universe (LeMasters, 1977).

For another, this approach expects parents to be experts—an expectation that can easily produce guilt. Parents can never learn all that psychologists, sociologists, and specialized educators know. Yet if anything goes wrong, teacher-counselor parents are likely to feel they have only themselves to blame (Skolnick, 1978b; LeMasters, 1977).

Finally, contemporary research increasingly suggests that this view greatly exaggerates the power of the parent and the passivity of children. Children also have inherited intellectual capacities and needs. Recent observers point instead to an **interactive perspective,** which regards the influence between parent and child as mutual and reciprocal, not just a "one-way street" (Lewis and Rosenblum, 1974). The "athletic coach" model proceeds from this perspective.

The Parent as Athletic Coach

Athletic-coach parenting incorporates aspects of the developmental point of view. The coach (parent) is expected to have sufficient ability and knowledge of the game (life) and to be prepared and confident to lead players (children) to do their best and, it is hoped, to succeed.

This parenting style recognizes that parents, like coaches, have their own personalities and needs. They establish team rules, or *house rules* (and this can be done somewhat democratically with help from the players), and teach these rules to their children. They enforce the appropriate penalties when rules are broken, but policing is not their primary concern. Children, like team members, must be willing to accept discipline and, at least sometimes, to subordinate their own interests to the needs of the family team.

Coaching parents encourage their children to practice and to work hard to develop their own talents. But they realize that they cannot play the game for their players.

The coach's position here is quite analogous to that of parents; once the game has begun it is up to the players to win or lose it.... [The coach] faces the same prospect as parents of sitting on the sidelines and watching players make mistakes that may prove disastrous [LeMasters, 1977:200]. ■

LeMasters also points out that coaches can put uncooperative players off the team or even quit, but no such option is available to parents. As we'll see in the next section, once individuals become parents, they remain in this role the rest of their lives. As we explore parenting over the course of life, we will apply principles and suggestions from the interactive and "athletic coach" perspectives on parenting.

STAGES OF PARENTING

People are accustomed to thinking of childhood as a developmental process. The early milestones of learning to walk, talk, and think abstractly, for example, are widely recognized. The developmental perspective also applies to adults, as we saw in Chapter 1, and it clearly applies to the parenting role, which is characterized by different tasks and needs at different stages.

According to one observer, the development of a parent has three stages: the new parent, who most often is inexperienced and feels incompetent; the "frantic, ambidextrous, and ambivalent parent of school-age children"; and the middle-aged parent with adolescents (Laws, 1978). We will discuss each of these, along with a fourth stage, the parent with adult children; and a fifth stage, the grandparent.

New Parents

The new-parent stage can be divided into three substages: the transition to parenthood, parents with babies, and parents with preschoolers.

The Transition to Parenthood A study by LeMasters in the late 1950s found that 83 percent of his white, middle-class sample experienced the birth of their first child as an "extensive" or "severe" crisis. This was true even though couples were well-adjusted individuals who had planned or desired the pregnancy and considered their marriages to be good. LeMasters attributed these parents' crises to a culturally romanticized view of parenthood and to society's failure to prepare people adequately for parenting (LeMasters, 1957). Other research has reached similar conclusions (Dyer, 1963).

More recently, scientists have argued that becoming a parent is not a crisis but a transition (Hobbs and Cole, 1976:729). Whether crisis or transition, the fact is that becoming a parent can be difficult, often more difficult than the parents had anticipated. New fathers and mothers report being bothered by the baby's interruption of such activities as sleeping, going places, and sexual expression. New mothers are distressed about their personal appearance, the additional amount of work required of them, and the need to change plans for their own lives and futures (Hobbs and Wimbish, 1977:681). There is some evidence that this transition is more difficult for black parents than for white parents, a finding that may be related to the more limited economic resources of this group as a whole (Hobbs and Wimbish, 1977).

Fathers as well as mothers are affected by new parenthood. A recent study of postpartum depression (symptoms of depression such as crying or "the blues" that follow childbirth) found that 62 percent of fathers reported some symptoms (compared with 89 percent of mothers). "Adaptation to parenthood isn't easy for men or for women," states Dr. Frank Pedersen of the National Institute of Child Health and Human Development.

Social scientist Alice Rossi has analyzed the transition to parenthood, comparing the parent role with other adult roles, such as worker or spouse. The transition to parenthood, Rossi asserts, is more difficult than the transition to either of these other roles for several reasons (1968). First, as Chapter 12 points out, cultural pressure encourages adults to become parents even though they may not really want to. But once a baby is born, especially to married couples, there is little possibility of undoing the commitment to parenthood.

Second, there is little preparation for parenting. Most mothers and fathers approach parenting with little or no previous experience in child care; nor is there much preparation during pregnancy itself. Fantasy often takes the place of realistic training for future parents. Romanticizing leads to disillusionment and often to the emotionally painful cycle one writer calls the "anger-depression-guilt-go-round" (McBride, 1973).

Third, unlike other adult roles, the transition to parenting is abrupt. "The new mother starts out immediately on a 24-hour duty, with responsibility for a fragile and mysterious infant totally dependent on her care" (Rossi, 1968); this is also true for fathers, although perhaps to a lesser degree.

Fourth, adjusting to parenthood necessitates changes in the couple's relationship, as was discussed in Chapter 12. Husbands can expect to receive less care from their wives. Employed wives who have established fairly egalitarian relationships with their husbands may find themselves in a different role, particularly if they quit working to become full-time homemakers.

Finally, as was pointed out earlier in this chapter, today's parents do not have clear guidelines about what constitutes good or successful parenting. They can inform themselves about the child's nutritional, medical, and other physical needs, and they can follow the general prescription that a child needs loving contact and emotional support. But what should parents do to guide their children toward adult competency? For the parents, there is little specific advice and a great deal of controversy, and they often feel like pioneers cutting their own trails. At the same time, the proliferation of "experts" in child rearing (Huber, 1980) leads parents to believe they could not possibly be competent. Some social scientists, in fact, see the experts as being in conflict with parents for control of the socialization process (Lasch, 1977).

Parents with Babies   It is often difficult for new parents to acquire a sense of perspective, because their experience is so new and there is little for them to compare it to. One kind of perspective comes with time itself. It helps to realize that the newborn will begin to mature, and that many of the frustrations associated with this stage, such as loss of sleep, worry about the umbilical cord, and so on, will soon disappear. Parents also need a sense of perspective in evaluating their own baby's personality. Babies are different from one another even at birth, and the fact that one baby cries a lot does not necessarily mean that it is receiving the wrong kind of care. Through the interactive perspective, parents can realize that their own ideas and attitudes are affected by the infant's appearance and behavior, and vice versa (Bell, 1974).

Infants have different "readabilities," that is, varying clarity in the messages or cues they give to tell caregivers how they feel or what they want (Bell, 1974). They also have different temperaments at birth: Some are "easy," responding positively to new foods, people, and situations, and transmitting consistent cues (such as a "tired cry" or a "hungry cry"). Other infants are more "difficult." They may have irregular habits of sleeping, eating, and elimination, which sometimes extend into childhood; they may adapt slowly to new situations and stimuli; and they may seem to cry endlessly, for no apparent reason. Still other babies, of course, are neither easy nor particularly difficult (Thomas et al., 1963; Thomas and Chess, 1977).

Whether a child is "easy" or "difficult" has a

TABLE 13·1 An Early Development Timetable		
Approximate Age	Baby's Development	Parents' Response
2 months	Develops visual skills and motor skills such as grasping	Provide visual-tactile stimulation: plastic mirror, toys, or other graspable objects
5–8 months	At first, babies are sociable; then they develop shyness or fear of strangers	Accept this change as natural
By 6 months	Learns familiarity with environment	Be predictable and consistent
8–14 months	Learns to crawl and walk	Provide safety; avoid unnecessary restrictions

Note: The following are good sources of information on early childhood development: Burton White, *The First Three Years of Life* (Englewood Cliffs, N.J.: Prentice-Hall, 1975); Jerome Kagan, "The psychological requirements for human development," pp. 400–11 in Arlene S. Skolnick and Jerome H. Sknolnick (eds.), *Family in Transition*, 2d ed. (Boston: Little, Brown, 1977); Haim G. Ginott, *Between Parent and Child* (New York: Macmillan, 1965).

great deal to do with a parent's self-esteem as a caregiver (Thomas et al., 1963; Thomas and Chess, 1977). Generally, an "easy" baby contributes to the caregiver's conviction that she or he is a good parent, while difficult babies may cause the parents to blame themselves. A parent's relationship with a difficult child may lack many of the expected rewards of parenthood. These parents may be tempted to treat the growing baby as a "problem child" or to respond by oversheltering the child, two reactions that may cause the child to internalize the sense that he or she is "different." Instead, they need to strike a balance between the child's needs for security and predictability and their own needs. These parents may also need more time away from their child than do parents of easier children (Thomas et al., 1968).

All infants have certain needs. Like anyone else, they need positive, affectionate, intimate relationships with others in order to develop feelings of self-esteem (Kagan, 1977). They need encouragement, conversation, and variety in their environment in order to develop emotionally and intellectually.

Babies also have particular needs associated with their stage of development, as Table 13·1 indicates. As in other situations discussed throughout this book, parenting through the new-baby stage requires both knowledgeable decision making and acceptance of certain developments as neither "bad" nor "good" but simply natural.

Parents with Preschoolers Preschool children continue to have many of the same needs they had as infants. They need opportunities to practice motor development. They need to be able to arrange objects and shapes, although these can be common household items rather than specially designed "educational" toys (Kagan, 1977). They also need wide exposure to language, especially when people talk directly to them. And they need to experience consistency in the standards they are trying to learn. Many parents today worry about whether the standards they set are too harsh or too lenient, but the content of the standards is less important than the consistency (Kagan, 1977).

During the preschool years parents will establish a parenting style similar to one (or a combination of more than one) of the styles described earlier. If parents have been influenced by the developmental perspective, they may be inclined to be lenient. Haim Ginott, author of *Between Parent and Child* (1965), distinguishes between permissiveness and overpermissiveness. Permissiveness is "an attitude of accepting the childishness of children"; it is fundamental to intimate parent-child relationships. Permissiveness means accepting that a clean, tucked-in shirt on a normal child will not stay clean or tucked in for long. Permissiveness is also "the acceptance of children as persons who have a constitutional right to have all kinds of feelings and wishes." Permissive parents do not admonish or restrict their children's wishes or feelings. They do, however, set limits on unacceptable actions. For example, it is permissible for a child to be angry, but it is never permissible for a child to hit his or her parents in anger. In contrast, *overpermissiveness* allows undesirable acts as expressions of feelings (Ginott, 1965:93–94).

Both parent and child need clear definitions of what is acceptable and what is unacceptable. Limits are best set as house rules and stated objectively in third-person terms. A parent can say, for example, "Chairs are for sitting in, not for jumping on" (Ginott, 1965:98). With preschoolers limits need to be set and stated very clearly: A parent who says "Don't go too far from home" invites the child to wander farther than she or he may intend. For this reason, "Don't go out of the yard at all" is a wiser rule. As the child develops and can distinguish between what is "too much" and what is not, the limits can be made more flexible.

Frantic, Ambidextrous, and Ambivalent Parents of School-Age Children

By the time children begin school, parents feel a bit more experienced. They have begun to see some positive results of their efforts and can take pride in their parental accomplishments. But they are still not completely confident: "They are humbled by much advice and many demands" (Laws, 1978:5).

American school-age children have many needs. First, they need to be encouraged to master the school's requirements and to accomplish learning goals appropriate to their abilities. Schools expect parents' cooperation and support in the form of helping the child acquire good study habits, showing interest in his or her work and progress, and perhaps assisting sometimes with school work—though parents should not *do* the homework or complete the projects. The extracurricular activities of school-age children also demand a significant amount of support and time from parents who are already overloaded. One result is that parents may push their children to excel and then not follow through with encouragement because their attention is needed elsewhere.

An alternative is to negotiate the child's needs for achievement, help, and encouragement with the parent's need for free time. A child can be told that if he or she wants to take music lessons, the parent will provide an instrument and transportation and will attend a negotiated number of performances, but the parent won't provide simultaneous support for soccer lessons. This strategy has the advantage of allowing the child a choice, but not overloading either parent or child.

Parents can protect their children by helping them structure their lives to avoid such an overload. Children today face demands for achievement from schools, church and recreational organizations, peers, and, of course, parents. This can produce the "hurried child" who is forced to assume too many challenges and responsibilities too soon. Parents may begin to push or "hurry" their children even before they begin school—when they are toddlers or earlier than that ("Toddlers," 1985; "Bringing up superbaby," 1983). Hurried children may achieve in adult ways at a young age, but they also acquire the stress induced by the pressure to achieve (Elkind, 1979). Or they may "drop out" and abandon goal-directed academic and extracurricular activity. Parents can help not only by checking on whether they have realistic expectations for their children but also by moderating any unreasonable outside demands on the children. A child may need active parental backing in negotiating with other institutions and organizations and in dealing with adults in positions of authority.

Besides functioning in the world of school and organizations, school children also need to feel that they are contributing members of their families. Children who are not given responsibility for their share of household chores may have trouble feeling they "belong," or they may become demanding because they have learned to "belong" as consumers rather than as productive family members.

One of the pluses of single-parent families as child-rearing institutions (discussed more extensively in Chapter 16) is that children's help is usually genuinely needed if the family is to survive.

Children not only need to be assigned tasks; they also need to be taught how to do them. Parents who choose not to patiently teach children how to change their beds or do dishes, for example, risk spending more time getting angry with and correcting an untrained child.

School children also need to learn how to choose and get along with friends and peers. In this area, as in others, however, they must be allowed to make mistakes and to learn from experience. Parents might point out alternative ways of relating to others, but they should not interfere much in peer quarrels and other troubles. As Chapter 9 illustrates, one must accept the inevitability of conflicts and learn how to deal effectively with them. This applies to children as well as to adults.

One particular area of conflict is between siblings. Parents should recognize the inevitability of sibling rivalry and make an effort *not* to overrespond either by punishing competitiveness or by creating an artificially equal environment (taking one child out for lunch, for instance, because the other has been invited to a birthday party). Children should be encouraged to work out disputes by themselves whenever possible. Often, in fact, the dispute loses its momentum when no parents are there to listen. Having said this, we need to emphasize that physical violence *should* be kept in check by parents. Research on family violence (Straus et al., 1980) indicates that violence between siblings, particularly boys, and some of it quite serious, is the most pervasive form of family violence. Parents should intervene to restrain siblings from physical violence and "provide children with an environment in which nonviolent methods of solving conflicts are learned" (Straus et al., 1980:93).

A further need of school-age children is for increasing recognition of their individuality and emerging autonomy. Like adults, children need some privacy. They can be assigned a spot in the house that is theirs and no one else's, or they can regularly be given some time alone when parents agree not to interrupt them. As growing individuals, children also need to practice making their own decisions. Sometimes a parent's need for social acceptance influences the parent to make decisions for the child, for example, when a child puts on the "wrong" shirt with the "wrong" pants. A way to compromise is for the parent to allow the child to

make choices within limits. For example, the parent may offer the child a choice between alternative pants or shirts.

In general, in recognizing school-age children's individuality, one should actively listen to what they are saying and try to respond to what they are feeling. The same general techniques as discussed in Chapter 9 can be applied, as we'll see later in this chapter. As children get older, parent-child dialogue can become a basis for negotiating house rules.

Middle-Aged Parents with Adolescents

Adolescence has the potential for being a time of conflict between parent and child, for in this stage both are involved in periods of transition (see Chapter 1). Both are experiencing biological shifts: The child is undergoing the physical and hormonal changes accompanying puberty; the parent, those of midlife. From a social-psychological viewpoint, the child is getting ready to move into the adult world, and the parent is increasingly aware of what he or she has yet to accomplish in life. A result may be an increased level of parent-child conflict as they struggle to accommodate the very different needs of each (Laws, 1978; Davis, 1974; Hatfield, 1985). The child needs to divest her- or himself of parental care and authority at the very time when the parent most needs the sense of self-worth that derives from the parenting role (Anthony, 1975).

Adolescents may use hostility to help free themselves from parents, sometimes with painful results. One mother described her feelings:

What bothered me was whether or not *I* would ever recover. I was convinced that I was the worst mother on earth. [According to my thirteen-year-old daughter] I understood nothing, I made demands surpassed in viciousness only by Adolf Hitler, I always looked so awful it would cause panic in the streets if I appeared in public, and I was prehistoric in my attitudes about dating. Thanks to the teen-ager I shared my home with, my self-image was not exactly at an optimum level [in LeShan, 1977:279]. ■

Another complicating factor is that our society offers no clear guidelines or prescriptions for relinquishing parental authority: The exact time when

■ "My mom's OK": high praise from a teenager. As children grow up, their perspective of their parents shifts. For a 7-year-old, Mom and Dad are wise authorities providing security; ten years later, he sees them as ignorant tyrants smothering him. Eventually, he may realize that the truth lies between these two extremes, but meanwhile the teen will probably find himself in conflict with his middle-age parents.

authority should be relinquished, or how much, is not culturally specified (Rossi, 1968; Davis, 1974).[2]

As Chapter 10 points out, the readjustment of authority between individuals is "always a ticklish process" (Davis, 1974:456). The process creates problems between parent and child for special reasons. Sociologist Kingsley Davis explains:

The parents have a vital stake in what the offspring will do. Because his acquisition of independence will free the parents of many obligations, they are willing to relinquish their authority; yet, precisely because their own status is socially identified with that of their offspring, they wish to insure satisfactory conduct on the latter's part and are tempted to prolong their authority.... The conflict of interest may lead to a struggle for power, the parents fighting to keep control in matters of importance to themselves, the son or daughter clinging to personally indispensable family services while seeking to evade the concomitant control [1974:456]. ■

_____

2. When to relinquish authority is, however, linked to certain economic factors. Upper middle-class families can afford to defer their children's financial independence, sending them off to college. Working-class parents, however, are experiencing a financial crunch (called the "life cycle crunch" by Oppenheimer) just at this time. Because blue-collar income typically decreases during late adulthood, children are pushed to earn their own living (Oppenheimer, 1974).

The struggle between parent and adolescent over when and how parental authority should be rescinded characteristically involves values. Because our society increasingly requires an adult to display a distinctly personal set of values, adolescents may feel the need to reject their parents' values, at least intellectually and for the time being, to gain adult status.

Collisions with adolescents over values are especially difficult to negotiate because they usually are not conflicts over specific behaviors. Teenagers wonder why they should change what they believe when it does not actually do the parent any harm (Gordon, 1970). If parents insist on having their own way, the adolescent does the same. Parent and child thereby may engage in a power struggle in which the adolescent feels honor bound to do just the opposite of what the parent demands (Ginott, 1965). For many parents, power struggles with teenagers tend to involve the child's style of dress and general appearance. Other decisions— whether homework will get finished, what school the youngster will attend, what career choices are available, what the consequences of experimentation with alcohol, other drugs, and premarital sex will be—do of course have far-reaching implications for the young person. These may be viewed by parents as intolerable risks, but by the children as valid choices to make for themselves.

Parents may take heart from the recent Middletown study. "Middletown," the name given by researchers to Muncie, Indiana, was the subject of a community study in the 1920s and 1930s (Lynd and Lynd, 1929, 1937). Sociologists returned to Middletown from 1976 through 1981 and, using the very same questionnaires employed earlier, obtained results that shatter our assumption that parents and adolescents are particularly prone to experience conflict in the United States. Our assumption has been that we have had rapid social change, so that youth grow up in a social milieu different from their parents. In reality, parent-child relations in Middletown changed very little between the 1920s and the 1970s, although there *had* been a marked shift in the previous generation (between 1890 and the 1920s). Apparently, once major urbanization took place in the late nineteenth and early twentieth centuries, families stabilized. Instead of an increased generation gap during this century, which we perceive as tumultuous, family patterns have remained stable; if anything, families have grown closer. Children's and parents' values are much alike, and relationships are warm (Caplow et al., 1982). We do not know how typical Muncie, Indiana, is— although the researchers make comparisons with national data to argue that it is reasonably typical.

Data from the "Youth in Transition" study, a longitudinal study of 1,628 boys (not girls!) in eighty-seven high schools conducted by researchers at the University of Michigan, revealed very little change in values and behaviors after age 15 (Bachman et al., 1978). This study suggests that drastic changes do not occur in later adolescence. Depending on the situation in the early teens, parents may feel encouraged to learn that chances of a sudden transformation of their adolescent are unlikely. Instead of engaging in power struggles, parents should recognize that by the very nature of their relationship, parents exercise decreasing control over what their children choose to do. Parents do continue to influence their adolescents as models and as consultants.

Parents as Models   Values are not just taught; they are caught from those around us whom we admire. That is why it is important for parents to "practice what they preach." Acting as the "right" kind of model can be more difficult than many parents expect. One authority notes that being aware of their power as models during the adolescent years "scares the hell out of some parents."

They are so conscious of themselves as models of good behavior, that they feel that they have to

be perfect all the time. They never admit to anything wrong and always have a dozen excuses for not being a "paragon of virtue" [Jurich, 1978:30]. ■

But this is neither necessary nor good parenting, for at least two reasons. First, it presents an unrealistic world to the growing child. It is too nearly perfect an example to follow, and in addition, the adolescent has no model for problem solving because he or she doesn't see parents struggling with their own imperfection. Second, this attitude takes away from the parent's freedom to make a mistake. "This puts tremendous pressure on the parents and reduces the 'humanness' of his parents in the adolescent's eyes" [Jurich, 1978:30–31].

Parents as Consultants   Besides acting as models, parents can influence adolescents by getting "hired as a consultant" (Gordon, 1970:263). Consultants, like athletic coaches, are prepared with facts and information about the alternatives under consideration; they inform their clients about the potential consequences of each alternative so that the client can make knowledgeable decisions. Consultants can offer their own opinions and viewpoints if they explain that this is what they are doing. But as the coach must allow the players to play the game, the consultant must allow the clients to make their own decisions.

An illustration of how this can be done is provided by psychologist James McCary in his well-known text about sexuality (1979). He explains how he would deal with the particularly tricky issue of helping his own adolescent children deal with premarital sex. McCary says he would tell his children his own beliefs, values, and attitudes, and outline the views on sex of his and other religions. He would also explain that young people are at the height of their physical sexual appetites at exactly the time when sex is forbidden them by social and religious standards. He would want his children "to have a kind and fair attitude toward other human beings.... I'd want them to understand that when their behavior in any way harms other persons or themselves, that behavior should be reconsidered" (McCary, 1979:13).

He would also want his children to know and value the normal methods and techniques of sexual outlet other than intercourse, such as masturbation and petting. He would tell his children about the possible outcomes of premarital sex, including feelings of guilt, possible pregnancy, and venereal diseases. If, with all this information, his son or daughter decided to have premarital intercourse, then he would provide information and access to contraceptive devices. If any of his children chose premarital sex, McCary said he

would want them to know that so long as they hurt neither themselves nor others, my respect and love for them would not change. And I would hope—and I believe it would follow—that if either of them ever needed a friend they would turn first to their parents and know that we would support them [1979:15]. ▪

With this last point McCary illustrates the growing belief among child-rearing authorities that developing and maintaining the parent-child relationship is the highest value an effective American parent can have today. In practice, this means that parents, particularly of adolescents and adult children, learn to accept what they cannot change and to pledge friendship and ongoing support even to children who reject their values.

In the case of premarital sex for teens, research shows that this approach can be of practical benefit. Teenage women whose mothers discuss sex with them are *less* likely to become pregnant than those whose mothers try to protect their children by withholding information (Inazu and Fox, 1980). Teenage mothers manage early parenthood better when their parents provide financial and emotional support; they are also more likely than others to return to school and to graduate from high school than those who move out of their parents' homes (Furstenberg and Crawford, 1978).

While parents of adolescents act primarily as consultants with regard to values and continue to love and support children even when these children choose to be different from them, they can continue to set limits on what they will allow in their own homes. Parents who believe that premarital sex is morally wrong, for example, can feel justified in refusing to allow their college-age son or daughter to sleep with a girlfriend or boyfriend in their own homes.

Setting Limits Through Democratic Discipline As children reach adolescence, limits can be based more and more on **democratic discipline,** in which all family members involved have some say. Rules are discussed ahead of time and both parents and children attempt to compromise whenever possible.

Social scientists and counselors hold that democratic or "authoritative" (Baumrind, 1971) discipline is more effective with adolescents than either laissez-faire or autocratic discipline. They also point out that parents need not feel guilty about occasionally setting limits without providing rational explanations. Parents should recognize that it is not always possible to give children watertight explanations for every limit they set. In some situations a parent has a vague feeling that he or she should not permit something but cannot give a rational explanation why, or the explanation does not stand up to teenagers' rebuttal. In these cases parents should recognize that it is all right simply to ask the child to accept and respect their feelings of anxiety. I-statements from parent to teenager, as discussed in Chapter 9, can help.

Adolescents and Work One factor affecting parents' actual and potential control and influence over children is whether or not the adolescent is working. In the past, critics of our family system (Holt, 1974) have faulted the exclusion of young people from our work system as contributing to adolescent malaise. In fact, studies of the impact of working on adolescent behavior indicate that the effect is not always positive, since an independent source of money removes one source of parental control and provides access to drugs and alcohol, as well as increasing freedom of movement away from home ("Teens' affluence," 1985). Grades are lower and drug use and delinquency higher for working teens. Money earned usually goes for consumption spending rather than saving for college or meeting family needs. Furthermore, working places pressure on teenagers, who have less time for activities, social lives, and just daydreaming. On the other hand, working teens learn something about the work world and its responsibilities and test some occupational ideas; they also learn to cope with emergencies and with difficult people and develop self-confidence. The bottom line seems to be that the benefits of working can be attained in fourteen hours (a week) or less; when teenagers work more than twenty hours, the costs outweigh the benefits.

Interestingly, families were quite involved in the teenager's job, by being consultants on making the decision to work, by serving as a means of transportation and filling in (on paper routes, for example), and through permitting deviations from normal family routines such as the family dinner (Cole, 1980).

Parents with Adult Children

The majority of American parents continue their relationship with their adult children, providing reciprocal services and living near them and visiting regularly. When they live too far apart for regular visiting, they maintain contact by telephone and letters and get together for extended visits (Troll et al., 1979). As parents grow older, they may move to be near one of their adult children (Bultena and Wood, 1969); middle-aged adult children may also return to the geographic area they grew up in to be near their aging parents (Troll et al., 1979).

Surveys show that parents over age 65 prefer to live in their own homes but near their adult children and grandchildren. They move in with children only when there is not enough money to live alone, when their health is so poor that self-care is impossible, or—to a lesser extent—when a spouse has died.

Those people over 65 who do live with a child are more likely to live with an unmarried than a married one. In most of these cases, furthermore, it is the parent who is "head of the household," with an unmarried son or daughter moving in with the parent or remaining with the parent rather than the older parent moving in with the children (Troll et al., 1979).

A modern trend is for parents of adult children to be concerned because their children either do not move out in young adulthood or return—after college or after divorce, for example. Unemployment, inflation, and related economic hazards make launching oneself into independent adulthood increasingly difficult (Glick and Lin, 1986a). Parents who awaited the increased intimacy of the empty-nest stage may be disappointed to find that the nest is not emptying as anticipated. One way to deal with this is to renegotiate the parent-child contract to stipulate that adult children pay their expenses, be responsible for their own child care, and contribute an appropriate effort to the maintenance tasks of the household. Whether or not parents continue to share their homes with their adult children, the relationship will probably be enhanced if parents relinquish parental authority, recognizing that their children's attitudes and values will differ from their own.[3] This is true even—or

---

3. Various groups have been formed to help parents accept adult children's different values and life-styles. One of these is Parents of Lesbians and Gay Men.

especially—when parents give adult children money. The "emotion" and desire to control needs to be separated from the gift as much as possible (Walker, 1984).

Grandparents

The grandparent role, like each of the other roles we have studied, is different from the image we have of it. For one thing, the role is shrinking: People are having fewer children today than in the past, and often those children live far away from their grandparents. So grandparents are usually only "part-time" grandparents at best.

Another reason the reality of the role differs from our image of it is that it may be a source of conflict, not just joy. In one study a majority of grandparents expressed comfort and pleasure with their role, but about a third were uncomfortable (Neugarten and Weinstein, 1964). Sources of discomfort and disappointment include the strain of thinking of oneself as old and conflicts with adult children over how to rear grandchildren. George Bach refers to this as part of the "senior generation gap," where adults differ from their own parents in opinions and attitudes about child rearing. A typical result, says Bach, is for adult children to try to "keep the old folks at a distance," and for grandparents to think that they aren't appreciated or welcome (Bach and Wyden, 1970; Wood and Robertson, 1976, 1978).

An alternative is for family members to realize that in order to be valued in the family, grandparents—like everyone else—have to earn recognition. They might do this by telling grandchildren about family history or customs, for example (grandparents are a primary source of family archive information), or by teaching them special skills, such as needlework, carpentry, or fishing (Wood and Robertson, 1976). Grandparents can invite their grandchildren over to fingerpaint, a simple activity but one that the children's parents find too messy. Such contributions can be a starting point for negotiating imaginative and mutually acceptable ways of being involved with one another.

Grandparents are not all alike. Grandparenting styles are myriad, and they are shaped by timing (whether one feels he or she became a grandparent too early, too late, or on time), health, employment status, personality, and other social responsibilities (Troll, 1985:135–49). One study (of grandmothers) found that some grandmothers, particularly older and more traditional ones, are heavily involved emotionally and in the socialization of their grandchildren. For others, grandmotherhood is a significant but primarily symbolic role; these tend to be younger grandmothers who are involved in work, leisure, or social activities of their own (Wood and Robertson, 1976, 1978). "There is a great amount of variation in the kinds of relationships that American grandparents have with their grandchildren. Some grandparents are actively involved in their grandchildren's lives, but many others are quite passive and distant" (Cherlin and Furstenberg, 1985:97). The younger the grandchild, the more involved the grandparent; as grandchildren approach late childhood and grandparents get older, there is less for them to enjoy together, although grandparenthood remains emotionally significant (Kahana and Kahana, 1970).

At all stages of life children provide one of the primary satisfactions in life for many people. Parents and children have a unique intimate relationship. Yet family relations are intense and difficult, and in some families tension and stress or learned patterns of behavior culminate in the unfortunate situation of child maltreatment, explored in the next section.

CHILD MALTREATMENT

Perceptions of what constitutes maltreatment have differed over history and in different cultures. Practices that we now consider abusive were accepted in the past as the normal exercise of parental rights or as appropriate discipline. Until the twentieth century children were mainly considered the property of parents. Aristotle wrote that a son or a slave is property, and there is no such thing as injustice to one's property. In ancient Rome a man could sell, abandon, or kill his child if he pleased. Infanticide has been practiced from earliest antiquity to limit family size, to assure crop growth, or to relieve the financial burdens (DeMause, 1975:87). In colonial Massachusetts and Connecticut filial disobedience was legally punishable by death.

Today, standards of acceptable child care vary according to culture and social class. What some groups consider mild abuse, others consider right and proper discipline. In 1974, however, Congress provided a contemporary definition of child maltreatment in the Child Abuse Prevention and Treatment Act. The act defines **child maltreatment** as

[the physical or mental injury, sexual abuse, or negligent treatment of a child] under the age of eighteen by a person who is responsible for the child's welfare under circumstances which indicate that the child's health or welfare is harmed or threatened thereby [U.S. Department of Health, Education, and Welfare, 1975:3]. ■

Abuse Versus Neglect

As the definition indicates, maltreatment of children takes many forms. People use the term **child abuse** to refer to overt acts of aggression, such as excessive verbal derogation, beating, or inflicting physical injury. Another form of physical child abuse that has received particular attention is *sexual abuse,* which includes exposure, fondling of sexual organs, intercourse, rape, and incest (sexual relations between related individuals, including step-relatives). Incest is the most emotionally charged form of sexual abuse; it is also the most difficult to detect.[4] Sexual abuse by paid caretakers as well as by family members is also a problem being addressed by policymakers and concerned child-care professionals.

Child neglect includes acts of omission—failing to provide adequate physical or emotional care. Abraham Levine regards physical neglect as "the failure to provide the essentials for normal life, such as food, clothing, shelter, care, supervision, and protection from assault" (1974:26). Physically neglected children are often hungry, show signs of malnutrition, lack proper clothing for weather conditions, have irregular school attendance, and are in obvious need of medical attention for such correctable conditions as poor eyesight, bad teeth, or needs for immunizations (U.S. Department of Health, Education, and Welfare, 1975:8).

Emotional Maltreatment   Child maltreatment can also be emotional: "the parent's lack of love and proper direction, inability to accept a child with his potentialities as well as his limitations . . .

---

4. The most common forms are father-daughter incest and incest involving a stepfather or older brother. Incest appears to be related to a variety of sexual, emotional, and physical problems among adult women who were abused as children.

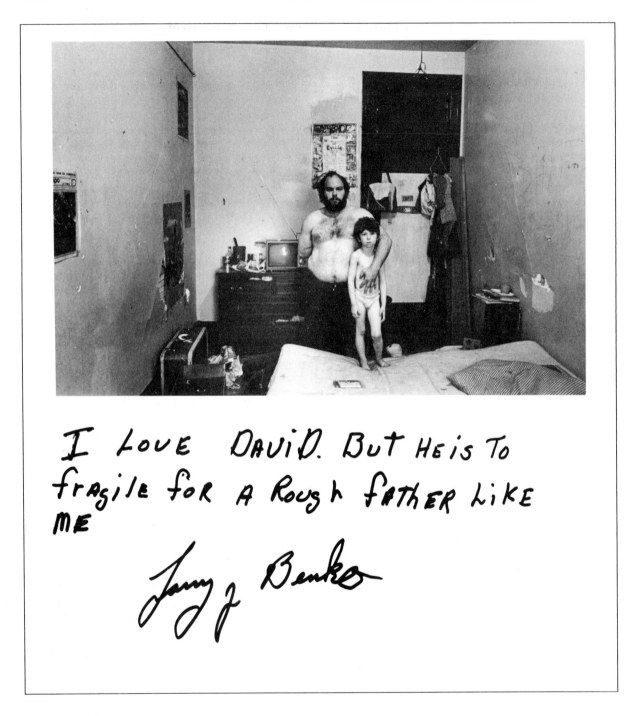

When David's father looked at this photo, he saw the obvious difference in size and power between himself and his small son. How might that difference help explain child abuse—and its existence in all socioeconomic, racial, ethnic, and religious groups?

[and] failure to encourage the child's normal development by assurance of love and acceptance" (in Mulford, n.d.:5). Parents who emotionally maltreat their children may be overly harsh and critical, demanding excessive academic, athletic, or social performance. They may simply withhold contact or fail to provide guidance. Or they may be unaware of or uninterested in their children's needs.

How Extensive Is Child Maltreatment?

Estimates of the number of child maltreatment incidents vary, but all suggest an extensive problem. According to one authority, some 10,000 children in the United States are severely battered each year; at least 100,000 to 500,000 are sexually abused (Watson, 1984); 100,000 are neglected physically, morally, or educationally; and another 100,000 suffer emotional maltreatment (DeFrancis, in Fontana, 1973:38). In 1983, according to the Criminal Justice Newsletter, over a million U.S. children suffered physical abuse, neglect, or sexual abuse. The American Humane Association announced in 1983 that the number of child-abuse cases reported to social service agencies had risen at a rate of about 10 percent each year since the mid-1970s (Straus and Gelles, 1986:466).

Statistics are probably not very accurate because of reporting biases and the overreliance on small samples to yield national estimates. (See Straus et al., 1980:3–28, for a discussion of measurement.) Moreover, interpreting rising rates of reported child abuse to mean that child abuse is rapidly increasing may be inaccurate.[5] For one thing, all states now have compulsory child-abuse reporting laws so that a growing proportion of previously unreported cases now come to the attention of child-welfare authorities. For another, "new standards are evolving in respect to how much violence parents can use in childrearing.... The definition of child abuse is being gradually enlarged to include acts that were not previously thought of as child abuse" (Straus and Gelles, 1986:466–67). There

is, in fact, some evidence that the incidence of child abuse has actually declined over the past ten to fifteen years (Straus and Gelles, 1986). Whatever the precise figures, maltreatment is a significant problem.

Whatever the actual figures, maltreated children live in families in all socioeconomic levels, races, nationalities, and religious groups, although—like all family violence—maltreatment is reported more frequently among poor and nonwhite families than among middle- and upper-class whites (Gelles, 1974).

Maltreatment Versus "Normal" Child Rearing: The Role of Social Expectations

It is not always easy to draw a line between "normal" child rearing and maltreatment. Regarding physical abuse, Arlene Skolnick stated: "Research has found nothing more striking than a pattern of child rearing merely exaggerating the usual one" (Skolnick, 1978a:286). For this reason, social scientists conclude that child maltreatment must be seen as a potential behavior in many families—even those we think of as "normal" (Gelles, 1977). Margo Fritz, director of Parent Assistance, a national self-help organization for abusive parents, makes a similar point:

Most people are conditioned to think of abuse in the terms in which the media have presented it for years—burned babies, critically abused children whose life hangs by a thread, malnourished infants.... There is a whole range of abuse that has never been dealt with that the public doesn't even acknowledge as being part of the problem at this point. When a parent is hitting a child and is out of control of himself, when he is dumping his own rage on his child—even if that child does not require treatment for inflicted trauma, that child has been abused and that parent is abusing [Fritz, in Sage, 1975:42]. ■

Another writer points out that hostile feelings toward children are normal, just as occasional feelings of hate between lovers are normal, as we saw in Chapter 9. Probably all parents lose self-control at times. Bearing this in mind, we will examine some society-wide beliefs and conditions that, when

---

5. There is speculation that some child-abuse charges are false. In some cases, according to family law experts and health professionals, fathers and stepfathers involved in divorce cases are being wrongly accused, usually as part of "the already emotionally charged atmosphere of court contests over child custody" (Dullea, 1987b:5).

exaggerated, can encourage well-intentioned parents to mistreat their children.

Parents' Misperceptions of Children One factor related to child maltreatment is the misperceptions of many parents about their children. They may have unrealistic expectations about what the child is capable of; often they lack awareness and knowledge of the child's physical and emotional needs.

Abusive parents tend to see their children as innately evil, deficient, or destructive, and as deliberately trying to thwart the parents' happiness. From a psychological perspective such feelings often stem from the parent's own feelings that he or she was "bad" as a child, too, or that the child has inherited undesirable characteristics from the partner or from a "problem" relative (U.S. Department of Health, Education, and Welfare, 1975:24).

Corporal Punishment A belief in physical punishment is also a contributing (but not sufficient) factor in child abuse. Abusive parents do not just discharge aggression impulsively. On the contrary, they have learned—probably in their own childhoods—to view children as requiring physical punishment. Parents who abuse their children were usually themselves abused or neglected as children (Zalba, 1974:409).

It is difficult to draw the line between "normal" discipline and child abuse. Also, parents are legally and culturally allowed to use corporal punishment to enforce rules. One writer observes that "a culturally defined concept of children as the 'property' of caregivers and of caregivers as legitimate users of physical force appears to be an essential component of child abuse" (Garbarino, 1977a:725). It is all too easy for parents to go beyond reasonable limits when angry or distraught or to have limits that include as "discipline" what most observers would define as "abuse."

Parental Stress Social scientists point out that parental stress and feelings of helplessness also play a significant part in precipitating child abuse (U.S. Department of Health, Education, and Welfare, 1975:21). This explanation emphasizes the importance of social situations. For instance, parents cast in social roles they are uncomfortable in may be more likely to mistreat their children. One psychologist argues that some mothers may be driven to mistreat their children because of the special problems women face in contemporary society. They have been taught that children are the center of a woman's life, and they may be frustrated because of limited opportunities to pursue their own interests away from their children (Keith-Spiegel, 1974).

Financial problems can cause stress, especially for single mothers; overload, so often related to financial problems, also creates stress that can lead to child abuse (Garbarino, 1976). Other causes of parental stress are children's misbehavior (Bell, 1974), rising inflation, changing life-styles and standards of living, and the fact that parents feel under pressure to do a "good" job but are often perplexed about how to do it.

Stress may be increased by a higher ratio of children to parents in a given household. A recent study of the ratio of children to parents in households, as reported in census data, found that fewer adults are directly involved in child rearing now, compared to 1960 (Zimmerman, quoted in Denzin, 1983). Stress may also be related to lessened social support. Denzin points out that "fewer adults [have] direct concern for the needs of children, such as day care, playgrounds, public schools, and immunization programs." Although adults who do not have children or whose children are grown may be concerned, it is also likely, Zimmerman thinks, that concern is more intense when children are present; and fewer than 40 percent of American households have children under 18.

Some households today—two-parent households—may have a child-parent ratio that is less stressful than in the past, as family size has declined. "In 1940, more than half of all children lived in households where there were more children than parents, [while] in 1980, fewer than half of all children lived in such arrangements" (Zimmerman, 1983). On the other hand, more single-parent households may mean a more intense child-parent ratio, as the one child–one parent ratio is probably more demanding than even two children to two adults because of the lack of shared parenting. In 1940, 11 percent of children lived in one-parent households; in 1984, 23 percent (U.S. Bureau of the Census, 1975; 1986b).

This study of the child-parent ratio and the percentage of the population who are active parents has not directly connected stress to child abuse, but it does have implications for parental stress. Public policy and private concern might be directed toward assisting parents who do seem to have greater responsibilities and thus more stress.

Family Privacy Another factor in child maltreatment is related to our way of life. Families have become less dependent on kinship and neighborhood relationships, placing more value on privacy. Anthropologists have pointed out that as a result, parents and children are alone together, shut off at home from the "watchful eyes and sharp tongues that regulate parent-child relations in other cultures" (Skolnick, 1978a:82). This privacy sets the stage not only for physical abuse but for the more common verbal and psychological abuse.

Social isolation also allows child maltreatment to get out of hand: Early incidents are often undetected, and even chronic neglect or battering may go unnoticed and may lead to severe physical and psychological damage, and even death. In neighborhoods that have support systems and tight social networks of community-related friends—where other adults are somewhat involved in the activities of the family—child abuse and neglect is much more likely to be noticed and stopped (Garbarino, 1977a, b).

Combating Child Maltreatment

Two approaches to combating child abuse and neglect exist: the *punitive approach*, which views maltreatment as a crime for which parents should be punished; and the *therapeutic approach*, which sees abuse and neglect as a family problem requiring treatment. While child maltreatment has by no means been decriminalized (all states have criminal laws against child maltreatment), the approach to child protection has gradually been shifting from punitive to therapeutic (Stewart, 1984). Not all who work with abused children are happy with this shift, preferring to hold one or both parents clearly responsible (particularly the father in incest cases). They reject the family system approach to therapy in principle because it implies distribution of blame or at least responsibility for change to all family members, including the child. The child protection worker may believe one or both parents is at fault and should not have custody or remain in the home (Stewart, 1984). Nevertheless, social workers and clinicians—rather than the police and the court system—increasingly investigate and treat abusive or neglecting parents (U.S. Department of Health, Education, and Welfare, 1975:29–31).

The therapeutic approach involves two interrelated strategies: increasing parents' self-esteem and their knowledge about children and involving the community and the larger society in child rearing. Because maltreating parents typically have low self-esteem, counselors and therapists who treat them begin by helping them build self-confidence.

One voluntary program, Parents Anonymous (PA), holds regular meetings to enhance self-esteem and educate abusive parents. Another voluntary association, CALM, attempts to reach stressed parents before they hurt their children. Among other things, CALM advocates obligatory high school classes on family life, child development, and parenting, and it operates a twenty-four hour hotline for parents in stress.

Involving the community and the larger society in combating child maltreatment means getting people other than parents to help with child rearing. One form of relief for abused and neglected children is to remove them from their parents' homes and place them in foster care. More and more, however, people are employing other alternatives, such as "supplemental mothers," who are available to baby-sit regularly with potentially maltreated children. Another form of relief is the community-based "crisis nursery" where parents can take their children when they feel the need to get away for a few hours. Ideally, crisis nurseries are open twenty-four hours a day and accept children at any hour without prearrangement, in order to relieve or divert a crisis in the parent-child relationship.[6]

Protecting Children from Others In the mid-1980s national attention turned to child molestation, kidnapping, and murder by strangers. Pictures of missing children appeared on grocery sacks and milk cartons ("How many," 1985:30). Nationwide programs were begun to fingerprint children—or to have identification information applied to children's teeth (McGrath, 1985)—in case they were abducted sometime in the future. Toy manufacturers made the most of a new, fear-motivated market and produced board games such as "Don't Talk To Strangers," in which the first player "home safely" wins. Books on personal safety and how to recognize potential or actual sexual abuse appeared for children of all ages. Magazine articles heralded the "epidemic of missing children" ("Vaccines," 1983:76) and coached parents on "how to teach children to resist assault" (Cooper, 1984).

Pediatricians and psychologists have begun to debate the prudence of this "national panic" (Tavris, 1985). For one thing, a child's statistical chances of being kidnapped or molested by a stranger are

---

6. Neighborhood and community groups can receive state or federal money to help develop crisis nurseries. The United States Department of Health, Education, and Welfare publishes a pamphlet on how to set up a crisis nursery.

minuscule compared to that same child's statistical chances of being physically or sexually abused by a family member or friend of the family (Scardino, 1985). According to pediatrician Benjamin Spock, we are "causing unnecessary fright in children—morbid fears. I don't see it doing any good, and I'm sure it's doing a lot of harm" (in *Newsweek*, Jan. 20, 1985, p. 13).

The campaign to teach children the harms of trusting strangers too much has unfortunate side effects. Teachers, day-care workers, and others who are occupationally involved with children are increasingly reluctant to hug or touch them for fear of being falsely accused of attempted molestation ("No hug," 1985). Children have been encouraged to reject the sincerely affectionate gestures not only of teachers but also of other community members. The following first appeared in the *Baltimore Sun*:

The elderly woman obviously meant no harm as she reached down to touch the curls on the head of the little girl standing in front of her in the supermarket checkout line. "What pretty curls you have," she said.

The little girl turned around with an expression that was as nasty as the woman's smile was sweet. "You better get your hands off me, lady," she said, "or I'm going to call the police" ["Experts," 1986]. ▪

It is ironic that while experts advise finding ways to involve the broader community in child rearing, some of our efforts designed to better protect children have discouraged just that. In any case, efforts to build parents' self-esteem and to involve the broader community in child rearing help not just abusive parents but all parents. The next section explores some ways that all parents can improve their relationships with their children by building self-confidence and sharing the child-rearing role with others.

TOWARD BETTER PARENT-CHILD RELATIONSHIPS

Probably more than in any other era, American parents today need to work to build their confidence and self-esteem. In Chapter 3 we suggested some ways to gain self-esteem. For parents in par-

ticular, building self-esteem means learning to let go of unnecessary guilt and self-doubt.

This may not be easy. As we've seen, parents are both beneficiaries and victims of social-scientific theories and research whose message is that parents can damage their children for life. From all the letters she has received over the years, columnist Ann Landers concludes: "If I were asked to select the one word that best describes the majority of American parents, that word would be *guilt-ridden*" (1977:2). A result of this guilt is not better parent-child relationships but rather uncertainty and doubt on the part of parents.

Building a High-Esteem Relationship

One antidote to parental guilt, doubt, and insecurity is to think of guiding children's development as a unique personal relationship between parent and child rather than as the application of some "expert" approach from active parent to passive and vulnerable child. As parents share their experiences, viewpoints, and values with their children and encourage their youngsters to share with them, parents' feelings of inadequacy are lessened and self-acceptance grows. Children can help nurture parents, too (Boulding, 1977:43). Using this approach, effective parenting is probably no more mysterious and difficult—albeit no easier—than developing continuing intimate relationships with others.

Also important in building parents' self-esteem is their learning to accept their own limitations and mistakes as inevitable and human. Instead of feeling guilty about how poorly he handled a fight between his children, for example, a father can praise himself for the patience he showed in helping his child with a homework assignment.

As parents gain self-acceptance, they will also become more accepting of their children. When parents make positive attributions to their children, such as "She [or he] wants to do the right thing," children internalize them (Laing, 1971). This sense of respect contributes to better parent-child relationships *and* improved self-images for both parents and children.

In recent years national organizations have emerged to help parents with the parent-child relationship. One of these is Thomas Gordon's Parent Effectiveness Training (PET), which applies

■ Two-paycheck and single-parent families often rely on relatives to assist with child rearing. These women—three sisters and a neighbor—are babysitters for an afternoon, as is this great-grandmother.

the guidelines for no-win intimacy described in Chapter 9 to the parent-child relationship. A similar, more recently developed program is Systematic Training for Effective Parenting (STEP). Both STEP and PET combine instruction on effective communication techniques with emotional support for parents.

Accepting Outside Help for Child Rearing

In addition to gaining self-acceptance and esteem, parents can also work to involve other members of their communities in child rearing. The first step, perhaps, is to insist that society recognize the positive achievements of conscientious parents, not just criticize parents and children for inadequacies. For example, a parent can remind an unnecessarily critical teacher that simply preparing a child for schooling—to learn to associate with others and to express him- or herself outside the family—is a significant accomplishment (Laws, 1978:5–6).

Parents and others can also begin to recognize

that in most societies and historical periods, several adults have been available to meet a child's emotional and physical needs. Efforts to emancipate isolated full-time mothers often involve urging them to find jobs outside the home, but this is not the only solution.

Kin Support Kin relationships in the urban white middle class have tended not to involve mutual services, but in the black community and in the white working class, kin play an important functional role. For example, the role of "extended parent" is relatively common; that is, the grandparent (usually grandmother) takes on the role of parent to the grandchildren and may run the house while the mother works (Clavan, 1978).

The role of grandmother in socializing black and working-class children has often been noted, but the cooperation between adult male and female siblings who share the same household or live near one another should also be mentioned (Stack, 1980:122). Often, responsibility for providing food, car, clothing, and shelter and for socializing children may be spread over several households:

Michael Lee grew up in The Flats and now has a job in Chicago. On a visit to The Flats, Michael described the residence and domestic organization of his kin. "Most of my kin in The Flats lived right here on Cricket Street, numbers sixteen, eighteen, and twenty-two, in these three apartment buildings joined together. My mama decided it would be best for me and my three brothers and sister to be on Cricket Street too. My daddy's mother had a small apartment in this building, her sister had one in the basement, and another brother and his family took a larger apartment upstairs. My uncle was really good to us. He got us things we wanted and he controlled us. All the women kept the younger kids together during the day. They cooked together too. It was good living" [Stack, 1980:117]. ■

People in the black community and in white working-class neighborhoods often feel they are involved in a network of kin and friends "whom they can count on" (Stack, 1980:118). As more middle-class whites become two-paycheck and single-parent families, they, too, come to rely more on kin support.

Cooperation Among Families Parents of young children can create child-care cooperatives in which a group of friends or neighbors periodically babysits with one another's children. The arrangement can be formalized so that caring time is recorded and balanced monthly, or it can be more informal. Another idea is to establish neighborhood play groups where a group of neighborhood children rotates from house to house regularly, one or more days a week. With older children, parents might exchange homework help—"I'll help Johnny with math on Tuesday evenings if you'll help Mary with English"—and of course form car pools for children's lessons and activities. Such practical services provide the occasion for children to form supportive relationships with other adults, and they are also a basis for shared parenting. Sometimes, parents find it easier to help someone else's children with homework and other problems.

Available Community Supports Another source of support is the community itself: teachers, school counselors and principals, police officers, adolescents' employers, and the public in general.

We have seen that many adults with whom children come into contact have different values and attitudes from their parents. On the other hand, the society at large often supports parental values, attitudes, and even house rules. When this is the case, parents can benefit from letting others—often even strangers—help socialize their children. For example, if a 3-year-old pushes the person who is ahead of her and her father in the grocery store check-out line, that person may tell the child crossly not to push. The father need not feel apologetic, nor does he have to scold the child himself. Rather, he can allow the child to learn from the consequences of her own behavior. The same rule applies to a careless child whose bicycle is stolen when he leaves it unlocked at a shopping center. His mother may help him call the police, but she can also let the police officer scold the boy for negligence. In both examples parents allow outsiders to help socialize their children, and thus they avoid getting involved in unnecessary nagging themselves. Programs such as Big Brothers/Big Sisters and Foster Grandparents involve volunteers who care about and can help with child rearing.

Day Care and Full-Time Caregivers Many parents use community networks to help in child rearing, but those who are employed have special needs. While a significant proportion of child care is provided by relatives—most often grandmothers—parents frequently hire nonrelatives who provide care either inside or outside their homes. Often these caregivers are neighbors, friends, retired persons, or full-time homemakers who choose to stay home with their own preschool children. The most satisfying arrangements are likely to be between families who have compatible values and life-styles and who live in the same neighborhood, although they need not be friends. Parents and the additional caregiver need to discuss and agree on their expectations beforehand. For example, they should negotiate the amount of payment, whether the hours of care will be flexible or fixed, whether the child is to take a daily nap, have a hot or a cold lunch, eat breakfast with the parents or other caregiver, and so on (Collins and Watson, 1976:22).[7]

---

7. The Day Care and Child Development Council of America publishes a pamphlet entitled "Checking Out Day Care: A Parent Guide," which is available by request. The pamphlet points out that there are no set rules for selecting a child-care program. What is important is to visit a number of facilities—with the child if possible—before making a final decision. See also Clarke-Stewart, 1982, in the Suggested Readings section of this chapter.

■ For working parents, day-care centers can supply a source of help in child rearing in a society that gives low priority to aiding families. Both government and business have been slow to provide assistance to workers with young children.

Relatives, friends, and neighbors are not always available to help, so working parents often place children in day-care facilities. Then, too, as parents have additional children and as their children get older, they are more likely to use day-care facilities. There are several types of day care, ranging from informal friendship networks to more formal arrangements.

Two types of more formal day care are available to parents: home-based care, in which one or more individuals care for several children in their own homes; and center-based care, in which children take part in a nursery school program or in an after-school program with a teaching staff and a classroom. Center-based facilities can be local operations or nationally affiliated franchises. Comprehensive and universal government-funded day care does not exist in the United States today, and it is a complicated and controversial issue. (Family policy issues such as day care and maternity or parental leave are discussed in Chapter 14.)

Working parents in several areas of the country have initiated neighborhood latchkey programs for school-age children who are too old for conventional day-care facilities. A 1982 estimate issued by the U.S. Department of Labor put the number of children age 10 or younger who care for themselves when not in school at 7 million (Robinson et al., 1986:4).

Bryan Robinson and his colleagues note that the term *latchkey* has taken on negative connotations, often meaning "unsupervised." This is not necessarily the case. Moreover, the term *latchkey* is not always applicable because many children care for themselves before school but have a parent at home afterward. Others stay home alone only during evenings or during the night, according to the hours their parent(s) are employed. "Additionally, other children cannot be considered unsupervised since parents supervise them in absentia by telephone or by supervisory rules during their absences" (Robinson et al., 1986:3). In some cases caregivers,

BOX 13·1

COMMUNICAT-ING WITH CHILDREN— HOW TO TALK SO KIDS WILL LISTEN, AND LISTEN SO KIDS WILL TALK

HELPING CHILDREN DEAL WITH THEIR FEELINGS

Children need to have their feelings accepted and respected.

1. *You can listen quietly and attentively.*
2. *You can acknowledge their feelings with a word.* "Oh … Mmm … I see …"
3. *You can give the feeling a name.* "That sounds frustrating!"
4. *You can give the child his wishes in fantasy.* "I wish I could make the banana ripe for you right now!"
5. *You can note that all feelings are accepted; but certain actions must be limited.* "I can see how angry you are at your brother. Tell him what you want with words, not fists."

TO ENGAGE A CHILD'S COOPERATION

1. *Describe what you see, or describe the problem.* "There's a wet towel on the bed."
2. *Give information.* "The towel is getting my blanket wet."
3. *Say it with a word.* "The towel!"
4. *Describe what you feel.* "I don't like sleeping in a wet bed!"
5. *Write a note.* (above towel rack)

    Please put me back so I can dry.

    Thanks!

    Your Towel

INSTEAD OF PUNISHMENT

1. *Express your feelings strongly—without attacking character.* "I'm furious that my saw was left outside to rust in the rain!"
2. *State your expectations.* "I expect my tools to be returned after they've been borrowed."
3. *Show the child how to make amends.* "What this saw needs now is a little steel wool and a lot of elbow grease."
4. *Give the child a choice.* "You can borrow my tools and return them or you can give up the privilege of using them. You decide."
5. *Take action.* Child: "Why is the tool box locked?" Father: "You tell me why."
6. *Problem-solve.* "What can we work out so that you can use my tools when you need them, and so that I'll be sure they're here when I need them?"

TO ENCOURAGE AUTONOMY

1. *Let children make choices.* "Are you in the mood for your gray pants today or your red pants?"

SOURCE:
Faber and Mazlish, 1980.

2. *Show respect for a child's struggle.* "A jar can be hard to open. Sometimes it helps if you tap the side of the lid with a spoon."
3. *Don't ask too many questions.* "Glad to see you. Welcome home."
4. *Don't rush to answer questions.* "That's an interesting question. What do you think?"
5. *Encourage children to use sources outside the home.* "Maybe the pet shop owner would have a suggestion."
6. *Don't take away hope.* "So you're thinking of trying out for the play! That should be an experience."

PRAISE AND SELF-ESTEEM

Instead of evaluating, describe.

1. *Describe what you see.* "I see a clean floor, a smooth bed, and books neatly lined up on the shelf."
2. *Describe what you feel.* "It's a pleasure to walk into this room!"
3. *Sum up the child's praiseworthy behavior with a word.* "You sorted out your pencils, crayons and pens, and put them in separate boxes. That's what I call *organization!*"

TO FREE CHILDREN FROM PLAYING ROLES

1. *Look for opportunities to show the child a new picture of himself or herself.* "You've had that toy since you were 3 and it looks almost like new!"
2. *Put children in situations where they can see themselves differently.* "Sara, would you take the screwdriver and tighten the pulls on these drawers?"
3. *Let children overhear you say something positive about them.* "He held his arm steady even though the shot hurt."
4. *Model the behavior you'd like to see.* "It's hard to lose, but I'll try to be a sport about it. Congratulations!"
5. *Be a storehouse for your child's special moments.* "I remember the time you . . ."
6. *When the child acts according to the old label, state your feelings and/or your expectations.* "I don't like that. Despite your strong feelings, I expect sportsmanship from you."

volunteer or paid, care for school-age children at neighborhood schools or churches before school in the morning and after school in the afternoon.

Is Day Care Good for Children? About 2 million children currently receive licensed day care. More than 5 million others age 3–5 attend nursery schools or kindergartens that often serve the same purpose. "In a wave of fundamental social change, day care is becoming a basic need of the American family" (Watson et al., 1984:14). Many Americans are ambivalent about day care for their children; the quality of some day-care centers leaves much to be desired. Nevertheless, most child-care experts agree that when day-care facilities are clean, safe, and adequately staffed, and when children are allowed to play together comfortably with some respect for individual needs, such environments are as healthy for children as home care.

Harvard psychologist Jerome Kagan compared middle- and working-class children (age 3½–30 months) reared at home with others attending a day-care center. The day-care group spent about eight hours a day at the center, five days a week. Kagan found that the day-care children did not seem to be much different emotionally or socially from children raised at home. Children from poorly educated and less privileged families, however, showed more intellectual growth when exposed to day care (Kagan, 1976; Kagan et al., 1978).

The common belief that it is harmful or at least not in a young child's best interest to spend long hours away from home every day is not supported by evidence. According to Urie Bronfenbrenner, there is no appreciable difference between day care and home care, provided the day care is of good quality. A child needs to spend a substantial amount of time "with somebody who's crazy about him," somebody "who thinks that kid is more important than other people's kids, someone who's in love with him and whom he loves in return." At the same time, a child needs or can benefit from "some day care, even some coolness toward him" such as objective evaluation (Bronfenbrenner, 1977).

The demand for day-care facilities has grown steadily in the last decade as more mothers join the labor force. Finding quality facilities at an affordable cost has become a serious problem for many parents ("What price," 1984). One response has been for corporations and other employers to offer child-care facilities at work (Collins, 1985).

Parents and Children: Maintaining Intimacy

Whether parents have full-time jobs and use day care or spend their days at home, being a parent involves a personal and intimate relationship. Like the marriage relationship, it is based on a culturally accepted "contract" between two parties: Parents expect some degree of achievement and loyalty from their children, and they reciprocate with support and commitment. And as in marriage, the parent-child relationship flows from a second, more personal contract between the individuals. That second contract is more likely to remain vital when participants recognize several factors.

First, society-wide conditions influence the relationship, and these factors can place extraordinary emotional and financial strains on parents. Formerly children were expected to become more help and less trouble as they grew older; today, many parents can expect just the opposite. Most of what children need costs more as they grow: clothes, transportation, amusement, and schooling. And as children grow older, they may adopt values their parents have trouble accepting.

Second, the parent-child relationship is more likely to be and remain vital when participants recognize and accept their own anger and frustrations with each other and work to have bonding fights that end in negotiation and compromise rather than denying negative feelings or playing power politics.

Third, many of the guidelines for bonding fights, discussed in Chapter 9, are also effective techniques for communicating with children and for guiding their development. Box 13·1, "Communicating with Children—How to Talk So Kids Will Listen, and Listen So Kids Will Talk," offers guidelines for supportively communicating with children. If children learn to relate well to other human beings and to take some personal responsibility for these relationships, they will be prepared to have good relationships as adults. In sum, the attitudes and practices helpful in maintaining intimacy— leveling, using I-statements, and presenting specific grievances and concrete suggestions—are just as effective in child rearing as they are in marriage.

And finally, satisfying parent-child relationships are based on personal contracts that are flexible and open rather than fixed, so that the participants can alter interpersonal agreements as the needs of one or both change.

Summary

Living with children is both exciting and frustrating. The mother's role and the father's role may be different from societal images, and both roles can be difficult, especially in our society, where attitudes have changed so rapidly and where there is little consensus about how to raise children. In addition, both children's and parents' needs change over the course of life.

Five styles of parenting can be described: the parent as martyr, as pal, as police officer, as teacher-counselor, and as athletic coach. This last style represents the interactive perspective, where the child's contributions and personality are recognized as fully as the parent's.

Child maltreatment is a serious problem in our society, and it is probably far more common than statistics indicate. One difficulty is drawing a clear distinction between "normal" child rearing and abuse.

To have better relationships with their children, parents need to recognize their own needs and to avoid feeling unnecessary guilt; to accept help from others (friends and the community at large as well as professional caregivers); and finally, to try to build and maintain flexible, intimate relationships using the same bonding techniques as those suggested (in Chapter 9) for marital partners.

Key Terms

laissez-faire discipline
    422
autocratic discipline
    422
developmental model of
    child rearing *423*
interactive perspective
    424
democratic discipline
    431
child maltreatment *433*
child abuse *433*
child neglect *433*

Study Questions

1. Discuss some effects of our society's romanticized, unrealistic image of motherhood and the "maternal instinct."
2. What negative and positive effects might mothers' employment have on children? What are your own views on this topic?
3. Do you think that fathers are less well equipped for parenting than are mothers? What are the relative contributions of biology and the social environment in determining the parenting ability of fathers?
4. What are the effects of employment on the father's role in parenting? How are these different from the effects of employment on the mother's role?
5. Compare the advantages and disadvantages of the five parenting styles discussed in this chapter.
6. Why might the transition to parenthood be more difficult than the transition to other adult roles, such as worker or spouse?
7. Compare the parenting difficulties of parents with babies, preschoolers, and school-age children. Which stage do you think would be the most difficult? The least difficult? Why?
8. Compare the different needs of babies, preschoolers, school-age children, and adolescents. How do these needs contribute to the difficulties of parenting at each of these stages?
9. Differentiate between child abuse and child neglect. Do you think that physical maltreatment is more, less, or equally damaging to children than emotional maltreatment?
10. It is not always easy to draw a line between "normal" child rearing and maltreatment. In your own opinion, at what point can this line be drawn?
11. Discuss some society-wide beliefs and conditions that, when exaggerated, can encourage well-intentioned parents to mistreat their children.
12. Explain the therapeutic approach to combating child maltreatment. Why do you think this approach is gradually overtaking the punitive approach to combating child maltreatment?

Suggested Readings

Bengston, Vern L., and Joan F. Robertson (eds.)
1985 *Grandparenthood.* Beverly Hills: Sage.
A collection of scholarly, readable articles on all aspects of grandparenthood.

Brazelton, T. Berry
1981 *On Becoming a Family: The Growth of Attachment.* New York: Delacorte.
Research-based information directed toward parents by one of America's foremost experts on child development.
1983 *Infants and Mothers: Differences in Development.* 2d ed. New York: Delacorte.
Child development made clear to parents.

Caplow, Theodore, Howard M. Bahr, Bruce A. Chadwick, Reuben Hill, and Margaret Holmes Williamson
1982 *Middletown Families: Fifty Years of Change and Continuity.* New York: Bantam.
A study of four generations of family life; attacks the myth of the "generation gap" and the "declining family."

Chess, Stella, Alexander Thomas, and Herbert G. Birch
1965 *Your Child Is a Person: A Psychological Approach to Parenthood Without Guilt.* New York: Viking.
Discussion of parent-child relationships based on a scientific, longitudinal study but addressed to a popular audience. Stresses the role of individual differences and how parents handle them at different ages. (Alexander Thomas, Stella Chess, Herbert G. Birch, M. Hertzig, and S. Korn, *Behavior Individuality in Early Childhood,* New York: New York University Press, 1963, is the scholarly presentation of this research.)

Clarke-Stewart, Alison
1982 *Daycare.* Cambridge, Mass.: Harvard University Press.
Research-based evaluation of the effects of day care on the child's development. Contains guidelines for parents making day-care choices.

Comer, James P., and Alvin F. Poussaint
1975 *Black Child Care: How to Bring Up a Healthy Black Child in America.* New York: Simon & Schuster.
Advice to parents from black psychiatrists at Yale and Harvard.

Daley, Eliot A.
1978 *Father Feelings.* New York: Morrow.
A father's moving journal of a year in the life of his family. Focuses on special ways fathers can encourage their children.

Dodson, Fitzhugh
1973 *How to Parent.* New York: New American Library.
Manual of child care centering on emotional and intellectual development. Very strong on educational play.

Faber, Adele, and Elaine Mazlish
1982 *How to Talk So Kids Will Listen and Listen So Kids Will Talk.* New York: Avon.
As the title says, how to communicate with children.

Finkelhor, David
1979 *Sexually Victimized Children.* New York: Free Press.
Exploratory study of victimization based on college student recollections.

Ginott, Haim G.
1965 *Between Parent and Child.* New York: Macmillan.
Techniques of parent-child communication.
1969 *Between Parent and Teen-ager.* New York: Macmillan.
Techniques of parent-teen communication, with sections on rebellion, anger, teenage sex, and driving, drinking, and drugs, among others.

Gordon, Thomas
1970 *Parent Effectiveness Training.* New York: Wyden.
Manual of widely used parenting techniques that also emphasizes communication techniques.

Lamb, Michael E. (ed.)
1986 *The Father's Role: Applied Perspectives.* New York: Wiley.
Readable, up-to-date collection of essays by social scientists on various aspects of fathering today.

Lamb, Michael, and Abraham Sagi (eds.)
1983 *Fatherhood and Family Policy.* Hillsdale, N.J.: Erlbaum.
Interesting articles toward policy strategies to enhance parenting by fathers.

LaRossa, Ralph, and Maureen M. LaRossa
1981 *Transition to Parenthood: How Infants Change Families.* Beverly Hills, Calif.: Sage.
New research by thoughtful observers of family dynamics.

LeMasters, E. E., and John DeFrain
1977 *Parents in Contemporary America: A Sympathetic View.* 4th ed. Homewood, Ill.: Dorsey.
Witty, readable discussion of parenting from the parents' point of view, emphasizing parents' roles in the current social context.

Lenz, Elinor
1983 *Once My Child, Now My Friend.* New York: Warner Books.
Advice on relationships with adult children.

Lewis, Michael, and Leonard A. Rosenblum (eds.)
1974 *The Effect of the Infant on Its Caregiver.* New York: Wiley.
As the title suggests, develops the point that

children socialize parents, just as parents socialize children.

Lightfoot, Sara Lawrence
1981 *Worlds Apart: Relationships Between Families and Schools.* New York: Basic Books. Discussion of the interplay between school and family.

Nurturing News: A Quarterly Forum for Nurturing Men.
Periodical for men who want to be active parents. Write 187 Casselli Avenue, San Francisco, Calif., 94114 for information.

O'Kane, Monica
1982 *Living with Adult Children: A Helpful Guide for Parents and Adult Children Sharing the Same Roof.* St. Paul, Minn.: Diction Books. New book of advice on a situation that is more common than it used to be.

Robinson, Bryan E., and Robert L. Barret
1986 *The Developing Father: Emerging Roles in Contemporary Society.* New York: Guilford Press.
Research on fatherhood includes theoretical perspectives, fathers' changing roles, issues surrounding teenage fatherhood, stepfatherhood, and gay fathers, among others.

Robinson, Bryan E., Bobbie H. Rowland, and Mick Coleman
1986 *Latchkey Kids: Unlocking Doors for Children and Their Families.* Lexington, Mass.: Heath/Lexington Books.
Scholarly research on the growing proportion of and problems confronted by latchkey children. Contains policy suggestions.

Schulenberg, Joy
1987 *Gay Parenting: A Complete Guide for Gay Men and Lesbians with Children.* New York: Anchor.
Excellent advice to parents.

Spock, Benjamin
1983 *Baby and Child Care.* New York: Pocket Books. Classic baby- and child-care manual, first published in 1946 and revised several times. It offers a great deal of solid and specific information and is very useful if read as a resource, not a bible.

Straus, Murray, Richard J. Gelles, and Suzanne K. Steinmetz
1980 *Behind Closed Doors.* New York: Doubleday. Major book on family violence, including child abuse. Chapter 3 takes a position against spanking.

White, Burton L.
1975 *The First Three Years of Life.* Englewood Cliffs, N.J.: Prentice-Hall.
Report of a research project at Harvard that has many practical implications for parents who wish to encourage their children's physical, emotional, social, and intellectual development during early childhood.

14 Managing Resources

*Work forty years of my
life, carry sacks on my
back, lard the earth with
my sweat, and pinch
and save my whole life
long for you, my
darlings, who made all
work easy for me and
every burden light.*
HONORÉ DE BALZAC, *Père Goriot*

The declining standard of living during recent years has made people more aware of the pragmatic functions of families in providing shelter, food, and health care. This chapter discusses how families meet these basic needs in today's changing economy. We will examine the effects of inflation and unemployment on a family's spending power and well-being. We'll discuss earning and spending over the course of family life. And we'll talk about budgets and credit, as well as family housing and health care.

As in other areas, many of the personal economic troubles people are experiencing reflect public issues. Families need to respond with knowledgeable decisions and actions. There are two things families can do: They can press for society-wide changes so that the economy in general—and energy, housing, food, and health-care industries in particular—better meet their needs. And people can work within their families to make the best use of the money and services that are available. Neither approach alone is sufficient; both are necessary. We begin with an examination of how our economy has changed in recent decades.

THE FAMILY IN A CHANGING ECONOMY

"It's a cold, hard fact that people's life styles are going to change," warned a Bank of America vice-president in late 1979. "We're entering an age of having to make do with less" (in Rankin, 1979:44). "The most recent period represents a decisive break with the past," claims a political economist (Blumberg, 1981:92). Since the mid-1970s the United States economy has been described as "slowing," "constricted," not "competitive." Whatever term is used, it implies a declining standard of living for the majority of Americans. For almost everyone, that realization comes as a shock because many Americans have become accustomed to abundance. But real income peaked in 1973 (after inflation is taken into account). Since then, average weekly earnings have declined by 14.3 percent, and median family income by 6 percent (Greenhouse, 1986).

The Rise and Fall of the Postwar Economy

After World War II the United States began a period of economic expansion that lasted through the 1960s. Family income more than doubled between

1939 and 1969. Unlike in the years after the Great Depression, most Americans no longer worried about having the basic necessities. They began to take needs for granted and set their sights on wants: new homes, new cars, television sets, wall-to-wall carpeting, electronic gadgets, travel. Americans believed that the economy could only continue to grow, and they developed a buy-now-pay-later mentality reflected in the new "credit-card economy."

Then in 1973 the rate of inflation began to spiral upward. An oil shortage in 1973 and 1974 raised energy costs astronomically, and energy costs, which rose 53 percent between 1978 and 1981, have continued to put additional economic pressures on families (U.S. Energy Information Administration, 1983).

Other economic difficulties (Thurow, 1980; Blumberg, 1981) contributed to the recession of the early seventies, and the twenty-eight months before December 1974 saw a drop in workers' real purchasing power (the value of one's money in terms of the goods it will buy, taking the declining worth of the dollar into account) of more than 20 percent. The economy continued to decline until, in 1975, unemployment reached levels not seen since before World War II (Becnel, 1979). In the late seventies unemployment rose still higher, to 10.1 percent in September 1982, the highest level in 42 years (Begley, 1982). While unemployment has now declined (6.0 percent in 1987; Hershey, 1987), many of the jobs lost in the 1970s and 1980s will not be restored even with an end to the recession, since they involve the long-term decline of our industrial sector due to inadequate investment and development, declining productivity, and increasing overseas competition, not only from foreign firms but from overseas branches of American corporations (Blumberg, 1981). Unions in foodprocessing and services areas as well as industrial unions are acquiescing to pay cuts; blue-collar wages, as a result, are unstable and declining. Companies are relocating, particularly from the industrial northeast to the "Sunbelt" or to third world countries, where labor is cheap.

Another feature of the seventies economy was double-digit inflation. While inflation has been under control in recent years—4 percent or less a year from 1983 to 1986 (Uchitelle, 1987)—generally high rates of interest continue to limit home ownership or make it more costly.

All in all, in the seventies and early eighties the combination of inflation, recession, and unemploy-

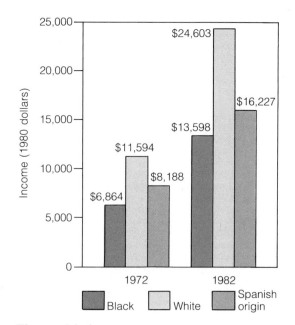

Figure 14·1

Median family income for black, Hispanic, and white families in 1972 and 1982. While middle-class black incomes have improved over the last twenty years, the economic situation of lower-class blacks has not. During this period the proportion of black families headed by women increased, while the proportion of black men with jobs fell. (Sources: U.S. Bureau of the Census, 1983c, d; Sternlieb and Hughes, 1984:96, 105)

ment put an end to the era of the postwar boom, as people realized that the economy would not keep on growing. For many, the 1970s and 1980s have been a time of "pinched possibilities, failed Utopian visions," and, as a result, "exhausted psychological resources" (Dickstein, 1977:272). As Figure 14·1 shows, this pinch has hurt minority families to an even greater extent than the white majority. Women—along with the disabled, retired, and non–property owners in general (Aldous et al., 1985)—have also been hit especially hard, particularly those who had recently entered the job market and fell into the "last hired, first fired" category.

The proportion of the population in poverty has increased in the eighties, peaking at 15.2 percent in 1983 (Pear, 1984) and dropping back to 13.6 percent in 1986—still "higher than in any year from 1969 through 1980" (Pear, 1987c: A12). There has been "a dramatic shift in the distribution of income

We are a contemporary family. We don't want to be ~~part~~ of the masses. We want to live with style!

JoAnn Roberts

away from lower- and middle-income groups toward the upper-income groups" (Chimerine, quoted in Arenson, 1983). Many families have managed to keep even with inflation only by having wives work (Blumberg, 1981), which reflects an economic necessity, not a life-style choice. It remains to be seen whether a restricted economy only limits our choices (as psychologist and pollster Daniel Yankelovich [1981] predicts) or whether in some cases these economic restrictions may contribute to changes that are viewed as desirable by family members.

After Affluence: Some Marriage and Family Questions

The changing economy poses several questions about marriage and family relationships. Some questions have to do with the conjugal balance of power: What will happen as more wives take on breadwinning responsibility along with their husbands? What will happen to a wife's gains in power if she is laid off? How issues such as these are decided has significant influence on marriage relationships. A contracting economy can mean opportunities for greater flexibility in roles as partners renegotiate their personal marriage contracts. Or it can mean a greater reliance on the hidden, traditional contract, with heavier work loads for already overloaded wives.

And what about the emotional implications of not finding work in one's profession or craft—or any work permitting one to be self-supporting? What about the need to move once or repeatedly in search of work? Or the need to live with relatives or other groups because one cannot maintain a separate home? Will some of this pressure end in family violence or other family turmoil? As we discuss family budgets and other issues, we will emphasize the need to openly negotiate these decisions.

Some clues to the impact of economic strain on the family come from an extensive study of 2,000 families interviewed in 1976 in New York, Detroit, Atlanta, and San Francisco (Caplovitz, 1979). Sociologist David Caplovitz asked whether married couples had been drawn closer together as a result of economic pressures, or whether there were more tensions and quarrels. In his overall sample 40 percent reported no change in their marriages, 28 percent reported that their marriages were better, 14 percent reported that their marriages were worse, and 19 percent reported a mixed response; all together, 33 percent reported at least some negative marital consequences. Respondents who were suffering from more economic strain—the poor, those low on the occupational hierarchy, blacks, and Hispanics—had much higher rates of marital turmoil. Recent statistical analysis (South, 1985) shows that the divorce rate tends to rise during periods of economic contraction, characterized by high unemployment. This is probably due to higher "levels of stress and tension" (South, 1985:38). Forty-six percent of Caplovitz's sample who reported that their economic situation was much worse also reported worsened general mental health. M. Harvey Brenner of Johns Hopkins University, an authority on economy and health, expected mental and physical health effects of the recession of the early 1980s to show up five to six years later (Slade and Roberts, 1984).

Economic needs and pressures vary over life and the next section explores earning and spending over the course of family life.

EARNING AND SPENDING OVER THE COURSE OF FAMILY LIFE

Chapter 12 discusses the "opportunity costs" of having children and also points to warnings by experts that our society will become increasingly stratified according to whether people choose to become parents. That is, child-free couples will not only earn more money but have considerably more discretionary income. Table 14·1 lists the 1982 median incomes of American families with and without children. For younger families—those whose household head is under 25—and also for families with heads of household age 25–44, the difference in earned income is considerable. A large part of this difference is due to the fact that childless wives may work full-time and/or pursue highly paid careers more avidly than do married mothers. Then, too, child-free husbands may devote more energy to their careers.

Most American families experience a series of financial ups and downs. The average couple feels relatively comfortable before they have children. As they raise and educate their children, they go through an extended period of constriction. The family economy expands as children become self-supporting, then usually contracts again when the parents retire (Troll et al., 1979; Gordon and Lee, 1977). In the following paragraphs we'll look at the changes in spending patterns that take place as families pass through these stages (see Figure 14·2).

Prenuptial Financial Planning

Partly because people are waiting until they are older to marry—and also because many marriages are remarriages—more and more weddings take place between individuals who have previously accumulated assets and/or debts. Financial advis-

TABLE 14·1 Median Incomes of Families with and Without Children by Age of Householder, 1982

Age	Families with Children	Families Without Children
All families	$25,340	$26,390
Under 25	13,140	18,780
25–34	21,440	28,090
35–44	28,410	33,230
45–54	31,260	32,940
55–64	28,720	29,640
65 +	19,580	18,910

SOURCE: Linden, 1984:5.

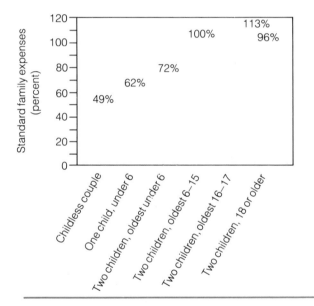

Figure 14·2

The family budget over the course of life: Family expenses. The bars illustrate how family expenses vary with the age and number of children. It takes as 100 percent a family with two children, the oldest age 6–15. Other figures indicate the amount of money needed for expenses in other family combinations, given as a percentage of the standard family's expenses. For example, a family with two children, the oldest age 16–17, needs 113 percent of the standard family's resources, while a childless couple needs only 49 percent of that amount. The estimate for children 18 and older is exclusive of college expenses and assumes that the children are largely self-supporting. If instead a child is in college, expenses will be sharply higher and will drop off after completion of his or her education. (Source: Adapted from Oppenheimer, 1974:230)

ers encourage couples to address money issues before they marry. One thing that needs to be discussed, for example, is how bank accounts will be set up. Whose will the money be—hers, his, theirs? A related question involves how to divide responsibility for household costs. Should each partner be accountable for half the expenses? Or should partners put in an equal percentage of their respective earnings even when one is making considerably more than the other? What about expenses one person can afford that the other cannot

(Goodman, 1983)? Box 14·1, "When Couple Splits Costs 50-50, It Isn't Necessarily Fair," points out that this is an issue for dating teens, cohabiting couples, and marrieds alike.

Along with determining who will be responsible for what expenses, partners need to inform each other regarding their assets and debts. If one plans to legally exclude certain assets from what will become joint property upon marriage, this needs to be discussed. Generally, partners are individually responsible for liabilities incurred before the

BOX 14 · 1

WHEN COUPLE SPLITS COSTS 50-50, IT ISN'T NECESSARILY FAIR

Columnist Ellen Goodman of the *Boston Globe* explains why:

The girl is suffering from lopsided change. She doesn't put it this way. Perhaps she hasn't even heard of the disease. At less than half my age, she sees the problem as part of her status quo. But let me explain the situation.

The girl, who is finishing her high school years with a certain measure of introspection, is going out to dinner on New Year's Eve. Having been raised according to equal-opportunity guidelines that favor shared roles and split costs, she expects to pay her own way.

Indeed, her boyfriend has the same expectation. This is what they do, after all: pizza down the middle, burgers 50-50, one movie ticket apiece.

But for New Year's Eve, they are planning a more upscale venture. For him, it will be a splurge. For her, it will be, she says frankly, a hardship. The difference between the two of them is not one of appetite but of paycheck.

The high school seniors each have after-school jobs, you see. She earns more than 59 cents to his dollar, but there is a gender gap of 30 cents an hour that adds up and up.

Their relationship to each other may be on equal footing and billing, but their relationship to the world is not. So, in a real-life sense, dinner will cost her more.

My young friend is describing a problem that occurs more than once every 365 days. She is talking about the unevenness of social change.

It has gradually become routine for young people to pay their own way. It's notably easier now for young men to become economic partners with their social partners. Young women feel some relief in and responsibility for paying their own way. But, to a large degree, the world still goes on valuing their work differently.

I also have two friends in their 20s, a young professional couple, who went searching for an apartment to share and came back with a similar problem. He was two years older and 50 percent better paid. Should they rent something that he could afford or that she could afford? Should each pay an equal amount of the rent or an equal percentage of their salaries?

SOURCE:
Goodman, 1983; p. 8.

---

marriage, but each should know the debt load of the other. Similarly, partners need to specify which credit cards they intend to keep separate and which they will share. Then, too, prospective spouses should have some idea of what will happen to the partner's personal possessions should one die (Card, 1984:74). If they haven't done so already, remarrying partners with children may want to negotiate wills. This can help prevent misunderstandings later

about whether certain personal property is to go to children upon one partner's death or to the surviving second spouse.

The Couple with No Children

Among married and cohabiting couples without children, both partners are usually employed, and

Their personal desire for equality conflicted with their sense of fairness. Their way, you see, was not the way of the world. Yet it is the way of more and more of us.

The authors of "American Couples" show in their research that cohabitation is "a pay-as-you-go system." But the researchers note an irony: "While both men and women insist that each partner's contribution to the household be as equal as possible, their ability to do so is hampered by the nature of the world of work. Most women cannot earn as much money as their male partners." When living costs are divided up 50-50, the women's 50 is a much larger percent of her income.

The couple I know decided to pay according to their means. But she struggles with the sense that her lifestyle is dependent on his income and he struggles against some resentment. In the year that they have lived together, he has been rewarded, perhaps unconsciously, with a larger voice in their decisions.

I don't believe that even married couples are immune from the symptoms that come when we change our minds before we change the world. Fewer couples today accept the idea of a female dependency. More have equality as a goal. But how much of that equality founders on unequal paychecks?

How many men want their own work to be valued more when it is paid more? How many women still overcompensate for smaller paychecks by doing larger amounts of unpaid household work? How many men get resentful if their wives don't have the paychecks to back up their demands for equity?

We like to think that we can create private lives that run according to our own rules. Our relationships, our families, can be a haven of our own principles. Ideally, money would make no difference to lovers and spouses; power and paychecks would be unrelated.

But the public world can undermine the foundation of our private lives. We take home attitudes with our take-home pay.

The high school senior will work out a solution for her New Year's Eve. But not a final solution. This is an issue that will linger with her, with us, through a host of lopsided new years until we change the world to match our minds.

thus their combined income may be relatively high even if their individual salaries or wages are low.

In any case, expenses at this stage are usually low, and couples are free to spend relatively large amounts on personal wants. They may decide to purchase a home and furnishings during this period. Some couples will choose to remain child-free; others will have children and move into the next stage.

The Family with Young Children

Having children is expensive, and the expenses of raising children increase as they grow older. A child age 12–17 costs about three times as much as one age 5 or younger. A family's standard of living typically declines until the oldest child reaches 18, even though in absolute terms income usually increases over this period (Espenshade, 1973).

Families with higher incomes spend more in dollars but less in percentage of income on raising children.

The Family with Older Dependent Children

The third stage may be the most expensive stage of all, and not just in families where children attend college. Blue-collar jobs often leave a family at a relatively low level of income just when children reach late adolescence and financial needs are higher. This results in an income "crunch" for many working-class families at this stage, and it helps explain why they tend to be more strict in emphasizing their offsprings' needs to become self-supporting (Oppenheimer, 1974).

Not many years ago, the majority of parents (middle-class parents, at least) believed they could safely look forward to a time when their children would finally be on their own, and accordingly, they would have additional money to spend as they wished until retirement. (The financial picture up to this point is depicted in Figure 14·2.) That expectation has become less realistic, however, for several reasons. For one thing, college costs and attendant student loan repayments have soared; tuition has risen twice as fast as inflation (Fiske, 1987). Some parents have remortgaged their homes to finance their children's college expenses. Furthermore, as we have seen in other chapters, the constricting economy forces young-adult children back into the homes of their parents (Glick and Lin, 1986a; Smith, 1986). Then, too, middle-aged couples may increasingly find themselves helping to support their own parents, because the aging population is now living longer and requiring more medical care (Gould, 1984); some states even require adult children to contribute to parent care (*Swoap* v. *Superior Court*, 1973; Callahan, 1985).

The Retired Couple

Some retired couples experience financial deprivation, finding themselves in tighter straits than their children and grandchildren (Troll et al., 1979). Income can decline as much as 50 percent after retirement (Parnes and Less, 1983).

Still, older persons were less hard hit by the economic troubles of the seventies and now have a poverty rate that is lower (14.1 percent in 1983) than the overall U.S. rate or the rate for children (22.2 percent) (Pear, 1985; Preston, 1984). Cost-of-living increases built into Social Security payments did a better job of keeping pace with inflation than did earned income. One study of retirees found that in 1980, 59 percent of married and 48 percent of unmarried retirees found their income "adequate" or "better than adequate," while only 9 percent and 15 percent, respectively, found they could not make ends meet (25 percent of black retirees fell into this category) (Parnes and Less, 1983). Serious illness, of course, can erode the savings and income of elderly persons and their families, and the papers have reported stories of spouses divorcing after long-term marriages so that their partner may receive government support for nursing home care (Williams, 1983). Health costs are rising, and health insurance programs, including Medicaid, are likely to be cut back, as is Social Security. While the present generation of elderly is unlikely to lose anything, it seems inevitable that taxes will be raised and benefits cut for future generations. Catastrophic health insurance could protect families against enormous health care debts likely to be accumulated during lengthy terminal illness, in the care of handicapped newborns, or, more and more likely, for the care of AIDS victims. We do not yet know if current government proposals will be acted on.

The ups and downs of family finances affect many aspects of a marriage. Social scientist Lillian Troll argues that

the amount of money couples have to spend on their own needs and desires clearly influences the way they live and the way they feel about their life.... Other things being equal, young couples raising children have a greater pinch than those who do not have children or those whose children have become relatively independent economically, and post-retirement couples are usually under greater economic deprivation than before retirement [Troll et al., 1979:43]. ■

One way to help ease these financial pinches at various stages of life is to plan ahead. During expansive stages couples might save toward anticipated future expenses. This is more readily accomplished when families operate on a budget, as the next section points out.

CREATING A WORKABLE BUDGET

As Box 14•2, "Budgeting Versus Romance: A Lesson in Realistic Planning in Marriage" suggests, **budgeting**—putting down on paper a spending plan for a definite time period (such as a month or a year)—can threaten many illusions about what married life will be like. That is one reason why people shy away from budgets (Gordon and Lee, 1977:365). Yet there are good reasons for budgeting.

Why Budget?

The word *budget* has an unfortunate connotation. To many Americans, it implies having *less* to spend. Actually, budgeting can mean having *more*. Americans think of their spending power in terms of how much money they make. But they can increase their real income—the amount of goods and services their money will buy—as much as 10 percent just by planning.

Besides the increase in real income, there are other good reasons to budget. First, budgeting encourages people to stop and think before they spend. Making conscious decisions about what they really want is one way to "minimize the influence of custom, conspicuous consumption, emulation, fashion, and advertising" (Gordon and Lee, 1977:365).

Second, budgeting makes it easier to adjust irregular income to regular expenses. Business executives who depend on fluctuating profits, professionals, salespeople on commission, and wage earners vulnerable to layoffs can never be sure of their annual or monthly incomes. Planning to reserve money in good months can help even things out during dry spells.

Third, budgeting helps when family income increases or decreases and when the amount families need to spend on certain things changes. For example, neglecting to plan ahead during an expansive period (such as just before retirement) can accustom a family to a life-style it may be surprised to find it can't sustain during the lean years that follow. Budgeting also helps during inflation and recession as real income falls.

Fourth, budgeting helps individuals and families discover and plug leaks in their expenditures. Shortly after receiving their paychecks, people often find they can't recall where the money went. With a budget, records show where it went and help people avoid spending carelessly. Using a budget helps families pinpoint just how much of their income is **discretionary income:** uncommitted money that can be spent as the family pleases. Being aware of that figure helps in making decisions about spending.[1]

Fifth, for two-paycheck families, budgeting encourages partners to decide whether the second wage earner's salary is to be considered permanent or temporary. Should one salary go toward buying a house, for example, or is it to be banked for emergencies and luxuries? If the second income goes to help buy a house, the family probably relinquishes the option of going back to living on one income.

Finally, budgeting encourages family members to reexamine their personal and family goals and values and to negotiate and cooperate about spending. "Budgeting is essentially a family project," write Leland Gordon and Stewart Lee. "Each member of the family should have a voice in determining the amount to be spent for all items, whether he or she contributes to the money income or not. And each member of the family must cooperate in keeping a record of expenditures" (1977:367). Budgeting is one avenue to renegotiating a couple's personal marriage contract. It can be used as a vehicle toward open discussion, fair fighting, and compromise. Because it helps get important issues into the open, budgeting can minimize power politics in a family and thereby help increase intimacy.

Planning a Budget: Five Steps

This section describes five steps to planning a workable budget in fairly general terms. Individual families can adapt the steps to their own interests and needs.

Step One: Estimating Income The first step is to make as accurate an estimate as possible of all income, including salaries, gifts, commissions, and so forth. At this stage it is important not to be

---

1. Don't feel you're in the minority, by the way, if you find yourself without discretionary money. According to one government-business report, only about one-third of American households have money left over after paying for a comfortable standard of living ("One-third," 1985).

BOX 14 · 2

BUDGETING VERSUS ROMANCE: A LESSON IN REALISTIC PLANNING IN MARRIAGE

Sociologist Carlfred Broderick, who teaches marriage and family courses, writes that "it is always an instructive experience to watch a class of unmarried undergraduate students draw up a budget for the first year of marriage."

Inevitably they assume two substantial incomes. One or possibly both are expected to bring a car with them into the marriage. They are scandalized to learn how much of their paychecks they never see due to deductions for various federal and state taxes. They are not aware that some companies also deduct substantial amounts for pension or retirement funds, insurance, or parking privileges. Even so, the diminished total is still substantial, and they plunge into the list of monthly expenditures with some zest. So much for a decent apartment and utilities, so much for food, so much for eating out, for entertainment or hobbies, for clothes, for insurance, for transportation, for medical and dental expenses, for personal allowances, for laundry, for subscriptions to newspapers and magazines, for church or charity, for gifts.

The married students in the class sit shaking their heads as the numbers are put on the board. Inevitably there is an overrun on the first approximation, so the class painfully and reluctantly cuts back on a few dollars here and there but finally comes up with a balanced budget and a feeling of relief that it is all really not so bad after all. Then someone says, "But what if the woman gets pregnant and they lose her income?" A grim silence settles over the class. Someone else says, "She just can't.... They can't afford a baby even on both incomes." "What? Not ever?" "Well, I don't see how . . . not on that budget." Yet it is clear that couples do it all the time. Eventually a married student will confess that he or she and spouse live on a fraction of the money listed. How? Well, they almost never eat out, and they drive only one car, and they don't have much furniture at all because they can't afford it. Not infrequently students accuse me of having set up this situation to discourage them from ever getting married. That is not true. But it is true that some of the toughest issues to face in the transition from romantic courtship to the realities of marriage are in the area of money.

SOURCE:
Broderick, 1979b:260–62.

overoptimistic about raises or projected commissions and profits. Unrealistic estimates can result in overspending.

Step Two: Compiling a Spending Inventory

The second step is to get a fairly accurate picture of current expenses. Overweight persons often insist they "never eat." But when they keep a daily record of the calories they take in, they are amazed. The same is true for spending money. A person might easily spend $20 a week on lunches but assume that he or she spends only about $10, for example.

Step Three: Preparing a Budget

The third step is to prepare a budget form similar to the list in Figure 14·3, which can be used for both one- and two-paycheck families. In adapting a personal budget, readers may want to omit some items and substitute others. Some items, of course, such as taxes and housing, cannot be eliminated. Intended expenses for each item should be written in for every month.

The sample budget in Figure 14·3 has nineteen items plus optional categories for "his" and "her" personal spending money. As a rule, more than twenty items makes a budget too cumbersome; up to that point, the more categories, the more accurate and useful the plan.

Because budgeting can sound like a disagreeable venture, a family may decide to work into it gradually. The budget can include relatively few items for expenditures, with a large amount designated "miscellaneous." As family members get used to the idea of budgeting, they can divide the miscellaneous category into specific expenditures.

When planning a budget today, it is important to take inflation into account. While less so than a few years ago, inflation is still a potential threat to economic well-being. A family has to increase its earnings by *more* than the rate of inflation to improve its standard of living. We are generally excited when we receive a raise, thinking of what we can do with that money. But if the rate of inflation reaches 13 percent, as it did in 1979, a family would need to increase its income more than 13 percent to remain at the same level of spending. People can calculate for inflation in their budgets. If income does not rise accordingly, families have to cut back on certain items in the plan. While cutting back is almost never enjoyable, it is easier with than without a budget.

Step Four: Keeping Records

The fourth step involves following through with the budget by keeping daily records of expenditures in a convenient notebook or in an account book bought for that purpose. The book can be set up with headings for common family expenses. At the end of the day, family members can go to the notebook and record what they've spent. Some families designate one member to make the daily recordings and also to write monthly checks for regular expenditures. This task can be rotated among family members. Older adolescents might periodically take this responsibility to gain valuable experience in handling money and also to feel that they are participating members of the family group.

Step Five: Rechecking

The fifth step is to compare records with the plan. At the end of each month, daily expenditure figures should be totaled for each item, then compared with the amounts planned in step three. If January had more food expenditures than were budgeted, either this expenditure would have to be cut back in February or more money allocated for food by taking it from some other category. If excessive expenses show up in successive months, the budgeter may decide to eliminate some expensive purchases. If expenditures for one account consistently fall below what was planned, the budget can be revised.

About Credit

In our country, credit cards and time purchases have become a way of life in recent years. Yet credit costs money, and it should be considered a purchase in its own right. In *Sylvia Porter's Money Book* (1976), financial writer Sylvia Porter offers some "right" and "wrong" reasons for borrowing. "Right" reasons include establishing a household or beginning a family, making major purchases, taking advantage of seasonal sales, financing college or other educational expenses, and genuine emergencies. Another "right" reason, according to Porter, is if the price of the wanted item is going up steeply and you know you will need one in the future. This last "right" reason made sense during the inflationary seventies, but such spending pressures do not exist at the moment.

"Wrong" reasons for using credit include buying to boost morale, to increase one's status, or on impulse. People misuse credit when they use it to

pawnshops. Interest rates vary widely among the different types of agencies. One of the most highly advertised sources of credit is the small loan company, which specializes in lending to borrowers who have little or no security. These sources serve a purpose, for without them many people with no security or poor credit ratings could not legally borrow money. But because of the risk small loan companies take, they charge extremely high interest rates.

Another way to borrow money is by arranging retail **installment financing,** in which people contract with a dealer to pay for major purchases over a period of time. The dealer receives the markup on the merchandise, and the interest on the unpaid balance. When making major purchases, people should study installment contracts with care and ask questions about anything they don't understand. Find out how much the item will *really* cost, that is, the price of the item plus the hidden cost of financing. Often people would not be willing to spend that much if the total cost were marked on the price tag. It is wise to compare interest rates and to consider whether a personal bank loan would be a less expensive way of paying for the item. Credit card rates have remained high compared to other forms of borrowing, although rate competition among bank cards is beginning to occur.

It is important to shop for credit as carefully as for any other major purchase. Furthermore, people should try to pay off one installment obligation before taking on a new one. Irwin Kellner, senior vice-president and economist with Manufacturers Hanover Trust Company in New York City, notes that installment debt has increased twenty-fold during the last two decades. He sees the increase in two-paycheck families as a major cause. "All this is fine when the economy is expanding," said Kellner, "but the economy is now in recession, with job prospects dwindling." If one wage-earner loses his or her job, the family may be in trouble because it has counted on the second income to help repay installment debts (in Rankin, 1979:98).

Consumers need to remember that using credit cards is the same as borrowing money, and credit-card purchases need to be budgeted the same way cash purchases are. Statistics on credit misuse are high. Of every twenty families that take out a loan to buy a new car or use a credit card to purchase a refrigerator, "one will wind up in trouble" (Rankin, 1979:44). In addition, winding up in financial

■ The high cost of living: Regardless of their income, most couples wish they had more money and fewer bills but find that spending takes priority over saving. Planning a budget—and following it—is one way to avoid being overwhelmed by expenses.

maintain an adequate cash reserve. Another misuse is financing purchases against an uncertain but hoped-for raise or future financial windfall—for example, "I know I'll get the Adams account, and that will mean lots of money, so I'll buy this now" (Porter, 1976:80–81).

People borrow money from many different sources. Some turn to their parents or, less often, to brothers and sisters; in such cases interest is likely to be low. Sometimes, relatives help each other by putting up security or cosigning bank loans, thereby taking advantage of lower interest rates.

Another source of credit is public lending agencies: credit unions, banks, finance companies, and

trouble can cause couples emotional stress and unhappiness (Rankin, 1979; Liebow, 1967; Udry, 1974). A good rule is to limit borrowing so that debt payments, excluding mortgage payments, account for no more than 10 percent of the family's take-home pay.

Financial Overextension and What to Do About It Optimally, families pay all their installment and other loans monthly, along with other regular expenses, and also set some money aside for savings (Daly, 1979). Some advisers suggest that a family is overextended if they have less than three months' take-home pay in savings for emergencies (Daly, 1979:31).

If an individual or a couple is financially overextended, the first step in solving the problem is to make a conscious choice to change things. Plan a budget jointly with a spouse or other family member who shares the budget responsibility. Look for places to cut expenses. Resolve not to use credit cards or take out new loans until things are better. If necessary, cut up all your credit cards—the first action credit counselors take for many of their clients (Rankin, 1979:102; Daly, 1979:32). Ask your creditors if they will agree to spread payments over a longer period. Usually, they will be willing to work out some temporary arrangement (Rankin, 1979:102–3).

If you feel it's necessary, consult a credit-counseling service in your area. Write the National Foundation for Consumer Credit or check the yellow pages of your phone book. Credit-counseling services associated with the national foundation provide free budget advice and charge a nominal fee—usually about ten dollars—for debt management. Often this involves working out a reduced-payment arrangement with your creditors (Rankin, 1979:103). It is important to make sure you're dealing with a legitimate credit counselor, though, because "some unscrupulous folks advertise debt counseling but actually keep a big slice of your funds as a fee for services—enough to push you over the brink if you're not there already" (Daly, 1979:32).

Some people aim to solve their credit problems by taking out a **consolidation loan**: a single loan large enough to cover all outstanding debts. Because the consolidation loan is repaid over an extended period of time, the monthly payments are smaller than they would be if a couple were making separate payments on a variety of shorter-term bills.

TOTAL INCOME
Breadwinner A
Breadwinner B

EXPENDITURES
"His" personal money
"Her" personal money
Family Expenses

ITEM
1. Food
2. Housing
3. Household operation
4. Household furnishings
5. Clothing:
Father
Mother
Child 1
Child 2
6. Transportation
Automobile
7. Taxes
Income (withholding)
Sales
Property
8. Personal care (shampoo, deodorant, cosmetics, and so on)
9. Medical care
10. Dental care
11. Insurance (life, Social Security, disability)
12. Savings
13. Vacation and recreation
14. Newspapers, magazines, postage
15. Education
16. Dues
17. Contributions
18. Gifts
19. Miscellaneous

Figure 14·3

Sample budget items for one- or two-paycheck families. (Source: Adapted from Gordon and Lee, 1977:369)

The total interest, however, is greater (Rankin, 1979:103). A problem with consolidation loans is that people tend to use them as a stopgap measure rather than changing their buying habits. "A consolidation loan is fine if you get religion," said one bank official. "The problem is that many people don't reform and are knocking on the bank door six or eight months later for another loan. For this reason you should avoid a consolidation loan and use it only as a last resort" (in Rankin, 1979:103).

Some people file for bankruptcy as a means of getting on their financial feet again. A recent federal law makes declaring bankruptcy much easier than it used to be, but declaring bankruptcy will seriously impair a credit rating and will remain on the credit record for up to fourteen years.[2]

Rising inflation has made it more important and at the same time less easy to manage family income. In the rest of this chapter, we'll examine three basic family necessities that are becoming increasingly difficult to procure.

MANAGING RESOURCES FOR HOUSING AND HEALTH CARE

We've seen in general terms how the combined factors of inflation and recession have created an economic pinch that affects most families today. In two areas in particular—housing and health care—people are finding that to keep up with costs, they must make a more conscious effort than ever before to be careful consumers and to change their lifestyles. We'll examine each of these areas and offer suggestions.

Housing in the 1980s

The family dwelling has psychological significance in virtually all cultures. In real and symbolic ways it marks off the family space and helps bind mem-

bers together. In addition, families need four basic things from housing: shelter from nature's elements, safety, provisions for sanitation, and access to fundamental resources such as water and food (Chilman, 1978b:105). How much can families expect to pay for these necessities?

A widely accepted rule is that a family, whether renting or buying, cannot afford a monthly housing expense of more than one week's take-home pay. This figure includes rent or the total of all house-payment expenses, such as interest, insurance, and taxes, but not utilities. As utility costs increase, it may be necessary to spend even less for rent or house payments. Of course, with increased housing and utility costs, many families have no choice but to take what they can get and must adjust the rest of their budget accordingly. Many low-income renters pay 50 percent or more of their income for housing (Kerr, 1986).

Housing Choices Throughout Life People's conceptions of their family housing needs change over the years. After marriage, Americans follow a **neo-local residence pattern** in which newlywed couples are expected to leave their parents' homes and set up their own households. In many other cultures newlyweds move in with the wife's or husband's family either permanently or until they are financially ready to establish their own household. Observers have pointed out that our pattern expects a lot from young couples, many of whom have not yet completed their education or occupational training. A widely accepted alternative, however, has been for young couples to rent an apartment. Apartment living is more feasible economically because it requires no large cash down payment.

People who are divorced also frequently live in apartments. Divorced people without children may choose apartments designed for singles. Single-parent families need apartments where children are accepted. Many divorced people have to adjust to apartment living after owning their own single-family home. Like young couples, single-parent families often choose apartment living because it is more economically accessible. Unfortunately, however, our contracting economy is beginning to limit apartment options, as we will discuss later.

When children begin to arrive, families often feel the need for larger quarters and think of renting or buying a house. Requirements of size depend, of course, on the size of the family.

Finally, when grown children begin their exo-

---

2. The Fair Debt Collection Practices Act provides important protection for overextended consumers. Among other things, the law prohibits independent collection agencies from making abusive or threatening phone calls, calling before 8 A.M. or after 9 P.M., or contacting friends or employers except to verify where you work or live (Rankin, 1979; Daly, 1979). Direct any questions or complaints to the Federal Trade Commission in Washington, D.C., or to a local Legal Aid Society.

dus, space needs decrease. The couple must choose between maintaining a family home that may be expensive and moving to a relatively maintenance-free apartment type of dwelling or a smaller house. Couples in retirement may, in fact, move to another geographic area, particularly if they are attracted to retirement communities, which have extensive activity programs for older adults. Considerations of health and physical mobility, such as the preference for a one-floor dwelling, also become important in housing choices. Housing for retired couples is usually smaller in scale, and it may vary considerably in economic equivalence from previous housing. Some couples can use a portion of their income for more luxurious accommodations when their children leave home. Others, particularly women without spouses or persons whose spouses require expensive nursing-home care, may have a diminished income that reduces their housing options. And, of course, the 1980s saw an increase in the number of families who were without any dwellings at all, due to unemployment, declining government support for low- or moderate-income housing, and gentrification, which is the replacement of low- or moderate-cost housing by commercial or high-income housing developments (Kerr, 1986).

Whatever the housing needs of the family, the realization of these needs is affected by trends in the apartment and home-buying markets.

Housing Discrimination Choice of housing may also be affected by housing discrimination. Even though federal laws prohibit discrimination in housing on the basis of race, religion, sex, and national origin, discrimination against blacks continues to exist. "A variety of recent local and national studies of the housing market show that if similar blacks and whites seek housing they are often treated differently.... Blacks are steered to all-black or largely-black areas" (Bianchi et al., 1982:50). This discriminatory pattern contributes to the somewhat higher rates of overcrowding and lower rates of home ownership among blacks, although housing for both blacks and whites improved dramatically between 1960 and 1977, with only 2 percent of housing units occupied by whites and 5 percent of housing units occupied by blacks now "structurally inadequate" (Bianchi et al., 1982).

Discrimination by marital status and sexual orientation remains an unknown factor. However, a striking new discriminatory pattern has emerged in the late seventies and early eighties—discrimination against families with children. Some owner-occupied housing (Press, 1984)and especially rental units will not accept occupants with children or will require childless couples to move upon becoming parents. A nationwide survey found that 25 percent of apartment units surveyed would not take children (Colten and Marans, 1982) and a study in Omaha, Nebraska—which certainly has a family-oriented image—discovered that 50 percent of apartment complexes surveyed would not accept children, while another 20 percent limited age or number of children (Himberger, 1982).

Some apartment owners have sexually harassed women tenants, especially those with children and low incomes, who are the most vulnerable.

The Apartment Squeeze This discrimination against children and harassment of tenants is partly the result of a limited supply of apartment housing, which permits owners to pick and choose among tenants. Far fewer rental apartments are available now than in the mid-1970s because of rising construction and operating costs. As a result, owners of apartment buildings increasingly have converted rental units to **condominiums** or cooperatives in which residents buy their living quarters. By so doing, landlords can reap a 20 percent profit or more on their investment. The move to apartment ownership is especially prevalent in large cities such as San Francisco, Houston, Atlanta, Chicago, New York, and Boston.

Owning a "condo" can be a hedge against inflation. But buying one's own apartment is largely an upper middle- or upper-class phenomenon. Many families don't have the necessary down payment, and mortgage and maintenance can cost as much as 50 percent more than renting the same space.

Such conversions drive out cash-shy young couples and singles, single-parent families, and older Americans. To fight this, some communities have legislated curbs on conversions or declared moratoriums on evicting tenants who refuse to buy ("Big switch," 1979, p. 59; "Houses," 1979, p. 55). Tenants' unions have been organized in some cities to resist conversions and to lobby for rent control and tenants' rights.

For those who are evicted or have other difficulties in maintaining their own apartments, an alternative in today's contracting economy may be to return to their parents' home. This is particularly true for never married singles and single-parent families, especially when family members live

■ This couple would like to expand their living quarters to accommodate their expanding family. But with the added expense of a child, they may find that the housing they can afford is not what they want. In many U.S. cities, home ownership is becoming an impossible dream for young families.

in the same geographical area. A return to extended-family living after a period of financial and emotional autonomy may cause conflict and stress, which can be alleviated by discussing attitudes and alternatives openly and making new house rules.

Another alternative is the shared apartment or house. Housemates may be personal friends or they may have answered an ad, a more and more common practice. Single parents may find shared housing especially attractive despite the complexities of working out relationships among several sets of adults and children (Anderson, J., 1984). In fact, there are benefits: "Children 'don't have to come home to an empty house. It's much more fun'" (Anderson, J., 1984:35).

Buying a House While many Americans rent apartments, home ownership is still an American ideal. For most people, owning a single-family house is a source of self-esteem (Chilman, 1978b:105). A house is an investment and provides protection against inflation; traditionally, house prices rise

faster than the inflation rate. A house is also a considerable expense. The buyer who pays 20 percent down and takes a 30–35-year mortgage will wind up paying interest on the mortgage that about equals the cost of the house.

In any case, home ownership is getting further and further out of the reach of many families, particularly younger ones (Cunniff, 1985; Olson, 1985). Housing prices have increased much faster than incomes in recent years (Rosenbaum, 1984). Figure 14-4 depicts the growth of housing prices relative to incomes from 1977 to 1985. In a 1983 Lou Harris poll, 91 percent of persons interviewed anticipated, probably correctly, that it would take two incomes in the family to make home ownership possible (Harris, 1983).[3] The demand for houses will soar as the full force of the baby boom that

---

3. In that year—1983—the typical home buyer was 33 years old and in a two-income marriage (Olson, 1984).

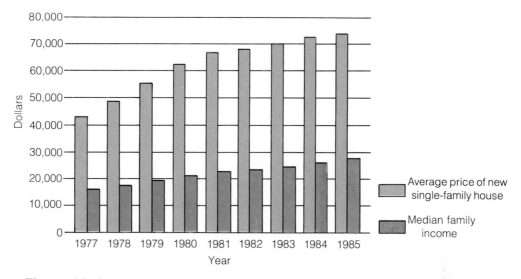

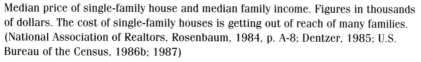

Figure 14-4

Median price of single-family house and median family income. Figures in thousands of dollars. The cost of single-family houses is getting out of reach of many families. (National Association of Realtors, Rosenbaum, 1984, p. A-8; Dentzer, 1985; U.S. Bureau of the Census, 1986b; 1987)

followed World War II hits the marketplace. And costs are going up. As a result, new single-family homes will be bought mainly by two-paycheck, intact families or by people with profits from selling a previous house. In fact, home ownership peaked in 1980 and has declined through 1985. "The drop may not seem dramatic to those who own a home, but the significance is that it was caused almost exclusively by younger people unable to buy their first homes" (Brown, in Olson, 1986, p. F-1). There is considerable local variation in housing prices—the median price of a house in Albany, New York, was $52,000 in 1984, while in the New York metropolitan area it was $100,600 (Rosenbaum, 1984).

Home ownership is economically advantageous because of tax savings (deduction of the interest portion of the monthly payment, which is considerable, especially in the early years of the loan), accumulated equity in the home, and appreciation of the value of the home. However, in the short term, renting is less costly; in fact, the cost of rent-

ing did not increase as rapidly as the cost of owning a house (Joint Center for Urban Studies, 1983, cited in Olson, 1983, p. F-1).

One consequence of high housing costs may be, as we have seen, that more young, divorced, and single-parent families live with their parents. One expected alternative is the building of smaller houses and more attached dwellings—duplexes and townhouses—as builders use higher density to keep prices in check. Another alternative is for two or more families to buy a duplex or a large house and share it. This last trend could develop into a new kind of communal living, one motivated by economics rather than ideology. There is some evidence that single-parents and also elderly singles are finding both financial and emotional benefits in sharing homes (Anderson, J., 1984; Fein, 1984). Finally, we can expect more and more young couples and single-parent families to borrow money for housing down payments from relatives. In fact, a survey conducted in Edmonton, Alberta, found that in areas where shelter costs were high (relative to income), young homeowners were more likely to have received financial assistance from their families. The study concluded that "people are meeting the rising costs of housing with informal familial support" (Kennedy and Stokes, 1982:315). The authors go on to raise questions about how this financial support affects relationships within the extended family and note that the "identification of priorities and compromises that parents make in deciding on their investments in their children constitutes an important area of further investigation" (Kennedy and Stokes, 1982:316). There are many interesting research questions concerning the impact of economic change on the family, and we can expect that more research will be done on "the evolution of family form and helping behavior as they adapt to changing social conditions, such as the increased cost of housing" (Kennedy and Stokes, 1982:316–17). A safe prediction is that if the economy contracts over the long term, more people will become aware of the mutual aid, financial and otherwise, that kin can offer.

Social scientist Arlene Skolnick has suggested that one consequence of the changing economic situation may be a society-wide reinvestment in extended family cooperation (Skolnick, 1978a:27). Families cooperating to purchase houses and family members undertaking financially rewarding household projects, such as adding insulation to attics or caulking and weather-stripping windows and doors, are two examples. Another is family members working to lower their health-care costs.

Family Health Care

Many families believe that they are up against an almost impossible challenge when they try to reduce the costs of health care. Health care is not only a family need, it is a responsibility prescribed by law; and it is one that becomes increasingly important with time—first in raising children, then later as couples age and have greater personal health concerns. Box 14·3, "The Family and America's High Medical Bill," describes how families have held down our nation's medical costs.

Health care has traditionally been seen primarily as the wife's concern. Mothers—even professional wives with full-time jobs—often take the main

responsibility not only for their children's health but also for their husband's care, especially as they age (Troll et al., 1979).

Getting Good Health Care: Some Modern Challenges Although health care is available in most areas, getting it can be a real challenge. Two critical observers point out at least four major problems in meeting the need for health care (Ehrenreich and Ehrenreich, 1979).

The first difficulty is cost. Health care is a commodity or a service that consumers purchase at unregulated, steadily increasing prices. By the mid-1970s the high cost of medical care in the United States had become a major economic factor in the lives of most American families (Porter, 1976:236). The cost of health-care services has increased much faster than the cost of living. Physicians' and dentists' fees, nursing home rates, and drug costs all soared. Some help is available through insurance plans, but as Barbara and John Ehrenreich point out, many people are "too rich for Medicaid, too poor for Blue Cross, and too young for Medicare" (1979:417). Private insurance plans and government programs are cutting benefits and increasing fees as health-care costs continue to rise precipitously in the eighties.

A second problem lies in the need to coordinate the services of a number of specialists to meet health-care needs. American medical care has become a fragmented aggregate of specialists who tend to see the patient only in terms of a specific health problem rather than as a whole person and family member. Also, the average consumer is not sufficiently informed to make efficient use of specialists.

A third, related problem is "figuring out what they are doing to you." Not only is the health-care industry dangerously fragmented, it usually offers its services "in an atmosphere of mystery and unaccountability" (Ehrenreich and Ehrenreich, 1979:416).

A fourth problem is "overcoming the built-in racism and male chauvinism of doctors and hospitals" (Ehrenreich and Ehrenreich, 1979:421). Blacks, Mexican-Americans, native Americans, and other racial minorities in the United States receive poorer medical care, die younger, and are ill more often than whites (Enos, 1976:242). Women also often receive discriminatory treatment (Dreifus, 1977; Boston Women's Health Book Collective, 1976).

These challenges are difficult ones, and because of the mystique of medical authority, many patients "feel helpless to question or complain . . . even when confronted with what seems to be irrational therapy" (Ehrenreich and Ehrenreich, 1979:421). Individuals can do some things to avoid making critical medical decisions by default, however. They can be informed and "energized," use a family physician, and keep family health records—and insist on being effectively included in medical decisions. Concern for informed consent and consumer rights in health care has made medical practitioners as well as patients more aware of these needs and has democratized the doctor-patient relationship somewhat. With advances in technology and doctors' awareness of their limits as decision makers for patients, patients and the families of patients who are not competent (that is, too ill) to make decisions may find themselves with many, and serious, decisions to make.

"Energized" Responses to Health-Care Challenges Social scientist Lois Pratt combines research results and theory to argue that families of all social classes can receive better health care when they put their minds to it. Pratt labels such families *energized.* **Energized families** "approach each encounter with the health care system ready for active engagement rather than passive submission" (Pratt, 1976:169). They get better response from the health-care industry because their members demand it and know how to shop for it. They refuse to be baffled by the medical mystique. Instead, they keep in mind that doctors "are independent entrepreneurs who see patients and charge fees for the services performed" (Schwartz, 1972:29). Energized families realize that, although there are many health-care problems they cannot change immediately, they can always challenge: They ask questions about fees, diagnoses, treatment, prescribed drugs, and so forth.

Enlisting Help from a Family Physician As Sylvia Porter points out, a doctor "should be a person who knows you and your family and is interested in your *health,* not just your illnesses" (Porter, 1976:260). A helpful adjunct to any family is a good general, or family, physician. Unlike specialists, family physicians see each family member's health within the family context. She or he can direct patients to specialists when necessary and can provide basic care when a specialist isn't needed.

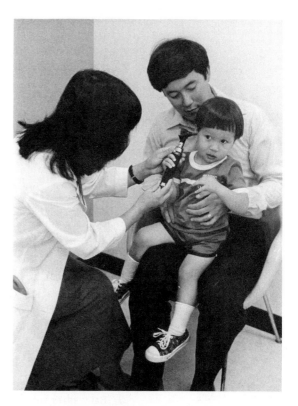

■ As medical care becomes increasingly technological and specialized, a reliable family doctor can help guide parents through the bewildering health care system. The family doctor can also give a valuable perspective by seeing each family member's health in the context of the whole family.

Pediatricians and internists also fill many of the same functions. Obviously, families should choose a family physician wisely. One clue to competence is membership on the medical staff of a good hospital, especially a hospital affiliated with a medical school (Porter, 1976:260).

Families may also consider health maintenance organizations (HMOs), which offer prepaid health care from their own staff of physicians (clients cannot choose their doctor). They have lower fees and an emphasis on preventive medicine. There is evidence, however, that the poor and ethnic minorities have difficulty with this system, particularly because the HMO's highly bureaucratic organization "requires verbal skills to argue for the symptoms that you have and for the care that you want"

BOX 14·3

THE FAMILY AND AMERICA'S HIGH MEDICAL BILL

By Boyd Littrell

Boyd Littrell, Ph.D., is professor of sociology at the University of Nebraska, Omaha.

Providing medical care has always been family work. Before the middle of this century, the family supplied most of America's medical care. In many parts of the world it still does. Especially mothers, but increasingly fathers, provide vast amounts of "nursing care." Go into a busy drugstore and watch people buying cough syrup, vaporizers, aspirin, and bandages. Not all, but many, of these customers are arranging medical care for their children, husbands, wives, or partners. Many adults also provide medical services for their aging parents. They act as advocates for ill or infirm parents as medical services become increasingly adversarial. They arrange hospital care, provide transportation to physicians' offices, and assist with complex insurance arrangements.

It would be enormously costly to purchase the medical services that the family provides. To see how important the family is to the rest of society, add up the costs of America's most commonly diagnosed illness: a cold. This is about what it would cost in a typical midwestern city:

1. Hire a semiskilled companion to take child to physician's office (2 hours at $10 per hour) — $ 20
2. Transportation (taxi or car and driver) — 15
3. Baby-sitter to provide round-the-clock care ($5 per hour) — 120
4. Delivery charge for prescription medicine — 5
5. Physician visit — 45
6. Prescription drugs — 25

$230

But we are interested in the cost to all of society, so we must multiply this cost. It would cost about $230 million to purchase 24 hours of care for 100,000

(Justice, 1986:5). Another health-care development is the free-standing "emergency" medical center, a sort of discount medical service that offers staff care on a walk-in basis for common complaints or emergencies on a fee-for-service basis, but without the traditional long-term doctor-patient relationships.

Keeping Family Health Records   A third way to meet health-care challenges is to keep records of the family's health history. Family physicians are

a great help to families, but the principal responsibility for maintaining members' health remains with families themselves. For this reason—and because a family may move to another region or change doctors and the previous doctor's records may not follow—it is a good idea to keep family health records at home. Health records should include a fairly complete medical history for each family member—such items as blood types, major illnesses, childhood diseases, allergies, immunizations, laboratory test results, and corrective devices

children with colds (allowing for differences in prices around the country). Fortunately for taxpayers, politicians, insurance companies, and for all of us consumers, the family donates most of this medical care. Families usually provide items 1 through 4 free of charge. In this example, that amounts to $160, or about 70 percent of the bill. That leaves a tax or an insurance bill of about $7 million—less than one-third of the original. And if we subtract the approximately 20 percent that many families pay in cash as their "deductible," the bill to society drops by another $1.4 million to $5.6 million.

In the last decade several factors have begun to limit the family's ability to donate medical care. Since the mid-1970s, median family income has declined, unemployment has risen, and more people go without health insurance. Americans also live in smaller dwellings. In addition, more mothers are employed outside their homes. In 1986, half of the mothers with infants under one year old were employed full-time.

As America's population ages, more medical services will be needed. Yet the reduced size of dwellings, the increase in two-paycheck families and single-parent families, and reduced earnings will make it more difficult for adults to care for their aging parents. Thus, the need for nursing home care for older Americans will increase. In addition, working parents will have to hire more child care for sick children. In short, changes in the family mean that families will be able to provide fewer medical services, which will add to the nation's medical bill. Unfortunately, the quality of health care will probably also decline.

Families are important to us personally. They provide our warmest and happiest moments. And with the death of parents, spouses, and children, they bring us our deepest feelings of sorrow. But important as they are to us and to our emotional lives, they are also crucial to the larger society, as we have seen in this example.

such as eyeglass prescriptions. Keeping records could be a family project in which all members participate.

Adapting to a Changing Economy In both law and tradition society commissions families to provide for their members' basic needs. In today's contracting economy families must make knowledgeable choices—must be "energized" not only in regard to health care but in other ways, too. Energized families apply their assertiveness to solving housing problems and managing their money wisely. Demographers have given a lot of thought not only to economic problems in general but to the limited places at the top for the large baby-boom generation. If economic opportunities are limited for many, it is "not unreasonable to assume that a key to living happily with less in the future will be to achieve heightened awareness of the things we already have but perhaps haven't savored before with such intensity" (Sifford, 1982:13).

Good financial management of one's resources

and a wholesome adaptation to less are not the only part of the picture for sociologists, however. As we have seen throughout this chapter, many of the personal or private troubles families have with finances, housing, food costs, or health care are really public issues. It is not just a family's personal problem if they cannot find or are evicted from a rental apartment because developers are converting apartment complexes to condominiums. Nor is the rising cost of food, energy, or health care purely a private trouble. These are public issues, and families can join together to change them.

FAMILIES AND SOCIETY

The larger society influences both individuals and families. For example, plant shutdowns and resulting layoffs or unemployment create personal problems and stress for families. High interest rates and building costs change a family's options so that people may have to settle for more crowded housing. The declining corporate commitment to a family wage (Ehrenreich, 1983) has imposed financial hardship as more couples become two-wage-earner families and as single parents struggle to make ends meet. The tightening of the American economy may also produce a greater number of extended families, especially families in which young adults (with or without children of their own) live with their parents.

Family members make choices within the larger social environment. As social scientists have begun to emphasize, society can be generally favorable toward families or not: It can either take them for granted or give them support and encouragement.

Observers of the family are growing more interested in family policy. Family policy addresses the problems families may face as they attempt to function in the context of the larger society. In a narrow sense **family policy** is all the procedures, regulations, attitudes, and goals of government that affect families. More broadly, family policy includes the effects that other social institutions—such as churches and corporations—have on families. For example, school administrators can take working parents into account by scheduling children's programs and parent-teacher conferences for evening hours when fewer parents are working. Some

schools are beginning "latchkey" programs with activities for children after school hours.

Working Parents

As more and more women in their childbearing years are employed, there is a crucial need for maternity or parental leave policies. Eighty percent of employed women become pregnant during their working lives, and over half of the women who work while pregnant return to work within a year of childbirth ("Background," 1985). As it stands, women must cope with pregnancy difficulties, recovery from childbirth, and early infant care as best they can on a usually minimal leave (Hewlett, 1986) or risk losing their jobs or seniority. A woman who filed suit in Montana lost her job after missing only five days of work due to pregnancy-related illness ("Background," 1985).

A recent Supreme Court decision reinstating a California mother in her job provides support for the notion that society must enable women to bear children without sacrificing their careers. But the decision itself only applies to pregnancy *disability* (not normal pregnancy) and only obliges employers to extend what disability protection they have to pregnancy; many employers have none. Moreover, another recent Supreme Court decision allows states to refuse unemployment compensation to women whose employers will not reinstate them after absence for pregnancy or childbirth (Taylor, 1987).

Important legislation has been proposed in Congress to remedy this situation. The Family and Medical Leave Act would require employers to provide eighteen weeks of unpaid leave for parents at the time of birth or adoption, for the care of seriously ill children, and, in some versions, for the care of aging parents. This **family leave** legislation would not only enable women to take maternity leave without losing job rights but would also permit men and women to take leave to care for families at times of crisis or special need.

European countries provide paid maternity leave in most cases, often for lengthy periods (Aldous and Dumon, 1980; Hewlett, 1986) and provide a stipend to parents for the support of the child. Indeed, our society needs to provide for child rearing as well as childbearing by working parents. William Brock, Secretary of Labor in the Reagan administration, remarks: " 'It's just incredible that we have seen the feminization of the work force with no more adaptation than we have had. . . . It is a problem of sufficient magnitude that everybody is going to have to play a role: families, individuals, businesses [and] government' " (quoted in O'Connell and Bloom, 1987).

Day care is a crucial need of working parents, who now spend $11 billion a year for child care. Preschool children may be in organized day care facilities (23 percent) or home day care—paid day care in the home of a nonrelative (22 percent). Some parents arrange for grandparents or other relatives to look after their children (15 percent), while 31 percent are cared for in their own homes, half by the father and half by someone else, perhaps a paid caretaker ("Families spend," 1987).

Corporations are beginning to respond to their employees' need for day care in a variety of ways. Some provide day care at or near the place of employment ("on-site" day care). Alternatively, corporate involvement includes referral service, inclusion of day care as an option in employee fringe benefit packages, or the provision of nursing services for sick children or arrangement of home child care. Much remains to be done. Although the number of corporations willing to assist with child care tripled between 1982 and 1985, only a small minority of corporations (1,800) are involved (Collins, 1985).

Some corporate representatives argue that child care is not their business (Meyers, 1985) but that of the parents or the society as a whole (Collins, 1985). Federal government assistance with child care has been problematic for years. Comprehensive child care legislation, providing for parent subsidies and a network of educationally oriented preschool centers, has often been proposed. It came close to realization three times, passing Congress in 1971 only to be vetoed by President Nixon (Steiner, 1981).

Because of this discouraging history, child care legislation is unlikely to be introduced in the foreseeable future. Instead, working parents' political agenda is now directed toward enabling parents to remain at home to care for their own children. The family leave bill in Congress in 1987 that would provide eighteen weeks of unpaid family care leave does not replace lost income. (Most parents are working precisely because they need the income.) But it does establish the principle that it is society's obligation to help workers meet their family obligations and that work can be interrupted for those obligations. The family leave bill makes no assumptions about who will take the leave; fathers, as well as mothers, are entitled to parental leave.

Employers are asked to help in other ways. Some proposals are intended to enable working parents to respond to the small emergencies and complex time schedule that is part of life with children. **Flextime** is a form of flexible scheduling that allows a worker to choose his or her working hours within some limits (such as being at work between 10:00 A.M. and 3:00 P.M.). *Block scheduling* permits an employee to concentrate the work week into three or four days. About 12 percent of full-time workers have flexible schedules, which can help parents share child care or be at home before and after an older child's school hours. The federal government is the largest employer committed to flexible scheduling, and 93 percent of participating federal workers rated flexible scheduling as "somewhat important" or "very important" (O'Connell and Bloom, 1987) in their lives.

Family Policy

Although "family policy" can include any government actions that affect families, such as tax policy, the Carter administration first articulated the need for government to formally develop policies to assist families. It shortly became clear that while almost everyone endorses the idea of a comprehensive family policy, Americans have little consensus on what that policy should be. Specific issues can be extremely controversial. At the 1980 White House Conference on Families, designed to give citizens an opportunity to help shape family policy, some people argued that only traditional nuclear families should be represented, while others saw the important task as finding ways of adapting to family change—by assisting single-parent families, for example.

Indeed, the diversity of family life-styles in the United States today makes developing a national family policy that would satisfy all or even most of us extremely difficult (Steiner, 1981). In the future we can expect increased competition for government resources, for example, between more traditional families with children and two-career, child-free couples (Hunt and Hunt, 1982).

Another issue is rooted in whether help for families should be based on need. Europeans tend to view family assistance as a social right belonging to all. They see child rearing as a socially important task that deserves public assistance, compensation, and support, and *not* just for parents who are poor or in some other way "below minimum standards" (Dumon and Aldous, 1979:498). In contrast, our government has tended to extend help only to people who "need" it—the poor, primarily, and families that do not meet minimum standards in being able to meet their own needs (Steiner, 1976:254–55).

Economic Support

And poverty *is* a real problem for many families in our society (Moynihan, 1986; McAdoo and McAdoo, 1985)—a problem so serious that one authority on child abuse believes that individual acts of violence against children are overshadowed by collective, society-wide maltreatment of children through poverty and discrimination (Gil, 1970). Young men's earnings have declined by almost one third in the past decade, exacerbating the problems of teen pregnancy and causing many young families to be living in poverty ("Economic shifts," 1987). Yet, economic and political developments of the 1980s have resulted in declining and inadequate governmental spending on social services (Piven and Cloward, 1982). We are far from establishing a program for minimum family income, in which single-parent families, intact families, and stepfamilies would be eligible for aid.

What to do about child support is another important policy issue affecting the financial adequacy of families. The idea of child support is that both parents will support their children after divorce or even if no marriage has taken place. Because over 90 percent of eligible children live with their mothers, fathers usually pay a court-determined amount toward the support of the child. But these amounts are small and not adjusted for rises in the cost of living. More importantly, compliance is minimal; fewer than half the fathers actually pay, regardless of their income (Weitzman, 1985).

This issue illustrates the significance of family policy. For many years collecting child support was left to the mother and her legal resources. Often the very poverty that inspired the hope of collecting also precluded retaining an effective lawyer. Further, state governments intervened only when the payment of welfare was at stake; no level of government assisted the individual client who was

not on welfare. Collecting child support has remained an individual problem that most individuals cannot solve.

Concern about the "feminization of poverty" (Pearce and McAdoo, 1981) and the inequity involved in unpaid child support has inspired legislation at the federal level. (Former husbands generally increase their standard of living by 42 percent following divorce, while women and dependent children experience a 73 percent decline [Weitzman, 1985].) States are presently implementing a 1983 law requiring wage withholding and interception of income tax refunds from parents who are more than thirty days behind in child support. This collective solution forged in the public policy process stands a good chance of benefiting the many American children of divorce.

Care of the Elderly and Dependent

It is perhaps worth considering that other families, such as families in crisis, may also need government help. Families that care for aging or mentally or physically handicapped members in their homes, for example, along with those who shelter unwed teenage mothers, may need financial assistance and specially designed services. It may be desirable, both for the persons involved and for society as a whole, to help families care for these dependent members, so that the burden will not become so overwhelming that families will give up, requiring the government to pay "outsiders" to provide the care (Moroney, 1979). Box 14•3 discusses the role the family plays in providing health care.

A more general issue is the provision of health care to all families. Some political leaders propose a national system of health insurance that will guarantee adequate health care at reasonable costs to all families. National health insurance would work somewhat the way our Social Security system does today. Citizens would pay into the system through taxes and collect during illness. One of the possible outcomes of the AIDS epidemic may be the development of national catastrophic health care insurance, as local and state governments and private and public hospitals will resist assuming the burden of costly health care for individuals who have exhausted their personal resources (Morganthau, 1986).

The aging of the American population has also

generated concern about the costs of health and dependent care. The "young old" (those under 75; Weeks, 1986), are relatively healthy, but the "old old" will compose an increasingly large proportion of the elderly population. Moreover, their children are likely to be senior citizens themselves. We face enormous costs for the care of chronic illness and of the infirm, costs beyond the reach of most families. Nursing home care, for example, exhausts the resources of the average family after only thirteen weeks (Tobin, 1980). Not only does cost make obtaining care problematic, but it also means that a surviving spouse is financially ruined, very likely losing home, savings, and retirement income. Working- and middle-class ill or elderly are also often distressed by the inability to leave something to their children.

In 1987, the federal government proposed the development of a catastrophic health care insurance program. States are considering legislation that would exclude a larger amount of a couple's assets from a means test (for state assistance for health care costs through Medicaid) so that individuals could pass on their homes to a spouse and retain a small amount of savings for the surviving spouse's support.

Corporations (Fernandez, 1986) as well as the government are taking an interest in freeing family members for extended elder care in times of crisis. The family leave bill intended for working parents was expanded to meet the increasing responsibility that individuals in an aging society have for the personal care of elderly parents.

Programmatic needs of the elderly include health care, long-term care facilities, transportation, subsidized housing, day care, prepared meals, and housekeeping assistance (Barberis, 1981), as well as maintenance of the social security program at its current level.

Government and Families

More government help to families, direct or indirect (by requiring leaves, for example) would be costly, of course. And it may be that Americans, with their individualistic values and economic difficulties, will not support costly family programs. On the other hand, the estimated costs of *not* having family programs may be higher. Disadvantaged children may eventually cost society more in unemployment compensation, welfare payments, imprisonment expenses, hospitalization for mental illness, and so forth than would preventive investments in support for their families (Schorr, 1979).

Another issue is whether federal, state, and local bureaucracies can deal effectively with families' needs without spending almost all their time and money in red tape. But not all government actions would have to be bureaucratically cumbersome. By providing a number of permanent, part-time or flexible-time positions, the government has significantly affected job and work-hour opportunities and set an example for private industry without adding to the bureaucracy.

Finally, past experience indicates that families have reason to be cautious about inviting the government to get involved. Programs created to be helpful may also provide the state with the power to intrude into family life in ways that are unwelcome (Donzelot, 1979). Still, many family challenges can be better met collectively than individually. The United States provides less help to families by far than any other industrialized nation, and Western Europe provides us with a number of examples of successful partnership between government and families in the interests of family support (Aldous and Dumon, 1980; Hewlett, 1986).

The idea of a national family policy may seem abstract, but if people are to shape the kinds of family living they want, they must not limit their attention to their own marriages and families. Making knowledgeable decisions about one's family increasingly means getting involved in national and local political campaigns, finding out what candidates have in mind for families, and writing and phoning government representatives once they are in office. One's role as a family member, as much as one's role as a citizen, has come to require participation in public policy decisions. While no family policy, of course, can guarantee "ideal" families (Tallman, 1979), such a policy may contribute toward a good foundation for family life.

Summary

The economic pinch that our society has been experiencing in the past few decades affects family life in significant ways. We saw in earlier chapters that more wives are going to work, partly to increase the family income; this chapter looked at things families can do to spend most efficiently the money they earn.

Budgets help families to manage expenditures wisely. Planning budgets is not all that's needed, though; daily and monthly records also should be kept as well. Buying wisely is also important, for informed consumers can get the most for their money. Credit expenditures should be budgeted, just like any other spending.

Two critical family needs are housing and health care. Costs of both have soared in recent years, posing real challenges to families. "Energized" families—those who make a serious effort to *not* make consumer decisions by default—are best able to meet those challenges.

Social resources are important for meeting family needs. Public and private sector programs are important resources for families, and political activity to shape family policy is important in creating the foundation for family life.

Key Terms

budgeting 457
discretionary income 457
installment financing 460
consolidation loan 461
neo-local residence pattern 462
condominium 463
energized family 467
family policy 470
family leave 470
flextime 471

Study Questions

1. What are some ways in which the contracting economy might affect marriage relationships?
2. Discuss the difference in the spending patterns of couples with no children, families with young children, families with older dependent children, and retired couples. How might you avoid financial pinches at various stages in your own future?
3. What are some reasons for budgeting?
4. What options are available to people who are overextended and don't want to be? Discuss the advantages and disadvantages of each option.
5. Discuss the changes that have taken place in our shrinking economy. How do these changes affect the housing situation and the life-styles of Americans?
6. What are some difficulties in getting good health care? How can individuals meet these challenges?
7. Are there any specific family policies you would like to see developed? What actions could you take toward this goal?

Suggested Readings

Barberis, Mary
1981 "America's Elderly: Policy Implications." *Population Bulletin* 35 (4). Washington, D.C.: Population Reference Bureau.
      Detailed forecast of the future needs of America's elderly along with some policy proposals.

Caplovitz, David
1979 *Making Ends Meet: How Families Cope with Inflation and Recession.* Beverly Hills, Calif.: Sage.
      Study of the impact of inflation and recession on the economy, mental health, and marital relations of families. Also reports on family coping strategies. Looks at demographic differentials, that is, families with different racial and class backgrounds, and so on.

Cassety, Judith (ed.)
1983 *The Parental Child-Support Obligation.* Lexington, Mass.: Heath.
      Presents all the important research and policy proposals regarding child support including broad questions about the financial support of all children.

Consumer Reports
      Magazine issues in which various brands of standard appliances and other products are tested. Available in most libraries.

Fernandez, John
1986 *Child Care and Corporate Productivity: Resolving Family/Work Conflicts.* Lexington, Mass.: Heath.
      Corporate ideas about policies for child and elder care.

Gordon, Leland, and Stewart Lee
1977 *Economics for Consumers.* New York: Van Nostrand.
      Useful information about spending strategies.

Keniston, Kenneth
1977 *All Our Children: The American Family Under Pressure.* New York: Harcourt Brace Jovanovich.
A utopian view of the possibilities for societal support for families. Useful because it tells about children's needs and how little we are doing to meet them with even our most ambitious proposals.

Moroney, Robert M.
1976 *The Family and the State: Considerations for Public Policy.* London: Longmans.
An academic book on family policy, still relevant. Especially good at noting the enormous contribution families make to social welfare.

Moynihan, Daniel Patrick
1986 *Family and Nation.* New York: Harcourt Brace Jovanovich.
The senator from New York argues a liberal agenda for the support of families, continuing his long-standing concern about children in poverty, especially children in single-parent families.

O'Connell, Martin, and David E. Bloom
1987 *Juggling Jobs and Babies: America's Child Care Challenge.* Population Reference Bureau Occasional Paper No. 12 (February). Washington, D.C.: Population Reference Bureau. Report containing statistical information, as well as a good discussion of issues in public policy for working parents.

Porter, Sylvia
1983 *Your Own Money.* New York: Avon.
Financial adviser's latest guidance.

Soldo, Beth
1981 "America's Elderly in the 1980s." *Population Bulletin* 35 (4). Washington, D.C.: Population Reference Bureau.
Much statistical and other information on America's elderly.

U.S. Department of Agriculture, Science and Education Administration
1976 *A Guide to Budgeting for the Family.* Home and Garden Bulletin No. 108. Washington, D.C.: U.S. Government Printing Office.
Brief government bulletin with forms for working out a budget.

U.S. Department of Health, Education and Welfare, Public Health Service and Health Resources Administration
1979 *How to Keep Your Family's Health Records.* DHEW Publ. No. (HRA) 79-636. Washington, D.C.: U.S. Government Printing Office.
Brief pamphlet outlining the medical records a family needs and how to keep them.

U.S. Department of Housing and Urban Development
1978 *Wise Home Buying.* HUD-267-H (8). Washington, D.C.: U.S. Government Printing Office.
Concise and readable pamphlet on many facets of buying a home.

U.S. Department of Labor, Bureau of Labor Statistics
1979 *Rent or Buy? Evaluating Alternatives in the Shelter Market.* Bulletin 2016. Washington, D.C.: U.S. Government Printing Office.
Detailed statistical comparison of renting and buying.

Weitzman, Lenore J.
1985 *The Divorce Revolution: The Unexpected Social and Economic Consequences for Women and Children.* New York: Free Press.
The legal aspects of divorce have an enormous effect on family finances and well-being. Weitzman presents an accurate and thorough analysis of the impact on families of the increase in divorce and divorce law reform.

V Family Change and Crises

With the expectation and the reality that people continue to change throughout their lives come the pressures that these individual changes exert on the family unit. External events may also require the partners to adapt. Intimate relationships may be simultaneously more meaningful and more difficult to maintain in the face of such changes.

Part Five examines how spouses and families manage change. Chapter 15 describes changing family situations, or crises, and what families can do to meet them creatively and effectively.

Chapter 16 discusses separation and divorce. Whether the decision to divorce is one partner's or both partners', divorce represents a move away from the marital commitment—emotionally, legally, socially, and psychologically separating oneself from the former spouse. Healing after divorce involves learning to commit oneself to being single again, if only temporarily.

Chapter 17 examines the making of new commitments in remarriage. As we shall see, more and more people who have been married before are committing themselves to building a family again. Such reconstituted families are different from traditional nuclear families in some important ways. In fact, because of the special challenges in stepfamily living, couples in a remarriage may need even stronger commitment to each other than those in first marriages. ▪

15 Family Crisis Management

God, grant me the
serenity to accept the
things I cannot change,
the courage to change the
things I can, and the
wisdom to know the
difference.
THE SERENITY PRAYER

A belief in romantic myths about marriages and families does not make families happy. Families are more likely to be happy when they work realistically toward more mutually supportive relationships. Nowhere does this become more apparent than in a discussion of family crises and transitions.

A **crisis** can be defined as a crucial change in the course of events, a turning point, an unstable condition in affairs. This definition encompasses three interrelated ideas: Crises necessarily involve change; a crisis is a turning point with the potential for either positive or negative effects, or both; and a crisis is a time of relative instability. Family crises share these characteristics. They are turning points that require some change in the way family members think and act in order to meet a new situation (Hansen and Hill, 1964).

When people live together over a period of time, they develop patterns of relating to one another. Members are fairly well aware of where each fits in and what each is expected to do, and the family functions smoothly when each member behaves according to the expectations of the other members. Any change that disrupts these expectations marks the onset of a crisis. For example, when a school-age child develops diabetes, parents must reorganize their morning, evening, and weekend routines to include testing the child's urine for sugar, injecting insulin, and making sure that the diabetic eats regularly (Benoliel, 1975).

Common events can also precipitate crises. Having a first baby or sending the youngest child off to college, for example, can bring about profound changes in family relationships and expectations. Some authorities have argued that *crisis* is too strong a word for such events, pointing out that partners anticipate such changes. Predictable changes in the course of family life can thus be viewed as **transitions** rather than as full-fledged crises.

The distinction between transitions and real crises, then, is blurred. This chapter examines family transitions as *predictable* crises. We will discuss how families define or interpret crises, both predictable and unpredictable, and how their definitions affect the course of a family crisis. We'll also look briefly at some of the predictable crises of the family life cycle, along with some ways families can meet crises more creatively.

THE COURSE OF A FAMILY CRISIS

Every family reacts somewhat uniquely to a crisis, but a family crisis ordinarily follows a fairly predictable course, similar to the "truncated roller

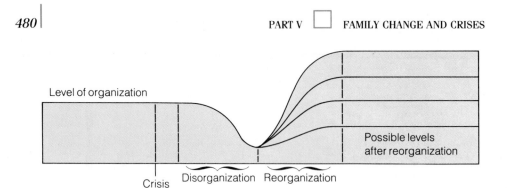

Level of organization

Possible levels
after reorganization

Crisis   Disorganization   Reorganization

FIGURE 15·1

Patterns of family adjustment to crisis. Families have a certain level of organization before a crisis; that is, they function at a certain level of effectiveness—higher for some families, lower for others. In the period of disorganization following the crisis, family functioning declines from its initial level. Families reorganize, and after the reorganization is complete (1) they may function at about the same level as before; (2) they may have been so weakened by the crisis that they function only at a reduced level; or (3) they may have been stimulated by the crisis to reorganize in a way that makes them more effective, as shown. (Source: Adapted from Hansen and Hill, 1964:810)

coaster" shown in Figure 15·1. Three distinct phases can be identified: the event that causes the crisis, the period of disorganization that follows, and the reorganizing or recovery phase after the family reaches a low point.

The Family Crisis: What Precipitates It?

Something has to happen to precipitate a crisis. That something is what social scientists call a **stressor,** a precipitating event that creates stress, (Hansen and Hill, 1964) or **strain** (Olson and McCubbin, 1983). Stressors and strains vary in both kind and degree, and their nature is one factor that affects how a family responds to crisis.

Types of Stressors and Strains   There are several types of stressors, as Figure 15·2 shows. Some involve the *loss of a family member* either permanently, such as through death or desertion, or temporarily, such as through hospitalization or wartime separation. Some research on stress has been based on families experiencing wartime separation during the Vietnam War, for example

(McCubbin and Patterson, 1983; see Suggested Readings).

A precipitating event can also involve the *addition of a member* or members to the family through birth or adoption or the addition of stepparents, siblings, and other kin through remarriage. Typical additions to the family are listed in Table 15·1. Some losses, including such less drastic ones as the entry of a child into elementary school, are also listed. Sociologist Pauline Boss, who composed the table, describes these entries and exits from the family as *boundary changes.* That is, family boundaries are shifting or contracting to include or exclude certain members. This may put stress on the family.

A third stressor is a *sudden change* in the family's income or social status. Most people think of stressors as negative. But positive changes, such as a move to a "better" neighborhood, a promotion, or sudden wealth or fame, can cause crises, too (Holmes and Rahe, 1967).

A fourth stressor that can precipitate family crises is less dramatic—ongoing *unresolved conflict* among members over the *familial roles.* We've seen that husbands' and wives' roles are changing. Today, many people view this change not as a crisis

Loss of
a family member

Addition of
a family member

Sudden change

Conflict over
family roles

Demoralizing event

FIGURE 15·2
Types of stressors.

but as a transition. Still, as Chapter 16 points out, people often report that conflict over changing roles was a reason for their divorce.

A fifth category of stressors includes *demoralizing events*—those that signal the gradual loss of family morale. Demoralization can accompany the precipitating events already described. But this category also includes such things as poverty, an illegitimate pregnancy, a runaway, a member's imprisonment, juvenile delinquency, suicide, mental illness, alcoholism, drug abuse, and chronic or crippling illnesses.

Crisis Overload A family can be demoralized not just by one serious, chronic problem but also by a series of small, unrelated crises that seem to build on each other too rapidly for the members to cope effectively. Sociologist and marriage counselor Carlfred Broderick explains:

Even small events, not enough by themselves to cause any real stress, can take a toll when they come one after another. First an unplanned pregnancy, then a move, then a financial problem that results in having to borrow several thousand dollars, then the big row with the new neighbors over keeping the dog tied up, and finally little Jimmy breaking his arm in a bicycle accident, all in three months, finally becomes too much [1979b:352]. ■

While it is difficult to point to any single precipitating factor, an unremitting series of small crises

can add up to a major demoralizing stress. Broderick terms this situation **crisis overload.**

Characteristically, crisis overload creeps up on people without their realizing it. In fact, people may fail to appreciate the crisis-precipitating potential of such common stress factors as, say, the energy shortage and rising inflation. In recent years most families have had to meet an increasing series of small crises related to energy and money, from changing their driving habits to lowering thermostats in winter and turning off air conditioners in summer. When other small stressors build on these, crisis overload can result.

External Versus Internal Stressors In addition to classifying crisis-precipitating events into types, we can distinguish between crises that begin outside and those that begin within the family (Hansen and Hill, 1964). **External stressors**— those that originate outside the family—include such things as hurricanes, tornadoes, and earthquakes as well as wars and threats of wars and economic decline. **Internal stressors,** in contrast, begin within the family itself and include such things as alcoholism, nonsupport, chronic gambling, or conflict over appropriate roles.

Internal and external stressors may have different effects. Crises precipitated by external factors often help to solidify a family. For example, families draw together when threatened by a hurricane or a blizzard. Internal crises, on the other hand, are more likely to divide and demoralize a family, primarily because family members tend to blame each

TABLE 15·1   Selected References to Illustrate Normative Life-Span Boundary Changes

Types of Life-Span Family Boundary Changes	Boundary Stressors Related to Physical and Psychological Membership in the System
Formation of the dyad	Acquisition of a mate Acquisition of in-laws Realignment with family of orientation Incorporating or rejecting former friendships
Birth of the first child	Acquisition of a new member Possible separation from extrafamilial work world If so, loss of working colleagues, and so on
Children first going to school	Separation of child from the family system to the world of school Acquisition of child's teacher, friends, and peers, that is, acceptance of them as part of the child's world
Job-related parent/spouse absence or presence	Fluctuating acquisition *and* separation due to extrafamilial role, for example, military service, or routine absence of the corporate executive. Stress results from repeated exit and reentry of the member. Also includes job changes such as return of mother to college or work after she's been a full-time homemaker or retirement of father from work back into the home.
Adolescent children leaving home	Separation of adolescent from the family system to his peers, school, or job system Acquisition of the adolescent's peers and intimates—same and opposite sex
Taking in child(ren) not your own or blending children from different dyads	Acquisition of another's offspring into the family system, for example, stepchildren, grandchildren, other nonrelated children
Loss of a spouse (through death, divorce, and so on)	Separation of mate from the dyad—therefore, dissolution of the marital dyad. Note: In case of divorce, the dyad may continue and function on other levels, such as coparenting.
Loss of parent(s)	Separation of child from parent(s) (child may likely be an adult)
Formation of a new dyad: remarriage	Acquisition of a new mate Acquisition of a new set of in-laws Realignment with family of orientation and former in-laws, children of former marriage, and so on Incorporating or rejecting former friendships, former spouses, and so on. Former spouse may still be in partnership with a member of the new dyad regarding parenting
Remaining single	Realignment with family of orientation If previously married, realignment with former in-laws Acquisition of friends, intimates, colleagues, and so on

SOURCE: Boss, 1980.

■ Most of us view involuntary change as a threat, not an opportunity. This man has not retired early—he's been laid off, unemployed for the first time in his adult life. Suddenly his world is out of balance, and adding to his disorientation is his feeling that no end to this crisis is in sight.

other, or to fight about which member is to blame, for their troubles. Yet focusing on blame greatly reduces a family's ability to cope with the crisis, as we shall see.

The "Double ABC-X Model" of Family Stressors and Strains

Figure 15•3 is a diagram of the "Double ABC-X Model of Family Stressors and Strains." About thirty years ago sociologist Reuben Hill proposed the ABC-X family crisis model, and much of what we've already noted about stressors, is based on Hill's insights and research. The **ABC-X model** states that A (the stressor event) interacting with B (the

family's ability to cope with a crisis, their "crisis-meeting resources") interacting with C (the family's definition of the event) produces X (the crisis).

Hill defined a stressor as a "situation for which the family has had little or no prior preparation" and crisis as "any sharp or decisive change from which old patterns are inadequate." Building on this ABC-X model, Hamilton McCubbin and Joan Patterson (1983) have advanced the double ABC-X model to better describe family adjustment to crises. In Hill's original model the "a" factor was the stressor event; in the **double ABC-X model** "a" factor becomes "Aa," or "family pile-up." Pile-up includes not just the stressor but also prior family hardships and strains that continue to affect family life (Olson and McCubbin, 1983:119).

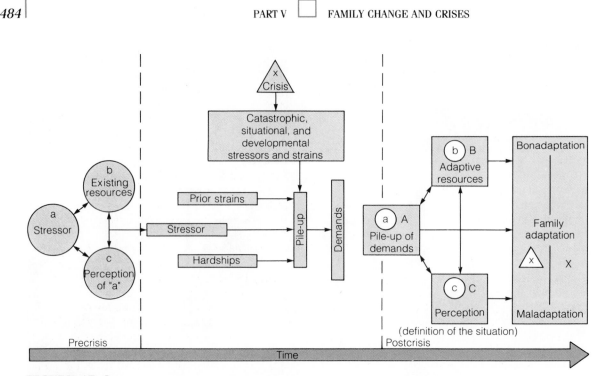

FIGURE 15·3
Double ABC-X model of family stressors and strains. (Source: Adapted from Olson
and McCubbin, 1983:119; Lavee et al., 1985:112)

According to the double ABC-X model, a stressor is a life event (normative or nonnormative), which affects the family at a discrete point in time and somehow produces or requires change in the family social system. Family hardships are demands on the family specifically associated with the stressor event. A parent's losing a job, for example, would be a stressor; it would soon be accompanied by hardships as bills begin to pile up. Prior strains are the residuals of family tension that linger from unresolved stressors or that are inherent in ongoing family roles such as being a parent or a spouse.

When a family experiences a new stressor, prior strains that may have gone unnoticed come to the fore. For example, ongoing-but-ignored marital conflict may intensify when parents suddenly face caring for a child diagnosed to have a chronic or terminal illness.

Unlike stressor events, which occur at discrete points in time, prior strains may not have a specific onset and may emerge more insidiously in the family. Just as their onset is unclear, the resolution of strains is often also unclear to families, which makes them even more difficult to deal with [Olson and McCubbin, 1983:119]. ■

Family stress, as distinct from a stressor, is the state of tension that often accompanies stressors and hardships. Stressors and hardships call for family coping and management skills. When family members do not have adequate resources for coping and managing—either because of prior strains or because of the character of the stressor event itself—stress emerges.

The "pile-up" concept of family-life stressors and strains (similar to Broderick's concept of "crisis overload") is important in predicting family adjustment over the course of family life. Scientists have hypothesized that an excessive number of life changes and strains occurring within a brief time, perhaps a year, are more likely to disrupt a family. "This would contribute to deterioration of the family unit and of the emotional and physical wellbeing of its members" (Olson and McCubbin, 1983:120). We have examined various characteristics of A, the stressor event, in double ABC-X model. Next we will look at C, how the family defines the event. We will discuss B, the family's crisis-meeting resources, later in this chapter.

Defining the Situation

The way in which a family interprets a crisis-precipitating event may have as much or more to do with members' ability to cope as with the character of the event itself.[1] Many events—unemployment or the accidental death of a child, for example—can be defined as either external or internal. One family might view a husband's unemployment as the result of a contracting economy (an external event), whereas another family might see the same situation as the result of the man's lack of initiative (an internal factor). Involuntary infertility (discussed in Chapter 12), getting AIDS, or a child's death can be interpreted as an accident or as the result of negligence or disloyalty.

Families who define a problem as their fault suffer more as individuals and also tend to provide less support than families who consider the cause to be external. For example, although it is almost impossible to distinguish degrees of anguish, parents who blame themselves for their child's developmental disability may be less able to cope with the situation than if they interpret the occurrence of the illness as beyond their control (Farber, 1959; Price-Bonham and Addison, 1978).

Several factors influence how family members will define a crisis. One is the nature of the precipitating event itself. War-induced separations are particularly difficult for families to deal with, because the ambiguity of the situation makes it hard to define. The unpredictability of the absent

member's return requires the family to develop two inconsistent modes of adaptation: one allowing for the absent member's return and a joyful reunion, the other allowing for the fact that he or she may not return (McCubbin et al., 1976; McCubbin, 1979).

Another factor that influences a family's definition of a crisis is the degree of hardship or the kind of problems the stressor creates. A mother's death may be harder on the family than is the news that she is seriously ill but may recover, for instance. At the same time, growing up with a blind, deaf, or otherwise disabled parent can seem to be not only an unfair situation but also a never-ending and hopeless one (Walker, L. A., 1985). Temporary unemployment is less of a hardship than a layoff in an area where there are few job prospects or a loss of a job at age 55. A third factor is the family's previous experience with crises, particularly those of a similar nature. If family members have had experience in nursing a sick member back to health, they will feel less bewildered and more capable of handling the situation.

A fourth factor is the way in which family members find out about a crisis. If parents are told tactfully and supportively that their child is disabled, for example, their adjustment is likely to be more positive, at least initially, than if they are told harshly and abruptly or misled with false encouragement (Price-Bonham and Addison, 1978; Power, 1979). Believing from the start that a crisis is insurmountable makes the adjustment even more difficult.

Death of a Child as a Stressor The likelihood of death in our society influences how we define a death in the family. In a society such as ours where death is statistically infrequent, not all deaths, but only unnecessary, preventable, or "premature" ones, are highly problematic (Parsons and Lidz, 1967). Under the mortality conditions that existed in this country in 1900, half of all families with three children could expect to have one die before reaching age 15. Parents defined the loss of a child, social historians believe, as an almost natural or predictable crisis and, consequently, suffered less pain than do parents today. By 1976, in contrast, the probability of a child/death was 6 in 100 (.06) (Uhlenberg, 1980:315). To illustrate this change, demographer Robert Wells asks readers to imagine themselves on a New Jersey village street in 1750:

As you sit by the roadside, you notice a [funeral procession] coming toward you.... The coffin

---

1. While we are discussing the *family's* definition of the situation, it is important to remember the possibility that each family member experiences a stressful event in a unique way. "These unique meanings may enable family members to work together toward crisis resolution or they may prevent resolution from being achieved. That is, an individual's response to a stressor may enhance or impede the family's progress toward common goals, may embellish or reduce family cohesion, may encourage or interfere with collective efficacy. From this perspective, what is important is not the 'family's' definition of the stressor but an understanding of individual perspectives regarding stressful situations, how these perspectives relate to behavior, and the influences of members' perspectives in combination" (Walker, L. A., 1985:832–33).

is . . . that of a child. This, also, you learn is not unusual, because children commonly died during this time period. The second thing that surprises you is that the individuals following the coffin to the graveyard seem to accept their loss relatively calmly. You will later learn that since so many children die at a relatively early age, parents do not invest significant amounts of emotional energy in their children until they have survived the first five or ten years of life. In addition, their religious beliefs encourage many colonists to view death not as an ending, but as a release from earthly miseries and sins.

As you watch the procession go by, you realize that about half the people in the procession are children, including several you later learn are brothers and sisters of the deceased [1985: 1–2]. ∎

Family members who lose a child today, by comparison, have not had much opportunity to witness death, dying, or grieving (Kübler-Ross, 1979). The death—defined as unnatural, irrational, uncalled-for—is an uncommonly painful event, especially in a rational progress- and action-oriented society such as ours.

Loss of potential children through miscarriage, still birth, or infant death has the added strain of ambiguity. It is unclear whether the incipient child is a member of the family or not. Attachment to the fetus or newborn may vary greatly so that the loss may be grieved greatly or little. Add to that the generally minimal display of bereavement customary in the United States and the omission of funerals or support rituals for perinatal (birth process) loss, and "all these ambiguities mean that a family may have to cope with sharply different feelings among family members . . . [and] the family as a whole may have to cope with the fact that they as a family have a very different reaction to loss than do the people around them" (Rosenblatt and Burns, 1986:238). In fact, a study of fifty-five instances of perinatal loss found that grief was still felt by some parents forty years later, while the majority reported no long-run grief and some had always defined their loss as a medical problem rather than a child death.

This study, because it dealt with an especially ambiguous situation, discovered a truth about death that is probably more general: "Loss through death may represent more than the person who has died" (251). Here "what is grieved may be the child, but it may also be subsequent childlessness, the absence of a desired additional child, an unpleasant medical or marital experience associated with the loss, a loss of innocence, the end to feelings of invulnerability, a loss of faith that life is fair, or something else" (251).

Family members' interpretations of a crisis event shape their responses in subsequent stages of the crisis.

The Period of Disorganization

The second phase of a crisis is a period of disorganization. At the beginning of this phase, it may seem that no adjustment is required at all. Family members may be numbed by the new or sudden stress and, in a process of denial, go about their business as if the event had not occurred.

Gradually, however, they begin to assimilate the reality of the crisis and to define the situation. Then the **period of disorganization** sets in: Family organization slumps, habitual roles and routines become nebulous and confused (Anthony, 1970), and members carry out their responsibilities with less enthusiasm. Typically, and legitimately, they begin to feel angry and resentful.

Expressive relationships within the nuclear family change. Some relationships grow stronger and more supportive; others weaken or grow more distant. Sexual activity, one of the most sensitive aspects of a relationship, often changes sharply. Patterns of sexual relations and expressiveness may alter or cease altogether for some couples (Komarovsky, 1940). Parent-child relations may also change.

Relations between family members and their outside friends, as well as extended kin network, may also change during this phase. Some families withdraw from all outside activities until the crisis is over; as a result, they may become more private or isolated than before the crisis began. As we shall see, withdrawing from friends and kin often weakens rather than strengthens a family's ability to meet a crisis.

For many families, however, the period of disorganization is a time when friends and especially kin gather and provide a network of support. This can be a highly visible effect, as when a family member dies and the extended family comes together during and after the funeral. But kin are also a source of support during other crises, providing aid during a financial emergency, helping with child care, or just "being there" to provide

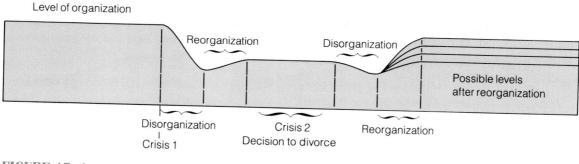

FIGURE 15.4
Divorce as a family adjustment to crisis and as a crisis in itself.

emotional support. It's easier to cope with crises when a person doesn't feel alone (e.g., Turner and Avison, 1985). For instance, studies have shown that unwed teenage mothers have a much better chance of resuming their education, becoming self-supporting, and coping with the tasks of parenting if their own parents provide initial help and support (Presser, 1978; Furstenberg and Crawford, 1978; Colletta and Gregg, 1979). A two-year study (Gore, 1978) of 100 unemployed married men recently laid off because of a plant shutdown found that those with more supportive social and kin relationships did not find jobs sooner, but they did exhibit fewer physical and mental stress symptoms.

While family support is important, it does not automatically come smoothly. At the nadir, or low point, of family disorganization, conflicts may develop over how the situation will be defined and how it should be handled. For example, in families with a seriously ill member, the healthy members are likely either to overestimate or to underestimate the sick person's incapacitation and, accordingly, to act either more sympathetically or less tolerantly than the ill member wants (Parsons and Fox, 1952; Strauss and Glaser, 1975). Reaching the optimal balance between nurturance and encouragement of the ill person's self-sufficiency may take time, sensitivity, and judgment.

During the period of disorganization family members face the decision of whether to express or to smother any angry feelings they may have. As Chapter 9 points out, people can express their anger either in primarily bonding or in alienating ways. Expressing anger as blame will almost always sharpen hostilities. When family members opt to

repress their anger, they risk converting it into destructive "anger insteads" or allowing it to smolder, thus creating tension and increasingly strained relations. The way in which members cope with conflict at this point will greatly influence the family's overall level of recovery.

Recovery

Once the crisis "hits bottom," things often begin to improve. Either by trial and error or (when possible) by thoughtful planning, family members usually arrive at new routines and reciprocal expectations. They are able to look past the time of crisis to envision a return to some state of normalcy and to reach some agreements about the future.

Some families do not recover intact, as today's high divorce rate illustrates. Divorce can be seen both as an adjustment to a family crisis and as a family crisis in itself (Figure 15.4).

Other families stay together, although at lower levels of organization or mutual support than before the crisis. As Figure 15.1 showed, some families remain at a very low level of recovery, with members continuing to interact much as they did at the low point of disorganization. This interaction often involves a series of circles in which one member is viewed as deliberately causing the trouble and the others blame and nag him or her to stop. This is true of many families in which one member is an alcoholic or otherwise chemically dependent, an overeater, or a chronic gambler, for example. Rather than directly expressing anger about being blamed and nagged, the offending member persists in the unwanted behavior. (Box 15·1, "Alcoholism as a Family Crisis: Seven Stages," defines stages in the response of an alcoholic's family to the crisis. Note that it is not uncommon for recovery to be arrested at any of the early stages.)

Some families match the level of organization they had maintained before the onset of the crisis, while others rise to levels above what they experienced before the crisis. For example, one partner's attempted suicide might motivate both spouses to reexamine their relationship. With the help of professional mental health and marriage therapists, they might develop a personal marriage contract that is more supportive to both.

Reorganization at higher levels of mutual support can also result from less dramatic crises. For example, partners in midlife might view their boredom with their relationship as a challenge and revise their life-style to add some zest—by traveling more, moving to a more hospitable community, or planning to spend more time together rather than in activities with the whole family. The next section reviews some fairly predictable transitions in the course of family living. We will discuss them here as crises, that is, as opportunities for creatively reorganizing a family's values, attitudes, roles, and relationships. Because it is impossible to adequately cover the various predictable and unpredictable crises that can arise, readers are urged to consult the suggested readings and the citations in this chapter.

FAMILY TRANSITIONS AS PREDICTABLE CRISES

The transitions that individuals make during their adult lives are discussed in Chapter 1, which points out, among other things, that partners' personal changes affect their marriage relationship. Families as a unit evolve as well. Over the course of family living, most families begin as child-free couples, later make the transition to parenthood, and still later make transitions to retirement and widow- or widowerhood. All these individual and family transitions can be viewed as **predictable crises.** They are crises because they require dramatic changes in family members' values, behavior, and attitudes and in family organization. During tran-

sitions, spouses can expect their relationship to follow the course of a family crisis, as described in the previous section. Yet they are predictable in that many families normally will experience them. Thus, there are some norms and some standard solutions and adaptations that already exist.

Transition to Parenthood

As we saw in Chapters 12 and 13, incorporating an infant into a formerly childless relationship can cause confusion, resentment, and conflict as the new parents struggle to redefine their own and each other's roles. Who gets up for the 2 A.M. feeding, for example? Who takes the baby to the doctor? Who takes responsibility for finding a baby-sitter when the couple wants to go out?

Reorganization begins as parents gradually accept, define, and adjust to the baby's many demands, but continuing adjustments must be made throughout the course of parenthood. Sometimes, crises involving the children turn into crises over each mate's expectations about their own relationship. For example, a child's illness might precipitate a crisis over husband-wife roles as new questions arise, such as which parent will stay home from work to care for the sick child.

Children's misbehavior at home or school can also disrupt the family. Adolescents' budding independence precipitates crises—some, like teenage pregnancy, juvenile delinquency, and drug abuse, more serious than others. When parents meet these crises as challenges, without blaming the child or each other, the crises can provide opportunities to develop more supportive family interaction. For example, parents who discover that one of their children regularly uses marihuana might obtain help from a counselor or other expert to increase their understanding of the young person and operate more effectively as parents than ever before.

Spouses' Midlife Transitions

Other predictable crises often accompany spouses' midlife transitions, and parents can expect to face conflicts during this period of life. Several conditions set the stage for heightened tension. Both spouses are beginning to experience the physical changes of aging, so their self-esteem may be unusually low. The husband's career (or both spouses' careers in a dual-career family) has probably reached its peak, and he faces either the emptiness that accompanies a lack of new goals or the disappointment that his accomplishments did not match his dreams. In some cases the husband's career has peaked while the wife is in the exciting and demanding beginning stage of her career, making for quite different time demands and career attitudes of the partners.

As children grow older and more independent, either parent may feel jealous of the young ones' new adult lives; they may also be on the receiving end of adolescent hostility. Parents may begin to fear that they did not raise their children well or influence them enough. In addition, parents in midlife are often expected to meet the growing needs of their own aging parents.

Against this backdrop couples often experience a degree of **role reversal,** which may be an inevitable aspect of human development (psychologist Carl Jung [1954] believes that we begin to develop other parts of our personalities at about age 40) or a result of social change. Formerly acquiescent wives may grow more assertive, while men develop their emotional side. Ironically, a husband may begin to place greater value on family togetherness at about the time his wife begins a search for personal fulfillment and recognition that takes her outside the home and to some extent separates her from her family (Robertson, 1978). A middle-aged husband who now wants to devote more time to relationships and less to work may encounter confrontations and experience feelings of isolation (Cohen, 1979), and a wife may fail to receive the support and enthusiasm for self-development she wants from her husband.

It is not difficult to see why many couples face transition problems when a full-time homemaker decides to work outside the home (Chapter 11 discusses this). Not surprisingly, a similar situation may occur when wives return to school after a period of full-time homemaking. In two recent studies a majority of husbands verbally approved of their wives' new student role (Hooper, 1979) or gave emotional support (Berkove, 1979), although only one-fourth of the men helped more with household chores (Hooper, 1979). But the longer the wife remained in school and the more involved she became, the more anxious her husband grew. The husbands wondered "where all this is going"; they frequently admitted to tense relations and to anger because more help was expected of them.

In crises precipitated by role reversal, couples can best achieve a high level of recovery if each partner maintains a flexible attitude. For instance, supportive husbands saw their wives' return to school as a positive event that broke their habitual life-style or gave them "something new to talk about" (Berkove, 1979). Role crises during midlife may offer a badly needed opportunity to rewrite the personal marriage contract to meet both partners' changing needs.[2] An awareness of what is happening can help couples to avoid conflict and instead truly enjoy the blossoming of previously neglected aspects of the personality.[3]

A homemaker wife's returning to work or school can precipitate a marital crisis, but it can also help a wife adjust to another critical transition, the so-called empty-nest stage of family life after the children leave home.

The Empty Nest

Empty nest, which refers to the postparental stage of family life, is a value-laden term based on the assumption that parents, particularly mothers, will feel lonely and depressed once their children have grown and left home; it is often associated with negative stereotypes of the menopausal woman. Hormonal changes do occur in both women and men in middle age, and to some extent these changes affect people's self-esteem, levels of energy, emotional stability, and so forth. But the hormonal changes that accompany menopause and the beginning of the empty nest have been exaggerated. Most women go through menopause without serious emotional upheaval, and studies show that many women today look forward to the time when their youngest child leaves home (Robertson, 1978).

---

2. Some authorities have pointed to the need for college and university programs to serve not only the individual student but also the families of adults returning to school. Counseling could help the husbands of student wives to understand the reasons for the wife's return to school and the new demands of her student role (Hooper, 1979).

3. We don't know yet what these midlife patterns will look like in the next generation, which has received more encouragement to develop androgynous qualities earlier in life.

BOX 15 · 1

ALCOHOLISM AS A FAMILY CRISIS: SEVEN STAGES

When one of the adults in a family becomes an alcoholic, the course of the crisis is similar to that described in this chapter. One authority, Joan Jackson, has described seven stages in the course of alcoholism. She points out that not all alcoholic families move through all seven stages, however: Many become mired in the early stages.

Stage 1: Attempts to Deny the Problem

Alcoholism rarely emerges full blown overnight. It is usually heralded by widely spaced incidents of excessive drinking, each of which sets off a small family crisis. The alcoholic may arrive home late with a ticket for reckless driving, for instance. Both mates try to account for such episodes as "perfectly normal." As the drinking becomes more frequent, the nonalcoholic mate may cover for the alcoholic, making excuses for missed engagements or absence from work.

Between drinking episodes, both mates feel guilty about the alcoholic's behavior. (It is common for nonalcoholic family members to blame themselves either consciously or unconsciously for the alcoholic's drinking.) So each spouse tries to be an "ideal mate" to the other, hiding conflicts. Gradually, not only the drinking problem but any other problems in the marriage may be sidestepped.

It takes some time for the sober spouse to realize that the drinking is neither normal nor controllable. Meanwhile, to protect themselves from embarrassment, the family may begin to eliminate outside activities and to become socially isolated.

Stage 2: Attempts to Eliminate the Problem

This stage begins when the family finally defines the drinking as "not normal" and tries to stop it alone. Lacking clear-cut guidelines, the nonalcoholic partner makes trial-and-error efforts. In rapid succession the sober mate threatens to leave, accommodates, nags, and makes excuses for the alcoholic. But these inconsistent efforts fail. The family gradually becomes so preoccupied with finding ways to keep the alcoholic sober that they lose sight of all other family goals. Almost all thought becomes centered on alcohol. Meanwhile, family isolation peaks.

Stage 3: Disorganization

This is a stage of "what's the use?" Nothing seems effective in stabilizing the alcoholic, and efforts to change the situation become sporadic. The family gives up trying to understand the alcoholic. The children may no longer be required to show the alcoholic parent affection or respect. The sober partner, recognizing his or her own inconsistent behavior, may become concerned about his or her sanity.

SOURCE:
Jackson, 1958:90–98.

Stage 4: Attempts to Reorganize in Spite of the Problem

Here the sober partner takes sole family leadership. The alcoholic is ignored or assigned the status of a recalcitrant child and is increasingly excluded from family activities. As a result, the drinking becomes less a family problem. Hostility diminishes and is replaced by feelings of pity, exasperation, and protectiveness.

The sober mate seeks assistance from public agencies and self-help groups such as Al-Anon. With an emerging new support network, the sober partner gradually regains his or her sense of worth. Some families remain at this stage indefinitely. But despite greater stabilization, subsidiary crises multiply. The alcoholic may become violent or get arrested for drunken driving. Each crisis temporarily disrupts the new family organization, but the realization that the events are caused by alcoholism often prevents the complete disruption of the family.

Stage 5: Efforts to Escape the Problem

When some major subsidiary crisis occurs—desertion or unemployment, for example—the family feels forced to take survival action. At this point many couples separate or divorce. First, however, the sober partner has to resolve the mental conflicts about deserting a sick mate. Separating from the alcoholic is further complicated by the fact that when the decision is about to be made, the alcoholic often gives up drinking for a while.

Some other events have made separation possible, however. By this time the sober partner has learned that the family runs more smoothly without the alcoholic. Taking over control has bolstered the sober mate's self-confidence, and his or her orientation has shifted from inaction to action. Also, the sober mate has become familiar with community agencies that can help.

Stage 6: Reorganization of the Family

Here the family reorganizes without the alcoholic. For the most part this goes relatively smoothly. The family has long ago closed ranks against the alcoholic and now feels free of the minor disruptions the drinker created in the family. Reorganization is impeded, however, if the alcoholic continues to attempt reconciliation or believes she or he must "get even" with the family for leaving or "kicking me out."

(continued)

BOX 15 · 1

Continued

Stage 7: Reorganization with Sobriety

If the partners have not divorced by the time the alcoholic recognizes that he or she has a drinking problem and makes serious efforts to stop drinking, hope is mobilized. The family attempts to open ranks again to give the alcoholic the maximum chance for recovery.

If treatment is successful, the couple can expect many other problems to appear, however. Both mates may have unrealistic expectations; the family may harbor built-up resentment; and it may require a major adjustment for both the spouse and the children to again respect the alcoholic as a responsible adult. Gradually, perhaps through counseling or membership in groups such as Alcoholics Anonymous and Al-Anon, the difficulties may be overcome and family adjustment and reorganization with sobriety can be achieved.

The empty-nest problem was highlighted by sociologist Pauline Bart's study of women who were hospitalized for depression. She found that many of these women had invested much of their lives in being mothers, and that they felt lost, unneeded, and depressed once the youngest child left home. Bart also found that women who devoted their time and energy in alternative roles or activities, such as employment, school, volunteer work, or their marital relationship, were better able to adjust (Bart, 1972).

More recent studies have questioned the current validity of the empty-nest notion (e.g., Borland, 1982). Family counselor Lillian Rubin interviewed 160 mothers whose children had recently left or were getting ready to leave home. She discovered that some mothers were momentarily sad, lonely, or frightened of an uncertain future, but they were not depressed. All except one responded to the actual or impending departure with feelings of relief. Many talked about new jobs and other opportunities for self-fulfillment (Rubin, 1978). Another study (Harkins, 1978) concluded that emptying the nest often has *positive* psychological effects for the mother. Changes in our society that offer middle-aged women encouragement to return

to work or school have made this a satisfying period of life for many women (Bird, 1979a).

In fact, research has indicated that if the children left home unexpectedly early or "too late," the transition to postparenthood was more stressful, and parents had more difficulty meeting the crisis. Indeed, having young-adult children who do not leave the nest as early as their parents had anticipated—or who return, perhaps after a divorce or because of financial difficulties—is a crisis that a growing number of families face today (Fleming, 1978).

Another possible strain on couples during this period is imposed by the failing health of their own aging parents (Robertson, 1978; Pillemer and Wolf, 1986). Paul Mattesich points out that the care of older persons (or other handicapped dependents) involves "great psychic, emotional, social, and economic costs" (1979:666; Van Meter and Johnson, 1985)—so the empty-nest stage may be far from a period of new freedom.

Rubin also noted the irony inherent in the persistence of the stereotype of the depressed empty-nest mother, since fathers may have transition pains, too. "There is often a keen sense of regret because fathering is over and the grown child appears to no longer need a father" (Robinson and Barret, 1986:72). This is especially true for men who are older, those who have fewer children, those who are more emotionally involved in fathering, and those who have a less satisfying marriage relationship (Lewis et al., 1979).

The need to readjust the couple's relationship and roles after parenthood is a crisis situation, and the outcome is often more positive when mothers, who at present do spend more time than fathers in nurturing children, have other meaningful roles, such as work, school, or other activities, to turn to. In fact, this is one transition with a high likelihood of a positive outcome, because marital happiness often increases when couples have time, energy, and financial resources to invest in their couple relationship (Aldous, 1978).

Retirement

Of all the transitions in later life, retirement probably represents the greatest change in the traditional masculine gender role (Atchley, 1977). Accustomed to seeing himself as principal breadwinner and head of the family, the retired husband faces his own kind of role loss. He may adapt in several ways.

A retired husband might devote more attention to family roles such as being a companionate husband and grandparent, and spend more time in homemaking tasks. Doing this can be problematic, however, for men who cling to the traditional masculine role that highly values work and achievement (Aldous, 1978).

The results of one study of seventy-four husbands with multiple sclerosis are applicable here, even though the study deals with an unexpected and much less common crisis than retirement (Power, 1979). All the men in the study had been their family's principal breadwinner and authority figure, but their illness upset this family organization because the husbands were no longer able to work. These men reacted in different ways. Most became "spectators" in their homes. Although they were physically able to perform many household, family, and leisure activities, they became inactive, tending to feel angry, deprived, and powerless. Some husbands remained "participants" in their families. Although they were unable to work, they found

new family activities, such as shopping with their wives and working in the kitchen. These husbands felt that working had been important but was not essential to their self-esteem. They also identified with avocational and family activities and considered these equally, if not more, important to their personal satisfaction.

Although this study looked at retirement forced by illness rather than by age, many of its conclusions apply to retirement in general. The more flexible home-bound men were in their outlook and role definitions, the more successful their adjustment tended to be. Retired husbands feel more useful when they take part in household activities, even traditionally feminine ones. A study of 100 retired men revealed that those who chose expressive roles emphasizing emotional support and companionship had higher morale (Lipman, 1960). Role flexibility for women was also important, and "both husbands and wives are happier in the aging period when they emphasize mutual help, companionship, and affection rather than trying to maintain the segregation of daily role activities characteristic of the retirement period" (Aldous, 1978:204).

Retirement often forces homemaking wives to adjust as well. Full-time homemakers may find it difficult to share the house that has become their exclusive territory during the day, and many don't want to share the housework with their retired husbands (Fengler, 1975).

Some observers have noted that as more and more women work outside the home, "the dual-retired couple that is now a somewhat innovative pattern will doubtless become a more popular family lifestyle in the future" (Keith and Brubaker, 1979:497). As this happens, couples' adjustments to retirement may go somewhat more smoothly. Each partner will be able to relate to the other's loss of occupational role, and the wife may not see the house or housework as her exclusive territory. Then, too, retired spouses who have developed common leisure activities can be expected to be happier together than those who have not (Kelley, 1981; 288–89). The majority of older couples today will experience considerable strain if they do not work out a new, mutually acceptable personal marriage contract.

Ironically, the better a couple adjusts to retirement together, the more painful may be a forthcoming transition to widow- or widowerhood.

Aging and Dying

Can death, however inevitable, ever be a predict-able family crisis? "Death disrupts the routine ongoingness [of the family]" (Marshall, 1986:127). It permanently removes a member and may bring the conjugal unit to an end. Yet, "we have to learn to accept the death of others—including others we love dearly—and keep living ourselves just as we have to learn to accept our own impending deaths and to keep on living" (127).

Death *is* now more predictable than in the past. We can expect a majority of people to live longer. This has changed death:

If it is necessary to make sense of death, then the nature of what [needs to] be made sense of has altered. Not capricious death, but predictable death; not death at an early age, but death as the culmination of life, calls out for meaning. In addi-tion, death now typically comes as the culmina-tion of a protracted period of time when the per-son can be viewed as "dying." By this [is meant] that death follows a period of chronic illness in a much larger proportion of cases than in earlier times [Marshall, 1986:132]. ■

Another consideration is that death is now for the most part removed from the family to the hos-pital and mourning removed from the home to the funeral parlor. "The dying are segregated among specialists for whom contact with death has become routine and even somewhat impersonal" (Blauner, 1966:379, quoted in Marshall, 1986:133).

Longevity and a gradual decline in health mean that individuals may be more aware of impending death. The process of death begins with an aware-ness, typically beginning in middle age and inten-sifying in the seventies. Death of the first and then the second parent makes the individual aware of the cycle of generations and may serve as a marker—years of life beyond the parental death ages are viewed as "extra" (Marshall, 1986).

Individuals vary in whether or not they calcu-late their remaining years. Those who do are more likely to view themselves as middle-aged (rather than old); to have plans for their time; and to have more favorable attitudes toward death (Keith, 1982), perhaps because they have begun a preparation process that reduces anxiety (Marshall, 1986). Marshall's research indicates that the "life review"—

evaluating and legitimating one's biography or progress through life—is a characteristic process: "In the normal case, a person will . . . complete the life review and reach a state of integrity" (141). "Most old people in our society do come to accept their deaths" (140).

Social relations are very significant to the older person, not only as life goes on but also during the dying process. The life review is most successful when it is social, and those who are able to talk intimately with at least one person, often a spouse, about their awareness of death are most accepting (Marshall, 1986). Fortunately—and contrary to some of our stereotypes—most older persons are in close contact with their families. Studies indi-cate that 84 percent of older parents with living children had seen them within the previous week, 90 percent within the last month (Shanas, 1968). Fifty-two percent of those not living with a child had seen one within the last week (Shanas, 1973). "Most old people see their siblings and relatives often" (Shanas, 1982:10 in Callahan, 1985:33). Of those elderly who were physically dependent (15 percent), two-thirds were cared for at home, mostly by relatives (Thornton and Freedman, 1983).

Only 5 percent of Americans 65 and older lived in nursing homes in 1985–86 (Hing, 1987). Fifty-four percent of Americans over 65 live with spouses (76 percent of men and 38 percent of women), 30 percent live alone (15 percent of men, 41 percent of women), and 14 percent live with other relatives (7 percent of men, 19 percent of women) (U.S. Bureau of the Census, 1986b).

Yet the aging do not want to be a burden to their families and do not want to live extremely inactive lives or linger in a severely disabled or vegetative state (Riley, 1970, cited in Marshall, 1986). Many fear the loss of control they experience in the hospital, where they cannot "control the very final stages of dying. . . . The ability to plan for the final settling of one's affairs—possible only if a person is in fact told a prognosis that he or she is dying—can enhance personal control. So can free-dom from pain. The spread of palliative care pro-grams [hospice], which offer open awareness and truth-telling, but also pain relief and social sup-port, may therefore do a great deal to increase the likelihood that an individual will be able to feel 'in control' during the final stages" (Marshall, 1986:143). Meanwhile, the partner, if there is a sur-viving spouse, must prepare for his or her future alone.

I LOOK AT THIS PICTURE AND I KNOW MY MOTHER KNEW THAT WE WERE THERE AND WE LOVED HER.

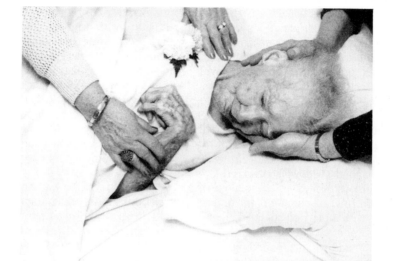

THIS IS MY MOTHER HELPLESS IN HER FINAL DAYS.
SHE WAS WAITING AND TRYING HARD TO DIE
SHE HAD LIVED TOO LONG

THE NURSING HOME GAVE HER THE CARE SHE REQUIRED,
BUT I WISH I COULD HAVE KEPT HER HOME WITH ME -
LIKE A ROSE KENNEDY.

IT IS ALL ECONOMICS AND TIME - IF ONLY I WERE RICH

Edna H. Sheely
DAUGHTER OF MARY G. SULLIVAN
1885 - 1985
8 CHILDREN
17 GRANDCHILDREN
28 GREAT GRANDCHILDREN

Widowhood and Widowerhood

Sociologist Talcott Parsons notes that "deaths, like other major points of transition in the personal life cycle, remain occasions upon which the central significance of the nuclear family in the personal attachments of the individual is conspicuously demonstrated, along with the solidarity of the more extended kin groups" (Parsons and Lidz, 1967:142). A final family crisis is the adjustment to widow- or widowerhood. Widowhood is usually a permanent status for older women. Only about 5 percent of women who are widowed after age 55 remarry (Cleveland and Gianturco, 1976, in Troll et al., 1979). "Remarriage is not possible for many older widows" (Streib and Beck, 1980:942). Indeed, for some women, widowhood may last longer than the child-rearing stage of life. This is not usually true for widowed men, who remarry far more often than women do. Living conditions have changed for the widowed over the last hundred years. In 1880, 9 percent of unmarried (widowed, divorced, and never married) persons over age 65 lived alone; in 1975, 66 percent. In 1880, 37 percent of the unmarried over 65 lived with a married son or daughter, while in 1975 only 7 percent did (Smith, 1981:110).

Typically, widow- and widowerhood begin with **bereavement,** a period of mourning (the period of disorganization in Figure 15•1), followed by gradual adjustment to the new, unmarried status and to the loss. Mates who lose a partner suddenly and without warning tend to have more difficulty adjusting to the loss than those who had warning, such as with a long illness (Newman, 1979). If the spouse's dying has been prolonged, much of the mourning may have preceded the actual death, so that grieving after the death is less intense. In a study of widows in Chicago, about half said they had recovered from their husband's death within a year, while 20 percent said they had never gotten over it and did not expect to (Lopata, 1973).

Bereavement manifests itself in physical, emotional, and intellectual symptoms. Physical reactions—shortness of breath, frequent sighing, tightness in the chest, feelings of emptiness in the abdomen, and loss of energy (Kalish, 1976)—are intense immediately following the onset of grief, but they diminish with time.

Emotional reactions include anger, guilt, sadness, anxiety, and preoccupation with thoughts of the dead spouse (Parkes, 1972). These responses, which also tend to diminish over time, are related to the quality of the marital relationship. If the surviving partner was emotionally reliant on the mate, he or she may experience greater grief. The surviving partner of a conflict-habituated union may suffer intensely, often to the surprise of family and friends. This is because conflict-habituated partners, unlike a devitalized couple, rely heavily on each other emotionally. There is some evidence that survivors of devitalized unions grieve less immediately after a mate's death but have greater difficulty with grief and guilt over more extended periods of time (Newman, 1979).

Intellectual reactions to a partner's death may include sanctifying the memory of the lost spouse, that is, retaining only positive memories of their time together. This idealization can be beneficial because it helps satisfy the survivor's need to believe that his or her past life and marriage were happy and meaningful. But such idealization can also make it harder to form new intimate relationships (Lopata, 1973).

These physical, emotional, and intellectual reactions to loss are characteristic of both women and men. Other reactions are more specifically associated either with a woman's loss of a husband or with a man's loss of a wife. We'll look at these sources of stress.

Loss of a Husband Becoming a widow can change the basis of a woman's identity, particularly if her role as wife has been central, as for many of the present generation of older women. Widows cope with this identity crisis in different ways. Some take a new job, participate in workshops for displaced homemakers, or involve themselves in civic or social organizations. Others become more involved with friends and family. Research suggests that strong relationships with friends are more often related to high morale among widows than family ties (Blau, 1973; Arling, 1976; Wood and Robertson, 1978). Peers are more apt to have shared interests and a sense that they chose each other, which can be more satisfying than relationships that are at least partly structured by obligation. Still, family ties, particularly with children, are important and provide continuity (Anderson, T., 1984; Houser and Berkman, 1984; Morgan, 1984).

The amount of personal and social disruption caused by widowhood depends to a large extent on the activities the couple had shared. Like divorced persons, widows often feel like "fifth wheels" among friends who are still couples. The kind of adjustment a woman makes may also be related to social class. Middle-class women are more likely than working-class women to have seen themselves as part of a husband-wife team and to have been involved with their husbands in a wide variety of activities. Therefore, the loss of companionship is often more traumatic for middle-class widows. At the same time, however, middle-class women tend to have a wider array of options: more friends and organizational activities, more education and job opportunities, and more financial resources for entertainment and travel. Working-class women have fewer friends and organizational memberships, less money, and less education, and on the whole they are much more likely to be lonely over a long period of time than are middle-class widows (Lopata, 1973).

Financial difficulties often plague widows, especially in the working class. In traditional marriages among older Americans today, the wife is often financially illiterate, that is, she is ignorant of the family finances and has no training in how to manage money (Lopata, 1973; Porter, 1976). The widow often finds herself in an ironic financial situation in which, because of changing times and expectations about women, she is expected to take care of herself but has neither the work experience nor the financial knowledge to do so. (Displaced-homemaker programs, discussed in Chapter 16, serve both divorced and widowed women who have problems like these.)

Loss of a Wife   Although it is not so financially stressful, widowerhood is at least as emotionally devastating for men as widowhood is for women. In fact, many authorities believe that being a widower is more difficult than being a widow. A man is likely to see a mate as an important part of himself and as the only person in whom he can confide (Glick et al., 1974); as Chapter 5 points out, women are more likely than men to have intimate friendships. Being a widower can also threaten a man's concept of himself and of life and retirement. One way in which the loneliness and sense of profound disruption are manifested is in higher suicide rates among widowers (Gove and Tudor, 1973:50–73). On the other hand, developing the grandfather role (provided that option is available) can help a man

to feel valued and involved (Robinson and Barret, 1986:74–75).

Widow- and widowerhood and the other family transitions or "predictable crises" we have been discussing can usually be anticipated and planned for. Partners can discuss what kind of funeral each wants and make sure each knows how to carry on financially after the other's death, for example. If they still have dependent children, they can decide how these would be cared for in case both parents died at the same time. They might discuss with the children their feelings about remarriage. Anticipating and planning ahead for crises whenever possible is an important aid to meeting them effectively and creatively.

FACTORS IN MEETING CRISES CREATIVELY

Meeting crises creatively means that after reaching the nadir in the course of the crisis, the family rises to a level of reorganization and emotional support that is equal to or higher than that which preceded the crisis. Social scientists have pointed out that most American families have some handicaps in meeting crises creatively, however.

The typical American family is under a high level of stress at all times. Providing family members with emotional security in an impersonal and unpredictable society is difficult even when things are running smoothly. Family members are trying to do this while holding jobs and managing other activities and relationships.

In addition, the average family has some weaknesses as an organization. Young and inexperienced dependents often outnumber more capable adults, and families can hardly reject their weak, ineffective, or problematic members to recruit more competent ones. Ironically, the principal function of today's family—offering a kind of unearned acceptance—makes the family less efficient in meeting crises (Parsons and Fox, 1952; Hansen and Hill, 1964): The family cannot tell a member to "shape up or ship out" as readily as an employer can. Families in crisis are very vulnerable to a breakup, perhaps more so than in the past (McCubbin, 1979).

For some families, breaking up is the most creative way to reorganize. And other families stay together and find ways to meet crises effectively. What differentiates families that reorganize creatively from those that do not? According to the ABC-X model, described earlier, successfully meeting crises depends partly on the family's resources (B in the model). These include family harmony, sound financial management and health practices, supportive communication patterns, a satisfying sexual relationship, healthy leisure activities, a supportive network of individual and family friends, and overall satisfaction with one's family and quality of life (Olson and McCubbin, 1983:211–14). As we have seen, families that meet crises effectively do not blame any one family member for the stressor event and define it as a challenge rather than as something that is necessarily bad. Other qualities, too, can help families recover from crises.

A Positive Outlook

Families that meet a crisis with an accepting attitude, focusing on the positive aspects of their lives, do better than those that feel they have been singled out for misfortune (Davis, 1972; Voysey, 1975). For example, many chronic illnesses have downward trajectories, so that both partners can realistically expect that the ill mate's health will only grow worse. Some couples are remarkably able to adjust to this, "either because of immense closeness to each other or because they are grateful for what little life and relationship remains" (Strauss and Glaser, 1975:64). Ironically, it is often easier for family members to focus on the positive when they accept their own and each other's negative feelings.[4]

Spiritual Values and Support Groups

Some researchers have found that strong religious faith is related to high family cohesiveness (Bahr

and Chadwick, 1985) and helps people meet crises, partly because it provides a positive way of looking at suffering (Voysey, 1975; McCubbin,1979:241). Many of the better-adjusted victims of multiple sclerosis described earlier belonged to charismatic religious groups, which acted as a source of strength (Power, 1979). Self-help groups, such as Al-Anon for families of alcoholics and Alateen for teenage children of alcoholics, can also help people take a positive approach to family crises.

High Self-Esteem

Families meet crises more creatively when members have high self-esteem. This is because when family members focus their energies to meet a crisis, they often have to cut down on their expression of affection and emotional support (Hansen and Hill, 1964:806). As a result, family members must stand alone emotionally until they work out new avenues for expressing mutual support and concern, and this requires high self-esteem. Also, family members with high self-esteem are more able to deal constructively with the conflict that characterizes families at the nadir of a crisis.

Open, Supportive Communication

Families whose members interact openly and supportively meet crises more creatively. For one thing, free-flowing communication opens the way to understanding. The better-adjusted husbands with multiple sclerosis, for example, believed that, even though they were embarrassed when they fell in public or were incontinent, they could freely discuss these situations with their families and feel confident that their families understood (Power, 1979).

Some research indicates that families who have difficulty coping with crises are far more inadequate in communicating with and supporting each other than they are in dealing with practical problems (Hansen and Hill, 1964:808). For example, moving can be considered a family crisis because it disrupts social networks (Lavee et al., 1985). The prolonged disruption or isolation that families experience after a move is often a result of strained relationships and inadequate supportive communication rather than of problems associated with the move itself (McAllister et al., 1973; Jones, 1973).

---

4. Three books written by Josh Greenfield, the father of a brain-damaged son named Noah, exemplify the capacity to accept both negative and positive feelings about an unfortunate situation. In *A Child Called Noah* (1972), *A Place for Noah* (1978), and *A Client Called Noah* (1987), Greenfield expresses bitterness, anger, frustration, and love for his son.

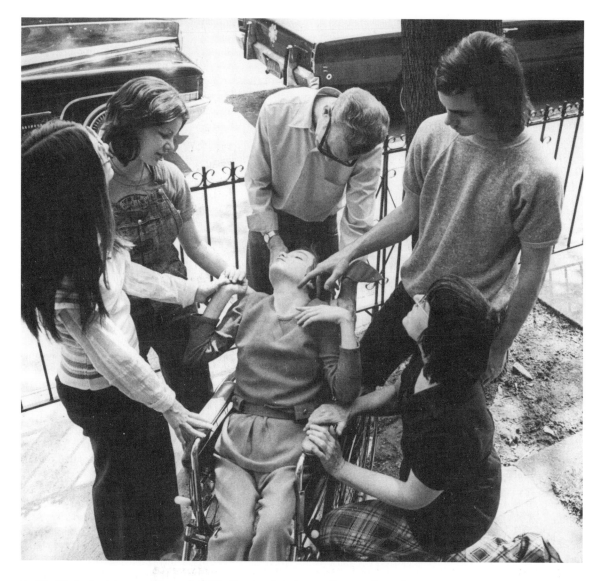

■ We think of *crisis* as synonymous with *disaster*, but the word comes from the Greek for *decision*. Although we cannot control the occurrence of many crises, we can decide how to cope with them. Recognizing that a chronic illness or disability will not improve, a family is challenged to adapt to the crisis.

Dying poses special communication problems, yet communication at this time is enormously important. Dying persons may become isolated or depressed when family members are only willing to talk in optimistic terms (Miller and Knapp, 1986). "Open" communication styles have even been correlated with longer survival of terminal patients (Shapiro, 1983).

Avoidance, confrontation, and reaction are three primary communication strategies that emerge in conversations with the dying. Avoidance, as the term implies, is an interaction with the patient that does not acknowledge death. "The motif is to carry on the interaction as if nothing were significantly different in the relationship.... In using this approach, persons try to focus on upbeat, positive topics—topics that center on current interests or news and topics that explore happy events of the patient's past" (Miller and Knapp, 1986:259).

The confrontive style, which focuses on the impending death, may not be well received by the patient. But it is intended to be helpful, motivated by "(1) an awareness that dying persons may have a need to ventilate their anger or thoughts about dying to someone; (2) an awareness that patients' clarifying their illness or feelings may have therapeutic value for patients; and (3) an awareness that the [family member] may have a desire to express feelings of affection or sorrow" (259).

The reactive approach is one of listening uncritically to the dying person. "By deeming whatever topics of conversation the dying person wishes to cover as appropriate, the [family member] is free to discover the norms of interaction with the particular individual, to assess the 'needs' of the dying person, to provide emotional support through the unqualified acceptance of the person's feelings, and to initiate any conversational topics that the patient has perceived to be appropriate. This approach seeks to help the patient by giving the patient control of the conversational agenda" (Miller and Knapp, 1986:260).

Miller and Knapp, who have done extensive research on communication with the dying based primarily on interviews with health care and clergy professionals, generally endorse a "dialectical" approach to these conversations. That is, rather than rely, as the professionals do, on one primary mode (usually reactive), the family member would do well to adapt the conversational strategy to the history of the family relationship, the nearness of death, the practical needs of the situation, and the emotional tone that seems intuitively appropriate at a particular time (Miller and Knapp, 1986). As with other family conversation, communication about death requires sensitivity, confidence in one's perception of the situation, and trust in one's instincts.

Adaptability

Adaptable families naturally adjust positively during crises. And families are more adaptable when they are more democratic and when conjugal power is fairly egalitarian (Patterson and McCubbin, 1984). In families in which one member wields authoritarian power, the whole family suffers if the authoritarian leader does not make effective decisions during a crisis—and allows no one else to move into a position of leadership (Hansen and Hill, 1964).

For example, a teenager may realize that his or her mother is addicted to drugs or is an alcoholic before either the mother or the father is willing to admit it. Although the whole family might benefit if the child goes to Alateen, an authoritarian father might forbid the youngster to attend or refuse transportation to the meetings. In a more democratic family the youngster would be allowed to attend Alateen meetings, even if the parents continued to disagree with the teenager's point of view.

It is true that in most families the conjugal power leader, usually the husband, tends to be replaced eventually by another member—the spouse or an older child—if he does not solve the problem effectively (Bahr and Rollins, 1971). Husbands who feel comfortable only as leaders may resent their loss of power, and this resentment may continue to cause problems when the crisis is over.

Just as traditional gender roles continue to affect most areas of family life, so, too, do they influence family crises. Social scientists Bryan Robinson and Robert Barret, in their book *The Developing Father* (1986), argue that "fathers, compared with mothers, have more difficulty coping with their severely retarded children, and they are especially vulnerable to social stigma and extrafamilial influences. Differences between fathers and mothers in coping can be problematic for their marriage. For example, a mother's primary coping style of using community and social support could increase the father's stress over potential social stigma and invasion of privacy. A father experiencing intense grief could be less responsive to the needs of his wife concerning the burden of physical care" (198–99).

Family adaptability in areas other than leadership is also important. As we noted earlier, disabled husbands who were able to adapt their family roles to their physical capacities were better adjusted. Families who can adapt their schedules and use of space, their family activities and rituals, and their connections with the outside world to the limitations and possibilities posed by the crisis will cope more effectively than families that are committed to preserving sameness.

Counseling and Informal Social Support

The success with which families meet crises may also depend on the community resources available to help. This may be particularly important for families caring for the disabled or chronically ill in their homes (Perlman, 1983; Brozan, 1984). We've seen in other chapters that the relationships family members cultivate with people outside their immediate family—with extended family and friends—can be of great value, especially during crises (McCubbin, 1979). One resource is marriage and family counseling.

Counseling can help families after a crisis occurs; it can also help when families foresee a family change or crisis. For instance, a couple might visit a counselor when expecting or adopting a baby, when the wife decides to find a job outside the home, when the youngest child is about to leave home, or when the husband or wife is about to retire. Marriage counselors now offer premarital counseling to help partners anticipate some of the problems associated with the transition to married life. Marriage counseling is not just for marriages that are in trouble but a resource that can help relationships.

An Extended Family

Kin networks are also a valuable source of support in times of crisis. They may provide financial help, child care, love and support, and a sense that responsibilities are shared.

Traditionally, extended-family networks have been stronger among black families and working-class families than in the white middle class in our society. But we have seen throughout this text that American society—and the American family—is changing. One important change seems to be a reaffirmation of kin networks among middle-class families. In the past social scientists have frequently noted the exchange of mutual aid among extended kin in black and white working-class families. But as middle-class wives have gone out to work, and families at all levels have experienced economic stress and high rates of divorce, middle-class families have begun to draw on the resources of extended kin as well (Clavan, 1978). Although three generations don't live under the same roof (they rarely have in America, even in colonial times), kin networks are still very important today, providing far more than a symbolic source of identity.

Grandparents, aunts, or other relatives may help with child rearing in two-career families, for instance. Unwed single parents, particularly teenagers, are often dependent on their parents to help them through difficult years. A study of federal government assistance and older persons found that families and friends provide 50 percent of services to the elderly and 70 percent of services to those elderly who are impaired (Laurie, 1978, in Smyer and Hofland, 1982). Families going through divorce often fall back on relatives for practical help and financial assistance. In other crises kin provide a "shoulder to lean on"—someone who can be asked for help without causing embarrassment—which can make a crucial difference in a family's ability to recover. Kin are such effective sources of assistance in a crisis that public policy is beginning to take kin networks into account in designing programs to help families in various kinds of crises (Furstenberg and Crawford, 1978; Moroney, 1979).

We need to note two reservations about extended kin as problem solvers. One is that recent demographic changes may make the assistance of adult children in caring for their parents much less likely in the future. For one thing, if couples or individuals remain childless, they will not have adult children to help them in old age. Children in small families will find the burden of caring for aging parents much heavier than when it was shared by a larger group of siblings. Parents may find that having one or two children, allowing for the inevitable frictions and misfortunes of life, does not ensure the availability of a child to take major responsibility for them later in life. This risk is aggravated by high divorce rates, as adult children may have their hands full coping with the divorce process, single-parent families, and reestablishment of careers and relationships (Smyer and Hofland, 1982). Children may even lose touch with noncustodial parents, develop anger toward either parent, or react negatively toward stepparents. Because of these weakened emotional bonds, children may not be sufficiently motivated to care for an aging parent or stepparent.

Another matter to consider is the burden that the extended family places on the family, which may have other responsibilities, such as coping with adolescent or younger children. Also, given present patterns of kinship relations and caring roles, it seems possible that adult women who have finished raising their children may be asked to give up self-development to devote themselves to aging relatives. Whether or not society's resources are made available through government support for families with problems is also a factor in the burden placed on the extended family, as Chapter 14 discussed.

CRISIS: DISASTER OR OPPORTUNITY?

A family crisis is a turning point in the course of family living that requires members to change how they have been thinking and acting. Sometimes, the event that precipitates a crisis is dramatic, unexpected, and unfortunate. Chronic illness, the death of a child or a spouse, a breadwinner's unemployment—all these require major alterations in the way family members think, feel, and act. "Good" changes can precipitate crises, too. Suddenly getting rich or, more commonly, moving to another city or state because of a promotion are examples.

The predictable changes of individuals and families—parenthood, midlife transitions, postparenthood, retirement, and widow- and widowerhood—are all family transitions that can be viewed as crises. From this point of view, crises can be regarded simply as logical results of the fact that people,

relationships, and marriages and families change.

Moreover, crises—even the most unfortunate ones—have the potential for positive as well as negative effects. One therapist cites cases in which death in a family with long-standing problems precipitated counselor-supported change enabling family members to function more effectively than they ever had (Gelcer, 1986). Whether a family emerges from a crisis with a greater capacity for supportive family interaction depends largely on how family members choose to define the crisis. A major theme of this text is that people create the kind of marriage and family they want by the choices they make. In times of crisis, family members make many choices, one of the most significant of which is whether to blame one member for the hardship. Casting blame, even when it is deserved, is less productive than viewing the crisis primarily as a challenge.

Put another way, choosing a positive outlook helps a person or a family to meet a crisis constructively. Electing to work toward developing more open, supportive family communication—especially in times of conflict—also helps individuals and families meet crises constructively. Chapter 16, for example, states that divorcing parents who interact cooperatively do their children—and themselves—a great favor. Then, too, families whose members choose to be flexible in roles and leadership meet crises creatively.

While they have options and choices, however, family members do not have absolute control over their lives. Many family troubles are really the results of public issues. The serious family disorganization that results from unemployment or poverty, for example, is as much a social as a private problem. Furthermore, many family tensions follow from changes in values held by the larger society (Hansen and Hill, 1964:795). In this text we have often suggested that the tension between individualistic and family values in our society creates personal and family conflict. And the society-wide movement toward equality and greater self-actualization may spark family crises as wives and children move toward more independence. Moreover, many family crises are harder to bear because communities lack adequate resources to help families meet them. Families must act collectively to obtain the social resources they need for effective crisis management in everyday living.

Summary

Family crises may be predictable, as when a new baby is born, or they may be unpredictable. In either case the event that causes the crisis is called the *stressor.*

A common pattern can be traced in families' reactions to crises. The three phases are the crisis itself, the period of disorganization, and the period of recovery or reorganization. The eventual level of reorganization a family reaches depends on a number of factors, including the type of stressor, the degree of stress it imposes, whether it is accompanied by other stressors, and the family's definition of the crisis situation. The ABC-X model of family crises recognizes all this.

Life transitions are more predictable than other crises, but they disrupt family patterns in a similar way. Predictable crisis phases in the course of family life include parenthood, midlife transitions, the empty-nest and retirement phases, and widow- and widowerhood.

Meeting crises creatively means resuming daily functioning at or above the level that existed before the crisis. Several factors can help: a positive outlook, spiritual values, the presence of support groups, high self-esteem, open and supportive communication within the family, adaptability, counseling, and the presence of a kin network.

Key Terms

crisis *479*	double ABC-X model *483*
transition *479*	period of
stressors *480*	disorganization *486*
crisis overload *481*	predictable crises *488*
external stressor *481*	empty nest *489*
internal stressor *481*	bereavement *496*
ABC-X model *483*	

Study Questions

1. Define *crisis* and explain how family crises fit this definition. How are family transitions the same as crises? How are they different?
2. Describe the three phases of a family crisis. Use an example to illustrate each phase.

3. Differentiate between the types of stressors. How are these single events different from crisis overload? How might a single crisis event affect a family differently from crisis overload?
4. Differentiate between external and internal stressors. How would they affect families differently? Which do you think would be the most difficult for families to cope with? Why?
5. Discuss the factors that influence how family members will define a crisis. How does the family's definition relate to the members' ability to adjust to the crisis?
6. Describe the period of disorganization in a family crisis situation. How can this phase of a crisis pull a family apart? How can it bring a family together?
7. What factors help some families recover from crisis while others remain in the disorganization phase?
8. Are family transitions, which are at least somewhat predictable, easier to adjust to than unpredictable crises? Why or why not?
9. Compare the transitions of parenthood, midlife, the empty nest, retirement, and widow- or widowerhood. Are there any similarities? Any differences? What factors would encourage adjustment to each transition? What factors would inhibit adjustment?

Suggested Readings

Caine, Lynn
1974   *Widow.* New York: Morrow.
        Personal account of a woman's reactions and adjustment to bereavement. Illustrates common problems of crises of loss.
Darling, Rosalyn B.
1979   *Families Against Society: A Study of Reactions to Children with Birth Defects.* Beverly Hills, Calif: Sage.
        Readable report of parents' responses and possible courses of action.
Davis, Fred
1963   *Passage Through Crisis: Polio Victims and Their Families.* Indianapolis, Ind.: Bobbs-Merrill.
        Classic research study based on observation of doctors, patients, and families. Provides a great deal of insight into how family dynamics are altered by the child's illness and disability.

Downs, William R.
1982 "Alcoholism as a developing family crisis." *Family Relations* 31:5–12.
Application of systems theory and Hill's ABC-X crisis theory to alcoholism.

Earhart, Eileen, and Michael J. Sporakowski
1984 *The Family with Handicapped Members.* Special issue of *Family Relations* 33 (Jan.).
Contains many useful articles based on research or clinical experience.

Figley, Charles R., and Hamilton T. McCubbin (eds.)
1983 *Stress and the Family, Vol. II: Coping with Catastrophe.* New York: Brunner/Mazel.
Part of a two-volume book on stress, covering current research in this field. Stressful family situations are divided into the transitions in family stages that are rather widely shared (Vol. I) and crises of various sorts that only some families experience (Vol. II).

Greenfield, Josh
1972 *A Child Called Noah.* New York: Holt, Rinehart & Winston.
1978 *A Place for Noah.* New York: Holt, Rinehart & Winston.
1987 *A Client Called Noah.* New York: Holt, Rinehart & Winston.
Accounts of a family's emotional response and attempts at coping with an autistic child. The author is honest about negative as well as positive feelings.

Journal of Health and Social Behavior
Academic journal that reports many studies of relationships between life events, stress, social supports and other coping mechanisms, and physical and mental health.

Kübler-Ross, Elisabeth
1969 *On Death and Dying.* New York: Macmillan.
Now classic conceptualization of death as a social and psychological experience. The stages of adjustment to death she identified have been applied to other losses and crises.

Lopata, Helena
1979 *Women as Widows: Support Systems.* Westport, Conn.: Greenwood.
Key research on women's experience of being widowed.

McCubbin, Hamilton I., and Charles R. Figley (eds.)
1983 *Stress and the Family, Vol. I: Coping with Normative Transitions.* New York: Brunner/Mazel.
Part of a two-volume book on stress, covering current research in this field. Stressful family situations are divided into the transitions in family stages that are rather widely shared (Vol. I) and crises of various sorts which only some families experience (Vol. II).

McCubbin, Hamilton I., and Joan M. Patterson
1983 "Family stress and adaptation to crisis: A double ABC-X model of family behavior." Pp. 87–106 in David H. Olson and Brent C. Miller (eds.), *Family Studies Review Yearbook.* Beverly Hills, Calif.: Sage.
Important synthesizing article that reviews and builds on previous theory and research on family crises. Authors' research is on families experiencing separation during the Vietnam War.

Perlman, Robert (ed.)
1983 *Family Home Care: Critical Issues for Services and Policies.* New York: Haworth Press.
Examines caring for the chronically ill or disabled family member at home as an ongoing crisis in "an unstable triad"—the sick or dependent person's demands, family resources, and community supports.

Price-Bonham, Sharon, and Susan Addison
1978 "Families and mentally retarded children: Emphasis on the father." *Family Coordinator* 27 (July):221–30.
Academic article summarizing relevant issues in the adjustment of a family to a mentally retarded child.

Reiss, David, and Mary Ellen Olivieri
1980 "Family paradigm and family coping: A proposal for linking the family's intrinsic adaptive capacities to its responses to stress." *Family Relations* 29:431–44.
Uses family systems theory to analyze family coping behavior. Builds on senior author's excellent work on family problem solving.

Steinem, Gloria
1983 *Outrageous Acts and Everyday Rebellions.* New York: Holt, Rinehart & Winston.
Autobiography of the well-known feminist and journalist, who grew up as the caretaker of a mentally ill mother; conveys the impact of coping with a major family burden as a child.

Steinglass, Peter, with Linda Bennett, Steven J. Wolin, and David Reiss
1987 *The Alcoholic Family.* New York: Basic Books.
Up-to-date analysis of the alcoholic family by family systems people and sociologists.

Vine, Phillis
1982 *Families in Pain: Children, Siblings, Spouses, and Parents of the Mentally Ill Speak Out.* New York: Pantheon.
Coping with "the tangible role responsibilities of having a mentally disabled relative." Based on interviews and written by an historian with a mentally disturbed relative.

Wedemeyer, Nancy Voight
1986 *Death and the Family.* Special issue of the *Journal of Family Issues* 7 (Sept.)

Articles on the emotional responses of families and on family relationships with the dying.

Wikler, Lynn

1983 "Chronic stresses of families of mentally retarded children." Pp. 143–50 in David H. Olson and Brent C. Miller (eds.), *Family Studies Review Yearbook*. Beverly Hills, Calif.: Sage.

Very specific assessment of these families' overload. Age-by-age comparison to families with "normal" children.

Wiseman, Jacqueline P.

1980 "The 'home treatment': The first steps in trying to cope with an alcoholic husband." *Family Relations* 29:541–49.

Sympathetic research on the wife's coping role. Suggests some behavioral clues to developing alcoholism.

16 Separation and Divorce

You cannot imagine how much we hoped in the beginning.
LIV ULLMANN, *Changing*

Divorce has become a common experience in the United States, in all social classes, age categories, and religious and ethnic groups. In this chapter we'll look at divorce in broad terms and analyze why so many couples divorce in our society today. In narrower terms we'll examine factors that affect people's decisions to divorce, the experience itself, and ways the experience can be made less painful and become the prelude to the future, alone or in a new marriage (remarriage is discussed in Chapter 17). We'll begin by looking at current divorce rates in the United States, the highest in the world.

DIVORCE RATES: HIGH BUT LEVELING OFF

The frequency of divorce has increased sharply through most of this century, with dips and upswings surrounding historical events (such as the Great Depression and major wars), as Figure 16•1 shows. Between 1960 and 1981 the divorce rate (per 1,000 married women age 15 or older) rose from 9.2 divorces to 22.5 (U.S. Bureau of the Census, 1985a), then dropped back to 21.5 by 1984 (U.S. National Center for Health Statistics, 1986a). The prevalence of divorce is also apparent in the incidence of single-parent families. Between 1970 and 1984 the number of children living with one parent increased 71 percent, while the number of children living with two parents declined by 21 percent (U.S. Bureau of the Census, 1985b:4). This increase in single-parent families is partly a result of factors other than divorce—rising illegitimacy rates and a greater tendency for unmarried mothers to establish independent households—but the major cause is divorce. In 1984 only 75 percent of American children under age 18 resided with both parents—81 percent of white children, 41 percent of black children, and 70 percent of Hispanic children (U.S. Bureau of the Census, 1985b:4).[1] By 1984 over one-fourth (25.7 percent) of all family groups were headed by one parent. Among whites this proportion was 20.1 percent, while among blacks it was 59.2 percent (U.S. Bureau of the Census, 1986b:43, Table 61). The majority of both black and white one-parent households currently are headed by women.

Although the divorce rate nearly doubled between 1965 and 1975, the rate of increase began to slow in the late seventies. The crude divorce rate (see Box 16•1, "How Divorce Rates Are Reported") peaked at 5.3 (per 1,000 population) in 1979 and

---

1. These data do not distinguish stepparents and biological parents in two-parent families.

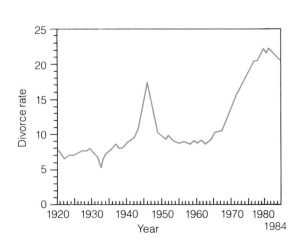

Figure 16·1

Divorce rates per 1,000 married women age 15 and older in the United States, 1920–84. (Sources: U.S. National Center for Health Statistics, 1979a, 1984a, 1986a; Thornton and Freedman, 1983)

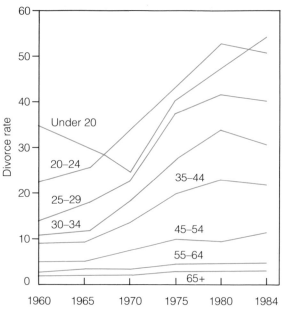

Figure 16·2

Divorce rate per 1,000 married women, by age at divorce, United States, 1960–1984. (Source: Glick and Lin, 1986b:739)

1981 and dropped to 5.0 in 1983, lower than it has been since 1977. From 1982 to 1985 it has remained at 5.0 or below (U.S. National Center for Health Statistics, 1986c). The same general trends in rates have occurred in all race and age groups. Blacks and younger persons thus continue to have rates that are higher than those of whites and older persons, although all rates have recently fallen. (Box 16·2, "Pressures on the Black Underclass," explores the differential divorce rate for blacks.)

Most observers conclude that the overall divorce rate has stabilized for the time being and may even drop by 1990 (Norton and Moorman, 1987). One reason is that fewer people are marrying at the vulnerable younger ages (Thornton and Freedman, 1983). Figure 16·2 compares divorce rates between 1960 and 1984 by women's age categories. As you can see from the figure, since 1980 the divorce rate has remained about the same or dropped among women over age 20, while rising sharply for those under 20. There are many reasons for the high divorce rate among teens (as Chapter 6 discusses), but most experts point to the interacting effects of economic hardship, low

education, premarital pregnancy (Teachman, 1983), and emotional immaturity.

While they have stabilized, the fact remains that divorce rates are higher than they have ever been in our society. One research project on outcomes of marriages of young women in their late 20s in 1985 concluded that over one-half (54 percent) of their first marriages and about the same proportion of remarriages would end in divorce (Norton and Moorman, 1987). Projections are that one out of three white children and two out of three black children born to a marriage will experience the dissolution of that parental marriage by the time they reach age 16 (Thornton and Freedman, 1983), compared to 25–30 percent of children born in the first half of the century.[2] We'll look at reasons for this striking change in family patterns in the next section.

The high divorce rate does not mean that Amer-

2. It should be noted that marriages can be dissolved by death as well as divorce. Until the mid-1970s increasing divorce and decreasing mortality (death was the most common cause of marital dissolution in past times) canceled each other out, so that no overall increase in marital dissolution occurred.

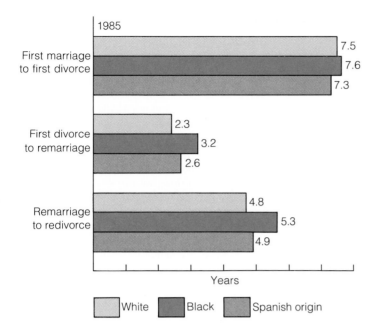

Figure 16·3
Interval between marriages for white, black, and Hispanic women age 15–74, United States, 1985. (Source: Adapted from Norton and Moorman, 1987:7)

icans have given up on marriage; it means that they find an unhappy marriage intolerable and hope to replace it with a happier one. In the 1970s, 80 percent of divorced persons eventually remarried. Although this rate of remarriage has declined somewhat in recent years, half of those who remarry do so relatively rapidly—within three years (Glick and Lin, 1986b; Norton and Moorman, 1987). Figure 16·3 depicts intervals between marriages for white, black, and Hispanic women in 1985. Divorced white women remarried, on average, in less than two-and-a-half years, black women in a little over three years, and Hispanic women in 2.6 years. Figure 16·3 also points to a more recent trend, redivorce. While divorced women spent an average of a little over seven years in their first marriages, the redivorced had been remarried for only about five years. (The stability of remarriages is addressed in Chapter 17.) Divorce thus represents, for many, a stage on the way to another marriage, not a permanent way of life. Consequently, many who divorce can expect several rapid and emotionally significant transitions in life-style and the family unit. They will feel stress and the need for adjustment,

but they will hope to establish a more permanent and a happier marital relationship. In the rest of this chapter we will concentrate on the decision to divorce and on the adjustment to divorce itself.

WHY MORE COUPLES ARE DIVORCING

Chapters 7 and 8 pointed to three factors that bind marriages and families together: economic interdependence; legal, social, and moral constraints; and the spouses' relationship. The binding strength of each factor is lessening, however, especially for marriages in the first four or five years. We'll examine how these changes affect the divorce rate.

Decreased Economic Interdependence

Traditionally, as we've seen, the family was a self-sufficient productive unit. Survival was far more

BOX 16 · 1

HOW DIVORCE RATES ARE REPORTED

Divorce rates are reported in many forms, some of which are more useful than others. Reports generally indicate rising rates no matter what measure is used, but the implications of these measures are frequently misunderstood.

1. *Number of divorces per year.* The number of divorces recorded per year is not an accurate measure of the rate, because it does not take into account the general increase in population. There may be more divorces in a population simply because there are more people.
2. *Ratio of current marriages to current divorces.* This measure is faulty because the marriages reported in the media have all taken place in the current year, whereas the divorces reported are of marriages that took place in many different years. The divorce rate then comes to depend on the marriage rate; that is, if the number of marriages goes down, the divorce rate will appear to rise, even if the number of divorces remains constant.
3. *Crude divorce rate.* The crude divorce rate is the number of divorces per 1,000 population. This measure takes into account changes in size of population, but includes portions of the population—children and the unmarried—not at risk for divorce.

SOURCES:
Crosby, 1980:51–68;
Scanzoni, 1972.

difficult outside of families, so members remained economically bound to one another. But today, since family members no longer need each other for basic needs, they are freer to divorce.

However, as Chapter 7 points out, families are still somewhat interdependent economically. As long as marriage continues to offer practical benefits, economic interdependence will help hold marriages together (Becker, 1981). The economic practicality of marriage varies according to several conditions. We'll look briefly at two: income and how it relates to divorce, and wives' employment.

Divorce and Income A positive relationship usually exists between marital stability and income; that is, up to a certain level, the higher the income, the less likely a couple is to divorce (Ross and Sawhill, 1975). A relative loss or lack of socioeconomic status seems important, too; men who are downwardly mobile—with less education than their parents—are more likely to divorce, as are those who fail to complete college. Both the stress of living without adequate economic resources and

the failure to meet one's expectations for economic or educational attainment seem to contribute to marital instability (Glick and Norton, 1979). This situation, together with the tendency of low-income groups to marry relatively early, helps explain why less well off families have the highest rates of marital disruption, including divorce, separation, and desertion (Glick, 1977; Hampton, 1975).

While economic stress is less in high-income marriages, the higher the income, the less economic impediment there is to divorce. As an old saying goes, there is not much difference between "enough" money and all the money in the world. But there is an enormous difference between "enough" and "not enough" money. Middle-income spouses who divorce can each expect to have "not enough" money, but upper-income partners may hope to divide their accumulated property and wealth so that each ends up with "enough." This relative economic independence, plus the fact that the pursuit of occupational success can erode marital intimacy, contributes to the divorce rate among high-income couples.

4. *Refined divorce rate.* This is the number of divorces per 1,000 married women over age 15. This measure compares the number of divorces with the total number of women eligible for divorce (adult married women) and hence is a more valid indicator of the propensity for divorce. It does not, however, predict one's chances of divorcing over a lifetime or for divorcing at any particular age. Age-specific divorce rates (number of divorces per 1,000 married women in each age group) are available, but they do not provide an overall rate.

Ideally, a cohort of married couples would be followed over a lifetime and their rate of divorce calculated. This sort of *longitudinal study* has never been done on a large scale and is unlikely ever to be done because of the expense and the length of time necessary for results. Of course, any rate calculated on this basis would be applicable only to those who married in the same year, since sociohistorical conditions (which affect divorce rates) would have changed over time.

On balance, the most useful and valid divorce rate appears to be the *refined divorce rate,* which we have presented in Figure 16·1.

Working Wives and Divorce Statistics show that divorce rates have risen as women's employment opportunities have increased. How directly does women's employment affect divorce?

A wife's taking a job outside her home does not necessarily mean she is likely to get divorced. According to one study of women in their late 20s, 84 percent of the employed wives remained married, while only 82 percent of the nonemployed wives did (Carlson, 1976). The transitional problems of conjugal power changes and task overload that couples experience when a wife takes a job can often be worked out, and most couples remain married. But although there is no conclusive evidence that a wife's working weakens a marriage, employment may contribute to a divorce by giving an *unhappily* married woman the economic power, the increased independence, and the self-confidence to help her decide on divorce (Booth, Johnson, and White, 1984). "Few writers believe that women's employment is a direct cause of marital dissolution; rather, they suggest that the widening opportunities for women allow couples to separate who are unhappy with their marriages for other reasons" (Cherlin 1981:53; Degler, 1980).

Decreased Social, Legal, and Moral Constraints

A second influence on the divorce rate has been the change in cultural values and attitudes. The social constraints that once kept unhappy partners from separating operate less strongly now (Ross and Sawhill, 1975), and divorce is more acceptable. For example, Ann Landers advises that "to remain in a loveless, sexless marriage is foolish" (June 18, 1984). Moreover, large corporations are more willing than before to hire divorced executives, and divorced politicians no longer feel the stigma that would have kept them from being elected to office a few decades ago.

No-fault divorce laws are one major factor in this shift, for they have legally abolished the concept of guilt (Weitzmann, 1985). Another factor is

BOX 16 · 2

PRESSURES
ON THE
BLACK
UNDERCLASS

Blacks have had higher divorce rates than whites and a lower proportion of two-parent families, even with education and income taken into account. Although slavery is often given as the explanation for this divergence, recent research suggests that the slave families for the most part had stable marriages. According to historian Herbert Gutman (1976), most slave children grew up in two-parent families, and black families were typically headed by two parents in the post–Civil War period—both in the South and in the urban North at least through 1925. The divergence between blacks and whites in two-parent households and marital stability is more recent. The table shows that the difference exists at all educational levels and that the gap has widened enormously in recent decades (Cherlin, 1981).

According to sociologist Andrew Cherlin, the increase in the divorce rate and in the number of female-headed households among blacks didn't occur until the Great Depression and has only become marked since the 1960s. By 1982, 22 percent of all children lived with one parent (17.2 percent of white children, 49.2 percent of black children, and 26.8 percent of Hispanic children). Cherlin believes that there is no evidence to support the common notion that differences are due to the slave experience or to the impact of urbanization on migrating blacks. He thinks that the worsening situation of the black underclass is probably an important factor, noting that "the gap between blacks and whites increased the most for the less well-educated" (Cherlin, 1981:107). However, to some extent this difference in marital stability between blacks and whites remains a puzzle.

the official posture of many American religions, which are less critical of divorce than they were in the past.[3] Fewer and fewer people now see divorce as a moral issue.

An even more basic factor has been the rise of individualistic values. Americans increasingly value personal freedom and happiness—gained, if necessary, at the cost of a marriage—over commitment to the family. They believe marriages ought to be happy if they are to continue. The definition of marriage as an emotional relationship rather than a practical one is a modern one (Shorter, 1975; Stone, 1980). For all societies undergoing the transition from traditional to modern, divorce rates have increased.

High Expectations: The "Ideal Marriage"

People increasingly expect marriage to provide a happy, emotionally supportive relationship, as both the Prologue and Chapter 7 pointed out. This is an essential family function; yet high expectations for intimacy between spouses push the divorce rate upward. Research shows that couples whose

---

3. But churches continue to have an influence on attitudes toward divorce (Glenn and Supancic, 1984). Catholics, Jews, and fundamentalist Christians have traditionally held stricter attitudes against marital dissolution than members of mainstream Protestant denominations, and they are less likely to divorce: Percentages of ever-divorced Protestants, Catholics, and Jews (1972 to 1980) were 24 percent, 17 percent, and 12 percent, respectively (William Petschek, 1986a:3). Between 1962 and 1980, however, the influence of the church on Catholics declined, while the influence of fundamentalist religions on their followers increased (Thornton, 1985).

Percentage Married With Husband Present for Women age 25–44, by Race and Educational Attainment, 1940 and 1979

Educational Status	Married, Husband Present (%)					
	1940			1979		
	White[a]	Black	Difference	White	Black	Difference
Less than high school diploma	75	64	11	74	36	38
High school diploma	73	61	12	81	49	32
At least one year of college	66	54	12	73	49	24

SOURCES:
For 1940, U.S. Bureau of the Census, Sixteenth Census of the United States, 1940: Population; Educational Attainment by Economic Characteristics and Marital Status, Tables 37 and 40; for 1979, unpublished tabulations from the public use tape of the March 1979 Current Population Survey. In Cherlin, 1981:107.
a. Data for whites in 1940 refer to native white population.

expectations are more practical are more satisfied with their marriages than those who expect more loving and expressive relationships (Troll et al., 1979). Indeed, many observers attribute our high divorce rate to the fact that Americans' expectations about marital happiness are *too* high.

In the words of one counselor, "marriages that end in divorce do not differ very much from other marriages" (Framo, 1978:79). Many people, he claims, end their unions not so much because of real misery as because of unrealized (often unrealistic) expectations and general discontent.

The Myth of the Romantic Divorce Along with the myth of the ideal relationship emerged what some observers have called the "myth of romantic divorce," in which divorcing couples "expect less stress and conflict, the joys of greater freedom, and the delights of self-discovery" (Hetherington et al.,

1977:46). During the 1960s and 1970s people emphasized divorce as "creative" (Krantzler, 1975) and a fairly predictable "rite of passage" as individuals changed over time (Sheehy, 1974). More recently, the emphasis has been on "living through" divorce (e.g., Rice and Rice, 1986). One reason some authorities give for the current leveling off of divorce rates is that stories of the expense, bitterness, and depression that often accompany divorce may be deterring some couples from parting.

The Changed Nature of Marriage Itself

To say that there are *no* societal constraints against divorce any more is probably an overstatement; nevertheless, as we have seen, they have weakened.

■ "What's wrong?" "Nothing." Even if this couple were willing or able to discuss what's wrong between them, such talk might not save their marriage. They have somehow traveled beyond moving forward together and may formally declare their estrangement by getting divorced.

A related issue is the changed nature of marriage itself. In the Prologue we argued that, due largely to our high divorce rate, marriage has been redefined as a nonpermanent—or, at best, a "semi-," "maybe," or "hopefully" permanent—relationship. In Chapters 6, 7, and 8 we note that marriage was originally perceived as a social institution for the practical purposes of economic support and responsible child rearing. But we have come to equate marriage with ongoing love, with "relationship." Emphasis on the relationship itself over the institutional benefits of marriage results in its being defined as not necessarily permanent. As Frederick Engels, a colleague of Karl Marx and an early family theorist, noted near the turn of the century, "If only the marriage based on love is moral, then also only the marriage in which love continues." Engels went on to argue—as have counselors and others over the last two decades—that "if affection definitely comes to an end or is supplanted by a new passionate love, separation is a benefit for both partners as well as for society" (Engels, 1942:73).

Self-Fulfilling Prophecy Defining marriage as semi-permanent becomes a self-fulfilling prophecy. Increasingly, spouses enter the union with reservations, making "no definitive gift" of themselves. But, "just as the person makes no definitive gift of himself, he has definitive title to nothing" (Durkheim, 1951:271). One result is that partners are encouraged to behave as if their marriage could end. In such a situation it is more than likely that it will.

Marital Conversation—More Struggle and Less Chitchat Besides being redefined as nonpermanent, marriage has changed in another way. No longer are the rules or normative role prescriptions for wives, husbands, or children taken for granted. Consequently, marriage entails continuous negotiation and renegotiation among members about trivial matters as well as important ones. When family roles were culturally agreed on, members were likely to "share the indifferent 'intimacies' of the day" (Simmel, 1950:127), to engage in relatively inconsequential conversation about events outside the family. Today, however, as family roles are less precisely defined, "marital conversation is more struggle and less chitchat.... The conversation turns inward, to the question of defining the makeup of the family,... [to the] forging and fighting for identities" (Wiley, 1985:23, 27). One result is that increasingly, marriage and family living feels like work, and living alone looks restful by comparison.

Shifts in these areas—the economic practicality of marriage, the morality of divorce, and expectations for marital happiness—have all had the effect of expanding the alternatives to marriage. The personal decision to divorce or not to divorce involves a process of balancing those alternatives against the practical and emotional satisfactions of one's present union. Case Study 16•1, "One Person's Decision to Divorce," gives an idea of what the process, discussed in the next section, can be like.

CHOOSING TO DIVORCE: WEIGHING THE ALTERNATIVES

One assumption behind the relative love and need theory, discussed in Chapter 10, is that spouses continually compare the benefits of their union with the projected consequences of not being married. As divorce becomes a more realistic option, this same weighing of alternatives takes place

(Lenthall, 1977; Levinger, 1965; Albrecht and Kunz, 1980; Udry, 1981). Unhappily married couples who eventually decide to divorce relate many marital complaints that weigh in this decision-making process.

Some Common Complaints

Table 16•1 lists the findings of a study in which divorced persons were asked what factors contributed to their divorce. If infidelity can be taken to indicate outside emotional investment of some sort, then the first three items have to do with the emotional quality of the marital relationship. Counselors suggest that common problems—with money, sex, and in-laws—are really arenas for acting out deeper conflicts, such as who will be the more powerful partner. Such problems often become routine, as we saw in Chapter 8, resulting in devitalized or conflict-habituated marriages. Many spouses choose to continue in such relationships. One of the first questions married people ask themselves is whether they would be happier if they were to divorce.

"Would I Be Happier?"

This is not an easy question to answer. Deciding whether one would be happier after divorce requires one to hypothesize about future alternatives. Some people may prefer to stay single after divorce, but many partners probably weigh their chances for a remarriage. According to an important national survey, divorced and separated individuals have lower levels of life satisfaction and a more negative general mood than married persons. Divorced or separated women report greater feelings of stress than either married or never married women (Campbell et al., 1976; Verbrugge, 1979). Divorced persons also have poorer physical health than married persons (Lynch, 1977), are more often depressed (Vega et al., 1984; Menaghan and Lieberman, 1986), and more inclined to suicide (Wasserman, 1984). Up to five years following a divorce, individuals report their lives as significantly less interesting than do marrieds and as more lonely, emptier, and discouraging. They indicate less happiness with life in general (Nock, 1981). Marriage can and often does provide emotional support, sexual gratification, companionship, and economic and

CASE STUDY
16·1

ONE PERSON'S
DECISION TO
DIVORCE

The narrator is a 30-year-old woman interviewed during the process of getting a divorce.

My husband and I met about eleven years ago. Joe managed a swimming pool, and I was a lifeguard. I was 19, and he was 23. It was love at first sight. We dated for about a year and were married August 18, 1968. I taught for almost three years and [then] . . . we had our first child, Stacey. [About two years later] . . . we had our second, Todd. I started substitute teaching once or twice a week after Todd was born. In the fall of 1977, I took a class toward getting my real estate license. I went to work selling real estate in January 1978. My husband and I had separated the previous December, and I filed for divorce in March 1978.

For me, deciding on separation and then divorce was not an overnight process. My husband and I had a seemingly idyllic marriage for about five years. We were very compatible. It is hard to pinpoint one thing as causing the deterioration of our marriage. I guess the popular statement that "we just grew apart" would apply. But I think that my growing and changing had more to do with it than anything else. I loved Joe, but in a very different way than when we were first married. It was definitely not a romantic love. . . .

I hold myself responsible for our breakdown in communication. I felt that if I was honest in my feelings, or rather my lack of feelings, he would be crushed and feel totally rejected. What could be worse than telling a person who loves you very much that your feelings have changed? . . .

So that was my dilemma: Be honest and make at least three other persons very unhappy or keep it to yourself and ride it out. On the surface we had a good marriage. We enjoyed doing things together and with the children. Joe

practical benefits. But unhappy marriages do not provide all (or in some cases, any) of these benefits. Compared with unhappily married people, divorced individuals display generally better physical and emotional health and higher morale (Renne, 1971).

Counselors advise that in many cases partners might be happier trying to improve their relationship than divorcing. They warn that frequently one's motive for divorce is really to solve an *individual* problem—one that stems from a period of transition, perhaps, or some personal inadequacies (Lager, 1977; Framo, 1978). If this is true, blaming one's partner and deciding to divorce will not be a solution unless personal growth also occurs. One

must decide whether divorce represents a healthy step away from an unhappy relationship that cannot be satisfactorily improved or is "an illusory means of solving an internal problem" (Framo, 1978:79). Going to a marriage counselor can help partners become more aware of the consequences of divorce so that they can make this decision more knowledgeably.

Considering the Consequences

Two subjects are often of special concern when the consequences of divorce are considered: how the

was a good friend and I cared for him, but I wasn't very happy either.

I finally decided that life is too short and it was his happiness or mine, and I asked for the separation. Again I was not being totally honest, because I told him I just needed some space. I was fairly sure we would never get back together. . . .

I am still trying to come to terms with my guilt. I know now that I made the right decision. But when I am really down and the problems seem to far outweigh the advantages, I have felt that I was only getting what I was due. It is pretty tough to feel otherwise when you are the only one who wants the divorce. . . .

I definitely still feel compassion for my husband, but it is very difficult to be friendly without him misunderstanding. I think some of this is because we have not yet gone to court finally. But the few times we have done something together with the kids, it has ended up the same way. At the end of the outing, Joe wants to be physically close to me. Then we're right back where we started with me not wanting that but being afraid to say anything because I know how it will hurt him. I am learning to avoid these situations. . . .

The toughest part for me has been knowing I made the right decision for myself but seeing the extreme pain the separation and divorce are causing my husband.

■ Why did this woman divorce her husband? Does it have anything to do with her expectations of love and marriage? Was the divorce a good decision for her? For the other members of the family? On what values did this woman base her decision? What values might she have had thirty years ago?

---

divorce will affect the children, and what the financial consequences will be.

The Effect on the Children   Estimates are that over 60 percent of all children will spend some time in a single-parent family as a consequence of marital disruption (Hofferth, 1983). As we noted earlier in this chapter, rates are much higher for black children.

How do separation and divorce affect children? Children's self-concepts are affected not so much by family structure as by the quality of familial relationships. Living in an intact family characterized by unresolved tension and alienating conflict causes greater emotional stress and lower self-esteem in children than living in a supportive single-parent family (Ross and Sawhill, 1975; Bane, 1976; Hess and Camara, 1979).

This is not to say that children do not suffer intensely when their parents divorce (which can be true for adult children of divorcing parents as well as for younger children [Garland, 1986]). They experience the loss of their identity as a member of an intact family, along with the loss of daily interaction with one of their parents. At school they may suffer from the cultural stigma of being from a "broken home," although this is lessening, and schools are instituting programs to help children cope with their parents' divorce (Sherman, 1985; Leerhsen, 1985b). Children whose parents have

TABLE 16·1 Major Reasons Given for Failure of First Marriage (490 respondents)

Reason	Number of Times Listed First	Reason	Total Number of Times Listed
Infidelity	168	Infidelity	255
No longer loved each other	103	No longer loved each other	188
Emotional problems	5?	Emotional problems	185
Financial problems	30	Financial problems	135
Physical abuse	29	Sexual problems	115
Alcohol	25	Problems with in-laws	81
Sexual problems	22	Neglect of children	74
Problems with in-laws	16	Physical abuse	72
Neglect of children	11	Alcohol	47
Communication problems	10	Job conflicts	20
Married too young	9	Other	19
Job conflicts	7	Communication problems	18
Other	7	Married too young	14

SOURCE: Albrecht, 1979:862.

divorced will more than likely have noticeably less money to live on, and the chances are fairly good that they will suffer economic deprivation.[4]

In addition, the experience is psychologically stressful. During and after divorce, children typically feel guilty, depressed, and anxious (Wallerstein and Kelly, 1980; Hetherington, 1973). Research has also shown that girls raised without a father may begin premarital sexual activity earlier (Kinnaird and Gerrard, 1986) and, more generally, have difficulty relating to men.[5]

Household disorder usually peaks about one year after divorce (Hetherington et al., 1977); after that, long-term effects depend on the family's adjustment, and there is no evidence that divorce necessarily makes children unhappy or unhealthy (Nock, 1982; Nelson, 1982; Ambert, 1984). One study interviewed all the members of fifty-eight divorced families over a five-year period (Wallerstein and Kelly, 1980). It found that although emotional adjustment varied, many of the 101 children had come through the experience fairly well. As Figure 16·4 shows, 63 percent were either in excellent or reasonably good psychological health (in this latter group, though, Judith Wallerstein and Joan Kelly noted that there were "islands of unhappiness and diminished self-esteem or anger" that still "hampered the full potential of their development"). Another 37 percent were not coping well, with anger playing a significant part in the emotional life of 23 percent. (In Figures 16·5 and 16·6 children's drawings suggest the ways the children have discovered to accommodate their parents' divorce.)

---

4. Because divorce settlements seldom include arrangements for how parents will pay for children's college education—and because family savings are often eroded by the costs involved with divorcing—financing the high costs of college for children of divorced parents can be especially problematic (Johnson, 1984). Some children of divorced parents who would otherwise have attended college may find that they cannot afford it. Others who would have gone away to college may find themselves attending a local school. College students with divorced parents may find themselves trying to negotiate for needed money from one parent, only to be told to "Ask your father, he has lots of money," and then later to "Ask your mother." This situation can be not only financially stressful but also lonely.

5. One study investigated the effects of father absence on adolescent daughters and found that diminished contact with

males caused some girls to be extremely shy and others to be sexually provocative when relating to males. All the girls in the study were without brothers as well as fathers, so their experience with the other sex was even more limited (Hetherington, 1973).

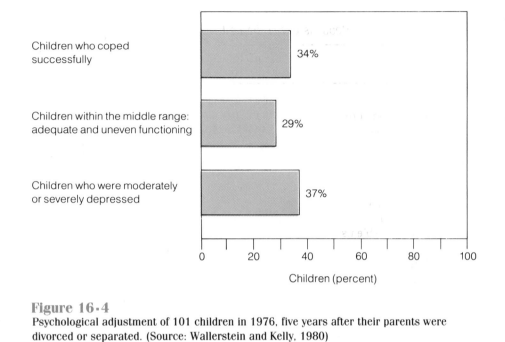

Figure 16·4
Psychological adjustment of 101 children in 1976, five years after their parents were divorced or separated. (Source: Wallerstein and Kelly, 1980)

By 1984 Wallerstein had been able to follow her sample of "children of divorce" for ten years. She found the majority of them to be approaching economic self-sufficiency, enrolled in educational programs, and, in general, to be responsible young adults. At the same time, many of them—especially the young women—were beset with "lingering sorrow" and seemed hesitant about marriage and childbearing for themselves. Said one of Wallerstein's respondents, "How can you expect commitment when anyone can change his mind?" Wallerstein writes:

These young women are attractive, intelligent and, in some instances, highly talented. Yet they are worried, even despairing, fearful of being rejected in their search for a man who would care for them and burdened by an anxiety, which they related directly to their parents' divorce.... A few of them were consumed with the anxiety that relationships could not be trusted from minute to minute [in "Years later," 1984]. ■

Because this study is based on a relatively small sample of children once in counseling, it has been interpreted in different ways. Even so, one conclusion about the effects of divorce on children is clear.

Children are most likely to adjust positively when parents cooperate during and after divorce and the child retains ties with the noncustodial parent (Wallerstein and Kelly, 1980). This is true among college students as well as younger children (Booth, Brinkerhoff, and White, 1984).

Counselors—who are now beginning to see children who have experienced divorce more than once—encourage divorced stepparents to maintain contact with their former stepchildren. According to Dr. Clifford Sager, a psychiatrist and director of family psychiatry at the Jewish Board of Family and Children's Services in New York, the dangers to the emotional health of both the stepchild and the stepparent when a remarriage breaks up have been overlooked—"woefully underestimated." In Sanger's words,

We have given too little thought to what kind of values we are demonstrating when we just walk away from these relationships or cut them off. The child is left with the fear that nobody can be trusted and perhaps he wasn't worth the love anyway. The stepparents must realize that after making all kinds of motions about being a caring love-parent or friend they can't suddenly disappear. They have a moral obligation. It's something

Figure 16·5
This drawing reveals the creative coping of a child whose parents are divorcing. She has figured out a way to include her father as well as keep within the bounds of reality as she knew it. (Source: Isaacs et al., 1986:280)

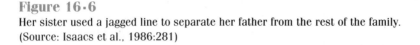

Figure 16·6
Her sister used a jagged line to separate her father from the rest of the family. (Source: Isaacs et al., 1986:281)

the biological parent must understand too [in Brooks, 1984b]. ▪

Going It Alone Sociologist Robert Weiss claims some real benefits to children from single-parent families (while acknowledging, of course, the pain of divorce and the disadvantages as well). If we suspend judgment long enough to look at the two-parent family and the one-parent family objectively, we see that the single-parent family offers the child, particularly the older child and adolescent, an opportunity for real responsibility. Single parents may discuss a wider range of matters with their children. Children share authority in both minor (what to watch on television and when to have dinner) and major (budgeting; where to live) matters. Weiss sees this as neither inherently desirable or undesirable, and defends these single-parent families and the child's independence.

Weiss also points out the painful side of the

emotional closeness between parent and children in a single-parent household. There may be an emotional vacuum when the children leave home, or at least a great deal of sadness. For the same reason, the tight bond of the single-parent family may make it difficult for the single parent to form a bond with a partner, and difficult for the children to adjust to a remarriage, which can seem intrusive (Weiss, 1979).

Financial Concerns   Besides its effects on children, the economic consequences of divorce must be considered. Divorce is costly, both the process itself and its aftermath. In many cases divorce precipitates a financial crisis. "Most Americans today live to the hilt of the breadwinner's income, and frequently beyond it!" notes a lawyer and family law professor. "For young families with little or no financial cushion, the sudden economic toll of divorce can be catastrophic" (in Porter 1976:715). Legal fees are high, and so are expenses incurred in the division of assets.

Even established families with equity in their houses suffer financially by divorcing (Espenshade, 1979). The cost of running the functioning household will not decrease unless the remaining members lower their standard of living. And it will cost about half again that much for one spouse to live separately.

Psychologist E. Mavis Hetherington compared seventy-two middle-class white couples who were still married with the same number of divorced couples in which the woman had custody of the children. She and fellow researchers found that money was a major source of stress and disagreement for both divorced mates (Hetherington et al., 1977). Because they had begun financing two households, their money didn't go as far as before. More divorced than married husbands had increased their work loads in an effort to raise their incomes. This financial strain was worsened in the first year after divorce because many felt immobilized by emotional troubles and were unable to work effectively. Particularly for women, divorce means a lowered standard of living, as is discussed later in this chapter.

Moral and Family Concerns   Another major influence on people's decisions about divorce is cultural proscriptions. While these have lessened in recent years, they still act as a powerful deterrent, especially for highly religious individuals, both black and white (Hampton, 1979). A person's family's feelings also play a role in the decision. It is difficult to be the first one in a family to divorce, and research shows that people more readily choose divorce as a solution to marital problems if their parents have previously done so (Mueller and Pope, 1977; Mott and Moore, 1979).

Even if they have themselves divorced, parents and other family members may have strong feelings against the divorce (Spanier and Castro, 1979). Parents are especially concerned about how the divorce will affect their relationship with their grandchildren (Framo, 1978).

Ambivalence, Vacillation, and Readiness for Divorce

As a couple moves toward divorce, they balance all of the anticipated moral, social, economic, and familial consequences against their satisfactions, securities, and unhappiness. As they weigh the alternatives, they can expect to go through "periods of agonizing, indecision, ambivalence and vacillation" (Framo, 1978:79). "Uncoupling," as sociologist Diane Vaughan (1986) puts it, is a long process during which former partners gradually redefine themselves and each other as single.

Once a person decides he or she wants a divorce, however, it is not always easy to wait: A sense of urgency often accompanies the decision. (As we saw in the Prologue, this feeling of "do it now" is a cultural trait.) Some people believe that failing to act decisively will mean they are denying their own needs.

Marriage counselors advise against making quick decisions, especially if partners are motivated by feelings of hate or anger. As pointed out in Chapter 3, the opposite of love is not hate but indifference. Research indicates that spouses with either strong positive or *negative* feelings toward their mates are more likely to experience high trauma with divorce than those with only friendly or indifferent feelings (Goode, 1956).

Because of this, counselors often suggest that intensely hostile couples who say they want a divorce try a period of **structured separation,** during which they live apart for a limited period, avoid securing lawyers or getting involved in new relationships, and continue in counseling together (Brooks, 1985). After such a separation, partners can usually determine more knowledgeably if they want to divorce.[6]

Readiness for divorce implies the willingness to take responsibility for one's own contribution to the breakup, along with seeing the alternatives to the marriage as somewhat appealing; it also means feeling comfortable with the decision over an extended period of time, without extreme vacillation (Pais and White, 1979:275).

Not all divorced persons wanted or were ready to end their marriage, of course. It may have been their mates' choice. Not surprisingly, research shows that the degree of trauma a divorcing person suffers usually depends on whether that person or the mate wanted the dissolution (Goode, 1956; Pais and White, 1979:275; Pettit and Bloom, 1984). Even for those who actively choose to divorce, however, divorce and its aftermath can be unexpectedly painful, as we shall see in the following section (Weiss, 1975:63–64; Hetherington et al., 1977).

THE SIX STATIONS OF DIVORCE

"One of the reasons it feels so good to be engaged and newly married," writes anthropologist Paul Bohannan, "is the rewarding sensation that out of the whole world, you have been selected. One of the reasons that divorce feels so awful is that you have been de-selected" (Bohannan, 1970b:33).

Bohannan has analyzed the contemporary American divorce experience in terms of six different facets, or "stations." He talks of the emotional, the legal, the economic, the coparental, the community, and the psychic divorce. The degree to which people feel "de-selected" in each of these realms of experience varies from one individual to another (some experiences, such as the coparental, do not characterize every divorce). Yet all are generally typical; we'll look at each.

The Emotional Divorce

Emotional divorce involves withholding bonding emotions and communications from the relation-

ship (Vaughan, 1986), typically replacing these with alienating feelings and behavior. Partners no longer reinforce but rather undermine each other's self-esteem through endless large and small betrayals: responding with blame rather than comfort to a spouse's disastrous day, for instance, or refusing to go to a party given by the spouse's family, friends, or colleagues. As emotional divorce intensifies, betrayals become greater (Framo, 1978:79).

In a failing marriage both spouses feel profoundly disappointed, misunderstood, and rejected. Because the other's very existence and presence is a symbol of failure and rejection, the spouses continually grate on each other (Bohannan, 1970b). The couple may want the marriage to continue for many reasons—continued attachment, fear of being alone, obligations to children, the determination to be faithful to marriage vows—yet they "hurt one another constantly as they communicate their frustration by look, posture, and tone of voice" (Weiss, 1975:24–25).

Divorce Counseling   For this reason, marriage counselors have begun to offer **divorce counseling,** in which partners try to negotiate various conflicts, grievances, and misunderstandings, as in marriage counseling (e.g., Rice and Rice, 1986). The goal of this kind of therapy is "to help a couple disengage from a marriage with a minimum of destructiveness to themselves and their children, and with the personal freedom to form new relationships" (Framo, 1978:77). A major concern of divorce counselors is to counteract the feelings of uncooperativeness and hostility that are particularly characteristic of the legal arrangements that accompany divorce.

The Legal Divorce

A **legal divorce** is the dissolution of the marriage by the state through a court order terminating the marriage. The principal purpose of the legal divorce is to dissolve the marriage bond so that emotionally divorced spouses can remarry.

Some couples are living apart, "separated," while still legally married. They may eventually resume the marriage, go on to divorce, or remain separated indefinitely. There are about half as many separated as divorced persons (Glick and Norton, 1979). Separation as a solution to an unhappy marriage has been declining relative to divorce, as persons

---

6. A danger with structured separation is that friends will define it, not as a "therapy technique" (Brooks, 1985), but as the beginning of the divorce process rather than as a time for decision making. When friends and colleagues know about the breakup, the process often accelerates.

who leave marriages are now more apt to resolve the situation legally.[7]

Two aspects of the legal divorce itself make marital breakup painful. First, "legal processes do not provide for the orderly and socially approved discharge of emotions that are elicited during the emotional divorce" (Bohannan, 1970b:42). Divorce, like death, creates the need to grieve. A widow helps plan and attends her husband's funeral, where she wears "mourning clothes" and weeps if she chooses. But the usual divorce in court is a rational, unceremonial exchange that takes only a few minutes. Many persons are disturbed by this anticlimax, wondering what to do with the rest of the day. And lawyers have been trained to solve problems "rationally" and to deal with clients in a detached, businesslike manner. Most are untrained in family psychology or sociology and many neither understand, care about, nor have time to listen to the anxieties, anger, and vacillations divorcing partners go through. While divorcing spouses might need and want them to, very few divorce attorneys view their role as helping with the grieving process (Bohannan, 1970b:39–40).

A second aspect of the legal divorce that aggravates the misery is the adversary system (Coogler, 1978). Under our judicial system a lawyer advocates his or her client's interest only. Eager to "get the most for my client" and "protect my client's rights," opposing attorneys are not trained to and ethically are not even supposed to *balance* the interests of the parties and strive for the outcome that promises most mutual benefit. Also, the divorcing individuals can feel frustrated by their lack of control over a process in which the lawyers are the principals.

Divorce Mediation **Divorce mediation** is a nonadversarial means of dispute resolution by which the couple, with the assistance of a mediator or mediators (frequently a lawyer-therapist team), negotiate the terms of their settlement of custody, support, property, and visitation issues (e.g., Blades, 1985). The couple work out a settlement best suited to the needs of their family. In the process it is hoped that they learn a pattern of dealing with each other that will enable them to work out future disputes. Data from the Denver Mediation Project, a research and intervention project dealing with divorcing couples, indicate that couples who use divorce mediation have less relitigation, feel more satisfied with the process and the results, and report better relationships with ex-spouses. Even couples who did not reach agreement in mediation show some positive effects from having gone through the process (Pearson and Thoennes, 1982).

The development of divorce mediation under court sponsorship or private auspices is part of a general modification of the legal divorce process occurring in the 1970s and 1980s.

No-Fault Divorce Before the 1970s the fault system predominated in divorce cases. A divorcing party had to prove she or he had "grounds" for divorce, such as the mate's adultery, mental cruelty, or desertion. Just discussing grounds increased hostilities and diminished chances for cooperative negotiation. To prove grounds required a determination of which partner was "guilty" and which partner "innocent." The one judged guilty rarely got custody of the children, and the judgment largely influenced property settlement and alimony awards. To the judge, the spouses, their friends, and the public, the one judged "guilty" was the loser.

Today, with **no-fault divorce,** a partner seeking divorce no longer has to prove grounds. Instead, a marriage is legally "dissolved" because the relationship is "irretrievably broken." No-fault divorce legally abolishes the concept of the "guilty party." But learning to think in terms of no-win/no-lose is difficult even for people in good marriages. One result, some observers suspect, is that divorcing spouses who are bent on publicly determining "guilt" or "innocence" fight the same court battle, but as a child-custody suit instead; we'll address this issue when we discuss coparental divorce. And as we shall see, a second, unanticipated result of no-fault

---

7. We have used the term *separation* to mean an informal separation; however, courts in many, though not all, states also grant **legal separations,** in which the couple remains legally married, but separate residences are sanctioned, and duties of child support and rights of visitation are established. Legal separation permits those who do not wish to break off their marriages formally for reasons such as religion or attachment to regularize their separate living arrangements. Some states view legal separation as an unnecessary halfway measure and have abolished this status.

Another form of legal dissolution of a marriage is **annulment** (civil annulment, not to be confused with the Catholic Church's procedures for dissolving a religious marriage). An annulment legally states that the marriage never existed and is commonly used with eloping underage couples, unconsummated marriages, or marriages in which the legal requirements for a valid marriage are not met—if there is close kinship, for example. Divorce statistics in the United States combine annulments (about 3 percent of divorces recorded) with other divorces (Glick and Norton, 1979).

statutes is that many divorced women are worse off economically.

The Economic Divorce

The third station of divorce is the **economic divorce,** the separation of the couple into distinct economic units, each with its own property, income, control of expenditures, and responsibility for taxes, debts, and so on. Behind the idea of fair property settlement run two contradictory legal assumptions. The first is that a family is an interdependent economic unit based on the basic exchange (see Chapter 6). That is, a man cannot earn the money he earns without the moral assistance and domestic services of his wife. A minority of states have community or joint property laws based directly on this premise. In those states family property legally belongs equally to both partners.

A second assumption is that a wife's work in the home is "nonproductive." If she is not employed outside the home, she does not contribute to the family's acquisition of property. When property is legally divided in divorce, these two legal points of view interplay. The result is that the wife gets some, but not always an equal share, of the family property (Weitzman, 1985).

In most settlements the wife receives from one-third to one-half of the property. But actually splitting household belongings and equipment can be difficult. In fact, an even split of the marital property may not be truly equitable if one partner has stronger earning power and benefits such as pensions and the other does not, and if one has a heavier child-support burden (Weitzman, 1985). Put another way, dividing property may be easy compared with ensuring that both partners and their children will have enough to live comfortably after divorce. Indeed, after divorce the economic status of former husbands often improves, while that of former wives usually deteriorates. Weitzman reports a 42 percent increase in standard of living for ex-husbands, compared with a 73 percent decline for ex-wives with minor children (1985). As we shall see, this situation is partly due to no-fault divorce laws.

The Divorce Revolution Sociologist Lenore Weitzman, in her important book *The Divorce Revolution* (1985), argues that no-fault divorce laws—the first of which was passed in California in 1970—have had unforeseen and unfortunate consequences for families. No-fault divorce laws were intended to mitigate hostilities between divorcing partners. But previously, financial awards—usually to the wife, who retained custody of the children—were subtly linked to "fault." (More often than not, the wife sued for divorce, proving her husband "at fault.")

Without the benefit of fault in a settlement—and with the changing attitudes toward traditional gender roles in which courts consciously sought to treat women and men equally—divorced women found themselves receiving less in terms of property settlements and alimony awards than had women prior to no-fault. While theoretically there is nothing wrong with this, the practical results have been hard on mothers and children. For one thing, the number of family homes being divided equally between ex-spouses has increased. This means either that the two parties maintain joint ownership after the divorce or that the house is sold and the proceeds divided equally. The number of California cases in which there was an explicit order to sell the family home rose from about one in ten in 1968 to about one in three by 1977 (Weitzman, 1985:78). Selling the family home—and adding the stress of moving and the loss of neighborhood, school, and friends to an already painful situation—is particularly difficult for families with minor children.

Another unforeseen consequence of no-fault legislation has been that increasingly, divorced mothers who are not trained to pursue jobs or careers have been thrust into the job market without skills or experience. (Chapter 11 notes the wage differential between women and men.) It should not be surprising, then, that for female-headed households income "drops precipitously" (Weiss, 1984). Sociologist Robert Weiss conducted a panel or longitudinal study of 5,000 households over a five-year period, beginning in 1968. He found that separation and divorce brought about household income reduction for single mothers in every income category, with the greatest reduction where marital income had been the highest. In the upper-income level, separation and divorce reduced income to about one-half of what it had been in the last year of marriage; in the middle-income level, to about two-thirds; and in the lower-income level, to about three-fourths (Weiss, 1984:116–17). Moreover, incomes tended to remain at those reduced levels throughout the time period of the study, that is, for at least five years after the divorce. While this is due largely to women's generally lower wages, it is also a result of changing attitudes about alimony.

Changing Attitudes About Alimony Until recently, the financial plight of divorced women went largely unnoticed: Popular myth had it that ex-wives lived comfortably on high alimony awards.[8] But the fact is that courts award alimony in only about 15 percent of all divorce cases (Weitzman, 1977:294). (Of those women who received alimony in 1979 in California, the median award was just $210 per month.) Alimony awards to wives in short marriages (less than five years) were virtually eliminated under the no-fault law (Weitzman, 1985:169).

The average award for child support is less than half of what it costs to maintain a child at poverty level. In addition, despite legal attempts to change the situation, less than half of eligible women received alimony or child support regularly (Espenshade, 1979). Some judges have even taken the new outlook on alimony as "a mandate to 'give those women what they ask for—if you want to be independent we'll give it to you with a vengeance' " (Weitzman, in Goodman, 1979). Elimination of alimony is probably unrealistic and unfair until job opportunities and career lines of men and women are comparable and women as well as men continue their careers. (Case Study 16•2, "One Woman's Reaction to Divorce," addresses these issues.)

Displaced Homemakers and Entitlement Older, full-time homemakers who suddenly find themselves divorced and without adequate support are called **displaced homemakers.** Typically, they have few or no marketable skills. When they married they expected the conditions and assumptions of the basic exchange to last for life.

The cruel joke is that both these women and their husbands never assumed that she would have to work. Rather, they assumed they had a contract: he would support her and she would care for him and their children. The problem, once again, is that society has changed the rules on her—and those new rules are most evident and most vigorously applied at the point of divorce [Weitzman, 1985:211]. ■

---

8. The word **alimony** comes from the Latin verb that means "to nourish." Historically, alimony rests on the assumption that a husband has the obligation to support his dependent wife even after divorce (Weitzman, 1985:167).

According to some observers, the results of divorce can be devastating for them (Williams, 1977). Although courts today usually award **rehabilitative alimony,** in which the ex-husband pays his ex-wife for a limited period while she goes to school or gets other retraining and finds a job, many displaced homemakers, particularly those in the upper middle class, are unlikely to be able to support themselves in the life-style of their marriage, nor are the older ones likely to remarry.

Opinions about ways to respond to the needs of displaced homemakers vary. The federal government has recognized their plight as a social problem and has funded and established programs to help them interview for jobs, return to school, solve credit problems, and so forth. Other groups argue that these wives and others deserve not alimony, but **entitlement.** Betty Friedan defines entitlement as the equivalent of severance pay for work done at home during the length of a marriage (Williams, 1977:75). An important basis for this argument is that the wife has contributed to her husband's employability through husband care, which can be extensive—as in the two-person single career discussed in Chapter 11. Therefore, she should be paid regularly after divorce for her interest and investment in his (that is, their) continuing earning power (Weitzman, 1977, 1985).

Child-Support Collection Families of women and children would be much better off after divorce, of course, if they received the child support due them. An important example of families acting to influence public policy so as to provide better support for families has been in the area of child support. Responding to grass-roots organizing of women's groups and other citizens' action groups, as well as to the obvious scale of the problem, states and now the federal government have passed legislation designed to facilitate and enforce child-support payments (1) through locator services for nonwelfare as well as welfare clients with benefits due them (nonwelfare clients hitherto had to pursue the matter in court with a private attorney) and (2) through provisions for interception of tax refunds and mandatory wage withholding to channel support payments to the custodial parent.

The Coparental Divorce

About two-thirds of couples who divorce have children. These spouses are involved in coparental

**CASE STUDY
16·2**

**ONE
WOMAN'S
REACTION
TO
DIVORCE**

Marsha gave this interview March 22, 1984. She had just been to an accountant who had prepared a 1983 joint income tax return for her and her ex-husband. Marsha had been divorced for five months at the time of the interview. She was 36 years old, with two children, ages 11 and 8. And she was angry and hurt.

I'm pissed! I'm crying and I'm hurt and I'm tired of all this—but mainly, tonight, I'm pissed. We just went to the accountant! Do you know how much Ben made last year? Do you KNOW how much he made? Twenty-eight thousand dollars! Do you know how much I made? Ten thousand dollars—that's working two jobs. That's working all day full-time at Firemen's Fund and weekends and two or three evenings a week clerking at the shopping center.

And he wants ME to pay for an eleven-dollar softball glove so that Amy can play ball this summer! I can't believe it. I can't believe it. He gives me six hundred dollars a month now, and that—do you know what that does?—that covers the house payment. Do you know that I paid out $594 to baby-sitters last year so I could go to work on days when they were off school and during the summer? I paid that out of my ten thousand dollars! What DOES he do with his money?

"Oh, Mom, we have to take good clothes Saturday when we go to see dad," Amy says.

"Oh really," I say.

"We're going out for lunch and then to the art museum."

So yesterday I called CETA [a government-funded job training program for low-income people]. I said, "Do you have anything I can be trained to do that pays?"

She said, "Well, almost all our funding's been cut; we hardly have anything anymore. We do do some clerical training though. What kind of job do you have now?"

I said clerical. She said, "Well, then why would you want to quit? Keep your job."

I said, "At $4.96 an hour!" She said that didn't sound so awful. Can you believe this? We used to—I mean I'm not saying I have to be rich or anything—but we used to have it comfortable. We paid our bills and took a vacation, things like that. Do you know I borrowed money from my credit union to

divorce, and a basic issue for them is determining which parent will take **custody,** or assume primary responsibility for making decisions about the children's upbringing and general welfare.[9]

---

9. Legal issues surrounding custody, visitation rights, and, sometimes, child-support payments in *re*divorces (i.e., divorcing stepfamilies) are just now beginning to emerge (Dullea, 1987a).

The **coparental divorce** is usually an extension of the basic exchange: Divorced fathers take legal responsibility for financial support, while divorced mothers continue the physical, day-to-day care of their children. With worsening economic prospects and changing attitudes and gender roles, however, a few mothers are voluntarily relinquishing custody (Rosenblum, 1984; Doudna, 1982) and more fathers are fighting for custody. Today, a small

pay my heat bill this winter? I still owe on that. So we probably won't run the air conditioner. Oh, but that's no big deal to him; what could he care?

She said, the CETA lady said, she said, "Well, how much do you make a year then?" I said, "Ninety-four hundred dollars." She said, "With only two dependents?" I said, "Yes." She said, "Well, that's too much; we couldn't help you anyway. That's too much!"

I said, "Well, what about a grant to go to school or something?" She said I'd have to contact the schools directly. But, you know, even if I went to four years of college, I couldn't ever have his earning capacity! And you know what the worst part is, what the meanest, dirtiest trick of all this is? He didn't want me to work when we were married!

I mean I met him when we were both working at the same place. When we got married and I got pregnant, he—well, we both—just assumed that I'd quit. But when the kids got a little older, I wanted to go back. "No," he said.

So he kept working and getting raises, and I kept the house and the budget, and I took care of the kids, and I sewed their clothes instead of buying them fancy, expensive ones—and now he's making $28,000 and the three of us are living on $10,000 plus the house payments. Even if you add up the $600 a month he gives me, we're living on $17,200 a year. That's the three of us and I'm working two jobs. And if you subtract the $600 a month from his salary, then he's living—*just he* is living—on $20,800. All alone, one job, no kids day in and day out, no baby-sitter expenses. I can't believe this!

But maybe, maybe the worst part is that I never wanted this divorce in the first place. You know that. I've told you that before. I looked at that $28,000 and at my $10,000 added on to it—I looked at the $38,000 that we made together, and I said, "Do you know what we could have done together with that kind of money?" Does he know what he's doing to us, to his children? Does he know?

■ How does Marsha's story illustrate anthropologist Paul Bohannan's concept of economic divorce? Do you think divorce counseling would have any impact on this woman's situation or on her feelings? Why or why not? How might this woman's husband feel in this situation? Does the fact that two children are involved have any impact on this woman's situation or feelings? How might Marsha's story help illustrate the concept of "his" and "her" divorce, discussed later in this chapter?

but growing number of fathers are awarded both custody and child support by ex-wives.

Under current laws a father and a mother who want to retain custody theoretically have equal chances, and judges try to assess the relationship between each parent and the child. However, because mothers are typically the ones who have physically cared for the child, and because of traditional attitudes about gender-appropriate behav- ior, some courts give preference to mothers (Robinson and Barret, 1986:87).

This is less often the case than is commonly thought, however. While custody is awarded to mothers in about 90 percent of cases, most often this has been agreed upon by the couple or the mother has custody by default. One study of 1977 cases found that two-thirds of fathers who requested sole physical custody received it. The mother had often agreed to this arrangement; nevertheless, in a third of the cases where custody was contested, the father was awarded custody (Weitzman and Dixon, 1979). In fact, women's advocates have expressed concern that in a supposedly gender-free legal context, fathers will receive priority because they have a greater ability to provide or because the working father who devotes some time to the children is perceived as a better parent than the working mother who does the same (Fisher, 1983; Polikoff, 1982).

Judith Fisher believes that women should not relinquish custody because they feel inadequate in comparison to their successful husbands. At the same time, she strongly supports the freedom of men and women to make choices about custody—including the woman's choice to live apart from her children—without guilt or stigma. She urges

1) the negation of the unflattering stereotypes of noncustody mothers; 2) sensitivity to the demands society places on mothers (as opposed to parents) and to the needs of all family members; 3) supportiveness of the woman's choice when it appears to have been well thought out; and 4) . . . prohibitions against blaming the mother when others (the children, the children's father, the courts) decide that the children should live apart from her [Fisher, 1983:357]. ■

A study comparing custodial mothers, fathers, and joint custody arrangements found no differences (Luepnitz, 1982); all were equally effective. Another study found that children do best in the custody of the same-sex parent (Santrock and Warshak, 1979). Extensive research comparing mother custody and father custody, and also joint custody, has yet to be done; however, the few careful studies and the numerous more anecdotal studies or studies with less satisfactory samples have found nothing to indicate serious problems with either father custody, joint custody, or with the more conventional maternal custody (Rosenthal and Keshet, 1980; Orthner et al., 1976; Mendes, 1976; Gasser and Taylor, 1976; Keshet and Rosenthal, 1978; Roman and Haddad, 1978; Grief, 1979).

The Visiting Parent Almost all the research and discussion to date on visiting parents have been about fathers, but research now suggests that the same findings apply to visiting mothers (Spanier and Castro, 1979:249). Fathers without custody

experience a sense of extreme loss.[10] For a time after the breakup, they feel depressed, sad, angry, lonely, and anxious about their children. New evidence suggests this can also be true for stepfathers and men who have cohabited with women and their children (Brooks, 1984b; Dullea, 1987a). They may have severe and frequent changes of mood (Keshet and Rosenthal, 1978). Hetherington's study, mentioned above, found that even two years after divorce, some fathers said they could not cope with seeing their children only occasionally. Ironically, one way fathers coped with this was to visit their children less often as time went by (Hetherington et al., 1977).

But just two months after the divorce, one-fourth of the fathers were seeing their children more than they had when they were married, for a variety of reasons:

a deep attachment to the child or the wife, feelings of duty or attempts to assuage guilt, an attempt to maintain a sense of continuity in their lives, or for some, a desire to annoy, compete with, or retaliate against the ex-spouse [Hetherington et al., 1977:45]. ■

These early visits often display what has been called the "Disneyland Dad" syndrome, in which the father indulges his child to make the visit as happy as possible (Hetherington et al., 1977). As time goes by, this phase generally passes. Often fathers become increasingly frustrated with their loss of influence over the children's upbringing, and they let themselves drift away from their children. Visiting, along with support payments, often becomes episodic.

Research indicates that fathers' decreased visiting can hurt children. A study of the self-esteem in boys age 9–14 whose parents had divorced showed considerably higher self-esteem among boys who saw their visiting parent at least once a month than among boys who saw the second parent less often (Lowenstein and Koopman, 1978). Wallerstein and Kelly's longitudinal study of children's adjustment to divorce found that "this sense of a continuing, close relationship [to the absent parent] was critical to the good adjustment of both boys and girls" (Wallerstein and Kelly, 1980:71).

Fighting Through the Children Another highly important factor in children's adjustment to divorce

---

10. So do grandparents, who in some states have organized to lobby for legal visitation rights ("Grandparents seek," 1985).

■ A common scenario of divorced parents: When the mother has custody of the children, the visiting father becomes the parent as pal. Part of the problem with this "Disneyland Dad" syndrome is that it sets up a "Martyred Mom" who hasn't the time or money to spare for fun and games with her children. We also see here a mutual enjoyment that is important to maintain. In time, visitation usually moves to a domestic setting and includes routine activities as well as special outings.

is the parents' relationship with each other. A divorced mother's negative comments about her ex-husband, for instance, can encourage the daughter to develop adverse feelings about her father and men in general (Hetherington, 1973).

Visitation is one frequent arena of parental disputes: The child isn't ready to go when visitation time starts or the visiting parent brings the child home late, for instance. Some mothers may try to stop visitation rights of fathers who let support payments lag. Visitation, like money and in-laws, can be an arena in which ex-spouses continue the basic conflicts they experienced before the divorce. Often the contest is one of values.

The good ex-husband/father feels, "My son is being brought up by his mother so that he is not my son." A divorced man almost always feels that his boy is being made into a different kind of man from what he himself is.... The good ex-wife/mother may be tempted to refuse the ex-husband his visitation rights because, from her point of view, "He is bad for the children" [Bohannan, 1970b:47–48]. ■

Counselors urge ex-spouses to work out irritations and conflict directly with each other rather than through their children. Parents need to communicate as openly as possible about their divorce *without* speaking negatively about the ex-mate. Counselors encourage the attitude "We had our problems, but that doesn't mean he (or she) is bad or that I'm bad." Some jurisdictions sponsor "visitation support groups," in which parents and stepparents discuss their problems with others, or provide court-supported conciliation of visitation disputes.

When parents refuse to assume a cooperative stance, their fighting through the children can become extreme, as in the practice of **child snatching:** kidnapping one's children from the other parent. Child snatching is frightening and confusing for the child and can even be physically dangerous. Yet even after custody has been determined by the courts, the snatching of a child by a biological parent is not legally considered kidnapping; in most states it has been a misdemeanor called *custodial interference.* Now, however, due to the passage of the federal **uniform child custody acts,** states recognize out-of-state custody decrees and do more to find and extradite offenders (Van Gelder, 1978:52). Child snatching is an extreme act, but it points up the frustration involved in arrangements regarding sole custody and visiting parents. An alternative is joint custody, which will be discussed at the end of this chapter.

Experts agree that adjusting to divorce is easier for children *and* parents when former spouses cooperate. Because they do not cooperate, however, "the most enduring pain of divorce is likely to come from coparental divorce" (Bohannan, 1970b:45). Significant but more short-lived pain accompanies the community divorce.

The Community Divorce

Important changes in one's life-style almost invariably mean changes in one's community of friends. When they marry, people usually replace their single friends with "couple friends," and couples also change communities when they divorce. Separating from one's former community of friends and in-laws is part of the pain of divorce.

Divorced persons often feel uncomfortable with their friends who are still married, like "fifth wheels" because activities are done in pairs (Lopata, 1973). One reason for discomfort is that their friends' divorce may challenge a couple to take another look at their own marriage, an experience that can cause a couple to feel anxious and uncomfortable with the divorced friend (Miller, 1970). Also, couple friends may be reluctant to become involved in a conflict over allegiances (Weiss, 1975).

In addition, friends of divorcing partners often experience their own sense of loss and grief: Their friendship circle will necessarily change. Friends of divorcing couples react to their own anxieties, fears, and sense of loss in different ways: One is a mutual withdrawal, during which the divorced person feels heightened loneliness and a sense of being "left" or "replaceable" (Anspach, 1976; Spicer and Hampe, 1975).

Finally, the scheduling of time is often a factor in the shift in friendship patterns. This is especially true of same-sex friendships, which may wane because the time available to get together no longer dovetails. For example, a newly divorced mother may have Sunday afternoons free while her children are visiting their father, but for her married friend, Sundays may be an important family time.

Like many newly married persons, those who are newly divorced have to find new communities to replace old friendships that are no longer satisfying. The initiative for change may in fact come not only from rejection or awkwardness in old friendships but from the divorced person's finding or wanting to find friends who share with him or her the new concerns and emotions of the divorce experience. Priority may also go to new relationships with persons of the opposite sex; for the majority of divorced and widowed persons, building a new community involves dating again.

Dating Again About 75 percent of separated people begin dating in the first year after their separation. Over 90 percent begin before the end of their second year (Hunt, 1966:110). While at first they may feel too emotionally distraught to risk new associations, gradually they see a date as one reassurance of their self-worth and as an antidote to loneliness (Weiss, 1975:280). One study found that separated persons who dated or cohabited had fewer adjustment problems than those who did not (Spanier and Castro, 1979:251). On the other hand, beginning to date early after divorce may disrupt relationships with one's children (Rodgers and Conrad, 1986).

Even though children may constrain their activities, the majority of those who are "single again" and dating engage in postmarital sex (Gebhard, 1970; Rosenthal and Keshet, 1978; Greenberg, 1979). In one sample 82 percent of divorced women and 43 percent of widows had postmarital coitus, usually during the first year after their marriage ended (Gebhard, 1970). The lower figure for widows reflects the double standard of aging, since widows as a group are older than divorcees. Another reason for the lower percentage among widows may be that they more often idealize their former husbands and take no interest in new sexual relationships (Gebhard, 1970:87).

Through the first year of dating, divorced persons tend to go out with several or many different people and be wary of commitment (Rosenthal and Keshet, 1978; Weiss, 1975). But sometimes during about the second year, dating takes on a new meaning; persons grow more desirous of developing one intimate relationship. "Increasingly a date will become for them an opportunity to see if something permanent might work out" (Weiss, 1975:293). Before this can take place, however, they must experience the sixth, and final, stage of divorce—the "psychic divorce."

The Psychic Divorce

Psychic divorce refers to the regaining of psychological autonomy through emotional separation from the personality and influence of the former spouse. In the process one learns to feel whole and complete again and to have faith in one's ability to cope with the world. In psychic divorce one must distance oneself from the still-loved aspects of the spouse, from the hated aspects, and "from the baleful presence that led to depression and loss of self-esteem" (Bohannan, 1970b:53).

Not all—and perhaps not even most—divorced persons fully succeed at psychic divorce. But counselors point out that this stage is a necessary prerequisite to a satisfying remarriage. Box 16·3, "Healing: Fifteen Suggestions," provides some guidelines.

To be successful, a psychic divorce requires a period of mourning. Like the death of a spouse, divorce means the end of a relationship. The experience of loss is as real as that suffered by people who are widowed. Just as a gradual process of emotional estrangement starts long before the actual legal event of divorce, the partners' emotional involvement often continues long after. This "persistence of attachment" (Weiss, 1975) is real for both spouses and should be understood and addressed.

There are at least three stages in the mourning process. The first, which typically occurs before the legal divorce, is shock and denial. Sometimes, a person's inability to accept the divorce manifests itself in physical illnesses, accidents, or even suicide attempts (Framo, 1978). Eventually, however, the frustration of emotional divorce leads partners to face facts. They may say to each other, "We can't go on like this."

A second stage, characterized by anger and depression, follows this realization. These feelings often alternate, so that recently divorced persons feel confused. (Whether, and if so, how, these feelings differ for people who experience a second [or a third] divorce will be a subject for future research.) Often their feelings resemble those of one ex-wife who asked a counselor, "How come I miss so terribly someone I couldn't stand?" (Framo, 1978:102). As we have seen, many former partners vent their anger in the coparental arena.

In the third stage ex-mates take responsibility for their own part in the demise of the relationship, forgive themselves and the mate, and proceed with their lives: The psychic divorce is then complete. As long as one views the ex-mate as an enemy or object of ongoing anger, however, the psychic divorce has not been accomplished, because bitterness and hate are emotions of a continuing relationship (Framo, 1978:102).

Unfortunately, our society does little to ease the healing process after divorce. Just as sexually segregated roles lead to husbands' and wives' marriages, they lead to husbands' and wives' divorces.

HIS AND HER DIVORCE

We have seen that gender roles diminish communication and understanding between women and men. Perhaps nowhere is the lack of understanding more evident than in the debate over which partner—the ex-wife or the ex-husband—is the victim of divorce. Both are victims. The first year after divorce is especially stressful for both ex-mates. Divorce wields a blow to each one's self-esteem. Both feel they have failed as spouses and, if there are children, as parents. They question their ability to get along well in a remarriage. Yet each has particular difficulties that are related to societal expectations.

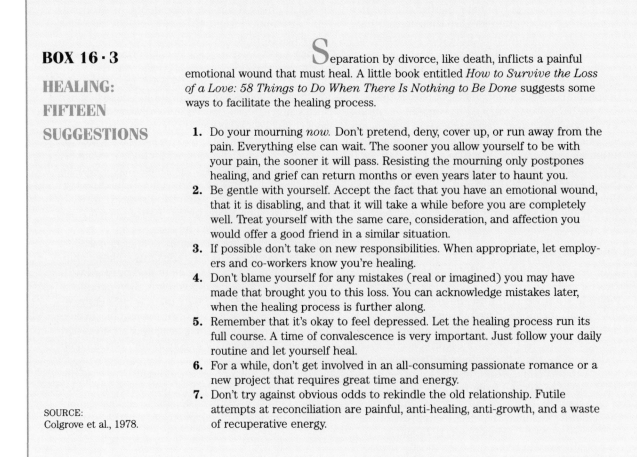

BOX 16 · 3

**HEALING:
FIFTEEN
SUGGESTIONS**

Separation by divorce, like death, inflicts a painful emotional wound that must heal. A little book entitled *How to Survive the Loss of a Love: 58 Things to Do When There Is Nothing to Be Done* suggests some ways to facilitate the healing process.

1. Do your mourning *now*. Don't pretend, deny, cover up, or run away from the pain. Everything else can wait. The sooner you allow yourself to be with your pain, the sooner it will pass. Resisting the mourning only postpones healing, and grief can return months or even years later to haunt you.
2. Be gentle with yourself. Accept the fact that you have an emotional wound, that it is disabling, and that it will take a while before you are completely well. Treat yourself with the same care, consideration, and affection you would offer a good friend in a similar situation.
3. If possible don't take on new responsibilities. When appropriate, let employers and co-workers know you're healing.
4. Don't blame yourself for any mistakes (real or imagined) you may have made that brought you to this loss. You can acknowledge mistakes later, when the healing process is further along.
5. Remember that it's okay to feel depressed. Let the healing process run its full course. A time of convalescence is very important. Just follow your daily routine and let yourself heal.
6. For a while, don't get involved in an all-consuming passionate romance or a new project that requires great time and energy.
7. Don't try against obvious odds to rekindle the old relationship. Futile attempts at reconciliation are painful, anti-healing, anti-growth, and a waste of recuperative energy.

SOURCE:
Colgrove et al., 1978.

Her Divorce

Ex-wives often feel helpless and physically unattractive. Women who were married longer, particularly those oriented to traditional gender roles, feel like "nobodies," having lost the identity associated with their husband's status (Hetherington et al., 1977:45–46). Getting back on their feet is particularly difficult for women in this group.

Divorced mothers who retain sole custody of their children also experience trouble. They often undergo severe overload as they attempt to provide not only for their financial self-support but also for the day-to-day care of their children (Johnson, 1983). Their difficulties are aggravated by discrimination in hiring, promotion, and salaries, by

the high cost of child care, and often by their less extensive work experience and training (Pais and White, 1979:277). All in all, custodial mothers frequently feel very much alone as they struggle with money, scheduling, and discipline problems, often passing up chances to meet people and, if they want to, even to marry again. Meanwhile, the ex-husband may seem to be reaping all the benefits with no unpleasant consequences. How accurate is this picture of the husband's divorce?

His Divorce

In fact, men take divorce much harder than many people—particularly their ex-wives—may think. "For a while, the man is totally devastated," explains

8. If you find photographs and mementos helpful to the mourning process, use them. If you find they bind you to a dead past, get rid of them. Put them in the attic, sell them, give them away, or throw them out.

9. Remember that it's okay to feel anger toward God, society, or the person who left you (even if through death). But it is *not* okay or good for you to hate yourself or to act on your anger in a destructive way. Let the anger out safely: hit a pillow, kick the bed, sob, scream. Practice screaming as loudly as you can. A car with the windows up makes a great scream chamber.

10. Use addictive prescription drugs like Valium wisely. Take them only if pre-scribed by your personal physician and only for a short period of time. *Don't* take them to mask your grief because your friends have grown tired of it.

11. Watch your nutrition. Take vitamins, eat good foods, and try to get plenty of rest.

12. Don't overindulge in alcohol, marijuana or other recreational chemicals, or cigarettes.

13. Pamper yourself a little. Get a manicure, take a trip, bask in the sun, sleep late, see a good movie, visit a museum, listen to music, take a long bath instead of a quick shower. As healing progresses, remember that it's okay *not* to feel depressed.

14. You might find keeping a journal or diary helpful. This way you can see your progress as you read past entries.

15. Heal at your own pace. The sadness comes and goes—though it comes less frequently and for shorter lengths of time as healing proceeds.

a family counselor. "He realizes how much his wife and children meant, he misses that feeling of walking into the house and saying, 'This is mine,' even if there has been tension and bitterness" (in *McCalls*, Nov. 1979, p. 85). Ex-husbands' loneliness is aggravated by the traditional male gender role, which discourages them from sharing their pain with other men. So they become more socially active to compensate for their feelings of low self-esteem, loss, and loneliness. As one said,

I'll do anything to avoid going home. Go to lousy movies, sit in a bar all night although I don't like to drink much, or talk to dull strangers. Anything to avoid the solitude. I used to work at home almost every night and come out to have a cup of coffee with my wife or read to the kids before

they went to bed [in Hetherington et al., 1977:45]. ■

Despite their increased activities, which custodial wives may envy, ex-husbands are often disappointed with their new freedom. Initially, they may be pleased with the sexual freedom of being single, but recreational relationships quickly seem empty and superficial. Also, newly divorced husbands may experience sexual problems that reflect a more general anxiety. Partly as a result, the "hip, Honda, and hirsute syndrome" of many new ex-husbands abates in the second year after divorce (Hetherington et al., 1977:45–46).

But they go on missing their families and children. At least one social worker maintains that divorced, noncustodial fathers have more radical readjustment to make in their life-styles than do custodial mothers. In return for the responsibilities and loss of freedom associated with single parenthood, custodial mothers escape much of the loneliness the loss of family status might otherwise offer and are somewhat rewarded by social approval for rearing their children. Noncustodial fathers, meanwhile, often retain the financial burden and obligations of fatherhood while experiencing few of its joys. Whether it takes place in the children's home, the father's residence, or at some neutral spot, visitation is typically awkward and superficial (Messinger, 1976:196). And the man may worry that if his ex-wife remarries, he will lose even more influence over his children's upbringing.

Many ex-husbands feel shut out and lost because women control access to emotional nurturance and also have a stronger influence on children. Yet for most women, men still hold the keys to economic security, and ex-wives suffer financially more than do ex-husbands. This interrelationship also applies to women's and men's separate experiences in divorce. The fact is that both men's and women's grievances could be alleviated by eliminating the economic discrimination toward women and the gender-role expectations that create husbands' and wives' divorces.

Joint Custody: Narrowing the Gap Between His and Her Divorce

As we have seen throughout this chapter, much of the anguish associated with divorce is related to the coparental station. This experience, say a growing number of separated parents and social scientists, is often more painful than it needs to be. Where parents live close to each other and where both are committed to the arrangement, joint custody or shared living arrangements, or both, can bring the experiences of both parents closer together, providing advantages to each. In **joint custody,** both divorced parents continue to take equal responsibility for important decisions regarding the child's general upbringing.

Miriam Galper, author of *Co-Parenting,* writes from her own four-year experience in sharing her children with her ex-husband and from interviews with other divorced families who are doing the same. She concludes that while there is a lack of understanding and support in the schools for shared custody arrangements, they can work. This is espe-

cially true when a small number of children are involved; when both parents are deeply committed to child rearing and get along well enough to work out details along the way; and when both parents are equally employable. There is some flexibility on this last point, but most joint custody arrangements involve fairly equal sharing of financial responsibility for the children, with each parent supporting himself and herself (Galper, 1978).

There are several advantages to arrangements for joint custody. (Table 16•2 lists advantages and disadvantages of joint custody from a father's perspective.) Shared custody gives children the chance for a more realistic and normal relationship with each parent. Furthermore, both parents can feel they have the opportunity to pass their own beliefs and values on to their children (Woolley, 1978:6–7). In addition, neither parent is overloaded with sole custodial responsibility and its concomitant loss of personal freedom. One study of 128 divorced or separated men concluded that shared custody was "the ideal arrangement" for parents and children. Fathers who shared custody reported that it enriched their lives and made them "more sensitive, expressive, flexible, and proud of their abilities as a parent," and they were even more comfortable with their children than were men with sole custody (Keshet and Rosenthal, 1978).

Despite its possibilities, joint custody arrangements remain limited in number and experimental in character ("Joint custody," 1984). Research that would clearly establish the effects of joint custody has not yet been done. The majority of attorneys and judges, along with some child psychiatrists, continue to favor sole custody. One reason is that ex-spouses may be no more able to agree on child-related decisions at this point than they were able to make joint decisions while married. Another reason is today's high rate of geographical mobility. When ex-mates move to separate regions, it would probably be harmful for the children to divide the year between two different schools and communities: The child becomes a six-month "visitor" in both homes (Jenkins, 1977). One alternative here is shared *legal custody*—in which both parents still have the right to participate in important decisions and retain a symbolically important legal authority—with *physical custody* (that is, residential care of the child) going to one parent. Some feminists oppose joint custody because they believe ex-husbands might use it to intervene excessively in the lives of their former wives (Bropy, 1985). Also, mothers, more than fathers, would find it dif-

---

TABLE 16·2 Advantages and Disadvantages of Joint Custody From a Father's Perspective

Advantages	Disadvantages
Fathers can have more influence on the child's growth and development—a benefit for men and children alike.	Children lack a stable and permanent environment, which can affect them emotionally.
Fathers are more involved and experience more self-satisfaction as parents.	Children are prevented from having a relationship with a "psychological parent" as a result of being shifted from one environment to another.
Parents experience less stress than sole-custody parents.	
Parents do not feel as overburdened as sole-custody parents.	Children have difficulty gaining control over and understanding of their lives.
Generally, fathers and mothers report more friendly and cooperative interaction in joint-custody than in visitation arrangements, mostly because the time with children is evenly balanced, and agreement exists on the rules of the system.	Children have trouble forming and maintaining peer relationships.
	Long-term consequences of joint-custody arrangements have not been systematically studied.
Joint custody provides more free social time for each single parent. Relationships with children are stronger and more meaningful for fathers.	
Parental power and decision making are equally divided, so there is less need to use children to barter for more.	

SOURCE: Robinson and Barret, 1986:89.

---

ficult to maintain a family household without child support, which is often not awarded when custody is shared.

Even without official joint custody or shared living arrangements, ex-mates can work to make both parents' relationships with children more realistic. Rather than being just a weekend visitor, the noncustodial parent can arrange visits that encourage routine parent-child interaction. For example, visiting parents might supervise after-school playtimes or homework sessions or take the child to the dentist. In this way children are able to "know that the noncustodial person is a whole person" (Bruch, 1978:26). By creating a practical arrangement that works for both ex-partners, divorced couples can lessen the emotional turmoil of divorce and reduce the differences between fathers' and mothers' experiences.

Summary

Divorce rates have risen sharply in this century, and divorce rates in the United States are now the highest in the world. In the past decade, however, they have begun to level off.

Reasons why more people are divorcing than in the past have to do with changes in society: economic interdependence and legal, moral, and social constraints are lessening; expectations for intimacy are increasing; and expectations for permanence are declining. People's personal decisions to divorce—or to redivorce—involve weighing marital complaints—most often communication problems—against the possible consequences of divorce. Two consequences that receive a great deal of consideration are how the divorce will affect children, if there are any, and whether it will cause serious financial difficulties.

The divorce experience is almost always far more painful than people expect. Bohannan has identified six ways in which divorce affects people. These six stations of divorce are the emotional divorce, the legal divorce, the economic divorce, the coparental divorce, the community divorce, and the psychic divorce. This last stage involves a healing process that individuals must complete before they can fully enter new intimate relationships.

Husbands' and wives' divorce experiences, like husbands' and wives' marriages, are still different. Both the overload that characterizes the wife's divorce and the loneliness that often accompanies the husband's divorce, especially when there are children, can be lessened in some cases by more androgynous settlements. Divorce counseling can help make the experience less painful and can also reduce high legal costs.

Key Terms

structured
   separation *521*
readiness for
   divorce *522*
emotional divorce *522*
divorce counseling *522*
legal divorce *522*
legal separation *523*
annulment *523*
divorce mediation *523*
no-fault divorce *523*

economic divorce *524*
displaced
   homemaker *525*
alimony *525*
entitlement *525*
custody *526*
coparental divorce *526*
child snatching *530*
psychic divorce *531*
joint custody *534*

Study Questions

1. What three factors bind marriages and families together? How have these factors changed and how has the divorce rate been affected?
2. Discuss the relationship of economics to marital stability.
3. Two reasons for the high divorce rate in the United States are the myth of the ideal relationship and the rise of individualistic values. Can we promote these and at the same time support the present institution of marriage?
4. What are the consequences of divorce on children? When is divorce a better alternative for the children than maintaining the marriage? A worse alternative?
5. Describe the six stations of divorce, and speculate on how each station might be made less difficult.
6. How is "his" divorce different from "her" divorce? How are these differences related to societal expectations?
7. Differentiate between *joint custody* and *shared living arrangements*. How can these narrow the gap between "his" and "her" divorces and help lessen the pain of divorce for some couples with children?

Suggested Readings

Cauhape, Elizabeth
1983   *Fresh Starts*. New York: Basic Books.
      Explores the effects of divorce for men and women at midlife, "examining the opportunities for growth as well as the problems that must be solved."
Gardner, Richard
1971   *Boys' and Girls' Book About Divorce*. New York: Bantam.
      A children's book aimed at helping children understand divorce. Child psychologists and other specialists who work with children of divorced parents consider this a valuable book. (For grades five and up.)
Haynes, John
1981   *Divorce Mediation: A Practical Guide for Therapists and Counselors*. New York: Springer.
      One of several manuals on divorce mediation.
Hootman, Marcia, and Patt Perkins
1983   *How to Forgive Your Ex-Husband*. New York: Doubleday.

The central theme is that this is a necessary prelude to "getting on with your life." Good tips, which could work for forgiving ex-wives, too.

Krantzler, Mel

1975 *Creative Divorce: A New Opportunity for Personal Growth.* New York: New American Library.
An optimistic self-help book that has been very influential. It helps divorced people see that some good can come of divorce—whether it was wanted or not.

Luepnitz, Deborah Anna

1982 *Child Custody.* Lexington, Mass.: Heath.
Research study on child custody comparing mother custody, father custody, and joint custody.

Napolitane, Catherine, with Victoria Pellegrino

1977 *Living and Loving After Divorce.* New York: Rawson, Wade.
This down-to-earth guide for women who are divorcing includes specific discussion of such topics as work, children, ex-husbands, lawyers, money, dating, sex, relatives, and living as a single person. It describes eight phases divorced women are likely to live through and is a good guide to understanding the emotional ups and downs of this experience.

Pearson, Jessica, and Nancy Thoennes

1982 "Mediation and divorce: The benefits outweigh the costs." *Family Advocate* 4:26–32.
Careful research study of divorce mediation.

Ricci, Isolina

1980 *Mom's House, Dad's House.* New York: Collier.
Very helpful, sensible advice manual for parents trying to manage the postdivorce family and for children adjusting to two households.

Salk, Lee

1978 *What Every Child Would Like Parents to Know About Divorce.* New York: Harper & Row.
Guidelines for parents in helping their children adjust to divorce. The author is a well-known pediatrician who obtained custody of his children after his recent divorce.

Teyber, Edward

1985 *Helping Your Children Through Divorce: A Compassionate Guide for Parents.* New York: Pocket Books.
Focuses on children's concerns and offers fairly realistic guidelines for parents.

Vaughan, Diane

1986 *Uncoupling: Turning Points in Intimate Relationships.* New York: Oxford University Press.
The sociological, theoretical core of Vaughan's work on this subject can be found in the essay, "Uncoupling: The social construction of divorce," in *Social Interaction,* H. Robboy and C. Clark (eds.), New York: St. Martin's Press, 1983. The book is an expanded version of the essay with more interview excerpts.

Wallerstein, Judith, and Joan Kelly

1980 *Surviving the Breakup.* New York: Basic Books.
Major longitudinal study of children's adjustment to divorce (based on a clinical sample in Marin County).

Ware, Chi

1984 *Sharing Parenthood After Divorce.* New York: Bantam.
Thoughtful book on how divorced couples can work together as parents.

Weiss, Robert S.

1975 *Marital Separation.* New York: Basic Books.
This book describes the experiences of divorcing and separating people through the use of excerpts from case studies. It is one of the best available on these subjects because it is based on research interviews and the author's experience conducting therapy groups and thus is grounded in the experience of real people.

1979 *Going It Alone.* New York: Basic Books.
Readable study of women parenting alone—how the job gets done, compromises, and joys.

Weitzman, Lenore J.

1981 *The Marriage Contract: Spouses, Love, and the Law.* New York: Free Press.
Legal aspects of the family, including much on divorce.

1985 *The Divorce Revolution.* New York: Free Press.
How no-fault laws have negatively affected the financial status of divorced women.

17 Remarriage

I have a hell of a lot fewer illusions about what sort of work it takes. But it's work that I enjoy.
REMARRIED MAN

It's a different sort of happiness now, . . . less innocent, more profound, less carefree, more wise.
REMARRIED WOMAN

Remarriage—marrying again after being divorced or widowed—is an alternative that more Americans are choosing. Remarriages have increased in number in recent decades, so that today they make up a significant proportion of all marriages. While they are becoming more accepted, society still tends to view them as abnormalities or aberrations of the "natural" family. The rites of remarriage, with their relative lack of ritual and ceremony, reflect this attitude.

Until about ten years ago, research and advice concerning remarriages was sparse, but more recently, social scientists, counselors, and journalists have given remarriage more attention. Some of their findings have shown that many remarried people consider themselves very happy. They are glad they chose to remarry and satisfied with their marital relationships and their lives. As many as 70 percent in one study believed that their husband-wife relationship had grown better over the years they have been remarried (Duberman, 1975:130). At the same time, remarriages are beset with special, often unforeseen, problems. More and more, counselors and agencies are recognizing and helping remarried couples and families deal with these difficulties.

This chapter explores remarriages today. We will discuss choosing a remarriage partner, noting some social factors that influence that choice. We'll examine happiness and stability in remarriage, as well as the fact that no cultural model exists to guide interactions among the often complex networks of kin. We'll focus on two particularly difficult problem areas in remarriages: stepchildren and finances. Finally, we will explore the writing of a remarriage contract. We'll begin with an overview of remarriage in the United States today.

REMARRIAGE: SOME BASIC FACTS

Remarriages have become increasingly common in the United States over the past twenty-five years. Figure 17·1 shows first marriage, divorce, and remarriage rates for American women from 1921 to 1984. The incidence of remarriage rose sharply during World War II, peaking as the war ended. During the 1950s both the divorce and remarriage rates declined and remained relatively low until the 1960s, when they began to rise again. The remarriage rate peaked again in about 1966 but has declined since then. Close examination of the graph reveals that while the remarriage rate declined along with the divorce rate in the late 1940s, the situation is not the same today. The divorce rate continued to climb after 1966 and has leveled off at a high point. But the remarriage rate has declined steadily since 1966. The decline is due in part to the contracting economy, which discourages people, particularly divorced men who may already be

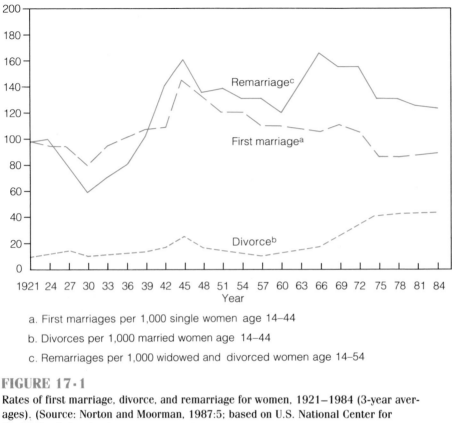

a. First marriages per 1,000 single women age 14–44

b. Divorces per 1,000 married women age 14–44

c. Remarriages per 1,000 widowed and divorced women age 14–54

FIGURE 17·1

Rates of first marriage, divorce, and remarriage for women, 1921–1984 (3-year averages). (Source: Norton and Moorman, 1987:5; based on U.S. National Center for Health Statistics data)

paying child support, from assuming at least partial financial responsibility for a new "instant family."

In spite of the changing trend, however, most people who divorce each year will probably remarry. Eighty-three percent of divorced men and 75 percent of divorced women remarry (Cherlin, 1981). Remarriages now comprise 46 percent of all marriages, compared with 31 percent in 1970 (U.S. National Center for Health Statistics, 1986b:11). By far the greatest majority of these remarriages are second marriages. Few people (only 2 percent of all adults in 1975) marry more than twice.[1] One result of the great number of remarriages is that

more Americans are living with other people's children. In 1980 about one-half (50.9 percent) of remarried households contained one or more stepchildren under age 18 (Cherlin and McCarthy, 1985:26).

There is no question that the increased incidence of divorce and remarriage has led to greater cultural tolerance of it. Fewer and fewer Americans view divorce and remarriage as a moral issue (Udry 1974:401). Remarriages have always been fairly common in the United States, but until this century almost all remarriages followed widowhood. Although as recently as the 1920s a majority of remarrying brides and grooms had been widowed, in 1984, 90 percent of remarrying brides and 91 percent of remarrying grooms were divorced (U.S. National Center for Health Statistics, 1987a). Today, the largest proportion of the remarried population are divorced persons who have married other divorced persons (U.S. National Center for Health

---

1. Some divorce lawyers and counselors, however, report having begun to see "regulars"—people who divorce, remarry, redivorce, then remarry and perhaps redivorce yet again (Leerhsen, 1985b). In 1985, 26 percent of those who had remarried had subsequently redivorced; this was about the same percentage as for those in first marriages (Norton and Moorman, 1987:4).

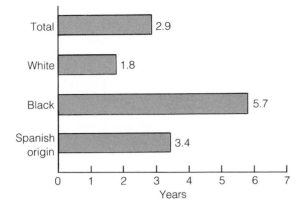

FIGURE 17·2

Median years separated after first marriage for white, black, and Hispanic women age 15 and older, 1985 (per 1,000 women). (Source: Norton and Moorman, 1987:8)

Statistics, 1986b: Table 5). In fact, remarriage is more than twice as likely to occur, age for age, among divorced women as among widowed women. Divorced men are two and one-half times more likely to marry again than never married men (U.S. National Center for Health Statistics, 1987a).

The average divorced person who remarries does so within about three years after divorce (Cherlin, 1981; Norton and Moorman, 1987). The averages differ, however, for women of different ethnic origins. Figure 17·2 depicts the median years white, black, and Hispanic women spent separated after the breakup of a first marriage. The relatively high number for blacks (5.7 years) reflects their lower rate of remarriage. While about 64 percent of white women remarry after divorce, a little less than 46 percent of black women, and about 55 percent of Hispanic women, remarry (Norton and Moorman, 1987:4). Do people choose partners differently the second time around? We'll explore the courtship process in the next section.

CHOOSING PARTNERS THE NEXT TIME: VARIATIONS ON A THEME

Courtship before remarriage may differ in many respects from courtship before first marriage. It may proceed much more rapidly, with the persons involved viewing themselves as mature adults who know what they are looking for (Hunt, 1966)—or it may be more cautious, with the partners needing time to recover from, or being wary of repeating, their previous marital experience (Krantzler, 1975). It is likely to have an earlier, more open sexual component—which may be hidden from the children through a series of complex arrangements. It may include both outings with the children and evenings at home as partners seek to recapture their accustomed domesticity.

Although courtship for remarriage has not been a major topic for research, Canadian sociologists Roy Rodgers and Linda Conrad have begun to remedy that. After reviewing the literature on divorce, stepfamilies, and family structure, they have posed several hypotheses for future testing. Generally, the hypotheses point up the complicated interrelationships between courting parents, their respective children, and their ex-spouses. For example, should one ex-spouse begin courtship while the other does not, conflict between the former spouses may escalate. Moreover, the noncourting partner may try to interfere with the ex-spouse's new relationship. A custodial ex-wife might do this by sabotaging her ex-husband's time with the children; ex-husbands might do this by threatening to withhold—or to legally change—financial support. Not only ex-spouses but children, too, can be expected to react negatively to a parent's dating. Generally, "The more the custodial parent's new partner displaces the child as a source of emotional support for the parent, the greater the probability of a negative reaction of the child to the new partner" and the more problems are likely to arise (Rodgers and Conrad, 1986:771).

All this suggests that remarriages are different for first marriages in important ways. Nevertheless, the basic structure of the remarriage process has much in common with initial marriage. We'll look at two significant factors that we first examined in Chapter 6 with regard to first marriages: the basic exchange and homogamy.

The Basic Exchange in Remarriage

We saw in Chapter 5 that, all else being equal, marriage favors husbands more than wives. Jessie Bernard pointed out that, as a whole, married life tends to place greater stresses on women who become mothers and, at the same time, reduces stress for men. This would suggest that ex-husbands more than ex-wives may want to remarry.

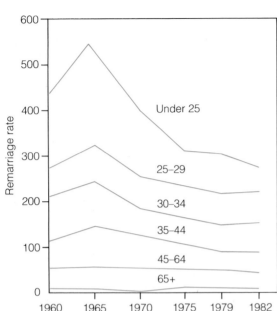

FIGURE 17·3

Remarriage rates per 1000 divorced women, by age at remarriage, 1960–1982. (Source: Glick and Lin, 1986b:739)

On the other hand, economists point out that women have more to gain financially from marriage than men (Ross and Sawhill, 1975). The following account by a single male in his late 20s illustrates this fact:

She was eyeing me and eyeing my house as a nice place to live with her son. It was the first thing she did. We went to my house one night and she says, "Boy, you've really got a nice back yard and a nice house here." And I'm thinking, "Why is she saying that?" It didn't click at the time, but she told this buddy of mine that her plan was to move in here with her kid—whatever his name was. Jason, that was the name, Jason. I could not stand that kid at all. So when I found this out, that I was her meal ticket, I thought, "Hea-a-a-vy." And that was the last time I saw her. She had great plans for me, but then I thought "Nah" [personal interview]. ■

From the discussion in Chapter 6 of the marriage market, the reader will remember that in recent years the basic exchange has become more lopsided than it was in the past. Both homemaking services and sex are more available to single men,

while women often still find it difficult to get good-paying jobs and support themselves. The scales are tipped even more in men's favor in the "remarriage market," where the remarriage rate is substantially lower for women than for men, particularly after age 30 (U.S. National Center for Health Statistics, 1986b:10).

Two factors influence the basic exchange to work against women's remarriage. One factor, age, works against women in several ways. Figure 17·3 shows the remarriage rates for divorced women in five age categories. Although the pattern of remarriage since 1960 has been similar for all age categories, the remarriage rate for younger women has been consistently higher (Glick and Lin, 1986b). Women live longer, on the average, than men do. After about age 30, there are more women than men in every age group, and by age 65 there are only 75 men for every 100 women. The "double standard of aging" also works against women in the remarriage market. In our society women are considered to be less physically attractive with age (e.g., Margolin and White, 1987), and they may also be less interested in fulfilling traditional gender-role expectations of being nurturant and submissive (Glenn and Weaver, 1977).[2]

A second factor that works against women in the remarriage market is the presence of children. As Chapter 16 indicated, the woman usually retains custody of children from a previous marriage. As a result, a prospective second husband may look on her family as a financial—and also an emotional and psychological—liability. Furthermore, children are often strongly loyal to the first family and may oppose or have strong reservations about the divorce for as long as five years afterward. In general, the more children a woman has, the less likely she is to remarry (Glick and Lin, 1986b).

Homogamy in Remarriage

Homogamy has traditionally been a second important factor influencing marriage choices. We saw in Chapter 6 that homogamy can be important in both the choice of a first marriage partner and the

---

2. Age works against both women's and men's remarriage in another way. Older people often face considerable social opposition to remarriage—both from restrictive pension and social security regulations and from their friends and children. Grown children may feel that marriage is inappropriate, or may be concerned about the natural parent's estate (Troll et al., 1979).

degree to which couples "live happily ever after." Does it affect second marriages in the same way? The answer to that question is, on the whole, no. Older people, particularly those who are widowed, are likely to remarry homogamously. Often, the new partner is someone who reminds them of their first spouse or is someone they've known for years (Troll et al., 1979). However, this rule does not apply to middle-aged or younger people who choose second marriage partners.

Choosing a remarriage partner differs from making a marital choice the first time inasmuch as there is a smaller pool of eligibles with a wider range of any given attribute. As prospective mates move from their late 20s into their 30s, they affiliate in occupational circles and interest groups that assemble people from more diverse backgrounds. There is also some evidence that divorced persons tend more toward heterogamy than nondivorced persons the first time around and that they simply accentuate this tendency when they remarry. As a result, remarriages are less homogamous than first marriages, with partners varying in age,[3] religious background, and educational background. Some observers note that homogamy increases the likelihood for marital stability and point to this preference for and increase in heterogamy as a partial explanation for the fact that the divorce rate is higher for second than for first marriages. The next section discusses stability and happiness in remarriages.

HAPPINESS AND STABILITY IN REMARRIAGE

As Chapter 6 points out, marital happiness and stability are not the same. *Marital happiness* refers to the quality of the marital relationship whether or not it is permanent; *stability* refers simply to the duration of the union. We'll look at both aspects.

Happiness in Remarriage

At least two important questions can be asked about happiness in remarriage. First, are remarried peo-

ple as happy in their relationship as people are in their first marriages? And second, how do remarried people compare their second marriage with their first?

To answer the first question, researchers compared the self-reported marital happiness of people who had divorced and remarried with that of never divorced couples, using data from three national surveys of white couples, conducted between 1973 and 1975 (Glenn and Weaver, 1977). Their findings are depicted in Figure 17·4. The marital happiness men reported was about the same for those who had never divorced and those who had remarried (71 percent to 68 percent). Among women there was a "small but significant" difference in reported happiness. Only 61 percent of divorced, remarried wives said they were "very happy," whereas 70 percent of never divorced women described themselves that way. Remarried women as a group evaluate their marriages less positively than do remarried men. The difference probably is related to remarried wives' increasing awareness of inequality in marriage and to the fact that the marriage gradient (described in Chapter 5) causes many women to marry second partners who are the right age but may not meet other standards (Glenn and Weaver, 1977).

One can easily exaggerate the importance of a small statistical difference, however, and the researchers concluded that, on the whole, the remarriages are probably about as happy as intact first marriages, which is remarkable considering their potential problems. But the question of how remarried people themselves compare their second marriages with their first marriages requires more research before an answer can be provided. A recent study in eight western states asked divorced and remarried men and women to compare their second union with their first. A large proportion (88 percent) said their second marriage was "much better" than their first, and an additional 7 percent rated it "a little better" (Albrecht, 1979). Another social scientist gives several reasons why such findings make sense:

There are many factors which contribute to the satisfaction which people find in second marriages. . . . The divorced person has probably learned something about marriage from his first failure. If age contributes anything to maturity, he should be able to make a more mature choice the second time. The significance of sex is transformed, since it can be more taken for granted in the approach to the second marriage. Second

---

3. The age difference between spouses is about four years in remarriages, compared to about two years for first marriages (U.S. National Center for Health Statistics, 1986b:13, Table 8).

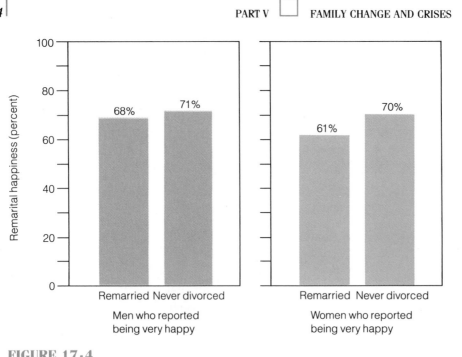

FIGURE 17·4

Remarital happiness compared to happiness in first marriages, for white men and women. (Source: Glenn and Weaver, 1977)

marriages have the advantages of being compared with a marriage which recently ended in bitterness and conflict. The second time around, the first-time loser has probably readjusted his expectations of marriage and is simply easier to please than those without previous marital experience [Udry, 1974:402]. ▪

This writer suggests that older, more experienced mates in remarriages are likely to be more mature than when they began their first marriages. (In 1984 the mean age at remarriage was 33.3 for brides and 36.8 for grooms, compared with 22.8 and 24.6 for first marriages; U.S. National Center for Health Statistics, 1987a.) Another authority questions this assumption, claiming that remarried people probably differ little from either first-married or unmarried persons in maturity, responsibility, and the ability to be supportive (Duberman, 1975). Some counselors add that people who ended troubled first marriages through divorce often are still experiencing personal conflicts, which they must resolve before they can expect to succeed in a second marriage. They may even be inclined to repeat the problems of the first marriage, marrying second spouses who seem superficially different (in appearance or political persuasion, for instance)

from their first spouses but who are similar in character. To counteract this situation and to allow the healing process described in Chapter 16 to run its course, many counselors advise waiting at least two years after divorce before entering into another serious relationship.

Stability of Remarriages

While remarriages are about as likely to be happy as intact first marriages, they differ in the likelihood of their stability. A number of studies dating back to the 1950s have found that remarriages are more likely to end in divorce than first marriages. It is projected that among young people in their 20s in the late seventies, 49 percent will end a first marriage by divorce; for remarriages, that figure rises to 60 percent (Glick, 1984).[4]

---

4. There is some evidence that for blacks remarriages may be *more* stable than first marriages. A 1973 survey of 10,000 women under age 45 found that the probability of separation and divorce during the first fifteen years of marriage was lower for blacks in remarriages than in first marriages (McCarthy, 1977, in Cherlin, 1978). This may be partly because blacks tend to be younger and less economically well off than whites at the time of first marriage.

Another statistic concerns the time it takes to decide on a second divorce, or "redivorce." People tend to get a second divorce in less time than it took them to obtain their initial divorce, about 4.9 years versus 7.5 years. The intervals between marriage, divorce, remarriage, and redivorce shortened during the seventies but have been lengthening again in the eighties (Norton and Moorman, 1987).

There are at least three reasons for the lower overall stability of remarriages. First, people who divorce in the first place are disproportionately from lower middle- and lower-class groups, which generally have higher divorce rates. When the divorce rate of first marriages is compared with that of second marriages *in the same part of the class structure,* "the difference is not striking" (Udry, 1974:401).

Second, persons who remarry after divorce are, as a group, more willing to choose divorce as a way of resolving an unsatisfactory marriage. In fact, Richard Udry points out, persons who are divorced may differ from those who have never divorced "more in their willingness to divorce than in the unhappiness of the first marriage.... By this fact alone it should be very surprising if more second marriages than first did not end in divorce" (1974:401).

Third, remarriages present some special stresses on a couple, stresses that are not inherent in first marriages. Our culture has not yet evolved norms or traditions that provide remarried partners and their families with models for appropriate behavior. As we gain experience with the problems of remarriage, which are discussed throughout this chapter, remarriages may become more stable. A recent projection expects eventual convergence of divorce rates for first and later marriages (Norton and Moorman, 1987).

Remarriage and Well-Being

Another comparison involves remarriage and continued singlehood as life-styles. A longitudinal study of 180 men and women divorced in Pennsylvania and followed for two and a half years found that those who had not remarried were as well off on eight measures of well-being as those who had remarried. "Many researchers and clinicians, as well as those who experience divorce, assume that remarriage following divorce may be a signifi-

cant—if not the most significant—alteration in social circumstance influencing enhanced well-being" and is the culturally preferred outcome (Spanier and Furstenberg, 1982:709). Yet there was virtually no difference in well-being in terms of satisfaction with one's life and health, suicide propensity, self-esteem, emotional balance, psychosomatic symptoms, and changes in habits between remarried persons and those who continued to be single, whether living with another adult or not. There was also no difference between men and women in the various categories, nor did presence or absence of children affect well-being.

It appears from this research that there are many routes to postmarital happiness. In fact, Graham Spanier and Frank Furstenberg pointed to the extreme diversity they encountered in the transition from divorce to remarriage.

This is highlighted very easily by the variations in living arrangements for both the children and adults involved. Some respondents had no children living with them born during the first marriage, have not remarried someone with children, and have borne no children following a remarriage. Other respondents may acquire children in any one of these three ways. In addition, there may be children from a previous marriage or stepchildren from a previous marriage of a new spouse or partner, who do not live in the same household as the respondent. This complex array of parent, stepparent, custodial, or noncustodial relationships makes it difficult to characterize marital disruption and its aftermath easily [1982:714]. ■

It is encouraging to learn that there are many ways of making a life after divorce, and that those who do not choose or have the opportunity to remarry can build a satisfying life. Given the sex ratio in the older years, many older women, in particular, will not find partners available. Individuals, both men and women, may come to prefer a single lifestyle.

The researchers found that people were not very accurate in predicting at the time of the divorce whether or not they would remarry. "Only 22 percent of those who had been eager to remarry had done so, compared with 30 percent who had said they were reluctant and 19 percent of those who said they would probably never remarry" (Spanier and Furstenberg, 1982:714). Nor was remarriage related to age, income, occupational status, education, religion, religiosity, or gender within the group, or to presence or absence of children. Partners who had initiated the divorce were more likely to have remarried, which the researchers attributed to greater readiness—since they had begun adjusting to the idea of divorce earlier—rather than to greater psychological health or development of a potential marriage relationship before the divorce. Among remarried persons, Spanier and Furstenberg did find that the quality of the remarriage was related to well-being.

REMARRIED FAMILIES: A NORMLESS NORM

When neither spouse in a remarriage has children, the couple's union is usually very much like a first marriage. But when at least one spouse has children from a previous marriage, family life often differs sharply from that of first marriages. A primary reason for this is the fact that our society offers members of **remarried families**[5] no *cultural script*, or set of socially prescribed and understood guidelines for relating to each other or for defining responsibilities and obligations.

Although society tends to broadly apply to second marriages the rules and assumptions of first marriages, these rules often ignore the complexities of remarried families and leave many questions unanswered. Three areas where these shortcomings are most apparent are within the remarried families, relationships with kin, and family law.

Characteristics of Remarried Families

The complexity of stepfamily structure, which affects family relationships, is illustrated in Table 17·1. It compares stepfamilies with the original nuclear family and with the single-parent family, which generally intervenes between marriages and remarriages. The repeated transitions from one family structure to another create a prolonged period of upheaval and stress. Yet sufficient adjustment to a single-parent household is likely to have occurred, so that a new adaptation to a two-parent remarried family is all the harder. A very tight emotional bond often exists in single-parent families (Weiss, 1979).

The unique characteristics of stepfamilies are pointed out by Emily Visher and John Visher (1979:29–33):

1. There is a biological parent outside the stepfamily unit and an adult of the same sex as the absent parent in the household.
2. Most children in stepfamilies hold membership in two households, with two sets of rules.
3. The role models for stepparents are poorly defined.
4. The fact that remarried families come together from diverse historical backgrounds accentuates the need for tolerance of differences. As one mother put it:

My children were used to saying grace before meals, using pretty good table manners when they are eating, and staying at the table until everyone was finished eating. My stepchildren, on the other hand, although they were similar in age to my own children, thought that saying grace was for the birds, pushed around in their food, couldn't wait to gulp it down, and then rushed off to watch TV. At least that's they way I saw it [Visher and Visher, 1979:32].

5. Step-relationships are new and untested and not a "given" as they are in intact families. Even when the new groups are in tune with each other, there is never the comfort of *knowing* that there is a bond of caring and love. Outward signals and signs are continuously needed in many stepfamilies to show that caring and loving really exist.
6. The children in stepfamilies have at least one extra set of grandparents.

5. After struggling with the terminology, we have concluded that the term *blended family* does not describe what happens; for the most part, persons involved in remarried families do not blend; that is, they do not lose the character and identity of the original family. Nor are families *reconstituted* or put back together. We do use the term *stepfamily* as a clearly descriptive one, which permits the negative as well as the positive feelings that usually exist to be acknowledged; however, we prefer the more neutral, less pejorative term *remarried family*.

TABLE 17·1 Major Structural Characteristics of Three American Family Patterns

Stepfamilies	Nuclear (intact) Families	Single-Parent Families
Biological parent is elsewhere.	Both biological parents present.	Biological parent is elsewhere.
Virtually all members have recently sustained a primary relationship loss.	——	All members have recently sustained a primary relationship loss.
An adult couple is in the household.	An adult couple is in the household.	——
Relationship between one adult (parent) and child predates the marriage.	Spousal relationship predates parental ones.	Parental relationship is the primary family relationship.
Children are members in more than one household.	Children are members in only one household.	Children may be members in more than one household.
One adult (stepparent) is not legally related to a child (stepchild).	Parents and child(ren) are legally related.	Parent and child(ren) are legally related.

SOURCE: Visher and Visher, 1979.

Kin Networks in the Remarried Family

Relationships with kin outside the immediate remarried family are complex and uncharted as well. One American anthropologist recently observed of the American scene:

Many people are married to people who have been married to other people who are now married to still others to whom the first parties may not have been married, but to whom somebody has likely been married [Tiger, 1978:14]. ■

The observation describes a large segment of American families, and the complexity it portrays is striking in several respects. One is the fact that our language has not yet caught up with the proliferation of new family roles. As family members separate and then join new families formed by remarriage, the new kin do not so much *replace* as *add* to kin from the first marriage. What are the new relatives to be called? There may be stepparents, stepgrandparents, and stepsiblings, but what, for instance, does a child call the new wife that her noncustodial father has married? Or if a child alternates between the new households of remarried parents in a joint custody arrangement, what does he call his "home" and where is his "family" (Cherlin, 1978:644)?

Anthropologist Paul Bohannan suggests a new term to define another previously unnamed relationship, the person one's former spouse remarries. He calls this person one's **quasi-kin** (Bohannan, 1970a). But he and other observers point to another way in which our culture has not yet caught up with the needs of the new remarried family. We have few mutually accepted ways of dealing with these new kinds of relationships. Interaction takes place between these families, often on a regular basis (about 60 percent of divorced parents' children have ongoing relationships with their noncustodial parent), yet there are no set ways of dealing with quasi-kin.

In one study a researcher presented hypothetical situations to ninety remarried men and ninety remarried women, all of whom had been divorced and had children from their previous marriages.

The couples showed no consensus about what would be appropriate behavior between quasi-kin. In situations involving conversations between a person's present spouse and his or her ex-spouse, for example, the only consensus among the respondents was that the two should say "hello." Beyond that, respondents did not agree on whether quasi-kin should engage in polite conversation or whether an ex-spouse should be invited into the new spouse's home while waiting to pick up her or his children (Goetting, 1979).

Because of the cultural ambiguity of remarried family relationships, social scientist Andrew Cherlin calls the remarried family an "incomplete institution" (1978). A second symptom of its "incompleteness" is the lack of legal definitions for roles and relationships in this institution.

Family Law and the Remarried Family

Because family law assumes that marriages are first marriages, there are no legal provisions for several remarried-family problems: balancing husbands' financial obligations to their spouses and children from current and previous marriages; defining a wife's obligations to husbands and children from the new and the old marriages; or reconciling the competing claims of current and former spouses for shares of the estate of a deceased spouse (Weitzman, 1981). Recent research suggests, incidentally, that remarried persons are reluctant to commit all their economic resources to a second marriage and take care to protect their individual interests and those of their biological children (Fishman, 1983).

Legal regulations concerning incest are also inadequate for stepfamilies. In all states marriage and sexual relations are prohibited between persons closely related by blood. But in many states these restrictions do not cover sexual relations or marriage between family members not related by blood—between stepsiblings or between a child and a stepparent for example. Margaret Mead pointed out that incest taboos serve the important function of allowing children to develop affection for and identification with other family members without risking sexual exploitation. She argued that current beliefs about incest, embodied in the law and social norms, fail to provide adequate security and protection for children in remarried families

(Mead, 1970). The complexity and uncertainty inherent in remarried families make stepparenting difficult. Many states are, however, reconsidering their laws about incest, adoption by stepparents, visitation rights of stepparents, and so on.

STEPPARENTING: A BIG PROBLEM IN REMARRIAGE

For most first-married couples, the biggest problems in their marriages are immaturity, sexual difficulties, and personal lack of readiness for marriage. For a remarried spouse, in contrast, stepchildren and finances present the greatest problems.

The results of one study of eighty-eight remarried families in Cleveland are shown in Table 17·2. The respondents were white, under age 45, had remarried between 1965 and 1968, and at that time had children under age 18 from a previous marriage (Duberman, 1975). From the table it can be seen that 35 percent of husbands and wives ranked child rearing as their number one problem, and that 20 percent of husbands and 16 percent of wives ranked money as the area of most serious conflict. These two categories thus combined to make up the major area of difficulty for over half of both husbands and wives. (Other problem areas included sexual relations, religion, political differences, relations with outsiders, and recreation, but these were ranked as far less important.) The findings of the Cleveland study were supported in a subsequent study by Messinger, who interviewed some seventy remarried couples (Messinger, 1976).

Several studies have found that children in stepfamilies are just as happy and well adjusted as children in intact families (Duberman, 1975; Wilson et al., 1975; Marotz-Baden et al., 1979; Bohannan and Erickson, 1978). But while stepchildren may turn out to be well adjusted, being a stepparent (or being married to one) often poses real problems for the marriage. The research on the eighty-eight stepfamilies in Cleveland indicated that children from a previous marriage increase both the likelihood of marital unhappiness and the chances of divorce for the remarried couple (Duberman, 1975). More recent research supports this conclusion and further suggests that, in some cases, remarried parents move teenagers out of the home as an alternative to further unhappiness and divorce

(White and Booth, 1985b). Yet the children a couple have from their new marriage seem to be associated with both increased happiness and stability (Becker et al., 1976; White and Booth, 1985b). According to Cherlin:

This is as we would expect, since children from a previous marriage expand the family across households and complicate the structure of family roles and relationships. But children born into the new marriage bring none of these complications. Consequently, only children from a previous marriage should add to the special problems of families in remarriage [1978:645]. ■

Stepparenting: Some Reasons It Is Difficult

There are many sources of difficulty associated with bringing families together under the same roof. In Lilian Messinger's study couples reported a diverse array of problems. For instance, ties with the noncustodial parent created a triangle effect that made the spouse's prior marriage seem "more real" than the second union; the children, upset after visits with the noncustodial parent, were required to make a major adjustment that made life difficult for everyone else; and the natural parents sometimes feel caught between loyalties to the biological child and their desire to please their partner (Messinger, 1976).

More specifically, three major problem areas can be identified in remarried families: financial burdens, role ambiguity, and negative feelings of the children, who often don't want the new family to "work."

Financial Strains   Observers point out that the problems that burden remarriages frequently begin with the previous divorce. This is particularly evident in the case of finances. Frequently, money problems arise because of obligations left over from first marriages. Remarried husbands are financially responsible for children from their first marriages and for their stepchildren. In the Cleveland sample discussed previously, a full 100 percent of the remarried husbands were the major family breadwinners (although 41 percent of the wives worked for wages), and over two-thirds of the husbands paid all the expenses of stepchildren under age 21 (Duberman, 1975:127–28). Even though

TABLE 17·2   Major Problems Found in Remarried Families

Problem	Husbands (%)	Wives (%)
Child rearing	35	35
Money	20	16
Sex relations	11	6
Religion	10	6
Political differences	9	11
Outsiders	9	14
Recreation	6	11
Total	100	100

SOURCE: Duberman, 1975.

disproportionately more second wives are employed outside their homes, remarried husbands report feeling caught between the often impossible demands of their former family and their present one. One said he felt like "a walking checkbook" (in Messinger, 1976:197). Some second wives also feel resentful about the portion of the husband's income that goes to his first wife to help support his natural noncustodial children. Or a second wife may feel guilty about the burden of support her own children place on their stepfather (Messinger, 1976).

The emotional impact of the previous divorce also causes money problems. Among Messinger's respondents, some women reported stashing money away in case of a second divorce, and some men refused to revise their wills and insurance policies for the same reason. For many couples, money became a sensitive issue that neither partner talked about (Messinger, 1976). As noted earlier, partners in remarriage are less likely to think and act in terms of "our" money (Fishman, 1983).

Role Ambiguity   Another basic problem in remarried families is that roles of stepchild and stepparent are neither defined nor clearly understood. Legally, the stepparent is a nonparent with no prescribed rights or duties: Case Study 17·1, "Being a Stepmother," discusses the frustrations this can cause. Indeed, the term *stepparent* originally meant a person who replaced a dead parent, not an acquired quasi-kin who becomes an additional parent. Uncertainties arise when the role of

**CASE STUDY
17·1**

**BEING A
STEPMOTHER**

Sharon, age 29, has been remarried to Dale for five years. It is a remarriage for both. They have three sons. Sharon has a son, Jeff, 7, from her first marriage. Dale has a son, Brian, 9, from his first marriage. Together they have a third boy, Mike, 3. Here Sharon talks about being a stepmother to Brian.

Brian had just turned 4 when we got married. His mother had met somebody else and just left. When we got married, she hadn't seen him for about a year or made any contact. But after we were married, she started coming back and saying, "I miss Brian."

She wanted visiting rights. Dale told her she could see Brian whenever she wanted. So she would pick him up on Tuesday night and bring him back Wednesday morning.

One day Brian was sick and I told her that. And she made the mistake of coming into the apartment—and she had lived there—. . . and saying, "I'm going to see for myself." She's never been in one of my houses since. I mean I'm the mother, and if she can't take my word for it. . . .

I would put good clothes on him [when he visited his mother], and she'd bring him back in raggy clothes. Pants up to here (*points to shin*) and shirts without buttons. She'd keep the good clothes so he could wear them over there. So I caught on, and I started sending him in crummy clothes, and she'd bring him back in the crummy clothes. But I wasn't gonna pay for clothes or mend shirts for him to wear over there. . . .

On the one hand, I think Brian should go see his mother because she is his mother. But on the other hand, when he comes back, the influence is so pronounced. He's really mean. He'll say mean things to Jeff; he won't obey me. He's really hostile. It's hard to put into words. She'd tell him he didn't have to mind me I think, and he wouldn't. There was a time when he'd come back and he'd wet the bed after being over there. Then we'd get that stopped and he'd have to go right back the next weekend. Then he'd come back and wet the bed again.

Oh, we've had lots of problems with this. Like when Brian started to go to school, I said, "He can't go over there any more week nights. He's got to be home in bed. During the weekend it's fine, but not on the week nights." Well,

parent is shared between stepparent and the non-custodial natural parent (Fast and Cain, 1966). As Bohannan points out, stepparents aren't "real," but "the culture so far provides no norms to suggest how they are different" (Bohannan, 1970a:119).

One result of this role ambiguity is that society seems to expect acquired parents and children to love each other in much the same way as biologically related parents and children do. In reality, however, this is not often the case. Interviews with remarried couples often reveal guilt about the lack of positive feelings (or even the presence of negative feelings) toward their partner's children. Delia Ephron, author of a book on remarriage based on personal experience, says discipline was a consistent source of family conflict:

she'd cry to Dale. But Dale wouldn't talk to her. He said he couldn't stand it after all the fights. And there *were* fights!

So she'd bring it up with me, and then she'd tell me it's none of my business. And I'd say, "I'm the only one thinking about Brian. You're thinking about the time you want with him, and Dale's over here not knowing what to do, and your folks are back there saying you've got to get him away from me, and I'm thinking about what's good for Brian."

But I found out that stepmothers have no rights whatsoever. In anything. I requested that Brian be psychologically tested at school. Well, when I went up there for the conference, they wouldn't tell me a thing. They said, "You're the stepmother, we can't tell you a thing." I said, "Can you give me the name of the test and the scores? I'll take them somewhere. I know people who will give me an evaluation." They couldn't even give me the name of the test. They had to talk with my husband and get a written consent that I was allowed to see the test.

It makes me very upset. If I sign a release for an operation or take him to emergency to get stitches, I am signing something I'm not supposed to sign.

That's the thing I don't like. Here I am the one who takes him to the dentist and does all this—I'm the one that takes him to the hospital—and then I don't have any rights. And if, if Dale were to die or something, Brian would probably go back there [to his mother]. I can't adopt him without her consent, and she won't let that happen. . . .

And then I get to regretting everything that I've put out. You know? Because I didn't cause all of it. I wasn't the one that was there in the beginning. . . .

The thing I resent is it's all on me. That's what gets me so upset. Here I am really a babysitter—someone who takes care of this child—and I get nothing out of it except all this guilt.

■ How does Sharon's story illustrate the fact that remarriage relationships are not institutionalized and therefore offer few guidelines for behavior? How does Dale's relationship with his ex-wife affect Sharon's relationship with Dale's son, Brian? What options does Sharon have and what choices can she make about her situation? About her resentment?

I thought my husband wasn't being strict enough, but what I found out was that stepfathers and stepmothers all think the real parent of the kids isn't being strict enough.

When you're a stepparent, you think you're an unbiased observer—when really you're an unbiased observer with a grudge, because you're an outsider and the very thing that's making you "unbiased" is something you resent [in Bennetts, 1986, p. 10-E]. ■

Similarly, stepchildren often don't react to their parent's new mate as though he or she were the "real" parent. The irony of expecting "real" parent-child love between acquired kin is further compounded by the fact that stepparents are not gen-

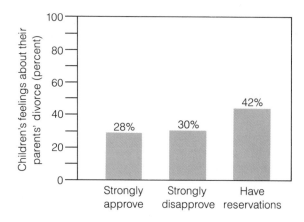

FIGURE 17·5

Children's feelings about their parents' divorce, five years later. If children have reservations about or strongly disapprove of their parents' past divorce, they may sabotage new relationships in the hope their parents will get back together. (Wallerstein and Kelly, 1980; adapted from p. 198)

erally expected to be "equal" in disciplining or otherwise controlling their stepchildren (Messinger, 1976).

Stepchildren's Hostility A third reason for the difficulty in stepparent-child relationships lies in children's lack of desire to see them work. Children often harbor fantasies that their original parents will reunite. Some recent research showed that five years after divorce, 30 percent of children or adolescents still strongly disapproved of their parents' divorce, and another 42 percent had reservations (see Figure 17·5) (Wallerstein and Kelly, 1980). Children who want their natural parents to remarry may feel that sabotaging the new relationship can help achieve that goal. In the case of remarriage after widowhood, children may have idealized, almost sacred memories of the parent who has died and may not want another to take his or her place. As a result, stepchildren can prove hostile adversaries. This is especially true for adolescents.

For a young teenager, a parent's remarriage may prove harder to accept than was the divorce (Krantzler, 1975:189). At puberty, when children are discovering their own sexuality, it is remarkable how conservative they can expect their parents to be with regard to *their* sexuality. As Chapter 13

points out, adolescence can be a trying time for parents. Teens tend to be impatient, self-centered, and argumentative. They can be especially distrustful, suspicious, and resentful toward a new parent, and they are sometimes verbally critical of a stepparent's goals, values, or personal characteristics (Fast and Cain, 1966).[6]

While virtually all stepchildren and stepparents are to some degree uncomfortable with some aspects of their family role, certain difficulties are more likely to trouble stepmothers, and others are more common to stepfathers. We'll look at each of these roles and the problems associated with them in more detail.

The Stepmother Trap

The role of stepmother is thought by clinicians and parents to be more difficult than that of stepfather. In the Cleveland study, for example, 45 percent of stepfathers (and only 18 percent of stepmothers) said their stepchildren felt loving toward them and vice versa (Duberman, 1975). The reason for this is a contradiction in expectations for the role of stepmother. Phyllis Raphael (1978) refers to it as the **stepmother trap:** on the one hand, society seems to expect romantic, almost mythical loving relationships between stepmothers and children (Maddox, 1975). On the other hand, stepmothers are seen and portrayed as cruel, vain, selfish, competitive, and even abusive (remember Snow White's, Cinderella's, and Hansel's and Gretel's). Stepmothers are accused of giving preferential treatment to their own children. As a result, writes Lucile Duberman, in our society "a stepmother must be exceptional before she is considered acceptable. No matter how skillful and patient she is, all her actions are suspect" (1975:50).

These conflicting expectations seem to come naturally with the stepmother role. To make matters worse, however, stepmothering situations often make the role even more complicated. We'll look briefly at the special circumstances of the "weekend stepmother."

---

6. Anger displacement, described in Chapter 9, may also play a part in the stepparent's difficulty. Many adolescents blame their parents or themselves, or both, because the first marriage broke up. The stepparent becomes a convenient scapegoat for their hostilities.

The Weekend Stepmother Special problems accompany the role of part-time or "weekend" stepmother when women are married to noncustodial fathers who see their children regularly. Generally, the remarried husband brings his children to the remarried family's home, which also causes problems. The part-time stepmother may try to establish a loving relationship with her husband's children only to be openly rejected, or she may feel left out by the father's ongoing relationship with his offspring. One study of women who were dating divorced fathers found that the woman would help the man with house and child care in an effort to free more of his time for intimacy and social life with her. To her frustration, however, the man often spent the extra free time with his children (Rosenthal and Keshet, 1978).

Part-time stepmothers can feel left out not only by the father's relationship with his children but also by his continued relationship with his ex-wife. Noncustodial fathers can spend long hours on the telephone with their ex-wives discussing their children's school problems, orthodontia, illnesses, and even household maintenance and repairs.

One stepmother summed up the feelings of many others in her role: "Considering all the negative influences at work, it's almost a miracle that anyone succeeds in the stepmother role" (Raphael, 1978:188). (Box 17•1, "Stepparenting: Some Tips," contains some advice that may make stepparenting easier.)

Stepfathering

Men who decide to marry a woman with children come to their new responsibilities with varied emotions. The motivations may be far different from those that make a man assume responsibility for his natural children. "I was really turned on by her," said one stepfather of his second wife. "Then I met her kids." This sequence is fairly common, and a new husband may have both positive and negative reactions, ranging from admiration to fright to contempt (Bohannan and Erickson, 1978:53). A stepfather's adjustment problems, therefore, are complex.

Research into the stepfather role suggests two contrasting conclusions. The first is that stepchildren tend to be well adjusted and to get along with their stepfathers as well as other children do with their natural fathers. The second is that stepfathers tend to view themselves as less effective than natural fathers view themselves (Bohannan and Erickson, 1978). Stepfathers' relatively low appraisal of their own performance may reflect the special problems and discomforts they experience in the stepfathering role. We'll look at a few of these.

Odd Man Out in an In-Group A new stepfather typically enters a household headed by a mother. When a mother and her children make up a single-parent family, the woman tends to learn autonomy and self-confidence, and her children may do more work around the house and take more responsibility in family decisions than other children. These are positive developments, but to enter such a family, a man must work his way into a closed group (Robinson and Barret, 1986:118–43). Paul Bohannan and Rosemary Erickson summarize: "Stepfathers take on a functioning in-group. The mother and children share a common history; the man coming to it has quite a different personal history" (1978:54).

Living arrangements can cause a new husband to feel like the "odd man out." One stepfather moved into his wife's house because she didn't want to move her children to a new school and neighborhood. But, he said, he "never felt at home there. . . . I'd sit someplace, and then I'd move someplace else. I didn't have a place there. I couldn't find a place there for the first few months" [Bohannan and Erickson, 1978:59].

The Hidden Agenda The new husband-father may feel out of place not only because of his different background but also because he has a different perspective on family life. After years of living as a single-parent family, for instance, both the mother and children are likely to have developed a heightened concern over the fairness of chore allocation. A newcomer who assumes the traditional male role may draw complaints that he is not contributing enough (Bohannan and Erickson, 1978). This last bone of contention is part of another source of potential conflict: the "hidden agenda."

The **hidden agenda** is one of the first difficulties a stepfather encounters: The mother or her children, or both, may have expectations about what the stepfather will do but may not think to give the new husband a clear picture of what those expectations are. The stepfather may have a hidden agenda of his own. For example, he may see his new stepchildren as unruly and decide they need

BOX 17 · 1

**STEP-
PARENTING:
SOME TIPS**

SOURCE:
U.S. Department of Health,
Education, and Welfare,
1978.

PREPARING TO LIVE IN STEP

In a stepfamily at least three and usually more individuals find themselves struggling to form new familial relationships while still coping with reminders of the past. Each family member brings to the situation expectations and attitudes which are as diverse as the personalities involved. The task of creating a successful stepfamily, as with any family, will be easier for all concerned if each member tries to understand the feelings and motivations of the others as well as his or her own.

It is important to discuss the realities of living in a stepfamily prior to the marriage, when problems that are likely to arise can be foreseen and examined theoretically. If you are contemplating entering a step-relationship, here are some points to consider:

1. Plan ahead! Some chapters of Parents Without Partners conduct "Education for Remarriage" workshops. Contact your local chapter or write to Parents Without Partners.
2. Examine your motives and those of your future spouse for marrying. Get to know him or her as well as possible under all sorts of circumstances. Consider the possible impact of contrasting life-styles.
3. Discuss the modifications that will be required in bringing two families together. Compare similarities and differences in your concepts of child rearing.
4. Explore with your children the changes remarriage will bring: new living arrangements, new family relationships, the effect on their relationship with their noncustodial parent.
5. Give your children ample opportunity to get to know your future spouse well. Consider your children's feelings, but don't allow them to make your decision about remarriage.
6. Discuss the disposition of family finances with your future spouse. An open and honest review of financial assets and responsibilities may reduce unrealistic expectations and resultant misunderstandings.
7. Understand that there are bound to be periods of doubt, frustration, and resentment.

discipline. Or he may find that after years of privacy, a bustling house full of children disrupts his routine. If the new stepfather does not measure up to the family's hidden agenda—or if his own hidden agenda conflicts with theirs—he may quickly be branded as unsatisfactory (Bohannan and Erickson, 1978).

A part of the stepchildren's hidden agenda, as we have seen, involves the extent to which they will let the new husband play the father role. Children may be adamant in their distaste for or jealousy of the stepfather, or they may be ready and anxious to accept the stepfather as a "new daddy." This last is particularly true of young children.

LIVING IN STEP

Any marriage is complex and challenging, but the problems of remarriage are more complicated, since more people, relationships, feelings, attitudes, and beliefs are involved than in a first marriage. The two families may have differing roles, standards, and goals. Because its members have not shared past experiences, the new family may have to redefine rights and responsibilities to fit the individual and combined needs.

Time and understanding are key allies in negotiating the transition from single-parent to stepfamily status. Consideration of the following points may ease the transition process:

1. Let your relationship with stepchildren develop gradually. Don't expect too much too soon—from the children or yourself. Children need time to adjust, accept, and belong. So do parents.
2. Don't try to replace a lost parent; be an additional parent. Children need time to mourn the parent lost through divorce or death.
3. Expect to deal with confusing feelings—your own, your spouse's, and the children's. Anxiety about new roles and relationships may heighten competition among family members for love and attention; loyalties may be questioned. Your children may need to understand that their relationship with you is valued but different from that of your relationship with your spouse and that one cannot replace the other. You love and need them both, but in different ways.
4. Recognize that you may be compared with the absent partner. Be prepared to be tested, manipulated, and challenged in your new role. Decide, with your mate, what is best for your children and stand by it.
5. Understand that stepparents need support from natural parents on child-rearing issues. Rearing children is tough; rearing someone else's is tougher.
6. Acknowledge periods of cooperation among stepsiblings. Try to treat stepchildren and your own with equal fairness. Communicate! Don't pretend that everything is fine when it isn't. Acknowledge problems immediately and deal with them openly.
7. Admit that you need help if you need it. Don't let the situation get out of hand. Everyone needs help sometimes. Join an organization for stepfamilies; seek counseling.

Young-adult children may be mature enough to think of the new addition to the family primarily as their mother's husband rather than as a stepfather (Bohannan and Erickson, 1978).

The hidden agendas of mother, children, and stepfather also involve supposedly simple matters of everyday living, such as food preferences, personal space, and the division of labor. Problems can arise when a meat-and-potatoes man joins a gourmet-dinner household, for example.

Discipline is likely to be a particularly tricky aspect of both the children's and the parents' hidden agenda. A few problem areas are notable. There are now two parents rather than one to establish

■ If at first you don't succeed: Most remarriages in the United States today involve divorced people marrying others who have been divorced. Such remarriages often start as families, with at least one partner bringing children from a previous marriage. Combining two previously established families often creates problems in the new family.

house rules and to influence children's behavior, but the parents may not agree. A second problem can be the holdover influence of the natural father. To the new father, there may sometimes seem to be *three* parents instead of two—especially if the noncustodial father sees the children regularly—with the natural father wielding more influence than the new father. Bohannan and Erickson compare such a situation to that in the old James Stewart movie about Harvey, the invisible rabbit: "You can't sit there, Harvey is sitting in that chair" (Bohannan and Erickson, 1978:59).[7] A third problem can be the development of children's responsibility and participation in decision making in single-parent families. The children may be unwilling

---

7. Bohannan and Erickson's study found no difference between natural families and stepfamilies in their division of disciplinary responsibility. Fathers and stepfathers both reported they were "in charge" in 37 percent of families, while the natural mother was responsible in 20 percent (Bohannan and Erickson, 1978).

to go back to being "children," that is, dependent on and subject to adult direction. The new parent may view them as spoiled and undisciplined rather than mature (Weiss, 1979).

Stepfathers react to these difficulties in finding a place in a new family in four ways. First, the stepfather can be driven away. Second, he may take control, establishing himself as undisputed head of the household, and force the former single-parent family to accommodate to his preferences. Third, he may be assimilated into a family with a mother at its head and have relatively little influence on the way things are done. And fourth, the stepfather, his new wife, and her children can all negotiate new ways of doing things (Bohannan and Erickson, 1978). This is the most positive alternative for everyone, and it is best achieved by writing a personal remarriage contract.

WRITING A PERSONAL REMARRIAGE CONTRACT

Reasons for writing a personal marriage contract were discussed in Chapter 8. To varying degrees, these reasons also apply to remarriage contracts. But additional reasons make it useful to negotiate a personal remarriage agreement or at least to talk over the issues involved. One reason is that remarriages are often beset with specific problems. Many times partners do not foresee these problems and are therefore not prepared to deal with them.[8]

A second reason for negotiating a remarriage contract is that partners who marry after divorce may want to try harder to make their marriage work but may be reluctant to fully commit themselves emotionally. Divorce and the struggles of the marriage prior to divorce can leave scars. When not openly acknowledged, past failure, rejection, loss, and guilt can undermine a new intimate relationship without either partner understanding what is happening. One way to counteract this is to share negative feelings about oneself, then to try to negotiate a relationship in which each partner feels as

secure, as positive about himself or herself, and as comfortable as possible.

A third, related reason for writing a remarriage agreement is that second-time spouses may feel the conflict taboo (described in Chapter 9) even more than do spouses in first marriages. Messinger reports that one woman's attitude reflected those of many respondents. In their desire to make their marriage work, the woman said, she and her spouse felt too "battle-scarred" to open "a can of worms." Accordingly, they glossed over differences that needed airing and resolution—differences they may not have hesitated to fight about in their first marriages (Messinger, 1976:197–98). As Chapter 9 points out, avoiding conflicts is a serious mistake.

Finally, remarriage contracts are important because, as we have seen, society has not yet evolved an effective cultural model for these complex relationships (Cherlin, 1978). Unless they discuss their expectations, new mates are likely to be unrealistic, says remarriage counselor Clifford Sager. "Ninety-five percent of people go into this with unrealistic expectations. They want to reproduce an intact family for the children, and of course that's not possible to do. It can't ever be the same" (Sager, in Bennetts, 1979, p. C-11). In fact, there are also complex legal issues involved in remarriage, which are best given careful consideration before the marriage (Weitzman, 1981). Inheritance is one: Do you want your money and property to go to your new spouse or your children? What does the law in your state permit on this? Obligation of a stepfather to support stepchildren is another important issue.

Custodial parents may want their new spouse to adopt the children. This generally involves a waiver of parental rights by the natural parent, who may not wish to do so. Recent court cases have addressed this issue; such termination of parental rights is extremely rare. Children above a certain age, perhaps 14, may or must give their own consent to stepparent adoption in some states.

Rights of stepparents to visitation or even custody of a stepchild in the event of death or divorce from the child's parent is a crucial issue these days, when so many people become closely attached to stepchildren. Stepchildren may have been raised by a stepparent who, as it turns out, has no legal parental rights. Law in this area—case law and legislation—is just being developed. It seems unlikely—and with reason—that natural parents

---

8. Lilian Messinger would like to see remarriage preparatory courses to alert remarrying couples to common problems and to help them find ways to discuss inevitable conflicts (Messinger, 1976).

will be legally replaced by stepparents, but it is important for the law to catch up with social change and find some way of including the stepparent as an authentic family member.

The most general point here is that people who remarry should not assume that they can do some of these things without checking with a lawyer. Individuals may also want to become active in relevant public policy areas that concern them.

Chapter 8 suggests some questions to address when creating a personal marriage contract; the majority of these apply to second marriages as well. In addition, remarriage contracts need to consider some other important areas, such as the responsibilities of the new partner to the children. Remarriage contracts, like other marriage agreements, should be revised as situations and partners change.

Divorce and remarriage, the subject of two of the chapters in Part Five, have only recently become commonplace in our society. Knowledgeably choosing to both divorce and remarry requires anticipating the consequences of those choices.

Summary

Although remarriages have always been fairly common in the United States, patterns have changed. Remarriages are far more frequent now, and they follow divorce more often than widowhood. The courtship process by which people choose remarriage partners has similarities to courtship preceding first marriages, but the basic exchange often weighs more heavily against older women, and homogamy tends to be less important.

Second marriages are usually about as happy as first marriages, but they tend to be less stable. An important reason is the lack of a cultural script. Relationships in immediate remarried families and with kin are often complex; yet there are virtually no social prescriptions and few legal definitions to clarify roles and relationships.

The lack of cultural guidelines is clearest in the stepparent role. Stepparents are often troubled by financial strains, role ambiguity, and stepchildren's hostility. Marital happiness and stability in remarried families seem, on the average, to be greater when the couple have a child from the new union. Personal remarriage contracts can help to establish an understanding where few social norms exist.

Key Terms

quasi-kin *547*
stepmother trap *552*
hidden agenda *553*

Study Questions

1. Discuss the similarities and differences between courtship before remarriage and courtship before first marriage.
2. How is the basic exchange in remarriage tipped against women? Compare this with the basic exchange in first marriages.
3. Why are remarriages less stable than first marriages even though they are about as likely to be happy as are intact first marriages?
4. The remarried family has been called an "incomplete institution." What does this mean? How does this affect the people involved in a remarriage? Include a discussion of kin networks and family law.
5. What are some problems faced by both stepmothers and stepfathers? What are some problems particularly faced by stepfathers? Why might the role of stepmother be more difficult than that of stepfather? How might these problems be resolved or alleviated?
6. What are some reasons for writing a personal remarriage contract? Is it more or less important to write a remarriage contract than a first marriage contract? Why? Discuss some topics that could be important to consider in a remarriage contract but not in a first marriage contract.

Suggested Readings

Einstein, Elizabeth
1982 *The Stepfamily: Living, Loving, and Learning.* New York: Macmillan.
This award-winning (award from the American Psychological Association) book chronicles the development stages of stepfamily living through experiences of the author (a stepchild and a stepmother), interviews with about fifty other stepfamilies, and discussions with professionals who work with stepfamilies.

Ephron, Delia
1986 *Funny Sauce: Us, the Ex, the Ex's New Mate, the New Mate's Ex, and the Kids.* New York: Viking.
How to live in stepfamilies, based on personal experience.

Inhinger-Tallman, Marilyn, and Kay Pasley
1987 *Remarriage.* Newbury Park, Calif.: Sage.
Comprehensive, concise review of research; intended for the classroom, but also useful to the general reader.

Robinson, Bryan E., and Robert L. Barret
1986 *The Developing Father.* New York: Guilford Press.
Includes a good chapter on stepfathers.

Roosevelt, Ruth, and Jeanette Lofas
1976 *Living in Step.* New York: Stein & Day.
Discussion of the complexities of stepfamily living for a popular audience (Jeanette Lofas is the founder of the Stepfamily Foundation).

U.S. Department of Health, Education, and Welfare, National Institute of Mental Health
1978 *Yours, Mine, and Ours: Tips for Stepparents.* Washington, D.C.: U.S. Government Printing Office.
Concise but meaty discussion and suggestions for making the most of the stepfamily situation through anticipating and preparing for change beforehand and knowing what to expect after remarriage.

Visher, Emily B., and John S. Visher
1979 *Stepfamilies: A Guide to Working with Stepparents and Stepchildren.* New York: Brunner/Mazel.
Solid, detailed discussion of problems of stepfamilies focused on having realistic expectations of stepfamilies, written by counselor-therapists who are also stepparents. The book refers to and is based on the research in this area and on the clinical and personal experience of the authors. Special problems of men, women, and children in various combinations—custodial and noncustodial—are discussed.

1982 *How to Win as a Stepfamily.* New York: Dembner.
More readable version of the authors' 1979 work on stepfamilies.

Weitzman, Lenore J.
1981 *The Marriage Contract: Spouses, Lovers, and the Law.* New York: Free Press.
Law and the family, including consideration of the complex legal and financial issues of stepfamilies.

Epilogue: Three Themes in Retrospect

There will inevitably be turning points in all of our lives. . . . We can't avoid change by resisting it or leaping ahead of it, but I think that we can go through it with less distress, if we keep open the dialogue between the past and the present, between the arguments we hold in both hands. We can shift our perspective from the fearful hope that things can stay the same to understanding the turning points around which life changes, people change.
ELLEN GOODMAN, *TURNING POINTS*

We have worked with three themes throughout this text: Marriage is changing so that relationship qualities are as important as, if not more important than, institutional characteristics; there is an interplay between individual families and the larger society; and individuals make family-related choices throughout their lives. Now it is time for some final thoughts about each of these themes.

A Change from Institution to Relationship

As families turn from emphasizing the utilitarian benefits of marriage, such as financial support, household maintenance, and child rearing, to focusing on intimate, supportive relationships, lov-ing becomes central to marriage and family life. Sex becomes less a physical act for procreation and more a potential source of pleasure and bonding. Individuals choose marriage partners not so much for their basic exchange values as for unique personal qualities.

With the transition to marriage as a relationship comes an emphasis on communicating effectively and supportively. As primary groups, contemporary families exist mainly because members see that being together is, in itself, good. One outcome of this attitude, ironically, is a high divorce rate. As families move from utilitarian arrangements to intrinsic relationships, expectations for intimacy rise, and divorce becomes available as an option.

The family, of course, continues to function as a supplier of practical needs. Families are no longer self-sufficient economic units, but they channel and mediate the practical, health, and educational needs of family members—needs that, in turn, are handled by entities such as stores, hospitals, and schools. The larger society greatly influences how families help members meet their practical needs and even, to a great extent, members' capacity for shaping a supportive familial environment.

Families and Society

Throughout this book we have pointed to the mutual influence of family and society. The larger society affects individuals and families by the economy's effect on the material base of family life, the societal values that pervade schools and other institutions, social definitions of appropriate family forms and sexual morality, the extent to which reproduction is encouraged or discouraged and child rearing is esteemed, and in many other ways. Society can be generally favorable toward families or not. It can take them for granted or give them support and encouragement. It can encourage some families and discourage others.

A Last Word About Family Policy If people are to shape the kinds of family living they want, they need to reach beyond their own marriages and families to get involved in electoral politics and federal and state legislation. One's role as a family member, as much as one's role as a citizen, has come to require participation in public policy decisions.

A Last Word About Myths One of the ways society works against an individual's knowledgeable decision making is by perpetuating harmful myths. One aim of our study has been to become aware of and debunk some dangerous myths about marriages and families. Myths are pernicious. Pictures of an "ideal" woman, man, wife, husband, mother, father, marriage, family, or sex life can eat away at one's self-esteem. This is because these idealized images present perfection as attainable, which it is not. Myths are shaky bases for decision making.

Choices Throughout Life

Making decisions about one's marriage and family begins in early adulthood and lasts into old age. People repeatedly make decisions about how to balance the need for individuality with that for commitment and togetherness. All individuals today, whether married or single, female or male, must determine the balance between caring for and about themselves and caring for and about others—their sisters and their brothers, the independent and the dependent, their own generation and future generations.

A Human Sexual Anatomy

If you are to understand sexual relations between individuals, you need to be aware of both the physiology of sex and the attitudes and emotions that shape people's feelings about their own sexuality and that of others. In Appendix A we will consider the first of these elements, the physiology of sex. We will look at female and male sexual anatomy and describe the **genitalia,** or external reproductive parts, and then the internal reproductive systems of each sex.

Female Genital Structures

The external genitalia of a woman are technically referred to as the **vulva.** The vulva is composed of several structures:

- the **mons veneris,** or pubic mound; an area of fatty tissue above the pubic bone;
- the **labia majora** (Latin for "greater lips"; the singular form of *labia* is *labium*), two rounded folds of skin; and, within them, the **labia minora** (or "lesser lips");
- **prepuce,** or clitoral hood: a fold of skin that covers the clitoris when it is not erect and is formed where the labia minora join;
- the **clitoris,** which consists of an internal shaft composed of **erectile tissue:** tissue

that becomes engorged with blood during arousal, causing it to increase in size; and a **glans,** a highly sensitive tip, about the size of a pea;

- the **urethra,** the opening through which urine passes from the bladder to the outside;
- the **vestibule,** or entryway to the vagina;
- the **perineum,** the area between the vestibule and the anus (the opening from the rectum and bowel);
- the **hymen,** a ring of tissue that partially covers the vaginal opening. The hymen contains small blood vessels that may bleed the first time the tissue is broken: at first intercourse, first insertion of a tampon, during masturbation, or as a result of some accidental injury.

The main internal structures of the female reproductive system are the vagina, the cervix, the uterus, the fallopian tubes, and the ovaries (see Figure A-1.)

The **vagina** is the passageway from the uterus to the external area. It is a potential space within a woman's body. Usually, the vaginal walls touch one another; but the vagina is elastic and capable of opening wide enough to allow a baby to pass through during birth. Such stretching would be extremely painful if the vagina had the same number of nerve endings as many of the structures of

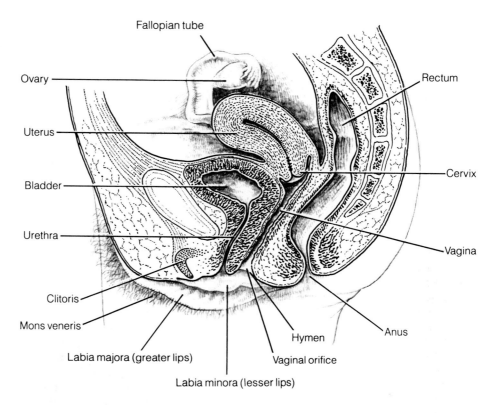

Fallopian tube

Ovary

Uterus

Bladder

Urethra

Clitoris

Mons veneris

Labia majora (greater lips)

Labia minora (lesser lips)

Rectum

Cervix

Vagina

Anus

Hymen

Vaginal orifice

FIGURE A·1
Female urogenital system.

the vulva have. Therefore, the vagina is almost insensitive to feeling.

At the top of the vagina is the **cervix:** the neck of the uterus (*cervix* means "neck" in Latin). The **uterus,** or womb, is a cavity whose purpose is to cradle a fetus until birth. Leading from the uterus are two passageways, called **fallopian tubes,** that connect a woman's uterus with her ovaries.

Ovaries are female **gonads,** or sex glands. Women have two ovaries, one on each side of their bodies. They produce reproductive cells (**ova,** or eggs) and two female sex hormones, estrogen and progesterone. Ordinarily, the ovaries alternate in producing one ovum per month, in a process called

ovulation.[1] The egg, barely visible, travels along the fallopian tubes to the uterus.

In preparing to receive the egg, the lining of the uterus, called the **endometrium,** thickens with a layer of tissue and blood (see Figure A-2). This tissue can nourish an embryo during the early stages of pregnancy, if the egg becomes fertilized during its passage from the ovaries. When fertilization does

---

1. Sometimes, women produce more than one egg at a time. This is one way that twins or multiple children are conceived.

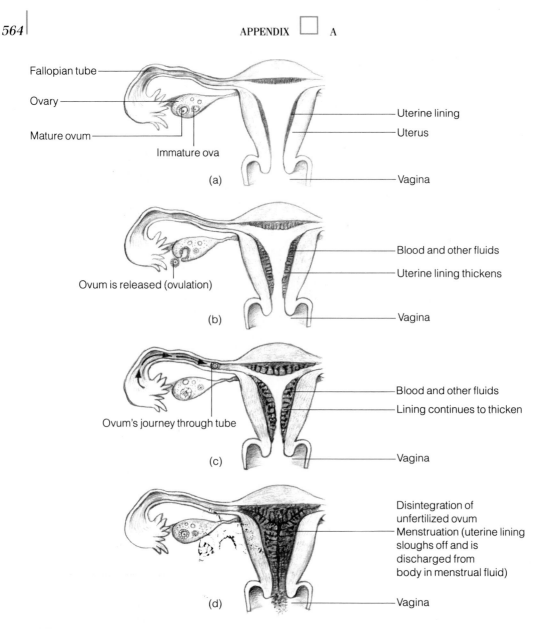

Fallopian tube

Ovary

Mature ovum

Immature ova

Uterine lining

Uterus

Vagina

(a)

Ovum is released (ovulation)

Blood and other fluids

Uterine lining thickens

Vagina

(b)

Ovum's journey through tube

Blood and other fluids

Lining continues to thicken

Vagina

(c)

Disintegration of
unfertilized ovum
Menstruation (uterine lining
sloughs off and is
discharged from
body in menstrual fluid)

Vagina

(d)

FIGURE A-2

The menstrual cycle: *(a)* During the early part of the
cycle, an ovum matures in an ovary; the endometrium
begins to thicken. *(b)* About fourteen days after the
onset of the last menstruation, a mature ovum is
released; the endometrium is thick and spongy. *(c)* The
ovum travels through one of the fallopian tubes; blood
and other fluids engorge the uterine lining. *(d)* If the
ovum is not fertilized, the endometrium breaks down
and sloughs off in a form of bleeding (menstruation).
(Source: Adapted from McCary, 1979:58)

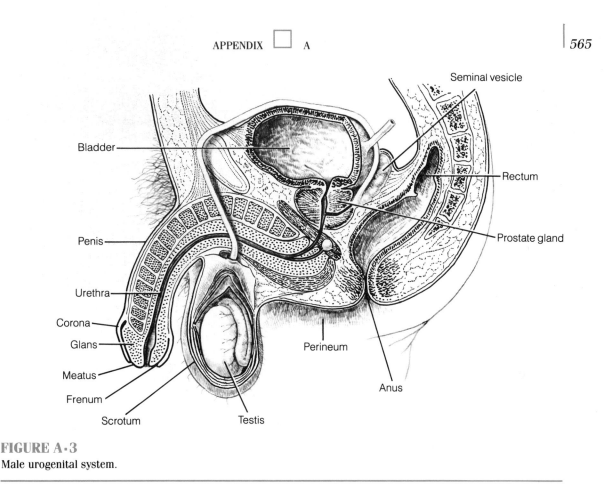

Seminal vesicle

Bladder

Rectum

Penis

Prostate gland

Urethra

Corona

Glans

Perineum

Meatus

Frenum

Anus

Scrotum   Testis

FIGURE A·3
Male urogenital system.

not occur, the egg and the unused endometrial tissue and blood are discarded during **menstruation.**[2]

Male Genital Structures

The external male genitalia are the **penis** and the scrotum (see Figure A-3). Like the female clitoris, the penis is composed of an erectile shaft and a sensitive tip, or glans. The glans is especially sensitive to touch at the **corona:** a crown-like ridge at its base. If a male has not been circumcised, the glans is covered by a thin membrane, the **foreskin,** when his penis is not erect (in circumcision, this foreskin is removed).[3] On the side of the penis,

which rests against the scrotum, is the **frenum,** the place where the foreskin is or was connected to the penis. The frenum, even more than the corona, is sensitive to tactile stimulation.

When a man is not sexually aroused, his penis is flaccid. When erect, penises vary somewhat in size and are usually about six inches in length and about an inch and a half in diameter. The **urethra** runs through the penis and carries male reproductive cells and urine, though never at the same time.[4] The opening at the tip of the penis is called the **meatus,** Latin for "passage."

2. Menstruation occurs in "monthly" cycles, ranging from about twenty-one to thirty-five days. Travel, anxiety, or change in diet can make periods more or less frequent.

3. In our society circumcision is usually performed shortly after a male baby's birth. Research on cancer rates suggests that circumcision helps prevent cancer of the cervix (Moore,

1980). For others, circumcision is an important sexual or religious ritual. In recent years the almost routine circumcision of male babies has been challenged by those who point to a slight medical risk as well as psychological trauma to the infant. We can expect to hear more about this issue in the future.

4. A man's urethra cannot carry urine while his penis is erect because erection automatically blocks the opening from his bladder to his urethra.

Behind the penis hangs a sac, the **scrotum,** which holds the two male gonads, the **testicles.** One testicle is usually lower than the other. Testicles, sometimes called *testes,* are the male counterpart to the female ovaries. They produce the male reproductive cells, called **sperm,** as well as male hormones such as testosterone. Unlike ovaries, however, testicles are external structures. That is because they must be maintained at a temperature lower than body temperature in order to produce living sperm. Between the scrotum and the anal opening is an area called the **perineum.** As in women, this area is sensitive to the touch.

The internal male reproductive structures are also shown in Figure A-3. Above the testicles, near the internal surface of the rectal walls, are two glands, the **seminal vesicles** and the **prostate.**

These glands produce **semen,** the milky fluid that carries the sperm through the urethra and out the meatus. There are usually between 200 million and 500 million sperm in a teaspoonful of semen. Sperm are ejaculated, or ejected, during the rhythmic contractions of **orgasm.**

If they are ejected into a woman's vagina, sperm move toward her fallopian tubes. Sperm can live in the fallopian tubes from two to five days. If one sperm cell fuses with a female egg, fertilization occurs and a fetus is conceived. There are a number of methods that can be used to prevent conception, and these are discussed in Appendix C.

The structures described above make up the male and female reproductive systems. Their reproductive functions are discussed in Appendix B.

B Conception, Pregnancy, and Childbirth

A female's ovaries alternate in releasing one egg, or ovum, each month, in a process called **ovulation.** Ovulation takes place about fourteen days before a menstrual period; so a woman's most fertile time is usually midway between menstrual periods, when the ovum is traveling through the fallopian tube to the uterus.

Conception

When sperm enter a female's vagina during coitus, they move into the fallopian tubes and can live there from two to five days. **Conception** takes place after **fertilization,** or the joining of the sperm cell with the ovum. If this takes place in the fallopian tube, the fertilized egg, or **zygote,** moves down to the uterus, where it embeds itself in the thickened lining, or endometrium (see Figure B-1), a process called **implantation.** Until an umbilical cord is formed during about the fifth week, the endometrial tissue provides nourishment for the developing fetus.

Pregnancy

The fertilization and implantation processes just described take place during the **germinal period,** or first two weeks of pregnancy. During this early period, the woman usually isn't aware that she is pregnant. By the fourth week, however, she may begin to notice some changes.

The first signs a woman often notices are a cessation of menstruation (because the endometrial tissue will not be sloughed off), nausea (a physical reaction to the zygote's embedding itself in the uterine wall), changes in the size and fullness of the breasts, darkened coloration of the **areolae** around the nipples, fatigue, and frequency of urination, a result of pressure on the bladder from the expanding uterus. Not all of these signs, including nausea and cessation of menstruation, are always present, so a woman who suspects she is pregnant should have a pregnancy test even if not all classical signs of pregnancy are present.

The Embryonic Stage The **embryonic stage** of pregnancy lasts from the third until about the eighth week. During this stage the head, skeletal system, heart, and digestive system begin to form. Also during this time a sac of salty, watery fluid called **amniotic fluid** surrounds the fetus to cushion and protect it. In later stages of pregnancy, doctors can detect some fetal diseases by withdrawing a tiny portion of this amniotic fluid through the mother's abdomen with a syringe and testing it in a laboratory. (See Box 12-1, "High-Tech Pregnancy: Ultrasound and Amniocentesis.") During this period, the **placenta,** which holds the fetus in place

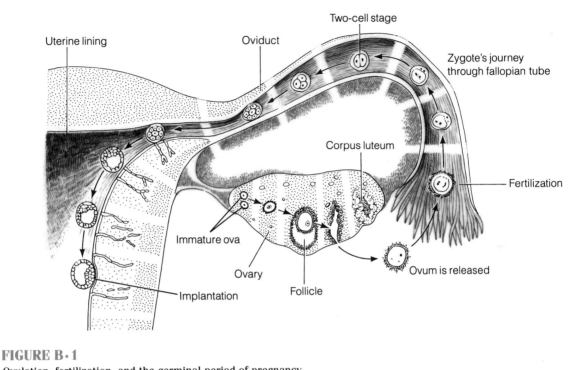

FIGURE B·1

Ovulation, fertilization, and the germinal period of pregnancy.

Labels in figure:

Uterine lining

Oviduct

Two-cell stage

Zygote's journey through fallopian tube

Corpus luteum

Fertilization

Immature ova

Ovum is released

Ovary

Follicle

Implantation

---

inside the uterus and functions in nourishment, develops. (The placenta will be discharged in childbirth.)

The Fetal Stage   The **fetal period** of development lasts from about eight weeks until birth. This span, including the germinal and embryonic periods, is often broken down into three three-month "trimesters." During the fetal period the organs and structural system that budded during the embryonic stage refine themselves and grow. Some of the changes that take place up to fifteen weeks are illustrated in Figure B-2.

In the third month the facial features become differentiated. The lips take shape, the nose begins to stand out, and the eyelids are formed, although they remain fused. The fingers and toes are well developed, and fingernails and toenails are forming.

During the fourth month most of the fetus's bones have formed, although they are still soft cartilage and will not be completely hardened into bone until many years after birth.

In the fifth month the fetal heartbeat can be heard through a stethoscope. Around this time, too, the **quickening**—the first fetal movements apparent to the mother herself—progresses from a mild fluttering to solid kicks against the side of the mother's abdomen. Any nausea the mother may have experienced usually disappears by now, and she is in the most comfortable period of her pregnancy.

In the sixth month the fetus grows to a foot in

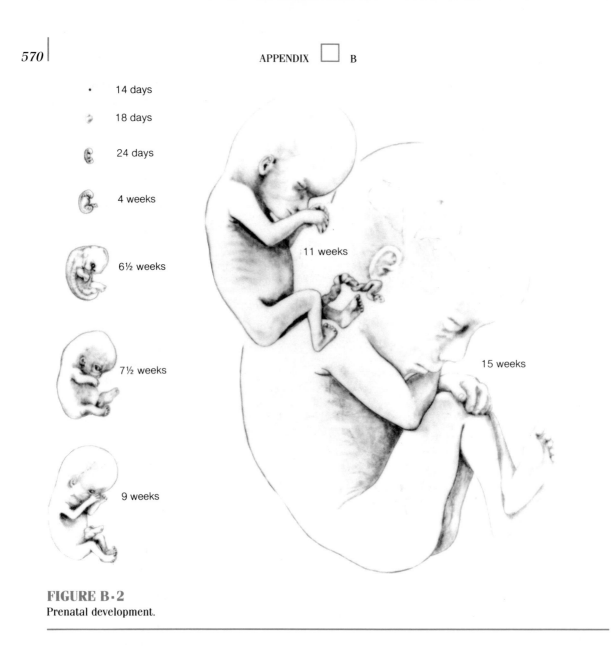

14 days

18 days

24 days

4 weeks

6½ weeks

7½ weeks

9 weeks

11 weeks

15 weeks

FIGURE B·2
Prenatal development.

length and about twenty ounces in weight. The fetus now has eyelashes; it can open and close its eyes and may even learn to suck its thumb. By the end of this month, its essential anatomy and physiology are almost complete; further development consists largely of an increase in size and of refinement and stabilization of the organs' functions. A fetus born or aborted at this time is likely to emerge alive and may live several hours. Survival beyond that will require constant medical attention, and the chances for survival are slim.

By seven months the fetus weighs about two and a half pounds. If it is born now, it will have a fair chance of survival with the aid of specialized attention and equipment. A baby born in the eighth month of pregnancy has a very good chance of survival, since its development is virtually complete.

In the eighth and ninth months of pregnancy, the fetus grows very rapidly, gaining an average of a half pound per week. At this time, the mother is likely to feel generally healthy but may also be uncomfortable because of the crowding in her expanding uterus and because weight increases may disrupt her equilibrium and her ability to get around. Toward the end of pregnancy, the fetus usually changes its position so that the head is in the lower part of the uterus. This marks the beginning of preparation for birth.

Childbirth

The process of childbirth takes place in three stages: labor, delivery, and afterbirth. Figure B-3 depicts the first two phases.

Labor   **Labor** is the process by which the baby is propelled from the mother's body through a series of contractions of the muscles of the uterus. Labor usually begins with mild contractions, at intervals of about fifteen to twenty minutes. The contractions increase steadily over the first phase of labor (usually from six to eighteen hours for the first birth, shorter for subsequent births); they also increase in intensity and duration until by the end of labor each contraction lasts a minute or more.

During labor some other changes usually take place. The cervix dilates from its normal size (about one-eighth inch) to approximately four inches in preparation for the baby's passage. A second occurrence is the expulsion of a bloody plug (sometimes called *show*) from the base of the uterus through the vagina. During pregnancy the plug helped prevent infectious bacteria from entering the uterus through the cervix. And third, the amniotic membrane (often called the *bag of waters*) ruptures, and amniotic fluid flows from the vagina. Show and breakage of waters are usually signs of imminent delivery. Together with these, full dilation of the cervix marks the beginning of the second, or delivery, stage of childbirth.

Delivery   The second phase of childbirth is the **delivery** of the baby. This phase extends from the time the cervix is completely dilated until the fetus is expelled—a process that may last from less than twenty minutes to (rarely) more than ninety minutes. The mother can often speed the birth process at this stage by tightening the muscles in her diaphragm, abdomen, and back so that the uterine muscles are aided in pushing the baby through the cervix. Her active participation at this point may also help reduce pain.

When the baby appears at the vaginal opening *(crowning),* its head usually turns so that the back of its skull emerges first, as is shown in Figure B-3. After the head emerges, the infant usually turns again to find the path of least resistance. This kind of delivery, in which the baby's skull emerges first,

occurs in about 95 percent of births. The remaining 5 percent of deliveries are more difficult: If the baby's buttocks, shoulder, foot, or face emerges first **(breech presentation),** the baby will not be able to take as compact a shape as it passes through the vagina.

Oversized babies (the average newborn weighs seven and a half pounds) can also cause problems because the baby's head must pass between the bones of the mother's pelvic arch. If the baby is too large, or if the mother's or baby's physical condition makes the stress of childbirth dangerous, a physician may decide to deliver the child by cesarean, or Caesarean, section (so called after Julius Caesar who was supposedly born in this way). A **cesarean section** is a surgical operation in which a physician makes an incision in the mother's abdomen and uterine wall to remove the infant.[1]

Another source of complications may be weak uterine contractions (often caused by anesthetics). If contractions are not strong enough to expel the baby, a physician may use forceps, tongs that fit around the baby's head, to draw the baby out through the vagina. This procedure is risky, however, for the inaccurate placement of forceps, along with the force necessary to pull the infant free, may cause disfigurement or brain damage.

Afterbirth   The third and final stage of childbirth takes place between two and twenty minutes after delivery. It consists of the expulsion of the **afterbirth:** the placenta, the amniotic sac, and the remainder of the umbilical cord.

"Natural" Childbirth   Hospitalization and a doctor's assistance have contributed greatly over the years to the sharp decrease in infant and maternal death during childbirth. The overwhelming majority, 98.5 percent, of babies born in 1984 were delivered in hospitals, as has been true for

---

1. An unprecedented 18 percent of the nation's infants are now born by cesarean section, and the rate is rising by about 1 percent annually. The National Center for Health Statistics reports that the cesarean rate rose from 4.5 percent of births in 1965 to 18 percent in 1981. There is no question that cesareans often are lifesaving procedures for both mothers and infants. But recently some women's and consumer's groups have warned against overdoing the practice. The trend alarms some because a cesarean section deprives a mother of the experience of normal childbirth. Cost is also a factor. One study showed that in 1977, the costs of a cesarean delivery ran an average of $2,300 more than a vaginal delivery ("C-section births," 1983).

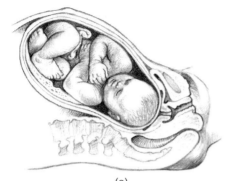

(a)

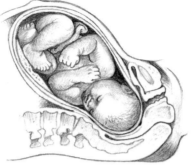

(b)

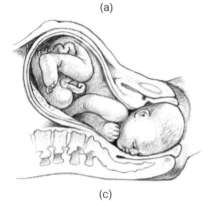

(c)

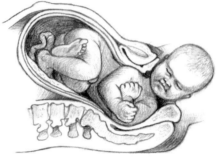

(d)

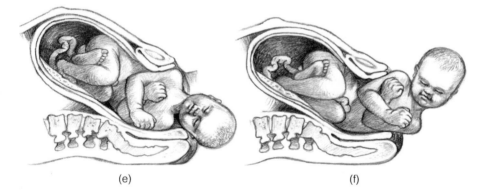

(e)

(f)

FIGURE B·3

Events in the childbirth process. (a) Before labor begins; (b) early stages of labor; cervix is dilating; baby's head starts to turn; (c) baby's head begins to emerge; (d) baby emerges and turns head to side; (e) delivery of anterior shoulder; (f) delivery of posterior shoulder.

many years (U.S. Bureau of the Census, 1986b). This reliance on hospitals and doctors, however, has given rise to a negative reaction against the treatment of childbirth as a medical problem rather than a natural event. Many physicians, nurses, and expectant mothers prefer not to rely on forceps, heavy anesthesia, or other often unnecessary procedures. They feel that more natural methods of delivery are more emotionally satisfying to both the mother and father and are often better for the infant.

Infants born under heavy sedation are less responsive and alert; they also have somewhat reduced chances for surviving a medical emergency. The parent-child bond is less easily established. Newer forms of birthing include "natural" childbirth, in which the use of anesthesia is minimized and the father's presence and participation are encouraged. The baby may be given to the mother for nursing or affectionate contact even before the umbilical cord is tied. A very recent development, still not legally or administratively permissible in all states, is the use of midwives rather than physicians as professional birth attendants. Midwives are paraprofessionals specially trained to assist mothers in the birth process; they provide both emotional support and professional expertise and recognize that the baby belongs to the family, not to the medical establishment. There is a small trend for more births delivered by midwives both in and out of hospitals. Although the numbers of such births are still relatively small, they have increased substantially in recent years (U.S. Bureau of the Census, 1986b).

C Contraceptive Techniques

Contraceptives, techniques and methods to prevent conception, can be divided into three groups. One group uses various chemical substances or mechanical devices, or both. These include the pill; the diaphragm; vaginal foam, cream, or jellies; vaginal suppositories; the contraceptive sponge (all used by females); and the condom, or "rubber" (used by the male). Chemical substances alter the biochemistry of the body, while mechanical devices form barriers between the sperm and ovum. Figure C-1 pictures some types of contraceptive devices. They are described in Table C-1.

A second method of contraception is the surgical sterilization of either the male (vasectomy) or the female (usually by tubal ligation). A vasectomy involves tying the tubes between the testicles (where sperm is produced) and the penis (through which the seminal fluid is ejaculated). The procedure can be done in a doctor's office and is safe. Following a vasectomy the male will be able to have erections, enjoy sex, and ejaculate as before the sterilization, but he will not be able to cause pregnancies. A tubal ligation involves cutting or scarring the fallopian tubes between a woman's ovaries and her uterus so that eggs cannot pass into the tubes to be fertilized. Tubal ligation must be done in a hospital and is more expensive than a vasectomy, but it is also safe. Unlike the techniques in the first group, which are generally reversible when one decides to have children, sterilization is a one-time procedure that is virtually 100 percent effec-

tive and usually permanent. Microsurgical techniques to restore fertility have been developed but are not always successful. Thus, couples should be certain about their decision to give up the capacity to have children.

The third type of conception control avoids all surgery, chemicals, and devices. Instead, it is based on controlling sexual behavior. One such method, the rhythm method, or periodic abstinence, depends on the couple's awareness of the woman's ovulation cycle: The couple refrains from intercourse for several days before and after the woman ovulates. The effectiveness of this technique, also described in Table C-1 depends on how correctly and diligently it is used.

Another method, withdrawal, is not included in Table C-1. It depends on the male's withdrawing his penis from the woman's vagina before he experiences orgasm. This technique is not effective: The male is tempted not to withdraw; and even if he does, the few drops of fluid that are emitted before orgasm may contain sperm, making it possible for the woman to become pregnant.

In order to choose which alternative or alternatives to use,[1] people need to consider how each method works, how effective it is, its advantages and disadvantages, its side effects, health impli-

---

1. Combining two (or more) methods—such as diaphragm and spermicidal cream—can often increase effectiveness greatly.

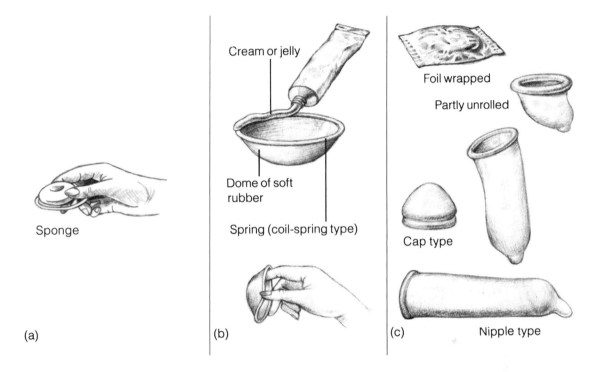

Sponge

(a)

Cream or jelly

Dome of soft rubber

Spring (coil-spring type)

(b)

Foil wrapped

Partly unrolled

Cap type

Nipple type

(c)

FIGURE C·1

Some types of contraceptive devices: (a) the sponge, which contains spermicide that is released in the woman's vagina; (b) a diaphragm—spermicidal cream is squeezed into the cup and around the rim before the diaphragm is inserted in the vagina; (c) condoms, placed over the man's penis.

cations for the user, and long-term effects on the ability to have children. Of the methods discussed, oral contraceptives and sterilization are the most frequently used, as Table C-1 shows.

We have not yet mentioned one means of controlling fertility: **abortion.** Abortion differs from the methods already discussed because it does not prevent conception but terminates the development of the fetus after conception.[2]

2. A new form of fertility regulation, menstrual extraction, cannot be classified as either abortion or contraception. In menstrual extraction the contents of the uterus are suctioned and scooped out at about the time of the expected menstrual period, whether or not a pregnancy has occurred. If this is performed regularly and under the assumption that there is no pregnancy, it can be viewed as a measure for health or convenience (avoiding debilitating periods), not as abortion. In effect, however, it would abort a zygote and may be performed with that purpose in mind.

TABLE C·1   A Comparison of Birth Control Methods

	What this is	What this does	How well this works[a]	Main advantages	Who can use this
The Pill	A monthly series of birth control pills. The ingredients are similar to hormones normally produced in a woman's body.	Most kinds of birth control pills keep your ovaries from releasing eggs. They do this only if you take a full monthly series on time. If you forget one or more pills, you may become pregnant.	Of 100 women on the Pill, about 2 may become pregnant during the first year of actual use. Women who never forget the Pill have less chance of getting pregnant.	It's a highly effective method, and convenient to use. Periods are more regular, with less cramps and less blood loss. There is less iron deficiency anemia, less acne, less pelvic inflammatory disease, and fewer ectopic pregnancies among users. It may offer some protection from non-cancerous breast tumors and ovarian cysts, as well as from ovarian and endometrial cancer.	Pill use is ruled out if you have, or have had, blood clots, or inflammation in the veins, serious liver diseases or unexplained bleeding from the vagina; also any suspicion of abnormal growth or cancer of the breast or uterus. You may need special tests to see whether you should take the Pill if you have certain other conditions that could get worse using the Pill.

More detailed information about the risks of birth control pills and who should not use them is provided in the package insert that accompanies each package of birth control pills. It is essential that you read and understand this additional information. |
| **Diaphragm** | A soft rubber cup with a flexible rim around the edge. It's used with contraceptive cream or jelly. | It's inserted into a woman's vagina before intercourse. The diaphragm covers the entrance to the uterus, and the cream or jelly halts sperm movement. | Of 100 women using diaphragms, about 19 may become pregnant during the first year of actual use. You may increase protection by checking that it covers the cervix every time you have intercourse. | Once it's learned, insertion is easy. It can be part of bedtime routine. Or it can be shared by both partners during lovemaking. Properly placed, it is not felt by either the woman or the man. | Diaphragm use is not recommended for women with poor muscle tone of the vagina or those who have a sagging uterus, or vaginal obstructions. |

How this is used	Possible problems		Warning signals
Take your particular pills as directed. You're protected as long as you take them on time and don't skip any. If you see a doctor for some other reason, be sure to say you're on the Pill. When you want to get pregnant, stop the pills. Use another method until your periods become regular. Normal cycles usually return in a few months, but a few women may have trouble getting pregnant for a while after pill use. After having a baby, get medical advice about when to go back on the Pill, especially if you plan to nurse. You must have regular medical checkups while taking the Pill.	Pill users have a greater chance than non-users of developing certain serious problems that may become fatal in rare cases, including blood clots, stroke, heart attack (to women age 35 and older), or liver tumors. Such chances increase with age, and when certain other health problems are present. The risks are magnified by smoking more than 15 cigarettes a day; by conditions such as high blood pressure, high levels of blood fat, or diabetes; or by being about a third above ideal weight or 35 years of age or over. To learn more about possible problems with pill use, talk to your clinician, and read the Pill package insert.	Some minor reactions include breast tenderness, nausea, vomiting, weight gain or loss, and spotting between periods. These often clear up after two to three months of use. Combining the Pill with other medicines such as antibiotics or drugs to control seizures may reduce the effectiveness of the Pill in preventing pregnancy. Talk to your doctor about what to do.	Report immediately any of the following symptoms: unusual swelling or pain in the legs; yellowing of skin or eyes; pain in the abdomen, chest or arms; shortness of breath; severe headache; severe depression; eye problems, such as blurred or double vision.
You must have the right size diaphragm prescribed for it to fit properly and work well. You will be shown how to put it in and take it out. Always use contraceptive cream or jelly with your diaphragm. And it must be in place every time you have sex. Check that the size needed is the same after a full-term pregnancy, or abortion or miscarriage beyond the first full three months of pregnancy, or pelvic surgery, or weight gain or loss of 10 pounds or more.	Most women have no side effects. Some women who use a diaphragm are more prone to develop bladder infections. Occasional mild allergic reactions to rubber or cream or jelly may occur. Women with very short fingers may need to use an inserter. A diaphragm may become dislodged during sex if the woman is on top or has a relaxed vagina as a result of childbirth. Check the diaphragm for weak spots or pin holes from time to time by holding to the light.		Report promptly any discomfort when the diaphragm is in place, irritation or itching in the genital area, frequent bladder infections, or unusual discharge from the vagina.

(continued)

TABLE C·1   Continued

	What this is	What this does	How well this works[a]	Main advantages	Who can use this
Contraceptive sponge	A soft, round-shaped sponge approximately two inches in diameter made of a synthetic substance impregnated with spermicide. A nylon loop is attached across the bottom of the sponge for ease of removal.	The sponge is moistened and inserted into the vagina (much like a diaphragm) before intercourse. The "dimple" fits over the cervix. The sponge continuously releases a spermicide that halts sperm activity and acts as a barrier to block sperm from entering a woman's uterus.	Research studies claim that of 100 women using the sponge, 9 to 11 percent will become pregnant. Pregnancy rates will likely be higher in actual use. An insert with detailed instructions for correct use is packaged with each sponge. Effectiveness can be further increased by using an additional method of contraception with the sponge, such as a condom.	It comes in one size. Once learned, insertion is easy. When inserted, there's no need to wait to have sexual intercourse and intercourse may be repeated within a twenty-four-hour period without additional preparation. There's little messiness or leakage. The spermicide contained in the sponge may offer some protection against certain sexually transmissible diseases. The sponge can be purchased without prescription.	Just about any woman who can use a tampon can use the sponge. However, a woman with short fingers may have difficulty placing and removing the sponge.

How this is used	Possible problems	Warning signals

Hold the sponge in one hand with the "dimple" side facing the body. The loop should dangle under the sponge away from the body. Wet it with a small amount of water (about two tablespoons) and squeeze to remove excess water. This activates the spermicide. Fold the sides of the sponge upward so the sponge looks long and narrow. Then slide the sponge into the opening of the vagina and as far back as your fingers will reach. When you let go of the sponge, it unfolds so as to cover the cervix. Check the position of the sponge by sliding a finger around the edge of the sponge to make sure the cervix is covered. You should be able to feel the ribbon loop across the bottom of the sponge. It may be worn for up to twenty-four hours without change, but it must be left in place for six hours after the last act of intercourse prior to removal. Put a finger inside the vagina, and hook it around the loop. Then slowly and gently pull the sponge out. The sponge is for one time use only, and should never be reused. Always discard the old sponge in a waste container. Do not flush down the toilet. Do not use during menstruation. If you have any questions, any problems, or are unsure about how to use the sponge, you should consult with your physician or local family planning clinic.

Rarely, irritation may occur with use of the sponge due to an allergic reaction. If this happens, discontinuing use of the sponge should clear up the problem. Removal problems can occur. If the loop cannot be located, or if the sponge cannot be found, or if found, cannot be removed, or if it fragments, a woman should call her physician or clinic for an examination and removal. There is some concern that sponge users may be at increased risk of toxic shock syndrome (TSS), which is associated with tampon use. Because the sponge is new, it is not known with certainty whether there is a definite relationship between TSS and sponge use. However, a few cases of TSS in which symptoms developed within twenty-four hours after sponge use have been reported. To minimize such a risk, do not leave the sponge in place longer than twenty-four hours, never use during menstruation, and avoid use after delivery of a baby or an abortion until your doctor approves. Also, promptly seek help with removal if such proves difficult.

Report promptly any itching or irritation in the genital area, persistent unpleasant odor, or unusual discharge from the vagina.

(continued)

TABLE C·1 Continued

	What this is	What this does	How well this works[a]	Main advantages	Who can use this
Condom	A sheath of thin rubber or animal tissue. It is put on a man's erect penis before intercourse.	A condom collects a man's semen and keeps sperm from entering a woman's vagina.	Of 100 couples relying on condoms, about 10 pregnancies may occur during the first year of actual use. When the woman uses a vaginal contraceptive at the same time, there is greater protection.	Condoms are easy to get. They help protect against sexually transmissible diseases. They're a reliable and handy backup or second method. They may help men with problems of premature ejaculation.	Just about any man who wishes to can use a condom. Men with sensitivity to rubber may be rare exceptions. Condoms may be purchased by men and women, and there are no age restrictions.
Vaginal contraceptives	Foams, creams, jellies and suppositories are chemical substances inserted before intercourse that stop sperm but don't harm vaginal tissue.	A vaginal contraceptive is inserted into a woman's vagina before intercourse. It spreads over the entrance to the uterus. It blocks sperm from entering the uterus, and the chemical halts sperm movement.	Of 100 women using a vaginal contraceptive, about 18 may become pregnant during the first year of actual use. When the man uses a condom at the same time, greater protection is possible.	Easy to buy in drug stores. Easy to use. May offer some protection against certain sexually transmissible diseases.	Almost any woman who wants to can use a vaginal contraceptive.
Fertility awareness	Several ways of checking a woman's changing bodily signs are designed to help her discover the days each month when an egg is likely to be released.	Knowing the several days before, during and right after an egg is released lets a woman avoid unprotected intercourse during her peak fertility, to prevent live sperm from meeting the egg.	Among 100 women limiting intercourse by these methods, about 24 may become pregnant during the first year of actual use. Keeping careful records can give better results.	No medication and little equipment is needed. Calendars, thermometers and charts are easy to get. These methods are acceptable to all religious groups.	Any woman in good health, who has been given careful instructions. Most successful users combine taking their temperature each day and checking vaginal mucus.

a. Careful and consistent use of methods can give better results than rates reported in actual use for users.

SOURCE: Reprinted courtesy of Planned Parenthood Federation of America, Inc., from a chart published in 1986. Source for information on the contraceptive sponge: Eagan, Jan. 1984:94 and *Planned Parenthood News*, Summer 1983.

How this is used	Possible problems		Warning signals
Either partner may roll a condom over the erect penis. About one-half inch at the tip is left slack to catch semen. After climax, but before losing erection, the rim of the condom must be held against the penis as the man withdraws. That way, the condom can't slip and spill semen. Then it's thrown away. A fresh one must be used for each act of intercourse.	Rough handling may tear rubber. Care is needed in withdrawing. Some couples object to the condom because it interrupts lovemaking. However, the man or woman can put the condom on as part of foreplay. Some users claim feeling is dulled.		None.
Some are to be inserted not more than an hour before intercourse, others about 10 minutes before. Dosage quantities vary. Each product has directions on the package. Usually, a woman lies down or squats, and gently inserts the product deep into the vagina. More must be inserted if sex is repeated.	No known side effect. In rare cases a woman or man may find these products produce a slight genital irritation. Changing brands may help. If not used exactly as directed, these products may not form a good barrier to the uterus. Some women complain of messiness or leakage.		None.
A woman's body temperature rises a little when an egg is released. Then it stays up until her next period. Her vaginal mucus increases just before an egg is released, and is clear and slippery. As it reduces in quantity it becomes cloudy and sticky, and may disappear. Every day, temperature must be taken and/or vaginal mucus checked, and records kept.	No bodily side effects to the user. Studies suggest there may be a slightly increased risk that a baby could have birth defects if an "aging" egg is fertilized. Care is needed in keeping records and interpreting signs. Illness or even lack of sleep can produce false temperature	signals. Vaginal infections or use of vaginal products or medication may alter changes in vaginal mucus.	None.

D Sexually Transmitted Diseases

More than a dozen diseases are transmitted through sexual contact. They affect people in every social class, occupation, education, and age category in the United States today.

Historically, the two most serious and widespread sexually transmitted diseases were syphilis and gonorrhea. Syphilis is eventually fatal and causes severe pain as well as dementia; it can be transmitted to the fetus during pregnancy. Gonorrhea can cause sterility in adults and also blindness-producing eye infections in infants during the birth process.

The introduction of antibiotic treatment, public health measures, and education enabling victims to identify symptoms and seek treatment appeared to almost eliminate syphilis and gonorrhea by the 1960s. Familiarity and the knowledge that the diseases could be treated reduced public anxiety considerably. But by the 1970s and early 1980s, the development of new antibiotic-resistant strains of these diseases, increased sexual activity, and increased vulnerability of some segments of the population because of increasing poverty, malnutrition, and drug use led to rising rates of these STDs, particularly in large urban centers. Recently, AIDS-inspired behavior changes toward more conservative sexual practices appear to have resulted in decreases in syphilis and gonorrhea.

Herpes simplex virus, Type II, developed as a new STD in the 1970s. Related to the herpes-I virus, which causes cold sores, HSV-II proved threatening to sexually active people because of its contagiousness and its debilitating symptoms of fever, headache, and general malaise. With the development of a pharmaceutical treatment for herpes and especially because of the emergence of AIDS in the eighties, herpes has come to seem much less fearful. Many people harbor the virus without incident. Danger to newborns from infection during the birth process still exists, however, and drug treatment is not totally effective.

AIDS is discussed in detail in Chapter 4. Always fatal and only minimally treatable thus far, it dominates our discussions of sexually transmitted diseases with good reason.

Still, a host of STDs that are less serious than AIDS, syphilis, and gonorrhea can be unpleasant and can also have a significant impact on fertility. Identification of new diseases and reclassification of old ones occurs frequently. Our STD chart includes chlamydial infections (nongonococcal urethritis and mucopurulent cervicitis and vaginitis—male and female genital tract inflammations), enteric diseases (infections of the digestive tract, particularly associated with male homosexual activity), and pelvic inflammatory disease, as well as genital warts, chancroid sores, and scabies and pubic lice. Hepatitis B is now classified as an STD.

Possible symptoms of STDs are unusual vaginal or penile discharges, genital tract itching, painful urination, nodules or growths, abdominal pain, or some combination of these, and possibly general symptoms such as headache, fever, chills, and digestive tract disturbances. These STDs can be treated by a physician, although considerable patience and experimentation with modes of treatment may be required. Treatment of the sexual partner or temporary abstinence from sex or both may also be necessary. Holistic health books or womens' health books (such as *Our Bodies, Ourselves*, Boston Women's Health Book Collective, 1976, 1984) may indicate helpful dietary, sexual, or clothing changes as well as home remedies that are not harmful and may help. However, medical treatment of these seemingly minor STDs is still important, not only because of discomfort, responsibility toward sexual partners, and potential reproductive complications but also because discoveries in recent years have hinted at the greater seriousness of STDs that were previously thought to be inconsequential. For example, pelvic inflammatory disease (a generic term for abdominal infections) can be a consequence of sexual activity and can have life-threatening complications.

Because of the serious consequences of these sexually transmitted disease if they are left untreated, they should be diagnosed and treated early. Persons who know that they have an STD should avoid sexual contact until they are completely cured. Doctors and clinics will offer more specific guidelines in individual cases. Moreover, persons who may have inadvertently exposed others to an STD should inform any partner or partners that they may have become infected. People who are sexually active with more than one partner should consider having a medical examination and blood tests frequently, even once a month. Anyone suspecting or finding symptoms of an STD should seek immediate diagnosis and treatment from a doctor or the free clinics available in most areas (Miller, 1988; Pierson and D'Antonio, 1974; Van Gelder, 1982; Clark, 1982; Seligman, 1980; Gagnon, 1977; Seligman, 1983; "Syphilis afflicts more newborns," 1984; "Syphilis cases drop sharply," 1985; Eckholm, 1986).

Table D-1 presents part of the 1986 sexually transmitted disease summary prepared by the U.S. Center for Disease Control in Atlanta, the premier U.S. public health agency. The terminology is technical and oriented to physicians, but we thought this technical information might prove helpful.

Table D · 1 Sexually Transmitted Disease Summary, 1986

Disease and Its Causes	Typical Symptoms	Complications and Aftereffects	Guidelines for Treatment
Nongonococcal Urethritis (NGU) *Chlamydia trachomatis* A human mycoplasma of the T-strain. Other sexually transmissible agents can cause NGU, these include: *Ureaplasma urealyticum, Trichomonas vaginalis, Candida albicans,* Herpes simplex virus.	Men usually have dysuria, frequency, and mucoid to purulent urethral discharge. Some men have asymptomatic infections. Steady female sexual partners of men with chlamydial NGU are likely to have chlamydial endocervicitis.	Urethral strictures. Prostatitis. Epididymitis. Chlamydial NGU may be transmitted to female sexual partners resulting in mucopurulent endocervicitis, PID and other adverse outcomes. (See below.)	Understand how to take any prescribed oral medications. If tetracycline is prescribed, take it 1 hour before or 2 hours after meals and avoid dairy products, antacids, iron or other mineral-containing preparations, and sunlight. Return for test-of-cure or evaluation 4-7 days after completion of therapy, or earlier if symptoms persist or recur. Refer sexual partner(s) for examination and treatment. Avoid sex until patient and partner(s) are cured. Use condoms to prevent future infections.
Mucopurulent Cervicitis (MPC) *Chlamydia trachomatis* is the principal pathogen, although *Neisseria gonorrhoeae,* herpes simplex virus, *Candida albicans,* and *Trichomonas vaginalis* can also produce cervicitus (see relevant panels).	The patient may be symptomatic or asymptomatic, and a yellow mucopurulent endocervical exudate may be present. Cervical ectopy appears to be correlated with cervical infection with this agent.	Ascending infections may lead to symptomatic or asymptomatic endometritis and salpingitis and subsequent infertility. Ascending infection during pregnancy may lead to adverse obstetric outcomes, conjunctivitis, or pneumonia in the infant, and puerperal infection.	Understand how to take any prescribed oral medications. If tetracycline is given, take it 1 hour before or 2 hours after meals, and avoid dairy products, antacids, iron or other mineral-containing preparations, and sunlight. Return for reevaluation 4-7 days after completion of therapy, or earlier if symptoms persist or recur. Refer sexual partner(s) for examination and treatment. Avoid sex until patient and partner(s) are cured. Avoid condoms to prevent future infections.

(continued)

Table D·1 Continued

Disease and Its Causes	Typical Symptoms	Complications and Aftereffects	Guidelines for Treatment
Gonorrhea *Neisseria gonorrhoeae* A Gram-negative diplococcus.	When symptomatic, men usually have dysuria, frequency, and purulent urethral discharge. Women may have abnormal vaginal discharge, abnormal menses, dysuria, or be asymptomatic. Anorectal and pharyngeal infections are common. These may be symptomatic or asymptomatic.	10-20 percent of women develop pelvic inflammatory disease (PID) and are at risk for its sequelae (see below). Men are at risk for epididymitis, sterility, urethral stricture, and infertility. Newborns are at risk for ophthalmia neonatorum, scalp abscess at the site of fetal monitors, rhinitis, pneumonia, or anorectal infections. All infected, untreated persons are at risk for disseminated gonococcal infection (includes septicemia, arthritis, dermatitis, meningitis, and endocarditis).	Understand how to take any prescribed oral medications. If tetracycline is prescribed, take it 1 hour before or 2 hours after meals and avoid dairy products, antacids, iron or other mineral-containing preparations, and sunlight. Return for test-of-cure 4-7 days after completing therapy. Refer sexual partners for examination and treatment. Avoid sex until patient and partner(s) are cured. Return early if symptoms persist or recur. Use condoms to prevent future infections.
Pelvic Inflammatory Disease (PID) *Neisseria gonorrhoeae* *Chlamydia trachomatis* An obligate intracellular organism of immunotypes A through K. Other microorganisms cause PID. Most of these have not been associated with sexual transmission.	The patient may present with pain and tenderness involving the lower abdomen, cervix, uterus, and adnexae, possibly combined with fever, chills, and elevated white blood cell (WBC) count and erythrocyte sedimentation rate (ESR). The diagnosis is more likely if the patient has multiple sexual partners, a history of PID, uses an intrauterine device (IUD), or is in the first 5-10 days of her menstrual cycle.	Potentially life threatening complications include ectopic pregnancy and pelvic abscess. Other complications are involuntary infertility, recurrent PID, chronic PID, chronic abdominal pain, pelvic adhesions, premature hysterectomy, and depression.	Understand how to take any prescribed oral medications. If tetracycline is given, take it 1 hour before or 2 hours after meals and avoid dairy products, antacids, iron or other mineral-containing preparations, and sunlight. Return 2-3 days after initiation of therapy for progress evaluation. Return for test-of-cure 4-7 days after completing therapy. Refer sexual partner(s) for evaluation and treatment. Avoid sexual activity until patient and partner(s) are cured. If an IUD is used, consult with family planning physician. Use condoms to prevent future infections.

(continued)

Table D·1   Continued

Disease and Its Causes	Typical Symptoms	Complications and Aftereffects	Guidelines for Treatment
Vaginitis *Trichomonas vaginalis vaginitis* A motile protozoan with an undulating membrane and four flagella. *Bacterial vaginosis (also called nonspecific vaginitis or Gardnerella vaginalis–associated vaginitis).* An infection of uncertain etiology: *Gardnerella vaginalis* (a small Gram negative pleomorphic coccobacillus), *Mobiluncus* spp. (motile, curved anaerobic rods), and other anaerobes have been implicated. *Fungal vaginitis (predominantly Candida albicans)* Dimorphic fungi which grow as oval budding yeast cells and as chains of cells (hyphae). Other vaginitides Other infectious, chemical, allergenic, and physical agents can cause vaginitis.	Presentations vary from no signs or symptoms to erythema, edema, and pruritus of the external genitalia. Excessive and/or malodorous discharge are common findings. Male sexual partners may develop urethritis, balanitis, or cutaneous lesions on penis.	Secondary excoriations. Recurrent infections are common. Bacterial vaginosis may be associated with infectious complications of pregnancy, such as chorioamnionitis and puerperal infection, and with polymicrobial upper genital tract infections in nonpregnant women, such as endometritis and salpingitis. Fungal vaginitis in pregnancy increases the risk of neonatal oral thrush.	Understand how to take or use any prescribed medications. Avoid alcohol until 3 days following completion of metronidazole therapy. Continue taking vaginally administered medications even during menses. Return if problems not cured or if it recurs. Use condoms to prevent trichomonas infections.
Genital Warts *Human papilloma virus* A small slowly growing DNA virus belonging to the papovavirus group.	Presents as single or multiple soft, fleshy, papillary or sessile, painless growths around the anus, vulvovaginal area, penis, urethra, or perineum.	Lesions may enlarge and produce tissue destruction. Giant condyloma, while histologically benign, may simulate carcinoma. Cervical lesions have been associated with neoplasia. In pregnancy, warts enlarge, are extremely vascular, and may obstruct the birth canal necessitating Cesarean section.	Return for weekly or biweekly treatment and followup until lesions have resolved. Partners should be examined for warts. Abstain from sex or use condoms during therapy.

(continued)

Table D·1 Continued

Disease and Its Causes	Typical Symptoms	Complications and Aftereffects	Guidelines for Treatment
Herpes Genitalis Herpes simplex virus (HSV) types 1 and 2 DNA viruses which cannot be distinguished clinically.	Single or multiple vesicles appear anywhere on the genitalia. Vesicles spontaneously rupture to form shallow ulcers which may be very painful. Lesions resolve spontaneously without scarring. The first occurrence is termed *initial infection* (mean duration 12 days). Subsequent, usually milder, occurrences are termed *recurrent infections* (mean duration 4.5 days). The interval between clinical episodes is termed *latency*. Viral shedding occurs intermittently during latency.	Males and females: Neuralgia, meningitis ascending myelitis, urethral strictures, and lymphatic suppuration may occur. Females: There is possibly an increased risk for cervical cancer and fetal wastage. Neonates: Virus from an active genital infection may be transmitted during vaginal delivery causing neonatal herpes infection. Neonatal herpes ranges in severity from clinically inapparent infections to local infections of the eyes, skin, or mucous membranes to severe disseminated infection which may involve the central nervous system. The infection has a high case fatality rate and many survivors have ocular or neurologic sequelae.	Keep involved area clean and dry. Since both initial and recurrent lesions shed high concentrations of virus, patients should abstain from sex while symptomatic. An undetermined but presumably small risk of transmission also exists during asymptomatic intervals. Condoms may offer some protection. Annual pap smears are recommended. Pregnant women should make their obstetricians aware of any history of herpes.
Syphilis *Treponema pallidum* A spirochete with 6-14 regular spirals and characteristic motility.	*Primary:* The classical chancre is painless, indurated, and located at the site of exposure. All genital lesions should be suspected to be syphilitic. *Secondary:* Patients may have a highly variable skin rash, mucous patches, condylomata lata, lymphadenopathy, or other signs. *Latent:* Patients are without clinical signs.	Both late syphilis and congenital syphilis are complications since they are preventable with prompt diagnosis and treatment of early syphilis. Sequelae of late syphilis includes neurosyphilis (general paresis, tabes dorsalis and focal neurologic signs), cardiovascular syphilis (thoracic aortic aneurism, aortic insufficiency), and localized gumma formation.	Understand how to take any prescribed oral medications. If tetracycline is given, take it 1 hour before or 2 hours after meals, and avoid dairy products, antacids, iron or other mineral-containing preparations, and sunlight. Return for followup serologies 3, 6, 12, and 24 months after therapy. Refer sexual partner(s) for evaluation and treatment. Avoid sexual activity until patient and partner(s) are cured. Use condoms to prevent future infections.
Chancroid *Haemophilis ducreyi* A pleomorphic Gram-negative bacillus commonly observed in small clusters along strands of mucous. On culture, the organism tends to form straight or tangled chains.	Usually a single (but sometimes multiple), superficial, painful ulcer appears and is surrounded by an erythematous halo. Ulcers may also be necrotic or severely erosive with ragged serpiginous borders. Accompanying adenopathy is usually unilateral. A characteristic inguinal bubo occurs in 25-60 percent of cases.	Systemic spread is not known to occur. Lesions may become secondarily infected and necrotic. Buboes may rupture and suppurate, resulting in fistulae. Ulcers on the prepuce may cause paraphimosis or phimosis.	Assure examination and treatment of sexual partner(s) as soon as possible. Return weekly or biweekly for evaluation until the infection is entirely healed. Use condoms to prevent future infections.

(continued)

Table D·1   Continued

Disease and Its Causes	Typical Symptoms	Complications and Aftereffects	Guidelines for Treatment
Pediculosis Pubis *Phthirus pubis* (pubic or crab louse) A grayish ectoparasite that is 1-4 mm long with segmented tarsi and claws for clinging to hairs.	Symptoms range from slight discomfort to intolerable itching. Erythematous papules, nits, or adult lice clinging to pubic, perineal, or perianal hairs are present and often noticed by patients.	Secondary excoriations. Lymphadenitis. Pyoderma.	Clothing and linen should be disinfested by washing them in hot water, by dry cleaning them, or by removing them from human exposure for 1-2 weeks. Avoid sexual or close physical contact until after treatment. Assure examination of sexual partners as soon as possible. Return if problem is not cured or recurs.
Scabies *Sarcoptes scabiei* The female mite is 0.3-0.4 mm; the male is somewhat smaller. The female burrows under the skin to deposit eggs.	Symptoms include itching, often worse at night, and the presence of erythematous, papular eruptions. Excoriations and secondary infections are common. Reddish-brown nodules are caused by hypersensitivity and develop 1 or more months after infection has occurred. The primary lesion is the burrow. When not obliterated by excoriations, it is most often seen on the fingers, penis, and wrists.	Secondary bacterial infection occurs, particularly with nephiritogenic strains of streptococci. Norwegian or crusted scabies (with up to 2 million adult mites in the crusts) is a risk for patients with neurologic defects and the immunologically incompetent.	Clothing and linen should be disinfected by washing them in hot water, by dry cleaning them, or by removing them from human exposure for 1-2 weeks. Avoid sexual or close physical contact until after treatment. Assure examination of sexual partners as soon as possible. Return if problem is not cured or recurs.
Hepatitis B Hepatitis B Virus (HBV) A DNA virus with multiple antigenic components.	Hepatitis B is clinically indistinguishable from other forms of hepatitis. Most infections are clinically inapparent. Clinical symptoms and signs include various combinations of anorexia, malaise, nausea, vomiting, abdominal pain and jaundice. Skin rashes, arthralgias, and arthritis can also occur.	Long-term sequelae include chronic persistent and chronic active hepatitis, cirrhosis, hepatocellular carcinoma, hepatic failure, and death. Rarely, the course may be fulminant with hepatic failure, resulting in early death. Infectious chronic carriers may be completely asymptomatic.	The frequency of clinical followup is determined by symptomatology and the results of liver function tests. Hepatitis B immune globulin (HBIG) and hepatitis B vaccine are available. Both are protective against hepatitis B infection.

(*continued*)

Table D·1 Continued

Disease and Its Causes	Typical Symptoms	Complications and Aftereffects	Guidelines for Treatment
Enteric Infections *Shigella*, hepatitis A virus, *Giardia lamblia*, *Entamoeba histolytica* and a variety of other organisms which produce enteric disease are sexually transmissible, particularly among male homosexuals.	Infections are frequently asymptomatic or minimally symptomatic. Symptoms include abdominal pain and cramping, diarrhea, fever, tenesmus, nausea, and vomiting; all in highly variable degrees of severity. Many cases give a history of frequent oral-genital and oral-anal contact, and/or a history of enteric illness in a recent sex partner.	Complications and sequelae vary with the disease agent, health of the host, therapy, and other factors. Spontaneous cures are common. Morbidity may be severe, requiring hospitalization and intravenous hydration. Infections may become systemic (such as Gram-negative septicemia) or distantly localized (amebic hepatic cyst). Some infections may rarely be fatal (hepatitis A, disseminated bacterial disease).	Follow dietary and medical regimens. Avoid oral-anal contact at least until infection is cleared. Refer sexual partner(s) for examination. Avoid sex until patient and partner(s) are cured. Return early if symptoms persist or recur.
AIDS (Acquired Immunodeficiency Syndrome) and HTLV-III/LAV INFECTIONS *Human T-lymphotropic virus type III*/lymphadenopathy associated virus and AIDS-related retrovirus. (All are agreed to be the same virus which contains RNA and is in the retrovirus family.)	The range of symptoms associated with HTL-III/LAV may extend from minimal to the full clinical syndrome of AIDS. Patients with the clinical syndrome of AIDS often give a history of nonspecific symptoms for months prior to diagnosis. These symptoms may include easy fatigue, poor appetite, weight loss, lymphadenopathy, diarrhea, fever and night sweats. Often symptoms specific to opportunistic diseases occur in patients with AIDS, such as purple to bluish skin lesions associated with Kaposi's sarcoma (KS) or shortness of breath and nonproductive cough resulting from *Pneumocystis carinii* pneumonia (PCP).	The outcome in patients with HTLV-III/LAV infection is not completely understood. Studies in a cohort of gay men whose serum contained antibody to HTLV-III/LAV showed about 5-10% of these patients were subsequently diagnosed with the clinical syndrome AIDS within 2-5 years, and another 25% had generalized lymphadenopathy or other AIDS-related conditions. The other two-thirds of the men were clinically well after 5 years.	Sexual contact with individuals who have had sex with multiple or anonymous partners increases risk of infection and should be avoided. For individuals who choose to initiate a new sexual relationship with a person at increased risk for HTLV-III/LAV infection or who maintain casual sexual relationships, sexual practices should be limited to those that do not permit any exchange of blood or bodily secretions. Condoms should be used consistently. Fisting is strongly discouraged. Do not inject illicit drugs. If such practices continue, do not share needles and syringes. Do not use inhalant nitrates ("poppers"). These have been implicated as a cofactor for Kaposi's sarcoma.

SOURCE: U.S. Department of Health and Human Services, Public Health Service, Centers for Disease Control, Center for Prevention Services, Division of Sexually Transmitted Diseases.

E Sexual Dysfunctions

Therapists distinguish six sexual dysfunctions: premature ejaculation, retarded ejaculation, and impotence among men; and general female dysfunction, female orgasmic dysfunction, and vaginismus among women (see Table E-1).

Premature Ejaculation

Premature ejaculation, the inability to control the ejaculatory reflex voluntarily, is one of the most common male sexual complaints. A man might ejaculate after several minutes of foreplay or just after entering his partner's vagina. In contrast, a man who has good ejaculatory control can continue to engage in sex play while in a highly aroused state.

The essential problem is not how quickly the man ejaculates but his inability to control the reflex. One way therapists deal with premature ejaculation is to teach a couple an exercise through which the man can gradually learn to control his orgasm. Therapists report that in most cases they have treated, premature ejaculation eventually disappears (Kaplan, 1974).

Retarded Ejaculation

A man afflicted with **retarded ejaculation,** or ejaculatory inhibition, cannot trigger orgasm. Cli-

nicians once thought that retarded ejaculation was relatively rare, but it now appears to be prevalent, at least in its mildest form.

In mild form ejaculatory inhibition is confined to specific anxiety-producing situations, such as when a man is with a new partner or when he feels guilty about the sexual encounter. In more severe cases a man may seldom experience orgasm during intercourse but may be able to achieve it by masturbation or by a partner's fondling or oral stimulation.

Treatment consists of marriage counseling sessions along with a series of progressive sexual exercises designed to relieve the man of his fears about intercourse. The rate of success with therapy is fairly high (Kaplan, 1974).

Impotence

A man suffering from **impotence,** or erectile inhibition, is unable to produce or maintain an erection. Although he may become aroused in a sexual encounter and want to have intercourse, he cannot. Clinicians and researchers estimate that half the male population has experienced at least temporary impotence. Unfortunately, our society tends to equate the capacity to have an erection with adult masculinity, so that even transient impotence may cause a man to feel almost unbearably anx-

TABLE E·1   Common Sexual Dysfunctions

Dysfunction	Symptoms	Usual Treatment
Premature ejaculation	Inability of a man to control ejaculatory reflex	Repeated stimulation to the point just before ejaculation
Retarded ejaculation	Inability of a man to trigger orgasm; may be situational or a general dysfunction	Sexual exercises combined with therapeutic counseling; temporary avoidance of intercourse and use of other means to elicit ejaculation
Impotence (erectile inhibition)	Inability of a man to produce or maintain an erection	Sexual exercises combined with therapeutic counseling; focus shifted away from *performance* aspect of sexual interaction
General female sexual dysfunction	Inability of a woman to derive erotic pleasure from sexual stimulation	Education about arousal techniques, creation of relaxed, sensuous environment free from pressure to have intercourse
Female orgasmic dysfunction	Difficulty of a woman in reaching orgasm	Focus on helping woman learn to reach climax by herself, then with husband in sexual exercises not initially aimed at intercourse
Vaginismus	Involuntary contraction of vaginal walls that prevents coitus	Correction of possible physical conditions; counseling plus exercises to recondition musculature

SOURCE: Kaplan, 1974:132–38.

NOTE: Treatment is preceded by a complete physical examination to identify any physiological causes for the disturbance.

ious, frustrated, and humiliated. In impotence, as in other sexual dysfunctions, the anxiety produced by one otherwise insignificant and transitory failure can initiate a downward spiral in which anxiety retards sexual responsiveness, leading to more anxiety about performance, less sexual success, and so on. Physicians estimate that between 40 and 60 percent of the impotence cases they see have physical causes ("Male Impotence," 1985). In some cases chronic impotence is successfully treated by surgically inserting an inflatable implant into the penis and scrotum ("Overcoming," 1984).

Although impotence can sometimes be a sign of deeper psychological problems, it is more often the result of more immediate causes, such as a fear of sexual failure, pressures created by an excessively demanding partner, or guilt (Kaplan, 1974:135). Depression or marital discord, or both, often accompany impotence, and these symptoms have to be at least somewhat relieved before a therapist can treat the impotence itself. Therefore, therapists combine sexual exercises at home with therapeutic counseling.

The exercises are designed to free the man from pressures to perform and let him simply enjoy his sexual feelings. Essentially, the couple is instructed to caress each other during sexual play but *not* to have intercourse. Permission to enjoy himself without having to perform allows the man to relax without worrying whether his body will respond. Paradoxically, the more he relaxes, the more likely his body *is* to respond. This same philosophy lies behind much of the treatment for female sexual dysfunction.

General Female Sexual Dysfunction

Women who experience **general female sexual dysfunction** derive little if any erotic pleasure from sexual stimulation. Some women have never experienced erotic pleasure; others have at one time but no longer do. Often they enjoyed petting before marriage but became unable to respond when intercourse was the expected goal of sex (Kaplan, 1974:136).

Help for a couple with this problem often begins with some basic information. Frequently, for instance, neither spouse knows where the clitoris is or recognizes its potential for eliciting erotic pleasure (Kaplan, 1974:133).

Besides giving the couple basic information, therapists encourage them to create a relaxed, sensuous atmosphere at home, one that allows for the natural unfolding of sexual responses. In one exercise the couple take turns caressing each other, but they do not progress to sexual intercourse and orgasm. Freed from the pressure to have intercourse, a woman can often experience erotic sensations, and the couple can gradually build on this sensation of pleasure until they are eventually ready for intercourse.

Female Orgasmic Dysfunction

Difficulty in reaching orgasm, or **female orgasmic dysfunction,** is the most common sexual complaint among women. Several variations are possible. Some women have never experienced orgasm,

while others experience the dysfunction after having been orgasmic. A few women cannot reach a climax under any circumstances. More often, a woman can reach orgasm, but only under specific conditions. Kaplan points out that many women with this dysfunction enjoy sex; they just "get stuck" at the plateau phase and cannot proceed to a climax (Kaplan, 1974). As in impotence, anxiety about performance can further inhibit a woman's sexual responsiveness.

Treatment for women who have never experienced orgasm usually begins by focusing on the woman alone. The therapist asks the woman to masturbate at home alone, stressing that the environment should be free from distractions and interruptions. Another approach for women who have never experienced orgasm is group education. Women meet together to learn about their bodies; they are then encouraged to masturbate at home until they become familiar and confident with their own response cycles (Barbach, 1975).

Once a woman can stimulate herself to climax, her husband enters the treatment program. The couple are told to make love as usual, except that after the husband ejaculates, he stimulates his wife to orgasm. The woman is told to be utterly "selfish," not to monitor her progress toward orgasm but to simply enjoy her sensations (Kaplan, 1974). Women are cautioned that watching one's own response to see if it's "right"—that is, headed toward orgasm—tends to inhibit physical responsiveness and to contribute to tension that sometimes develops into long-term sexual problems (Masters and Johnson, 1970). Rather, each partner is to enjoy the pleasurable sensations produced by the caresses of the partner.

This treatment is helpful in letting couples see beyond the myth of the simultaneous orgasm—the erroneous idea that true love or really great sex means that both partners must reach orgasm at the same time. Sometimes partners do climax simultaneously, but not usually. The belief that they *should* can leave the woman, who is typically slower to become aroused, frustrated; it may even encourage her to "fake it." It may be better to take turns in being pleasured to orgasm.

Direct Clitoral Versus Vaginal Stimulation

One reason it may be better to take turns is that many women report they do not reach orgasm through vaginal stimulation in intercourse, despite the earlier myth that vaginal orgasms are more "mature" than clitoral orgasms. As Chapter 4 pointed out, there is a much greater concentration of nerve endings in the clitoral prepuce than in the vagina itself. In one physician's research only about 20 percent of the women sampled said they never require a final "push" from direct clitoral stimulation to attain orgasm during intercourse. Sixty-four percent said that if they had to choose between clitoral and vaginal stimulation, they would settle for the clitoral (Fisher, 1973:247–48). One possible pattern is for the husband to stimulate his wife's clitoris until she reaches orgasm and then to enter her vagina to attain his own climax.

One sex therapist estimates that of the 90 percent of women who have experienced orgasm, only about half do so regularly during intercourse. While some therapists still treat women who cannot reach orgasm without direct clitoral stimulation, others do not attach importance to how a woman reaches a climax. They see the need for direct clitoral stimulation as a normal variant of female sexuality (Kaplan, 1974).

Recent research reported in Chapter 4 notes that some women are quite responsive vaginally. The best strategy, it would seem, would be for the individual woman to be aware and make her partner aware of her own response pattern.

Fear of Loss   Some women never achieve orgasm with a partner even with direct clitoral stimulation, although they are able to climax by masturbating. Typically, this situation reflects a woman's anxiety about the relationship. As sexual excitement builds, so does the feeling of loss of control over one's environment. If a woman consciously or unconsciously fears that the love object is undependable, she may find this loss of control so threatening that she "turns it off" (Fisher, 1973:195). Fear of loss can be rooted in a loss suffered in childhood, through the death or emotional absence of a parent, for example. Or it can be a realistic response to a partner's characteristics.

Treating inorgasm caused by fear of loss typically involves individual or marital therapy or both.

A therapist may try to uncover hidden fears left over from childhood and may also try to determine whether the husband behaves in ways that suggest a lack of dependability. For example, is he away for long periods? Does his acceptance of his wife fluctuate? If behaviors such as these are called to the couple's attention, they may be able to change their interaction so that the wife feels more secure and thus less anxious about reaching orgasm (Fisher, 1973:249).[1]

Vaginismus

Vaginismus is relatively rare. A woman with this dysfunction is anatomically normal, but whenever her partner attempts to penetrate her vagina, the vaginal muscles involuntarily contract so that intercourse is impossible. Typically, vaginismic women are, at least unconsciously, afraid of vaginal penetration and intercourse.

After any physical conditions have been corrected, therapists treat vaginismus by seeking in counseling sessions to uncover the basis for the woman's fear of vaginal entry. Then progressive exercises are used to recondition the muscles at the entrance to the vagina. The length of the treatment varies, but therapists report excellent results (Kaplan, 1974).

In all the dysfunctions we have described, a common thread is the emotional climate of a couple's relationship. This emotional relationship may be a cause of the dysfunction or it may be affected by the dysfunction or both. While therapists help a couple overcome their immediate sexual difficulties, they also try to help partners recognize and avoid alienating practices that can become obstacles to mutually pleasurable sex.

---

1. While fear of loss is usually associated with female orgasmic dysfunction, it often plays a part in male dysfunction, too.

F Some Facts About Sex Therapy

In traditional approaches to treating sexual dysfunctions, therapists looked for subtle and profound psychological sources, such as unresolved emotional conflicts from childhood or severe marital power struggles. These causes still exist, but today therapists focus on more immediate and obvious reasons for the dysfunction: anxieties about sexual failure or fear that the partner expects too much or that the partner will reject sexual advances. These fears create various sexual defenses, introduce conscious control into lovemaking, and thus inhibit persons from abandoning themselves to the experience. One important feature of Masters and Johnson's therapy is its attempt to remove performance pressure by insisting that the couple *not* strive for orgasm or even have intercourse but rather focus on all-over body pleasure and pleasuring.

Masters and Johnson laid down some ground rules for sex therapy in their book *Human Sexual Inadequacy* (1970). They said that therapists should work in male-female teams and with both partners in the relationship. They stressed that the team should be comfortable with their own sexuality and nonjudgmental about the full range of human sexual activity. Since then, some therapists—Helen Singer Kaplan, head of the Sex Therapy and Education Program in New York, for example—have successfully treated couples without a cotherapist. However, many contemporary therapists follow the Masters and Johnson guidelines.

Because Masters and Johnson used cameras and other observational equipment during their research on human sexual response, many people believe that therapy clinics use everything from hidden camera equipment in mirrored rooms to sexual surrogates. But legitimate therapists do not use hidden cameras or other observational equipment. A few use surrogates, but only when an individual comes for therapy without a spouse or partner and prefers this form of therapy. Masters and Johnson, in keeping with their focus on the couple's *relationship,* have given up the use of surrogates in therapy.

Therapy normally begins with a physical and psychological examination of both partners. Although it is commonly held that only about 10 percent of sexual dysfunctions have a physiological basis, the last decade has, in fact, witnessed some return to physical treatments. Recent research found that 34 percent of 105 impotent men studied had low levels of testosterone and related pituitary and thyroid problems. Some 92 percent of them responded to hormone treatments. This compares to a usual 60 to 70 percent success rate in treating impotence with psychotherapy. Any sex therapy, then, should begin only after a physician has ruled out any physical cause.

In addition, a legitimate therapist will give a couple a clear picture of what to expect during treatment and will probably make a "therapeutic contract" with them that clearly establishes the couple's responsibility for treatment.

Masters and Johnson concentrate therapy into twelve or fourteen consecutive days in a motel. But this is unrealistic for many couples, and other therapists schedule sessions over a period of twelve or fifteen weeks while the couple lives at home. Either way, sex therapy can be very expensive. Masters and Johnson were charging $2,500 in 1976 for two weeks of therapy, and unfortunately, their imitators are also charging high fees. Working with a single therapist instead of a team is less expensive.

With the help of qualified therapists, Masters and Johnson claim that sex is one form of marital communication that may be altered in a relatively short time. Masters and Johnson report "nonfailure" rates of 80 percent. This claim has been challenged, however, with other therapists reporting success rates of a little less than 50 percent. This discrepancy has led to serious questioning and controversy over the adequacy of Masters and Johnson's methods and the validity of their research reports. For example, did Masters and Johnson attain such high success rates by screening out the more difficult cases and using the term "nonfailure," so that any glimmer of sexual response might include the subject among the successful cases (Zilbergeld and Evans, 1980; reply by Kolodny, 1981; for an excellent discussion of this controversy see Mahoney, 1981:555–56)? All in all, the reported rate of success in legitimate sex-therapy programs remains encouraging and therapists continue to use Masters and Johnson's methods. But the word *legitimate* is crucial.

One way to check therapists' qualifications is to find out whether they belong to either EAST or AASEC. EAST (Eastern Association of Sex Therapists) is a group of approximately 100 legitimate practitioners. AASEC (American Association of Sex Educators and Counselors) has developed a certification program that requires academic training, supervised therapy experience, and a written examination. In the absence of membership in either association, therapists are more likely to be legitimate if they are accountable to a community agency, teaching hospital, medical school, or university.

If a couple cannot find a therapist with these qualifications, or if costs are prohibitive, there are other choices. Group therapy for sex problems has developed; this approach is especially effective for women, who may, indeed, not respond as well to couples therapy. Another choice for couples is to recognize that sexual problems often reflect the general relationship and to seek help from a qualified marriage counselor.

Sexuality textbook writer E. R. Mahoney points out a final caution: "It can be stated without doubt that *we do not have enough knowledge about human sexuality to say with any degree of certainty what definitely causes sexual problems*" (Mahoney, 1983:556). Sex therapy, as with therapy or social action in other areas of life, has often been in advance of scientific research. This does not necessarily mean therapy programs should not be developed or that people should not seek sex therapy; however, we need to keep in mind the limits of our certainty about it.

Glossary

AAMFT American Association for Marriage and Family Therapy. Membership requires a graduate degree in medicine, law, social work, psychiatry, psychology, or the ministry; special training in marriage or family therapy or both; and at least three years of clinical training and experience under a senior counselor's supervision.

ABC-X model A model of family crisis in which A (the **stressor** event) interacts with B (the family's resources for meeting a crisis) and with C (the definition the family formulates of the event) to produce X (the crisis). See also **double ABC-X model, strain.**

abortion The expulsion of the fetus or embryo from the uterus either naturally (*spontaneous abortion* or *miscarriage*) or medically (*induced abortion*).

abstinence The standard that maintains that regardless of the circumstances, nonmarital intercourse is wrong for both women and men. Many religions espouse abstinence as a moral imperative. See also **double standard, permissiveness with affection,** and **permissiveness without affection.**

abuse Behavior aimed primarily at hurting another person either verbally or physically.

acquaintance rape Forced or unwanted sexual contact between acquaintances. See also **date rape.**

adoption The process by which an individual or a couple become the legal parents of a child not biologically theirs.

adult life cycle The sequence throughout adulthood of structuring one's life followed by self-examination.

A-frame relationship A relationship style (symbolized by the capital letter A) in which partners have a strong couple identity but little **self-esteem;** therefore, they are dependent on each other rather than interdependent. See also **H-frame relationship** and **M-frame relationship.**

afterbirth The **placenta,** amniotic sac, and the remainder of the umbilical cord, all of which are expelled during delivery after the actual birth of the baby.

agape The love style that emphasizes unselfish concern for the beloved in which one attempts to fill the other's needs even when that means some personal sacrifice. See also **eros, ludus, mania, pragma, storge.**

age expectations Societal expectations about how people should think and behave because of their age. For instance: Women over_____(you fill in the blank) should not wear bikinis; men over_____should not wear muscle shirts.

age-thirty transition An adult transition period that usually occurs when a person is between 28 and 32 years old. During this time people ask themselves: What is my life all about now that I'm doing what I'm supposed to be doing? See also **midlife transition.**

aggressive behavior Behavior in which a person acts in a hostile fashion, launching a verbal or physical attack on another. See also **abuse** and **assertive action.**

AIDS (acquired immune deficiency syndrome) A sexually transmitted disease involving breakdown in the manufacture of white blood cells, which resist viruses, bacteria, and fungi.

alienating fight tactics Tactics in fighting that tend to create distance between intimates: They don't resolve conflict; they increase it. See also **gaslighting, gunnysacking, kitchen-sink fight.**

alimony Derived from the Latin verb meaning "to nourish" or "to give food to"; the traditional condition in which the breadwinning husband undertook the obligation to support his dependent wife and children even after divorce. Alimony laws that require *only* husbands to pay alimony to wives have been declared unconstitutional by the United States Supreme Court.

ambivalence The existence of mutually conflicting feelings or thoughts about some person, object, or idea; having "mixed emotions" about an occurrence or issue; believing one thing "in your head" and feeling quite differently "in your guts."

amniotic fluid Salty, watery fluid that surrounds the developing fetus within the mother's **uterus,** cushioning and protecting it; also called *amnion.*

androgyny The social and psychological condition in which individuals can think, feel, and behave in ways that express both **instrumental** and **expressive character traits.** Androgyny is the combination of both "masculine" and "feminine" qualities in one individual. Androgynous persons will probably be better equipped to deal with industrial society. Moreover, androgynous partners may find greater intimacy in marriage than do more traditional spouses.

anger "insteads" Ways people deal with their anger rather than expressing it directly. Some substitutes for open anger are overeating, boredom, depression, physical illness, and gossip.

annulment A dissolution of a marriage that legally states the marriage never existed.

antinatalism The structural, or societal, condition in which bearing and rearing children is discouraged either overtly or—as may be the case in the United States—covertly through subtle economic discrimination against parents.

archival family function The creating, storing, preserving, and passing on of particular objects, events, or rituals that family members consider relevant to their personal identities and to maintaining the family as a unique existential reality or group.

areolae The pigmented areas of the breasts surrounding the nipples.

artificial insemination A process in which a physician injects live **sperm** into a woman's **vagina** when she is ovulating.

assertive action Behavior that expresses positively, affirms, defends, or maintains one's position or feelings about an issue. See also **abuse** and **aggressive behavior.**

assignment The designation of gender identity to a **hermaphrodite** shortly after birth. The person is then treated accordingly.

attribution Assigning or attributing character traits to other persons. Attributions can be positive or negative, such as when a spouse is told he or she is an interesting or a boring person.

authority Power based on the recognition of its legitimacy by those over whom the power is exercised. The United States government has authority in this country but not in Iran.

autocratic discipline Discipline of children that places the power of determining rules and limits entirely in the hands of the parent, with little or no input from the growing child. See also **democratic discipline** and **laissez-faire discipline.**

autonomy The experience of self-control and self-direction. Autonomy is important to building **self-esteem.** Once a person achieves a degree of **independence** and autonomy, he or she can consider moving toward **interdependence** or **intimacy.**

B

baby boom The dramatically rising birth rate from after World War II until 1960.

basic exchange The idea that women, historically and even today, have traded their ability to bear and rear children and to perform domestic duties for man's physical protection and economic support. Men exchange breadwinning for women's house care, husband care, and child care.

bereavement A period of mourning after the death of a loved one.

black polygamous family A family in which two or more women maintain separate households and are independently pair-bonded to a man whom they share and who moves between households as a husband to both women.

blue-collar workers Individuals employed as mechanics, truckers, police officers, and so forth—jobs typically requiring uniforms.

bonding fighting Fighting that brings intimates closer together rather than leaving them just as far apart or pushing them even farther apart. See also **alienating fight tactics.**

breech presentation In childbirth, a delivery in which the baby's buttocks, shoulder, foot, or face emerge first. This makes for a more difficult delivery than the **vertex presentation.**

budgeting Putting on paper a plan of spending for a definite period, such as one month or one year.

C

case study A written summary and analysis of data gained by psychologists, psychiatrists, counselors, and social workers when working directly with individuals and families. Case studies are often used as sources in **scientific investigation.**

catharsis myth Cultural myth that holds that if family members routinely express verbal or mild physical aggression toward one another, tension is released and therefore reduced. It is true that family members should be **assertive** toward one another, but they should not be **aggressive.**

cervix At the top of the **vagina** in the female, the "neck" of the **uterus.**

cesarean section A surgical operation in which a physician makes an incision in the mother's abdomen and uterine wall to remove the infant. Named after Julius Caesar, who was supposedly delivered this way.

checking-it-out A communication or fighting technique in which a person asks the other whether her or his perceptions of the other's feelings or thoughts are correct.

child abuse Overt acts of aggression against a child, such as excessive verbal derogation, beating, or inflicting physical injury. Sexual abuse is a form of physical child abuse.

child-free family Married or cohabiting adults who choose not to have children.

child maltreatment Defined by the Child Abuse Prevention and Treatment Act of 1974 as the physical or mental injury, sexual abuse, or negligent treatment of a child "under the age of eighteen by a person who is responsible for the child's welfare."

child neglect Failure to provide adequate physical or emotional care for a child.

child snatching Kidnapping one's own children from the other parent after divorce.

choosing by default Making semiconscious or unconscious choices when one is not aware of all the possible alternatives or when one pursues the path of least resistance. From this perspective, doing nothing about a problem or issue, or making no choice, is making a serious choice— that is, the choice to do nothing.

choosing knowledgeably Making choices and decisions after (1) recognizing as many options or alternatives as possible; (2) recognizing the social pressures that can influence personal choices; (3) considering the consequences of each alternative; and (4) becoming aware of one's own values.

clitoris Part of the female **genitalia:** female **erectile tissue,** consisting of an internal shaft and a tip, or **glans,** which contains concentrations of nerve endings and is highly sensitive.

closed marriage A synonym for **static marriage.**

cohabitation Living together in an intimate, sexual relationship without traditional, legal marriage. Sometimes referred to as "living together" or "marriage without marriage." Cohabitation can be a courtship process or an alternative to legal marriage, depending on how partners view it.

coitus Sexual intercourse.

commitment to intimacy The determination to develop relationships in which experiences cover many areas of per-

sonality, problems are worked through, conflict is expected and seen as a normal part of the growth process, and there is an expectation that the relationship is basically viable and worthwhile.

common-law marriage A legal concept whereby cohabiting partners are considered legally married if certain requirements are met, such as showing intent to enter into a marriage. Few states recognize common-law marriage today, but a small minority do, such as Alabama, Rhode Island, and Kansas.

communal family A family form that includes several monogamous couples, who share everything except sexual relations, and their children. See also **commune.**

commune A group of adults and perhaps children who live together, sharing aspects of their lives. Some communes are **group marriages,** in which members share sex; others are **communal families,** with several monogamous couples, who share everything except sexual relations, and their children.

community divorce The concept that people tend to lose old friends of the couple and make new friends—that is, change communities—when they divorce.

commuter marriage A marriage in which couples live apart. Also called **two-location family.**

conception The moment in which an **ovum** (egg) joins with a **sperm** cell and a fetus begins to develop.

condominium Apartment or townhouse owned by an individual and paid for by obtaining a mortgage (*not* a rented apartment). Apartment ownership is becoming increasingly common.

conflict-habituated marriage A marital relationship characterized by ongoing tension and unresolved conflict. See also **devitalized, passive-congenial, total,** and **vital marriage.**

conflict taboo The cultural belief that conflict and anger are wrong, which thereby discourages people from dealing with these "negative" emotions openly.

congestion The engorgement of the genital blood vessels, which causes the affected tissues to swell. Occurs during the excitement phase of sexual response.

conjoint marriage counseling Counseling in which the counselor sees the husband and wife together rather than one at a time.

conjugal power Power exercised between spouses.

connections Nena O'Neill's concept of the family network, usually provided by extended kin, who with marriage "connect" the intimate couple to the larger society and thereby help support the relationship. One problem social scientists see with interracial marriages is that they often lack these supportive connections. Connections also imply ties created by a marriage to other families, past and future.

consensual validation The process whereby people depend on others, especially **significant others,** to help them affirm their definitions of and attitudes and feelings about reality. Consensual validation is important in modern society because social reality is no longer just taken for granted as "the way things are."

consolidation loan A single loan large enough to cover all outstanding debts.

contraceptives Techniques and devices that prevent **conception.**

cooperative Group of families who agree to pool their resources to provide certain goods or services they all need. (2) A system of condominium or apartment ownership.

coparental divorce An arrangement in which divorced fathers take legal responsibility for financial support, while divorced mothers continue the physical, day-to-day care of their children.

corona A crownlike ridge at the base of the **glans** on the **penis.**

courtly love Popular during the twelfth century and later, courtly love is the intense longing for someone other than one's marital partner—a passionate and sexual longing that ideally goes unfulfilled. The assumptions of courtly love influence our modern ideas about **romantic love.**

courtship The process whereby a couple develops a mutual commitment to marriage.

crisis A crucial change in the course of events, a turning point, an unstable condition in affairs.

crisis overload A situation in which an unremitting series of small crises adds up to a major crisis.

crude birthrate The number of births per thousand population. See also **total fertility rate.**

cultural model A system or set of socially prescribed and understood guidelines for doing many things. There is no adequate cultural model for *remarried families*. The traditional cultural model for **"natural" families** is changing along with **gender roles.**

cunnilingus Oral stimulation of a woman's genital area

custody Primary responsibility for making decisions about the children's upbringing and general welfare.

D

date rape Forced or unwanted sexual contact between people who are on a "date." See also **acquaintance rape.**

dating A form of **courtship** in which, through a series of appointed meetings, an exclusive relationship between two persons often evolves.

deference customs Symbols of subordination in which, by gestures and words, people show that they recognize and accept their dependence and lower status vis-à-vis someone of higher status. In patriarchal families wives and children observe deference customs.

defining a crisis The subjective process of determining the nature and meaning of a crisis-provoking situation. For example, one husband might view his wife's return to school as a result of changing cultural values and attitudes about women's roles; another husband might define the situation

as an indication that he has begun to bore her and she no longer loves him.

delivery The second phase (after labor) of childbirth, lasting from the time the **cervix** is completely dilated until the fetus is expelled.

democratic discipline A parenting attitude and method in which all family members have some input into family and discipline decisions; whenever possible, rules are discussed ahead of time, with both children and parents participating. See also **autocratic discipline** and **laissez-faire discipline.**

democratic family One that emphasizes egalitarian decision making and the individual development of family members.

dependence The general reliance on another person or on several others for continuous support and assurance, coupled with subordination to that other. A dependent partner probably has low **self-esteem** and is having **illegitimate needs** met by the partner on whom he or she is dependent. See also **independence** and **interdependence.**

developmental model of child rearing Popularized by many child-rearing experts, this view sees the child as an extremely plastic organism with virtually unlimited potential that the parent is called on to tap and encourage. The model ignores or de-emphasizes parents' personal rights. See also **interactive perspective of parenting.**

devitalized marriage A marital relationship in which a couple have lost the original zest, **intimacy,** and meaningfulness that were once a part of their relationship. See also **conflict-habituated marriage, passive-congenial marriage, total marriage, vital marriage.**

dimorphism The condition in which males tend to be taller, more muscular, and hairier than females.

discretionary income Uncommitted income that persons or families can spend as they please.

discrimination Unfavorable treatment of groups of people for arbitrary, nonrational reasons. Women and racial minorities are discriminated against in jobs outside the home, in access to political power, and in other, more subtle ways. See also **prejudice.**

displaced homemaker A full-time housewife who, through divorce or widowhood, loses her means of economic support.

displacement A passive-aggressive behavior in which a person expresses anger with another by being angry at or damaging people or things the other cherishes. See also **passive-aggression.**

divorce counseling Counseling in which partners go together to negotiate conflicts, grievances, and misunderstandings. The goal of divorce counseling is to help a couple separate with a minimum of destructiveness to themselves and to their children.

divorce mediation A nonadversarial means of dispute resolution by which the couple, with the assistance of a mediator or mediators (frequently a lawyer-therapist team), negotiate the terms of their settlement of custody, support, property, and visitation issues.

divorce readiness   See **readiness for divorce.**

double ABC-X model   A variation of the **ABC-X model** of family crises that emphasizes the impact of unresolved prior crises. In this model A becomes Aa and represents not only the current **stressor** event but also "family pile-up," or residual **strains** from prior crises.

double messages   See **mixed messages.**

double standard   The standard according to which premarital sex is more acceptable for males than for females. Reiss subdivided the double standard into **orthodox** and **transitional.** See also **abstinence, permissiveness with affection,** and **permissiveness without affection.**

double standard of aging   A sociological concept describing the situation that men are not considered old or sexually ineligible as early in their lives as women are. Americans view older men as "distinguished" and older women as just plain "old."

dowry   A sum of money or property brought to the marriage by the female.

dual-career family   Family in which both partners have a strong commitment to the lifetime development of careers.

dual-earner family   Family in which the wife is working but her work is *not* viewed as a lifetime career. Her work is considered secondary in importance and in psychological involvement to her family role, and it does *not* serve as an important source of identity. Also called *two-paycheck marriage.*

E

economic divorce   The separation of the couple into separate economic units, each with its own property, income, control of expenditures, and responsibility for taxes, debts, and so on.

economic interdependence   The situation in which spouses need each other's labor and special skills to survive better as members of a cooperative group than as separate individuals. Historically, economic interdependence was grounded in the **basic exchange.** Today, with increased fear of unemployment and rising inflation, economic interdependence remains important for families as spouses pool their separate earning abilities to maintain a standard of living neither could achieve alone.

economic maturity   The ability to support oneself and a partner if necessary. In our society, economic maturity has been considered a prerequisite for a stable, happy marital relationship.

egalitarian relationship   Sometimes referred to as **equalitarian,** an egalitarian relationship is one in which partners share equally in practical responsibilities and decision making.

ejaculation   The rhythmic discharge of seminal fluid containing **sperm** from the **penis** during **orgasm.**

embryonic stage   The period of pregnancy after the first two weeks **(germinal period)** until about eight weeks, during which the fetal head, skeletal system, heart, and digestive system begin to form. See also **fetal period.**

embryo transplant   The implantation of a fertilized egg, donated by a fertile woman, into an infertile woman.

emotion   A strong feeling arising without conscious mental or rational effort, such as joy, reverence, anger, fear, love, or hate. Emotions are neither bad nor good and should be accepted as natural. People can and should learn to control what they *do* about their emotions.

emotional divorce   Withholding any bonding emotions and communication from the relationship, typically replacing these with alienating feelings and behavior. Emotional divorce usually begins before actual legal divorce.

emotional maturity   Having high **self-esteem** and the ability not to become emotionally paralyzed when a disappointment occurs; having the ability to feel sufficiently autonomous, coupled with the willingness to negotiate and compromise with a loved one. Emotional maturity is one prerequisite for a stable, happy marriage.

empty nest   An old (some say outdated) sociological term referring to the postparental stage of family life. With the contracting economy, the trend to stay single longer, and the high divorce rate, more and more parents are complaining that their nests won't seem to empty.

endogamy   Marrying within one's own social group. See also **exogamy.**

endometrium   The lining of the **uterus,** which thickens with a layer of tissue and blood in order to nourish an embryo should an egg become fertilized. If no egg is fertilized, the endometrial tissue and blood are discarded during **menstruation.**

energized family   A family that approaches consumer encounters, particularly with the health-care system, ready for active engagement rather than passive submission. Energized families demand quality products and services and know how to shop for them.

entering the adult world   The first stage in the adult life cycle, which for middle-class individuals lasts roughly from age 18 to age 28, during which the individual begins to structure an adult life-style.

entitlement   In divorce, the equivalent of severance pay for work done at home during the length of the marriage, paid to a wife upon divorce instead of traditional **alimony.**

Equal Credit Opportunity Act   United States federal law passed in 1975 that allows a married woman's good credit rating to continue to belong to her after divorce or widowhood or if she wants to establish credit in her name only. The law forbids discrimination on the basis of sex or marital status in any legal transaction.

equalitarian relationship   One in which partners share equally in practical responsibilities, such as breadwinning and housekeeping, and decision making. A synonym is **egalitarian relationship.**

erectile tissue   Genital tissue that becomes engorged with blood during **sexual arousal,** causing it to increase size. In women, erectile tissue composes the **clitoris;** in men, the **penis.**

erogenous zones   Areas of the body most sensitive to **sexual arousal** through touch.

eros   The love style characterized by intense emotional attachment and powerful sexual feelings or desires. See also **agape, ludus, mania, pragma, storge.**

ethologists   People who study human beings as an evolved animal species. Ethologists compare human behavior with that of other primates.

exchange theory   The theory that people tend to marry others whose social class, education, physical attractiveness, and even **self-esteem** are similar to their own.

excitement phase   One of the four phases of **sexual arousal** described by Masters and Johnson. The excitement phase begins when people begin to feel sexually aroused and is characterized by increased breathing, blood pressure, and pulse rates; **vasocongestion** of the **penis** and **clitoris;** and vaginal lubrication in women. See also **orgasmic phase, plateau phase, resolution phase.**

exogamy   Marrying a partner from outside one's own social group. See also **endogamy.**

experiment   One tool of **scientific investigation,** in which behaviors are carefully monitored or measured under controlled conditions; also called *laboratory observation.*

expressive character traits   Such traits as warmth, sensitivity to the needs of others, and the ability to express tender feelings, traditionally associated with women. Expressive character traits and roles complement **instrumental ones.**

expressive sexual script   The view of human sexuality in which sexuality is basic to the humanness of both women and men; all individuals are free to express their sexual selves; and there is no one-sided sense of "ownership." Also called *expressive sexuality.*

extended family   Family including relatives besides parents and children, such as aunts or uncles. See also **nuclear family.**

extended parent   A grandparent or other adult relative who wholly or partially takes over the role of parent.

external stressor   An event that precipitates a family **crisis** and that originates from outside the family itself. See also **internal stressor.**

F

Fair Debt Collection Practices Act   A United States federal law that prohibits, among other things, independent collection agencies from making abusive or threatening phone calls, calling before 8 A.M. or after 9 P.M., or contacting friends or employers except to verify where a person works or lives.

fallopian tubes   The tubes that connect a female's **uterus** with her **ovaries.** Named after sixteenth-century Italian anatomist Gabriel Fallopius, who first described them.

familism   The valuing of traditional family living; also, cherishing **family values,** such as family togetherness, cohesiveness, and loyalty.

family   Any sexually expressive or parent-child relationship in which people live together with a commitment, in an intimate interpersonal relationship. Family members see their identity as importantly attached to the group, which has an identity of its own. Families today take several forms: **single-parent, remarried, dual-career, communal, homosexual,** traditional, and so forth. See also **extended family, nuclear family.**

family boundaries   Barriers, both physical and psychological, that families in virtually all cultures establish to mark themselves off from the rest of society.

family cohesion   That intangible emotional quality that holds groups together and gives members a sense of common identity.

family functions   What families do for members of society. Family functions include responsible reproduction and child rearing; providing economic support for members, including health maintenance; and providing emotional security in an **impersonal society.**

family policy   All the actions, procedures, regulations, attitudes, and goals of government that affect families.

family values   Values that focus on the family group as a whole and on maintaining family identity and cohesiveness. See also **familism.**

feedback   The communication technique of stating in different words what another person has said or revealed nonverbally.

fellatio   Oral stimulation of the male's genital area.

female orgasmic dysfunction   A female **sexual dysfunction** in which a woman becomes sexually aroused but cannot reach **orgasm.**

fertility rate   The number of births per 1,000 women in their childbearing years.

fertilization   The joining of an ovum (egg) with a **sperm** cell.

fetal period   The period of pregnancy lasting from about eight weeks until birth. See also **embryonic stage** and **germinal period.**

flexible marriage   One that allows and encourages partners to grow and change both as individuals and in the relationship. A synonym is **open marriage.**

flexible monogamy   The condition in which a couple allows each other some degree of sexual freedom with outside partners, but also expects that each will remain the other's primary sexual partner. See also **primariness** and **sexual exclusivity.**

foreskin   A thin membrane covering the **glans** of the **penis** at birth and removed by circumcision.

frenum   The place where the **foreskin** is or was connected to the **penis.**

G

gaslighting   An alienating tactic in which one partner chips away at the other's perception of her- or himself and at the other's definitions of reality. Gaslighting can literally drive people insane. See also **consensual validation.**

gender Attitudes and behavior associated with and expected of the two sexes. Persons are born with a **sex,** but as a result of **socialization,** they grow up with a gender.

gender roles Masculine and feminine prescriptions for behavior. The masculine gender role demands **instrumental character traits** and behavior, while the feminine gender role demands **expressive character traits** and behavior. Traditional gender roles are giving way to **androgyny,** but they're by no means gone.

general female sexual dysfunction A female **sexual dysfunction** in which a woman experiences very little if any erotic pleasure from sexual stimulation.

general sexual unresponsiveness See **general female sexual dysfunction.**

genitalia The external reproductive parts of women and men.

germinal period The first two weeks of pregnancy. See also **embryonic stage, fetal period.**

getting together A **courtship** process different from **dating,** in which groups of women and men congregate at a party or share an activity.

glans The sensitive tip at the end of the **clitoris** in women and of the **penis** in men.

gonads Sex glands, or glands secreting sex hormones: the **ovaries** in women, the **testicles** in men.

"good provider" role A specialized masculine role that emerged in this country in about the 1830s and that emphasizes the husband as the only or the primary economic provider for "his" family.

group marriage A family form in which several couples share a household and sexual relations. See also **commune.**

gunnysacking An **alienating fight tactic** in which a person saves up, or "gunnysacks," grievances until the sack gets too heavy, bursts, and lets ancient hostilities pour out.

H

head of household One who exercises decision-making authority and is also responsible for family breadwinning. This social status was traditionally allocated to the husband in patriarchal societies, but today many single women are heads of households.

hermaphrodite A person whose **genitalia** cannot be clearly identified as either female or male at birth. Attending physicians assign a sex identity to hermaphrodites at birth or shortly thereafter.

heterogamy Marriage between partners who differ in race, age, education, religious background, or social class. Compare with **homogamy.**

heterosexuals Individuals who prefer sexual partners of the opposite sex.

H-frame relationship Relationships that are structured like a capital H: Partners stand virtually alone, each self-sufficient and neither influenced much by the other. An

example would be a **devitalized, dual-career marriage.** See also **A-frame relationship** and **M-frame relationship.**

hidden agenda Associated with stepfathers who, with remarriage, assume functioning single-parent families of a mother and her children. The family may have a *hidden agenda,* or assumptions and expectations about how the stepfather will behave—expectations and assumptions that are often not passed on to the new stepfather.

hidden marriage contract The traditional legal-social marriage contract, which encourages strict monogamy, permanence, rigid husband-wife roles, and static marriage relationships.

holistic view of sex The view that conjugal sex is an extension of the whole marital relationship, which is not chopped into compartments, with sex reduced to a purely physical exchange.

homogamy Marriage between partners of similar race, age, education, religious background, and social class. See also **heterogamy.**

homosexual family A family in which partners of the same sex live together and share sexual and emotional commitment.

homosexuals Persons who prefer same-sex partners.

hormones Chemical substances secreted into the bloodstream by the endocrine glands.

house husband A husband who stays home to care for the house and family while his wife works outside the home for pay.

husband-dominant power A form of **conjugal power** in which the husband has more power than the wife.

hymen In the female, a ring of tissue that partly covers the vaginal opening.

hypergamy Marrying up socioeconomically on the part of the white woman who, in effect, trades her socially defined superior racial status for the economically superior status of a middle- or upper middle-class black partner.

I

idealization Seeing loved ones as extraordinary, remarkable, and unique.

identification A strong emotional attachment for a person, coupled with the desire to be like that person.

identity A sense of inner sameness developed by individuals throughout their lives: They "know who they are" throughout their various endeavors and pursuits, no matter how different these may be.

illegitimate needs Needs that arise from feelings of self-doubt, unworthiness, and inadequacy. Loving partners cannot fill each other's illegitimate needs no matter how much they try. One fills one's illegitimate needs best by personally working to build one's **self-esteem.** A first step might be doing something nice for oneself rather than waiting for somebody else to do it.

imaging Choosing to look and behave in ways that one imagines one's partner will consider attractive. An imaging partner complements a **romanticizing** one. Imaging is the opposite of **authenticity.**

implantation   The process in which the fertilized egg, or **zygote,** embeds itself in the thickened lining of the **uterus.**

impotence   A **sexual dysfunction** in which a male is unable to produce or maintain an erection.

independence   Self-reliance and self-sufficiency. To form lasting intimate relationships, independent people have to choose to become **interdependent.**

individualistic values   Values that encourage **self-fulfillment,** personal growth, "doing one's own thing," **autonomy,** and **independence.** Individualistic values can conflict with **family values.**

influence   The ability to change another's attitudes or behavior in such a way that the overpowered person undergoes an authentic change in preferences. Committed intimate relationships rest on mutual influence.

installment financing   Contracting with a dealer to pay for major purchases over a period of time.

institution   See **social institution.**

institutional behavior   The dutiful and responsible performance of accepted social roles, such as wife, husband, parent, provider, and housekeeper. Institutional behavior characterized marriage of the 1950s.

instrumental character traits   Traits that enable one to accomplish difficult tasks or goals—for example, rationality, leadership. Traditionally, people thought men were born with instrumental character traits. See also **expressive character traits.**

interactional marriage pattern   Marriage pattern in which partners emphasize companionship and expressions of love, rather than the **basic exchange** or simple **economic interdependence.** Contrast with **parallel relationship.**

interactive perspective   A perspective of parenting that considers the influence between parent and child reciprocal rather than just from parent to child. This perspective postdates the **developmental perspective.**

intercourse   The insertion of the **penis** into the **vagina,** also called **coitus.**

interdependence   A relationship in which people who have high **self-esteem** make strong commitments to each other, choosing to help fill each other's **legitimate,** but not **illegitimate, needs.**

intermediate conjugal relationship   A marital relationship in which spouses value the middle-class ideal of couple togetherness and therefore limit their separate leisure pursuits. This ideal of togetherness does not carry with it the emphasis on active sharing and **intimacy,** so such a relationship is similar to a **devitalized** or **passive-congenial marriage.** See also **joint conjugal relationship, segregated conjugal relationship.**

internalize   To make a cultural belief, value, or attitude one's own. When internalized, an attitude becomes a part of us and influences how we think, feel, and act. Internalized attitudes become valued emotionally and therefore are difficult to change. When people do begin to change them, they can expect to go through a period of **ambivalence.**

internal stressor   An event that precipitates a family **crisis** and that originates from within the family. See also **external stressor.**

intimacy   Committing oneself to a particular other and honoring that commitment in spite of some personal sacrifices while sharing one's inner self with the other. Intimacy requires **interdependence.**

intrinsic marriage   A marriage in which the emphasis is on the intensity of feelings about each other and the centrality of the spouse's welfare in each mate's scale of values. Intrinsic marriages are primary, intimate relationships. See also **utilitarian marriage.**

in vitro fertilization   A process in which a baby is conceived outside a woman's body, in a laboratory dish or jar, but develops within the woman's uterus.

involuntary infertility   The condition of wanting to conceive and bear a child but being physically unable to.

involuntary stable singles   Older divorced, widowed, and never married people who wanted to marry or remarry, but have not found a mate and have come to accept being single as a probable life situation.

involuntary temporary singles   Singles who would like, and expect, to marry. These can be younger never marrieds who do not want to be single and are actively seeking mates, as well as somewhat older people who had not previously been interested in marrying but are now seeking mates.

isolation   The result of engineering distance between oneself and others and of generally avoiding relationships that could lead to disclosure of inner feelings. **Imaging** often accompanies and sometimes masks isolation.

J

joint conjugal relationship   A marital relationship in which couples share their leisure time and are highly involved emotionally with each other. Similar to **total** and **vital** marital relationships. See also **intermediate conjugal relationship** and **segregated conjugal relationship.**

joint custody   A situation in which both divorced parents continue to take equal responsibility for important decisions regarding their child's general upbringing.

K

kitchen-sink fight   An alienating type of fight that does not focus on specific, here-and-now issues: Everything but the kitchen sink gets into the battle.

L

labia majora   Two rounded folds of skin, the external "lips" in the female **genitalia.**

labia minora   Latin for "lesser lips"; two folds of tissue within the **labia majora** in the female **genitalia.**

labor   In childbirth, the process by which the baby is propelled from the mother's body.

laissez-faire discipline Discipline in which parents let children set their own goals, rules, and limits. See also **autocratic discipline** and **democratic discipline.**

legal divorce The dissolution of a marriage by the state through a court order terminating the marriage.

legal separation A separation in which a couple remains legally married, but separate residences are sanctioned, and duties of child support and rights of visitation are established.

legitimate needs Needs that arise in the present rather than out of the deficits accumulated in the past.

leisure phobia The psychological malady or "handicap" in which a person is afraid of or has trouble enjoying free time.

leveling Being transparent, authentic, and explicit about how one truly feels, especially concerning the more conflictive or hurtful aspects of an intimate relationship. Among other things, leveling between intimates implies **self-disclosure** and **commitment to intimacy.**

life cycle A sequence of stages and transitions during which a person structures and intermittently evaluates his or her life course; sometimes referred to as **adult life cycle.**

life spiral An alternative to the **life cycle** model of the adult life course; the life spiral model stresses the incorporation by individuals of both traditional and alternative roles throughout their lifetime.

liking A feeling not as powerful as loving. It may be more rational, a result of thinking rather than feeling. A positive appraisal of someone.

longitudinal study One technique of **scientific investigation,** in which researchers study the same individuals or groups over an extended period of time, usually with periodic surveys.

looking-glass self The concept that people gradually come to accept and adopt as their own the evaluations, definitions, and judgments of themselves that they see reflected in the faces, words, and gestures of those around them.

love A deep and vital emotion resulting from significant need satisfaction, coupled with a caring for and acceptance of the beloved, and resulting in an intimate relationship. Love may make the world go 'round, but it's a lot of work too.

love style A distinctive character of personality that loving or lovelike relationships can take. One social scientist has distinguished six: **agape, eros, ludus, mania, pragma,** and **storge.**

ludus The love style that focuses on love as play and on enjoying many sexual partners rather than searching for one serious relationship. This love style emphasizes the recreational aspect of sexuality. See also **agape, eros, mania, pragma, storge.**

M

male dominance The cultural idea of masculine superiority; the idea that men exercise the most control and influence over society's members.

mania The love style that combines strong sexual attraction and emotional intensity with extreme jealousy and moodiness, in which manic partners alternate between euphoria and depression. See also **agape, eros, ludus, pragma, storge.**

manipulating Seeking to control the feelings, attitudes, and behavior of one's partner or partners in underhanded ways rather than by assertively stating one's case.

marital rape A husband's compelling a wife against her will to submit to sexual contact that she finds offensive.

marital stability The ability of a marriage to last, regardless of whether the relationship is happy.

marriage gradient The sociological concept that men marry down in educational and occupational status and women marry up. As a result, never married women may represent the "cream of the crop," whereas never married men may be the "bottom of the barrel." The marriage gradient is easy to observe in the way American couples match their relative heights and ages, with the men slightly taller and older.

marriage market The sociological concept that potential mates take stock of their personal and social characteristics and then comparison shop or bargain for the best buy (mate) they can get.

marriage premise By getting married, partners accept the responsibility to keep each other primary in their lives and to work hard to ensure that their relationship continues. See **primariness.**

marriage squeeze The sociological concept that, among people born during the baby boom following World War II, women reached their most marriageable age range two or three years before men born in the same year. As a result, there was an excess of young women when marriage rates were highest. Because of the **double standard of aging,** the marriage squeeze also affects choices in remarriage: Older men have a larger pool of women from which to choose a wife.

married women's property acts Laws passed in most states during the nineteenth century that for the first time recognized the right of wives to hold property separately from their husbands.

martyring Giving others more than one receives in return to maintain relationships. Martyrs often "punish" the person to whom they are martyring by letting her or him know "just how much I put up with."

masturbation Self-stimulation to provide sexual pleasure.

meatus The opening at the tip of the **penis.**

menstruation The (about monthly) process of discarding an unfertilized **ovum,** unused tissue, and blood through the vaginal opening.

M-frame relationship Relationship based on couple **interdependence.** Each partner has high **self-esteem,** but they mutually influence each other and experience loving as a deep emotion. See also **A-frame relationship** and **H-frame relationship.**

midlife transition   The transition that begins at about age 35 for women and 45 for men; the most dramatic and potentially turbulent of the adult **life-cycle transitions.** At this time people in our culture realize their lives are "half over" and consequently reevaluate them, sometimes making dramatic and sweeping changes. It is fairly common during the midlife transition for husbands to decide to concentrate less on career and more on family, while many wives make the opposite shift. See also **age-thirty transition.**

mixed message   Two simultaneous messages that contradict each other; also called a **double message.** For example, society gives us mixed messages regarding **family values** and **individualistic values** and about premarital sex. People, too, can send mixed messages, as when a partner says, "Of course I always like to talk with you" while turning up the TV.

modern societies   Social scientists refer to advanced industrial societies as modern because these tend to encourage individualism, social and personal change, and flexibility. See also **traditional societies.**

monogamy   The sexually exclusive union of a couple.

mons veneris   The female pubic mound, an area of fatty tissue above the pubic bone.

multiorgasmic   Capable of experiencing several successive orgasms during one sexual encounter.

myotonia   Increased muscle tension, often as a result of **sexual arousal.**

myth   A cultural belief, often inaccurate, about the way things are.

N

narcissism   Concern chiefly or only with oneself, without regard for the well-being of others. Narcissism is selfishness, not self-love. People with high **self-esteem** care about and respect themselves *and* others. Narcissistic, or selfish, people, on the other hand, have low self-esteem, are insecure, and therefore worry unduly about their own well-being and very little about that of others.

natural family   A traditional cultural view in which the "normal," "typical," or "right" family consisted only of two monogamous heterosexual parents and their children. Husbands were primary breadwinners; wives were homemakers. See also **nuclear family.**

naturalistic observation   A technique of **scientific investigation** in which a researcher lives with a family or social group or spends extensive time with them, carefully recording their activities, conversations, gestures, and other aspects of everyday life.

neo-local residence pattern   The socially approved practice and cultural expectation that newlyweds will leave their parents' homes and set up their own. (Other residence patterns in other cultures are *matrilocal* and *patrilocal,* in which newlyweds reside with the bride's or groom's family, respectively.)

neutralizing power   The practice of weakening a powerful person's control by refusing to cooperate.

no-fault divorce   The legal situation in which a partner seeking a divorce no longer has to prove "grounds." Virtually all states now have no-fault divorce.

no-power   A situation in which partners are equally able to influence each other and, at the same time, are not concerned about their relative power vis-à-vis each other. No-power partners negotiate and compromise instead of trying to "win."

nuclear family   A family group comprising only the wife, the husband, and their children. See also **extended family, natural family.**

nymphomaniac   A mythical impression of women from the **patriarchal sexual script.** Classically, a nymphomaniac is defined as a woman with persistently high levels of sexual tension who continually searches for orgasmic relief but fails to attain it.

O

open marriage   A synonym for **flexible marriage,** in which partners allow and encourage each other to grow and change over the years. Open marriages need not be sexually open; they can, by mutual agreement, be sexually exclusive.

opportunity costs (of children)   The economic opportunities for wage earning and investments that parents forego when rearing children.

orgasm   The climax in human sexual response during which sexual tension reaches its peak and is suddenly discharged. In men, **ejaculation** almost always accompanies orgasm.

orgasmic phase   The third of four progressive phases of **sexual arousal** described by Masters and Johnson. The orgasmic phase is characterized by extremely pleasurable sexual sensations and by involuntary rhythmic contractions in the **vagina** and **penis.** See also **excitement phase, plateau phase, resolution phase.**

ova   Plural of **ovum.**

ovaries   Two female **gonads,** or sex glands, that produce reproductive cells called **ova,** or eggs.

overload   The objective condition or subjective feeling resulting from having to juggle too many roles or demands simultaneously. Wives who work outside the home typically experience overload as they try to keep up with both work and household responsibilities.

ovulation   The process by which the female ovary produces an **ovum,** or egg. Usually, the two **ovaries** alternate, so that one ovulates each month.

ovum   An egg produced by the female ovary. Usually the two **ovaries** alternate in producing one ovum each month in a process called **ovulation.** The plural of **ovum** is **ova.**

ovum transplant   A process in which a fertilized egg is implanted into an infertile woman. See also **embryo transplant.**

P

paradoxical pregnancy The concept that the more guilty and disapproving a sexually active woman is about premarital sex, the less likely she is to use contraceptives regularly, if at all.

parallel relationship A marital relationship based on gender-role segregation in which the husband is expected to be a good provider and the wife a good housekeeper. Companionship and **intimacy** are not considered important. See also **interactional marriage pattern.**

passive-aggression Expressing anger at some person or situation indirectly, through nagging, nitpicking, or sarcasm, for example, rather than directly and openly. See also **sabotage** and **displacement.**

passive-congenial marriage A marital relationship in which spouses accent things other than emotional closeness; unlike **devitalized** partners, passive-congenial spouses have always done so. See also **conflict-habituated, devitalized, total,** and **vital marriage.**

paterfamilias A term from seventeenth-century England for the male head of the family household, who was solely responsible for the economic and spiritual welfare of his family and represented in his person the supposed unity and integrity of the family. Associated with historical *patriarchy.*

patriarchal sexual script The view of human sexuality in which men own everything in the society, including women and women's sexuality, and males' sexual needs are emphasized while females' needs are minimized.

penis The penis and the **scrotum** together make up the external male **genitalia.** The penis is composed of an erectile shaft and a sensitive tip, or **glans.**

penis envy Sigmund Freud's assumption that girls (and women) are envious of the male's penis and therefore devalue themselves and all other women.

perineum In the female, the area between the **vestibule** to the **vagina** and the anus. In the male, the area between the **scrotum** and the anus.

period of disorganization That period in a family **crisis,** after the stressor event has occurred, during which family morale and organization slump and habitual roles and routines become nebulous. See also **external stressor, internal stressor.**

permissiveness with affection The standard that permits premarital sex for women and men equally, provided they have a fairly stable, affectionate relationship. See also **abstinence, double standard,** and **permissiveness without affection.**

permissiveness without affection The standard that allows premarital sex for women and men regardless of how much stability or affection there is in their relationship. Also called the *recreational* standard. See also **abstinence, double standard,** and **permissiveness with affection.**

personal marriage contract An articulated, negotiated agreement between partners about how each will behave in many or all aspects of the marriage. Personal marriage contracts need to be revised as partners change. A synonym is **relationship agreement.**

personal power Power exercised over oneself. See also **autonomy.**

petting Physical contact that is directed toward **sexual arousal** and does not involve **intercourse;** includes kissing, fondling, and sometimes cuddling.

pink-collar jobs Low-status, low-pay jobs still reserved primarily for women. The "pink-collar job ghetto" includes secretaries, beauticians, clerks, domestic workers, bookkeepers, waitresses, and so forth.

placenta Tissue and membrane that hold the fetus in place inside the **uterus** and function in nourishment; discharged in childbirth.

plateau phase The second phase of **sexual arousal,** during which the bodily changes begun during the excitement phase intensify and pelvic thrusting, which begins voluntarily, grows more rapid and becomes involuntary, especially among men. See also **excitement phase, orgasmic phase, resolution phase.**

pleasure bond The idea, from Masters and Johnson's book by the same name, that sexual expression between intimates is one way of expressing and strengthening the emotional bond between them.

pleasuring Spontaneously doing what feels good at the moment during a sexual encounter; the opposite of **spectatoring.**

polygamy A man's having more than one wife.

pool of eligibles A group of individuals who, by virtue of background or birth, are most likely to make compatible marriage partners.

power The ability to exercise one's will. **Personal power,** or autonomy, is power exercised over oneself. **Social power** is the ability to exercise one's will over others.

power politics Power struggles between spouses in which each seeks to gain a power advantage over the other; the opposite of a **no-power** relationship.

pragma The love style that emphasizes the practical, or pragmatic, element in human relationships and involves the rational assessment of a potential (or actual) partner's assets and liabilities. See also **agape, eros, ludus, mania, storge.**

predictable crisis Fairly predictable **transitions** over the course of family living that can be considered crises or critical opportunities for creatively reorganizing a family's values, attitudes, roles, or relationships.

premature ejaculation A **sexual dysfunction** in which a man is unable to control his ejaculatory reflex voluntarily.

prepuce Part of the female **genitalia;** the fold of skin that sometimes covers the **clitoris,** formed where the **labia minora** join; the clitoral hood.

primariness Commitment to keeping one's partner the most important person in one's life. See also **commitment to intimacy.**

primary group A group, usually relatively small, in which there are close, face-to-face relationships. The family and a friendship group are primary groups. See also **secondary group.**

principle of least interest The postulate that the partner with the least interest in the relationship is the one who is more apt to exploit the other. See also **relative love and need theory.**

programmatic postponers Couples who postpone parenthood, so as to arrive at late first-time parenthood, by a deliberate, self-conscious process of mutual intention, negotiation, and planning.

pronatalist bias A cultural attitude that takes having children for granted.

prostate A male internal reproductive organ that, along with the **seminal vesicles,** produces **semen.**

psychic divorce Regaining psychological autonomy after divorce; emotionally separating oneself from the personality and influence of the former spouse.

psychic intimacy The sharing of people's minds and feelings. Psychic intimacy may or may not involve **sexual intimacy.**

Q

quasi-kin Anthropologist Paul Bohannan's term for the person one's former spouse remarries. The term is also used more broadly to refer to former in-laws and other former and added kin resulting from divorce and remarriage.

quickening The first fetal movements apparent to the pregnant woman.

R

readiness for divorce A state combining a willingness to take responsibility for one's own contribution to the breakup, seeing the alternatives to the marriage as somewhat appealing, and feeling comfortable with the decision to divorce without extreme vacillation over an extended period of time.

real income The amount and number of goods and services a person's money will buy.

recreational sex See **permissiveness without affection.**

refractory period A time after **orgasm** during which a man cannot become sexually aroused; it usually lasts at least twenty minutes and may be considerably longer, particularly in older men.

rehabilitative alimony A plan under which a man pays his former wife support for a limited period after their divorce while she goes to school or otherwise gets retraining and finds a job.

relationship agreement See **personal marriage contract.**

relationship maturity The ability to understand a partner's point of view, make decisions about how one might change his or her own behavior that a partner doesn't like, explain one's own point of view to the partner and ask for changes in the partner's behavior when one feels this is appropriate.

relative love and need theory Theory of **conjugal power** which holds that the spouse with the least to lose if the marriage ends is the more powerful in the relationship.

remarried family A family consisting of a husband and wife, at least one of whom has been married before, and one or more children from the previous marriage of either or both spouses. There are more remarried families in the United States today, and they usually result from divorce and remarriage.

repression The involuntary, unconscious blocking of painful thoughts, feelings, or memories from the conscious mind. Repressed feelings of anger often come out in other ways, such as overeating and feeling bored or depressed. See also **suppression.**

resolution phase The final phase of **sexual arousal** described by Masters and Johnson, during which partners' bodies return to their unstimulated state. See also **excitement phase, plateau phase,** and **orgasmic phase.**

resource hypothesis Hypothesis by Blood and Wolfe that since **conjugal power** was no longer distributed according to sex, the relative power between wives and husbands would result from their relative "resources" (for example, age, education, job skills) as individuals.

retarded ejaculation A **sexual dysfunction** in which a man, although sexually aroused, cannot trigger **orgasm.**

role reversal The exchange of traditional **sex roles** so that, for example, the wife works outside the home and the husband stays home to care for their children. During and after middle age, wives and husbands tend to experience some degree of role reversal as men grow more nurturant and woman become more assertive.

romanticizing Imagining or fabricating many qualities of a person the romanticizer wants to love, as well as many sentimentalized aspects of loving, marriage, parenthood, sexual expression, and so forth.

romantic love An encompassing attraction between two persons, based on sexual attraction, companionship, mutual need satisfaction, some degree of **self-disclosure,** and the belief that the beloved is special. Americans today associate romantic love with marriage. The danger is the temptation to think that romantic love is natural and takes no work.

S

sabotage A passive-aggressive action in which a person tries to spoil or undermine some activity another has planned. Sabotage is not always consciously planned. See also **passive-aggression.**

scapegoating A negative family interaction behavior in which one family member is consistently blamed for everything that goes wrong in the household.

scientific investigation The systematic gathering of information—using **surveys, experiments, naturalistic observation,** and **case studies**—from which it often is possible to generalize with a significant degree of predictability.

script A culturally written and directed pattern or "plot" for human behavior. A social or cultural script includes the words, facial expressions, and costuming of the actors.

scrotum A sac behind the **penis** that holds the two male gonads or sex glands, the **testicles.**

secondary group A group, often large, characterized by distant, practical relationships. An **impersonal society** is characterized by secondary groups and relations. See also the opposite, **primary group.**

segregated conjugal relationship A marital relationship in which each spouse has sex-segregated roles and separate leisure pursuits and friends. This style of relationship is similar to a **parallel relationship** and is more common in the working or lower classes. See also **intermediate conjugal relationship** and **joint conjugal relationship.**

self-actualization Developing one's own personal interests and talents; **self-fulfillment.**

self-concept The basic feelings people have about themselves, their abilities, and their worth; how people think of or view themselves.

self-disclosure Letting others see one as one really is. Self-disclosure demands **authenticity.**

self-esteem Feelings and evaluations people have about their own worth.

self-fulfillment Developing one's individual talents and interests. A popular synonym is **self-actualization.**

self-sufficient economic unit A situation in which family members cooperatively produce what they consume. The American rural family of the eighteenth century tended to be a self-sufficient economic unit; virtually no American family is one today.

semen The milky fluid that carries the **sperm** through the **urethra** and out the **meatus.**

seminal vesicles Internal male reproductive glands that, with the **prostate,** produce **semen,** the milky fluid that carries the **sperm** through the **urethra** and out the **meatus.**

sensuality A more general term than *sexuality*, conveying a general awareness and readiness to respond to experiences from all the sense organs.

settling down The process occurring at about age 30 whereby people invest themselves in whatever they have decided is important to them.

sex The different chromosomal, hormonal, and anatomical components of males and females at birth.

sex ratio The ratio of men to women in a given society or subgroup of society.

sex roles The biologically based aspects of behaviors of men and women. Sex roles are essentially unchangeable by social forces.

sexual arousal The process of awakening, stirring up, or exciting sexual desires and feelings in ourselves or others.

sexual dysfunction Any sexual inadequacy that inhibits a person's achievement of **orgasm,** either alone or with a partner.

sexual exclusivity Expectations for strict monogamy in which a couple promise or publicly vow to have sexual relations only with each other. See also **flexible monogamy.**

sexual expression The way people act out or otherwise manifest the sexual aspects of themselves.

sexual intercourse The insertion of the penis into the vagina. Also called **coitus.**

sexual intimacy A level of interpersonal interaction in which partners have a sexual relationship. Sexual intimacy may or may not involve **psychic intimacy.**

sexually transmitted diseases (STDs) Highly contagious diseases transmitted from one person to another through sexual contact. There are more than a dozen STDs, but the most serious are **AIDS,** syphilis, gonorrhea, and herpes simplex virus, type 2 (HSV-2).

sexual preference The preference an individual has for a sexual partner of the same or opposite sex.

sexual responsibility The assumption by each partner of responsibility for his or her own sexual response.

shared functions (of the family) Performing activities necessary for maintaining families by a cooperative effort of families, including extended kin, and other institutions, such as the government, public education, and so forth.

shared living arrangements The situation in which, after his or her parents divorce, a child spends fairly equal amounts of time residing with each parent; often accompanies **joint custody.**

sibling rivalry Inevitable jealousy and conflict between sisters and brothers.

significant others Persons whose opinions about one are very important to one's **self-esteem.** Good friends are significant others, as are family members.

single Any person who is divorced, separated, widowed, or never married.

single-parent family A family consisting of a never married, divorced, or widowed parent and biological or adopted children. The majority of single-parent families in the United States today are headed by women and result from divorce.

social institution A system of patterned and predictable ways of thinking and behaving—beliefs, values, attitudes, and norms—concerning important aspects of people's lives. The five major social institutions are family, religion, government or politics, economics, and education.

socialization The process by which society influences members to **internalize** attitudes, beliefs, values, and expectations.

social penetration The process through which persons gradually share intimate information about themselves, allowing each other to penetrate toward their innermost secrets.

social power The ability to exercise one's will over others.

spectatoring A term Masters and Johnson coined to describe the practice of emotionally removing oneself from a sexual encounter in order to "watch" oneself and see how one is doing. See also **pleasuring.**

sperm Male reproductive cells.

static marriage A marriage that does not change over the years and does not allow for changes in the partners. Static marriage partners rely on their formal, legal bond to enforce permanence and sexual exclusivity. Static marriages are more inclined to become devitalized than are **flexible marriages.**

stepfamily A family containing a man and a woman, at least one of whom has been married before, and one or more children from the previous marriage of either or both spouses.

stepmother trap The conflict between two views: Society sentimentalizes the stepmother's role and expects her to be unnaturally loving toward her stepchildren but at the same time views her as a "wicked witch."

storge An affectionate, companionate style of loving. See also **agape, eros, ludus, mania, pragma.**

strains The tension and problems that linger from prior unresolved **stressors** and become factors in family crises. See also **ABC-X model, double ABC-X model.**

stressor A precipitating event that causes a crisis—it is often a situation for which the family has had little or no preparation. See also **ABC-X model, double ABC-X model, strain.**

strict monogamy The sexual exclusivity of a couple.

structured separation A limited period during which spouses live apart, avoid securing lawyers for a divorce, avoid getting involved in new relationships, and continue in marriage counseling together.

surrogate mother A woman who carries within her **uterus** a developing fetus for a couple who cannot conceive and carry an infant naturally. The surrogate mother delivers the infant, then turns it over to the couple.

survey A technique of **scientific investigation** using questionnaires or brief face-to-face interviews or both. An example is the United States Census. See also **longitudinal study.**

symbiotic relationship A relationship based on the mutual meeting of **illegitimate needs.** See also **legitimate needs.**

T

territoriality The defense of objects and places against their use by others.

testicles Male **gonads,** or sex glands, which hang in the **scrotum** behind the **penis** and produce male reproductive cells **(sperm)** and the hormone testosterone.

total fertility rate For a given year, the number of births that women would have over their reproductive lifetimes if all women at each age had babies at the rate for each age group that year.

total marriage A marital relationship in which partners are intensely bound together psychologically; an **intrinsic** rather than a **utilitarian** marriage. Total relationships are similar to **vital** relationships but are more multifaceted. See also **conflict-habituated, devitalized, passive-congenial,** and **vital marriage.**

traditional societies Social scientists refer to agricul-tural-patriarchal societies as traditional because they tend to value obedience, inheritance, and tradition over flexibility and changes. See also **modern societies.**

traditional wife role As delineated by sociologist John Scanzoni, the situation in which a wife places her husband's and children's interests before her own. See also **wife self-actualization.**

transition Predictable changes in the course of family life.

trust The feeling that one can rely on oneself and others to provide for one's needs. Trust is an important building block to **self-esteem.**

two-career couple See **dual-career family.**

two-career marriage See **dual-career family.**

two-location families See **commuter marriage.**

two-paycheck family See **dual-earner family.**

two-person single career The situation in which one spouse, usually the wife, encourages and participates in the other partner's career without direct recognition or personal remuneration.

two-stage marriage An alternative to more formal dating proposed by the late anthropologist Margaret Mead. Americans would first enter into *individual marriages* involving no children but a serious though not necessarily lifelong commitment. Couples who were compatible in individual marriages might choose to move into the second stage, *parental marriage,* which would presume lifelong commitment and the ability to cooperatively support and care for a child or children.

U

uniform child custody acts Passed in many, but not all, states, these acts recognize out-of-state custody decrees.

urethra The opening in women and men through which urine passes from the bladder to the outside.

uterus A cavity inside the female in which a fetus grows until birth; also called *womb.*

utilitarian marriage A union begun or maintained for primarily practical purposes. See also **intrinsic marriage.**

V

vagina The passageway in the female from the **uterus** to the outside; the "birth canal."

vaginismus A **sexual dysfunction** in which anatomically normal vaginal muscles involuntarily contract whenever a partner attempts penetration, so that intercourse is impossible.

value maturity The quality that allows people to recognize and feel comfortable and sure about their own personal values. See also **values clarification.**

values clarification Becoming aware of one's values and choosing to act in a way that is consistent with them.

vertex presentation In childbirth, a delivery in which the baby's skull emerges first. Ninety-five percent of births occur in this way. See also **breech presentation.**

vital marriage A marital relationship in which partners are intensely bound together psychologically; an **intrinsic,** as opposed to a **utilitarian,** marriage. See also **conflict-habituated, devitalized, passive-congenial,** and **total marriage.**

voluntary stable singles Singles who are satisfied to have never married, divorced persons who do not want to remarry, cohabitants who do not intend to marry, and those whose life-styles preclude marriage, such as priests and nuns.

voluntary temporary singles Younger never-marrieds and divorced persons who are postponing marriage or remarriage. They are open to the possibility of marriage, but searching for a mate has a lower priority than other activities, such as career.

vulva The female external genitalia.

W

wheel of love An idea developed by Ira Reiss in which love is seen as developing through a four-stage, circular process, including rapport, self-revelation, mutual dependence, and personality need fulfillment.

white-collar workers Professionals, clerical workers, salespeople, and so forth, who have traditionally worn white shirts to work.

wife beating Difficult to define explicitly, but formally, a blow with a clenched fist (not a slap) that is repeated over time.

wife-dominant power A form of **conjugal power** in which the wife has more power than the husband.

workaholic A person whose work has become addictive; someone whose work has taken over such a major portion of his or her identity as to interfere with bodily health, personal happiness, interpersonal relationships, and often even effective work performance itself.

Z

zygote A fertilized **ovum** (egg). See also **embryonic stage, fetal period, germinal period.**

References

Adams, Bert N., and Ronald Cromwell
 1978 "Morning and night people in the family: A preliminary statement." *Family Coordinator* 27:5–13.

Adams, Virginia
 X 1980 "Getting at the heart of jealous love." *Psychology Today* 13 (May):38–47, 102–6.
 1984 "After contraception: dispelling rumors about later childbearing." *Population Reports*, Series J (28) (Sept.-Oct.).

"AIDS called potential no. 2 killer of men."
 1987 *Omaha World-Herald*, June 2.

"AIDS cases in the United States."
 1987 U.S. Center for Disease Control. Reported in *Omaha World-Herald*, June 4.

"AIDS cost of $16 billion is possible in U.S. by 1991."
 1986 *Omaha World-Herald*, June 17, p. 1.

"AIDS disability payments limited."
 1987 *New York Times*, June 2.

"AIDS is felt on campus, but many ignore danger."
 1987 *Omaha World-Herald*, Apr. 6.

"AIDS is predicted to spread tenfold by 1991."
 1986 *Omaha World-Herald*, June 13, p. 1.

Alan Guttmacher Institute
 1976 *Eleven Million Teenagers: What Can Be Done About the Epidemic of Adolescent Pregnancies in the United States?* New York: Alan Guttmacher Institute.

Albrecht, Stan L.
 1979 "Correlates of marital happiness among the remarried." *Journal of Marriage and the Family* 41 (Nov.):857–67.

Aldous, Joan
 1978 *Family Careers: Developmental Change in Families.* New York: Wiley.

Aldous, Joan (ed.)
 1982 *Two Paychecks: Life in Dual-Earner Families.* Beverly Hills, Calif.: Sage.

Aldous, Joan, Lawrence Marsh, and Scott Trees
 1985 "Families and inflation." Paper prepared for presentation at the 80th Annual Meeting of the American Sociological Association, Aug. 26–30.

Aldous, Joan, and Wilfried Dumon, eds.
 1980 *The Politics and Programs of Family Policy.* Notre Dame, Ind.: University of Notre Dame Press.

"The all-American blood-soaked family."
 1976 *Human Behavior* 5 (Feb.):34–35.

Allen, C., and M. Straus
 1980 "Resources, power, and husband-wife violence." Pp. 188–208 in M. Straus and G. Hotaling (eds.), *The Social Causes of Husband-Wife Violence.* Minneapolis: University of Minnesota Press.

Allen, W., and B. Abasegbe
 1980 "A comment on Scotts' 'Black polygamous family formation.' " *Alternative Lifestyles* 3:375–81.

Allgeier, E. R.
 1983 "Sexuality and gender roles in the second half of life." Pp. 135–37 in Elizabeth Rice Allgeier and Naomi B. McCormick (eds.), *Changing Boundaries: Gender Roles and Sexual Behavior.* Palo Alto, Calif.: Mayfield.

Altman, I., and W. W. Hayhorn
 1965 "Interpersonal exchange in isolation." *Sociometry* 28:411–26.

Altman, Irwin, and Dalmas A. Taylor
 1973 *Social Penetration: The Development of Interpersonal Relations.* New York: Holt, Rinehart & Winston.

Altman, Lawrence K.
 1987a "Anxiety allayed on heterosexual AIDS." *New York Times*, June 5.
 1987b "Data suggest AIDS risk rises yearly after infection." *New York Times*, March 3.
 1987c "Does the AIDS virus work alone?" *New York Times*, May 26.
 1987d "Health experts find no evidence to link AIDS to kissing." *New York Times*, June 8.
 1987e "New virus tied to AIDS is found in Africa." *New York Times*, June 2.
 1987f "2 virtually identical AIDS viruses present new problems in research." *New York Times*, Apr. 9.

Alwin, Duane, Philip Converse, and Steven Martin
 1985 "Living arrangements and social integration." *Journal of Marriage and the Family* 47 (May):319–34.

Ambert, Anne-Marie
1984   "Longitudinal changes in children's behavior toward
        custodial parents." *Journal of Marriage and the
        Family* 46 (2) (May):463–67.
Anderson, Jane
1984   "Shared housing gives financial and moral support to
        single parents." *Christian Science Monitor*, Sept. 17,
        p. 35.
Anderson, Trudy B.
1984   "Widowhood as a life transition: Its impact on kinship
        ties." *Journal of Marriage and the Family* 46 (1)
        (Feb.):105–14.
Anspach, Donald F.
1976   "Kinship and divorce." *Journal of Marriage and the
        Family* 38 (May):323–30.
Anthony, E. James
1970   "The impact of mental and physical illness on family
        life." *American Journal of Psychiatry* 127:138–46.
1975   "The reactions of adults to adolescents and their
        behavior." Pp. 105–21 in John J. Conger (ed.),
        Contemporary Issues in Adolescent Development.
        New York: Harper & Row.
Arafat, I., and Betty Yorburg
1973   "On living together without marriage." *Journal of Sex
        Research* 9:21–29.
Ard, Ben N., Jr.
1977   "Sex in lasting marriages." *Journal of Sex Research*
        13:274–85.
Arditti, Rita, Renate Duelli Klein, and Shelley Minden (eds.)
1984   *Test-Tube Women: What Future for Motherhood?*
        London: Routledge & Kegan Paul (Pandora).
Arenson, Karen W.
1983   "Sagging sales puzzle economists." *Omaha World-
        Herald*, March 28, p. 12.
Ariès, Phillipe
1962   *Centuries of Childhood: A Social History of Family
        Life.* New York: Knopf.
Arling, Greg
1976   "The elderly widow and her family, neighbors, and
        friends." *Journal of Marriage and the Family* 38
        (Nov.):757–68.
Atchley, Robert C.
1977   *The Social Forces in Later Life: An Introduction to
        Social Gerontology.* 2d ed. Belmont, Calif.: Wadsworth.
Athanasiou, Robert, Wallace Oppel, Leslie Michelson, Thomas
Unger, and Mary Yager
1973   "Psychiatric sequelae to term birth and induced early
        and late abortion: A longitudinal study." *Family
        Planning Perspectives* 5:227–31.
Babbie, Earl
1982   *The Practice of Social Research.* 2d, 3d eds. Belmont,
[1977] Calif.: Wadsworth.
Bach, George R., and Ronald M. Deutsch
1970   *Pairing.* New York: Avon.
Bach, George R., and Peter Wyden
1970   *The Intimate Enemy: How to Fight Fair in Love and
        Marriage.* New York: Avon.
Bachman, Jerald, Patrick O'Malley, and Jerome Johnston
1978   *Adolescence to Adulthood—Change and Stability.*
        Ann Arbor, Mich.: Institute for Social Research.
Bachrach, Christine A.
1986   "Adoption plans, adopted children, and adoptive
        mothers." *Journal of Marriage and the Family* 48
        (May):243–53.
Bachrach, Christine A., and William D. Mosher
1984   "Use of contraception in the United States, 1982."
        Advance data. *Vital and Health Statistics of the
        National Center for Health Statistics,* No. 102, Dec. 4.
"Background on the Parental and Disability Leave Act of 1985."
1985   *National NOW Times* (Aug.-Sept.).
Bagarozzi, Dennis A., and Paul Rauen
1983   "Premarital counseling: Appraisal and status." Pp.

580–97 in David H. Olson and Brent C. Miller (eds.),
        Family Studies Review Yearbook, v. 1. Beverly Hills,
        Calif.: Sage.
Bahr, Howard M., and Bruce A. Chadwick
1985   "Religion and family in Middletown, USA." *Journal of
        Marriage and the Family* 47 (2) (May):407–14.
Bahr, Stephen J., and Boyd C. Rollins
1971   "Crisis and conjugal power." *Journal of Marriage and
        the Family* 33 (May):360–67.
Bailyn, Lotte
1970   "Career and family orientations of husbands and wives
        in relation to marital happiness." *Human Relations* 23
        (Apr.):97–114.
Baker, Susan W.
1980   "Biological influences on human sex and gender. *Signs*
        6:80–96.
Ball, Richard E., and Lynn Robbins
1986   "Marital status and life satisfaction among black
        Americans." *Journal of Marriage and the Family* 48
        (May):389–94.
Balswick, Jack O., and Charles W. Peek
1977   "The inexpressive male: A tragedy of American society."
        Pp. 222–29 in Arlene S. Skolnick and Jerome H.
        Skolnick (eds.), *Family in Transition: Rethinking
        Marriage, Sexuality, Child Rearing, and Family
        Organization.* 2d ed. Boston: Little, Brown.
Bandura, Albert
1965   "Influence of models: Reinforcement contingencies on
        the acquisition of imitative responses." *Journal of
        Personality and Social Psychology* 1:589–95.
Bane, Mary Jo
1976   "Marital disruption and the lives of children." *Journal
        of Social Issues* 32:103–17.
Barbach, Lonnie Garfield
1975   *For Yourself: The Fulfillment of Female Sexuality.*
        New York: Doubleday.
Barberis, Mary
1981   "America's elderly: Policy implications." *Population
        Bulletin* 35(4), Supplement, Jan. Washington, D.C.:
        Population Reference Bureau.
Barden, J. C.
1987   "Marital rape: Drive for tougher laws is pressed." *New
        York Times,* May 13.
Bardwick, Judith M.
1971   *Psychology of Women: A Study of Biocultural
        Conflicts.* New York: Harper & Row.
Barker-Benfield, G. J.
1975   *The Horrors of the Half-Known Life: Male Attitudes
        Toward Women and Sexuality in Nineteenth-
        Century America.* New York: Harper & Row.
Baron, Robert A., and Donn Byrne
1984   *Social Psychology.* 4th ed. Boston: Allyn & Bacon.
Barron, James
1987   "In ads for condoms, a new focus on women." *New York
        Times,* June 3.
Bart, Pauline
1972   "Depression in middle-aged women." Pp. 163–86 in
        Vivian Gornick and Barbara K. Moran (eds.), *Women in
        Sexist Society: Studies in Power and Powerlessness.*
        New York: New American Library.
Baucom, Donald H., and Paige K. Besch
1985   "Personality processes and individual differences."
        Journal of Personality and Social Psychology 48
        (5):1218–26.
Baumrind, Diana
1971   "Current patterns of parental authority."
        Developmental Psychology Monographs 4:1–102.
Bayer, Ronald
1983   "Gays and the stigma of bad blood." *Hastings Center
        Report* 13 (Apr.):5–7.
Beach, Frank A.
1977a   "Cross-species comparisons and the human heritage."

Pp. 296–316 in Frank A. Beach (ed.), *Human Sexuality in Four Perspectives*. Baltimore, Md.: Johns Hopkins University Press.

Beach, Frank A. (ed.)
1977b *Human Sexuality in Four Perspectives*. Baltimore, Md.: Johns Hopkins University Press.

Bean, Frank D., Russell L. Curtis, and John P. Marcum
1977 "Familism and marital satisfaction among Mexican-Americans." *Journal of Marriage and the Family* 39 (Nov.):759–67.

de Beauvoir, Simone
1952
[1949] *The Second Sex*. New York: Bantam.

Beck, Joan
1984 "Benefits for part-time workers pose new tax problems." *Omaha World-Herald*, May 1.

Becker, Gary S.
1981 *A Treatise on the Family*. Cambridge, Mass.: Harvard University Press.

Becker, Gary S., Elizabeth M. Landes, and Robert T. Michael
1976 "Economics of marital instability." Working paper no. 153, Stanford, Calif.: National Bureau of Economic Research. Cited in Andrew Cherlin, "Remarriage as an incomplete institution," *American Journal of Sociology* 84:634–50.

Becnel, Barbara
1979 "Black workers: Progress derailed." Pp. 149–60 in Jerome H. Skolnick and Elliott Curie (eds.), *Crisis in American Institutions*. 4th ed. Boston: Little, Brown.

Bedard, Virginia S.
1978 "Wife-beating." *Glamour*, Aug., pp. 85–86.

Beer, William R.
1983 *Househusbands: Men and Housework in American Families*. New York: Praeger.

Begley, Sharon
1982 "Jobs—putting America back to work." *Newsweek*, Oct. 2, pp. 78–82.
1986 "Moving target: Searching for a vaccine and a cure." *Newsweek*, Nov. 24, p. 36.

Belkin, Lisa
1985 "Parents weigh costs of children." *New York Times*, May 23.

Bell, Alan
1981 *Omaha World-Herald*, Aug. 29, p. 5-A.

Bell, Alan P., Martin S. Weinberg, and Sue Kiefer Hammersmith
1981 *Sexual Preference: Its Development in Men and Women*. Bloomington: University of Indiana Press.

Bell, Joseph N.
1977 "Rescuing the battered wife." *Human Behavior* 6 (June):16–23.

Bell, Richard Q.
1974 "Contributions of human infants to caregiving and social interaction." Pp. 11–19 in Michael Lewis and Leonard A. Rosenblum (eds.), *The Effect of the Infant on its Care Giver. Origins of Behavior Series*, v. 1. New York: Wiley.

Bell, Robert R.
1966 *Premarital Sex in a Changing Society*. Englewood Cliffs, N.J.: Prentice-Hall.
1975 "Swinging: Separating the sexual from friendship." Pp. 150–68 in Nona Glazer-Malbin (ed.), *Old Family/New Family*. New York: Van Nostrand.
1981 *Worlds of Friendship*. Beverly Hills, Calif.: Sage.

Bell, Robert R., and Jay B. Chaskes
1970 "Premarital sexual experience among coeds, 1958 and 1968." *Journal of Marriage and the Family* 32 (Feb.):81–84.

Bell, Robert R., and Kathleen Coughey
1980 "Premarital sexual experiences among college females, 1958, 1968, and 1978." *Family Relations* 29 (July):353–57.

Bellah, Robert N., Richard Madsen, William M. Sullivan, Ann Swidler, and Steven M. Tipton
1985 *Habits of the Heart: Individualism and Commitment in American Life*. Berkeley: University of California Press.

Bem, Sandra
1975 "Androgyny vs. the tight little lives of fluffy women and chesty men." *Psychology Today* 9 (Sept.):58–62.

Benenson, Harold
1984 "Women's occupation and family achievement in the U.S. class system: A critique of the dual-career family analysis." *British Journal of Sociology* 35 (March):19–41.

Bennett, Neil G., and David E. Bloom
1986 "Why fewer American women marry." *New York Times*, Dec. 13.

Bennetts, Leslie
1979 "Guidance for stepfamilies suffering from togetherness." *New York Times*, Aug. 28, p. C-11.
1986 "Stepparenting." *Omaha World-Herald*, Dec. 7, p. 10-E.

Benoliel, Jeanne Q.
1975 "Childhood diabetes: The commonplace in living becomes uncommon." Pp. 89–98 in Anselm L. Strauss and Barney G. Glaser (eds.), *Chronic Illness and the Quality of Life*. St. Louis: Mosby.

Berardo, Felix M.
1985 "Age heterogamy in marriage." *Journal of Marriage and the Family* 47:553–66.

Berardo, Felix, and Hernan Vera
1981 "The groomal shower: A variation on the American bridal shower." *Family Relations* 30:395–401.

Berg, Barbara
1984 "Early signs of infertility." *Ms.*, May, pp. 68ff.

Berger, Brigitte, and Peter L. Berger
1983 *The War over the Family: Capturing the Middle Ground*. Garden City, N.Y.: Anchor Press/Doubleday.

Berger, Michael, Martha Foster, and Barbara Strudler Wallston
1978 "Finding two jobs." Pp. 23–35 in Robert Rapoport and Rhona Rapoport (eds.), *Working Couples*. New York: Harper & Row.

Berger, Peter L., Brigitte Berger, and Hansfried Kellner
1973 *The Homeless Mind: Modernization and Consciousness*. New York: Random House.

Berger, Peter L., and Hansfried Kellner
1970 "Marriage and the construction of reality." Pp. 49–72 in Hans Peter Dreitzel (ed.), *Recent Sociology No. 2*. New York: Macmillan.

Berger, Peter L., and Thomas Luckmann
1966 *The Social Construction of Reality: A Treatise in the Sociology of Knowledge*. New York: Doubleday.

Berk, Richard A., and Phyllis J. Newton
1985 "Does arrest really deter wife battery? An effort to replicate the findings of the Minneapolis spouse abuse experiment." *American Sociological Review* 50:253–62.

Berk, Richard A., Phyllis J. Newton, and Sarah Fenstermaker Berk
1986 "What a difference a day makes: An empirical study of the impact of shelters for battered women." *Journal of Marriage and the Family* 48 (Aug.):481–90.

"Berkeley makes unwed partners eligible for employee benefits."
1984 *Omaha World-Herald*, Dec. 16.

Berkove, Gail Feldman
1979 "Perceptions of husband support by returning women students." *Family Coordinator* 28 (Oct.):451–57.

Bernard, Jessie
1964 "The adjustments of married mates." Pp. 675–739 in Harold T. Christensen (ed.), *The Handbook of Marriage and the Family*. Chicago: Rand McNally.
1982
[1972] *The Future of Marriage*. 2d ed. New York: Bantam.
1986 "The good-provider role: Its rise and fall." Pp. 125–44 in

Arlene S. Skolnick and Jerome H. Skolnick (eds.), *Family in Transition: Rethinking Marriage, Sexuality, Child Rearing, and Family Organization.* 5th ed. Boston: Little, Brown.

Berscheid, Ellen, and Elaine H. Walster
1969   *Interpersonal Attraction.* Reading, Mass.: Addison-Wesley.

Bianchi, Suzanne, Reynolds Farley, and Daphne Spain
1982   "Racial inequality in housing: An examination of recent trends." *Demography* 19:30–51.

Bianchi, Suzanne M., and Daphne Spain
1986   *American Women in Transition.* New York: Russell Sage.

"Big switch to condos and co-ops."
1979   *Time,* March 5, p. 59.

Bird, Caroline
1978   *The Two-Paycheck Marriage: How Women at Work Are Changing Life in America.* New York: Rawson, Wade.
1979a   "The best years of a woman's life." *Psychology Today* 13 (June):20–26.
1979b   "Sex and power." *Women's Day,* June 26, pp. 64–74, 156.
1979c   *The Two-Paycheck Marriage.* New York: Simon & Schuster.

Black, Carolyn, Kathleen L. Norr, Susanne Meyering, James L. Nom, and Allen O. Charles
1981   "Husband gatekeeping in childbirth." *Family Relations* 30:97–204.

"Blacks face higher risk than whites."
1987   *Omaha World-Herald,* June 4.

Blades, Joan
1985   *Family Mediation: Cooperative Divorce Settlement.* Englewood Cliffs, N.J.: Prentice-Hall.

Blake, Judith
1974   "Can we believe recent data on birth expectations in the U.S.?" *Demography* 11:25–44.
1979   "Is zero preferred? American attitudes toward childlessness in the 1970s." *Journal of Marriage and the Family* 41:245–57.

Blau, Peter M.
1964   *Exchange and Power in Social Life.* New York: Wiley.

Blau, Peter M., and Otis D. Duncan
1967   *The American Occupational Structure.* New York: Wiley.

Blau, Zena S.
1973   *Old Age in a Changing Society: New Viewpoints.* New York: Franklin Watts.

Blauner, R.
1966   "Death and the social structure." *Psychiatry* 29:378–94.

Bleier, Ruth
1984   *Science and Gender: A Critique of Biology and Its Theories of Women.* Elmsford, N.Y.: Pergamon.

Blood, Robert O., Jr.
1969   *Marriage.* 2d ed. New York: Free Press.

Blood, Robert O., Jr., and Donald M. Wolfe
1960   *Husbands and Wives: The Dynamics of Married Living.* New York: Free Press.

Bloom, David E., and Neil G. Bennett
1985   "Marriage patterns in the United States." Harvard University, National Bureau of Economic Research, Working Paper 1701 (Sept.).

Blumberg, Paul
1981   *Inequality in an Age of Decline.* New York: Oxford University Press.

Blumstein, Philip, and Pepper Schwartz
1983   *American Couples: Money, Work, Sex.* New York: Morrow.

Boffey, Philip M.
1987   "Health officials fear 'sideshow' in AIDS efforts." *New York Times,* June 8.

Bohannan, Paul
1970a   "Divorce chains, households of remarriage, and multiple divorces." In Paul Bohannan (ed.), *Divorce and After.* New York: Doubleday.
1970b   "The six stations of divorce." Pp. 29–55 in Paul Bohannan (ed.), *Divorce and After.* New York: Doubleday.

Bohannan, Paul, and Rosemary Erickson
1978   "Stepping in." *Psychology Today* 12 (Jan.):53–54.

Bolger, Niall, Phyllis Moen, and Geraldine Downey
1985   "Family transitions and work decisions: A life course analysis of labor force re-entry for mature married women." Paper prepared for presentation at the 80th Annual Meeting of the American Sociological Association, Aug. 26–30.

Bonham, Gordon Scott
1977   "Who adopts: The relationship of adoption and social demographic characteristics of women." *Journal of Marriage and the Family* 39 (May):295–306.

Booth, Alan
1977   "Wife's employment and husband's stress: A replication and refutation." *Journal of Marriage and the Family* 39 (Nov.):645–50.

Booth, Alan, David B. Brinkerhoff, and Lynn K. White
1984   "The impact of parental divorce on courtship." *Journal of Marriage and the Family* 46 (1) (Feb.):85–94.
1985   "Sibling structure and parental sex-typing of children's household tasks." *Journal of Marriage and the Family* 47 (2) (May):265–73.

Booth, Alan, and Elaine Hess
1974   "Cross-sex friendship." *Journal of Marriage and the Family* 36:38–74.

Booth, Alan, David R. Johnson, and Lynn K. White
1984   "Women, outside employment, and marital instability." *American Journal of Sociology* 90 (3):567–83.

Booth, Alan, and John Edwards
1985   "Age at marriage and marital instability." *Journal of Marriage and the Family* 47 (1) (Feb.):67–75.

Borland, Dolores Cabric
1982   "A cohort analysis approach to the empty-nest syndrome among three ethnic groups of women: A theoretical position." *Journal of Marriage and the Family* (Feb.):117–28.

Boss, Pauline G.
1980   "Normative family stress: Family boundary changes across the lifespan." *Family Relations* 29:445–52.

Bossard, James H., and E. S. Boll
1943   *Family Situations.* Philadelphia: University of Pennsylvania Press.

Boston Women's Health Book Collective
1976   *Our Bodies, Ourselves: A Book by and for Women.* 2d ed. New York: Simon & Schuster.
1984   *The New Our Bodies, Ourselves.* New York: Simon & Schuster.

Bott, Elizabeth
1957   *Family and Social Network: Roles, Norms, and External Relationships.* London: Tavistock.

Bould, Sally
1980   "Unemployment as a factor in early retirement decisions." *American Journal of Economics and Sociology* 39:123–36.

Boulding, Elise
1976   "Familial constraints on women's work roles." Pp. 95–117 in Martha Blaxall and Barbara Reagan (eds.), *Women and the Workplace.* Chicago: University of Chicago Press.
1977   "Children's rights." *Society* (Nov.-Dec.):39–43.

Bowers v. *Hardwick*
1986   478-, 92L Ed 140, 106 S Ct.

Bracken, Michael, Lorraine Klerman, and Maryann Bracken
1978   "Abortion, adoption, or motherhood: An empirical study of decision-making during pregnancy." *American Journal of Obstetrics and Gynecology.* 130:251–62.

Brandt, Anthony
1982   "Avoiding couple karate: Lessons in the marital arts."
        Psychology Today 16:38–43.
Brazelton, T. Berry
1976   *Toddlers and Parents.* New York: Dell.
1981   *On Becoming a Family: The Growth of Attachment.*
        New York: Delacorte.
1983   *Infants and Mothers: Differences in Development.* 2d
        ed. New York: Delacorte.
Brecher, Ruth, and Edward Brecher (eds.)
1966   *An Analysis of Human Sexual Response.* New York:
        New American Library.
Brehm, Jack
1966   "A theory of psychological reactance." In *Social
        Psychology: A Series of Monographs, Treatises, and
        Texts.* New York: Academic Press.
"Bringing up superbaby."
1983   *Newsweek,* March 28, pp. 62–67.
Brod, Harry
1986   "Why is this men's studies different from all other
        men's studies?" *Journal of the National Association
        for Women Deans, Administrators, and Counselors*
        49 (4) (Summer):44–49.
Brodbar-Nemzer, Jay Y.
1986   "Marital relationships and self-esteem: How Jewish
        families are different." *Journal of Marriage and the
        Family* 48 (Feb.):89–98.
Broderick, Carlfred B.
1971   "Beyond the five conceptual frameworks: A decade of
        development in family theory." *Journal of Marriage
        and the Family* 33:39–159.
1978   "Up with marriage." Paper presented at the Building
        Family Strengths Symposium, University of Nebraska,
        Lincoln, May.
1979a   *Couples: How to Confront Problems and Maintain
        Loving Relationships.* New York: Simon & Schuster.
1979b   *Marriage and the Family.* Englewood Cliffs, N.J.:
        Prentice-Hall.
Broderick, Carlfred, and James Smith
1979   "The general systems approach to the family." Pp.
        112–29 in Wesley R. Burr et al., *Contemporary
        Theories About the Family,* v. 2. New York: Free Press.
Brody, Charles J., and Lala Carr Steelman
1985   "Sibling structure and parental sex-typing of children's
        household tasks." *Journal of Marriage and the
        Family* 47 (2) (May):265–73.
Bronfenbrenner, Urie
1958   "Socialization and social class through time and space."
        Pp. 400–25 in Eleanor E. Maccoby, T. N. Newcomb, and
        E. L. Hartley (eds.), *Readings in Social Psychology.*
        New York: Holt.
1977   "Nobody home: The erosion of the American family."
        Psychology Today 10 (May):41–47.
Brooks, Andrée
1984a   "Child-care homes divide communities." *New York
        Times,* July 19.
1984b   "Stepparents and divorce: Keeping ties to children."
        New York Times, July 29, p. 46.
1985   "Trial separation as a therapy technique." *New York
        Times Style,* Sept. 6.
1986   "When studies mislead." *New York Times,* Dec. 29.
Brophy, Beth
1986   "Children under stress." *U.S. News & World Report,*
        Oct. 27:58–63.
Brophy, Julia
1985   "Child care and the growth of power: The status of
        mothers in custody disputes." Pp. 97–116 in Julia
        Brophy and Carol Smart (eds.), *Women in Law:
        Explorations in Law, Family, and Sexuality.* London:
        Routledge & Kegan Paul.
Broverman, Inge K., S. R. Vogel, D. M. Broverman, F. E. Clarkson,
and P. S. Rosencrantz

1972   "Sex roles stereotypes: A current appraisal." *Journal of
        Social Issues* 28 (2):59–78.
Brown, Kathy
1982   "Sharing opens window on secrets of adoption." *Omaha
        World-Herald,* Dec. 5, p. 16-E.
Browne, Angela
1987   *When Battered Women Kill.* New York: Free Press.
Brozan, Nadine
1984   "A respite for families of disabled children." *New York
        Times,* Aug. 6.
Bruch, Carol S.
1978   "Making visitation work: Dual parenting orders."
        Family Advocate 1 (Summer):22–26, 41–42.
Buchanan, Patrick J.
1983   "Nature exacts awful penalty from gays." *Omaha
        World-Herald,* May 25, p. 36.
Bukstel, Lee R., Gregory D. Roeder, Peter R. Kilmann, James
Laughlin, and Wayne M. Sotile
1978   "Projected extramarital sexual involvement in un-
        married college students." *Journal of Marriage and
        the Family* 40 (May):337–40.
Bultena, Gordon L., and Vivian Wood
1969   "The American retirement community: Bane or
        blessing?" *Journal of Gerontology* 24:209–17.
Bumpass, Larry L., and Ronald R. Rindfuss
1979   "Children's experience of marital disruption."
        American Journal of Sociology 85:49–65.
Burchell, R. Clay
1975   "Self-esteem and sexuality." *Medical Aspects of Human
        Sexuality* (Jan.):74–90.
Burgess, Ernest, and Harvey Locke
1953   *The Family: From Institution to Companionship.*
[1945] New York: American Book Co.
Burgess, Ernest, and Paul Wallin
1953   *Engagement and Marriage.* Philadelphia: Lippincott.
Burke, Ronald J., and Tamara Weir
1976   "Relationship of wives' employment status to husband,
        wife and pair satisfaction and performance." *Journal of
        Marriage and the Family* 38 (May):279–87.
Burr, Wesley R.
1973   *Theory Construction and the Sociology of the
        Family.* New York: Wiley.
Burris, Beverly H.
1983   "The human effects of underemployment." *Social
        Problems* 31 (Oct.):96–110.
Byrne, Donn E.
1971   *The Attraction Paradigm.* New York: Academic Press.
1977   "A pregnant pause in the sexual revolution." *Psychology
        Today* 11 (July):67–68.
Bytheway, William R.
1981   "The variation with age of age differences in marriage."
        Journal of Marriage and the Family 43:923–27.
Cadden, Vivian
1973   "The politics of marriage: A delicate balance." Pp.
        296–302 in Marcia E. Lasswell and Thomas E. Lasswell
        (eds.), *Love, Marriage, Family: A Developmental
        Approach.* Glenview, Ill.: Scott, Foresman.
Caine, Lynn
1974   *Widow.* New York: Morrow.
Callahan, Daniel
1985   "What do children owe elderly parents?" *Hastings
        Center Report* 15 (Apr.):32–37.
Campbell, Angus A.
1975   "The American way of mating: Marriage, si; children,
        maybe." *Psychology Today* 8 (May):37–43.
Campbell, Angus A., P. L. Converse, and W. L. Rodgers
1976   *The Quality of American Life: Perceptions,
        Evaluations, and Satisfactions.* New York: Russell
        Sage.
Campbell, Meg
1984   "On having a second child." *Ms.,* Sept., p. 140.
Cancian, Francesca M.
1985   "Gender politics: Love and power in the private and

public spheres." Pp. 253–64 in Alice S. Rossi (ed.), *Gender and the Life Course.* New York: Aldine.

Caplovitz, David
1979   *Making Ends Meet: How Families Cope with Inflation and Recession.* Beverly Hills, Calif.: Sage.

Caplow, Theodore, Howard M. Bahr, Bruce A. Chadwick, Reuben Hill, and Margaret Holmes Williamson
1982   *Middletown Families: Fifty Years of Change and Continuity.* New York: Bantam.

Card, Emily
1984   "Before—or even after—you say 'I do'." *Ms,* June, pp. 72–78.

Card, Josefina J.
1981   "Long-term consequences for children of teenage parents." *Demography* 18 (2) (May):137–56.

Card, Josefina, and L. L. Wise
1978   "Teenage mothers and teenage fathers: The impact of early childbearing on the parents' personal and professional lives." *Family Planning Perspectives* 10:199–205.

Cargan, Leonard, and Matthew Melko
1982   *Singles: Myths and Realities.* Beverly Hills, Calif.: Sage.

Carlson, Elwood
1976   "Don't blame the divorce rate on working wives." *Psychology Today* 10 (July):17.

Carol, Arthur
1983   "Pay gaps: Worry not for women but humdrum households." *Wall Street Journal,* Aug. 12.

Carro, Geraldine
1983   "Stay-home fathers' superkids." *Psychology Today* 7:71.

Carson, Rubin
1978   *The National Love, Sex, & Marriage Test.* Garden City, N.Y.: Doubleday/Dolphin.

Cassety, Judith (ed.)
1983   *The Parental Child-Support Obligation.* Lexington, Mass.: Heath.

Catholic Theological Society of America
1977   *Human Sexuality: New Directions in American Catholic Thought.* New York: Paulist Press.

Cauhape, Elizabeth
1983   *Fresh Starts: Men and Women After Divorce.* New York: Basic Books.

"Census shows family wealth skewed."
1986   *Omaha World-Herald,* July 19.

Chafetz, Janet Saltzman
1978   *Masculine, Feminine, or Human? An Overview of*
[1974] *the Sociology of the Gender Roles.* 2d ed. Itasca, Ill.: Peacock.

Chaikin, Alan L., and Valerian J. Derlega
1976   "Self-disclosure." Pp. 177–210 in J. W. Thibaut, J. T. Spence, and R. C. Carson (eds.), *Contemporary Topics in Social Psychology.* Morristown, N.J.: General Learning Press.

"Changing women."
1984   *American Demographics* (Jan.):16.

Charny, Israel
1974   "Marital love and hate." In Suzanne K. Steinmetz and Murray A. Straus (eds.), *Violence in the Family.* New York: Dodd, Mead.

Cherlin, A.
1978   "Remarriage as incomplete institution." *American Journal of Sociology* 84:634–50.
1981   *Marriage, Divorce, Remarriage.* Cambridge, Mass.: Harvard University Press.

Cherlin, Andrew, and Frank F. Furstenberg
1985   "Styles and strategies of grandparenting." Pp. 97–116 in Vern L. Bengston and Joan F. Robertson (eds.), *Grandparenthood.* Beverly Hills, Calif.: Sage.

Cherlin, Andrew, and James McCarthy
1985   "Remarried couple households: Data from the June 1980 Current Population Survey." *Journal of Marriage and the Family* 47 (1) (Feb.):23–30.

Chesler, Phyllis
1972   *Women and Madness.* New York: Doubleday.

Chess, Stella, Alexander Thomas, and Herbert G. Birch
1965   *Your Child Is a Person: A Psychological Approach to Parenthood Without Guilt.* New York: Viking.

Chilman, Catherine
1978a   "Families of today." Paper presented at the Building Family Strengths Symposium, University of Nebraska, Lincoln, May.
1978b   "Habitat and American families: A social-psychological overview." *Family Coordinator* 27 (Apr.):105–11.

Chodorow, Nancy
1978   *The Reproduction of Mothering: Psychoanalysis and the Sociology of Gender.* Berkeley: University of California Press.

Christensen, Harold, and Christina F. Gregg
1970   "Changing sex norms in America and Scandinavia." *Journal of Marriage and the Family* 32 (Nov.):616–27.

Cimbalo, R. S., V. Faling, and P. Mousaw
1976   "The course of love: A cross-sectional design." *Psychological Reports* 38:1292–94.

Clark, Matt
1982   "Herpes: The VD of the '80s." *Newsweek,* Apr. 12.

Clarke-Stewart, Alison
1977   "The father's impact on mother and child." Paper presented at the meeting of the Society for Research in Child Development, New Orleans, La., March.

Clatworthy, Nancy M.
1975   "Living together." Pp. 67–89 in Nona Glazer-Malbin (ed.), *Old Family/New Family.* New York: Van Nostrand.

Clavan, Sylvia
1978   "The impact of social class and social trends on the role of grandparent." *Family Coordinator* 27:351–57.

Clayton, Richard R.
1979   *The Family, Marriage, and Social Change.* 2d ed. Lexington, Mass.: Heath.

Clayton, Richard R., and Harlan L. Voss
1977   "Shacking up: Cohabitation in the 1970's." *Journal of Marriage and the Family* 39 (May):273–83.

Clemens, Audra W., and Leland J. Axelson
1985   "The not-so-empty nest: The return of the fledgling adult." *Family Relations* 34:259–64.

Cleveland, Martha
1981   "Sexuality in the middle years." Pp. 121–28 in Peter J. Stein (ed.), *Single Life.* New York: St. Martin's Press.

Cleveland, William P., and Daniel T. Gianturco
1976   "Remarriage probability after widowhood: A retrospective method." *Journal of Gerontology* 31 (1):99–103.

Clifford, M., and Elaine H. Walster
1973   "The effect of physical attractiveness on teacher expectation." *Sociology of Education* 46:248.

Cockerham, William C.
1981   *Sociology of Mental Disorder.* Englewood Cliffs, N.J.: Prentice-Hall.

Cohen, Debra Rae
1978   "Sexuality: Children of homosexuals seem headed straight." *Psychology Today* 12 (Nov.):44–45.

Cohen, Gaynor
1977   "Absentee husbands in spiralist families." *Journal of Marriage and the Family* 39 (Aug.):595–604.

Cohen, Jessica Field
1979   "Male roles in mid-life." *Family Coordinator* 28 (Oct.):465–71.

Cole, Sheila
1980   "Send our children to work?" *Psychology Today* 14 (July):44–68.

Cole, Thomas
1983   "The 'enlightened' view of aging." *Hastings Center Report* 13:34–40.

Colgrove, Melba, Harold Bloomfield, and Peter McWilliams
1978   *How to Survive the Loss of a Love: 58 Things to Do When There Is Nothing to Be Done.* New York: Bantam.

"College students: Who they are, what they think."
1986   *Chronicle of Higher Education,* Feb. 5.

Colletta, Nancy Donohue, and Carol Hunter Gregg
1979   "The everyday lives of adolescent mothers: Variables related to emotional stress." Paper presented at the annual meeting of the National Council on Family Relations, Boston, Aug.

Collins, Alice H., and Eunice L. Watson
1976   *Family Day Care: A Practical Guide for Parents, Caregivers, and Professionals.* Boston: Beacon.

Collins, Glenn
1979   "The good news about 1984." *Psychology Today* 12 (Jan.):34.
1985   "More corporations are offering child care." *New York Times Style,* June 21, p. 25.

Colten, Mary Ellen, and Robert W. Marans
1982   "Restrictive rental practices and their impact on families." *Population Research and Review* 1:43–58.

Comer, James P., and Alvin F. Poussaint
1975   *Black Child Care.* New York: Simon & Schuster.

Comfort, Alex
1972   *The Joy of Sex.* New York: Crown.

Coogler, O. J.
1978   *Structured Mediation in Divorce Settlement: A Handbook for Marital Mediators.* Lexington, Mass.: Lexington Books.

Cooke, Cynthia W., M.D., and Susan Dworkin
1981   "Good health: The age of high tech pregnancy." *Ms.,* Apr., pp. 15–16.

Cooley, Charles
1902   *Human Nature and the Social Order.* New York: Scribners.
1909   *Social Organization.* New York: Scribners.

Cooney, Rosemary, Lloyd H. Rogler, Rose Marie Hurrell, and Vilma Ortiz
1982   "Decision making in intergenerational Puerto Rican families." *Journal of Marriage and the Family* 44:621–31.

Cooper, Sally
1984   "Confronting a near and present danger," *Ms.,* Apr., p. 72.

Coopersmith, Stanley
1967   *The Antecedents of Self-Esteem.* San Francisco: Freeman.

Coser, Lewis
1956   *The Functions of Social Conflict.* New York: Free Press.

"Court-martial of soldier is urged for sex after positive AIDS test."
1987   *New York Times,* May 9.

Coverman, Shelley, and Joseph F. Sheley
1986   "Change in men's housework and child-care time, 1965–1975." *Journal of Marriage and the Family* 48 (May):413–22.

Cowan, Connell, and Melvyn Kinder
1987   *Women Men Love, Women Men Leave.* New York: Crown.

Crano, William D., and Joel Aranoff
1975   "A re-examination of cross-cultural principles of task segregation and sex role differentiation in the family." *American Sociological Review* 40:12–20.

Crewdson, John
1987   "Fears, hopes mingle as America intensifies fight to conquer AIDS." *Omaha World-Herald,* June 4.

Crimmins, Eileen M.
1984   "Life expectancy and the older population: Demographic implications of recent and prospective trends in old age mortality." *Research on Aging* 6 (Dec.):490–514.

Critelli, Joseph W., Emilie J. Myers, and Victor E. Loos
1986   "The components of love: Romantic attraction and sex role orientation." *Journal of Personality* 54:354–76.

Cromwell, Ronald E., P. Keeney Bradford, and Bert N. Adams
1976   "Temporal planning in the family." *Family Process* 15:343.

Cromwell, Ronald E., and David H. Olson (eds.)
1975   *Power in Families.* New York: Wiley.

Cromwell, Vicky L., and Ronald E. Cromwell
1978   "Perceived dominance in decision-making and conflict resolution among Anglo, black, and chicano couples." *Journal of Marriage and the Family* 40 (Nov.):749–59.

Crosby, John F.
1976   *Illusion and Disillusion: The Self in Love and Marriage.* 2d ed. Belmont, Calif.: Wadsworth.
1980   "A critique of divorce statistics and their interpretation." *Family Relations* 29 (Jan.):51–68.

Cuber, John, and Peggy Harroff
1965   *The Significant Americans.* New York: Random House. (Published also as *Sex and the Significant Americans,* Baltimore: Penguin, 1965.)

Cunniff, John
1985   "Ownership slide greatest for young." *Omaha World-Herald,* Oct. 21.

"Cupid's arrows strike at random."
1981   *St. Louis Post-Dispatch,* Feb. 15, p. 2-B.

Cutler, Beverly R., and William G. Dyer
1965   "Initial adjustment processes in young married couples." *Social Forces* 44 (Dec.):195–201.

Dahms, Alan M.
1976   "Intimacy hierarchy." Pp. 85–104 in Edward A. Powers and Mary W. Lees (eds.), *Process in Relationship: Marriage and Family.* 2d ed. New York: West.

Daly, Margaret
1979   "What to do if you're overextended." *Better Homes and Gardens,* Nov., pp. 31–32, 37.

Daniels, Pamela, and Kathy Weingarten
1980   "Postponing parenthood: The myth of the perfect time." *Savvy Magazine,* May, pp. 55–60.
1982   *The Timing of Parenthood in Adult Lives.* New York: Norton.

Dannefer, Dale
1984   "Adult development and social theory." *American Sociological Review* 49:100–116.

D'Antonio, William V., and Joan Aldous (eds.)
1983   *Families and Religion: Conflict and Change in Modern Society.* Beverly Hills, Calif.: Sage.

Darling, Carol A., David J. Kallen, and Joyce E. VanDusen
1984   "Sex in transition, 1900–1980." *Journal of Youth and Adolescence* 13 (5):385–99.

Darling, Jon
1981   "Late-marrying bachelors." Pp. 34–40 in Peter J. Stein (ed.), *Single Life.* New York: St. Martin's Press.

Darling, Rosalyn B.
1979   *Families Against Society: A Study of Reactions to Children with Birth Defects.* Beverly Hills, Calif.: Sage.

David, Deborah S., and Robert Brannon (eds.)
1976   *The Forty-Nine Percent Majority: The Male Sex Role.* Reading, Mass.: Addison-Wesley.

Davis, Angela Y.
1981   *Women, Race, and Class.* New York: Random House.

Davis, Fred
1963   *Passage Through Crisis: Polio Victims and Their Families.* Indianapolis: Bobbs-Merrill.
1972   *Illness, Interaction, and the Self.* Belmont, Calif.: Wadsworth.

Davis, J. A.
1980   *General Social Surveys, 1972–1980: Cumulative Data.* Chicago: National Opinion Research Center.

Davis, Kingsley
1974   "The sociology of parent-youth conflict." Pp. 446–59 in

Rose L. Coser (ed.), *The Family: Its Structures and Functions*. 2d ed. New York: St. Martin's Press.

Davis, Peter.
1987 "Exploring the kingdom of AIDS." *New York Times Magazine*, May 31, pp. 32ff.

Dean, Gillian, and Douglas T. Gurak
1978 "Marital homogamy the second time around." *Journal of Marriage and the Family* 40 (Aug.):559–70.

DeBold, Joseph F., and Zella Luria
1983 "Gender identity, interactionism, and politics: A reply to Rogers and Walsh. *Sex Roles* 9:1101–8.

Deckard, Barbara Sinclair
1983 *The Women's Movement: Political Socioeconomic, and Psychological Issues*. 3d ed. New York: Harper & Row.

Decter, Midge
1976 "Toward the new chastity." Pp. 380–95 in Sol Gordon and Roger W. Libby (eds.), *Sexuality Today and Tomorrow*. North Scituate, Mass.: Duxbury.

Deegan, Mary Jo
1986 Personal communication.

Degler, Carl N.
1980 *At Odds: Women and the Family in America from the Revolution to the Present*. New York: Oxford University Press.

DeMause, Lloyd
1975 "Our forebears made childhood a nightmare." *Psychology Today* 8 (Apr.):85–88.

Dentzer, Susan
1985 "When a house can't be home." *Newsweek*, Apr. 8, pp. 53–54.

Denzin, Norman K.
1970 *Sociological Methods*. Chicago: Aldine.

DeRosis, Helen A., and Victoria Y. Pellegrino
1976 *The Book of Hope: How Women Can Overcome Depression*. New York: Macmillan.

"Desperate victims scrape up cash and hope to get the latest drugs."
1987 *Omaha World-Herald*, June 4.

DeWolf, Rose
1982 "Feelings mixed on life as single." *New York Times*, Sept. 16, p. 20.

Dickstein, M.
1977 *Gates of Eden*. New York: Basic Books.

"Difficulty in finding husbands drives single women to counseling."
1986 *Omaha World-Herald*, Dec. 30.

Dion, Karen
1972 "Physical attractiveness and evaluations of children's transgressions." *Journal of Personality and Social Psychology* 24:207–13.

Dion, Karen, and Ellen Berscheid
1972 "Physical attractiveness and social perception of peers in preschool children." Mimeographed.

Dodson, Fitzhugh
1973 *How to Parent*. New York: New American Library.

Donzelot, Jacques
1979 *The Policing of Families*. New York: Random House.

Doudna, Christine
1981 "Where are the men for the women at the top?" Pp. 21–34 in Peter J. Stein (ed.), *Single Life*. New York: St. Martin's Press.

1982 "The weekend mother." *New York Times Magazine*, Oct. 3, pp. 72–75, 84–88.

Douvan, Elizabeth
1979 Quoted in *IRS Newsletter*, v. 7. University of Michigan, Ann Arbor.

Dreifus, Claudia (ed.)
1977 *Seizing Our Bodies: The Politics of Women's Health*. New York: Vintage.

Dressel, Paula L.
1980 "Assortative mating in later life: Some initial considerations." *Journal of Family Issues* 1:379–96.

Driscoll, Richard, Keith E. Davis, and Milton E. Lipetz
1972 "Parental interference and romantic love: The Romeo and Juliet effect." *Journal of Personality and Social Psychology* 24:1–10.

"Dr. Koop: AIDS may 'explode' among heterosexuals."
1987 *Omaha World-Herald*, Apr. 20.

Dryfoos, Joy G.
1984 "A new strategy for preventing unintended teenage childbearing." *Family Planning Perspectives* 16 (July-Aug.):193–95.

Duberman, Lucile
1975 *The Reconstituted Family: A Study of Remarried Couples and Their Children*. Chicago: Nelson-Hall.

1977 *Marriage and Other Alternatives*. 2d ed. New York: Praeger.

Dullea, Georgia
1987a "Divorces spawn confusion over stepparents' rights." *Omaha World-Herald*, March 18.

1987b "False child-abuse charges seem to be on the increase." *New York Times*, reprinted in *Omaha World-Herald*, Jan. 19, p. 5.

1987c "Wives confront spouses' homosexuality." *New York Times*, Apr. 27.

Dumon, Wilfried, and Joan Aldous
1979 "European and United States political contexts for family policy research." *Journal of Marriage and the Family* 41 (Aug.):497–505.

Duncan, Otis Dudley
1982 "Recent cohorts lead rejection of sex-typing." *Sex Roles* 8:127–33.

Duncan, R. Paul, and Carolyn Cummings Perrucci
1976 "Dual occupation families and migration." *American Sociological Review* 41 (Apr.):252–61.

Dunning, Jennifer
1986 "Women and AIDS: Discussing precautions." *New York Times*, Nov. 3.

Durkheim, Émile
1933 *Division of Labor in Society*. George Simpson (trans.).
[1893] New York: Macmillan.

1951 *Suicide*. John A. Spaulding and George Simpson (trans.). Glencoe, Ill.: Free Press.

Duvall, Evelyn
1957 *Marriage and Family Development*. Philadelphia: Lippincott.

1977 *Marriage and Family Development*. 5th ed. Philadelphia: Lippincott.

Duvall, Evelyn Mills, and Brent C. Miller
1985 *Marriage and Family Development*. 6th ed. New York: Harper & Row.

Dyer, Everett D.
1963 "Parenthood as crisis: A re-study." *Marriage and Family Living* 25 (May):196–201.

Dyer, Wayne W.
1977 "How to put more love in your life." *Family Circle*, Nov. 15, pp. 6, 88–90.

Easterlin, Richard
1978 "What will 1984 be like?" Presidential Address to the Population Association of America, Apr.

1987 *Birth and Fortune: The Impact of Numbers on Personal Welfare*, 2d rev. ed. Chicago: University of Chicago Press.

Easterlin, Richard A., and Eileen M. Crimmins
1985 *The Fertility Revolution: A Supply-Demand Analysis*. Chicago: University of Chicago Press.

Eaton, William W.
1980 *The Sociology of Mental Disorders*. New York: Praeger.

Eckholm, Erik
1986 "Genital herpes is more common, but the alarm is diminishing." *New York Times*, July 8.

"Economic shifts cutting earnings for young men."
1987 *Omaha World-Herald*, June 12.

Edelman, Marian Wright
1985 "The sea is so wide and my boat is so small." Pp. 72–82

in Harriette Pipes McAdoo and John Lewis McAdoo (eds.), *Black Children: Social, Educational, and Parental Environments*. Beverly Hills, Calif.: Sage.

Edwards, John N., and Alan Booth
1976 "Sexual behavior in and out of marriage: An assessment of correlates." *Journal of Marriage and the Family* 38:73–81.

Eggebeen, David, and Peter Uhlenberg
1985 "Changes in the organization of men's lives: 1960–1980." *Family Relations* 34 (Apr.):251–57.

Ehrenreich, Barbara
1983 *The Hearts of Men: American Dreams and the Flight from Commitment*. Garden City, N.Y.: Anchor/ Doubleday.

Ehrenreich, Barbara, and John Ehrenreich
1979 "The American health empire: The system behind the chaos." In Jerome H. Skolnick and Elliott Curie (eds.), *Crisis in American Institutions*. 4th ed. Boston: Little, Brown.

Ehrlich, Carol
1971 "The male sociologist's burden: The place of women in marriage and family texts." *Journal of Marriage and the Family* 33:421–30.

Eiduson, Bernice T., Madeleine Kornfein, Iria Lee Zimmerman, and Thomas E. Weisner
1982 "Comparative socialization practices in traditional and alternative families." Pp. 315–46 in Michael E. Lamb (ed.), *Nontraditional Families: Parenting and Child Development*. Hillsdale, N.J.: Erlbaum.

Elder, Glen
1974 *Children of the Great Depression*. Chicago: University of Chicago Press.

Elder, Glen H., Jr.
1977 "Family history and the life course." *Journal of Family History* 2 (Winter):279–304.

Elder, Glen H., Jr., and Richard C. Rockwell
1976 "Marital timing in women's life patterns." *Journal of Family History* 1:34–53.

Elkind, David
1979 "Growing up faster." *Psychology Today* 12 (Feb.):38–45.

"Embryo freezing cited in a 2nd birth."
1984 *New York Times*, July 7, p. 44-A.

Emerson, R. M.
1962 "Power-dependence relations." *American Sociological Review* 27:31–41.

Engels, Friedrich
1942 *The Origin of the Family, Private Property, and the State*. New York: International.

Enos, Daryl D.
1976 "Blacks, chicanos, and the health care system." Pp. 242–62 in Donald H. Zimmerman et al. (eds.), *Understanding Social Problems*. New York: Praeger.

Equal Rights Monitor
1976 " 'Landmark decision' in murder case." Oct., p. 17.

Erikson, Erik
1963 *Childhood and Society*. New York: Norton.
1964 "Inner and outer space: Reflections on womanhood." *Daedalus* 93:582–606.
1979 Interview in *Omaha World-Herald*, Aug. 5.

Espenshade, Thomas J.
1977 "The value and cost of children." *Population Bulletin* 32 (1). Washington, D.C.: Population Reference Bureau.
1979 "The economic consequences of divorce." *Journal of Marriage and the Family* (Aug.):615–25.

Etaugh, C.
1974 "Effects of maternal employment on children: A review of recent research." *Merrill-Palmer Quarterly* 20:71–98.

Etzkowitz, Henry, and Peter Stein
1978 "The life spiral: Human needs and adult roles." *Alternative Lifestyles* 1:434–46.

Evans, Sara
1978 *Personal Politics*. New York: Knopf.

"Experts debate effects of missing-child work."
1986 *Omaha World-Herald*, Feb. 14.

Faber, Adele, and Elain Mazlish
1982 *How to Talk So Kids Will Listen and Listen So Kids Will Talk*. New York: Avon.

Falbo, T.
1976 "Does the only child grow up miserable?" *Psychology Today* 9 (May):60–65.

"Families spend $11 billion each year for child care."
1987 *Omaha World-Herald*, May 8.

Farber, Bernard
1959 "Effects of a severely mentally retarded child on family integration." *Monographs of the Society for Research in Child Development* 24 (71):80–94.

Farrell, Warren
1974 *The Liberated Man*. New York: Random House.

Fast, I., and A. C. Cain
1966 "The stepparent role: Potential for disturbances in family functioning." *American Journal of Orthopsychiatry* 36 (Apr.):485–91.

Fein, Esther B.
1984 "Lonely elderly singles finding major benefits in sharing homes." *New York Times*, Aug. 6.

Feldman, Larry B.
1975 "Effect of anger and resentment on sexual expression." *Medical Aspects of Human Sexuality* (Dec.):10–21.

Fengler, Alfred P.
1973 "The effects of age and education on marital ideology." *Journal of Marriage and the Family* 35:264–71.
1975 "Attitudinal orientation of wives toward their husbands' retirement." *International Journal of Aging and Human Development* 6:139–52.

Ferber, Marianne, and Joan Huber
1979 "Husbands, wives, and careers." *Journal of Marriage and the Family* 41 (May):315–25.

Fernandez, John
1986 *Child Care and Corporate Productivity: Resolving Family/Work Conflicts*. Lexington, Mass.: Heath.

Ferree, Myra Marx
1976 "Working-class jobs: Housework and paid work as sources of satisfaction." *Social Problems* 23 (Apr.):431–41.
1983 "The women's movement in the working class." *Sex Roles* 9:493–505.

"Fertility study cites exercise."
1985 *New York Times*, May 29.

Fidell, Linda, and Jane Prather
1976 "Women: Work isn't always the answer." *Psychology Today* 10 (Sept.):78.

Figley, Charles R., and Hamilton T. McCubbin (eds.)
1983 *Stress and the Family*, v. 2. *Coping with Catastrophe*. New York: Brunner/Mazel.

Findlay, Steven
1985 "Jobs sap couples' craving for sex." *USA Today*, May 8.

Finklehor, David
1979 *Sexually Victimized Children*. New York: Free Press.

Firestone, Shulamith
1970 *The Dialectic of Sex: The Case for Feminist Revolution*. New York: Morrow.

"First anti-AIDS bias suit decided in favor of dead complainant."
1986 *Omaha World-Herald*, Aug. 7.

"First 'ovum transfer' baby born."
1984 *Chronicle of Higher Education* (Feb. 15):7, 9.

Fisher, Judith L.
1983 "Mothers living apart from their children." *Family Relations* 32:351–57.

Fisher, Seymour
1973 *Understanding the Female Orgasm*. New York: Bantam.

Fisher, W. A., M. Edmunds, C. T. Miller, K. Kelley, and L. A. White
1979 "Psychological and situation-specific correlates of

contraceptive behaviors among university women."
Journal of Sex Research 15:38–55.

Fishman, Barbara
1983 "The economic behavior of stepfamilies." *Family Relations* 32:359–66.

Fiske, Edward
1987 "Tuitions at new peak heating cost debate." *New York Times,* May 12.

Flaim, Paul O.
1979 "The effect of demographic changes on the nation's unemployment rate." *Monthly Labor Review* 102 (3):13–23.

Fleming, A.
1978 "When the kids *don't* leave home." *Women's Day,* July 10, pp. 59–63.

"Florida's top ranking in syphilis cases is linked to use of drugs."
1987 *New York Times,* May 26.

Fontana, Vincent J.
1973 *Somewhere a Child Is Crying: Maltreatment—Causes and Prevention.* New York: Macmillan.

Foote, Nelson
1954 "Sex as play." *Social Problems* 1:159–63.

Ford, Clellan A., and Frank A. Beach
1971 "Human sexual behavior in perspective." Pp. 155–71 in Arlene S. Skolnick and Jerome H. Skolnick (eds.), *Family in Transition: Rethinking Marriage, Sexuality, Child Rearing, and Family Organization.* Boston: Little, Brown.

Framo, James L.
1978 "The friendly divorce." *Psychology Today* 11 (Feb.):77–80, 99–102.

Franklin, Clyde W.
1984 *The Changing Definition of Masculinity.* New York: Plenum Press.

Freedman, Deborah S., and Arland Thornton
1979 "The long-term impact of pregnancy at marriage on the family's economic circumstances." *Family Planning Perspectives* 11 (Jan.-Feb.):6–21.

Freedman, Samuel G.
1986 "New York offers help to unmarried fathers." *New York Times,* reprinted in *Omaha World-Herald,* Dec. 7.

Freeman, Derek
1983 *Margaret Mead in Samoa: The Making and Unmaking of an Anthropological Myth.* Cambridge, Mass.: Harvard University Press.

Freeman, Ellen
1978 "Abortion: Subjective attitudes and feelings." *Family Planning Perspectives* 10 (May-June):150–55.

Friedan, Betty
1963 *The Feminine Mystique.* New York: Dell.
1978 "Where are women in 1978?" *Cosmopolitan,* Aug., pp. 196, 206–11.

Frieze, Irene H., Jacquelynne E. Parsons, Paula B. Johnson, Diane N. Ruble, and Gail L. Zellman
1978 *Women and Sex Roles: A Social Psychological Perspective.* New York: Norton.

Fromm, Erich
1956 *The Art of Loving.* New York: Harper & Row.
1975 *Man for Himself: An Inquiry into the Psychology of*
[1947] *Ethics.* New York: Ballantine.

Fuller, Doris Byron
1984 "Working women's impact on economy is 'beyond belief'." *Omaha World-Herald,* Nov. 25.

Furstenberg, Frank F., Jr.
1976 *Unplanned Parenthood: The Social Consequences of Teenage Childbearing.* New York: Macmillan.

Furstenberg, Frank, Jr., and Alfred Crawford
1978 "Family support: Helping teenage mothers to cope." *Family Planning Perspectives* 10 (Nov.-Dec.):322–33.

Gagnon, John H.
1977 *Human Sexualities.* Glenview, Ill.: Scott, Foresman.

Gallup, George
1978 "Poll shows abortion backed under 'certain conditions'." *Omaha World-Herald,* Jan. 22.

Gallup, George, Jr.
1986 Gallup Poll, "Americans find family life satisfying." *San Francisco Chronicle,* Dec. 25, p. 8.

Galper, Miriam
1978 *Co-Parenting: Sharing Your Child Fully: A Sourcebook for the Separated or Divorced Family.* Philadelphia: Running Press.

Gans, Herbert J.
1962 *The Urban Villagers: Group and Class in the Life of Italian-Americans.* Glencoe, Ill.: Free Press.

Garbarino, James
1977a "The human ecology of child maltreatment: A conceptual model for research." *Journal of Marriage and the Family* 39 (Nov.):721–35.
1977b "The price of privacy in the social dynamics of child abuse." *Child Welfare* 56 (Nov.):565–75.

Gardner, Richard
1971 *Boys' and Girls' Book About Divorce.* New York: Bantam.

Garland, Susan A.
1986 "Emotional, financial burdens of divorce: Adult children often forgotten." Newhouse News Service, in *Omaha World-Herald,* May 13, p. 5.

Garrett, Betty
1978 "A den mother goes back to work." *Working Mother,* Oct., pp. 60–67.

Gasser, Rita D., and Claribel M. Taylor
1976 "Role adjustment of single parent fathers with dependent children." *Family Coordinator* 25:397–401.

Gayford, J. J.
1975 "Battered wives." *Medicine, Science, and the Law* 15:237–45.

Gebhard, Paul
1970 "Postmarital coitus among widows and divorcees." Pp. 81–96 in Paul Bohannan (ed.), *Divorce and After.* Garden City, N.Y.: Doubleday.

Geist, William E.
1987 "In AIDS era, a new club for singles." *New York Times,* Apr. 15.

Gelcer, Esther
1986 "Dealing with loss in the family context." *Journal of Family Issues* 7:315–36.

Gelles, Richard J.
1974 *The Violent Home: A Study of Physical Aggression Between Husbands and Wives.* Beverly Hills, Calif.: Sage.
1976 "Abused wives: Why do they stay?" *Journal of Marriage and the Family* 38 (Nov.):659–68.
1977 "Power, sex, and violence: The case of marital rape." *Family Coordinator* 26 (Oct.):339–47.
1979 *Family Violence.* Beverly Hills, Calif.: Sage.

Gelles, Richard J., and Claire Pedrick Cornell
1985 *Intimate Violence in Families.* Beverly Hills, Calif.: Sage.

Gerard, Jeremy
1987 "Creative arts being reshaped by the epidemic." *New York Times,* June 9.

Gerson, Kathleen
1985 *Hard Choices: How Women Decide About Work, Career, and Motherhood.* Berkeley: University of California Press.

Gerstel, Naomi
1977 "The feasibility of commuter marriages." Pp. 357–67 in P. J. Stein, J. Richmond, and N. Hannigan (eds.), *The Family: Functions, Conflicts, and Symbols.* Reading, Mass.: Addison-Wesley.

Giddings, Paula
1984 *When and Where I Enter: The Impact of Black*

Women on Race and Sex in America. New York: Morrow.

Gil, David G.
1970   *Violence Against Children: Physical Child Abuse in the United States*. Cambridge, Mass.: Harvard University Press.

Gillespie, Dair
1971   "Who has the power? The marital struggle." *Journal of Marriage and the Family* 33:445–58. Reprinted in Jo Freeman (ed.), *Women: A Feminist Perspective*. Palo Alto, Calif.: Mayfield.

Gilligan, Carol
1982   *In a Different Voice: Psychological Theory and Women's Development*. Cambridge, Mass.: Harvard University Press.

Ginott, Haim G.
1965   *Between Parent and Child*. New York: Macmillan.

Glass, Jennifer, Vern L. Bengston, and Charlotte Chorn Dunham
1986   "Attitude similarity in families." *American Sociological Review* 51:685–98.

Glass, Shirley P., and Thomas L. Wright
1977   "The relationship of extramarital sex, length of marriage, and sex differences in marital satisfaction and romanticism: Athanasiou's data reanalyzed." *Journal of Marriage and the Family* 39 (Nov.):691–703.

Glazer-Malbin, Nona (ed.)
1975   *Old Family/New Family*. New York: Van Nostrand.

Glenn, Norval D.
1982   "Interreligious marriage in the United States: Patterns and recent trends." *Journal of Marriage and the Family* 44:555–68.

Glenn, Norval, Andrea A. Ross, and Judy Corder Tully
1974   "Patterns of intergeneralization mobility of females through marriage." *American Sociological Review* 39:683–99.

Glenn, N. D., and Charles N. Weaver
1977   "The marital happiness of remarried divorced persons." *Journal of Marriage and the Family* 39 (May):331–37.
1979   "A note on family situation and global happiness." *Social Forces* 57:960–67.

Glenn, Norval D., and Michael Supancic
1984   "The social and demographic correlates of divorce and separation in the United States: An update and reconsideration." *Journal of Marriage and the Family* 46 (3) (Aug.):563–75.

Glenn, N. D., S. K. Hoppe, and D. Weiner
1974   "Social class heterogamy and marital success: A study of the empirical adequacy of a textbook's generalization." *Social Problems* 21:539–50.

Glenn, Norval D., and Sara McLanahan
1981   "The effects of offspring on the psychological well-being of older adults." *Journal of Marriage and the Family* 43:409–21.
1982   "Children and marital happiness: A further specification of the relationship." *Journal of Marriage and the Family* 44:63–72.

Glennon, Lynda M.
1979   *Women and Dualism: A Sociology of Knowledge Analysis*. New York: Longman.

Glick, Ira O., Robert S. Weiss, and C. Murray Parkes
1974   *The First Year of Bereavement*. New York: Wiley.

Glick, Paul C.
1977   "Updating the life cycle of the family." *Journal of Marriage and the Family* 39 (Feb.):5–13.
1984   "Marriage, divorce, and living arrangements." *Journal of Family Issues* 5:7–26.

Glick, Paul C., and Arthur J. Norton
1973   "Perspectives on the recent upturn in divorce and remarriage." *Demography* 10 (Aug.):301–14.
1979   "Marrying, divorcing, and living together in the U.S.

today." *Population Bulletin* 32 (5). Washington, D.C.: Population Reference Bureau.

Glick, Paul C., and Graham Spanier
1980   "Married and unmarried cohabitation in the United States." *Journal of Marriage and the Family* 42 (Feb.):19–30.

Glick, Paul C., and Sung-Ling Lin
1986a   "More young adults are living with their parents: Who are they?" *Journal of Marriage and the Family* 48 (Feb.):107–12.
1986b   "Recent changes in divorce and remarriage." *Journal of Marriage and the Family* 48 (4) (Nov.):737–47.

Goetting, Ann
1979   "The normative integration of the former spouse relationship." *Journal of Divorce* 2:395–414.

Goffman, Erving
1959   *The Presentation of Self in Everyday Life*. Garden City, N.Y.: Doubleday.

Goldberg, Steven
1973   *The Inevitability of Patriarchy*. New York: Morrow.

Goldstine, Daniel, Katherine Larner, Shirley Zuckerman, and Hilary Goldstine
1977   *The Dance-Away Lover and Other Roles We Play in Love, Sex, and Marriage*. New York: Morrow.

Goleman, Daniel
1985a   "New studies examine sexual guilt." *New York Times*, Aug. 20.
1985b   "Patterns of love charted in studies." *New York Times*, Sept. 10.

Goode, William J.
1956   *After Divorce*. Glencoe, Ill.: Free Press.
1959   "The theoretical importance of love." *American Sociological Review* 24:38–47.
1963   *World Revolution and Family Patterns*. New York: Free Press.
1971   "Force and violence in the family." *Journal of Marriage and the Family* 33 (Nov.):624–35.
1982   "Why men resist." Pp. 131–50 in Barrie Thorne and Marilyn Yalom (eds.), *Rethinking the Family: Some Feminist Questions*. New York: Longmans.

Goodman, Ellen
1979   "Fairness is the problem." *Northwest Sun* (Omaha), Sept. 13, p. x.
1983   "When couple splits costs 50/50, it isn't necessarily fair." *Omaha World-Herald*, Dec. 27, p. 8.
1987a   "Mandatory tag hurts effectiveness of AIDS tests." *Omaha World-Herald*, June 9, p. 10.
1987b   "M is for money, not mother." Boston Globe Newspaper Company/Washington Post Writers Group. In *The Daily Nebraskan*, Feb. 17.

Gordon, Henry A., and Kenneth C. W. Dammeyer
1980   "The gainful employment of women with small children." *Journal of Marriage and the Family* 42:327–36.

Gordon, L.
1970   "Functions of the family." In L. B. Tanner (ed.), *Voices from Women's Literature*. New York: New American Library.

Gordon, Leland J., and Stewart M. Lee
1977   *Economics for Consumers*. New York: Van Nostrand.

Gordon, Michael, and Penelope Shankweiler
1968   "Difference equals less: Female sexuality in recent marriage manuals." *Journal of Marriage and the Family* 33 (Aug.):459–66.

Gordon, Thomas
1970   *Parent Effectiveness Training*. New York: Wyden.

Gore, Susan
1978   "The effect of social support in moderating the health consequences of unemployment." *Journal of Health and Social Behavior* 19 (June):157–65.

Gore, Susan, and Thomas W. Mangione
1983   "Social roles, sex roles, and psychological distress:

Additive and interactive models of sex differences."
Journal of Health and Social Behavior 24:300–312.

Gottlieb, Annie
1979   "The joyful marriage." *Redbook*, Nov., pp. 29, 194–96.

Gottman, John
1979   *Marital Interaction: Experimental Investigations.*
New York: Academic Press.

Gottman, John, Howard Markman, and Cliff Notarius
1977   "The topography of marital conflict: A sequential
analysis of verbal and nonverbal behavior." *Journal of
Marriage and the Family* 39 (Aug.):461–77.

Gottman, John, C. Notarius, J. Gonso, and H. A. Markman
1976   *A Couple's Guide to Communication.* Champaign, Ill.:
Research Press.

Gould, Carole
1984   "Helping to support mom and dad." *New York Times*,
July 15.

Gould, Roger L.
1977   "The phases of adult life: A study in developmental
psychology." Pp. 12–19 in Lawrence R. Allman and
Dennis T. Jaffe (eds.), *Readings in Adult Psychology:
Contemporary Perspectives.* New York: Harper & Row.

Gould, Stephen Jay
1987   "The terrifying normalcy of AIDS." *New York Times
Magazine*, Apr. 19, pp. 32–33.

Gove, Walter
1979   "Sex, marital status, and psychiatric treatment: A
research note." *Social Forces* 58:89–93.

Gove, Walter R., and Jeanette Tudor
1973   "Adult sex roles and mental illness." *American Journal
of Sociology* 78 (Jan.):50–73.

Gove, Walter R., and Michael Hughes
1979   "Possible causes of apparent sex differences in physical
health." *American Sociological Review* 44
(Feb.):126–46.

Gove, Walter R., Michael Hughes, and Omar R. Galle
1979   "'Overcrowding in the home: An empirical investigation
of its possible pathological consequences." *American
Sociological Review* 44 (Feb.):59–80.

"Grandparents seek visitation law."
1985   *Omaha World-Herald*, March 26.

Gray-Little, Bernadette
1982   "Marital quality and power processes among black
couples." *Journal of Marriage and the Family*
44:633–46.

Green, Eric
1982   Personal communication.

Greenblatt, Cathy Stein
1983   "The salience of sexuality in the early years of
marriage." *Journal of Marriage and the Family*
45:289–99.

Greenfield, Josh
1972   *A Child Called Noah: A Family Journey.* New York:
Holt, Rinehart & Winston.
1978   *A Place for Noah.* New York: Holt, Rinehart & Winston.
1987   *A Client Called Noah.* New York: Holt, Rinehart &
Winston.

Greenfield, Sidney J.
1969   "Love and marriage in modern America: A functional
analysis." *Sociological Quarterly* 6:361–77.

Greenhouse, Steven
1986   "The average guy takes it on the chin." *New York
Times*, July 13, p. 1-F.

Gregg, Gail
1986   "Putting kids first." *New York Times Magazine*, Apr.
13, pp. 47ff.

Grief, J. B.
1979   "Fathers, children, and joint custody." *American
Journal of Orthopsychiatry* 49:311–19.

Griffith, Janet
1973   "Social pressures on family size intentions." *Family
Planning Perspectives* 5 (Fall):237–42.

Gross, Harriet Engel
1980   "Dual-career couples who live apart: Two types."
Journal of Marriage and the Family 42:567–76.

Gump, J. P.
1975   "Reality and myth: Employment and sex role ideology
in black women." Paper presented at the Conference for
New Directions for Research on the Psychology of
Women, Madison, Wisconsin.

Gundle, Ruth
1986   "Civil liability for police failure to arrest: *Nearing
v. Weaver." Women's Rights Law Reporter*
9 (3, 4):259–64.

Gurin, Gerald, Joseph Veroff, and Sheila Feld
1960   *Americans View Their Mental Health.* New York: Basic
Books.

Gutman, Herbert G.
1976   *The Black Family in Slavery and Freedom,
1750–1925.* New York: Pantheon.

Guttentag, Marcia, and Paul Secord
1983   *Too Many Women: The Sex Ratio Question.* Beverly
Hills, Calif.: Sage.

Haas, Linda
1980   "Role-sharing couples: A study of egalitarian
marriages." *Family Relations* 29:289–96.

Hacker, Andrew (ed.)
1983   *U/S: A Statistical Portrait of the American People.*
New York: Viking.

Hacker, Andrew
1986   "Women and work." *New York Review of Books*, Aug.
14, pp. 26–32.

Haggstrom, Gus W., Linda J. Waite, David E. Kanouse, and
Thomas J. Blaschke
1985   "A look at the consequences of childbearing . . .
Advancement may be temporarily derailed, but ultimate
careers are not." *Rand Checklist* 337 (Apr.).

Hall, Trish
1987   "Infidelity and women: Shifting patterns." *New York
Times*, June 1.

Hall, Francine S., and Douglas T. Hall
1979   *The Two-Career Couple.* Reading, Mass.: Addison-Wesley.

Halleck, Seymour
1969   "Sex and power." *Medical Aspects of Human Sexuality*
(Oct.):8–24.

Hallenbeck, Phyllis N.
1966   "An analysis of power dynamics in marriage." *Journal
of Marriage and the Family* 28 (May):200–203.

Haller, Max
1981   "Marriage, women, and social stratification: A
theoretical critique." *American Journal of Sociology*
86:766–95.

Hamachek, Don E.
1971   *Encounters with the Self.* New York: Holt, Rinehart &
Winston.

Hampton, Robert L.
1975   "Divorcees and dollars." *Human Behavior* 4 (Sept.):61.
1979   "Husband's characteristics and marital disruption in
black families." *The Sociological Quarterly* 20
(Spring):255–66.

Handy, Charles
1978   "Going against the grain: Working couples and greedy
occupations." Pp. 36–46 in Robert Rapoport and Rhona
Rapoport (eds.), *Working Couples.* New York: Harper &
Row.

Hansen, Donald A., and Rueben Hill
1964   "Families under stress." Pp. 782–819 in Harold
Christensen (ed.), *The Handbook of Marriage and the
Family.* Chicago: Rand McNally.

Hargrove, Barbara
1983   "The church, the family, and the modernization
process." Pp. 113–40 in William U. D'Antonio and Joan
Aldous (eds.), *Religions and Families: Conflict and
Change in Modern Society.* Beverly Hills, Calif.: Sage.

Haring-Hidore, Marilyn, William A. Stock, Morris A. Okun, and Robert A. Witter
1985 "Marital status and subjective well-being: A research synthesis." *Journal of Marriage and the Family* 47 (4) (Nov.):947–53.

Harkins, Elizabeth B.
1978 "Effects of empty nest transition on self-report of psychological and physical well-being." *Journal of Marriage and the Family* 40 (Aug.):549–56.

Harlap, Susan, Patricia Shionoj Savitri Ramcharan, Heinz Berendes, and Frederick Pellegrin
1979 "A prospective study of spontaneous fetal losses after induced abortions." *New England Journal of Medicine* 301 (Sept. 27):677–81.

Harmetz, Aljean
1987 "Films from Hollywood enter the AIDS era." *New York Times,* June 25.

Harris, Louis
1983 Poll reported on radio station KOIL, Omaha, Nebr.
1986 Poll, Sept.-Oct. 1986, commissioned by Planned Parenthood Federation of America and reported in Dennis Hevisi, "Teen-agers back birth-control clinics." *New York Times,* Dec. 17, p. 16.

Harry, Joseph
1983 "Gay male and lesbian relationships." Pp. 216–34 in Eleanor D. Macklin and Roger H. Rubin (eds.), *Contemporary Families and Alternative Lifestyles: Handbook on Research and Theory.* Beverly Hills, Calif.: Sage.
1984 *Gay Couples.* New York: Praeger.

Hatfield, Julie
1985 "Adolescents have need to try their wings." *Boston Globe,* reprinted in *Omaha World-Herald,* May 6.

Hatkoff, T. S.
1977 "Personal communication to Robert Ryder." Cited in Bernard Murstein, "Mate selection in the 1970s." *Journal of Marriage and the Family* 42:777–92.

Hawke, Sharryl, and David Knox
1978 "The one-child family: A new life-style." *Family Coordinator* 27 (July):215–19.

Hawkes, Glenn R., and Minna Taylor
1975 "Power structure in Mexican and Mexican-American farm labor families." *Journal of Marriage and the Family* 37 (Nov.):807–11.

Hayden, Dolores
1981 *The Grand Domestic Revolution: A History of Feminist Designs for American Homes, Neighborhoods, and Cities.* Cambridge, Mass.: MIT Press.

Hayes, S. W., and L. J. Oziel
1976 "Homosexuality: Behavior and attitude." *Archives of Sexual Behavior* 5:283–89.

Hayghe, Howard
1982 "Dual earner families: Their economic and demographic characteristics." Pp. 27–40 in Joan Aldous (ed.), *Two Paychecks.* Beverly Hills, Calif.: Sage.

Heer, David M.
1963 "The measurement and bases of family power: An overview." *Marriage and Family Living* 25:133–39.
1974 "The prevalence of black-white marriage in the United States, 1960 and 1970." *Journal of Marriage and the Family* 36 (May):246–58.

Heer, David, and Amyra Grossbard-Schectman
1981 "The impact of the female marriage squeeze and the contraceptive revolution on sex roles and the women's liberation movement in the United States, 1960 to 1975." *Journal of Marriage and the Family* 43:9–65.

Heilbrun, Alfred B., Jr.
1976 "Identification with the father and sex-role development of the daughter." *Family Coordinator* 25 (Oct.):411–17.

Henry, Jules
1971 *Pathways to Madness.* New York: Random House.

Henshaw, Stanley K.
1987 "Characteristics of U.S. women having abortions, 1982–1983." *Family Planning Perspectives* 19 (Jan.-Feb.):5–9.

Henshaw, Stanley K., Jacqueline Darroch Forrest, and Jennifer Van Wort
1987 "Abortion services in the United States, 1984 and 1985." *Family Planning Perspectives* 19 (Mar.-Apr.):63–70.

Henshaw, Stanley K., and Kevin O'Reilly
1983 "Characteristics of abortion patients in the United States, 1979 and 1980." *Family Planning Perspectives* 15 (Jan.-Feb.):5–16.

Hernandez, Donald J.
1986 "Demographic and socioeconomic circumstances of minority families and children." Paper presented at the conference on "Minority Families and Children," National Institute of Child Health and Development, Bethesda, Md., May 28–29.

Hershey, Robert D.
1987 "Jobless rate at lowest point since '79." *New York Times,* July 3.

Hess, Beth B.
1984 "Protecting the American family: Public policy, family, and the new right." Pp. 11–21 in Rosalind G. Genovese (ed.), *Families and Change.* South Hadley, Mass.: Bergin & Garvey.

Hess, Robert D., and Kathleen A. Camara
1979 "Post-divorce family relationships as mediating factors in the consequences of divorce for children." *Journal of Social Issues* 35:79–96.

"Heterosexual spread of AIDS causes worry."
1986 *Omaha World-Herald,* Oct. 22.

Hetherington, E. Mavis
1973 "Girls without fathers." *Psychology Today* 6:47–52.

Hetherington, E. Mavis, Martha Cox, and Roger Cox
1977 "Divorced fathers." *Psychology Today* 10 (Apr.):42–46.

Hevesi, Dennis
1986 "Teen-agers back birth control clinics." *New York Times,* Dec. 17, p. 16.

Hewlett, Sylvia Ann
1986 *A Lesser Life: The Myth of Women's Liberation in America.* New York: Morrow.

Heyman, Andrea
1976 "Legal challenges to discrimination against men." Pp. 297–320 in Deborah S. David and Robert Brannon (eds.), *The Forty-Nine Percent Majority: The Male Sex Role.* Reading, Mass.: Addison-Wesley.

Hicks, Mary W., Sally Hansen, and Leo Christie
1983 "Dual career/dual work families: A systems approach." Pp. 164–79 in Eleanor A. Macklin and Roger H. Rubin (eds.), *Contemporary Families and Alternative Lifestyles.* Beverly Hills, Calif.: Sage.

Hill, Charles T., Letitia Ann Peplau, and Zick Rubin
1976 "Breakups before marriage: The end of 103 affairs." *Journal of Social Issues* 32:147–68.

Hiller, Dana V., and William W. Philliber
1980 "Necessity, compatibility, and status attainment as factors in the labor force participation of married women." *Journal of Marriage and the Family* 42:347–54.
1986 "The division of labor in contemporary marriage: Expectations, perceptions, and performance." *Social Problems* 33 (3) (Feb. 1986):191–201.

Hilsdale, Paul
1962 "Marriage as a personal existential commitment." *Marriage and Family Living* 24:137–43.

Himberger, Tim
1982 "Finding rental housing difficult for parents." *CAUR Review* X (Jan.-Mar.):1–4.

Hing, Esther
1987 "Use of nursing homes by the elderly: Preliminary data from the 1985 national nursing home survey." National Center for Health Statistics, Advance Data, No. 135, May 14.

Hite, Shere
1976 *The Hite Report.* New York: Macmillan.

Hobart, C. W.
1958 "The incidence of romanticism during courtship." *Social Forces* 36:362–67.

Hobbs, Daniel F., Jr., and Sue Peck Cole
1976 "Transition to parenthood: A decade replication." *Journal of Marriage and the Family* 38 (Nov.):723–31.

Hobbs, Daniel F., Jr., and Jane Maynard Wimbish
1977 "Transition to parenthood by black couples." *Journal of Marriage and the Family* 39 (Nov.):677–89.

Hochschild, Arlie R.
1975 "Inside the clockwork of male careers." Pp. 47–80 in Florence Howe (ed.), *Women and the Power to Change.* New York: McGraw-Hill.
1983 *The Managed Heart: Commercialization of Human Feeling.* Berkeley: University of California Press.

Hock, Ellen, M. Therese Gnezda, and Susan L. McBride
1984 "Mothers of infants: Attitudes toward employment and motherhood following birth of the first child." *Journal of Marriage and the Family* (May):425–31.

Hofferth, Sandra L.
1983 "Updating children's life course." Washington, D.C.: National Institute of Child Health and Human Development.
1984 "Kin networks, race, and family structure." *Journal of Marriage and the Family* 46:791–806.

Hofferth, Sandra L., Joan B. Kahn, and Wendy Baldwin
1987 "Premarital sexual activity among U.S. teenage women over the past three decades." *Family Planning Perspectives* 19 (Mar.-Apr.):46–53.

Hoffman, Lois W., and Martin Hoffman
1973 "The value of children to parents." Pp. 19–76 in James T. Fawcett (ed.), *Psychological Perspectives on Population.* New York: Basic Books.

Hoffman, Lois W., and Jean B. Manis
1979 "The value of children in the United States: A new approach to the study of fertility." *Journal of Marriage and the Family* 41 (Aug.):583–96.

Hogan, Dennis P.
1985 "The demography of life-span transitions: Temporal and gender comparisons." In Alice Rossi (ed.), *Gender and the Life Course.* New York: Aldine.

Hogan, Dennis P., and Evelyn M. Kitagawa
1985 "The impact of social status, family structure, and neighborhood on the fertility of black adolescents." *American Journal of Sociology* 90:825–55.

Hogan, Dennis P., and Nan Marie Astone
1986 "The transition to adulthood." *Annual Review of Sociology* 12:109–30.

Hogue, Carol
1977 "An evaluation of studies concerning reproduction after first trimester induced abortion." *International Journal of Gynecology and Obstetrics* 15:167–71.

Hogue, Carol J. Rowland, Willard Cates, Jr., and Christopher Tietze
1983 "Impact of vacuum aspiration on future childbearing: A review. *Family Planning Perspectives* 15:119–26.

Holmes, Thomas S., and Richard H. Rahe
1967 "The social readjustment rating scale." *Journal of Psychosomatic Research* 11:213–18.

Holmstrom, Lynda Lytle
1972 *The Two-Career Family.* Cambridge, Mass.: Schenkman.

Holt, John
1974 *Escape from Childhood.* New York: Dutton.

Homans, George
1961 *Social Behavior: Its Elementary Forms.* Harcourt, Brace & World.

Hooker, Evelyn
1963 "The adjustment of the male overt homosexual." In
[1957] Hendrik M. Ruitenbeek (ed.), *The Problems of Homosexuality in Modern Society.* New York: Dutton.

Hooper, Judith Oakey
1979 "My wife, the student." *Family Coordinator* 28 (Oct.):459–64.

Hootman, Marcia, and Patt Perkins
1983 *How to Forgive Your Ex-Husband.* New York: Doubleday.

Hopkins, June, and Priscilla White
1978 "The dual-career couple: Constraints and supports." *Family Coordinator* 27 (July):253–59.

Horn, Jack C.
1978 "Unbalanced relationships: Who becomes jealous of whom?" *Psychology Today* 11 (Feb.):26, 29.

Hornick, J. P., L. Doran, and S. H. Crawford
1979 "Premarital contraceptive usage among male and female adolescents." *Family Coordinator* 28:181–90.

Houser, Betsy B., and Sherry L. Berkman
1984 "Aging parent/mature child relationships." *Journal of Marriage and the Family* 46 (2) (May):295–99.

"Houses in the 80's: Smaller, fewer, costlier."
1979 *U.S. News & World Report,* Apr. 2, pp. 54–56.

"How many missing kids?"
1985 *Newsweek,* Oct. 7.

Howard, Jane
1973 *A Different Woman.* New York: Dutton.

Huber, Joan
1980 "Will U.S. fertility decline toward zero?" *Sociological Quarterly* 21:481–92.

Huber, Joan, and Glenna Spitze
1980 "Considering divorce: An expansion of Becker's theory of marital instability." *American Economic Review* 86:75–89.
1983 *Sex Stratification.* New York: Academic.

Hughes, Michael, and Walter R. Gove
1981 "Living alone: Social integration and mental health." *American Journal of Sociology* 87:48–74.

Hunt, Janet G., and Larry L. Hunt
1977 "Dilemmas and contradictions of status: The case of the dual-career family." *Social Problems* 24 (Apr.):407–16.
1982 "Dual-career families: Vanguard of the future or residue of the past?" Pp. 41–62 in Joan Aldous (ed.), *Two Paychecks.* Beverly Hills, Calif.: Sage.
1986 "The dualities of careers and families: New integrations or new polarizations?" Pp. 275–89 in Arlene S. Skolnick and Jerome H. Skolnick (eds.), *Family in Transition: Rethinking Marriage, Sexuality, Child Rearing, and Family Organization.* 5th ed. Boston: Little, Brown.

Hunt, Morton
1966 *The World of the Formerly Married.* New York: McGraw-Hill.
1974 *Sexual Behavior in the Seventies.* Chicago: Playboy Press.
1984 "Sex never ages." *Psychology Today* (Jan.):16–17.

"Impact of AIDS: Patterns of homosexual life changing."
1985 *New York Times Style,* July 22, p. 15.

Inazu, J. K., and G. L. Fox
1980 "Maternal influence on the sexual behavior of teenage daughters: Direct and indirect sources." *Journal of Family Issues* 1 (March):81–102.

"J" (Joan Garrity)
1977 *Total Loving.* New York: Simon & Schuster.

Jackson, Joan J.
1958 "Alcoholism and the family." *Annals of the American Academy of Political and Social Science* 315 (Jan.):90–98.

Jacob, T.
1975   "Family interaction in disturbed families: A meth-
        odological and substantive review." *Psychological
        Bulletin* 82:33–65.
Jacoby, Susan
1975   "49 million singles can't be all right." Pp. 115–23 in Saul
        D. Feldman and Gerald W. Thielbar (eds.), *Life Styles:
        Diversity in American Society.* 2d ed. Boston: Little,
        Brown.
Jacques, Elliot
1977   "Death and the mid-life crisis." Pp. 315–25 in Lawrence
        R. Allman and Dennis T. Jaffe (eds.), *Readings in
        Adult Psychology: Contemporary Perspectives.* New
        York: Harper & Row.
Jeffords, Charles R., and R. Thomas Dull
1983   "Demographic variations in attitude toward marital rape
        immunity." *Journal of Marriage and the Family*
        44:755–62.
Jenkins, R. L.
1977   "Maxims in child custody cases." *Family Coordinator*
        (Oct.):385–89.
Johnson, Beverly I.
1980   "Marital and family characteristics of the labor force,
        March, 1979." *Monthly Labor Review* 103 (Apr.):48–51.
Johnson, Colleen L.
1975   "Authority and power in Japanese-American marriage."
        Pp. 182–96 in Ronald E. Cromwell and David H. Olson
        (eds.), *Power in Families.* Beverly Hills, Calif.: Sage.
Johnson, Dirk
1987   "Fear of AIDS stirs new attacks on homosexuals." *New
        York Times,* Apr. 24.
Johnson, Frank, Eugene Kapelan, and Donald Tusel
1979   "Sexual dysfunction in the 'two career' family." *Medical
        Aspects of Human Sexuality* (Jan.):7–17.
Johnson, Phyllis J.
1983   "Divorced mothers' management of responsibilities:
        Conflicts between employment and child care."
        Journal of Family Issues 4 (1) (March):83–103.
Johnson, Sharon
1984   "In divorced families, paying for college." *New York
        Times,* Aug. 1.
*Johnson v. Transportation Agency, Santa Clara County,
California*
1987   748 F.2nd 1308 (9th Circ.).
"Joint custody can be difficult."
1984   *Omaha World-Herald,* Aug. 22, p. 3.
Jones, Stella
1973   "Geographic mobility as seen by the wife and mother."
        Journal of Marriage and the Family 35:210–18.
Jorgensen, Stephen R.
1977   "Social heterogamy, status striving and perceptions of
        marital conflict: A partial replication and revision of
        Pearlin's contingency hypothesis." *Journal of Marriage
        and the Family* 39 (Nov.):653–60.
Jorgensen, Stephen R., and Janis C. Gaudy
1980   "Self-disclosure and satisfaction in marriage: The
        relation examined." *Family Relations* 29 (July):281–87.
Joseph, Gloria
1984   "Common differences." Lecture at Women's Festival,
        University of Nebraska at Omaha, Feb. 25.
Joseph, Gloria, and Jill Lewis
1981   *Common Differences: Conflict in Black and White
        Feminist Perspectives.* New York: Anchor/Doubleday.
Jourard, Sidney M.
1964   *The Transparent Self: Self-Disclosure and Well-
        Being.* New York: Van Nostrand.
1976   "Reinventing marriage." Pp. 231–37 in Edward A.
        Powers and Mary W. Lees (eds.), *Process in
        Relationship: Marriage and Family.* 2d ed. New York:
        West.
1979   "Marriage is for life." Pp. 230–37 in Carl E. Williams and
        John F. Crosby (eds.), *Choice and Challenge:*

Contemporary Readings in Marriage. 2d ed.
        Dubuque, Iowa: Wm. C. Brown.
"Judge: Breaking doctor's orders not against law."
1987   *Omaha World-Herald,* Feb. 27.
Jung, C. G.
1954   *The Development of Personality.* London: Routledge &
        Kegan Paul.
Jurich, Anthony
1978   "Parenting your adolescent." Paper presented at the
        National Symposium on Building Family Strengths,
        University of Nebraska, Lincoln, May 3–5.
Justice, Eric
1986   "HMO fails the poor: Do logistics baffle them?" *Medical
        News* (Oct. 6):5.
Kafka, John S., and Robert G. Ryder
1974   "Notes on marriages in the counter culture." Pp. 304–12
        in Arlene S. Skolnick and Jerome H. Skolnick, (eds.),
        Intimacy, Family, and Society. Boston: Little, Brown.
Kagan, Jerome
1977   "The psychological requirements for human
        development." Pp. 400–411 in Arlene S. Skolnick and
        Jerome H. Skolnick (eds.), *Family in Transition:
        Rethinking Marriage, Sexuality, Child Rearing, and
        Family Organization.* 2d ed. Boston: Little, Brown.
Kagan, Jerome, Richard Kearsley, and Philip Zelazo
1978   *Infancy: Its Place in Human Development.*
        Cambridge, Mass.: Harvard University Press.
Kahana, Boaz, and Eva Kahana
1970   "Grandparenthood from the perspective of the
        developing grandchild." *Developmental Psychology*
        13:98–105.
Kalish, Richard A.
1975   *Late Adulthood: Perspectives on Human
        Development.* Monterey, Calif.: Brooks/Cole.
1976   "Death and dying in a social context." In Robert H.
        Binstock and Ethel Shanas (eds.), *Handbook of Aging
        and the Social Sciences.* New York: Van Nostrand.
Kalmuss, Debra S., and Murray A. Straus
1982   "Wife's marital dependency and wife abuse." *Journal of
        Marriage and the Family* 44:277–86.
Kamerman, Sheila
1980   *Parenting in an Unresponsive Society: Managing
        Work and Family Life.* New York: Free Press.
Kamerman, Sheila, and Alfred J. Kahn
1981   *Child Care, Family Benefits, and Working Parents.*
        New York: Columbia University Press.
Kanin, E. J., and D. H. Howard
1958   "Postmarital consequences of premarital sex
        adjustments." *American Sociological Review*
        23:556–60.
Kanin, E. J., K. D. Davidson, and S. R. Scheck
1970   "A research note on male-female differentials in the
        experience of heterosexual love." *Journal of Sex
        Research* 6:64–72.
Kann, Mark E.
1986   "The costs of being on top." *Journal of the National
        Association for Women Deans, Administrators, and
        Counselors.* 49 (Summer):29–37.
Kantor, David, and William Lehr
1975   *Inside the Family: Toward a Theory of Family
        Process.* San Francisco: Jossey-Bass.
Kantrowitz, Barbara
1986   "Fear of sex." *Newsweek,* Nov. 24, pp. 40–42.
1987   "The year of living dangerously." *Newsweek on
        Campus,* Apr., pp. 12–21.
Kapel, Saul
1978   "Boundaries give teen a sense of security." *Omaha
        World-Herald,* March 9. New York News Service.
Kaplan, Helen Singer
1974   "No-nonsense therapy for six sexual malfunctions."
        Psychology Today 8 (Oct.):132–38.

1975   The Illustrated Manual of Sex Therapy. New York: Times Books.

Kaplan, Marion A.
1985   *The Marriage Bargain: Women and Dowries in European History*. New York: Harrington Park Press.

Kassel, V.
1966   "Polygyny after 60." *Geriatrics* 21:214–18.

Kassorla, Irene
1973   *Putting It All Together*. New York: Brut Publications; Hawthorn/Dutton.

Katz, Mitchell H., and Chaya S. Piotrowski
1983   "Correlates of family role strain among employed black women." *Family Relations* 32:331–39.

Keith, Patricia M.
1982   "Perceptions of time remaining and distance from death." *Omega* 12:307–18.

Keith, Patricia M., and Timothy H. Brubaker
1979   "Male household roles in later life: A look at masculinity and marital relationships." *Family Coordinator* 28 (Oct.):497–502.

Keith-Spiegel, P.
1974   "Child abuse as a feminist concern." UCLA Colloquium Series on Sex Roles and Sex Differences, Los Angeles, June 3.

Kelley, Harold H.
1981   "Marriage relationships and aging." Pp. 275–300 in James G. March (ed.), *Aging: Stability and Change in the Family*. New York: Academic Press.

Kennedy, Leslie W., and Dennis W. Stokes
1981   "Extended family support and the high cost of housing." *Journal of Marriage and the Family* 44:311–18.

Kenny, D. T.
1952   "An experimental test of the catharsis hypothesis of aggression." Ph.D. dissertation, University of Washington.

Kenrick, Douglas, and Robert B. Cialdini
1977   "Romantic attraction: Misattribution vs. reinforcement explanations." *Journal of Personality and Social Psychology* 35:381–91.

Kephart, William
1971   "Oneida: An early American commune." Pp. 481–92 in Arlene S. Skolnick and Jerome H. Skolnick (eds.), *Family in Transition: Rethinking Marriage, Sexuality, Child Rearing, and Family Organization*. Boston: Little, Brown.

Kerchoff, Alan, and Keith E. Davis
1962   "Value consensus and need complementarity in mate selection." *American Sociological Review* 27 (June):295–303.

Kern, Louis J.
1981   *An Ordered Love: Sex Roles and Sexuality in Victorian Utopias—the Shakers, the Mormons, and the Oneida Community*. Chapel Hill: University of North Carolina Press.

Kernberg, Otto
1978   "Why some people can't love." *Psychology Today* 12 (June):50–59.

Kerr, Carmen
1977   *Sex for Women Who Want to Have Fun and Loving Relationships with Equals*. New York: Grove.

Kerr, Peter
1986   "The new homelessness has its roots in economics." *New York Times*, March 16.

Keshet, Harry F., and K. M. Rosenthal
1978   "Fathering after marital separation." *Social Work* 23 (Jan.):11–18.

Kimmel, Michael S.
1986   "Teaching about men: Retrieving womens studies' long lost brother." *Journal of the National Association for Women Deans, Administrators, and Counselors* 49 (Summer):13–21.

King, Karl, Jack O. Balswick, and Ira E. Robinson
1977   "The continuing premarital sexual revolution among college females." *Journal of Marriage and the Family* 39 (Aug.):455–59.

Kinnaird, Keri L., and Meg Gerrard
1986   "Premarital sexual behavior and attitudes toward marriage and divorce among young women as a function of their mothers' marital status." *Journal of Marriage and the Family* 48 (4) (Nov.):757–66.

Kinsey, Alfred, Wardell B. Pomeroy, and Clyde E. Martin
1948   *Sexual Behavior in the Human Male*. Philadelphia: Saunders.
1953   *Sexual Behavior in the Human Female*. Philadelphia: Saunders.

Kirk, H. David
1964   *Shared Fate: A Theory of Adoption and Mental Health*. New York: Free Press.
1977   "A new bill of sexual rights and responsibilities." Pp. 7–9 in *Annual Editions 77/78 Focus: Human Sexuality*. Guilford, Conn.: Dushkin.

Kline, Jennie, Zena Stein, Mervyn Susser, and Dorothy Warburton (eds.)
1986   "Induced abortion and the chromosomal characteristics of subsequent miscarriages (spontaneous abortions)." *American Journal of Epidemiology* 123:1066–79.

Klott, Gary
1987   "Unemployment declines to 6.2%, reaching lowest level in 7 years." *New York Times*, May 9.

Knox, David H., Jr.
1971   "The love attitude inventory." Saluda, N. C.: Family Life Publications.
1975   *Marriage: Who? When? Why?* Englewood Cliffs, N.J.: Prentice-Hall.

Knox, David H., Jr., and K. Wilson
1978   "The differences between having one and two children." *Family Coordinator* 27 (Jan.):23–27.

Knupfer, Genevieve, Walter Clark, and Robin Room
1966   "The mental health of the unmarried." *American Journal of Psychiatry* 122 (Feb.).

Koch, Joanne, and Lew Koch
1976   "A consumer's guide to therapy for couples." *Psychology Today* 9 (Mar.):33–38.

Komarovsky, Mirra
1940   *The Unemployed Man and His Family*. New York: Dryden.
1962   *Blue-Collar Marriage*. New York: Vintage.
1976   *Dilemmas of Masculinity: A Study of College Youth*. New York: Norton.
1977   "Cultural contradictions and sex roles." Pp. 229–41 in Arlene S. Skolnick and Jerome H. Skolnick (eds.), *Family in Transition: Rethinking Marriage, Sexuality, Child Rearing, and Family Organization*. 2d ed. Boston: Little, Brown.

Koop, C. Everett
n.d.   *Surgeon General's Report on Acquired Immune Deficiency Syndrome*. Washington, D.C.: U.S. Department of Health and Human Services.

Korman, Sheila
1983   "Nontraditional dating behavior: Date-initiation and date-expense-sharing among feminists and non-feminists." *Family Relations* 32:575–81.

Korman, Sheila, and G. Leslie
1982   "The relationship between feminist ideology and date expense-sharing to perceptions of sexual aggression in dating." *Journal of Sex Research* 18:114–29.

Kornfein, Madeleine, Thomas S. Weisner, and Joan C. Martin
1979   "Women into mothers: Experimental family life-styles." Pp. 259–91 in Jane Roberts Chapman and Margaret Gates (eds.), *Women into Wives: The Legal and Economic Impact of Marriage*. Beverly Hills, Calif.: Sage.

Krantzler, Mel
1975   *Creative Divorce: A New Opportunity for Personal Growth.* New York: New American Library.
Kreps, Juanita M., and R. John Leaper
1977   "The future for working women." *Ms.,* March, pp. 56–57.
Kübler-Ross, Elisabeth
1979   *On Death and Dying.* New York: Macmillan.
Kuhn, Manfred
1955   "How mates are sorted." In Howard Becker and Reuben Hill (eds.), *Family, Marriage, and Parenthood.* Boston: Heath.
Ladner, Joyce A.
1971   *Tomorrow's Tomorrow: The Black Woman.* Garden City, N.Y.: Doubleday.
Lager, Eric
1977   "Parents-in-law: Failure and divorce in a second chance family." *Journal of Marriage and Family Counseling* 3 (Oct.):19–23.
Laing, Ronald D.
1971   *The Politics of the Family.* New York: Random House.
Laing, Ronald, and A. Esterson
1964   *Sanity, Madness, and the Family.* Baltimore: Penguin.
Lamanna, Mary Ann
1977   "The value of children to natural and adoptive parents." Ph.D. dissertation, Department of Sociology, University of Notre Dame.
Lamanna, Mary Ann, and Agnes Riedmann
1981   *Marriage and Families: Making Choices Throughout the Life Cycle.* Belmont, Calif.: Wadsworth.
Lamb, Michael E.
1976   "The role of the father: An overview." Pp. 1–63 in Michael Lamb (ed.), *The Role of the Father in Child Development.* New York: Wiley.
1978   "The father's role in the infant's social world." Pp. 87–108 in Joseph H. Stevens, Jr., and Marilyn Matthews, *Mother/Child, Father/Child Relationships.* Washington, D.C.: National Association for the Education of Young Children.
Lamb, Michael E. (ed.)
1981   *The Role of the Father in Child Development.* 2d ed. New York: Wiley.
1982   *Nontraditional Families: Parenting and Child Development.* Hillsdale, N.J.: Erlbaum.
Lamb, Michael, Majt Frodi, Carl-Philip Hwang, and Ann Frodi
1983   "Effects of paternal involvement on infant preferences for mothers and fathers." *Child Development* 54:450–58.
Lamb, Michael E., and Jamie E. Lamb
1976   "The nature and importance of the father-infant relationship." *Family Coordinator* 25 (Oct.):379–85.
Lamb, Michael, and James A. Levine
1983   "The Swedish parental insurance policy: An experiment in social engineering." Pp. 39–51 in Michael Lamb and Abraham Sagi (eds.), *Fatherhood and Family Policy.* Hillsdale, N.J.: Erlbaum.
Lamb, Michael, and Abraham Sagi (eds.)
1983   *Fatherhood and Family Policy.* Hillsdale, N.J.: Erlbaum.
Lambert, Bruce
1987   "Rise in AIDS sparks debate over testing and tracing of victim's contacts." *New York Times,* Jan. 27.
Lampe, Philip
1976   "Adultery and anomie." *Human Behavior* 5:14–15.
Landers, Ann
1977   "Parents: What do you owe your children?" *Family Circle,* Nov. 15, pp. 152–54.
1986   "She's too young to be stuck in a loveless marriage." *Omaha World-Herald,* June 18.
LaRossa, Ralph
1977   *Conflict and Power in Marriage: Expecting the First Child.* Beverly Hills, Calif.: Sage.
LaRossa, Ralph, and Maureen M. LaRossa

1981   *Transition to Parenthood: How Infants Change Families.* Beverly Hills, Calif.: Sage.
Lasch, Christopher
1977   *Haven in a Heartless World: The Family Beseiged.* New York: Basic Books.
1980   *The Culture of Narcissism.* New York: Warner Books.
Laslett, Barbara
1973   "The family as a private and public institution." *Journal of Marriage and the Family* 35 (Aug.):480–94.
Laslett, Peter
1971   *The World We Have Lost: England Before the*
[1969] *Industrial Age.* 1st, 2d eds. New York: Scribner.
Laslett, Peter, and R. Wall (eds.)
1972   *Household and Family in Past Times.* London and New York: Cambridge University Press.
Lasswell, Marcia, and Norman Lobsenz
1976   *No-Fault Marriage.* New York: Ballantine.
1977   "Why some marriages can survive an affair and others can't." *McCall's,* Nov., pp. 50, 54, 296.
1979   "What being faithful really means." *McCall's,* Apr., pp. 60–62.
Laurie, W. F.
1978   "Employing the Duke OARS methodology in cost comparisons of home services and institutionalization." *Center Reports on Advances in Research* 2 (2). Duke University Center for the Study of Aging and Human Development.
Lavee, Yoav, Hamilton I. McCubbin, and Joan M. Patterson
1985   "The double ABCX model of family stress and adaptation: An empirical test by analysis of structural equations with latent variables." *Journal of Marriage and the Family* 47 (4) (Nov.):811–26.
Laws, Duane M.
1978   "How to survive as a parent." Paper presented at the National Conference on Building Family Strengths, University of Nebraska, Lincoln, May 3–5.
Laws, Judith Long
1971   "A feminist review of marital adjustment literature: Or rape of the locke." *Journal of Marriage and the Family* 33:483–516.
Laws, Judith Long, and Pepper Schwartz
1977   *Sexual Scripts: The Social Construction of Female Sexuality.* Hinsdale, Ill.: Dryden.
Lawson, Carol
1986   "Surrogate births and the familiy." *New York Times,* Dec. 8.
Leashore, Bogart R.
1979   "Human services and the unmarried father: The 'forgotten half'." *Family Coordinator* 28 (Oct.):529–34.
Lederer, William J., and Don D. Jackson
1968   *The Mirages of Marriage.* New York: Norton.
Lee, Gary R.
1977   "Age at marriage and marital satisfaction: A multivariate analysis and implications for marital stability." *Journal of Marriage and the Family* 39 (Aug.):493–504.
Lee, John Alan
1973   *The Colours of Love.* Toronto: New Press.
Leerhsen, Charles
1985   "Reading, Writing and Divorce." *Newsweek,* May 13, p. 74.
Leik, Robert K., and Reuben Hill
1979   "What price a national policy for families." *Journal of Marriage and the Family* 41 (Aug.):457–59.
Lein, Laura
1979   "Male participation in home life: Impact of social supports and breadwinner responsibility on the allocation of tasks." *Family Coordinator* 28 (Oct.):489–95.
Leishman, Katie
1987   "Heterosexuals and AIDS: The second stage of the epidemic." *Atlantic Monthly* 259, Feb., pp. 39–58.

Lemann, Nicholas
1986   "The origins of the underclass." *Atlantic Monthly,* July, pp. 31–35.
LeMasters, E. E.
1957   "Parenthood as crisis." *Marriage and Family Living* 19 (Nov.):352–55.
1975   *Blue-Collar Aristocrats: Life Styles at a Working Class Tavern.* Madison: University of Wisconsin Press.
LeMasters, E. E., and John DeFrain
1983   *Parents in Contemporary America: A Sympathetic View.* 4th ed. Chicago: Dorsey.
Lennard, Henry L., and Arnold Bernstein
1969   *Patterns in Human Interaction: An Introduction to Clinical Sociology.* San Francisco: Jossey-Bass.
Lenthall, Gerard
1977   "Marital satisfaction and marital stability." *Journal of Marriage and the Family* (Oct.):25–32.
Lenz, Elinor
1983   *Once My Child, Now My Friend.* New York: Warner Books.
Lenz, Elinor, and Barbara Myerhoff
1985   *The Feminization of America.* Los Angeles: Tarcher (St. Martins Press).
LeShan, Eda
1977   "A four-letter word for parents: Wait." *Woman's Day,* Nov. 15, pp. 277–79.
Levin, A., S. C. Schoenbaum, R. R. Monson, and K. J. Ryan
1978   "Induced abortion: The risk of spontaneous abortions." *Family Planning Perspectives* 11 (Jan.-Feb.):39–40.
Levin, Robert J.
1975   "The *Redbook* report on premarital and extramarital sex: The end of the double standard?" *Redbook,* Oct., pp. 38–44, 190–192.
Levine, Abraham
1974   "Child neglect: Reaching the parent." *The Social and Rehabilitation Record* 1 (July-Aug.):26–27, 33.
Levinger, George
1965   "Marital cohesiveness and dissolution: An integrative review." *Journal of Marriage and the Family* 27 (Feb.):19–28.
Levinger, George, and S. D. Snoek
1972   *Attraction in Relationships: A New Look at Interpersonal Attraction.* Morristown, N.J.: General Learning Press.
Levinson, Daniel J.
1978   *The Seasons of a Man's Life.* New York: Knopf.
Lewis, Lionel S., and Dennis Brissett
1967   "Sex as work: A study of avocational counseling." Social Problems 15 (1):8–17.
Lewis, Michael
1972   "Culture and gender roles: There's no unisex in the nursery." *Psychology Today* 5 (May):54–57.
Lewis, Michael, and Leonard A. Rosenblum (eds.)
1974   *The Effect of the Infant on Its Caregiver.* New York: Wiley.
Lewis, Robert A., Phillip J. Freneau, and Craig L. Roberts
1979   "Fathers and the postparental transition." *Family Coordinator* 28 (Oct.):514–20.
Libby, Roger W.
1976   "Social scripts for sexual relationships." In Sol Gordon and Roger W. Libby (eds.), *Sexuality Today and Tomorrow.* North Scituate, Mass.: Duxbury.
1977   "Creative singlehood as a sexual life-style." Pp. 37–61 in Roger W. Libby and Robert N. Whitehurst (eds.), *Marriage and Alternatives: Exploring Intimate Relationships.* Glenview, Ill.: Scott, Foresman.
Liebow, Elliot
1967   *Tally's Corner.* Boston: Little, Brown.
Lightfoot, Sara Lawrence
1981   *Worlds Apart: Relationships Between Families and Schools.* New York: Basic Books.

Linden, Fabian
1984   "Families with children." *American Demographics* (Apr.).
Lindsey, Karen
1982   *Friends as Family.* Boston: Beacon Press.
Lipman, Aaron
1960   "Role conceptions of couples in retirement." Pp. 475–85 in Clark Tibbitts and Wilma Donahue (eds.), *Social and Psychological Aspects of Aging.* New York: Columbia University Press.
Lipmen-Blumen, Jean
1984   *Gender Roles and Power.* Englewood Cliffs, N.J.: Prentice-Hall.
1985   "Little or no change in attitudes on abortion; Clinic bombings are universally condemned." *Family Planning Perspectives* 17:76–78.
Littrell, Boyd
1986   "Industrialization and the family: Female labor force participation." Unpublished paper.
Locke, Robert
1982   "Questions, controversy surround growth of 'in vitro' birth centers." *Omaha World-Herald,* Jan. 19.
Locksley, Anne
1980   "On the effects of wives' employment on marital adjustment and companionship." *Journal of Marriage and the Family* 42:337–46.
"Log, said to list AIDS test-takers, is lost."
1987   *New York Times,* Apr. 23.
Lopata, Helena Znaniecki
1971   *Occupation: Housewife.* New York: Oxford University Press.
1973   "Living through widowhood." *Psychology Today* 7 (July):87–92.
Lowenstein, Joyce S., and Elizabeth J. Koopman
1978   "A comparison of the self-esteem between boys living with single-parent mothers and single-parent fathers." *Journal of Divorce* 2 (Winter):195–208.
Luepnitz, Deborah Anna
1982   *Child Custody.* Lexington, Mass.: Heath.
Lukas, J. Anthony
1985   *Common Ground: A Turbulent Decade in the Lives of Three Families.* New York: Knopf.
Luker, Kristin
1975   *Taking Chances: Abortion and the Decision Not to Contracept.* Berkeley and Los Angeles: University of California Press.
1984   *Abortion and Politics of Motherhood.* Berkeley: University of California Press.
Lumiere, Richard, and Stephani Cook
1983   *Healthy Sex: And Keeping It That Way.* New York: Simon & Schuster.
Lyman, Stanford M., and Marvin B. Scott
1975   *The Drama of Social Reality.* New York: Oxford University Press.
Lynch, James J.
1977   *The Broken Heart: The Medical Consequences of Loneliness.* New York: Basic Books.
Lynd, Robert S., and Helen Merrell Lynd
1929   *Middletown: A Study in American Culture.* New York: Harcourt & Brace.
1937   *Middletown in Transition: A Study in Cultural Conflicts.* New York: Harcourt & Brace.
Lynn, David B.
1969   *Parental and Sex-Role Identification: A Theoretical Formulation.* Berkeley, Calif.: McCutchan.
1976   "Fathers and sex-role development." *Family Coordinator* 25 (Oct.):403–9.
1977   "Fathers and America in transition." Pp. 378–85 in Arlene S. Skolnick and Jerome H. Skolnick (eds.), *Family in Transition: Rethinking Marriage, Sexuality, Child Rearing, and Family Organization.* 2d ed. Boston: Little, Brown.

McAdoo, John L.
1981 "Involvement of fathers in the socialization of black children." Pp. 225–37 in Harriette Pipes McAdoo, *Black Families*. Beverly Hills, Calif.: Sage.

McAllister, Ronald J., Edgar W. Butler, and Edward J. Kaiser
1973 "The adaptation of women to residential mobility." *Journal of Marriage and the Family* 35:197–204.

McBride, Angela Barron
1973 *The Growth and Development of Mothers*. New York: Harper & Row.

McCarthy, J. F.
1977 "A comparison of dissolution of first and second marriages." Paper presented at the annual meeting of the Population Association of America, St. Louis, Apr. 21–23.

McCary, James Leslie
1979 *Human Sexuality*. 2d ed. New York: Van Nostrand.

Maccoby, Eleanor E., and Carol Nagy Jacklin
1974 *The Psychology of Sex Differences*. Stanford, Calif.: Stanford University Press.

McClelland, David C.
1986 "Some reflections on the two psychologies of love." *Journal of Personality* 54:334–53.

McCormick, Naomi B., and Clinton J. Jessor
1983 "The courtship game: Power in the sexual encounter." Pp. 64–86 in Elizabeth Rice Allegier and Naomi B. McCormick (eds.), *Changing Boundaries: Gender Roles and Sexual Behavior*. Palo Alto, Calif.: Mayfield.

McCubbin, Hamilton I.
1979 "Integrating coping behavior in family stress theory." *Journal of Marriage and the Family* 41 (May):237–44.

McCubbin, Hamilton I., Barbara B. Dahl, Gary R. Lester, Dorothy Benson, and Marilyn L. Robertson
1976 "Coping repertoires of families adapting to prolonged war-induced separations." *Journal of Marriage and the Family* 38 (Aug.):461–72.

McCubbin, Hamilton I., and Charles R. Figley (eds.)
1983 *Stress and the Family*. v. I. *Coping with Normative Transition*. New York: Brunner/Mazel.

McCubbin, Hamilton I., and Joan M. Patterson
1983 "Family stress and adaptation to crisis: A double ABCX model of family behavior." Pp. 87–106 in David H. Olson and Brent C. Miller (eds.), *Family Studies Review Yearbook*, v. 1. Beverly Hills, Calif.: Sage.

Macdonald, Charlotte
1979 "The stunted world of teen parents." *Human Behavior* 8 (Jan.):52–55.

McDonald, Gerald W.
1977 "Parental identification by the adolescent: A social power approach." *Journal of Marriage and the Family* 39 (Nov.):705–19.
1980 "Family power: The assessment of a decade of theory and research, 1970–1979." *Journal of Marriage and the Family* 42:841–54.

McDonald, Gerald W., and Marie Withers Osmond
1980 "Jealousy and trust: Unexplored dimensions of social exchange dynamics." Paper presented at the National Council on Family Relations Workshop on Theory Construction and Research Methodology. Portland, Ore., Oct. 21.

McDonald, Kim
1986 "Researchers urge mandatory screening for AIDS virus in high-risk groups." *Chronicle of Higher Education* (June 4).

Macfarlane, Aidan
1977 *The Psychology of Childbirth*. Cambridge, Mass.: Harvard University Press.

McFarlane, Allan H., Geo Stray, R. Norma, David L. Streiner, and Ranian G. Roy
1983 "The process of social stress: Stable, reciprocal, and mediating relationships." *Journal of Health and Social Behavior* 24:160–73.

McGill, Michael E.
1985 *The McGill Report on Male Intimacy*. New York: Holt, Rinehart & Winston.

McGrath, Mary
1985 "Youngster's tooth serves as I.D. card." *Omaha World-Herald*, May 17.

McGuinness, Diane, and Karl Pribram
1979 "The origins of sensory bias in the development of gender differences in perception and cognition." Pp. 3–56 in Morton Bortner (ed.), *Cognitive Growth and Development: Essays in Honor of Herbert G. Birch*. New York: Brunner/Mazel.

McIntosh, Mary
1968 "The homosexual role." *Social Problems* 16 (Fall):192.

Macke, Anne S., George W. Bohrnstedt, and Ilene N. Bernstein
1979 "Housewives' self-esteem and their husbands' success: The myth of vicarious involvement." *Journal of Marriage and the Family* 41 (Feb.):51–57.

McLain, Raymond, and Andrew Weigert
1979 "Toward a phenomenological sociology of family: A programmatic essay." Pp. 160–205 in Wesley R. Burr, Reuben Hill, F. Ivan Nye, and Ira L. Reiss (eds.), *Contemporary Theories About the Family*, v. 2. New York: Free Press.

Macklin, Eleanor D.
1972 "Heterosexual cohabitation among unmarried students." *Family Coordinator* 21:463–72.
1983 "Nonmarital heterosexual cohabitation: An overview." Pp. 49–74 in Eleanor D. Macklin and Roger H. Rubin (eds.), *Contemporary Families and Alternative Lifestyles: Handbook on Theory and Research*. Beverly Hills, Calif.: Sage.

Macklin, Eleanor D., and Roger H. Rubin (eds.)
1983 *Contemporary Families and Alternative Lifestyles: Handbook on Theory and Research*. Beverly Hills, Calif.: Sage.

McMurty, John
1977 "Monogamy: A critique." Pp. 3–13 in Roger W. Libby and Robert N. Whitehurst (eds.), *Marriage and Alternatives: Exploring Intimate Relationships*. Glenview, Ill.: Scott, Foresman.

McNulty, Faith
1981 *The Burning Bed*. New York: Bantam.

Maddox, Brenda
1975 *The Half-Parent: Living with Other People's Children*. New York: M. Evans.
1982 "Homosexual parents." *Psychology Today* 15 (Feb.):62–69.

Mahoney, E. R.
1978 "Gender and social class differences in changes in attitudes toward premarital coitus." *Sociology and Social Research* 62:279–86.
1983 *Human Sexuality*. New York: McGraw-Hill.

Makepeace, James M.
1981 "Courtship violence among college students." *Family Relations* 30:97–102.

Malabre, Alfred L., Jr.
1978 "Women at work: As their ranks swell, women holding jobs reshape U.S. society." *Wall Street Journal*, Aug. 30, cited in Linda J. Waite, "U.S. women at work." *Population Bulletin* 36 (May). Washington, D.C.: Population Reference Bureau.

"Male impotence has emotional, physical roots."
1985 *Los Angeles Daily News*, in *Omaha World-Herald*, Oct. 20.

"Many victims of violent crime know attackers."
1987 AP, in *Omaha World-Herald*, Jan. 19, p. 18.

Marciano, Teresa Donati
1977 "Middle-class incomes, working-class hearts." Pp. 465–76 in Arlene S. Skolnick and Jerome H. Skolnick

(eds.), *Family in Transition: Rethinking Marriage, Sexuality, Child Rearing, and Family Organization*. 2d ed. Boston: Little, Brown.

1979   "Male influences on fertility: Needs for research." *Family Coordinator* 28 (Oct.):561–68.

Marcus, Philip M.
1977   "Knowledge and power in bargaining for a marriage partner." Pp. 25–32 in Jacqueline P. Wiseman (ed.), *People as Partners*. 2d ed. New York: Harper & Row.

Marcuse, Herbert
1964   *One-Dimensional Man: Studies in the Ideology of Advanced Industrial Society*. Boston: Beacon.

Margolin, Leslie, and Lynn White
1987   "The continuing role of physical attractiveness in marriage." *Journal of Marriage and the Family* 49 (Feb.):21–27.

Margolis, Maxine L.
1984   *Mothers and Such: Views of American Women and Why They Changed*. Berkeley: University of California Press.

Marks, Stephen R.
1977   "Multiple roles and role strain: Some notes on human energy, time, and commitment." *American Sociological Review* 42 (Dec.):921–36.

Marotz-Baden, Ramona, Gerald Adams, Nancy Bueche, Brenda Munro, and Gordon Munro
1979   "Family form or family process? Reconsidering the deficit family model approach." *Family Coordinator* 28 (Jan.):5–13.

Marshall, Victor
1986   "A sociological perspective on aging and dying." Pp. 125–46 in Victor M. Marshall (ed.), *Later Life: The Social Psychology of Aging*. Beverly Hills, Calif.: Sage.

Martinson, Floyd M.
1955   "Ego deficiency as a factor in marriage." *American Sociological Review* 20:161–64.

Martz, Larry
1987   "New panic over AIDS." *Newsweek*, March 30.

Marvin v. *Marvin*. 18 Cal. 3rd 660
1976   P. 50 in Walter Wadlington and Monrad O. Paulsen, *Domestic Relations: Cases and Materials*. 3d ed. Mineola, N.Y.: The Foundation Press, 1978.

Marwell, Gerald
1975   "Why ascription? Parts of a more or less formal theory of the functions and dysfunctions of sex roles." *American Sociological Review* 40:445–55.

Maslow, Abraham H.
1943   "A theory of human motivation." *Psychological Review* 50:370–96.
1956   "Self-actualizing people: A study of psychological health." Pp. 160–94 in Clark E. Moustakas (ed.), *The Self: Explorations in Personal Growth*. New York: Harper & Row.

Masters, William H., and Virginia E. Johnson
1966   *Human Sexual Response*. Boston: Little, Brown.
1970   *Human Sexual Inadequacy*. Boston: Little, Brown.
1973   "Orgasm, anatomy of the female." In Albert Ellis and Albert Abarbanel (eds.), *The Encyclopedia of Sexual Behavior*. New York: J. Aronson.
1976   *The Pleasure Bond: A New Look at Sexuality and Commitment*. New York: Bantam.
1979   *Homosexuality in Perspective*. Boston: Little, Brown.

Mathews, Vincent D., and Clement S. Mihanovich
1963   "New orientations on marital maladjustment." *Marriage and Family Living* (Aug.):300–305.

Mattesich, Paul W.
1979   "Review of Robert M. Moroney, the family and the state: Considerations for social policy." *Journal of Marriage and the Family* 41 (Aug.):665–66.

Matthews, Ralph, and Anne Martin Matthews
1986   "Infertility and involuntary childlessness: The transition to nonparenthood." *Journal of Marriage and the Family* 48 (Aug.):641–49.

May, Clifford D.
1987   "Friends link McKinney and homosexuality." *New York Times*, May 9.

May, Rollo
1969   *Love and Will*. New York: Norton.

Mazor, Miriam D.
1979   "Barren couples." *Psychology Today* 12 (May):101.

Mazur, Ronald
1977   "Beyond jealousy and possessiveness." Pp. 181–87 in Gordon Clanton and Lynn G. Smith (eds.), *Jealousy*. Englewood Cliffs, N.J.: Prentice-Hall.

Mead, George Herbert
1934   *Mind, Self, and Society*. Chicago: University of Chicago Press.

Mead, Margaret
1928   *Coming of Age in Samoa*. New York: New American Library/Mentor.
1935   *Sex and Temperament in Three Primitive Societies*. New York: Morrow.
1949   *Male and Female: A Study of the Sexes in a Changing World*. New York: Morrow.
1966   "Marriage in two steps." *Redbook*, July.
1970   "Anomalies in American postdivorce relationships." Pp. 107–25 in Paul Bohannan (ed.), *Divorce and After*. New York: Doubleday.

Mead, Margaret, and Rhoda Metraux
1979   "A better mother, a better wife, a better person." *Redbook*, Feb., pp. 79–81.

Meer, Jeff
1985   "Loneliness." *Psychology Today* 19 (7) (July):28–33.

Mehrabian, Albert
1972   *Nonverbal Communication*. New York: Aldine-Atherton.

Meislin, Richard J.
1977   "Poll finds more liberal beliefs on marriage and sex roles, especially among the young." *New York Times*, Nov. 27.

Meissner, M., E. Humphreys, C. Meis, and J. Scheu
1975   "No exit for wives: Sexual division of labor and the cumulation of household demands." *Canadian Review of Sociology and Anthropology* 12:424–39.

Menaghan, Elizabeth, and Morton Lieberman
1986   "Changes in depression following divorce: A panel study." *Journal of Marriage and the Family* 48 (May):319–28.

Mendes, Helen
1976   "Single fathers." *Family Coordinator* 25:439–44.

Merton, Robert K.
1976   *Sociological Ambivalence and Other Essays*. New York: Free Press.

Messinger, Lilian
1976   "Remarriage between divorced people with children from previous marriages: A proposal for preparation for remarriage." *Journal of Marriage and Family Counseling* 2 (Apr.):193–200.

Meyer, John W.
1986   "The self and the life course: Institutionalization and its effects." Pp 199–245 in A. B. Sorensen, F. E. Weinert, and L. R. Sherrod (eds.), *Human Development and the Life Course: Multidisciplinary Perspectives*. Hillsdale, N.J.: Erlbaum.

Meyer, Thomas J.
1984   " 'Date rape': A serious campus problem that few talk about." *Chronicle of Higher Education* XXIX (15) (Dec. 5):1, 12.

Meyers, William
1985   "Child care finds a champion in the corporation." *New York Times*, Aug. 4.

Middlebrook, Patricia N.
1974   *Social Psychology and Modern Life*. New York: Knopf.

Milano, Elyce, and Stephen F. Hall
1986   "Sex-roles in dating: Paying vs. putting out." Unpublished paper.

Miller, Arthur A.
1970   "Reactions of friends to divorce." Pp. 56–76 in Paul
        Bohannan (ed.), *Divorce and After.* New York:
        Doubleday.
Miller, G. Tyler, Jr.
1988   *Living in the Environment.* 5th ed. Belmont, Calif.:
        Wadsworth.
Miller, Seymour
1977   "On men: The making of a confused middle-class
        husband." Pp. 241–51 in Arlene S. Skolnick and Jerome
        H. Skolnick (eds.), *Family in Transition: Rethinking
        Marriage, Sexuality, Child Rearing, and Family
        Organization.* 2d ed. Boston: Little, Brown.
Miller, Vernon D., and Mark L. Knapp
1986   "Communication paradoxes and the maintenance of
        living relationships with the dying." *Journal of Family
        Issues* 7:255–76.
Mills, C. Wright
1973   *The Sociological Imagination.* New York: Oxford
[1959] University Press.
Minuchin, Salvatore
1974   *Families and Family Therapy.* Cambridge, Mass.:
        Harvard University Press.
Mishler, Elliot G., and Nancy E. Waxler (eds.)
1968   *Interaction in Families: An Experimental Study of
        Family Processes and Schizophrenia.* New York:
        Wiley.
Mitchell, Juliet, and Ann Oakley (eds.)
1986   *What Is Feminism?* New York: Pantheon.
Mithers, Carol Lynn
1986   "A mortgage of one's own." *Ms.,* Apr., pp. 42ff.
Monahan, Thomas P.
1970   "Are interracial marriages really less stable?" *Social
        Forces* 48:461–73.
1976   "An overview of statistics on interracial marriage in
        the United States, with data on its extent from 1963–
        1970." *Journal of Marriage and the Family* 38
        (May):223–31.
Money, John, and Anke A. Ehrhardt
1974   *Man and Woman, Boy and Girl: Differentiation and
        Dimorphism of Gender Identity from Conception to
        Maturity.* New York: New American Library/Mentor.
Monmaney, Terence
1987   "AIDS: Who should be tested?" *Newsweek,* May 11.
Monroe, Pamela A., Janet L. Bokemeier, J. Morley Kotchen, and
Harlley McKean
1985   "Spousal response consistency in decision-making
        research." *Journal of Marriage and the Family* 47
        (Aug.):733–38.
Montagu, Ashley
1971   *Touching: The Human Significance of the Skin.* New
        York: Columbia University Press.
Moore v. *City of East Cleveland*
1977   431 U.S. 494, 9: S. Ct. 1932.
Moore, Kristin
1978   "Teenage childbirth and welfare dependency." *Family
        Planning Perspectives* 10:233–35.
Moore, Kristin A., Margaret C. Simms, and Charles L. Betsey
1986   *Choice and Circumstance: Racial Differences in
        Adolescent Sexuality and Fertility.* New Brunswick,
        N.J.: Transaction Books.
Moorman, Jean
1985   "More U.S. women are deferring first birth till their
        mid- or late 30s." *Family Planning Perspectives* 17
        (1) (Jan.-Feb.):41.
1986   "History and future of the relationship between
        education and marriage." Unpublished paper.
        Washington, D.C.: Bureau of the Census.
Morgan, Barrie S.
1981   "A contribution to the debate on homogamy,
        propinquity, and segregation." *Journal of Marriage
        and the Family* 43:909–21.

Morgan, Leslie A.
1984   "Changes in family interaction following widowhood."
        Journal of Marriage and the Family 46 (2)
        (May):323–31.
Morganthau, Tom
1986   "Future shock." *Newsweek,* Nov. 24, pp. 30–39.
Moroney, Robert M.
1979   "The issue of family policy: Do we know enough to take
        action?" *Journal of Marriage and the Family* 41
        (Aug.):461–63.
Moss, J. Joel, and Ruth Brasher (eds.)
1981   "Family life education." Special issue of *Family
        Relations,* v. 30 (Oct.).
"Most Americans remain opposed to abortion ban and continue
to support woman's right to decide."
1984   *Family Planning Perspectives* 16:233–34.
"Mother's reactions are called natural."
1987   *Omaha World-Herald,* Feb. 26.
Mott, Frank L., and Sylvia F. Moore
1979   "The causes of marital disruption among young
        American women: An interdisciplinary perspec-
        tive." *Journal of Marriage and the Family* 41
        (May):355–65.
Moynihan, Daniel Patrick
1986   *Family and Nation.* New York: Harcourt Brace
        Jovanovich.
Mueller, Charles W., and Hallowell Pope
1977   "Marital instability: A study of its transmission between
        generations." *Journal of Marriage and the Family* 39
        (Feb.):83–92.
Mulford, Robert M.
n.d.   *Emotional Neglect of Children: A Challenge to
        Protective Services.* Denver: The American Humane
        Association, Children's Division.
Murray, Charles
1984   *Losing Ground: American Social Policy, 1950–1980.*
        New York: Basic Books.
Murstein, Bernard I.
1971   *Theories of Attraction and Love.* New York: Springer.
1980   "Mate selection in the 1970s." *Journal of Marriage
        and the Family* 42:777–92.
1986   *Paths to Marriage.* Beverly Hills, Calif.: Sage.
Murstein, Bernard I., Mary Cerreto, and Maria Macdonald
1977   "A theory and investigation of the effect of exchange
        orientation on marriage and friendship." *Journal of
        Marriage and the Family* 39 (Aug.):543–48.
Nason, Ellen M., and Margaret M. Poloma
1976   *Voluntarily Childless Couples: The Emergence of a
        Variant Life Style.* Beverly Hills, Calif.: Sage.
Nassau County School Board. v. *Arline*
1987   55 U.S. L.W. 4547 (Mar. 3).
National NOW Times
1979   July, p. 12.
National Organization for Changing Men
1986   "Brother: The newsletter of the national organization
        for changing men." Vol. 4 (3) (June).
Nelson, Geoffrey
1982   "Coping with the loss of father." *Journal of Family
        Issues* 3 (1) (March):41–60.
Neugarten, Bernice L.
1977   "Adult personality: Toward a psychology of life cycle."
        Pp. 41–48 in Lawrence R. Allman and Dennis T. Jaffe
        (eds.), *Readings in Adult Psychology: Contemporary
        Perspectives.* New York: Harper & Row.
Neugarten, Bernice L., and Karol Weinstein
1964   "The changing American grandparent." *Journal of
        Marriage and the Family* 26 (May):199–204.
"New AIDS virus detected as it spreads from Africa."
1987   *New York Times,* June 5.
Newcomb, Paul R.
1979   "Cohabitation in America: An assessment of
        consequences." *Journal of Marriage and the Family*
        41 (Aug.):597–603.

Newman, Jill
1976 "How battered wives are fighting back." *Parade*, Apr. 11.
Newman, Robert
1979 "For women only: Warning of widowhood eases adjustment period." United Feature Syndicate, in *Omaha World-Herald*, Apr. 11, p. 32.
Newsweek
1979 "Equalimony," *Orr* v. *Orr*, March 19, p. 40.
New York Times/CBS News Poll
1984 *New York Times*, Sept. 19, p. 80. Cited in "Most Americans remain opposed to abortion ban and continue to support woman's right to decide." *Family Planning Perspectives* 16:233–34.
Nieto, Consuelo
1974 "The chicana and the women's rights movement." Source unknown.
Nimkoff, Meyer, and Russell Middleton
1960 "Types of family and types of economy." *American Journal of Sociology* 66:215–25.
"1984 brides spend more."
1984 UPI, in *Omaha World-Herald*, March 11.
Nock, Steven L.
1979 "The family life cycle: Empirical or conceptual tool." *Journal of Marriage and the Family* 41 (Feb.):15–26.
1981 "Family life cycle transitions: Longitudinal effects on family members." *Journal of Marriage and the Family* 43:703–34.
1982 "Enduring effects of marital disruption and subsequent living arrangements." *Journal of Family Issues* 3 (1) (March):25–40.
"No hug; adults fear charges of sex abuse."
1985 *Omaha World-Herald*, May 26.
Nordheimer, Jon
1986 "With AIDS about, heterosexuals are rethinking promiscuity." *New York Times*, March 22.
1987 "AIDS specter for women: The bisexual male." *New York Times*, Apr. 3.
Norton, Arthur
1983 "Family life cycle: 1980." *Journal of Marriage and the Family* 45:267–75.
Norton, Arthur J., and Jeanne E. Moorman
1987 "Current trends in marriage and divorce among American women." *Journal of Marriage and the Family* 49:3–14.
Norton, Eleanor Holmes
1985 "Restoring the traditional black family." *New York Times Magazine*, June 2, pp. 43ff.
Nye, F. Ivan, with Howard M. Bahr, Stephen J. Bahr, John E. Carlson, Viktor Gecas, Steven McLaughlin, and Walter L. Slocum
1976 *Role Structure and Analysis of the Family*. Beverly Hills, Calif.: Sage.
Oakley, Ann
1974 *Woman's Work: The Housewife, Past and Present*. New York: Random House.
O'Brien, John E.
1971 "Violence in divorce-prone families." *Journal of Marriage and the Family* 33:692–98.
O'Brien, Patricia
1980 "How to survive the early years of marriage." Pp. 51–54 in Robert H. Walsh and Ollie Pocs (eds.), *Marriage and Family 80/81*. Guilford, Conn.: Dushkin.
O'Connell, Martin, and David E. Bloom
1987 *Juggling Jobs and Babies: America's Child Care Challenge*. Occasional Paper No. 12 (Feb.). Washington D.C.: Population Reference Bureau.
Ogden, Annegret S.
1986 *The Great American Housewife: From Helpmate to Wage Earner, 1776–1986*. Westport, Conn.: Greenwood Press.
O'Kane, Monica
1982 *Living with Adult Children: A Helpful Guide for Parent and Adult Children Sharing the Same Roof*. St. Paul, Minn.: Diction Books.
Olson, Chris
1983 "Renting vs. owning: If you are settled, think about buying." *Omaha World-Herald*, Feb. 12, p. F-1.
1984 "Builders' survey describes typical buyer of new home." *Omaha World-Herald*, Feb. 26, p. F-1.
1985 "Costs of owning weigh heavily on young buyer." *Omaha World-Herald*, Nov. 9, p. F-1.
1986 "Percentage of homeowners continues its downhill slide." *Omaha World-Herald*, Nov. 9, p. F-1.
Olson, David H., and Hamilton I. McCubbin
1983 *Families: What Makes Them Work*. Beverly Hills, Calif.: Sage.
Olson, David H., Candyce S. Russell, and Douglas H. Sprenkle
1980 "Marital and family therapy: A decade review." *Journal of Marriage and the Family* 42:973–93.
Olson, David H., Douglas H. Sprenkle, and Candyce S. Russell
1979 "Circumplex model of marital and family systems: I. Cohesion and adaptability dimensions, family types, and clinical adaptations." *Family Processes* 18:3–28.
"One-third have discretionary money."
1985 *Omaha World-Herald*, Dec. 1.
O'Neill, Nena, and George O'Neill
1972 *Open Marriage: A New Life Style for Couples*. New York: M. Evans.
Oppenheimer, Valerie Kincaide
1974 "The life cycle squeeze: The interaction of men's occupational and family life cycles." *Demography* 11 (May):227–45.
Orthner, Dennis, Terry Brown, and Dennis Ferguson
1976 "Single-parent fatherhood: An emerging lifestyle." *Family Coordinator* 25:429–37.
Osmond, Marie W., and P. Martin
1978 "A contingency model of marital organization in low income families." *Journal of Marriage and the Family* 40:315–29.
Otto, Luther B.
1979 "Antecedents and consequences of marital timing." Pp. 101–26 in Wesley Burr et al., *Contemporary Theories About the Family*, v. 1. New York: Free Press.
Pais, Jeanne, and Priscilla White
1979 "Family redefinition: A review of the literature toward a model of divorce adjustment." *Journal of Divorce* 2 (Spring):271–81.
Papanek, Hanna
1973 "Men, women, and work: Reflections on the two-person career." Pp. 90–110 in Joan Huber (ed.), *Changing Women in a Changing Society*. Chicago: University of Chicago Press.
Parke, Ross D.
1986 "Fathers: An intrafamilial perspective." Pp. 59–68 in Michael W. Yogman and T. Berry Brazelton (eds.), *In Support of Families*. Cambridge, Mass.: Harvard University Press.
Parke, Ross D., and Douglas B. Swain
1976 "The father's role in infancy: A reevaluation." *Family Coordinator* 25 (Oct.):365–71.
Parkes, C. M.
1972 *Bereavement*. New York: International Universities Press.
Parkes, Colin M., and Robert S. Weiss
1983 *Recovery from Bereavement*. New York: Basic Books.
Parnes, Herbert, and Lawrence Less
1983 *From Work to Retirement: The Experience of a National Sample of Men*. Columbus: Ohio State University Center for Human Resource Research.
Parsons, Talcott
1955 "The American family: Its relations to personality and to the social structure." Pp. 3–33 in Talcott Parsons and R. F. Bales (eds.), *Family, Socialization and Interaction Process*. Glencoe, Ill.: Free Press.

Parsons, Talcott, and Robert F. Bales
1955   *Family, Socialization, and Interaction Process.* Glencoe, Ill.: Free Press.

Parsons, Talcott, and Renee Fox
1952   "Illness, therapy, and the modern American family." *Journal of Social Issues* 8:31–44.

Parsons, Talcott, and Victor Lidz
1967   "Death in American society." Pp. 133–70 in Edwin Scheidman (ed.), *Essays On Self Destruction.* New York: Science House.

Patterson, Joan M., and Hamilton I. McCubbin
1984   "Gender roles and coping." *Journal of Marriage and the Family* 46 (1) (Feb.):95–104.

Peach, Ceri
1974   "Homogamy, propinquity, and segregation: A re-evaluation." *American Sociological Review* 39:636–46.

Pear, Robert
1984   "Rate of poverty found to persist in the face of gains." *New York Times,* Aug. 3.
1985   "Increase found in child poverty in study done by U.S." *New York Times,* May 23.
1987a   "Experts on AIDS urge more testing on optional basis." *New York Times,* May 11.
1987b   "Problems seen in Reagan's plan on AIDS testing." *New York Times,* June 3.
1987c   "Poverty rate dips as median family income rises." *New York Times,* July 31.

Pearce, Diana, and Harriette McAdoo
1981   *Women and Children: Alone and in Poverty.* Washington, D.C.: National Advisory Council on Economic Opportunity.

Pearlin, Leonard I.
1975   "Status inequality and stress in marriage." *American Sociological Review* 40:344–57.

Pearlin, Leonard I., and Joyce S. Johnson
1981   "Marital status, life-strains, and depression." Pp. 165–78 in Peter J. Stein (ed.), *Single Life.* New York: St. Martin's Press.

Pearson, Jessica, and Nancy Thoennes
1982   "Meditation and divorce: The benefits outweigh the costs." *Family Advocate* 4:26–32.

Peck, M. Scott, M.D.
1978   *The Road Less Traveled: A New Psychology of Love, Traditional Values and Spiritual Growth.* New York: Simon & Schuster.

Peplau, Letitia A.
1979   "Power in dating relationships." Pp. 106–21 in Jo Freeman (ed.), *Women: A Feminist Perspective.* 2d ed. Palo Alto, Calif.: Mayfield.
1981   "What homosexuals want in a relationship." *Psychology Today* 15:28–29.

Peplau, Letitia A., and S. Cochran
1981   "Value orientations in the intimate relationships of gay men." *Journal of Homosexuality* 6:1–29.

Peplau, Letitia A., and Steven L. Gordon
1983   "The intimate relationships of lesbians and gay men." Pp. 226–44 in Elizabeth Rice Allgeier and Naomi B. McCormick (eds.), *Changing Boundaries: Gender Roles and Sexual Behavior.* Palo Alto, Calif.: Mayfield.

Perlman, Robert (ed.)
1983   *Family Home Care: Critical Issues for Services and Policies.* New York: Haworth Press.

Peterman, D. J., C. A. Ridley, and S. M. Anderson
1974   "A comparison of marriage and heterosexual cohabiting and noncohabiting college students." *Journal of Marriage and the Family* 36 (May):344–54.

Peters, Marie F., and Harriette P. McAdoo
1983   "The present and future of alternative lifestyles in ethnic American cultures." Pp. 288–307 in Eleanor D. Macklin and Roger H. Rubin (eds.), *Contemporary Families and Alternative Lifestyles: Handbook on Research and Theory.* Beverly Hills, Calif.: Sage.

Pettit, Ellen J., and Bernard L. Bloom
1984   "Whose decision was it? The effects of initiator status on adjustment to marital disruption." *Journal of Marriage and the Family* 46 (3) (Aug.):587–95.

Pierson, Elaine C., and William V. D'Antonio
1974   *Female and Male Dimensions of Human Sexuality.* Philadelphia: Lippincott.

Pietropinto, Anthony, and Jacqueline Simenauer
1977   *Beyond the Male Myth: What Women Want to Know About Men's Sexuality, A National Survey.* New York: Times Books.

Pillemer, Karl A., and Rosalie S. Wolf (eds.)
1986   *Elder Abuse: Conflict in the Family.* Dover, Mass.: Auburn House.

Pines, Maya
1979   "A head start in the nursery." *Psychology Today* 13 (Sept.):56–58.
1981   "Only isn't lonely (or spoiled or selfish)." *Psychology Today* 15 (Feb.):15–19.

Piven, Frances Fox, and Richard A. Cloward
1982   *The New Class War: Reagan's Attack on the Welfare State and Its Consequences.* New York: Pantheon.

Pleck, Elizabeth H., and Joseph H. Pleck
1980   *The American Man.* Englewood Cliffs, N.J.: Prentice-Hall.

Pleck, Joseph H.
1977   "The work-family role system." *Social Problems* 24:417–27.
1979   "Men's family work: Three perspectives and some new data." *Family Coordinator* 28 (Oct.):481–88.
1981   *The Myth of Masculinity.* Cambridge, Mass.: MIT Press.
1985   *Working Wives/Working Husbands.* Beverly Hills, Calif.: Sage.
1986   "Employment and fatherhood: Issues and innovative policies." Pp. 385–412 in Michael E. Lamb (ed.), *The Father's Role: Applied Perspectives.* New York: Wiley.

Pocs, O., and A. G. Godow
1977   "Can students view parents as sexual beings?" *Family Coordinator* 26:31–36.

Pocs, O., A. G. Godow, W. L. Tolone, and R. H. Walsh
1977   "Is there sex after 40?" *Psychology Today* 11:54ff.

Pogrebin, Letty Cottin
1977   "Househusbands." *Ladies Home Journal,* Nov., p. 30.
1983   *Family Politics: Love and Power on an Intimate Frontier.* New York: McGraw-Hill.

Polikoff, Nancy D.
1982   *Why Are Mothers Losing: A Brief Analysis of Criteria Used in Child Custody Determinations.* Washington, D.C.: Women's Legal Defense Fund.

"Poll showed AIDS ahead of career as 'most feared'."
1987   *Omaha World-Herald,* May 11.

Poloma, Margaret M., and T. Neal Garland
1971a   "Jobs or careers: The case of the professionally employed married woman." Pp. 126–42 in André Michel (ed.), *Family Issues of Employed Women in Europe and America.* Leiden, Netherlands: Brill.
1971b   "The married professional woman: A study in the tolerance of domestication." *Journal of Marriage and the Family* 33 (Aug.):531–40.
1971c   "On the social construction of reality: Reported husband-wife differences." *Sociological Focus* 5:40–54.

Poloma, Margaret M., Brian Pendleton, and T. Neal Garland
1982   "Reconsidering the dual career marriage." Pp. 173–88 in Joan Aldous (ed.), *Two Paychecks.* Beverly Hills, Calif.: Sage.

Porter, Sylvia
1976   *Sylvia Porter's Money Book.* New York: Avon.
1979   *Sylvia Porter's New Money Book.* New York: Doubleday.
1983   *Your Own Money.* New York: Avon.

Porterfield, Ernest
1982   "Black-American intermarriages in the United States."

Pp. 17–34 in Gary Crester and Joseph J. Leon (eds.), *Intermarriages in the United States*. New York: Haworth.

Poussaint, Alvin
1982 "What every black woman should know about black men." *Ebony* 37 (Aug.):36–40.

Powell, Brian, and Lala Carr Steelman
1982 "Testing and undertested comparison: Maternal effects on sons' and daughters' attitudes toward women in the labor force." *Journal of Marriage and the Family* 44:349–55.

Power, Paul W.
1979 "The chronically ill husband and father: His role in the family." *Family Coordinator* 28 (Oct.):616–21.

Powers, Edward A., and Mary W. Lees (eds.)
1976 *Process in Relationship: Marriage and Family*. 2d ed. New York: West.

Powledge, Tabitha M.
1983 "Windows on the womb." *Psychology Today* 17 (May):37–42.

Pratt, Lois
1976 *Family Structure and Effective Health Behavior: The Energized Family*. Boston: Houghton Mifflin.

"Pregnant question."
1987 *The Nation*, Jan. 31.

Press, Aric
1984 "Suffer the little children." *Newsweek*, Jan. 2, p. 4.

Presser, Harriet B.
1978 "Sally's corner: Coping with unmarried motherhood." Paper presented at the annual meeting of the American Sociological Association, Sept. 4–7. Reported in *Family Planning Perspectives* 11 (Jan.-Feb. 1979):43–44.

Preston, Samuel
1984 "Children and the elderly: Divergent paths for America's dependents." *Demography* 21:435–57.

Price-Bonham, Sharon, and Susan Addison
1978 "Families and mentally retarded children: Emphasis on the father." *Family Coordinator* 27 (July):221–30.

"Protesters pushing president to intensify his AIDS efforts."
1987 *Omaha World-Herald*, June 2.

Queen, Stuart A., Robert W. Habenstein, and Jill S. Quadagn
1985 *The Family in Various Cultures*. 5th ed. New York: Harper & Row.

Quinn, Jane Bryant
1983 "Women and the gender gap." *Newsweek*, Sept. 26.

Rainwater, Lee
1965 *Family Design*. Chicago: Aldine.
1968 "Social class and conjugal role relations." In Marvin B. Sussman (ed.), *Source Book on Marriage and the Family*. 3d ed. Boston: Houghton Mifflin.

Rankin, Deborah
1979 "How not to get too deep in debt." *Redbook*, Nov., pp. 98–103.

Ransford, H. Edward, and Jon Miller
1983 "Race, sex, and feminist outlooks." *American Sociological Review* 48:46–59.

Raphael, Phyllis
1978 "The stepmother trap." *McCall's*, Feb., pp. 188–94.

Rapoport, Rhona
1962 "Normal crisis, family structure, and mental health." *Family Process* 2:68–80.

Rapoport, Rhona, and Robert Rapoport
1964 "New light on the honeymoon." *Human Relations* 17:35–56.
1971 *Dual-Career Families*. Baltimore: Penguin.
1975 "Men, women, and equity." *Family Coordinator* 24:421–32.

Rapoport, Robert, and Rhona Rapoport (eds.)
1978 *Working Couples*. New York: Harper & Row.

Rausch, Harold L., Ann C. Greif, and Jane Nugent.
1979 "Communication in couples and families." Pp. 468–89 in Wesley R. Burr, Reuben Hill, F. Ivan Nye, and Ira L.

Reiss, *Contemporary Theories About the Family*, v. 1. New York: Free Press.

Reicheit, P. A.
1978 "Changes in sexual behavior among unmarried women utilizing oral contraception." *Journal of Population* 1 (Spring):57–68.

Reid, John
1982 "Black America in the 1980s." *Population Bulletin*, v. 37. Washington, D.C.: Population Reference Bureau.

Reinke, Barbara J., David S. Holmes, and Rochelle L. Harris
1985 "The timing of psychosocial changes in women's lives: The years 25 to 45." *Journal of Personality and Social Psychology* 48 (5):1353–54.

Reiss, David
1971a "Varieties of consensual experience: I. A theory for relating family interaction to individual thinking." *Family Process* 10:1–28.
1971b "Varieties of consensual experience: III. Contrasts between families of normals, behavior disorders and schizophrenics." *Journal of Nervous and Mental Disorders* 152:73–95.
1981 *The Family's Construction of Reality*. Cambridge, Mass.: Harvard University Press.

Reiss, Ira L.
1960 "Toward a sociology of the heterosexual love relationship." *Marriage and Family Living* 22 (May):139–45.
1967 *The Social Context of Premarital Permissiveness*. New York: Holt, Rinehart & Winston.
1975 "Premarital contraceptive usage: A study and some theoretical explanations." *Journal of Marriage and the Family* 37 (Aug.):619–30.
1976 *Family Systems in America*. 2d ed. Hinsdale, Ill.: Dryden.
1981 "Some observations on ideology and sexuality in America." *Journal of Marriage and the Family* 43:271–83.
1986 "A sociological journey into sexuality." *Journal of Marriage and the Family* 48 (May):233–42.

Rempel, Judith
1985 "Childless elderly: What are they missing?" *Journal of Marriage and the Family* 47 (2) (May):343–48.

Renne, Karen S.
1970 "Correlates of dissatisfaction in marriage." *Journal of Marriage and the Family* 32 (Feb.):54–67.
1971 "Health and marital experience in urban population." *Journal of Marriage and the Family* 33:338–50.

Renvoize, Jean
1985 *Going Solo: Single Mothers by Choice*. Boston: Routledge & Kegan Paul.

"Researchers confirm induced abortion to be safer for women than childbirth: Refute claims of critics."
1982 *Family Planning Perspectives* 14 (Sept.-Oct.):271–72.

"Researchers of smoking report risk of senility and female infertility."
1985 *Omaha World-Herald*, May 24.

"Researchers test birth control injection for men."
1987 *New York Times*, Feb. 24, p. 19.

Reynolds v. *United States*
1878 98 v. s. 145, 25 L. Ed. 244 vs. S. C.

Rheingold, H. L., and K. Cook
1975 "The content of boys' and girls' rooms as an index of parents' behavior." *Child Development* 46:459–63.

Rhodes, Jewell Parker, and Edwardo Lao Rhodes
1984 "Commuter marriage: The toughest alternative." *Ms.*, June, pp. 44–48.

Ricci, Isolina
1980 *Mom's House, Dad's House*. New York: Collier.

Rice, Joy E., and David G. Rice
1986 *Living Through Divorce: A Developmental Approach to Divorce Therapy*. New York: Guilford Press.

Richards, Michelle
1987   National Public Radio Report, "Morning edition," May 2.
Richards-Ekeh, Kaylene
1984   Personal communication.
Richardson, John G.
1979   "Wife occupational superiority and marital troubles: An examination of the hypothesis." *Journal of Marriage and the Family* 41 (Feb.):63–72.
Richardson, Laurel Walum
1981   *The Dynamics of Sex and Gender: A Sociological Perspective.* 2d ed. New York: Houghton Mifflin.
1985   *The New Other Woman: Contemporary Single Women in Affairs with Married Men.* New York: Free Press.
Ridley, Carl, Dan J. Peterman, and Arthur W. Avery
1978   "Cohabitation: Does it make for a better marriage?" *Family Coordinator* 27 (Apr.):129–36.
Riley, John W.
1970   "What people think about death." Pp. 30–41 in O. G. Brim, Jr., H. E. Freeman, S. Levine, and N. A. Scotch (eds.), *The Dying Patient.* New York: Sage.
Riley, Matilda White
1987   "On the significance of age in sociology." *American Sociological Review* 52:1–14.
Risman, B. J., C. T. Hill, Z. Rubin, and L. A. Peplau
1981   "Living together in college: Implications for courtship." *Journal of Marriage and the Family* 43:77–83.
Robbins, Catherine C.
1987   "Expanding power for Indian women." *New York Times,* May 25.
Robbins, Cynthia, Howard B. Kaplan, and Steven S. Martin
1985   "Antecedents of pregnancy among unmarried adolescents." *Journal of Marriage and the Family* 47 (3) (Aug.):567–84.
Robertson, Joan F.
1978   "Women in mid-life: Crisis, reverberations, and support networks." *Family Coordinator* 27 (Oct.):375–82.
Robinson, Bryan E., and Robert L. Barret
1986   *The Developing Father: Emerging Roles in Contemporary Society.* New York: Guilford Press.
Robinson, Bryan E., Bobbie H. Rowland, and Mick Coleman
1986   *Latchkey Kids: Unlocking Doors for Children and Their Families.* Lexington, Mass.: Heath/Lexington Books.
Robinson, Bryan, Patsy Skeen, and Lynda Walters
1987   "The AIDS epidemic hits home." *Psychology Today* (Apr.):48–52.
Robinson, Ira E., and Davor Jedlicka
1982   "Change in sexual attitudes and behavior of college students from 1965 to 1980: A research note." *Journal of Marriage and the Family* 44:237–40.
Robinson, John
1977   *How Americans Use Time: A Social Psychological Analysis of Everyday Behavior.* New York: Praeger.
Robinson, John, Thomas Juster, and Frank Stafford
1976   *Amerians' Use of Time.* Ann Arbor, Mich.: Institute for Social Research.
Rodgers, Roy H., and Linda M. Conrad
1986   "Courtship for remarriage: Influences on family reorganization after divorce." *Journal of Marriage and the Family* 48 (Nov.):767–75.
Rodman, Hyman
1970   *Marital Power and the Theory of Resources in Cultural Context.* Detroit: Merrill-Palmer Institute.
1977   "Lower-class family behavior." In Arlene S. Skolnick and Jerome H. Skolnick (eds.), *Family in Transition: Rethinking Marriage, Sexuality, Child Rearing, and Family Organization.* 2d ed. Boston: Little, Brown.
Rogers, Carl R.
1961   *On Becoming a Person.* Boston: Houghton Mifflin.
Rogers, Lesley J.
1983   "Hormone theories for sex differences–politics disguised as science: A reply to DeBold and Luria." *Sex Roles* 9:1109–13.
Rogers, L., and J. Walsh
1982   "Shortcomings of the psycho-medical research of John Money and co-workers into sex differences on behavior: Social and political implications." *Sex Roles* 8:269–81.
Rokeach, Milton, and Louis Mezei
1966   "Race and shared beliefs as factors in social choice." *Science* 14:167–72.
Rollins, Boyd, and Harold Feldman
1970   "Marital satisfaction over the family life cycle." *Journal of Marriage and the Family* 32 (Feb.):20–28.
Roman, Mel, and William Haddad
1978   "The case for joint custody." *Psychology Today* 12:96–105.
Roper Poll
1987   March 30. Reported on National Public Radio.
Rosenbaum, David E.
1984   "The $100,000 house: Getting smaller every year." *New York Times,* Aug. 1, p. A-8.
Rosenblatt, Paul C., and Linda Hammer Burns
1986   "Long-term effects of perinatal loss." *Journal of Family Issues* 7:237–54.
Rosenblum, Karen E.
1984   "The route to voluntary non-custody: How mothers decide to relinquish child custody." *Alternative Lifestyles* 6 (3) (Spring):175–85.
Rosenkrantz, Paul, Susan Vogel, Helen Bee, Donald M. Broverman, and Inge Broverman
1968   "Sex-role stereotypes and self-concepts in college students." *Journal of Consulting and Clinical Psychology* 32:287–95.
Rosenthal, A. M.
1987   "Individual ethics and the plague." *New York Times,* May 28.
Rosenthal, Kristine, and Harry F. Keshet
1978   "The not quite stepmother." *Psychology Today* 12 (July):82–86.
1980   *Fathers Without Partners.* New York: Rowman & Littlefield.
Ross, Catherine, John Mirowsky, and Patricia Ulrich
1983   "Distress and the traditional female role." *American Journal of Sociology* 89:670–82.
Ross, Heather, and Isabel Sawhill
1975   *Time of Transition.* Washington, D.C.: Urban Institute.
Ross, L.
1971   "Mode of adjustment of married homosexuals." *Social Problems* 18:385–93.
Rossi, Alice S.
1968   "Transition to parenthood." *Journal of Marriage and the Family* 30 (Feb.):26–39.
1977   "A biosocial perspective on parenting." *Daedalus* 106 (Spring):1–31.
1984   "Gender and parenthood." *American Sociological Review* 49 (Feb.):1–19.
Rothman, Barbara Katz
1982   *In Labor: Women and Power in the Birthplace.* New York: Norton.
1984   *Giving Birth: Alternatives in Childbirth.* New York: Penguin.
1986   *The Tentative Pregnancy: Prenatal Diagnosis and the Future of Motherhood.* New York: Viking.
Rotkin, K.
1973   "The phallacy of our sexual norm." *Loaded* 1 (Feb.), Santa Cruz, Calif.
Rubin, Isadore
1976   "Sex over 65." Pp. 226–28 in Jacqueline P. Wiseman (ed.), *The Social Psychology of Sex.* New York: Harper & Row.
Rubin, Lillian B.
1976   *Worlds of Pain: Life in the Working-Class Family.* New York: Basic Books.

1978   *Women of a Certain Age: The Midlife Search for Self.*
        New York: Harper & Row.
1983   *Intimate Strangers: Men and Women Together.* New
        York: Harper & Row.

Rubin, Zick
1973   *Liking and Loving: An Invitation to Social
        Psychology.* New York: Holt, Rinehart & Winston.

Rubin, Zick, Charles T. Hill, Letitia A. Peplau, and Christine D.
Dunkel-Schetter
1980   "Self-disclosure in dating couples: Sex roles and the
        ethic of openness." *Journal of Marriage and the
        Family* 42:305–17.

Ruble, Thomas L.
1983   "Sex stereotypes: Issues of change in the 1970s." *Sex
        Roles* 9:397–402.

Rule, Sheila
1984   "Couples taking unusual paths for adoptions." *New
        York Times,* July 26, p. A-B4.

Russell, Candyce Smith
1974   "Transition to parenthood: Problems and gratifica-
        tions." *Journal of Marriage and the Family* 36
        (May):294–302.

Sabatelli, Ronald M., and Erin F. Cecil-Pigo
1985   "Relational interdependence and commitment in
        marriage." *Journal of Marriage and the Family* 47
        (Nov.):931–37.

Safilios-Rothschild, Constantina
1967   "A comparison of power structure and marital
        satisfaction in urban Greek and French families."
        Journal of Marriage and the Family 29:345–52.
1969   "Family sociology or wives' family sociology? A cross-
        cultural examination of decision-making." *Journal of
        Marriage and the Family* 31 (May):290–301.
1970   "The study of family power structure: A review
        1960–1969." *Journal of Marriage and the Family* 32
        (Nov.):539–43.
1975   "Family and stratification: Some macrosociological
        observations and hypotheses." *Journal of Marriage
        and the Family* 37 (Nov.):855–60.
1976   "A macro- and micro-examination of family power and
        love: An exchange model." *Journal of Marriage and
        the Family* 38 (May):355–61.
1983   "Toward a social psychology of relationships." Pp.
        306–12 in Arlene S. Skolnick and Jerome H. Skolnick
        (eds.), *Family in Transition: Rethinking Marriage,
        Sexuality, Child Rearing, and Family Organization.*
        4th ed. Boston: Little, Brown.

Sage, Wayne
1975   "Violence in the children's room." *Human Behavior* 4
        (July):41–47.

Saint Paul Maternal and Infant Care Project, High School Clinic,
Education and Day Care Program, 1980–81 School Year
        Unpublished paper. Saint Paul, Minn., n.d., cited in Joy
        G. Dryfoos, "A new strategy for preventing unintended
        teenage childbearing." *Family Planning Perspectives*
        16 (July-Aug.):195.

Salk, Lee
1978   *What Every Child Would Like Parents to Know About
        Divorce.* New York: Harper & Row.

Salmon, Marylynn
1986   *Women and the Law of Property in Early America.*
        Chapel Hill and London: University of North Carolina
        Press.

Sampson, Ronald V.
1965   *The Psychology of Power.* New York: Pantheon.

Sanders, Alvin J.
1986   "Differentials in marital status between black and white
        males." *Population Today* 14 (Nov.):6–7.

Santrock, John W., and Richard A. Warshak
1979   "Father custody and social development in boys and
        girls." *Journal of Social Issues* 35:112–15.

Sarrel, Philip
1977   "Sexual anatomy and physiology." In *Annual Editions,
        Focus: Human Sexuality 77/78.* Guilford, Conn.:
        Dushkin.

Satir, Virginia
1972   *Peoplemaking.* Palo Alto, Calif.: Science and Behavior
        Books.

Saxton, Lloyd
1977   *The Individual, Marriage, and the Family.* 3d ed.
        Belmont, Calif.: Wadsworth.

Scanzoni, John H.
1970   *Opportunity and the Family.* New York: Free Press.
1972   *Sexual Bargaining: Power Politics in the American
        Marriage.* Englewood Cliffs, N.J.: Prentice-Hall.
1975   *Sex Roles, Life Styles, and Childbearing: Changing
        Patterns in Marriage and the Family.* New York: Free
        Press.
1976   "Gender roles and the process of fertility control."
        Journal of Marriage and the Family 38
        (Nov.):677–91.
1979   "Social processes and power in families." Pp. 295–316
        in Wesley Burr et al., *Contemporary Theories About
        the Family,* v. 1. New York: Free Press.

Scanzoni, Letha, and John H. Scanzoni
1976   *Men, Women, and Change: A Sociology of Marriage
        and Family.* New York: McGraw-Hill.

Scardino, Albert
1985   "Experts question data about missing children." *New
        York Times,* Aug. 18.

Scarf, Maggie
1979   "The more sorrowful sex." *Psychology Today* 12
        (Apr.):45–90.
1987   *Intimate Partners: Patterns in Love and Marriage.*
        New York: Random House.

Schafer, Robert B., and Patricia M. Keith
1981   "Equity in marital roles across the family life cycle."
        Journal of Marriage and the Family 43:359–67.

Schaie, K. Warner, and Iris A. Parham
1976   "Stability of adult personality traits: Fact or fable?"
        Journal of Personality and Social Psychology
        34:146–58.

Schneider, Elizabeth
1986   "Describing and changing: Women's self-defense work
        and the problem of expert testimony." *Women's Rights
        Law Reporter* 9 (3, 4):195–222.

Schooler, Carmi, Joanne Miller, Karen A. Miller, and Carol N.
Richtand
1984   "Work for the household: Its nature and consequences
        for husbands and wives." *American Journal of
        Sociology* 90 (1) (July):97–124.

Schorr, Alvin L.
1979   "Views of family policy." *Journal of Marriage and the
        Family* 41 (Aug.):465–67.

Schulz, David A., and Stanley F. Rodgers
1975   *Marriage, the Family, and Personal Fulfillment.*
        Englewood Cliffs, N.J.: Prentice-Hall.

Schwartz, Harry
1972   *The Case for American Medicine: A Realistic Look at
        Our Health Care System.* New York: McKay.

Schwartz, Richard D.
1954   "Social factors in the development of legal control."
        Yale Law Journal 63:471–91.

Scott, Joseph W.
1980a   "Black polygamous family formulation." *Alternative
        Lifestyles* 3:41–64.
1980b   "Conceptualizing and researching American po-
        lygyny—and critics answered." *Alternative Lifestyles*
        3:395–404.

Seifer, Nancy
1973   *Absent from the Majority: Working Class Women in
        America.* New York: National Project on Ethnic America
        of the American Jewish Community.

Seligman, Jean
1980   "The misery of Herpes II." *Newsweek*, Nov. 10, p. 105.
1983   "The AIDS epidemic: The search for a cure."
       Newsweek, Apr. 18, pp. 73–79.
Sena-Rivera, Jaime
1979   "Extended kinship in the United States: Competing
       models and the case of La Familia Chicana." *Journal of
       Marriage and the Family* 41:121–29.
Sennett, Richard, and Jonathan Cobb
1974   *The Hidden Injuries of Class*. New York: Random
       House.
"Sense of identity, melting pot in U.S. portrait."
1985   *New York Times*, reprinted in *Omaha World-Herald*,
       Feb. 24.
Shahan, Lynn
1981   *Living Alone and Liking It!: A Complete Guide to
       Living on Your Own*. New York: Stratford Press (dist.
       by Harper & Row).
Shain, Merle
1978   *When Lovers Are Friends*. Philadelphia: Lippincott.
Shanas, Ethel
1968   "A note on the restriction of life space: Attitudes of
       older cohorts." *Journal of Health and Social Behavior*
       9:86–90.
1973   "Family-kin networks and aging in cross-cultural
       perspective." *Journal of Marriage and the Family*
       35:505–11.
1982   "The family relations of old people." *The National
       Forum* 62 (Fall).
Shanas, Ethel, and Marvin Sussman
1978   "The family in later life." *The Annals of the Ameri-
       can Academy of Political and Social Sciences*
       (July):13–27.
Shange, Ntozake
1985   *Betsey Brown: A Novel*. New York: St. Martin's Press.
Shapiro, Johanna
1983   "Family reactions and coping strategies in response to
       the physically ill or handicapped child: A review." *Social
       Science and Medicine* 17:913–31.
Shapiro, Stephen A.
1984   *Manhood: A New Definition*. New York: Putnam.
Sharff, Jagna Wojcicka
1981   "Free enterprise and the ghetto family." *Psychology
       Today* (March):41–47.
Sheehy, Gail
1974   *Passages: Predictable Crises of Adult Life*. New York:
       Dutton.
1979   "Introducing the postponing generation: The truth
       about today's young men." *Esquire*, Oct., pp. 25–33.
1981   *Pathfinders*. New York: Morrow.
Sherman, Beth
1985   "Helping the child of divorce." *New York Times*, Apr.
       14, p. 20.
Sherman, Lawrence W., and Richard A. Berk
1984   "Deterrent effects of arrest for domestic assault."
       American Sociological Review 49:261–72.
Shipler, David K.
1984   "Israel's kibbutzim look to needs of the individual." *New
       York Times*, June 27, p. A-6.
Shoehigh, Lori
1985   Personal communication.
Shorter, Edward
1975   *The Making of the Modern Family*. New York: Basic
       Books.
Shostak, Arthur
1979   "Abortion as fatherhood lost: Problems and reforms."
       Family Coordinator 28 (Oct.):569–74.
Shostak, Arthur, and Gary McLouth (eds.)
1984   *Men and Abortion: Losses, Lessons, and Love*. New
       York: Praeger.
Sievers, Stephen, Ollie Pocs, and William Tolone
1983   "Premarital sexual experience and marital sexual

adjustment." Paper presented at the Annual Meeting of
       the Midwest Sociological Society, Kansas City, Mo., Apr.
Sifford, Darrell
1982   "Happiness is not to be found in shrinking
       pocketbooks." *Omaha World-Herald*, March 11, p. 13.
Sigusch, Volkmar, Gunter Schmidt, Antje Reinfeld, and Ingeborg
Wiedemann-Sutor.
1970   "Psychosexual stimulation: Sex differences." *Journal of
       Sex Research* 6 (Feb.):10–24.
Silvern, Louise E., and Victor L. Ryan
1983   "A reexamination of masculine and feminine sex role
       ideals and conflicts among ideals for the man, woman,
       and person." *Sex Roles* 9:1223–48.
Simmel, Georg
1950   *The Sociology of Georg Simmel*. Kurt H. Wolfe (trans.
       and ed.). Glencoe, Ill.: Free Press.
Singer v. Hara
1974   11 Wash. App. 247, 522 P 2d 1187.
"Single people are buying more homes."
1981   *Omaha World-Herald*, Apr. 27.
Singh, R. Krishna, Bonnie L. Walton, and L. Sherwood Williams
1976   "Extramarital sexual permissiveness: Conditions and
       contingencies." *Journal of Marriage and the Family*
       38 (Nov.):701–12.
"A singular forecast for women."
1986   *Newsweek*, Dec. 29.
Skolnick, Arlene S.
1978a *The Intimate Environment: Exploring Marriage and
       Family*. 2d ed. Boston: Little, Brown.
1978b "The myth of the vulnerable child." *Psychology Today*
       11:56–65.
Slade, Margot, and Katherine Roberts
1984   "Public health's economic pulse." *New York Times*,
       July 1.
Slaff, James I., and John K. Brubaker
1985   *The AIDS Epidemic*. New York: Warner.
Slater, Philip
1976   *The Pursuit of Loneliness: American Culture at the
       Breaking Point*. 2d ed. Boston: Beacon.
Smith, Daniel Scott
1981   "Historical change in the household structure of the
       elderly in economically developed societies." In James
       C. March (ed.), *Aging*. New York: Academic Press.
Smith, Marcia
1986   "Homeward odyssey... Economic, personal crises bring
       adult kids back to nest." *Omaha World-Herald*, March
       18.
Smyer, Michael A., and Brian Hofland
1982   "Divorce and family support in later life: Emerging
       concerns." *Journal of Family Issues* 3:61–77.
"Soldier to stand trial in AIDS assault case."
1987   *New York Times*, June 5.
Soldo, Beth
1980   "America's elderly in the 1980s." *Population Bulletin*
       35(4) (Jan.). Washington, D.C.: Population Reference
       Bureau.
Sonkin, Daniel Jay, Del Martin, and Lenore E. Auerbach Walker
1985   *The Male Batterer: A Treatment Approach*. New York:
       Springer.
Sontag, Susan
1976   "The double standard of aging." Pp. 350–66 in Sol
       Gordon and Roger W. Libby (eds.), *Sexuality Today
       and Tomorrow*. North Scituate, Mass.: Duxbury.
South, Scott
1985   "Economic conditions and the divorce rate: A time-
       series analysis of the postwar United States." *Journal
       of Marriage and the Family* 47 (1) (Feb.):31–41.
Spanier, Graham B.
1972   "Romanticism and marital adjustment." *Journal of
       Marriage and the Family* 34:481–87.
Spanier, Graham B., and Robert F. Castro
1979   "Adjustment to separation and divorce: An analysis

of 50 case studies." *Journal of Divorce* 2 (Spring):241–53.

Spanier, Graham B., and Frank F. Furstenberg, Jr.
1982 "Remarriage after divorce: A longitudinal analysis of well-being." *Journal of Marriage and the Family* 44:709–20.

Spanier, Graham B., Robert A. Lewis, and Charles L. Cole.
1975 "Marital adjustment over the family life cycle: The issue of curvilinearity." *Journal of Marriage and the Family* 37 (May):263–75.

Spencer, Herbert
1945 *Principles of Sociology.* Cited in E. Burgess and H.
[1876] Locke, *The Family: From Institution to Companionship.* New York: American Book Co.

Spicer, Jerry, and Gary Hampe
1975 "Kinship interaction after divorce." *Journal of Marriage and the Family* 35 (Feb.):113–19.

Spiro, Melford
1956 *Kibbutz: Venture in Utopia.* New York: Macmillan.
1958 *Children of the Kibbutz.* New York: Macmillan.
1979 *Gender and Culture: Kibbutz Women Revisited.* Durham, N.C.: Duke University Press.

Spitze, Glenna
1984 "Black family migration and wives' employment." *Journal of Marriage and the Family* (Nov.):781–90.

Spitze, Glenna D., and Linda J. Waite
1981 "Wives' employment: The role of husbands' perceived attitudes." *Journal of Marriage and the Family* 43:117–24.

Spock, Benjamin
1983 *Baby and Child Care.* Rev. ed. New York: Pocket Books.

Sproat, Kezia
1983 "How do families fare when the breadwinner retires?" *Monthly Labor Review* 106 (Dec.):40–43.

Srole, Leo, and Anita K. Fisher (eds.)
1978 *Mental Health in the Metropolis: The Midtown Manhattan Study.* Rev. ed. New York: New York University Press.

Srole, Leo, J. S. Langer, S. T. Michael, M. K. Opler, and T.A.C. Rennie
1962 *Mental Health in the Metropolis: The Midtown Manhattan Study.* New York: McGraw-Hill.

Stabenau, James R., Joe Tupin, Martha Werner, and William Pollin
1968 "A comparative study of families of schizophrenics, delinquents, and normals." Pp. 221–44 in Elliot G. Mishler and Nancy E. Waxler (eds.), *Family Processes and Schizophrenia.* New York: Science House.

Stacey, Judith
1986 "Are feminists afraid to leave home? The challenge of conservative pro-family feminism." Pp. 208–37 in Juliet Mitchell and Ann Oakley (eds.), *What Is Feminism?* New York: Pantheon.

Stack, Carol B.
1974 *All Our Kin: Strategies for Survival.* New York: Harper & Row.
1980 "Domestic networks: Those you count on!" Pp. 117–23 in *Annual Editions: Anthropology 80/81.* Guilford, Conn.: Dushkin.

Stafford, Frank P.
1980 Women's use of time converging with men's." *Monthly Labor Review* 103 (Dec.), Table 2, p. 58.

Stafford, Rebecca, Elaine Backman, and Pamela Dibona
1977 "The division of labor among cohabiting and married couples." *Journal of Marriage and the Family* 39 (Jan.):43–57.

Stanley, Elizabeth
1977 "Emergence of strong sexual drives in women past thirty." *Medical Aspects of Human Sexuality* 11:18–27.

Staples, Robert
1971 "Toward a sociology of the black family: A theoretical

and methodological assessment." *Journal of Marriage and the Family* 33 (Feb.):119–35.
1978 "Race, liberalism-conservatism and premarital sexual permissiveness: A bi-racial comparison." *Journal of Marriage and the Family* (Nov.):730–41.
1981a "Black singles in America." Pp. 40–51 in Peter J. Stein (ed.), *Single Life.* New York: St. Martin's Press.
1981b *The World of Black Singles: Changing Patterns of Male-Female Relationships.* Westport, Conn.: Greenwood.
1982 *Black Masculinity: The Black Male's Role in American Society.* Santa Barbara, Calif.: Black Scholar Press.
1983 *The Black Woman in America: Sex, Marriage, and the Family.* Chicago: Nelson-Hall.
1985 "Changes in black family structure: The conflict between family ideology and structural conditions." *Journal of Marriage and the Family* 47 (Nov.):1005–13.

Staples, Robert (ed.)
1986 *The Black Family: Essays and Studies.* 3d ed. Belmont, Calif.: Wadsworth.

Staples, Robert, and Alfredo Mirande
1980 "Racial and cultural variations among American families: A decennial review of the literature on minority families." *Journal of Marriage and the Family* 42:887–903.

Stein, Peter J.
1976 *Single.* Englewood Cliffs, N.J.: Prentice-Hall.
1984 "Men in families." Pp. 143–62 in Beth B. Hess and Marvin B. Sussman (eds.), "Women and the family: Two decades of change." *Marriage and Family Review* 7 (3, 4) (Fall-Winter).

Stein, Peter J. (ed.)
1981 *Single Life: Unmarried Adults in Social Context.* New York: St. Martin's Press.

Stein, Robert B., Lorn Polk, and Barbara Bovee Polk
1975 "Urban communes." Pp. 171–88 in Nona Glazer-Malbin (ed.), *Old Family/New Family.* New York: Van Nostrand.

Steinem, Gloria
1983 *Outrageous Acts and Everyday Rebellions.* New York: Holt, Rinehart & Winston.

Steiner, Gilbert
1976 *The Children's Cause.* Washington, D.C.: The Brookings Institution.
1981 *The Futility of Family Policy.* Washington, D.C.: The Brookings Institution.

Steinglass, Peter
1987 *The Alcoholic Family.* New York: Basic Books.

Steinmetz, Suzanne K.
1977 *The Cycle of Violence: Assertive, Aggressive, and Abusive Family Interaction.* New York: Praeger.

Steinmetz, Suzanne K., and Murray A. Straus (eds.)
1974 *Violence in the Family.* New York: Dodd, Mead.

Stephens, William N.
1963 *The Family in Cross-Cultural Perspective.* New York: Holt, Rinehart & Winston.

Stern, Gabriella
1985 "Hispanics' swelling ranks to alter economy, society." *Omaha World-Herald,* Nov. 10, p. 11-A.

Sternlieb, George, and James W. Hughes
1984 *Income and Jobs: USA: Diagnosing the Reality.* Rutgers: State University of New Jersey, Center for Urban Policy Research.

Stevens, William K.
1987 "Fear of AIDS brings explicit advice to campus, caution to the singles bar." *New York Times,* Feb. 17.

Stewart, Mary White
1984 "The surprising transformation of incest: From sin to sickness." Paper presented at the annual meeting of the Midwest Sociological Society, Chicago, Ill., Apr. 18.

Stinnett, Nick
1978 "Strengthening families." Paper presented at the National Symposium on Building Family Strengths, University of Nebraska, Lincoln, May 3–5.
Stoll, Clarice Stasz
1978 *Female and Male: Socialization, Social Roles, and Social Structure.* 2d ed. Dubuque, Iowa: Wm. C. Brown.
Stone, Lawrence
1980 *The Family, Sex, and Marriage in England, 1500–1800.* New York: Harper & Row.
Storms, M. D.
1980 "Theories of sexual orientation." *Journal of Personality and Social Psychology* 38:783–92.
Strachan, Elizabeth Walter
1957 *A Mother's Wages.* Chicago: Moody Press.
Straits, Bruce C.
1985 "Factors influencing college women's responses to fertility decision-making vignettes." *Journal of Marriage and the Family* 47 (3) (Aug.):585–96.
Straus, Murray A.
1974 "Leveling, civility, and violence in the family." *Journal of Marriage and the Family* 36 (Feb.):13–20.
Straus, Murray A., Richard J. Gelles, and Suzanne K. Steinmetz
1980 *Behind Closed Doors: Violence and the American Family.* New York: Doubleday.
Straus, Murray A., and Richard Gelles
1986 "Societal change and change in family violence from 1975 to 1985 as revealed by two national surveys." *Journal of Marriage and the Family* 48 (Aug.):465–79.
Strauss, Anselm, and Barney Glaser
1975 *Chronic Illness and the Quality of Life.* St. Louis: Mosby.
Streib, Gordon F., and Rubye Wilkerson Beck
1980 "Older families: A decade review." *Journal of Marriage and the Family* (Nov.):937–56.
Strober, M. H.
1977 "Wives' labor force behavior and family consumption patterns." *American Economic Review* 67:410–17.
Stubblefield, P. G., R. R. Monson, S. C. Schoenbaum, C. E. Wolfson, D. J. Cookson, and K. C. Ryan
1984 "Fertility after induced abortion: A prospective follow-up study." *Obstetrics and Gynecology* 62:186.
"Study probes single women's sex habits."
1986 *Omaha World-Herald,* June 1.
"Study sees low AIDS risk for women in single episode."
1987 *New York Times,* June 6.
"Study: Success costlier for women workaholics."
1984 Cox News Service, in *Omaha World-Herald,* Apr. 14.
Sullivan, Ronald
1987 "Insurers to limit policies of buyers refusing AIDS test." *New York Times,* June 5.
Suransky, Valerie Polakow
1982 *The Erosion of Childhood.* Chicago: University of Chicago Press.
"Survey: Many collegians hold conservative views."
1986 *Omaha World-Herald,* Aug. 5.
Switzer, Ellen
1977 "The sex problem nobody talks about: An interview with Dr. Helen Singer Kaplan." *Family Circle,* Nov., pp. 54–60.
Swoap v. Superior Court of Sacramento County
1973 10 Cal. 3d 490, 111 Cal. Rpts. 136, 516 P.2d 840.
"Syphilis afflicts more newborns."
1984 *Omaha World-Herald,* Dec. 2
"Syphilis cases drop sharply."
1985 *Omaha World-Herald,* Aug. 11.
Szasz, Thomas S.
1976 *Heresies.* New York: Doubleday/Anchor.
Tallman, Irving
1979 "Implementation of a national family policy: The role of

the social scientist." *Journal of Marriage and the Family* 41 (Aug.):469–72.
Tavris, Carol, and Susan Sadd
1977 *The* Redbook *Report on Female Sexuality.* New York: Dell.
Taylor, Patricia Ann, and Norval D. Glenn
1976 "The utility of education and attractiveness for females' status attainment through marriage." *American Sociological Review* 41 (June):484–98.
Taylor, Robert Joseph
1986 "Receipt of support from family among black Americans: Demographic and familial differences." *Journal of Marriage and the Family* 48 (Feb.):67–77.
Taylor, Stuart
1987 "State bar to jobless pay after pregnancy upheld." *New York Times,* Jan. 22.
Teachman, Jay T.
1983 "Early marriage, premarital fertility, and marital dissolution." *Journal of Family Issues* 4:105–26.
"Teen ignorance on AIDS shows."
1987 *Omaha World-Herald,* May 5.
"Teens' affluence keeps cash registers full."
1985 *Omaha World-Herald,* May 11.
Terkel, Studs
1977 *Working.* New York: Pantheon.
Tevis, Cheryl
1979 "How does the law cut the cake—Equal partner or marital helpmate?" *Successful Farming* 77:30–31.
"Texas bill allows quarantine for AIDS."
1987 *Omaha World-Herald,* June 2.
Thibaut, John, and Harold H. Kelley
1959 *The Social Psychology of Groups.* New York: Wiley.
Thomas, Alexander, and Stella Chess
1977 *Temperament and Development.* New York: Brunner-Mazel.
Thomas, Alexander, Stella Chess, and Herbert G. Birch
1968 *Temperament and Behavior Disorders in Children.* New York: New York University Press.
Thomas, Alexander, Stella Chess, Herbert G. Birch, M. Hertzig, and S. Korn.
1963 *Behavior Individuality in Early Childhood.* New York: New York University Press.
Thomas, Darwin, Victor Gecas, Andrew Weigert, and Elizabeth Rooney
1974 *Determinants of Self-Concept, Conformity, Religiosity, and Counter Culture Values. Family Socialization and the Adolescent.* Lexington, Mass.: Heath.
Thompson, E. P.
1982 "Time, work-discipline, and industrial capitalism." Pp. 299–309 in Anthony Giddens and David Held (eds.), *Classes, Power, and Conflict.* Berkeley: University of California Press.
Thornton, Arland
1977 "Children and marital stability." *Journal of Marriage and the Family* 39 (Aug.):531–40.
1985 "Changing attitudes toward separation and divorce: Causes and consequences." *American Journal of Sociology* 90 (4):856–72.
Thornton, Arland, and Deborah Freedman
1983 "The changing American family." *Population Bulletin,* v. 38. Washington, D.C.: Population Reference Bureau.
Thurman, Judith
1982 "The basics: Chodorow's theory of gender." *Ms.,* Sept., pp. 35–36.
Thurow, Lester C.
1980 *The Zero Sum Society.* New York: Basic Books.
Tiger, Lionel
1978 "Omnigamy: The new kinship system." *Psychology Today* 12 (July):14.

Tilly, Louise A., and Joan W. Scott
1978   *Women, Work, and Family.* New York: Holt, Rinehart & Winston.
Tobin, S. S.
1980   "The family and services." Pp. 370–99 in C. Eisdorfer (ed.), *Annual Review of Gerontology and Geriatrics,* v. 1. New York: Springer.
"Toddlers on the fast track."
1985   *New York Times,* Oct. 26.
Tomasson, Robert E.
1987   "Number of women in state legislatures rises steadily." *New York Times,* May 26.
"Too Late for Prince Charming?"
1986   *Newsweek,* June 2, pp. 54–58.
"Transfusions to still play AIDS role."
1987   *Omaha World-Herald,* May 10.
"Treating AIDS: The economic toll."
1987   Data from the U.S. Public Health Service, reported in *New York Times,* May 30.
Troll, Lillian E.
1975   *Early and Middle Adulthood: The Best Is Yet to Be—Maybe.* Monterey, Calif.: Brooks/Cole.
1985   "The contingencies of grandparenting." Pp. 135–50 in Vern L. Bengston and Joan F. Robertson (eds.), *Grandparenthood.* Beverly Hills, Calif.: Sage.
Troll, Lillian E., and Eugenia M. Parron
1981   "Age changes in sex roles amid changing sex roles: The double shift." *Annual Review of Gerontology and Geriatrics* 2:118–43.
Troll, Lillian E., Sheila J. Miller, and Robert C. Atchley
1979   *Families in Later Life.* Belmont, Calif.: Wadsworth.
Turner, Ralph H.
1976   "The real self: From institution to impulse." *American Journal of Sociology* 81 (5) (Mar.):989–1016.
Turner, R. Jay, and William R. Avison
1985   "Assessing risk factors for problem parenting: The significance of social support." *Journal of Marriage and the Family* 47 (4) (Nov.):881–92.
"Two more laws relating to retirement plans and TDA benefits."
1985   *The Participant* (Dec.):1–2.
Uchitelle, Louis
1987   "How to gauge the inflation rate." *New York Times,* July 8.
Udry, J. Richard
1974   *The Social Context of Marriage.* 3d ed. Philadelphia: Lippincott.
1981   "Marital alternatives and marital disruption." *Journal of Marriage and the Family* (Nov.):889–97.
1980   "Death and the family." *Journal of Family History* (Fall):313–20.
U.S. Bureau of the Census
1975   *Historical Statistics of the United States, Colonial Times to 1970.* Washington, D.C.: Government Printing Office.
1979   *Statistical Abstract of the United States.* Washington, D.C.: Government Printing Office.
1981   *Statistical Abstract of the United States, 1981.* Washington, D.C.: Government Printing Office.
1982   *Statistical Abstract of the United States, 1982–83.* Washington, D.C.: Government Printing Office.
1983a   "Marital status and living arrangements: Mar. 1, 1982." *Current Population Reports,* Series, P-20, No. 380. Washington, D.C.: Government Printing Office, May.
1983b   *Statistical Abstract of the United States, 1984.* Washington, D.C.: Government Printing Office.
1983c   "Money income and poverty status of families and persons in the United States, 1982" (advance data from the March 1983 *Current Population Survey*). *Current Population Reports,* Series P-60, No. 140. Washington, D.C.: Government Printing Office.
1983d   "Money income of households, families and persons in the United States: 1981." *Current Population Reports,*

Series P-60, No. 137. Washington, D.C.: Government Printing Office.
1985a   "Household and family characteristics: March, 1984." *Current Population Reports,* Series P-20, No. 398. Washington, D.C.: Government Printing Office.
1985b   "Marital status and living arrangements: March, 1984." *Current Population Reports,* Series P-20, No. 399 (July). Washington, D.C.: Government Printing Office.
1986a   "Marital status and living arrangements: March, 1985." *Current Population Reports,* Series P-20, No. 410 (Nov.). Washington, D.C.: Government Printing Office.
1986b   *Statistical Abstract of the United States, 1986.* Washington, D.C.: Government Printing Office.
1986c   "Households, families, marital status, and living arrangements, March, 1986: Advance report." *Current Population Reports,* Series P-20, No. 412. Washington, D.C.: Government Printing Office.
1987   *Statistical Abstract of the United States, 1987.* Washington, D.C.: Government Printing Office.
U.S. Bureau of Labor Statistics
1986a   "Employment in perspective: Women in the labor force, third quarter, 1986," Report 733. Washington, D.C.: Department of Labor.
1986b   "Employment in perspective: Women in the labor force, fourth quarter, 1986." Report 738, Washington, D.C.: Department of Labor.
1986c   "Half of mothers with children under 3 now in labor force." Press release, Aug. 20. Washington, D.C.: Department of Labor.
1987   "Employment and earnings characteristics of families: First quarter, 1987." Press release, Apr. 21. Washington, D.C.: Department of Labor.
U.S. Congress Subcommittee on Human Resources, Civil Service Compensation, and Employee Benefits
1983   *Pay Equity: Equal Pay for Work of Comparable Value.* Washington, D.C.: Government Printing Office.
U.S. Department of Health, Education, and Welfare
1975   *Child Abuse and Neglect: Volume I, An Overview of the Problem.* Publication #(OHD) 75-30073. Washington, D.C.: Government Printing Office.
U.S. Department of Health, Education, and Welfare, National Institute of Mental Health
1978   *Yours, Mine, and Ours: Tips for Stepparents.* Washington, D.C.: Government Printing Office.
U.S. Department of Health, Education, and Welfare, Health Resources Administration
1979   *How to Keep Your Family's Health Records.* DHEW Publ. No. (HRA) 79-636. Washington, D.C.: Government Printing Office.
U.S. Energy Information Administration
1983   Cited in *Omaha World-Herald,* Dec. 3.
U.S. National Center for Health Statistics
1979   "Advance report—Final divorce statistics, 1977." *Monthly Vital Statistics Report* 28(2), Supplement.
1982a   "Advance report of final natality statistics, 1980." *Monthly Vital Statistics Report* 31(8), Supplement, Nov. 30.
1982b   "Annual summary of births, deaths, marriages, and divorces: United States, 1981." *Monthly Vital Statistics Report* 30(13), Dec. 20.
1984a   "Advance report of final divorce statistics, 1981." *Monthly Vital Statistics Report* 32(9), Supplement (2), Jan. 17.
1984b   "Advance report of final natality statistics, 1982." *Monthly Vital Statistics Report* 33(6), Supplement, Sept. 28.
1985a   "Advance report of final marriage statistics, 1982." *Monthly Vital Statistics Report* 34(3), Supplement, June 28.
1985b   "Advance report of final natality statistics, 1983." *Monthly Vital Statistics Report* 34(6), Supplement, Sept. 20.

1985c "Marriage and first intercourse, marital dissolution, and remarriage: United States, 1982." No. 107, Apr. 12.

1986a "Advance report of final divorce statistics, 1984." *Monthly Vital Statistics Report* 35(6), Supplement, Sept. 25.

1986b "Advance report of final marriage statistics, 1983." *Monthly Vital Statistics Report* 35(1), Supplement, May 2.

1986c "Annual summary of births, marriages, divorces, and deaths: United States, 1985." *Monthly Vital Statistics Report* 34(13), Sept. 19.

1986d "Advance report of final mortality statistics, 1984." *Monthly Vital Statistics Report* 35(6), Supplement (2), Sept. 26, Table 12, p. 34.

1987a "Advance report of final marriage statistics, 1984." *Monthly Vital Statistics Report* 36(2), Supplement (2), June 3.

1987b "Advance report of final natality statistics, 1985." *Monthly Vital Statistics Report* 36(4) (Supp.), July 17.

U.S. v. *Dege*
1960 364 U.S. 51.

"Vaccines for the epidemic of missing children."
1983 *Psychology Today* (May):76.

Van den Haag, Ernest
1974 "Love or marriage." Pp. 134–42 in Rose Laub Coser (ed.), *The Family: Its Structures and Functions.* 2d ed. New York: St. Martin's Press.

Vander Zanden, James
1977 *Social Psychology.* New York: Random House.
1981 *Social Psychology.* 2d ed. New York: Random House.

Van Fossen, Beth E.
1977 "Sexual stratification and sex role socialization." *Journal of Marriage and the Family* 39 (Aug.):563–74.

Van Gelder, Lindsy
1978 "Beyond custody: When parents steal their own children." *Ms.* 11, May, p. 62.
1982 "The terrible curse of herpes." *Rolling Stone,* Mar. 4, pp. 23–24.

Van Gelder, Lindsy, and Carrie Carmichael
1975 "But what about our sons?" *Ms.* 4 Oct. pp. 52–56, 94–95.

Van Meter, Mary Jane S., and Patricia Johnson
1985 "Family decision making and long-term care for the elderly." *Journal of Religion and Aging* 1 (4) (Summer):59–88.

Vaughan, Diane
1986 *Uncoupling: Turning Points in Intimate Relationships.* New York: Oxford University Press.

Veevers, Jean E.
1974 "The life style of voluntary childless couples." In Lyle Larson (ed.), *The Canadian Family in Comparative Perspective.* Toronto: Prentice-Hall.

Vega, William A., George J. Warheit, and Kenneth Meinhardt
1984 "Marital disruption and the prevalence of depressive symptomatology among Anglos and Mexican Americans." *Journal of Marriage and the Family* 46 (4) (Nov.):817–24.

Ventura, Stephanie J.
1982 "Trends in first births to older mothers, 1970–1979." *Monthly Vital Statistics Report* 31(2), Supplement (2), May 27.
1983 "Births of Hispanic parentage, 1980." *Monthly Vital Statistics Report* 32 (6), Supplement, U.S. National Center for Health Statistics, Washington, D.C., Sept. 23.
1987a "Births of Hispanic parentage, 1983 and 1984." *Monthly Vital Statistics Report* 36(4), Supplement (2), July 24.
1987b "Trends in marital status of mothers at conception and birth of first child: United States, 1964–66, 1972, and 1980." *Monthly Vital Statistics Report* 36(2), Supplement, May 29.

Verbrugge, Lois M.
1979 "Marital status and health." *Journal of Marriage and the Family* 41 (May):267–85.

Veroff, Joseph, Richard A. Kulka, and Elizabeth Douvan
1981 *The Inner American: A Self-Portrait from 1957 to 1976.* New York: Basic Books.

Vincent, Clarke E.
1976 "Prerequisites for marital and sexual communication." Pp. 134–57 in Edward A. Powers and Mary W. Lees (eds.), *Process in Relationship: Marriage and Family.* 2d ed. New York: West.

Vine, Phyllis
1982 *Families in Pain: Children, Siblings, and Parents of the Mentally Ill Speak Out.* New York: Pantheon.

Visher, Emily B., and John S. Visher
1979 *Stepfamilies: A Guide to Working with Stepparents and Stepchildren.* New York: Brunner/Mazel.

Vogel, Ezra F., and Norman W. Bell
1960 "The emotionally disturbed child as family scapegoat." Pp. 382–97 in Norman W. Bell and Ezra F. Vogel, *A Modern Introduction to the Family.* Glencoe, Ill.: Free Press.

Voydanoff, Patricia
1980 "Work-family life cycles." Paper presented at the Workshop on Theory Construction and Research Methodology, National Council on Family Relations, Oct.

Voysey, Margaret
1975 *A Constant Burden: The Reconstitution of Family Life.* London: Routledge & Kegan Paul.

Wachowiak, Dale, and Hannelore Bragg
1980 "Open marriage and marital adjustment." *Journal of Marriage and the Family* 42:57–62.

Waite, Linda J.
1981 "U.S. women at work." *Population Bulletin* 36 Washington, D.C.: Population Reference Bureau.

Waldman, Elizabeth
1983 "Labor force statistics from a family perspective." *Monthly Labor Review* 106:16–19.

Walker, Alexis J.
1985 "Reconceptualizing family stress." *Journal of Marriage and the Family* 47 (4) (Nov.):827–38.

Walker, Kathryn E.
1970 "Time spent by husbands in household work." *Family Economics Review* 7:8–13.

Walker, K., and M. Woods
1976 *Time Use: A Measure of Household Production of Family Goods and Services.* Washington, D.C.: American Home Economics Association.

Walker, Lou Ann
1984 "Adult children and family money." *New York Times,* July 12.
1985 "When a parent is disabled." *New York Times,* June 20.

Wallace, Michele
1979 *Black Macho and the Myth of the Superwoman.* New York: Warner Books.

Waller, Willard
1937 "The rating and dating complex." *American Sociological Review* 2:727–34.
1951 *The Family: A Dynamic Interpretation.* New York: Dryden. (Revised by Reuben Hill.)

Wallerstein, Judith, and Joan Kelly
1980 *Surviving the Break-Up: How Children Actually Cope with Divorce.* New York: Basic Books.

Walsh, Froma
1982 *Normal Family Processes.* New York: Guilford.

Walsh, Robert, William Ganza, and Tim Finefield
1983 "A fifteen year study about sexual permissiveness." Paper presented at the annual meeting of the Midwest Sociological Society, Apr. 16.

Walster, Elaine H.
1965 "The effects of self-esteem on romantic liking." *Journal of Experimental and Social Psychology* 1:184–97.

1974   "Passionate love." Pp. 277–89 in Arlene S. Skolnick and Jerome H. Skolnick (eds.), *Intimacy, Family, and Society.* Boston: Little, Brown.

Walster, Elaine, E. Aronson, D. Abrams, and L. Rottman
1966   "Importance of physical attractiveness in dating behavior." *Journal of Personality and Social Psychology* 4:508–16.

Walster, Elaine, Ellen Bersheid, and G. William Walster
1974   "New directions in equity research." *Journal of Personality and Social Psychology* 25:151–76.

Walster, Elaine, and G. William Walster
1978   *A New Look at Love.* Reading, Mass.: Addison-Wesley.

Walster, Elaine, G. William Walster, and Ellen Berscheid
1978   *Equity Theory and Research.* Boston: Allyn & Bacon.

Walster, Elaine, G. William Walster, and Jane Traupman
1978   "Equity and premarital sex." *Journal of Personality and Social Psychology* 37:82–92.

Walter, Carolyn Ambler
1986   *The Timing of Motherhood.* Lexington, Mass.: Heath.

Warbelow, Kathy
1979   "Auto wives: The lonely queens." *Monthly Detroit,* Aug., pp. 42–49.

Wasserman, Ira A.
1984   "A longitudinal analysis of the linkage between suicide, unemployment, and marital dissolution." *Journal of Marriage and the Family* 46 (4) (Nov.):853–59.

Watson, Roy E. L.
1983   "Premarital cohabitation vs. traditional courtship: Their effects on subsequent marital adjustment." *Family Relations* 32 (Jan.):139–48.

Watson, Russell
1984   "A hidden epidemic." *Newsweek,* May 14, pp. 30–36.

Weber, Max
1948   *The Theory of Social and Economic Organization.* Talcott Parsons (ed.). New York: Free Press.

Wedemeyer, Nancy Voigt
1986   *Death and the Family.* Special issue of the *Journal of Family Issues* 7 (Sept.).

Weeks, Jeffrey
1985   *Sexuality and Its Discontents: Meanings, Myths, and Modern Sexualities.* London: Routledge & Kegan Paul.

Weeks, John R.
1986   *Population: An Introduction to Concepts and Issues.* 3d ed. Belmont, Calif.: Wadsworth.

Weigert, Andrew, and Ross Hastings
1977   "Identity loss, family and social change." *American Journal of Sociology* 28 (May):1171–85.

Weiler, Stephen J.
1981   "Aging and sexuality and the myth of decline." Pp. 317–27 in James G. March (ed.), *Aging: Stability and Change in the Family.* New York: Academic Press.

Weinberg, Thomas S.
1983   *Gay Men, Gay Selves: The Social Construction of Homosexual Identities.* New York: Irvington.

Weiss, Robert S.
1969   "The fund of sociability." *Transaction* 7 (July-Aug.):36–43.
1975   *Marital Separation: Managing After a Marriage Ends.* New York: Basic Books.
1979   *Going It Alone.* New York: Basic Books.
1981   "The study of loneliness." Pp. 152–64 in Peter J. Stein (ed.), *Single Life.* New York: St. Martin's Press.
1984   "The impact of marital dissolution on income and consumption in single parent households." *Journal of Marriage and the Family* 46 (Feb.):115–27.

Weitzman, Lenore J.
1977   "To love, honor, and obey?" Pp. 288–313 in Arlene S. Skolnick and Jerome H. Skolnick (eds.), *Family in Transition: Rethinking Marriage, Sexuality, Child Rearing, and Family Organization.* 2d ed. Boston: Little, Brown.
1981   *The Marriage Contract: Spouses, Lovers, and the Law.* New York: Free Press.

1985   *The Divorce Revolution: The Unexpected Social and Economic Consequences for Women and Children in America.* New York: Free Press.

Weitzman, Lenore J., and Ruth B. Dixon
1979   "Child custody awards: Legal standards and empirical patterns for child custody, support, and visitation after divorce." *University of California at Davis Law Review* 12:473–521.

Wekerle, Gerda
1975   "Vertical village: Social contacts in a single highrise complex." Faculty of Environmental Studies, York University, Toronto.

Weller, Robert H., and Leon F. Bouvier
1983   *Population: Demography and Policy.* New York: St. Martin's Press.

Wells, Robert V.
1985   *Uncle Sam's Family: Issues in and Perspectives on American Demographic History.* Albany, N.Y.: State University of New York Press.

West, Gilly
1985   "The belateds: A grounded theory about older women going to college while they raise their children." Paper prepared for presentation at the 80th Annual Meeting of the American Sociological Association, Aug. 26–30.

"What price day care?"
1984   *Newsweek,* Sept. 10, pp. 14–23.

White, Lynn K.
1979   "The correlates of urban illegitimacy in the United States, 1960–1970." *Journal of Marriage and the Family* 41 (Nov.):715–26.

White, Lynn K., and Alan Booth
1985a   "The transition to parenthood and marital quality." *Journal of Family Issues* 6 (4) (Dec.):435–49.
1985b   "The quality and stability of remarriages: The role of stepchildren." *American Sociological Review* 50 (Oct.):689–98.

White, Lynn K., Alan Booth, and John N. Edwards
1986   "Children and marital happiness." *Journal of Family Issues* 7 (2) (June):131–47.

White, Lynn K., and David B. Brinkerhoff
1981   "The sexual division of labor: Evidence from childhood." *Social Forces* 59 (Sept.):170–81.

Whitehurst, Robert N.
1977   "The monogamous ideal and sexual realities." Pp. 14–21 in Roger W. Libby and Robert N. Whitehurst (eds.), *Marriage and Alternatives: Exploring Intimate Relationships.* Glenview, Ill.: Scott, Foresman.

Wiley, Norbert F.
1985   "Marriage and the construction of reality: Then and now." Pp. 21–32 in Gerald Hantel (ed.), *The Psychosocial Interior of the Family.* 3d ed. Hawthorne, N.Y.: Aldine.

Will, Jerrie, Patricia Self, and Nancy Datan
1975   "Sex roles: Stereotyping—it starts early and dies hard." *Psychology Today* 8 (Jan.):85, 91.

William Petschek National Jewish Family Center of the American Jewish Committee
1986a   "Divorce." *Newsletter,* v. 5 (4) (Winter).
1986b   "Intermarriage." *Newsletter,* v. 6 (1) (Spring).

Williams, Carl E., and John F. Crosby
1979   *Choice and Challenge: Contemporary Readings in Marriage.* 2d ed. Dubuque, Iowa: Wm. C. Brown.

Williams, Robin M.
1951   *American Society.* New York: Knopf.

Williams, Roger
1977   "Alimony: The short goodbye." *Psychology Today* 10 (July):71.

Williams, Susan Darst
1983   "Ill husband's care needs ending 65-year marriage." *Omaha World-Herald,* May 19.

Willie, Charles Vert
1981   *A New Look at Black Families.* Bayside, N.Y.: General Hall.

1985   *Black and White Families: A Study in Complementarity.* Bayside, N.Y.: General Hall.

Willie, Charles V., and Susan L. Greenblatt
1978   "Four 'classic' studies of power relationships in black families: A review and look to the future." *Journal of Marriage and the Family* 40 (Nov.):691–94.

Wilson, Kenneth L., Louis A. Zurcher, Diana Claire McAdams, and Russell L. Curtis
1975   "Stepfathers and stepchildren: An explanatory analysis from two national surveys." *Journal of Marriage and the Family* 37 (Aug.):526–36.

Winch, Robert F.
1952   *The Modern Family.* New York: Holt.

Winn, Marie
1983   "The loss of childhood." *New York Times Magazine,* May 8, pp. 18–28.

Winter, David G., David McClelland, and Abigail Stewart
1977   "Husband's motives and wife's career level." *Journal of Personality and Social Psychology* 35:159–66.

Wiseman, Jacqueline P.
1981   "The family and its researchers in the eighties: Retrenching, renewing, and revitalizing." *Journal of Marriage and the Family* 43:263–66.
1985   "Individual adjustments and kin relationships in the 'new immigration': An approach to research." Paper presented at the Annual Meeting of the American Sociological Association.

Wolf, Deborah
1979   *The Lesbian Community.* Berkeley and Los Angeles: University of California Press.

"Women given higher odds of marriage."
1986   *Omaha World-Herald,* Oct. 7.

Wood, Vivian, and Joan F. Robertson
1976   "The significance of grandparenthood." In Jaber F. Gubrium (ed.), *Time, Roles, and Self in Old Age.* New York: Human Sciences Press.
1978   "Friendship and kinship interaction: Differential effects on the morale of the elderly." *Journal of Marriage and the Family* 40 (May):367–75.

Woodward, Kenneth
1982   "The Bible in the bedroom." *Newsweek,* Feb. 1, p. 71.

Woolley, Persia
1978   "Shared custody." *Family Advocate* 1 (Summer):6–9, 33–34.

Wortis, Rochelle Paul
1974   "The acceptance of the concept of the maternal role by behavioral scientists." In Arlene S. Skolnick and Jerome H. Skolnick (eds.), *Family in Transition: Rethinking Marriage, Sexuality, Child Rearing, and Family Organization.* 2d ed. Boston: Little, Brown.

Wright, Gwendolyn
1981   *Building the Dream: A Social History of Housing in America.* New York: Pantheon.

Wright, James D.
1978   "Are working women *really* more satisfied? Evidence from several national surveys." *Journal of Marriage and the Family* 40 (May):310–13.

Yankelovich, Daniel A.
1974   "The meaning of work." Pp. 19–48 in Jerome M. Rosow (ed.), *The Worker and the Job: Coping with Change.* Englewood Cliffs, N.J.: Prentice-Hall.
1981   *New Rules: Searching for Self-Fulfillment in a World Turned Upside Down.* New York: Random House.

"Years later, 'children of divorce carrying the burden'."
1984   UPI, in *Omaha World-Herald,* Feb. 16, p. 29.

Yllo, Kersti A.
1978   "Non-marital cohabitation beyond the campus." *Alternative Lifestyles* 1:37–54.

Yogev, Sara, and Jeanne Brett
1985   "Perceptions of the division of housework and child care and marital satisfaction." *Journal of Marriage and the Family* 47 (Aug.):609–18.

Zablocki, Benjamin
1977   *Alienation and Investment in the Urban Commune.* New York: Center for Policy Research.

Zalba, Serapio
1974   "Battered children." Pp. 407–14 in Arlene S. Skolnick and Jerome H. Skolnick (eds.), *Intimacy, Family, and Society.* Boston: Little, Brown.

Zelnik, Melvin, and John F. Kantner
1977   "Sexual and contraceptive experience of young unmarried women in the United States, 1976 and 1971." *Family Planning Perspectives* 9:55–71.
1978a   "Contraceptive patterns and premarital pregnancy among women aged 15–19." *Family Planning Perspectives* 10:135–42.
1978b   "First pregnancies to women aged 15–19: 1976 and 1971." *Family Planning Perspectives* 10 (Jan.-Feb.):11–20.
1980   "Sexual activity, contraceptive use, and pregnancy among metropolitan area teenagers, 1971–1979." *Family Planning Perspectives* 12:230–37.

Zelnik, Melvin, and Young J. Kim
1982   "Sex education and its association with teenage sexual activity, pregnancy, and contraceptive use." *Family Planning Perspectives* 14 (May-June):117–26.

Zimmerman, Mary K.
1977   *Passage Through Abortion: The Personal and Social Reality of Women's Experiences.* New York: Praeger.

Zussman, Shirley, and Leon Zussman
1979   "Making time for intimacy." *McCall's,* Feb., p. 75.

Acknowledgments

We wish to thank the following for permission to reprint, abridge, or adapt. **Addison-Wesley Publishing Company: [pp. 331, 334, 374, 375, 376]** Quotations from *Two Career Couple* by Francine S. Hall and Douglas T. Hall. Copyright © 1979 Addison-Wesley Publishing Company, Inc. Reading, MA. Reprinted by permission. **Aldine de Gruyter, Publishers: [pp. 321, 323]** Quotations from Francesca M. Cancian, "Gender Politics: Love and Power in Private and Public Spheres" in Alice S. Rossi (ed.), *Gender and the Life Course,* Aldine de Gruyter, Publishers, New York. Copyright © 1985 by the American Sociological Association. Reprinted by permission. **American Academy of Political and Social Science: [pp. 490–492]** Abridgment of "Alcoholism and Family" by Joan J. Jackson in volume no. 315 of *The Annals* of The American Academy of Political and Social Science. Copyright © 1958 AAPSS. Used by permission. **American Demographics, Inc.: [p. 453]** Table 14-1 adapted from Fabian Linden, "Families with Children," *American Demographics,* April 1984. Used by permission. **American Psychological Association: [p. 294]** Figure 9-3 adapted from Albert Bandura, "Influence of Models: Reinforcement Contingencies on the Acquisition of Imitative Responses," *Journal of Personality and Social Psychology* 1:589–95. Copyright 1965 by APA. Used by permission. **American Sociological Association: [p. 101]** Figure 3-2 adapted from Irwin Altman and William W. Haythorn, "Interpersonal Exchange in Isolation," *Sociometry* 28:422. Copyright 1965 by ASA. Used by permission. **Bantam Books: [pp. 532–533]** Abridged from *How to Survive the Loss of a Loved One: 58 Things to Do When There Is Nothing to Be Done* by Melba Colgrove, Harold Bloomfield, and Peter McWilliams, 1976, Bantam. Used by permission. **Basic Books: [pp. 120, 268–270, 362]** Quotations from *Worlds of Pain: Life in the Working-Class Family* by Lillian Rubin, 1976, Basic Books, **[p. 520]** Figures 16-5 and 16-6 from *The Difficult Divorce: Therapy for Children and Families* by Marla Beth Isaacs, Braulio Montalvo, and David Abelson. Copyright © 1986 by Basic Books, Inc. **[pp. 519, 552]** Figures 16-4 and 17-5 adapted from *Surviving the Breakup: How Children and Parents Cope with Divorce* by Judith Wallerstein and Joan Berlin Kelly. Copyright © 1980 by Judith S. Wallerstein and Joan Berlin Kelly. Reprinted by permission of Basic Books, Inc., Publishers. **Brunner/Mazel: [pp. 546, 547]** Table 17-1 and excerpt adapted from *Stepfamilies: A Guide to Working with Stepparents and Stepchildren* by Emily B. Visher and John S. Visher, 1979, Brunner/Mazel. Used by permission. **I. W. Charny: [pp. 290, 302–303]** Excerpts adapted from *Marital Love and Hate* by Israel W. Charny, 1972, Macmillan. Copyright © Israel W. Charny. Used by permission. **Doubleday & Company: [pp. 522, 523, 529, 530, 531, 550]** Excerpts from *Divorce and After* by Paul Bohannan. Copyright 1968, 1970 by Paul Bohannan. **[p. 304]** Excerpt from *No-Fault Marriage* by Marcia Laswell and Norman Lobsenz, 1976, Ballantine. **[p. 336]** Figure 10-1 adapted from *Behind Closed Doors* by Murray A. Straus, Richard J. Gelles, and Suzanne K. Steinmetz. Copyright © 1980 by Richard J. Gelles and Murray A. Straus. **[pp. 68–79]** Excerpts from *Black Macho and the Myth of Superwoman* by Michele Wallace. Copyright © 1978, 1979 by Michele Wallace. Reprinted by permission of Doubleday & Company. **E. P. Dutton: [pp. 124–125, 218, 255, 263, 264, 266, 267, 270, 271]** Quotations from *The Significant Americans* by John F. Cuber and Peggy B. Haroff. Copyright © 1965 by John F. Cuber. A Hawthorn book. **[p. 291]** Figure 9-2 based on *Putting It All Together* by Dr. Irene Kassorla. Copyright © 1973 by Brut Productions, Inc. A Hawthorn book. Reprinted by permission of E. P. Dutton, a division of NAL Penguin Inc. **M. Evans and Company: [p. 30]** Figure 1-1 adapted from *Shifting Gears* by Nena O'Neill and George O'Neill. Copyright © 1974 by Nena O'Neill and George O'Neill. Reprinted by permission of the publisher, M. Evans and Co., Inc., New York, NY 10017, p. 167. **Grove Press: [p. 123]** Excerpts from *Sex for Women Who Want to Have Fun and Loving Relationships with Equals* by Carmen Kerr. Copyright © 1967 by Carmen Kerr. Reprinted by permission of Grove Press, Inc. **Guilford Press: [pp. 492–493, 500–501, 535]** Quotations and Table 16-2 from *The Developing Father: Emerging Roles in Contemporary Society* by Bryan E. Robinson and Robert L. Barret, 1986. Reprinted by permission of The Guilford Press. **Guttmacher Institute: [p. 402]** Table 12-1 adapted from "Most Americans Remain Opposed to Abortion Ban and Continue to Support Women's Right to Decide," *Family Planning Perspectives,* vol. 16, no. 5, 1984. Reprinted with permission from Family Planning Perspectives, published by The Alan Guttmacher Institute, New York, 1984. **Harper & Row: [p. 129]** Table 4-3 from "Sex Over 65" by I. Rubin in *Advances in Sex Research,* Hugo Beigel (ed.), 1963. **[pp. 236, 237]** Excerpts from *All Our Kin: Strategies for Survival in the Black Community* by Carol B. Stack. Copyright © by Carol B. Stack. Used by permission of Harper & Row Publishers, Inc. **Harvard University Press: [p. 513]** Table in Box 16-2 from *Marriage, Divorce, Remarriage* by A. Cherlin, 1981. Used by permission. **Haworth Press: [p. 192]** Table 6-3 from *Intermarriage in the United States,* Gary Crester and Joseph

Leon, eds. Copyright 1982 by Haworth Press, Inc. **[p. 484]** Figure 15-3 adapted from *Social Stress and the Family,* H. I. McCubbin, M. B. Sussman, and J. M. Patterson, eds. Copyright 1983 by Haworth Press, Inc. Reprinted by permission. All rights reserved. **Dana Hiller: [pp. 232, 233]** Table 7-2 and excerpts from "Role Expectations and Perceptions of Partner's Role Expectations in Contemporary Marriage" by Dana Hiller and William W. Phillber. Paper presented at 80th Annual Meeting of the American Sociological Association, August 26–30, 1985. Used by permission. **Henry Holt and Company: [p. 183]** "The Pasture" from *The Poetry of Robert Frost* edited by Edward Connery Lathem. Copyright 1939, © 1967, 1969 by Holt Rinehart and Winston. Reprinted by permission of Henry Holt and Company, Inc. **Holt, Rinehart and Winston: [pp. 94–95, 96–97]** Excerpts from *Encounters with the Self* by Don E. Hamachek. Copyright © 1971 by Holt, Rinehart and Winston, Inc. Reprinted by permission of Holt, Rinehart and Winston, Inc. **Ann Landers: [p. 255–256]** Excerpt from *Omaha World Herald,* March 1979, Field Newspaper Syndicate. Used by permission. **Little, Brown and Company: [pp. 231, 435]** Table 7-1 and quotation from *The Intimate Environment: Exploring Marriage and the Family,* 2nd ed., by Arlene Skolnick. Copyright © 1978 by Little, Brown and Company (Inc.). Reprinted by permission. **Longman: [pp. 48, 75, 321, 330]** Quotations from "Why Men Resist" by William J. Goode in *Rethinking the Family: Some Feminist Questions,* Barrie Thorne and Marilyn Yalom, eds. Copyright © 1982 by Longman, Inc. All rights reserved. Used by permission. **Mayfield: [pp. 122, 318–319]** Excerpts from "The Courtship Game: Power in the Sexual Encounter" by N. B. McCormick and C. J. Jessor in *Changing Boundaries: Gender Roles and Sexual Behavior,* E. R. Allegier and N. B. McCormick, eds., 1983, Mayfield Publishing Company. Used by permission. **William Morrow & Company: [pp. 86–87]** Excerpts from *The Dance-Away Lovers* by D. Goldstine, K. Larner, S. Zuckerman, and H. Goldstine. Copyright © 1977 by Daniel Goldstine, Katherine Larner, Shirley Zuckerman, and Hilary Goldstine. **[pp. 315, 324, 325]** Excerpts from *American Couples: Money, Work, Sex* by P. Blumstein and P. Schwartz. Copyright © 1983 by Philip Blumstein and Pepper Schwartz. Reprinted by permission of William Morrow & Company. **National Association for Women Deans, Administrators, and Counselors: [p. 73]** Quotations from "The Costs of Being on Top" by Mark E. Kann, *Journal of the National Association for Women Deans, Administrators, and Counselors,* 49 (Summer) 1986. Reprinted by permission. **National Council on Family Relations: [pp. 100, 103]** Figure 3-1 and excerpt from "Toward a Sociology of the Heterosexual Love Relationship" by Ira L. Reiss, *Marriage and Family Living,* May 1960. Copyright 1960 by NCFR. **[pp. 127]** Table 4-2 from "The Salience of Sexuality in the Early Years of Marriage" by Cathy S. Greenblatt, *Journal of Marriage and the Family,* May 1983. Copyright 1983 by NCFR. **[pp. 74, 154, 155]** Tables 5-1 and 5-2 and excerpts from "Changes in the Organization of Men's Lives" by David Eggebeen and Peter Uhlenberg, *Family Relations,* April 1985. Copyright 1985 by NCFR. **[p. 197]** Table in Box 6-1 adapted from "Interreligious Marriage in the United States: Patterns and Recent Trends" by Norval Glenn, *Journal of Marriage and the Family,* August 1982. Copyright 1982 by NCFR. **[p. 206]** Table 6-5 from "Heterosexual Cohabitation Among Unmarried Students" by Eleanor Macklin, *Family Coordinator,* October 1972. Copyright 1972 by NCFR. **[pp. 208–209, 210–211]** Box 6-3 and Table 6-6 adapted from "Cohabitation: Does It Make for a Better Marriage?" by Carl A. Ridley, Dan J. Peterman, and Arthur W. Avery, *Family Coordinator,* April 1978. Copyright 1978 by NCFR. **[pp. 335, 340, 341, 435]** Table 10-1 and excerpts from "Societal Change and Change in Family Violence from 1975 to 1985" by Murray Straus and Richard Gelles, *Journal of Marriage and the Family,* August 1986. Copyright 1986 by NCFR. **[p. 339]** Table 10-2 from "Abused Wives: Do They Stay?" by Richard Gelles, *Journal of Marriage and the Family,* November 1976. Copyright 1976 by NCFR. **[p. 482]** Table 15-1 from "Normative Family Stress: Family Boundary Changes Across the Life-Span" by Pauline Boss, *Family Relations,* October 1980. Copyright 1980 by NCFR. **[pp. 508, 542]** Figures 16-2 and 17-3 from "Recent Changes in Divorce and Remarriage" by Paul C. Glick and Lin Sung-Ling, *Journal of Marriage and the Family,* November 1986. Copyright 1986 by NCFR. **[pp. 509, 540, 541]** Figures 16-3, 17-1, and 17-2 adapted from "Current Trends in Marriage and Divorce Among American Women" by Arthur J. Norton and Jeanne E. Moorman, *Journal of Marriage and the Family,* February 1987. Copyright 1987 by NCFR. **[p. 518]** Table 16-1 adapted from "Correlates of Marital Happiness Among the Remarried" by Stan L. Albrecht, *Journal of Marriage and the Family,* November 1979. Copyright 1979 by NCFR. **[p. 544]** Figure 17-4 adapted from "The Marital Happiness of Remarried Divorced Persons" by Norval D. Glenn and Charles H. Weaver, *Journal of Marriage and the Family,* May 1977. Copyright 1977 by NCFR. **[p. 545]** Excerpts from "Remarriage After Divorce: A Longitudinal Analysis of Well-Being" by Graham B. Spanier and Frank F. Furstenberg, *Journal of Marriage and the Family*, November 1982. Copyright © 1982 by NCFR. All items reprinted by permission of the authors and the National Council on Family Relations, 1910 West County Road B, Suite 147, St. Paul, MN 55113. **Nelson-Hall: [p. 549]** Table 17-2 reprinted from *The Reconstituted Family* by Lucile Duberman, p. 40. Copyright 1975 by Lucile Duberman. Used by permission of Nelson-Hall Publishers, Chicago. **Newsweek: [p. 361]** Table 11-2 from *Newsweek* Magazine, March 31, 1986. Copyright © 1986 by Newsweek, Inc. Reprinted by permission. **New York Times: [pp. 71, 356]** Figure 2-3 and Table 11-1 from *New York Times* poll of December 4, 1983. Copyright © 1983 by the New York Times Company. **[pp. 170–171]** Excerpts from "Why Fewer American Women Marry" by Neil G. Bennett and David E. Bloom, December 13, 1986. Copyright © 1986 by The New York Times Company. Reprinted by permission. **W. W. Norton: [pp. 55, 377]** Figure 2-1 and Table 11-3 adapted from *Women and Sex Roles: A Social Psychological Perspective* by Irene H. Frieze et al. Copyright © 1978 by W. W. Norton & Company, Inc. Reprinted by permission. **Omaha World Herald: [pp. 410–412]** From "Sharing Opens Window on Secrets of Adoption," *Omaha World Herald*, December 5, 1982. Reprinted by permission of Omaha World Herald and the author. **Pi Kappa Phi Fraternity: [pp. 202–203]** "Statement of Position on Sexual Abuse" and reproduction of poster reprinted by permission of Pi Kappa Phi Fraternity. **Population Association of America: [p. 453]** Figure 14-2 adapted from "The Life Cycle Squeeze: The Interaction of Men's Occupational and Family Life Cycles" by Valerie K. Oppenheimer, *Demography*, May 1974. Used by permission of the Population Association of America. **Prentice-Hall: [pp. 189, 190, 214–215, 218]** Excerpts from *Marriage: Who? When? Why?* by David H. Knox, Jr. © 1975. **[pp. 308, 458, 481]** Excerpts from *Marriage and the Family* by Carlfred B. Broderick. © 1979. **[pp. 311, 323]** Excerpts from *Gender Roles and Power* by Jean Lipman-Blumen. © 1984. Reprinted by permission of Prentice-Hall, Inc., Englewood Cliffs, New Jersey. **Psychological Reports: [p. 92]** Table from *The Course of Love: A Cross-Sectional Design* by R. S. Cimbalo, V. Faling, and P. Mousaw, *Psychological Reports*, 38:1292–1294, 1976. Reprinted with permission of the authors and publisher. **Rand McNally: [p. 480]** Figure 15-1 adapted from *The Handbook of Marriage and the Family* by Donald A. Hansen and Reuben Hill, Harold Christensen (ed.), p. 810. Copyright © 1964 by Rand McNally & Company. Reprinted by permission of the publisher. **Random House: [pp. 16–17]** Excerpt from *Pathways to Madness* by Jules Henry. Copyright © 1972 by Random House, Inc. **[p. 72]** Figure 2-4 adapted from *New Rules: Searching for Self-Fulfillment in a World Turned Upside Down* by Daniel Yankelovich. Copyright © 1981 by Random House, Inc. Reprinted by permission. **Rawson Associates: [pp. 442–443]** Excerpted from *How to Talk So Kids Will Listen and Listen So Kids Will Talk* by Adele Faber and Elaine Mazlish. Copyright © 1980 by Adele Faber and Elaine Mazlish. Reprinted with the permission of Rawson Associates. **Sage Publications: [pp. 151, 152–153, 160, 164, 166, 167, 168]** Excerpts and Figures 5-6 and 5-8 from *Singles: Myths and Realities* by Leonard Cargan and Matthew Melko. Copyright © 1982. **[p. 494]** Excerpts from *Later Life: The Social Psychology of Aging* by Victor Marshall. Copyright © 1986. **[p. 500]** Excerpts from "Communication Paradoxes and the Maintenance of Living Relationships with the Dying" by Vernon D. Miller and Mark L. Knapp, *Journal of Family Issues* 7:255–276. Copyright © 1986. Reprinted by permission of Sage Publications, Inc. **St. Martin's Press: [pp. 157, 158, 161]** Excerpts and Table 5-3 from *Single Life: Unmarried Adults in Social Context*, edited by Peter J. Stein. Copyright © 1981 by St. Martin's Press. Reprinted with permission of the publisher. **Science and Behavior Books: [pp. 93, 95]** Excerpts from *Peoplemaking* by Virginia Satir, 1972. Reprinted by permission of the author and publisher, Science and Behavior Books, Inc., Palo Alto, California. **Scott, Foresman: [pp. 107, 113, 115, 122]** Excerpts from *Human Sexualities* by John Gagnon, 1977. Used by permission of Scott, Foresman & Company. **Simon & Schuster: [pp. 212–213]** Excerpt from *Total Loving* by "J." Copyright © 1977 by Joan Garrity. **[pp. 300–301, 328–329]** Excerpts from *Couples: How to Confront Problems and Maintain Loving Relationships* by Carlfred B. Broderick. Copyright © 1979 by Dr. Carlfred B. Broderick. **[p. 396]** Excerpt from *The New Our Bodies, Ourselves* by The Boston Women's Health Book Collective. Copyright © 1984 by The Boston Women's Health Book Collective, Inc. Reprinted by permission of Simon & Schuster, Inc. **Society for the Study of Social Problems: [p. 113]** Table 4-1 from "The Homosexual Role" by Mary McIntosh, *Social Problems*, Vol. 16, No. 2, Fall 1968, p. 190. © 1968 by the Society for the Study of Social Problems. Reprinted by permission of the Society. **State University of New York Press: [p. 485–486]** Excerpt from *Uncle Sam's Family: Issues and Perspectives on American Demographic History* by Robert V. Wells. Copyright © 1985 State University of New York Press. Reprinted by permission. **Peter Stein: [pp. 149, 151, 161, 179]** Excerpts and Table 5-5 from *Single* by Peter J. Stein, 1976, Prentice-Hall, Inc. Copyright © Peter J. Stein. Reprinted by permission of Peter J. Stein. **Judith Thurman: [pp. 62–63]** Abridgment of "The Basics: Chodorow's Theory of Gender" by Judith Thurman, *Ms.* Magazine, September 1982. Copyright © 1982 by Judith Thurman. Used by permission of Judith Thurman. **University of California Press: [pp. 36, 37]** Excerpts from *Hard Choices: How Women Decide about Work, Career and Motherhood* by Kathleen Gerson, 1985, University of California Press. Used by permission. **D. Van Nostrand: [pp. 457, 461]** Excerpts and Figure 14-3 from *Economics for Consumers*, 7th Edition, by Leland J. Gordon and Stewart M. Lee. © 1977 by Litton Educational Publishing, Inc. **[pp. 564]** Figure A-2 adapted from *Human Sexuality*, 2nd Edition, by James L. McCary, 1979. Published by D. Van Nostrand Company. Used by permission of Litton Educational Publishing, Inc. **Wadsworth: [pp. 12, 271, 294, 302, 308]** Excerpts from *Illusion and Disillusion: The Self in Love and Marriage*, 2nd ed. by John F. Crosby. © 1976 by Wadsworth Publishing Company, Inc. Reprinted by permission of Wadsworth Publishing Company, Belmont, CA 94002. **Washington Post Writers Group: [pp. 454–455]** Excerpt from "When Couple Splits Costs 50/50, It Isn't Necessarily Fair" by Ellen Goodman. © 1983 The Boston Globe Newspaper Company/Washington Post Writers Group. Reprinted with permission. **Wyden Books: [pp. 198–199]** Excerpt from *Pairing* by George R. Bach and Ronald M. Deutsch, 1970. Reprinted by permission of Wyden Books. **Ziff-Davis: [pp. 528, 533]** Excerpt from "Divorced Fathers" by E. Mavis Heatherington, *Psychology Today*, April 1977. Reprinted with permission from *Psychology Today* Magazine, copyright © 1977 Ziff Davis Publishing Company.

Photo Credits

21 Jim Goldberg/Archive Pictures Inc.; **35** © Jim Goldberg; **41** Randy Matusow/Archive Pictures Inc.; **49** Bruce Davidson/Magnum Photos Inc.; **53** Sepp Seitz/Woodfin Camp & Associates; **57** Raymond Depardon/Magnum Photos Inc.; **67** Max Ramirez/Archive Pictures Inc.; **85** Jean-Claude Lejeune/Stock, Boston; **90** Abigail Heyman/Archive Pictures Inc.; **93** Henri Cartier-Bresson/Magnum Photos Inc.; **98** Jim Goldberg/Archive Pictures Inc.; **102** Abigail Heyman/Archive Pictures; **114** © Jim Goldberg; **116** © Nathan Lyons; **126** Barbara Alper/Stock, Boston; **128** Ferdinando Scianna/Magnum Photos Inc.; **134** © Marshall Rheiner; **150** Jim Goldberg/Archive Pictures Inc.; **157** Lamnite E. Druskis/Jeroboam, Inc.; **165** © Ken Heyman; **173** bottom: Mark Godfrey/Archive Pictures Inc.; **190** Alan Carey/The Image Works; **217** Jim Goldberg/Archive Pictures Inc.; **224** bottom: Hazel Hankin/Stock, Boston; **225** bottom: Frances B. Johnston: *A Hampton Graduate at Home*, 1899–1900. Platinum print, $7\frac{1}{2} \times 9\frac{1}{2}$". Collection, The Museum of Modern Art, New York. Gift of Lincoln Kirstein; **230** Jane Scherr/Jeroboam, Inc.; **235** Eve Arnold/Magnum Photos Inc.; **239** Kent Reno/Jeroboam, Inc.; **244** Rose Skytta/Jeroboam, Inc.; **256** © Ken Heyman; **265** © Jim Goldberg; **267** Jill A. Cannefax/EKM-Nepenthe; **285** Karin Rosenthal/Stock, Boston; **291** Jill Freedman/Archive Pictures Inc.; **307** © Ken Heyman; **321** Jane Scherr/Jeroboam, Inc.; **322** Jim Goldberg/Archive Pictures Inc.; **326** Michael Weisbrot & Family/Stock, Boston; **337** Michael O'Brien/Archive Pictures Inc.; **349** Earl Dotter/Archive Pictures Inc.; **355** Danny Lyons/Magnum Photos Inc.; **360** Michal Heron/Woodfin Camp & Associates; **363** Charles Gatewood/Stock, Boston; **367** Michal Heron/Woodfin Camp & Associates; **390** Suzanne Wu/Jeroboam, Inc.; **395** Joan Liftin/Archive Pictures Inc.; **399** Mary Ellen Mark/Archive Pictures Inc.; **423** Leonard Freed/Magnum Photos Inc.; **434** © Jim Goldberg; **441** Elizabeth Crews/Stock, Boston; **451** Jim Goldberg/Archive Pictures Inc.; **460** Michael Malyszko/Stock, Boston; **464** Frederick D. Bodin/Stock, Boston; **467** © Elizabeth Crews; **483** Charles Harbutt/Archive Pictures Inc.; **495** © Jim Goldberg; **499** © Abraham Menashe; **514** Susan Rothenberg/Photo Researchers; **529** Henk Lebo/Jeroboam, Inc.; **556** Lynne Jaeger Weinstein/Woodfin Camp & Associates.

Snapshot Credits

10 Nellie Revit; **19** Gary Mcdonald; **31** Nellie Revit; **43** top left, center, and bottom left: Nellie Revit; top right: Helene Podgorski; bottom right: Jenny Collins; **53** right: Katherine Wilmot; **66** both photos: Suzanne Gooding; **173** top: Suzanne Gooding; center: Jim Lenoir; **177** top left: Sandra Craig; top right: Lynda Frattaroli; center: Jenny Collins; bottom: Nellie Revit; **193** Patricia Rose; **200** top left: Andrew Ogus; top right: Eleanor Sviatopolk-Mirsky; bottom: Sandra Craig; **224** top left: Nellie Revit; top right: MaryEllen Podgorski; **225** top: Sandra Craig; **277** Sandra Craig; **298** Gary Mcdonald; **314** Lindsay Kefauver; **364** top: Nellie Revit; bottom: Tom Nerney; **392** Jerilyn Emori; **417** both photos: MaryEllen Podgorski; **429** Gary Mcdonald; **439** both photos: Nellie Revit.

Name Index

Subject Index